Organizational Behavior

A Practical, Problem-Solving Approach

Third Edition

Angelo Kinicki
Arizona State University
Kent State University

McGraw Hill

ORGANIZATIONAL BEHAVIOR: A PRACTICAL, PROBLEM-SOLVING APPROACH, THIRD EDITION

Published by McGraw-Hill Education, 2 Penn Plaza, New York, NY 10121. Copyright © 2021 by McGraw-Hill Education. All rights reserved. Printed in the United States of America. Previous editions © 2018 and 2016. No part of this publication may be reproduced or distributed in any form or by any means, or stored in a database or retrieval system, without the prior written consent of McGraw-Hill Education, including, but not limited to, in any network or other electronic storage or transmission, or broadcast for distance learning.

Some ancillaries, including electronic and print components, may not be available to customers outside the United States.

This book is printed on acid-free paper.

1 2 3 4 5 6 7 8 9 LWI 24 23 22 21 20

ISBN 978-1-260-07507-6 (bound edition)
MHID 1-260-07507-9 (bound edition)
ISBN 978-1-260-51625-8 (loose-leaf edition)
MHID 1-260-51625-3 (loose-leaf edition)

Executive Portfolio Manager: *Michael Ablassmeir*
Lead Product Developer: *Kelly Delso*
Product Developer: *Anne Ehrenworth*
Executive Marketing Manager: *Debbie Clare*
Content Project Managers: *Harvey Yep (Core) / Keri Johnson (Assessment)*
Buyer: *Susan K. Culbertson*
Design: *Matt Diamond*
Content Licensing Specialist: *Carrie Burger*
Cover Image: *© malerapaso/Getty Images*
Compositor: *Aptara®, Inc.*

All credits appearing on page or at the end of the book are considered to be an extension of the copyright page.

Library of Congress Control Number: 2019920084

The Internet addresses listed in the text were accurate at the time of publication. The inclusion of a website does not indicate an endorsement by the authors or McGraw-Hill Education, and McGraw-Hill Education does not guarantee the accuracy of the information presented at these sites.

DEDICATION

To the thousands of students I encountered during my career. Thank you for making me a better teacher and writer.

— *Angelo*

Courtesy of Angelo Kinicki

Angelo Kinicki is an emeritus professor of management and held the Weatherup/Overby Chair in Leadership from 2005 to 2015 at the W.P. Carey School of Business at Arizona State University. He joined the faculty in 1982, the year he received his doctorate in business administration from Kent State University. He was inducted into the W.P. Carey Faculty Hall of Fame in 2016. Angelo currently is the Dean's Scholar in Residence at Kent State University. He is teaching in the MBA program and serves on the Dean's National Advisory Board.

Angelo is the recipient of six teaching awards from Arizona State University, where he taught in its nationally ranked MBA and PhD programs. He also received several research awards and was selected to serve on the editorial review boards for four scholarly journals. His current research interests focus on the dynamic relationships among leadership; organizational culture; organizational change; and individual, group, and orga-

nizational performance. Angelo has published over 95 articles in a variety of academic journals and proceedings and is co-author of eight textbooks (32 including revisions) that are used by hundreds of universities around the world. Several of his books have been translated into multiple languages, and two of his books were awarded revisions of the year by McGraw-Hill. Angelo also was identified as being among the top 100 most influential (top .6%) Organizational Behavior authors in 2018 out of a total of 16,289 academics.

Angelo is a busy international consultant and is a principal at Kinicki and Associates, Inc., a management consulting firm that works with top management teams to create organizational change aimed at increasing organizational effectiveness and profitability. He has worked with many Fortune 500 firms as well as numerous entrepreneurial organizations in diverse industries. His expertise includes facilitating strategic/operational planning sessions, diagnosing the causes of organizational and work-unit problems, conducting organizational culture interventions, implementing performance management systems, designing and implementing performance appraisal systems, developing and administering surveys to assess employee attitudes, and leading management/executive education programs. He developed a 360^0 leadership feedback instrument called the Performance Management Leadership Survey (PMLS) that is used by companies throughout the world.

Angelo and his wife of 37 years, Joyce, have enjoyed living in the beautiful Arizona desert for 36 years. They are both natives of Cleveland, Ohio. They enjoy traveling, hiking, and spending time in the White Mountains with Gracie, their adorable golden retriever. Angelo also has a passion for golfing.

We are pleased to share these exciting updates and new additions to the third edition of *Organizational Behavior*!

Features

In this new edition, we have better integrated the **3-Step Problem-Solving Approach** throughout, and clarified its relationship to the **Organizing Framework for Understanding and Applying OB.** In addition:

- **Winning at Work** boxes at the beginning of every chapter offer career-readiness guidance for students on a variety of timely, pertinent topics.

- **OB in Action** boxes illustrate OB concepts or theories *in action* in the real world, featuring well-known companies and individuals.

- **Applying OB** boxes offer students "how-to" guidance on applying OB knowledge in their lives. The importance of career readiness is stressed in many of these boxes throughout the book, indicated with a "Career Readiness" label.

- **Problem-Solving Application** boxes provide a minicase for students to analyze, using the 3-Step Problem-Solving Approach.

- **Takeaways for Me** and **Takeaways for Managers conclude each chapter,** explaining in direct terms practical applications of the chapter content from the student's perspective as an employee and a manager.

- **Problem-Solving Application Cases** at the end of each chapter provide a complex and current case with one or more problems that pertain to concepts discussed in the chapter.

- **Legal/Ethical Challenges** provide a concluding exercise in each chapter and ask students to choose from several courses of action or invent their own to resolve a business situation involving ethics at work.

Connect

In our continuing efforts to help students move from comprehension to application, and to ensure they see the personal relevance of OB, we have included a variety of new exercises to our already robust Connect offering:

- **Problem-Solving Application Case Analyses:** All problem-solving application mini-cases and end-of-chapter cases are now assignable as case analyses in Connect. These exercises give students the opportunity to analyze a situation and to apply the 3-Step Problem-Solving Approach. Student knowledge and proficiency are assessed using high-level multiple-choice questions that focus on both the problem-solving approach and on the key topics of each chapter.

- **Application-Based Activities:** Students can gain valuable practice using problem-solving skills to apply their knowledge to realistic scenarios. Included in this edition are two types of Application-Based Activities: *Role-Playing mini-simulations* that allow students to make decisions and see, in real time, the impact of those decisions; and *Self-Assessments,* which are research-based surveys that students can take to gain further introspection into how organizational behavioral concepts apply to them.

- **Cumulative Case:** This capstone activity provides students the opportunity to apply the 3-Step Problem-Solving Approach on an actual situation affecting a specific firm (Tesla). Because the case examines issues at the individual, group, and organizational levels of analysis at Tesla, it can be used in parts or as a comprehensive assignment or exam. All told, this activity presents students with a rich and practical example to apply their OB knowledge and problem-solving skills.

- **iSeeIt Videos:** Brief, contemporary introductions to key course concepts that often perplex students, this series will enhance your student-centered instruction by offering your students dynamic illustrations that guide them through the basics of core OB concepts such as motivation, leadership, socialization, and more.

- **Manager's Hot Seat Videos:** These vignettes allow students to assume the role of a manager as they immerse themselves in real-life situations. Students see how managers deal with employees and complex issues, and use critical-thinking skills in defining their approach and course of action–while learning from the manager's mistakes.

Chapters

In each chapter we have refreshed examples, research, figures, tables, statistics, and photos, as well as streamlined design to ease navigation and improve readability. We have also largely replaced the topics in such popular features as Winning at Work, Legal/Ethical Challenges, Problem-Solving Application mini cases, and Problem-Solving Application Cases. New in this edition, each chapter concludes with a section entitled "Making Connections," in which we provide a list of specific applications of chapter content for students and managers. Beyond these valuable changes, the following outlines some of the more notable changes by chapter.

CHAPTER 1

- New content on the implications of OB for students' jobs and careers.

- Expanded and enhanced section on ethics, including expanded treatment on the prevalence of cheating and other forms of unethical conduct at school and work; revised and further developed section on ethical dilemmas and whistleblowers; revised and enhanced content on the importance of soft versus hard skills; expanded explanation of the importance of self-awareness for personal development and job and career success.

- Updated survey results outlining skills most sought by employers.

- New Winning at Work feature provides insight and guidance on how to deal with challenges in the hiring process, including the growing role of artificial intelligence and how to effectively get past these virtual gatekeepers.

- New Applying OB feature on how self-awareness can help one build a fulfilling career.

- Updated and refined the 3-Step Approach to Solving Problems Using OB.

CHAPTER 2

- New content on the factors that shape the values of Generation Z; increasing employee commitment, with best practices used by Hilton, Salesforce, and Cisco.

- New examples clarify content about Schwartz's value theory and explain cognitive dissonance.

- Updated statistics on employee engagement around the world; new data on employee satisfaction in the U.S.; new statistics on telecommuting; new research on accounting/financial performance and customer service/satisfaction as outcomes of job satisfaction.

- New Winning at Work feature on creating your own sense of employee engagement.

- New Problem-Solving Application features on McDonald's workers protesting sexual harassment at work; Netflix's approach to sexual harassment in the workplace.

- New OB in Action feature on how companies foster employee engagement.

- New Applying OB features on ways to implement telecommuting for employees; using job satisfaction to reduce employee turnover.

- New end-of-chapter Problem-Solving Application Case on Walmart's values under scrutiny.

CHAPTER 3

- New section on the dark side of personality, the dark triad: narcissism, psychopathy, and Machiavellianism; new coverage of emotional intelligence, including the most recent research and ways in which to develop one's EI; new content on the potential and actual success of introverts in the workplace; new content on how to manage emotions during the job search process.

- Expanded section on brain training, using current research findings and applications; streamlined treatment of multiple intelligences with new, compelling examples; updated and streamlined material related to core self-evaluations.

- Updated research and practical implications of intelligences, linking Big 5 personality dimensions to performance.

- New Winning at Work feature illustrating the career implications of OB, with guidance on which interview questions students should be prepared to answer and ask.

- New Applying OB features on what to look for in a manager; managing emotions during the job search.

- New OB in Action features on intelligence testing; one of the richest self-made women in America (who also epitomizes self-efficacy).

- New Problem-Solving Application on Uber's former CEO, Travis Kalanick.
- New end-of-chapter Problem-Solving Application Case on the fall of John Schnatter, founder of Papa John's Pizza.
- New Legal/Ethical Challenge on drug testing with the recent legalization of marijuana in some states.

CHAPTER 4

- New, expanded discussion and illustration of the four stages of social perception; new content on diversity, including new discussion of assumptions about diversity and new examples about the use of quotas when it comes to hiring practices; new example to elaborate on the self-serving bias.
- New research on how a person's appearance affects our perception and their ability to get hired; updated research on stereotypes; new results of gender research; updated trends and statistics related to diversity, including the topic of pay equity for men and women and research on unwelcoming workplace environments.
- New Applying OB features on developing cultural awareness to enhance perception; the best companies for Millennial workers.
- New OB in Action features on the use of virtual technologies for job interviews and recruitment; how U.S. companies are using product design to reach a diverse customer base.
- New Problem-Solving Application about firefighters suing for age discrimination.
- Updated end-of-chapter Problem-Solving Application Case on the diversity profile of technology companies.
- New Legal/Ethical Challenge about patient requests versus employees' civil rights.

CHAPTER 5

- New content on equity sensitivity.
- New illustrations of extrinsic and intrinsic motivation; new examples to illustrate key theories including Maslow's theory, self-determination theory, and equity/justice theory; new examples to illustrate the concept of goal setting and the application of the job characteristics model.
- New research on employees' opinions about performance feedback and pay; updated

research and examples on job design, job crafting, and i-deals.
- New Winning at Work feature on how to negotiate for a pay raise at work.
- New Problem-Solving Applications about employee benefits at Walmart; symphony orchestra members going on strike.
- New OB in Action feature about job swapping and job rotation opportunities.
- New end-of-chapter Problem-Solving Application Case on why Amazon workers are not feeling motivated.
- New Legal/Ethical Challenge about whether Sears executives should receive bonuses while taking the company through bankruptcy.

CHAPTER 6

- New content on the primary outputs and functions of performance management; applied goalsetting to jobs and careers; the major reasons performance management is criticized; the growing role of technology in performance management; contemporary performance management, highlighting that it is now continual and includes more coaching and ongoing feedback; how to improve performance monitoring.
- Revised Winning at Work feature on best practices for productivity.
- New Applying OB features on goal-setting; responding to negative feedback; effective coaching.
- New OB in Action features on ID checks; monitoring for performance; compensation.
- New Problem-Solving Application on incentivizing teachers in one underperforming school district.
- New end-of-chapter Problem-Solving Application Case on the consequences resulting from Wells Fargo's use of incentives.
- New Legal/Ethical Challenge on the practice of employers' asking about current salary.

CHAPTER 7

- New content on positive and negative deviance; how students can increase their flourishing at school; turning rejection in the job search process into positive motivation.

- Updated and expanded section on doing well and doing good, including three qualifying criteria and further development of how this occurs across levels of OB (individual, group, and organizational); expanded material on how to insert more positivity in one's work; organizational climate; revised material on the history and current role of positivity in OB; prosocial behaviors.

- Refined, updated, and expanded research, applications, and benefits of mindfulness at work; updated research and applications of resilience, optimism, and signature strengths at work.

- New Winning at Work feature on boosting performance with productivity.

- New Applying OB features on how managing internal responses can improve performance; boosting positivity with a fun work environment; fostering positive candidate experiences during job interviews.

- New OB in Action features on socially-responsible investing; mindfulness at major healthcare, biotech, and industrial companies; employee wellness via resistance training at a major health system; how one fast-casual health food business fosters positive culture

- New Problem-Solving Application on Amazon's acquisition of Whole Foods and reckoning of the two companies' values.

- New end-of-chapter Problem-Solving Application Case on how aggressive marketing created an opioid epidemic.

- New Legal/Ethical Challenge on hiring those with criminal pasts.

CHAPTER 8

- New section differentiating groups and teams using three characteristics: dependence, accountability, and time.

- Revised and updated content on formal and informal groups and their respective functions; group and team norms; types of teams, especially related to virtual team challenges and solutions; updated and expanded content on trust: what it is, why it is important, and how to repair it when damaged.

- Expanded and refined content on team effectiveness, including new material on the characteristics of high performing teams and how to use conflict to improve teamwork.

- Revised and expanded research and application related to social-loafing (how to prevent and overcome it); updated research and content on team adaptive capacity.

- New Applying OB features on cultivating cohesiveness to improve the function of groups and teams; the benefits of microinternships for both employers and students.

- New OB in Action features on how T-Mobile has changed their customer service approach by working in teams; how conflict and tension can be the key to better teams.

- New end-of-chapter Problem-Solving Application Case on the predicaments that Boeing faces with its 737 Max airliner.

CHAPTER 9

- New content on media richness; social listening; generational differences regarding the role of digital devices and communication expectations and norms; social media and OB.

- New subsection on phubbing (phone snubbing) and FOMO (fear of losing out); new discussion on nondefensive communication.

- New research on media richness, managers' use of empathy; tips on managing e-mail; statistics on social media and OB.

- New OB in Action features on communication transparency at a skin-care company; how empathy is good for business; crowdsourcing success stories at Lego and Frito-Lay.

- New Applying OB feature on how to ace a video job interview.

- New end-of-chapter Problem-Solving Application Case about United Airlines' turbulent communications strategy.

- New Legal/Ethical Challenge on whether social media posts impact the cost of life insurance premiums.

CHAPTER 10

- New section on harassment—what it is and how to prevent it at work.

- New content on functional versus dysfunctional conflict: causes and outcomes; intergroup conflict material; creating the climate for psychological safety; framing negotiation as a skill, task, or even a game—with the goal of improving your attitude related to negotiation and thus improving the outcomes.

- Revised and updated content related to conflict avoidance, including reasons why people avoid conflict, how to avoid avoiding conflict, and the desired outcomes of conflict management.

- Expanded and updated sections related to work-life conflict, with a new focus on harmony or integration of life's; modern conflict at work; civility at work, including its forms, prevalence, and costs; programming functional conflict and conflict handling styles; ethics and negotiations.

- New Applying OB features on how to explain your departure from one job while interviewing for another; psychological safety at Google; how to ask for a larger salary or a raise.

- New OB in Action features on dealing with conflict; the battle between two unions involved in the creation of shows and movies.

- New Problem-Solving Application on the Fair Food Program.

- New Problem-Solving Application Case on Facebook's struggles with protection of data and privacy.

- New Legal/Ethical Challenge on arbitration versus litigation.

CHAPTER 11

- New section on artificial intelligence and its increasing use in decision making.

- Expanded discussion of Kahneman's two ways of thinking; updated information on data analytic jobs and majors; new examples for the four types of decision-making styles; new examples of bounded rationality, intuition, big data, analytical decision making, and creativity.

- New data on use of heuristics by physicians; new statistics about use of big data;

new research on the importance of creativity and curiosity within organizations.

- New Winning at Work feature about how to practice critical thinking skills for decision making.

- New OB in Action features on improving an airport terminal under bounded rationality; how big data helps advance the health care industry; how shaking up your routine may spark creativity.

- New Problem-Solving Application on how cognitive bias was partly to blame for California's devastating wildfires.

- New end-of-chapter Problem-Solving Application Case on Airbus's decision to cease production of its A380 airliner.

- New Legal/Ethical Challenge on whether college students should be expelled if their parents cheated to get them into school.

CHAPTER 12

- Revised content on common influence tactics, including current and compelling examples of students, #MeToo, and employees; political tactics, highlighting the increasing activism by employees, students, and other groups; political behavior, uncertainty, performance, and change; the tactic of blame and levels of political action; apologies—when and how to use them effectively.

- Updated and expanded research on the five bases of power, with a focus on negative legitimate and referent power.

- New Applying OB features on social media influencers; etiquette in the hiring process; body art in the workplace.

- New OB in Action features on giving tax breaks and other incentives to billion-dollar companies; employee activism; the effects of student activism on companies and corporations.

- New end-of-chapter Problem-Solving Application Case on Nike and the MeToo Movement.

- New Legal/Ethical Challenge on companies who impose their leaders' values on employees.

CHAPTER 13

- New section on abusive supervision and what strategies organizations can implement to eliminate such behavior.

- New content on the leadership model developed by Kouzes and Posner; the four ways of creating psychological empowerment; the four behaviors demonstrated by transformational leaders.

- New statistics on why leadership is so important in today's organizations; new research on leadership traits and task and relational leadership; new research about leader-member exchange model of leadership.

- New OB in Action features on how one university used task leadership to help reclaim the national college football championship; abusive leadership at a local pharmacy.

- New Problem-Solving Application on Barnes & Noble's search for a new CEO.

- New end-of-chapter Problem-Solving Application Case on Elon Musk and his leadership behavior.

- New Legal/Ethical Challenge on whether store managers should force employees to pierce childrens' ears against their wishes.

CHAPTER 14

- Expanded discussion of sustainability as a key driver of organizational success.

- New examples for the three levels of organizational culture; the four cultural types in the competing values framework; the 12 mechanisms to change organizational culture; the three stages of socialization; the career and psychosocial functions of mentoring; how human and social capital enhance the benefits of mentoring.

- Updated research for the three stages of socialization; new illustrations on the importance of organizational culture; new examples of the career and psychosocial functions of mentoring.

- New OB in Action feature about companies that demonstrate sustainability leadership.

- New Problem-Solving Application about Sprouts Farmers Market and its organizational culture.

- New Applying OB feature about key strategies for cultivating a network and mentoring relationship.

- New end-of-chapter Problem-Solving Application Case about the culture clashes at Ford Motor Company.

CHAPTER 15

- New introductory section and illustration that provide an overview of how organizational structure and innovation impact organizational effectiveness.

- Shifted discussion of assessing organizational effectiveness to the end of the chapter to provide a clearer link between implementing organizational design and evaluating its effectiveness using various metrics, including the Balanced Scorecard.

- Updated examples on learning organizations; the seven types of organizational structure; innovation in organizations.

- New research on the effects of open-office design on individual, group, and organizational outcomes; updated research related to learning organizations and innovation in organizations.

- New Problem-Solving Applications about gig workers' growing influence in the labor market; AMD and its struggles to innovate.

- New end-of-chapter Problem-Solving Application Case about one major bookseller and the challenges it faces to stay in business.

- Updated Legal/Ethical Challenge about universities' tax-exempt status and the response from their local communities.

CHAPTER 16

- New section on confronting and effectively overcoming failures at work.

- New material contrasting fatigue versus tiredness and consequences at work; the role and characteristics of change agents; tips on overcoming resistance to change.

- Revised and expanded content on forces for change; updated material on using missions to motivate change; revised content on resistance to change—its causes and how to overcome it; revised content on stress at work, including statistics, causes, and costs.

- Streamlined and updated research and examples related to common models of change; forces for change; managing stress.
- New Winning at Work feature on relocating.
- New OB in Action features on turnover among CEOs; improving lives with shoes.

- New Applying OB features on answering behavioral interview questions; how to rant productively.
- New Problem-Solving Application on the AT&T/Time Warner merger.
- New end-of-chapter Problem-Solving Application Case on the reinvention of Toys R Us.

- *"I want a good job, one that I like and is fulfilling. How do I know which job and company are a good fit for me?"*

- *"I know that this job and company provide good opportunities for me, but what can I do to be sure I actually realize these opportunities?"*

- *"I can't stand my job, but I need the money. Should I talk to my boss or just quit?"*

- *"I am taking a class with 50 percent of the grade due to teamwork. My team has four members and two of us are doing all the work. I've been talking to the team, but the two members still aren't doing their share. I am at a loss for what to do."*

- *"How do I negotiate a salary and benefits for my new job, or a raise for the one I have?"*

Each of these scenarios presents a *problem*. We all are faced with problems every day, and our ability to solve problems can set us apart from others in our jobs and careers. In fact, surveys consistently show that problem solving is one of the skills most valued by employers. For this reason, we designed *Organizational Behavior*, 3e, to help students become more effective problem solvers. *Students who are effective problem solvers today become valued leaders tomorrow.*

The third edition of *Organizational Behavior* relies on three key strategies to help students use OB knowledge to solve problems:

- Consistent 3-Step Problem-Solving Approach.

- Applied, practical features.

- User-centric design.

3-Step Problem-Solving Approach

Given *problem solving* is one of the skills most sought by employers, we help students develop instead of hone this skill. We teach them to use a **3-Step Problem-Solving Approach**—(1) define the problem, (2) identify the causes, and (3) recommend a solution. This approach is introduced in Chapter One and used multiple times in each subsequent chapter. To complement the 3-Step Approach, we also developed the **Organizing Framework for Understanding and Applying OB.** This framework is used in two ways. First, it provides students a means for organizing OB concepts into three categories (inputs, processes, and outcomes) as they learn them. This facilitates student learning and shows how concepts relate to each other. Second, it is an important and complementary tool for problem solving. Problems are often defined in terms of outcomes in the Organizing Framework, and the causes are commonly found in the inputs and processes elements. Students use this framework in every chapter to solve problems confronted by real organizations and employees.

We provide many opportunities for students to practice using the 3-Step Problem-Solving Approach. Problem-Solving Application mini cases are inserted throughout each chapter. These provide numerous opportunities for students to apply their OB knowledge and practice their problem solving skills to real companies and people. The longer **Problem-Solving Application Case** at the end of each chapter presents more complex and current business cases containing one or more problems that illustrate OB concepts included in a particular chapter. A version of the Organizing Framework is presented in each chapter and is populated with relevant concepts from that chapter, which students use to define and solve problems presented in the various features. This capstone **Cumulative Case** activity provides students the opportunity to apply the 3-Step Problem-Solving Approach on an actual situation affecting a specific firm (Tesla) in **Connect.**

We carry the 3-Step Problem-Solving Approach into **Connect,** McGraw-Hill's market-leading digital platform, and provide students with numerous opportunities to observe how different decisions can lead to different outcomes. We also offer *new* critical-thinking application exercises tied to the Problem-Solving Application boxes and Problem-Solving Application Cases, giving students additional practice with applying the 3-Step Approach. These activities are a

"My students have embraced the problem-solving approach . . . and are excelling as a result. They tell me in their feedback that they 'get it.' To me, that proves success and that learning has taken place."

David D. Mull
—Columbia College of Missouri

combination of **case analyses, video cases, and click-and-drag exercises.**

Applied, Practical Approach

The third edition repeatedly demonstrates the practical value of OB concepts in solving real-world problems in students' professional and personal lives. **OB in Action** boxes illustrate OB concepts or theories *in action* in the real world, featuring well-known companies. **Applying OB** boxes offer students "how-to" guidance on applying their knowledge in both their professional and personal lives. Appearing at the end of each chapter are *new* **Takeaway** features that explain to students the practical value of OB concepts—one for their personal use now (**Takeaways for Me**) and the other for managers (**Takeaways for Managers**).

Legal/Ethical Challenges ask students to choose from several proposed courses of action or invent their own to resolve a business situation that falls into a gray area of ethics at work.

Connect provides a multitude of opportunities for active practice and application of concepts learned during class or while completing assigned reading. **SmartBook** is another key component. This adaptive and data-driven reading experience gives students ample opportunity to develop mastery of key learning objectives tied to core OB concepts, while also providing instructors real-time snapshots of student comprehension.

User-Centric Approach

It is important for us to offer *users,* whether students or instructors, a tool that is easy to navigate, easy to digest, and exceptionally practical. We therefore have taken great care to create content, craft our writing, and include features that focus on the needs and interests of the user. To that end, **Learning Objectives** and **"The Bigger Picture"** feature open the main sections of each chapter and immediately place students in a practical learning mode.

We also present content in **digestible chunks** of text, with frequent opportunities to engage with or reflect on the material. The **Winning at Work** feature opens each chapter with a list of practical tips related to a highly relevant topic for work and/or school, such as negotiating a salary for a new job or a pay raise, or how to manage meetings more effectively. **Self-Assessments** in **Connect** allow students to evaluate personal characteristics related to OB concepts, as well as to reflect on their own characteristics and behavior. **What Did I Learn** provides students with a review of the chapter's key concepts, an invitation to answer important questions relating to chapter content, and a summary of the Organizing Framework for a given chapter.

Connect gives instructors the foundations for creating a **course** that fits their individual teaching needs. The **Teaching Resource Manual** offers a playbook for creating and delivering a discussion-based learning environment in which students practice and apply concepts in a more active manner. The extensively revised **Test Bank** offers greater opportunity to assess students on OB concepts at a higher level, with essay and scenario-based questions to engage students' problem-solving skills. Finally, a comprehensive set of **PowerPoint** slides provide guidance in addressing key concepts.

Developing Effective Problem Solvers Today, Valued Leaders Tomorrow

Organizational Behavior, 3e, explicitly addresses OB implications for students' jobs and careers, showing how OB provides them with the higher-level soft skills employers seek, such as problem solving, critical thinking, leadership, and decision making. We strongly believe that applying OB theories and concepts provides tremendous value to students' lives today and throughout their careers. The understanding and application of OB enhances student effectiveness at school and work, both today and tomorrow.

> *"(This) is a text with a practical approach . . . Theory is there, but explained in a hands-on manner, which fits well into the way I present the course."*
>
> **Dr. Floyd Ormsbee**
> **—Clarkson University**

> *"Practical, student centered, highly relevant to both students and employers needs. (It) hits all of the most critical topics of OB in an engaging and visually appealing way, and includes a critical thinking approach that is easy to learn and use."*
>
> **Jody Tolan**
> **—University of Southern California Marshall School of Business**

You're in the driver's seat.

Want to build your own course? No problem. Prefer to use our turnkey, prebuilt course? Easy. Want to make changes throughout the semester? Sure. And you'll save time with Connect's auto-grading too.

65%

Less Time Grading

Laptop: McGraw-Hill; Woman/dog: George Doyle/Getty Images

They'll thank you for it.

Adaptive study resources like SmartBook® 2.0 help your students be better prepared in less time. You can transform your class time from dull definitions to dynamic debates. Find out more about the powerful personalized learning experience available in SmartBook 2.0 at **www.mheducation.com/highered/connect/smartbook**

Make it simple, make it affordable.

Connect makes it easy with seamless integration using any of the major Learning Management Systems—Blackboard®, Canvas, and D2L, among others—to let you organize your course in one convenient location. Give your students access to digital materials at a discount with our inclusive access program. Ask your McGraw-Hill representative for more information.

Padlock: Jobalou/Getty Images

Solutions for your challenges.

A product isn't a solution. Real solutions are affordable, reliable, and come with training and ongoing support when you need it and how you want it. Our Customer Experience Group can also help you troubleshoot tech problems—although Connect's 99% uptime means you might not need to call them. See for yourself at **status.mheducation.com**

Checkmark: Jobalou/Getty Images

FOR STUDENTS

Effective, efficient studying.

Connect helps you be more productive with your study time and get better grades using tools like SmartBook 2.0, which highlights key concepts and creates a personalized study plan. Connect sets you up for success, so you walk into class with confidence and walk out with better grades.

Study anytime, anywhere.

Download the free ReadAnywhere app and access your online eBook or SmartBook 2.0 assignments when it's convenient, even if you're offline. And since the app automatically syncs with your eBook and SmartBook 2.0 assignments in Connect, all of your work is available every time you open it. Find out more at **www.mheducation.com/readanywhere**

"I really liked this app—it made it easy to study when you don't have your text-book in front of you."

- Jordan Cunningham,
Eastern Washington University

No surprises.

The Connect Calendar and Reports tools keep you on track with the work you need to get done and your assignment scores. Life gets busy; Connect tools help you keep learning through it all.

Learning for everyone.

McGraw-Hill works directly with Accessibility Services Departments and faculty to meet the learning needs of all students. Please contact your Accessibility Services office and ask them to email accessibility@mheducation.com, or visit **www.mheducation.com/about/accessibility** for more information.

Acknowledgments

We could not have completed this product without the help and support of a great number of people. It all began with the vision of our director, Michael Ablassmier. He assembled a fantastic team to help create a truly unique product and pushed us to create new and applied features valued by the market. Among our first-rate team at McGraw-Hill, we want to acknowledge key contributors: Senior Product Developer Anne Ehrenworth's assistance was instrumental in structuring the editorial process; Cate Rzasa, content developer, Debbie Clare, Senior Marketing Manager, helped us implement our vision for creative and proactive marketing; Harvey Yep lead content project manager, and Keri Johnson, senior content project manager, led the core and Connect components through the production process; Matt Diamond, designer, and Debra Kubiak, design manager, worked with us to streamline the design and come up with a creative new cover concept; and Allison Marker, editorial coordinator, provided tremendous support behind the scenes.

We also want to thank Patrick Soleymani, George Mason University, for his work on the Teaching Resource Manual. Patrick also contributed in many other ways to help us achieve our vision. We are also grateful to Lara Hobson for her work on the Test Bank, and to Jake Heller for his work on the PowerPoints. Deep gratitude goes to Ravi Shanmugam for his work on Connect, and Ken Carson, Grove City College, for all his work on researching and developing the Self-Assessment feedback.

We would like to acknowledge the following instructors for providing feedback to shape this product. Special thanks goes to:

Tim Basadur,
Concordia University Chicago

James Bishop,
New Mexico State University–Las Cruces

B.D. Boardman,
University of Phoenix

Adeline Boomgaard,
University of Phoenix

Brenda D. Bradford,
Missouri Baptist University

Chris Bresnahan,
University of Southern California

Mark Burdsall,
University of Pittsburgh

E. Holly Buttner, PhD.,
University of North Carolina at Greensboro–Bryan School of Business & Economics

Dr. Bill Carnes,
Metropolitan State University of Denver–College of Business

Ileene Chernoff,
University of Phoenix

Donna Chlopak,
Montclair State University

Amanda L. Christensen,
University of Cincinnati

Dean Cleavenger,
University of Central Florida

Elizabeth Cooper
University of Rhode Island

Dana M. Cosby,
Western Kentucky University

Matthew Cronin,
George Mason University

Joe Daly,
Appalachian State University

Caitlin A. Demsky,
Oakland University

Diane Denslow,
University of North Florida

Dr. Anant Deshpande,
SUNY Empire State College

John DeSpagna,
Nassau Community College

Kristen DeTienne,
Brigham Young University

Ken Dunegan,
Cleveland State University

Steven M. Elias,
New Mexico State University

Aimee Ellis,
Ithaca College

W. Randy Evans,
University of Tennessee at Chattanooga

Michelle H. Feller,
Weber State University

Martin L. Fogelman,
SUNY Albany

Charla S. Fraley,
Columbus State Community College

John D. Fuehrer,
Baldwin Wallace University

Allison S. Gabriel,
University of Arizona

Jane Whitney Gibson,
Nova Southeastern University

Cynthia Gilliand,
University of Arizona

Lydia Gilmore,
Columbus State Community College

Simona Giorgi,
Boston College

Early Godfrey,
Gardner Webb University

Roy Lynn Godkin,
Lamar University

Connie Golden,
Lakeland Community College

Nora Alicia González,
University of Phoenix

Dr. Deborah Good,
University of Pittsburgh

Christina Goodell,
Florida State College at Jacksonville

Meghan Griffin,
Daytona State College

Samuel Hazen,
Tarleton State University

Kim Hester,
Arkansas State University

Lara Hobson,
Western Michigan University

Wayne Hochwarter,
Florida State University

Madison Holloway,
Metropolitan State University of Denver

Brooks Holtom,
Georgetown University

Jenni Hunt,
Southern Illinois University–Edwardsville

Teresa Hutchinson,
University of Phoenix

Kendra Ingram,
Texas A&M University–Commerce

Hank Karp,
Hampton University

Stacey R. Kessler,
Montclair State University

Anthony J. Kos,
Youngstown State University

Michael Kosicek,
Indiana University of Pennsylvania

Christine L Krull,
IUPUI

Mika Tatum Kusar,
Fort Lewis College

Caroline Leffall,
Bellevue College

Fengru Li,
University of Montana Business School

Katie Liljequist,
Brigham Young University

Gregory P. Lucht,
University of Phoenix

Douglas Mahony,
Lehigh University

Jennifer Malarski,
Metropolitan State University

Laura Martin,
Midwestern State University

J. J. Massey,
The University of Texas at Tyler

Merrill A. Mayper,
University of Phoenix

Douglas McCabe,
Georgetown University–McDonough School of Business

Lorianne D. Mitchell,
East Tennessee State University

Dan Morrell,
Middle Tennessee State University

Paula C. Morrow,
Iowa State University

Robert Muliero,
University of Phoenix

David D. Mull,
Columbia College of Missouri

Daniel F. Nehring,
Morehead State University

Jeananne Nicholls,
Slippery Rock University

Dr. Floyd Ormsbee,
Clarkson University

Bradley P. Owens,
State University of New York at Buffalo

John Pepper,
The University of Kansas

Jeff Peterson,
Utah Valley State College

Don Powell,
University of North Texas

Gregory R. Quinet,
Southern Polytechnic State University

Samuel Rabinowitz,
Rutgers University–Camden

Jude A. Rathburn,
University of Wisconsin–Milwaukee

Alicia J. Revely,
Miami University

Herb Ricardo,
Indian River State College

Katherine Robberson,
Southern Illinois University–Edwardsville

Joe Rode,
Miami University–Oxford

Matt Rodgers,
The Ohio State University

Deborah Roebuck,
Kennesaw State University

Kristie Rogers,
University of Kansas

Hannah R. Rothstein,
CUNY Baruch College

Christopher Roussin,
Suffolk University

David Ruderman,
University of Colorado at Denver

Frances McKee Ryan,
University of Nevada–Reno

Gordon Schmidt,
Indiana Purdue University–Fort Wayne

Dr. Marina Sebastijanovic,
University of Houston

Holly Schroth,
University of California

Ravi Shanmugam,
University of Kansas

Richard G. Sims,
University of Phoenix

Kenneth Solano,
Northeastern University

Patrick Soleymani,
George Mason University

Dan Spencer,
University of Kansas

Dr. Atul Teckchandani,
California State University–Fullerton

Mussie T. Tessema,
Winona State University

Linda Thiede Thomas,
Bellevue University

Jody Tolan,
University of Southern California–Marshall School of Business

Mary L. Tucker,
Ohio University

Brian Usilaner,
University of Maryland–University College

Wellington Williams, Jr.,
University of Phoenix

Robert M. Wolter,
IUPUI School of Engineering and Technology

John G. Zappala,
Central Michigan University

Finally, I hope you enjoy this textbook. Best wishes for happiness, health, and success!

Angelo Kinicki

brief contents

contents

3   INDIVIDUAL DIFFERENCES AND EMOTIONS

4   SOCIAL PERCEPTION AND MANAGING DIVERSITY

5 FOUNDATIONS OF EMPLOYEE MOTIVATION

6 PERFORMANCE MANAGEMENT

7 POSITIVE ORGANIZATIONAL BEHAVIOR

PART TWO
Groups 295

8 GROUPS AND TEAMS

9 COMMUNICATION IN THE DIGITAL AGE

10 MANAGING CONFLICT AND NEGOTIATIONS

11 DECISION MAKING AND CREATIVITY

12 POWER, INFLUENCE, AND POLITICS

13 LEADERSHIP EFFECTIVENESS

PART THREE
Organizational Processes   547

14 ORGANIZATIONAL CULTURE, SOCIALIZATION, AND MENTORING

15 ORGANIZATIONAL DESIGN, EFFECTIVENESS, AND INNOVATION

16 MANAGING CHANGE AND STRESS

Organizational Behavior

A Practical, Problem-Solving Approach

PART ONE

Individual Behavior

Making OB Work for Me

After reading this chapter, you should be able to:

LO 1-1 Describe the value of OB to your job and career.

LO 1-2 Identify factors that influence unethical conduct and how it affects performance.

LO 1-3 Utilize OB to solve problems and increase your effectiveness.

LO 1-4 Explain the practical relevance and power of OB to help solve problems.

LO 1-5 Utilize the Organizing Framework for Understanding and Applying OB.

LO 1-6 Apply the Organizing Framework to the 3-Step Problem-Solving Approach.

LO 1-7 Describe the implications of OB knowledge and tools for you and managers.

In this chapter you'll learn that the study and practice of OB often organizes the workplace into three levels—the individual, the group or team, and the organization. We therefore structured this book the same way—Part One is devoted to individual-level phenomena (job satisfaction), Part Two to groups and teams (team cohesiveness), and Part Three to the organizational level (innovation). Make sure you read the final section of Chapter 1 for a preview of the many concepts you'll learn in the book. You'll also find a summary and application of the Organizing Framework for Understanding and Applying OB and the 3-Step Problem-Solving Approach. These are fundamental tools we created not only to help you learn more effectively, but also to help you apply and realize the true value of OB for you personally.

Winning at Work

Your Future

Your future starts with your next job, whether it is your very first or your tenth. Once you've identified a desirable job to apply for, the challenge becomes—how do you get that job? Part of the answer is to give employers what they want, and as you'll learn employers want employees who possess and effectively use OB knowledge and tools.

Employers Want OB

This is supported by the findings of countless surveys, such as one by ManpowerGroup with thousands of employers, which found 61 percent rate people (OB) skills as the most important trait in new hires.[1] Research by the National Association of Colleges and Employers (NACE) routinely shows the three skills most valued by employers are critical thinking, problem solving, and teamwork.[2] Building your skills in these areas and others is the overarching goal of this book. The Applying OB box later in this chapter differentiates and describes hard and soft skills in greater detail, but what we cover here Is how to emphasize these on your resume.

Talking to Robots

As you likely know, many companies use applicant tracking software (ATS) that not only organizes the hundreds or even thousands of applications received, but also makes them searchable. ATS scans for key words inserted by humans, scores them accordingly, and then pares the applications based on these scores. This means you need to put points on the board with the robot. Even if you are indeed the best candidate, if you're not seen—no interview, no offer, no job. And for the human eyes that ultimately review your resume, some estimates suggest a recruiter spends approximately 6 seconds reviewing your resume.[3] So, what can you do?

First, it is your responsibility to communicate to the prospective employer (both their ATS robots and humans) what you can do for them. Tell them in direct and specific terms what they want to know and what you can do for them.

Use Their Language and Tell Them What You Can Offer

1. *Use the Same Language.* You are well served to use the same words a prospective employer uses in their job ads. To ensure your spellings match theirs consider writing things in multiple forms. Your degree, for instance, "I have a bachelor's in management (BS in management)," includes two different versions and increases likelihood of being "picked."

2. *Identify Key Skills for the Job.* If the most Important skills are not listed or evident in the job posting, then what do you do? Ask! Whomever you can communicate with simply ask, "I know the posting notes a number of important skills, but what are the two or three that are most important?"

3. *Don't Overlook Other Key Words.* Your skills of course matter, but also do your research and include key words for Important customers, how they are served, as well as key products and services.

4. *Don't Just List or Tell—Illustrate!* Better than simply listing are descriptions of how you've used these at school (team

projects, practice, sports, or clubs) and/or work (internships, full-time jobs, or volunteer work). Problem solving, critical thinking, creativity, teamwork, collaboration, communication, active listening, self-awareness, attention to detail, strategic thinking.

5. *Your Commitment to Development.* Be sure to Include training or workshops (outside of school) you've done, as it will show you are aware of the importance of these skills and are committed to developing them.

6. *Position Matters.* Like real estate, location matters so be thoughtful as to where you put key words. Education-related information is obvious enough, in the education section, but others depend on the resume format you choose. For instance, skills-based resumes are now more popular compared to old-school chronological resumes, especially if you don't have much experience yet or are changing careers.

7. *Don't Overlook the Cover Letter.* This is an opportunity to include and highlight the most Important key skills, if you've identified them as suggested in #1 above.

8. *What's in a Name?* A lot! Just as you expect to be addressed by your name in an interview, assume the ATS and humans who ultimately get involved in the hiring process also value names. Specifically, be sure to include the company name and job title. Don't be generic, such as: "I want to join a company that _____," or "I want to contribute to a valuable company . . ."[4]

Bottom line: Whether your major or job experience is accounting, finance, marketing, IT/IS, or something else, the fact is that jobs increasingly require OB knowledge and skills. "Everyone has to work across silos," says Becky Frankiewicz, president of Manpower Group North America. And since OB skills "are not usually taught in business schools or undergraduate programs, they are qualities that you have to burnish on your own, preferably in the early stages of your career."[5]

What's Ahead in This Chapter

You'll learn how OB can drive your job and career success. You'll grasp the difference between hard and soft skills and the value of developing both, as well as the importance of self-awareness. We'll show how ethics are integral to long-term individual and organizational success, and we'll introduce a problem-solving approach you can use in a wide variety of situations at school, at work, and in life. What really powers this book is our Organizing Framework for Understanding and Applying OB, which we introduce mid-chapter. This framework will help you organize and apply OB concepts and tools as you learn them. To show you the power of the Organizing Framework, we conclude the chapter with a preview of the many concepts, theories, and tools you will learn. We then show you how to apply this knowledge using our 3-Step Problem-Solving Approach. We think you'll be intrigued by this glimpse into all you will learn in this book and course. Let's get started!

1.1 USE KNOWLEDGE OF OB TO ENHANCE YOUR PERFORMANCE AND CAREER

THE BIGGER PICTURE

Are you uncertain about the value of organizational behavior (OB) and how it fits into your school curriculum or your professional life? This section will explain how OB can be valuable to you. You'll see how OB knowledge and tools go far beyond common sense and can enhance your personal job performance and career success. For instance, you will learn what it takes to get hired versus what it takes to get promoted, the importance of both hard and soft skills, and the role of self-awareness in your success.

LO 1-1

Describe the value of OB to your job and career.

The term *organizational behavior (OB)* describes an interdisciplinary field dedicated to understanding and managing people at work. To achieve this goal, OB draws on research and practice from many disciplines, including:

- Anthropology
- Economics
- Ethics
- Management
- Organizational theory
- Political science
- Psychology
- Sociology
- Neuroscience
- Vocational counseling

From this list you can see that OB is very much an applied and broad discipline that draws from many sources. Throughout this book we will help you see the relevance and value of OB for your own job and career.

Let's begin by looking at how OB compares to your other courses, explaining the contingency perspective, which is the premise of contemporary OB, and exploring the importance of both hard and soft skills.

How OB Fits into My Curriculum and Influences My Success

Organizational behavior is an academic discipline focused on understanding and managing people at work. This includes managing yourself and others both inside and outside the organization, but unlike jobs associated with functional disciplines, such as accounting, marketing, and finance, you will not get a job in OB.

What then is the benefit of learning about OB? The answer is that the *effective application* of OB is critical to your success in all disciplines of work and all job levels. As you'll learn, technical knowledge associated with any given job is important, but your ability to influence, get along with, manage, and get things done through others is what makes the difference. Put more simply—people skills!

Our professional lives are extremely busy and challenging and effectiveness will require a host of both hard and soft skills. Your understanding and application of OB concepts and tools will help you meet the many challenges, perform better, and create more attractive opportunities throughout your career.

Somos Images LLC/Alamy Stock Photo

Applying OB knowledge and tools gives you opportunities, sets you apart from your peers and competition, and contributes to your success. An important part of your success is ability to know which tools to use and under what circumstances. This is described as a contingency approach to managing people and is the foundation of contemporary OB.

A Contingency Perspective—The Contemporary Foundation of OB

A *contingency approach* calls for using the OB concepts and tools that best suit the situation, instead of trying to rely on "one best way." This means there is no single best way to manage people, teams, or organizations. A particular management practice that worked today may not work tomorrow. What worked with one employee may not work with another. The best or most effective course of action instead depends on the situation.

Harvard's Clayton Christensen put it this way: "Many of the widely accepted principles of good management are only situationally appropriate."[6] Put differently, don't use a hammer unless the job involves nails. You'll learn in Chapter 13, for instance, no single leadership style is best and works in all situations. This makes OB very different from many of your other courses in that answers here are rarely black and white, right or wrong, but instead the best answer—the most appropriate behavior—*depends on the situation*. Directly considering situational factors is fundamental to OB and is emphasized throughout this book.

Therefore, to be effective you need to understand and do what is appropriate given the situation, rather than adhering to hard-and-fast rules or defaulting to personal preferences or organizational norms. Organizational behavior specialists, and many effective managers, embrace the contingency approach because it helps them consider the many factors that influence the behavior and performance of individuals, groups, and organizations. Taking a broader, contingent perspective like this is a fundamental key to your success in the short and the long term.

Effectively applying the contingency approach requires self-awareness, which means knowing your own skills, abilities, values, weaknesses, strengths, preferences, and fit with the environment. It also includes knowing how others see you in terms of these same factors. Not surprisingly, self-awareness is key to your success in both the short and long term.[7] The following Applying OB box explains in some detail what self-awareness is and how to build It.

To help increase your self-awareness we include multiple Self-Assessments in every chapter. These are an excellent way to learn about yourself and see how you can apply OB at school, at work, and in your personal life. Go to Connect, complete the assessments, then answer the questions included in each of the Self-Assessment boxes.

Let's start with your motivation to manage others. Many employees never manage others. Some choose not to and some don't get the chance, but what about you? How motivated are you to manage others? Go to conect.mheducation.com and Self-Assessment 1.1 to learn about your motivation for managing others. What you learn might surprise you. Surprised or not, more precisely understanding your motivation to manage others can guide your course selection in college and your job choices in the marketplace.

A central feature of almost any successful development program is self-awareness. Knowing who you are and knowing your preferences are important considerations in personal development.

Lana Isabella/Moment/Getty Images

Applying OB

Self-Awareness Can Help You Build a Fulfilling Career

Employers Care—So Should You. The Stanford Graduate School of Business asked the members of its Advisory Council which skills are most important for their MBA students to learn. The most frequent answer was self-awareness.[8] Self-awareness has been identified as one of the key attributes of successful leaders, as they tend to get along better with others and their companies are more profitable.[9]

Key to Your Development. Larry Bossidy (former CEO of Honeywell) and Ram Charan (world-renowned management expert) said it best in their book *Execution*: "When you know yourself, you are comfortable with your strengths and not crippled by your shortcomings. Self-awareness gives you the capacity to learn from your mistakes as well as your successes. It enables you to keep growing."[10]

Influencing Others. They also argue that you need to know yourself in order to be authentic—real and not fake, the same on the outside as the inside. Authenticity is essential to influencing others, which we discuss in detail in Chapter 12. People don't trust fakes, and it is difficult to influence or manage others if they don't trust you (trust is covered in Chapter 8). The implication is that to have a successful career you need to know who you are, what you want, *and* how others perceive you.

Experience + Power (does not equal) Self-Awareness. Unfortunately, some people's experience and success lead them to be overconfident about their abilities and become less self-aware. Making matters worse, the same research revealed the more senior the leadership position the greater the overconfidence, and only 10 to 15 percent of employees actually meet the criteria of self-awareness, despite nearly all believing they are![11]

Building Your Self-Awareness. Research and practice provide excellent practical guidance:

1. Practice mindfulness daily. We'll explore mindfulness in detail in Chapter 7, but for our purposes here mindfulness involves purposefully focusing your attention on the here and now, yourself, the environment, and those around you in the present moment.
2. Take timeouts. Even if it is just a minute or two, stop what you are doing and do nothing. Don't check your phone, e-mails, or go talk to a coworker. Self-awareness requires time and space, and when you're working under (time) pressure you are most likely to go with your habits and usual ways of thinking, feeling, and acting. This is why true timeouts can foster self-awareness.
3. Keep a diary of strengths and weaknesses. Make and periodically revise a list of your strengths and weaknesses.
4. Take self-assessments. Many tests exist, for example the Myers-Briggs, that measure various personal characteristics and help you learn about yourself. Better still, there are multiple self-assessments in every chapter of this book.
5. Keep ears open, mouth shut. In other words, listen! Self-awareness requires insight and some of the best insights come from others. Seek feedback, listen, and learn.[12]

SELF-ASSESSMENT 1.1

How Strong Is My Motivation to Manage?

Please be prepared to answer these questions if your instructor has assigned Self-Assessment 1.1 in Connect.

1. Does this instrument accurately assess your potential as a manager? Explain.
2. Which of the seven dimensions do you think is likely the best predictor of managerial success? Which is the least? Explain.
3. The instrument emphasizes competition with others in a win-lose mentality. Describe the pros and cons of this approach to management.

"OB Is Just Common Sense"   As professors and consultants we often hear, "OB is just common sense." We can easily refute this inaccurate claim, but instead we simply say— "Even if it is common sense it certainly isn't common practice!" If common sense were all that mattered, managers would always treat employees fairly, businesses would never make "stupid" decisions, and you and other employees would make very few mistakes. Everyone would perform better and be happier.

Moreover, common sense is largely based on experience or logic, both of which have limits, and it suffers three major weaknesses you need to be aware of and avoid:

- **Overreliance on hindsight.** Common sense works best in well-known or stable situations with predictable outcomes—what worked before should work again. But modern business situations are complex and uncertain and require adapting to change, which are exactly the conditions under which common sense is likely to fail. And because it focuses on the past, common sense lacks vision for the future.

- **Lack of rigor.** People comfortable with common-sense responses may not apply the effort required to appropriately analyze and solve problems. If you lack rigor, and aren't especially thorough or precise, then you are unlikely to define the problem accurately, identify the true causes, or recommend the right courses of action.

- **Lack of objectivity.** Common sense can be overly subjective and lack a basis in science. In such cases we are not always able to explain or justify our reasoning to others, which is a sign that common sense lacks objectivity.

OB is a scientific means for overcoming the limits and weaknesses of common sense. The contingency approach in OB means you don't settle for options based simply on experience or common practice if another solution may be more effective. The goals of OB are to give you *more* than common sense, enhance your understanding of situations at work, and guide your behaviors. This in turn will make you more attractive to potential employers and more effective once hired. Let's explore this idea in greater detail, beginning with the importance of possessing and developing both hard and soft skills.

Employers Want Both Hard and Soft Skills

Most of us know the difference between hard and soft skills.

- *Hard skills* **are the technical expertise and knowledge required to do a particular task or job function,** such as financial analysis, accounting, or operations.

- *Soft skills* **relate to human interactions and include both interpersonal skills and personal attributes.**

Susan Vitale, chief marketing officer for iCIMS, an HR software provider described them this way: "Hard skills are what you do, and soft skills are how you do it."[13] Research has long showed people may excel based on hard skills but they often fail because of soft skills.[14] Maybe that's why firms tend to weigh soft skills so heavily when hiring. The *Future of Jobs* report by the World Economic Forum provides compelling supporting evidence. They found the most sought-after skills for graduates in 2020 are problem solving, critical thinking, creativity, and people management.[15]

What do you notice about these four skills? Which are hard skills? None! Instead, all are soft skills, the skills you need to interact with, influence, and perform effectively when working with others.

This is a good news/bad news story. The good news—all of these skills are key topics in this book and can be developed. The bad news is 33 percent of recruiting professionals feel candidates' skills in these areas have declined in the past five years.[16] "Many claim that college grads are lacking in people skills and have trouble solving problems and thinking creatively. . . . Having a college degree and technical skills isn't enough to land their first job."[17]

TABLE 1.1   Four Skills Most Desired by Employers for Workforce 2020[18]

SKILL	DESCRIPTION	THIS BOOK
1. Problem solving	Identifying complex problems and reviewing related information to develop and evaluate options then implement solutions.	Our problem-solving approach is used throughout the book. We repeatedly ask you to apply your knowledge to solve problems at school, at work, and in life.
2. Critical thinking	Using logic and reasoning to identify the strengths and weaknesses of alternate solutions, conclusions, or approaches to problems.	Critical thinking is fundamental to this book and woven throughout. We designed features and exercises to help you think critically and apply your OB knowledge and tools.
3. Creativity	Applying new ideas, processes, and technology to improve products, services, and other outcomes.	Creativity is a function of person and situation factors and can result In new processes and outcomes. All of these are fundamental elements of OB and described in more detail later In this chapter and throughout the book.
4. People management	Motivating, developing, and influencing others to meet individual, group, and organizational goals.	OB is people management which means every chapter provides knowledge and tools to make you a more effective people manager.

Table 1.1 shows four sought-after skills, along with a brief explanation of how we directly address them in this book.

One key aspect of soft skills is that they are *not* job specific. Instead they are **portable skills, more or less relevant in every job, at every level, and throughout your career.**[19] All of these and many more soft skills are represented by OB topics covered in this book, whether as personal attributes or interpersonal skills:

Personal attributes
(with which you build goodwill and trust and demonstrate integrity)

- **Attitudes** (Chapter 2)
- **Personality** (Chapter 3)
- **Teamwork** (Chapter 8)
- **Leadership** (Chapter 13)

Interpersonal skills
(with which you foster respectful interactions)

- **Active listening** (Chapters 12 and 13)
- **Positive attitudes** (Chapters 2 and 7)
- **Effective communication** (Chapter 9)

The takeaway for you? Good interpersonal skills can make a candidate with a less-marketable degree an appealing hire, while a lack of people skills may doom a college grad to unemployment, low pay, or otherwise undesirable and limited opportunities.[20]

How OB Fits into My Career

Hard skills are of course important. Accountants, for instance, need to understand debits and credits, financial analysts must calculate net present value, and both need to understand cash flows. However, to be competitive and give employers what they want, you must develop soft skills too. Some soft skills will even *increase* in importance over your career and help set you apart from the competition. To highlight this point, think about the criteria used for hiring workers versus promoting them.

How to Ace Your Next Interview

Everyone knows that jobs are won or lost during interviews. Here are a few simple tips to help you finish on top.

1. **Create an elevator pitch.** Imagine you're in the elevator with the interviewer and have only 60 seconds to sell yourself. Select your three best-selling points (strengths) and *concisely* explain how each would benefit the company. Stay focused—keep your pitch short and meaningful.

2. **Finish strong.** At the end of the interview state and show your enthusiasm for the opportunity. Also restate your one or two best-selling points and how they will benefit the company.

3. **Prepare for situational questions.** Anticipate questions like, "Why do you want this job?" and, "Tell me about a time when you had a conflict at work and what you did about it." Be prepared to answer them by describing the situation, your behavior, and the resulting impact. Also consider describing what you learned in that situation.

4. **Make your research social.** Reach out to your network *privately* (you don't want everyone to know you're looking) and learn whether anyone has worked for or interviewed with your target company. Learn about the person you're interviewing with on LinkedIn—education, past jobs, positions within the target company. Glassdoor.com and other sites can be a wealth of information on employee experiences and compensation.

5. **Don't trip up on the money.** It's generally best to wait until you have a formal offer in hand before discussing pay. If asked about your salary requirement during the interview, respond by saying, "Are you making me an offer?" The answer will likely be, "No, not yet." But if the interviewer persists, say, "I would prefer to have all the details in hand in order to determine what would be most appropriate and fair. Once I have those, I will happily discuss compensation."[21]

What It Takes to Get Hired   Regardless of where you are in your career today, ask yourself: What criteria were used to hire you for your first job? What factors did your hiring manager consider? (If your first job is still ahead of you, what factors do you think will be most important?) You and most of your peers will identify things like college major, GPA, and internship or other experience. In short, for most jobs you are selected for your technical skills, your ability to do the given job. Whatever the selection criteria, you need to perform during the interview process in order to receive the offer. The Applying OB box provides some useful insights on how to ace interviews.

What It Takes to Get Promoted   Now ask yourself what criteria are used for promotions? Of course, performance in your current job is often a primary consideration. However, you and many other employees may fail to realize that your perceived ability to get things done through others and to manage people will be another important deciding factor. If you and three of your coworkers are all vying for an open management position, then it's likely all four of you perform at a high level. This means performance isn't the only

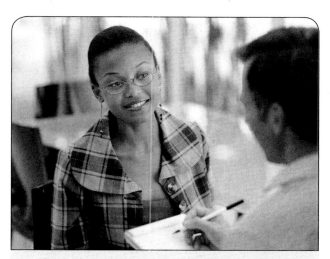

An understanding of OB can provide extremely valuable knowledge and tools to help "sell" yourself during job interviews.
Chris Ryan/OJO Images/age fotostock

deciding factor—all of you are top performers. Instead, it may be your perceived ability to directly or indirectly manage others!

Roxanne Hori, an associate dean at New York University's Stern School of Business, echoes this argument: "Yes, your knowledge of the functional area you're pursuing is important. But to succeed longer term . . . having strong team skills and knowing how to build and manage relationships were seen as just as important." One executive she interviewed suggested that students should "take as much organizational behavior coursework as possible . . . because as you move into leadership roles, the key skills that will determine your success will be around your ability to interact with others in a highly effective fashion."[22] As authors of this book, we agree, but more Importantly we hope after learning the power of OB you'll agree too.

Some career experts, such as Chrissy Scivicque, the CEO of a career coaching and training firm and writer for *Forbes* and *The Wall Street Journal,* go so far as to say that most people have the technical skills to succeed at higher-level jobs. And even if some new technical knowledge is needed it generally is easy to learn. However, as you rise through the hierarchy your job generally will require a more developed set of soft skills, such as communication, emotional intelligence, ethics, and stress management.[23]

We make this point visually in Figure 1.1. It illustrates how technical or job-specific skills decline in importance as you move to levels of higher responsibility, while personal skills increase.

Performance Gives Me Credibility   Performance matters because it gives you credibility with your peers and those you may manage. Be aware that early in your career your bosses will be looking for more than your job performance. They also will evaluate your management potential, and their opinion will affect your future opportunities. So even in a non-management position you need to know how to:

- Apply different motivational tools (Chapter 5).
- Provide constructive feedback (Chapter 6).
- Develop and lead productive teams (Chapters 8 and 13).
- Understand and manage organizational culture and change (Chapters 14 and 16).

Knowledge of OB, therefore, is critical to your individual performance, your ability to work with and manage others, and your career success (promotions, pay raises, increased opportunities). As you may already know, ethics can similarly make or break you at every step of your career, which is why we cover it next.

FIGURE 1.1   Relative Importance of Different Skills Based on Job Level

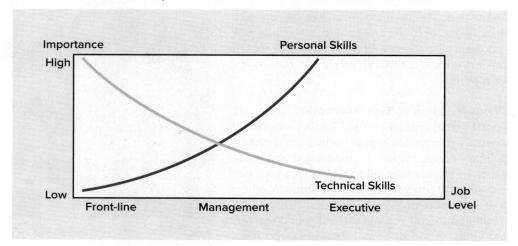

SOURCE: Lombardo, Michael, and Robert Eichinger. *Preventing Derailment: What To Do Before It's Too Late.* North California: Center for Creative Leadership, 1989.

1.2 RIGHT VS. WRONG—ETHICS AND MY PERFORMANCE

THE BIGGER PICTURE

If you were asked, "Do you know right from wrong? Are you secure in your ethics?" of course you would answer yes to both questions. What's interesting is that most people who suffer ethical lapses also answer yes. OB can teach you about the drivers of unethical behavior, and in the process improve your awareness while enabling you to reduce your risk. You'll learn that even though most unethical behavior is not illegal, it still causes tremendous damage to people, their jobs and careers, and their employers. Fortunately, the OB concepts and tools you learn through this course will help you recognize and navigate ethical challenges.

Ethics guides our behavior by identifying right, wrong, and the many shades of gray in between. We will weave discussions of ethics throughout the book for three key reasons.

LO 1-2

Identify factors that influence unethical conduct and how it affects performance.

1. Employees are confronted with ethical challenges at all levels of organizations and throughout their careers.
2. Unethical behavior damages relationships, erodes trust, and thus makes it difficult to influence others and conduct business.
3. Unethical behavior reduces cooperation, loyalty, and contribution, which hurts the performance of individuals, teams, and organizations.

Ethics also gets priority because many OB topics have a direct and substantial influence on the conduct of individuals and organizations. Notably, reward systems (Chapter 6), decision making (Chapter 11), leader behavior (Chapter 13), and organizational culture (Chapter 14) all can powerfully challenge our ethical standards at work. Let's begin by describing cheating, a common form of unethical conduct at school and work.

Cheating

Cheating is a persistent part of reality in sports, school, and business. For instance, with some regularity it seems a marathon runner either enters a race somewhere after the start line or cuts the course (Rory O'Connor in London 2018), a ball is doctored to provide unfair advantage (Cameron Bancroft of the Australia National cricket team), or an individual athlete throws games or shaves points. An investigation of professional tennis revealed a "tsunami" of fixed matches (hundreds) in the 2000s.[24] Then there was the systematic use and cover-up of performance enhancing drugs (PEDs) rampant in major league baseball in the early 2000s, Lance Armstrong and his seven Tour de France victories, and more recently the Russian Olympic team.[25] PEDs are even used by card players! The world champion bridge player Geir Helgemo tested positive for banned substances and was suspended for one year and required to forfeit his title, awards, and points.[26]

Student Cheating   If cheating is common in sports, it is rampant in high school and college. Fifty-one percent of high school students participating in a national survey reported cheating on exams. And besides typical school cheating, such as looking on another student's paper, using a cheat sheet, or plagiarism, countless examples exist of students sharing answers via social media, text messages, Bluetooth technology, and various devices.[28] Sixty-two percent of U.S. college students reported knowledge of another student using a connected device to cheat on an assignment, exam, or project.[29]

Some describe cheating in marathons as rampant. Large races, like the Boston Marathon, can have nearly forty thousand competitors. And in some marathons hundreds have been accused of cheating in some fashion, from falsifying qualifying times to riding a bicycle twice during one race![27]

Marty Schwalm/MediaNews Group/Boston Herald/Getty Images

And then there is contract cheating, paying someone else to do your work. Countless websites advertise these services, and this type of cheating is at epidemic proportions according to some.[30] A survey of students worldwide found 16 percent paid for at least one assignment during their college studies.[31] Well-intentioned or not, some services can get students in trouble, such as twelve Texas Christian University students who were suspended for using the Quizlet app to cheat on exams.[32] These are just a few examples and statistics of a very long list or cheating in grade school and college, increasingly assisted by technology. What percentage of students at your school do you think cheat on homework assignments? Exams? Take-home finals?

Administrators, Teachers, and Parents Too   Cheating isn't limited to students. T.M. Landry, a college prep school in rural Louisiana, which received incredible recognition for sending underprivileged students to elite universities, was caught falsifying transcripts and college application materials.[33] This is just another example of systematic and illegal efforts by schools and school systems to falsely elevate performance.[34] Temple University's business school dean was dismissed for submitting inaccurate data (e.g., GPA, admissions, and GMAT scores) to improve the school's rankings.[35]

We now know some number of parents, college admissions consultants, counselors, coaches, and many others also engage in cheating, as revealed by the college admissions scandal unveiled in early 2019. William Singer, the college consultant at the center of the scandal, facilitated admissions for scores of students to numerous universities, such as the University of Southern California, Stanford, and Yale. Parents paid him nearly $25 million for his services, which included bribes to administrators, counselors, and coaches; faking student profiles, sometimes as elite athletes for sports they didn't even play; and having other people take SAT and ACT exams. Dozens of people have been charged with a host of crimes—money laundering, fraud, racketeering, and obstruction of justice—with many pleading guilty.[36]

If winning a game or receiving good grades are strong temptations, then of course people cheat to get ahead at work too, and sometimes misconduct seems contagious and infects an industry. A notable example is the emissions and fuel economy cheating perpetrated by numerous automakers—VW (including Audi and Porsche), Nissan, Mitsubishi, Suzuki, and Subaru. These companies engaged in widespread systematic falsification of measures of fuel economy to meet and beat various environmental standards.[37]

These examples highlight the frequency and destructiveness of cheating. Now, let's explore other forms of unethical conduct and their legality, frequency, causes, and solutions.

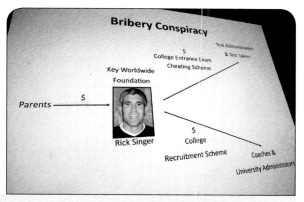

Students aren't the only ones who cheat in high school and college, Tracey and Michael Landry, founders of T.M. Landry College Prep in Louisiana, were accused of orchestrating a very intricate scheme to get the school's students into some of the most elite universities. William Singer, a college consultant, implemented his own elaborate and far-reaching practices to ensure his clients' (parents) children admission to colleges of their choice.

(Left) Brian Snyder/Reuters/Newscom; (right) Steven Senne/AP Images

Ethical Lapses—Legality, Frequency, Causes, and Solutions

The vast majority of founders, leaders, and managers mean to run ethical organizations, yet corporate corruption is widespread. Some of the executives whose unethical behavior bankrupted the organizations they led, destroyed the lives of many employees, and caused enormous financial losses for employees, investors, and customers in the last few decades are:

Michael Milken (Drexel Burnham Lambert, 1990)

Kenneth Lay and Jeff Skilling (Enron, 2001)

Bernie Ebbers (WorldCom, 2002)

Bernie Madoff (Madoff Investment Securities LLC, 2009)

Hisao Tanaka (Toshiba, 2015)

Sepp Blatter (FIFA, 2015)

Shigehisa Takada (Takada, 2017)

Elizabeth Holmes (Theranos, 2018)

Indictments and verdicts are a matter for the courts, and our point is that each of these disgraced executives led companies or organizations that in most cases employed thousands of other people. Surely these organizations did not advertise for and hire the criminally minded to assist the leaders in their unethical endeavors. Most employees probably knew little or nothing about any unethical or illegal activities, while others were deeply involved. How does the work environment produce unethical conduct, sometimes on an extreme scale, from people who are otherwise good, well-intentioned, and on the right side of the law? Knowledge of OB helps you answer this question.

Unethical Does *Not* Mean Illegal   While extreme examples of unethical and illegal conduct make headlines, they are the exception. The truth is that very few unethical acts are illegal, most are not punished in any way, and even if illegal, few are prosecuted.

This means you should *not* rely on the legal system to manage or assure ethical conduct at work. For instance, conflicts of interest are very common across industries and most are not illegal. *The New York Times* reported that Dr. Jose Baselga, a top cancer researcher, didn't disclose millions of dollars in compensation received from pharmaceutical companies for whom he conducted and published research related to their drugs. Dr. Baselga also served on the boards of these same companies, was an editor for one that published this work, and promoted the benefits of these drugs at conferences. Worse still,

Dr. Jose Baselga was accused of numerous conflicts of interest related to his research.

Eligio Paoni/Contrasto/Redux Pictures

some of this occurred while he was president of the Association of Cancer Research which made policies regarding researcher conflicts, and he was the chief medical officer at Sloan Kettering where some of the research was conducted.[38]

Southwest Airlines mechanics provided another example in 2019 when they created widespread slowdowns in flights to pressure the company in negotiations with their union. The mechanics slowed their work and grounded planes in the name of safety concerns, causing the cancellation of approximately 100 flights per day for several weeks.[39] Such actions are not uncommon and rarely judged illegal, but they do raise ethical concerns given the costs and inconveniences to customers. The nearby OB in Action box provides another notable instance of how widespread unethical behavior has resulted in virtually no legal consequences.

Why Ethics Matters to Me and My Employer   Criminal or not, unethical behavior harms not only the offending employee but also his or her coworkers and employer. Unethical behavior by your coworkers, including company executives, can make *you* look bad and tarnish *your* career.

OB in Action

Wrong? Absolutely! Illegal? Seemingly Not.

Zero. That is the number of senior Wall Street Executives that went to jail because of the 2008–2009 financial crisis. This is baffling to many, as Wall Street firms were central to the creation, packaging, and sales of faulty financial products that cost millions of people their homes, jobs, and savings. It is estimated that $30 trillion of the world's wealth was destroyed during the crisis, in large part due to the behaviors of financial institutions overseen by executives. Put simply, the crisis would not have happened without the firms and their leaders. Many of the biggest firms were saved by the government in what became known as "too big to fail."[40]

Although over 300 people were convicted in relation to the crisis, most of these were community bankers, mortgage lenders, and real estate brokers and developers. The lack of consequences for the Wall Street executives is perhaps even more astounding when over $150 billion In fines were levied and paid by their firms. Put differently, their firms were fined enormous sums of money, which means the firms were held accountable but the executives who led them were not. This contrasts with other countries, notably Iceland, which is far smaller than the U.S., but prosecuted the CEOs of three large banks and 23 other bankers.[41]

Two central figures in the U.S. during the crisis had telling and damning comments. Eric Holder, the U.S. attorney general at the time, said the conduct that led to the crisis was "unethical and irresponsible." And "some of this behavior—while morally reprehensible—may not necessarily have been criminal."*[42] Ben Bernanke, the chair of the Federal Reserve Bank during the financial crisis, said, ". . . more corporate executives should have gone to jail for their misdeeds . . . since everything that went wrong or was illegal was done by some individual, not by an abstract firm."[43]

YOUR THOUGHTS?

1. If you think executives (and perhaps other employees) of financial institutions should be punished for their roles in the crisis, describe what punishment you think is appropriate.

2. If you think they should not be punished, explain why.

3. Is it appropriate for the firms to pay fines, but for the executives to avoid consequences? Justify your answer.

Steven A. Cohen's SAC Capital Advisors eventually shut down after numerous employees pled guilty and/or were convicted of misconduct. But this didn't stop Cohen, and he simply opened another firm (Point72 Asset Management) and continued trading.
(Left) Seth Wenig/AP Images; (right) Suzanne DeChillo/Redux Pictures

SAC Capital Advisors, for example, was one of the most successful hedge funds in the 2000s. But the fund and its founder, Steven A. Cohen, were dogged throughout 2012–2016 by suspicions of insider trading, and many traders with ties to SAC were convicted. Before any formal charges were made against the firm itself or its founder, clients withdrew nearly $2 billion in assets.[44] SAC investors ultimately withdrew even more money, nearly $2 billion in fines were levied, and the fund was ordered to close.

That didn't stop Cohen, however, who reopened the company as a "family office," named Point72, and traded only his personal fortune. He ultimately settled charges brought against him personally, without admitting guilt, which resulted in his paying no personal fines and being banned only from trading other people's money for two years.[45] In early 2018 his ban completed, Cohen opened a new fund and began to raise and invest other people's money again.[46]

"Point72" and Steven A. Cohen are infamous. The financial returns of his former firm SAC Capital were legendary. Many of the most senior people in the firm were convicted or pled guilty to financial crimes. How about others in the firm who were perhaps uninvolved or even unaware of the insider trading?

To make this more real for you, imagine you are interviewing for a job. How would you explain your past employment history if it included jobs at SAC, Enron, Countrywide, MF Global, Madoff Investment Securities, Takada, or Theranos? It certainly is possible and even likely that you did nothing wrong. However, it *is* likely you would always be concerned about what others thought or suspected about your involvement. Would suspicions remain in the back of your future colleagues' minds? Sometimes ethical choices are clear—right or wrong—but sometimes they are more complicated and pose dilemmas.

Ethical Dilemmas   *Ethical dilemmas* **are situations with two choices, neither of which resolves the situation in an ethically acceptable manner.** Such situations surround us at work and school and highlight that choosing among available options is not always a choice between right and wrong. Since such dilemmas are so frequent and potentially conse-quential, we include an Ethical/Legal Challenge feature at the end of each chapter that asks you to consider what you might do if confronted with difficult ethical choices at work.

An excellent example is the #MeToo movement. The women who have and will come forward are confronted with a true dilemma—speak out about the inappropriate, unaccept-able, and in some instances illegal behavior they have experienced, or say nothing and take a chance the behavior will continue with themselves and/or others. The first choice can be

Martin Shkreli earned a dubious reputation for purchasing existing pharmaceuticals with little competition, and then hiking the prices hundreds or even thousands of percent. Even while in prison on fraud and other charges, he is rumored to be attempting to run a pharmaceutical company, Illegally.[50]

(Left) Craig Ruttle/AP Images; (right) Ryan Remiorz/The Canadian Press/AP Images

devastating to their jobs, careers, and reputations, and the second allows the bad behavior to continue.[47] The stories in the headlines have seemingly wrecked the careers of the many famous and often wealthy men implicated,[48] but what we don't yet know and maybe never will is what will happen to the opportunities and careers of the accusers and victims? What costs will be borne by them? Similar considerations are highlighted in the OB in Action box related to whistleblowers.

An eternal dilemma confronts pharmaceutical companies. On the one hand they need to make a profit to reward shareholders and invest in research and development; however, in many instances how much profit is "enough"? What about denying life-saving medicines to those who cannot afford them? What about charging widely different prices for the same product to different patients based on their insurance or country? The difficulty with such dilemmas at least in part has contributed to some of the very public scandals related to drug pricing in recent years.[49]

OB in Action

The Whistle-Blower's Dilemma

Whistle-blowing often creates a particularly challenging type of ethical dilemma. People do wrong, unethical, and even illegal things at work, and you and other employees know about the misconduct and may have even witnessed it firsthand. The dilemma is what to do about it—should you keep quiet or do you notify management or the authorities? Sharing your knowledge may indeed seem like the "right thing to do," and depending on the situation you may even profit, but it might cost you dearly.

Whistle-blowers can have many motives. Some are inspired by their personal sense of fairness or morality, while others may act out of greed or revenge. The Government Accountability Project (GAP) is a whistle-blower protection organization, whose director, Tom Devine, makes recommendations for those inclined to speak out.

1. Think of Yourself. What are the potential benefits and costs to you personally?

2. Test Internally. Raise the Issue within the organization before going to the authorities or media. Most organizations have mechanisms in place (such as hotlines) and chains of command. Use them, even if you don't expect them to work.

3. Recognize That It Will Be Personal. Many organizations will attack you and your character, regardless of what they do about the issue. Retaliation often occurs, and not just by the accused and offending individual(s), but by others too.[51] HR and legal departments are there to "protect" the organization, not you.

Whistle-Blowing for Profit   The Dodd-Frank Act of 2010 and some regulatory agencies provide incentives for whistle-blowers who report financial fraud which is both illegal and unethical. Some can receive up to 30 percent of any settlement if regulators collect more than $1 million due to the infraction.[52] The largest awards to date were paid in 2018 when $83 million were paid to three whistle-blowers from Merrill Lynch who reported the misuse of funds.[53]

The Costs   Although whistle-blower protection laws exist, they often do not sufficiently protect employees. For instance, a vice president at Chase Bank, Linda Almonte, was asked to review more than 20,000 past-due credit card accounts before they were sold to another company. Almonte's team reported back to her that nearly 60 percent contained some sort of major error, including discrepancies about the amount or whether the court had indeed ruled for the bank. Concerned, Almonte went up the chain of command, flagging the errors and encouraging management to halt the sale. Instead, the bank fired Almonte and completed the deal.[54] Nobody would hire her, which ruined her professionally and financially. She and her family ultimately moved to another state, where they lived in a hotel while she continued to look for work.

Ultimately, Chase was ordered to pay $200 million in fines and restitution. The company also settled a suit for an undisclosed amount with Almonte.[55]

What's the Lesson?   Doing the right thing is just that, doing the right thing. While it is noble, doing the

Protesters calling for the protection of whistleblowers.

Christophe Forestier/Alamy Stock Photo

right thing can also be very costly. Losing your job or suffering other forms of retaliation are unfortunately common, and there isn't much recourse. Suing your employer, even if legitimate, rarely results in future job offers for the whistle-blower.

YOUR THOUGHTS?

1. What can employers do to encourage whistle-blowers?

2. How can organizations ensure that whistle-blowers are protected, other than simply making it a policy (just words)?

3. What can you do as an individual employee when you witness or become aware of unethical conduct?

What Causes Unethical Behavior?   Harvard professor Max Bazerman and Ann Tenbrunsel of the University of Notre Dame have studied ethical and unethical conduct extensively. They concluded that while criminally minded people exist in the workplace, most employees are good people with good intentions. Bazerman and Tenbrunsel contend that instead of ill intent, cognitive biases and organizational practices "blind managers to unethical behavior, whether it is their own or that of others."[56] Table 1.2 summarizes their findings and outlines causes of unethical behavior as well as what we can do to address that behavior as employees and managers.

Many possible reasons for unethical behavior at work exist, beyond those listed in Table 1.2, such as:

1. Personal motivation to perform ("I must be No. 1").
2. Pressure from a supervisor to reach unrealistic performance goals along with threats for underperforming.
3. Reward systems that honor unethical behavior.
4. Employees' perception of little or no consequences for crossing an ethical line.[57]

What about Unethical Behavior in College and When Applying for Jobs?   A study of graduate students in the United States and Canada, including MBAs, found that

TABLE 1.2   Causes of Unethical Behavior at Work and What to Do About It

ILL-CONCEIVED GOALS	MOTIVATED BLINDNESS	INDIRECT BLINDNESS	THE SLIPPERY SLOPE	OVERVALUING OUTCOMES
Description:				
We set goals and incentives to promote a desired behavior, but they encourage a negative one.	We overlook the unethical behavior of another when it's in our interest to remain ignorant.	We hold others less accountable for unethical behavior when it's carried out through third parties.	We are less able to see others' unethical behavior when it develops gradually.	We give a pass to unethical behavior if the outcome is good.
Example:				
The pressure to maximize billable hours in accounting, consulting, and law firms leads to unconscious padding.	Baseball officials failed to notice they'd created conditions that encouraged steroid use.	A drug company deflects attention from a price increase by selling rights to another company, which imposes the increases.	Auditors may be more likely to accept a client firm's questionable financial statements if infractions have accrued over time.	A researcher whose fraudulent clinical trial saves lives is considered more ethical than one whose fraudulent trial leads to deaths.
Remedy:				
Brainstorm unintended consequences when devising goals and incentives. Consider alternative goals that may be more important to reward.	Root out conflicts of interest. Simply being aware of them doesn't necessarily reduce their negative effect on decision making.	When handing off or outsourcing work, ask whether the assignment might invite unethical behavior and take ownership of the implications.	Be alert for even trivial ethical infractions and address them immediately. Investigate whether a change in behavior has occurred.	Examine both "good" and "bad" decisions for their ethical implications. Reward solid decision processes, not just good outcomes.

SOURCE: Bazerman, Max H., and Ann E. Tenbrunsel. "Ethical Breakdowns: Good People often Let Bad Things Happen. Why?" *Harvard Business Review* 89, no. 4 (April 2011). https://www.hbs.edu/faculty/Pages/item.aspx?num=39125.

peer behavior was by far the strongest predictor of student cheating, followed by severity of penalties and certainty of being reported.[58] Students are more likely to cheat if their classmates cheat, and/or they think the probability of being caught is small, and if caught the penalties will not be severe.

However, don't be too quick to blame this bad behavior on your lying, cheating classmates. The same researchers acknowledge that there are many other potential reasons for cheating, such as perceived unfairness in grading. It also is possible that students see different degrees of cheating—for instance, in homework assignments versus on exams.

As for job hunting, an analysis of 2.6 million job applicant background checks by ADP Screening and Selection Services revealed that "44 percent of applicants lied about their work histories, 41 percent lied about their education, and 23 percent falsified credentials or licenses."[59] Sadly, it's seemingly getting worse. More recent data shows 85 percent of employers caught false information on resumes or applications, up from 66 percent five years earlier.[60]

Figure 1.2 highlights some of the most common and most outrageous lies told on resumes. Can you imagine being a recruiter? If you believe these numbers, more than half the people you interview could be lying to you about something!

FIGURE 1.2 Examples and Prevalence of Lies on Resumes

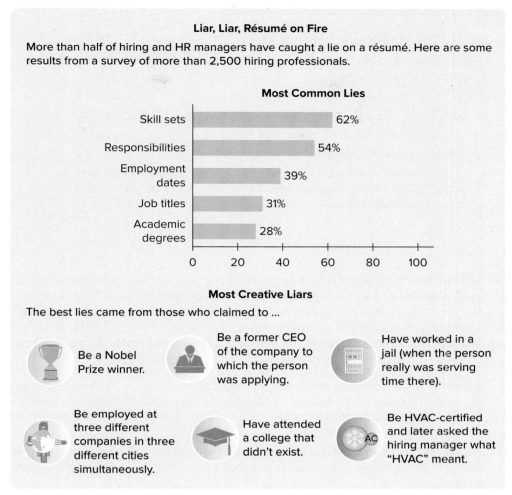

Liar, Liar, Résumé on Fire

More than half of hiring and HR managers have caught a lie on a résumé. Here are some results from a survey of more than 2,500 hiring professionals.

Most Common Lies

- Skill sets — 62%
- Responsibilities — 54%
- Employment dates — 39%
- Job titles — 31%
- Academic degrees — 28%

Most Creative Liars

The best lies came from those who claimed to ...

- Be a Nobel Prize winner.
- Be a former CEO of the company to which the person was applying.
- Have worked in a jail (when the person really was serving time there).
- Be employed at three different companies in three different cities simultaneously.
- Have attended a college that didn't exist.
- Be HVAC-certified and later asked the hiring manager what "HVAC" meant.

SOURCE: Gurchiek, Kathy. "Liar, Liar, Resume on Fire." *SHRM,* September 2, 2015. https://www.shrm.org/resourcesandtools/hr-topics/talent-acquisition/pages/lying-exaggerating-padding-resume.aspx.

Employers are getting more sophisticated and thus are more likely to catch you by utilizing skills assessments as part of the hiring process for some jobs. Also coding or design skills can be assessed using simple behavioral questions during an interview. If dates and facts on your social media sites don't align with your resume and other communications, this may also raise a red flag. Background checks are another way "alternative facts" are revealed, including not just contacting the references you provided, but perhaps even colleagues from past employers too. Finally, keep in mind you're never off the hook for the false information provided during the hiring process.[61] Many news stories describe high-level individuals who have been called out and terminated.

Whether at work or school, some people don't see their actions as unethical. Despite being convicted, the top two executives at Enron proclaim their innocence to this day, Jeff Skilling as well as Ken Lay until he died. Nevertheless, it will be helpful for you to learn more specifically about your own ethical tendencies. Some people view ethics in ideal terms, which means that ethical principles or standards apply universally across situations and time. Others, however, take a relativistic view and believe that what is ethical depends on the situation. Take Self-Assessment 1.2 to learn about your own views.

What Can You Do about It? You have or likely will witness questionable or even blatantly unethical conduct at work and you may be tempted to think, *This is common practice, the incident is minor, it's not my responsibility to confront such issues,* or *loyal workers don't confront each other.* While such rationalizations for not confronting unethical conduct are common, they have consequences for individuals, groups, and organizations. What can you do instead? Here are a few suggestions:

1. **Recognize that it's business and treat it that way.** Ethical issues are business issues, just like costs, revenues, and employee development. Collect data and present a convincing case against the unethical conduct just as you would to develop a new product or strategy.

2. **Accept that confronting ethical concerns is part of *your* job.** Whether it is explicit in your job description or not, ethics is everyone's job. If you think something is questionable, act.

3. **Challenge the rationale.** Lapses occur despite policies against them. If this is the case, then ask, "If what you did is common practice or OK, then why do we have a policy forbidding it?" Alternatively, and no matter the rationale, you can ask, "Would you be willing to explain what you did and why in a meeting with our superiors, customers, or during an interview on the evening news?"

4. **Use your lack of seniority or status as an asset.** While many employees rely on their junior status to avoid confronting ethical issues, being junior can instead be an advantage. It enables you to raise issues by saying, "Because I'm new, I may have misunderstood something, but it seems that what you've done may be out of bounds or could cause problems."

5. **Consider and explain long-term consequences.** Many ethical issues are driven by temptations and benefits that play out in the short term. Frame and explain your views in terms of long-term consequences.

6. **Suggest solutions—not just complaints.** When confronting an issue, you will likely be perceived as more helpful and be taken more seriously if you provide an alternate course or solution. Doing so will also make it more difficult for the offender to disregard your complaint.[62]

Now that you have a good understanding of the importance of ethics at school and work, we'll turn our attention to using OB to solve problems. The ability to apply OB to solve problems is a major part of what makes this knowledge so valuable.

1.3 OB AND PROBLEM SOLVING

THE BIGGER PICTURE

Now that you know that OB is not just common sense, the challenge is to find a way to organize and apply its many concepts and theories. In this section, we explain how you can apply OB to effectively solve problems at work, at school, and in your life. We use a 3-Step Problem-Solving Approach.

A *problem* is a difference or gap between an actual and a desired state or outcome, and *problem solving* is a systematic process for closing such gaps.

Problem-solving skills are increasingly needed in today's complex world. Loren Gary, former associate director at Harvard's Center for Public Leadership, supports this assertion: "The ability to identify the most important problems and devising imaginative responses to them is crucial to superior performance in the modern workplace, where workers at all levels of the organization are called upon to think critically, take ownership of problems, and make real-time decisions."[63]

For example, Jeff Bezos, CEO and founder of Amazon, has long downplayed the importance of meeting quarterly numbers to please Wall Street investors. He instead defines his problem as delivering superior service to customers, today, tomorrow, and forever. His problem-solving efforts are thus more likely to focus on innovative products and delivery times than on profit margins and earnings per share.

To help increase your personal performance and well-being at school, work, and home, we created an informal approach to apply OB tools and concepts to solving problems. It's simple, practical, and ready to use now!

LO 1-3

Utilize OB to solve problems and increase your effectiveness.

A 3-Step Approach

There are many approaches to problem solving, and knowing this, it was important for us as professors and authors to provide an approach that is both practical and effective across a variety of situations. The 3-Step Approach presented in this book is the result of our combined consulting experience of applying our knowledge of OB to help real-world employees and organizations solve problems. Our intent is to help you apply your OB knowledge and tools to boost your own effectiveness in school, at work, and in life.

Basics of the 3-Step Approach Here are the three steps in our applied approach to problem solving.

Step 1: Define the problem. Most people identify problems reactively—after they happen—which causes them to make snap judgments or assumptions. These are often plagued by a reliance on common sense and result in defining the problem incorrectly, which in turn leads to identifying inaccurate causes and

Few CEOs have faced more scrutiny in the recent past than Facebook's Mark Zuckerberg. He has been challenged over concerns about privacy, sharing and selling access and data, and allowing the platform to influence election outcomes.

Saul Loeb/Getty Images

ineffective solutions. All of us could benefit from Albert Einstein's comment, "If I were given one hour to save the planet, I would spend 59 minutes defining the problem and one minute resolving it." Let's take Professor Einstein's advice and learn how to improve our ability to define problems throughout this course and in your professional life.

- **Define problems in terms of desired outcomes, then test each one by asking, "Why is this a problem?"** First think of what you want, what is the desired outcome or state, then compare it to what you have or the current situation. It is important to resist snap judgements and quickly conclude you "know" the problem and underlying causes. You are better served to start with available facts and details. Then ask yourself, "Why is this gap a problem?" For example, suppose you are disengaged from your work. How do you know this? What is the evidence? Perhaps you no longer go out of your way to help your coworkers and stop responding to e-mails after work hours. You've defined your problem using evidence (or data). Now ask, "Why is this a problem?" Because when you are engaged, your coworkers benefit from you sharing your knowledge and experience. Coworkers and customers benefit from your responsiveness and willingness to respond to e-mails on their timeline, even when it isn't necessarily convenient for you (after hours). We find that asking "why" multiple times helps refine and focus your definition of the problem.

Step 2: Identify potential causes using OB concepts and theories. Essential to effective problem solving is identifying the appropriate underlying causes. So far you have OB concepts like the contingency perspective and ethics—and many more are coming—to use as potential causes. The more knowledge you have to choose from, the more likely you will identify the appropriate cause(s) and recommendation(s). To improve your ability to accurately identify potential causes, we provide the following tip for Step 2.

- **Test your causes by asking, "Why or how does this cause the problem?"** Once you have confidently defined the problem in Step 1—disengagement—you need to identify potential causes (Step 2). Ask, "Why am I disengaged?" One common reason, backed by science, is that you perceive you were evaluated unfairly in your recent performance review. "Why or how did this cause disengagement?" If you feel unappreciated for what you've done, then you are unmotivated to go the extra mile to help your coworkers or customers. Asking "why" multiple times and following the line of reasoning will lead you to define and identify problems and causes more accurately.

Step 3: Make recommendations and (if appropriate) take action. Whether planning and/or implementing recommendations, it is important to map or link recommendations to the causes and problems. The following is a simple and helpful suggestion.

- **Map recommendations onto causes.** Be certain to link recommendations to causes which are linked to the problem. The rationale is good recommendations address the causes, and when causes are removed or improved the underlying problem is solved or at least mitigated. Returning to our engagement example, the perceived fairness of performance reviews can be improved if managers use multiple raters, such as peers and the employee him- or herself (you'll learn about multiple raters in Chapter 6). Now, map or link this recommendation to the cause (an unfair performance review) to ensure it is appropriate and will effectively address the cause identified in Step 2 and the problem defined in Step 1. Fixing the cause eliminates the problem.

How This Problem-Solving Approach Develops Throughout the Book   As you learn more OB concepts and tools, the 3-Step Approach will become richer and more useful. Later, in Chapter 11, you'll learn this approach to problem solving is an abbreviated version of the rational approach to decision making.

Tools to Reinforce My Problem-Solving Skills

Because of our strong belief in the value of problem solving at school, work, and life more generally, we created numerous opportunities throughout the book to help you master this skill by applying OB. Each chapter, for instance, includes the following features:

- **Problem-Solving Application Mini-Cases**—These mini-cases present a problem or challenge for you to solve. You are asked to apply the 3-Step Approach to each.
- **Self-Assessments**—Validated instruments allow you to immediately assess your personal characteristics related to OB concepts, frequently with a personal problem-solving focus (see below).
- **End-of-Chapter Problem-Solving Application Cases**—The full-length cases require you to apply the OB knowledge gained in a particular chapter to define the problem, determine the causes, and make recommendations.
- **Ethical/Legal Challenge**—Mini-cases present provocative ethical dilemmas in today's workplace. You are asked to consider, choose, then justify different courses of action.

How good are your problem-solving skills? For a preliminary idea complete Self-Assessment 1.3 which measures your problem-solving skills and will help you understand:

- What types of things you consider when solving problems.
- How you think about alternate solutions to problems.
- Which approach you prefer when solving problems.

Tip: Take this assessment again at the end of the course to see whether your skills have improved.

SELF-ASSESSMENT 1.3   CAREER READINESS

Assessing Your Problem-Solving Potential

Please be prepared to answer these questions if your instructor has assigned Self-Assessment 1.3 in Connect.

1. What do items 1–3 tell you about your ability to define problems?
2. Do your scores on items 4–6 match your perceptions of your ability to generate effective solutions?
3. Using the individual items, describe the pros and cons of your tendencies toward implementing solutions.

1.4 STRUCTURE AND RIGOR IN SOLVING PROBLEMS

THE BIGGER PICTURE

When struggling to solve a problem, have you ever felt the solution was beyond your reach? Sometimes the solution is a matter of organizing or structuring the problem and its elements. OB can help. We'll show you useful tools to assist in organizing and applying your OB knowledge as it grows. You can use these same tools to solve problems more rigorously and more effectively.

LO 1-4

Explain the practical relevance and power of OB to help solve problems.

It's easier to understand and apply OB if you categorize or organize your knowledge as you learn it. The first and most fundamental distinction is between elements that are related to you and those related to the situation.

The Person–Situation Distinction

OB concepts and theories can be classified into two broad categories—person factors and situation factors. The person–situation distinction is foundational to OB.[64]

* *Person factors* **are the infinite characteristics that give individuals their unique identities.** These characteristics combine to influence every aspect of your life. In your job and career, they affect your goals and aspirations, the plans you make to achieve them, the way you execute such plans, and your ultimate level of achievement. Part One of this book is devoted to person factors.

This is simple and makes perfect sense, but as we all know reality is seldom simple. *Things* get in the way, and these "things" often are situation factors.

* *Situation factors* **are all the elements outside us that influence what we do, the way we do it, and the ultimate results of our actions.** A potentially infinite number of situation factors can either help or hinder your efforts and outcomes, such as job satisfaction, performance, and turnover.[65] This is why situation factors are fundamental to OB and critically important to your performance. Parts Two and Three of this book are devoted to situation factors.

Which Influences Behavior and Performance More—Person or Situation Factors?   Researchers and managers have debated for decades whether person or situation factors are more influential. They ask, for instance, about the relative impact of "nature versus nurture" and whether leaders are "born or made." We address these debates in Chapters 3 and 13, respectively.

Many believe that some people are *by their nature* better suited than others to perform well at work ("born winners"). In contrast, others believe some people are clearly better in *a given job or situation*. No particular person could outperform every other person in every possible job! No one is the best at everything.

This second view is supported by research in psychology and OB. **The *interactional perspective* states that behavior is a function of interdependent person and situation factors.**[66] The following quotation captures this reality: "Different people may perceive similar situations in different ways and similar people may perceive different situations in the same way."[67]

People and Situations Are Dynamic People change, situations change, and the two change each other. To illustrate:

- People bring their abilities, goals, and experiences to each and every situation, which often changes the situation.
- Conversely, because situations have unique characteristics, such as opportunities, rewards, and coworkers, they change people. What you value in a job will likely differ between now and the time you are trying to make a move to senior management.
- It is also true the current job market and employer expectations differ from those at the height of the technology bubble in the late 1990s or those in of the Great Recession of 2007–2009. In the first scenario employees changed, and in the second the situation changed.
- Finally, your manager—a situation factor—can change what you do, how you do it, and your effectiveness. You too can exert influence on your manager. In fact, many of the concepts and tools in this book can be applied to manage up (influence your manager and other superiors).

What is the bottom-line for your personal effectiveness? *You need to understand both person and situation factors and the interplay between the* two. Knowledge and consideration of one without the other is insufficient.

How Does the Person–Situation Distinction Help Me Apply OB Knowledge?
Categorizing your knowledge in terms of person and situation factors is immensely helpful when applying OB knowledge to solve problems. Consider downsizing.

Many companies restructure indiscriminately and cut a large percentage from their employee ranks, such as a 20 percent across the board reduction. Assume you and five coworkers, all of whom do the same job, are downsized. Each of you experience the same event, but your reactions will vary. You might not feel too bad if you didn't like the job and were considering going to graduate school anyway. Two of your coworkers, however, may be devastated and depressed.

Aside from the cyclical nature of its industry, U.S. automakers have felt intense competitive pressures for decades, resulting in persistent waves of layoffs—often tens of thousands per year. These industry and economic characteristics are important situation factors for these employees.

(Left) Jim West/Alamy Stock Photo; (right) Darren McCollester/Getty Images

Nevertheless, because the downsizing event was the same for all of you (the situation factors were identical), we can assume that the differences in everyone's reactions were due to things about you as individuals (person factors), such as other job opportunities, how much each of you liked the job you just lost, your financial situation, and whether you have kids, mortgages, or a working partner. The person–situation distinction, therefore, provides a means for classifying OB concepts and theories into causes of behavior and problems.

The Three Levels of OB

We explained above that OB distinguishes among three levels at work: individual, group/team, and organizational. Let's think about the varied reasons people quit their jobs as an Illustration of how considering levels helps in solving real-world problems.

- Some people quit because their job doesn't fulfill what they value at work, for example, providing a challenging and stimulating work (an individual-level input).
- Others quit because of conflict with their boss or because they have nothing in common with their coworkers (a group/team-level process).
- A common reason people quit is a faulty reward system which unfairly distributes raises, bonuses, recognition, and promotion opportunities (an organizational-level process).

Understanding and considering levels increases your problem-solving effectiveness and performance. This is highlighted in the problem-solving example in Section 1.6.

Applying OB Concepts to Problem Solving

Nothing causes more harm than solving the wrong problem. Assume, for instance, that several people in your department have quit in the past year. What could be the reason? The person–situation distinction allows you to consider unique individual factors as well as situation factors that might be the source of the problem. Considering the levels of individual, group, and organization will allow you to look at each for possible causes. For example:

- **Person factors.** Do your departing coworkers have something in common? Is there anything about their personalities that makes working in your department unfulfilling, for example, a preference to work collaboratively rather than independently? What about their ages? Gender? Skills?
- **Situation factors.** Has the job market improved and now offers more attractive opportunities at better wages elsewhere?
- **Individual level.** Has the job itself become boring and less meaningful or rewarding to the employees who quit?
- **Group/team level.** Did a new manager take over your department, one who micromanages and is less interested in developing you and your coworkers? How does turnover in your department compare to that in other departments in the organization? Depending on the answers, the new manager or other factors may explain these differences?
- **Organizational level.** Has the organization changed or restructured such that the most desirable positions are now at the headquarters in another state?

By following this approach and asking these questions, you widen your focus and review a larger number of possible causes, increasing the likelihood you will identify the right problem. If you don't quite follow this example, then have no fear because we'll analyze a turnover scenario in the last section of this chapter and provide a more detailed application. Stay tuned!

We now move on to the Organizing Framework for Understanding and Applying OB. This tool is not only helpful for learning OB, but it is incredibly valuable when using OB to solve problems.

1.5 THE ORGANIZING FRAMEWORK FOR UNDERSTANDING AND APPLYING OB

THE BIGGER PICTURE

You're about to learn about the single best tool for understanding and applying OB's many concepts and tools—the Organizing Framework for Understanding and Applying OB. The framework will help tremendously in improving your problem-solving abilities at school, work, and in your larger life space. In the final section, we give you practical and effective guidance on how to choose among alternate solutions to problems.

Given your knowledge of the person–situation distinction and levels (individual, group/team, and organizational), you are now ready to learn about the Organizing Framework for Understanding and Applying OB. We created this framework (see Figure 1.3) for two reasons. The first is to help you organize OB concepts and theories into three causally related categories–Inputs, Processes, and Outcomes. Students often ask, "How do these concepts fit together?" The Organizing Framework helps answer this question. The second reason for creating the Organizing Framework is its value in helping to solve problems. It enhances your problem-solving skills and marketability to employers. Now let's explore this valuable tool in more detail.

A Basic Version of the Organizing Framework

The foundation of the Organizing Framework is a systems model wherein inputs influence outcomes through processes. The person and situation factors are inputs, and processes and outcomes are divided into the three levels of OB–individual, group/team, and organizational.

This framework implies that person and situation factors are the initial drivers of all outcomes, such that inputs affect processes and processes affect outcomes. This is a dynamic process which means many outcomes will in turn affect inputs and processes. See Figure 1.3. The relationships between outcomes at one point in time and inputs and processes at another are shown as feedback loops in the Organizing Framework (the black arrows at the bottom of the figure).

FIGURE 1.3   Organizing Framework for Understanding and Applying OB

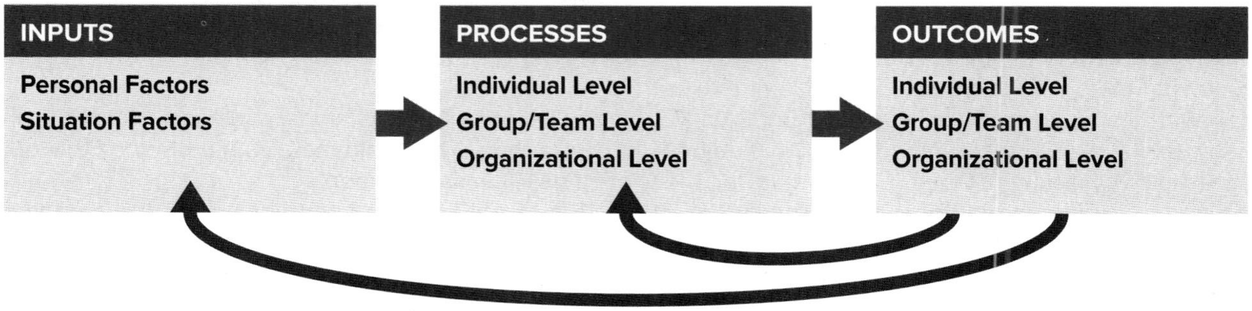

INPUTS	PROCESSES	OUTCOMES
Personal Factors	Individual Level	Individual Level
Situation Factors	Group/Team Level	Group/Team Level
	Organizational Level	Organizational Level

As you work through this book notice that each chapter begins with a version of the Organizing Framework that helps introduce the concepts discussed in that particular chapter. Each chapter repeats the same version of the framework at the end as part of the chapter review. If you add up the content of all the chapters, you'll end up with something that looks like the fully populated or complete Organizing Framework shown in the next section of this chapter. The fully populated framework is a useful preview of all you will learn, a powerful tool for solving problems throughout the course, and an effective review tool for preparing for a comprehensive final exam.

By definition, frameworks (and models) are simplifications of reality and necessarily exclude information. This means the complete Organizing Framework will not show every OB concept that might affect employee behavior, performance, and other outcomes. However, the basic elements of the framework will help you understand, organize, and apply any OB topic you encounter. The following OB in Action box illustrates the value of the Organizing Framework and its components—inputs, processes, and outcomes. Be sure to answer the "Your Thoughts?" questions, as they will show you how to apply your new OB knowledge and tools.

Applying OB

Mars: The World We Want Tomorrow

You likely associate Mars Company with its candy products (Snickers, M&Ms, Lifesavers), for which it's been known for more than 100 years. But what you likely don't know is that today about half of the company's $35 billion in revenues and more than half of its 115,000 member workforce is dedicated to pet foods, such as Pedigree and Whiskas, and pet care, Banfield Pet Hospitals and Veterinary Centers of America (VCA), to name but a few. Mars is not only in the business of catering to your sweet tooth and your sweet dog or cat, but it also puts a high priority on catering to its employees.[68] The company made the Fortune 100 Best Companies to Work For again in 2019 (#98),[69] and the Organizing Framework of Understanding and Applying OB can help us understand how they do It.

Inputs The environment at Mars lacks the perks touted by many tech companies—no Foosball tables, no free gourmet lunches, and no premier health clubs. More than this, some work practices are downright old school. For instance, all employees, including the president, have to punch a time clock each day and are docked 10 percent of their pay for the day if late.[70]

But what Mars may seem to lack in style it makes up for with its culture. Former President Paul S. Michaels explains how the company aligns its values and practices by asking: "Does it add value for the consumer to pay for marble floors and Picassos?" If it doesn't, then the company doesn't provide it. Employees seem to love the place and have very positive relationships at work; many families have three generations working at Mars. The culture seems to be one big

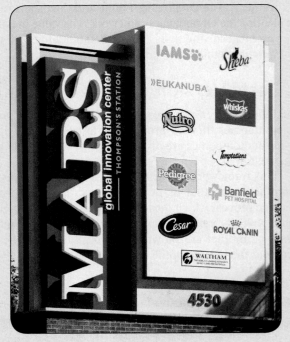

James R. Martin/Shutterstock

family interested in cats, dogs, and candy. At one facility more than 200 employees bring their dogs to work each day. (Leash rules apply.)[71]

This family environment flows from the founding Mars family, which still tightly controls the company according to the "Five Principles of Mars": quality, responsibility, mutuality, efficiency, and freedom. Employees can recite these principles and live them.[72]

The focus on values reflects the purpose-driven nature of Mars and its leadership. Current CEO, Grant Reid, put It succinctly: "The way we do business today creates the world we want tomorrow."[73]

Processes While some practices may seem frugal, the company reportedly awards bonuses of 10 to 100 percent of employees' salaries. The company also invests heavily in the community via its Mars Volunteers and Ambassador Programs. For instance, associates at their Banfield facilities impacted more than 144,000 people and pets In 2018, and other associates assisted those affected by earthquakes and hurricanes in Mexico and Puerto Rico, respectively.[74]

The company believes in and fosters sustainable practices across its businesses, including its suppliers and product development. For Instance, Mars created a product to address malnutrition in collaboration with the Tata Group In India.[75]

Outcomes Mars posts a very low turnover rate (5 percent),[76] a sign that employees are highly satisfied with their jobs. And the fact that the company has managed to grow consistently for decades and remain private is compelling evidence of its strong financial performance. Moreover, the CEO has plans to double revenues in the next 10 years and to do so sustainably.[77]

Let's now consider the details of the Organizing Framework and apply it to the 3-Step Problem-Solving Approach.

Using the Organizing Framework for Problem Solving

You can use the Organizing Framework at all three steps of the problem-solving process to add rigor, intelligently apply your OB knowledge, and in turn improve your performance.

> **Step 1: Define the problem.** Problems can be defined in terms of gaps in outcomes at three levels in the Organizing Framework.
>
> **Step 2: Identify causes.** Causes are often best thought of in terms of inputs (person or situation) or processes at various levels (individual, group/team, organizational).
>
> **Step 3: Generate recommendations.** Consider the most appropriate recommendations using your OB knowledge and tools, then map these onto the causes (inputs or processes).

The ultimate effectiveness of your problem-solving efforts will be determined by the impact of your recommendations on the underlying causes and problem. Let's discuss this next.

Selecting a Recommendation and Taking Action (if appropriate) Selecting recommendations (solutions) is both art and science. In fact, this is the decision-making part of the problem-solving process and is discussed in greater detail in Chapter 11. Choosing the appropriate course of action is critically Important as research shows nearly 50 percent of decisions fail.[78] Part of the explanation is some managers rely largely on intuition (also discussed in Chapter 11) and experience. While these approaches can work, others use more analytical or systematic methods to select a solution.

Don't Forget to Consider Constraints As a matter of practicality, most people lack the time, knowledge, or access to data to routinely follow such a rigorous procedure. Therefore, your selection most often requires you to consider various constraints—on time, money, your own authority, and information—that can occur at different levels. Let's now consider a few practical pointers on how to select the best solution.

Applied Approaches to Selecting a Solution

You can save time and hassle with the following practical advice from renowned problem-solving expert and professor Russell Ackoff. Ackoff recommends first deciding how complete a response you are looking for. Do you want the problem to be *resolved*, *solved*, or *dissolved*?

- **Resolving** problems is arguably the most common action managers take and simply means choosing a satisfactory solution, one that works but is less than ideal. Putting a "doughnut" or temporary spare tire fixes a flat, but it is certainly not ideal and is unlikely to last.
- **Solving** problems is the optimal or ideal response. For instance, you could buy a new, high-quality, full-size spare to keep in your trunk (not the typical doughnut or the "run-flats" that manufacturers frequently provide).
- **Dissolving** problems requires changing or eliminating the situation in which the problem occurs. Keeping with our example, the city you live in could build and utilize effective public transportation and remove the necessity of having cars (and tires) altogether.[79]

Making this decision first helps guide your choice among alternatives. In addition, it helps you decide what you need, whether it is realistic, and what level of effort and resources to use.

Basic Elements for Selecting an Effective Solution

After deciding whether to resolve, solve, or dissolve the identified problem, you need to select the most effective solution. A problem-solving expert says: "The essence of successful problem solving is to be willing to consider real alternatives."[80] To help you choose among alternatives identified in Step 2, we distilled three common elements that will help you qualify the best solution:

1. **Selection criteria.** Identify the criteria for the decision you must make, such as its effect on:
   - Bottom-line profits.
   - You and your classmates or coworkers.
   - Your organization's reputation with customers or the community.
   - Your values.
   - Ethical implications.

2. **Consequences.** Consider the consequences of each alternative, especially trade-offs between the pros and the cons, such as:
   - Who wins and who loses.
   - Ideal vs. practical options.
   - Perfection vs. excellence.
   - Superior vs. satisfactory results.

3. **Choice process.** Decide who will participate in choosing the solution. (If more than one person, agree on the method. Will you vote? Will the vote be public or secret? Unanimous or simple majority?):
   - You
   - Third party
   - Team

In every case, consider the necessary resources, including which people will be key sources of support for (and resistance to) your ultimate selection. Consider who can help and who can hurt your efforts—what's in it for them?

Putting it all together, the OB knowledge and tools you'll learn in this book will help tremendously in selecting and implementing the best solution given the situation you face. The final section of this chapter provides a preview of what you will learn in this book, along with an example application of the Organizing Framework and the 3-Step Problem-Solving Approach.

1.6 PREVIEW AND APPLICATION OF WHAT YOU'LL LEARN

THE BIGGER PICTURE

This section provides a high-level overview of what you will learn in this book, and it shows a summary Organizing Framework for Understanding and Applying OB. A thorough application of the 3-Step Problem Solving Approach is also provided to illustrate its power and applicability.

We wrote this preview to serve three primary functions: (1) It is a sneak peek and foreshadows all you will learn in this book; (2) it illustrates how to use the Organizing Framework when solving problems with the 3-Step Problem-Solving Approach; and (3) it serves as a review for a comprehensive final exam for this course.

LO 1-6

Apply the Organizing Framework to the 3-Step Problem-Solving Approach.

We begin this section by briefly reviewing the 3-Step Problem-Solving Approach and the components of the Organizing Framework. We will apply these tools to an example problem-solving scenario. The purpose is to be a tutorial of how you are expected to apply your knowledge and these tools throughout the rest of the book.

The 3-Step Problem-Solving Approach

This chapter began by demonstrating that common sense often is not common practice. We instead showed you how to think critically and add rigor and structure to your problem solving by using three steps, recapped as follows:

Step 1: Define the problem. To be an effective problem solver, you must define the problem accurately. It all starts here.

Step 2: Identify potential causes using OB concepts and theories. The many OB theories and concepts you will learn are extremely useful in helping identify the underlying causes of the problem you defined in Step 1.

Step 3: Make recommendations and (if appropriate) take action. Once you have identified the problem and its causes, you can plan and implement recommendations, applying your OB knowledge and tools.

Improving your problem-solving abilities will lead to better performance for you, your team, and your organization. This is important given that problem solving is one of the most sought after skills of employers across jobs and industries.

The Organizing Framework

Figure 1.4 illustrates a summary version of the Organizing Framework. It shows the OB concepts and theories you will learn and includes chapter references for finding details about them. The framework further illustrates how the various concepts are related to each other: Inputs affect processes, which in turn influence outcomes. Remember, problems are generally identified by looking for gaps in desired versus actual outcomes, and causes can be found in inputs and processes.

Here are a few important insights from Figure 1.4.

- There are more person factors that affect processes than situation factors. Pay particular attention to person factors when looking for causes of problems.

- Solving problems requires you to think across levels. Notice the many different concepts listed under individual, group/team, and organizational processes and outcomes.

- OB concepts are both inputs and processes. Leadership is a good example. This reinforces the dynamic nature of organizational behavior and underscores the consideration of connections between inputs and processes when solving problems.

FIGURE 1.4   Summary of Organizing Framework for Understanding and Applying OB

INPUTS

Personal Factors (associated chapters)

Hard and soft skills: 1
- Ethical behavior: 1
- Values: 2
- Attitudes: 2
- Intelligence: 3
- Cognitive abilities: 3
- Personality: 3
- Core self-evaluations: 3
- Emotional intelligence: 3
- Stereotypes: 4
- Diversity: 4
- Motivation: 5, 6, 7
- Positive OB: 7
- Emotions: 3, 7
- Mindfulness: 7
- Psychological capital: 7
- Communication: 9
- Social media: 9
- Decision making: 11
- Creativity: 11
- Resistance to change: 16

Situation Factors
- Ethical behavior of others: 1, 10, 12
- Leadership: 1, 8, 13
- Job design: 5
- Competition, regulators, and leadership: 6
- Human resource policies, practices, and procedures: 6, 9, 14
- Relationship quality: 8
- Decision making: 11
- Organization culture and climate: 7, 10, 13, 14, 15
- Mentoring: 14
- Organizational design: 15
- Forces for change: 16
- Resistance to change (coworker and organizational): 16
- Organizational mission and vision: 16

PROCESSES

Individual Level (associated chapters)
- Emotions: 3, 7
- Perceptions: 4, 6
- Attributions: 4
- Motivation: 5, 6, 7
- Job design: 5
- Performance management practices: 6
- Communication: 7, 8, 9
- Trust: 8
- Decision making: 11, 15
- Creativity: 11
- Leadership: 1, 8, 13
- Mentoring: 14

Group/Team Level
- Group/team dynamics: 3, 4, 8, 11, 14, 16
- Communication: 7, 8, 9
- Group roles and norms: 8
- Group development: 8
- Trust: 8
- Team effectiveness: 8
- Conflict and negotiation: 10
- Decision making: 11
- Creativity: 11
- Power, influence, and politics: 12
- Structural and psychological empowerment: 12
- Impression management: 12
- Organizational culture and climate: 7, 10, 13, 14, 15
- Organizational socialization: 14
- Mentoring: 14
- Organizational design: 15

Organizational Level
- Managing diversity: 4
- Human resource policies, practices, and procedures: 6, 8, 14
- Communication: 7, 8, 9
- Organizational culture and climate: 7, 10, 13, 14, 15
- Decision making: 11
- Creativity: 11
- Leadership: 1, 6, 8, 13
- Organizational socialization: 14
- Organizational design: 15
- Leading and managing change and stress: 16

OUTCOMES

Individual Level (associated chapters)
- Task performance: all but 15
- Work attitudes: all but 11, 15
- Turnover: all but 11, 15
- Career outcomes: 1, 3, 4, 8, 10, 11, 12, 13, 14, 16
- Well-being/flourishing: 2, 3, 4, 7, 13, 16
- Citizenship behavior/ counterproductive behavior: 2, 5, 6, 7, 8, 10, 12, 13, 16
- Intrinsic and extrinsic motivation: 5
- Creativity: 6, 7, 8, 10, 11, 13, 15
- Physical health: 7
- Stress (physical and emotional): 12, 15, 16
- Resistance to change: 15, 16
- Accidents: 16
- (Un)Ethical behavior: all but 3, 7, 15

Group/Team Level
- Group/team performance: all but 1, 2
- Group satisfaction: 3, 4, 6, 8, 9, 10, 12, 13, 16
- Group/team cohesion and conflict: 6, 7, 8, 10, 11, 12, 14, 16
- Group/team collaboration: 13, 15
- Innovation: 6, 8, 10, 11, 14, 15, 16
- Resistance to change: 16
- (Un)Ethical behavior: all but 3, 7, 15

Organizational Level
- Accounting/financial performance: 2, 3, 6, 7, 8, 9, 10, 11, 12, 13, 14, 15, 16
- Customer service/satisfaction: 2, 4, 5, 6, 7, 8, 9, 10, 11, 12, 13, 14, 16
- Survival: 3, 6, 16
- Reputation: 3, 4, 6, 9, 10, 12, 16
- Employer of choice: 4, 6
- Innovation: 6, 8, 10, 11, 14, 15, 16
- Organizational effectiveness: 7, 15, 16
- Legal liability: 9, 11, 12
- Product/service quality: 14
- Operational efficiency: 14, 15
- (Un)Ethical behavior: all but 3, 7, 15

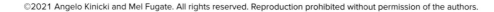

- Knowledge about OB is important. Simply look at the outcomes box! Over two dozen different outcomes are affected by OB-related inputs and processes. The framework further shows the frequency with which various outcomes are important to managers. Notice the number of chapters where individual task performance, work attitudes, turnover, group/team performance, innovation, accounting/financial performance, and customer service/satisfaction are discussed. And more personally, observe that career outcomes (an individual-level outcome) are related to concepts included in nearly every chapter.

Using the Framework for Learning   When you first read or learn about a new concept we recommend you attempt to categorize it in terms of whether it is a person factor, such as values and work attitudes (Chapter 2), personality and emotions (Chapter 3), perceptions and diversity (Chapter 4); or a situation factor like human resource policies, practices, and procedures (Chapter 6), leader behavior (Chapter 13), and organizational culture (Chapter 14). Doing this will improve your understanding and help you learn how they are related to each other.

We also encourage you to consider the issue of levels as you progress in learning about OB. Not only do many OB concepts exist at particular levels, such as personality at the individual level, but some concepts like performance management and conflict are processes that can affect outcomes across all levels.

Breadth and Power of OB   You should conclude from this that OB matters in business. More importantly it matters to you—your job and your career. And anyone (other textbooks, classmates, coworkers, bosses) who says OB is simply common sense, or that it only affects employee commitment, satisfaction, and performance, clearly does not understand the full and true power and value of OB. At the conclusion of this course you'll know better and won't make such mistakes!

Problem-Solving Application

Technology: A Situation Factor That Affects Your Performance

Since the Blackberry Quark in 2003, the iPhone 2007, and the first Android in 2008, smartphones have become extensions of our hands, which means they go with us and are used everywhere.[81] Approximately 31 percent of adults with smartphones report being online nearly constantly as do 39 percent of those 18–29 years old.[82] Many employers allow employees to bring-their-own-devices (BYOD) and access work e-mail and other resources via their personal phones. Walmart, for instance, adopted such a policy and now allows employees to check inventory, prices, review sales data, and sign in and out for their shifts from their own devices. This is a reversal of previous policies that banned the use of personal devices at work.[83]

Martin Novak/Shutterstock

Benefits. Walmart obviously expects to save money and boost performance, and they like other employers are promoting the benefits to employees. Employers claim smartphone use at work, and connectivity more generally, provides employees greater flexibility in terms of where they work, how, and when.[84] Flexible work arrangements, such as telecommuting, have ballooned in the past decade as a result and are now benefits highly valued by employees. On the surface this scenario appears to be a win-win, but the benefits are not without costs.

Costs. Besides privacy and security concerns, which are very real, always being connected has real costs. The statistics are overwhelming and troubling. For instance, more than half of Americans don't take all of their allotted vacation time. This happens for many reasons, but the most common are concerns (1) work will pile up while away, (2) only they can do their jobs, and (3) they could be replaced while away.[85]

Employees who don't unplug are far more likely to report lower commitment (Chapter 2), lower engagement (Chapter 2), feel less valued (multiple chapters), and experience higher levels of stress (Chapter 16), anxiety (Chapters 3 and 16) and work-life conflicts (Chapter 10). Moreover, laws govern what constitutes work, overtime, and compensation, and our always connected society puts more and more companies at legal risk.[86]

Causes. Organizational cultures are part of the cause (Chapter 13). Company values, policies, and practices are more or less supportive of unplugging. Besides the culture, your direct supervisor's expectations and behavior (role modeling) determine to a large degree the extent to which employees suffer the pitfalls of always being plugged-in. One study found only 14 percent of managers unplug when they take time off and just 7 percent of senior level managers. This does not bode well for most of us.

More troubling still is that it seems the mere expectation you'll check e-mail after hours causes anxiety, stress, and decreased well-being, even if you don't actually check It! This suggests you don't even have to actually work after hours to experience negative effects.[87]

Apply the 3-Step Problem-Solving Approach

Step 1: Define the problem(s) described in this example. Remember, problems are gaps between what exists and what is desired. Consider outcomes that are undesirable and for whom.

Step 2: Identify potential causes to the problem(s) defined In Step 1. Be sure to link the causes to the problem you identified.

Step 3: Make a recommendation aimed at each cause you feel will improve or remove the problem. Be sure your recommendations link to the causes identified in Step 2.

Hypothetical Problem-Solving Scenario

Observation and practice are two excellent ways to learn. Let's do both. We will work through a problem-solving scenario and show you how to use the Organizing Framework and the 3-Step Approach.

The scenario involves the problem of employee turnover, an individual-level outcome we used earlier in the chapter. For this application assume you are a valued junior employee who is thinking of quitting, and many other talented junior employees have quit your department in the past couple of years.

Step 1: Define the Problem   To reiterate, a problem is a gap between a current situation and a desired situation or outcome. First review the outcomes box in the Organizing Framework, because many problems are gaps between one or more current and desired outcomes. For instance, in this hypothetical scenario your organization has a turnover problem. Why is this a problem? Because the company wants to have the appropriate number of talented people in its most crucial jobs. Note that defining the problem this way is different from saying more people quit your company this year than last year, or that your employer has higher turnover than its competitors. (Note: If your worst performers quit instead of your best, then you could argue your organization is better off due to the reduction in "dead wood" rather than having a problem.) It isn't necessarily a problem to lose people, especially underperformers or those with obsolete skills, but if your organization's most valuable and high-performing people (like you) quit, then a problem exists. This sort of reasoning highlights the importance of defining the problem accurately.

Now that we've confidently completed the first step and defined the problem accurately—turnover of talented, high-performing, junior employees—let's continue the process and identify the potential causes of this turnover problem.

Step 2: Use OB to Highlight the Causes   While people quit for a variety of reasons, a good place to start is to consider both person and situation inputs, then various processes as potential causes of your organization's turnover problem. Look at the summary Organizing Framework for guidance (see Figure 1.4).

- **Potential Cause 1**—Person factors often represent key causes of turnover. Possibly the junior employees are quitting because their jobs don't fulfill their personal values (see Chapter 2). Low job satisfaction (Chapter 2) and demotivating job characteristics (see Chapter 5) also might cause turnover.

- **Potential Cause 2**—Situation factors frequently are causes of turnover. For example, people may be quitting because they have poor relationships with their bosses (see Chapter 13) or are working in a culture (see Chapter 14) characterized by damaging political behavior (see Chapter 12).

- **Potential Cause 3**—Individual, group/team, and organizational processes can also cause turnover. Conflict (with your boss), a team-level process (see Chapter 10), may constitute a cause of turnover. Another is a faulty performance management system (an organizational-level process—Chapter 6), one that unfairly distributes raises, bonuses, and recognition. As you will learn in Chapter 5, perceived injustice can be a powerful driver of employee turnover.

Notice the potential causes are located in different components (inputs and processes) and different levels within the Organizing Framework. Using the Organizing Framework to identify potential causes increases the likelihood that you'll identify the appropriate ones, essential to creating and implementing the best solution in Step 3.

Step 3: Generate Effective Recommendations Using OB   Now it's time to review the potential causes and identify the most likely and significant ones for the problem you defined in Step 1. Returning to our scenario, we list brief recommendations for each of the potential causes outlined above. We'll address all three to highlight how much you will learn and the practical value of that knowledge.

- **Response to Cause 1: Recommendations for Improving Person Factors.** OB provides a host of ideas for solving problems. The needs of your most valuable employees could be better satisfied if they were allowed to work on projects that satisfy their values of self-direction or achievement (Chapters 2 and 5). Job satisfaction might be increased through rewards that equitably meet employees' needs. Finally, motivation can be enhanced if people are allowed to assume more responsibility for projects (job enrichment) and the ability to decide how and when to do their work (autonomy).

- **Response to Cause 2: Recommendations for Improving Situation Factors.** Manager–employee relationships can suffer for many reasons, but let's assume some key and more junior employees in your department feel they are in the "out group," instead of the "in group," consisting of older and more senior employees who have known and worked with your manager for many years. This cause sounds like poor leader–member exchange (LMX in Chapter 13), which can be remedied if managers are trained to be more inclusive and implement formal mentoring and development programs. Managers can improve the political behavior driving a negative culture by acknowledging its existence and discontinuing the practice of rewarding people who are too political. Finally, team building (see Chapter 8) can reduce conflict among employees.

- **Response to Cause 3: Recommendations for Improving Processes.** Along with the knowledge you will gain related to justice and goal setting, Chapter 6 provides a host of ideas for improving performance management practices. A good place to start is to use Table 6.1 and clearly define and communicate performance goals and expectations. If these goals are SMART, then they are more likely to be achieved. Finally, rewards are more effective if the links between particular levels of performance and rewards are made clear. Rewards and their consequences should be fair and based on accurate performance evaluations.

Are you surprised by the many causes and potential solutions for this problem? As we just illustrated, the 3-Step Approach, combined with the Organizing Framework, can help you to more effectively solve problems. This, in turn, will contribute to your professional (and personal) effectiveness and potentially increase your opportunities.

1.7 MAKING THE CONNECTION: WHAT IS OB AND WHY IS IT IMPORTANT?

THE BIGGER PICTURE

To reflect on and apply your new knowledge, we provide a few notable examples of how you can benefit as both an employee and a manager.

LO 1-7

Describe the implications of OB knowledge and tools for you and managers.

Takeaways for Me

1. **Be sure you develop and apply both hard and soft skills.** Effective employees can no longer solely rely on technical expertise to get a job and advance once you do.

2. **Consider the skills most sought after by employers (like critical thinking, problem solving, decision making, active listening) and decide which are your strengths and weaknesses.** Use this knowledge along with the self-assessments in this book to improve your self-awareness and guide your development.

3. **Give your employers what they want!** Be sure to highlight the valued skills you possess during interviews and explore and seize opportunities to develop the others.

4. **Identify the most common forms of unethical conduct in your job, determine possible causes using Table 1.2, and confront and/or avoid them.** Unethical conduct can be so damaging to you and your career. Most unethical conduct is not illegal, which means legal action is rarely a viable solution. Also, be aware of the possible consequences of whistle-blowing—doing the "right thing" can be costly. Finally, applying rigor and structure to problem solving can help you avoid the pitfalls of common sense and make you more successful at work, at school, and in life.

Takeaways for Managers

1. **Identify the key skills needed to be top performers in the jobs you manage.** You may consider an existing or past top performer, but we also suggest determining to what extent your current employees possess soft skills and the other skills noted as determined by the most current research. Select and develop employees focusing on these skills.

2. **Determine the most common forms of unethical conduct for managers like you, as well as for those you manage.** Identify the likely causes (see Table 1.2) and explain clearly what you expect from your employees when they are confronted with such situations.

3. **Realize that performance and all other employee behavior is a function of both the person and the situation.** Don't be too quick to attribute bad (or good) behavior to the employee as situation factors may also be at play.

4. **Improve your effectiveness and that of those you manage by applying the 3-Step Problem-Solving Approach.** Be sure to define problems accurately and look for causes at multiple levels—individual, group/team, and organizational. Organizations and people are complex and managing them requires you to consider this complexity and deal with it effectively. Models like the Organizing Framework can help.

Our Wishes for You

Knowledge by itself is not an advantage; to get ahead you must apply your knowledge. This is why we wrote this book with a primary emphasis on application and provide numerous opportunities for practice in every chapter. We encourage you to continually apply your new OB knowledge as you learn it. Applying knowledge is the key to achieving a more successful and fulfilling career, which is our ultimate wish for you and our goal for writing this book. Enjoy the rest of your journey!

What Did I Learn?

You learned OB is a multidisciplinary field of study focused on behavior at three levels—individuals, groups/teams, and organizations. Understanding and applying OB knowledge and tools are valuable means for Increasing your performance at school and work, as well as advancing your career. Like most every OB concept, (un)ethical behavior is determined by both person and situation factors. More generally, OB knowledge is a powerful problem-solving tool and can make you more satisfied and effective in many arenas of your life—school, work, and home.

Key Points for Understanding Chapter 1

You learned the following key points.

1.1 THE VALUE OF OB TO YOUR JOB AND CAREER

- OB is an applied discipline focused on managing the behaviors of individuals, groups/ teams, and organizations.
- The contingency approach says the best or most effective approach depends on the situation.
- Self-awareness is critically important to your short and long-term success.
- Employers want employees who possess both hard and soft skills.

1.2 FACTORS THAT INFLUENCE UNETHICAL CONDUCT AND HOW IT AFFECTS PERFORMANCE

- Ethics is concerned with behavior—right, wrong, and the many shades of gray in between.
- The vast majority of unethical conduct at work is *not* illegal.
- Unethical conduct negatively affects the individual targets, the perpetrators, coworkers, and entire organizations.

- Ethical dilemmas are situations in which none of the potential solutions are ethically acceptable.

1.3 USING OB TO SOLVE PROBLEMS AND INCREASE YOUR EFFECTIVENESS

- A problem is a difference or gap between a current and a desired outcome or state.
- Problem solving is a systematic means for closing such differences or gaps.
- The 3-Step Problem Solving Approach includes defining the problem, identifying the causes using OB concepts, and making recommendations and action plans.

1.4 THE PRACTICAL RELEVANCE AND POWER OF OB TO HELP SOLVE PROBLEMS

- The person–situation distinction is a fundamental way to organize, understand, and apply OB concepts.
- Person factors are the many characteristics that give individuals their unique identities.
- Situation factors consist of all the elements outside us that influence what we do.

1.5 THE ORGANIZING FRAMEWORK FOR UNDERSTANDING AND APPLYING OB

- The Organizing Framework is a tool that helps you organize, understand, and apply your OB knowledge and tool.
- The systems approach—inputs, processes, outcomes—is the basis of the Organizing Framework.
- The Organizing Framework is extremely valuable when applied to the 3-Step Problem-Solving Approach.

1.6 APPLYING THE ORGANIZING FRAMEWORK TO THE 3-STEP PROBLEM-SOLVING APPROACH

- The Organizing Framework is a powerful tool to use with the 3-Step Problem-Solving Approach.
- The fully populated Organizing Framework is an excellent preview of the breadth, depth, and practical knowledge you will gain during this course.

1.7 WHAT IS OB AND WHY IS IT IMPORTANT?

- OB knowledge and tools are powerful means for enhancing your job performance and career opportunities.
- Understanding and applying OB concepts are critical for manager success.

The Organizing Framework for Chapter 1

In this chapter we introduced our first application of the Organizing Framework, demonstrating the basic structure of inputs, processes, and outcomes (see Figure 1.5). The basic framework shown here will help you organize new concepts, theories, and tools as they are introduced, as well as help you retain and apply them. We'll use the Organizing Framework at the end of each chapter as an aid to review and apply what you've just learned.

We hope you are impressed by all that you will learn, as illustrated in the Summary Organizing Framework (Figure 1.4). The same framework can help you understand and manage behavior and solve problems in many different organizational contexts (clubs, sports teams, and other social groups).

FIGURE 1.5 Organizing Framework for Understanding and Applying OB

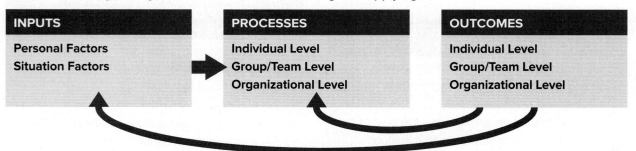

INPUTS	PROCESSES	OUTCOMES
Personal Factors	Individual Level	Individual Level
Situation Factors	Group/Team Level	Group/Team Level
	Organizational Level	Organizational Level

Blood, Brilliance, Blind Ambition, and Fraud

How can you change the world of medicine, or at least medical testing, monitoring, and diagnosis? One potential way is to invent a device that performs more than 240 tests with just a couple of drops of blood, faster, more effectively, and with less pain than existing approaches.[88] Coming up with the idea is one thing, but raising the funds and assembling the necessary talent is another. It's not enough to have an idea, you need to bring it to life. If you were to do this it would help to be extremely intelligent, even more driven, and be willing to do anything it takes. Anything. This describes Elizabeth Holmes and the company she founded, Theranos, which aimed to revolutionize medicine with a new blood testing technology.

FORECLOSURE OF A DREAM

Unfortunately, the technology didn't work. But that didn't stop Holmes from telling investors, customers, employees, the press, and everyone else it did. Her ambition transformed to fraud and resulted in the death of Theranos. The testing that supposedly certified the efficacy of the company's product has since been discredited, and it is now known that some of the demonstrations of prototypes of the company's products were rigged.

The billions of dollars in estimated value of Theranos are gone, along with It the accolades once showered on Holmes as being the youngest self-made billionaire at age 30. At one point $9 billion but now $0. Also gone is the $700 million of investors' actual money, and the jobs of many very talented employees who were either fired or quit during the company's existence. These employees, along with the unfortunate few who stayed to the end, may have tarnished reputations for years to come as a result of their association with Holmes and her company. Holmes is now faced with the fallout and is confronted with criminal charges related to defrauding investors, customers, employees, and most anyone else connected to the company. Her ex-boyfriend, and Theranos's president and COO, Ramesh Balwani is also facing many of the same charges. He acted as confidant, advisor, and as many insiders eventually learned, was seemingly the only other person within the company besides Holmes how knew the truth.[89]

HOW DID THIS HAPPEN?

She went from Stanford undergraduate engineering student and celebrated female entrepreneur, to the founder and leader of one of the most astounding frauds in science and business in the recent past. Theranos was the company she founded with the hopes and claims that its technology would revolutionize blood testing and in the process medicine. Holmes always wanted to make an impact, and at 19 saw this as her path. She spent the next several years assembling the necessary talent, money, influence, and notoriety to realize her vision. But as we now know it was a sham.

Holmes was single-minded and unwavering in pursuit of her vision. She ruled the company like a dictator, making all critical decisions herself, sharing information on a need to know basis, and expressing enthusiasm and positivity even in instances of flat out failures, such as demonstrations and presentations to investors and potential customers. She quickly soured on, then avoided, and even retaliated against those who questioned her or her ways. Absolute loyalty, which meant agreement and obedience, was demanded by Holmes. Individuals and groups who spoke out or otherwise fell out of favor were quickly dismissed, as was any feedback that was inconsistent with Holmes's desired message or outcome,[90]

Although it was Holmes's company, and she hoarded authority, other factors supported her ultimately disastrous approach. Her vision, charisma, conviction, and delivery persuaded many wealthy and otherwise powerful people and organizations to support her cause. For Instance, two of the largest Investors were Betsy DeVos, now education secretary and part of the founding family of Amway, as well as Rupert Murdoch (the media mogul who owns Fox among many others). The board was stacked with celebrities from government (Henry Kissinger and George Schultz, both former secretaries of state). Along with others with impressive track records from Apple and other tech companies, these prominent Individuals gave Holmes and Theranos credibility.[91]

WHAT ABOUT THE BOARD?

The company also had a board of directors, which, as in other companies public or private, was charged with ultimate oversight and responsibility. Members of the Theranos board had impressive resumes and should have been up to the task, such as Avie Tevanian, who was Steve Jobs's righthand man at Apple and head of software engineering, and Don Lucas (chair of the board) a long-time and successful venture capitalist. However, they were relatively silent or when they did speak up, as Tevanian did, they were dismissed. Apparently, Holmes grew tired of his increasingly confrontational insistence she "open the books" and justify her seemingly wildly and overly optimistic revenue projections.[92]

But the real truth is coming to light from books, documentaries, and legal proceedings. Walgreens, one of Theranos's marquee customers, is suing for $140 million, the SEC has charged Holmes and Balwani with fraud, and other investors are sure to follow. This raises the question: how could this have been avoided? How can this be prevented in the future?

Assume you are the chair of the Theranos board of directors back in 2003 at the founding of the company. Apply the 3-Step Problem-Solving Approach to preventing the debacle.

APPLY THE 3-STEP PROBLEM-SOLVING APPROACH TO OB

STEP 1: Define the problem.

A. Look first at the Outcomes box of the Organizing Framework to help identify the important problem(s) in this case. Remember that a problem is a gap between a desired and current state. State your problem as a gap and be sure to consider problems at all three levels. If more than one desired outcome is not being accomplished, decide which one is most important and focus on it for steps 2 and 3.

B. Cases have key players, and problems are generally viewed from a particular player's perspective. You need to determine from whose perspective—employee, manager, team, or the organization—you're defining the problem. In this case you're asked to assume the role of chair of the board of directors at Theranos.

C. Use details in the case to determine the key problem. Don't assume, infer, or create problems not included in the case.

D. To refine your choice, ask yourself, *why is this a problem?* Explaining why helps refine and focus your thinking. Focus on topics in the current chapter, because we generally select cases illustrating concepts specifically located within the current chapter.

STEP 2: Identify causes.

Using material from this chapter and summarized in the Organizing Framework, identify the causes of the problem you identified in Step 1? Remember, causes tend to appear in either the Inputs or Processes boxes.

A. Start by looking at the Organizing Framework (Figure 1.4) and decide which person factors, if any, are most likely causes of the defined problem. For each cause, explain why this is a cause of the problem. Asking *why* multiple times is more likely to lead you to root causes of the problem. For example, do executive characteristics help explain the problem you defined in Step 1?

B. Follow the same process for the situation factors. For each ask yourself, *why is this a cause?* By asking why multiple times you are likely to arrive at a complete and more accurate list of causes. Again, look to the Organizing Framework for this chapter for guidance. Did particular policies or practices play a role?

C. Now consider the Processes box in the Organizing Framework. Are any processes at the individual, group/team, or organizational level potential causes of your defined problem? For any process you consider, ask yourself, *why is this a cause?* Again, do this for several iterations to arrive at the root causes.

D. To check the accuracy or appropriateness of the causes, be sure to map them onto the defined problem and confirm the link or cause and effect connection.

STEP 3: Recommend solutions.

Make your recommendations for solving the problem. Consider whether you want to resolve it, solve it, or dissolve it (see Section 1.5). Which recommendation is desirable and feasible?

A. Given the causes you identified in Step 2, what are your best recommendations? Use material in the current chapter that best suits the cause. Consider the OB in Action and Applying OB boxes, because these contain insights into what others have done.

B. Be sure to consider the Organizing Framework—both person and situation factors—as well as processes at different levels.

C. Create an action plan for implementing your recommendations and be sure your recommendations map onto the causes and resolve the problem.

What Would You Do?

Assume you are a nursing director for a nursing home. You've been working at the facility for a few short months when you learn the company that owns the home has been improperly overbilling Medicare for the care and services provided to the residents. You bring this to the attention of the company's managers, but they do nothing. You then notify the appropriate authorities (becoming a whistle-blower) and, dismayed by the fraud and other problems, you quit.

Several months later you interview for a new position as nursing director at another facility. The interview is with a panel of 10 decision makers, including the CEO, medical director, and other administrators, who will decide whether or not you get the job.

One other important detail: This facility is just two miles from the one you reported to the authorities before quitting. Nursing, like some other industries, tends to be a closed circle of people who often cross paths repeatedly in different jobs over time. This means one or more of the interviewers may know about you and the other facility before the interview, or one or more of them will likely learn after if they don't know already.

What would you do about divulging information regarding the allegations made against your previous employer? Choose your answer from the options below. Be sure to explain and justify your choice.

Your Response

1. Do not divulge the whistle-blowing. Justify.
2. Wait until you learn the outcome of the interview; if you don't get the offer, don't share the information. Justify.
3. Wait until you learn the outcome of the panel interview; if you get a job offer, then tell the person who makes you the offer about the allegations. Explain your reasoning.
4. Tell all members of the panel during your interview. Explain your reasoning, Including anticipating their potential reaction and what you might do as a result.
5. Create and explain another course of action.

2 Values and Attitudes

After reading this chapter, you should be able to:

LO 2-1   Describe the role values play in influencing your behavior.

LO 2-2   Explain how personal attitudes affect workplace behavior and work-related outcomes.

LO 2-3   Discuss the importance of four key workplace attitudes.

LO 2-4   Discuss the five causes of job satisfaction.

LO 2-5   Describe work-related outcomes associated with job satisfaction.

LO 2-6   Describe the implications of values and attitudes for you and managers.

Caia Image/Image Source

The Organizing Framework for Understanding and Applying OB shown in Figure 2.1 summarizes what you will learn in this chapter. Chapter 2 begins your study of the way values, personal attitudes, and intentions serve as inputs to a host of individual- and organizational-level outcomes. Remember, we generally define problems as gaps between the current and the desired state of one or more outcomes. In this chapter, pay attention to the way values and personal attitudes might become causes of problematic outcomes, such as low task performance, poor workplace attitudes, low well-being/flourishing, low citizenship behavior/counterproductive behavior, and high turnover. These inputs also might contribute to explaining the organizational-level outcomes of poor firm performance and low customer service or satisfaction.

FIGURE 2.1   Organizing Framework for Understanding and Applying OB

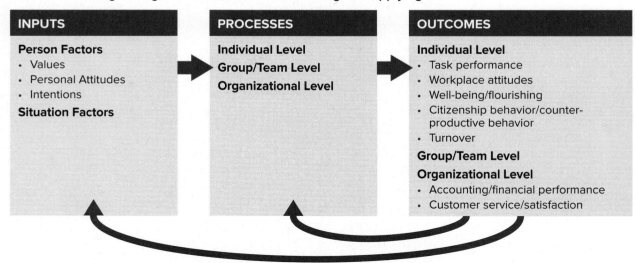

INPUTS	PROCESSES	OUTCOMES
Person Factors • Values • Personal Attitudes • Intentions **Situation Factors**	**Individual Level** **Group/Team Level** **Organizational Level**	**Individual Level** • Task performance • Workplace attitudes • Well-being/flourishing • Citizenship behavior/counter-productive behavior • Turnover **Group/Team Level** **Organizational Level** • Accounting/financial performance • Customer service/satisfaction

Winning at Work

Creating Your Own Sense of Engagement

We'll see in this chapter that employee engagement is a workplace attitude that motivates people to identify with and immerse themselves in their work, actively applying a sense of urgency, focus, intensity, and enthusiasm. That sounds like a positive and rewarding approach to bring to the job every day, doesn't it?

Managers have a number of tools at their disposal to help foster engagement at work, like maintaining supportive relationships with employees and reducing factors that can create stress and frustration. The good news for those starting out in their careers, however, is that whether your manager uses these tools or not, you can foster your own sense of engagement no matter what kind of work you do.

Here are some ways to be sure you are bringing your best and most deeply engaged self to the job each day:[1]

- *Know your job and what is expected of you.* Ask well-informed questions, seek out training you may need, volunteer for extra assignments, and look for new roles you can play in your organization to increase your sense of competence and skill. These all contribute to engagement at work and increase your visibility as well.

- *Speak up when you have appropriate opportunities.* Those who are heard are usually more emotionally committed to the organization and are more likely to feel they are valued. Offer positive suggestions or constructive feedback in team or committee meetings, for example.

- *Ask for frequent feedback.* Make it a habit to ask your boss, your coworkers, and your peers in other departments how well you're performing, so you know what you're doing well and what to improve on. Recognition and praise build engagement, as does constructive criticism.

- *Work on developing mindfulness.* Mindfulness is a strategy that allows you to readily focus on the task at hand. Some immediate steps you can take are limiting your time online, checking your e-mail only once or twice a day and at specific times, and avoiding your cellphone during the work day except for emergencies. Don't try to multitask. Instead, work on your ability to focus so you can enjoy the satisfaction of completing each task.

- *Avoid coworkers who are actively disengaged.* Disengaged workers can sometimes be influential people in the organization and are often vocal about their feelings, but their negative attitudes about the workplace are contagious and can spread dissatisfaction even among those who are otherwise ready to be fully engaged.

- *Take charge of your health.* To be sure you are working at your best performance level, eat healthy foods, drink plenty of water, exercise, get enough sleep, and spend a little time each day recharging through a quiet activity like yoga or meditation.

If you're still struggling to feel engaged, try these additional steps:

- *Revisit the big picture.* Refresh your understanding of your organization's larger mission and how your work contributes to achieving it. What's the larger picture, and what role does your work play? How can you close any gap that might exist between the two?

- *Challenge yourself.* If you're just coasting along at work, look for a task that needs doing or a committee or work team to which you can contribute, and ask your manager to let you tackle this new opportunity. Emphasize your desire to learn and grow, and be ready to demonstrate that you'll continue doing your current work to the highest standards.

- *Take a break.* If you haven't taken any time off in a while, consider a short break or even a vacation to replenish your emotional resources. Try to physically and mentally disconnect from work as much as possible while away, and use the time to regain your focus and enthusiasm.

- *Do something for yourself.* Add a meaningful spark to your life outside work by volunteering in your community, learning a new skill unrelated to work, going to a professional networking event, or simply making more time for socializing with family and friends.

Gallup's *State of the Global Workplace* report says that only 15 percent of employees around the world are engaged at work, which could be costing U.S. employers alone as much as $550 billion in lost productivity every year.[2] Rather than interpreting this data to mean you don't stand a chance of maintaining your connection to work, realize that you actually have a unique opportunity to stand out from the crowd. Fully engaged employees are widely acknowledged to be a company's most valuable asset. That asset can be you.

What's Ahead in This Chapter

Now that you have new tools to make OB work for you—tools like the Organizing Framework and the 3-Step Problem Solving Approach—you're ready to put them to work. With this chapter we begin exploring how individual-level factors influence a host of important outcomes. Specifically, we look at the way individual-level factors such as values affect workplace attitudes and behavior. We help you explore how your personal values affect your own workplace attitudes and behavior. We'll outfit you with OB concepts to understand key work-related attitudes—organizational commitment, employee engagement, and perceived organizational support—which lead to important outcomes at the individual and organizational levels. Before you're done, you will understand the causes and consequences of job satisfaction, an important outcome for both employees and managers.

2.1 PERSONAL VALUES

THE BIGGER PICTURE

You may already have a good understanding of your personal values and the role they play in your life. In an organization, personal values contribute to workplace attitudes and behavior. So it's important to understand how the full range of potential human values affects our attitudes and behavior at work. Then you can use this knowledge to influence outcomes in the Organizing Framework for Understanding and Applying OB.

Values are abstract ideals that guide our thinking and behavior across all situations. They stem from our parents' values, our experiences in childhood and throughout life, and our religious or spiritual beliefs. Values are relatively stable and can influence our behavior without our being aware of it.

Understanding the way values affect our behavior matters for two reasons. First, values guide our actions across all situations. Knowing this helps you to self-manage, such as by choosing a major or career for which you are well suited. Second, you will be more effective at influencing others' attitudes and behaviors when you are armed with an understanding of values and their effects.

Renowned researcher Shalom Schwartz created a theory of personal values that many managers and OB professionals find useful for understanding the motivational impact of our values. Let's look at this theory.

Schwartz's Value Theory

Schwartz proposed that broad values motivate our behavior across any context. He categorized these values into two opposing or bipolar dimensions, as outlined in Table 2.1. The first dimension ranges from concern for the welfare of others (which Schwartz calls *self-transcendence*) to pursuit of one's own interests (*self-enhancement*). The second dimension ranges from self-directed independence (which Schwartz calls *openness to change*) to

TABLE 2.1 Bipolar Dimensions in Schwartz's Model

FIRST BIPOLAR DIMENSION	
Self-Transcendence	**Self-Enhancement**
Concern for the welfare and interests of others (universalism, benevolence).	Pursuit of one's own interests and relative success and dominance over others (power, achievement).
SECOND BIPOLAR DIMENSION	
Openness to Change	**Conservation**
Independence of thought, action, and feelings and readiness for change (stimulation, self-direction).	Order, self-restriction, preservation of the past, and resistance to change (conformity, tradition, security).

conformity (*conservation*). Schwartz stressed that it is the relative importance we give to these two dimensions of opposing values that drives our behavior.[3] For example, if you value achievement (self-enhancement) over universalism (self-transcendence), you will spend your evening studying hard to get an A in this class rather than attending a meeting about fighting climate change. Our values help us to make these types of choices.

Schwartz categorized 10 broad values within these two opposing dimensions. Figure 2.2 shows those 10 values as the slices of a pie, with the underlying opposing dimension shown outside the circle. Schwartz placed the 10 values in a circular-motivation structure to illustrate their compatibility. In general, adjacent values (like self-direction and universalism) are more compatible. That is, these values share a common focus that promotes their acceptance within an individual. Values that are farther apart (like self-direction and power) are less compatible or in conflict. Opposing values (such as self-direction and conformity) are less likely to be held by the same individual.

Schwartz noted that one set of values is in opposition to the other set, as suggested by the use of color in Figure 2.2. Notice the unique treatment of several values: Tradition and conformity share a single wedge, supporting the same broad motivational goal. Conformity is toward the center because it does not conflict with the opposing value quite as much as does tradition, which is toward the outside. Also notice that hedonism shares elements of both openness to change and self-enhancement.

Protesting is often driven by values-based issues such as ending gun violence. These protesters might be expressing the self-transcendence value of universalism and the self-direction value associated with openness to change. In contrast, completing a college degree might reflect values associated with achievement, power, and stimulation.

(Left): Rena Schild/Shutterstock; (right): Digital Vision/SuperStock

FIGURE 2.2 Values and Motives in Schwartz's Theory

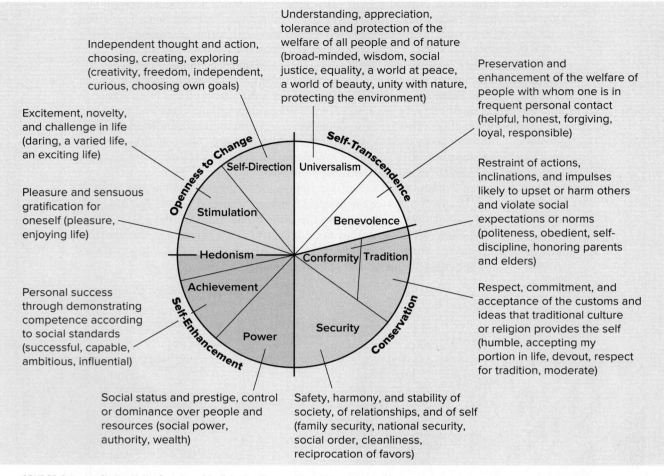

Independent thought and action, choosing, creating, exploring (creativity, freedom, independent, curious, choosing own goals)

Understanding, appreciation, tolerance and protection of the welfare of all people and of nature (broad-minded, wisdom, social justice, equality, a world at peace, a world of beauty, unity with nature, protecting the environment)

Excitement, novelty, and challenge in life (daring, a varied life, an exciting life)

Preservation and enhancement of the welfare of people with whom one is in frequent personal contact (helpful, honest, forgiving, loyal, responsible)

Pleasure and sensuous gratification for oneself (pleasure, enjoying life)

Restraint of actions, inclinations, and impulses likely to upset or harm others and violate social expectations or norms (politeness, obedient, self-discipline, honoring parents and elders)

Personal success through demonstrating competence according to social standards (successful, capable, ambitious, influential)

Respect, commitment, and acceptance of the customs and ideas that traditional culture or religion provides the self (humble, accepting my portion in life, devout, respect for tradition, moderate)

Social status and prestige, control or dominance over people and resources (social power, authority, wealth)

Safety, harmony, and stability of society, of relationships, and of self (family security, national security, social order, cleanliness, reciprocation of favors)

Self-Transcendence · Universalism · Benevolence · **Openness to Change** · Self-Direction · Stimulation · Hedonism · **Self-Enhancement** · Achievement · Power · Conformity · Tradition · Security · **Conservation**

SOURCE: Schwartz, Shalom H. "An Overview of the Schwartz Theory of Basic Values." *Online Readings in Psychology and Culture* 2, no.1 (2012): 9. https://doi.org/10.9707/2307-0919.1116. Bardi, Anat, and Shalom H. Schwartz. "Values and Behavior: Strength and Structure of Relations." *Personality & Social Psychology Bulletin* 29, no. 10 (October 2003): 1207–220. https://doi:10.1177/0146167203254602.

Workplace Applications of Schwartz's Theory   You can feel comfortable applying this theory because research supports its basic structure and its prediction of behavior. For example, suppose you and several classmates are working together on a sustainability project for an earth sciences course. You volunteer to assign specific tasks to the three other classmates on the project. Paul, one of the team members, tells you he's not convinced that climate change is a real issue, so it may not be a good idea to ask him to come up with ideas to protect the earth's natural resources, because he may not value the importance of protecting the environment (universalism). Instead, he might be better suited to prepare the project's final report because he's motivated to get an A for the assignment because success is important to him (achievement).

In the workplace, managers can better supervise workers by using Schwartz's model to understand their values and motivation. For example, if a manager knows that an employee values universalism and benevolence, then it would be wise to assign this employee to projects or tasks that have social value. Managers can also use Figure 2.2 to reduce the chances of employees' experiencing conflict between their values and their work assignments, when options are available. An employee who values tradition and conformity over achievement, for example, will not be happy about being asked to work on a holiday or to miss a child's school play for work.

Research also confirms the theory's relevance cross-culturally for both children and adults. As you might expect, the priorities given to Schwartz's values do vary across countries.[4]

Personal Application of Schwartz's Theory   Schwartz's model can help you determine whether your values are consistent with your goals and whether you are spending your time in a meaningful way. Complete the Self-Assessment that measures the worth to you of Schwartz's 10 values, and whether your goals align with these values.

SELF-ASSESSMENT 2.1	CAREER READINESS

What Are My Core Values?

Please be prepared to answer these questions if your instructor has assigned Self-Assessment 2.1 in Connect.

1. Rank your scores for the values from high to low. Do you agree with this rank order?

2. What are your top five values? Which do you think has the greatest impact on your personal goals?

3. Do you think you may want to focus more on any of the five lowest-rated values as you graduate from school and pursue a career? Explain.

The Dynamics of Values

In general, our values are relatively stable across time and situations. This means that positive employee attitudes and motivation are greatest when the work environment is consistent with employee values. For example, Airbnb, the global lodging website, tries to attract and motivate employees by offering them an annual travel and experiences credit of $2,000 to visit anywhere around the world where the company offers accommodations. The company does this because it believes Airbnb employees are driven to "embrace the adventure" and experience personal growth through traveling to different countries and communities.[5]

Values tend to vary across generations because they are influenced by events in childhood and youth. For example, the author's parents lived through the Depression, which lasted through the 1930s and part of the 1940s. This experience led them to value security and to be conservative with their money. They did not like debt, and they opposed the use of credit cards. Do you know anyone with values like these? In contrast, the values held by baby boomers, people born between 1946 and 1964, are influenced by events like the assassination of President John F. Kennedy, the Vietnam War, and the shooting deaths of student protesters at Kent State University in Ohio. In contrast, Millennials, people born between 1980 and 2001, have been influenced by events like September 11, the wars in Iraq and Afghanistan, the founding of Google, and the rise of social media. What shapes the values of Generation Z? Born between 1997 and 2012, Gen Zers have been influenced by growing up during a recession (focus on saving money); making connections on their mobile devices more than 10 hours a day; and fighting for racial equality and inclusion.[6] We discuss generational differences thoroughly in Chapter 4.

2.2 PERSONAL ATTITUDES AND THEIR IMPACT ON BEHAVIOR AND OUTCOMES

THE BIGGER PICTURE

Closely related to values are personal attitudes, which also operate as an input in the Organizing Framework for Understanding and Applying OB. (In contrast, *workplace* attitudes are defined as outcomes in the framework.) Personal attitudes have three components—affective, cognitive, and behavioral. Knowing these components helps us understand how and when personal attitudes affect behavior. Have you ever been stopped short by something that didn't seem to make sense? When personal attitudes collide with reality, the result is cognitive dissonance. From an OB perspective, your personal attitudes affect your behavior via your intentions.

LO 2-2

Explain how personal attitudes affect workplace behavior and work-related outcomes.

In this section, we discuss the components of personal attitudes and examine the connection between personal attitudes and behavior.

Personal attitudes affect behavior at a different level than do values. While values represent *global* beliefs that influence behavior across *all* situations, personal attitudes relate only to behavior directed toward *specific* objects, persons, or situations. We summarize the differences between the two in Table 2.2.

Attitudes represent our feelings or opinions about people, places, and objects and range from positive to negative. They are important because they influence our behavior. For example, you are more likely to select chocolate ice cream over vanilla if you are more positively disposed toward chocolate. In contrast, **workplace attitudes are an outcome of various OB-related processes, including leadership.** In this chapter we reserve the term *workplace attitudes* for attitudes that have resulted from the interaction of various individual, group, and organizational processes. We examine the effects of workplace attitudes later in Section 2.3.

As predictors of likely behavior, attitudes attract serious attention. Hardly a day goes by without the popular media reporting the results of another effort to take the pulse of public opinion (attitudes). Political consultants use poll results, for instance, to draft messages meant to nudge the public's attitudes toward desired results. In the workplace, managers conduct attitude surveys to monitor workplace attitudes like job satisfaction and employee engagement, and to identify the causes of employee turnover.

TABLE 2.2   Differences between Values and Personal Attitudes

CONCEPT	SCOPE	INFLUENCE	AFFECTS BEHAVIOR
Personal Values	Global	Broad: All situations	Variously
Personal Attitudes	Specific	Targeted: Specifically	Via intentions

OB in Action

Hospitality Industry Uses Attitude Surveys to Target Causes of Turnover

The hospitality industry is using attitude surveys to identify the causes of employee dissatisfaction and turnover—and perhaps discover why there is a shortage of good cooks. A recent survey conducted by Culinary Agents revealed that career development opportunities were very important to kitchen and dining room employees. Managers use results from surveys like this to make organizational changes. One restaurant, for instance, implemented a Sous Chef Supper Series, in which under-chefs can introduce original dishes to the public. Others are making it easier for their cooks to stay healthy. Chef Tony Maws of Craigie on Main in Cambridge, Massachusetts, offers company-sponsored yoga classes for employees. At SPQR in San Francisco, executive chef Matthew Accarrino has led his kitchen staff on bike rides to the Napa Valley to visit the restaurant's partnering farm.[7] Blue Apron, the meal kit delivery service, uses customized software to regularly survey employees with quick polls.[8]

YOUR THOUGHTS?

1. What are the pros and cons of using results from attitude surveys to create organizational changes?

2. Do you think the changes described above will reduce employee turnover for cooks? Explain.

Personal Attitudes: They Represent Your Consistent Beliefs and Feelings about Specific Things

Consider a work example. If you have a positive attitude about your job (specifically, you like what you are doing), you should be more willing to extend yourself by working longer and harder. This example illustrates that attitudes propel us to act in a specific way in a specific context.

Values and attitudes are generally in harmony, but not always. A manager who strongly values helpful behavior may have a negative attitude toward helping an unethical coworker.

This pastry chef seems to be enjoying her job. Not only does this attitude positively impact her performance, but it is contagious to others in the kitchen. Do you think we have a choice in our work attitudes?

Echo/Image Source

The Three Components of Attitudes: Affective, Cognitive, and Behavioral

Our overall attitudes toward someone or something are a function of the combined influence of three components of attitudes:

1. **The affective component—"I feel." The *affective component* of an attitude contains our feelings or emotions about a given object or situation.** For example, how do you *feel* about people who talk on their cell phones in restaurants? If you feel annoyed with such people, you are experiencing a negative affect toward them.

2. **The cognitive component—"I believe." The *cognitive component* of an attitude reflects our beliefs or ideas about an object or situation.** What do you *think* about people who talk on cell phones in restaurants? Your idea that such behavior is rude (or not) represents the cognitive component of your attitude.

3. **The behavioral component—"I intend." The *behavioral component* refers to the way we intend or expect to act toward someone or something.** For example, how would you intend to respond to someone talking on a cell phone during dinner at a restaurant if this individual were sitting near you and your guest?

All three components influence behavior. You are unlikely to say anything to someone using a cell phone in a restaurant if you are not irritated by this behavior (affective), if you believe cell phone use helps people manage their lives (cognitive), and if you have no intention of confronting the individual (behavioral).

When Attitudes and Reality Collide: Consistency and Cognitive Dissonance

Have you ever been accused of being a hypocrite—saying one thing and then behaving differently? Like most people, you probably want to maintain consistency between your attitudes and your behavior.

But sometimes attitudes conflict with reality. Suppose Megan has a positive attitude about helping others. One day in class, Megan's instructor announces there will be a contest to come up with the best social media campaign to increase enrollment at the school. The prize for winning the contest is $500, which would go a long way to helping Megan purchase a new laptop. The rub is that Rob, one of her classmates, has come to her seeking help on *his* contest entry, agreeing to split the cash prize with her if they win. Although Megan would like to help Rob, she feels it would take time away from completing her own entry. Should she make time to help her classmate or focus solely

We are more likely to purchase a car when we have positive attitudes toward it. These attitudes might pertain to make, model, color, price, and quality. Which component of attitudes would most strongly affect your overall attitude toward buying a sleek new convertible?

John Lund/Marc Romanelli/Blend Images LLC

on finishing her own contest entry? According to social psychologist Leon Festinger, Megan's situation is creating *cognitive dissonance.*

Cognitive dissonance **represents the psychological discomfort a person experiences when simultaneously holding two or more conflicting cognitions (ideas, beliefs, values, or emotions).**[9] Festinger was fascinated by the way people are motivated to maintain consistency (and avoid dissonance) among their attitudes and beliefs, and the way they resolve inconsistencies that drive cognitive dissonance. From observation, he theorized that we can reduce cognitive dissonance in three ways:

1. *Change your attitude or behavior or both.* Megan could either (a) tell herself that she can't help Rob because she wants to win the contest and the much-needed prize money or (b) schedule a little extra time to help her classmate and split the prize money.

2. *Belittle the importance of the inconsistent behavior.* Megan could belittle (in the sense of "make small") the belief that she needs to help her classmates every time they ask for assistance.

3. *Find consonant elements that outweigh dissonant ones.* Megan could tell herself that she can't help because she could really use the prize money to buy a new laptop.

Attitudes Affect Behavior via Intentions

Psychologists I. Ajzen and M. Fishbein further explored the reasons our attitudes and behavior can be misaligned. Based on this work, Ajzen developed and refined a model focusing on intentions as the key link between attitudes and planned behavior. See Figure 2.3.

Determinants of Intention Figure 2.3 suggests that three key general motives (in the three gold circles) predict or at least influence intention and behavior.

1. *Attitude toward the behavior:* the degree to which a person has a favorable or unfavorable evaluation of the behavior in question.

FIGURE 2.3 Ajzen's Theory of Planned Behavior

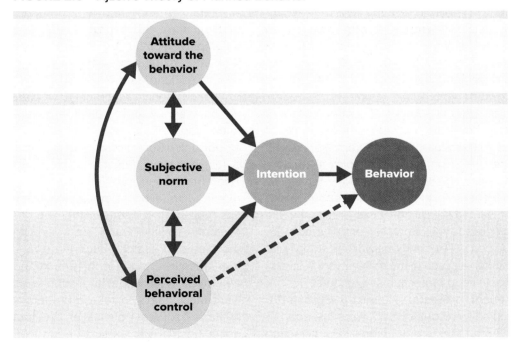

SOURCE: Ajzen, Icek. "The Theory of Planned Behaviour." *Organizational Behavior and Human Decision Processes* 50, no. 2 (December 1991): 179–211.

2. *Subjective norm:* a social factor representing the perceived social pressure for or against the behavior.

3. *Perceived behavioral control:* the perceived ease or difficulty of performing the behavior, assumed to reflect past experience and anticipated obstacles.[10]

Consider the intention of donating blood. You would have a positive intention if you thought donating was valuable for society (attitude toward the behavior), if your friends were going to join you (subjective norm), and if you had the time to participate (perceived control).

Putting the Theory into Practice We provide a case regarding McDonald's as a context for applying this theory. Once you identify the problem in the case, Ajzen's theory can be used to explain why the McDonald's employees went on strike. You do this by considering whether or not the three determinants of intentions are influencing the employees' behavior of walking off their shifts. If you conclude that one or more of these determinants is a cause for the strike, then propose what management can do to change the situation. For example, if you believe that the McDonald's workers have a positive attitude about going on strike, then what should management do to change these attitudes?

Problem-Solving Application

McDonald's Workers Protest Sexual Harassment: What Should Management Do?

Hundreds of McDonald's employees in 10 U.S. cities recently staged a series of strikes to call attention to the prevalence of sexual harassment at work and to urge the company to take more active steps to prevent it. "This is more important than work," said one Kansas City employee who experienced harassment and skipped her shift to participate in that city's rally. "We have the strength to protect one another and demand the justice we deserve," she told the crowd.[11]

With historically low wages and a large share of the workforce, one that consists predominantly of women and young adults, the restaurant industry and the fast-food industry in particular employ many people typically vulnerable to rights violations. Four in 10 female employees in these sectors report having received unwanted sexual advances, and nearly 3 in 10 report various forms of harassment. The majority, including 90 percent of immigrant workers, keep quiet about such offenses, and many are unaware that they are legally entitled to protection and recourse.

The recent protests, organized by a labor rights group called Fight for $15, were intended to draw public attention to employees' dissatisfaction with McDonald's response to complaints. "What McDonald's does on this issue, how they choose to treat it, how they act on it proactively, will have influence on other stores," said a lawyer for the workers.[12] Among workers' demands are better training, more effective ways to file complaints, and an employee committee specifically empowered to look into sexual misconduct issues at the company's 14,000 stores.

Ten McDonald's workers have already filed sexual harassment and retaliation complaints against male supervisors with the Equal Employment Opportunity Commission (EEOC). Nearly 30 other employees claim they have been harassed at work. Two enforcement problems specific to the restaurant industry are that employees often depend on tips, making it difficult for them to challenge poor customer behavior, and the franchise structure of the fast-food sector, which large companies may feel absolves them from any responsibility for employee relations at individual stores. Workers want McDonald's to take a bigger role in setting human resource policies at the franchise level, believing this will extend needed protections to employees of franchise businesses that may not have a human resource department or a safe process for handling complaints about workplace harassment. As the lawyer quoted above observed, McDonald's is a huge company and easily capable of doing this effectively if it chooses to.

McDonald's statement said, "We have strong policies, procedures and training in place specifically designed to prevent sexual harassment. To ensure we are doing all that can be done, we have engaged experts in the areas of prevention and response."[13] Employees, however, say nothing is being done.[14]

Apply the 3-Step Problem-Solving Approach

Action 1: What is the problem in this case?

Action 2: Identify the causes of the problem.

Action 3: Make a recommendation to correct the situation.

Research and Practical Applications   According to the Ajzen model, someone's intention to engage in a given behavior is a strong predictor of that behavior. For example, if you want a quick way to determine whether a worker will quit his or her job, have an objective third party ask the worker what he or she intends. The answer is likely to be accurate. Research supports this conclusion[15] and the prediction that intentions are influenced by the three general motives in Ajzen's model.[16]

So if we want to change behavior, we should look at intentions and ways we might modify them by working on the three general motives shown in Figure 2.3. Managers may be able to influence behavioral change by doing or saying things that affect the three determinants of employees' intentions to exhibit a specific behavior: attitude toward the behavior, subjective norms, and perceived behavioral control. In your own life, if you want to exercise more, you should start by changing your intentions about exercising and your associated beliefs about it.

Let's consider another practical illustration. Have you ever wanted a classmate to increase the quality of his or her work on a team project? If so, Ajzen's model can help you. Start by trying to create a *positive attitude* toward contributing high-quality work. You might do this by telling the person that getting a good grade on the project will increase everyone's chances of getting higher grades for the course and ultimately a better job upon graduation. Next, model the desired behavior by producing good work yourself and recognizing others who do the same. This should strengthen the *subjective norm* about doing high-quality work. Finally, talk to the individual about any obstacles getting in the way of high-quality work and discuss solutions for overcoming them. This should increase the person's *perceived behavioral control.*

2.3 KEY WORKPLACE ATTITUDES

THE BIGGER PICTURE

Of the many workplace attitudes we might see as outcomes in the Organizing Framework for Understanding and Applying OB, researchers have identified a small number that are especially potent. These *key* attitudes allow you to track a limited number of workplace attitudes to gauge how the organization is doing. When you try to make sense of the workplace on either side of a manager's desk, these are the important attitudes to follow.

LO 2-3

Discuss the importance of four key workplace attitudes.

Savvy managers will track four key workplace attitudes:

1. Organizational commitment
2. Employee engagement
3. Perceived organizational support
4. Job satisfaction

These attitudinal measures serve a dual purpose. First, they represent important outcomes that managers may be working to enhance directly. Second, they link to other significant outcomes that managers will want to improve where possible. For example, low job satisfaction and low employee engagement imply lower task performance and higher employee turnover.[17] This is why managers should track key workplace attitudes and understand their causes and consequences.

> **EXAMPLE** Facebook sends out employee surveys on a regular basis to gauge work attitudes and employee engagement. The company discovered these surveys not only give employees the chance to be heard but also provide management with important information when it comes to how long people intend to stay at the social networking giant. For example, according to Facebook's head of people analytics, individuals who don't fill out employee surveys are 2.6 times more likely to leave the company over the next six months.[18]

This section specifically examines the first three of the four attitudes: organizational commitment, employee engagement, and perceived organizational support. Job satisfaction, the most studied workplace attitude, will be covered in a later section.

Organizational Commitment

OB researchers define *commitment* as "a force that binds an individual to a course of action of relevance to one or more targets."[19] This definition highlights the way OB researchers link commitment to behavior and the way workers can commit to multiple targets or entities. For example, an individual can be committed to his or her job, family, girl- or boyfriend, faith, friends, career, organization, and/or a variety of professional associations. Let us now consider the application of commitment to a work organization.

Organizational commitment **reflects the extent to which an individual identifies with an organization and commits to its goals.** Committed individuals tend to display two outcomes:

- Likely continuation of their employment with the organization.
- Greater motivation toward pursuing organizational goals and decisions.

What Drives Organizational Commitment?   Many factors inspire organizational commitment, but let's start with a basic one. Organizational commitment exists to the degree that your personal values match the values that pervade your company's organizational culture. For example, if you value achievement and your employer rewards people for accomplishing goals, you are more likely to be committed to the company. This consistency between personal and company values is called person–culture fit and is discussed in Chapter 14.

Throughout this book we will cover other drivers of organizational commitment, including:[20]

- Personality.
- Meaningfulness of the work being performed.
- Organizational climate.
- Leader behavior.
- Organizational culture.

Finally, commitment depends on the quality of an employee's psychological contracts. ***Psychological contracts*** **represent an individual's perception about the reciprocal exchange between him- or herself and another party.** In a work environment, the psychological contract represents an employee's beliefs about what he or she is entitled to receive in return for what he or she provides to the organization. Research shows that an employer breach of the psychological contract is associated with lower organizational commitment, job satisfaction, and performance and with greater intentions to quit.[21]

How Can Managers Increase Employees' Commitment?   To highlight how managers can increase employees' commitment, we review three general best practices and then discuss approaches used by Hilton, Salesforce, and Cisco.

General Best Practices

- Hire people whose personal values align with the organization's.
- Make sure that management does not breach its psychological contracts.
- Treat employees fairly and foster trust between managers and employees.

Example Company: Hilton

- *Fortune* listed it as the No. 1 best company to work for in 2019.
- Launched new team member benefits including parental leave and adoption assistance.
- Implemented a companywide immersion program requiring every executive leader to spend one week on the front lines working alongside cooks, housekeepers, and front desk personnel.
- Invested heavily in redesigning employee spaces with better lighting, more comfortable furnishings, and an updated cafeteria.
- Worked with Under Armour to introduce lighter, more comfortable work wear for service employees.
- Increased expenditures for continuous learning and career development programs through its Hilton University program.[22]

Example Company: Salesforce

- *Fortune* listed it as No. 2 best company to work for in 2019.
- Spent nearly $9 million over three years to address differences in pay across gender and race for its more than 21,000 employees.
- Built company culture around *Ohana*—the Hawaiian concept of family, with 10 employee resource groups to encourage employees to be their "full authentic self" at work.
- Asks new employees to spend part of their first day doing service work in the local community.
- Gives employees seven paid days of volunteer time off annually to make the world a better place in addition to a generous amount of paid time off and sick leave.
- Established the role of Chief Philanthropy Officer to oversee the millions of dollars in grants the company provides to support education in underserved neighborhoods, homelessness organizations, and other local community initiatives.[23]

Example Company: Cisco

- *Fortune* listed it as the sixth best company to work for in 2019.
- Outlines company and employee expectations and benefits in "Our People Deal," a manifesto detailing what Cisco can do for its employees and what the company expects in return.
- Flextime helps employees achieve work–life balance. **Flextime is a policy of giving employees flexible work hours so they can come and go at different times, as long as they work a set number of hours.**
- Employees get 40 hours of paid time off to volunteer, and the company matches this time with financial contributions to the volunteers' programs.
- To encourage new ideas, launched global pitch contest to its 37,000-plus employees to come up with innovative solutions to technology problems with a $50,000 prize.
- Employees get 36 days of holiday and vacation time following one year of employment.[24]

Employee Engagement

Observing workers at a summer camp and an architecture firm in 1990, William Kahn defined **employee engagement** as **"the harnessing of organization members' selves to their work roles; in engagement, people employ and express themselves**

This employee looks highly engaged in her work. Note the attention and focus she uses to uncover this fossil. Would you find this type of work meaningful?

Arpad Benedek/Getty Images

physically, cognitively, and emotionally during role performance."[25] The essence of this definition is the idea that engaged employees "give their all" at work. Further study identified its components as four feelings:

- Urgency
- Focus

- Intensity
- Enthusiasm[26]

Have you ever felt at work or school that time seems to fly by? If yes, then you understand why academics, consultants, and managers want to understand how they can harness the power of employee engagement.

How Much of the U.S. Workforce Is Actively Engaged?   The U.S. workforce appears to be achieving close to the global average. Consulting firm Aon has traced data on employee engagement around the globe for more than 15 years, studying millions of employees. Recent figures for North America (of which the United States is the largest component) and other global regions are shown in Table 2.3.[27] Although the U.S. workforce leads Europe, it is outpaced by Latin America, Africa-Middle East, and Asia Pacific.

What Contributes to Employee Engagement?   Let's use the Organizing Framework for Understanding and Applying OB to identify key drivers of employee engagement.

Person Factors

- Personality.
- Positive psychological capital.
- Human and social capital.[28]

Situation Factors

- Job characteristics. People are engaged when their work contains variety and when they receive timely feedback about performance.
- Leadership. People are more engaged when their manager is supportive and maintains a positive, trusting relationship with them.[29]
- Organizational climate can range from positive and inspiring to negative and depleting. Positive climates obviously foster engagement.
- Stressors. **Stressors are environmental characteristics that cause stress.** Engagement is higher when employees are not confronted with a lot of stressors.[30]

What Outcomes Are Associated with Employee Engagement?   Consulting firms such as Gallup, Hewitt Associates, and Blessing White have been in the forefront of collecting proprietary data supporting the practical value of employee engagement. For example, Gallup estimates that an organization whose employees are highly engaged can

TABLE 2.3   Employee Engagement Around the World

LOCATION OF EMPLOYEES	PERCENT OF HIGHLY OR MODERATELY ENGAGED EMPLOYEES
1. The World	65%
2. North America	64
3. Europe	60
4. Asia Pacific	65
5. Latin America	75
6. Africa-Middle East	66

achieve 10 percent higher customer loyalty/engagement; 20 percent more productivity; and 21 percent greater profitability.[31] Other recent academic studies similarly showed a positive relationship between employee engagement, performance, and physical and psychological well-being and corporate-level financial performance and customer satisfaction.[32]

Now that you know engagement is correlated with performance at work, try the following Self-Assessment to measure your level of engagement with your studies. Can you improve your performance in the classroom?

SELF-ASSESSMENT 2.2   CAREER READINESS

To What Extent Are You Engaged in Your Studies?

Please be prepared to answer these questions if your instructor has assigned Self-Assessment 2.2 in Connect.

1. Is your level of engagement what you expected?
2. How might you increase it?
3. To what extent do your professors influence your level of engagement? How might they foster more engagement from you?

How Can Managers Increase Engagement? As a manager you will have many opportunities to improve employee engagement, even if you can't offer the lavish perks of the richest corporations. One way is to make sure inputs in the Organizing Framework are positively oriented. Organizations do this by measuring, tracking, and responding to surveys of employee engagement.

> **EXAMPLE** The Ritz-Carlton hotel chain significantly lowered employee turnover (to 28 percent vs. an industry average of more than 55 percent) and increased both customer satisfaction and customer spending by assessing potential candidates against the company's 12 employee values related to its gold standards for customer service.[33]

Other ideas include creating career and developmental opportunities for employees, recognizing people for good work, effectively communicating and listening, allowing people to exercise during the workday, creating a physically attractive and stimulating work environment, giving employees meaningful work to do, and empowering them.

OB in Action

Companies Foster Employee Engagement in Different Ways

- **Freese and Nichols** This Texas engineering firm fosters engagement with generous development opportunities. When engineer Kim Patak wanted the company to adopt greener water engineering, her bosses gave her $10,000 and time off for a training program on environmentally sound infrastructure practices. "It felt like I was getting a graduate degree," says Patak of her experience. "It felt amazing to have that support of the company, to have the trust in me." Since then, the company's expertise and leadership in sustainable water practices have grown rapidly.[34]

- **T-Mobile** In hiring Ivan Beltran to manage its flagship New York City store, T-Mobile gambled on a candidate with "passion and love for the brand" but no experience as a director. Beltran explains why that paid off. "What

Chip Bergh, Levi Strauss CEO
Richard Drew/AP Images

president of retail channels, "We tell people, 'We want you to be you.' We think people do their best work when they can be themselves."[35]

- **Levi Strauss** "If we can identify much earlier people who are at risk of developing cancer, then go into hyper care for them to make sure that, if they do get the disease, you catch it at stage zero or stage 1—where the cost of care is much, much less . . . it's much better for everyone." That's not a doctor talking. It's Chip Bergh, CEO of jeans maker Levi Strauss, which recently offered employees an optional free DNA test. Says Bergh, "The more we can do to keep our employees engaged and give them benefits that are meaningful for them, the better it is for us."[36]

it means to me is I work for a company that truly values their employees, a company willing to take risks." Ranked among the best workplaces in the nation's largest city, T-Mobile continues to embrace employees' individuality. Says Jon Frier, executive vice

YOUR THOUGHTS?

1. What do you think about these approaches to engagement?

2. Which company approach would be most effective for you as an employee? Explain.

Perceived Organizational Support

Perceived organizational support **(POS) reflects the extent to which employees believe their organization values their contributions and genuinely cares about their well-being.** Your POS would be negative if you worked for a bad boss or a company that did not provide good health benefits or career opportunities. It would more likely be positive if you worked for outdoor gear retailer REI (Recreational Equipment, Inc.) in one of its more than 150 stores across the country. REI fully funds the company profit-sharing plan (without employees needing to contribute their own pay); awards annual incentive pay based on reaching individual, department, and company goals; subsidizes the majority of employees' medical plan costs; offers a referral bonus of $100 to $2,000; and gives generous discounts (30 to 50 percent) on REI gear and apparel.[37]

How Does POS Affect Employees? People are willing to work hard and commit to their organizations when they believe the company truly cares about their best interests. Quite simply, we are motivated by the *norm of reciprocity* to return the favor when someone treats us well. This is why we are more likely to reciprocate with hard work and dedication when our employer treats us favorably. But the favorable treatment must be voluntary, not imposed by external constraints such as government or union rules. Voluntary actions demonstrate that the giver genuinely values and respects us.

Benefits of POS Managers cannot go wrong in providing organizational support. Research shows that it is positively associated with employee engagement, organizational commitment, job satisfaction, organizational citizenship behavior, greater trust, innovation, and lower tendency to quit.[38]

How can managers foster positive POS?

They can treat employees fairly, avoid political behavior, provide job security, empower employees, reduce stressors in the work environment, eliminate abusive supervision, and fulfill the psychological contract.[39]

2.4 THE CAUSES OF JOB SATISFACTION

THE BIGGER PICTURE

Job satisfaction is the most frequently studied outcome in the Organizing Framework. To help you understand it better, this section provides you with the five major models of job satisfaction. These models can help you manage others and yourself, leading to an increased sense of satisfaction at work or school for you and others.

LO 2-4

Discuss the five causes of job satisfaction.

Job satisfaction essentially reflects the extent to which an individual likes his or her job. Formally defined, *job satisfaction* **is an affective or emotional response toward various facets of your job.** Notice that job satisfaction is not a monolithic concept. Rather, a person can be relatively satisfied with one aspect of her or his job and dissatisfied with one or more others.

Managers and organizations measure job satisfaction in one of two ways. The simplest is to use a single overall rating, such as, "How satisfied are you with your job?" People respond on a rating scale that might run from (1) very dissatisfied to (5) very satisfied. Have you ever completed a survey like this? The second method assess satisfaction along a series of facets. For example, researchers at Cornell University developed the Job Descriptive Index (JDI) to assess satisfaction with the following: work, pay, promotions, coworkers, and supervision.[40] This type of assessment provides more detailed and actionable information about job satisfaction. If desired, managers or researchers can add the ratings across facets to arrive at a total score.

We use a facet measure of job satisfaction in the following Self-Assessment. Completing it will inform you about your level of satisfaction for a current or past job and make the rest of the chapter more practical for you. Are you curious about where you stand?

SELF-ASSESSMENT 2.3   CAREER READINESS

How Satisfied Are You with Your Present Job?

Please be prepared to answer these questions if your instructor has assigned Self-Assessment 2.3 in Connect.

1. What are your relative levels of satisfaction with recognition, compensation, and supervision?

2. Which of these three aspects of satisfaction is most important to you? Explain.

3. What can you do to increase your level of job satisfaction?

Source: Adapted from D.J. Weiss, R.V. Dawis, G.W. England and L.H. Lofquist, *Manual for the Minnesota Satisfaction Questionnaire* (Minneapolis: Industrial Relations Center, University of Minnesota, 1967). Used with permission.

Do you think job satisfaction across the United States has been going up or down over the past few years? A national survey conducted by the Conference Board attempted to answer this question by asking 1,500 employed individuals to rank their job satisfaction based on 23 components. Results revealed 51 percent were satisfied with their jobs in

2018, the seventh straight year that overall job satisfaction had increased among U.S. workers.[41] The significance of this finding will become more apparent after you read the final section of this chapter.

At a Glance: Five Predominant Models of Job Satisfaction

If you want insight into the drivers of your own job satisfaction or that of others, consider five models of these causes, summarized as follows. We look at each in more detail in Table 2.4.

TABLE 2.4   Five Models of Job Satisfaction

MODEL	HOW MANAGEMENT CAN BOOST JOB SATISFACTION
Need fulfillment	Understand and meet employees' needs.
Met expectations	Meet employees' expectations about what they will receive from the job.
Value attainment	Structure the job and its rewards to match employee values.
Equity	Monitor employees' perceptions of fairness and interact with them so they feel fairly treated.
Dispositional/genetic components	Hire employees with an appropriate disposition. (See qualifications below.)

Brief Review: Five Predominant Models of Job Satisfaction

Let's take a closer look at these models. It will increase your understanding if you personalize each model to your own past experiences.

Need Fulfillment   Need fulfillment models propose that satisfaction is determined by the extent to which the characteristics of a job allow an individual to fulfill her or his needs. **Needs are physiological or psychological deficiencies that arouse behavior.** All of us have different needs, which means that managers need to learn about employees' needs if they want to increase employees' job satisfaction.

> **EXAMPLE** A recent annual survey of 600 individuals by the Society for Human Resource Management asked employees to choose the aspects of their jobs that were very important to their job satisfaction. For the third year in a row, the top choice was respectful treatment of employees at all levels of the organization. Other important contributors to job satisfaction included compensation/pay; trust between employees and senior management; job security; and opportunities to use skills and abilities.[42] Are any of these aspects important to you?

Research generally supports the conclusion that need fulfillment is correlated with job satisfaction.[43]

Met Expectations   *Met expectations* **represent the difference between what an individual expects to receive from a job, such as good pay and promotional opportunities, and what she or he actually receives.** When expectations are greater than what is received, a person will be dissatisfied. On the other hand, he or she will be satisfied when outcomes are above and beyond expectations. Research strongly supports the conclusion that met expectations are significantly related to job satisfaction.[44]

Value Attainment   The idea underlying *value attainment* is that satisfaction results from the perception that a job allows for fulfillment of an individual's important values. Research consistently supports this perspective. Managers can enhance employee satisfaction by providing work assignments and rewards that reinforce employees' values.

Equity   Equity theory builds on the notion that satisfaction rests on how "fairly" an individual is treated at work. If we perceive that our work outcomes, relative to our inputs, compare favorably with someone else's outcomes and inputs, we will be satisfied. Research has strongly supported the theory behind this model.[45] Managers thus are encouraged to monitor employees' fairness perceptions and to interact with employees in such a way that they feel equitably treated. Chapter 5 explores how this can be accomplished.

Dispositional/Genetic Components   Ever notice that some coworkers or friends remain satisfied in situations where others always seem dissatisfied? The dispositional/genetic model posits that job satisfaction is a function of both personal traits and genetic factors. Indeed, the model implies that stable individual differences are at least as powerful as characteristics of the work environment in their impact on satisfaction.

Few studies have tested these propositions in depth, but they do show that dispositional factors are significantly associated with only selected aspects of job satisfaction. Dispositions had stronger relationships with intrinsic aspects of a job (such as having autonomy) than with extrinsic aspects (such as the receipt of rewards).[46] Genetic factors also were found to significantly predict life satisfaction, well-being, and general job satisfaction.[47] Overall, researchers estimate that 30 percent of an individual's job satisfaction is associated with dispositional and genetic components.[48]

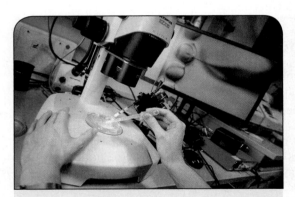

As technology continues to advance, it's likely scientists will be able to edit the genes of human embryos to alter genetic makeup including personal traits. Is this a good thing?
Gregor Fischer/Getty Images

EXAMPLE Recent gene-editing experiments conducted in China may have an impact on personal traits and genetic factors in the future. A Chinese scientist recently announced he and his team had used a powerful gene-editing technique called Crispr to alter the genes of human embryos that were implanted in female volunteers. One of the volunteers gave birth to twin girls and another volunteer is now pregnant. In addition to the ethical issues raised by such experiments, the worldwide scientific community is questioning the long-term effects of such alterations, which if successful, would be inherited by future generations and likely change individuals' genetic makeup and personal traits.[49]

A Shorter Walk to Work

Now that we have looked at the predominant models of job satisfaction, let's highlight one element that allows people to balance their work and family lives: the opportunity to telecommute. *Telecommuting* allows employees to do all or some of their work from home, using advanced telecommunications technology and Internet tools to send work electronically from home to the office, and vice versa.

- About half of the U.S. workforce telecommutes for at least part of the time spent working.

- The number of people telecommuting has grown 140 percent between 2005 and 2016. Experts estimate that 50 percent of the U.S. workforce has a job compatible with teleworking.
- The need for flexibility is a key reason people like telecommuting.[50]
- Studies confirm telecommuting enhances productivity and retention and decreases absenteeism.[51]

These positive statistics imply that the opportunity to telecommute could improve job satisfaction. To make such programs successful, consider the recommendations in the Applying OB box below.

Applying OB

Best Practices for Implementing Telecommuting

1. Assess the readiness of both people and jobs for telecommuting. Not all employees or all jobs are ready for this step.
2. Ensure employees have the proper technology and support, and that the communications network is secure.
3. Establish clear expectations about the goals of the program and how it will work. For example, encourage telecommuters to keep regular work hours and to set up a dedicated office space.
4. Make it a priority to establish trust on both sides. Communicate regularly, give credit when due, and avoid micromanaging.
5. Evaluate the program's effectiveness with regular and fair assessments of employee performance.[52]

More and more employees are telecommuting from their homes on a regular basis. Managers need to encourage regular communications, ensure employees keep regular work hours, and insist on workers setting up a dedicated office space.
Jupiterimages/Getty Images

2.5 MAJOR CORRELATES AND CONSEQUENCES OF JOB SATISFACTION

THE BIGGER PICTURE

The documented relationship between job satisfaction and other positive organizational outcomes is good news. It means that employers have economic reasons for fostering job satisfaction to improve results. You're about to learn four key attitudinal and behavioral outcomes and two organizational-level outcomes associated with this relationship.

LO 2-5

Describe work-related outcomes associated with job satisfaction.

Thousands of studies have examined the relationship between job satisfaction and other organizational variables. We consider a subset of the most important variables from the standpoint of managerial relevance. Ten key outcomes correlate to job satisfaction—four attitudinal and four behavioral, and two organizational-level outcomes. Job satisfaction has significant correlations with:

Attitudes

- Motivation
- Job involvement
- Withdrawal cognitions
- Perceived stress

Behavior

- Job performance
- Organizational citizenship behavior (OCB)
- Counterproductive work behavior (CWB)
- Turnover

Organizational Level

- Accounting/financial performance
- Customer service/satisfaction

Attitudinal Outcomes of Job Satisfaction

We examine four attitudinal outcomes of job satisfaction that are important to OB researchers and managers: motivation, job involvement, withdrawal cognitions, and perceived stress.

Motivation   Employee motivation represents a psychological process that arouses our interest in doing something, and it directs and guides our behavior. As you might expect, employee motivation positively correlates to job satisfaction. Managers can enhance employees' motivation with a host of techniques and recommendations discussed throughout this book.

Job Involvement *Job involvement* **represents the extent to which an individual is personally engaged in his or her work role.** Many years of research have demonstrated that job involvement is moderately related to job satisfaction.[53] Managers can foster satisfying work environments to fuel employees' job involvement.

Withdrawal Cognitions Although some people quit their jobs impulsively or in a fit of anger, most first go through a process of thinking about whether they should quit. *Withdrawal cognitions* **capture this thought process by representing an individual's overall thoughts and feelings about quitting.** Low job satisfaction is believed to be one of the most significant contributors to thoughts of quitting.

> **EXAMPLE** A recent survey of more than 1,000 employed U.S. workers conducted by Bamboo HR revealed that 31 percent of respondents left a job within the first six months of being hired because they thought their new boss was a jerk; the job was different from what they expected in the interview; or they felt alone and not engaged with coworkers. Results suggest managers can help increase job satisfaction by ensuring that new employees understand their new job tasks and feel connected to others in the organization.[54]

Have you ever felt like this when studying for exams? Unfortunately, too much stress impairs our ability to perform at school or at work.
Kdonmuang/Shutterstock

Perceived Stress Stress has negative effects on many different OB-related outcomes. For instance, it is positively related to absenteeism, turnover, coronary heart disease, and viral infections. As you would expect, it also has a strong negative relationship to job satisfaction and employee engagement. Managers should attempt to reduce the negative effects of stress by improving job satisfaction and by encouraging employees to detach from work during off-job time (stop thinking about work and don't "take it home with you").[55]

Problem-Solving Application

What to Do, or Not to Do, about Sexual Harassment

When actor Kevin Spacey was accused of sexual misconduct, Netflix was among the companies that responded unequivocally, removing him as executive producer and star of its acclaimed series "House of Cards" and then abandoning another deal with him, despite losing $39 million in the process. When it came to setting an internal sexual harassment policy for its own employees, however, Netflix drew a more confused reaction.

The new policy reportedly forbids employees to ask each other for their phone numbers without prior permission, to flirt, or to ask a colleague for a date again if he or she has already said no. It encourages employees to shout, "Stop! Don't do that again," if a colleague behaves inappropriately. But rumors about a rule that said employees should not stare at each other for more than five seconds at a time drew particular mockery in the media, and among Netflix employees as well. They reportedly began deliberately staring at each other, counting to five, and looking away.

Critics also wondered how employees could network with each other for business purposes without sharing phone numbers and questioned why Netflix seemed to presume that every such request was made for the purpose of dating or in pursuit of sex.

Netflix responded by issuing this statement: "We're proud of the anti-harassment training we offer to our productions. We want every Netflix production to be a safe and respectful working environment. We believe the resources we offer empower people on our sets to speak up, and shouldn't be trivialized."[56]

Some, however, felt the policies themselves trivialized the very real problems of sexual harassment at work, which have been in especially sharp focus since the rise of the #MeToo movement. A later statement from Netflix said the five-second "rule" was not a rule but rather a suggestion raised in a training session about the new policy.[57]

Apply the 3-Step Problem-Solving Approach

Step 1: Define the problem in this case.

Step 2: Identify the OB concepts or theories that help explain the situation Netflix faced and its reaction.

Step 3: State what you would do if you were a human resource officer at Netflix responsible for setting harassment policies.

Behavioral Outcomes of Job Satisfaction

Job satisfaction has a positive association with two constructive individual-level behavioral outcomes—job performance and organizational citizenship behavior (OCB). It also has a negative relationship with two potentially negative behaviors—counterproductive work behavior (CWB) and turnover. The following discussion is more practical when you consider that these individual-level outcomes in the Organizing Framework are driven by processes at the group and organizational level, which, further upstream, are influenced by environmental characteristics.

Job Performance   One of the biggest controversies within OB research centers on the relationship between job satisfaction and job performance. This is more complicated than it might first appear; OB experts have identified at least eight ways in which these variables are related. Here is what we know from research.[58]

A team of researchers analyzed data involving nearly 7,000 individuals over a three-year period.[59] They made two key findings:

- **Job satisfaction and performance are *moderately* related.** This supports the belief that employee job satisfaction is a key workplace attitude managers should consider when attempting to increase employees' job performance.

- **The relationship between them is complex.** Researchers now believe **both variables indirectly influence each other** through a host of person factors and environmental characteristics contained in the Organizing Framework.

Organizational Citizenship Behavior   *Organizational citizenship behavior (OCB)* **is defined as "individual behavior that is discretionary, not directly or explicitly recognized by the formal reward system, and that in the aggregate**

promotes the effective functioning of the organization."[60] This definition highlights two key points:

- OCBs are voluntary.
- OCBs help work groups and the organization to effectively achieve goals.

Examples of organizational citizenship behavior include such gestures as:

- Constructive statements about the department.
- Expression of personal interest in the work of others.
- Suggestions for improvement.
- The training of new people.
- Respect for the spirit as well as the letter of housekeeping rules.
- Care for organizational property.
- Punctuality and attendance well beyond standard or enforceable levels.[61]

Managers certainly would like employees to exhibit these behaviors, and research clearly supports their value. OCBs have a moderately positive correlation with job satisfaction.[62] Moreover, they are significantly related to both individual-level consequences (performance appraisal ratings, intentions to quit, absenteeism, and negative job attitudes) and organizational-level outcomes (productivity, efficiency, lower costs, customer satisfaction, and unit-level satisfaction and turnover).[63]

These results are important for two reasons. First, exhibiting OCBs is likely to create positive impressions about you among your colleagues and manager. In turn, these impressions affect your ability to work with others, your manager's evaluation of your performance, and ultimately your promotability. Second, the aggregate amount of employees' OCBs affects important organizational outcomes. It is thus important for managers to foster an environment that promotes organizational citizenship behaviors.

Volunteerism is a form of discretionary citizenship behavior that promotes a positive organizational image. What personal values lead someone to volunteer to tend to a local community garden?
John Lund/Marc Romanelli/Blend Images LLC

Counterproductive Work Behavior You already know from personal experience and OB research that the absence of satisfaction may be associated with some types of undesirable behavior, such as low employee engagement and performance. In contrast to the helping nature of OCBs, *counterproductive work behavior (CWB)* **harms other employees, the organization as a whole, and/or organizational stakeholders such as customers and shareholders.** CWBs represent a particularly negative work-related outcome. Examples include bullying, theft, gossiping, backstabbing, drug and alcohol abuse, destruction of organizational property, violence, deliberately poor or incorrect work, Internet surfing for personal reasons, excessive socializing, tardiness, sabotage, and sexual harassment.[64]

> **EXAMPLE** Mastering the company's mail order system, an IKEA worker issued himself nearly $400,000 in refunds for purchases made by customers.

> **EXAMPLE** A former manager at a lab testing company created fake invoices and expense reports to get reimbursed for more than $1.2 million.

> **EXAMPLE** A U.S. postal worker in Washington, DC, bilked the Postal Service out of nearly $40,000 in unearned wages by claiming he was serving jury duty on a lengthy federal trial. The worker fabricated court paperwork to support his reimbursement claims.[65]

CWB has a strong negative relationship with job satisfaction, so managers should find ways to reduce it. Here are three key ways.

1. Hire individuals who are less prone to engage in counterproductive behavior. Cognitive ability is associated with many measures of success, so it is a logical quality to screen for in hiring decisions. Personality tests also may be relevant.

2. Design jobs that promote satisfaction, and root out and eliminate managers who treat others in an abusive manner.[66]

3. Respond quickly and appropriately if an employee does engage in CWBs, defining the specific behaviors that are unacceptable and the requirements for acceptable behavior.

Turnover Turnover can be a good thing when a low-performing person like George Costanza from *Seinfeld* quits or is fired. This result enables managers to replace the Georges of the world with better or more diverse individuals or to realign the budget. In losing a good employee, however, the organization loses valuable knowledge and experience and it can be costly. Experts estimate that the cost of turnover for an hourly employee is roughly 20 percent of his or her annual salary, higher for professional employees with specialized skills.[67]

Job satisfaction has a moderately strong negative relationship with turnover. Managers are well served by enhancing employees' job satisfaction, especially in today's competitive labor market.[68] For example, global HR consulting firm Mercer surveyed more than 160 large employers recently and found that voluntary turnover was at more than 15 percent.[69]

All these considerations suggest several practical steps employers can take to tackle a turnover problem. See the Applying OB box.

Organizational-Level Outcomes of Job Satisfaction

Job satisfaction is positively associated with the organizational-level outcomes of accounting/financial performance and customer service/satisfaction.

Accounting/Financial Performance   Earlier we noted that job satisfaction was moderately associated with an individual's performance. It thus makes sense to hypothesize that the aggregate level of employee job satisfaction should be positively associated with a company's accounting/financial performance. A study of 448 small- to medium-sized business units supported this prediction. However, the association between job satisfaction and this outcome is lower than between job satisfaction and productivity.[74] This makes sense because many other factors besides job satisfaction impact accounting/financial performance.

Customer Service/Satisfaction   Why do we expect satisfied employees to provide higher-quality service to customers? The answer is the spillover effect. Spillover occurs when attitudes in one part of our lives spill over to another. Employees' positive work attitudes might spill over to improve their behaviors toward customers. In support of this idea, research supports a positive association between job satisfaction and customer satisfaction.[75]

2.6 MAKING THE CONNECTION: HOW DO VALUES AND ATTITUDES AFFECT WORK-RELATED OUTCOMES?

Personal values, attitudes, and intentions play a significant role in affecting individual and organizational outcomes at work. Here are some key points to consider.

LO 2-6

Describe the implications of values and attitudes for you and managers.

Takeaways for Me

Here are five additional things you can do to turn this chapter's lessons into positive change in your personal and professional life.

1. **Identify your core values:** This can help you make decisions about careers, companies to work for, relationships, and ways to manage others.

2. **Realize the power of your beliefs and intentions:** Your intentions will drive your behavior, but it is beliefs that create your intentions. If you want to change a behavior, such as losing weight or studying more, the first step is to analyze and change your beliefs about the behavior.

3. **Engagement is partly a choice on your part, and it all starts with doing meaningful work:** Identify what types of work you find meaningful.

4. **If your manager or organization is not providing support, consider moving on:** There are many great companies that understand the value of organizational support.

5. **Before quitting a job, consider doing a cost–benefit analysis:** Write down the costs of staying and compare them to the perceived benefits of leaving. Making an emotional decision might feel good in the short run, but it is less likely to lead to positive results.

Takeaways for Managers

There are five key implications for managers.

1. **Hire people whose values match the values that underlie the organization's culture:** Such employees are more likely to be productive and to stay.

2. **Influence employees' behavior by reinforcing appropriate beliefs:** For example, if you want to improve employee retention, underscore the value of staying at the company.

3. **Employee commitment is strongly associated with emotional connections at work:**[76] Create positive team spirit and engage in social activities that promote friendships among employees.

4. **Employees won't be engaged if you display negative emotions:** Stay positive and model engagement.

5. **There is a trend for employees to quit less than one year on the job:** Discuss their expectations when you hire and socialize new employees effectively. Socialization is discussed in Chapter 14.

What Did I Learn?

You learned that employee engagement is a workplace attitude that motivates people to identify with and immerse themselves in their work. Values and attitudes directly affect a variety of organizational outcomes, and companies pay attention to them to achieve improved performance. Companies track the work attitude of job satisfaction because it positively correlates with other positive workplace attitudes (motivation, job involvement, reduced stress) and behavior (job performance, OCB, customer satisfaction, reduced CWB and turnover). Reinforce your learning with the chapter's Key Points below. Next, consolidate your learning using the Organizing Framework, shown in Figure 2.4. Then, challenge your mastery of the material by answering the chapter's Major Questions in your own words.

Key Points for Understanding Chapter 2

You learned the following key points.

2.1 PERSONAL VALUES

- Values are abstract ideals that guide your thinking and behavior across all situations.
- Schwartz proposed that 10 core values guide behavior across contexts and time (see Figure 2.2).
- The 10 core values each relate to one of four themes: self-transcendence, conservation, self-enhancement, and openness to change (see Figure 2.2).
- Managers can use the Schwartz model to motivate employees and to reduce the chances of employees' experiencing conflict between their values and their work assignments.

2.2 PERSONAL ATTITUDES AND THEIR IMPACT ON BEHAVIOR AND OUTCOMES

- Attitudes represent your feelings or opinions about people, places, and objects and range from positive to negative. Workplace attitudes are outcomes in the Organizing Framework for Understanding and Applying OB.
- The three components of attitudes are affective, cognitive, and behavioral.
- Cognitive dissonance represents the psychological discomfort an individual experiences when his or her attitudes or beliefs are incompatible with his or her behavior.
- Intentions are the key link between attitudes and behavior in Ajzen's model. Three determinants of the strength of an intention are attitude toward the behavior, subjective norms, and perceived behavioral control (Figure 2.3).

2.3 KEY WORKPLACE ATTITUDES

- Organizational commitment reflects how strongly a person identifies with an organization and is committed to its goals. It is influenced by a host of factors in the Organizing Framework, including personality, leader behavior, organizational culture, meaningfulness, organizational climate, and psychological contracts.
- Employee engagement occurs when employees give it their all at work. It includes feelings of urgency, focus, intensity, and enthusiasm.
- Employee engagement is influenced by personal factors and environmental characteristics contained in the Organizing Framework.
- Perceived organizational support reflects how much employees believe their organization values their contributions and cares about their well-being. Employees are happier and work harder when they feel supported.

2.4 THE CAUSES OF JOB SATISFACTION

- Job satisfaction is an affective or emotional response toward various facets of the job. It is a key OB outcome.
- The five major causes of job satisfaction are need fulfillment, met expectations, value attainment, equity, and dispositional/genetic components.

- Telecommuting allows people to balance their work and family lives. It uses telecommunication technology and Internet tools to send and receive work between home and office.

2.5 MAJOR CORRELATES AND CONSEQUENCES OF JOB SATISFACTION

- Job satisfaction is significantly associated with the following attitudinal variables: motivation, job involvement, withdrawal cognitions, and perceived stress.
- Job satisfaction is significantly related to five key behavioral outcomes: job performance, organizational citizenship behavior, counterproductive work behavior, turnover, and customer satisfaction.

2.6 HOW DO VALUES AND ATTITUDES AFFECT WORK-RELATED OUTCOMES?

- Identifying your core values will help you make smart decisions about career moves and relationships in both your personal and professional life.
- Recognizing the power of your beliefs and how they influence behavior will help you zero in on the type of work you find meaningful.
- Hiring people whose values and attitudes align with an organization's culture encourages employee motivation, productivity, and retention.

The Organizing Framework for Chapter 2

As shown in Figure 2.4, values, personal attitudes, and intentions serve as inputs that lead to a host of outcomes. Although this chapter focused on workplace attitudes as an outcome, future chapters will look at other outcomes in more detail.

Challenge: Major Questions for Chapter 2

You should now be able to answer the following major questions. If you can't, have you really processed and internalized the lessons in the chapter? Refer to the Key Points, Figure 2.4, the chapter itself, and your notes to revisit and answer the following major questions:

1. What role do play in influencing my behavior?
2. How do personal attitudes affect workplace behavior and work-related outcomes?
3. Why should management pay attention to workplace attitudes?
4. How can changes in the workplace improve job satisfaction?
5. What work-related outcomes are associated with job satisfaction?

FIGURE 2.4 Organizing Framework for Understanding and Applying OB

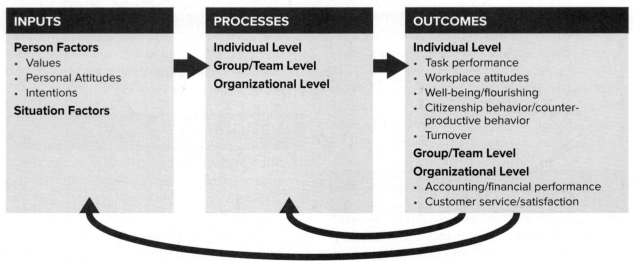

Walmart's Values Come under Scrutiny

Sam Walton founded Walmart in Rogers, Arkansas, and the company grew from that single store in 1962 to more than 11,300 locations spanning 27 countries by 2019. Today, the multinational retailer is the world's largest company by revenue—generating over $500 billion in 2018—and the largest private employer with more than 2.2 million employees. The retailer also owns Sam's Club, a chain of warehouse clubs that sell groceries and general merchandise in bulk.[77]

Walmart is known for its "everyday low prices," but critics say prices are not all that's low at the retailer. Individual employees, advocacy groups, and government agencies have brought numerous labor-related lawsuits against the company, scrutinizing its internal values. Let's take a closer look at what's going on at the massive retailer.

A SERIES OF WORKPLACE ABUSES

Walmart prides itself on its values. The retailer states that, "We define culture as our values in action. It's how we deliver superior customer service, create a great front-line work environment and improve performance . . ." Moreover, Walmart's stated values are centered on being "guided by good," which includes "respect for the individual" and "acting with integrity."[78] Allegations against the company suggest a different story.

Consider a report by a workers' advocacy group that says Walmart "routinely refuses to accept doctors' notes, penalizes workers who need to take care of a sick family member and otherwise punishes employees for lawful absences." The report is based on a survey of more than 1,000 Walmart employees and accuses Walmart of violating the American with Disabilities Act and Family Medical Leave Act, among other labor laws.[79]

Katie Orzehowski was a cashier at the Walmart in North Huntingdon, Pennsylvania, and completed the employee survey. She suffered a miscarriage in 2016 and provided doctors' notes and hospitalization records to excuse her missed shifts, but the company refused to excuse her absences. She was so worried that another absence would get her fired that she returned to work, while still in recovery. "I still had a lot of bleeding going on, and that's embarrassing," Orzehowski told *The New York Times*.[80]

Walmart's focus on the bottom line over its employees' welfare didn't end with those who suffered from an illness. The Equal Employment Opportunity Commission (EEOC) filed a lawsuit against the retailer in September 2018 alleging it unlawfully discriminated against pregnant workers in Wisconsin. The complaint was filed on behalf of Alyssa Gilliam, who became pregnant in 2015. Gilliam requested light duty or transfer to a less physically demanding job in which she would avoid heavy lifting due to her pregnancy. The company declined to accommodate her in any way, including providing her with a chair, shorter work days, or additional breaks. The EEOC alleges that Walmart retaliated by cutting Gilliam's benefits, reducing her work hours, and eventually forcing her to take unpaid leave. Interestingly, Walmart had a robust light duty program that allowed workers with lifting restrictions to be accommodated, "But Walmart deprived pregnant workers of the opportunity to participate in [this] program. This amounted to pregnancy discrimination, which violates federal law," said the EEOC.[81]

Gilliam wasn't the only employee denied a chair. Adam Catlin, who suffers from cerebral palsy, has been a Walmart greeter in Selinsgrove, Pennsylvania, for almost ten years. Catlin was told in 2019 that due to a change in corporate policy, he would need to stand for his entire eight-hour shift and lift up to 25 pounds or be fired. Caitlin's mother urged Walmart customers on Facebook to support her son. "I know corporate decisions are corporate decisions, if [that's] where this originated from, but does anyone ever make any decisions anymore by putting any heart or care into it?" she wrote.[82]

WALMART'S ALLEGED BAIT AND SWITCH

Walmart CEO Doug McMillon's compensation for fiscal 2018 was $22.8 million, which is 1,188 times the annual compensation of its median employee. In contrast, CEO pay at S&P firms averaged 361 times more than the average employee in 2018.[83] Overall, the company "has been the defendant in scores of cases, including class actions, or group suits, accusing the company of wage-law violations," according to Jonathan Tasini, president of the Economic Future Group.[84]

Walmart decided to raise its minimum wage from $10 to $11 in 2018. With much fanfare, CEO McMillon stated, "Today, we are building on investments we've been making in associates, in their wages and skills development . . . It's our people who make the difference and we appreciate how they work hard to make every day easier for busy families."[85] Now consider that Walmart closed dozens of its Sam's Club warehouses on the same day it announced the pay increases.[86] This brings into question whether the retailer had positive intentions in raising employee pay. The United Food and Commercial Workers International Union, for example, called the wage increase a "public relations stunt" meant to distract from the closing of 63 stores.[87] The closures resulted in approximately 10,000 workers losing their jobs.[88] The timing of the announcement wasn't the only issue as many Sam's Club employees had no idea their stores would be closed until the day of the announcement. According to *The Times*, some workers showed up for work only to be informed that their stores were closed.[89]

POOR JOB SATISFACTION IMPACTS CUSTOMER SERVICE

Walmart's minimum wage hikes may raise the pay of some of its workers, but they may not be enough to solve the retailer's continued customer service problem, according to *Forbes*.[90] Walmart's American Customer Satisfaction Index (ACSI) score dropped between 2016 and 2017. The ASCI measures the quality of products and services American consumers receive by major department and discount retailers. The drop placed Walmart at the bottom of a list of department and discount retailers (even below a bankrupt Sears).

Making Change at Walmart (MCAW), an organization dedicated to transforming the lives of Walmart employees, believes the company's poor customer service ratings are related to the way it treats its workers. "Walmart lacks the ability to improve its customer experience when it refuses to focus on what we all know to be true—quality jobs create quality experiences for both shoppers and workers," says MCAW director Randy Parraz.[91] Walmart needs to do more for its employees if it wants to improve their attitudes with customers. For example, wages and benefits are so poor at Walmart that thousands of its employees qualify for food stamps, Medicaid, and other government assistance programs, according to MCAW.[92]

Walmart says it has a "common purpose of saving people money so they can live better."[93] It seems its employees will need to live better as well if the company wants to continue its success.

APPLY THE 3-STEP PROBLEM-SOLVING APPROACH TO OB

STEP 1: Define the problem.

A. Look first at the Outcome box of the Organizing Framework in Figure 2.4 to identify the important problem(s) in this case. Remember that a problem is a gap between a desired and a current state. State your problem as a gap, and be sure to consider problems at all three levels. If more than one desired outcome is not being accomplished, decide which one is most important and focus on it for steps 2 and 3.

B. Cases have protagonists (key players), and problems are generally viewed from a particular protagonist's perspective. You need to determine from whose perspective—employee, manager, team, or the organization—you're defining the problem.

C. Use details in the case to identify the key problem. Don't assume, infer, or create problems that are not included in the case.

D. To refine your choice, ask yourself, *Why is this a problem?* Answering this question helps refine and focus your thinking. Focus on topics in the current chapter, because we generally select cases that illustrate concepts in the current chapter.

STEP 2: Identify causes of the problem by using material from this chapter, which has been summarized in the Organizing Framework shown in Figure 2.4. Causes will tend to appear in either the Inputs box or the Processes box.

A. Start by looking at Figure 2.4 to decide which person factors, if any, are most likely causes of the defined problem. For each cause, ask yourself, *Why is this a cause of the problem?* For example, if you think personal attitudes—an input in the Organizing Framework—are a cause, ask yourself why. This might lead you to the conclusion that Mayer's attitudes about telecommuting are related to her prior work experience. This may have led her to make decisions that are adversely affecting employees. Asking why several times will lead you to a more complete list of causes.

B. Follow the same process for the situation factors.

C. Because no processes were specifically discussed in this chapter, you can skip an analysis of this component of the Organizing Framework.

D. To check the accuracy or appropriateness of the causes, be sure to map them onto the defined problem.

STEP 3: Make recommendations for solving the problem. Consider whether you want to resolve it, solve it, or dissolve it (see Section 1.5). Which recommendation is desirable and feasible?

- Given the causes identified in Step 2, what are your best recommendations? Use the material in Chapter 2 (or in Chapter 1) to propose a solution.

- Find potential solutions in the OB in Action and Applying OB boxes within the chapter. These features provide insights into what other individuals or companies are doing regarding the topic at hand.

- Create an action plan for implementing your recommendations.

What Should Management Do About an Abusive Supervisor?

This challenge involves the behavior of Bernadine Pearce. Pearce was the supervisor of Michelle Ruppert, a clerk in the Office of the Tax Collector in the Borough of Point Pleasant, New Jersey. Pearce worked at the local government for about 40 years.

Ruppert filed a lawsuit claiming that her boss and the office allowed a hostile work environment to exist. She had worked at the office for about three years at the time of the suit.

The hostility allegedly began on Ruppert's first day at work. Upon arriving, Pearce showed her the "Wall of Shame." Placed conspicuously in the main office, it contained a funeral urn with the "ashes of problem employees." Ruppert noted that it resembled "the way Adolf Hitler treated the disabled and the Jews during the Holocaust," with "various nameplates of the employees who were 'exterminated'" or fired by Pearce.

The lawsuit alleges that Pearce stated "that all personnel of her office should be 'perfect humans,' as she believed she was."[94]

Media reports about the situation allege that "Pearce threw papers at Ruppert and called her a 'waste of a human being,' encouraged Pearce's daughter and coworker to give Ruppert the middle finger, and referred to Ruppert as a 'mess up' who should just 'quit her job.'"[95]

Ruppert ultimately experienced stress and anxiety and took sick leave for medical and psychiatric treatment. When she returned to work, Ruppert alleges that Pearce relocated her desk so that she had to look at the Wall of Shame, which now contained her name along with the others.[96]

Addressing the Challenge

What would you do if you were the manager responsible for the entire office?

1. Settle the lawsuit and allow Bernadine Pearce to retire. While Pearce's behavior is bad, she did give the city 40 years of her life.

2. According to what we learned about counterproductive behavior, you would settle the lawsuit and fire Pearce. Assuming the allegations are accurate, Pearce's behavior deserves to be punished.

3. Settle the lawsuit and then retire because you allowed this abusive situation to exist.

4. Fight the lawsuit. If nothing else, this may help you reduce the payment that will be awarded to Ruppert.

5. Invent other options.

3

Individual Differences and Emotions

After reading this chapter, you should be able to:

LO 3-1   Distinguish individual differences based on their relative stability.

LO 3-2   Explain how multiple intelligences affect your performance.

LO 3-3   Illustrate ways in which personality can affect your performance at school and work.

LO 3-4   Describe the impact of core self-evaluations on performance.

LO 3-5   Realize the benefits of emotional intelligence.

LO 3-6   Explain how understanding emotions makes people more effective.

LO 3-7   Describe the implications of individual differences and emotions for you and managers.

The Organizing Framework for Understanding and Applying OB shown in Figure 3.1 summarizes the key concepts in Chapter 3. This chapter builds on Chapters 1 and 2 and explores numerous additional person factors, such as intelligence, personality, proactive personality, self-efficacy, self-esteem, locus of control, and emotional intelligence. We add to this an important individual-level process—emotions. Personality and the other person factors are related not only to emotions, but to a host of other processes and outcomes across levels in the Organizing Framework. While reading this chapter pay attention to the way these person-factor inputs influence individual-level outcomes, such as task performance, workplace attitudes (job satisfaction), well-being/flourishing, citizenship behaviors/counterproductive behaviors, turnover, and career outcomes. These inputs might contribute to explaining group/team conflict and performance, as well as organizational-level outcomes such as poor firm performance and low customer satisfaction.

FIGURE 3.1 Organizing Framework for Understanding and Applying OB

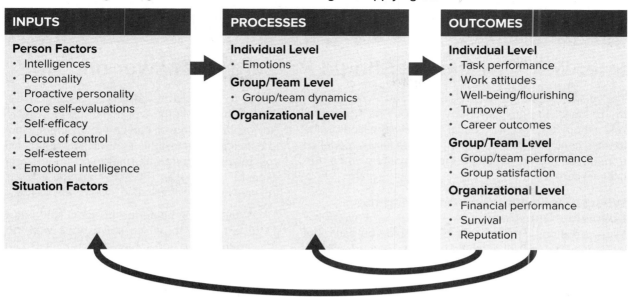

INPUTS	PROCESSES	OUTCOMES
Person Factors • Intelligences • Personality • Proactive personality • Core self-evaluations • Self-efficacy • Locus of control • Self-esteem • Emotional intelligence **Situation Factors**	**Individual Level** • Emotions **Group/Team Level** • Group/team dynamics **Organizational Level**	**Individual Level** • Task performance • Work attitudes • Well-being/flourishing • Turnover • Career outcomes **Group/Team Level** • Group/team performance • Group satisfaction **Organizational Level** • Financial performance • Survival • Reputation

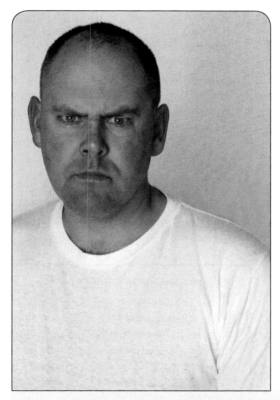

A seemingly infinite number of characteristics make us who we are as individuals. It therefore is helpful to organize these individual differences so we can better understand and use them to manage people at work. One method is to categorize characteristics in terms of their malleability. These photos illustrate this method. For instance, just by looking we can determine the gender of these two people. We also can approximate their ages. Your height and age are fixed traits, characteristics we cannot change. These photos also show very different emotions. The woman appears to be surprised and the man angry. Unlike height and age, our emotions can and do change easily and often. Managers can use that knowledge in multiple ways, such as selecting and hiring people on relatively fixed traits (intelligence), and training them on the appropriate or most effective emotions to display with customers. (left): Ingram Publishing; (right): Gulfimages/Alamy Stock Photo

Winning at Work

Interview Questions I Should Prepare to Answer *and ASK*

You've likely heard that interviews are a two-way street—the prospective employer interviews you and vice versa. And although the list of potential interview questions is limitless, a combination of research, practice, and experience from experts can help narrow the list and help you determine what to ask and how to prepare your resume.

What to Consider When Answering the Following Questions

Many questions you can anticipate, some you can't, but either way the following should help. First, we provide the questions or requests from the interviewer, followed by what she or he presumably wants to know and how you might respond.

1. "What are your strengths?" Identify two or three key skills noted in the job description and provide examples. Also use your OB knowledge and consider sharing some individual differences (Chapter 3) along with a brief Illustration, such as: "I am an extrovert and thrive in groups and teams." Or, "I am a motivated and skilled problem solver." This book will definitely help.

2. "What are your weaknesses?" Don't dare say, "My strengths are my weaknesses," "I work too hard," or "I'm a perfectionist." Interviewers want to check you're honest, humble, and ensure you are motivated to work on your weaknesses. Be honest without torpedoing your opportunity. Whatever you choose, be sure to explain how you became aware of it and what you are doing to address it.

3. "Describe yourself." Two approaches to consider. One, describe the professional path leading to where you are now. What piqued your interests and how did your studies or (work) experiences influence your path? Or, you might pick 2 or 3 key attributes you possess and explain how they will benefit the organization if hired.

4. "Tell me how you dealt with a challenge." Interviewer wants to learn how you deal with pressure and conflict. Think of and describe a situation, task, action, and result (STAR method). Example situations to consider: (a) difficult team member for a school project, sports team, or at work; (b) pressure situation where you performed well; or (c) met a tight and consequential deadline.

5. "Describe your dream job." The prospective employer is trying to determine fit, that is, do your interests align with the job and organization for which you are interviewing. Accordingly, be sure whatever you choose is relevant to and emphasizes *both* what you would receive from the "dream job" and what you would provide. Put differently, the dream job is not all about you. Also explain what the employer would get in return.[1]

What to Consider Asking

You of course will think of many questions of your own. However, you are well served to consider including these to gain important insights that will help you decide should you receive an offer, and help you understand what to expect if you accept. The questions you ask also provide the interviewer with valuable insights about you.

1. "Why are you hiring for this job?" Is it a new position due to growth, which could bode well for you, the organization, and future opportunities? Or, are they trying to fill an existing position due to a promotion or turnover? It could be valuable to learn which—promotions are good (you'll likely want one yourself) and if turnover is because the boss is a nightmare you may want to reconsider, especially if it is a pattern.

2. "What is the career path?" Essentially you want to know where do employees go after this role, what is the next step? It's likely you prefer to see opportunities beyond this job, and asking this question can help you learn whether that is the norm within the organization.

3. "What are the performance expectations and how are they measured?" Clarity and specifics are preferred and wish-washy, unclear answers may be cause for concern. You don't want surprises when it comes time for your performance review, as money, promotions, and opportunities may be at stake.

4. "What do you like and dislike about working here?" Just like the interviewer wants to know your strengths and weaknesses, you want to know theirs. Do their strengths align with or conflict with your interests, such as development, teamwork, and collegiality?[2]

What's Ahead in This Chapter

In this chapter you'll explore individual differences (IDs), which are the many attributes that distinguish all of us from one another. Recognizing and understanding IDs is critical to effectively applying OB knowledge and tools. For managers, it is fundamental to attracting, motivating, retaining, and improving the performance of others.

Your exploration of IDs begins with an explanation of the relative stability of these differences. Next, you'll delve into a subset of individual differences researchers have found to be particularly important in the work context: (1) intelligence, (2) cognitive abilities, (3) personality, (4) core self-evaluations, (5) attitudes (also covered in Chapter 2), and (6) emotions (including emotional intelligence).

3.1 THE DIFFERENCES MATTER

THE BIGGER PICTURE

You undoubtedly notice that your friends behave differently in different situations, whether in class, watching a sporting event, cramming for an exam, or coping with a new job. However, what you probably don't pay much attention to are the characteristics and behaviors that don't change. To help you understand and use this knowledge, we'll arrange the individual attributes on a continuum based on their relative stability. At one end are relatively fixed or stable *traits* (like intelligence), and at the other end are more flexible *states* (like emotions), with various *trait-like* and *state-like* characteristics in between.

Individual differences (IDs) are the many attributes, such as traits and behaviors, that describe each of us as a person. IDs are a big part of what gives each of us our unique identities, and are fundamental to the understanding and application of OB. So, what is it that makes us different? Is it our genetics or our environment? The answer is both.[3] And while the way you are raised, along with your experiences and opportunities, helps shape who you are, a large volume of research on twins suggests genetics matters more. But what is more important at work is recognizing the many attributes that make us unique individuals, regardless of whether they are due to nature or nurture.

LO 3-1

Distinguish individual differences based on their relative stability.

To help you understand and apply the knowledge you will gain about IDs, we organize and discuss them according to Figure 3.2.

On the left-hand side of Figure 3.2 we arrange individual differences on a continuum. At the top of the continuum are intelligence and cognitive abilities, which are relatively fixed. This means they are stable over time and across situations and are difficult to change. At the bottom are attitudes (which we discussed in Chapter 2) and emotions, which are relatively flexible. Emotions change over time and from situation to situation, and thus can be altered more easily. To elaborate, you aren't more or less intelligent at school than you are at work or home, although your emotions commonly change within and between all these places. Both your intelligence and emotions, as well as many other individual characteristics influence the many outcomes included in the right side of Figure 3.2.

The distinction between relatively fixed and flexible individual differences has great practical value. Wise managers know they have little or no impact on fixed IDs. You can't change an employee's level of intelligence or remake an employee's personality.[4] But you can help employees manage their attitudes and emotions. For instance, many effective managers (and their employers) select employees based on positive, job-relevant, but relatively stable IDs. This hiring strategy enables managers to capitalize on the personal strengths someone brings to a job because these stable strengths affect behavior and performance in almost every work situation.[5] Intelligence and analytical abilities, for example, are beneficial in front of customers, in teams with coworkers, and when working alone on a project.

In contrast, managers can have greater influence on the relationships between relatively flexible IDs and individual-level work outcomes, like performance and job satisfaction. They can do this by implementing policies that raise employees' core self-evaluations, attitudes, and emotions. For example, as a manager you'll likely see better results from

FIGURE 3.2 Relative Stability of Individual Differences

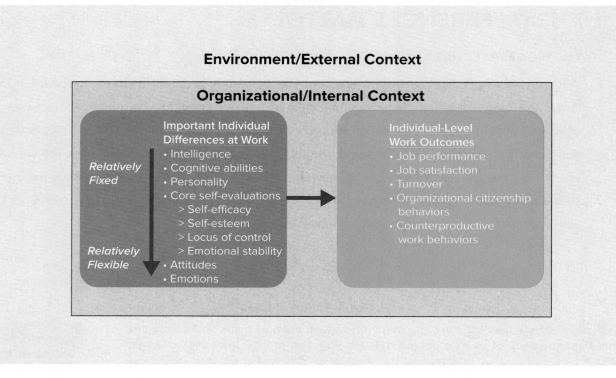

assigning work with new products and new markets to employees who are open to experience than to employees with low levels of this attribute. Similarly, you could help build new employees' confidence about selling to tough customers if you role-model how to do this effectively, give them experience presenting to easy customers first, and provide verbal encouragement before and constructive feedback after.

Managers are wise to pay attention to the effect of employee attitudes and emotions on turnover. Low job satisfaction and high negative emotions can predict which employees are likely to quit. Thankfully, however, attitudes and emotions can be changed more easily than other IDs. You can apply the same knowledge in reverse during job interviews, to help determine whether you'd like to work for that person. Read the following Applying OB box and find out how.

Applying OB   CAREER READINESS

Does Your Potential Boss Get the Job?

You may have heard "People quit managers, not their jobs or companies." Of course, employees quit for a host of reasons, but managers are a major one for most. A Gallup poll of more than 1 million employees who quit revealed 75% did so because of their bosses, not the job itself.[6] This means you should do your best to determine if turnover is an issue at any prospective employer, especially in the area in which you will work.

And if it is you should be concerned that they have (bad) manager issues.

We encourage you to look out for potential "bad" bosses, and to help in that endeavor we describe four common types:

- *Marionette* managers are puppets to their own bosses or to the organization. They don't challenge any policies or practices and won't stand up for you. They are loyal to themselves, not you, and follow orders and expect you to do the same.

- *King Kong* managers feel superior to you and other subordinates; they have reached the top and expect you to bow down.
- Keeping with the superiority theme, *Superman* bosses believe the world and everyone in it (you) revolves around them. They are the best and thus most qualified to make decisions. And making matters worse, they not only feel entitled to recognition and credit, they will steal it if possible.
- Then, there are *Taskmasters* who micromanage and often suffocate and kill employee creativity. They are consumed with bottom line results and will grind you up to achieve them.[7]

Now that we've described several versions of nightmare bosses, we offer the following tips and questions to help you learn whether the interviewer is worthy of being your manager.

1. **Determine what you want.** If you simply want a job or aren't sure what you want in a job and where you want it to lead, you are obviously more likely to accept a position with a bad boss. To gain more clarity about your boss, ask yourself what kind of relationship you want with him or her. Do you want someone hands-on, nurturing, and developmental? Or do you want a boss who is hands-off and will let you do your own thing? Asking these questions is a critical first step in evaluating your potential new boss.

2. **Look for good *and* bad.** While signing on with a bad boss can make you miserable, missing the opportunity to work with a good boss is costly too. Don't wear rose-colored glasses and overlook red flags, but don't be overly harsh either. Finding a boss willing to be a real advocate and champion for you and your career is invaluable. Make a list of your prospective boss's pros and cons and review it honestly.

3. **Learn what is expected of you.** Learning what the job entails seems obvious but is often overlooked. Ask, "What are your key expectations of me?" And, "If I'm a top performer, which I expect to be, what should my track record look like in 30, 60, or 90 days?" Ask, "How do people get ahead here? How do they fall behind?"

4. **Ask where others have gone.** Assuming your manager has been in the position for a while, he or she has likely managed other employees in the position for which you are interviewing. Ask: "Where have others you've managed gone?" You want to know whether they have been promoted or quit the organization. The first is encouraging, the second a potential red flag. It may be a sign of a miserable boss, or at least one who is not especially developmental.

5. **Meet people like you.** Do what you can to meet and learn from other employees—those doing the same job today or in the recent past. Sometimes you can find information online, and other times the company's interview process may provide opportunities to meet and interact with these employees. Learn what was good, bad, ugly. Ask, "If you were me, what would you want to know?" And, "If I'm going to be successful, then *what do I need to do and not do* with this person as my manager?" You may not get much detail, but it is worth trying to learn this information. Your own future may depend on it.

Next, let's discuss an individual difference which has historically received considerable attention at school and less at work—intelligence.

3.2 INTELLIGENCES: THERE IS MORE TO THE STORY THAN IQ

THE BIGGER PICTURE

You may be smarter than you think. You may already know your IQ, and your grades may reflect intellectual intelligence. But you can be intelligent in other ways too. We explain various forms of intelligence because all are inputs to the Organizing Framework, and all affect your performance.

LO 3-2

Explain how multiple intelligences affect your performance.

Although experts do not agree on a specific definition, many say *intelligence* **represents an individual's capacity for constructive thinking, reasoning, and problem solving.** Most people think of intelligence in terms of intelligence quotient or IQ, the famous score on tests we often take as children. Many people view intelligence and IQ as one big attribute of brainpower. However, intelligence, intelligence testing (for IQ), and related research are more complex.

The concept of intelligence has expanded over the years and is now thought of and discussed in terms of general mental abilities. People are different in terms of such abilities, but this isn't what is important at work. What is important is to understand intelligence or mental abilities in order to manage people more effectively. Put another way, the reason we highlight intelligence and mental abilities is they are related to performance at work.[8] This section provides a brief overview of intelligence and mental abilities and highlights practical implications.

Intelligence Matters . . . and You Have More Than You Might Think

Historically, intelligence was believed to be purely genetic—passed from one generation to another—you were either born "smart" or not. Do you agree with this belief? What are the implications of believing intelligence is a gift of birth? Regardless of your personal views, research has shown intelligence, like personality, can be altered or modified in several ways.[9] Think about it. No matter who you are or where your starting point in education or experience is, if you engage in more constructive thinking, reasoning, and problem solving, you will get better at these skills. You'll be more intelligent. If you buy this argument, then after reading this book and studying OB you'll be more intelligent due to the practice in critical thinking and problem solving you'll gain.

Am I More Intelligent than My Parents? If you answer yes to this question, research may support your claim. A steady and significant rise in average intelligence among those in developed countries has been observed over the last 70 years. Why? Experts at an American Psychological Association conference concluded, "Some combination of better schooling, improved socioeconomic status, healthier nutrition, and a more technologically complex society might account for the gains in IQ scores."[10] If you think you're smarter than your parents and your teachers, despite them saying you don't know important facts they do, you're probably right!

Mayim Bialik not only plays a neuroscientist on the blockbuster TV show *The Big Bang Theory,* but she actually has a PhD from UCLA (she also was accepted to Harvard and Yale). Reports put her IQ between 150 and 163. Matt Damon has a similarly impressive IQ of 160. It would seem the brainpower of his character in *Good Will Hunting* didn't require much "acting."[11] (left): Amanda Edwards/WireImage/Getty Images; (right): Michel Euler/AP Images

Multiple Intelligences (MI) While many people think of intelligence in general terms, such as IQ, it is more common and more practical to think in terms of multiple intelligences, or an intelligence for something specific. Howard Gardner, a professor at Harvard's Graduate School of Education, investigated the nature of intelligence for years and summarized his findings in his 1983 book *Frames of Mind: The Theory of Multiple Intelligences.*[12] The eight intelligences he identified, listed in Table 3.1, include not only mental abilities but social and physical abilities and skills as well.

Dr. Anne-Marie Imafidon was names one of the Top 50 Women Tech before turning 30. Stuart C. Wilson/Getty Images

EXAMPLE Named one of the Top 50 Women in Tech before turning 30, Dr. Anne-Marie Imafidon is the cofounder and CEO of Stemettes which helps girls develop and realize their potential in science, technology, engineering, and math—STEM, Stemettes, get it? Clever. To help inspire and guide teenaged girls, she and her company have developed apps and created mentoring programs and collaborations with large multi-national tech and media companies, such as Salesforce and BBC. Imafidon's intelligence in notable, as she is the youngest girl ever to pass A-level computing (age 11) and one of the youngest to earn a computer science masters from Oxford University.[15] But this belies her introversion. In an interview she said, "My dream in life is to be a hermit. Clubbing, festivals, and travelling are too much. . . . If I'm there it's for other people, not me. I'd rather spend a quiet night in front of the TV."[16]

Many believe the concept of multiple intelligences has important implications for employee selection, training, and performance. For example, one-size-fits-all

TABLE 3.1   Gardner's Eight Intelligences

TYPE OF INTELLIGENCE	EXAMPLE
Linguistic intelligence: potential to learn and use spoken and written languages.	Madeline Johnson, CEO of marketing and PR firm Market Council, speaks Spanish, Italian, Portuguese, along with her native English. She consults for multinational companies, and linguistic intelligence enables her to develop richer and more productive relationships quicker.[13]
Logical-mathematical intelligence: potential for deductive reasoning, problem analysis, and mathematical calculation.	Did this intelligence help or hurt you on your college entrance exam?
Musical intelligence: potential to appreciate, compose, and perform music.	Do you play the drums? Have you heard Marco Minnemann? He is widely considered a virtuoso drummer, one of the best on the planet. If you were to measure this form of intelligence, Minneman's musical intelligence score would likely be very high.
Bodily-kinesthetic intelligence: potential to use mind and body to coordinate physical movement.	Serena Williams, tennis player extraordinaire, says her mind helps her realize her tremendous physical talent.
Spatial intelligence: potential to recognize and use patterns.	Fighter pilots are excellent examples of people gifted with spatial intelligence.
Interpersonal intelligence: potential to understand, connect with, and effectively work with others.	Compare Warren Buffett (CEO of Berkshire Hathaway) to Larry Ellison (former CEO of Oracle). Critics see the first as approachable and friendly, the second as arrogant.
Intrapersonal intelligence: potential to understand and regulate yourself.	As the only woman assistant general manager of an NBA team, Kelly Krauskopf must have enormous self-awareness and control to endure the constant criticism and conflict in the job and for being a woman in that job.
Naturalist intelligence: potential to live in harmony with your environment.	Rose Marcario, the CEO of clothing and outdoor sports retailer Patagonia, supports the company's famous ad—"don't buy this jacket." The company has a long tradition of environmental responsibility in which it encourages customers not to buy more than they need to limit the strain on Earth's resources.[14]

training programs often fall short when diversity of intelligences is taken into consideration. When clinical training for undergraduate nursing students was designed to draw upon and apply their eight intelligences, for example, they acquired greater proficiency in clinical skills. This type of training also enabled them to utilize and develop interpersonal intelligence, extremely important for effective patient care.[17]

Near the end of this chapter, you will encounter the concept of *emotional intelligence,* which managers can apply for employee selection and other purposes. Future breakthroughs in the area of multiple intelligences will attract more OB researchers and practicing managers.

Practical Intelligence   We can draw practical benefits from Gardner's notion of multiple intelligences. For instance, Cornell University's Robert J. Sternberg applied Gardner's "naturalist intelligence" to the domain of leadership under the heading *practical intelligence.* He explains: **"*Practical intelligence* is the ability to solve everyday problems by utilizing knowledge gained from experience in order to purposefully adapt to, shape, and select environments.** It involves changing oneself to suit the environment (adaptation), changing the environment to suit oneself (shaping), or finding a new environment within which to work (selection). One uses these skills to (*a*) manage oneself, (*b*) manage others, and (*c*) manage tasks."[18]

Class action attorney Elizabeth Cabraser epitomizes the concept of multiple intelligences. Jeff Chiu/AP Images

EXAMPLE Attorney Elizabeth Cabraser has led some of the largest class-action lawsuits of our time, such as against big tobacco, makers of silicone breast implants, BP (for the Deepwater Horizon oil spill), and Toyota, GM, Takata, and VW for safety violations. Cabraser is an introvert and soft-spoken in court and outside of work. Her acclaim and success undoubtedly reflect considerable practical intelligence. Her success in class-action suits highlights her linguistic as well as intra- and interpersonal intelligences. These skills help immensely both in and out of court with clients and other attorneys. She also appears to have considerable musical intelligence; in college she played drums and toured with bands. But now she plays and collects drums only in her spare time.[19]

Practical Implications

Many educators and parents have embraced the idea of multiple intelligences because it helps explain how a child could score poorly on a standard IQ test yet be obviously gifted in other ways such as music, sports, or relationship building. It then follows we need to help each child develop in his or her own unique way and pace. Many people make the same arguments about college students and employees, but what is important as a matter of practice is to identify intelligences relevant to the job, and then to select, place, and develop individuals accordingly.

The Business of Brain Training   The interest in improving intelligence goes far beyond children and school. A number of companies, including Lumosity, Cogfit, and Elevate are in the business of brain training, claiming that adult intelligence can be increased by playing the company's games. Like other games, players improve their performance on these brain games over time, and some have also improved scores on IQ and other related tests.

Proof Is Lacking   Researchers, however, recommend caution. More research refutes the improvement claims made by such companies than supports them.[20] In fact, the Federal Trade Commission fined Lumosity $2 million for falsely claiming its training could prevent memory loss, dementia, and Alzheimer's disease.[21] The links between IQ and performance in school and on the job are also inconclusive. Part of the criticism is because IQ tests measure things taught in school, like linguistics (language) and analytics (math). This means if you do well in school, you're likely to do well on the test and vice versa (we're testing what is taught and teaching what is tested).[22]

What We Know   Improving intelligence through training is difficult, and you are well served to consider carefully before investing your time, money, or energy. But if you're going to do it, experts say in order to be effective such training needs three characteristics:

1. *Adaptive.* In intellectual training, much like physical training, improvement occurs when you exert yourself just beyond your limits. Easy should be avoided; constant and increasing challenge is what you need.

2. *Variety.* Given you have multiple intelligences, you'll need a variety of activities to improve. Memory, for instance, involves multiple areas of your brain which is why it is

best to include a host of stimuli (e.g., sights and sounds) to improve it. Training only your mathematical skills will improve just your mathematical skills, not your linguistic intelligence or more general IQ.

3. *Generalizability.* Most games and intelligence tests do not involve what you actually do in your job or everyday life. Therein lies the problem—you improve on a game or a test, but it has no relevance or impact on your performance at work. This is part of the reason why in 2014 more than 70 scientists "signed a statement warning consumers about commercial 'brain training' programs." Because you improve on the games doesn't mean you're smarter or will be a better performer at school or work.[23]

Regardless of your personal view on the practical value of intelligence at school or work, the following OB in Action box offers an interesting illustration of how intelligence testing is used in professional sports.

OB in Action

Smarts and Performance in Sports

Intelligence in its various forms is important because of its link to performance. Research and experience do not always support this link—the smartest are not necessarily the best performers in any arena. However, most believe it influences performance enough to test and select candidates based on IQ and other measures of intelligence. Perhaps you should consider it too.

Intelligence Testing in Football   Not only does the National Football League have an intelligence test for players, but it has been using it since the 1970s! The Dallas Cowboys began the practice with the popular Wonderlic test (50 questions with a 12-minute time limit). The test is administered at the Combine where new recruits are "interviewed" to assess physical and intellectual capabilities. Player scores are one factor considered by teams in the draft.

Only one player has had a perfect score so far—wide receiver Pat McInally of the Cincinnati Bengals from 1976 to 1985. Quarterback Ryan Fitzpatrick seemingly has "smarts" no matter how you measure it. He scored 48 on the Wonderlic (the third-best score of all time), completed the test in the shortest time ever and also scored 1580 out of 1600 on his SAT.[24]

Smarts aren't limited to QBs. Sam Acho, a linebacker in the NFL, speaks three languages and was awarded the Campbell Trophy for college football's top scholar-athlete when he attended the University of Texas.[25] Christian Wilkins, while a defensive lineman at Clemson also won this award, and he finished his bachelor's degree in only two and half years—and completed a masters too![26]

New Test and Other Sports   Multiple NFL, NBA, and MLB teams have recently trialed a new test—the Athletic Intelligence Quotient (AIQ). This test assesses how fast a player can acquire, process, and apply information. The idea or hope is these characteristics are better predictors of performance in sports, compared to a more general aptitude test such as the Wonderlic.[27] Baker Mayfield was reported to have the second highest score of the 63 college quarterbacks who have now taken the AIQ.[28]

YOUR THOUGHTS?

1. If you were a coach of a professional sports team would you favor intelligence testing? Why or why not?

2. Assume your employer uses such tests, and you are a hiring manager, how much weight would you give intellectual intelligence? Explain.

3. If you owned your own company justify *both* why you would and why would not use intelligence tests in the hiring process.

Let's now explore the ever-popular way that distinguishes people at work and in life—personality.

3.3 PERSONALITY, OB, AND MY EFFECTIVENESS

THE BIGGER PICTURE

You probably feel you know yourself better than anyone else, but you're about to learn some tools that will help you see how others perceive you. One such tool is the Big Five personality profile, which summarizes hundreds of personality traits into five categories. Another useful approach centers on *proactivity*. These tools will help you understand the managerial implications of other people's views of you. We explore these topics because personality is a fundamental driver of your behavior and performance at work, and an important input in the Organizing Framework for Understanding and Applying OB.

Personality **is the combination of relatively stable physical, behavioral, and mental characteristics that gives individuals their unique identities.** These characteristics or traits—including the way we look, think, act, and feel—are the product of interacting genetic and environmental influences and are stable over time and across situations and cultures.[29] Personality is a person input in the Organizing Framework.

Karen Sparck Jones was a highly regarded scientist whose work in the 1960s and 70s laid the foundation for search engines decades later. She was a self-taught programmer who combined statistics and linguistics to help computers interpret words. Jones was an advocate for women in science, fond of sailing, and wore a similar "uniform" most days—jeans, sweater, and a blouse.

LO 3-3

Illustrate ways in which personality can affect your performance at school and work.

There Is More to Personality Than Liking and Fit

Like most people, you may often think of personality in terms of whether you like or dislike someone. For instance, if you're asked to describe your professor for this class you might say: "She's great. I love her personality." Or if asked to describe your boss you might say: "He's a difficult individual, he's unethical, many of his colleagues won't associate with him, and he is widely disrespected and should be fired." If you are recruiting someone for a job (or your fraternity or sorority) you might say: "I really like his/her personality . . . I think he/she will fit in great with the rest of us."

What Can I Do with "Like"? While "liking" and "fit" matter (recall our discussion of fit from Chapter 2), these general and evaluative types of descriptions aren't very useful from a management standpoint. If you think of personality only in these terms, then what type of guidance would you give your recruiters for hiring new employees? "Go find people you like and be sure they fit" won't take you very far. And because you like someone doesn't mean you should hire that person, he or she will perform well, or he or she will be a good addition to your organization.

Be Precise to Be Effective To be effective at managing people you need to be more precise and scientific about personality. This challenge has motivated a tremendous amount of research about personality in psychology and in OB and provides

TABLE 3.2　Characteristics of Persons Scoring High on the Five Dimensions

THE BIG FIVE PERSONALITY DIMENSIONS	PERSONALITY CHARACTERISTIC
1. Extroversion	Outgoing, talkative, sociable, assertive
2. Agreeableness	Trusting, good-natured, cooperative, softhearted
3. Conscientiousness	Dependable, responsible, achievement-oriented, persistent
4. Emotional stability	Relaxed, secure, unworried
5. Openness to experience	Intellectual, imaginative, curious, broad-minded

SOURCE: Barrick, Murray R., and Michael K. Mount. "Autonomy as a Moderator of the Relationships between the Big Five Personality Dimensions and Job Performance." *Journal of Applied Psychology* 78, no. 1 (February 1993): 111–18. http://dx.doi.org/10.1037/0021-9010.78.1.111.

specific definitions of what personality is, provides tools to measure it, and data as to the effect it has on important processes and outcomes across all levels of the Organizing Framework.

The Big Five Personality Dimensions

Defining something as complex as personality is a challenge. Fortunately, psychologists and researchers have simplified this work into the **Big Five Personality Dimensions: extroversion, agreeableness, conscientiousness, emotional stability, and openness to experience.**[30] Table 3.2 details the five personality dimensions. For example, someone scoring high on extroversion will be an extrovert—outgoing, talkative, sociable, and assertive. Someone scoring low on emotional stability will likely be nervous, tense, angry, and worried.

A person's scores on the Big Five reveal a personality profile as unique as their fingerprints. To discover your own Big Five profile, complete Self-Assessment 3.1 and you'll learn there is more to personality than being likable or fitting in. This Self-Assessment will increase your self-awareness and illustrate some of the concepts described. Many companies use personality profiles for hiring and promotions, so your profile should provide practical insights.

SELF-ASSESSMENT 3.1　　　CAREER READINESS

What Is My Big Five Personality Profile?

Please be prepared to answer these questions if your instructor has assigned Self-Assessment 3.1 in Connect.

1. What are your reactions? Do you agree with the scores on your Big Five profile?

2. Which dimension(s) is (are) your highest? In which situations would they be most beneficial?

3. Which one or two dimensions do you think are likely the best predictors of managerial success? Which is the least? Explain.

4. What are the implications of your Big Five profile for working in teams at school or work?

One important question lingers: Are personality models unique to the culture in which they were developed? Cross-cultural research on the Big Five suggests the answer is no. Specifically, the Big Five personality structure held up very well in a study of women and men from Russia, Canada, Hong Kong, Poland, Germany, and Finland.[31] As a comprehensive analysis of Big Five studies revealed, "To date, there is no compelling evidence that culture affects personality structure."[32]

Hail the Introverts

Personality is not monolithic. Every person is a combination of the various dimensions—no one is 100 percent of one and zero of the others. This means, for instance, you and everyone else has some amount of introversion. Unfortunately, however, introverts get a bad rap in terms of performance and often are stereotyped and seen as less effective than extroverts or those who are conscientious. (You'll learn much more about stereotyping and perceptions more generally in Chapter 4.)

If this is your own view, you have more to learn. Founders of some of the most iconic tech companies of all time—Bill Gates, Larry Page, and Mark Zuckerberg—are perceived as introverts, and yet their accomplishments are legendary. Regardless of your own level of introversion, the nearby Applying OB box provides guidance on how to thrive as an introvert.

You could be on the Supreme Court! Ruth Bader Ginsburg is a self-described introvert, and given what we know about her work and what those who know her personally have shared, it is safe to assume she is highly conscientious, intelligent, and open to experience. These seemingly would be very beneficial traits in a Supreme Court justice. Her impact on gender equality and the legal history of America cannot be overstated, as are her many accomplishments. She was one of the first nine women admitted to Harvard Law School, made the *Law Review* in her first year, but despite these accomplishments had difficulties getting a job.[33] She obviously overcame these challenges and eventually made it to the highest court in the land, and since then has overcome multiple bouts of cancer.[34] It certainly seems like introversion didn't get in her way.

The iconic Supreme Court member's life has been chronicled on TV and in movies, providing vivid insight into her personality. TCD/Prod.DB/Alamy Stock Photo

Proactive Personality

A *proactive personality* is an attribute of someone "relatively unconstrained by situational forces and who effects environmental change. Proactive people identify opportunities and act on them, show initiative, take action, and persevere until meaningful change occurs."[35] In short, people with proactive personalities are hard-wired to change the status quo. It is no surprise this particular individual difference has received growing attention from both researchers and managers. Think about it. Companies, and their managers, routinely say they want employees who take initiative and are adaptable, as today's hypercompetitive and fast-changing workplace requires such characteristics.

Research shows those with proactive personalities positively influence many of the work outcomes shown in Figure 3.2 (and later in Figure 3.5). For example, proactivity is related to increased performance, satisfaction, affective organizational commitment (genuine desire to remain a member of an organization), and social networking.[36] Particularly interesting is the finding that those with proactive personalities tend to increase the supportiveness of their supervisors (a true benefit), and they also modify their work situations so they have more control. You likely are not thinking of retirement yet, but if you have a proactive personality then you will be more likely to be satisfied in your retirement, regardless of whether you were satisfied with your career or not.[37]

Applying OB

How to Thrive as an Introvert

Having an introverted personality is an individual difference that you, Larry Page, J. K. Rowling, Rosa Parks, Bill Gates, Mark Zuckerberg, and many other successful people share. Regardless of your own level of success, you can benefit from the advice of Russ Fujioka, entrepreneur and former president of the Americas for cloud accounting company Xero. Fujioka is a self-proclaimed and successful introvert.

1. **Be self-aware.** Be aware that introverts can be perceived as disinterested or aloof when they seem less engaged in conversations and social interactions. They may or may not be disinterested, of course, but are more likely to show it if they are. And in business situations, they must make the effort necessary to appear interested and force themselves to be engaged.

2. **Calibrate your intensity.** When engaging others, especially groups of people or teams at work, try to push your personal intensity level to 10 on a 10-point scale. If you feel your volume, body language, and interactions are maxed out, realize that if you were an extrovert, you'd probably be playing at only 7 instead of 10. Your perception of intense and loud is lower than what others will perceive. (Soliciting feedback, which is discussed in Chapter 6, is a good way of calibrating your intensity.)

3. **Play to your strengths.** Because engaging others is typically quite draining for introverts, it is a good idea to talk about and stick to topics you know and care about. This will enable you to naturally feel more energized and comfortable.

4. **Get team practice.** Join a team. Whether you join a recreational sports team or a club of some sort, being a member will help you practice and become comfortable with interacting with others. If it is a non-work team, the pressure and stress of work won't be part of the experience, making it easier to engage. This will help build your skills for when they really count—at work![38]

Proactive Managers What about your manager? An interesting study showed the ideal scenario is for both you and your manager to be proactive. This results in a better fit and better relationship between the two of you, and it also increases your level of job performance, job satisfaction, and affective commitment.[39] The same study also showed that the worst scenario in terms of performance was low proactivity for both you and your manager, followed by a highly proactive manager and a low proactivity follower. Employers are well-served to value and seek out employees and managers with high levels of proactive personality.

Given these insights, how proactive do you believe you are? How might you increase your proactivity? To help answer these questions, learn about your own proactivity, and explore the potential benefits for you by completing Self-Assessment 3.2.

SELF-ASSESSMENT 3.2　　CAREER READINESS

How Proactive Am I?

Please be prepared to answer these questions if your instructor has assigned Self-Assessment 3.2 in Connect.

1. Do you see a pattern among the questions on which you scored the highest? The lowest?

2. What are the implications of your highest-scoring answers for your success in school? In other words, how can these aspects of your proactivity help you?

3. How can knowledge of your proactive personality score help you when you look for a job? Be specific.

Proactivity and Entrepreneurs   Besides leading to increases in job performance, job satisfaction, and affective commitment (as discussed in Chapter 2), proactive personality is also linked to intentions to be entrepreneurial. This really should not be surprising, but it is helpful to know that scientific OB research substantiates this belief. Building on this, we can say employees with proactive personalities are more likely to be engaged (again, see Chapter 2) and creative at work.[40]

Successful entrepreneurs often exemplify proactive personality. Consider Dan Goldie, former professional tennis player and successful financial adviser. Goldie's youthful passion was tennis and his talent led him to junior championship titles, a scholarship at Stanford, and a ranking of 27th on the pro tour. Now he considers himself more successful at managing money than he ever was at tennis. Impressive to be sure.

Perhaps the more interesting aspect of Goldie's story is that proactivity has been a hallmark of his entire journey. He knew he wanted to attend college and the only way to pay for it was with a scholarship. He trained, competed, and earned it. He dreamed of playing professionally, so he looked at colleges with top tennis programs (like Stanford). He valued money and turned professional as soon as possible. Realizing he would not be a top player and tennis would not last forever, he completed an MBA while on tour. He utilized his standing to associate with and learn about finance from top professionals in that industry. Later he leveraged his tennis relationships to land some of his first and most significant clients as a money manager.[41]

Another entrepreneurial example is Sal Khan's Khan Academy. Now world famous, this organization provides Internet-based learning for nearly every scholastic subject under the sun. Here's how it started. Khan, who has three graduate degrees, offered to help his cousin with one of her classes via the Internet. She learned, the word spread, and a company was born. Khan Academy now has 18 million monthly users, more than 150 employees, and its courses are translated into 36 languages.[42]

Sal Khan's influence in online learning is epic. It is likely that a number of his individual differences (e.g., intelligence and proactivity) contribute to his entrepreneurial success.
Larry Busacca/Getty Images

Fascinating statistics, shown in Table 3.3, highlight other notable individual differences of entrepreneurs. How do you match up?

TABLE 3.3   Taking the Measure of Entrepreneurs

40	Average and median age
95.1%	Have bachelor's degrees
47%	Have advanced degrees
71.5%	Come from middle-class backgrounds
< 1%	Come from extremely rich or extremely poor backgrounds
70%	Used own savings as major source of funding
42.5%	Were firstborn
3.1	Average number of siblings
51.9%	First in family to start a business
69.9%	Married when they launched first business
59.7%	Had at least one child
73%	Think luck is an important factor in the success of their venture

SOURCE: *The Wall Street Journal.* "By the Numbers: Taking the Measure of Entrepreneurs." November 12, 2012.

Table 3.3 contains only averages. Even if you don't possess these qualities, you can still succeed as an entrepreneur. To help make this point, let's explore the link between personality and performance.

The Dark Side of Personality

Most of the individual differences covered in this book are positive or desirable, and Chapter 7 is devoted entirely to Positive Organizational Behavior. However, there are three individual differences that are universally considered undesirable, as they negatively affect outcomes across individual, group, and organizational levels: **narcissism, psychopathy, and Machiavellianism. These are referred to as the *Dark Triad*,**[43] but before saying any more, it is important to note at least the first two are considered clinically as personality disorders, which is not our interest here, but instead it is the prevalence and consequences at work that is our concern. That said, you may have already encountered people with one or more of these traits, and when this happens in the form of a manager, colleague, partner, advisor, or mentor the effects can be devastating. Let's explore in a bit of detail and learn how to identify if not also avoid them.

Narcissists **are characterized as (1) having a grandiose sense of self-importance; (2) requiring or even demanding excessive admiration; (3) having a sense of entitlement; (4) lacking empathy; and (5) tending to be exploitative, manipulative, and arrogant.**[44] Although most OB research investigates this trait in leaders (Chapter 14), narcissists inhabit every arena of our lives and at all levels and positions at work. Part of the problem with narcissists is they can be charismatic or even charming to many, reach high levels of status in organizations, especially in the short term, but once something is at stake for them, they can turn and throw you to the curb.

How do you identify a narcissist? For one, pay attention to your emotions—how do they make you feel? These people can prop you up with praise to win you over (manipulation), but then they make you feel stupid or inadequate. Narcissists are good at making you feel that all problems or bad outcomes are your fault, and their contributions are the most significant or valuable. Second, pay attention to what they do more than what they say. They can say good things about you then throw you under the bus. Remember, they are skilled at making themselves look good and viewed in a favorable light, so they may not show their true colors in a group setting. Third, someone else is always the target of blame. You will rarely hear a narcissist say, "I was wrong, it was my fault," especially if the outcomes are consequential and may make them look bad.[45]

Psychopaths **can be aggressive and lack concern for others, guilt, or remorse when their own actions do others harm.** The key here is when *they* harm others. Research shows psychopaths are likely to engage in and cause counterproductive work behaviors (CWBs from Chapter 2) and damage morale of those with whom they work.[46] One way to identify such people, for example, a prospective boss or business partner, is to learn about their relationships over time. Does he or she have any or many true long-term friends? What about people they've managed or led in some meaningful way over time, are these relationships still intact, do these people speak fondly of this person? Like narcissism, you need to beware, as this trait can be difficult to detect. Psychopaths may use words that suggest empathy and concern, but they are a false front.

Machiavellians **believe the ends justify the means, often maintain emotional distance, and are manipulative.** These individuals may climb the corporate ladder quite quickly, but they rarely make or keep friends along the way. Like the other traits, they show little regard for you or others beyond your benefit or value to achieving their goals. They also are prone to more CWBs and rarely succeed over time.

Employees with one or more of these characteristics tend to leave destroyed relationships in their wake over time. You are best served to identify and avoid any one of the three, especially if they are in positions of power and may exert influence over your job, career, and well-being.

Personality and Performance

Instead of simply assuming personality affects performance, let's see what research has to say and how this knowledge can make you more effective. First, and most generally, your personality characteristics are likely to have the greatest influence and effect on performance when you are working in situations that are unstructured and with few rules.[47] This makes sense. You're more likely to show your true colors (your personality) when the situation is open and lacks constraints.

As for the Big Five, knowledge of these stable personality dimensions can assist in selecting the right people and assigning responsibilities to them that will set them up to win.

- *Conscientiousness* has the strongest and most positive effects on performance across jobs, industries, and levels. Individuals who exhibit traits associated with a strong sense of purpose, obligation, and persistence generally perform better than those who do not. They also tend to have higher job satisfaction.[48] This trait has consistently been shown to be the most influential when it comes to performance at work.[49]
- *Extroversion*, not surprisingly, is beneficial if the job involves interpersonal interaction. It is also a stronger predictor of job performance than agreeableness, across all professions.
- *Agreeable* employees are likely to fit and excel in jobs requiring interpersonal interaction, such as customer service. These same employees are more likely to stay with their jobs, be kind and get along with others, and thus have positive relationships and experiences at work.[50]
- *Openness* is linked with higher levels of creativity compared with other traits, but open employees may be more likely to quit. Such people are curious and may seek and find new opportunities, even when they are satisfied with their current jobs.[51] This characteristic seems like a double-edged sword for employers. On the one hand they want open and flexible employees, but these are also the same employees who are likely to quit. How might you deal with this as a manager or the owner of a business?
- *Emotional stability* is associated with higher job satisfaction and well-being. Those low in emotional stability (high on neuroticism) have opposite experiences, including higher levels of burnout. It is difficult to find a downside to emotional stability in the workplace. If you are a hiring manager, perhaps you'd consider including this trait in your recruiting and selecting efforts.

Finally, if employee engagement is the desired outcome, then proactive personality was found to be the strongest predictor, followed by conscientiousness and extraversion. Agreeableness and openness were the weakest.[52]

Personality Testing at Work

Personality testing is a commonly used tool for making decisions about hiring, training, and promotion. Roughly 90 percent of Fortune 500 companies use some form of pre-employment testing, including personality tests.[53] A few of the major reasons organizations use such tests are:

1. Reduce time and cost of recruiting and hiring.
2. Reduce biases in the interview process.
3. Increase the pool of candidates (because such tests can be administered electronically and remotely).
4. Complement candidate information found in resumes and interviews.[54]

Personality tests, in particular, are more widely used at the management level than at the entry level. However, despite this widespread use, many experts argue that the typical personality test is not a valid predictor of job performance.[55] One reason might be that many test takers don't describe themselves accurately but instead try to guess what answers the employer is looking for.[56] With this in mind, consider the recommendations of the following Applying OB box the next time you take such a test.

Applying OB

Acing Employment Tests

Employment tests can be far more consequential than those you take in school, since getting hired or promoted may depend on It. This may tempt you to provide answers you think the employer wants, but faking is ill-advised. Many tests are intended to assess fit, and if you don't answer honestly, you might get a job but perhaps it will be one you hate! Instead consider the following tips:

1. **Practice.** Yes, like other tests (GMAT, SAT, MCAT, LSAT) you can practice for employment tests, and practicing can help increase scores by 20 percent. Practicing works because you become more comfortable taking such tests, you develop effective test-taking strategies, and you learn what you're being tested on. This is why so many students take GRE practice exams, as doing so helps sharpen reasoning, numerical, and verbal skills.

2. **Play to your own rhythms.** If you are sharpest in the afternoon try to avoid taking employment tests in the morning. Also, beware of what you eat and drink. Don't overdo the caffeine, unless that is what you've done for every test you've ever taken.

3. **Be yourself . . . sort of.** Don't lie. Well-designed tests can often detect inaccuracies, and most skilled interviewers unveil inconsistencies with ease. But also, beware of being too extreme. Ambition is generally good, but extreme ambition can be dysfunctional. A strong work ethic is preferred, but too high a level is a red flag. In a word—moderation. Don't be too much of even good things. And when interviewing, take the lead from what others have said about you. If someone has recommended or endorsed you, learn what they said and emphasize those same attributes. Sell yourself the way your endorsers are selling you. You want the interviewer's data points to align.

SOURCE: D. Meinert, "Heads Up: Personality Assessments Are Being Used More Often in the Hiring Process. But What Do They Really Tell You?" *HR Magazine*, June 2015, 88–98.

Another reason for inaccurate results is that personality tests are typically bought off the shelf and often given indiscriminately by people who aren't trained or qualified. And while rigorous research shows personality is related to performance, the effects are small. Moreover, and perhaps more importantly, personality tests are designed to measure personality, not to identify the individual differences needed to *perform at a high level in a particular job*. This means managers need different and better ways to measure personality if they want to select employees based on performance-conducive personality traits.

An excellent example is the very popular Myers-Briggs Type Indicator (MBTI). Although helpful for self-awareness purposes, or discussing preferences related to communicating and making decisions with colleagues, rigorous science largely shows it is a poor predictor of job performance. To be fair, the test is not designed or intended to be a predictor of performance, but rather offer insights for you and colleagues. Keith McNulty, People Science Leader at McKinsey, says: "There is no place for the MBTI in organizations. The issue is using it and other measures in ways in which they were not intended and for which science doesn't support."[57]

To help overcome these shortcomings, researchers have used technology and advances in brain science to create a new breed of tests. Companies such as Pymetrics and Knack use games to help assess cognitive abilities, thought processes, and other characteristics.

TABLE 3.4   Advice and Words of Caution about Personality Testing in the Workplace

Researchers, test developers, and organizations that administer personality assessments offer the following suggestions for getting started with testing or for evaluating whether tests already in use are appropriate for forecasting job performance:

- Determine what you hope to accomplish. If you are looking to find the best fit between job and applicant, analyze the aspects of the position that are most critical for it.

- Look for outside help to determine if a test exists or can be developed to screen applicants for the traits that best fit the position. Industrial psychologists, professional organizations, and several Internet sites provide resources.

- Insist any test recommended by a consultant or vendor be validated scientifically for the specific purpose you have defined. Vendors should be able to cite *independent*, credible research supporting a test's correlation with job performance.

- Ask the test provider to document the legal basis for any assessment: Is it fair? Is it job-related? Is it biased against any racial or ethnic group? Does it violate an applicant's right to privacy under state or federal laws? Get legal advice to assure that a test does not adversely affect any protected class.

- Make sure every staff member administering tests or analyzing results is educated about how to do so properly and will keep results confidential. Use the scores on personality tests with other factors you believe are important to the job—such as skills and experience—to create a comprehensive evaluation of the merits of each candidate and apply those criteria identically to each applicant.

SOURCE: Bates, Steve. "Personality Counts." *SHRM*, February 1, 2002. https://www.shrm.org/hr-today/news/hr-magazine/pages/0202covstory.aspx.

The intended advantage is that prospective employees will be assessed on how they play or what they actually do, rather than on their answers to multiple-choice questions or a self-report instrument.

Wise managers learn about personality and the tools used to measure it before investing in and/or utilizing the data they yield. Table 3.4 provides some insights.

There Is No "Ideal Employee" Personality

Given the complexity of today's work environments, the diversity of today's workforce, and recent research evidence, the quest for an ideal employee personality profile is sheer folly. Just as one shoe does not fit all people, one personality profile does not fit all job situations. Good managers take the time to get to know *each employee's unique combination* of personality traits, abilities, and potential and to create a productive and satisfying person–job fit. In other words, a contingency approach to managing people is best (recall the discussion of contingency in Chapter 1).

3.4 CORE SELF-EVALUATIONS: HOW MY EFFICACY, ESTEEM, LOCUS, AND STABILITY AFFECT MY PERFORMANCE

THE BIGGER PICTURE

You can significantly improve your self-awareness by understanding your core self-evaluations (CSEs). These self-evaluations provide broad and useful ways to describe personality in terms of four important individual differences: self-efficacy, self-esteem, locus of control, and emotional stability. CSEs and their component dimensions are more flexible than IQ but more stable than emotions. Your knowledge of CSEs can improve your performance at work, in your career, and in your life.

LO 3-4

Describe the impact of core self-evaluations on performance.

When studying individuals, we either consider narrow or broad concepts. Narrow concepts tend to be better for describing individuals because they are more precise, for instance, when identifying musical intelligence, whereas broad concepts (the Big 5) are better for predicting behavior and outcomes included in Figure 3.2 and the Organizing Framework. The rationale is that broad concepts are more likely to include the complexity in both individuals and situations than those that are narrow. With this in mind we, explore core self-evaluations (CSEs), which is an especially broad personality trait.

Core self-evaluations (CSEs) **represent four narrow and positive individual traits: (1) generalized self-efficacy, (2) self-esteem, (3) locus of control, and (4) emotional stability.** (See Figure 3.3.) People with high core self-evaluations see themselves as capable, competent, and valuable. This section discusses the component traits and highlights research and managerial implications for each.

Why should you care about CSEs? CSEs have desirable effects on many outcomes in the Organizing Framework, such as increased job performance, job and life satisfaction, motivation, organizational citizenship behaviors, and better adjustment to international assignments. CEOs with high core self-evaluations positively influence their organization's drive to take risks, innovate, and seek new opportunities, especially strong in dynamic business environments.[58] Better still, CSEs can be developed and improved.[59]

Now let's learn about the component dimensions.

FIGURE 3.3   The Core Self-Evaluation and Its Components

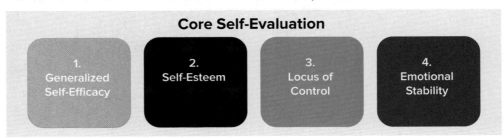

Core Self-Evaluation

| 1. Generalized Self-Efficacy | 2. Self-Esteem | 3. Locus of Control | 4. Emotional Stability |

Self-Efficacy—"I Can Do That"

Have you noticed that those who are confident about their ability tend to succeed, while those who are preoccupied with failing tend to fail? At the heart of such performance differences is self-efficacy. **Self-efficacy is a person's belief about his or her chances of successfully accomplishing a specific task.**

Self-Efficacy Can Be Developed   Helpful nudges in the right direction from parents, role models, and mentors are central to the development of high self-efficacy. For example, a study of medical residents showed guidance and social support from their mentors improved the residents' clinical self-efficacy.[60]

Mechanisms of Self-Efficacy   A detailed model of self-efficacy is shown in Figure 3.4. To apply this model, imagine you have been told to prepare and deliver a 10-minute talk to an OB class of 50 students on how to build self-efficacy. How confident are you that you can complete this task? Part of your self-efficacy calculation is to evaluate the interplay between person and situation factors described in the Organizing Framework.

FIGURE 3.4   **Self-Efficacy Paves the Way for Success or Failure**

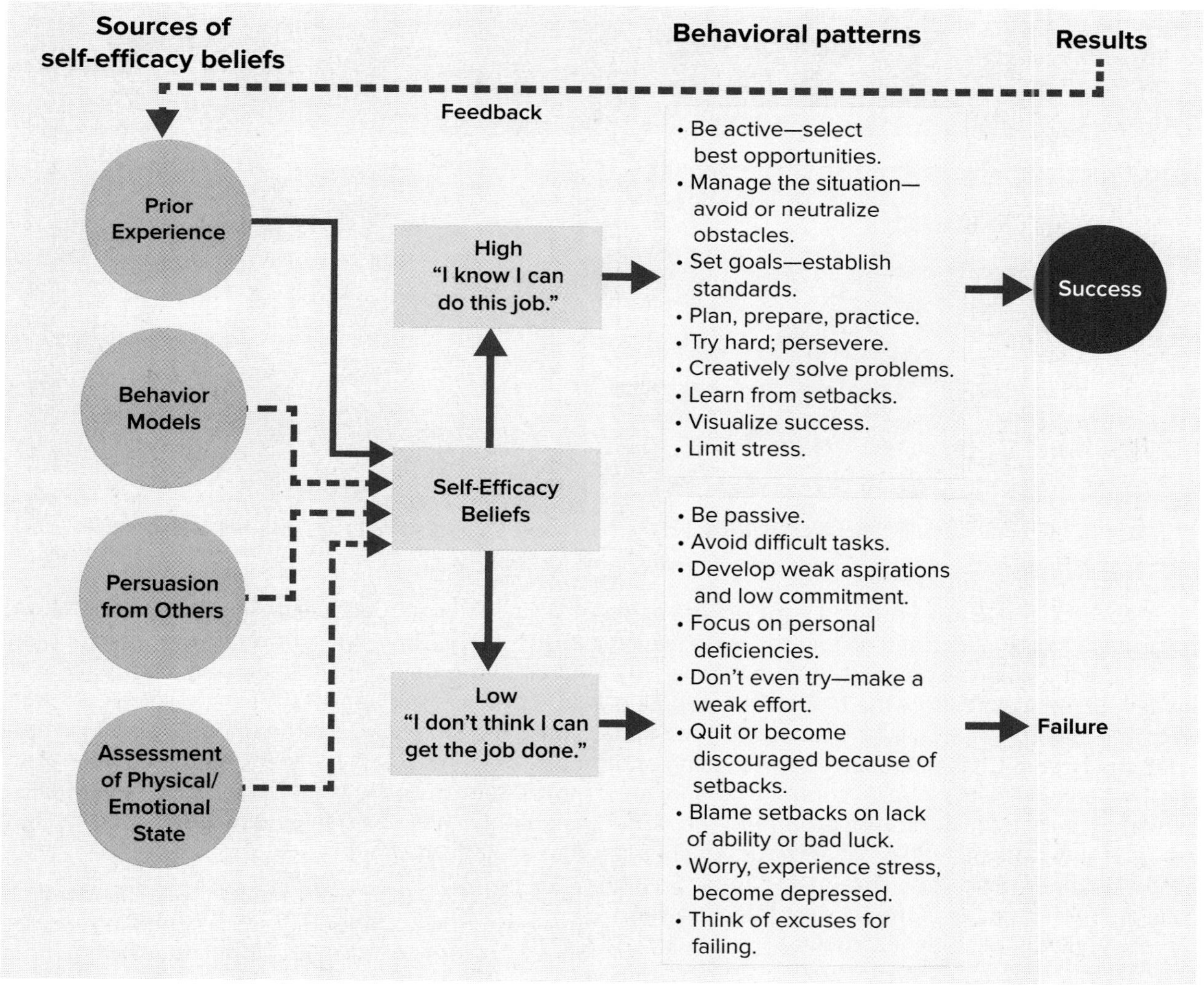

SOURCE: Bandura, Albert. "Perceived Self-Efficacy in Cognitive Development and Functioning." *Developmental Psychology* 25, no. 5 (1993): 117–148. http://dx.doi.org/10.1037/0012-1649.25.5.729; and Wood, Robert, and Albert Bandura. "Social Cognitive Theory of Organizational Management." *The Academy of Management Review* 14, no. 3 (July 1989): 361–384. https://DOI: 10.5465/AMR.1989.4279067.

On the left-hand side of Figure 3.4, among the sources of self-efficacy beliefs, prior experience takes first position as the most potent of the four sources. This is why it connects to self-efficacy beliefs with a *solid* line. Past success in public speaking would boost your self-efficacy, and poor experiences would diminish it. Other sources of your beliefs about yourself—behavior models, persuasion from others, and physical and emotional factors—might also affect your self-confidence. As weaker sources, they connect to beliefs with *dashed* lines in the figure.

Your evaluation of the situation yields your self-efficacy level—ranging from high to low expectations for success. High expectations are not mere bravado; but instead are deep convictions supported by experience. Your self-efficacy beliefs affect your *behavioral patterns* (right-hand portion of Figure 3.4). If you have high self-efficacy about giving a 10-minute speech, you will work harder, longer, and more creatively when preparing for your talk than would a low-self-efficacy classmate. Better performance will follow.

People program themselves for success or failure by enacting their self-efficacy beliefs. Positive or negative results subsequently act as feedback and become the basis of personal experience and future levels of self-efficacy. The OB in Action box provides an excellent illustration.

OB in Action

You Can Go to the Moon and Beyond, If You Believe in Yourself

(left): NASA/Ken Ulbrich.; (right): Helen H. Richardson/MediaNews Group/The Denver Post/Getty Images

Eren Ozmen is #19 on Forbes' list of richest self-made women in America and epitomizes self-efficacy. She and her husband's company (she is the majority owner), Sierra Nevada (*not* the beer), are competing to create and operate reusable spacecraft. Their first craft, the Dream Chaser, crashed upon landing and the company lost the NASA contract to SpaceX. However, that setback did not stop her. The company is now part of a $14 billion effort to shuttle cargo between Earth and the International Space Station. The company is the biggest female-owned government contractor in the country.

Her Own Journey Began Far Away   She came to the U.S. from Turkey for graduate school in the 1980s and later bought Sierra Nevada, her employer at the time. They have now turned their original investment of $5 million into a company with $1.6 billion in sales and 4,000 employees in 33 locations. The story is one of an underdog and tremendous personal risk for Ozmen, as the company has never been in space exploration. But it nevertheless acquired other companies and developed its way into the industry.

It Was Not a Clear or Straight Path   This parallels her own journey. A journalism and public relations major, she knew nothing about technology, and moved through numerous jobs in America after graduating. She and her husband worked at Sierra

Nevada for several years, which nearly went bankrupt, before taking it over and transforming it into what it is today—a major competitor in the race to space.[61]

YOUR THOUGHTS?

1. How do you think Ms. Ozmen's self-efficacy influenced her decisions along the way?

2. Although by most any measure she seems to be successful now, how do you think her challenges along the way shaped her self-efficacy?

3. What can you learn from her story and apply to building your own self-efficacy?

Managerial Implications   Self-efficacy has been extensively studied in the workplace. The data supports several recommendations. As a rule, managers are encouraged to nurture self-efficacy in themselves and others because it is related to improved job performance and job satisfaction (both are important individual-level outcomes). Table 3.5 provides a few specific means for building self-efficacy. Nearly all are explained in detail in other chapters of this book.

Self-Esteem—"Look in the Mirror"

Self-esteem **is your general belief about your self-worth.** Personal achievements and praise bolster self-esteem, while prolonged unemployment and destructive feedback erode it. Researchers measure self-esteem by having people indicate their agreement with positive and negative statements about themselves. An example of a positive statement is,

TABLE 3.5   **Ways to Apply Knowledge of Self-Efficacy at Work**

APPLICATION	EXPLANATION	
1. Job Design	Complex, challenging, and autonomous jobs tend to enhance perceived high self-efficacy. Boring, tedious jobs generally do the opposite.	
2. Training and Development	Managers can improve employees' self-efficacy expectations for key tasks through guided experiences, mentoring, and role modeling.	
3. Self-Management	Training linked to goal setting, action planning, and self-motivation enhance self-efficacy expectations.	
4. Goal Setting and Quality Improvement	Goal difficulty needs to match the individual's perceived self-efficacy.[62] As self-efficacy and performance improve, goals and quality standards can be made more challenging.	
5. Creativity	Supportive managerial actions—encouraging risk taking and providing "blue sky time"—can augment the strong link between self-efficacy beliefs and workplace creativity.[63]	
6. Coaching	Those with low self-efficacy and employees hampered by learned helplessness need lots of constructive pointers and positive feedback.[64]	
7. Leadership	Leadership talent surfaces when top management gives high self-efficacy managers a chance to prove themselves under pressure.	

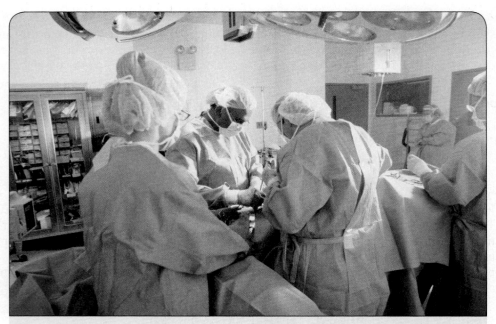

Many individual differences influence performance. Of those discussed so far in this chapter, which do you think are most important for surgeons? Would you rather have a surgeon with high self-efficacy or high self-esteem? Michael N. Paras/Pixtal/age fotostock

"I feel I am a person of worth, the equal of other people." An example of a negative statement is, "I feel I do not have much to be proud of." Those who agree with the positive statements and disagree with the negative statements have high self-esteem. They see themselves as worthwhile, capable, and accepted. People with low self-esteem view themselves in negative terms. They do not feel good about themselves and are hampered by self-doubts.[65]

Although research suggests self-esteem is relatively consistent within cultures, over time, and among men and women, we can still ask: *Can it be improved?*

Can Self-Esteem Be Improved?   The short answer is yes. If your self-esteem is lower than you'd like now, don't despair. It has been shown, for example, that supportive clinical mentors improved medical residents' self-esteem.[66] But not everyone is convinced.

Researchers have found one method especially effective for improving self-esteem. Low self-esteem can be raised more by having the person think of *desirable* characteristics *possessed* rather than of undesirable characteristics from which he or she is free.[67]

Some researchers believe performing at a high level boosts your self-esteem, not the other way around. Thus, they reason it's a mistake to focus on self-esteem. We all know people who "talk big" but "deliver small" and thus seem to suffer from delusions of competency.

Our Recommendation: Apply yourself to things important to you. If getting an A in your OB course affects your sense of self-worth, then you will be motivated to work harder and presumably perform better.

Locus of Control: Who's Responsible— Me or External Factors?

Locus of control is a relatively stable personality characteristic that describes how much personal responsibility we take for our behavior and its consequences. We tend to attribute the causes of our behavior primarily to either ourselves or environmental factors. (Recall our discussion of the person–situation distinction in Chapter 1.) Locus of control thus has two forms—internal and external.

Internal Locus of Control

People who believe they control the events and consequences that affect their lives are said to possess an *internal locus of control.* Such people, called internals, tend to attribute positive outcomes to their own abilities and negative outcomes to their personal shortcomings. Many entrepreneurs eventually succeed because their internal locus of control helps them overcome setbacks and disappointments. They see themselves as masters of their own fate and not as simply "lucky."

Those who willingly take high-stakes jobs in the face of adversity (such as pulling a company back from scandal or bankruptcy) likely have a high internal locus of control. Dara Khosrowshahi, for instance, took over at Uber after a slew of scandals and bad press damaged the company's reputation and resulted in the ouster of then CEO, Travis Kalanick.[68]

External Locus of Control

In contrast, **those who believe their performance is the product of circumstances beyond their immediate control possess an *external locus of control*** and tend to attribute outcomes to environmental causes, such as luck or fate. An "external" would attribute a passing grade on an exam to something external like an easy test and attribute a failing grade to an unfair test or distractions at work.

Locus in the Workplace

The outcomes of internals and externals differ widely at work.

Internals

- Display greater work motivation.
- Have stronger expectations that effort leads to performance.
- Exhibit higher performance on tasks that require learning or problem solving, when performance leads to valued rewards.
- Derive more job satisfaction from performance.

Externals

- Demonstrate less motivation for performance when offered valued rewards.
- Earn lower salaries and smaller salary increases.
- Tend to be more anxious.[69]

Don't mistakenly assume, however, that internal locus is always good and external is always bad. High internals can implode, burn out, or otherwise underperform in situations offering them little or no control, such as during organizational changes in which they have no input or influence. An external locus would be more helpful here. Encouragingly, research shows managers can increase the degree of one's internal locus of control over time by providing more job autonomy (something you'll learn about in Chapter 5).[70]

Emotional Stability

As described in our discussion of the Big Five and in Table 3.2, **individuals with high levels of *emotional stability* tend to be relaxed, secure, unworried, and less likely to experience negative emotions under pressure.** In contrast, if you have low levels of emotional stability, you are prone to anxiety and tend to view the world negatively. How is this knowledge useful at work?

Employees with high levels of emotional stability have been found to have higher job performance and to perform more organizational citizenship behaviors. Emotionally stable employees also exhibit fewer counterproductive work behaviors (CWBs), actions that undermine their own or others' work. Both OCBs and CWBs were discussed in Chapter 2 and are individual-level outcomes illustrated in Figure 3.2 and the Organizing Framework.

Three Practical Considerations for Core Self-Evaluations

Before leaving core self-evaluations let's briefly touch on three areas of interest:

- Is having more of a CSE component always better?
- Is the whole of the CSE components greater than its parts?
- How can managers use CSEs?

Is More Always Better?   Like having more self-esteem, having greater emotional stability is not always better. Researchers found curvilinear, or inverted-U, relationships between emotional stability and outcomes. This suggests that as your emotional stability increases, so too will your job performance and organizational citizenship behaviors, *but only to a point*.

It seems as emotional stability continues to increase, OCBs decline, likely because you focus your attention on the task at hand and *not* on your coworkers. Typically, that's a good thing, but at a certain level emotional stability becomes problematic if you begin obsessing over details and lose sight of the larger objectives and those with whom you work.

Emotional stability can also protect against stressors at work, such as trouble with supervisors, unfair policies, and too much work. It also reduces the likelihood employees will act out by committing CWBs. But there may come a tipping point when the stress becomes too much and emotional stability cannot prevent counterproductive behaviors.[71]

What is the lesson for you? Emotional stability is an asset for many types of jobs, but it will take you only so far.

The USA women's national soccer team has won four Women's World Cup titles, most recently in 2019. And although Megan Rapinoe was awarded the FIFA Best Player Award, neither she nor any of her teammates could have won a single game alone. Can you think of non-sports examples where the whole is greater than the sum of the parts?

Is the Whole of CSE Greater than Its Parts?   To clarify the value of CSE as a whole, versus that of its component traits, think of basketball as a metaphor. Clearly a team outperforms any individual playing alone. Even the greatest player would have no chance against an entire team. And the five greatest players ever, playing individually, still have no chance against an entire team. The sum of their solo efforts would be zero.

However, if you assembled a *team* of the five greatest players, then those individuals playing as a team would be able to do things and perform in ways they couldn't otherwise do on their own (more on teams in Chapter 8). CSE and its component traits are much the same. Core self-evaluation is the team and the traits are the individual players—the whole is greater than the sum of the parts.

How Can I Use CSEs?   Especially in a managerial role, you can use your knowledge of CSEs in many practical ways, such as:

- **Employee selection.** It is more efficient to select employees using CSEs as one broad personality characteristic rather than using its four component traits. Employers can determine the link between one characteristic (CSE) and performance in a particular job, rather than having to determine the relationships between each of the four components' parts and performance. This is one relationship versus four. Doing so enables managers and employers to take advantage of the various beneficial outcomes described above.
- **Training.** The training potential of CSEs is limited because most of its components are trait-like or relatively fixed (self-esteem, locus of control, and emotional stability). That said, self-efficacy is more flexible than the other three components and can be enhanced as explained above. (Figure 3.4 is an excellent "how to" guide.)

Before moving on, we encourage you to assess your own core self-evaluations in Self-Assessment 3.3. Knowledge of your CSEs helps you understand other components of your personality beyond the Big Five discussed and assessed earlier. Awareness of your self-esteem, self-efficacy, locus, and emotional stability can help guide many aspects of your work life, such as what types of jobs to look for and what types of development opportunities may be most useful for you.

SELF-ASSESSMENT 3.3   CAREER READINESS

How Positively Do I See Myself?

Please be prepared to answer these questions if your instructor has assigned Self-Assessment 3.3 in Connect.

1. What is your CSE score? A score greater than 48 is high, between 36 and 48 moderate, and less than 36 low.
2. What are the implications for your performance in school? Work?
3. Now consider this scenario: You're on a three-member team for a project in this class that requires research, a paper, and a presentation. Your CSE score is high, one team member's is moderate, and the other's is low. Describe the potential implications for the three of you working together and your ultimate performance on the paper and presentation.

Let's continue our discussion of individual differences and learn about emotional intelligence (EI) next. EI is a popular OB concept and relatively more flexible than CSEs and the others discussed thus far.

3.5 THE VALUE OF BEING EMOTIONALLY INTELLIGENT

THE BIGGER PICTURE

You likely already know that intelligence doesn't tell us everything we need to know about performance. The smartest student doesn't always get the best grades, and the smartest candidate for a job is not necessarily the best choice. While you almost certainly agree with both of these statements, what is even more certain is that people perform better if they have emotional intelligence—smart or not. When you understand the concept of emotional intelligence from an OB perspective, you'll understand why it is an important person-factor input in the Organizing Framework.

LO 3-5

Realize the benefits of emotional intelligence.

As we know, people deal with their emotions in a variety of ways, which is one reason we are discussing emotions in the chapter on individual differences. For a long time many people considered skill in managing emotions as simply a matter of maturity. However, since the mid-1990s researchers, consultants, and managers have increasingly described emotional maturity by using the phrase *emotional intelligence (EI)*. Today, EI is big business. Hundreds of consulting companies provide EI products and services, and estimates suggest approximately 75 percent of Fortune 500 companies use them.[72]

What Is Emotional Intelligence?

Emotional intelligence **is the ability to monitor your own emotions and those of others, to discriminate among them, and to use this information to guide your thinking and actions.** Referred to by some as EI (used in this book) and by others as EQ, emotional intelligence is a mixture of personality and emotions and has four key competencies (see also Table 3.6):

1. Self-awareness

2. Self-management

3. Social awareness

4. Relationship management[73]

The first two dimensions constitute *personal competence* and the second two feed into *social competence*. Recall the discussion earlier in the chapter of inter- and intra-personal intelligences described by Howard Gardner. EI builds on this work.

Before learning more about emotional intelligence, complete Self-Assessment 3.4. Self-awareness is fundamental to EI and having this knowledge in hand is helpful in exploring the benefits of EI and learning how to develop it.

TABLE 3.6 Developing Emotional Intelligence

Personal Competence	HOW WE MANAGE OURSELVES	
	Capability	**Description**
Self-Awareness	Emotional self-awareness	Reading one's own emotions and recognizing their impact; using "gut sense" to guide decisions
	Accurate self-assessment	Knowing one's strengths and limits
	Self-confidence	A sound sense of one's self-worth and capabilities
Self-Management	Emotional self-control	Keeping disruptive emotions and impulses under control
	Transparency	Displaying honesty and integrity; trustworthiness
	Adaptability	Flexibility in adapting to changing situations or overcoming obstacles
	Achievement	The drive to improve performance to meet inner standards of excellence
	Initiative	Readiness to act and seize opportunities
	Optimism	Seeing the upside in events

Social Competence	HOW WE MANAGE RELATIONSHIPS	
	Capability	**Description**
Social Awareness	Empathy	Sensing others' emotions, understanding their perspective, and taking active interest in their concerns
	Organizational awareness	Reading the currents, decision networks, and politics at the organizational level
	Service	Recognizing and meeting follower, client, or customer needs
Relationship Management	Inspirational leadership	Guiding and motivating with a compelling vision
	Influence	Wielding a range of tactics for persuasion
	Developing others	Bolstering others' abilities through feedback and guidance
	Change catalyst	Initiating, managing, and leading in a new direction
	Conflict management	Resolving disagreements
	Building bonds	Cultivating and maintaining a web of relationships
	Teamwork and collaboration	Cooperation and team building

SOURCE: Goleman, Daniel, Richard E. Boyatzis, and Annie McKee. *Primal Leadership: Realizing the Power of Emotional Intelligence.* Boston: Harvard Business School Press, 2002.

SELF-ASSESSMENT 3.4   CAREER READINESS

What Is Your Level of Emotional Intelligence?

Please be prepared to answer these questions if your instructor has assigned Self-Assessment 3.4 in Connect.

1. Which of the four competencies is highest for you? What are the implications for you at school and/or work?

2. Which competency is the lowest? What are the implications for you at school and/or work?

3. Do you have greater personal or social competence? What are the implications for you at school and/or work?

You can gain considerable Insights regarding EI by observing those who seem to possess and lack this valuable ID. Uber's former CEO provides an excellent example of the latter. See the Problem-Solving Application.

Problem-Solving Application

Darkness in the C-Suite at Uber

Do you remember Travis Kalanick, the founder and former CEO of Uber? Ample evidence from an employee survey, testimonials from other executives (both inside and outside of Uber), and business partners provide compelling evidence for a number of troubling traits exhibited by Uber's founder and former CEO.

When public opinion of the company took major hits due to numerous scandals—sexual harassment at corporate, allegations of rape and other illegal behavior by drivers, and a perception of greed and exploitation when it implemented surge pricing during a taxi strike at JFK airport—Kalanick claimed Uber had a public relations problem, instead of acknowledging the company he founded and created had a serious culture problem. This was further exacerbated by his seeming disregard, If not outright encouragement, for rampant sexual harassment.

In addition, there is the infamous video of him arguing with an Uber driver during a ride he took. You may recall the driver expressed his concerns about the company and the challenges faced by drivers. Instead of taking these concerns as feedback, Kalanick showed a blatant lack of empathy and a great deal of arrogance by blaming the driver, and people like him, by stating they didn't take enough personal responsibility for their own lives. And later, when convinced by others to meet with the driver and apologize, he doubled down and argued the same points again! Another employee who witnessed the meeting described his own reaction as deeply troubling. The lack of willingness to accept responsibility for negative behaviors and events (e.g., sexual harassment) was exacerbated further still by bullying and retaliation against those who complained to HR.[74]

Kalanick has also been described as unrelentingly combative. In meetings he routinely switched between praising and tearing down individuals. Jeff Jones, Uber's former president, quit after only a few months and was so eager to leave he didn't even negotiate an exit package, leaving millions of dollars behind. Adding insult to injury, Uber employees were asked to rank specific business leaders, both inside and outside the company, for a survey and Kalanick ranked last in tech company CEOs![75]

Using a quick checklist:

Grandiose self-importance. Check.

Lack of empathy. Check.

Arrogant. Check.

Sense of entitlement. Check.

Demand excessive admiration. Perhaps.

Although Travis Kalanick has already stepped down as CEO, assume he hasn't, and apply the 3-Step Problem-Solving Approach below.

Apply the 3-Step Problem-Solving Approach

Step 1: Define the problem in the confronting Uber's board of directors.

Step 2: Identify the OB concepts and theories that may point to the cause(s) of the problem. What role did emotional intelligence play in the problem you defined? Which personality attributes are evident, and how might they have contributed?

Step 3: Assume Kalanick was still the CEO and make a recommendation to correct the situation. Think both short-term and long-term.

Now that you have some knowledge of your EI you might wonder, *why another type of intelligence, and how is EI different from IQ?* Those who developed the concept of EI argue that traditional models of IQ are too narrow, failing to consider interpersonal competence. They also argue from a practical perspective that EI is more flexible than IQ and can be developed throughout your working life. This is consistent with Figure 3.2 and the practical benefits of relatively flexible IDs. Let's explore the benefits of EI and how to develop yours.

Benefits of EI

What Research Tells Us EI has been linked to better social relationships, well-being, and satisfaction across all ages and contexts, including work.[76] For instance, store managers' EI was shown to foster greater team cohesiveness (covered in Chapter 8) among sales associates, and this in turn boosted sales.[77] EI has also been linked with creativity, helping employees manage their emotions amid the challenges of the creative process to stay on task and remain in the creative space. EI further enables individuals to apply positive emotions to their work, improving their creative outcomes.[78]

EI also seems to have a dark side. In a study with undergraduates, researchers found those with higher EI were more effective at faking pre-employment personality tests. Participants were better able to change their answers to align with the characteristics

Tillman Fertitta is a self-made billionaire and now owns the NBA's Houston Rockets, Golden Nugget Casinos, and the Landry's Restaurant Group. He learned to cook in his father's restaurant in Galveston, dropped out of the University of Houston, and is now the president of its Board of Regents.[82] Donna Ward/Getty Images

listed in the job description.[79] And sadly, some people use their EI skills to manipulate others, faking empathy or supporting another only to make yourself look good, rather than authentically caring and helping.[80] He says, "People want to be led, but you've got to know how to lead different people. . . . I treat everybody differently . . . and if you do that in business, you're going to be successful."[81]

Figure 3.5 summarizes the relationships between EI and several individual differences we've covered as well as several outcomes. EI does not contain any strong relationships with other inputs or outcomes contained in the Organizing Framework. In fact, there are an equal number of weak and moderate relationships. Most importantly, EI was not found to be the big driver of performance as suggested by some consultants and academics.

How to Develop Your EI? Dan Goleman, the person whose book helped take EI mainstream, highlights the importance of self-awareness—both how you see yourself and how others see you (recall our discussion from Chapter 1). He and his colleague, Michelle Nevarez, recommend using the following three questions to build your EI. We think you'll notice, what they recommend sounds much like the problem-solving approach used in this book.

1. What are the differences between how you see yourself and others see you? This means you need to do a self-assessment on the competencies in Table 3.6, as well

FIGURE 3.5 Relationships between Emotional Intelligence and Individual Differences and Outcomes

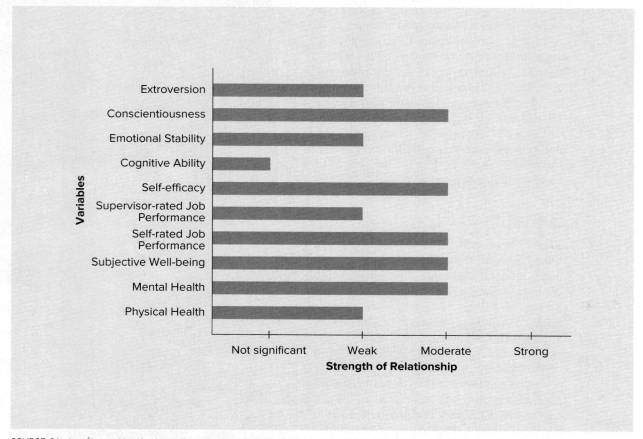

SOURCE: Sánchez-Álvarez, Nicolás, Natalio Extremera, and Pablo Fernández-Berrocal. "The Relation between Emotional Intelligence and Subjective Well-Being: A Meta-Analytic Investigation." *The Journal of Positive Psychology* 11, no. 3 (August 2015): 276–85. http://dx.doi.org/10.1080/17439760.2015.1058968; Joseph, Dana L., Jing Jin, and Daniel A. Newman. "Why Does Self-Reported Emotional Intelligence Predict Job Performance? A Meta-Analytic Investigation of Mixed EI." *Journal of Applied Psychology* 100, no. 2 (2015): 298–342. http://dx.doi.org/10.1037/a0037681; and Martins, Alexandra, Nelson Ramalho, and Estelle Morin. "A Comprehensive Meta-Analysis of the Relationship between Emotional Intelligence and Health." *Personality and Individual Differences* 49, no. 6 (October 2010): 554–64. https:doi:10.1016/j.paid.2010.05.029.

as get feedback on how others see you in terms of the same competencies. Feedback can come from friends, coworkers, customers, classmates, your boss, or a personal coach.

2. What matters to you? Once the information from #1 is in hand, sift through and decide what is important to you. Put differently, ascertain your goals and use the information to help determine which aspects of your EI need development.

3. What changes will you make to achieve these goals?[83] This is the planning part; you have a goal, information to help, now you need a plan. Make a plan, implement, review, and revise. (You'll learn much more about goal setting and how to make your EI development efforts more successful in Chapter 6.)

Practical Takeaways   EI certainly makes common sense and is appealing on the surface. However, despite its popularity and the millions of dollars spent on EI programs every year, the research results are mixed. Proceed with caution.[84] Beware of individuals and companies claiming EI is the silver bullet of performance. It is but another individual difference, and no single attribute explains all behavior. Nevertheless, you should identify and develop your own EI to realize the clear interpersonal benefits. Table 3.6 can serve as a guide.

Now that you've learned about emotional intelligence, let's explore emotions themselves.

3.6 UNDERSTAND EMOTIONS TO INFLUENCE PERFORMANCE

THE BIGGER PICTURE

The human experience is awash in emotions, and you won't be surprised to learn emotions are important both at work and as an individual-level process in the Organizing Framework. We'll explore the difference between felt versus displayed emotions and how emotions serve as an important means of communication with ourselves and others. Most of your experiences elicit a mix of positive and negative emotions, and these emotions are tightly related to your goals.

Many people believe employees should check their emotions at the door when they come to work. This is unrealistic and simply impossible. Like personality and the other IDs discussed thus far, emotions are an integral part of who we are as people, a fundamental part of the human experience, and greatly influence our performance. Given this reality, you will want to understand emotions so you can manage them *as a process* to benefit you, your team, and your employer. This will help make emotions a practical tool to use, rather than something to avoid, ignore, or suppress.

LO 3-6

Explain how understanding emotions makes people more effective.

Emotions—We All Have Them, but What Are They?

Emotions are complex, relatively brief responses aimed at a particular target, such as a person, information, experience, or event. They also change psychological and/or physiological states.[85] Researchers distinguish between *felt* and *displayed* emotions. For example, if your boss informs you that you've been passed over for a promotion, you might feel disappointed and/or angry (felt emotion). You might keep your feelings to yourself or you might begin to cry. Both reactions are instances of displayed emotions. It's just that in the first case you are choosing not to show emotion, which means your display is "no emotion." Your display can affect the outcomes, in this case your manager's reactions. Taxi drivers, waiters, and hairdressers all received higher tips when they were trained to manage what they felt and the way they displayed these feelings.[86]

Emotions may also motivate your behavior and are an important means for communicating with others.[87] A smile on your face signals you are happy or pleased, while a scowl and a loud, forceful tone of voice may reflect anger. We also know our emotions can and often do change moment to moment and thus are more flexible than the other IDs discussed so far. For these reasons, emotions have important implications for you at school, at work, and in every other social arena of your life. They can even be the root cause of why you procrastinate. Read the Applying OB box and learn how to combat your tendencies.

Applying OB

Do You Procrastinate? Blame Your Emotions!

Most people procrastinate at least occasionally, which means we irrationally delay an action despite expecting to be worse off. We often attribute procrastination to poor time management or even laziness, but it seems research has revealed a true cause—emotions.[88] Researchers say procrastination is a way to deal with stress. That's right. Putting off studying for your next exam is one way of dealing with the stress of preparing for it.

The rationale is many things you do while procrastinating are often things that make you feel good or you enjoy, such as shopping, going out with friends, watching TV, or playing video games. They help ease the anxiety associated with the task you need to do (study for an exam). Compounding this further, it seems that people who are more impulsive tend to be more anxious, and the more anxiety they experience, the more likely they are to procrastinate to make themselves feel better. With this in mind, what can occasional and chronic procrastinators do to help themselves?

1. *Set subgoals.* Whatever the needed or dreaded task is, break it into smaller parts or subgoals and specify a start and end time for each. Doing this will help the task seem less daunting, which will reduce your associated anxiety and the temptation to do something else more enjoyable (procrastinate).

2. *Just do it.* We're not talking about going for a run or playing sports, which while healthy may be another form of procrastination. Instead, we're saying to get started and do part of the task. Once you've begun, completing it will seem less difficult.

3. *Envision the benefits and feelings.* How will you feel when you're finished? What will you be able to do? This seems obvious enough, but research has shown that people rarely think of such benefits when they are procrastinating.

4. *Reward yourself.* Building on No. 3, reward yourself for achieving the subgoals, as well as the overall goal or task.

Blaming your emotions won't get your term paper done or help you prepare sufficiently for the upcoming client presentation. Understanding the role emotions play may help you recognize and overcome your tendencies. With this advice in mind, get to work!

Adapted from S. Wang, "To Stop Procrastinating, Start by Understanding the Emotions Involved," *The Wall Street Journal*, August 31, 2015, http://www.wsj.com/articles/to-stop-procrastinating-start-by-understanding-whats-really-going-on-1441043167.

Emotions as Positive or Negative Reactions to Goal Achievement

You'll notice from the definition you can think of emotions, whether positive, negative, or mixed, in terms of your goals.[89]

- **Positive.** If your goal is to do well in school and you graduate on time and with honors, you are likely to experience positive emotions, such as *joy, gratitude, pride, satisfaction, contentment,* and *relief.* These emotions are positive because they are *congruent* (or consistent) with your goal.

- **Negative.** Negative emotions are triggered by frustration and failure to meet goals. They are said to be goal *incongruent.* Common negative emotions are *anger, fright, anxiety, guilt, shame, sadness, envy, jealousy,* and *disgust.* Which of these are you likely to experience if you fail the final exam in a required course? Failing would be incongruent with your goal of graduating on time with a good GPA. Typically, the more important the goal, the more intense the emotion.

- **Mixed.** Meeting or failing to meet our goals can also generate *mixed* emotions. Let's say you receive a well-earned promotion that brings with it positives—increased responsibility and higher pay—but only if you relocate to another state, which you don't want to do.

Besides Positive and Negative, There's Past vs. Future

The negative–positive distinction matters—you're happy, you're sad. However, another characteristic of emotions can be especially useful for managers. Assume you're a manager in a company that just downsized 15 percent of its employees. This is stressful for all those who lost their jobs, but let's focus on two fictitious employees who survived the cuts—Shelby and Jennifer. Both feel negatively about the job cuts, but in different ways.

Shelby: Her dominant emotion is anger. People are typically angry about things that happened (or didn't happen) in the past. Anger is a backward-looking or retrospective emotion.

Jennifer: Her dominant emotion is fear. People are typically fearful of things that might happen in the future. Fear is a forward-looking or prospective emotion.

Practical implications for managers: Knowing these emotions tells you that Shelby is likely most concerned with something that happened in the past, perhaps the way decisions were made about whom to terminate. She may think the process was unfair and caused three of her favorite colleagues to be let go. As for Jennifer, knowing she is dominated by fear tells you that uncertainty about the future—perhaps her job might be cut next—concerns her most. As their manager, you can use knowledge of Shelby's and Jennifer's emotions to guide your own actions.

How Can I Manage My Negative Emotions at Work?

Theoretically, to manage your emotions at work you could simply translate felt emotions into displayed emotions—unfiltered. Besides being unrealistic this would be disastrous. To help, we explore emotion display norms, how to handle a host of negative emotions, and the emotions related to a job search.

Organizations have *emotion display norms or expectations* regarding the types of emotions that are appropriate for employees to show in different situations.[90] For instance, to always act happy and positive in front of customers or your boss, remain calm in meetings, and don't show anger. What about crying? Many people think this is taboo and a reputation killer, but not as many people feel this way as you might think. For instance, 38 percent of participants in a recent study reported crying is okay occasionally, but if it is frequent then your career could suffer. This compares to 31 percent who said crying had no effect. However, 32 percent thought it is never okay and if you do cry, then people will perceive you as weak or immature.[91]

But what can you do when you feel negative emotions at work? The OB in Action box describes the costs and benefits of displaying anger at work.

OB in Action

The Good and Bad of Anger at Work

Andrew Cornell, CEO of Cornell Iron Works, understands the days of the screaming boss are, or at least should be, a thing of the past. He deals with anger toward his employees by holding frequent and brief meetings, "rather than 'waiting until the end, throwing a nuclear bomb and leaving blood all over the wall.'"[92]

Screaming takes other forms too. At work you might receive a hostile e-mail berating you, which was copied to your coworkers in ALL CAPS. Science supports the many people who believe yelling, whether by e-mail or face-to-face, is inappropriate and counterproductive. You may have been in a group meeting when someone was so angry he or she began to scream and bully another person. Both are unprofessional and uncalled for, and they damage the reputation of the perpetrator.

Costs of Negative Emotions Growing research evidence confirms the suspected undesirable outcomes of negative emotions. For instance, managers need to be careful about generating feelings of shame and/or anger when giving feedback to employees because these particular emotions have been linked to counterproductive work behaviors such as abuse of others and theft.[93]

Unhappy Customers May Suffer Twice Customers' negative emotional displays, such as verbal aggression, have been shown to negatively affect employee job performance. Specifically, receivers of the aggression made more mistakes recalling and processing the customers' complaints.[94] You may want to think twice before venting on a customer service representative.

What About the Benefits of Anger? Expressing your anger sometimes can actually help solve the problem. Your message is communicated, though forcefully, which can lead to better understanding. Displays of anger are more likely to be beneficial if they are directed at organizational issues and problems instead of at individuals. Being angry at the problem rather than the person is likely to be perceived more constructively and less defensively.[95]

YOUR THOUGHTS?

1. What advice would you give to managers on how to handle their own anger and other negative emotions at work?

2. What advice would you give to managers on how to handle the anger and negative emotions felt (and expressed) by their direct reports?

3. What has been the most productive way for you to deal with your negative emotions?

Anger isn't the only negative emotion. Table 3.7 provides guidance on a variety of others and how to deal with them. As you study the table, think of your own experiences and reactions and how the recommendations could have helped you handle them.

TABLE 3.7   Common Negative Emotions and How to Handle Them

IF YOU'RE FEELING . . .	THEN YOU MIGHT WANT TO . . .
Fearful	Step back and try to see the situation objectively. Ask yourself: "Is my business or career truly at risk?" If not, you may be feeling nervous and excited rather than fearful.
Rejected	Do you respect the opinion of the person rejecting you? If the comment came from someone you don't respect, rejection may instead be a backhanded compliment. If you do respect the person, you may want to clarify by asking: "The other day you said _____ and I felt hurt. Can you explain what happened?"
Angry	Get some distance from the situation to avoid blowing your top in the heat of the moment. Once you calm down, pinpoint the reason you are angry. Most often the reason is someone violated a rule or standard that is deeply important to you. Find a way to communicate the importance of the rule or standard to the person so it doesn't happen again.
Frustrated	We all get frustrated at work when results don't meet our expectations, given the amount of time and energy we've applied. The goal often is achievable, but progress is slow. First, reassess your plan and behavior. Do they need modification? If not, perhaps you simply need to be patient.
Inadequate	Even those with the highest self-esteem feel they don't measure up at times. Our discussion of self-efficacy and how to build it in Table 3.5 can guide your solution to this emotion.
Stressed	Time constraints are a major source of stress. Too many commitments, too little time. You need to prioritize! Do what is important rather than what is urgent. For example, most e-mail is urgent but not important.

SOURCE: James, Geoffrey. "Feeling Negative? How to Overcome It." *Inc.*, November 26, 2012. https://www.inc.com/geoffrey-james/how-to-handle-negative-emotions-at-work.html.

Finally, searching for a job can be an emotional experience, the proverbial rollercoaster—up and down and up and down again. The mixture of positive and negative emotions can be daunting, so what can you do? The following advice may help, but before we get to the emotions it is important to do two things first. Become organized and be disciplined. A job search can be overwhelming, time consuming, and often happens over a long period of time. It therefore is important to create a system to keep track of your efforts, establish a routine, and stick to both![96] Now let's address some of the common emotions in the Applying OB box.

Applying OB

CAREER READINESS

Managing Emotions During Job Search

You cannot see the future, but you can anticipate potential scenarios or outcomes in your job search. Include in your planning, "If X happens, then I'll do Y." This may help reduce the uncertainty of the negative emotions that go along with it.

Fear. Yes, once again fear rears its head. Although often justified it is rarely helpful. There is no single or best way to deal with it, but knowing that fear is future-oriented can help create different scenarios for interviews and outcomes. Doing so will reduce the uncertainty and hopefully your fear too.

Frustration. Some job descriptions read like autobiographies, and the only thing missing is your picture. Yet, you don't get an interview. Or, you feel you nailed the interview but don't get the job offer. Besides disappointment, this can be frustrating. The best advice here is the cliché that "you must be in it to win it." Don't take the process personally. The employer may have made the wrong decision, or they may have had an internal candidate already picked out and are just going through the motions with you. Whatever the reason, pick yourself up and try again. Look at these occurrences not as setbacks, but as learning opportunities to further hone your resume, and communications and interviewing skills.

Excitement. Yes, the job search has positive emotions too, and you must also manage them. Envision passing the screening call, nailing the first interview, and feeling even better about the second. Wonderful! But don't become complacent and stop your search. Continue to work the process. This opportunity may stall or fall through, or you may even find a more appealing opportunity.

We'll conclude the chapter by distilling some specific applications of what you just learned.

3.7 MAKING THE CONNECTION: HOW DO INDIVIDUAL DIFFERENCES AND EMOTIONS AFFECT MY PERFORMANCE?

THE BIGGER PICTURE

We conclude this chapter with practical applications of knowledge and tools related to individual differences, intended to improve your effectiveness as both an employee and manager.

LO 3-7

Describe the implications of individual differences and emotions for you and managers.

Takeaways for Me

Use your new knowledge of personality, intelligences, CSEs, emotions, and EI, along with the self-assessments and concepts learned in Chapter 3 to:

1. **Enhance your self-awareness.**
2. **Identify the pros and cons of particular IDs for you at school and work.**
3. **Create profiles of the managers and leaders where you work (or where you want to work if you're not currently employed).** Profiling the "important people" in this way will not only illustrate the concepts you've learned, but serve as a template or prototype of what is valued by a particular employer. In other words, create a profile of what successful people look like in terms of individual differences and use this knowledge to highlight the same qualities you possess during job interviews and to guide your own development.
4. **Use your knowledge of emotional intelligence,** because despite mixed research results, it can make or break an individual in any given job and have implications for the larger career.

Takeaways for Managers

IDs have great practical significance for managers.

1. **Explicitly include the individual differences that matter most in job descriptions.** This means you are well served to list job responsibilities *and* the employee characteristics you think are most important to be successful in a specific job.
2. **Use your knowledge of the continuum when selecting and training employees.** Realize you often will want to hire and test for relatively fixed traits (intelligence and personality), because these are not easy to change, and consider training or coaching the others.
3. **Assess your own emotional intelligence, paying explicit attention to *both* personal and social competence.** Don't simply make a summary judgment— "I have high EI," or "My EI is pretty good." Given the potential consequences of low EI, you are wise to put in the effort to learn about and improve both aspects of yours (if needed). After doing this, you will be better prepared to assess the emotional intelligence of those you manage and those you consider hiring. These actions will benefit you, them, other coworkers, and the larger organization.

Individual differences are fundamental to who you are as an employee and as a person. Understanding the many concepts presented here will assist you in better understanding yourself and others, and perhaps enhance your problem-solving skills too. Recall the person-situation inputs in the Organizing Framework? You have learned a great deal about person inputs and yourself in the process!

What Did I Learn?

You learned that who you are affects performance because individual differences (IDs) play an important and often fundamental role in the way you perform at school, at work, and in other contexts. Reinforce and consolidate your learning with the Key Points and Organizing Framework. Then challenge your mastery of the material by completing the Problem-Solving Application Case and Legal/Ethical Challenge.

Key Points for Understanding Chapter 3

You learned the following key points.

3.1 DISTINGUISHING INDIVIDUAL DIFFERENCES BASED ON THEIR RELATIVE STABILITY

- Individual differences (IDs) is a broad category used to describe the vast number of attributes (traits and behaviors) that describe a person.
- It is helpful to think of IDs in terms of their relative stability.

3.2 HOW MULTIPLE INTELLIGENCES AFFECT MY PERFORMANCE

- Intelligence Is more than IQ and represents an individual's capacity for constructive thinking, reasoning, and problem solving.
- Multiple intelligences are linguistic, logical, musical, kinesthetic, spatial, interpersonal, intrapersonal, and naturalist.
- Identifying the intelligences relevant to particular jobs can be used to select, place, and develop individuals accordingly.

3.3 WAYS IN WHICH PERSONALITY CAN AFFECT MY PERFORMANCE AT SCHOOL AND WORK

- Personality is the combination of stable physical, behavioral, and mental characteristics that give individuals their unique identities.

- The Big Five personality dimensions are extroversion, agreeableness, conscientiousness, emotional stability, and openness to experience.
- People with proactive personalities identify opportunities and act on them, show initiative, take action, and persevere until meaningful change occurs.
- Employers use personality tests to select and place employees, but no "ideal personality" exists and tests are often misused.

3.4 THE IMPACT OF CORE SELF-EVALUATIONS ON PERFORMANCE

- Managers can realize the practical value of CSEs by selecting employees based on them and then training them to enhance elements of their CSEs.
- Self-efficacy is a person's belief about his or her chances of successfully accomplishing a specific task.
- Self-efficacy beliefs can be improved via experience, behavior models, persuasion from others, and emotional state.

3.5 THE BENEFITS OF EMOTIONAL INTELLIGENCE

- Emotional intelligence (EI) is the ability to monitor your own and others' feelings and emotions and use this information to guide your thinking and actions.
- EI is associated with higher sales and improved retention, as well as leadership effectiveness.
- EI can be developed by building personal and social competence.

3.6 HOW UNDERSTANDING EMOTIONS MAKES PEOPLE MORE EFFECTIVE

- Emotions are complex, relatively brief responses aimed at a specific target.

- Most experiences are a mixture of positive and negative emotions, rather than purely one or the other.
- Emotions can be distinguished in terms of a future or a past orientation.
- Emotion display norms dictate which types of emotions are expected and appropriate in particular organizational situations.

3.7 HOW DO INDIVIDUAL DIFFERENCES AND EMOTIONS AFFECT MY PERFORMANCE?

- Knowledge of IDs is abundant and a useful way for leveraging your strengths and developing your weaknesses.

- IDs are insightful for understanding, motivating, and otherwise managing employees.
- Awareness and management of your and others' emotions can enhance performance.

The Organizing Framework for Chapter 3

As shown in Figure 3.6, you learned how individual differences can present themselves through the process of emotions (both felt and expressed) at the individual level, affecting many workplace outcomes across individual, group/team, and organizational levels.

FIGURE 3.6 Organizing Framework for Understanding and Applying OB

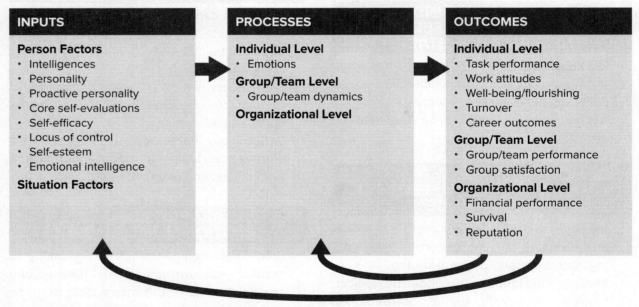

Better Ingredients. Better Pizza. Worst Spokesperson.

John Schnatter founded Papa John's Pizza in a broom closet in his father's tavern in 1984. The restaurant is now the fourth largest pizza delivery chain in the United States with more than 5,300 corporate and franchisee owned establishments worldwide.[97] Papa John's revenues exceeded $1.5 billion in 2018 but were down for the first time in almost ten years.[98] The company is also down a spokesperson. Schnatter, better known as "Papa John," was ousted by the organization after a series of controversial statements.[99]

Let's take a closer look at the issues facing Papa John's and its founder.

PROBLEMATIC STATEMENTS

Schnatter told college students in 2013 that he "has a real problem with the English language" while discussing his poor score on the verbal portion of the SAT. Those who know him seem to agree with that sentiment, but don't believe grammar is the underlying problem. For example, Steve Coomes, a restaurant industry journalist who has interviewed Schnatter a dozen times, wrote a blog post in 2018 titled "A tale of a man who couldn't tame his tongue" in which he profiled a CEO he claims "has always said too much."[100]

One of Schnatter's first controversial statements was in 2012 when he discussed the passage of President Obama's Affordable Care Act. What caught the public's attention was not his political opposition to the law, but the fact that he complained to shareholders that it would increase the cost of a large pizza by 14 cents. Papa John's social media was soon inundated with outraged customers claiming they would pay a couple extra cents so Papa John's employees had health insurance. Others said they would take their business to a restaurant that has empathy and ". . . doesn't begrudge their employees the ability to seek a doctor when they're ill."[101]

Schnatter found a new target in 2017, the National Football League (NFL). Papa John's was a significant sponsor of the league at the time that many players were kneeling during the national anthem to raise awareness of police brutality and social injustice. Again, Schnatter caused controversy because he could not keep his emotions and impulses under control. According to the *Washington Post* he said that the NFL's "poor leadership" and inability to stop the protests hurt the league's TV ratings, which in turn hurt sales of his pizza because it is advertised heavily during games. To make matters worse, a white supremacist group embraced the remarks and dubbed Papa John's as the official pizza of the alt-right. Papa John's condemned the group and distanced itself from the endorsement, but the damage was already done and the company had to apologize for Schnatter's "divisive" remarks.[102] The NFL also broke ties with the company, according to the *New York Times*.[103]

Schnatter was forced to resign as the company's CEO after making the controversial comments about the NFL, but that did not stop him from continuing to cause public outrage with his statements. In May 2018 Schnatter, who was still serving as Papa John's chairman at the time, used the n-word on a conference call with executives and a marketing agency when referring to African Americans. The marketing agency terminated its contract with Papa John's and Schnatter was forced to resign as the company's chairman.[104]

PAPA JOHN BATTLES PAPA JOHN'S

Schnatter's comments gravely injured the restaurant chain he founded. Sales at North American stores fell more than 7% in 2018 and the organization's stock lost a third of its value.[105] Papa John's tried to distance itself from Schnatter to stop the bleeding. The board of directors evicted Schnatter from the company's Louisville, Kentucky, headquarters, took him off pizza boxes and commercial materials, and directed him to cease all communications with internal and external stakeholders.[106]

Papa John would not go quietly though. He hurled multiple lawsuits at his former company and took out a full-page newspaper ad directing Papa John's 120,000 employees to a website he set up. The website includes press releases, news articles, and public filings in support of Schnatter.[107]

Papa John's and Schnatter reached an agreement in 2019 to resolve many of their points of contention. As a result of the agreement, Schnatter will resign from the Papa John's board of directors and cease litigation against his former company. However, the matter is far from closed. Schnatter's spokesperson says he still "retains his ability to assert new legal claims" in the future related to his ouster.[108] Moreover, the founder is still the company's largest individual shareholder, owning a 19% stake.[109]

THE COMPANY'S CONTINUED STRUGGLES

Papa John's continues to reel under negative publicity even after Schnatter's exile. The company has closed over 100 locations in the past year while competitors such as Dominos and Pizza Hut have opened new ones.[110] It has also been forced to assist suffering franchisees by providing royalty relief and other types of subsidies, further deteriorating the company's bottom line.[111]

APPLY THE 3-STEP PROBLEM-SOLVING APPROACH TO OB

Use the Organizing Framework in Figure 3.6 and the 3-Step Problem-Solving Approach to help identify inputs, processes, and outcomes relative to this case.

STEP 1: Define the problem.

A. Look first at the Outcome box of the Organizing Framework in Figure 3.6 to help identify the important problem(s) in this case. Remember, a problem is a gap between a desired and current state. State your problem as a gap and be sure to consider problems at all three levels. If more than one desired outcome is not being accomplished, decide which one is most important and focus on it for steps 2 and 3.

B. Cases have key players, and problems are generally viewed from a player's perspective. You need to determine from whose perspective— employee, manager, team, or the organization— you're defining the problem. As in other cases, whether you choose the individual or organizational level in this case can make a difference.

C. Use details in the case to determine the key problem. Don't assume, infer, or create problems that are not explicitly included in the case itself. Only use what is provided in the case.

D. To refine your choice, ask yourself, *why is this a problem?* Explaining why helps refine and focus thinking. Focus on topics in the current chapter, because we generally select cases that illustrate concepts in the current chapter.

STEP 2: Identify causes.
Using material from this chapter and summarized in the Organizing Framework, identify what are the causes of the problem you identified in Step 1. Remember, causes tend to appear in either the Inputs or Processes boxes.

A. Start by looking at the Organizing Framework (Figure 3.6) and determine which person factors, if any, are most likely causes of the defined problem. For each cause explain why or how it causes the problem. Asking why multiple times is more likely to lead you to root causes of the problem. For example, do particular individual differences John Schnatter possesses help explain the problem you defined in Step 1?

B. Follow the same process for situation factors. For each ask yourself, *why is this a cause?* By following the process of asking why multiple times, you are likely to arrive at a more complete and accurate list of causes. Again, look to the Organizing Framework for guidance.

C. Now consider the Processes box in the Organizing Framework. Are any processes at the individual, group/team, or organizational level potential causes of your defined problem? It certainly seems Schnatter's emotions are notable aspects of his experience and predicament. Do they help explain the problem defined in Step 1? What about the board and their governance of Papa John's? What about the fact that Schnatter is still a significant shareholder in the company? For any process you consider, ask yourself, *why is this a cause?* Again, do this for several iterations to arrive at the root causes.

D. To check the accuracy or appropriateness of the causes, be sure to map them onto the defined problem and confirm the link or cause and effect connection.

STEP 3: Recommend solutions.
Make recommendations for solving the problem, considering whether you want to resolve it, solve it, or dissolve it. Which recommendation is desirable and feasible?

A. Given the causes identified in Step 2, what are your best recommendations? Use material in the current chapter that best suits the cause. Remember to consider the OB in Action and Applying OB boxes, because these contain insights into what others have done. Details of this case, for instance, describe how Papa John's board is concerned and has legitimate authority to make changes at the organization and repair its reputation. What might they do?

B. Be sure to consider the Organizing Framework— both person and situation factors, as well as processes at different levels.

C. Create an action plan for implementing your recommendations and be sure your recommendations map onto the causes and resolve the problem.

To Test or Not to Test, That Is a Problem

Companies across industries have tested for drugs for many years, and depending on the job and the drug, few would argue against such practices. For instance, no one wants pilots, air traffic controllers, or surgeons to be altered in any way while performing their duties. In the past when there was ambiguity about drugs and jobs the law made it easier—if the drug is illegal for recreational use then it is reasonable to include it in testing, pre- and post-employment. This is why few people today or in the past would support the use of heroin or cocaine at work, and thus testing for these Is still widely accepted.

But Now There Is Recreational Pot (Not Medicinal)

Although still illegal at the federal level, marijuana is legal for medicinal uses in 39 states and for recreational use in 10 (as of early 2019), and a Gallup poll showed 64 percent of Americans favor its legalization.[112] These changing attitudes and legal complexities are forcing owners, managers, and employees to reconsider their positions and policies related to drugs and drug testing in the workplace.

Some argue testing is obsolete while others claim the current situation requires even greater diligence.[113] The state of Maine, as an example, has outlawed pre-employment testing and dismissal for a first positive test for pot use at work, which has led companies there and elsewhere to eliminate or at least reduce testing. Vermont also legalized recreational use but does not require employers to tolerate possession or use at work, nor does it forbid them from testing for it.[114]

On the other hand, many argue employers have a responsibility to provide a safe and productive workplace, and to the extent policies and practices related to marijuana (or any other substance) undermine these responsibilities, then such policies are difficult to defend. The failure to establish and enforce such policies erodes employee morale and potentially increases legal liability for employers. Additionally, since opioids and other prescription drug misuse is epidemic, many think drug policies and practices need to be tougher at work, not more relaxed. Further support for this position is that 4.2 percent of urine tests done on employees in 2016 were positive, the highest level in more than a decade.[115]

What About Unreliable Tests?

As before and still, those who test positive almost always claim their exposure was indirect, a situation factor, and it was the secondhand smoke of a partner, friend, person sitting next to them at a concert or in a car. Experts and processes today reduce the likelihood of false positives to nearly zero, and many processes automatically use a second and more stringent testing method when the initial test comes back positive. Furthermore, testing today allows for a threshold level for all drugs, and the thresholds are now high enough to require being stuck in a closet with four friends smoking pot heavily for hours in order for a bystander to register positive.[116]

This poses quite a dilemma for owners, managers, and employees. Let's explore your own views and recommended actions with the following questions.

1. What is your position on drug testing at work, both pre- and post-employment? Explain.

2. Assume you are a manager of employees across multiple states, some with recreational drug legalization and others not, what would you do?

3. Employees in most companies are allowed to take smoke breaks, historically for cigarettes, but what if now they want to include pot-breaks in those states where marijuana is legal? Assume you own the company, does that change your views?

4

Social Perception and Managing Diversity

After reading this chapter, you should be able to:

LO 4-1   Describe how you form perceptions of others.

LO 4-2   Discuss how awareness of stereotypes helps you make better decisions.

LO 4-3   Explain how causal attributions help managers interpret employee performance.

LO 4-4   Describe the four layers of diversity and how they help organizations manage diversity effectively.

LO 4-5   Discuss the business rationale for managing diversity.

LO 4-6   Discuss the most common barriers to implementing successful diversity programs.

LO 4-7   Explain what organizations are doing to manage diversity effectively.

LO 4-8   Describe the implications of social perception and managing diversity for you and managers.

The Organizing Framework shown in Figure 4.1 summarizes the key concepts discussed in Chapter 4. We discuss the impact of three important person factors—diversity, demographics, and stereotypes, and the situation factor of diversity climate on a host of processes at the individual, group/team, and organizational levels. These person and situation factors affect the individual level processes pertaining to perception, attributions, and psychological safety. They also influence processes at the group/team and organizational levels. One of the biggest takeaways from this chapter is the fact that the combination of inputs and processes shown in Figure 4.1 have a broad effect on individual, group/team, and organizational level outcomes. Try to observe how the inputs and processes affect individual level outcomes such as task performance, work attitudes, well-being, flourishing, turnover, and career outcomes such as promotions. At the same time, you should learn that concepts discussed in this chapter also affect group/team level outcomes of performance and satisfaction as well as organizational outcomes like being an employer of choice, customer satisfaction, and reputation.

FIGURE 4.1 Organizing Framework for Understanding and Applying OB

INPUTS	PROCESSES	OUTCOMES
Person Factors • Diversity • Demographics • Stereotypes **Situation Factors** • Diversity climate	**Individual Level** • Perceptions • Attributions • Psychological safety **Group/Team Level** • Group/team dynamics **Organizational Level** • Options to manage diversity	**Individual Level** • Task performance • Work attitudes • Well-being/flourishing • Turnover • Career outcomes **Group/Team Level** • Group/team performance • Group satisfaction **Organizational Level** • Employer of choice • Customer satisfaction • Reputation

This team of professionals is focused on finalizing plans for a new office space. Success in this effort requires coordination among a diverse set of people, and this is not always an easy task. Research and anecdotal evidence reveals that diversity can promote greater performance once people learn to work effectively with people different from themselves.

stockbroker/123RF

Winning at Work

Perception Plays a Key Role in Getting a Job

More recruiters than ever are using social media to find good employees. A recent U.S. survey of 800 recruiters by Jobvite revealed that 25 percent of hiring companies overall are developing recruiting methods that rely on Instagram; the rate is 63 percent among technology companies. Results also showed that nearly half the companies surveyed (43 percent) have used texting to communicate with job applicants, and they report a high approval rating for those communications.[1]

Panther Media GmbH/Alamy Stock Photo

Another survey reveals that nearly 3 in 4 Millennial job seekers (aged 18 to 34) found their most recent job through social media. That's not too surprising if you consider that 82 percent of hiring organizations report using social media to recruit "passive" candidates; that is, those who are not actively looking for a job.[2]

Perceptions Start with Social Media Posts

A national CareerBuilder survey of more than 1,000 hiring and HR managers found that 7 in 10 research job candidates online, using their social network profiles to assess their potential fit with the company. Nearly half said if they couldn't find a candidate online, they would hesitate to get in touch for an interview. Although the Internet is a gold mine of information for recruiters, a poorly managed online image can hurt your chances of finding a job. Forty percent of employers in the CareerBuilder survey report forming a negative impression of candidates who posted "provocative or inappropriate" photos; 36 percent disliked online revelations of alcohol or drug use; and 31 percent were turned off by expressions of race, gender, or religious bias.[3]

Consider the experience of Pete Maulik, chief strategy officer at Fahrenheit 212. Maulik was ready to make an offer to an applicant, but after checking out the man's LinkedIn profile he decided the applicant was not a team player. "He took credit for everything short of splitting the atom," Maulik said. "Everything was 'I did this.' He seemed like a lone wolf. He did everything himself."

Maulik recalls another seemingly good applicant who used his Twitter account "to disparage just about every new innovation in the marketplace." Maulik concluded the applicant "was much more comfortable as the critic than the collaborative creator."[4] This candidate was not hired either.

Recommended Tips

The following suggestions can help you manage the impression you are projecting based on the information you post on social media.

Do's

- Be aware of each platform's policies and procedures because they tend to vary.
- Focus on the quality of your posts rather than the quantity.
- Use Twitter and LinkedIn to play up your professional interests (like sharing relevant news articles).
- Cross-check your résumé and LinkedIn profile to make sure there are no discrepancies.
- Share information about your volunteer activities and work with professional associations.
- Make sure there are no typos or grammatical errors in your materials.
- Remember to continuously update your profiles.

Don'ts

- Don't bad-mouth a current or former employer, colleague, or company.
- Avoid foul language and negative remarks.
- Don't post when you are impaired, or even when you are overly tired or emotional.
- Don't post anything that might be perceived as racist, biased, sexually oriented, or illegal.[5]

What's Ahead in This Chapter

We want to help you enhance your understanding of the perceptual process so you won't fall victim to common perceptual errors—yours or other people's. This chapter will show you, for instance, how perception influences the way managers manage diversity. Diversity should matter to you because the way a business deals with diversity affects the way you are perceived as an individual. Diversity matters to your organization too, because it allows you to take advantage of the fullest range of human skill and talent. We also discuss barriers and challenges to managing diversity, and the practices organizations use to overcome them.

4.1 THE PERCEPTION PROCESS

THE BIGGER PICTURE

Understanding how you process information will help you see how perception affects a variety of important processes and outcomes within the Organizing Framework for Understanding and Applying OB. It can also assist in managing the perceptions people form about you.

Imagine you are driving on a winding mountain road at dusk and suddenly see something in the road. Is it an animal, a rock, or a person? Should you stop or just maneuver around it? Suppose you're in a team meeting and one of your teammates makes a negative statement about your work. Is the person being political or just having a bad day? Your mind is trying to quickly answer these questions before you respond.

Perception is key to resolving the above questions. **Perception is a cognitive process that enables us to interpret and understand our surroundings.** Recognition of objects is one of this process's major functions. But because organizational behavior's (OB's) principal focus is on people, our discussion will emphasize *social* perception rather than object perception.

Perception is important to OB because it affects our actions and decisions. It is based on our perception of reality, not on reality itself. Our exploration of this important process begins with a discussion of social perception and the four stages of processing information. We then consider a model of person perception, which provides a practical framework for understanding how we form perceptions of others. Finally we consider the managerial implications of person perception.

Stages of Social Perception

You can learn to avoid making perceptual errors by understanding the process that guides perception. As shown in Figure 4.2, there are four stages of social perception:

- *Stage 1:* Selective attention/comprehension
- *Stage 2:* Encoding and simplification
- *Stage 3:* Storage and retention
- *Stage 4:* Retrieval and response

FIGURE 4.2   Social Perception: A Social Information Processing Model

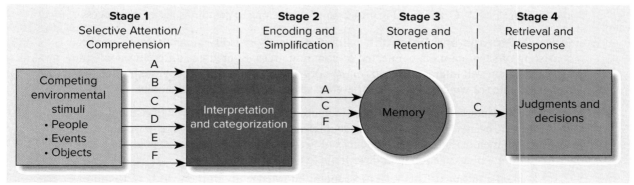

McGraw-Hill Global Education Holdings, LLC

The first three stages describe how specific social information is observed and stored in memory. The fourth and final stage, retrieval and response, involves turning mental representations into real-world judgments and decisions.

Let's look at the four stages of social perception by following a simple example. Suppose you were thinking of taking a personal finance course. Three professors teach the same course, using different types of instruction and testing procedures. Through personal experience, you now prefer good professors who rely on the case method of instruction and essay tests. According to social perception theory, you would likely arrive at a decision regarding which course to take based on the instructor, following the steps outlined in the following sections.

Stage 1: Selective Attention/Comprehension

People are constantly bombarded by physical and social stimuli. To avoid being overwhelmed, they selectively perceive subsets of environmental stimuli. This is where *attention* plays a role. **Attention is the process of becoming consciously aware of someone or something.** Research has shown that people tend to pay attention to *salient stimuli*—that is, something that stands out from its context. For example, a 250-pound man would certainly be salient in a women's aerobics class but not at a meeting of NFL players.

One's needs and goals often dictate which stimuli are salient. In our personal finance example, you would begin your search for the "right" professor by asking friends who have taken classes from the three available professors. You might also interview the professors who teach the course to gather additional information. In Figure 4.2, all the information you obtain shows as competing environmental stimuli labeled A through F. You interpret and categorize your notes.

Stage 2: Encoding and Simplification

Our memory does not store observed information in its original form; encoding is required. Our brains interpret or translate raw information into mental representations. To accomplish this, individuals assign pieces of information to **cognitive categories, groups of objects that are considered equivalent.** For example, categories are generally designated by names—for example, *dog, animal.*[6]

In social information processing theory, a particular category builds on a *schema*. A *schema* **represents a person's mental picture or summary of a particular event or type of stimulus.** For example, picture a sports car. Does the picture show a small vehicle with two doors? Is it red? If you answered yes, you would tend to classify all small, two-door, red vehicles as sports cars because this type of car possesses characteristics consistent with your sports car schema. We interpret and evaluate people, events, and objects by comparing their characteristics with information contained in *schemata* (the plural form of schema).

Relying on encoding helps us to simplify what might be a bewildering range of inputs. Encoding and schemata make the world more manageable. In our personal finance example, let's say you simplify by focusing on categories most salient to you: the method of instruction, testing procedures, and past grade distributions. Figure 4.2 shows these three salient pieces of information as lines A, C, and F.

Having collected relevant information about the three professors and their approaches, you compare this information with other details contained in schemata. This comparison leads you to form an impression of what each professor's course might be like. In turn, the relevant information (lines A, C, and F in Figure 4.2) are passed along to the third stage of the process.

Stage 3: Storage and Retention

Long-term memory is like an apartment complex consisting of separate units connected to common areas. Sometimes different people in each apartment will interact. Long-term memory similarly consists of separate but related compartments (or wings), one each for events, semantic materials, and people.[7]

- **Event memory:** This compartment includes categories with information about both specific events (relying on unique details) and general events (relying on schemata). These memories describe sequences of events in familiar situations: going to a restaurant, going on a job interview, going to a movie, etc.

- **Semantic memory:** This refers to general knowledge about the world, as a kind of mental dictionary of concepts. Each concept includes a definition (e.g., a good leader) and associated traits (outgoing), emotional states (happy), physical characteristics (short), and behaviors (works hard). These concepts are stored as schemata and are often subject to cultural differences.

- **Person memory:** Categories within this compartment supply information about a single individual (your professor) or groups of people (professors). You are more likely to remember information about a person, event, or advertisement if it contains characteristics that are similar to something stored in the compartments of memory.

As time draws near for you to decide which personal finance professor to choose, your schemata of them are stored in the three categories of long-term memory and are available for immediate retrieval and comparison.

Stage 4: Retrieval and Response   People retrieve information from memory when they make judgments and decisions, and these ultimately come about in one of two ways: (1) we draw on, interpret, and integrate categorial information stored in long-term memory or (2) we retrieve a summary judgment that has already been made.

On course registration day, you have to choose which professor to take for personal finance. After retrieving your schemata-based impressions from memory, you select a good professor who uses the case method and gives essay tests (line C in Figure 4.2). In contrast, you may choose your preferred professor by simply recalling the decision you made two weeks ago.

A Model of Person Perception

Figure 4.1 showed that perception is an important *process* in the Organizing Framework for Understanding and Applying OB because it affects our actions and decisions. Consider dieting. Recently Weight Watchers International stopped using the word *diet* in its advertising because of the word's negative perception. In fact, the company slimmed down its own name to WW and is adding the word *wellness* to its brand. Company president and CEO Mindy Grossman noted that "We are becoming the world's partner in wellness."[8] Weight Watchers clearly is trying to use the perception process to increase sales.

Music artist DJ Khaled is one of many celebrities who endorse Weight Watchers and its wellness approach to a healthy lifestyle. Do you think more people will join WW's programs because of celebrity endorsements?
Lu Chau/AP Images

Perception is influenced by three key components: the characteristics of the *perceiver,* of the *target*—the person or group being observed—and of the *situation* (see Figure 4.3).[9] Let's take a closer look at how these components work.

Characteristics of the Perceiver   Figure 4.3 shows six key perceiver characteristics that affect our perceptions of others.[10] As you read, consider how they might have influenced your perceptions in the past.

- **Direction of gaze.** Gaze is the first step in the perception process because it focuses your attention and tells the brain what you think is important in the immediate environment. When scanning people, we also tend to pay attention to others who are gazing at us. We usually remember people when we make direct eye contact with them.

- **Needs and goals.** We are more likely to perceive whatever is related to our goals and needs. For example, we perceive examples of food if we are hungry. If we are looking for a friend at a party, we scan the room for familiar faces and fail to perceive strangers.

- **Experience with target.** Our perception of a target is influenced by our past experience with him or her. You might perceive someone's firm handshake negatively, for instance, if you know this person has attempted to exert power and control over you in the past. The same handshake is positive if you remember the target as a friendly, caring person.

FIGURE 4.3   A Model of Person Perception

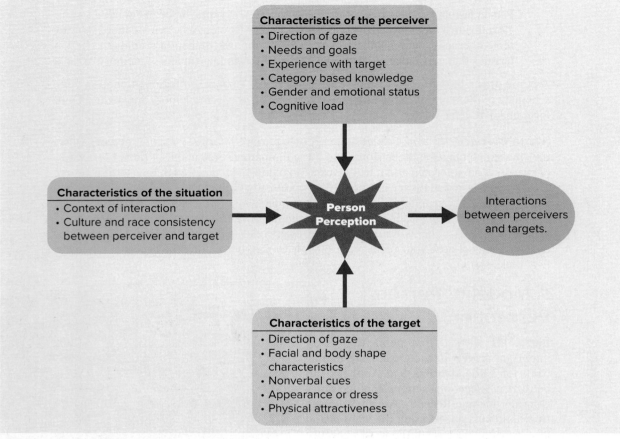

McGraw-Hill Global Education Holdings, LLC

- **Category-based knowledge.** Category-based knowledge consists of perceptions, including stereotypes, that we have stored in memory about various categories of people (professors, singers, artists, police, politicians, and so on). We use this information to interpret what we see and hear. For instance, if you believe professors in general are intelligent, you are more likely to perceive that those teaching your current courses are intelligent. If your memory tells you that people who lie cannot be trusted, you are likely to perceive a politician as untrustworthy who is caught in a lie. We discuss stereotypes in the next section.

- **Gender and emotional status.** Women recognize emotions more accurately than men, and both men and women are more likely to recognize a target's emotions when they are consistent with their own. Experiencing negative emotions such as anger and frustration is likely to make your perceptions more negative. The opposite is true for positive emotions such as optimism and love.

- **Cognitive load.** Cognitive load represents the amount of activity going on in your brain. If you are tired and distracted after working a long day, your perceptions are more likely to be distorted and susceptible to stereotypical judgments.

Characteristics of the Target   Figure 4.3 identifies five important characteristics of the target that affect our person perception.[11] The characteristics are:

- **Direction of gaze.** We form different perceptions of people based on whether they are looking at us while conversing. Direct eye contact suggests interest, whereas eyes darting across a room suggests the opposite.

- **Facial features and body shape.** We often use faces as markers for gender, race, and age, but face and body characteristics can lead us to fall back on cultural stereotypes.

For example, height has been associated with perceptions of prosperity—high income—and occupational success. Excess weight can be stereotypically associated with negative traits such as laziness, incompetence, and lack of discipline.

- **Nonverbal cues.** Communication experts tell us that nonverbal actions are highly influential in perception. Gestures, touching, facial expressions, eye contact, and body movements like slouching all convey messages. You might perceive that someone is defensive if you observe folded arms, a facial scowl, or crossed legs. In many cultures appropriate touching conveys an impression of warmth and caring.

- **Appearance or dress.** We all are susceptible to being influenced by appearance. We may conclude someone who shows up for work with tattoos or other body art may not be serious about doing a good job or may wonder how the person even got hired. However, research doesn't support this perception. In a recent survey of more than 2,000 individuals, those with tattoos were no less likely to be employed than their uninked counterparts and average earnings were the same for both groups.[12]

- **Physical attractiveness.** While attractiveness is culturally determined, the beauty-is-good stereotype leads us to perceive attractive people positively. High attractiveness has been associated with better job opportunities, higher performance ratings, and the potential for increased earnings. One team of researchers concluded, "The effects of facial attractiveness are robust and . . . attractiveness is a significant advantage for both children and adults in almost every domain of judgment, treatment, and behavior."[13]

Characteristics of the Situation   Figure 4.3 shows two key situational characteristics that affect perception: the context of the interaction, and the culture and race consistency between perceivers and targets.

- **Context of interaction.** Perceptions are affected by the social context in which the interaction occurs. For example, your parent will likely perceive your eating food from the kitchen when you visit home differently than will a coworker whose food you take from the office refrigerator. Texting someone while eating dinner with friends is perceived differently than texting during a business meeting. Context matters!

- **Culture and race consistency.** We more accurately recognize emotions displayed by people from our own culture or from other familiar cultures. We also better understand and remember facial expressions displayed by people from our own race. For instance, both authors do consulting around the world, and we find it harder to accurately perceive group dynamics in foreign than in U.S. companies. Angelo recalls telling a joke to a group of Finnish managers. No one laughed or made any facial expressions, and he thought the joke had bombed until someone told him at a break that he was really funny. What a perceptual surprise! The Applying OB box provides some tips on how to develop your own cultural awareness.

Applying OB
CAREER READINESS

Developing Cultural Awareness to Enhance Perception

Our cultural backgrounds and expectations are just some of many factors that affect our own perceptions of a person or situation. For example, "Americans see an apology as an admission of wrongdoing, whereas Japanese see it as an expression of eagerness to repair a damaged relationship, with no culpability necessarily implied."[14] To build your own cultural awareness and enable you to form more accurate perceptions of unfamiliar people and situations, consider the following:[15]

1. **Know what you don't know.** Begin by acknowledging that you may not have good or sufficient information about another person's culture, and that there are probably gaps in your knowledge that you can fill.

2. **Try not to judge prematurely.** Once you've recognized that you may have some cultural biases, withhold judgment of others whose motivations, words, or actions you may not immediately understand, and of situations that are new to you.
3. **Do some homework.** Even if your organization doesn't provide formal diversity training, there are almost unlimited resources in libraries and online for finding information about other cultures on your own. Do some research and consider using your company's suggestion box or other feedback framework to propose diversity training if there isn't any.
4. **Rely on good manners.** Always err on the side of cordiality and respect and give others the benefit of the doubt whenever appropriate. Use informality with care; it is not valued equally in all cultures, particularly in business relationships.
5. **Reach out to others as a way to learn.** Get to know coworkers from other cultures than your own. Invite them to share coffee or a meal, listen carefully, and be ready to share information about what you have in common as well as how you may differ. Give these new relationships time to develop.
6. **Build diverse teams.** Include different kinds of people on any team you are asked to build and make an active effort to work with them on teams to which you are assigned.

Managerial Implications of Person Perception

Person perception is the window through which we all observe, interpret, and prepare our responses to people and events. It affects a wide variety of managerial activities, organizational processes, and quality-of-life issues. We'll touch on hiring, performance appraisal, and leadership.

Hiring   Interviewers make hiring decisions based on their impression of how an applicant fits the perceived requirements of a job. Unfortunately, many of these decisions are

Do you think these diners have any implicit cognitions when it comes to choosing their menu selections? Do you think their choice of rosé wine activates a preference for a certain type of entrée?
Image Source

made on the basis of implicit cognition. ***Implicit cognition* represents any thoughts or beliefs that are automatically activated from memory without our conscious awareness.** The existence of implicit cognition, or implicit bias, leads people to make biased decisions without realizing they are doing so.[16] A recent study of letters of recommendation for academic job positions, for instance, demonstrated that people recommend female versus male candidates in different ways, probably based on gender role stereotypes. The letters described female applicants as caring, friendly, and nice, while male applicants were strong, decisive, and outstanding.[17]

Experts recommend three solutions for reducing the biasing effect of implicit cognition. First, managers can be trained to understand and recognize this type of hidden bias. Second, they can use structured rather than unstructured interviews. Interviewers ask the same sequence of questions to all applicants in a structured interview, which leads to more reliable evaluations. Finally, managers can rely on evaluations from multiple interviewers rather than just one or two people. More companies now are using virtual interviews as a tool for reducing problems associated with implicit cognition (see the OB in Action box).

Performance Appraisal   Faulty perceptions about performance can lead to inaccurate performance appraisals, which can erode morale and thwart some women from seeking formal leadership roles in an organization. Consider the results of a recent study of how former CEOs influence the success of their female successors.

The research looked at all of the CEO successions involving female successors over a 20-year period across the largest companies in the United States. Findings suggest that women CEOs were successful when their mostly male predecessors promoted gender-neutral work environments and functioned as "gatekeepers," meaning the male CEOs were closely involved in hiring, selecting, and socializing the women within the company's organizational culture, and providing them with ongoing feedback about their performance—both formally and informally.[18]

Perceptual biases in performance appraisals can be reduced by the use of more objective measures of performance. While this is a good idea, it is hard to implement for jobs that require interdependent work, mental work, or work that does not produce objective outcomes.

Companies can also reduce bias by providing managers a mechanism for accurately recalling employee behavior, such as a performance diary. Finally, it would be useful to train managers about perceptual biases and about how they can avoid them in performance evaluations.[19]

OB in Action

Virtual Interviews Can Improve the Accuracy of Job Interviews and Reduce Costs

What do Doctors Without Borders, Yelp, Trivago, ExxonMobil, Porsche Consulting, and ClubMed have in common? According to WebEmployed.com, these organizations and others use Skype to conduct virtual interviews with qualified job candidates around the world.[20] Among the benefits are speed and cost savings, since the time and expense to get candidate and interviewer to the same place are eliminated. Not only can hiring companies interview more candidates; multiple interviewers can participate, yielding more and better information for selecting a new hire. Job candidates benefit, too. They don't need to take time off for travel to be considered for a job, and they can widen the pool of organizations to which they apply.

In a variation on virtual interviewing that demonstrates another of its advantages, Matt Mullenweg, CEO of Automattic (the parent company of Word-Press), tries to eliminate hidden bias by using text-only Skype and messaging for the final stage of interviewing. "I don't know the gender or ethnicity of anyone I interview," he says. "I see only the words on the screen. It's as close to a double-blind process as

you can get. I'm looking mainly for passion and cultural fit. Of the people who make it to the final interview, 95 percent get a job offer—a testament to the effectiveness of our approach."[21]

Even before the interview, some companies are using virtual technologies in recruiting. Jet.com, the New Jersey-based shopping site owned by Walmart, has created a virtual reality simulation to let potential job candidates try out its workplace culture wherever they happen to be. They can observe a meeting with the CEO, sample the company's happy hour, and even play games. The company hopes this opportunity will allow it to attract the best candidates to compete against its main rival, Amazon.com.[22]

YOUR THOUGHTS?

1. The above discussion focuses on the positive aspects of virtual interviews. Are there negative aspects of this strategy? If so, what are they?

2. How would you prepare for a virtual interview?

3. If you were relying on virtual interviews to select job candidates, what would you look for?

Leadership Research demonstrates that employees' evaluations of leader effectiveness are influenced strongly by their categorical knowledge of what constitutes good and poor leaders. For example, a team of researchers found that the following behaviors are representative of effective leadership:

1. Assigning specific tasks to group members.
2. Telling others they have done well.
3. Setting specific goals for the group.
4. Letting other group members make decisions.
5. Trying to get the group to work as a team.
6. Maintaining definite standards of performance.[23]

4.2 STEREOTYPES

THE BIGGER PICTURE

Don't say you don't use stereotypes; they help us process information faster and thus are part of the way we humans think. But stereotypes can also lead to bad decisions and undermine personal relationships. Being aware of them can save you from such pitfalls.

LO 4-2

Discuss how awareness of stereotypes helps you make better decisions.

"A *stereotype* is an individual's set of beliefs about the characteristics or attributes of a group."[24] We need to recognize how stereotypes affect our perception because we use them without intending to or even being consciously aware that we are.[25]

Stereotypes are not always negative. For example, the belief that engineers are good at math is certainly part of a stereotype and is positive. Stereotypes also may or may not be accurate. Engineers may in fact be better at math than the general population.

Unfortunately, stereotypes can lead to poor decisions. Consider people diagnosed with cancer, about 38 percent of men and women living in the United States.[26] A recent study showed that managers continue to make discriminatory decisions about employees who are cancer patients.[27] All told, stereotypes can create barriers for women, older individuals, people of color, and people with disabilities, all while undermining loyalty and job satisfaction. Let's look at examples.

Gender.   A summary of research revealed that:

- Men were preferred for male-dominated jobs (e.g., firefighters), but there was no preference for either gender in female-dominated jobs (e.g., nurse).
- Female entrepreneurs looking for funding for their start-ups have a more difficult time than their male counterparts in obtaining venture capital due to gender bias on the part of investors.
- Women are more likely than men to hire other women.
- Women of color are more negatively affected by sex-role stereotypes than white women or men in general.[28]

Race.   Studies of race-based stereotypes demonstrated that people of color experienced more perceived discrimination and less psychological support than whites.[29] Perceived racial discrimination was also associated with more negative work attitudes, physical health, psychological health, and organizational citizenship behavior.[30]

Age.   Another example of an inaccurate stereotype is the belief that older workers are less motivated, more resistant to change, less trusting, less healthy, and more likely to have problems with work–life balance. A recent study refuted all these negative beliefs about age.[31]

Stereotype Formation and Maintenance

We build stereotypes through a four-step process:

1. **Categorization.** We categorize people into groups according to criteria (such as gender, age, race, and occupation).
2. **Inferences.** Next, we infer that all people within a particular category possess the same traits or characteristics: women are nurturing, older people have more job-related accidents, African Americans are good athletes.

3. **Expectations.** We form expectations of others and interpret their behavior according to our stereotypes.

4. **Maintenance.** We maintain stereotypes by:
   - Overestimating the frequency of stereotypic behaviors exhibited by others.
   - Incorrectly explaining expected and unexpected behaviors.
   - Differentiating minority individuals from ourselves.

Research shows that it takes accurate information and motivation to reduce the use of stereotypes.[32]

Managerial Challenges and Recommendations

The key managerial challenge is to reduce the extent to which stereotypes influence decision making and interpersonal processes throughout the organization. We suggest three ways that this can be achieved.

1. **Managers should educate people about stereotypes and how they can influence our behavior and decision making.** Many people may not understand how stereotypes unconsciously affect their perception. For example, in a recent LinkedIn report on gender insights, data revealed that when recruiters are searching for job candidates and they see a list of men and women, they tend to open the men's LinkedIn profiles more frequently than the women's profiles. To combat the initial selection bias, more companies are implementing anonymous hiring and removing key identifiers (for example, names and photos) from candidates' applications.[33]

2. **Managers should create opportunities for diverse employees to meet and work together in cooperative groups of equal status.** Social scientists believe positive interpersonal contact among mixed groups is the best way to reduce stereotypes because it provides people with more accurate data about the characteristics of others.

3. **Managers should encourage all employees to increase their awareness of stereotypes.** Awareness helps reduce the application of stereotypes when making decisions and interacting with others.

What do you notice in this photo? The woman working from a wheelchair? Do you think some people have negative stereotypes about those with disabilities? Research shows that many people do.

Pixtal/age fotostock

4.3 CAUSAL ATTRIBUTIONS

THE BIGGER PICTURE

Consciously or unconsciously, you use *causal attributions* when you seek to explain the causes of behavior. So do most managers. You can avoid the *fundamental attribution bias* and *self-serving bias* if you learn how they distort our interpretation of observed behavior.

LO 4-3

Explain how causal attributions help managers interpret employee performance.

Attribution theory is based on a simple premise: Rightly or wrongly, people infer causes for their own and others' behavior. Formally defined, **causal attributions are suspected or inferred causes of behavior.** Managers need to understand how people formulate these attributions because they profoundly affect organizational behavior. Consider Table 4.1, in which the manager's understanding of observed behavior leads to very different actions.

Kelley's Model of Attribution

Current models of attribution build on the pioneering work of the late Fritz Heider. Heider, the founder of attribution theory, proposed that **behavior can be attributed either to *internal factors* within a person (such as ability) or to *external factors* within the environment (such as a difficult task).** Following Heider's work, Harold Kelley attempted to pinpoint some specific antecedents of internal and external attributions. Kelley hypothesized that people make causal attributions by observing three dimensions of behavior: *consensus, distinctiveness,* and *consistency.*[34] These dimensions vary independently, forming various combinations and leading to differing attributions.

- *Consensus* **compares an individual's behavior with that of his or her peers.** There is high consensus when someone acts like the rest of the group and low consensus when he or she acts differently.
- *Distinctiveness* **compares a person's behavior on one task with his or her behavior on other tasks.** High distinctiveness means the individual has performed the task in a significantly different manner than he or she has performed other tasks.
- *Consistency* **judges whether the individual's performance on a given task is consistent over time.** Low consistency is undesirable for obvious reasons and implies that a person is unable to perform a certain task at some standard level. High consistency implies that a person performs a certain task the same way, with little or no variation over time.

TABLE 4.1   The Link between Attributions and Managerial Actions

OBSERVED BEHAVIOR	MANAGER'S ATTRIBUTION	MANAGERIAL ACTION
Employee fails to meet minimum standards	Lack of effort	Reprimand
Employee fails to meet minimum standards	Lack of ability	Training

FIGURE 4.4 Sample Charts of Consensus, Distinctiveness, and Consistency in Performance

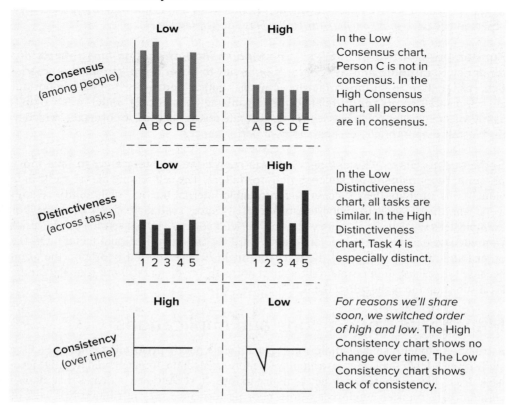

In the Low Consensus chart, Person C is not in consensus. In the High Consensus chart, all persons are in consensus.

In the Low Distinctiveness chart, all tasks are similar. In the High Distinctiveness chart, Task 4 is especially distinct.

For reasons we'll share soon, we switched order of high and low. The High Consistency chart shows no change over time. The Low Consistency chart shows lack of consistency.

SOURCE: Brown, Karen A. "Explaining Group Poor Performance: An Attributional Analysis." *Academy of Management Review* 9, no. 1 (January 1984): 54–63. https://DOI: 10.2307/258232.

Figure 4.4 provides sample charts of these dimensions in both low and high incidence.

How do these three dimensions of behavior lead to specific attributions? Kelley theorized that people attribute behavior to either *internal* causes (personal factors) or *external* causes (environmental factors) depending on the way they rank consensus, distinctiveness, and consistency as shown in Table 4.2:

EXAMPLE You would make an internal attribution to Mary if she displayed extraordinary performance relative to her peers and this level of performance was typical for Mary over the past year. In contrast, you would arrive at an external attribution if Mary's performance was similar to her peers, but the performance on the task you observed was lower than usual for Mary over the past year.

While other combinations are possible, the two options shown below have been most frequently studied.[35] **Note:** For another view of Kelley's theory, return to Figure 4.4. In the figure, we provided charts that, taken together, indicate internal attributions on the left-hand side and external attributions on the right-hand side.

TABLE 4.2 Formation of Internal and External Attributions

ATTRIBUTION	CONSENSUS (PEOPLE)	DISTINCTIVENESS (TASKS)	CONSISTENCY (TIME)
Internal	Low	Low	High
External	High	High	Low

Attributional Tendencies

Researchers have uncovered two attributional tendencies that distort our interpretation of observed behavior—*fundamental attribution bias* and *self-serving bias.*

Fundamental Attribution Bias   The *fundamental attribution bias* **reflects our tendency to attribute another person's behavior to his or her personal characteristics, rather than to situation factors.** This bias causes perceivers to ignore important environmental factors (again refer to the Organizing Framework), which often significantly affect behavior. Such bias leads to inaccurate assessments of performance, which in turn fosters inappropriate responses to poor performance.

Self-Serving Bias   The *self-serving bias* **represents our tendency to take more personal responsibility for success than for failure.** The self-serving bias suggests individuals will attribute their success to controllable internal factors (high ability or hard work) and their failures to uncontrollable external factors (bad luck or lack of sleep). For example, let's say you ace a test in your most difficult course. The self-serving bias suggests your success occurred because you studied hard for the exam (internal factor). On the other hand, let's say you failed the test. You might believe you did poorly on the exam because the teacher didn't explain the subject correctly or you had to work your shift at the local sub shop the night before the test.[36]

Managerial Applications and Implications

Attribution models can explain how managers handle poorly performing employees. One study revealed that managers gave employees more immediate, frequent, and negative feedback when they attributed their performance to low effort. Another indicates that managers tended to transfer employees whose poor performance they attributed to a lack of ability. These same managers also decided to take no immediate action when poor performance was attributed to external factors beyond an individual's control.[37]

These observations offer useful lessons for all of us:

- **We tend to disproportionately attribute behavior to internal causes.** This bias can result in inaccurate evaluations of performance, leading to reduced employee motivation. The Organizing Framework for Understanding and Applying OB offers a simple solution for overcoming this tendency. You must remind yourself that behavior and performance are functions of both person and situation factors.

- **Other attributional biases may lead managers to take inappropriate actions.** Such actions could include promotions, transfers, layoffs, and so forth. Inappropriate responses can dampen motivation and performance.

- **An employee's attributions for his or her own performance have dramatic effects on motivation, performance, and personal attitudes such as self-esteem.** For instance, people tend to give up, lower their expectations of future success, and experience decreased self-esteem when they attribute failure to lack of ability. Employees are more likely to display high performance and job satisfaction when they attribute success to internal factors such as ability and effort.[38]

4.4 DEFINING AND MANAGING DIVERSITY

THE BIGGER PICTURE

Like seashells on a beach, people come in a variety of shapes, sizes, and colors. All of us need to be aware of the different layers of diversity and to know the difference between affirmative action and diversity management.

Do you have any preconceived notions about diversity that are worth considering? Let's take a reality check:

- **Assumption: Gender diversity on boards of directors does not affect firm performance.** Wrong, says a team of researchers who aggregated results from 140 research studies. Findings showed that firms were more profitable when women were members of the board of directors. As of 2018, there were only 12 Fortune 500 companies with zero women on their boards, and 11 of the 12 firms performed poorly over the past five years when compared to other Fortune 500 companies (the other firm is privately held).[39]

- **Assumption: Organizations are losing Baby Boomers to retirement—can Millennials fill the gap?** Yes, in terms of sheer numbers, but no, in terms of skills. According to Pew Research data, of the 75 million strong Baby Boom generation, 44 million are still working, with the youngest in their early 50s. Millennials contribute nearly 53 million workers to the labor force but because of their ages, they don't necessarily have the job experience or skills yet to fill the roles of the retiring Boomers.[40]

- **Assumption: Whites will constitute the majority among U.S. racial groups through 2060.** No, according to the U.S. Census Bureau. Today whites represent 61 percent of the population, but that will drop below 45 percent by 2060.[41]

> **LO 4-4**
>
> Describe the four layers of diversity and how they help organizations manage diversity effectively.

The United States is becoming more diverse in its gender, racial, educational, and age makeup. For example, there are now more working parents, more nonwhites, and more older people, and the consequences are not always what you might expect. **Demographics are the statistical measurements of populations and their qualities (such as age, race, gender, or income) over time.** The study of demographics helps us better appreciate diversity and helps managers develop human resource policies and practices that attract, retain, and develop qualified employees. In the remainder of this chapter we will further your understanding of diversity and its managerial challenges.

Layers of Diversity

Diversity represents the multitude of individual differences and similarities that exist among people, making it an input in the Organizing Framework for Understanding and Applying OB. As you will learn, however, managing diversity also affects a variety of processes and outcomes within the Organizing Framework.

Moreover, diversity pertains to everybody. It is not just an issue of age, race, or gender; of being heterosexual, gay, or lesbian; or of being Catholic, Jewish, Protestant, or Muslim. Diversity pertains to the host of individual differences that make each of us unique and different from all others.

FIGURE 4.5 The Four Layers of Diversity

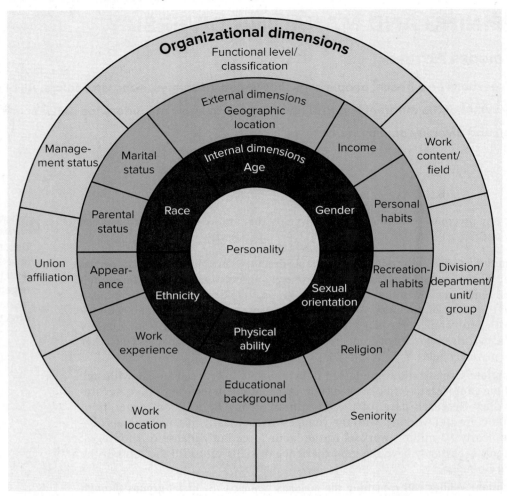

SOURCE: Gardenswartz, Lee, and Anita Rowe. *Diverse Teams at Work: Capitalizing on the Power of Diversity.* Virginia: Society For Human Resource Management, 2003.

Lee Gardenswartz and Anita Rowe, a team of diversity experts, identified four layers of diversity to help distinguish the important ways in which people differ (see Figure 4.5). Taken together, these layers define our personal identities and influence the way each of us sees the world.

Figure 4.5 shows that *personality* is at the center of the diversity wheel because it represents a stable set of characteristics responsible for a person's identity. These are the dimensions of personality discussed in Chapter 3. The next layer of diversity is composed of *internal dimensions,* also referred to as surface-level dimensions of diversity. **"Surface-level characteristics are those that are quickly apparent to interactants, such as race, gender, and age."**[42] Because we view these characteristics of others as unchangeable, they strongly influence our attitudes, expectations, and assumptions about them, which, in turn, influence our behavior. Take the experience of an African American middle manager sitting by the pool while vacationing at a resort. As she recalls, "A large 50-ish white male approached me and demanded that I get him extra towels. I said, 'Excuse me?' He then said, 'Oh, you don't work here,' with no shred of embarrassment or apology in his voice."[43] Stereotypes regarding one or more of the internal dimensions of diversity most likely influenced this man's behavior.

Figure 4.5 shows that the next layer of diversity consists of *external influences*. These are individual differences over which we have more control, such as where we live, our religious affiliation, our marital and parental status, and our work experience. These dimensions also exert a significant influence on our perceptions, behavior, and attitudes.

The final layer of diversity is *organizational dimensions* such as seniority, job title and function, and work location. Integrating these last two layers yields deep-level characteristics of diversity. **"Deep-level characteristics are those that take time to emerge in interactions, such as attitudes, opinions, and values."**[44] These characteristics are definitely under our control.

Affirmative Action vs. Diversity Management

Affirmative action and diversity management are driven by very different values and goals. This section highlights these differences.

Affirmative Action Affirmative action is not a law in and of itself. It is an outgrowth of equal employment opportunity (EEO) legislation. The goal of this legislation is to outlaw discrimination and to encourage organizations to proactively prevent discrimination. **Discrimination occurs when employment decisions about an individual are based on reasons not associated with performance or related to the job.** For example, organizations cannot legally discriminate on the basis of race, color, religion, national origin, sex, age, physical and mental disabilities, and pregnancy. **Affirmative action is an intervention aimed at giving management a chance to correct an imbalance, injustice, mistake, or outright discrimination that occurred in the past.**

Does the number of white males stand out in this picture of the U.S. Congress? Criticized for its lack of diversity, the U.S. Congress recently added over 120 women to its ranks.

Saul Loeb/Getty Images

Affirmative action

- Can refer to both voluntary and mandatory programs.
- Does not legitimize quotas. Quotas are illegal and can be imposed only by judges who conclude that a company has engaged in discriminatory practices.
- Does not require companies to hire unqualified people.
- Has created tremendous opportunities for women and minorities.
- Does not foster the type of thinking needed to manage diversity effectively.

In an effort to encourage diversity and combat gender inequity, former California governor Jerry Brown signed legislation in 2018 to require companies based in the state to add women to their board of directors.

Jae C. Hong/AP Images

Is the last point surprising? Research uncovered the following tendencies of affirmative action plans. They are

1. Perceived more negatively by white males than by women and minorities, because white males see the plans as working against their interests.

2. Viewed more positively by people who are liberals and Democrats than by conservatives and Republicans.

3. Not supported by people who hold racist or sexist attitudes.[45]

4. Found to negatively affect the women and minorities expected to benefit from them. Supposedly hired on the basis of affirmative action, these groups feel negatively stigmatized as unqualified or incompetent.[46]

Recently California became the first state in the nation to legally require women on boards for companies based in the state. Although seen as a conscious effort to even out the gender inequity in corporate boardrooms, some female leaders say they worry the new regulation could result in women being named to boards to comply with the regulation rather than to bring new skills and business experience to company boards. According to Bonnie Gwin, co-managing partner of executive search firm Heidrick & Struggles, "We've got to fix it [the gender imbalance], but I'm personally not a huge fan of quotas."[47]

Managing Diversity *Managing diversity* **enables people to perform to their maximum potential.** Diversity management focuses on changing an organization's culture and infrastructure such that people work to the highest productivity possible. Ann Morrison, a diversity expert, attempted to identify the types of initiatives 16 companies used to successfully manage diversity. Her results found three key strategies at work: education, enforcement, and exposure. She describes them as follows:

- **The educational component.** Education "has two thrusts: one is to prepare nontraditional managers for increasingly responsible posts, and the other is to help traditional managers overcome their prejudice in thinking about and interacting with people who are of a different sex or ethnicity."

- **The enforcement component.** Enforcement "puts teeth in diversity goals and encourages behavior change."

- **The exposure component.** Exposing people to others with different backgrounds and characteristics "adds a more personal approach to diversity by helping managers get to know and respect others who are different."[48]

In summary, both consultants and academics believe organizations should strive to *manage* diversity rather than being forced to use affirmative action.

4.5 BUILDING THE BUSINESS CASE FOR MANAGING DIVERSITY

THE BIGGER PICTURE

After reviewing the business case for managing diversity, we also look at demographic changes in the U.S. workforce that make the need to manage diversity all the more urgent. These demographic changes have major implications for OB.

The growing diversity in the United States is not a business initiative; it is a reality. Businesses can consciously choose to manage diversity or get caught short by the demographic changes facing the country.

LO 4-5

Discuss the business rationale for managing diversity.

Business Rationale

The rationale for managing diversity is more than the fact that it's legally, socially, or morally desirable. Quite simply, it's good business. The OB in Action box illustrates how companies can gain competitive advantage by using product design to reach a diverse market.

OB in Action

Using Product Design to Reach a Diverse Market

Can building diversity into your organization's purpose be good for business? More companies today believe it is. Product designers and marketers are looking for ways to make products and services "inclusive" so they can serve a broader market, or "universal" so they can reach just about everyone, rather than limiting their use to a narrower market such as the able-bodied. For example, voice-activated computer technology such as Google Voice makes social media more accessible to people with limited dexterity for typing, and those with limited or no vision. Alzheimer's patients might someday rely on a device such as Amazon's artificial intelligence–assisted DeepLens camera, currently in development, to recognize and interact with family and friends they no longer remember. Because this "smart camera" relies on universal design principles, however, anyone else can use it as well. People who communicate via sign language can confidently rely on the superior screen resolution of Apple's Facetime video chat feature, as other sighted users do too.[49]

The idea behind inclusive design is to begin with outliers, such as people with disabilities or other limitations, and design for them first, ideally resulting in a product or service that is ultimately better for everyone. As Kat Holmes, a former Microsoft staffer who heads her own product design company, recently told *Fast Company*, the process matters as much as the result. The right question to ask, she says, is, "Did you involve someone in your design process who was previously unable to participate? How you get there is what makes it inclusive, not that it's targeted at an underrepresented or underserved community."[50]

Inclusive marketing took hold at Hyatt Hotels when Hyatt recognized that half of all business travelers are women. Acknowledging women's preferences and concerns, the hotel chain remedied issues it had not seen as problems before, such as male employees making late-night room-service deliveries, mirrors and bathrobes designed for larger and taller male guests, and dark parking lots that made women feel less safe. All the chain's guests benefited from the changes, not just women.[51]

Managing diversity also gives an organization the ability to grow and maintain its business in an increasingly competitive marketplace. Here's what Alex Gorsky, current Chairman and CEO of Johnson & Johnson, said:

> Our people are one of a kind—the way they think, feel, speak, and work; what they've experienced, and where they're from. Harnessing these unique perspectives and experiences gives us great problem-solving potential—the ideas, solutions, and strategies that, when mobilized, brings health to billions of people.[53]

Research supports the logic of this strategy. For example, a recent study of 739 retail stores found reinforcement for the *access-and-legitimacy* perspective, defined in the following manner:

> An *access-and-legitimacy perspective* on diversity is based in recognition that the **organization's markets and constituencies are culturally diverse.** It therefore behooves the organization to match the diversity in parts of its own workforce as a way of gaining access to and legitimacy with those markets and constituent groups.[54]

Companies increasingly recognize the value of having a workforce that matches the race of their customers. Why would customers prefer to be helped by someone like them?

Steve Hix/Getty Images

This particular study discovered that customer satisfaction and employee productivity were higher when the racial-ethnic composition of store employees matched that of customers.[55]

These favorable results were taken one step further by another team of researchers, who wanted to know whether customers would spend more money in stores when they perceived themselves as similar to the sales representatives. Results from 212 stores supported the idea that customer–employee similarity leads to more spending.[56] Clearly it pays to manage diversity, but organizations cannot use diversity as a strategic advantage if employees fail to contribute their full talents, abilities, motivation, and commitment. Thus organizations must create an environment or culture that allows all employees to feel included and valuable. Managing diversity is a critical component of creating this environment.

Trends in Workforce Diversity

For managers, the study of demographics suggests unique ways of managing diverse employees. For organizations, it helps signal whether human resource policies and procedures are appropriate to the characteristics of a diverse employee population. Let's examine five categories on the internal dimension of the diversity wheel in Figure 4.5—gender, race, sexual orientation, physical/mental abilities, and age—and one category on the external dimension, educational level.

Women Break the Glass Ceiling—but Navigate a Labyrinth   Coined in 1986, **the term *glass ceiling* identifies an invisible but absolute barrier that prevents women**

from advancing to higher-level positions. Various statistics support the existence of the glass ceiling. Take the pay gap between men and women, for example. In 2018, the median weekly income in full-time management, professional, and related occupations was $1,468 for men but $1,078 for women. Even among female and male MBA graduates who made about the same upon graduation over the past 15 years, by 2017 a 28 percent pay gap had opened with women earning an average of $59,000 less per year than their male counterparts.[57]

Some people think these pay differences come about because women leave the workforce to raise children, or because men perform better on the job. Although women are more likely than men to take time off to raise children, recent research continues to demonstrate that pay differences and productivity gaps were not due to performance evaluations, particularly in the STEM (science, technology, engineering, and mathematics) fields.[58] Other unknown causes are behind the gender pay gap.

Alice Eagly and Linda Carli conducted a thorough investigation into the organizational life of women and in 2007 published their conclusions that women had finally broken through the glass ceiling.[59] We've updated the data reported in Eagly and Carli's book that led them to their conclusion. In late 2018 there were more female CEOs (24 within the Fortune 500) and more women in managerial, professional, and related occupations than in the 1990s and 2000s.[60] Statistics further showed that women had made strides along several measures.

1. **Educational attainment:** Women earned the majority of bachelor's and master's degrees in 2018.

2. **Seats on boards of directors of Fortune 500 firms:** Women held 9.6 percent of seats in 1995 and 21.2 percent in 2018.

3. **Leadership positions in educational institutions and Congress:** In 2017 women represented 30 percent of college presidents, and in 2019, 131 women served in Congress—the largest number ever.

4. **Federal court appointments:** In 2019, more than 36 percent of federal courts of appeals judges were female.[61]

You can interpret the above statistics in one of two ways.

- **No Change.** On the one hand, you might see proof that women remain underpaid and underrepresented in leadership positions, victims of discriminatory organizational practices.

- **Positive Change.** Or you can agree with Eagly and Carli's conclusion that "men still have more authority and higher wages, but *women have been catching up. Because some women have moved into the most elite leadership roles, absolute barriers are a thing of the past.*"[62]

Sometimes a woman's career is thought to resemble a labyrinth like this—with twists and turns needed to get through the maze. Have you experienced such twists and turns in your career?
Sergey Nivens/Shutterstock

Eagly and Carli propose that a woman's career follows a pattern more characteristic of a path through a labyrinth. They believe a woman's path to success is neither direct nor simple but rather contains twists, turns, and obstructions, particularly for married women with children.

Racial Groups Face Their Own Glass Ceiling and Perceived Discrimination
The U.S. workforce is becoming increasingly diverse. Between 2016 and 2060, the Census Bureau predicts the following changes in ethnic representation:

- Growth: The Asian population will grow from 5.7 percent to 9.1 percent of the total.

- Growth: The Hispanic population will grow from 17.8 percent to 27.5 percent.

- Mild Growth: The African American population will rise from 13.3 percent to 15.0 percent.

- Decline: Non-Hispanic whites will drop from 61.3 percent to 44.3 percent.[63]

In 2060 so-called minority groups will constitute approximately 57 percent of the work-force, according to the Census Bureau.[64] And yet three additional trends suggest that current-day minority groups are stalled at their own glass ceilings:

Smaller percentage in the professional class. Hispanics, or Latinas/os, and African Americans have a smaller relative hold on managerial and professional jobs compared with whites. Women of color generally do better than men of color.

More discrimination cases. The number of race-based charges of discrimination that were deemed to show reasonable cause by the U.S. Equal Employment Opportunity Commission increased from 294 in 1995 to 723 in 2017. Companies paid a total of $355.6 million to resolve these claims without litigation in 2017.[65]

Lower earnings. Minorities also tend to earn less personal income than whites. In 2018, median weekly earnings for workers 16 years and older were $916, $694, $1,095, and $680 for whites, blacks, Asians, and Hispanics, respectively. Asians had the highest median income.[66]

Sexual Orientation: LGBTQ People Become More Visible

The term **LGBT is a widely recognized acronym to represent lesbian, gay, bisexual, and *transgender.*** However a fifth letter has been gaining acceptance—Q—which according to the Human Rights Campaign can mean either "questioning" or "queer."

Q for "questioning" refers to someone in the process of exploring his or her sexual iden-tity. "People use the term *queer* because it's not specific to sexual orientation or to gender identify but is more of an umbrella term that can encompass a lot of people." You may want to avoid using the term *queer* because it is offensive to some in the LGBT community.[67]

We are discussing sexual orientation because organizations cannot afford to allow between 3.9 and 5.1 percent of the workforce to feel disenfranchised. This represents the estimated number of people who identify as LGBT.[68]

Because LGBTQ employees often experience a lack of inclusion, their engagement, performance, and retention can be affected. A recent study by the Human Rights Cam-paign Foundation, for instance, revealed that unwelcoming environments can lead to close to half of LGBT workers remaining closeted at work (meaning they don't acknowledge their sexual orientation); 31 percent feeling unhappy at work; 20 percent searching for a different job; and 10 percent leaving a job because the work environment was not very accepting of LGBT people.[69]

The good news is that over 90 percent of Fortune 500 companies offer workplace protections on the basis of sexual orientation and gender identity. In contrast, 21 states do not offer such protections.[70]

Physical and Mental Abilities: People with Disabilities Face Challenges

Approximately 20 percent of Americans have a physical or cognitive disability, according to the U.S. Census Bureau. The ***Americans with Disabilities Act* prohibits discrimina-tion against those with disabilities and requires organizations to reasonably accom-modate an individual's disabilities.**[71]

Not surprisingly, some people with disabilities have difficulty finding work. The U.S. Bureau of Labor Statistics found that 8.0 percent were unemployed in 2018, more than twice the rate of those with no disability (3.7 percent).[72] Contrary to negative stereotypes about hiring the disabled, such as that making reasonable accommodation is expensive, many organizations are finding this group of people to be a valuable source of talent. Micro-soft, for example, has two programs that encourage inclusion for disabled workers: the autism hiring program and the supported employment program, as well as local partners who share information on Microsoft's inclusive hiring practices with the community.[73]

Generational Differences in an Aging Workforce

The U.S. population and work-force are getting older, and the workforce includes greater generational differences than ever before. In a recent poll by Frank N. Magid Associates, more than half of the respon-dents said they were least likely to get along with someone from another generation compared to 30 percent with a different racial background and 19 percent with the opposite sex. According to the company's executive director, "Generational understanding is the new diversity training."[74] We already see four generations of employees working together, soon to be joined by a fifth (see Table 4.3). Managers need to deal effectively with generational differences in values, attitudes, and behaviors. Many companies, including IBM, Lockheed Martin, Ernst & Young LLP, and Aetna, address this issue by providing training workshops on generational diversity.

Table 4.3 summarizes generational differences using common labels: traditionalists, baby boomers, Gen Xers, Millennials/Gen Ys, and Gen Zers. We use such labels (and resulting generalizations) for sake of discussion. There are always exceptions to the characterizations shown in Table 4.3.[75]

Millennials account for the largest block of employees in the workforce, followed by baby boomers. Thus Millennials are often managed by boomers, who possess very different values and personal traits. Conflicting values and traits are likely to create friction between people.

TABLE 4.3 **Generational Differences**

	TRADITIONALISTS	BABY BOOMERS	GEN XERS	MILLENNIALS (GEN Y)	GEN ZERS
Birth Time Span	1928–1945	1946–1964	1965–1980	1981–1996	1997–
Current Population	25.7 million	73 million	65 million	71 million	86 million
Key Historical Events	Great Depression, World War II, Korean War, Cold War era, rise of suburbs	Vietnam War; Watergate; assassinations of John and Robert Kennedy and Martin Luther King, Jr.; women's movement; Kent State killings; first man on the moon	MTV, AIDS epidemic, Gulf War, fall of Berlin Wall, Oklahoma City bombing, 1987 stock market crash, Bill Clinton–Monica Lewinsky scandal	September 11 terrorist attack, Google, Columbine High School shootings, Enron and other corporate scandals, wars in Iraq and Afghanistan, Hurricane Katrina, financial crisis of 2008 and high unemployment	Social media, election of Barack Obama, financial crisis of 2008 and high unemployment
Broad Traits	Patriotic, loyal, disciplined, conformist, possessed of a high work ethic and respect for authority	Workaholic, idealistic, competitive, materialistic, possessed of a high work ethic, in search of personal fulfillment	Self-reliant, adaptable, cynical, independent, technologically savvy, distrustful of authority, in search of work–life balance	Entitled, civic minded, close parental involvement, cyberliteracy, appreciate diversity, multitasking, in search of work–life balance, technologically savvy	Multitasking, digital natives, independent learners, cyberliteracy, communicate fast and online
Defining Invention	Fax machine	Personal computer	Mobile phone	Google and Facebook	Social media and iPhone apps

SOURCES: Parker, Kim, Nikki Graf, and Ruth Igielnik. "Generation Z Looks a Lot Like Millennials on Key Social and Political Issues." *Pew Research Center,* January 17, 2019. https://www.pewsocialtrends.org/2019/01/17/generation-z-looks-a-lot-like-millennials-on-key-social-and-political-issues/; Massot, Dolors. "15 Ways Generation Z Could Change the World." *Aleteia SAS,* May 09, 2018. https://aleteia.org/2018/05/09/15-ways-generation-z-could-change-the-world/; "Resident population in the United States in 2017, by generation." *Statista*; Meister, Jeanne C, and Karie Willyerd. *The 2020 Workplace: How Innovative Companies Attract, Develop, and Keep Tomorrow's Employees Today.* Harper Business, 2010; and Alsop, Ron. *The Trophy Kids Grow Up: How the Millennial Generation is Shaking Up the Workplace.* Jossey-Bass, 2008.

Millennials also tend to change jobs more frequently than other categories of workers. For example, the median job tenure of people between 20 and 24 is less than 16 months. This puts pressure on companies to find ways to retain this talented segment of the workforce.[76]

Goldman Sachs Group Inc. is addressing the issue head on. According to *The Wall Street Journal* the firm is "rethinking the way it structures bankers' early years at the firm. The bank is dangling carrots, including promises to speed the path to promotions and eliminating some of the grunt work that often falls to younger employees." In addition to lightening workloads, the company started having "town-hall-style meetings to address grievances to keep young people on board." And just in case some workers jump ship and need to be replaced, Goldman is advertising on Spotify to attract more Millennial and Gen Z employees both in the United States and the UK.[77] Will other groups of employees view these changes as unfair? Time will tell.

Have age-related differences at school or work caused any conflicts for you? The following Self-Assessment was created to assess your attitudes toward older employees. Because the term *older* is relative, define *older employees* in your own terms when completing the assessment.

SELF-ASSESSMENT 4.1   CAREER READINESS

What Are Your Attitudes Toward Working with Older Employees?

Please be prepared to answer these questions if your instructor has assigned Self-Assessment 4.1 in Connect.

1. What is your attitude about working with older employees? Are you surprised by the results?

2. What is your level of satisfaction when working with older employees?

3. Based on your results, what can you do to improve your satisfaction when working with older employees?

Educational Levels: Mismatch between Education and Organizational Needs

There are three potential education–work mismatches:

- **College graduates may be in jobs for which they are overqualified.** The U.S. Census Bureau estimates that 22 percent of the U.S. workforce has at least a college degree.[78] Unfortunately, even with a strong economy, nearly 300,000 college graduates are working minimum-wage jobs—148,000 with bachelor's degrees and 146,000 with associate's degrees.[79] These graduates are **underemployed, working at jobs that require less education than they have** such as waiting tables, tending bar, painting, and other work that someone with less education could perform. Underemployment is associated with poorer work attitudes, job performance, job satisfaction, motivation, and psychological well-being.[80]

- **College graduates may not have the skills desired by employers.** Recent studies show that college graduates, while technically and functionally competent, lack teamwork skills, critical-thinking ability, oral communication skills, and analytic reasoning.[81] There is also a shortage of college graduates in technical fields related to science, math, technology, and engineering.

- **High-school dropouts and others may not have the literacy skills needed for many jobs.** A recent study revealed that 6.1 percent of all U.S. students between 16 and 24 dropped out of high school in 2016.[82] The dropout rate is higher for males. This statistic, along with the fact that 32 million U.S. adults read below a basic level, is a real problem for employers, because about 50 percent of on-the-job reading materials are written at or above a ninth-grade level.[83]

4.6 BARRIERS AND CHALLENGES TO MANAGING DIVERSITY

THE BIGGER PICTURE

Wouldn't you rather know what obstacles lay ahead, instead of discovering them too late? We share 11 common challenges to effectively managing diversity.

The following is a list of the most common barriers to implementing successful diversity programs:[84]

1. **Inaccurate stereotypes and prejudice.** Mistaken perceptions manifest themselves in the belief that differences are weaknesses and that diversity hiring means sacrificing competence and quality. As a reporter for *The Wall Street Journal* noted, "Studies show that negative stereotypes about aging—for example, that older people inevitably grow less productive and more depressed—are as pervasive as they are inaccurate."[85] Inaccurate stereotypes like this limit the promotability and job satisfaction of older workers.

2. **Ethnocentrism.** The ethnocentrism barrier is based on the feeling that our cultural rules and norms are superior to or more appropriate than the rules and norms of another culture.

3. **Poor career planning.** Lack of opportunities for diverse employees to get work assignments that qualify them for senior management positions can stunt careers.

> **LO 4-6**
>
> Discuss the most common barriers to implementing successful diversity programs.

There are more than 11 different types of lightning. This type is called an anvil crawler, because it travels horizontally and generally at high altitudes. A lightning storm like this can be dangerous, and we must be careful to avoid being struck. The same is true for an organization's diversity climate—which signals the extent to which the organization's "internal climate" supports diversity initiatives. Bad organizational climates, like bad lightning storms, result in people taking cover by withholding effort and skills.

Menno van der Haven/Shutterstock

4. **A negative diversity climate.** We define organizational climate in Chapter 7 as employee perceptions about an organization's formal and informal policies, practices, and procedures. *Diversity climate* **is a subcomponent of an organization's overall climate and is defined as the employees' aggregate "perceptions about the organization's diversity-related formal structure characteristics and informal values."**[86] Diversity climate is positive when employees view the organization as being fair to all types of employees, which promotes employee loyalty and overall firm performance.[87] It also enhances psychological safety. *Psychological safety* **reflects the extent to which people feel free to express their ideas and beliefs without fear of negative consequences.** As you might expect, psychological safety is positively associated with outcomes in the Organizing Framework like innovation.[88]

5. **A hostile working environment for diverse employees.** Hostile work environments are characterized by sexual, racial, and age harassment and can be in violation of Equal Employment Opportunity law, such as Title VII of the Civil Rights Act.[89] Whether perpetrated against women, men, older individuals, or LGBTQ people, hostile environments are demeaning, unethical, and appropriately called "work environment pollution." You certainly won't get employees' best work if they believe the work environment is hostile toward them. The Applying OB box highlights the companies recognized for creating a work environment supportive of Millennials.

Applying OB

Best Companies for Millennials

Indeed.com, the popular job posting site, has released its list of the U.S. employers that Millennials rate as the best to work for. Now in their twenties and thirties and open to job changes, Millennials make up about a third of the U.S. workforce, and they place "opportunity to learn and grow" at the top of their wish-list for employers. Many are disillusioned about the business community, finding that companies could act more ethically and do more to help make the world a better place. Millennials want flexibility in where and when they work, and they want to prioritize their health and their families. Parental leave and tuition assistance are also prized.[90]

An analysis of the list by *Forbes* found that the top companies recommended by Millennials had a few things in common: "a focus on education, working mothers, work–life balance, compensation, and giving back."[91] The top 10 companies were Northrop Grumman, Discover Financial Services, Kaiser Permanente, Delta, Southwest Airlines, Apple, Pfizer Inc., Capital One, EY (one of the big four global accounting firms), and Dow Chemical.

Among the highlights: Kaiser Permanente makes leadership training and mentoring programs available; Delta and Southwest both offer profit sharing and free travel to all their destinations; Discover hosts on-site fitness centers and mother's rooms; and Apple provides generous parental leave plans. Most of the top ten companies offer adoption assistance and some form of tuition assistance. At Discover, that means full payment for an online bachelor's degree.[92]

6. **Diverse employees' lack of political savvy.** Diverse employees may not get promoted because they do not know how to "play the game" of getting along and getting ahead in an organization. Research reveals that women and people of color are excluded from organizational networks that could help them rise.[93] Some organizations attempt to overcome this barrier by creating employee resource groups that encourage individuals with similar backgrounds to share common experiences and success strategies. American Express has 16 network groups and Cisco has 13.[94]

7. **Difficulty balancing career and family issues.** Women still assume most of the responsibilities associated with raising children. This makes it harder for them to work evenings and weekends or to travel. Even without children in the picture, household chores take more of a woman's time than a man's.

8. **Fear of reverse discrimination.** Some employees believe diversity management is a smoke screen for reverse discrimination. This belief leads to very strong resistance because it makes people feel one person's gain is another's loss.

9. **Lack of organizational priority for diversity.** Low priority for diversity leads to subtle resistance in the form of complaints and negative attitudes. Employees may complain about the time, energy, and resources devoted to diversity that could have been spent doing "real work."

10. **A poor performance appraisal and reward system.** Performance appraisals and reward systems must reinforce the need to effectively manage diversity. Success must thus be based on a new set of criteria. For example, AT&T evaluates the extent to which its managers are inclusive of employees with different backgrounds. These evaluations are used in salary and promotion decisions.[95]

11. **Resistance to change.** Effectively managing diversity entails significant organizational and personal change. Sometimes this resistance is a function of cross-cultural values. In Japan, for example, women have a difficult time being promoted to senior management positions because of the practice of lifetime employment and age-based promotions. This tradition still holds at both large and small companies.[96]

Are you curious about the diversity climate in a current or former employer? If yes, take the Self-Assessment below. It measures the components of an organization's diversity climate and will enable you to determine whether your employer has or had a favorable one.

SELF-ASSESSMENT 4.2

Assessing an Organization's Diversity Climate

Please be prepared to answer these questions if your instructor has assigned Self-Assessment 4.2 in Connect.

1. What were the three highest- and lowest-rated survey items? What does this tell you about your employer?

2. Based on these scores, what advice would you give the human resources officer at the company you evaluated?

In summary, managing diversity is a critical component of organizational success. It is a challenge, but it is necessary if you want to create an environment that engages employees and motivates them to do their best.

4.7 ORGANIZATIONAL PRACTICES USED TO EFFECTIVELY MANAGE DIVERSITY

THE BIGGER PICTURE

Whether you manage a diverse work group or find yourself managed within a diverse work group, you'll do better by understanding the various ways in which organizations attempt to manage diversity. You'll be able to review eight options in the following section. *Hint:* We recommend mutual adaptation.

LO 4-7

Explain what organizations are doing to manage diversity effectively.

What are organizations doing to effectively manage diversity? We can answer this question by first providing a framework for categorizing organizational initiatives.

Framework of Options

One especially relevant framework was developed by R. Roosevelt Thomas Jr., a diversity expert. Thomas identified eight generic action options that organizations can use to address any type of diversity issue. After describing each option, we discuss relationships among them.[97]

Option 1: Include/Exclude   Include/exclude is an outgrowth of affirmative action programs. Its primary goal is to either increase or decrease the number of diverse people at all levels of the organization. Big 5 Corporation is a sporting goods retailer that operates 435 stores in 11 western states. Recently it was fined $165,000 to settle a racial discrimination and retaliation lawsuit filed by the EEOC. According to the lawsuit, Big 5's store manager and assistant managers in a store on Whidbey Island, Washington, subjected an African American management trainee to ongoing racial harassment and death threats. The trainee was forced to go on several leaves due to stress from ongoing racial harassments and threats, as well as retaliatory work assignments and discipline. Ultimately Big 5 terminated the trainee. In addition to the fine, Big 5 agreed to review and revise its current policies regarding discrimination and to provide training to its employees, supervisors, managers, and investigators on how to keep the workplace free of harassment, discrimination, and retaliation.[98]

Option 2: Deny   People may deny differences exist, saying that all decisions are color-, gender-, and age-blind and that success is determined solely by merit and performance. Seasons 52, a national restaurant chain, agreed to settle a $2.85 million federal lawsuit that alleged age discrimination when it came to hiring employees. In the suit filed with the EEOC, the agency said managers at the restaurant chain tried to portray a young and hip image by hiring younger servers and hosts. The initial complaint alleged that the company wouldn't hire two men in their mid-40s and early 50s because of their age. After contacting thousands of people over 40 who had applied for positions with Seasons 52, EEOC determined that more than 250 additional people claimed they were treated with bias during the interview process. Seasons 52 admits no liability and continues to deny the allegations but will be required to hold new training for all hiring managers regarding "non-discriminatory recruiting, interviewing, and hiring."[99]

Option 3: Assimilate   The idea behind assimilation is that, given time and reinforcement, all diverse people will learn to fit in or become like the dominant group. Organizations initially assimilate employees through their recruitment practices and through orientation programs that describe their preferred values and standard operating procedures. Employees then are encouraged to refer to policies and procedures when confused about what to do in a specific situation. These practices create behavioral homogeneity among employees.

Option 4: Suppress   Differences are squelched or discouraged when suppression is the diversity strategy. Managers and peers tell employees to quit whining and complaining about issues. Saying, "You've got to pay your dues" is another way to suppress differences and promote the status quo.

Option 5: Isolate   Isolation maintains the status quo by setting the diverse person off to the side. Then he or she is unable to influence organizational change. Managers can isolate people and entire teams and departments by putting them on special projects, creating functionally independent entities often referred to as silos.

These volleyball players illustrate the idea of assimilation. Note the common uniforms and the structured approach toward acknowledging their opponents. Assimilation techniques used by some organizations create levels of homogeneity and behavioral expectations, which can be reinforced by corporate policies and procedures.
Christopher Futcher/Getty Images

Option 6: Tolerate   Toleration entails acknowledging differences but not valuing or accepting them. This live-and-let-live approach allows organizations to give lip service to the issue of managing diversity. It differs from isolation in that it allows for the inclusion of diverse people, but differences are still not truly valued or accepted.

Option 7: Build Relationships   Relationship building is based on the premise that good relationships can overcome differences. It addresses diversity by fostering high-quality relationships—characterized by acceptance and understanding—among diverse groups. For example, financial services firm Baird has paired a group of senior leaders with junior Millennial employees so they can capitalize on their strengths and differences when it comes to developing competitive business strategies and building relationships with each other and their client base.[100]

Option 8: Foster Mutual Adaptation   Mutual adaptation allows people to change their views for the sake of creating positive relationships with others. Employees and managers alike must be willing to accept differences and, most important, agree that everyone and everything is open for change. Diversity training is one way to kick-start mutual adaptation. Research shows that such training can positively enhance people's attitudes and feelings about working with diverse employees.[101]

Conclusions about Action Options   Although the action options can be used alone or in combination, some are clearly more effective than others. Exclusion, denial, assimilation, suppression, isolation, and toleration are the least preferred options. Inclusion, building relationships, and mutual adaptation are preferred. That said, Thomas reminds us that mutual adaptation is the only approach that unquestionably endorses the philosophy behind managing diversity.

Choosing how to best manage diversity is a dynamic process and is influenced by the context. For instance, some organizations are not ready for mutual adaptation. The best they might be able to achieve is the inclusion of diverse people.

How Companies Are Responding to the Challenges of Diversity

We close this chapter by sharing some examples and models that demonstrate how companies are responding to the emerging challenges of managing diversity. Compare these to Thomas's framework and you'll find the greatest activity around Options 7 and 8, building relationships and fostering mutual adaptation.

Response: Paying Attention to Sexual Orientation   The Transgender Law Center estimates that about 2 percent of the population is transgender. The term *transgender* **applies to anyone whose gender identity or gender expression is different from sex at birth.** Although 83 percent of Fortune 500 firms forbid discrimination based on gender identity, transgender people are protected against discrimination in only 18 states and the District of Columbia.[102] More companies recognize that they don't want to alienate this segment of the population, however, and are implementing programs to help them transition. The Coca-Cola Company, for example, began offering transgender-inclusive health insurance coverage nearly a decade ago and also assists with the costs of taxes imposed on eligible U.S. employees whose same-sex spouse or partner was enrolled in health benefits in states that do not recognize same-sex marriage. Other companies, including PayPal, Hyatt, Microsoft, and IKEA, address the needs of transgender employees by trying to create an inclusive culture—where individuals can be their authentic selves.[103]

Unfortunately, the U.S. military does not appear to be trying to maintain an inclusive culture for transgender service personnel. In early 2019, the U.S. Supreme Court allowed President Trump's ban on transgender persons in the military to proceed, which means most transgender persons—for now—are disqualified from military service.[104]

Response: Addressing Changing Customer Demographics   Recognizing that its core demographic is changing, Target recently launched a campaign called #SinTraducción ("without translation") targeting Spanish-speaking customers, which used words with no English equivalent. For example, words such as "sobremesa," a period of time after a meal conversing among family and friends, and "estrenar," the act of using or wearing something for the first time, were used in the social media campaign to strike up conversations between Target and its Hispanic customers. The marketing approach underscored Target's acknowledgment that the Spanish language plays an important role in today's American culture, particularly among its many Hispanic customers.[105]

Response: Helping Women Navigate the Career Labyrinth   Organizations can make career navigation easier by providing flexible work schedules and the developmental assignments that prepare women for promotional opportunities. According to a business writer, the Boston Consulting Group "focuses heavily on recruiting and retaining women, offering part-time options, mentoring and professional-development programs." *On-ramping* **programs encourage people to reenter the workforce after a temporary career break.** Companies such as Credit Suisse and Goldman Sachs Group offer these to women in particular. Goldman, for example, instituted "returnship" programs that offer short-term job assignments to former employees.[106]

Response: Helping Hispanics Succeed   Medical device maker Arthrex and Shaw Industries Inc. hope to raise employee productivity, satisfaction, and motivation by developing customized training programs to improve the communication skills of their Spanish-speaking employees. Research reveals that retention and career progression of minorities can be significantly enhanced through effective mentoring.[107]

Response: Providing Community and Corporate Training to Reduce the Mismatch between Education and Job Requirements   To combat education gaps on a more global level, JPMorgan Chase started The Fellowship Initiative (TFI) in

New York in 2010 and expanded it to Chicago, Los Angeles, and Dallas. The goal is to provide intensive academic and leadership training to young men of color. Jamie Dimon, chair and CEO of JPMorgan Chase, is committed to the program. "These young men need access to high quality education and positive role models in and outside the classroom," he said. Michael Bloomberg, then New York City's mayor, applauded JPMorgan's effort by concluding, "We need more civic-minded companies and organizations to step up and join this work, and I congratulate JPMorgan Chase for being a leader in this effort and for making a real difference in the lives of young men of color in our city."[108]

At the individual corporate level, companies, including Wheeler Machinery Co. in Salt Lake City, have instituted specialized training programs that enable less-qualified people to perform more technically oriented jobs. Lockheed Martin and Agilent Technologies also offer paid apprenticeships or internships to attract high-school students interested in the sciences.[109]

Response: Retaining and Valuing Skills and Expertise in an Aging Workforce

Here are seven initiatives that can help organizations to motivate and retain an aging workforce:

1. Provide challenging work assignments that make a difference to the firm and employees.
2. Give employees considerable autonomy and latitude in completing a task.
3. Provide equal access to training and learning opportunities when it comes to new technology and job processes.
4. Provide frequent recognition for skills, experience, and wisdom gained over the years.
5. Offer mentoring opportunities whereby older workers can pass on accumulated knowledge to younger employees.
6. Offer short sabbaticals to help the workforce stay fresh and current.
7. Design a work environment that is both stimulating and fun.[110]

You'll see a number of these tactics being used by BAE, a multinational defense and aerospace company, according to a writer for *Bloomberg Businessweek*. "When BAE learns that an employee with deep institutional knowledge plans to retire, whether in a few months or a couple of years, a knowledge-transfer group of about a half-dozen people of varying ages working in the same area is formed. The teams meet regularly over months to talk and exchange advice. Younger workers elicit tips, and in some cases older ones gradually hand off tasks to junior employees."[111]

Some organizations, such as fire departments, have encountered problems managing older employees; see the Problem-Solving Application box.

Problem-Solving Application

Firefighters, 46 and 54, Sue for Age Discrimination

Firefighters John Guido and Dennis Rankin were only 46 and 54, respectively, when they were fired by the Mount Lemmon fire district, a department of the state of Arizona. Each had put in nine years of employment. The fire district claimed the two were fired for budget reasons, and because they had not volunteered for wildland duty. But one of the people chosen to replace them had also not served on any wildland firefighting assignments for the last two years.

Guido and Rankin then filed an age discrimination suit with the Equal Employment Opportunity Commission (EEOC), charging they had been let go simply because they were the two oldest full-time members of the department. The EEOC agreed there was "reasonable cause" for their claim that in dismissing them Mount Lemmon had violated the Age Discrimination in Employment Act (ADEA).

A federal trial judge sided with the fire district's attorneys, who argued that federal anti-discrimination law applied only to private organizations with at least 20 employees. Appealing the ruling, Guido and Rankin, who had meanwhile found other employment, watched as their case finally made its way to the U.S. Supreme Court several years later. In its 8-0 ruling in late 2018 (newly appointed Justice Brett Kavanaugh did not participate), the Supreme Court decided in favor of the two firefighters.

Justice Ruth Bader Ginsberg's opinion in the case said Mount Lemmon's reading of the law was inconsistent with precedent and with EEOC rulings and that, while the ADEA does not in fact apply to private companies with fewer than 20 employees, it sets no size limit on public employers, including local government entities like the Mount Lemmon fire department. Thus these entities are required to obey the Age Discrimination Act regardless of size. With that ruling, Guido and Rankin were entitled to sue their former employer for damages. While the law does not guarantee they will win their case, they plan to ask for their lost past and future wages.[112]

Apply the 3-Step Problem-Solving Approach

Step 1: Identify the problem in this case.

Step 2: Identify the OB concepts or theories that may be causing the problem. For example, are stereotypes, diversity climate, or frameworks for managing diversity causes of the problem?

Step 3: Recommend what you would do to correct the situation. Think both short term and long term.

Response: Resolving Generational Differences Traditional and boomer managers are encouraged to consider their approach toward managing the technologically savvy Gen Xers and Millennials. Gen Xers and Millennials, for instance, are more likely to visit social networking sites during the workday, often perceiving this activity as a "virtual coffee break." In contrast, traditional and boomer managers are more likely to view this activity as wasted time, leading them to adopt policies that attempt to prevent it. Experts suggest that restricting access to social media will not work in the long run if an employer wants to motivate younger employees.

Would you like to improve your working relationships with diverse people? If yes, Self-Assessment 4.3 can help. It asks you to compare yourself with a group of other people you interact with and then to examine the quality of the relationships between yourself and these individuals. This enables you to gain a better understanding of how similarities and differences among people influence your attitudes and behavior.

SELF-ASSESSMENT 4.3 | CAREER READINESS

How Does My Diversity Profile Affect My Relationships with Other People?

Please be prepared to answer these questions if your instructor has assigned Self-Assessment 4.3 in Connect.

1. Which diversity dimensions have the greatest influence on the quality of your interpersonal relationships?

2. Consider the person with whom you have the most difficulty working. Which dimensions of diversity may contribute to this relationship? What can you do to improve it?

4.8 MAKING THE CONNECTION: WHY IS UNDERSTANDING PERCEPTION AND DIVERSITY ESSENTIAL TO MY SUCCESS?

THE BIGGER PICTURE

Understanding the concepts of perception and diversity will play a significant role in being successful at work. Here are some key points to consider.

Takeaways for Me

Here are four additional things you can do to turn this chapter's lessons into positive change in your personal and professional life.

LO 4-8

Describe the implications of social perception and managing diversity for you and managers.

1. **Remember your personal and professional success depends on others' perceptions of you:** Because perceptions can override your good work, it is important to gather feedback on what others think of you.

2. **It is normal to be affected by stereotypes:** It would be helpful to reflect on your stereotypes and try to avoid letting them bias your decisions and perceptions of others.

3. **Consider how you will respond when you hear negative or disparaging things about diverse people:** It's going to happen, and your response can make the difference in stopping such comments.

4. **Celebrate your uniqueness, but remember some people are uncomfortable with individual differences among people:** We encourage you to just be yourself.

Takeaways for Managers

There are three key implications for managers.

1. **Because managers make many types of judgments about people, it is important to try and make these judgments without being biased or using stereotypes:** This can be difficult because such cognitive errors are a natural and normal part of how we process information.

2. **The fundamental attribution bias can lead to inaccurate interpretations of someone's suitability for a job or a performance evaluation:** Be aware of this attributional error and try to consider both personal and situational factors when evaluating others.

3. **Managing diversity is good for individual employees, managers, and organizations as a whole:** Whether local or global, organizations will compete more effectively when all employees feel included, supported, and valued. We all should try our best to be understanding and supportive of people who are different from the majority.

What Did I Learn?

You learned that perception and managing diversity are essential for success. Why? Because *social* and *person perception* help you better understand the perception process, improve the way you are perceived, and adjust your own perception to avoid common perceptual errors. *Managing diversity* (represented by both diversity and demographics in our Organizing Framework) lets you better optimize diversity's effect on individual and group/team outcomes. Reinforce your learning with the Key Points below. Then consolidate your learning using the Organizing Framework. Finally, challenge your mastery of the material by answering the Major Questions in your own words.

Key Points for Understanding Chapter 4

You learned the following key points.

4.1 THE PERCEPTION PROCESS

- Perception is a mental and cognitive process that enables us to interpret and understand our surroundings.
- Social perception is a four-stage process. The four stages are selective attention/comprehension, encoding and simplification, storage and retention, and retrieval and response (see Figure 4.2).
- Person perception is influenced by three components: characteristics of the perceiver, characteristics of the target, and characteristics of the situation.
- Person perception affects a wide variety of organizational activities including hiring decisions, performance appraisals, and leadership.

4.2 STEREOTYPES

- Stereotypes represent generalized beliefs about the characteristics of a group.
- Stereotypes are not always negative, and they are not always inaccurate.
- Common stereotypes exist about gender, race, and age.
- Stereotyping is a four-step process that consists of categorization, inference, expectation formation, and maintenance.
- We maintain stereotypes by (a) overestimating the frequency of stereotypic behaviors exhibited by others, (b) incorrectly explaining expected and unexpected behaviors, and (c) differentiating minority individuals from ourselves.

4.3 CAUSAL ATTRIBUTIONS

- Causal attributions are suspected or inferred causes of behavior.
- According to Kelley's model of causal attribution, we make external attributions when consensus and distinctiveness are high and consistency is low. We make internal (personal responsibility) attributions when consensus and distinctiveness are low and consistency is high.
- The fundamental attribution bias emphasizes personal factors more than situation factors while we are formulating attributions. In the self-serving bias we personalize the causes of our success and externalize the causes of our failures.

4.4 DEFINING AND MANAGING DIVERSITY

- Diversity represents the individual differences that make people unique from and similar to each other.

- Diversity varies along surface-level characteristics like race, gender, and age and along deep-level characteristics such as attitudes, opinions, and values.
- Affirmative action is an outgrowth of equal employment opportunity legislation and is an intervention aimed at giving management a chance to correct past discrimination.
- Managing diversity entails enacting a host of organizational changes that enable all people to perform to their maximum potential.

4.5 BUILDING THE BUSINESS CASE FOR MANAGING DIVERSITY

- Managing diversity is predicted to be good business because it aims to engage employees and satisfy customers' unique needs.
- There are six key demographic trends: (a) women are navigating a labyrinth after breaking the glass ceiling, (b) racial groups are encountering a glass ceiling and perceived discrimination, (c) recognition of sexual orientation is growing in importance, (d) people with disabilities face challenges, (e) generational differences are growing in an aging workforce, and (f) a mismatch exists between workers' educational attainment and organizational needs.

4.6 BARRIERS AND CHALLENGES TO MANAGING DIVERSITY

- There are 11 barriers to successfully implementing diversity initiatives: (a) inaccurate stereotypes and prejudice, (b) ethnocentrism, (c) poor career planning, (d) a negative diversity climate, (e) a hostile working environment for diverse employees, (f) diverse employees' lack of political savvy, (g) difficulty balancing career and family issues, (h) fears of reverse discrimination, (i) lack of organizational priority, (j) the need to revamp the organization's performance appraisal and reward systems, and (k) resistance to change.

4.7 ORGANIZATIONAL PRACTICES USED TO EFFECTIVELY MANAGE DIVERSITY

- Organizations have eight options for addressing diversity issues: (a) include/exclude the number of diverse people at all levels of the organization, (b) deny that differences exist, (c) assimilate diverse people into the dominant group, (d) suppress differences, (e) isolate diverse members from the larger group, (f) tolerate differences among employees, (g) build relationships among diverse employees, and (h) foster mutual adaptation to create positive relationships.

4.8 WHY IS UNDERSTANDING PERCEPTION AND DIVERSITY ESSENTIAL TO YOUR SUCCESS?

- Your overall success depends on other people's perceptions of you—gathering feedback from them will help you grow and mature.
- Your ability to recognize and avoid stereotypes will help you make unbiased decisions.
- Managing diversity at all levels of an organization will ensure that employees feel included, supported, and valued.

The Organizing Framework for Chapter 4

As shown in Figure 4.6, you learned that diversity, demographics, and stereotypes serve as key person factors, while diversity climate is an important situation factor. You also know there are relevant processes across the individual level (perception, attributions, and psychological safety), the group/team level (group/team dynamics), and the organizational level (options to manage diversity). These inputs and processes have critical outcomes.

FIGURE 4.6 Organizing Framework for Understanding and Applying OB

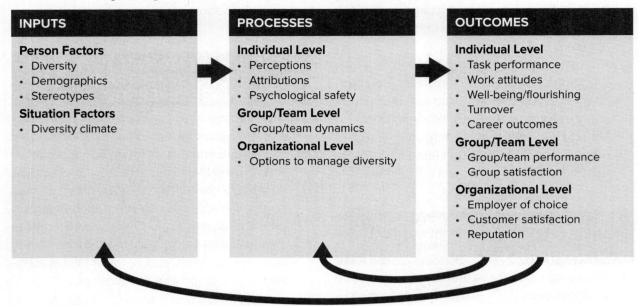

Challenge: Major Questions for Chapter 4

1. How do I form perceptions of others?
2. How can I use awareness of stereotypes to make better decisions and manage more effectively?
3. How do I tend to interpret employee performance?
4. How does awareness about the layers of diversity help organizations effectively manage diversity?
5. What is the business rationale for managing diversity?
6. What are the most common barriers to implementing successful diversity programs?
7. What are organizations doing to effectively manage diversity, and what works best?

White, Male, and Asian: The Diversity Profile of Technology Companies

Managing diversity is a hot topic among technology companies, some of which have started to display transparency by publishing their diversity profiles.

Google's diversity report reveals its workforce is 69.1 percent male and 30.9 percent female. Ethnicity data for Google's U.S. workforce indicates 53.1 percent white, 36.3 percent Asian, 4.2 percent of two or more races, 3.6 percent Latinx, and 2.5 percent black.[113] This pattern is similar to Apple (32 percent female and 54 percent white, and U.S. ethnicity data showing 21 percent Asian, 13 percent Hispanic, 9 percent black, 3 percent of two or more races, and 1 percent other)[114] and Facebook (36 percent female, and U.S. ethnicity data of 46.6 percent white, 41.4 percent Asian, 4.9 percent Hispanic, and 3.5 percent black).[115]

Executives within the technology industry have started to implement a variety of programs and policies to change the demographic profiles of their companies. For example, Pinterest established a 2018 goal to have 25 percent of new hires in engineering roles be female and 8 percent from underrepresented ethnic groups.[116] Intel established a hiring goal of full representation of underrepresented minorities and women in its U.S. workforce by 2020.[117]

Is setting diversity hiring goals fair? While companies that set them note the hiring goals are not meant to be quotas, some managers may perceive them that way. This would likely create feelings of reverse discrimination, fueling resistance to hiring diverse employees.

What has led to the skewed demographics at technology companies? Some experts believe the root cause goes back to patterns and norms in elementary and high school, where girls are not encouraged to focus on the STEM subjects (science, technology, engineering, and math). If this is true, female high-school students are not developing the proficiency that would help them major in STEM subjects in college. Further, a writer for *Forbes* concluded that an unconscious bias exists "that science and math are typically 'male' fields while humanities are primarily 'female' fields, and these stereotypes further inhibit girls' likelihood of cultivating an interest in math and science."[118]

A related issue is the "information gap." High-school students simply do not know which jobs are in high demand. For example, research shows that 24 percent of high-school seniors "have no idea of what career they want to pursue. Of high school seniors who have pinpointed a desired profession, 23 percent said they made their career choice based on something they saw on TV or in a movie."[119] This is a problem because TV shows often depict technology-oriented people as geeky males. Who wants to be a geek?

Others claim the tech industry has a pipeline problem. In other words, not enough females and minorities are majoring in STEM subjects in college. Statistics conflict on this subject. Some data indicate that females earn fewer than 20 percent of college degrees in computer science and engineering, even though they achieve the majority of bachelor's degrees in the United States.[120] In contrast, other studies suggest there is not a pipeline issue. According to *EdSource* writer Carolyn Jones, about half of the students in high-school science and math courses are female.[121] Data from the National Science Foundation indicate that women earn approximately 50 percent of science and engineering bachelor's degrees.[122] A *USA Today* study further showed that "top universities graduate black and Hispanic computer science and computer engineering students at twice the rate that leading technology companies hire them."[123] There must be some reason these students are not being hired.

If the above data are accurate, then it is possible that companies have a systemic problem based on hiring managers' beliefs, stereotypes, or unconscious biases. This occurred at Pinterest, for example, when it tried to increase the number of women and minorities being hired. Although recruiters found qualified applicants "from nontraditional backgrounds, managers often continued to prioritize people from places like Stanford and MIT, which have less broad student bodies. And while Adam Ward, Pinterest's head of recruiting, and Abby Maldonado, its diversity-programs specialist, had encouraged colleagues to pass along résumés from a range of candidates, most of the referrals were still white or Asian," according to *Fast Company*.[124] Pinterest founder Evan Sharp believes technology companies may not be giving diversity the same type of attention they give to product development initiatives.

There may also be more overt causes of the underrepresentation of female and minority tech employees. Consider results from a survey of 1,000 women who had held technology positions. These women explained why they believe females leave the tech field at a rate 45 percent higher than males. A perceived lack of career growth/trajectory was the most common factor in females' decisions to leave tech. Further, almost 50 percent of the women interviewed believed they had been paid less than their male counterparts. Other top reasons, particularly among women in tech aged 25–34, were difficulties breaking into management and leadership roles, perceived bias and discrimination, and a lack of female leadership representation in the company.[125]

Could something as subtle as gender-based communication contribute to the problem? The answer is yes, according to a recent report presented in *Fortune*. A study of 1,100 technology resumes from 512 men and 588 women uncovered gender-related differences that may affect a recruiter's perceptions. For example, "women's résumés are longer, but shorter on details. . . . Yet when it comes to providing details about previous jobs, the men present far more specific content than the women do," according to the *Fortune* report. Women were also found to "lead with their credentials and include more personal background. On average, the women's résumés cite seven personal distinctions apiece, while the men's cite four." Overall, women tend to use more narrative while men are more precise about their experiences.[126]

Assume you are a senior leader at a technology company. What does the information in this case tell you about managing diversity?

APPLY THE 3-STEP PROBLEM-SOLVING APPROACH TO OB

STEP 1: Define the problem.

A. Look first at the Outcome box of the Organizing Framework in Figure 4.6 to help identify the important problem(s) in this case. Remember that a problem is a gap between a desired and current state. State your problem as a gap and be sure to consider problems at all three levels. If more than one desired outcome is not being accomplished, decide which one is most important and focus on it for steps 2 and 3.

B. Cases have protagonists (key players), and problems are generally viewed from a particular protagonist's perspective. You need to identify the perspective—employee, manager, team, or the organization—from which you're defining the problem.

C. Use details in the case to identify the key problem. Don't assume, infer, or create problems that are not included in the case.

D. To refine your choice, ask yourself, *Why is this a problem?* Explaining why helps refine and focus your thinking. Focus on topics in the current

chapter, because we generally select cases that illustrate concepts in the current chapter.

STEP 2: Identify causes of the problem by using material from this chapter, which has been summarized in the Organizing Framework shown in Figure 4.6. Causes will appear in either the Inputs box or the Processes box.

A. Start by looking at Figure 4.6 to identify which person factors, if any, are most likely causes of the defined problem. For each cause, explain why this is a cause of the problem. Asking why multiple times is more likely to lead you to root causes of the problem. For example, if you think demographics—an input in the Organizing Framework—is a cause, ask yourself why. This might lead to the conclusion that there are not enough females and minorities who are taking STEM majors in college. In turn, this might lead to the conclusion that a poor pipeline is a root cause of demographics at technology companies. Then ask yourself why this is happening. The cause might go all the way back to elementary and high school. By following this process of asking why multiple times, you will be more likely to arrive at a more complete list of causes.

B. Now consider the Processes box shown in Figure 4.6. Consider whether perception, attributions, psychological safety, group/team dynamics, or options to manage diversity are causes of the problem. For any concept that might be a cause, ask yourself, *Why is this a cause?* Again, do this for several iterations to arrive at root causes.

C. Follow the same process for the situation factors.

D. To check the accuracy or appropriateness of the causes, be sure to map them onto the defined problem.

STEP 3: Make recommendations for solving the problem. Consider whether you want to resolve it, solve it, or dissolve it (see Section 1.5). Which recommendation is desirable and feasible?

A. Given the causes identified in Step 2, what are your best recommendations? Use the content in Chapter 4 or one of the earlier chapters to propose a solution.

B. Potential solutions may be found in the OB in Action and Applying OB boxes within the chapter. These features provide insights about how other individuals or companies are handling the topic at hand.

C. Create an action plan for implementing your recommendation.

Should Patient Requests Trump Health Care Employees' Civil Rights?

This case describes an incident that occurred at Beaumont Hospital in Dearborn, Michigan, and resulted in a lawsuit.

Teoka Williams, a 10-year veteran black nurse at Beaumont, overheard her patient comment in a racially charged manner that she did not want to be cared for by a black nurse. Williams reported the incident to the hospital's clinical manager who proceeded to bar the nurse from treating both the patient and the other patients sharing her room.[127]

Williams filed a complaint with the hospital's human resources department and was told that "patient requests are honored all the time and the next time it happens she would simply be taken off the assignment altogether." She felt "humiliated, embarrassed, and disappointed" by the experience. Her attorney Julie Gafkey said that health care facilities should not consent to patient requests at the expense of their employees' civil rights. Williams sued the hospital for federal and state civil rights violations.[128]

The American Medical Association's ethics code expressly prevents physicians from discriminating against patients based on race, gender, sexual orientation, gender identity, or other clinically irrelevant characteristics.[129] Official policies and guidelines for dealing with patient discrimination against health care providers, however, are virtually nonexistent.[130] Further, a survey of "emergency physicians found patients often make such requests, and they are routinely accommodated. A third of doctors who responded said they felt patients perceive better care from providers of shared demographics, with racial matches considered more important than gender or religion."[131]

Some hospitals are beginning to address this issue. For example, the Mayo Clinic in Rochester, Minnesota, has developed policies and procedures to protect its staff from patient discrimination. The policies allow staff members to deny discriminatory patient requests, extend guidance for handling such requests, and outline official reporting mechanisms.[132]

Your Views

What would you have done if you were a medical administrator at the time the request was made?

1. I would not have honored the patient's request. I would have explained why Teoka Williams and other African American nurses are best suited to take care of the patient.

2. I would have done exactly what the hospital did. The patient has a right to be taken care of by someone with a preferred race or gender.

What would you do about the lawsuit?

1. Fight it. It's ridiculous that someone would feel emotional stress and humiliation from simply being reassigned.

2. Settle it and create a policy that prohibits honoring future requests like this.

3. Settle it but hold a hospitalwide meeting explaining the rationale for continuing to accommodate such requests.

5

Foundations of Employee Motivation

After reading this chapter, you should be able to:

LO 5-1   Define motivation and how it affects your behavior.

LO 5-2   Compare and contrast the content theories of motivation.

LO 5-3   Compare and contrast the process theories of motivation.

LO 5-4   Describe three approaches to motivating employees through job design.

LO 5-5   Describe the implications of employee motivation for you and managers.

The Organizing Framework for Understanding and Applying OB shown in Figure 5.1 summarizes what you will learn in this chapter. Although Chapter 5 focuses on motivation, an individual-level process, a host of person and situation factors influence it. There are more situation than person factors in the figure. This reinforces the simple fact that managers significantly affect our motivation because they have more control over situation than person factors. Figure 5.1 further shows that processes across the individual, group/team, and organizational level influence a variety of important outcomes.

FIGURE 5.1   Organizing Framework for Understanding and Applying OB

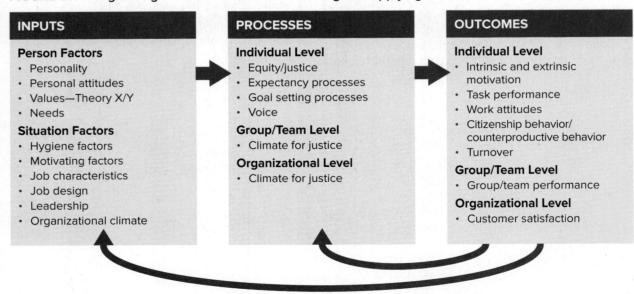

Winning at Work

Negotiating for a Raise

Among the many things you'll discover about motivation in this chapter is that money is not the only incentive leading to high performance. However, there's no question that equitable salaries and well-deserved bonuses are motivating, and that, conversely, inequities in pay can hurt job satisfaction and performance.

Ahlapot/iStockphoto/Getty Images

What can you do if you feel your performance merits a bump in your compensation? What is the most effective way to ask for a raise? Here are a few suggestions from the experts.

1. **Know what you want.** One writer who has researched the special frustrations that Millennial women in particular feel about compensation offers this three-word mantra: "Wish, want, walk." That is, know what your ultimate *wish* is, know what you would *want* if you couldn't get your wish, and know what offer you would reject or *walk* away from.[1]

2. **Know what you're worth.** Do your homework, on sites like Glassdoor.com and Salary.com, to find out what people with your level of experience are earning to do similar work in the same or related industries. Your chances of succeeding in a salary negotiation are much higher if your demands are realistic for your circumstances, including any factors particular to your firm that you should take into account.[2]

3. **Enlist support if possible.** If a mentor or sponsor will champion your request for a raise (and if you can seek his or her advice as well), all the better. If you are a gig worker looking to raise your rates, this person could be a supportive client or clients. However, a word of caution: Transparency about pay has some advantages, but it is not the universal standard. Avoid referring to what your colleagues make, even if you know it, as a reason you should make more. The conversation you want to have is about *you,* not about others.[3]

4. **Build your story.** Be prepared to offer concrete evidence of accomplishments and contributions that prove your worth. Document results above expectations, successful projects, or responsibilities outside the normal scope of your job, and praise and commendations from your manager, customers, colleagues, and other influential voices. These will bolster your argument that you deserve a pay increase. Have you saved your organization time, money, or other resources; offered successful new ideas or initiatives; brought new clients in; or increased revenue? Get in the habit of regularly documenting your tangible achievements to clearly demonstrate what you're worth to your firm.

5. **Consider your options.** If a raise isn't possible just now, consider accepting another form of compensation instead, such as added vacation time, a one-time bonus, or work-life options like flextime or occasional telecommuting privileges. This is the "want" part of "Wish, want, walk." "Think of things [the company] may have the ability to give you instead of money," advises Allison Hutton, chief talent officer at Allavanti Group. "Coming up with alternatives is usually viewed as positive."[4]

6. **Be patient.** It's unlikely you'll get an answer right away, so don't expect one. Your boss will need to consider the department's budget, the organization's overall performance, the case you've presented, and your compensation relative to that of comparable others in the group or company. Keep your case factual, don't oversell it, and choose your moment carefully to be sure of finding a receptive audience. If just-released quarterly results reflect poorly on your manager, for instance, hold your fire for a couple of weeks.

7. **Stay positive, and don't give up!** At the very least, you can walk away with a plan you and your manager agree will eventually bring you the increase you want.[5] Above all, if you've done a good job and can demonstrate just how good, don't be afraid to make your case. Good luck!

What's Ahead in This Chapter

There are far too many dysfunctional organizations where managers don't seem to have a clue about how to motivate workers. OB supplies proven methods of how to motivate employees. These aren't just abstract theories. All spring from observation and study of the workplace, and they have been validated in real-life testing. Business professionals treasure them as tools for making work better and more productive. We'll show you how these methods operate and give practical tips and suggestions for implementing them.

5.1 THE WHAT AND WHY OF MOTIVATION

THE BIGGER PICTURE

Motivation is a key process within the Organizing Framework for Understanding and Applying OB. Understanding the principles of motivation can help you both achieve personal goals and manage others in the pursuit of organizational goals.

LO 5-1

Define motivation and how it affects your behavior.

Motivation theories help us understand our own behaviors in organizational settings and provide us tools for motivating others.

Motivation: What Is It?

Motivation explains why we do the things we do. It explains why you are dressed the way you are right now, and it can account for what you plan to do this evening.

How Does It Work?   The term *motivation* derives from the Latin word *movere,* meaning "to move." In the present context, **motivation describes the psychological processes "that underlie the direction, intensity, and persistence of behavior or thought."**[6] "Direction pertains to *what* an individual is attending to at a given time, intensity represents the *amount* of effort being invested in the activity, and persistence represents *for how long* that activity is the focus of one's attention."[7]

There are two types of motivation: extrinsic and intrinsic.

- *Extrinsic motivation* **results from the potential or actual receipt of external rewards.** Extrinsic rewards such as recognition, money, or a promotion represent a payoff we receive from others for performing a particular task. For example, in 2018 Southwest Airlines paid its employees $544 million in profit-sharing bonuses, increasing every employee's annual compensation by nearly 10.8 percent. This is the 45th consecutive year that the airline has paid out profit-sharing bonuses to employees. According to Southwest CEO Gary Kelly, "Our people are our greatest asset and they deserve all the credit for our continued success." Such recognition from management is certainly a motivating factor for Southwest workers.[8]

- *Intrinsic motivation* **occurs when an individual is inspired by "the positive internal feelings that are generated by doing well,** rather than being dependent on external factors (such as incentive pay or compliments from the boss) for the motivation to work effectively."[9] We create our own intrinsic motivation by giving ourselves intrinsic rewards such as positive emotions, satisfaction, and self-praise. Consider the intrinsic motivation of Millennials Kory and Mallory Stevens, who started the Taft shoe company out of their apartment several years ago. They were recently named to *Forbes* 30-under-30 list of people to watch in the coming years for their passion, motivation, and entrepreneurship. Per the company website, "As Taft continues to grow, our vision for the brand remains the same—we believe in making beautiful shoes at beautiful prices and offering the best service

Intrinsic motivation helps Taft founders Kory and Mallory Stevens fulfill their vision of making beautiful shoes at competitive prices and offering the best possible service to their customers.

Courtesy of Taft Clothing

and value possible." With NBA ballers James Harden and Dwayne Wade, as well as action star Dwayne Johnson as super fans, this dynamic couple has turned athletes and celebrities into shoe ambassadors via social media and are motivated to continue their success.[10]

The Two Fundamental Perspectives on Motivation: An Overview

Researchers have proposed two general categories of motivation theories: content theories and process theories. **Content theories** identify internal factors such as needs and satisfaction that energize employee motivation. **Process theories** explain the process by which internal factors and situational factors influence employee motivation.[11] It's important to understand both motivational perspectives because they offer different solutions for handling motivational problems. The following two sections discuss several theories for each theoretical perspective.

5.2 CONTENT THEORIES OF MOTIVATION

THE BIGGER PICTURE

Five OB theories deal with the internal factors that motivate individuals. Several come from other disciplines. So you may have already encountered Maslow's hierarchy of needs and related content theories such as McGregor's Theory X and Theory Y, acquired needs theory, self-determination theory, and Herzberg's motivator-hygiene theory.

LO 5-2

Compare and contrast the content theories of motivation.

Most *content theories of motivation* are based on the idea that an employee's needs influence his or her motivation. Content theorists ask, "What are the different needs that activate motivation's direction, intensity, and persistence?" *Needs are defined as physiological or psychological deficiencies that arouse behavior.* They can be strong or weak and are influenced by environmental factors. This tells you that human needs vary over time and place.

Content theories include:

- McGregor's Theory X and Theory Y.
- Maslow's need hierarchy theory.
- Acquired needs theory.
- Self-determination theory.
- Herzberg's motivator-hygiene theory.

McGregor's Theory X and Theory Y

Douglas McGregor outlined his theory in his book *The Human Side of Enterprise*.[12] Drawing on his experience as a management consultant, McGregor formulated two sharply contrasting sets of assumptions about human nature. *Theory X is a pessimistic view of employees: They dislike work, must be monitored, and can be motivated only with rewards and punishment ("carrots and sticks").* McGregor felt this was the typical perspective held by managers. To help them break with this negative tradition, McGregor formulated his own Theory Y. *Theory Y is a modern and positive set of assumptions about people at work: They are self-engaged, committed, responsible, and creative.*

Consider the value of adopting a Theory Y approach toward people. One recent study demonstrated that employees and teams had higher performance when their managers displayed Theory Y behaviors. A second study uncovered higher levels of job satisfaction, organizational commitment, and organizational citizenship when managers engaged in Theory Y behaviors.[13]

Maslow's Need Hierarchy Theory: Five Levels of Needs

In 1943, psychologist Abraham Maslow published his now-famous need hierarchy theory of motivation. Although the theory was based on his clinical observation of a few neurotic individuals, it has subsequently been used to explain the entire spectrum of human behavior. **The *need hierarchy theory* states that motivation is a function of five basic needs: physiological, safety, love, esteem, and self-actualization.** See Figure 5.2 for an explanation.

FIGURE 5.2 Maslow's Need Hierarchy

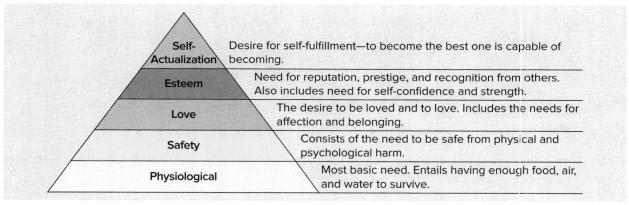

McGraw-Hill Global Education Holdings, LLC

The Five Levels   Maslow proposed that the five needs are met sequentially and relate to each other in a "prepotent" hierarchy (see Figure 5.2). Prepotent means the current most-pressing need will be met before the next need becomes the most powerful or potent. In other words, Maslow believed human needs generally emerge in a predictable stair-step fashion. Thus when physiological needs have been met, safety needs emerge, and so on up the need hierarchy, one step at a time. Once a need has been satisfied, it activates the next higher need in the hierarchy. This process continues until the need for self-actualization has been activated.[14]

Using Maslow's Theory to Motivate Employees   Although research does not clearly support its details, Maslow's theory does offer practical lessons. It reminds us, for instance, that employees have needs beyond earning a paycheck. In addition to offering health care benefits, which fills a physiological need, Wisconsin–based consumer products company SC Johnson has an on-site employee concierge service to help employees with some of life's chores. Concierges send packages and flowers, pick up groceries, shop for the best deals on car insurance, take employees' cars in for service, and even stand in line for concert tickets.[15]

This theory tells us that a "one style fits all" approach to motivation is unlikely to work. Studies show that different motivators are needed for employees working at small firms, whose owners may not have the money to spend on extensive benefits and perks. There are several strategies that will help keep employees motived at start-up or small businesses:

- Offer flexibility when it comes to work hours;
- Recognize and reward good performance; and
- Involve employees in decision making.[16]

A final lesson of Maslow's theory is that satisfied needs lose their motivational potential. Therefore, managers are advised to motivate employees by devising programs or practices aimed at satisfying emerging or unmet needs.

Acquired Needs Theory: Achievement, Affiliation, and Power

David McClelland, a well-known psychologist, began studying the relationship between needs and behavior in the late 1940s. He proposed the *acquired needs theory,* **which states that three needs—for achievement, affiliation, and power—are the key drivers of employee behavior.**[17] McClelland used the term "acquired needs" because he believes we are not born with our needs; rather we learn or acquire them as we go about living our lives.

FIGURE 5.3 McClelland's Three Needs

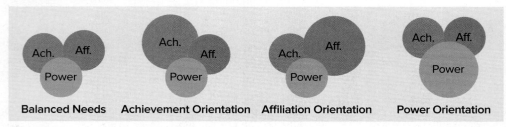

| Balanced Needs | Achievement Orientation | Affiliation Orientation | Power Orientation |

The Three Acquired Needs   McClelland's theory directs managers to drive employee motivation by appealing to three basic needs:

- **Need for achievement,** the desire to excel, overcome obstacles, solve problems, and rival and surpass others.

- **Need for affiliation,** the desire to maintain social relationships, be liked, and join groups.

- **Need for power,** the desire to influence, coach, teach, or encourage others to achieve.

People vary in the extent to which they possess these needs, and often one need dominates the other two (see Figure 5.3).

McClelland identified a positive and negative form of the power need. The positive side is called the need for *institutional power.* It manifests in the desire to organize people in the pursuit of organizational goals and help people obtain the feeling of competence. The negative face of power is called the need for *personal power.* People with this need want to control others, and they often manipulate people for their own gratification.

You can use this theory to motivate yourself, assuming you are aware of your need states. Can you guess which of the three needs is most dominant? Would you like to know which is helping or hindering the achievement of your personal goals? Check your perceptions by taking the acquired needs Self-Assessment.

SELF-ASSESSMENT 5.1   CAREER READINESS

Assessing Your Acquired Needs

Please be prepared to answer these questions if your instructor has assigned Self-Assessment 5.1 in Connect.

1. Which of the three needs is dominant for you? Are you surprised by this result?

2. Which is/are helping you to achieve your goals?

3. Are any of the needs affecting your level of well-being? Should you make any changes in your need states?

Using Acquired Needs Theory to Motivate Others   The following OB in Action box illustrates how Cameron Mitchell's acquired needs affected the way he ran his successful restaurant business.

You can apply acquired needs theory by appealing to the preferences associated with each need when you (1) set goals, (2) provide feedback, (3) assign tasks, and (4) design the job.[18] Let's consider how the theory applies to Cameron Mitchell.

- **Need for achievement.**   People motivated by the need for achievement, like Cameron Mitchell, prefer working on challenging, but not impossible, tasks or projects. They like situations in which good performance relies on effort and ability rather

OB in Action

Cameron Mitchell has achieved his childhood dream of running a successful restaurant business. He currently runs 32 upscale themed restaurants, such as Hudson 29 and Ocean Prime, in 12 states. His business earns about $300 million in annual revenue.[19]

Mitchell's primary goal was "to create an extraordinary restaurant company known for great people delivering genuine hospitality." He says, "In order to achieve this goal, I could not do it on my own! In fact, our past, present, and future success is directly attributed to our associates."[20]

You might not have foreseen Mitchell's success based on his difficult childhood. His parents divorced when he was 9, and he began drinking alcohol and trying drugs in middle school. When he started dealing drugs in high school, his mom threatened to call child protective services. Mitchell decided to run away.

He moved into a one-room apartment with other teens and sometimes went days without food. He decided to return home at 16 when he found himself thinking about suicide. He went back to high school and took a job as a dishwasher at a local steak house. He loved the job and concluded, "The restaurant business was where I wanted to be the rest of my life."

When Mitchell's application to the Culinary Institute of America was rejected due to his poor grades, he became more driven. He started working double shifts so he could pay for community college. He eventually graduated from culinary school and began working as a sous chef. Mitchell opened his first restaurant in 1993 in Columbus, Ohio. It was a success![21]

Mitchell's business puts people first. "Our associates are the core and foundation of our company," he says, "and they are my number one priority. If they aren't happy at work, it will show in the food they produce, the way they treat our guests and the way they treat each other. . . . We treat them great and, in turn, they take great care of the company."[22]

The company's commitment to its employees shows in the wide array of benefits it offers, which

Cameron Mitchell
Courtesy of Cameron Mitchell Restaurants

exceed industry standards. It also rewards restaurant managers who support and develop their teams. Mitchell believes associates should have trusting, caring relationships with each other. He encourages managers' autonomy by allowing them to provide input on menu and wine selection decisions. The company further reinforces the value of autonomy and effective decision making with leadership training programs. Managers are taught "how to think (rather than 'how to do'). The goal is to encourage creative, appropriate problem-solving and idea generation," according to the company's website."[23]

YOUR THOUGHTS?

1. Which of the three acquired needs is most pronounced in this example?

2. Would you like to work for someone like Cameron Mitchell? Why?

than luck, and they like to be rewarded for their efforts. High achievers also want to receive a fair and balanced amount of positive and negative feedback. This enables them to improve their performance.

- **Need for affiliation.** People motivated by the need for affiliation like to work in teams and in organizational climates characterized as cooperative and collegial.[24] You clearly see this theme at work in Cameron Mitchell's restaurants.

- **Need for power.** People with a high need for power like to be in charge. They enjoy coaching and helping others develop. Cameron Mitchell seems to exemplify this need.

Self-Determination Theory: Competence, Autonomy, and Relatedness

Self-determination theory was developed by psychologists Edward Deci and Richard Ryan. In contrast to McClelland's belief that needs are learned over time, this theory identifies *innate* needs that must be satisfied for us to flourish. **Self-determination theory assumes that three innate needs influence our behavior and well-being—the needs for competence, autonomy, and relatedness.**[25]

Self-Determination Theory Focuses on Intrinsic Motivation Self-determination theory focuses on the needs that drive intrinsic motivation. Intrinsic motivation is longer lasting and has a more positive impact on task performance than extrinsic motivation.[26] The theory proposes that our needs for competence, autonomy, and relatedness produce intrinsic motivation, which in turn enhances our task performance. Research supports this proposition.[27]

The Three Innate Needs An innate need is a need we are born with. The three innate needs are:

1. **Competence—"I need to feel efficacious."** This is the desire to feel qualified, knowledge-able, and capable to complete an act, task, or goal.

2. **Autonomy—"I need to feel independent to influence my environment."** This is the desire to have freedom and discretion in determining what you want to do and how you want to do it.

3. **Relatedness—"I want to be connected with others."** This is the desire to feel part of a group, to belong, and to be connected with others.

Although the above needs are assumed to be innate, according to Deci and Ryan their relative value can change over our lives and vary across cultures.

Using Self-Determination Theory to Motivate Employees Managers can apply self-determination theory by trying to create work environments that support and encourage the opportunity to experience competence, autonomy, and relatedness. Here are some specific suggestions:

- **Competence.** Managers can provide tangible resources, time, contacts, and coaching to improve employee competence. They can make sure employees have the knowledge and information they need to perform their jobs. For example, e-commerce giant Amazon offers new hires an intensive, month-long training and leadership program before they begin their job, and its "virtual contact center" trains employees to work from home. According to the company's corporate communications manager, "We want our employees to be owners from day one, so we train them to take ownership over products and services that impact millions of customers."[28]

At Amazon, managers apply the self-determination theory by trying to create a work environment that supports and encourages the opportunity to experience competence, autonomy, and relatedness. New hires undergo an intensive, month-long training and leadership program before they start their new job, which helps them take ownership of the products and services delivered to millions of customers every day.
Jeramey Lende/Shutterstock

- **Autonomy.** Managers can empower employees and delegate meaningful assignments and tasks to enhance feelings of autonomy. This in turn suggests they should support decisions their employees make. A recent study confirmed this conclusion. Employees' intrinsic motivation was higher when they perceived that their manager supported them.[29] Schneider Electric is a global company specializing in energy management and automation and it offers dedicated courses for leadership, customer education, energy solutions, sales excellence, and functional skills to its more than 160,000 employees worldwide. Company executives believe providing high-potential, early-career opportunities for its workforce encourages autonomy and paves the way for strong and future leaders of the organization.[30]

- **Relatedness.** Many companies use fun and camaraderie to foster relatedness. In addition, a positive and inspiring corporate vision can create a feeling of commitment to a common purpose. At 23andMe, a consumer genetic testing company, founder and CEO Anne Wojcicki believes in using her influence to further the position of women in the biotech industry, which has long been a male-dominated field. The company has a policy of hiring equal numbers of men and women, maintains a balance of men and women at the leadership level, and fosters a workplace culture that supports liberal parental leave policies, a robust employee onboarding process, and a strong sense of belonging and relatedness.[31]

Herzberg's Motivator-Hygiene Theory: Two Ways to Improve Satisfaction

Frederick Herzberg's theory is based on a landmark study in which he interviewed 203 accountants and engineers.[32] These interviews, meant to determine the factors responsible for job satisfaction and dissatisfaction, uncovered separate and distinct clusters of factors associated with each. This pattern led to the *motivator-hygiene theory,* **which proposes that job satisfaction and dissatisfaction arise from two different sets of** factors—satisfaction comes from *motivating factors* and dissatisfaction from *hygiene factors.*

- **Hygiene factors—What makes employees dissatisfied?** Job dissatisfaction was associated primarily with factors in the work *context* or environment. Herzberg hypothesized that such *hygiene factors*—**including company policy and administration, technical supervision, salary, interpersonal relationships with supervisors, and working conditions—cause a person to move from a state of no dissatisfaction to dissatisfaction.** He did not believe their removal created an immediate impact on satisfaction or motivation (for that, see motivating factors following). At best, Herzberg proposed that individuals will experience the *absence* of job dissatisfaction when they have no grievances about hygiene factors.

- **Motivating factors—What makes employees satisfied?** Job satisfaction was more frequently associated with factors in the work *content* of the task being performed. Herzberg labeled these *motivating factors* or *motivators* because each was associated with strong effort and good performance. He hypothesized that such *motivating factors, or motivators*—**including achievement, recognition, characteristics of the work, responsibility, and advancement—cause a person to move from a state of no satisfaction to satisfaction.** Therefore, Herzberg's theory predicts managers can motivate individuals by incorporating motivators into an individual's job.

For Herzberg, the groups of hygiene and motivating factors did not interact. "The opposite of job satisfaction is not job dissatisfaction, but rather no job satisfaction; and similarly, the opposite of job dissatisfaction is not job satisfaction, but no dissatisfaction."[33] Herzberg conceptualizes dissatisfaction and satisfaction as two parallel continuums. The starting point is a null state in which *both* dissatisfaction and satisfaction are absent. Theoretically an organization member could have good supervision, pay, and working conditions (no dissatisfaction) but a tedious and unchallenging task with little chance of advancement (no satisfaction), as illustrated in Figure 5.4.

Managerial View of Job Satisfaction and Dissatisfaction   Insights from Herzberg's theory allow managers to consider the dimensions of both job content and job context so they can manage for greater overall job satisfaction. There is one aspect of this theory we think is wrong, however. We believe you can satisfy and motivate people by providing good hygiene factors. REI (Recreational Equipment Inc.), regularly rated one of the top companies to work for by *Fortune,* is a good example. The company routinely pays both part- and full-time employees significantly more than regulatory minimums and

FIGURE 5.4   **Role of Job Content and Job Context in Job Satisfaction and Dissatisfaction**

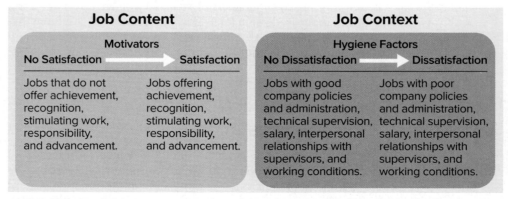

SOURCE: Whitsett, David A., and Erik K. Winslow. "An Analysis of Studies Critical of The Motivator-Hygiene Theory." *Personnel Psychology,* Winter (1997): 391–415.

provides benefits to part-timers who work 20 hours a week (industry threshold for benefits is typically 30 hours a week). In addition, company contributions to the employee retirement plan are considered very generous compared to other retailers—employees may receive up to an additional 15 percent of their pay contributed by the company. And its employee turnover rate is almost half that of other retailers.[34]

Other companies seem to agree with our conclusion, because they have been offering a host of hygiene factors in an attempt to attract and retain Millennials. A recent survey of 5,000 Millennials revealed they are looking for better workplace benefits, including flexible work arrangements, generous matches to their 401(k) plans, pet insurance, and help with paying down their student loan debt. In this tight labor market, many companies are taking a closer look at their benefits packages to attract and maintain a competitive workforce.[35]

Using Herzberg's Theory to Motivate Employees   Although research does not support the two-factor aspect of Herzberg's theory or the proposition that hygiene factors are unrelated to job satisfaction, three practical applications of the theory help explain why it remains important in the study of OB.

1. **Hygiene first.** There are practical reasons to eliminate dissatisfaction before trying to use motivators to increase motivation and performance. You will have a harder time motivating someone who is experiencing pay dissatisfaction or otherwise struggling with Herzberg's hygiene factors.

2. **Motivation next.** Once you remove dissatisfaction, you can hardly go wrong by building motivators into someone's job. This suggestion represents the core idea behind the technique of job design that is discussed in the final section of this chapter.

3. **A few well-chosen words.** Finally, don't underestimate the power of verbal recognition to reinforce good performance. Savvy managers supplement Herzberg's motivators with communication. Positive recognition can fuel intrinsic motivation, particularly for people who are engaged in their work.

Problem-Solving Application

Walmart Adds Sick-Leave Pay. Problem Solved?

Early in 2019, the giant retailer Walmart instituted a sweeping revision of some core human resource policies affecting its 1.1 million hourly workers in the United States. The move was undertaken in response to the fact that an increasing number of states and cities now require employers to offer paid sick leave. As of February 2019, Walmart's store and warehouse workers can earn one hour of paid leave for every 30 hours worked, up to 48 hours total. The time can be used for any purpose without infringing on vacation time. Since the new policy consolidates and unifies a number of earlier rules, the company expects it will simplify administration and compliance, as well as reduce absenteeism. Management also hopes the policy change will help continue a decline in turnover that started the year before, when, it says, an improved wage scale, relaxed dress codes, and more generous parental leave helped reduce turnover by more than 10 percent.[36]

At the same time, however, the company has tightened up some of its other employment policies. For instance, workers can now be fired for accumulating only five attendance violations within six months, whereas the limit was nine in the past. Short of firing, attendance has new financial consequences too. Although workers with perfect attendance can earn higher quarterly bonuses, they currently make up fewer than a third of Walmart's hourly employees. Those who miss more than a handful of shifts will now see their bonuses cut by as much as half. Before the policy revamp, employee bonuses were based solely on store performance.[37]

"Walmart is responding to our call for change with a new policy. But what they are giving with one hand, they are taking with the other," said Shashauna Phillips, a Walmart employee in South Carolina and a leader in OUR Walmart, a worker group. Phillips also worries that one result of offering a financial incentive for perfect attendance is that employees will come to work sick.[38]

Others share her concern that Walmart has a way to go before it can claim to be doing everything possible to support and retain its workers. Vermont's Senator Bernie Sanders, for example, issued a statement saying that Walmart's new sick-leave policy was "a small step forward but not enough," noting that "Walmart . . . is not a poor company" and urging it to raise its starting pay to $15 an hour (as a public outcry and legislation introduced by Sanders recently forced Amazon to do). Walmart currently starts its hourly workers at $11 an hour, up from only $9 as recently as 2017.[39] Writing in *The Hill*, Congressional representative Ro Khanna of California and Marc Perrone, International President of the United Food and Commercial Workers Union, also urged Walmart to increase its basic wage, saying that Congress should take action again to compel Walmart and other large employers to pay their workers enough to feed their families and avoid forcing the "taxpayer-funded safety net" to make up the difference. Amazon faced a choice between raising wages and paying the government for the social safety net benefits its workers claimed. It opted to raise wages; Khanna and Perrone feel Walmart should make the same decision.[40]

Walmart's sales are growing steadily and are expected to near $530 billion for fiscal 2019.[41]

Apply the 3-Step Problem-Solving Approach

Step 1: Define the problem in this case.

Step 2: Identify the key causes of this problem.

Step 3: Make your top two recommendations for fixing the problem at Walmart.

Figure 5.5 illustrates the overlap among the need and satisfaction theories discussed in this section. As you can see, the acquired needs and self-determination theories do not include lower-level needs. Remember, higher-level need satisfaction is more likely to foster well-being and flourishing.

FIGURE 5.5   A Comparison of Need and Satisfaction Theories

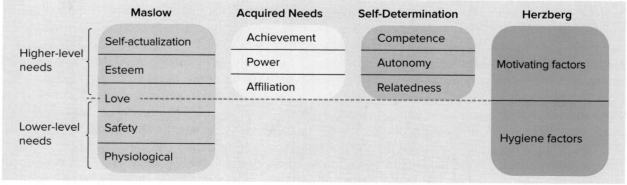

McGraw-Hill Global Education Holdings, LLC

5.3 PROCESS THEORIES OF MOTIVATION

THE BIGGER PICTURE

Process theories examine the way personal factors and situation factors influence employee motivation. You'll be considering three major process theories: equity/justice theory, expectancy theory, and goal-setting theory. Each offers unique ideas for motivating yourself or employees.

Process theories of motivation **describe** *how* **various person factors and situation factors in the Organizing Framework affect motivation.** They go beyond content theories by helping you understand *why* people with different needs and levels of satisfaction behave the way they do at work.

In this section we discuss three process theories of motivation:

LO 5-3

Compare and contrast the process theories of motivation.

- Equity/justice theory
- Expectancy theory
- Goal-setting theory

Equity/Justice Theory: Am I Being Treated Fairly?

Defined generally, **equity theory is a model of motivation that explains how people strive for** *fairness* **and** *justice* **in social exchanges or give-and-take relationships.** According to this theory, people are motivated to maintain consistency between their beliefs and their behavior. Perceived inconsistencies create cognitive dissonance (or psychological discomfort), which in turn motivates corrective action. When we feel victimized by unfair social exchanges, the resulting cognitive dissonance prompts us to correct the situation. This can result in a change of attitude or behavior.

Consider what happened when workers at several U.S. poultry processing plants were forced to wear adult diapers during their work shifts as a result of being denied bathroom breaks by supervisors. A report by Oxfam America revealed supervisors repeatedly mocked workers and ignored their requests and threatened punishment or firing in an effort to keep the processing line running to meet production quotas. In the U.S. poultry industry, less than a third of all plants are unionized, which leaves most workers without crucial safety protections.[42] In addition, another investigation found that the more than half a million men and women who work in meat-processing plants have some of the most dangerous factory jobs in America.[43]

As a result of pressure from worker advocate groups and unions, as well as growing consumer awareness about the hazards experienced by poultry workers, Tyson Foods announced it would provide regularly scheduled bathroom breaks, give more attention to the line speeds at its processing plants, offer training on workers' rights, and establish safety councils that would include employees.[44]

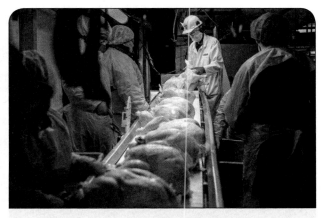

Working the processing line at a U.S. poultry plant is a dangerous and challenging job, fraught with near-impossible work goals. Intense pressure from worker advocate groups, labor unions, and even consumers has resulted in companies improving conditions for their workers.
USDA photo by Preston Keres.

Psychologist J. Stacy Adams pioneered the use of equity theory in the workplace. Let us begin by discussing his ideas and their current application. We then discuss the extension of equity theory into *justice theory* and conclude by discussing how to motivate employees with both these tools.

The Elements of Equity Theory: Comparing My Outputs and Inputs with Those of Others   The key elements of equity theory are outputs, inputs, and a comparison of the ratio of outputs to inputs (see Figure 5.6).

- **Outputs—"What do I perceive that I'm getting out of my job?"** Organizations provide a variety of outcomes for our work, including pay/bonuses, medical benefits, challenging assignments, job security, promotions, status symbols, recognition, and participation in important decisions. Outcomes vary widely, depending on the organization and our rank in it.

- **Inputs—"What do I perceive that I'm putting into my job?"** An employee's inputs, for which he or she expects a just return, include education/training, skills, creativity, seniority, age, personality traits, effort expended, experience, and personal appearance.

FIGURE 5.6   Elements of Equity Theory

Equity theory compares how well you are doing to how well others are doing in similar jobs. Instead of focusing just on what you get out of the job (outputs) or what you put into the job (inputs), equity theory compares your ratio of outputs to inputs to those of others.

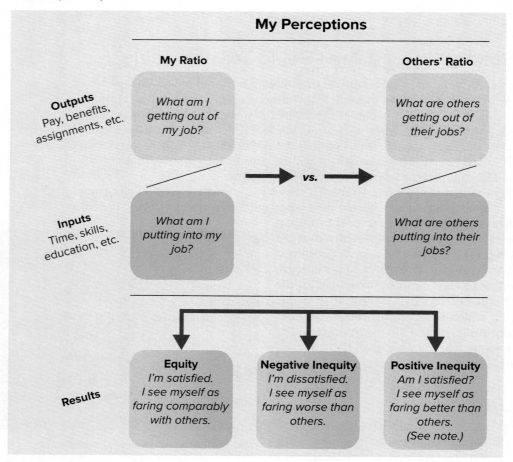

Note: Does positive inequity result in satisfaction? Some of us may feel so. But J. Stacy Adams recognized that employees often feel guilty about positive inequity, just as they might become angry about negative inequity. Your positive inequity is others' negative inequity. If your coworkers saw you as being favored unfairly in a major way, wouldn't they be outraged? How effective could you be in your job then?

McGraw-Hill Global Education Holdings, LLC

- **Comparison—"How does my ratio of outputs to inputs compare with those of relevant others?"** Your feelings of equity come from your evaluation of whether you are receiving adequate rewards to compensate for your collective inputs. In practice people perform these evaluations by comparing the perceived fairness of their output-to-input ratio to that of relevant others (see Figure 5.6). They divide outputs by inputs, and the larger the ratio, the greater the expected benefit. This comparative process was found to generalize across personalities and countries.[45]

People tend to compare themselves to other individuals with whom they have close interpersonal ties, such as friends, and to whom they are similar, such as people performing the same job or individuals of the same gender or educational level, rather than to dissimilar others. For example, we work for universities, so we consider our pay relative to that of other business professors, not the head football coach.

The Outcomes of an Equity Comparison

Figure 5.6 shows the three different equity relationships resulting from an equity comparison: equity, negative inequity, and positive inequity. Because equity is based on comparing *ratios* of outcomes to inputs, we will not necessarily perceive inequity just because someone else receives greater rewards. If the other person's additional outcomes are due to his or her greater inputs, a sense of equity may still exist. However, if the comparison person enjoys greater outcomes for similar inputs, *negative inequity* will be perceived. On the other hand, a person will experience *positive inequity* when his or her outcome-to-input ratio is greater than that of a relevant comparison person.

People tend to have misconceptions about how their pay compares to that of their colleagues. These misconceptions can create problems for employers. Consider the implications of results from a recent PayScale study of more than 500,000 employees. Close to 90 percent of those who were paid *above the market—positive inequity*—believed they were underpaid, while only 10 percent correctly perceived they were overpaid. In addition, 11 percent of the people paid *at the market rate—equity*—believed they were underpaid. When it comes to employee satisfaction, study results revealed that how employees *feel* about the pay process is more than five times more impactful on how satisfied they are than how they are paid relative to the market.[46] In both these cases, significant numbers of equitably treated people perceived a state of inequity. If management fails to correct these perceptions, it should expect lower job satisfaction, commitment, and performance.

The Elements of Justice Theory: Distributive, Procedural, and Interactional Justice

Beginning in the later 1970s, researchers began to expand the role of equity theory in explaining employee attitudes and behavior. This led to a domain of research called *organizational justice*. Organizational justice reflects the extent to which people perceive they are treated fairly at work. This, in turn, led to the identification of three different components of organizational justice: distributive, procedural, and interactional.[47]

- **Distributive justice reflects the perceived fairness of the way resources and rewards are distributed or allocated.** Do you think fairness matters when it comes to the size of people's offices? Robert W. Baird & Co., a financial services firm ranked as *Fortune's* 16th best place to work in 2019, did. The company decided to make everyone's office the same size in its newly renovated corporate headquarters.[48]

- **Procedural justice is the perceived fairness of the process and procedures used to make allocation decisions.**

- **Interactional justice describes the "quality of the interpersonal treatment people receive when procedures are implemented."[49]** Interactional justice does not pertain to the outcomes or procedures associated with decision making. Instead it focuses on whether people believe they are treated fairly when decisions are being implemented.

Tools exist to help us improve our ability to gauge the level of fairness or justice that exists in a current or past job. Try Self-Assessment 5.2. It contains part of a survey developed to measure employees' perceptions of fair interpersonal treatment. If you perceive your work organization as interpersonally unfair, you are probably dissatisfied and have contemplated quitting. In contrast, your organizational loyalty and attachment are likely greater if you believe you are treated fairly at work.

SELF-ASSESSMENT 5.2

Measuring Perceived Interpersonal Treatment

Please be prepared to answer these questions if your instructor has assigned Self-Assessment 5.2 in Connect.

1. Does the level of fairness you perceive correlate to your work attitudes such as job satisfaction and organizational commitment?

2. What is causing your lowest level of perceived fairness? Can you do anything to change these feelings?

3. What do these results suggest about the type of company you would like to work for after graduation?

The Outcomes Associated with Justice   Doesn't it make sense that your perceptions of justice are related to outcomes in the Organizing Framework? Of course! This realization has generated much research into organizational justice over the last 25 years. We created Figure 5.7 to summarize these research findings. The figure shows the strength of relationships between nine individual-level outcomes and the three components of organizational justice. By and large, distributive and procedural justice have consistently stronger relationships with outcomes. This suggests that managers would be better off paying attention to these two forms of justice. In contrast, interactional justice is not a leading indicator in any instance.

You can also see that certain outcomes, such as job satisfaction and organizational commitment, have stronger relationships with justice. All told, however, the majority of relationships between justice and important OB outcomes are weak. This reinforces the conclusion that motivating people via justice works for some outcomes but not for others.

Equity Sensitivity   In the study of equity theory, researchers have put forth the notion that not all individuals prefer an equal ratio of inputs to outcomes. This concept is known as *equity sensitivity.*[50] For example, individuals who are high in equity sensitivity place more importance on inputs (what they can give in a specific situation) versus those who place more importance on outcomes (what rewards they can get in a certain situation).[51] Recent research supports this concept, suggesting that equity sensitivity can help predict certain workplace outcomes, including organizational citizenship behaviors and inappropriate workplace behaviors.[52]

Using Equity and Justice Theories to Motivate Employees   Figure 5.7 notwithstanding, managers can't go wrong by paying attention to employees' perceptions of equity and justice at work. Here are five practical lessons to help you apply equity and justice theories.

1. **Employee perceptions count.** No matter how fair management thinks the organization's policies, procedures, and reward system are, each employee's *perception* of the equity of those factors is what counts. For example, male employees were found to be more sensitive toward pay inequity and procedural justice than female employees.[53] Further, justice perceptions can change over time.[54] This implies that it is important for managers to regularly assess employees' justice beliefs. Companies tend to do this by using employee work attitude surveys.

FIGURE 5.7 Outcomes Associated with Justice Components

The three components of organizational justice have varying effects on workplace outcomes, listed here in rough order from strongest to weakest. Note that job satisfaction and organizational commitment lead the list and most strongly align with justice components.

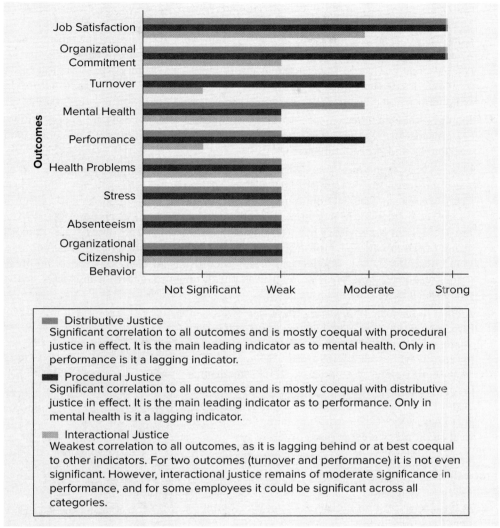

Distributive Justice
Significant correlation to all outcomes and is mostly coequal with procedural justice in effect. It is the main leading indicator as to mental health. Only in performance is it a lagging indicator.

Procedural Justice
Significant correlation to all outcomes and is mostly coequal with distributive justice in effect. It is the main leading indicator as to performance. Only in mental health is it a lagging indicator.

Interactional Justice
Weakest correlation to all outcomes, as it is lagging behind or at best coequal to other indicators. For two outcomes (turnover and performance) it is not even significant. However, interactional justice remains of moderate significance in performance, and for some employees it could be significant across all categories.

SOURCES: Pan, Xiaofu, Mengyan Chen, Zhichao Hao, and Wenfen Bi. "The Effects of Organizational Justice on Positive Organizational Behavior: Evidence from a Large-Sample Survey and a Situational Experiment." *Frontiers in Psychology* 8 (January 2018). https://doi:10.3389/fpsyg.2017.02315; Robbins, Jordan M., Michael T. Ford, and Lois E. Tetrick. "Perceived Unfairness and Employee Health: A Meta-Analytic Integration." *Journal of Applied Psychology* 97, no. 2 (March 2012): 235–72. https://DOI: 10.1037/a0025408; Fassina, Neil E., David A. Jones, and Krista L. Uggerslev. "Meta-Analytic Tests of Relationships between Organizational Justice and Citizenship Behavior: Testing Agent-System and Shared-Variance Models." *Journal of Organizational Behavior* 29, no. 6 (August 2008): 805–28. https://dx.doi.org/10.1002/job.494; Cohen-Charash, Yochi, and Paul E. Spector. "The Role of Justice in Organizations: A Meta-Analysis." *Organizational Behavior and Human Decision Processes* 86, no. 2 (November 2001): 278–321. http://dx.doi.org/10.1006/obhd.2001.2958; and Colquitt, Jason A., Donald E. Conlon, Michael J. Wesson, Christopher O. L. H. Porter, and K. Yee Ng. "Justice at the Millennium: A Meta-Analytic Review of 25 Years of Organizational Justice Research." *Journal of Applied Psychology* 86, no. 3 (2001): 421–45. https://DOI: 10.1037//0021-9010.86.3.425.

2. **Employees want a voice in decisions that affect them.** Employees' perceptions of justice are enhanced when they have a voice in the decision-making process. **Voice is "the discretionary or formal expression of ideas, opinions, suggestions, or alternative approaches directed to a specific target inside or outside of the organization with the intent to change an objectionable state of affairs and to improve the current functioning of the organization."**[55] Managers are encouraged to seek employee input on organizational issues that are important to employees, even though many employees

are reluctant to use their "voice." Consider how Saleforce's CEO Marc Benioff addressed the issue of employees wanting their voices heard on an important topic. Faced with employee objections to the company's recent work with the U.S. Border Patrol (which has been separating children of illegal immigrants from their parents), Benioff created Silicon Valley's first-ever Office of Ethical and Humane Use of Technology. With advisers from Georgetown, Harvard, Amnesty International, and other organizations, this initiative provides Salesforce and its employees with a solid framework for discussing the thorny ethical issues that technological advances can raise. "We may not all agree," Benioff said, "but we can have that discussion and figure out how to move forward together."[56] Managers can overcome issues such as these by creating a voice climate. **A *voice climate* is one in which employees are encouraged to freely express their opinions and feelings.**[57]

3. **Employees should have an appeals process.** Employees should be given the opportunity to appeal decisions that affect their welfare. This opportunity fosters perceptions of distributive and procedural justice.

4. **Leader behavior matters.** Employees' perceptions of justice are strongly influenced by their managers' leadership behavior and the justice-related implications of their decisions, actions, and public communications.[58] For example, Kenneth Frazier, CEO of pharmaceutical giant Merck, took a stand against extremism when he resigned from President Trump's advisory business council after the president refused to criticize a group of white nationalist protesters in Charlottesville, Virginia. The grandson of a man born into slavery, Frazier said he resigned from the council because the president's response, "was one that I felt was not in concordance with my views or the views we claim to hold as a country."[59]

5. **A climate for justice makes a difference.** Team performance was found to be higher in companies that possessed a climate for justice.[60] Do you think it's OK for customers to yell at retail or service employees or treat them rudely? We don't! A climate for justice incorporates relationships between employees and customers. Employees are more likely to provide poor customer service when managers allow customers to treat employees rudely or disrespectfully.[61]

And as for you? You can work to improve equity ratios through your behavior or your perceptions. For example, you could work to resolve negative inequity by asking for a raise or a promotion (raising your outputs) or by working fewer hours or exerting less effort (reducing your inputs). You could also resolve the inequity cognitively, by adjusting your perceptions of the value of your salary or other benefits (outcomes) or the value of the actual work you and your coworkers do (inputs).

Expectancy Theory: Does My Effort Lead to Desired Outcomes?

***Expectancy theory* holds that people are motivated to behave in ways that produce desired combinations of expected outcomes.** Generally, expectancy theory can predict behavior in any situation in which a choice between two or more alternatives must be made. For instance, it can predict whether we should quit or stay at a job, exert substantial or minimal effort at a task, and major in management, computer science, accounting, marketing, psychology, or communication.

Shaquem Griffin, a linebacker with the Seattle Seahawks, has all the motivation he needs to become a successful player in the NFL. A congenital birth defect resulted in his left hand being amputated when he was 4 years old, but Griffin sees that life-changing event as the reason he continues to work so hard to succeed.

Otto Greule Jr/Getty Images

FIGURE 5.8 Major Elements of Expectancy Theory

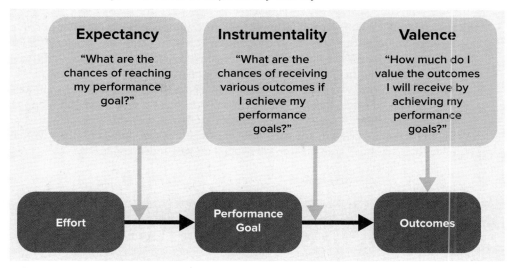

McGraw-Hill Global Education Holdings, LLC

The most widely used version of expectancy theory was proposed by Yale professor Victor Vroom. We now consider the theory's key elements and recommendations for its application.

The Elements of Vroom's Expectancy Theory: Expectancy, Instrumentality, and Valence Motivation, according to Vroom, boils down to deciding how much effort to exert in a specific task situation. This choice is based on a two-stage sequence of expectations—moving from effort to performance and then from performance to outcome. Figure 5.8 shows the major components of this theory.

Let us consider the three key elements of Vroom's theory.

1. **Expectancy—"Can I achieve my desired level of performance?" An *expectancy* represents an individual's belief that a particular degree of effort will be followed by a particular level of performance.** Expectancies take the form of subjective probabilities. As you may recall from a course in statistics, probabilities range from zero to one. An expectancy of zero indicates that effort has no anticipated impact on performance, while an expectancy of one suggests performance is totally dependent on effort.

   > **EXAMPLE** Suppose you do not know how to use Excel. No matter how much effort you exert, your perceived probability of creating complex spreadsheets that compute correlations will be zero. If you decide to take an Excel training course and practice using the program a couple of hours a day for a few weeks (high effort), the probability that you will be able to create spreadsheets that compute correlations will rise close to one.

   Research reveals that employees' expectancies are affected by a host of factors. Some of the more important ones include self-efficacy, time pressures, task difficulty, ability and knowledge, resources, support from peers, leader behavior, and organizational climate.[62]

2. **Instrumentality—"What intrinsic and extrinsic rewards will I receive if I achieve my desired level of performance?" *Instrumentality* is the perceived relationship between performance and outcomes.** It reflects a person's belief that a particular outcome is contingent on accomplishing a specific level of performance. Passing exams, for instance, is instrumental in graduating from college, or put another way, graduation is contingent on passing exams. In this tight labor market, even the U.S. military is offering bonuses to entice individuals to join. For example, the U.S. Navy offers enlistment bonuses (including money for college degrees) from $5,000 to more

than $25,000, depending on prior experience.[63] The Problem-Solving Application box illustrates what happens when classical musicians find instrumentality out of balance.

3. **Valence—"How much do I value the rewards I receive?"** *Valence* **describes the positive or negative value people place on outcomes.** Valence mirrors our personal preferences. For example, most employees have a positive valence for receiving additional money or recognition. In contrast, being laid off or being ridiculed for making a suggestion would likely be negative valence for most individuals. In Vroom's expectancy model, *outcomes* are consequences that are contingent on performance, such as pay, promotions, recognition, or celebratory events. For example, Aflac hosted a six-day appreciation week for employees that included theme park visits, movie screenings, and daily gifts.[64] Would you value these rewards? Your answer will depend on your individual needs.

Problem-Solving Application

Symphony Orchestras on Strike

The rarified world of classical music is often perceived as calm, even staid, and above the hassles of the workaday world. But with the cost of producing performances rising and ticket sales and donor support slumping in many markets, this picture is far from the truth. In recent years musicians of more than one symphony orchestra have gone on strike for better pay and other benefits. Among the latest are the players of the Chicago Symphony Orchestra, one of the top (and best-paid) U.S. classical ensembles. The musicians' union had been negotiating a new contract for almost a year when players recently began picketing Orchestra Hall in Chicago in an attempt to hang on to disputed employment benefits, including their prized defined-benefit pension plan.

The orchestra's management says the cost of maintaining this retirement benefit has skyrocketed, making it unsustainable for the group's future, and proposes substituting a less expensive defined-contribution plan. This would follow the example of organizations in many other industries, which have switched to defined-contribution plans for their employees and thus shifted the investment risk to workers as well. But Chicago's defined-benefit plan "has been the hallmark of the orchestra's benefits package (and those of other leading orchestras) for over 50 years," says a member of the musicians' negotiating committee, and members want to keep it that way.[65]

While defined-benefit plans, in which benefits are essentially guaranteed, are still common in major U.S. orchestras, many such plans are underfunded, putting benefits for both current and future retirees in jeopardy. Management says its current offer will "put the musicians in as good if not a better state upon their retirements," but Chicago's players counter that attracting and retaining world-class musicians will grow ever more difficult "if our benefits continue to fall."[66] Meanwhile, the orchestra's famed director Ricardo Muti urged management to consider the welfare of the musicians, even visiting the picket line, though some performances had to be canceled while talks continued.[67]

Apply the 3-Step Problem-Solving Approach

Step 1: Define the problem in this case.

Step 2: Identify the cause of the problem. Do the parties featured in this case use the principles of expectancy theory?

Step 3: Make a recommendation to the orchestra's management. Should the musicians be allowed to keep their defined-benefit pension plan?

TABLE 5.1   Managerial and Organizational Implications of Expectancy Theory

FOR MANAGERS	FOR ORGANIZATIONS
• Determine the outcomes employees value.	• Reward people for desired performance, and do not keep pay decisions secret.
• Identify good performance so appropriate behaviors can be rewarded.	• Design challenging jobs.
• Make sure employees can achieve targeted performance levels.	• Tie some rewards to group accomplishments to build teamwork and encourage cooperation.
• Link desired outcomes to targeted levels of performance.	• Reward managers for creating, monitoring, and maintaining expectancies, instrumentalities, and outcomes that lead to high effort and goal attainment.
• Make sure changes in outcomes are large enough to motivate high effort.	• Monitor employee motivation through interviews or anonymous questionnaires.
• Monitor the reward system for inequities.	• Accommodate individual differences by building flexibility into the motivation program.

According to expectancy theory, your motivation will be high when all three elements in the model are high. If any element is near zero, your motivation will be low. Whether you apply this theory to yourself or managers apply it to their employees, the point is to simultaneously consider the status of all three elements.

Using Expectancy Theory to Motivate Employees   There is widespread agreement that attitudes and behavior are influenced when organizations link rewards to targeted behaviors. For example, in this era of #MeToo and other social initiatives, many companies, including Microsoft, Intel, and Facebook, have begun to link bonuses to how well senior leaders champion the firm's anti-discrimination objectives and diversity efforts.[68]

Expectancy theory has important practical implications for individual managers and organizations as a whole (see Table 5.1). Three additional recommendations are often overlooked. First, establish the right goal. Our consulting experience reveals that people fail at this task more often than you might imagine. Second, remember that you can better keep behavior and performance on track by creating more opportunities to link performance and pay. Recent research supports this point. A survey of more than 2,500 HR and office professionals suggests there is a growing divide between management and employees when it comes to performance feedback and pay. While 94 percent of the executives surveyed are confident employees are satisfied with their company's performance review process, more than two-thirds of employees believe the process is outdated, happens too infrequently, and is often incomplete. In addition, to help link performance with pay, some organizations have implemented variable pay plans with individual incentive bonuses being the most common type of incentive awarded.[69] Finally, monetary rewards must be large enough to generate motivation, and this may not be the case for annual merit raises in the U.S. The average merit raise has been around 3 percent over the past five years, although recent studies suggest employees are anticipating larger increases based on strong company performances over the past year. To overcome this limitation, organizations are starting to eliminate merit raises and replace them with discretionary bonuses for special projects or one-time achievements.[70]

The following Problem-Solving Application illustrates expectancy theory in action at Westwood High School in Mesa, Arizona.

Problem-Solving Application

A High School Principal Uses Principles of Expectancy Theory to Motivate Students

Tim Richard, principal at Westwood High School, decided to use a motivational program he called "Celebration" to improve the grades of 1,200 students who were failing one or more courses. The school has a total of 3,000 students.

How Does the Program Work? "Students are allowed to go outside and have fun with their friends for 28 minutes on four mornings a week," the principal explained to the local newspaper. "But those who have even one F must stay inside for 'remediation'—28 minutes of extra study, help from peer tutors, or meetings with teachers." Richard, who successfully implemented the program at a smaller high school, believes the key to motivating students is to link a highly valued reward—socializing with friends outside—with grades. Socializing includes playing organized games, dancing and listening to music, eating snacks, and just plain hanging out. Results suggest the program is working.

Positive results were found within two to three months of the motivation program's start. The number of students with failing grades dropped to 900. The principal's goal is to achieve zero failing grades by the end of the year.

What Is the Student Reaction? Students like the program. Ivana Baltazar, a 17-year-old senior, said, "You really appreciate Celebration after you have been in remediation." She raised an F in economics to a B after receiving help. Good academic students like Joseph Leung also like the program. Leung is a tutor to students with failing grades. He believes that "the tricky part is getting people out of the mind-set that they can't succeed. . . . A lot of times they just haven't done their homework. I try to help them understand that the difference between a person passing and failing is their work ethic."[71]

Apply the 3-Step Problem-Solving Approach

Step 1: Define the problem Tim Richard is trying to address.

Step 2: Identify the causes. What OB concepts or theories are consistent with Richard's motivational program?

Step 3: Make recommendations for fixing the problem. Do you agree with Richard's approach to improving student performance? Why or why not?

Goal-Setting Theory: How Can I Harness the Power of Goal Setting?

Regardless of the nature of their specific achievements, successful people tend to have one thing in common: Their lives are goal-oriented. This is as true for politicians seeking votes as it is for world-class athletes like Simone Biles. Research also supports this conclusion. The results of more than 1,000 studies from a wide range of countries clearly show that goal setting helps individuals, teams, and organizations to achieve success.[72]

Next we review goal setting within a work context and then explain the mechanisms that make goal setting so effective. We will discuss the practical applications of goal setting in Chapter 6.

U.S. gymnast Simone Biles won a medal in every event she entered in the 2019 world championships competition. Biles has now set her sites on winning gold in multiple events at the 2020 Summer Olympics in Tokyo, Japan.

Francois Nel/Getty Images

Edwin Locke and Gary Latham's Theory of Goal Setting   After studying four decades of research on goal setting, two OB experts, Edwin Locke and Gary Latham, proposed a straightforward theory of goal setting. Here is how it works.[73]

- **Goals that are specific and difficult lead to higher performance than general goals like "Do your best" or "Improve performance."** This is why it is essential to set specific, challenging goals. ***Goal specificity* means whether a goal has been quantified.** For example, a goal of increasing the score on your next OB test by 10 percent is more specific than the goal of trying to improve your grade on the next test.

- **Certain conditions are necessary for goal setting to work.** People must have the ability and resources needed to achieve the goal, and they need to be committed to the goal. If these conditions are not met, goal setting does not lead to higher performance. Be sure these conditions are in place as you pursue your goals.

- **Performance feedback and participation in deciding how to achieve goals are necessary but not sufficient for goal setting to work.** Feedback and participation enhance performance only when they lead employees to set and commit to a specific, difficult goal, even when that goal is to delegate other activities to colleagues. For example, managing partners, clients, and colleagues vie for time with Julia Lamm, a director at PwC in New York. With the help of her boss, Lamm has learned to prioritize her projects; reimagine routine status meetings with managers to focus on problem solving; and forgo nonessential meetings by delegating them to associates.[74] Goals lead to higher performance when you use feedback and participation to stay focused and committed to a specific goal.

- **Goal achievement leads to job satisfaction, which in turn motivates employees to set and commit to even higher levels of performance.** Goal setting puts in motion a positive cycle of upward performance.

In sum, it takes more than setting specific, difficult goals to motivate yourself or others. You also want to fight the urge to set impossible goals. They typically lead to poor performance or unethical behavior, as they did at Volkswagen. The company admitted installing software on more than 11 million cars that manipulated emission test results.[75] Company engineers claimed they tampered with the software because targets set by the CEO at the time, Martin Winterkorn, were too difficult to achieve. To date, the emissions scandal has cost the company more than $35 billion.[76] Set challenging but attainable goals for yourself and others.

What Are the Mechanisms Behind the Power of Goal Setting?   Edwin Locke and Gary Latham, the same OB scholars who developed the motivational theory of goal setting just discussed, also identified the underlying mechanisms that explain how goals affect performance. There are four.

1. **Goals direct attention.** Goals direct our attention and effort toward goal-relevant activities and away from goal-irrelevant activities. If, for example, you have a term project due in a few days, your thoughts and actions tend to revolve around completing that project. In reality, however, we often work on multiple goals at once. Prioritize your goals so you can effectively allocate your efforts over time.[77] For example, fast-food giant KFC recently announced plans to ensure that all plastic-based, consumer packaging across its global businesses will be recoverable or reusable by 2025. In addition, the chain said the goal of having 100 percent of chicken within its U.S. supply chain raised without antibiotics important to human medicine has been met—two years after announcing its pledge.[78]

2. **Goals regulate effort.** Goals have an energizing function in that they motivate us to act. As you might expect, harder goals foster greater effort than easy ones. Deadlines also factor into the motivational equation. We expend greater effort on projects and tasks when time is running out. For example, an instructor's deadline for turning in your term project would prompt you to complete it instead of going out with friends, watching television, or studying for another course.

3. **Goals increase persistence.** Within the context of goal setting, persistence represents the effort expended on a task over an extended period of time. It takes effort to run 100 meters; it takes persistence to run a 26-mile marathon. One of your textbook authors—Angelo Kinicki—knows this because he ran a marathon. What an experience! His goal was to finish in 3 hours 30 minutes. A difficult goal like this served as a reminder to keep training hard over a three-month period. Whenever he wanted to stop training or run slow sprints, his desire to achieve the goal motivated him. Although he missed his goal by 11 minutes, it still is one of his proudest accomplishments. This type of persistence happens when the goal is personally important.

4. **Goals foster the development and application of task strategies and action plans.** Goals prompt us to figure out how we can accomplish them. This begins a cognitive process in which we develop a plan outlining the steps, tasks, or activities we must undertake. For example, the city of Memphis, Tennessee, recently announced a five-year plan called the 800 Initiative with the goal of growing the revenue of 800 minority-owned businesses by $50 million and helping them add paid employees to scale their operations. Funded partly by the city and commitments by other organizations including FedEx, the program offers business coaching, technical assistance, education, and access to loans and grants to help businesses grow.[79] Setting and using action plans also reduces procrastination. If this is sometimes a problem for you, break your goals into smaller and more specific subgoals.[80] That will get you going.

5.4 MOTIVATING EMPLOYEES THROUGH JOB DESIGN

THE BIGGER PICTURE

Job design focuses on motivating employees by considering the situation factors within the Organizing Framework for Understanding and Applying OB. Objectively, the goal of job design is to structure jobs and the tasks needed to complete them in a way that creates intrinsic motivation. We'll look at how potential motivation varies depending on who designs the job: management, you, or you in negotiation with management.

"Ten hours [a day] is a long time just doing this. . . . I've had three years in here and I'm like, I'm going to get the hell out. . . . It's just the most boring work you can do."

—Ford autoworker

"I love my job. . . . I've learned so much. . . . I can talk with biochemists, software engineers, all these interesting people. . . . I love being independent, relying on myself."

—Corporate headhunter

"We see about a hundred injuries a year and I'm amazed there aren't more. The main causes are inexperience and repetition. . . . People work the same job all the time and they stop thinking."

—Slaughterhouse human resources director

LO 5-4

Describe three approaches to motivating employees through job design.

These quotations reflect the different outcomes that can result from job design.[81] **Job design, also referred to as *job redesign* or *work design*, refers to any set of activities that alter jobs to improve the quality of employee experience and level of productivity.** As you can see from this definition, job design focuses on motivating employees by considering the situation factors within the Organizing Framework.

Figure 5.9 summarizes the approaches to job design that have developed over time.[82]

- **Top-down.** Managers changed employees' tasks with the intent of increasing motivation and productivity. In other words, job design was management led.
- **Bottom-up.** In the last 10 years, the top-down perspective gave way to bottom-up processes, based on the idea that employees can change or redesign their own jobs and boost their own motivation and engagement. Job design is then driven by employees rather than managers.

FIGURE 5.9 Historical Models of Job Design

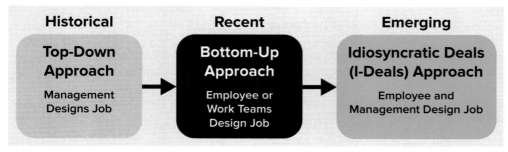

McGraw-Hill Global Education Holdings, LLC

- **I-deals.** The latest approach to job design, *idiosyncratic deals,* attempts to merge the two historical perspectives. It envisions job design as a process in which employees and individual managers jointly negotiate the types of tasks employees complete at work.

This section provides an overview of these three conceptually different approaches to job design.[83] We give more coverage to top-down techniques and models because they have been used for longer periods of time and more research is available to evaluate their effectiveness.

Top-Down Approaches— Management Designs Your Job

In top-down approaches, management creates efficient and meaningful combinations of work tasks for employees. If it is done correctly, in theory, employees will display higher performance, job satisfaction, and engagement, and lower absenteeism and turnover. The five principal top-down approaches are scientific management, job enlargement, job rotation, job enrichment, and the job characteristics model.

Scientific Management Scientific management draws from research in industrial engineering and is most heavily influenced by the work of Frederick Taylor (1856–1915). Taylor, a mechanical engineer, developed the principles of scientific management based on research and experimentation to determine the most efficient way to perform jobs. **Scientific management is "that kind of management which conducts a business or affairs by standards established by facts or truths gained through systematic observation, experiment, or reasoning."**[84]

This automotive assembly line, which is using robotics, is a great example of scientific management. The principles of scientific management have aided auto manufacturers to produce cars more efficiently and with higher quality.

Glow Images

Designing jobs according to the principles of scientific management has both positive and negative consequences. Positively, employee efficiency and productivity are increased. On the other hand, research reveals that simplified, repetitive jobs also lead to job dissatisfaction, poor mental health, higher levels of stress, and a low sense of accomplishment and personal growth.[85] Recognition of these negative consequences paved the way for the next four top-down approaches.

Job Enlargement Companies first used job enlargement in the late 1940s in response to complaints about tedious and overspecialized jobs created from the principles of scientific management. **Job enlargement puts more variety into a worker's job by combining specialized tasks of comparable difficulty.** Some call this strategy *horizontally loading* the job. Researchers recommend using job enlargement as part of a broader approach that uses multiple motivational methods, because by itself job enlargement does not have a significant and lasting positive effect on job performance.[86]

Job Rotation Like job enlargement, job rotation gives employees greater variety in their work. **Job rotation calls for moving employees from one specialized job to another.** Rather than performing only one job, workers are trained and given the opportunity to perform two or more separate jobs on a rotating basis. Proposed benefits of job rotation include the following:[87]

- Increased engagement and motivation because employees have a broader perspective on the organization.

- Increased worker flexibility and easier scheduling because employees are cross-trained to perform different jobs.
- Increased employee knowledge and abilities, which improves employees' promotability and builds a pipeline of internal talent.

More companies are now hiring new college graduates into "rotational programs," which allow them to work in different functional areas for short periods and learn many different parts of the business along the way. Finally, the technique of job rotation has evolved into *job swapping,* with increased opportunities both here and abroad. (See the OB in Action box.)

OB in Action

Job Swapping and Job Rotation Opportunities Abound

How would you like to work all over the country without the hassle of changing jobs? At Abbott, the health care company, new graduates with appropriate majors from partner universities who are selected for the two- to three-year corporate development program are asked to rotate among different jobs at company offices around the country. The focus areas are finance, information technology, manufacturing, quality assurance, engineering, and environmental health.

Similarly, the Global Fellows Program at Edelman, a global communications marketing company, chooses strong employees with high potential to work at international locations like Shanghai, Moscow, and Abu Dhabi for as long as 18 months. HSBC Holdings, one of the world's largest banking companies, has comparable opportunities that range from 10 weeks to 2 years and places interns and entry-level employees in locations as wide-ranging as Argentina, the UK, Singapore, and France. There they work in relationship management, global trade, and receivables finance in the Commercial Banking Global Graduate Program, and in retail banking and wealth management in the Digital Global Graduate Program.

Emerson, a global technology and engineering company, runs an Engineers in Leadership Program that rotates as many as 18 candidates every year through a two-year program exposing them to one domestic and one international assignment. Benefits for the chosen employees include training, mentorship, and network building. Even the NFL runs a Junior Rotational Program that cycles employees through 6- to 12-month projects at different departments including Events, Communications and Public Affairs, Football Operations and Officiating, and International.[88]

Job swapping, in which employees actually switch with one another for a time, can take place internally or externally. One good example of external swapping was forged by Travis York, CEO of a marketing firm called GYK Antler, who decided he could better understand how to work with his client, technology firm Dyn Industries, if he took CEO Jeremy Hitchcock's place for a typical day. "We thought it would be good to be in each other's shoes so we could understand each other better and gain a deeper perspective," York says. The experiment was so rewarding that York has repeated it three times with other clients, including the CEO of an art school, the founder of a men's fashion company, and a professional basketball player. Everything is "fair game" during the swap day except raises, hires, and firings. Several weeks later, York will follow up with the CEO and then make it a point to check in with the person on a regular basis thereafter.[89]

Common features of many successful job swaps and rotations are planning, goal setting, the possibility of benefit for participants on both sides, mentors to offer direction and answers, and written (or posted) documentation about the job to lower the learning curve.[90]

YOUR THOUGHTS

1. What are the pros and cons of job swaps and rotations?

2. What would be your ideal job swap or rotation?

3. If you managed a business, would you offer this option to your employees? Why or why not?

Job Enrichment   Job enrichment is the practical application of Frederick Herzberg's motivator-hygiene theory of job satisfaction, discussed earlier in this chapter. Specifically, *job enrichment* **modifies a job such that an employee has the opportunity to experience achievement, recognition, stimulating work, responsibility, and advancement.** These characteristics are incorporated into a job through *vertical loading*. Rather than giving employees additional tasks of similar difficulty (*horizontal loading*), vertical loading gives them more autonomy and responsibility. For example, "Final Friday" is a big hit with employees at Hot Dog Marketing, a branding and digital marketing agency in the Austin, Texas area. According to CEO Jessica Scanlon, six times a year, employees are encouraged to use the last Friday of the month as a free day to work on personal projects or to pursue skills to further their professional development.[91]

The Job Characteristics Model   Two OB researchers, J. Richard Hackman and Greg Oldham, played a central role in developing the job characteristics approach. They proposed that intrinsic motivation was determined by three psychological states. In turn, these psychological states were fostered by the presence of five core job characteristics (see Figure 5.10).

The goal of **the *job characteristics model* is to promote high intrinsic motivation by designing jobs that possess the five core job characteristics.** The five characteristics are as follows:

- **Skill variety.** The extent to which the job requires an individual to perform a variety of tasks that require him or her to use different skills and abilities.

- **Task identity.** The extent to which the job requires an individual to perform a whole or completely identifiable piece of work. Task identity is high when a person works on a product or project from beginning to end and sees a tangible result.

FIGURE 5.10   The Job Characteristics Model

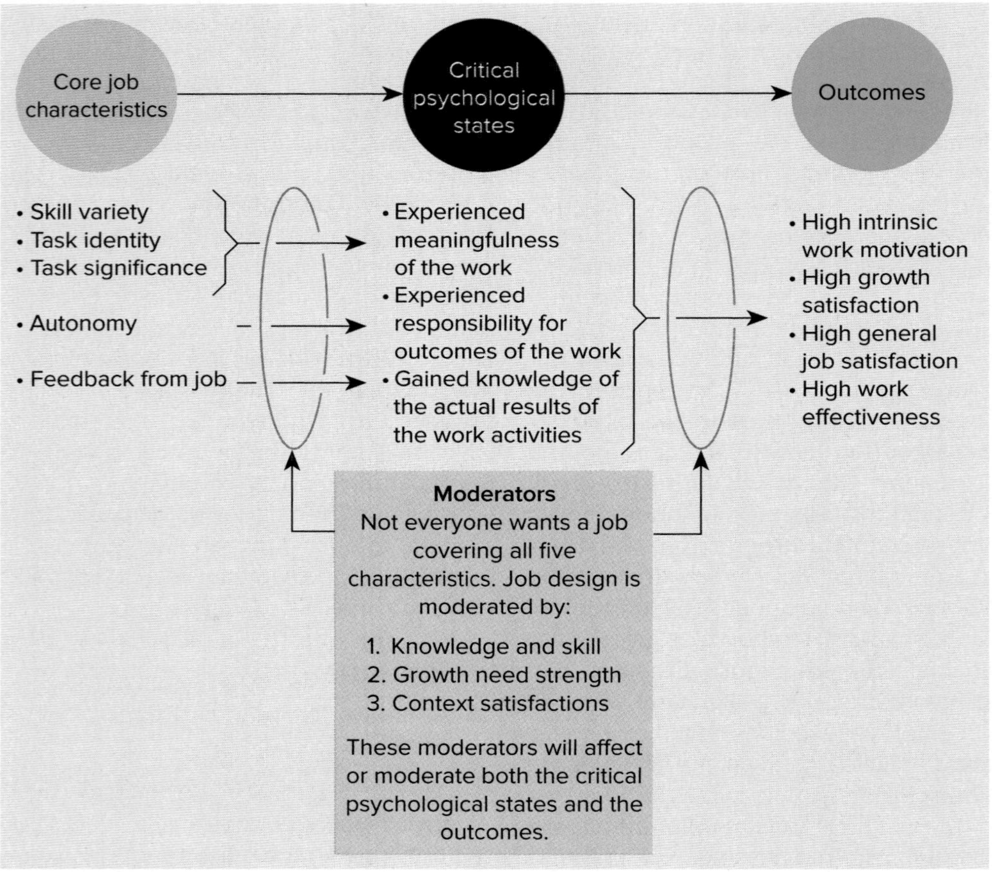

SOURCE: Hackman, J. Richard, and Greg R. Oldham. *Work Redesign.* Massachusetts: Addison-Wesley, 1980.

- **Task significance.** The extent to which the job affects the lives of other people within or outside the organization.
- **Autonomy.** The extent to which the job enables an individual to experience freedom, independence, and discretion in both scheduling and determining the procedures used in completing the job.
- **Feedback.** The extent to which an individual receives direct and clear information about how effectively he or she is performing the job.[92]

Moderators. A moderator is a variable that changes the relationship between two other variables. Hackman and Oldham proposed that there are moderators that affect the success of job design, and they are shown in the moderator box of Figure 5.10.

- *Knowledge and skill* (representing whether or not the person has the knowledge and skills to perform the enriched job).
- *Growth need strength* (representing the desire to grow and develop as an individual).
- *Context satisfactions* (representing the extent to which employees are satisfied with various aspects of their job, such as pay, coworkers, and supervision).

The takeaway is that job design is more likely to work when people have the required knowledge and skills, when they want to develop, and when they are satisfied with their jobs. Job design is not for everyone.

In Practice. Research identifies three practical implications of applying the job characteristics model.

1. Managers can increase employee job satisfaction.[93]
2. Managers can enhance employees' intrinsic motivation and performance, while reducing absenteeism and stress.[94]

   EXAMPLE File-sharing company Dropbox increases employee autonomy and motivation by its unlimited vacation policy, explaining "we provide generous time off policies for everything life throws your way." Adobe's frequent "check-in" conversations, which take the place of annual performance reviews, enable managers and employees to discuss performance and opportunities on an informal basis and provide real-time feedback to promote growth and development.[95]

3. Managers can find noticeable increases in the quality of performance after a job redesign program. Results from 21 experimental studies revealed that job redesign resulted in a median increase of 28 percent in the quality of performance.[96]

Bottom-Up Approaches—You Design Your Own Job

As its name suggests, bottom-up job design is driven by employees rather than managers; it is also referred to as job crafting. **Job crafting represents employees' attempts to proactively shape their work characteristics.**[97] The concept is largely based on the theories of empowerment and intrinsic motivation, and its goal is to help employees experience a sense of meaning in their jobs. A recent survey of more than 2,200 professionals revealed that 90 percent of them would be willing to earn less money (roughly 23 percent of future earnings) for more meaningful work.[98]

This employee of Swiss-based computer device producer Logitech is working on a computer mouse. He looks very focused on the task at hand. It may be that job crafting is partly behind his engagement. The company is using job crafting to increase employee engagement and job satisfaction. As part of this effort the company created a 90-minute workshop to help employees learn how to align their strengths and interests with tasks contained in their jobs.

Gaetan Bally/Keystone/AP Images

TABLE 5.2 Forms of Job Crafting

CHANGES IN APPROACH	EXAMPLE	CHANGES IN RESULTS
Task boundaries: Number, scope, and type of job tasks.	Design engineers engage in relational activities that move a project to completion.	Engineers are now guardians or movers of projects; they complete work in a more timely fashion.
Relational nature: Quality and/or amount of interaction with others encountered in a job.	Hospital cleaners actively care for patients and families and integrate themselves into the workflow of their floor units.	Cleaners are now helpers of the sick; they see the work of the floor unit as a vital part of an integrated whole.
Cognitive crafting: Perception of or thinking about tasks and relationships in your job.	Nurses take responsibility for all information and "insignificant" tasks so they can care more appropriately for a patient.	Nurses are now patient advocates; they provide high-quality, technical care.

SOURCE: Wrzesniewski, Amy, and J. E. Dutton. "Crafting a Job: Revisioning Employees as Active Crafters of Their Work." *Academy of Management Review* 26, no. 2 (2001): 179–201. https://DOI: 10.2307/259118.

Forms of Job Crafting   Employees are viewed as "job crafters" according to the bottom-up model because they are expected to define and create their own job boundaries. Table 5.2 illustrates three forms of job crafting. The first changes the job's *task boundaries*. You can do this by taking on more or fewer tasks or by altering their scope or nature. The second form changes the *relational nature* of the job. Specifically, you can alter the quantity or quality of interactions you have with others at work, or you can establish new relationships. The third method is *cognitive crafting*. In this strategy you perceive or think differently about the existing tasks and relationships associated with your job.

Outcomes of Job Crafting   The right-hand column in Table 5.2 outlines the potential impact of job crafting on employee motivation and performance. You can see that job crafting is expected to change the way employees perceive their jobs. It should also result in more positive attitudes about the job, which is expected to increase employee motivation, engagement, and performance. Preliminary research supports this proposition.[99]

Computer accessories maker Logitech Inc. successfully implemented a job crafting pilot program. Jessica Amortegui, senior director of learning and development, said, "The company hopes helping employees find more intrinsic motivation in their work will be a powerful hiring draw. Logitech plans to begin using the [program] with all 3,000 of its workers."[100]

Given that job crafting can lead to higher levels of engagement and satisfaction, you may be interested in understanding how you can apply the technique to a former, current, or future job. The Self-Assessment 5.3 explores the extent to which you are applying job crafting to reduce job demands, seek resources, or seek challenges.

Idiosyncratic Deals (I-Deals)— You Negotiate the Design of Your Job

The last approach to job design, idiosyncratic deals, represents a middle ground between top-down and bottom-up methods and attempts to overcome their limitations. For example, top-down approaches are constrained by the fact that managers cannot always create changes in task characteristics that are optimal for everyone. Similarly, job crafting is limited by the amount of latitude people have to change their own jobs. **Idiosyncratic deals (i-deals) represent "employment terms individuals negotiate for themselves, taking myriad forms from flexible schedules to career development."**[101] Although "star performers" have long negotiated special employment contracts or deals, demographic trends and the changing nature of work have created increased opportunities for more employees to negotiate i-deals.

I-deals tend to affect task and work responsibilities, schedule flexibility, location flexibility, and compensation.[102] The goal of such deals is to increase employee intrinsic motivation and productivity by allowing employees the flexibility to negotiate employment relationships that meet their own specific needs and values. RSM promotes and encourages the creation of i-deals among its more than 9,600 employees. The focus of its program is to create innovative and flexible ways of working.[103]

This relatively new approach to job design has begun to generate much research. Results confirm that i-deals are associated with higher perceived organizational support, job satisfaction, and perceived voice. Employees also are less likely to quit when they negotiate i-deals.[104] Future study is needed to determine the generalizability of these encouraging results.

Consider how you might one day create an i-deal for yourself. Self-Assessment 5.4 will help you think through the process.

5.5 MAKING THE CONNECTION: HOW CAN I APPLY MOTIVATION THEORIES?

THE BIGGER PICTURE

Motivation explains why we do the things we do and is an important process that affects behavior in both our personal and professional lives. Here are some key points to consider.

Takeaways for Me

Here are five things you can do to turn this chapter's lessons into positive change in your personal and professional life.

1. **Identify the needs that are important to you today, recognizing they may change over time:** This can help you identify the type of work you would like to do before and after graduation.

2. **If your current job is low on hygiene or motivating factors, reflect on what you can do to change this situation:** You may be able to create change by talking to your boss, asking for new work assignments, or getting a different job.

3. **Festering feelings of inequity are not good for you or those you interact with on a regular basis:** Make a plan to correct any feelings of inequity that exist in your life.

4. **Set specific, measurable goals for things you want to accomplish in your life:** Develop an action plan that outlines the path to success, then be sure to reward yourself for accomplishing the goals.

5. **If your current job is unfulfilling, try to find ways to incorporate job crafting or i-deals into your work:** If this doesn't work, you might consider changing jobs.

Takeaways for Managers

There are seven key implications for managers.

1. **Recognize that intrinsic motivation can have longer-lasting effects than extrinsic motivation:** Try to build Herzberg's motivators into employees' work experiences.

2. **Acknowledge that needs drive employee motivation:** Find a way to determine employee needs, such as employee surveys or one-on-one meetings.

3. **Because some needs are innate, consider people's needs when they are first hired:** Validated tests exist that will identify these needs.

4. **Uncover employees' perceptions about equity and justice:** Then correct any deficiencies by administering employee surveys or exit interviews.

5. **Incorporate the principles of expectancy theory:** By ensuring employees believe they can accomplish their goals and linking performance to rewards that individual employees value.

6. **Work with employees to set challenging yet attainable goals and then establish action plans:** Be sure employees have the resources they need to achieve these goals.

7. **Consider different ways to design jobs:** Doing so will ensure that jobs foster intrinsic motivation and meaningfulness.

What Did I Learn?

You learned that motivation, a key individual-level process, is influenced by inputs such as needs, perceptions of justice, expectancies and instrumentalities, goals, and job design. You learned how various theories and models of motivation can be applied by managers to improve multiple outcomes. Reinforce your learning with the Key Points below. Consolidate your learning using the Organizing Framework. Then challenge your mastery of the material by answering the Major Questions in your own words.

Key Points for Understanding Chapter 5

You learned the following key points.

5.1 THE WHAT AND WHY OF MOTIVATION

- There are two types of motivation: intrinsic and extrinsic.
- Extrinsic motivation results from the potential or actual receipt of external rewards.
- Intrinsic motivation is driven by positive internal feelings generated by doing well.

5.2 CONTENT THEORIES OF MOTIVATION

- Content theories are based on the idea that an employee's needs influence motivation. There are five key content theories.
- Douglas McGregor proposed a theory of motivation based on two opposing views of employees. Theory X people believe employees dislike work and are motivated by rewards and punishment. Theory Y people believe employees are self-engaged, committed, and responsible.
- Abraham Maslow proposed that motivation is a function of five basic needs—physiological, safety, love, esteem, and self-actualization—arranged in a prepotent hierarchy.
- David McClelland's acquired needs theory is based on the idea that motivation is a function

of three basic needs: achievement, affiliation, and power.
- Self-determination theory assumes that three innate needs influence motivation: competence, autonomy, and relatedness.
- Frederick Herzberg's motivator-hygiene theory is based on the premise that job satisfaction comes from motivating factors and dissatisfaction from hygiene factors.

5.3 PROCESS THEORIES OF MOTIVATION

- Process theories attempt to describe how various person factors and situation factors affect motivation.
- Equity theory explains how people strive for fairness and justice in social exchanges. Fairness or equity is determined by comparing our outputs and inputs with those of others.
- Three key types of justice are distributive, procedural, and interactive.
- Expectancy theory assumes that motivation is determined by our perceived chances of achieving valued outcomes. The three key elements of this theory are expectancies, instrumentalities, and valence of outcomes.
- Goal-setting theory proposes that goals affect performance because they (1) direct our attention, (2) regulate effort, (3) increase persistence, and (4) encourage the development of action plans.

5.4 MOTIVATING EMPLOYEES THROUGH JOB DESIGN

- Job design theories are based on the idea that motivation is primarily influenced by the tasks people perform and the characteristics of the immediate work environment.
- Three broad approaches to job design are top-down, bottom-up, and emerging.
- The premise of top-down approaches is that management is responsible for creating efficient and meaningful combinations of work tasks for employees. Top-down approaches

include scientific management, job enlargement, job rotation, job enrichment, and the job characteristics model.

- Bottom-up approaches, also referred to as job crafting, are driven by employees rather than managers. Employees create their own job boundaries.
- Emerging approaches include idiosyncratic deals (i-deals). This approach views job design as a process in which employees and managers jointly negotiate the types of tasks employees complete at work.

5.5 HOW CAN I APPLY MOTIVATION THEORIES?

- Identifying needs important to you helps pinpoint the type of work you might find meaningful.
- Talking with your boss about possible changes in work activities may increase your motivation to perform at a higher level.
- Setting specific, measurable goals in your personal life and career help keep you focused and moving forward.

The Organizing Framework for Chapter 5

As shown in Figure 5.11, both person and situation factors influence the process of motivation.

You can also see that there are more situational than personal factors influencing motivation. This underscores the importance of leadership and creating a work environment that reinforces voice and justice. Figure 5.11 further illustrates that motivational processes affect outcomes across the individual, group/team, and organizational levels.

Challenge: Major Questions for Chapter 5

You should now be able to answer the following questions. Unless you can, have you really processed and internalized the lessons in the chapter? Review relevant portions of the text and your notes to answer the following major questions. With Figure 5.11 as your guide, look for inputs, processes, and outputs specific to each:

1. What is motivation and how does it affect my behavior?
2. How would I compare and contrast the content theories of motivation?
3. How would I compare and contrast the process theories of motivation?
4. How are top-down approaches, bottom-up approaches, and "idiosyncratic deals" similar and different?

FIGURE 5.11 Integrative Framework for Understanding and Applying OB

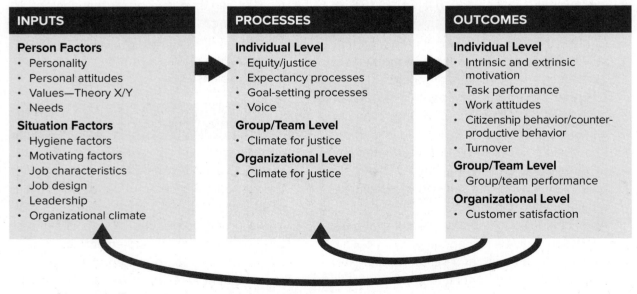

Workers at Amazon Are Not Feeling Motivated

Across the globe at over 175 fulfillment centers, more than 125,000 workers frantically "pick, pack, and ship millions of Amazon.com customer orders to the tune of millions of items per year."[105] Amazon's innovations, like free 2-day shipping for Prime members, dash buttons, and in-home delivery, have made the retail giant a standout in customer service. The company has consistently received award-winning customer satisfaction ratings.[106] Amazon became the most valuable public company and second largest e-commerce company in the world in 2019 by being hyper-focused on customer experiences.[107]

But many of Amazon's fulfillment center workers are unhappy with what they are required to do to assure these esteemed customer experiences.[108] The result has been public outcry, boycotts, poor attitudes and health, and extremely high turnover rates among workers. What's making employees so miserable inside Amazon fulfillment centers?

WORKING AT AN AMAZON FULFILLMENT CENTER

Amazon designs its fulfillment center jobs for efficiency, with managers constantly monitoring and tracking employees in three primary areas. First, workers are monitored for productivity as they race to fill as many orders as possible to meet or exceed daily quotas. Those who don't meet their quotas are written up, and excessive write-ups can lead to termination.[109] A recent undercover investigation revealed that some employees are so fearful of missing their quotas that they forego taking necessary bathroom breaks and instead urinate in bottles and trash cans inside the warehouses.[110] The company is so dedicated to its productivity goals that workers reportedly don't speak to one another during their shifts, saying that managers strongly discourage any kind of camaraderie.[111]

Second, management monitors fulfillment center workers for security purposes. One employee described the environment as resembling a prison, noting time-consuming scans for contraband (e.g., sunglasses, phones, hoodies) and stolen items at the beginning and end of shifts.[112] There's also a custom of publicly shaming employees who steal from the company on flat-screen TVs and bulletin boards around the warehouses.[113]

Third, fulfillment center managers track employee attendance. Workers can be fired for excessive missed work days, or, as Amazon calls it, going into negative unpaid time off (UPT). Employees have reported being so terrified of missing work that they show up even when they are too sick or injured to work safely, in spite of the extremely physically demanding nature of the job.[114]

HOW DOES AMAZON ATTRACT FULFILLMENT CENTER WORKERS?

How is it that news of a new Amazon fulfillment center is still seen as cause for celebration, given what has been reported about working conditions? Employment opportunities are one key explanation. The company tends to locate fulfillment centers on the outskirts of major metropolitan areas, often in regions that have yet to recover from the recent economic recession and are desperate for increased jobs.[115] In other words, if Amazon opens a fulfillment center in your town, chances are your employment prospects will be better than those you've got right now.

Even so, many Amazon fulfillment center employees feel the compensation they receive is not commensurate with the extreme working conditions and job demands. Worker retention thus seems to be a function of a lack of viable alternatives rather than positive employee attitudes toward the company. As one worker stated, "that's what makes people not want to quit—the pay" . . . "you can treat me any type of way, since this is the best money we can get out here . . ."[116]

Amazon does provide some additional incentives to increase productivity at its fulfillment centers. For example, managers often hold competitions that reward employees with "swag bucks"—tokens to spend inside the warehouse on things like t-shirts, water bottles, or cafeteria meals.[117] Other rewards reportedly include small gift cards and even cookies. Said one employee, "I don't want a cookie or a gift card. I'll take it, but I'd rather a living wage. Or not being timed when you're sitting on the toilet."[118] Another worker found these incentives insulting, saying that "around this time of year the managers, if their targets are met or exceeded, they get a bonus."[119]

Amazon implemented a policy guaranteeing a minimum wage of $15 per hour after receiving such negative attention in the press. This resulted in raises as small as 25 cents per hour, which many viewed as "damage control."[120] For some tenured workers, the new policy meant their wages became compressed and they lost important benefits they previously received, such as stock options and bonus opportunities.[121]

WHAT'S NEXT?

Stacy Mitchell, co-director of the Institute for Local Self-Reliance, said, "There's this way in which Amazon's warehouses are perceived to be a good thing for a community, but that's only because the context in which they are being proposed and built is so devoid of better opportunities." Said a current employee, "They're walking a fine line in the community—everybody knows someone who's worked there, and no one says it's a good place to work."[122]

Some Amazon workers have attempted to generate interest in union representation but have been unable to gain the momentum necessary for an organizing campaign. This is likely due to two main causes. First, the fact that Amazon has one of the highest turnover rates in the United States means that employees aren't around long enough for a movement to take shape. Second, workers have expressed they are afraid to speak up and participate in organizing campaigns for fear of retaliation from the company.[123]

It's unlikely we'll see any sweeping changes to the way Amazon manages its fulfillment center workers in the near future. This is because Amazon already loses money on e-commerce and subsidizes the losses with other segments of its business. Any changes to the current state of affairs could mean a loss of our coveted cheap wares and free two-day shipping.[124]

APPLY THE 3-STEP PROBLEM-SOLVING APPROACH TO OB

STEP 1: Define the problem.

A. Look first at the Outcome box of the Organizing Framework in Figure 5.11 to help identify the important problem(s) in this case. Remember that a problem is a gap between a desired and a current state. State your problem as a gap and be sure to consider problems at all three levels. If more than one desired outcome is not being accomplished, decide which one is most important and focus on it for steps 2 and 3.

B. Cases have protagonists (key players), and problems are generally viewed from a particular protagonist's perspective. Identify the perspective from which you're defining the problem—is it the perspective of Amazon or its workers?

C. Use details in the case to identify the key problem. Don't assume, infer, or create problems that are not included in the case.

D. To refine your choice, ask yourself, *Why is this a problem?* Explaining why helps refine and focus your thinking. Focus on topics in the current chapter, because we generally select cases that illustrate concepts in the current chapter.

STEP 2: Identify causes of the problem by using material from this chapter, summarized in the Organizing Framework shown in Figure 5.11. Causes will appear in either the Inputs box or the Processes box.

A. Start by looking at Figure 5.11 to identify which person factors, if any, are most likely causes to the defined problem. For each cause, ask, *Why is this a cause of the problem?* Asking why multiple times is more likely to lead you to root causes of the problem.

B. Follow the same process for the situation factors.

C. Now consider the Processes box in Figure 5.11. Consider concepts listed at all three levels. For any concept that might be a cause, ask yourself, *Why is this a cause?* Again, do this for several iterations to arrive at root causes.

D. To check the accuracy or appropriateness of the causes, be sure to map them onto the defined problem.

STEP 3: Make recommendations for solving the problem. Consider whether you want to resolve it, solve it, or dissolve it (see Section 1.5). Which recommendation is desirable and feasible?

A. Given the causes identified in Step 2, what are your best recommendations? Use the content in Chapter 5 or one of the earlier chapters to propose a solution.

B. You may find potential solutions in the OB in Action boxes and Applying OB boxes within this chapter. These features provide insights into what other individuals or companies are doing in relationship to the topic at hand.

C. Create an action plan for implementing your recommendations.

Should Senior Executives Receive Bonuses for Navigating a Company through Bankruptcy?

Consider the case of Sears Holdings, which filed for bankruptcy protection in October 2018. The company closed several hundred stores in recent years and cut over 50,000 jobs between January 2017 and March 2018.[125] Still, Sears sought and received approval to pay up to $25.3 million in bonuses for key executives and other employees.[126] Does this seem appropriate from a justice or expectancy theory perspective?

A federal law was established in 2005 to restrict companies from paying bonuses to executives before and during a bankruptcy process. The law does allow for companies to dole out executive bonuses while simultaneously seeking bankruptcy protection, but only in cases where companies are seeking to rebound and could thus be irreparably harmed by the loss of key executives.[127] In the case of Sears, a judge ruled that the bonuses were legal because they were tied to the company meeting specific financial milestones.[128] U.S. bankruptcy trustee William Harrington formally objected to the bonus proposal saying that "the bonuses do not feel like an effort to retain top talent through a difficult period, but a final extraction of cash before the ship sinks."[129]

The practice of giving bonuses to senior executives who navigate a company through bankruptcy is quite common. A *Wall Street Journal* study of 12 of the 100 biggest corporate bankruptcies revealed that CEOs from these firms were paid more than $350 million in various forms of compensation. "Over the past few years, fights have erupted during a handful of Chapter 11 bankruptcy cases," the newspaper reported. "The central argument has been over whether companies are adhering to federal laws when giving their executives the extra pay." While judicial decisions regarding this issue have been mixed, consider the ethics of paying executives large bonuses when laying off workers, closing plants, and eliminating health care and retirement benefits to retirees.[130] Does this seem fair or just?

Finding Answers to Solve the Challenge

Is it ethical to pay these bonuses? Respond to each of the following options.

1. Yes. Navigating a company through bankruptcy is hard work and requires hard decisions. Executives at Sears, for example, are expected to earn those bonuses by staying with the company to shepherd it through tough times, helping to turn it around.

2. Yes, if all employees receive some sort of bonus for staying through a bankruptcy process. In other words, executives should be paid the same as other surviving employees. If everyone took a 10 percent pay cut or gets a 10 percent bonus, so should executives. What's fair for one is fair for all.

3. Absolutely not. It just is not right to close stores, displace employees, and eliminate retirement benefits while simultaneously giving executives hefty bonuses.

What is your ideal resolution to the challenge?

6 Performance Management

After reading this chapter, you should be able to:

LO 6-1 Summarize the elements of effective performance management.

LO 6-2 Explain how and why goal setting gives you an advantage.

LO 6-3 Describe how monitoring and evaluation can improve your performance and ability to manage others.

LO 6-4 Apply knowledge of feedback and coaching to review and improve performance.

LO 6-5 Implement rewards to generate desired outcomes.

LO 6-6 Use reinforcement and consequences to improve performance.

LO 6-7 Describe the implications of performance management for you and managers.

Figure 6.1 summarizes what you will learn in this chapter. The main focus is performance management, which we position as an individual process in the Organizing Framework for Understanding and Applying OB. It could easily be considered a group- or organizational-level process, but we put it at the individual level because it is the performance of individuals that determines the performance of groups and organizations. Performance management is an umbrella phrase that includes a number of important OB concepts, such as goal setting, performance measurement and appraisals, feedback, and rewards. Performance management therefore is an especially important topic in OB.

FIGURE 6.1   Organizing Framework for Understanding and Applying OB

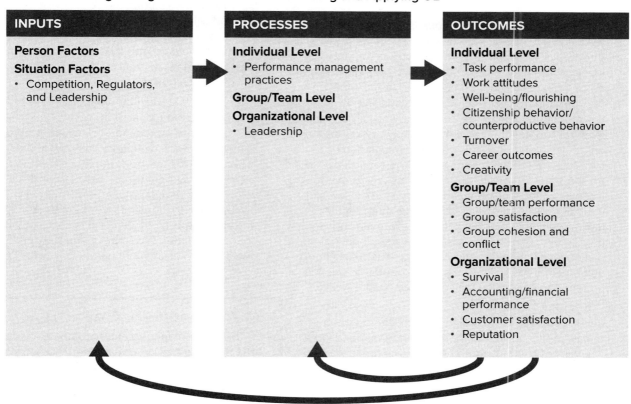

INPUTS	PROCESSES	OUTCOMES
Person Factors	**Individual Level**	**Individual Level**
Situation Factors	• Performance management practices	• Task performance
• Competition, Regulators, and Leadership	**Group/Team Level**	• Work attitudes
	Organizational Level	• Well-being/flourishing
	• Leadership	• Citizenship behavior/ counterproductive behavior
		• Turnover
		• Career outcomes
		• Creativity
		Group/Team Level
		• Group/team performance
		• Group satisfaction
		• Group cohesion and conflict
		Organizational Level
		• Survival
		• Accounting/financial performance
		• Customer satisfaction
		• Reputation

Winning at Work

Busy vs. Productive—Productive Wins

Many people are busy but far fewer are productive. Given that everyone has the same number of hours in a day, one way to beat the competition is to spend your time more productively than others. We assembled the following collection of best practices to help make you more productive, which should in turn Improve your job performance and career opportunities.

1. **Learn how you spend your time.** Create a time log by tracking your time and the way you spend it for two or three days to capture the things you commonly do. Ideally, you'll pause every hour or two and record how much time you've spent on particular tasks. If this isn't feasible, then be sure you record your time twice in the morning, twice in the afternoon, and once in the evening.[1] (Note: You cannot accurately document the entire day at the end. This doesn't work so don't even try.) When you have two or three days recorded, add up the time you spent on various tasks. Identify the three activities that consume the greatest amounts of your time. It is especially useful to determine how much time you spend on social media, e-mailing, texting, playing games, and surfing the web, then, determine how much of this effort is really related to school and/or work. You'll likely be shocked, and if so this will hopefully motivate you to use your time more wisely.

2. **Never touch things twice.** This means you should never put tasks in a holding pattern.[2] If you open an e-mail, for instance, and then decide to respond later, you will have to look at it at least one more time. This advice also applies to phone calls and other items on your to-do list. You need to decide the first time you touch it—take action now, delegate it, or delete it. At first you may think this isn't possible. But being decisive is key to increasing productivity. You may have to do some less desirable or even undesirable tasks immediately instead of putting them off. Or you'll have to figure out how to do certain things, like texting, only at certain times of the day.

3. **Schedule e-mail, text, and phone time.** Turn off notifications—all of them. Then set specific times in the day when you'll check and tend to other distracting tasks. For instance, you are wise to always *look at and respond to e-mail* in the same space of time, such as at 11:00 each morning and 4:00 each afternoon. When the phone rings, you don't have to answer it. If it's important the caller will leave a message, which you can listen to during the time you've allocated. Set times for particular tasks and stick to them.

4. **Take regular breaks.** Recharging with a walk, music, or a brief chat has been shown to improve your concentration

and boost productivity during the time you're on task. Some research suggests that 90-minute intervals of work are best. This means you should set a plan for what you'll accomplish in 90 minutes, then take a break. A series of intense, focused, and energized intervals is more productive than long stretches of uninterrupted work.[3]

5. **Eat the frog.** This phrase was famously used by a renowned sales trainer, Brian Tracy, which means do the most undesirable item on your to-do list first, at the beginning of the day. Thus it doesn't get postponed, your least desirable task is finished, making the rest of your day that much better.[4]

6. **Not always yes.** Busy people arguably say "yes" too often, but productive people say "yes" more judiciously. When approached or invited to participate in something that is voluntary, instead of deciding say: "Thank you for the opportunity, but do you mind if I consider it overnight and get back in touch?" Most will see this as acceptable, and then you have the opportunity to consider your other commitments, determine the fit of your skills to the task, and of course consider the impact you can make before deciding and giving your answer.[5]

What's Ahead in This Chapter

Performance management encompasses many of the topics and tools you've learned thus far. In many ways this chapter serves as a summary. And in other ways it serves as a rationale for taking the course. If you want to know why OB is important, and why its theories, models, and tools matter, the answer comes down to improving performance at all three levels of OB—individual, team, and organizational. The discussion in this chapter focuses on several of the critical components of effective performance management: goal setting, feedback, rewards, and reinforcement. To effectively manage performance, managers and organizations need to identify and communicate clear expectations or goals, monitor and provide feedback regarding progress toward these goals, and then link and deliver appropriate consequences (rewards) for goal achievement. We highlight how performance management serves as a powerful tool for motivating, developing, and retaining talent. We hope you will appreciate why effective performance management policies and practices often dramatically affect many aspects of your work life.

6.1 PERFORMANCE MANAGEMENT PROCESSES

THE BIGGER PICTURE

Performance management occurs in many arenas of your life, notably school and work. Because it is a process that generates grades at school and pay and promotions at work, it is important to understand how it works. You'll learn why performance management is one of the most critical and far-reaching processes in the Organizing Framework. You'll see why opinions about the usefulness and effectiveness of performance management practices are often negative. However, you'll also learn how performance management practices can be beneficial, such as by helping signal and reinforce desired behaviors and outcomes across all levels of OB.

This chapter focuses on improving individual job performance, notably yours, as well as on your ability to improve the performance of others. To do this, you need to draw on and apply many of the concepts and tools you've learned thus far, such as hard and soft skills, personality, perceptions, and of course, motivation. The integration and application of this knowledge for the purposes of improved outcomes is called *performance management.*

Performance management (PM) is a set of processes and managerial behaviors that include defining, monitoring, measuring, evaluating, and providing consequences for performance expectations.[6] Defined in this way, PM is far more than performance appraisal. Appraisals typically consist only of the actual performance review, an event. Effective PM, in contrast, is a continual process and a critically important individual-level process of which appraisals are a subset.[7] Performance management typically operates through an organization's managers and human resources policies and practices. You will learn how it affects outcomes across all levels in the Organizing Framework, such as individual (job satisfaction, OCBs, and turnover), team (cohesiveness, conflict, and performance), and organizational (reputation, performance, survival, innovation, and employer of choice).

But before we dive in, it is helpful to frame exactly what is in store with a quote from Elaine Pulakos, a renowned PM expert and CEO of PDRI, a leading human resource development consulting company, and her colleagues who described it this way: "No other talent management system has been the subject of such great debate, change, and emotion as PM."[8] This means you'll learn about the good, the bad, and the ugly of this important individual-level process.

Effective Performance Management

As illustrated in Figure 6.2, effective PM has four components:

1. Defining performance.
2. Monitoring and evaluating performance.
3. Reviewing performance.
4. Providing consequences.

Please note the double-headed arrows. They signify the systems part of PM, which means the various components affect each other. How performance is defined

LO 6-1

Summarize the elements of effective performance management.

FIGURE 6.2 Effective Performance Management System

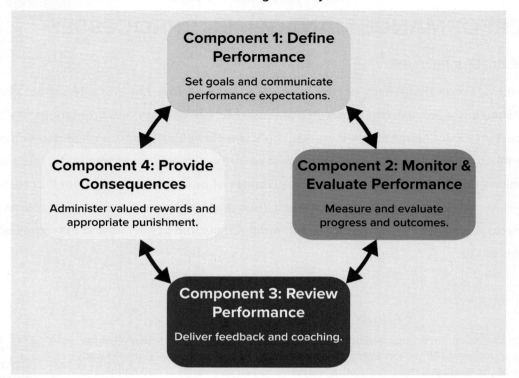

SOURCE: Kinicki, Angelo J., Kathryn J. L. Jacobson, Suzanne J. Peterson, and Gregory E. Prussia. "Development and Validation of the Performance Management Behavior Questionnaire." *Personnel Psychology* 66, no. 1 (Spring 2013): 1–45. https://doi.org/10.1111/peps.12013.

(Component 1) obviously impacts how it is measured (Component 2), at least it should, but how it is measured helps refine the performance expectations themselves.

Successfully managing performance is a powerful means for improving individual, group/team, and organizational effectiveness. Effective performance management influences important outcomes such as greater employee engagement and better organizational performance.[9] Managers who practice effective performance management generate exceptional results compared to those who don't:

- 48% higher profitability.
- 22% higher productivity.
- 30% higher employee engagement scores.
- 17% higher customer engagement scores.
- 19% lower turnover.[10]

Common Uses of Performance Management

Most performance management systems have six primary outputs and functions.

1. Performance ratings. High, low, better, or worse than before or others.
2. Feedback. Generating the content and delivering it.
3. Development and performance improvement plans. Underperformers need to improve or be moved out.
4. Career planning. Linking expectation and performance to increased responsibilities.
5. Recommendations for employee-related decisions. Rewards, promotions, training, or termination.
6. Documentation for legal purposes. Sound decisions need appropriate supporting data.[11]

The extent to which organizations effectively practice performance management can have enormous impact on outcomes across all levels. This greatly impacts your personal opportunities, job satisfaction, engagement, and turnover among other aspects of your career. That said, only 3 percent of PM studies since the early 2000s investigated career planning.[12] What does this mean for you? It means researchers likely aren't the ones offering the best insights for your career planning and this is why we draw on insights from career coaches, counselors, and other professionals. See the following Applying OB box for an example.

Applying OB

CAREER READINESS

Apply Goal Setting to Your Job and Career

Although most people have desires, wishes, and preferences for their jobs and careers, and most also set a goal or two from time to time, such as to get a raise or a promotion, relatively few people make career plans. The four components of performance management can serve as a useful guide to career planning, and this begins with goal setting.

1. *Set long-term goals.* It is good to start far into the future, at least as far as you can reasonably think, such as 10 years, when you're 30, or some other marker.

   I want to get: _____ by (date) _____.

   I will need these skills: a, b, and c.

   Which require the following experiences:

2. *Break these into shorter-term goals.* Think of these as steps along the way to the long-term goal noted above. Take each skill, for instance, and determine the necessary sub-goals and steps to achieve them.[13]

Note: You'll be far more likely to achieve each of the goals above if you apply the SMART and other goal setting tools explained later in this chapter.

3. *Action plans for each goal.* Most good plans contain who, what, where, when, and how. Be sure you at least consider all of these elements for each goal in #2.

4. *Implement.* If you do the previous steps correctly and thoroughly this should be clear. It is of course helpful if you practice, consult a coach, or at least get advice from appropriate others. Informational interviews or shadowing someone for a day can be immensely helpful.

5. *Review, revise, and re-engage.* Like effective performance management, you need to review your progress *and* outcomes. Don't focus only on the outcomes but monitor your progress as well. Did you implement the plan you created, did you do it on time, and what did you learn along the way? Use this information to revise your plan and get back to it!

What Goes Wrong with Performance Management

Volumes of research and employee surveys report that the majority of managers and organizations do a poor job of managing employee performance. According to extensive research done by Gallup:

- 20% of employees feel their performance is managed in a way that motivates them.

- 29% perceive their employers' PM system as fair.

- 26% agree they are accurate.[14]

- Less than 40% of employees say their systems do *not* provide clear goals or generate honest feedback.[15]

- 66% of employees say it actually interferes with their productivity.

- 58% of 576 HR executives surveyed graded their company's performance management systems as a C or worse.[16]

The meeting in this photo is typical of many performance reviews: Once a year a manager and a subordinate sit on opposite sides of a table, the manager does most of the talking, both are uncomfortable, and each walks away less than happy with the results. This chapter will help you understand how and why you and your managers can do better.

Chris Ryan/OJO Images/age fotostock

These unfortunate perceptions raise the question: Why do companies often do so poorly with performance management? The most common reasons employees feel performance management doesn't measure up are:

Feedback is rare. You will learn much more about feedback later in the chapter, but the most fundamental problem is that feedback is in frequent. If your performance is reviewed only once a year, as is still common, there's little chance that feedback shared will in any way be linked to the behaviors that produce the performance. Moreover, unless the person providing the feedback has a photographic memory its accuracy may be questionable.

Lack of clarity on how to improve. The various scores and rankings provide little detail or guidance on how to actually improve. For example, if you rated on a 1 to 5 scale, strongly disagree to strongly agree, how do you really translate that into actionable performance improvement? This highlights that everyone is rated using the same scale, yet we know not all jobs and employees are the same.

Manager bias. As you learned in Chapter 4, biases are very real and can be especially problematic in the context of PM. Nothing undermines the effectiveness of a PM system faster than a lack of perceived fairness. Making matters worse, many managers do not really understand the responsibilities of the jobs they are reviewing, which makes the process difficult and the outcomes suspect.

Negative reactions. Due to the above and other reasons, employees often react very negatively. This is no surprise. Such reactions can undermine motivation and if the review occurs only once a year, then it can take a long time for you to recover.

Too much focus on pay and incentives. The performance evaluation component of PM is often linked to rewards (consequences), which means any issues you may have with the process are likely to impact these important individual level outcomes. Moreover, the hyper-focus on pay can blind you to the developmental aspects of an otherwise fair and constructive review.[17]

Pervasive poor views of performance management practices have led many notable companies including Accenture, Netflix, Microsoft, GE, and Eli Lilly to scrap their old practices.[18] The following OB in Action box illustrates how Deloitte has tackled the challenges of performance management.

OB in Action

The Deloitte Way: "Snapshots" and "Check-ins"

As part of a renewed commitment to developing its high-caliber workforce, Deloitte made a $100 million investment in The Leadership Center (called Deloitte University). In the process it reviewed the role played by its performance management practices.

The internal review and research revealed two things. First, performance, retention, and client satisfaction were all better when employees felt they were playing to their strengths in their jobs.[19] Second, current PM practices were interfering. The company then embarked on a dramatic transformation of its practices, and its new approach is as interesting for what it excludes as for what it includes. Gone are once-a-year performance reviews, 360-degree feedback tools, and cascading goals.[20] Included are the four components of effective performance management outlined above and described below.

Key Elements of Deloitte's Approach

1. **Setting Goals and Objectives.** Like its many clients, Deloitte has objectives, financial and otherwise, it must achieve. All are important and consequential for employees. However, instead of being set centrally by senior management and cascading down through the organization, goals are now set per client, per team, per employee. This means that goal setting and expectations are much more local and are handled by team leaders, rather than global and done by senior executives at headquarters.

2. **Monitoring and Measuring Performance.** The company still tracks and measures performance, but now it does so in the form of Snapshots. These are questions each team leader answers for each team member, whether quarterly, monthly, at the end of a project, or at any other meaningful point. Instead of ranking the team member, leaders indicate to what extent they agree with statements like, "Given what I know of this person's performance, I would always want him or her on my team," "This person is at risk for low performance," and "If it were my money, I would award this person the highest possible compensation increase in bonus."[21]

3. **Reviewing Performance and Providing Feedback.** Performance reviews and feedback happen not once or twice a year but at regular check-ins. Check-ins are one-on-one, real-time discussions between team leaders and their team members. Their purpose is to discuss progress, expectations, feedback, and any other relevant details related to current or near-term work. The rationale is that performance is driven through conversations, and check-ins give frequent opportunities for managers and employees to meet and talk. Check-ins are not mandated or tracked. Deloitte simply prompts all employees via periodic e-mails that ask, "Did you have a check-in conversation with your team leader this week? Yes or No."[22] Snapshot responses are aggregated every quarter, and HR reviews and discusses the results with business leaders. Along with other metrics, such as revenue per employee, Snapshots give leaders a more holistic and timely view of individual and unit performance.

4. **Rewarding Performance.** Snapshots provide regular and ongoing opportunities to recognize and correct performance, and the quarterly reviews provide yet another opportunity. All of this culminates in annual compensation decisions, which are now based on a wealth of information consistently captured throughout the year.

YOUR THOUGHTS?

1. From an employee's perspective, what do you think are some of the pros and cons of Deloitte's PM system? Explain.

2. Assuming you are a team leader at Deloitte, describe one benefit and one challenge of the PM system for you.

3. What do you think are the major challenges in implementing Deloitte's new PM practices?

Given the still largely negative views of PM practices and outcomes, what are enlightened and successful individuals and organizations doing to improve PM?

Contemporary PM Is Continual

The starting point and the fundamental problem to overcome is that most organizations and their managers treat PM as a bureaucratic chore, a box to be checked, rather than treating it as a critically important and continuing development process.[23] For instance, Gallup recommends reframing the entire system as progress improvement and highlights three qualities that make PM more effective:

- Establish expectations that are clear, collaborative, and aligned. Of course, clarity is important, but as you'll learn later in the chapter there are benefits to you being involved in setting goals, including performance goals. And it is nothing new to say it is important to align employees' goals with those of the organization, but research underscores the importance of doing so. Companies with effective PM ensure this alignment happens.

- Continually coach. Annual or quarterly reviews fall far short of continual. You'll learn more about feedback later, but even the best feedback is of little value only once a year. You accomplish tasks every day at work, encounter challenges regularly, which means you'd likely benefit from more frequent feedback and coaching.

- Create accountability. Besides being critical to performance, accountability is what gives value to goals and coaching. You'll learn many different ways to hold people accountable throughout this course, and whatever you choose it is important to ensure the means are achievement-oriented, fair and accurate, and developmental.[24]

Johnson and Johnson (J&J), the behemoth consumer products company, tried a more contemporary program in which employees, peers, and bosses used an app to provide real-time feedback. The initial uptake was slow, but when the company offered training to show managers the benefits of effective feedback nearly 50 percent of managers participated and approximately 3,000 pieces of feedback were shared.[25] The new approach was real-time and linked behaviors, outcomes, and feedback, as well as providing numerous and timely opportunities for coaching.

Now that you have a general understanding of the performance management process and its importance, let's take a closer look at how to define performance expectations and goals.

6.2 DEFINE PERFORMANCE— EXPECTATIONS AND GOALS

THE BIGGER PICTURE

Not all goals are the same, and you're about to learn the difference between performance goals and learning goals. More importantly, you'll pick up tips on how to manage the goal-setting process. You'll also benefit from practical guidance on what types of goals to use in particular circumstances.

LO 6-2

Explain how and why goal setting gives you an advantage.

It makes sense that improving goal setting is a way to boost both your own performance and your ability to manage the performance of others. But once again, common sense is not common practice. Let's make this personal. Do you set goals? Do you write them down? Do you revisit and revise them periodically? If you answered yes to all three then you are truly exceptional! But the fact is that even those that consider themselves goal-setters rarely do a good job of it, and the same can be said for organizations.

According to Gallup's "State of the American Manager" report, only 12 percent of employees strongly agreed that their manager helps them set performance goals.[26] To improve your own goal setting, let's begin by differentiating two general types of goals—performance and learning.

Do You Want to Perform or Learn?

One way to organize or differentiate your many goals is to categorize them as performance or learning. **A *performance goal* targets a specific end result, and a *learning goal* promotes enhancing your knowledge or skill.** Managers typically overemphasize the former and ignore the latter as they try to motivate greater effort and achieve results.

If you lack necessary skills, experience, or direction from your manager, then performance goals can be more frustrating than motivating. A performance goal can deflect attention from the discovery of task-relevant capabilities (learning goals); as such it often is helpful to set learning goals first and then set performance goals once you've developed some level of proficiency. Let's illustrate using a tennis analogy.

If a novice tennis player focuses on getting 100 percent of her first serves in (a performance goal), this may prevent her from concentrating on the fundamental elements of an effective serve (learning goals). Both goals are ultimately important, but the novice player must learn how to play the game before becoming concerned about reaching challenging performance outcomes, such as a high first serve percentage and aces.

This insight may also have implications for college graduation rates. The U.S. Department of Education reports that 59 percent and 66 percent of students graduate from public and private institutions, respectively.[27] Of

Learning about and applying goal setting has been shown to improve one's academic achievement.

Edwin Remsberg/Alamy Stock Photo

course, many factors can contribute to these outcomes, but one person factor that could help are students' goal-setting skills. A study of students who were struggling academically demonstrated the power of teaching people how to skillfully set and integrate both learning and performance goals. The students participated in an intensive online tutorial on how to write and achieve personal goals, which led to significant improvement in academic achievement four months later.[28]

What about at work? A study of nearly 900 managers across industries showed those with learning goals performed better at their jobs and were more adaptive to change.[29] You should assume your employer would like you to do both—perform and adapt—and now you know your goals can make the difference.

The lesson? Learn about and apply goal setting to improve your grades at school and your performance at work.

Managing the Goal-Setting Process

There are four general steps to follow when implementing a goal-setting program (for yourself or others). Deficiencies in one step cannot be made up for with strength in the others, which means you need to diligently execute all four steps.

Step A: Set goals.

Step B: Promote goal commitment.

Step C: Provide support and feedback.

Step D: Create action plans.

TABLE 6.1   Guidelines for Writing Smart Goals

Specific	State goals in precise rather than vague terms. For example, I will participate in 20 hours of training this quarter, versus I will do more training this year. Quantify your goals whenever possible.
Measurable	You need to track progress *and* verify whether a goal has been achieved or not. This requires some form of measurement or verification—quantity, quality, completed (yes or no), and other relevant details. If, for instance, the goal is to assess the characteristics of your company's top-performing sales teams, then you likely will need to include both quantitative (sales) and qualitative (methods for building customer relationships) measures. Also be sure to consider the interplay between quantity and quality of output—trade-offs matter.
Attainable	Goals should be realistic, challenging, and attainable. Impossible goals reduce motivation because people do not like to fail. It helps to remember people have different levels of ability and skill, and what is easy and second nature for one person may be very difficult for another.
Results oriented	To focus on desired end results, goals should start with the word *to* followed by verbs such as *complete, acquire, produce, increase,* and *decrease.* Corporate goals should focus on desired end results that support the organization's strategy. In turn, an individual's goals should directly support the accomplishment of corporate goals. Activities that support the achievement of goals are outlined in action plans.
Time bound	Specify target dates for goal completion. Getting a job is an outcome, but there are several sub-goals you must accomplish first. You're more likely to achieve them and get the job if you put dates on the calendar.

SOURCE: Schroedera, Juliana, and Ayelet Fishbachb. "How to Motivate Yourself and Others? Intended and Unintended Consequences." *Research in Organizational Behavior* 35 (2015): 123–41. https://doi.org/10.1016/j.riob.2015.09.001.

Step A: Set Goals   Whether your manager sets your goals for you, or you set them together, the goals should be "SMART." **SMART** **applied to goals is an acronym for** **specific, measurable, attainable, results** oriented, and **time** bound. Goals with these qualities are clearer and more actionable than those that aren't. And when SMART goals are set from the top to the bottom of an organization, it is easier to link employee goals to those at higher levels—the department and organization. This could help you and your colleagues understand how your work and performance affects others, including the strategy of the company.[30] Table 6.1 lists practical guidelines for writing SMART goals.

Step B: Promote Goal Commitment   Goal commitment boosts motivation to achieve any particular goal, and commitment can be increased by ensuring goals are personally relevant, obtainable, and fair. Table 6.2 provides additional practical advice for increasing your goal commitment, while at the same time improving the quality of your goals and boosting your likelihood of success.

Step C: Provide Support and Feedback   This step is about helping employees achieve their goals. (More detail related to feedback is provided later in this chapter.) Practical suggestions include:

- Make sure each employee has the necessary skills and information to reach his or her goals. Provide training if necessary, because it can boost people's expectancy (recall expectancy theory from Chapter 5).

TABLE 6.2   Tips for Increasing Goal Commitment and Success

Write Your Goals Down	You've heard it before, but writing your goals down makes a real difference. The process of writing them helps refine and imprint them in your mind, and it provides a record that you can go back to and revise as you make progress. It is more efficient since you don't have to keep the goals and details in your head.
Identify Key Obstacles and Sources of Support	Be proactive and try to identify who or what might get in your way. Conversely, think of who or what might be able to help you reach your goal.
Ask What's in It for YOU?	List the benefits of achieving the goal, and keeping your eyes on the prize will help you stay motivated over time.
Break It Down	Some goals are big and/or take considerable effort and time to achieve. It is helpful to break them down into smaller, sub- or intermediate goals.
Visualize	If you haven't tried this—it works! Imagine not only how you will benefit by achieving your goal, but also how you will feel. Adding the positive emotional component can boost your motivation.
Organize	Preparation is key. It gives you clarity, makes you more efficient, and helps you avoid wasting energy and time.
Reward Yourself	Reward yourself both for making progress while pursuing your goal and for attaining the ultimate outcome. It is important to reinforce your efforts. Building in small wins and rewards along the way can help motivate you and keep you on track.[31]

- Similarly, pay attention to employees' expectations about their perceived relationship between effort and performance (Chapter 5), their perceived self-efficacy, and their reward preferences, and adjust accordingly.
- Give employees timely and task-specific feedback (knowledge of results from job characteristics in Chapter 5) about what they are doing right and wrong.
- Provide monetary and nonmonetary incentives and be sure to reward meaningful progress—not just goal accomplishment.

Step D: Create Action Plans What use is a goal without a plan for realizing it? For instance, planning the amount of time you intend to devote to training, rather than simply attending a session or doing it when you can, greatly improves the effectiveness of your learning. The same applies to studying—plan your study time and what you will study during that time, and research says you are more likely to stick with it and increase your learning.[32]

The first three steps all help tremendously in formulating your actions plans. Table 6.2 offers additional useful tips. We also encourage you to look to your experience—what's worked in the past when pursuing a similar goal? If you can't rely on your own experience, then learn what others have done and follow their plan. No need to reinvent the wheel. See the nearby OB in Action box to learn how the goal-setting plan worked in a restaurant.

OB in Action

I Need to See Some ID[33]

The owner of two restaurants wanted to help guard against credit card theft as it costs both customers and the business. A simple way of doing this is to ensure cashiers compare IDs with names and and signatures on the credit cards presented by customers. The owner did an experiment and set a compliance goal and an intervention at one restaurant but not the other. Before the experiment began, the baseline ID check rate at both restaurants was about 3 percent. At the target restaurant the manager met with employees, set a 50 percent ID check goal, posted signs next to the registers, and provided a verbal reminder at the beginning of each shift, "let's meet our goal of 50 percent."

The results were remarkable! ID checks rose to nearly 40 percent at the target restaurant and even remained above 30 percent many weeks after the prompts were stopped. The other restaurant without the goal and prompt saw no change in ID checks.

This goal-setting strategy is simple and effective. Put this knowledge to use.

YOUR THOUGHTS?

1. What is a way you could apply this simple goal-setting and prompt intervention to improve your performance at school?

Simply setting goals and offering reminders can have a dramatic impact on behaviors, as happened in the restaurants described in this box.
Chuck Savage/Corbis/Getty Images

2. Why do you think this worked at the restaurant? Why do you think it would work for the personal example you provided in #1?

3. At your current job, or one you had in the past, describe how you or the manager could apply a similar intervention. Be sure to describe desired behavior and both the goal and the prompt or reminder.

Next, visualize what achieving the goal looks like and work backward. This is another instance when the characteristics of SMART goals are extremely valuable. Being specific, results oriented, and time bound are fundamental characteristics of solid action plans. Finally, if you run into difficulties we've already provided you with an excellent tool—the 3-Step Problem-Solving Approach. This can help you identify and remedy roadblocks in your goal setting and action plans.

Applying a contingency approach to goal setting is another way to be more effective and boost performance. Let's explore this next.

Contingency Approach to Defining Performance and Setting Goals

Recall the discussion in Chapter 1 about how effective employees and managers (you!) should use a *contingency approach*. Do what the situation requires rather than applying a one-size-fits-all approach, relying on personal preferences, or doing something "the way it's always been done." Fit the behavior, policy, or practice to the situation. You can apply this same wisdom to goal setting.

Learning and performance goals have their place, and SMART goals can give you a significant advantage over your competitors. However, another way to define goals is in terms of *behavioral, objective,* and *task/project* (see Table 6.3). Defining goals in this manner helps you ensure your goals *match the situation.* For instance, not all performance can or should be defined and measured in dollars and cents.

Once you've clarified expectations and set effective goals, it is necessary to monitor and evaluate your progress and ultimate level of achievement. This is the focus of the next section.

TABLE 6.3   Contingency Approach to Defining Performance

BEHAVIORAL GOALS	OBJECTIVE GOALS	TASK OR PROJECT GOALS
Can be used in most jobs.	Best for jobs with clear and readily measured outcomes.	Best for jobs that are dynamic, but in which nearer-term activities and milestones can be defined.
Most relevant for knowledge work.	Measure what matters, not just what can be measured.	Similar to SMART goals.
Example: Treat others with professionalism and respect; communicate clearly.	Examples: sales quotas, production rates, error rates.	Example: Complete your portion of the team project by Tuesday.

SOURCE: Adapted from M. Schrage, "Reward Your Best Teams, Not Just Star Players," *Harvard Business Review,* June 30, 2015, https://hbr.org/2015/06/reward-your-best-teams-not-just-star-players.

6.3 PERFORMANCE MONITORING AND EVALUATIONS

THE BIGGER PICTURE

To ensure success, you'll need to accurately measure and evaluate both your progress and the ultimate completion of the goals you set in component 1—defining expectations. In this section you'll learn numerous practical tips to help with monitoring and evaluating performance. This includes learning how perceptual errors can influence your evaluation of performance, and why 360-degree feedback is commonly used to help overcome shortcomings in the measurement and evaluation of performance.

LO 6-3

Describe how monitoring and evaluation can improve your performance and ability to manage others.

Once you have defined and communicated performance expectations (goals), you are ready to monitor and evaluate progress and ultimate performance. We emphasize the need to monitor and evaluate *both* progress toward the goal and ultimate level of goal achievement. Doing both instead of simply focusing on the final outcome boosts both motivation and performance.

For instance, at school you prefer to learn how you're performing sometime before your final grade report, such as a midterm exam and/or homework assignments. If the only score you receive and the only time you learn this is on the final, then you have no opportunity to take corrective action and improve the outcome. Moreover, your final exam may not appropriately capture all that you've done throughout the course. Despite this common-sense argument, many, many organizations and entire industries focus only on one final outcome, such as sales target (pharmaceuticals), wins (sports), and rankings (business schools).

This is why accurately and appropriately monitoring and evaluating *both progress and outcomes* are critical components of effective performance management and your personal effectiveness.

Monitoring Performance— Measure Goals Appropriately and Accurately

Monitoring performance means measuring, tracking, or otherwise verifying progress and ultimate outcomes. You use the information gathered through monitoring to identify problems and successes and to find opportunities for enhancing performance during the pursuit of a goal. To be effective, you need to use or even create accurate and appropriate measures. Table 6.3 showed that many goals can be categorized as behavioral, objective, or task-oriented, and the way you measure these goals should match their character.

Final ACADEMIC MARKS						
1st Qtr	2nd Qtr	1st Sem	3rd Qtr	4th Qtr	Fnl Exm	Fnl Mrk
A	A		B+	B		B+
B+	C+		C+	C		C+
B+	B+		B+	B		B+
B	D+		C	C+		C
B+	C		C	C+		C+
B+	C					C+
			B+	B		B
B	B+					B+
			B+	A		B+

Grades are the dominant if not sole way performance is monitored and evaluated at school. Mid-term exams and homework grades are a means for monitoring your progress toward your overall or final grade.

rjp85/E+/Getty Images

Monitoring   Your measurement and monitoring can improve further still if you consider the following (you'll notice some overlap with Table 6.3):

Timeliness. Was the work completed on time? Many customer service roles require representatives to answer calls within a certain number of rings, or to respond to customer requests in a certain number of hours or days.

Quality. How well was the work done? A behavioral goal that could fit here is greeting customers warmly, personally, and with a smile. Measurement consists of observing and/or reporting that these actually occurred.

Quantity. How much? Sales goals are common examples here, such as dollars or number of units sold.

Financial metrics. What are the profits, returns, or other relevant accounting/financial outcomes? For instance, some law firms measure the performance of attorneys and the larger firm by calculating profits in dollars per partner.[34]

Like many other elements of our lives, technology is revolutionizing performance management. Employers can and often do track computer and phone usage, install cameras in most places, and review social media activity. Now, however, employers are capturing employee facial expressions, tone of voice, emotions, location, interactions, and bio/health data, and the list is growing.[35] ***Electronic performance monitoring* (EPM) uses technology to gather, store, analyze, and report employee behavior.**[36] The OB in Action box illustrates some interesting applications and the associated pros and cons.

OB in Action

Monitoring for Performance Becomes More Sophisticated and Pervasive

There was a time when some employers used tape measures to plot the distance and paths nurses followed on their patient rounds in hospitals.[37] Today, such monitoring is done with hardware and software that provides real-time location and activity logs for employees. Patty Jo Toor, the chief nursing officer at Florida Hospital Celebration Health, uses electronic badges to monitor how often nurses and other care providers visit patient rooms.[38] One result was the hospital found it could increase time with patients by stocking more medication on the floors during the night shift, cutting the time nurses had to spend ordering it. In a similar way, United Parcel Service (UPS) has used GPS to make drivers' routes more efficient, saving time, gas, emissions, and money (millions of dollars every year).[39]

Benefits to the Employer Supporters outline a number of benefits, such as reducing theft, improving safety and productivity, and limiting liability. If you're being watched you're less likely to take extra-long or unsanctioned breaks, spend work time shopping online, or tending to your fantasy sports standings. Basically, monitoring ensures you're

doing what you're expected to do, and do the expected things better.[40]

Some companies equip their vehicles with video cameras in case of theft or accidents. Shuttle Express Inc., for example, used dashboard camera video to show that its driver was not at fault in an accident. It saved the company an estimated $100,000.[41]

Most employees would not fault employer monitoring that guards against improper sharing of trade secrets or other proprietary information, but as monitoring becomes more capable and more pervasive we might ask: Just because employers *can* monitor, *should* they, and what are the boundaries?

Costs and Cautions for Employers Dissenters argue such monitoring is demoralizing, unfair, violates privacy, and decreases job satisfaction. And some studies show links between electronic performance monitoring (EPM) and decreased job performance and increased counterproductive work behaviors (CWBs).[42] Still others reveal it increases stress, fatigue, and negative emotions.[43]

Employers also are tracking the time lost to non-work activities. College basketball's March Madness is estimated to cost employers approximately $4 billion In lost productivity,[44] which is due to the nearly 51 million employees who participate in and thus fill out pools, watch, and talk about the games. Consider also Cyber Monday, when nearly half of U.S. workers say they shop online while at work. Great news for the retailers; not so much for other businesses and their managers who suffer the lost productivity.

Individual opinions will vary about each of these, but such constant monitoring has the potential to cause stress, undermine employee morale and trust, and even be the grounds for lawsuits.

One of the early challenges to tracking employees using GPS technology involved Intermex Wire Transfer. Employees were required to download an app to their phones and keep them on 24/7. An employee asked her manager about nonwork hours tracking, and he told her, "yes," the employer would track her both on and off duty. She "likened it to wearing a house arrest bracelet," protested, uninstalled the app, and was fired. She and the company ultimately settled out of court.[45]

YOUR THOUGHTS?

1. Assuming you own your company, make the case for monitoring your employees.

2. If you are working (or have worked), does your employer monitor employees? If yes, describe the costs and benefits to that employer.

3. If your employer does not monitor employees, what type of monitoring might be beneficial from the employer's perspective?

4. Whether you are working or not, describe a type of monitoring that would be useful for your school.

Companies have considerable legal discretion to monitor employees, including for performance, but along with the benefits come challenges. Here are helpful tips to consider when utilizing monitoring for performance at work.

- **Be Transparent.** Explain the what, where, how, and why. Tell employees what is monitored, where, how, and especially why. Justify! The primary motive should be performance improvement. But if guarding against theft is another goal, say so. Employees may raise potential pitfalls you didn't consider. Many negative reactions happen because employees are unaware of the motives and practices.

- **Monitor Only Work.** Make work and nonwork boundaries clear and the ensure both parties abide by them. For instance, do not track employees' locations during nonwork hours.

- **Focus on Development, Not Punishment or Deterrence.** Avoid blocking everything and instead collect, analyze, share, and act on information that contributes to performance. If you're simply monitoring to catch employees doing the wrong things, then you are undermining employee trust and will spur an eternal game of cat and mouse.

- **Make it Fit and Fair.** Be sure monitoring fits particular jobs and situations to the extent necessary and feasible. If some employees' and their jobs require more flexibility and access, then consider this. However, be sure that all employees across levels are expected to comply with policy.[46]

After you've defined your performance goals and monitored them using accurate and appropriate measures, it is time to evaluate the level and/or quality of performance.

Evaluating Performance

Your measures of performance should be both relevant and accurate. There is nothing more discouraging than being measured on criteria that don't matter or not being measured on those that do. *Evaluating performance* **is the process of comparing performance at some point in time to a previously established expectation or goal.** To do this, you obviously need something to compare, which is why measurement or verification is needed in some form.

Your midterm grade, for instance, helps you monitor your performance so far, but it isn't the end of the story. You then evaluate it—did you perform as you expected? Why or why not? How will your midterm performance affect your grade for the course? The answers to these questions are important and are often influenced by your perceptual processes.

As you learned in Chapter 4, your attributions and perceptions can greatly influence the way you evaluate the information you gathered via monitoring. Table 6.4 lists common perceptual errors in monitoring employee performance and recommended solutions.

The best-laid goals can be completely undermined if performance toward them is not measured appropriately, or if performance is evaluated with bias. Many organizations and their managers have tried to overcome such problems using 360-degree feedback.

In *360-degree feedback,* individuals compare perceptions of their own performance with behaviorally specific (and usually anonymous) performance information

TABLE 6.4   Common Perceptual Errors Related to Performance Evaluation

PERCEPTUAL ERROR	TENDENCY	EXAMPLE	RECOMMENDED SOLUTION: KEEP PERFORMANCE NOTES
Halo effect	To form an overall impression about a person or object and then use that impression to bias ratings about same.	Rating an employee positively across all dimensions of performance because the employee is so likable.	Record examples of positive and negative employee performance throughout the year. Remember employee behavior tends to vary across different dimensions of performance.
Leniency	To consistently evaluate other people or objects in an extremely positive fashion.	Rating an employee high on all dimensions of performance regardless of actual performance.	Provide specific examples of both good and poor behavior so you can help the employee improve. Remember it does not help employees when they are given positive but inaccurate feedback. Be fair and realistic in evaluations.
Central tendency	To avoid all extreme judgments and rate people and objects as average or neutral.	Rating an employee as average on all dimensions regardless of actual performance.	Define an accurate profile, with high and low points, so you can help the employee improve. Remember it is normal to provide feedback that contains both positive and negative information.
Recency effect	To over-rely on the most recent information. If it is negative, the person or object is evaluated negatively.	Rating an employee based only on the last portion of the review period.	Accumulate examples of performance over the entire rating period. Remember to look for trends but accept some variance as normal.
Contrast effect	To evaluate people or objects by comparing them with characteristics of recently observed people or objects.	Rating an employee as average, from a comparison of the employee's performance with the exceptional performance of a few top performers.	Evaluate employees against a standard, rather than against the performance of your highest-performing employees. Remember that each employee deserves the objectivity in evaluation that a standard can provide.

from their manager, subordinates, and peers. Such *multi-rater feedback* can also come from outsiders, such as customers or suppliers. These participants can help overcome positive or negative biases due to perceptions or manager-employee relationships.[47]

HCL Technologies, one of India's three largest IT services companies, implements a 360-degree feedback program for the CEO and 3,800 managers. The CEO's reviews are transparent, posted on the company's internal website for all 50,000 employees to see. The managers' results are posted too. Vineet Nayar, the former CEO who created the system, described the system as "reverse accountability," wherein managers are accountable to employees, the opposite of the business norm.[48]

Collecting performance information from multiple sources helps the person being evaluated get a broad view of his or her performance, and it also highlights any biases and perceptual errors that might be occurring. Finally, using multiple raters also makes it much more difficult for managers to unfairly favor or punish particular employees (recall our discussion of equity and fairness in Chapter 5).

A study of 360-degree feedback for 69,000 managers and 750,000 employees revealed fascinating results. Managers *dramatically overrated* their own capabilities—perhaps this is not a surprise. But those who *underrated* their prowess were viewed by employees as the most effective leaders. The underraters also had the most engaged employees (an important individual-level outcome).[49]

Research on 360-degree feedback, combined with your author's consulting experience, leads us to *favor* anonymity and also to *discourage* use of 360-degree feedback for pay and promotion decisions. When it is used for pay and promotions managers often resist and/or try to manipulate the process. However, multi-source feedback can be extremely helpful for training and development purposes.

Now that you have a sense of the importance of monitoring and evaluating performance, as well as tips for doing this accurately, let's move on to the next component and review performance. This includes the critically important and dramatically underutilized skill: feedback.

Vineet Nayar, former CEO of HCL Technologies and world-renowned management expert, believes in realizing employees' full potential. He energetically advocates that organizations put employees first and invest in their development.

Stephane Audras/REA/Redux Pictures

6.4 PERFORMANCE REVIEW, FEEDBACK, AND COACHING

THE BIGGER PICTURE

You're about to learn how different forms of feedback influence performance and how to deliver feedback more effectively. You'll also see how combining feedback with coaching is a powerful means for managing and improving your performance and that of others.

Most people agree that feedback has the potential to boost performance. However, most people also admit that they neither receive nor provide feedback as often or as well as they would like. Forty-seven percent of employees surveyed by Gallup indicated they receive feedback a few times or less per year from their managers, while 19 percent reported receiving it zero times or once (likely in an annual review). This contrasts with the 7 percent who said they receive feedback daily.[50] We'll help you understand some reasons this happens and what you can do about it. It is safe to say your feedback skills are some of the most valuable tools you can develop and use throughout your career. Now let's convince you that this bold statement is true.

What Effective Feedback Is . . . and Is Not

Many if not most students and employees alike appreciate feedback. Both want to know how they're doing and how their performance compares to that of their peers. Feedback is an important, but not always present, cousin of goal setting. It enables you to learn how your performance compares to the goal, which you can then use to modify your behaviors and efforts. We therefore define **feedback as information about individual or collective performance shared with those in a position to improve the situation.**

Effective feedback is only information—it is not an evaluation. Subjective assessments such as "You're lazy" or "You have a bad attitude" do not qualify as effective feedback. They are simply opinions and often have little value. But hard data such as units sold, days absent, dollars saved, projects completed, customers satisfied, and quality rejects are all examples of effective feedback. Christopher Lee, author of *Performance Conversations: An Alternative to Appraisals,* clarifies the concept of feedback by contrasting it with performance appraisals:

> Feedback is the exchange of information about the status and quality of work products. It provides a road map to success. It is used to motivate, support, direct, correct, and regulate work efforts and outcomes. Feedback ensures that the manager and employees are in sync and agree on the standards and expectations of the work to be performed. Traditional appraisals, on the other hand, *discourage* two-way communication and treat employee involvement as a bad thing. Employees are discouraged from participating in a performance review, and when they do, their responses are often considered "rebuttals."[51]

Mike Duke, former president and CEO of Walmart, is a strong advocate of linking goal setting and feedback.

> Leadership is about . . . listening and getting feedback from a broad array of constituents. . . . It's about setting aggressive goals and not being afraid to go after very

aggressive goals and targets. I think it's even better for a leader to set an aggressive goal and come up a little short than it would be to set a soft goal and to exceed it. . . . Hard feedback is in some environments viewed in a very threatening way, and people don't want to hear feedback. In our environment, I think there is a desire to hear candid feedback. When we leave a meeting, before we'll even drive away, I'll ask, "Well, give me feedback." I think a leader asking for feedback sets a good tone.[52]

Clearly, feedback can affect outcomes across levels of the Organizing Framework.

If Feedback Is So Helpful, Why Don't We Get and Give More?

This obvious question is worth answering. After surveying thousands of students and employees, researchers offer the most common responses:

1. **Potential strain on relationships.** It is easy for most people to deliver good news: "Susan, great job on the project. The customer was very pleased, and you made the team look good." However, very few people like to deliver negative feedback (or bad news in general): "Susan, you were ill-prepared and really hurt our chances with that customer." We worry about making the person feel bad and wonder how that person will act in the future because of it. After all, we often make friends at work, we genuinely like many of our coworkers, and we don't want to make them feel bad, make ourselves and others uncomfortable, or harm our relationships.

2. **Too little time.** We're all busy. Even true believers in the value of feedback often let it slide: "This week I plan to talk to Mark about how impressed I am with his fast start at the company." But the week passes and you still haven't done it. Next week. But then that passes too, and so on, and so on.[53]

3. **Lack of confidence.** Very few people are trained to give effective feedback and so lack confidence in their abilities. This problem is compounded if the feedback is going to include negative content and/or will be tied to a performance evaluation. After reading this chapter and book, you won't have such an excuse. You'll be equipped with both knowledge and tools to boost your confidence.

4. **No consequences.** As you'll learn or may already be aware, the trend is toward giving more frequent and considerably different forms of feedback than in the past. However, if managers are not evaluated on whether they provide feedback—effective or not—they are less likely to give it.

With these common obstacles in mind, let's learn how to overcome them and do better, beginning with the two primary functions of feedback—to instruct and to motivate.

Two Functions of Feedback

Experts say feedback serves two functions for those who receive it: one is *instructional* and the other *motivational*. Feedback instructs when it clarifies roles or teaches new behavior. For example, an assistant accountant might be advised to handle a certain entry as a capital item rather than as an expense item. Feedback motivates when it serves as a reward, such as recognition for a job well done, or promises a reward (remember the discussion in Chapter 5). Hearing the boss say, "You've completed the project ahead of schedule; take the rest of the day off," is a pleasant reward for hard work. More generally, however, many employees appreciate the attention and interest expressed by the very act of providing feedback, regardless of content.

Assume you're one of the students learning CPR in the photo. Which type of feedback do you think would be more helpful and you would appreciate more—instructional or motivational? Regardless of your preference, you certainly would agree that both forms would be more effective than the instructor simply saying you did it wrong and that she is

Assume you're one of the students learning CPR in the photo. Which type of feedback do you think would be more helpful and you would appreciate more—instructional or motivational? Regardless of your preference, you certainly would agree that both forms would be more effective than the instructor simply saying you did it wrong and that she is unhappy with your performance. Keep this in mind when you provide feedback to others. Keep it instructional or motivational and you'll keep it appreciated and effective!

Hero Images/Getty Images

unhappy with your performance. Keep this in mind when you provide feedback to others. Keep it instructional or motivational and you'll keep it appreciated and effective!

We also think you'll find this example especially interesting. A study showed that undergraduate students who used peer-to-peer feedback on writing assignments improved the quality and performance of their work. This likely isn't a surprise, but what is notable is that either giving or receiving both resulted in similar improvements. This suggests simply giving feedback can boost your performance.[54]

Important Sources of Feedback—Including Those Often Overlooked

The three common sources of feedback are

1. Others
2. Task
3. Self

It almost goes without saying that you receive feedback from *others* (peers, supervisors, lower-level employees, and customers). Perhaps less obvious is the fact that the *task* itself is a common source of objective feedback. For instance, many tasks—writing code, landing a plane, or driving a golf ball—provide a steady stream of feedback about how well or poorly you are doing. A third source of feedback is *you,* but self-serving bias and other perceptual problems can contaminate this source (recall Chapter 4).

NO SURPRISES!   Whoever conducts a performance review should ensure there are no surprises—good or bad! As a general rule, if you are surprised by something shared during your review, your manager is doing a poor job of managing your performance. It also is a sure sign that he or she is not giving you the appropriate quantity and quality of feedback. Most often such surprises occur in performance management systems structured around an annual review. This means that regardless of how frequently performance information is collected, it is communicated and discussed only once a year.

To avoid surprises in your own reviews, check in with your manager periodically and informally ask, "Is there anything I should be aware of? I know we'll have my review later this year, and I want to be sure there are no surprises . . . even positive ones." If you punctuate your question with a smile it is likely your manager will clearly understand your intent.

The OB in Action box describes the progressive and effective approach to employee feedback at Zappos.

OB in Action

How Do You Spell Feedback and Self-Improvement? Z-A-P-P-O-S!

One of the key elements that enables Zappos to have rock star status with its customers and employees is the company's approach to performance management. The company has led rather than followed trends in PM and puts a premium on feedback, which it sees as fundamental to continuous improvement.

Form of Feedback For starters, the company is largely organized in teams and each with a coach rather than manager. And much like coaches of sports teams, Zappos coaches focus on the development and performance of team members. They rely heavily on instructional feedback, such as how long customers had to wait on hold and what percentage indicated their problem was resolved during a call, rather than evaluative or punitive judgements. Zappos team member Lori Johnson, who has been at Zappos since 2017 and in customer service roles for more than 30 years, described the sessions with coaches as 1-on-1 conversations and 2-way, rather than the conventional manager-subordinate performance meeting. Metrics are used, but not exclusively, and conversations tend to include specific examples of particular behaviors witnessed versus simple numeric ratings.[55]

Linked to Values The nature of the coach-team member conversations, and thus the feedback, are directly linked to the company's 10 core values: deliver WOW through service, embrace and drive change, create fun and a little weirdness, be creative and open-minded, pursue growth and learning, build open and honest relationships with communication, build a positive team and family spirit, do more with less, be passionate and determined, be humble. The company's performance

Zappos employees are not only allowed but encouraged to personalize their workspaces. This aligns with the company's values—create fun and a little weirdness—and is believed to foster excellent customer service.
Ronda Churchill/Bloomberg/Getty Images

management and associated feedback are all driven by and based on these values.[56]

Use and Frequency of Feedback The company long ago abandoned the traditional once-a-year review. Team members, like Ms. Johnson, commonly meet with their coach every couple of weeks to discuss job-related issues in real-time. They also meet once a month more formally to review the trailing three months of performance. She described these as formal only in the sense metrics are pulled and reviewed, but the actual conversation is informal, free-flowing, and a casual back-and-forth. These frequent interactions provide numerous opportunities for feedback and enable desirable behaviors to be recognized and reinforced, as well as take corrective action, as it happens.[57]

Not Meeting Expectations? If someone's performance is not up to standards, the company provides numerous free, on-site courses aimed at skill building and improvement.[58]

YOUR THOUGHTS?

1. What are the advantages to the Zappos approach to feedback?

2. What disadvantages are possible?

3. Explain why you would or would not want to be an employee with such a PM system.

4. Assume you are a manager at a company using a similar approach. What may be the pros and cons of this system for you?

Your Perceptions Matter

Another reason people don't give or get more feedback is that they don't want it. What are your attitudes toward feedback? Do you seek it out? Do you want to hear it only if it is positive? To answer these questions and better understand your desire for feedback, complete Self-Assessment 6.1 and read the following section.

Factors that Affect Your Perceptions of Feedback   Many factors influence the way we perceive feedback. For instance, all managers and employees are susceptible to the fundamental attribution bias (your manager attributes your poor performance entirely to you and things you control) and the self-serving bias (you are likely to take credit for positive performance outcomes and attribute poor performance to extrinsic factors). The following also can influence your perceptions of feedback:

1. *Accuracy.* A common criticism of PM systems is that they measure the wrong things or measure the right things the wrong way. Either way, the feedback is inaccurate.

2. *Credibility of the sources.* If a member of your project team points out shortcomings in your work, you are likely to put more weight on the feedback if he or she is an "A" student or top performer. Trust is critical here too. If you don't trust the person delivering the feedback, you will likely be suspicious of his or her intentions and discount its value.

3. *Fairness of the system.* If you perceive the process or outcomes as unfair—recall equity theory from Chapter 5—you are likely not only to discount the feedback but also to be outraged, withdraw, commit counterproductive work behaviors, and/or quit. Performance appraisals are one of the aspects of organizational life that most commonly reveal issues of fairness.

4. *Performance-reward expectancies.* Effective performance management, particularly ongoing and open feedback between you and your supervisors, is an important means of managing such expectancies.

5. *Reasonableness of the goals or standards.* When it comes to goals, challenging is good, unattainable bad. If your manager says, "You can earn a bonus of up to 50 percent of your salary," ask whether anyone has actually ever earned that much. If not, you may be the first, but more likely the goal is unreasonable.

Any feedback that fails to clear one or more of these cognitive hurdles will be rejected or discounted by the employee.

Negative Feedback   Remember, feedback itself is simply information. It becomes positive or negative only when you compare it to a goal or expectation. Such comparisons are the basis for improvement. (Note: Negative feedback is *not* negative reinforcement. You'll learn the important difference later in this chapter.)

People tend to perceive and recall positive feedback more accurately than they do negative feedback. But negative feedback, such as being told your performance is below average, can have a *positive* motivational effect. One study showed that those who were told they were below average on a creativity test subsequently outperformed those who were led to believe their results were above average. The subjects apparently took the negative feedback as a challenge and set and pursued higher goals. Those receiving positive feedback were less motivated to do better.[59]

However, as you likely know, negative feedback needs to be used with discretion because it is perceived and processed differently. For instance, a study of employees in a company with a transparent peer-review process—each employee knew both the ratings and the associated raters—showed that after receiving negative feedback employees tended to distance themselves from the sources of that feedback, and then "shopped around" for and associated with colleagues who provided positive feedback. As you might expect, some employees had to work with those providing negative feedback, and over time they developed more and richer relationships with members outside of their group. So how do you balance the benefits and costs? The same Harvard researchers suggested the key is in ensuring employees feel valued and they also make positive contributions.[60]

It thus seems research is mixed on negative feedback, but you will undoubtedly receive it throughout your working life. It therefore is a good idea to learn how to deal with it effectively, which is the purpose of the nearby Applying OB box.

Applying OB   CAREER READINESS

Making Lemonade from Lemons—How to Respond to Negative Feedback

Although research is mixed, all of us receive negative feedback, and in most Instances the person providing the feedback has genuinely positive intentions. The goal of course in most instances is to improve your performance, which means your challenge is how to avoid getting defensive or having your self-esteem or self-efficacy crushed. The following tips can help.

1. **Hit the Brakes.** Oftentimes our first reaction is quick and defensive. A better approach is to pause, listen, and then take time to process. When processing it helps to frame it as "what can I learn from this? How was this intended to help me?" It also can help to then think of a positive way you contribute in the same task or relationship.

2. **Confirm.** Don't immediately discount or accept the feedback, but instead seek other unbiased sources. Even if done informally they can help confirm or refute the negative feedback. This is one reason why multi-rater or 360 feedback is so valuable—you can compare. But from whom? It is a good idea to identify a small group of people you trust both to share such information with and hear the truth in return. One executive referred to such people as "loving critics."

3. **Approach and Cultivate, Don't Avoid.** As you learned above, and likely understand, people tend to avoid those who delivered the bad news. But if you're serious about improving your self-awareness and effectiveness, then you need to cultivate relationships with people who will give it to you straight. Try thanking those who provide such Information and ask whether they would mind your following up periodically.

4. **Assess and Own?** In addition to and as a result of the above advice, you may learn some of the negative feedback pertains to individual differences, some of which might be relatively more fixed than others (recall from Chapter 3). In such instances you may communicate to those who provided the feedback, such as that you are not especially likeable, and tell them that their feedback helped raise your awareness. And even though you seem kind of stand-offish, you genuinely like to interact with people. Then, ask for their understanding and help as you work on breaking down and resetting their perceptions.[61]

Negative feedback of course has its place at work. Sometimes it is necessary, but be very careful when using it to avoid doing more harm than good.
Photographee.eu/Shutterstock

Nonetheless, feedback with a negative message or threatening content needs to be administered carefully to avoid creating insecurity and defensiveness. Both negative and positive feedback need to provide clear guidance to improve performance. Feedback is most likely to be perceived accurately, and thus more likely to be acted on, when it is instructional and helps achieve an important or valued outcome.

Table 6.5 lists important and fundamental do's and don'ts for giving feedback. In addition to these, the following tips further improve your feedback skills and provide pointers on how to deliver it:

1. **Reflect.** Before giving feedback you are well served to identify what change you want to see, what is the context or experiences of the target person (person or situation factors influencing his or her performance), and whose needs you are meeting by giving the feedback. Answering these three questions helps clarify your motives and intended outcomes.

2. **Cultivate Trust.** By reflecting on and sharing the information in #1, you will help the receiver understand your intentions are for her or his development. You might say, for instance, "I know you want to be the number one performer and get promoted, and I would like to offer some feedback that might help."

3. **Be Action-Oriented.** Sharing information isn't the end. Feedback is more effective if it is accompanied by suggested actions.[62] When done in this way, providing feedback is a form of problem-solving—what is the problem, likely causes, accompanied by recommended actions.

TABLE 6.5 Feedback Do's and Don'ts

DON'T[63]	DO[64]
Don't use feedback to punish, embarrass, or put someone down.	Keep feedback relevant by relating it to existing goals.
Don't provide feedback that is irrelevant to the person's work.	Deliver feedback as close as possible to the time the behavior was performed.
Don't provide feedback too late to do any good.	Provide specific and descriptive feedback.
Don't provide feedback about something beyond the individual's control	Focus the feedback on things employees can control.
Don't provide feedback that is overly complex or difficult to understand.	Be honest, developmental, and constructive.

Today's Trends in Feedback

Like PM more generally, feedback is becoming more informal, continual, and inclusive. It also is increasingly taking place between other employees and not just between managers and subordinates. These new developments hold the promise of making feedback truly more developmental and effective.

It is worth noting, however, that another trend is for direct if not also critical feedback. Netflix, for instance, is practicing what is called "radical transparency" in feedback and other elements of its operations. Most generally, says CEO Reed Hastings, the intent is to get employee input and feedback in every aspect of the company. Performance evaluations are one example and are visible to all employees, and salary information for all employees is available to approximately 500 employees at the director level and above. But that's not all. Constant and even blunt feedback is encouraged—employees should always be looking for and offering ways to improve. The "keeper test" is one especially interesting example of direct feedback. Managers are expected to ask themselves when evaluating employees: Would I keep this person? Would I fight to have them on my team?[65]

Just as feedback practices are evolving in PM, so too are those related to coaching.[66]

Coaching—Turning Feedback into Change

Coaching **is a customized process between two or more people with the intent of enhancing learning and motivating change.** Coaching can occur at any component in the PM process, but it most often follows the review and consequences of performance.

One way to look at coaching is that it is an individualized and customized form of PM. It is different from training, which typically consists only of skill

Donna Morris, Chief Human Resource Officer & Executive Vice President of Employee Experience at Adobe Systems, spearheaded a dramatic transformation in the way her company manages performance. Regular "check-ins" and "snapshots" are mini and continual opportunities to provide and receive feedback.

building with the same content delivered to a group of people. It differs from mentoring, which typically has a career rather than a performance focus and most often flows from more senior to more junior employees. All these processes differ from counseling, which usually aims to overcome a problem, conflict, or dysfunctional behavior.[67]

With these differences in mind, effective coaching is developmental, has specific performance goals, and typically includes considerable self-reflection, self-assessment, and feedback. In fact, "research from Gallup, McKinsey, and Harvard recommends that giving feedback should be the most used tool in a coach's toolbox."[68] Research shows employees who received continual development conversations with their managers were nearly three times more likely to be engaged at work! This reinforces volumes of studies which show goal setting to be more effective when it is accompanied by continue coaching related to progress monitoring and feedback.[69]

Some venture capitalists see the benefits of coaching. Felicis Ventures, a VC firm founded by a former Google employee, is changing venture capital by investing 1 percent of the money invested into the coaching and mental health of the founders of the firms in which they invest. The firm realizes the founders and other leaders of startups are both underskilled and overstressed, and by helping in both areas they are increasing the chances for their investments to perform.[70] You too can be a more effective coach by applying the advice in the nearby Applying OB box.

Felicis Ventures is changing venture capital by investing in the coaching and mental health of the founders of the firms in which they invest.

Peter DaSilva/The New York Times/Redux Pictures

Applying OB

An "F" in Coaching Signals Success

We're not talking grades, but instead some fundamental elements to practice when coaching others: frequency, focus, and future orientation.[71]

Frequent. Consistent with trends in PM, the most effective coaches engage others regularly, whether it be face-to-face, e-mail, phone, text, video conferences, etc. The point isn't so much the channel but the frequency. Although the appropriate frequency is contingent on many person and situation factors, research by Gallup suggests that at least once a week is a good goal. And remember, feedback does not need to be formal. Check-ins can work: "How are you doing today?" "What worked well in the presentation or meeting?" Simple encouragement or recognition works too.

Focused. Frequency can allow communications to wander, so be sure to stay on point. It thus helps to identify and assign specific tasks and priorities. Outlining purposes and outcomes is a good place to start; however, coaching is most effective when it is a two-way street. Try not to tell and prescribe, but to discuss, identify, and recommend—problem solve collaboratively.

Future-Oriented. At the heart of coaching is development, and development is all about improving for the future. Therefore, beware of focusing too much on past performance and instead spend most of your efforts on what to do going forward. Think of coaches in sports. They of course use past games and matches for learning, but most of the attention is on improving skills and performance for the next competition. Be sure your coaching does the same.

The Self-Assessments throughout this book can serve as important elements for your own coaching, helping you identify your development opportunities.[72] When coaching is approached in this way, it is not only an important aspect of effective performance management, but it is also consistent with positive organizational behavior (Chapter 7). Consider this: If coaching is done in the way described, who wouldn't appreciate or benefit from it?

6.5 PROVIDING REWARDS AND OTHER CONSEQUENCES

THE BIGGER PICTURE

You of course like being rewarded, but some rewards are more effective than others. Next, you'll learn common types of rewards and the potential outcomes of specific reward systems. You'll see how organizations use various criteria, such as results and behaviors, to distribute rewards, as well as why rewards can fail to motivate as intended.

LO 6-5

Implement rewards to generate desired outcomes.

Rewards are a critical component of performance management, and just as particular motivational approaches affect people differently, so do rewards. Some employees see their job as the source of a paycheck and little else. Others derive great pleasure from their job and association with coworkers. Even volunteers who donate their time to charitable organizations, such as Habitat for Humanity, walk away with rewards in the form of social recognition and having done something meaningful for themselves and impactful to others. Hence, the subject of organizational rewards includes but goes far beyond monetary compensation. We begin by outlining key factors of organizational reward systems.

Key Factors in Organizational Rewards

Despite the fact that reward systems vary widely, they do share some common components. The model in Figure 6.3 diagrams the relationship of three components:

1. Types of rewards
2. Distribution criteria
3. Desired outcomes

Let us examine these components and then discuss pay for performance.

Types of Rewards

Financial, material, and social rewards qualify as *extrinsic rewards* because they come from the environment. Psychic rewards, however, are *intrinsic rewards* because they are self-granted. If you work primarily to obtain rewards such as money or status, you are extrinsically motivated. If you derive your primary reward from the task itself, or the feeling that your work is meaningful and gives you a sense of responsibility, then you are motivated by intrinsic rewards (recall extrinsic and intrinsic motivation from Chapter 5).

Responders to the devastating 2018 Camp Fire in Butte County, California, certainly had a difficult job to do. For firefighters, police, medical, and other emergency personnel, such work is their occupation, which means they have formal responsibilities and are paid. However, it was clear that many of them were motivated by and received intrinsic rewards far beyond pay. They were saving their own homes and communities, and like the many volunteers, they were saving lives.

The relative importance of extrinsic and intrinsic rewards is a matter of culture and personal preferences, so it is critically

Thankfully for all of us, many people perform their jobs for reasons other than money and other extrinsic rewards. Some of the best examples are first responders to disasters who do more than simply "punch the clock."

Justin Sullivan/Getty Images

FIGURE 6.3   Key Factors in Organizational Reward Systems

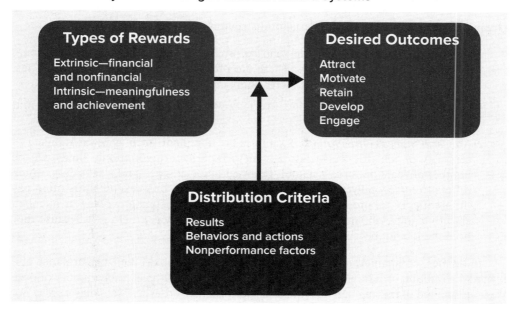

important to know what types of rewards you and others value most. This knowledge can make the difference in your getting what you want personally, as well as in your ability to effectively manage others. It can also assist you in identifying employers with whom you fit.[73]

For example, if you're hard-charging, a high income is very important to you, and you like to be rewarded based on your own efforts, then it would be advisable to look for companies whose reward systems align with these preferences. You also can use your self-knowledge to "manage up." The author of this book routinely told his managers shortly after he was hired which of the rewards available for that particular job he valued most. This helped his managers choose and provide rewards that would have the most positive impact.

Kaiser Permanente, an integrated health care system in California, is opening its own medical school in 2020. To attract high caliber students and encourage them not to avoid relatively low-paying specialties (family medicine and pediatrics), it is not charging tuition for students in the first five years. These motives and actions are similar to those of New York University and Columbia's medical schools, which also are eliminating tuition for their students. These are extremely valuable, as the median debt for medical school graduates in 2017 was just under $200,000. And it seems to be working. NYU reported overall med school applications increased 47 percent, and those from applicants who identified as black increased 142 percent![74]

Self-Assessment 6.2 will help you identify the rewards you value most and show you what a survey of employees revealed they valued most.

SELF-ASSESSMENT 6.2   CAREER READINESS

What Rewards Do I Value Most?

Please be prepared to answer these questions if your instructor has assigned Self-Assessment 6.2 in Connect.

1. Were your perceptions accurate? Why or why not?

2. What would Vroom's expectancy theory (covered in Chapter 5) suggest you should do?

3. Would you generalize the actual survey results to all nonmanagerial employees? Why or why not?

Distribution Criteria

Organizations use three general criteria for distributing rewards:

- *Results.* Tangible results include quantity produced, quality, and individual, group, or organizational performance. These are often accounting-type measures—sales, profit, or error rate. Employers increasingly include customer satisfaction.

- *Behavior and actions.* Examples are teamwork, cooperation, risk taking, and creativity.

- *Nonperformance considerations.* Examples are abundant, such as rewards linked to seniority or job title. Associate attorneys' salaries are commonly linked to the number of years out of law school—first-year associates get paid a set salary, which differs from second-year associates, and so on. Night or weekend shifts often pay differently. Perks provided to executives, like use of a company plane or membership to a golf club, are nonperformance rewards. They get them just because they hold the job not because of what they do.

Industries, companies, and jobs all differ, and so too should their performance and reward-distribution criteria. Many Internet companies, for example, track number of page views, registered users, and app downloads as performance criteria. These may or may not be relevant to individual employee, team, or organizational performance. Netscape founder, and now legendary tech investor, Marc Andreessen is leading a charge to do away with what he calls "vanity" or "bull#$!% metrics." He argues that many common metrics are meaningless and don't capture performance. "Download counts can easily be inflated if an app developer is willing to pay."[75]

Digital and social media companies therefore have struggled to develop and utilize effective PM metrics, which are necessary to gauge performance and allocate rewards. Some examples for marketing via digital and social media are:

- Reach and Impressions. Reach is the number of different people who view your post, while impressions are the number of times a given person views it. Think of it as breadth and depth.

- Platform Engagement. This can be likes, retweets, shares, comments, etc.

- Conversions. Of those that click or view how many actually take action, such as buy your product. This is an obvious way for many to measure return on investment (ROI) for investments in online advertising.

- Relevancy Score. This is used to compare or test the relative interest of one potential customer to others. You essentially present the same ad content to multiple customer groups, perhaps via different channels, and then focus your future resources on the one that showed the greatest interest.[76]

In sum, effective PM includes measures, rewards, and distribution criteria that are linked.[77]

Desired Outcomes of the Reward System

As Figure 6.3 showed, a good reward system should not only attract and motivate talented people, but it should also foster development and keep talented people from leaving. A prime example is Tulsa-based QuikTrip, a gas station and convenience store chain. Good employee wages and benefits, training, and a friendly and supportive culture result in an annual turnover rate of just 13 percent. The industry average is 59 percent! An employee was quoted as saying, "We actually have to open new markets to create movement to give our employees an opportunity to advance because no one leaves."[78]

The Applying OB box addresses the important topic of rewards and teams.

Put the "I" in Team with Appropriate Incentives

Many companies and leaders trumpet the importance of teamwork—we win or lose together. Yet most of these same companies reward individuals and not teams. Such inconsistencies undermine teamwork and the effectiveness of PM. If teamwork is truly important, then the following recommendations can ensure that PM practices send consistent signals.

1. *Split 50-50.* Awards, bonuses, and recognition should be split evenly. If there is an employee of the year, then be sure to have a team of the year. If money is allocated too, be sure teams and individuals get the same.

2. *Acknowledge assistance.* Don't take team members' help for granted. The supporting cast needs to be explicitly recognized.

3. *Show enthusiasm and fanfare.* Be sure energy and attention for team incentives matches that for individuals.

4. *Measure both!* If teams are indeed valuable, create and utilize effective means for measuring team performance, just as you do for individuals.

Be Sure You Get the Outcomes You Desire

Rewards come in many forms, both financial and nonfinancial. But most fundamentally rewards are exchanges—you are given this for doing that. At work you may be paid a cash bonus or your commission rate may increase for performing above and beyond your sales quota. While you are at school professors sometimes give you extra credit for doing well in an assignment or course. But whatever the case, whoever provides the reward should get what is desired or intended in exchange. There are three potential outcomes from rewards:

1. *Desired outcome.* You get more of what you intended and for which you are rewarding people.

2. *Nothing.* The reward can have no effect.

3. *Undesired side effects.* Rewards reinforce or motivate the wrong behaviors.

For example, doctors and hospitals in the U.S. health care system have historically been compensated for the services they provide. This means providers make more money when they run more tests and provide more treatments—postoperative infections and procedure-related strokes are on average twice as profitable as cases that go smoothly. A study by Harvard Medical School, Bain Consulting Group, and Texas Health Systems found:

> Private-insurance and Medicare payments soared when surgeries went awry, outpacing extra treatment costs. In one example, a complication during an intestinal surgery . . . could lead to an intensive care stay, boosting payments five-fold. . . . On average, procedures with complications netted $15,700 versus $7,600 for procedures that went well.[79]

People should get paid for their expertise and work. But performance management is part of both the cause and the solution to this enormous challenge. This example illustrates how the distribution of rewards can be both an input and a process in the Organizing Framework.

The takeaway: Be sure your performance management system and associated rewards produce the desired outcomes and be mindful of undesirable side effects.

Total and Alternative Rewards

Historically, rewards programs were simply a matter of combining compensation with some mix of health insurance and vacation time. These of course still matter, but today leading organizations are offering far more complex and personalized packages.[80] Besides the usual paycheck, the variety and magnitude of organizational rewards have evolved into a mind-boggling array, such as fertility services, child adoption assistance, college tuition reimbursement, college loan repayment, stock grants and options, and pet insurance. All these are extrinsic rewards, and it is common for nonwage benefits to be 50 percent or more of total compensation.

The current and broader perspective on compensation is referred to as "total rewards." **Total rewards encompass not only compensation and benefits, but also personal and professional growth opportunities and a motivating work environment that includes recognition, job design, and work–life balance.** Table 6.6 lists and describes the key components of a total rewards perspective.

This broader view of rewards has grown partly in reaction to stiffer competition and challenging economic conditions, which have made it difficult for cost-conscious organizations to offer higher wages and more benefits each year. Employers have had to find alternative forms of rewards that cost less but still motivate employees to excel.

Fortune's 100 Best Places to Work list provides a treasure trove of some of the most generous and interesting awards currently offered. Biotech giant Genentech was number one in the salary category in 2019 at $205,000 per year (up from $180,000 in 2018). This is far ahead of number two in the salary category, Atlassian, a software developer, and the most valuable tech firm in Australia, which pays an average of $167,000. Although that kind of money is certainly appealing, enterprise software company Work-Day (#4 in 2019) is quite creative with alternative rewards. They provide unlimited time off and onsite manicures, bike repairs, and car washes. And Wegman's Food Markets, a grocery store chain and #3 on *Fortune*'s list of Best Places to Work, spent $50 million on employee development, $5 million on scholarships, and filled half of its open jobs internally. Baptist Health South Florida also was a clear believer in employee development opportunities, as they filled 75 percent of their leadership positions with internal candidates.[82] See the OB in Action box for an especially generous and long-term performance-oriented plan at Hilcorp.

TABLE 6.6 Components of a Total Rewards Perspective[81]

COMPONENT	DESCRIPTION
Compensation	Base pay, merit pay, incentives, promotions, and pay increases
Benefits	Health and wellness care, savings and retirement planning, and paid time off
Work–life effectiveness	Policies and practices to help employees thrive at work and home
Recognition	Formal and informal programs that acknowledge employee efforts and behaviors that support the organization's strategies and objectives
Talent development	Training, career development, and other support necessary to improve performance and advance careers

OB in Action

Hilcorp is the largest independent energy exploration and production company in the U.S. One of the company's core values is alignment. "When Hilcorp wins, we all win" is how they state it on their website.[84] The company certainly seems to walk the talk when it comes to compensation. CEO Greg Lalicker describes it this way, "We want it to be in everybody's best interest that Hilcorp succeeds and, when we do succeed, that everybody shares the rewards equitably."[85] Sounds like he took this OB course.

Goal Alignment The company sets goals over periods of five years, and oil exploration and production projects typically occur over the course of years. And if the company meets those targets everybody is compensated very generously. For instance, from 2006 to 2011, the goal was to double production from 40,000 barrels per day to 80,000, reserves from 125 million to 250 million, and double the value of the business from $1 billion to $2 billion. Hilcorp met all of these targets!

Perhaps the only thing more impressive than doubling these key performance metrics were the associated rewards. Every employee received $50,000 to spend on a car. When the company met the goals for 2011 to 2015 each employee received $100,000 cash to spend how they wish. The rewards are prorated for employees not at Hilcorp the entire period.

And That's Not All Besides production goals, Hilcorp rewards employees with annual bonuses up to 60 percent of an employee's salary which are linked to overall company performance, measured with production rate, midstream income, operating costs, and reserves.

Since safety is so fundamentally important In many industries, especially oil and gas production, you'd think the company would provide incentives or bonuses linked to this. Nope. When asked about this Mr. Lalicker said, "Safety is a requirement, not an upside. If people aren't working hard to operate safely, then they are fired."

YOUR THOUGHTS?

1. Describe three benefits of the reward practices at Hilcorp. Explain not only the benefit but how or why it works.

2. What are the downsides or potential challenges with this program's emphasis on organization-level rewards?

3. Assume you are a founder and CEO of Hilcorp, what you would you do when individual employees don't perform in this system? Describe and justify your actions.

Bottom line: The most effective reward programs tend to align with employee preferences. But we know that rewards often don't work as intended—let's explore why and what to do about it.

Why Rewards Often Fail and How to Boost Their Effectiveness

Here are some of the reasons rewards often fail to motivate.

1. Too much emphasis on monetary rewards.
2. Sense in recipient that extensive benefits are entitlements.
3. Fostering of counterproductive behavior (as discussed in Chapter 2).
4. Long delay between performance and reward.
5. One-size-fits-all rewards.
6. Use of one-shot rewards with short-lived motivational impact.
7. Continued use of demotivating practices such as layoffs, across-the-board raises and cuts, and excessive executive compensation.[86]

One way to use these findings is as a checklist and determine to what extent your employer's, or another company's, practices suffer from these shortcomings. Then apply your new knowledge and help ensure that managers and employers get more for their reward bucks!

How to Boost the Effectiveness of Rewards One means for improving the effectiveness of almost any reward system is to involve employees in devising the system. Recall the discussion of motivation and procedural justice in Chapter 5. Including employees in the design, selection, and assessment of rewards programs increases the chance employees will perceive the rewards as fair and valuable. (Valuable rewards are the valence outcomes in expectancy theory from Chapter 5.) Involvement also fosters employee engagement—discussed in Chapter 2—because it makes them feel valued.

A major and common problem with rewards is they don't always work as intended. The Problem-Solving Application provides an excellent example and opportunity to apply your knowledge and build your skill.

Problem-Solving Application

Incentives, Performance, and Schools

Like organizations in other industries, the Houston Independent School District (HISD) believed it could direct, motivate, and improve performance with monetary rewards. The goal was to improve the skills and test scores of students at 40 underperforming schools.

Officials thought the underlying reasons for the underperformance were low performing teachers, as those at the target schools were twice as likely to be rated "ineffective" or "needs improvement" than in well-performing schools. Worse still, teachers at these same schools were half as likely to be rated "highly effective." School district leaders reasoned that offering money—$5000 signing bonuses—would attract better teachers to the poor performing schools.

Officials spent nearly $7 million to incentivize highly rated teachers to move to the target schools in the 2017–18 school year, and they planned to spend a similar amount in 2018–2019. But there was a problem—it didn't work. The 40 schools experienced tremendous turnover—40–60 percent of teachers at worst schools quit—but the teachers who replaced them had nearly identical (poor) ratings when they arrived.

This left officials scratching their heads. The dismal results might have been due to the fact they had no performance criteria for teachers to qualify for the bonus and move to one of the 40 schools. Moving to the worst performing schools could be perceived as very risky, as highly rated teachers' performance could drop in a more challenging, underperforming school. Adding to the risk, some teachers would presumably be giving up a position at a "better" school. Of course, it also was possible $5000 just wasn't enough for many.[87]

Apply the 3-Step Problem-Solving Approach

Step 1: Define the problem HISD officials wanted to fix.

Step 2: Identify the potential causes of this problem. (Consider also the common reasons rewards fail to motivate.)

Step 3: Make your recommendations.

Pay for Performance

Pay for performance **comprises merit and/or bonus pay based on individual-, group-, or organization-level measures and involving individual, group, or organization rewards.**[88] Therefore, it is compensation above and beyond basic wages and salary, and its use is consistent with the expectancy theory of motivation.[89]

Most often pay for performance is referred to as *variable pay* because it most depends or varies based on some behavior or outcome, and variable pay has grown as a percentage of total compensation for decades. PayScale's Compensation Best Practices Report of 2018 revealed 71 percent of companies surveyed used some form of variable pay, and 79 percent of companies considered top-performing did.[90] This means that over the course of your career an increasing portion of your pay will be variable.

Pay for performance is used to align employees' interests and behaviors with those of the department and organization, as it links your behaviors and outcomes to objectives or goals at some level.[91] Figure 6.4 outlines the most commonly used types today, along with the frequency of use according to size and type of company, and Figure 6.5 displays the most common variable pay by job type.

FIGURE 6.4   **Different Types of Variable Pay and Percentage and Size of Company That Uses Each**[92]

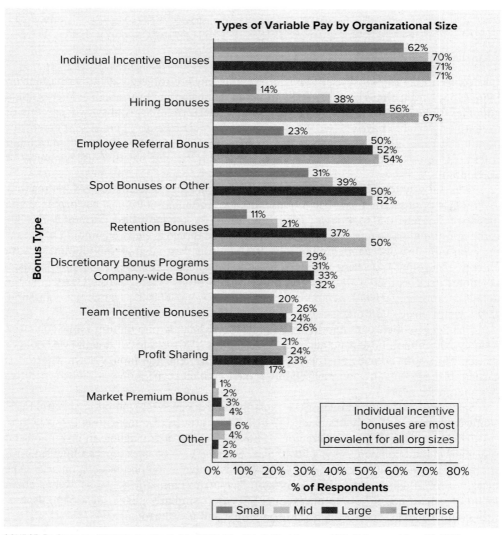

SOURCE: PayScale, Inc. "Variable Pay Trends into 2018: Who Gets It, What Types and Why?" Accessed June 14, 2019. https://www.payscale.com/compensation-today/2018/04/variable-pay-trends.

FIGURE 6.5 Variable Pay by Type and Organizational Level

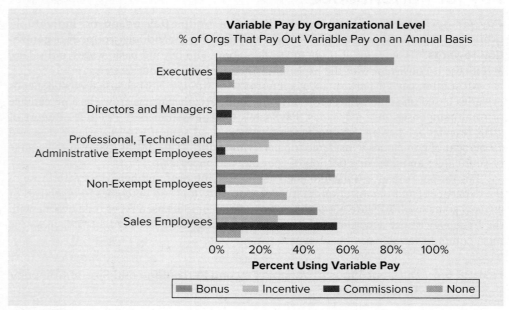

SOURCE: PayScale, Inc. "Variable Pay Trends into 2018: Who Gets It, What Types and Why?" Accessed June 14, 2019. https://www.payscale.com/compensation-today/2018/04/variable-pay-trends.

You'll notice the most used types of variable pay are targeted at individual performance, but as you climb in the organization and manage others variable pay increasingly becomes linked to team and organization-level performance. Eighty-two percent of executives' variable pay is based on organizational performance, versus 43 percent for nonmanagers. It also is more common for certain types of roles. Sales and management roles are more likely to have outcomes appropriate for variable pay than are engineers or accountants.[93]

A useful way to differentiate between types of pay for performance is whether they reward past or future performance. Bonuses are most often given for past performance and incentives are intended to motivate future performance. The most basic form of bonus pay is the traditional piece-rate plan, wherein an employee is paid a specified amount of money for each unit of work. Many online jobs are paid this way, such as the amount of data entered, recordings transcribed, or customer service calls taken.[94] Freelancer, for instance, promotes itself as the "world's largest online platform for finding jobs." Users post the details of work they want done and others bid on the work. This is a classic but contemporary form of piece-rate work.[95]

Girl Scout cookies are another example. Approximately one million Girl Scouts sell roughly 200 million boxes and generate $776 million. This is a lot of dough (we couldn't resist). Thin mint cookies are the perennial top seller, and the money stays where it is earned. If the Scouts in your area sell more, their council keeps more for their own activities and projects.[96]

Sales commissions are one of the most popular incentives, wherein a specified percentage or amount of money is paid for particular or groups of transactions.

Jen Tadin, National Sales Director for Small Business at Gallagher, an insurance and risk management company, uses a 60-40 plan. Sixty percent of sales rep's compensation is guaranteed in the form of salary, and 40 percent is available in commissions on sales. She takes it a step further and links commission payouts to company goals, as well as client retention, client count, and total revenue. Microsoft similarly aligns sales commissions with company goals, specifically cloud computing and new customers.[97]

A word of caution regarding sales incentives is offered by Jason Jordan, of Vantage Point Performance (sales consulting and coaching). Effective incentives should do two

Selling Girl Scout cookies is a famous form of piece-rate work. Each year Girl Scouts sell approximately 200 million boxes and take in $776 million.

Andy Matsko/AP Images

things: motivate the right behaviors and reward successful outcomes. Too often leadership designs incentive plans to do a third thing: discourage bad behaviors. Sales incentives cannot take the place of sales management, so don't try to use them as 'managers in absentia.'"[98]

Making Pay for Performance Work

As we've done throughout the book, we use research and practice to guide your learning. Research shows mixed results for pay for performance—sometimes it increases performance as intended, other times not, and like other rewards sometimes it creates undesirable outcomes. For instance, executives and the organizations they lead are increasingly expected to deliver not only financial performance but also corporate social performance. The little research that exists shows that simply setting social goals for executives is not enough to improve the organization's social performance outcomes. However, if the targets are quantifiable (target percentage, amount, or other clear measures) and linked to compensation, then social performance tends to improve.[99] Although the researchers did not examine this directly, it seems that making these goals SMART makes a difference.

Companies with the best pay-for-performance results tend to:

- Pay top performers substantially more than their other employees.
- Reduce "gaming" of the system by increasing transparency.
- Utilize multiple measures of performance.
- Calibrate performance measures to ensure accuracy and consistency.[100]

Most experts agree it is critically important to ensure pay for performance practices fit the situation and align with the organization's strategy and culture.[101]

Now let's learn the mechanisms by which rewards change our behavior, along with how and when they are administered can make a difference.

6.6 REINFORCEMENT AND CONSEQUENCES

THE BIGGER PICTURE

In this section, you'll learn about three especially effective and practical means for influencing your behavior and that of others: (1) the law of effect and the way it relates to respondent and operant conditioning; (2) common types of reinforcement; and (3) the way managers can increase the effectiveness of reinforcement using a variety of reinforcement schedules.

LO 6-6

Use reinforcement and consequences to improve performance.

Providing consequences is the last component of the performance management process, and the way rewards and consequences more generally are administered can make or break performance management efforts. Effective use of these OB tools is particularly important given that pay raises and promotions are often powerful career outcomes in the Organizing Framework. They often influence perceptions of fairness, intentions of quitting, emotions, and a range of behaviors at work. For instance, have you ever worked your butt off and gotten results, yet neither your effort nor performance were acknowledged? Have you ever witnessed a colleague, teammate, or friend be rewarded handsomely when you think they didn't deserve it? The answer to both questions is undoubtedly "yes," and as you thus know the resulting impact on your motivation and future performance can be significant and negative.

To help you understand and use consequences effectively, we begin with behavior modification and reinforcement techniques.

The Law of Effect—Linking Consequences and Behaviors

In the early 1900s psychologist Edward L. Thorndike observed in his lab that a cat would behave randomly when placed in a small box with a secret trip lever that opened a door. However, once the cat had accidentally tripped the lever and escaped, it would go straight to the lever when placed back in the box. This observation led to Thorndike's now famous *law of effect,* **which says behavior with favorable consequences tends to be repeated, and behavior with unfavorable consequences tends to disappear.**[102] This was a dramatic departure from previous notions that behavior was the product of instincts.

Using Reinforcement to Condition Behavior

B. F. Skinner refined Thorndike's work and developed what came to be known as *behaviorism* as he dealt strictly with observable behavior. He believed it was pointless to explain behavior in terms of unobservable inner states, such as needs, drives, attitudes, or thought processes. He instead drew an important distinction between two types of behavior: respondent and operant behavior.[103]

Respondent behavior **describes automatic reactions to stimuli, or stimulus-response (S-R),** like when you are startled by an unexpected loud noise or yank your hand from a hot surface. These behaviors are obviously important, but not nearly as common and consequential as *operant behavior,* **behaviors that are learned and occur when we "operate on" the environment to produce desired consequences.** It can be helpful to think of this as *response-stimulus (R-S) model* or *operant conditioning*, as it describes things we do to generate desired behaviors and are the essence of much of OB.

Contingent Consequences

According to Skinner's operant theory, contingent consequences control behavior in one of four ways:

1. Positive reinforcement.
2. Negative reinforcement.
3. Punishment.
4. Extinction.

Of critical importance is the term *contingent*, which means there is a purposeful if-then link between the target behavior and the consequence. You therefore should first think of the target behavior and whether you want to increase or decrease it, and then choose the appropriate consequence (see Figure 6.6). We next look more closely at the four types of consequences.

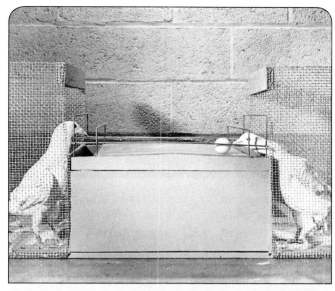

B. F. Skinner taught pigeons how to pace figure eights and how to bowl by reinforcing the underweight (and thus hungry) birds with food whenever they more closely approximated target behaviors.
Bettmann/Getty Images

Increase Desired Behaviors *Positive reinforcement* **is the process of strengthening a behavior by contingently presenting something appealing.** A behavior is strengthened when it increases in frequency and weakened when it decreases in frequency. An excellent example comes from BP in the years immediately following the horrific Deep Water Horizon oil spill in the Gulf of Mexico. Newly appointed CEO Bob Dudley based 100 percent of employees' variable pay (bonuses) on safety for the fourth quarter of 2010.[104] This was a reward or reinforcer for safe behaviors—better safety, more money.

Negative reinforcement **also strengthens a desired behavior by contingently withdrawing something displeasing.** Many probationary periods for new hires are applications of negative reinforcement. During probation periods, often your first 30, 60, or 90 days on a new job, you need to have weekly meetings with your boss or have somebody sign off on your work. Once you've demonstrated your skill these requirements are removed.

FIGURE 6.6   Contingent Consequences in Operant Conditioning

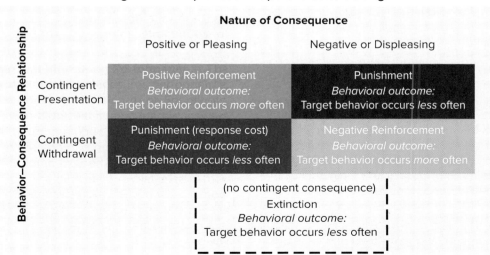

Unfortunately, most people confuse *negative reinforcement* with *negative feedback,* which is a form of punishment. Negative reinforcement, as the word *reinforcement* indicates, *strengthens a desirable behavior* because it provides relief from something undesirable (paperwork, meetings, or yelling).

Decrease Undesired Behaviors **Punishment is the process of weakening behavior through either the contingent presentation of something displeasing or the contingent withdrawal of something positive.** The U.S. Department of Transportation now fines airlines up to $27,500 per passenger for planes left on the tarmac for more than three hours. This policy reduced reported cases from 535 to 12 in the first year it was implemented.[105] Similarly, Allegiant Airlines was fined $225,000 for not keeping their planes cool enough during tarmac delays.[106]

However, remember the possibility of unintended consequences mentioned earlier. A study of the tarmac delay rule found it resulted in more cancelled flights, as airlines tried to avoid fines. This of course requires passengers to find another flight costing even more time.[107]

Approximately 51 percent of employers providing health insurance use money to motivate employees to participate in wellness programs and health screening. For instance, a form of negative reinforcement commonly used is the reduction of insurance premiums for employees who participate. You'd rather not pay insurance premiums, which means reducing premiums when you participate (get healthy) is contingently removing or limiting those undesirable payments.[108] Figure 6.7 shows the percentage of employers that offer various types of incentives for health exams.

Be sure to remember punishment needs to be used sparingly and wisely. Perceptual errors and biases you've learned about in previous chapters also apply to punishment. Specifically:

1. Negative events are far more impactful on people than positive events. People typically exert more energy to avoid losses and negative events than they do to receive positive outcomes.

FIGURE 6.7

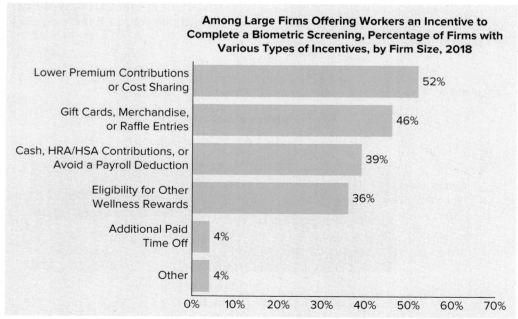

SOURCE: Kaiser Family Foundation. "2018 Employer Health Benefits Survey." Accessed June 14, 2019. https://www.kff.org/report-section/2018-employer-health-benefits-survey-summary-of-findings/.

2. Negative events stick with us much longer than positive events. This means you are likely to remember and be affected by punishment (demotion) or negative feedback (poor performance review) much longer than a promotion or positive review.

3. Punishment is more likely to be informal, unless of course you are put on a performance improvement plan or fired, and thus at the discretion of your manager. To elaborate, organizations most often have established policies and practices for allocating rewards, but they rarely devote as much attention and formality to punishments. One important implication is the use of punishments will be far more variable.[109]

Weakening a behavior by ignoring it or making sure it is not reinforced is referred to as *extinction.* Not returning calls, unfriending, or otherwise not responding are extinction tactics. A good analogy for extinction is the fate of your houseplants if you stopped watering them. Like a plant without water, a behavior without occasional reinforcement eventually dies. Although they are very different processes, both punishment and extinction have the same weakening effect on behavior.

The bottom line: Knowing the difference between these various forms of contingent consequences provides you with numerous powerful tools with which to manage yourself and others. Put another way, you just learned four tools for influencing behavior. Most people think of and use only two—positive reinforcement and punishment (negative feedback). Apply your knowledge and get ahead!

Positive Reinforcement Schedules

You can supercharge or at least enhance the effectiveness of positive reinforcement (rewards) by managing the timing or schedule of reinforcement. Continuous and intermittent reinforcement schedules are two common means for timing the administration of reinforcers.

Continuous Reinforcement **If every instance of a target behavior is reinforced, then a *continuous reinforcement* (CRF) schedule is in effect.** Just as you train your dog to do a new trick by providing a reward each time he or she does it successfully, CRF

Like dogs, humans respond to reinforcement. To make this work for you, identify a behavior you want somebody to perform, and when they do be sure to shower them with praise, recognition, or some other form of reward they value and tell them it is because of what they did. The behavior will likely happen again.

Darkcloud/iStock/Getty Images

TABLE 6.7 Reinforcement Schedules, Examples, Advantages, and Disadvantages

REINFORCEMENT SCHEDULE	EXAMPLES	ADVANTAGES	DISADVANTAGES
Fixed ratio	Piece-rate pay; bonuses tied to the sale of a fixed number of units	Clear and predictable link between the behavior and the reinforcer	Costly to monitor performance and administer reinforcers (like money); reinforcers lose effect over time
Variable ratio	Slot machines that pay after a variable number of pulls; lotteries that pay after a variable number of tickets sold	Strong motivation to continue until reinforcer is received; less costly than fixed ratio	Some desired behaviors will not be rewarded; potentially long periods between reinforcers (such as payouts)
Fixed interval	Paychecks (every two weeks or once a month); annual bonuses; probationary periods	Clear and predictable link between the behavior and reinforcer; less costly than fixed ratio	Inconsistent effort and performance over the interval (majority of effort/performance occurs near reinforcer)
Variable interval	Random supervisor "pats on the back"; spot rewards; random audits (financial); random drug tests of athletes and employees; pop quizzes	Consistent and strong motivation to perform over time; least costly schedule due to relatively little monitoring and administration	Some desired behaviors will not be reinforced; potentially long periods between reinforcers (payouts)

schedules are especially useful when employees learn a new task or skill. Assume, for instance, you are asked to conduct an analysis of the individual purchasing patterns of your employer's largest customers. Your manager could help you develop this skill by giving you feedback as you complete the analysis for each customer. This feedback and recognition reinforce your performance on this new task. However, you can see that while this reinforcement is especially helpful and appreciated for the first few customer analyses, it likely loses its effect after the 10th, 20th, and 30th customer. Enough already! This scenario shows how CRF is susceptible to perceptions of entitlement and rapid extinction if the link is broken.

One way to help guard against the fading benefit of reinforcers is to use intermittent schedules. *Intermittent reinforcement* **consists of reinforcement of some but not all instances of a target behavior.** Table 6.7 shows four subcategories of intermittent schedules along with examples.

EXAMPLE Of the many reasons people don't save enough money, one is motivation. One way banks can motivate people to save is to utilize variable schedules in the same way slot machines and lotteries do—provide an opportunity to win big. To illustrate, assume your savings account balance averages $1,000 per month, and you earn 5 percent interest. One way to get you to maintain this balance and save even more is to offer you an opportunity to win prizes of $50, $500, or $5,000 if you do. The trade-off, however, is you only earn 3 percent guaranteed. Like the gambling games, people are motivated to behave in ways with the potential to earn more. Of course, the devil is in the details, but when managed appropriately by the bank, people are not gambling away their money, but instead are maintaining higher average savings balances and earning approximately the same guaranteed return (in this example, 5 percent). Researchers at the University of Maryland have run experiments with similar results.[110]

Applying knowledge of biases and reinforcement you've learned in this course has tremendous potential, as the Federal Reserve Bank reported 24 percent of Americans don't have access to $400, and not all of these people are poor.[111]

Organizations Typically Rely on the Weakest Schedule

Variable ratio and variable interval schedules of reinforcement generally produce the strongest behaviors and are most resistant to extinction. As gamblers will attest, variable schedules hold the promise of reinforcement after the next roll of the dice, spin of the wheel, or pull of the lever. Continuous and fixed schedules, in contrast, are the least likely to elicit the desired response over time. Nevertheless, the majority of work organizations rely on fixed intervals of reinforcement, such as hourly wages and annual reviews and raises.

Reinforcement Schedules and Performance   Figure 6.8 illustrates the relative effect of the schedules on performance over time. Consider three professors who teach different sections of the same OB course. Assume their students are essentially equal in age, experience, and GPAs across the three sections. This is the scenario:

- Professor Blue bases student grades solely on short quizzes given at the beginning of every class (continuous reinforcement).
- Professor Black bases grades on a midterm and final exams of equal weight (fixed interval).
- Professor Red uses a number of unannounced or pop quizzes (variable interval).

We expect the level of preparation for each class and overall academic performance (preparation and learning) to follow the patterns in Figure 6.8. Professor Blue's students will start fast and prepare diligently for each class. However, they will then settle into a routine and a common level of preparation. Over time they will figure out what is required and do less. Some may even quit preparing once they have a clear sense of what their overall grade will be.

The pattern for Professor Black's students is all too common. They start slowly, knowing there is plenty of time before the midterm. When it grows near the intensity of their preparation increases and some begin cramming. Once the midterm passes they disconnect for a while until they ramp up again for the final.

In contrast, Professor Red's students will likely maintain a higher average level of preparation throughout the course, because there is a chance they will have a pop quiz and be graded in every session.

The bottom line: Students generally don't like unannounced or pop quizzes. However, if the professor's goal is increased student preparation and learning, then variable-interval grading is one means for generating a higher average level of student performance.

These same patterns and results apply in business settings too. For instance, many sales and professional service jobs such as accounting and law have monthly numbers to meet, like sales or billable hours. This often means employees get far more work done in the last few days of the month than in the beginning (see Figure 6.8).

Practical Implications for Using the Strongest Schedule   In general, any type of consequence—whether reward or punishment—is more effective when administered near the time of the behavior. Effectiveness wears off as time passes. You are unlikely to change your professor's grading format or the timing of your employer's pay and bonus schedules; however, there are many ways you can put your knowledge of positive reinforcement schedules to use within the confines of existing practices.

   Spot Rewards. Spot rewards are highly effective. If your coworker has worked hard to make your project a success, recognize her efforts via an e-mail to the

FIGURE 6.8 Reinforcement Schedules and Performance

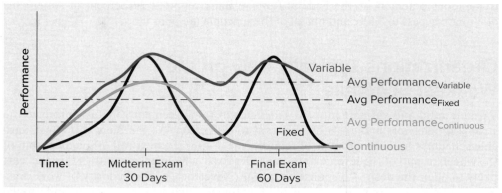

SOURCE: ©2014 Mel Fugate

entire team including your manager. Your manager, in turn, may decide to give Friday off to those who complete their current work satisfactorily and ahead of schedule.

Variable Rewards/Bonuses. Entrepreneurs can especially benefit from applying knowledge of reinforcement schedules. Assume you started your own business and, like many new business owners, you are short on cash. You would like to provide regular bonuses and pay raises, but you can afford monetary rewards only when your company secures a new customer or a big order. The variable nature of these rewards not only recognizes employees' efforts and success, but also motivates them to work hard in the future because they know that such efforts are recognized and reinforced.

Celebrations. When it comes to school, we advocate celebrating and thus reinforcing "victories," such as completing a paper, achieving a good score on an exam, and ending a semester in which you worked hard and performed well. Scattering these reinforcers throughout the semester can help reenergize you to work hard in the future, especially if you make these rewards contingent on good behavior and outcomes.

All three of these examples apply to variable schedules, and we encourage you to think of your own examples and consider their effectiveness. Reinforcement schedules, like the larger process of performance management, are often limited only by your creativity and willingness to apply your knowledge.

6.7 MAKING THE CONNECTION: HOW CAN I USE GOALS, FEEDBACK, REWARDS, AND POSITIVE REINFORCEMENT TO BOOST EFFECTIVENESS?

THE BIGGER PICTURE

We conclude this chapter with a number of practical applications of PM knowledge and tools to improve your effectiveness as both an employee and manager.

Applying knowledge and best practices related to PM is a way to get ahead throughout your career, and to help you, we've distilled some pointed applications.

LO 6-7

Describe the implications of performance management for you and managers.

Takeaways for Me

There are five notable ways to excel as an employee.

1. **Look for companies and managers with PM practices that align with your personal values, preferences, and aspirations:** If you like continual feedback and large differentials between top and low performers, find opportunities that match.

2. **Compare what managers and organizations say they value and what they reward:** Many will say they value and reward performance, but they give everyone the same 3 percent raise or promote people based on tenure rather than performance.

3. **Use Table 6.2 to build your own goal commitment:** This alone can set you apart from the competition.

4. **Ask for regular feedback if you're not already given it:** This step will help you avoid surprises during your reviews and boost your performance in between.

5. **Using Self-Assessment 6.2, identify the rewards you value most, then tell your managers which available rewards you value most:** Be sure to think broadly about rewards, and don't think only about the money. If you value time (vacation), autonomy (flexibility to work from home), or development (tuition benefits), making these part of your total rewards can enhance the value of your compensation.

Takeaways for Managers

There are seven takeaways that will prove useful as a manager.

1. **Immediately increase your management effectiveness:** Ensure that you set clear expectations and provide regular and effective feedback for those you manage.

2. **Make explicit and clear links between the rewards you provide and the behaviors and/or outcomes the rewards are intended to signal.**

3. **Practice the recommendations in Table 6.2 to boost goal commitment:** This, along with ensuring your people set SMART goals, will help set them up to win.

4. **Guard against common perceptual errors when evaluating performance:** Be sure you effectively measure the appropriate elements of performance (both quantitative and qualitative) for a particular job and individual.

5. **Provide more feedback:** Apply what you learned here to make it more effective (see Table 6.5) and focus on development more than evaluation. Feedback is a skill; practice it and you'll get better.

6. **Be certain your rewards are delivering the intended outcomes:** Clearly linking them to expectations helps.

7. **If teamwork is important and truly valued, then be certain your PM practices send such signals.**

What Did I Learn?

In our coverage of performance management, you learned how you can use goals, feedback, rewards, and reinforcement to boost effectiveness. Reinforce and consolidate your learning with the Key Points and Organizing Framework. Then challenge your mastery of the material by completing the Problem-Solving Application Case and Legal Challenge/Ethical.

Key Points for Understanding Chapter 6

You learned the following key points.

6.1 THE ELEMENTS OF EFFECTIVE PERFORMANCE MANAGEMENT

- Effective performance management (PM) is a process of defining, monitoring, reviewing, and providing consequences.
- PM is often used for employee-related decisions and development.
- Employee perceptions of the value and effectiveness of PM are often very low.

6.2 HOW AND WHY GOAL SETTING GIVES YOU AN ADVANTAGE

- Goal setting is critical to effective PM.
- Both learning and performance goals can be used.
- SMART goals are more likely to be achieved.
- Goal commitment, support and feedback, and action plans foster goal achievement.
- PM can be improved using behavioral, objective, and task/project goals.

6.3 HOW MONITORING AND EVALUATION CAN IMPROVE YOUR PERFORMANCE AND ABILITY TO MANAGE OTHERS

- Monitoring performance requires making effective measurements of progress and outcomes.

- Evaluation requires comparing performance measures to expectations or goals.
- Performance evaluation is often hampered by perceptual errors.
- Multi-rater or 360-degree feedback can make performance evaluation more accurate.

6.4 APPLYING KNOWLEDGE OF FEEDBACK AND COACHING TO REVIEW AND IMPROVE PERFORMANCE

- Two basic functions of feedback are to instruct and motivate.
- Sources of feedback include others, the task, and yourself.
- The effectiveness of positive and negative feedback is greatly influenced by the receiver's perceptions.
- Coaching helps translate feedback into desired change.

6.5 IMPLEMENTING REWARDS TO GENERATE DESIRED OUTCOMES

- Rewards can be extrinsic or intrinsic.
- Rewards are commonly distributed based on results, behavior, and nonperformance considerations.
- Total and alternative rewards are increasingly common practices.

6.6 USING REINFORCEMENT AND CONSEQUENCES TO IMPROVE PERFORMANCE

- Providing contingent consequences is fundamental to effective reinforcement.
- Both positive and negative reinforcement increase desired behaviors.
- Punishment and extinction both decrease undesirable behaviors.
- The schedule on which reinforcers are administered can increase their effectiveness.

- Knowledge and application for PM can guide your efforts and set you apart from others.
- PM tools are invaluable for managers who seek to realize the performance potential for their employees and themselves.

The Organizing Framework for Chapter 6

As shown in Figure 6.9, performance management practices are associated with nearly every outcome across the three levels of OB. At the individual level these outcomes are task performance, work attitudes, well-being/flourishing, citizenship and counterproductive behaviors, turnover, career outcomes, and creativity. Group and team-level performance, along with group satisfaction, cohesion, and conflict, are similarly related. As for the organizational level, performance management practices link to accounting/financial performance, customer satisfaction, reputation, and even an organization's overall survival. Please observe the roles of regulators, competition, and leadership as inputs and processes affecting PM and its associated outcomes.

FIGURE 6.9   Organizing Framework for Understanding and Applying OB

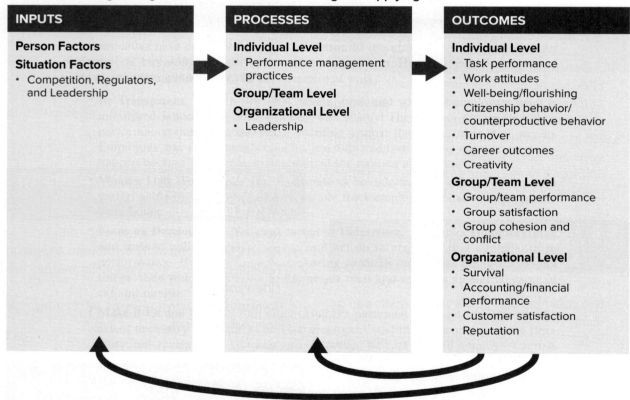

INPUTS	PROCESSES	OUTCOMES
Person Factors	**Individual Level**	**Individual Level**
Situation Factors	• Performance management practices	• Task performance
• Competition, Regulators, and Leadership	**Group/Team Level**	• Work attitudes
	Organizational Level	• Well-being/flourishing
	• Leadership	• Citizenship behavior/ counterproductive behavior
		• Turnover
		• Career outcomes
		• Creativity
		Group/Team Level
		• Group/team performance
		• Group satisfaction
		• Group cohesion and conflict
		Organizational Level
		• Survival
		• Accounting/financial performance
		• Customer satisfaction
		• Reputation

Incentives Gone Wrong, Then Wrong Again, and Wrong Again

Money is an important tool for both attracting and motivating talent. If you owned a company or were its CEO, you would likely agree and choose performance management practices to deliver such outcomes. It also is possible you'd use incentives to help align your employees' interests, behaviors, and performance with those of the company. After all, countless companies have used incentives very successfully, but not all. The incentives used by Wells Fargo had disastrous consequences for employees, customers, and the company itself.

THE SCENARIO AND BEHAVIORS

A client enters a bank branch and opens a checking account. The performance expectations of the banker that helped open the account were to open eight accounts for each customer, which meant he or she needed to persuade that customer to open seven additional accounts! This resulted in the banker then attempting to open a savings account and maybe a credit card account, simple enough. But the problem happened when the customer left without opening additional accounts and many bankers went ahead and did so anyway without the customer's consent. Customers who had mortgages with the bank sometimes had insurance policies opened without their knowledge. The bank also financed automobiles for many customers, and insurance was also often added unknowingly to these. Small business customers were frequently overcharged for credit cards and other services. More generally, customers for one product were cross-sold other products, and along with many of these additional accounts there were fees. The increased number of accounts helped employees meet their numbers, and the fees provided still more income for the bank.[112]

Even after all of these efforts, many bankers still fell short of their goals and opened accounts in family members' names. One branch manager opened 24 accounts in her teenage daughter's name and 21 in her husband's. Other reports include Wells Fargo bankers canvassing employees at stores in which they shopped.[113] Pet insurance was added in some instances![114]

Some sham accounts were closed once the employee received credit, but many remained open, charging fees and affecting customers' credit.

THE DAMAGE TO CUSTOMERS AND EMPLOYEES

Wells employees created approximately 3.5 million fake accounts; even now precise numbers are difficult to obtain. But it seems as if 1.5 million deposit and 500,000 credit card accounts were opened without customer consent, and it erroneously foreclosed on over 400 mortgages and repossessed thousands of cars. Over 800,000 customers with auto loans were charged for auto insurance.[115] The list goes on.

The negative consequences within Wells Fargo also have been enormous. CEO John Stumpf was ousted along with former head of community banking, Carrie Tolstedt. Seventy-five million dollars in compensation was clawed back from these two executives, as it was considered ill-gotten and due to illegal or at least unprofessional behaviors. The same executives lost additional millions in compensation, and approximately 5,300 employees were fired. Numerous regulatory agencies fined Wells Fargo for nearly $200 million, the company's stock underperformed its competitors', and it is difficult to estimate the cost of damage to the company's reputation and the resulting lost business.[116] Above all, there are the incalculable costs to customers in money, frustration, ruined credit, lost vehicles, and lost homes.

THE CULPRITS

Much of this carnage has now been attributed to perverse incentives and poor leadership. Investigations revealed that both Stumpf and Tolstedt were well aware of these unethical behaviors, but they turned a blind eye or even encouraged these behaviors. It was reported that Tolstedt repeatedly denied and resisted complaints about goals being unachievable and problematic.[117] But what about the thousands of employees that actually opened the accounts? When writing about the Wells Fargo scandal, Professor Elizabeth Tippett noted, "Research suggests that ethical behavior is not about who you are or the values you hold. Behavior is often a function of the situation in which you make the decision, even factors you barely notice."[118]

Another interesting detail regarding performance expectations is that the eight-account expectation for every customer was only three 10 years earlier. It also is important to note that this sort of cross-selling (multiple products to the same customer) was something Wells was known for and contributed to its past success. It's been reported that the reason for eight instead of another number was that CEO Stumpf said it rhymed with "great."

ACTIONS

To be fair, numerous examples exist of Wells Fargo management explicitly instructing employees not to engage in such activities, including ethics training and the deployment of risk professionals to identify and correct inappropriate conduct. But this obviously wasn't enough, and even though employees were expected to report any misdeeds, they didn't. Incentives stayed in place and employees continued to be pressured and even fired if they did not make their sales quotas. Some involved in the scandal argued it isn't the employees' fault, they needed a paycheck and this is what their employer required.[119] Tim Sloan, who worked at Wells for decades, was inserted as the new CEO and charged with cleaning up the mess, restoring the bank's reputation, and warding off a potential new $1 billion fine.[120]

Sloan worked in the role for two years before stepping down in 2019, presumably for not being able to turn things around.[121] Whoever replaces him has the same challenges. Assume you are the new CEO, what would you do?

APPLY THE 3-STEP PROBLEM-SOLVING APPROACH TO OB

Use the Organizing Framework in Figure 6.9 and the 3-Step Problem-Solving Approach to help identify inputs, processes, and outcomes relative to this case.

STEP 1: Define the problem.

A. Look first to the Outcome box of the Organizing Framework in Figure 6.9 to help identify the important problem(s) in this case. Remember that a problem is a gap between a desired and current state. State your problem as a gap and be sure to consider problems at all three levels. If more than one desired outcome is not being accomplished, decide which one is most important and focus on it for steps 2 and 3.

B. Cases have key players, and problems are generally viewed from a particular player's perspective. You need to determine from whose perspective—employee, manager, team, or the organization—you're defining the problem. As in other cases, whether you choose the individual or organizational level in this case can make a difference. In this case you're asked to assume the role of the new CEO.

C. Use details in the case to determine the key problem. Don't assume, infer, or create problems that are not explicitly included in the case itself.

D. To refine your choice, ask yourself, *why is this a problem?* Explaining why helps refine and focus your thinking. Focus on topics in the current chapter, because we generally select cases that illustrate concepts in the current chapter.

STEP 2: Identify causes.
Using material from this chapter and summarized in the Organizing Framework, identify what are the causes of the problem you identified in Step 1? Remember, causes tend to appear in either the Inputs or Processes boxes.

A. Start by looking at the Organizing Framework (Figure 6.9) and determine which person factors, if any, are most likely causes to the defined problem. For each cause, explain why this is a cause of the problem. Asking why multiple times is more likely to lead you to root causes of the problem. There may be few or no person factors but be sure to consider them. For example, did attributes of the leaders or other employees contribute to the problems defined in Step 1?

B. Follow the same process for the situation factors. For each ask yourself, *Why is this a cause?* For example, leadership at the executive and other levels might have some effect on the problem you defined. Aside from performance management, did other HR practices contribute to the problem? If you agree, which specific practices and why? By following the process of asking why multiple times you are likely to arrive at a more complete and accurate set of causes. Again, look to the Organizing Framework for this chapter for guidance.

C. Now consider the Processes box in the Organizing Framework. Performance management processes are clearly part of the story, but are any other processes at the individual, group/team, or organizational level that caused your defined problem? For any process you consider, ask yourself, *why is this a cause?* Again, do this for several iterations to arrive at the root causes.

D. To check the accuracy or appropriateness of the causes, be sure to map them onto the defined problem and confirm the link or cause and effect connection.

STEP 3: Recommend solutions.
Make your recommendations for solving the problem, considering whether you want to resolve it, solve it, or dissolve it (see Section 1.5). Which recommendation is desirable and feasible?

A. Given the causes identified in Step 2, what are your best recommendations? Use material in the current chapter that best suits the cause. Remember to consider the OB in Action and Applying OB boxes, because these contain insights into what others have done.

B. Be sure to consider the Organizing Framework—both person and situation factors, as well as processes at different levels.

C. Create an action plan for implementing your recommendations, and be sure your recommendations map onto the causes and resolve the problem.

LEGAL/ETHICAL CHALLENGE

What Is Your Current Salary?

For eons it's been standard operating procedure to ask job candidates: "What is your current salary?" The motives for this question are obvious. If your current salary is beyond that budgeted for the job you're interviewing for, then employers often and quickly exclude you from the candidate pool, while those with lower current salaries are assumed to be more likely to accept an offer.

This Practice Is Damaging

This is changing, however, as legislators in multiple states have outlawed companies from asking about job candidates' salary histories. Policymakers' motives are to help eliminate one factor contributing to persistent gender and minority compensation disparities. In support, Susie Clark, director of undergraduate studies at the University of Indiana's Kelley School of Business, says: "Gender pay inequality will go on forever if we don't do something." Eliminating the question about salary is expected to focus employers' attention on job qualifications, such as skills, abilities, and experience, and to use market data to set pay. Put differently, the argument by some is employers should not be making offer decisions based on a candidate's current or past pay.

Such Changes Would Be Ineffective

Many HR experts and executives disagree and argue banning the box will not have the desired effect of reducing unwarranted pay disparities. They further argue it is reasonable and necessary for employers to learn during the interviewing process if they can reasonably expect to meet a candidate's pay expectations.

Alternatives Already Exist

Some companies and HR managers have already devised and implemented alternatives, particularly in instances when considerable and accurate market data exists. This information enables them to confidently "price" jobs. Still other employers determine and implement pay ranges which allow for some adjustment based on an individual's qualifications.[122] But neither of these provide insights into candidate expectations.

What Would You Do?

Assume you are the person responsible for setting the practices at your company, what would you recommend?

1. Would you eliminate such questions from your hiring process? Defend your choice.

2. Describe how you would implement this practice, and explain your rationale.

3. Given your response to #1, assume the law changed in your state and requires you do the opposite. Describe how you would effectively implement that practice.

7

Positive Organizational Behavior

After reading this chapter, you should be able to:

LO 7-1   Explain the benefits of positive organizational behavior.

LO 7-2   Apply knowledge of positive emotions to enhance your effectiveness.

LO 7-3   Understand how to foster mindfulness.

LO 7-4   Describe how psychological capital and signature strengths can improve outcomes at work.

LO 7-5   Develop a climate that promotes positive organizational behavior.

LO 7-6   Create the conditions for flourishing in your job and career.

LO 7-7   Describe the implications of positive organizational behavior for you and managers.

Figure 7.1 summarizes what you will learn in this chapter. The focus is on *positive organizational behavior* and how positive inputs and processes influence a host of outcomes across levels of OB. The Organizing Framework for Understanding and Applying OB illustrates how person factors such as mindfulness, psychological capital, and signature strengths form the basis for positive functioning at work. A variety of situation factors also affect the positivity of an organization's processes. They include organizational culture, organizational climate, organizational values, virtuous leadership, and organizational practices. In turn the inputs and processes shown in the Organizing Framework influence a host of outcomes at the individual, group/team, and organizational level. Most importantly, you will learn about a valuable new individual-level outcome labeled flourishing. Flourishing is a contemporary way of describing success or positive functioning at work.

FIGURE 7.1 Organizing Framework for Understanding and Applying OB

INPUTS	PROCESSES	OUTCOMES
Person Factors • Emotions • Mindfulness • Psychological capital • Signature strengths **Situation Factors** • Organizational culture • Organizational climate • Organizational values • Virtuous leadership • Organizational practices	**Individual Level** • Communication • Decision making discretion • Interpersonal conflict **Group/Team Level** • Communication • Civility • Group Dynamics **Organizational Level** • Communication	**Individual Level** • Task performance • Work attitudes • Flourishing • Physical health • Citizenship behavior/ counterproductive behavior • Turnover • Creativity **Group/Team Level** • Group/team performance • Group/team cohesion and conflict **Organizational Level** • Accounting/financial performance • Organizational performance • Customer satisfaction

Flourishing is at the core of positive organizational behavior. We flourish when our lives contain positive emotions, engagement in our work, positive relationships with others, meaningfulness, and a sense of achievement. It is safe to assume that many people working for and with NASA were flourishing when the Insight Lander successfully landed on Mars in late 2018. The flight was 300 million miles over six months, but the journey was much longer. Numerous employees have been working on this project for decades, including one member of the NASA team who helped conceive of this project 40 years ago![1]
Source: NASA/Bill Ingalls.

Winning at Work

Boosting Your Performance with Positivity[2]

Engagement is a key driver of performance at all levels—you, your team, and your organization. Key drivers of engagement are relationships, and positivity is an excellent way to cultivate productive relationships, so you are well served to learn how to use positivity. The rationale behind this approach is best explained in Shawn Anchor's TED Talk, wherein he describes how happiness leads to success, rather than the other way around. Further, as you have already learned, he explains how emotions are contagious and people like positivity. So, how do you use positivity to improve relationships, engagement, and performance?

1. Smile. It's that simple and the best place to start. Anchor illustrates how the 10 & 5 tool is used widely within the hotel industry to foster positive interactions with guests. In short, if a guest is within 10 feet make eye contact and smile. If a guest is within five feet make eye contact, smile, and say hello or, how are you? Research in the hospital setting showed doctors and nurses who practice the 10 & 5 rule boosted employee and patient satisfaction.

2. Have Purpose. "Happiness Is working hard at work worth doing." Influence yourself and others by ensuring you have a clear and compelling reason for doing what you're doing. As you learned in Chapter 5, meaningfulness and impact on others are two ways to boost intrinsic motivation. If you don't know how or why your own work makes an impact, then work with your supervisor to better understand. When asking someone else to help or to assist with something, be sure to communicate the purpose and potential impact they and their work will have.

3. Encourage and Praise. Feedback is one form, recognition is another, but what is important is to observe and acknowledge the efforts and outcomes of others.

4. Say Thank You. It is that simple. Be polite and say thank you.

5. Celebrate. Celebrate wins big and small, as well as progress and accomplishments. It is important to acknowledge and celebrate progress and accomplishments. As you learned about goal setting In Chapter 6, don't wait until the final outcome is known, but instead congratulate people for their efforts along the way. These small celebrations can help motivate you and others to stay the course and perform better.

LWA/Larry Williams/Blend Images

Your performance at work and throughout your career is dependent in large part on influencing others (a primary focus of Chapter 12), and people are attracted to positivity. It is energizing to you, your work, and to others. Be an energizing force and improve your own performance and ability to influence others.

What's Ahead in This Chapter

We're concluding Part One of the book and our discussion of the individual level by introducing you to one of the most exciting and fastest-growing areas of OB, *positive organizational behavior (POB)*. Research suggests you can enhance your life and job satisfaction by following some of the ideas presented in this chapter. We explore the value of positive organizational behavior and expand on several elements to help you foster personal positivity. Positive emotions are one such element (an individual-level process), as are mindfulness (a person input), positive psychological capital (a person input), and organizational climate (a situation factor). Combined, these elements create a positive workplace environment and enable people, teams, and organizations to flourish. Flourishing is the ultimate individual-level outcome of POB and consists of positive emotions, engagement, constructive relationships, meaningfulness, and achievement.

7.1 THE VALUE OF POSITIVITY

THE BIGGER PICTURE

You can benefit at school and at work by understanding positive organizational behavior (positive OB or POB), a purposefully positive approach to managing the behavior of individuals, groups, and organizations. You'll see some of these potential benefits when you explore three ways in which positive OB affects a broad set of outcomes contained in the Organizing Framework of OB.

Positive OB focuses on positive human characteristics that can be measured, developed, and effectively managed for performance improvement.[3] It Is an offshoot of positive psychology and positive organizational scholarship, and like these, focuses on building positive qualities in and positive outcomes for individuals, groups, and organizations. Positive OB contrasts with the historical concentration in these disciplines on sickness and dysfunction in people and organizations.[4] The differences are highlighted in the following hypothetical scenarios.

LO 7-1

Explain the benefits of positive organizational behavior.

Two Scenarios—Which Do You Prefer?

Let's set the stage by describing two scenarios included in an early presentation of positive organizational behavior (POB).

First Scenario   "Imagine a world in which almost all organizations are typified by greed, selfishness, manipulation, secrecy, and a single-minded focus on winning."[5] Wealth is the ultimate measure of success, feelings of distrust, anxiety, self-absorption, fear, burnout, and abuse are common. Members often experience conflict, treat each other disrespectfully, and break agreements with each other. Employees in this context focus on problem solving, managing uncertainty, overcoming resistance, achieving profitability, and figuring out how to beat the competition.

Second Scenario   Now imagine a world in which appreciation, collaboration, virtuousness, vitality, and meaningfulness are the rule. Well-being and thriving are the markers for success among individuals, groups, and organizations alike. Trustworthiness, resilience, wisdom, humility, and positive energy are common features. Relationships and interactions are described as compassionate, loyal, honest, respectful, and forgiving. Employees emphasize excellence, positive deviance, extraordinary performance, and positive spirals of flourishing.

A Matter of Emphasis Rather than Rejection of Business Realities   Many professionals who first encounter positive organizational behavior assume it simply rejects the realities in the first scenario: the need to solve problems, manage uncertainty, overcome resistance, achieve profitability, and compete successfully. But something else is happening.

Positive organizational behavior "does not reject the value and significance of the phenomena in the first worldview. Rather, it *emphasizes* the phenomena represented in the second."[6] We will show you how identifying and applying the many positive attributes of individuals, groups, and organizations is yet another powerful way of increasing your effectiveness professionally and personally.

FIGURE 7.2   A Framework of Positive OB

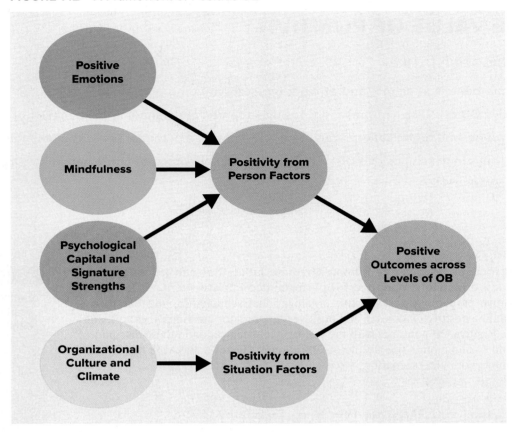

A Framework for Positivity

We created Figure 7.2 to help organize, understand, and apply your knowledge of POB. As you recall from the Organizing Framework of OB, person and situation factor inputs influence processes and outcomes across levels. Similarly, in Figure 7.2, positive emotions, mindfulness, psychological capital, and signature strengths are the inputs that help create positivity from person factors, and organizational climate is an input that helps create positivity from situation factors. Positivity from these two sources contribute to positive outcomes across levels of OB.

Taking this a step further, positive outcomes are generated through three processes: the amplifying effect, the buffering effect, and the positivity effect. Let's discuss each.

Amplifying Effect   In the *amplifying effect,* **positive practices from one individual result in additional positive practices by others, which spur positivity in others, which generate other positive outcomes.** The amplifying effect is often conveyed via positive emotions and social capital (your relationships and network). The idea is positivity fuels more positivity, such that both the receiver and witnesses of kind acts are likely to perform kind acts of their own. This results in reinforcing cycles or *upward spirals of positivity.* Such behaviors can then transform organizations into more compassionate and harmonious places, while improving interpersonal interactions, collaboration, information sharing, and efficiency.[7]

This perspective on positive emotions is called the *broaden-and-build theory,* which proposes positive emotions broaden our attention and make us more open to experience.

These are self-reinforcing—more creates more—resulting in upward spirals of additional positive emotions and actions. For instance, employees who supported and trusted their coworkers received support and trust in return. This may not surprise you; we all hope to reap what we sow. However, the positive spiral is notable. Support and trust resulted in even more support and trust in return.[8] One implication for you is if you want something, then give something. If you want more, give more. Do your own experiment and find out.

People are more likely to exhibit *prosocial* behaviors when positive OB is taking place in their work environments. **Prosocial behaviors are positive acts performed without the expectation of anything in return.[9]** A striking and heart-warming example was provided by Laura Mazur and Jessica Robertson in the 2019 Pittsburgh Marathon. The two women who did not know each other were the last runners on the course when they joined hands at about mile 25. They supported each other to the finish line in an exhibition of prosocial behavior that went viral. Another racer who finished already and watched Mazur and Robertson said, "it isn't about finishing first, it's about helping each and every person change their lives for the better."[10]

Laura Mazur and Jessica Robertson, two strangers, finished the final mile of the Pittsburgh Marathon holding hands. They were the last runners on the course and bonded together to help each other complete the race. Helping others, especially when you expect nothing in return, has been shown both to make you feel better and motivate those people to help others.

Courtesy of Daniel Heckert

Buffering Effect   To buffer means to reduce or counteract the effects of a negative force. **In the *buffering effect,* positive practices and resources reduce the impact of negative events and stressors.** When we are confronted with stressors or otherwise undesirable experiences, we utilize various social and personal resources to buffer or cope with them.[11] At work, we use social support from helpful coworkers to cope, and/or we may use personal resources such as *psychological capital* described later in this chapter.

Positivity Effect   The *positivity effect* "is the attraction of all living systems toward positive energy and away from negative energy, or toward that which is life giving and away from that which is life depleting."[12] Organizations using positive practices are more likely to create an atmosphere of positive energy, which in turn fuels performance,[13] such as financial, work climate (more on this later in the chapter), turnover, patient satisfaction, employee participation, and managerial support.[14]

The Benefits of Positive OB Extend Beyond Good Performance

Positive OB is more than seeing the good side of people, sharing examples of good performance, or treating employees well. Positive OB focuses on creating *exceptionally positive* inputs, processes, and outcomes at all levels in the Organizing Framework. Exceptionally positive means above and beyond expectations, more than making the grade. This level of achievement is referred to as *positive deviance*. Gretchen Spreitzer and Kim Cameron from the University of Michigan describe **positive deviance** as **"successful performance that dramatically exceeds the norm in a positive direction."**[15] The relative effects of deviance at the individual and organizational levels are illustrated in Figure 7.3.

FIGURE 7.3   A Continuum Illustrating Positive Deviance

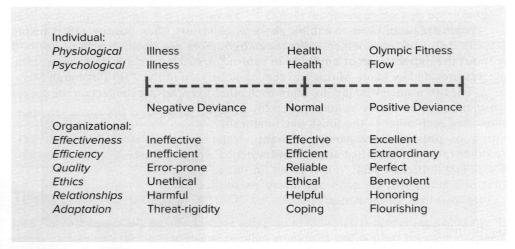

SOURCE: M. Meyer, "The Evolution and Challenges of the Concept of Organizational Virtuousness in Positive Organizational Scholarship," *Journal of Business Ethics,* 153, 2018, 245–264. IN Cameron and Caza (2002, p. 35)

The Applying OB box describes ways you can insert positivity into your life, generally, and at work.

Applying OB

How to Build Positivity and Your Success

Because behavior is a product of our emotions, thoughts, beliefs, and experiences, it makes sense that managing these internal responses can improve our performance. Try these suggestions:

- **Set intentions.** *Intentions* **are the end point or goal you want to achieve. They drive your behavior.**[16] If you want to accomplish a specific result on a given day, start your day with a positive intention to do so. Set your intentions around tasks and people that matter to you.

- **Express gratitude to someone.** We are healthier both physically and mentally when we express gratitude. People receiving gratitude report these same positive outcomes.[17] Your expression of thanks might be a small gesture, like thanking someone for holding a door open while you pass, or it can also be bigger like starting a college scholarship to assist others in financial need. You can keep a gratitude journal at your bedside and write down one or two things each day that went well or write a thank-you note to someone. The point is to look for positive actions by others and acknowledge them.

- **Do something helpful or positive for other people.** You do not have to give a tangible gift, but instead offer someone a kind or positive gesture as a smile, a compliment, or words of encouragement. Volumes of research show helping others is one of the most fulfilling things you can do. The more you give, the more you'll get.[18]

- **Become more hopeful.** *"Hope* **is believing the future will be better than the present and you have some power to make it happen."**[19] The following process was found to increase hopefulness for college students: Identify an important goal, identify different ways to achieve the goal, identify obstacles to each pathway and develop a plan for overcoming these roadblocks, and work the plan.[20] Taking these steps should give you a sense of hope and control.

- **Focus on the positive side of life.** Negative thoughts and worry are prime enemies of staying focused in the present moment. We often worry about things we can't control, including events in the past. Don't worry about the past or what you can't control, instead try to stay focused on what is happening in the present moment.
- **Be aware of negative thoughts and beliefs.** The brain has a built-in negativity bias. This allows negative events to have more impact on us than positive ones, and we often think bad information about someone is more important than positive information.[21] If you find yourself focusing on negativity, try to reframe your thoughts in a positive direction. For example, rather than worrying about your level of performance on an exam, tell yourself you are prepared and will do just fine.

Positively Deviant Employees Aren't Just Happy and Satisfied—They Are Much, Much More Job satisfaction is an important outcome in the Organizing Framework. However, you have also learned job satisfaction is not the strongest or best predictor of job performance. Positive OB provides you with additional useful insights beyond job satisfaction and other attitudes that predict performance. For instance, a study published in the *Harvard Business Review* showed employees who *flourish* (a key positive outcome of positive OB shown in Figure 7.2 and discussed later) reported:

- 16 percent higher overall performance.
- 125 percent less burnout.
- 32 percent more commitment to their employers.
- 46 percent more job satisfaction.
- Fewer sick days.[22]

These outcomes are compelling. Organizations can foster positive deviance in employees in a number of ways, such as those described in Table 7.1.[23]

Doing Well and Doing Good Positive businesses *do well, and they do good*. They *do well* by being profitable and performing at a high level, but they also *do good* by making the well-being of their employees and other stakeholders (suppliers, customers, and communities) a priority.

TABLE 7.1 Positive OB Practices That Foster Employee Positivity

ORGANIZATIONAL PRACTICE	DESCRIPTION AND BENEFIT
Provide decision-making discretion	Allowing employees to make decisions gives them a sense of control and greater opportunities for learning.
Share information	Information helps employees see the impact of their work and how it fits into the big picture, like the vision and goals of the organization.
Minimize incivility	Poor treatment, for example bullying and rude behavior, has dramatic negative effects on outcomes in the Organizing Framework and often leads to uncivil behavior by the victims. Organizations need to select employees based on civility and take swift and appropriate action when incivility occurs.
Provide feedback	Feedback can be motivational and instructional.

SOURCE: Spreitzer, Gretchen, and Christine Porath. "Creating Sustainable Performance." *Harvard Business Review,* January 2012. https://hbr.org/2012/01/creating-sustainable-performance.

This positive approach to business is now mainstream. For example, *Fortune* magazine has published a list of companies that are not altruistic—doing good for goodness's sake—but that are nevertheless solving major problems profitably. These meet three criteria:

1. **Measurable Social Impact**. *Fortune* assessed the magnitude and lasting nature of the company's impact on a notable societal problem.

2. **Business Results**. How does the company benefit? Shareholder return factors heavily. It isn't enough to receive good PR and reputational benefits.

3. **Degree of Innovation**. It isn't enough to do good and do so profitably, it also is important to do so creatively, differently from others.[24]

Good to Employees = Good to Shareholders   Positive organizations empower, support, and develop employees not just because leaders believe doing so is valuable in and of itself, but because it helps meet shareholder expectations. Kip Tindell, founder of the Container Store, reflects this belief in his philosophy about the value of employees:

> One great employee is equal to three good ones. If you really believe that, a lot of things happen. We try to pay 50 to 100 percent above industry average. That's good for the employee, that's good for the customer, but it's good for the company too, because you get three times the productivity at only two times the labor cost.[25]

Doing good can enhance well-being, even in the absence of a monetary reward, and it can happen at all levels in the Organizing Framework.

- *Individual Level*   Joe Ryan started his own company, and rather than the common label of CEO he instead chose CFE—chief fun engineer. He thought this label aligned better with the nature of the company—party-games—and his actual responsibilities. It also is a great conversation tool, enabling him to explain and promote his business to others.[26]

- *Team/Unit Level*   CSAA Insurance Group from California has a unique proposition for employees. If you work for us you'll spend multiple weekends per year volunteering in some of the nation's best national parks. Hundreds of the company's employees travel in teams to help with beautification and cleanup projects. For this they get Friday as a paid day off and spend the weekend camping and helping. This aligns with the company mantra—"taking care of business means taking care of each other." Volunteering is included in leaders' performance expectations, and in 2018 the goal was 80 percent employee participation in volunteering. They achieved 99 percent![27]

- *Organizational Level*   Walmart has made reducing waste a major focus, so much so it has diverted approximately 78 percent of the waste it produces away from landfills.[28] It has done this via recycling, packaging design and materials, and food disposal, and is influencing its suppliers to do the same. The company's philosophy is that any waste is bad, and it is trying to close the loop by making products circular, meaning the energy, packaging, and products themselves are captured and put back into the system.[29]

Give in Order to Get   Giving financially doesn't necessarily detract from outcomes. Researchers studied the links between the amount of discounted care and the quality of all care provided by a number of hospitals in Southern California. Discounted care is given to those who cannot pay or can pay only a reduced rate; sometimes it amounts to a financial loss for the hospital. The researchers found hospitals that provided more discounted care also reported lower incidences of pneumonia and heart failure, as well as better surgical outcomes and fewer readmissions.[30] This seems to suggest altruism and high performance are not mutually exclusive.

Notions of positivity are catching on with Wall Street too, as illustrated in the OB in Action box.

OB in Action

How Do You Spell Green? ESG.

Socially responsible investing is nothing new, it's decades-old in fact. However, it's finally lost its stigma and is now recognized as a viable and profitable approach to investing. Financial instruments with a green and responsible focus are referred to as environmental, social, and governance (ESG). Ample evidence now exists showing that companies can be very profitable by considering the environment, communities, and employees in their decisions.[31]

Bank of America and Merrill Lynch found that approximately 20% of all investors, and 50% of those with a longer time horizon, consider ESG issues in their decisions, demonstrating there is sufficient demand for such considerations. In support of this focus, McKinsey studied mid-large companies between 2001 in 2014 who manage with a long-term approach, which means they consistently invest profits back into their business through people and R&D. They found these companies performed substantially better than their peer group: 47% greater revenue growth and 36% greater profit. As one investor put it, "investments chosen with social concerns in mind proved 'more resilient and less risky.'"[32]

ESG investing is no longer just for do-gooders and tree huggers. Some titans of the investment world have gotten behind it, including billionaire investor Paul Tudor Jones II. In 2012 he started a foundation, Just Capital, to develop a series of corporate performance measures including things other than dollars and cents, like how workers are treated and job creation.

In the beginning, Just Capital produced only a list, but then Goldman Sachs used these metrics to create a new exchange traded fund as part of its social impact efforts. The fund includes a selection of Russell 1000 companies and tracks the top performers in each industry based on Just Capitals' measures, which now include metrics related to workers, customers, products, environment, jobs, communities, and management. In its first year the top performers were only tech companies: Intel, Texas Instruments, NVidia, Microsoft, and IBM.

Just Capital says the companies in the fund outperformed their peer group impressively and in socially conscious ways. They paid 71 percent less in fines for consumer complaints and violations, 94 percent less in equal employment opportunity commission fines, and produced 45 percent lower greenhouse gases. And to top it off, they created 20 percent more jobs in their peer group.[33]

YOUR THOUGHTS?

1. What are the pros and cons of ESG investing?

2. Assume you are a money manager, explain why you would or would not consider ESG factors in your investing? Be sure to include at least two reasons for each argument.

3. Do you think this approach will continue to be effective over time? Explain.

Balancing the needs of multiple stakeholders—employees, customers, communities, and investors—is a major challenge. Despite what particular leaders may say, most give clear priority to one, often at the expense of the others. But some truly attempt to satisfy all stakeholders. A glowing example is Salesforce, which ranked #2 on *Fortune*'s Best Places to Work list in 2019.[34] This company continues to deliver impressive results for many of its stakeholders. For employees, it spent $3 million to help establish pay equity, and it provides unlimited vacation time and paid sabbaticals among many other attractive benefits. It invests in communities by providing each employee seven days per year to devote to a cause they choose, and it matches up to $5,000 in charitable giving.[35] Whether these practices have actually attracted investors isn't exactly clear, but what is clear is it hasn't scared them away. The company's stock is a long-time favorite among tech investors.

However, positive approaches to doing business aren't without difficulties. The following Problem-Solving Application describes challenges Whole Foods has had maintaining its doing well by doing good philosophy since being acquired by Amazon in 2017.

Problem-Solving Application

Whole Foods vs. Whole Amazon

Investigative journalist Michael Blanding put it best, "Amazon's acquisition of Whole Foods . . . was the corporate equivalent of mixing tap water with organic extra virgin olive oil. You'd be hard-pressed to find two companies with more different value propositions."[36] Stories quickly emerged about Whole Foods customers unhappy about the changes at their favorite organic retailer, and they weren't the only ones complaining. Similar negative stories emerged from employees regarding the new performance-driven expectations imposed by Amazon.

Immediate Impact After the acquisition, Amazon's presence was immediately felt. In addition to plastering its logo everywhere In Whole Foods stores, it also used its strengths in data and data analysis to determine appropriate product mixes and bring efficiencies to many processes. After all, Amazon is known for its efficiencies, low costs, and low prices.

Clash This is a stark contrast to Whole Foods' highly empowered approach to doing business, wherein individual stores and their employees had autonomy regarding decisions about product selection, inventory, and how best to serve customers. This employee-centric focus is what earned the company a spot-on *Fortune*'s Best Places to Work list for 20 consecutive years, and the reason its customers enjoyed personalized intensive, hands-on service. Although this decentralized, high-touch approach had real benefits, it also had considerable inefficiencies that Amazon was keen to address.

Amazon and its employees utilized data, rigorous analysis and controls, and demanding performance management practices. In the eyes of Amazon, customers were faceless digital profiles of purchasing history and preferences. This environment was a good fit for some employees but incredibly stressful and negative for others. Evidence for this was Whole Foods dropping from *Fortune*'s list in 2018 (it didn't make the list in 2019 either).

Unrealized Potential? These differences have the potential to undermine the hopes and goals of the merger, which were to bring Amazon's efficiencies and operating prowess to Whole Foods' unique approach and loyal customers, enabling it to scale up and make an even larger impact in the market. Leaders at Amazon, and to a lesser extent at Whole Foods, now have decisions to make. Problems exist, and the success of the marriage depends on solving them.

Assume you're a consultant, what would you recommend to Amazon's leadership?

Apply the 3-Step Problem-Solving Approach

Step 1: Define the problem as described in the case.

Step 2: Identify the causes of the problem. Which inputs and processes from the Organizing Framework are evident?

Step 3: Make recommendations to Amazon's leadership regarding how to realize the potential of the merger.

7.2 THE POWER OF POSITIVE EMOTIONS

THE BIGGER PICTURE

OB recognizes emotions as an important and ever-present individual-level process. In the section ahead you can see whether your positive emotional experience matches our list of the 10 most common positive emotions. Positivity is more than feeling happiness and painting a smile on your face. You'll also find tips on how to foster positive emotions and how to apply them at school, work, and home.

Referring to Figure 7.2, note that positive emotions help drive positivity from person factors. Recall in Chapter 3 we introduced emotions as relatively brief psychological and physiological reactions having a particular target, such as a person (an unethical, bullying boss), a situation (a night out with your closest friends), or an event (scoring well on an exam). Our discussion then focused on negative emotions and how to manage their expression. We now turn to positive emotions.

Like their negative cousins, positive emotions are relatively flexible individual differences and are important processes in the Organizing Framework. You may think of emotions in terms of positive or negative; however, there is much more to the story.

LO 7-2

Apply knowledge of positive emotions to enhance your effectiveness.

Beyond Happy vs. Sad

Positive and negative emotions are not polar opposites. The world of emotions is not happy versus sad. Negative emotions spur you to act in quite narrow or specific ways. Fear may motivate you to flee and anger may motivate you to fight. Positive emotions, in contrast, tend to broaden your mind-set and allow you to consider new, different, and possibly better alternatives when trying to solve a problem.

Positive Emotions as Resources   If you think of emotions in this way, you can see negative emotions are limiting and positive emotions are resources that fuel individual, group, and organizational flourishing. (*Flourishing* is discussed in detail in the last section of this chapter.) Psychology professor Barbara Fredrickson explains positive emotions this way:

> To get a feel for the ways positive emotions can build life resources, envision for a moment something that made you feel joyful, playful, or intensely alive—when you wanted to smile, cheer, or jump up and dance around. Maybe it was . . . sharing a meal with lots of laughter with a friend you haven't seen in ages . . . maybe it was dancing with the group of friends as your favorite band played. Whatever comes to mind for you, take a moment to relive the experience in your mind, letting joy rekindle. Consider how you felt and what you felt like doing. What we've learned about

joyful experiences like these is that the playful urges they carry build resources, and in times of trouble, these gains in resources can help you in important ways—strengthen relationships, boost performance at school and work, and improve your health.[37]

The bottom line is positive emotions help you build resources in the form of:

- Social relationships that are supportive, fulfilling, and lasting.
- Psychological well-being that leads to personal growth, meaningful goals, and self-acceptance.[38]
- Physical well-being in the form of lower stress and a healthy heart.

These resources support your efforts and effectiveness in all arenas of life—school, work, and family.

Benefits of Positive Emotions   Positive emotions are processes influencing many outcomes in the Organizing Framework, and they have desirable effects on:

- Organizational commitment
- Creativity
- Decision making
- Intentions to quit
- Performance[39]
- Stress[40]

Table 7.2 lists the 10 most common positive emotions from the most to the least frequently experienced. Love is a special case, however. Despite being at the bottom of the list, it is the most frequently experienced positive emotion. After reading about each of the other positive emotions, you'll understand why it was inserted last in the table.

Positive Emotions Are Contagious

It has been shown time and again, if you help someone in a meaningful or even a small way, that person is more likely to help others. As Barbara Fredrickson says, "Beyond the dance of positivity between you and the person you helped, those who witness your good deed may well feel inspired, their hearts uplifted and elevated."[41]

This means not only do you reap the benefits of helping somebody else, but that person also benefits, and so does the person he or she helps, and so on. This self-reinforcing and perpetuating aspect of positive emotions, and positivity more generally, is what leads to **upward spirals of positivity, in which your positive behaviors, feelings, and attitudes generate the same in others in a continually reinforcing process.**

Positivity spirals may also work in the other direction. In diverse customer service jobs—such as financial consulting, medical care, retail banking, hair care, and grocery stores—customers who showed delight with the service generated positive emotions in the provider and a subsequent increase in that person's organizational commitment and job satisfaction. We're often pleased when we help somebody and they in turn show appreciation. However, better still, the benefits extend to future customers via improved service behaviors.[42] This illustrates the lasting or enduring effects of positivity.

This contagion occurs in teams too. Positive emotions spread to create team-level emotions that help members new and old feel safe, welcome, and truly part of the team. These benefits lead to improved team performance.[43]

TABLE 7.2   Description of the 10 Most Frequent Positive Emotions

POSITIVE EMOTION	DESCRIPTION
Joy	Visualize this: Your surroundings are safe and familiar. Things are going your way, even better than you expected. Choice requires little effort on your part. Colors are more vivid. There's a spring in your step and your face lights up with a smile and an inner glow.
Gratitude	Imagine you've realized someone has gone out of his or her way to do something different. Your mentor gently steers your career in the right direction, or your physician meets you at the office after hours or on the weekend. Gratitude opens your heart and generates an urge for you to give back, to do something good in return, either for the person who helped you or for someone else.
Serenity	Like joy, serenity includes safe and familiar surroundings and requires little effort on your part. But unlike joy, serenity is low key. It comes when you go on a long, leisurely ride or walk, engage in fulfilling conversation, or get wrapped up in a good book while relaxing on vacation.
Interest	Something novel or different draws your attention, filling you with a sense of possibility or mystery. Unlike the case for joy and serenity, the circumstances call for effort on your part. You're pulled to immerse yourself in what you're discovering.
Hope	Hope is different from most other positive emotions you experience when you're safe and/or satisfied. You are hopeful when something isn't going your way, but you believe that it can.
Pride	You know pride's evil cousins—shame and guilt—and the painful feelings that overcome you when you are to blame for something. Pride is the opposite; you're responsible for something good, something for which you can take credit or that made a positive difference to someone else. (However, unchecked pride is hubris.)
Amusement	Sometimes something unexpected happens that makes you laugh. Amusement is social; it most often occurs in the company of and as a result of others. Heartfelt laughter often accompanies amusement.
Inspiration	When you're inspired you are moved to do something extraordinary, something you might otherwise feel is beyond your abilities. This same feeling rivets your attention, warms your heart, and draws you in. Inspiration doesn't just feel good; it makes you want to act, to improve, or even to be the best you can be.
Awe	Closely related to inspiration is awe which happens on a grand scale. You feel overwhelmed, small, and humble. Awe makes you stop in your tracks. Sometimes people are awed by the beauty of nature (Grand Canyon or Niagara Falls).
Love	Love is not a single positive emotion but incorporates many of the others. When these good feelings stir our hearts within a safe, often close relationship, we call it love. Early stages of romantic relationships involve intense interest in everything and anything the person says. You share amusements and laughter together and as the relationship builds great joy, you begin to share your hopes and dreams for the future together. When the relationship becomes more solid, you experience serenity and can be proud of your partner's achievements, as if they are your own.

SOURCE: Fredrickson, Barbara L. *Positivity.* New York: Three Rivers Press, 2009.

We often think of service encounters from the customer's perspective, but research shows positive customers help generate positive feelings and behaviors in employees. These positive effects can "spiral" beyond a particular encounter to positively affect the employee's other behaviors.

Peathegee Inc/Blend Images

How Much Positivity Is Enough?

Don't overlook the valuable role of negative emotions—life is not all sunshine and roses. Negative emotions can motivate you to try harder and improve, and they can also protect you against harmful situations and communicate to others your need for help or support.[44] Forcing yourself to feel or act as if everything is great all the time is absurd and would certainly undermine your effectiveness, health, and overall well-being. Even the most positive person feels the intense emotional pain associated with experiences of loss and betrayal, and positive people get angry when they or others are treated unfairly. So how much positivity is enough?

Multiple Positives for Every Negative   Some researchers have argued for specific optimal ratios of positive to negative which others have disputed. Yet, all agree that positive and negative experiences are not equivalent. You cannot remedy a negative experience by simply adding a positive one—it's not one for one.

Instead, to flourish and experience the benefits of positive OB discussed in this chapter, you must have three, five, or more positive experiences for every negative.[45] You don't need to focus on which positive emotions you feel at a particular time, but be sure you have multiple positives for every negative one.

Why? Because it has been well-established that our brains respond differently to positive and negative experiences.

- **Negative experiences** activate a survival orientation and lead us to be more responsive to negative information. Our brains actually look harder for negative than for positive information during daily activities.[46] This might help explain why managers tend to give more negative than positive feedback to employees.

- **Positive experiences** activate a supportive orientation and lead us to be more responsive to positive information. This is part of the reason managers, and people more generally, seem receptive to new ideas when in a good mood. The following Applying OB box describes how to boost positivity by injecting some fun.

Applying OB

Boost Positivity with Fun

Of course, everyone likes to have fun, including at work. Thanks to researchers in the 2000s we have scientific support for its benefits in the workplace. Fun in the workplace is defined as: "characteristics or features of the work environment of a social, playful, and humorous nature, which have the potential to trigger positive feelings of enjoyment, amusement, and lighthearted pleasure."[47]

Situation Factor When viewed this way fun is a situation factor, which means it is an input in the Organizing Framework and is something you and your coworkers can control. Some companies are well known for cultivating fun as an important value or part of their culture. For instance, Marriott famously says, "work hard, yet keep it fun." Google leaders have been known to espouse "fun comes from everywhere,"[48] and Southwest Airlines Is well known for its "fun-LUVing" culture and encourages employees to be "creative and add a touch of levity and laughter whenever possible."[49]

Benefits Fun for fun's sake, is fine, but purposefully building a fun work environment has many benefits, such as helping coworkers make new connections while learning something new because of the interactions. Employees also have been found to support one another, be more creative, resilient, and optimistic, all due to fun.[50]

How to Build It Several factors can help cultivate a fun work environment, including:

- Supportive Practices. Be a fun promoter, not a damper. Manager encouragement, participation, and other supportive behaviors help.
- Employee autonomy. Let them play!
- Events. Activities, stimulating job responsibilities, and socializing are ways of building fun. To help ensure your efforts have the desired results, consider the type of activity, those involved In the activity, and make it voluntary. You can't force fun; you can only present the opportunity. Research has found employees generally appreciate mainstream activities aligning with their interests (celebrations for birthdays or achievements) rather than something wacky or with narrow appeal.[51]

This discussion reveals why managers should focus on the good things employees are doing, and why all of us should focus on the positive qualities of coworkers, classmates, business partners, friends, and significant others. You're likely thinking, "sounds good, but how?"

Strategies to Increase Your Positivity The following activities can help increase positive experiences and decrease your negative ones.[52]

Create high-quality connections. Any social interaction, whether with family, coworkers, classmates, or the person ahead of you in line, is a chance to create a high-quality connection. These connections are energizing and enhance your positivity. To transform ordinary interactions into high-quality connections, try the following tips:

1. **Make someone the only person in the room.** Engage the other person by being present, attentive, and affirming. Act as though he or she is the only person in the room.

2. **Support.** Encourage the person and help him or her achieve a goal or attain success.

3. **Give trust.** Believe you can depend on this person to meet your expectations, and let it show.

4. **Goof off,** play, have fun! Have no goals or intentions other than to goof off with others.

Cultivate kindness. Set a goal of performing five new acts of kindness in a single day. Aim for actions that make a difference and come at no cost to you. Assess what those around you might need most and make a plan, but execute your plan so acts of kindness occur on the same day to further enhance the impact.

Develop distractions. One of the best ways to break from negativity is to distract yourself. Brainstorm and think of ways—old and new—to distract yourself from negative thoughts. Be sure to think of things you can do at school, at home, or at work. Make two lists: healthy distractions and unhealthy distractions. Healthy distractions can be going for a run, taking a bike ride, or playing your favorite sport. Unhealthy distractions might be drinking, eating junk food, watching TV, or playing video games. For each unhealthy distraction, challenge yourself to add another healthy distraction to your list. Negativity can creep in anywhere and at any time, so keep your lists of distractions handy and practical.

For example, Sam Kendricks may not be household name, but he is a renowned pole vault champion. He won bronze in the 2016 Olympics, five consecutive national titles, a world championship, and was undefeated in meets in 2017. Obviously, he is a world class talent but what is equally notable is his determination to spread positivity by making friends with and helping support his fellow competitors. The pole vault is one of the loneliest of sports—just you, the pole, and bar—and you either win or lose. Yet during competitions Kendricks gives pointers, coaches, and cheers for his competitors. His positivity was captured in an interview: "They probably thought I seemed a little strange. I really pushed on these other guys that I wanted to be their friend and help them. . . . I had an undefeated season last year, but what good is victory if you can't share it?"[53]

Dispute negative self-talk and thoughts. Write on 3×5-inch cards your most frequent negative thoughts or emotions about yourself, a relationship, or a situation at school, work, or home. Then, in a private place where no one can hear you, read the cards aloud one at a time. After reading each, immediately dispute or counter it. Don't stop to think but beat it down and disprove it with something positive about yourself,

Sam Kendricks treats the pole vault like a team sport. He helps and cheers on his competitors in the middle of meets. He believes friendship and positivity benefit his performance and that of his competitors, and that's how he likes it.
David Emm/Getty Images

the situation, or the facts. Be sure to do this with enthusiasm, to build your conviction. Practice. Your goal is to learn to dispute negative thoughts as quickly as they enter your mind.

Platitudes = Fake = Bad Outcomes   Uttering positive words or forcing a smile isn't enough. Humans are excellent detectors of insincerity.[54] If your positivity is not heartfelt and genuine, you will not reap any of the benefits of improved performance, relationships, and health we've discussed. Disingenuous attempts at positivity may even do harm, because your lack of authenticity may erode others' trust in you and reduce your influence and credibility with them.

Your Level of Positivity   To make this discussion come to life for you, find out the relative frequency of your positive to negative emotions. This knowledge can help you understand many things about yourself, such as how likely you are to reap the benefits of positive emotions and positive OB. Emotions are short-lived, and any measure of your emotions captures your feelings about a specific event, person, or dimension of your life at only a particular point in time. We encourage you to take Self-Assessment 7.1 for the past day of your life, which is intended to capture your positivity more generally. Then take it again, focusing on school or work as your target. Now calculate your ratio of positive to negative emotions for work or school, and compare it to your ratio for life more generally. This will provide knowledge of your positivity in various arenas of life and help you better understand this important personal resource.

SELF-ASSESSMENT 7.1

Learn Your Positivity Ratio

Please be prepared to answer these questions if your instructor has assigned Self-Assessment 7.1 in Connect.

1. What is your reaction to the results?
2. Considering the individual differences (IDs) we discussed in Chapter 3, which ones do you think are contributing to your ratio?
3. Do others see you as more or less positive than your ratio suggests? Why?
4. If you conduct this self-assessment for two different dimensions of your life (school and work), to what do you attribute the differences in the ratios if any?
5. Describe three things you can do to improve your positivity ratio for school.

SOURCE: Barbara Fredrickson, *Positivity: Groundbreaking Research Reveals How to Embrace the Hidden Strength of Positive Emotions, Overcome Negativity, and Thrive,* Crown Publishers, 2009.

Next, we'll explore an approach to positivity and well-being that has received enormous attention, and practice, in the past several years.

7.3 FOSTERING MINDFULNESS

THE BIGGER PICTURE

You may be more aware of mindfulness by its absence, such as when you're saying something you feel is important, yet the person you're speaking to isn't paying attention. In this section, you'll find you can improve your focus and attention through practice, and how doing so can be tremendously beneficial to you, those around you, and your employer.

Mindfulness is "the awareness that emerges through paying attention on purpose, in the present moment, and nonjudgmentally to the unfolding of experience moment by moment."[55] We can be mindful of our inner world (our feelings and thoughts), and our outer world, including the feelings, thoughts, and interactions of others. Everyone has the ability to be mindful, but it takes effort. The default setting in our minds is to judge or evaluate our current internal and external situation,[56] and it is this mental chatter that detracts from the inner quiet we need to stay focused on and aware of what is going on around us.

Mind Full, or Mindful?

Figure 7.2 shows mindfulness is another person factor that creates positivity in work environments, along with a growing number of desirable outcomes for individuals, teams, and organizations. This is why we study it in OB and explore some of the details next.

Big Business

The interest in mindfulness, and meditation more generally, at work has grown tremendously in recent years. Mindfulness is now mainstream and widely practiced by employees and in workplaces everywhere. A study by the Centers for Disease Control and Prevention revealed a two- to three-fold increase in the number of people practicing some sort of mindfulness since 2012.[57] A survey of 163 employers of different sizes and industries found that greater than 52 percent planned to provide mindfulness classes within the next year, and another 25 percent planned to do so within the next two years.[58]

Many companies now sponsor mindfulness training for employees (Google, Nike, Fidelity) and others have cashed in by providing apps and other forms of mindfulness training. Insight Timer, for instance, claims it is the world's most used meditation app with over 6 million users[59] and more than 50,000 hours of meditation per day. This is one small part of the more than $1 billion mindfulness industry.[60] A competitor, Headspace, anticipates doubling its corporate clients in just one year.[61]

Like many other things at work, it helps if senior leaders buy in and are believers in mindfulness. The following OB in Action box describes how the former CEO of Aetna brought mindfulness to his employees, along with the experiences of other companies.

OB in Action

Biotech, Insurance, and Industrials . . . They're All Mindful. What About You?

CEO Is a Believer Mark Bertolini, the former CEO of Aetna Health (which merged with CVS), credits mindfulness with changing his life after a horrible skiing accident before becoming CEO. He used it to help manage the pain and recover from his injuries, and once becoming CEO, he was determined that employees should reap similar benefits. But it wasn't easy. In an interview with *The New York Times* he recalls the CFO at the time saying, "'We're a profit-making entity. This isn't about compassion and collaboration.' I said, 'Well, I actually think it is. And I'm in charge, so we're going to do it.'"[62]

Bertolini also credits mindfulness with boosting the minimum wage at the company. The company's yoga instructor heard numerous complaints regarding pay from employees during the training sessions; these were then shared with Bertolini. He was deeply troubled by the dire financial situations of many employees, which he then acted on by increasing the minimum wage at the company from $12 to $16 per hour.[63] Although mindfulness did not directly cause the change, the classes provided the opportunity for him to learn about employees' plight and open his mind to listen and thus sparked his compassion to act.

Scientists Proved It to Themselves Scientists at biotech company Genentech felt happier and more content at both work and home after using a mindfulness app. Like true scientists, they conducted

Mark Bertolini attributes much of his recovery from a severe skiing accident to mindfulness. He then promoted it throughout the company when CEO at Aetna Health.
Cindy Ord/Getty Images

experiments and used the data to convince HR to offer the Headspace app to all of the company's 14,000 employees. It seems to work, as 2,500 of them now use the app at least four times per week.

Nancy Vitale, senior vice president of human resources at Genentech, said: "Headspace is giving us an opportunity to focus on the health and well-being of our employees. . . . Our mission is bringing breakthrough medicines to patients, and it's critical to foster an environment where employees feel they can give their best."

Industrial Well-Being Industrial giant GE also uses mindfulness training as a part of its employee health and well-being efforts. The company provides one month free and then 60 percent discounts for employees who want to continue. So far feedback has been very positive, according to Global Wellness Leader Adam Malinkoski, and more than 5,000 employees have tried it.[64]

YOUR THOUGHTS?

1. If your employer provided mindfulness training would you participate? Why or why not?

2. If you were CEO would you be willing to give mindfulness training a try? Why or why not?

3. Have you meditated or done yoga? If yes, what are the benefits you experienced? If you haven't personally, what have others you know told you about their experience?

Benefits of Mindfulness

Although mindfulness was originally used as a means for guarding against negative work-related outcomes, such as stress and burnout, now it is promoted for improving a wide range of cognitive, emotional, behavioral, and physical outcomes.[65]

The American Psychological Association has compiled several scientifically supported mindfulness benefits:

1. Less rumination. If you dwell on past or current challenges, you are likely ruminating. Mindfulness can help reduce this often destructive emotional vicious circle.

2. Reduced stress. Stress can have many undesirable effects, which will be explored in more detail in Chapter 16. But there are clear benefits for mindfulness.

3. Improved memory. Many forms of meditation have been shown to improve retention and working memory, beyond the benefits of reducing stress.

4. Better focus. Mindfulness training has been shown to improve focus and decision making.

5. Self-awareness. Mindfulness fosters self-observation and introspection.

6. Greater interpersonal effectiveness and satisfaction. It is likely the other benefits noted contribute to better relationships, but mindfulness helps reduce conflict and lessen the negative effects when it occurs.[66]

Each of these companies has created a climate that fosters positive OB. Do you agree that industry leaders have a larger responsibility to make the world a better place?

Top Left: Michael Lucia/The Oakland Tribune/ZUMA Press, Inc./Alamy Stock Photo; Top Right: Kristoffer Tripplaar/Alamy Stock Photo; Bottom Left: Bjorn Bakstad/Shutterstock; Bottom Right: Asif Islam/Shutterstock

Evidence is accumulating as to the many benefits of mindfulness at work, especially in the areas of performance, interpersonal relationships, and overall well-being. Mindfulness interventions have been shown to increase job performance, organizational citizenship behaviors (OCBs from Chapter 2), and safety behaviors. It's also been shown to improve communications, leadership, and teamwork, while reducing conflict.[67]

It's no wonder so many organizations have explored the benefits of mindfulness. But what about you? Would you like to improve your interpersonal interactions and experience less stress? If yes, then you'll gain insight about your current level of mindfulness by completing Self-Assessment 7.2. Then, in the next section we will walk you through a mindfulness exercise with the hope you'll get some sense of the benefits for your personally. But first, be sure to take the assessment and answer the questions.

SELF-ASSESSMENT 7.2

What Is My Level of Mindfulness?

Please be prepared to answer these questions if your instructor has assigned Self-Assessment 7.2 in Connect.

1. What questions identified your greatest inhibitors? (Select the three items with the lowest scores.)
2. What is the cause of these inhibitors?
3. Examine the techniques listed in the next section and decide which one might be best suited for your needs. Start using the technique on a daily basis.

Practicing Mindfulness

The goal of practicing mindfulness is to help you become more calm-and-collected in all circumstances. An influential book, *The Leader's Way*, explains: "When the mind is disturbed by anger, jealousy, hate, impatience, fear, lack of self-confidence, or negative emotions about things that happened in the past, it is wasting valuable time that instead should be used for constructive thinking."[68] Practicing mindfulness helps you focus your mind on productive activities while constraining counterproductive thinking and mind wandering.

The good news is you can learn mindfulness by practicing a variety of simple meditation techniques on a regular basis. Although there are many good books, articles, and helpful apps,[69] we review two approaches that are easily learned: a breathing meditation and a walking meditation. Research shows practicing short meditative techniques reduces stress and negative emotions and increases emotional regulation, task performance, and memory.[70] Give the techniques a try and note how you feel!

Breathing Meditation   Breathing meditations are easy and can be done almost anywhere. Focusing on breath reminds us of the here and now because it brings us back to a fundamental and vital function of life. This technique requires nothing more than tuning in to the physical sensations associated with breathing in and out. Two experts recommend the following simple approach for getting started:

- Place your hand on your stomach a couple of inches beneath the upside-down V at the center of your rib cage. Look down, breathe normally, and watch your hand. You'll probably see it move only a little bit, and more-or-less up and down. Your abdomen should expand when you inhale and contract on the exhale.
- Leaving your hand in place, now breathe in such a way that your hand moves out and back, perpendicular to your chest. Try to breathe into your hand with real oomph, so that it travels back and forth half an inch or more with each breadth.[71]

Start by trying these two steps for about 10 to 20 breaths. Once you are comfortable with this form of diaphragm breathing, you can take your practice to the next level with these additional instructions:

- Sit comfortably in a chair, feet firmly on the ground and your back relatively erect. Feel like you are a "proud mountain" of stability. Close your eyes and take a deep inhale that fills your belly and lungs. Now exhale, noticing how your belly contracts. Do this twice.

- Add counting to four or five as you both inhale and exhale, to ensure you are taking deep breaths. Try doing this for five minutes twice a day. You can extend the length of time you practice breathing meditations as you become more comfortable with the technique.

Your mind is likely to wander during these exercises. You will also notice sounds around you. That's normal. Acknowledge the thoughts and sounds and return your focus to your breath. Don't try to chase the thoughts away or give the sounds much attention. Just recognize them and let them pass. The thoughts will move away like a white cloud being blown by the wind in a blue sky.

Walking Meditation   This can be done any time you are walking, and no one will know you are doing it. Start this technique by forming an intention or desired goal. Doing this sends a signal to the mind that guides its attentiveness and awareness during the meditative practice.[72] A sample intention is, "I will focus on the act of walking while ignoring other sounds and thoughts."

Experiencing nature can be very meditative and has been found to improve our mood and general outlook. If you want to make a walk like this meditative, take breaks now and then to focus on what you are seeing, hearing, or smelling.

Tananya pitiwatsombat/Shutterstock

Begin walking and keep your intention in mind. Concentrate on placing one foot after the other. Feel the rhythmic nature of your steps. Focus on how it feels to lift and place your feet on the surface. Train your mind to be aware of your footsteps. Notice the speed at which you walk and the pressure being felt by your feet. Consider changing the length of your stride and notice how it feels. If your mind starts to wander or you begin thinking about something you have to do, just recognize the thought and then drop it. Return your attention and awareness to your intention, which is the act of walking. You will be amazed at what you can observe.[73] Try this for five minutes every day for three weeks and observe the effects.

A variation on this technique is to focus your intention on sound or smell. For example, "I will focus on all sounds during my walk," and "I will focus on all smells during my walk." If you use an intention aimed at sound, begin walking and concentrate on what you hear. Listen for all types of sounds like footsteps, birdsong, mechanical objects operating, wind, tree branches rustling, voices, clanging of objects, airplanes overhead, and so on. The key is to allow your mind to focus on anything that can be heard. Again, recognize stray or wandering thoughts, and let them passively go away by returning to your intention. Try this for five to 10 minutes.

Practice Makes Perfect   Mindfulness can be learned via practice, and though it takes time and commitment, the benefits are substantial. The techniques above can get you started, and helpful apps can also guide you through meditative experiences.[74] In addition, your local gym might offer classes. For example, 24 Hour Fitness is exploring the use of special meditative pods that use sound and light to help people meditate.[75]

7.4 PSYCHOLOGICAL CAPITAL AND SIGNATURE STRENGTHS

THE BIGGER PICTURE

Positive psychological capital is part of the positive OB movement and is a key person input in the Organizing Framework (Figure 7.2). You'll often find it explained in terms of its components: hope, efficacy, resiliency, and optimism (HERO). You're about to learn how to develop and benefit from your "inner HERO" or psychological capital. We also explore signature strengths, which are another way to utilize individuals' positive attributes instead of attempting to overcome weaknesses.

Individuals with high levels of *positive psychological capital (PsyCap)* possess considerable hope, efficacy, resilience, and optimism (HERO). To elaborate:

LO 7-4

Describe how psychological capital and signature strengths can improve outcomes at work.

H	**Hope.** Persevering toward goals and, when necessary, redirecting paths in order to succeed.
E	**Efficacy.** Having the confidence to take on challenging tasks and put in the effort necessary to succeed.
R	**Resilience.** When hampered by problems and adversity, sustaining and bouncing back and even beyond to attain success.
O	**Optimism.** Making a positive attribution about succeeding now and in the future.[76]

Besides being positive PsyCap can be developed.[77] Recall from Chapter 3 when we discussed the relative flexibility of individual differences, such as attitudes and emotional intelligence (Figure 3.2). Flexible individual differences are opportunities for you and managers to develop and improve. This means training and practice can increase your PsyCap.

Not only is your PsyCap flexible, but it also has been shown to improve many outcomes in the Organizing Framework, such as increasing job satisfaction, organizational commitment, and well-being, and decreasing intentions to quit, job stress, anxiety, and counterproductive work behaviors.[78]

PsyCap has also been shown to guard against negative experiences and events. One study found employees who were subjected to abusive supervisors, who also had high levels of PsyCap, still performed OCBs.[79] Although these findings are interesting, we would likely advocate for improving or removing the abusive supervisor, instead of developing the PsyCap of employees so they can deal with it better. PsyCap also reduced the degree to which stockholders sold shares due to a negative earnings surprise.[80] Not sure who benefits—the shareholders or the company?

Let's learn how to develop your PsyCap and that of others by focusing on the HERO traits.

Hope = Willpower + Waypower

You're probably thinking, "Of course I know what hope is; what else is there to know?" You may even see yourself as more hopeful than the average person. If this is your view, you might be surprised to learn that hope actually has two components, and knowing this can help you understand why hope works, when it doesn't, and how to build it.

The two components of hope are *willpower* and *waypower*. This means **to have *hope* you need to have a goal and the determination to achieve it—willpower. You also need to see one or more paths to achieve your goal, even when faced with adversity—waypower.**[81] Hope requires both a goal and a means for achieving that goal.

Ben Horowitz, the renowned technology entrepreneur and venture capitalist, puts a high premium on the willpower of entrepreneurs. Willpower, along with genius, are in his mind the two most crucial characteristics of successful entrepreneurs. "Building a company is hard and lonely. It demands relentless focus. And no matter how well you do, you must be ready to be pummeled again and again."[82] It takes willpower to persist. Horowitz himself demonstrated enormous willpower when Loudcloud, an earlier venture with Marc Andreessen, nearly failed half a dozen times before ultimately being revived, strengthened, and sold to HP for $1.6 billion. Horowitz used "force of personality and willpower to make a business out of it," said Herb Allen III, the CEO of Allen & Co.[83]

In a practical sense, hope supports adaptability and change.[84] A series of studies showed hope led to increased adaptability for police officers and insurance sales agents, and in the case of the agents, it also led to increased sales commissions.[85] You can build hope in yourself and others via effective goal setting (Chapter 6).[86] The problem-solving approach can help too, because it can assist you in identifying potential obstacles, sources of support, and feasible alternate paths by which to reach your goal.

Efficacy

We discussed efficacy in Chapter 3; remember efficacy also is a component of your core self-evaluations (CSEs) and represents your confidence in your ability to achieve. It therefore influences the way you perceive the world around you and your ability to deal with challenges and opportunities. Figure 3.4 provides a guide for improving your self-efficacy. Applying your knowledge of self-efficacy will help you realize its important role in positive psychological capital—greater efficacy makes you more confident, more positive, and more effective.

Resilience

If you're *resilient* you have the capacity to consistently bounce back from adversity and to sustain yourself when confronted with challenges. Resilience helps you when things go your way and when they don't—it is your built-in shield and recovery characteristic. Fred Luthans, the father of psychological capital, and his colleagues stated that resilience "is arguably the most important positive resource to navigating a turbulent and stressful workplace."[87]

What gives resilience its power? Resilient people are open to new experiences, flexible to changing demands, and emotionally stable when confronted with adversity.[88] It is no wonder that resilience is a component of psychological capital and positive OB. Resilience can be improved with support, such as coaching or help from others during trying times or experiences. The work climate, discussed in the next section of this chapter, can make employees feel safe enough to take risks and to make mistakes, thus enhancing their resilience.[89] The following OB in Action box illustrates how resilience is used at one of the nation's largest health systems and how to build a resilience program at work.

Optimism

Optimists are both realistic and flexible. Think about it—if you aren't realistic you are setting yourself up to fail. And if you fail too often, even the most optimistic of us loses our motivation and inspiration. True optimists are flexible and willing to revise their views as situations change. (Recall the contingency approach to management discussed in Chapter 1.) However, optimists don't see everything as positive; if so, they would be unrealistic or delusional.

OB in Action

Resilience Is Organizational at Kaiser

Kaiser Permanente is one of the largest health systems in the United States, employing approximately 200,000 employees. Employee wellness is a primary focus for this organization and is led by Kathy Gerwig, VP of employee safety, health, and wellness. Ms. Gerwig is a member of the American Heart Association CEO Roundtable, which has studied the matter and produces the Resilience in the Workplace Report.[90]

Ms. Gerwig and Kaiser address a broad range of issues confronted by workers today: relationships at work, emotional well-being, how we handle stress, and the increasingly dynamic and uncertain career landscape. Kaiser approaches these issues by focusing on six elements of employee well-being: physical health and safety, mental health and wellness, financial well-being, career development, other relationships, and community involvement.[91]

VP Gerwig believes resilience threads through all of these elements, and as such she and Kaiser promote resilience at the individual, department, and organizational levels. For instance, Kaiser offers extensive resilience training not only for its employees, but also for partners in the communities in which it operates, such as schools.

The Resilience in the Workplace Report showed nearly three-quarters of those who participated in resilience training found it beneficial, in part by reducing stress and improving sleep. The AHA report also made recommendations for implementing a workplace resilience program that includes five practices:[92]

1. Understand the problem. Much like our own 3-Step Approach, the AHA recommendation is to identify the problems, find causes, and determine to what extent resilience can help.

2. Create a culture supporting resilience. Develop the appropriate training and other practices to support resilience and stress reduction (paid time off, breaks, wellness programs, and employee development). And very importantly, ensure leadership support and participation.

3. Assess resilience and outcomes at baseline. Measure resilience and other outcomes (job satisfaction, job stress, and sick time used) before implementing interventions, so you have a baseline against which to compare progress.

4. Determine program design. What are the components, who will deliver, who will participate, when, and where?

5. Implement and continuously improve.[93] Just as you learned about performance management in Chapter 6: set goals, measure and evaluate, review and improve, and provide consequences.

This course provides knowledge and tools of great value for each element. Now that you've learned what Kaiser does and the AHA recommends, what are your thoughts?

YOUR THOUGHTS?

1. What is the likelihood you would participate in resilience training if offered by your employer? Why or why not? Explain.

2. Assume you are a manager and a believer in the benefits of resilience at work, what might you do to persuade your employees to participate in resilience training?

3. What are the potential downsides to employability resilience? Explain.

Also recall from Chapter 4 that optimists perceive the causes of events in a particular way. **Optimists often attribute successes to "personal, permanent, and pervasive causes, and negative events to external, temporary, and situation-specific ones."**[94] Scientists argue humans actually have an optimism bias which, in part, alters our views of the likely outcomes in our lives and motivates us to act.[95]

Have you ever wondered why people are optimistic in the first place? What function does optimism serve? One school of thought claims it is self-inspiration, our mind's way of motivating us to move forward even if the future is uncertain. The rationale is if humans didn't think the future would be bright—an improvement over today—they might be crippled with fear and uncertainty, never take risks, and never try to better themselves or their situation. After all, humans have the unique ability to think ahead and to realize they will die some day. If the mind didn't have some way of combating this, then many people would be preoccupied with gloom and wouldn't save money or invest in their children.

Therefore, a belief that things can or will be better in the future not only helps keep our minds at ease, but it reduces stress (discussed in Chapter 16) and helps us color our decisions in a positive, appealing light and keeps us moving forward.

How I Can Develop My PsyCap

Like other more conventional forms of capital (cash, facilities, patents, equipment), PsyCap is a resource you invest in or develop with the expectation of future returns or benefits. It can help you flourish in your professional and personal life. Its components are mutually reinforcing—developing one often helps develop the others.[96] Try putting the following recommendations into practice and develop your PsyCap.

- **Hope development.** Generate a work-related goal important to you and attainable yet challenging. Then, create multiple plans for achieving this goal, share them with others—coworkers or classmates, and get their feedback and recommendations.

- **Efficacy development.** Besides recommendations from Chapter 3, break your larger goal into smaller sub-goals as discussed in Chapter 6. Create plans for achieving the sub-goals and share them with others to gain feedback and recommendations.

- **Resilience development.** Make a list of your personal talents, skills, and social connections. Specify how these can help you achieve your goal, identify potential obstacles, and decide how to avoid them or reduce their impact.[97]

- **Optimism development.** Hope development bolsters your optimism, but it may be helpful to identify obstacles and negative expectations. On your own, check to see whether the obstacles you identify are valid, and have others challenge your assumptions.

Complete Self-Assessment 7.3 to learn your personal PsyCap score, as it can help you understand and improve your ability to find a job, increase your creativity and innovativeness, and reduce the stress in your life.[98] Your score will also serve as the basis for developing hope, efficacy, resiliency, and optimism, as described above.

SELF-ASSESSMENT 7.3   CAREER READINESS

What Is My Level of PsyCap?

Please be prepared to answer these questions if your instructor has assigned Self-Assessment 7.3 in Connect.

1. Which score is the highest? The lowest? Complete the PsyCap development steps and be sure to utilize your highest or strongest component. Pay extra attention to developing the lowest or weakest component.

2. In the Organizing Framework identify a process at all three levels—individual, group, and organizational—that PsyCap is likely to influence.

3. Describe one thing you can do to further develop each component of your PsyCap.

Adapted from F. Luthans, C. M. Youseff, and B. J. Avolio, *Psychological Capital: Developing the Human Competitive Edge* (Oxford, UK: Oxford University Press, 2006).

Let's conclude this section with an exploration of signature strengths.

Signature Strengths

Signature strengths **"are positive human traits that influence thoughts, feelings, and behaviors and provide a sense of fulfillment and meaning."**[99] Signature strengths are a subset, typically three to seven for most individuals, of a larger collection of 24 character strengths (see Table 7.3). What helps differentiate signature strengths from the rest is that "a person owns, celebrates, and frequently exercises"[100] them, and these strengths are "core to people's identities, and feel authentic, exciting, and invigorating when used."[101] Signature strengths can be developed, too.[102]

TABLE 7.3 The 24 Character Strengths

Creativity	Zest	Modesty
Curiosity	Love	Prudence
Judgment	Kindness	Self-regulation
Love of learning	Social intelligence	Beauty
Perspective	Teamwork	Gratitude
Bravery	Fairness	Hope
Perseverance	Leadership	Humor
Honesty	Forgiveness	Religiousness

SOURCE: Harzer, Claudia, and Willibald Ruch. "The Application of Signature Character Strengths and Positive Experiences at Work." *Journal of Happiness Studies* 14, no. 3 (June 2012): 965–83. https://doi.org/10.1007/s10902-012-9364-0.

A Departure from Past and Present   The strengths movement represents a dramatic departure from conventional management research and practice. As noted earlier, the vast majority of writing, research, and managing focuses on how to fix what is wrong and who is underperforming or otherwise not meeting expectations.

Many large and successful organizations have used a strengths approach, for example, VMware, Wayfair, and the Boston Consulting Group. The primary focus is now on employee successes and potential, rather than on missteps and deficiencies.[103] Research by the Gallup organization on employee strengths shows some impressive findings. Employees who report using their strengths every day at work are:

- Three times more likely to feel as though they have an excellent quality of life.
- Six times more likely to be engaged at work.
- 8 percent more productive.
- 15 percent less likely to quit.[104]

Would you like to be more engaged with school, work, and leisure activities? If yes, your signature strengths are very likely the key. Self-Assessment 7.4 will help identify your signature strengths. Use your scores to assess how you might build your strengths into daily activities at school, work, and life.

Applying Strengths at Work   Consultants who work for Gallup, a firm instrumental in the strengths movement, said: "Giving employees a chance to excel by doing what they do best every day seems like a no-brainer. In too many organizations, though, encouraging employees to know and use their strengths at work is limited to a guerrilla movement."[105] This quotation highlights that the fundamental obstacles to realizing the benefits associated with signature strengths are situation factors, such as leaders, managers, performance management practices, and organizational culture. Put another way, of course it is necessary to be aware of your strengths, but it also is necessary to be in situations allowing you to use them.

Recent research should help persuade reluctant employees and leaders. Interventions, or activities and practices designed to identify and use peoples' signature strengths, showed desirable results for a number of outcomes in the Organizing Framework for OB, such as increases in positive emotions, satisfaction, goal attainment, and academic performance, along with decreases in depression and counterproductive work behaviors.[106]

To help with this, we provide the following guidance on how organizations can create environments that foster and utilize employees' strengths:

1. **Look in the mirror.** Like most work endeavors, a strengths approach requires leader support to succeed. Begin with leaders learning their own strengths and being open about them. Leaders, for instance, who show vulnerability and admit to their own mistakes and limitations can serve as powerful role models for the larger organization.

2. **Build strengths into performance management.** Strengths need to be supported by expectations, measurement, review, and rewards. It is an uphill battle to talk about, encourage, and celebrate strengths if performance management practices do not support them.

3. **Know your purpose.** Leaders need to be clear on why they and the organization are focusing on strengths—what is the intended benefit? Is it greater collaboration, increased customer satisfaction, innovation, or reduced turnover? Employees need to understand why and how strengths are important to the organization and its objectives.

4. **Coach and develop strengths-oriented managers.** A strengths approach is not common, and implementing it effectively requires effort. Set your managers up to win by providing appropriate coaching and support.[107]

Since you now have a sense of two flexible and very important positive individual differences—psychological capital and signature strengths—we move to the group/team level in the next section and discuss organizational climate. You'll learn how policies and practices can help foster and realize the positive attributes of employees.

7.5 POSITIVE ORGANIZATIONAL CLIMATES

THE BIGGER PICTURE

Organizational climate describes the way you and your cohorts evaluate the school you attend or the workplace you share. A positive climate is one component that makes positive organizational behavior work, and you're about to discover how organizations and managers can foster such a climate.

You may be the most positive person you know, but to flourish you need the right environment. Figure 7.2 shows organizational culture and climate are the key situation factors that promote positive work environments, meaning they are critical to reaping the benefits of POB. We focus on organizational climate in this section (again in Chapter 10) and organizational culture in Chapter 14.

Organizational climate **consists of employees' shared perceptions of organizational policies, practices, procedures, and routines.**[108] Simply put, organizational climate reflects employees' beliefs about what they see going on at work and what is happening to them. These perceptions can range from positive and uplifting to negative and debilitating. Positive climates, such as one that supports safety, lead to positive outcomes like fewer accidents at work.[109] Supportive climates—those in which employees believe the organization values their contributions, provides support, and cares about their well-being—can serve as a buffer against the demands and stressors in wide range of jobs.[110] In contrast, negative climates that condone abusive supervision or fear are associated with negative outcomes, like less cooperation, less citizenship behavior, and lower performance.[111] What type of climate do you think is most likely to promote positivity from situation factors? The OB in Action box describes how fast-fresh restaurant Sweetgreen does it.

LO 7-5

Develop a climate that promotes positive organizational behavior.

OB in Action

Sweetgreen . . . Sweet Indeed

Sweetgreen is in the fast-casual health food business and focuses on what's good *for* you and what's good *to* you. It sells nourishment, natural and made to order, which is consistent with its mission to "build healthier communities by connecting people to real food."[112] Combine these elements (focus on employees, quality product, and an enormous social media presence) and you have the recipe for success. But the most important ingredient of their success is the company's positive culture. How they do this is quite remarkable.

Emergency Fund. Employees make voluntary donations to an emergency fund used to support other employees in times of need, such as a being displaced by a house fire or for travel to care for a sick family member.

Gratitude. Positive comments from customers are collected and used for personal notes of gratitude from the owners. These are celebrated during Gratitude Nights where employees get together to share and be recognized.

Community Impact. Employees are encouraged and given time to support local causes, and in some cases the efforts are in coordination with larger agencies like the LA Food Policy Council.[113]

Also notable is such positivity does not require vast resources, meaning it isn't just for large, public multinationals companies. Sweetgreen was started by three Georgetown University graduates who started small, but after 11 years have 90 locations and have attracted piles of venture capital. But how did they get here?

What if you want to do something similar? The following advice may help.

- **Job #1—Employee Wellness.** A positive culture isn't possible without tending to employee well-being at work and in their larger life space. Ensure employees have resources for professional development and health.

- **Make It Mean Something.** Like those at Sweetgreen, employees prefer to have a clear purpose in their work, they want to see a meaningful impact. Mission and vision statements can help, but what matters most is how they are put into practice, beginning with the leaders at every level.

- **Goals with Impact.** Include employee development, community involvement, and customers in your goals. The knowledge and skills learned in Chapter 6 can help.

Jeffrey MacMillan/The Washington Post/Getty Images

- **Be Positive.** Positivity needs to be part of daily practice, so express gratitude, smile, be optimistic. Remember, emotions are contagious, make yours positive and infectious.[114]

YOUR THOUGHTS?

1. What is most compelling to you about the Sweetgreen approach?

2. What do you think are the 2 or 3 biggest challenges for managers of Sweetgreen restaurants?

3. Assume you started a business, what do you think would be the challenges of implementing a similarly positive approach? How might you address such challenges?

Figure 7.4 presents a model showing positive climates are a function of organizational values, organizational practices, and virtuous leadership. We'll explore each of these situation factors next.

Organizational Values

We defined *values* in Chapter 2 as abstract ideals that guide our thinking and behavior across all situations. In the context of organizational climate, organizational values represent ideals endorsed, shared, and supported by the organization as a whole. Three global values essential for promoting positive organizational behavior are described next (see Figure 7.4).[115]

1. ***Restorative justice* reflects "a shared belief in the importance of resolving conflict multilaterally through the inclusion of victims, offenders, and all other stakeholders."**[116] Organizations subscribing to restorative justice tend to resolve conflict by giving all parties a chance to express their thoughts and feelings. This in turn leads to healing when there has been hurt or offense, thereby producing solutions focusing on the greater good.

2. **Compassion is a shared value that drives people to help others who are suffering.** It is associated with behaviors related to sympathy, kindness, tenderness, warmth, and love.[117]

3. **Temperance is a shared belief in showing restraint and control when faced with temptation and provocation.** Temperance promotes self-control, humility, and prudence. It helps people avoid egocentric and heated emotional responses and practice patience and restraint.[118]

Organizational Practices

Organizational practices **are the procedures, policies, practices, routines, and rules that organizations use to get things done.** Figure 7.4 shows training programs, support programs, and human resource practices and policies represent three key sets of practices that shape organizational climate.[119] Employees have greater commitment, satisfaction, citizenship behavior, and performance—and lower absenteeism and intentions to quit—when they believe organizational practices support them professionally or personally.[120]

Marc Benioff, CEO and co-founder of Salesforce, has created a company climate that fosters positive OB. Many would consider him a virtuous leader. He exudes benevolence and often speaks of how leaders in all industries, but especially technology, have a larger responsibility to make the world a better place. Certainly not at the expense of profits, but while making them.

Salesforce's organizational practices are clearly employee focused. It provides exceptional benefits and rewards for its employees, such as bonuses for employee referrals. It paid out over $5 million for such referrals in 2017. It also uses its software to identify employees who have not been promoted within the past year and a half and actively seeks new challenges and opportunities for them. All employees are given 56 hours of paid leave each year to volunteer in the community. No wonder it was number two on *Fortune*'s 2019 list of Best Places to Work.[121]

Benioff's conduct and the company's practices reflect underlying values of compassion, temperance, and restorative justice. For instance, Benioff is outspoken and addresses social issues often, including those related to LGBTQ rights, pay equity, and the downsides of social media.[122]

Virtuous Leadership

Virtuousness represents "what individuals and organizations aspire to be when they are at their very best."[123] The focus of virtuous leadership is to help individuals, groups, and organizations to elevate, enrich, and flourish. Although Chapter 12 provides a broad discussion of leadership, we consider it here as well due to its significant relationship with organizational climate.[124]

OB scholars have proposed a variety of traits and individual differences that underlie virtuous leadership. The four shown in Figure 7.4 were selected because they are most frequently discussed in OB research. Virtuous leaders are more focused on the *greater good* than on self-interest.

Virtuous leaders tend to promote *trust* by making sure their words match their actions, and by treating people with respect and dignity. *Integrity,* which comes from being guided by morals and honesty, fosters positive OB. For example, people who lied less over 10 weeks were found to have improved mental and physical health than people who lied more frequently.[125]

The final component of virtuous leadership, **forgiveness,** is "the capacity to foster collective abandonment of justified resentment, bitterness, and blame, and, instead, it is the adoption of positive, forward-looking approaches in response to harm or damage."[126] In addition to promoting positive outcomes, forgiveness can affect your health. Research shows that *unforgiveness* is associated with bitterness, anger, health problems, and premature death.[127]

7.6 FLOURISHING: THE DESTINATION OF POB

THE BIGGER PICTURE

If asked what you want out of life, you might reply you want to be happy. One early leader in the positive psychology movement eventually went beyond that goal and proposed another: *Flourishing*. You may find this broadened goal to include even more of your true aspirations. Flourishing, a key individual-level outcome in the Organizing Framework, includes five elements: positive emotions, engagement, relationships, meaning, and achievement (PERMA).

Martin Seligman, a renowned psychologist from the University of Pennsylvania, has studied happiness and well-being for over 30 years. He is credited as the driver of today's positive psychology movement, which is the forerunner of POB.[128] Seligman originally believed happiness was the most important outcome in our lives but has changed his mind over the years. He now believes people equate happiness with being cheerful, and you don't have to be cheerful to be physically or psychologically healthy.

LO 7-6

Create the conditions for flourishing in your job and career.

Seligman proposed that **well-being was the combined impact of five elements—positive emotions, engagement, relationships, meaning, and achievement (PERMA).** Well-being comes from freely pursuing one or more of these five elements.[129]

Flourishing represents the extent to which our lives contain PERMA. PERMA is the most important outcome from the process of positivity shown in Figure 7.2 When we flourish, our lives are characterized by "goodness . . . growth, and resilience."[130] We should all strive to flourish because of its association with other positive outcomes like lower cardiovascular risk, lower levels of inflammation, longer life, greater REM sleep, and positive mental health.[131] PERMA elements are also positively related to important outcomes in the Organizing Framework—task performance, career satisfaction, organizational commitment, and low turnover.[132]

An interesting study of first-year university students found the following experiences contributed most to their flourishing:

- Socializing with new and old friends.
- Enjoying their academic subjects.
- Having more free time.
- Understanding and performing well in class.[133]

This demonstrates the importance of positive emotions, relationships, and achievement—PERMA—in college.

Flourishing is also profitable. Many investors now include social responsibility and a focus on the greater good when it comes to employees and communities as key criteria in their investment decisions.

Positive Emotions

Although we thoroughly discussed positive emotions earlier in this chapter, one aspect of Barbara Fredrickson's "broaden and build" theory bears repeating because it enhances your ability to experience the other components of PERMA. Positive emotions *broaden* your perspective as to how to overcome challenges in life. For example, the emotion of joy is more likely to lead you to envision creative ideas during a brainstorming session. Positive emotions also *build* on themselves, resulting in a spreading of positive emotions within yourself and to those around you.

Some companies understand the power of positive emotions and the significant damage possible from negative emotions. The Applying OB box shows how this knowledge is applied in the context of recruiting—not to those that are hired but to those that are not.

Applying OB

CAREER READINESS

Converting Rejection into Business, or Not

The reality when interviewing for a job is only one person can get it. If it isn't you, then you join the often hundreds of other applicants who were rejected. How you feel about this is in part a function of how you were treated by the prospective employer. Feeling disappointed about the outcome is one thing; however, your feeling disrespected or even scorned can make an enormous difference to that company's bottom line.

Talent Board, a nonprofit devoted to improving job candidate experience, has a "candidate experiences resentment calculator" to help organizations estimate how much mistreated candidates can cost. They approach each candidate as though they were a potential or current customer for a given company's products or services, with the potential to spend $100 per year. Let's say this same company has 100 applicants for 10 jobs. This equates to 1,000 people to delight, or at the very least not disappoint. You can see how the numbers can get large, really large. Multiply those numbers year after year and you can clearly see the potential for both positive and negative impact. Talent Board has also showed that nearly three-quarters of candidates would be inclined to do business with a company which treated them well in the interview process, and 46 percent said they would end the relationship if treated poorly.[134]

Kimberly-Clark understands this potential. The enormous consumer goods company (Huggies, Cottonelle, and Kleenex) sends coupons to candidates who are interviewed via phone, and also requires managers to send thank you notes to those who interview face-to-face. More importantly, they keep candidates informed of the process.[135]

Research shows candidates expect and appreciate interviews to be conducted as scheduled and for hiring decisions to be made and communicated as intended. Not surprisingly, the top reason candidates withdraw from the process is prospective employers not being respectful of their time. The classic and all too common example is: "We plan to hold interviews in two weeks and will get in touch," but six weeks pass by and still no communication or action.[136]

So, how do you and your employer foster positive candidate experiences? The following advice can help you in evaluating the care and respect you have or have not bestowed on candidates (or you have experienced as a candidate).

1. **Manage Expectations.** This seems so obvious, yet is too often ignored. Organizations need to give thought to and communicate the details, and make good on them, such as content and length of resumes, what to expect during interviews (phone, Skype, or face-to-face), timing, and other details related to the process. If prospective employers don't provide them, candidates will, thus increasing the chances of unmet expectations and undesirable outcomes.

2. **Listen.** In almost any search and hiring process candidates want to ask questions and to be heard. It is helpful to train those involved in the process to listen, ask if there are questions, and give candidates opportunities to make their case.

3. **Be Accountable.** The hiring organization needs to apply performance management techniques (see Chapter 6), to ensure the goals and expectations are clear, measured, evaluated, and reinforced. A good hiring process requires more than filling the position; importantly, data needs to be collected on those not hired too. This information can provide valuable insights, such as identifying candidates for future jobs and revising the recruiting messaging to attract better candidates.

4. **Manage Decision Time and Communication.** Most processes involve a series of cuts or rounds, and candidates should be informed promptly when they are no longer being considered. For candidates who make it far into the process, the courtesy of a phone call should be given and for others a promptly sent e-mail will do. Don't wait weeks and months to do this. Communicate final decisions promptly as many candidates are not sitting around waiting. Her or his application to your company is unlikely to be the only one awaiting a decision.
5. **Fairness.** You've learned about fairness many times in this book already, and it is no surprise it can make or break a candidate's experience and thus add to or subtract from the company's bottom line. If candidates feel they did not get a fair chance, or were not appropriately considered, there is a problem.
6. **Be Sure to Include This Question.** Regardless of the job or process, consider asking every candidate, "Is there anything else you would like us to know?"[137]

Apply this knowledge if you're ever in the position of hiring others because tending to these details can have a significant impact on you and your organization's ability to make good hires in the short and long term, as well as impact the potential to gain or lose customers. Keep these factors in mind when interviewing for positions, as the way in which prospective employers tend to these details may assist you in determining whether they are worthy of your talents and/or your business.

Engagement

You recall from Chapter 2 that employee engagement reflects the extent to which you are physically, cognitively, and emotionally engaged in an activity, task, or project. This state is sometimes called being "in the zone" or in a state of "flow." **Flow "is the state of being completely involved in an activity for its own sake."**[138] Flow is a positive state because our well-being benefits from our deep attention to and engagement with an activity.

Engagement and positive emotions are not one and the same. When we are *in flow,* we are not necessarily thinking about anything; we are just doing! Our concentration is so high during flow that we use all the cognitive and emotional resources normally needed for thought and feelings.

How can you create engagement or flow for yourself? Seligman and others suggest this is a two-part sequence consisting of (1) identifying your signature strengths and (2) learning to use them in daily personal and work activities.[139] For us, working on this book, teaching, and playing golf are activities that put us into flow. Once you have identified your strengths, you can work with your manager to determine how to incorporate them into your job.

Relationships

Think of the last time you had a belly-laugh, felt joyous, were inspired, or experienced awe. Were you with someone else at the time? We suspect so, because positive emotions are often associated with activities that include others.

Biologists explain that humans are creatures of the hive. After studying insects like wasps, termites, and ants, researchers concluded the group is a natural unit of selection. In other words, both insects and people prefer to be in groups and to work collaboratively with others to get things done. For insects it is building a fortress or hive and for us it is completing tasks and projects, socializing, sharing memories, and traveling.

While others may on occasion annoy us, positive relationships are a strong contributor to our well-being. They buffer us from stressors and provide resources enabling us to more effectively accomplish tasks. Positive relationships fuel the giving and receiving of social support. **Social support is the amount of perceived helpfulness we derive from social relationships.** There are four types.

- *Esteem support:* reassurance a person is accepted and respected despite any problems or inadequacies.
- *Informational support:* help defining, understanding, and coping with problems.
- *Social companionship:* time spent with others in leisure and recreational activities.
- *Instrumental support:* financial aid, material resources, or needed services.[140]

You can enhance your level of flourishing by seeking social support, but you will also flourish by providing support to others, particularly in the form of kindness. Research shows us the exhibition of kindness produces significant increases in well-being.[141] Conduct a kindness exercise by doing a completely unexpected thing for someone else. It can be as simple as holding a door open for another to pass through or helping someone with directions. Notice how you feel. You should experience one or more positive emotions.

Meaningfulness

Viktor Frankl, an Austrian neurologist and psychiatrist who survived the Holocaust, was a strong proponent of using meaningfulness to promote well-being. His best-selling book *Man's Search for Meaning* chronicled his experiences in concentration camps and summarized what he learned from these events. Frankl's conclusion was "striving to find a meaning in one's life is the primary motivational force" for people.[142] In other words, it is the drive to find meaning in our lives that instills in us a sense of purpose and motivation to pursue goals.

First responders, and the many others that assist in the recovery of natural disasters, work for more than just a paycheck. It is safe to assume they find tremendous meaningfulness in their work.

Frederic J. Brown/AFP/Getty Images

Meaningfulness is the sense of "belonging to and serving something that you believe is bigger than the self."[143] In our case, for instance, we derive meaning from writing this book because we believe it can enrich your life and help you manage others more effectively. We have three suggestions for building meaning into your life.

1. **Identify activities you love doing.** Try to do more of these activities or find ways to build them into your work role. Employees at Stryker, a medical devices company headquartered in Michigan, are encouraged to witness the impact of their work. They observe surgeries, interact with doctors and patients, and some have even performed procedures on cadavers to get a different perspective. Stryker is #11 on *Fortune*'s 2019 Best Places to Work.[144]

2. **Find a way to build your natural strengths into your personal and work life.** You assessed your signature strengths earlier in Self-Assessment 7.4. Kimley-Horn, a planning and design company (e.g., hospitals, resorts, and sports facilities) and #18 on *Fortune*'s list, asks and allows employees to set up their own "mini-practices" where they identify new locations for developing new projects for their diverse customers.[145] The company's website states: "Employees know our culture and approach to business are built on a desire to see our staff flourish, one and all."[146]

3. **Go out and help someone.** Research shows people derive a sense of meaningfulness from helping others.[147] Accounting and consulting firm Crowe-Horwath clearly believes in helping others; for instance, it provides its employees with 96 paid hours to volunteer annually. That's 12 eight-hour work days for each employee totaling about 30,000 hours of community, pro-bono, and volunteer service![148] Helping others creates the upward spiral of positivity we discussed earlier in this chapter.

Achievement

The final component of PERMA, achievement, pertains to the extent to which you have a self-directed "achieving life." In other words, we flourish when we pursue achievement for its own sake. Doing so fosters feelings of competence and mastery, which in turn enhances our self-esteem and self-efficacy. Companies help employees achieve by providing skills-based training and professional developmental activities. *Training* magazine created a list of the top 125 U.S. companies that invest in such training. The top five in 2018 were Leading Real Estate Companies of the World, New York Community Bancorp, Sonic Automotive, BNSF Railway Company, and Dollar General Corporation.[149]

Let's conclude this chapter with a few explicit applications of the knowledge and tools from this chapter.

7.7 MAKING THE CONNECTION: HOW CAN I FLOURISH AT SCHOOL, WORK, AND HOME?

THE BIGGER PICTURE

We conclude this chapter with a number of practical applications of POB knowledge and tools to improve your effectiveness as both an employee and manager.

LO 7-7

Describe the implications of positive organizational behavior for you and managers.

Takeaways for Me

There are six ways you can apply the material in this chapter:

1. **Share important information and provide effective feedback. Since positive practices amplify positive outcomes, you can improve your work environment by identifying and emphasizing such practices, like sharing important information and providing effective feedback.**

2. **If you are upset with your partner or coworker, try to think of at least three things you like or appreciate about him or her.** Similarly, if someone is upset with you, realize you need several positive interactions or actions to compensate for each negative.

3. **Develop a plan to be more mindful.** Techniques like meditation and yoga can enhance your ability to focus and hold your attention. Many good books and apps can help in this pursuit.

4. **Making your goals SMART *and* formulating effective action plans will help build your level of hope (goal + path = hope).** Hope should boost your goal commitment and success.

5. **You can contribute to a positive organizational climate by adhering to the values your employer endorses and by trying to be more virtuous.**

6. **Develop a plan to build PERMA into your life by focusing on those components over which you have more control.** You can make a choice to be more positive, you can work on building more positive relationships in your life, and you can strive for achievement.

Takeaways for Managers

There are seven key implications for managers:

1. **Identify existing positive practices, such as appropriately and regularly recognizing performance, and emphasize them.** Role-model these practices and watch your people flourish.

2. **Realize your emotions are contagious.** To build a positive environment for your people, be positive yourself. Random acts of kindness can go a long way (give someone a spot bonus or an afternoon off or throw an impromptu celebration in the office).

3. **Model mindfulness by being focused on the present moment whenever you are talking or meeting with others.** You can also establish a policy of not using web-based or mobile technologies during meetings.

4. **Encourage your employer to train employees in mindfulness techniques.**

5. **Learn about and utilize your strengths and those of the people you manage.** Be sure to verbally acknowledge others' strengths and create opportunities for them to be used.

6. **Endorse and model your employer's stated corporate values and engage in more virtuous leadership.**

7. **Support your employees' level of PERMA by engaging in one or more of the following:** (1) display positive emotions at work, (2) identify the tasks or responsibilities that engage your employees and find ways to design them into their jobs, (3) provide the four sources of social support when possible, (4) use I-deals, discussed in Chapter 5, to help employees find meaning in their work, and (5) encourage creative approaches to achieving goals.

We hope you now have a greater understanding of the tangible and far-reaching benefits of positivity and positive OB. Use this knowledge to improve not only your own well-being and performance, but that of your coworkers and friends.

What Did I Learn?

In this chapter, you learned positive OB focuses on creating work environments in which people flourish, and a number of techniques that can help increase your positivity at school and home. Reinforce and consolidate your learning with the Key Points and Organizing Framework. Then challenge your mastery of the material by completing the Problem-Solving Application Case and Legal/Ethical Challenge below.

Key Points for Understanding Chapter 7

You learned the following key points.

7.1 THE VALUE OF POSITIVITY

- Positive OB emphasizes positive inputs, processes, and outcomes across all three levels of OB.
- Positive OB operates via *amplifying, buffering,* and *positivity.*
- Positivity is more than positive thinking and improves health, relationships, performance, and many other aspects of your jobs and career.

7.2 THE POWER OF POSITIVE EMOTIONS

- Negative emotions cause you to narrow your focus, while positive emotions cause you to broaden your thinking.
- Positive emotions are contagious and can be actively increased.
- Research shows you need multiple positive experiences to overcome or compensate for each negative.

7.3 FOSTERING MINDFULNESS

- Mindfulness is fostered by paying attention to the present moment in a nonjudgmental way.
- Mindfulness can be learned through a variety of simple "meditative" techniques practiced on a regular basis.

7.4 PSYCHOLOGICAL CAPITAL AND SIGNATURE STRENGTHS

- Positive psychological capital (PsyCap) consists of hope, efficacy, resilience, and optimism (HERO).
- Hope includes not only a goal and determination to achieve it, but also one or more clear paths for achieving it.
- Resilience is your ability to bounce back after adversity and sustain yourself.
- Optimism attributes positive events to personal, permanent, and pervasive factors.
- Signature strengths are a handful of personal attributes influencing your thoughts, feelings, and behaviors.

7.5 POSITIVE ORGANIZATIONAL CLIMATES

- Organizational climate represents employees' perceptions of an organization's policies, practices, procedures, and routines.
- Positive organizational climates are a function of organizational values, organizational practices, and virtuous leadership.
- The key components of virtuous leadership are a focus on the greater good, trust, integrity, and forgiveness.

7.6 FLOURISHING: THE DESTINATION OF POB

- Flourishing reflects the extent to which our lives contain positive emotions, engagement, relationships, meaning, and achievement (PERMA).
- Positive emotions are contagious.
- You can increase engagement by using your signature strengths in everyday activities.
- Four key types of social support are esteem support, informational support, social companionship, and instrumental support.

7.7 HOW CAN I FLOURISH AT SCHOOL, WORK, AND HOME?

- Well-being Is comprised of positive emotions, engagement, relationships, meaning, and achievement (PERMA).
- Flourishing reflects the extent to which our lives contain PERMA.
- Meaningfulness can be enhanced by doing things you love, utilizing your strengths, and helping others.

The Organizing Framework for Chapter 7

Figure 7.5 shows four person factors and five situation factors contribute to positive outcomes across the three levels of OB. You can also see there are processes at the individual, group/team, and organizational level that affect outcomes. As for outcomes affected by the inputs and processes shown in Figure 7.5, individual-level ones include task performance, work attitudes, flourishing, physical health, citizenship behavior/counterproductive behavior, turnover, and creativity. At the group/team level, outcomes include group/team performance and group cohesion and conflict. Finally, at the organizational level, outcomes include financial performance, overall organizational performance, and customer satisfaction.

FIGURE 7.5 Organizing Framework for Understanding and Applying OB

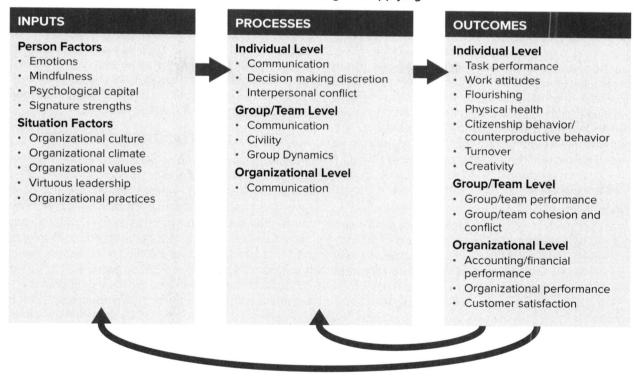

INPUTS	PROCESSES	OUTCOMES
Person Factors • Emotions • Mindfulness • Psychological capital • Signature strengths **Situation Factors** • Organizational culture • Organizational climate • Organizational values • Virtuous leadership • Organizational practices	**Individual Level** • Communication • Decision making discretion • Interpersonal conflict **Group/Team Level** • Communication • Civility • Group Dynamics **Organizational Level** • Communication	**Individual Level** • Task performance • Work attitudes • Flourishing • Physical health • Citizenship behavior/counterproductive behavior • Turnover • Creativity **Group/Team Level** • Group/team performance • Group/team cohesion and conflict **Organizational Level** • Accounting/financial performance • Organizational performance • Customer satisfaction

Opioids: Pain Relief, Grief, and Purdue

HISTORY OF OPIOIDS AND MEDICAL USE

The human experience contains both joy and pain, and physical forms of the latter have many causes, from disease to trauma. Since the 1800s humans have been treating pain with opioids, a class of very powerful painkillers extracted and created from the opium poppy, such as heroin, morphine, and codeine. To provide a sense of the long history and use of opioids, it is interesting to note the Bayer Company manufactured heroin for commercial sale in 1898. One of the major uses at the time was as a cough suppressant, and not just for pain relief. The addictive properties became well known by the 1920s and the sale of heroin was banned.[150]

World War II was a turning point in opioid use. The scale of the war resulted in enormous numbers of injuries and soldiers who suffered from both acute and chronic pain, but physicians then had a limited arsenal with which to treat such conditions. Oxycodone, manufactured from a chemical in opium, was one of the drugs used in what was then the early days of what we now refer to as pain management. New drugs entered the market in the 1970s, like Percodan (oxycodone and aspirin) and Percocet (oxycodone and acetaminophen), but most physicians were taught to avoid prescribing such highly addictive medications to patients.[151]

CHANGING VIEWS

The scenario began to change in the 1980s when an article printed in the *New England Journal of Medicine* pushed back against the perceived dangers of prescribing opioids. The physician author claimed addictions were rare in patients with no history of addiction, and adverse effects were no greater than those of other drugs.[152]

People with chronic pain, such as those with terminal illnesses, became the new patients for opioids. In a few short years, physicians' perceptions had changed, and the risks of abuse and addiction were seen as relatively low compared to the benefits for patients in otherwise dire circumstances.[153]

Although addiction and abuse were very real, by the 1990s medical opinions were shifting and prioritizing pain management as a primary motive and responsibility for physicians everywhere.[154] This resulted in a much greater use of opioids, which to this point had all been very fast-acting. This was problematic for millions of patients whose pain was more or less constant, such as those with cancer, since fast-acting pain relievers had to be taken about every four hours. Longer-acting and safer alternatives were desperately needed.[155]

ENTER PURDUE PHARMA AND OXYCONTIN

Purdue Pharma is a private company founded by three Sackler brothers in 1952, and it has been run or at least controlled by Sacklers ever since. The family has amassed an enormous fortune, estimated at approximately $13 billion by *Forbes* in 2016, and have donated generously to universities, medical schools, and museums around the world:[156] Tuft's University, University of Nebraska, National Academy of Sciences, New York Presbyterian Hospital, Dia Art Foundation, Global Poverty Project, Victoria and Albert Museum in London, the Guggenheim, and the Brooklyn Museum.[157]

Purdue Pharma began testing OxyContin, an extended release version of oxycodone (in use since the early 1900s), in 1994 with the hopes of filling the need in the market: effective and extended pain relief with reduced addictive qualities. The drug was approved and brought to market in 1996 as a safe alternative to existing opioids. During the same space of time painkiller prescriptions increased from 2 million to over 10 million per year.[158] One current estimate puts total sales of OxyContin at $35 billion for Purdue.[159]

CONDUCT AND CONSEQUENCES

Purdue's marketing efforts were aggressive and effective. For instance, a doctor in a promotional video stated: "These drugs, which I repeat, are our best, strongest pain medications, should be used much more than they are for patients in pain." Only a year later painkiller prescriptions had jumped by 11 million, not to 11 million but an additional 11 million. Sales grew from $48 million in 1996 to nearly $1.1 billion in 2000, and this was spurred by dozens of pain management and speaker training conferences across the U.S., attended by more than 5,000 physicians, pharmacists, and nurses (all-expenses-paid). In 2001 alone, Purdue was said to have spent $200 million on promoting the use of opioids and OxyContin.[160] The goal of course was to educate, and boost prescriptions.

After OxyContin's launch in 1996, Purdue more than doubled its number of sales reps and provided extremely generous sales incentives. Average annual salaries for reps were $55,000 and annual bonuses averaged over $70,000 (ranging from $15,000 to more than $200,000). To spur sales further still, representatives provided coupons for physicians to offer to patients a free month's supply.[161] Purdue didn't just incentivize sales, it pressured them too. Court documents show that a sales VP sent a message chastising the representatives in the

Boston sales district. He threatened that if sales of opioids didn't increase then those representatives should be fired; he wanted to send a message. The sales manager allegedly agreed.[162]

By 2003 nearly half of all OxyContin prescriptions came from primary care physicians, rather than anesthesiologists and other specialists who previously dominated pain management and treatment.

WHERE ARE THE LEADERS IN ALL OF THIS?

Amid the growing evidence of abuse in the early 2000s, Richard Sackler, then chairman and president of Purdue, fought back, advising the company and its representatives to push the blame onto the addicts themselves. He was quoted as saying, "We have to hammer on abusers in every way possible. . . . They are the culprits in the problem. They are reckless criminals."[163]

These aggressive tactics ultimately cost the company over $600 million in fines, when in 2007 three executives pled guilty for misrepresenting the dangers of OxyContin. The Sacklers, however, were not accused and faced no personal repercussions. The Sacklers and Purdue Pharma pressed on and explored selling the product in countries with no controls on such medications while at the same time expanding promotions in the U.S.

OTHER CONTRIBUTORS

At the turn of the millennium some regulatory changes accelerated the popularity of prescription painkillers. The Joint Commission, a major governing body that reviews and accredits hospitals and medical centers, began requiring all patients to be assessed for pain and failing to do so effectively would result in a sanction. The Joint Commission printed a book in 2000 to be used by physicians in continuing education seminars, citing the evidence for opioid addiction was limited and their use effective. (Note: The book was sponsored by Purdue Pharma, and the Joint Commission removed this standard in 2009.)[164]

In 2010 Purdue Pharma released a new formulation of OxyContin, one which was reformulated to make it more difficult to crush and snort, as was commonly done by those that abused it. This was done in response to the growing evidence of abuse, but research and clinicians continued to question the efficacy of this reformulation.

WHERE ARE WE NOW?

By 2016 the director of the Centers for Disease Control, Dr. Tom Frieden, wrote in the *New England Journal of Medicine*, "We know of no other medication routinely used for a nonfatal condition that kills patients so frequently." He noted that data on long-term opioid use was still lacking, but what he did know at the time was that perhaps as many as 26 percent of patients using opioids for chronic noncancer pain become dependent on it.[165]

In early 2019, Massachusetts Attorney General Maura Healy charged Purdue Pharma and eight members of the Sackler family with exacerbating the opioid epidemic. The indictment accuses them of personally micromanaging a long-term deceptive marketing campaign to encourage hundreds of employees and tens of thousands of physicians to inappropriately prescribe Oxycontin.

Citing the CDC, AG Healy claimed approximately 400,000 people died from opioid overdoses between 1999 and 2017, and the family's role was central and thus they should be held accountable. Thirty-five other states are also suing Purdue Pharma for downplaying the risks and promoting Oxy as a less additive alternative opioid.[166]

Assume you are the CEO and chair of the board of Purdue, but not a member of the Sackler family. What would you do?

APPLY THE 3-STEP PROBLEM-SOLVING APPROACH TO OB

STEP 1: Define the problem.

Use the Organizing Framework in Figure 7.5 and the 3-Step Problem-Solving Approach to help identify inputs, processes, and outcomes relative to this case.

A. Look first at the Outcomes box of the Organizing Framework to help identify the important problem(s) in this case. Remember that a problem is a gap between a desired and current state. State your problem as a gap and be sure to consider problems at all three levels. If more than one desired outcome is not being accomplished, decide which one is most important and focus on it for steps 2 and 3.

B. Cases have key players, and problems are generally viewed from a particular player's perspective. You need to determine from whose perspective—employee, manager, team, or the organization—you're defining the problem. In this case, you're asked to assume the role of CEO and chair of the board of directors for Purdue (but not a member of the Sackler family).

C. Use details in the case to determine the key problem. Don't assume, infer, or create problems not included in the case.

D. To refine your choice, ask yourself, *why is this a problem?* Explaining why helps refine and focus your thinking. Focus on topics in the current chapter, because we generally select cases illustrating concepts specifically located within the current chapter.

STEP 2: Identify causes.

Using material from this chapter and summarized in the Organizing Framework, identify the causes of the problem you identified in Step 1. Remember, causes tend to appear in either the Inputs or Processes boxes.

A. Start by looking at the Organizing Framework (Figure 7.5) and decide which person factors, if any, are most likely causes of the defined problem. For each cause, explain why this is a cause of the problem. Asking *why* multiple times is more likely to lead you to root causes of the problem. For example, do executive characteristics help explain the problem you defined in Step 1?

B. Follow the same process for the situation factors. For each ask yourself, *why is this a cause?* By asking why multiple times you are likely to arrive at a complete and more accurate list of causes. Again, look to the Organizing Framework for this chapter for guidance. Did particular policies or practices play a role?

C. Now consider the Processes box in the Organizing Framework. Are any processes at the individual, group/team, or organizational level potential causes of your defined problem? For any process you consider, ask yourself, *why is this a cause?* Again, do this for several iterations to arrive at the root causes.

D. To check the accuracy or appropriateness of the causes, be sure to map them onto the defined

problem and confirm the link or cause and effect connection.

STEP 3: Recommend solutions.
Make your recommendations for solving the problem. Consider whether you want to resolve it, solve it, or dissolve it (see Section 1.5). Which recommendation is desirable and feasible?

A. Given the causes you identified in Step 2, what are your best recommendations? Use material in the current chapter that best suits the cause. Consider the OB in Action and Applying OB boxes, because these contain insights into what others have done.

B. Be sure to consider the Organizing Framework—both person and situation factors—as well as processes at different levels.

C. Create an action plan for implementing your recommendations and be sure your recommendations map onto the causes and resolve the problem.

LEGAL/ETHICAL CHALLENGE

Is Hiring Candidates with Criminal Records Wise or Risky?

Let's start with some perspective: 33 percent. That is the proportion of working-age Americans with a criminal record.[167] Each year approximately 650,000 people are released from prison,[168] which is about the same as the population of Memphis, TN, or Portland, OR. All of their offenses are not equal of course, but before hastily deciding whether you would hire somebody with a record or not it helps to consider just how many people have this label.

Many hiring managers and companies have knee-jerk reactions to exclude such candidates, as reflected on many applications with the infamous box, "Have you ever been convicted of a crime? Yes or No." When job markets are flush with candidates, excluding these candidates may not be such a problem. However, when the job market is hot and labor is tight, many companies across industries might think differently. And of course, some companies, industries, and geographies are confronted with seemingly eternal talent shortages regardless of the economy. This means such exclusionary policies may shrink an already small talent pool.

Putting the economy and labor market aside, individuals and companies excluding those with records typically do so on the grounds of limiting their liability and/or ensuring employee and customer safety. On the other side of this argument are those who feel people should be given a second chance: they've paid their debt to society. Research done by the Society of Human Resource Management found the three top

reasons reported for hiring candidates with criminal records were: (1) desire to hire the best available candidate, (2) give workers a second chance, and (3) improve the community.[169]

Many have argued it is unfair for criminals to be forever handicapped in the job market because of a past offense. This has led many states and cities to "ban the box" and require companies to wait until a hiring decision has been made before doing a criminal record check. On the other side of this argument is that waiting until late in the hiring process costs companies and individuals time and money, and therefore they should be allowed to gather and consider that information at the beginning.[170]

What Would You Do?

What would you do regarding candidates with criminal records if you owned your company?

1. Would you use the "box" to identify and exclude candidates with records if the law allows it in your city and state? Justify your decision.

2. How would you justify the decision to not use criminal records in the hiring criteria. Justify your decision.

3. Would you take a middle-ground position and use criminal records in some way or to some extent? Explain how and why.

4. Invent other options.

PART TWO

Groups

8

Groups and Teams

After reading this chapter, you should be able to:

LO 8-1 Describe the key characteristics of groups and differentiate them from those of teams.

LO 8-2 Explain the group development process.

LO 8-3 Apply your knowledge of teams to increase your value as an employee and a team player.

LO 8-4 Build and repair trust.

LO 8-5 Illustrate your ability to foster team effectiveness.

LO 8-6 Describe the implications of groups and teams for you and managers.

Figure 8.1 summarizes what you will learn in this chapter. The main focus is on groups and teams and the associated processes within the Organizing Framework. You'll see that group and team dynamics affect outcomes across all levels of OB. For instance, groups and teams powerfully affect the individual-level outcomes of their members, for instance, task performance, work attitudes, turnover, flourishing, and creativity. Groups and teams similarly affect their own collective outcomes, such as group/team performance, group satisfaction, and group cohesion and conflict. Finally, because many organizations consist of teams, they also affect organization-level outcomes like financial performance, organizational performance, customer satisfaction, and innovation.

FIGURE 8.1   Organizing Framework for Understanding and Applying OB

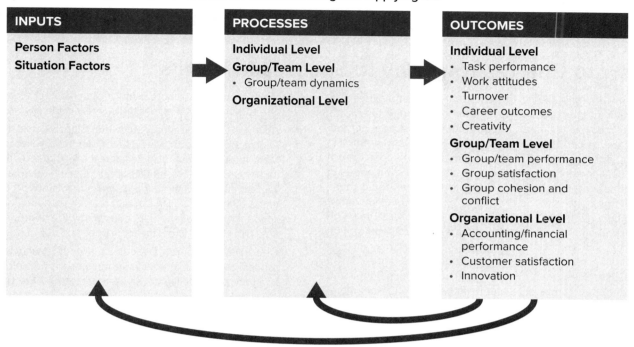

INPUTS	PROCESSES	OUTCOMES
Person Factors **Situation Factors**	**Individual Level** **Group/Team Level** • Group/team dynamics **Organizational Level**	**Individual Level** • Task performance • Work attitudes • Turnover • Career outcomes • Creativity **Group/Team Level** • Group/team performance • Group satisfaction • Group cohesion and conflict **Organizational Level** • Accounting/financial performance • Customer satisfaction • Innovation

In addition to being responsible for important outcomes, like rescuing the injured or even saving their lives, military medical teams illustrate most, if not all, of the team concepts covered in this chapter. For instance, they serve both organizational and individual functions, complete complex tasks that individuals acting alone cannot, and confirm individual team members' self-esteem and sense of identity. The members of military medical teams fulfill various task and maintenance roles essential to effective team dynamics and functioning, such as information seeker and encourager. Fundamental to all of this are the teamwork competencies of the team members—possessing and applying their relevant knowledge and skills in constructive ways for the benefit of the soldiers they save and the overall team. Source: Sgt. Daniel Schroeder/U.S. Army

Winning at Work

How to Charter Your Way to Success in Teams

When working in teams, most students and employees simply dive in and tackle the task at hand. Although this works sometimes, many times it doesn't. There are a variety of reasons teams underperform and you will learn about many in this chapter. Some of the most fundamental causes are a lack of alignment on what needs to be done, how it needs to be done, and by whom. One way to help overcome these challenges is to create a **team charter, which is a document detailing members' mutual expectations about how the team will operate, allocate resources, resolve conflict, and meet its commitments.**[1] Creating the charter may include identifying member strengths, setting goals, agreeing on processes for communication and decision making, and deciding how to measure and use contributions from members. The process of creating a charter gives the team an opportunity to consider the capabilities of its members along with important contextual factors that can either help or hinder the team's efforts.[2]

Experts recommend including the following elements:[3]

1. *Mission statement:* Like organization mission statements (Chapter 16), team charter mission statements describe why a team exists—its overarching purpose. Be careful not to describe this mission in terms of a goal, for example, "get a good grade." Missions focus on and articulate a higher purpose. For example, the American Humane Society's is: "Celebrating animals, confronting cruelty." This statement tells people why the organization exists, not how it achieves this mission.

2. *Team vision:* Vision statements are forward-looking and describe what the team looks like when functioning at its best. A vision has more detail than a mission statement and describes how its actions and deliverables (products and services) affect specific outcomes and stakeholders, like other team members, customers, professors, other students and coworkers, and suppliers. The Humane Society's team mission is "to promote the human-animal bond, protect street animals, advance farm animal welfare, stop wildlife abuse, curtail and eliminate painful animal testing, respond to natural disasters and confront animal cruelty in all its forms."[4]

3. *Team identity:* It helps to create a team name and perhaps a logo to help signify membership. These can serve as important ways for team members to connect to the team and to distinguish the team and its members from other individuals and teams. Think of the names and mascots of sports teams and the functions they serve. It can be helpful to use the same elements in your own teams at school and work. Team rosters including each member's name, e-mail address, phone number, and schedule can assist in making communication and planning teamwork much more efficient. This task becomes even more useful if each member's team-related strengths and responsibilities are included as well.

4. *Boundaries:* Boundaries identify the values, such as timely and quality work, to which team members will commit. Many effective teams also describe the legitimate activities of the team, which are details about what the team will and will not do and what members will and will not do in the name of the team. It is also important to agree to and describe the key stakeholders affected by the team's activities. This clarifies whom the team does and does not serve.

5. *Operating guidelines:* Describe the team structure and processes, including how leadership and other roles will function, how decisions will be made, how work will be allocated, and how members will communicate with each other and with those outside the team. It can be very helpful to describe how conflict will be managed, insofar as processes and consequences.

6. *Performance norms and consequences:* Team researchers have shown that effective teams often outline the performance expectations, including: how team and member performance will be assessed; how members are expected to interact with each other; how dysfunctional behaviors will be managed; how team members will be disciplined for not adhering to team norms; the process for terminating a member from the team; expectations for team meetings; expectations for member contributions to team projects; consequences for work that is late or of poor quality; how tasks for team projects will be allocated to individual team members.[5]

7. *Charter endorsement:* Every team member should sign an endorsement signifying commitment to the elements of the charter.

What's Ahead in This Chapter

We begin Part Two of this book with a discussion of groups and teams. Your performance at work and school improves when you understand the differences between formal and informal groups, because the two have different functions, roles, norms, and dynamics. Next, we describe the group and team development process, and we'll differentiate groups from teams and explore important team concepts, such as different types of teams and the nature of their interdependence. A number of key team characteristics also are explored, including team competencies and teamwork. The value of trust is covered next, because trust is a critical element for group and team functioning. We close by exploring facilitators for team effectiveness—common purpose, composition, collaboration, and rewards.

8.1 GROUP CHARACTERISTICS

THE BIGGER PICTURE

Groups are different from teams, can be formal or informal, and serve multiple functions. Group roles and norms are the means by which expectations are communicated to groups and their members, and they are powerful forms of social control influencing group and member behavior. They may also influence several important outcomes across the levels in the Organizing Framework.

Most fundamentally, we use groups and teams at work because the complexity and demands are simply too great to be managed by individuals.[6] Although we'll address teams separately later in the chapter, it is easiest and best if we define and differentiate groups and teams upfront. It will eliminate the suspense, head off some obvious questions, prevent you from looking ahead for the answer, and keep you focused on groups for the moment.

Groups and teams can be described using three characteristics:[7]

1. **Dependence** is the extent to which one member's tasks and responsibilities are linked to those of other members.
2. **Accountability** involves who is responsible for the tasks and related outcomes.
3. **Time** is the duration members spend to together completing tasks and responsibilities.

Using these characteristics, groups and teams are differentiated in Table 8.1.

Drawing on Table 8.1, we define **_groups_** as collections of two or more individuals with low or no task dependency, who are not accountable to each other for their work, and who may or may not assemble for a specified period of time. _Teams_ are collections of two or more individuals whose tasks and responsibilities depend on the other members, are collectively accountable for the performance and outcomes associated with their work, and work together for the time required for task completion.

To add more clarity, let's use as an example an airplane's passengers and crew.[9] Passengers are a group and the crew are a team. Despite being on the same flight, passengers have a variety of goals and reasons for flying. Your reasons are more often than not independent of my reasons. The crew of the plane, however, is a team as their tasks and

LO 8-1

Describe the key characteristics of groups and differentiate them from those of teams.

TABLE 8.1 Three Characteristics for Describing and Differentiating Groups and Teams.[8]

DIFFERENTIATING CHARACTERISTICS	GROUPS	TEAMS
Task Dependency	Independent. Members' tasks and responsibilities are independent from each other.	Interdependent. Members' tasks and responsibilities are interdependent.
Accountability	Individual. Performance and other outcomes are the responsibilities of individual members.	Shared. Performance and other outcomes are shared responsibilities among members.
Time Together	Unspecified. May be unspecified as most often not linked to a specific task or goal.	Specific. Generally, for a specific amount of time required to complete a task or goal.

SOURCE: Nemeth, Bianka. "Group vs team: What's the difference?" _Session Lab_, January 13, 2018. https://www.sessionlab.com/blog/working-with-groups-and-teams/.

responsibilities are linked or interdependent. If a pilot or flight attendant doesn't show up for a flight, then other members of the crew are affected and unable to do their jobs, either appropriately or at all.

Passengers are only accountable for their own actions. If you miss your flight, then it is only you who is accountable for your actions and must pay for the consequences. Crew members, in contrast, are accountable for each other as noted above. Pilots can't do their jobs without the flight attendants and vice versa. If one attendant doesn't meet his responsibilities, then another needs to pick up the slack (shared accountability).

Once the flight lands passengers may connect to other flights and continue their travels, or not. Either way it has nothing to do with the other passengers. As for the crew, they delivered the passengers from city A to city B, a common goal, and their job is done.

Groups are commonly further differentiated in terms of formal and informal, which you'll learn about next.

Formal and Informal Groups

Individuals join or are assigned to groups for various purposes. **A *formal group* is assigned by an organization or its managers to accomplish specific goals.** Such groups often have labels: work group, team, committee, or task force. **An *informal group* exists when the members' overriding purpose in getting together is friendship or a common interest.**[10] Formal and informal groups often overlap, for instance, when a team of analysts play tennis after work.

Functions of Informal Groups   Informal groups often form around particular interests or causes and typically do not have goals or objectives. This is not surprising as they operate without formal rules or authority, and members generally come and go as they please. Nearly all of your social media groups (people and causes you follow) are examples of informal groups. The 120 million-plus people who follow Cristiano Ronaldo on Instagram constitute an informal group, as do the 100 million that follow Dwayne Johnson and another 100 million for Beyoncé.[11]

A particularly valuable and increasingly common informal group is former employees, or what companies variously call comeback colleagues, boomerang employees, or simply alumni. When treated well former employees can be extremely valuable, providing quality job candidate referrals, partnering opportunities, and rehires. Some companies have truly seized such opportunities. Sedexo, the food service company, has 9,000 management-level former employees registered in its alumni network. And this group is the source of approximately 20 percent of the hires it makes each year![12]

Deloitte, an early adopter who launched its alumni program in 2000, has hundreds of thousands of former employees in its alumni group, from which it made 2,800 hires in 2017. This makes perfect sense—former employees know the culture, know the work, and ramp up very quickly.[13]

Functions of Formal Groups   Formal groups fulfill two basic functions: *organizational* and *individual* (see Table 8.2). Complex combinations of these functions can be found in formal groups at any given time.

Next, let's learn about roles and norms, two of the most powerful influences on individual behavior in groups.

Roles and Norms: The Social Building Blocks of Group and Organizational Behavior

Groups transform individuals into functioning organizational members through subtle yet powerful social forces. These social forces, in effect, turn "I" into "we" and "me" into "us." Group influence weaves individuals into the organization's social fabric by communicating and enforcing both role expectations and norms. That is, group members positively

TABLE 8.2 Formal Groups Fulfill Organizational and Individual Functions

ORGANIZATIONAL FUNCTIONS	INDIVIDUAL FUNCTIONS
1. Accomplish complex, interdependent tasks that are beyond the capabilities of individuals.	1. Satisfy the individual's need for affiliation.
2. Generate new ideas and solutions.	2. Develop, enhance, and confirm the individual's self-esteem and sense of identity.
3. Coordinate inter-departmental and inter-organizational efforts.	3. Give individuals an opportunity to test and share their perceptions of (social) reality.
4. Provide a problem-solving mechanism for complex problems requiring varied information and assessments.	4. Reduce the individual's anxieties and feelings of insecurity and powerlessness.
5. Implement complex decisions.	5. Provide a problem-solving mechanism for personal and interpersonal problems.
6. Socialize and train newcomers.	

SOURCE: Schein, Edgar H. *Organizational Psychology.* New Jersey: Prentice-Hall, 1988.

reinforce those who adhere to roles and norms with friendship and acceptance. Nonconformists, in contrast, experience criticism and even ostracism or rejection by group members. Anyone who has experienced the "silent treatment" from a group of friends knows what a potent social weapon ostracism can be. Let's look at how roles and norms develop and why they are enforced.

What Are Roles and Why Do They Matter?

A *role* is a set of expected behaviors for a particular position, and a ***group role* is a set of shared expected behaviors for members of the group as a whole.** Each role you play is defined in part by the expectations of that role.[14] In the role of student, you are expected to be motivated to learn, conscientious, participative, and attentive. Professors are expected to be knowledgeable, prepared, and genuinely interested in student learning. Sociologists view roles and their associated expectations as a fundamental basis of human interaction and experience.

Two types of roles are particularly important—*task* and *maintenance*. Effective groups ensure that both are being fulfilled (see Table 8.3). **Task roles enable the work group to define, clarify, and pursue a common purpose;** and *maintenance roles* **foster supportive and constructive interpersonal relationships.** Task roles keep the group *on track,* while maintenance roles keep the group *together.* Members can play more than one role at a time, or over time.

To illustrate, think of a team for one of your classes, perhaps a team case analysis. When the team meets and a member clarifies the deliverables for the assignment, that person is playing a task role (information seeker/giver in Table 8.3). If another member solicits input from all other members, to ensure their voices are heard, then this person is playing a maintenance role (gatekeeper in Table 8.3). The group's leader or any of its members can play any of the task and maintenance roles in combination or in sequence.

The task and maintenance roles listed in Table 8.3 can serve as a handy checklist for managers and group leaders who wish to ensure group development (discussed in the next section of this chapter) and effectiveness (the last section of this chapter).

Learn about your own group role preferences by completing Self-Assessment 8.1. This knowledge can help you understand why you might have been more or less satisfied with a particular group or team of which you've been a member. Playing roles that don't match your preferences is likely to be less satisfying. Furthermore, understanding your own preferences will enable you to set yourself up to be happy and productive in future groups, because you can volunteer for or position yourself to play the roles you prefer.

TABLE 8.3 Task and Maintenance Roles[15]

TASK ROLES	DESCRIPTION
Initiator	Suggests new goals or ideas
Information seeker/giver	Clarifies key issues
Opinion seeker/giver	Clarifies pertinent values
Elaborator	Promotes greater understanding through examples or exploration of implications
Coordinator	Pulls together ideas and suggestions
Orienter	Keeps group headed toward its stated goal(s)
Evaluator	Tests group's accomplishments with various criteria such as logic and practicality
Energizer	Prods group to move along or to accomplish more
Procedural technician	Performs routine duties (handing out materials or rearranging seats)
Recorder	Performs a "group memory" function by documenting discussion and outcomes

MAINTENANCE ROLES	DESCRIPTION
Encourager	Fosters group solidarity by accepting and praising various points of view
Harmonizer	Mediates conflict through reconciliation or humor
Compromiser	Helps resolve conflict by meeting others halfway
Gatekeeper	Encourages all group members to participate
Standard setter	Evaluates the quality of group processes
Commentator	Records and comments on group processes/dynamics
Follower	Serves as a passive audience

SOURCE: Porteus, Ann. "Roles People Play in Groups." Stanford University. Accessed April 4, 2019. https://web.stanford.edu/group/resed/resed/staffresources/RM/training/grouproles.html

SELF-ASSESSMENT 8.1

Group and Team Role Preference Scale

Please be prepared to answer these questions if your instructor has assigned Self-Assessment 8.1 in Connect.

1. Does your preferred role (the one with the highest score) match your perceptions? Justify your answer using examples of your behavior.

2. Given your preferred role, how can you be most effective in group assignments? What challenges might playing your preferred role cause for you? For your group?

3. Describe how playing your least preferred role (the one with the lowest score) has been problematic for you and one of your teams. Explain two ways you could improve your performance and that of your team by working on this deficiency.

What Are Norms and Why Do They Matter? *Norms* are shared attitudes, opinions, feelings, or behaviors that guide individual and group behavior. Norms are more encompassing than roles, which tend to be at the individual level in the Organizing Framework and pertain to a specific job or situation. Norms are shared and apply to the group, team, or organization. They help create order and allow groups to function more efficiently because they save groups from having to figure out how to do the same things each time they meet. Norms also help groups move through the development process you'll learn about in the following section.

Although norms are typically unwritten and are seldom discussed openly, they have a powerful influence on group and organizational behavior. Like organizational culture, individual members and group behavior are guided in part by shared expectations and norms. For example, the 3M Co. has a norm whereby employees devote 15 percent of their time to thinking big, pursuing new ideas, or further developing something spawned from their other work. The "15 percent time" program, as it is called, was started in 1948 and supports the culture of innovation for which 3M is known. Terry Ceulemans, 3M's Global Director for Automotive and Aerospace Solutions, views this practice as the company investing 15 percent of its labor costs into innovation, and the returns have been enormous. Products like Post-It Notes, reflective traffic lights, and Scotchguard might have never been invented otherwise.[16]

Although Google has abandoned its 20% practice, Gmail, AdSense, and Google Talk were all attributed to projects employees developed during this time.[17] Twitter and others who do hack-a-thons provide other successful examples.

Researchers and others have utilized "blue sky" time with great success, such as Andre Geim and Konstantin Novoselov, who won the Nobel Prize in physics with experiments they did on Friday (on their "own time"). The idea is simply to be disciplined and be sure to allocate time to think freely, pursue pet projects, or explore other ideas.[18]

Norms serve many purposes and are thus reinforced by the group. Some of these reasons are listed in Table 8.4.

Norms can emerge on their own over time. For instance, think of the group of friends you socialized with on Friday night. What were some of the norms of behavior? Were these norms the result of discussion and explicit agreement? That's highly unlikely. They just happened.

In contrast, norms can also be purposefully created, which is what we advocate. Why leave things to chance when you can directly influence them for the better? The World Health Organization (WHO) sets norms, as described in the OB In Action box related to the Safe Surgery Checklist. Although the 19 items are an actual written list, they typically are not formally required, which would make them rules.

TABLE 8.4 Why Norms Are Reinforced

NORM	REASON	EXAMPLE OF REINFORCEMENT
"Make our department look good in top management's eyes."	Group/organization survival	A staff specialist vigorously defends the vital role of her department at a divisional meeting and is later complimented by her boss.
"Work hard and don't make waves."	Clarification of behavioral expectations	A senior manager takes a young associate aside and cautions him to be a bit more patient with coworkers who see things differently.
"Be a team player, not a star."	Avoidance of embarrassment	A project team member is ridiculed by her peers for dominating the discussion during a progress report to top management.
"Make customer service our top priority."	Clarification of central values	Two sales representatives are given a surprise Friday afternoon party for winning best-in-the-industry customer service awards from an industry association.

OB in Action

The mission of the World Health Organization (WHO) is to improve health for people around the world, including improving surgical outcomes. This mission is reflected in the Safe Surgery Checklist which outlines three stages of surgery and the important tasks associated with each. The aim is to reduce the most common and avoidable surgical risks. To do this, the checklist recommends that a surgery coordinator (a specific task role) be assigned to ensure that each task is complete before the surgical team moves to the next stage.[19]

Stage 1—(Sign In) Before Administering Anesthesia: Confirm patient identity, site, procedure, and consent; mark the site of the surgery; perform anesthesia safety check; turn pulse oximeter on.

Stage 2—(Time Out) Before Incision: Confirm all team members have introduced themselves by name and role; surgeon, anesthesiologist, and nurse confirm patient, procedure, and site; surgeon reviews critical steps and potential challenges; anesthesiologist checks for potential problems; nursing team reviews that all equipment and personnel are in place. Confirm appropriate medications have been administered.

Stage 3—(Sign Out) Before Patient Leaves Operating Room: Nurse verbally confirms with the team— name of procedure has been recorded; instrument, sponge, and needle counts are correct; specimen is labeled and includes patient's name; surgeon, anesthesiologist, and nurse review post-op concerns, medications, and pain management.

The list was created by a broad interdisciplinary team of surgeons, gynecologists, anesthetists, nurses, infection control experts, public health personnel, patient advocates, and biomedical engineers. Central to the Safe Surgery Checklist's development and implementation is teamwork. The intention is to improve surgical outcomes by embedding norms related to communication and teamwork, regardless of the location of a clinic or available resources, such as technology and clinical training.[20]

Results have been impressive with studies reporting a 47 percent reduction in mortality and a 36 percent reduction in complications.[21] However, other research has shown consistent and effective implementation varies dramatically, depending on individual, procedural, and contextual factors. Those that helped facilitate effective use were well-informed specialists, supporters for use of the list, along with teams who are genuinely focused on the intended benefits and content of the list.[22]

YOUR THOUGHTS?

1. Think of an effective team of which you are or have been a member. What are some of the norms to which you would attribute the team's effectiveness?

2. Now think of a team that is ineffective. What norms do you think contribute to its lower performance?

3. Now think of a team you belong to currently. What are two norms you feel would improve its effectiveness?

Finally, another way to think about roles and norms is as peer pressure. Peer pressure is about expectations, and we all know how effective or problematic expectations can be. At its root, peer pressure is simply the influence of the group on the individual, and the expectations of associated roles and norms are the means of this influence.

8.2 THE GROUP DEVELOPMENT PROCESS

THE BIGGER PICTURE

You'll find working in groups and teams much easier when you recognize that they often follow a development process. One such process has five stages, and the other is called *punctuated equilibrium*. We explore both and help you understand the problems and benefits common to groups and teams as they evolve. Your application of this knowledge will enable you to more effectively manage individual- and group-level outcomes in the Organizing Framework and perform more successfully in work and school groups.

At work and school groups and teams go through a development process. Sometimes this development is like the life cycle of products in marketing or like human development in biology. That is, it consists of stages of a specific number, sequence, length, and nature. Other kinds of groups form, progress in a stable manner for a while, but then respond to an event by radically changing their approach.[23] We discuss both development processes, beginning with the most popular—Tuckman's five-stage model (see Figure 8.2).

LO 8-2

Explain the group development process.

FIGURE 8.2 Tuckman's Five-Stage Model of Group Development

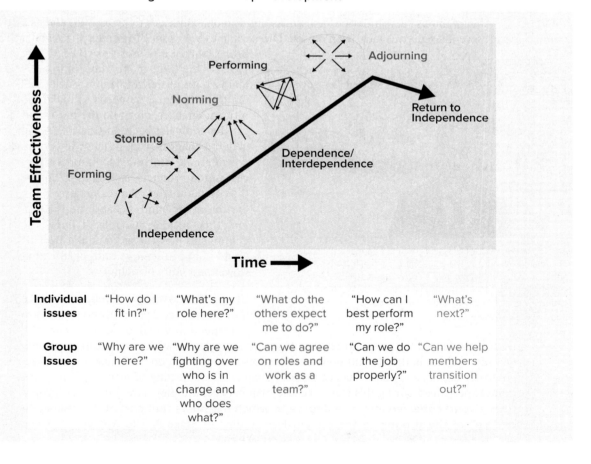

Individual issues	"How do I fit in?"	"What's my role here?"	"What do the others expect me to do?"	"How can I best perform my role?"	"What's next?"
Group Issues	"Why are we here?"	"Why are we fighting over who is in charge and who does what?"	"Can we agree on roles and work as a team?"	"Can we do the job properly?"	"Can we help members transition out?"

Tuckman's Five-Stage Model of Group Development

Tuckman's five-stage model of group development—forming, storming, norming, performing, adjourning—has great practical appeal because it is easy to remember and apply.[24] Notice in the top part of Figure 8.2 how individuals give up an increasing amount of their independence as a group develops. The lower box in the figure also describes some of the issues faced by individual members and the larger group as it develops.

The five stages are not necessarily of the same duration or intensity. For instance, the storming stage may be practically nonexistent or painfully long, depending on the goal clarity, commitment, and maturity of the members.

Stage 1: Forming   During the ice-breaking forming stage, group members tend to be uncertain and anxious about the unknowns such as their roles, the people in charge, and the group's goals. Mutual trust is low, and there is a good deal of holding back to see who takes charge and how.

Some research shows that conflict among group members is actually beneficial during this stage. For instance, early conflict in product development teams can boost creativity.[25] However, the results can also be quite different. For example, in the life-and-death situations sometimes faced by surgical teams and airline cockpit crews, the uncertainty inherent in the early stages of development (forming and storming) can be dangerous.

Stage 2: Storming   The storming stage is a time of testing. Individuals test the leader's policies and assumptions as they try to decide how they fit into the power structure. Subgroups may form and resist the current direction of a leader or another subgroup. In fact, some management experts say the reason many new CEOs don't survive is they never get beyond the storming stage. Yet still other executive changes are made because the board feels things need to be stirred up, as was the case at Volkswagen in 2018 when it inserted Herbert Diess as the new CEO.

The infamous "defeat device" and emissions scandal continues to haunt VW, and as a result several executives have been ousted. Diess came to VW from BMW after the scandal broke, thus he is not ensnared in the mess. This will make developing his teams both easier and more difficult.[26] On the one hand, he needs to make significant changes, clean up the mess, and get the company back on track. Presumably the changes he'll initiate will involve considerable storming to improve processes and products, as well as to ensure the company stays on a scandal-free path. On the other hand, because he is not a long-time insider, he doesn't know the culture and how things work at VW. This could make norming and performing slower and more difficult.

As CEO of VW, Herbert Diess has both the benefit and handicap of coming from outside the company. He benefits from not being entrenched in many of the norms and culture to which the emissions scandal is attributed, but he also lacks the knowledge of how to get things done effectively within the company.

Odd Andersen/AFP/Getty Images

Stage 3: Norming   Groups that make it through Stage 2 generally do so because a respected member, other than the leader, challenges the group to resolve its power struggles so work can be accomplished. Questions about authority and power are best resolved through unemotional, matter-of-fact group discussion, and soft influence tactics (Chapter 12). A feeling of team spirit is sometimes experienced during this stage because members believe they have found their proper roles. **Group cohesiveness, the degree to which members feel part of the collective or "we" of the group,**[27] is the principal by-product of Stage 3. The Applying OB box describes some practical tips for cultivating cohesiveness.

How to Cultivate Cohesiveness and Success[28]

Cohesiveness can greatly improve the functioning of groups and teams, and it thus is important to your success as a team member and team leader. Foundational to group cohesion are trust and cooperation, topics you'll learn about in different places in this chapter. But here, several members of the Forbes Coaches Council shared advice from their own experiences to help you.

1. **Clarify commitments.** Individual and collective roles and responsibilities must be determined, communicated, measured, and reinforced. Accountability is key, as team members not following through or delivering as they are expected to build resentment and erode cohesiveness.

2. **Give trust to get trust.** Most team members understand the importance of trust, and leaders commonly emphasize this point. However, before expecting and lecturing others on trust you should assess how trusting you've been. Have you allowed others to take on important responsibilities and do their part without your oversight?

3. **Share and welcome.** It's one thing to offer your insights, talents, and experiences for the benefit of the team, but it is equally important, regardless of your role, to welcome, expect, and facilitate the same from others. You don't have all the answers or the best Ideas, so be aware and don't act as though you do.

4. **Disagree respectfully.** Disagreements are expected and can be functional and desirable, as you'll learn In Chapter 10. However, few things undermine cohesiveness faster than disrespectful language and behaviors. Model it and don't tolerate it.

5. **Eat, play, love.** You don't have to love each other to have a cohesive, high-performing group, but engaging in social activities together can break down barriers and loosen people up, enabling them to reveal more about themselves and be more vulnerable. This may lead to greater cohesiveness within the group at work or school.

There are other ways to cultivate cohesiveness, but give some of these a try with a team from one of your classes and make note of the benefits.

Stage 4: Performing Activity during this vital stage is focused on solving task problems, as contributors get their work done without hampering others. This stage is characterized by a climate of open communication, strong cooperation, and lots of helping behavior. Conflicts and job boundary disputes are handled constructively and efficiently. Cohesiveness and personal commitment to group goals help the group achieve more than could any one individual acting alone.

Stage 5: Adjourning The group's work is done; it is time to move on to other things. The return to independence can be eased by rituals such as parties or award ceremonies celebrating the end and new beginnings. During the adjourning stage, leaders must emphasize valuable lessons learned.

Punctuated Equilibrium

In contrast to the discrete stages of Tuckman's model, some groups follow a form of development called **punctuated equilibrium, as groups establish periods of stable functioning until an event causes a dramatic change in norms, roles, and/or objectives; the group then establishes and maintains new norms of functioning, returning to equilibrium** (see Figure 8.3). Extreme examples of punctuated equilibrium often occur because of disruptive technologies, like Apple's introduction of iTunes. This innovation caused all players in the music industry to radically change their approaches from digital to streaming and from purchasing entire albums to buying individual songs and subscriptions. Something similar happened when Netflix started renting out DVDs through the mail, then streaming, and now they are the global streaming colossus.[29]

In such scenarios, companies and teams that adapt will realize tremendous new opportunities, but those that don't often find themselves obsolete and go out of business. This phenomenon plays out at all levels of OB, such that punctuated equilibrium at the organizational level drives significant change, development, and opportunity at the group and individual levels too. Many careers have been extinguished and others ignited due to punctuated equilibrium. Apply your new knowledge of OB to be sure yours is one that benefits.

Although much of what you have learned thus far also applies to teams, they have important differences and unique characteristics that we'll explore next.

FIGURE 8.3   Punctuated Equilibrium

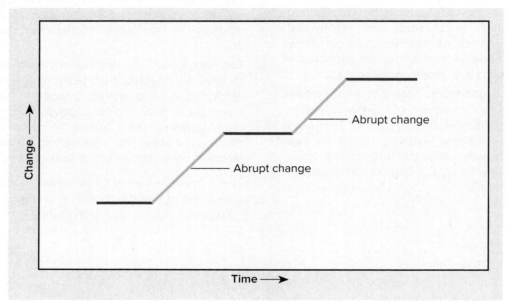

8.3 TEAMS AND THE POWER OF COMMON PURPOSE

THE BIGGER PICTURE

When you better understand the difference between groups and teams, you'll be well equipped to perform better in both. You'll find practical tips in our discussion of critical teamwork competencies, along with a description of various types of teams. This section concludes with a discussion of team interdependence, a characteristic that is fundamental to the functioning of teams.

As noted previously, teams are a collection of individuals whose tasks and responsibilities depend on the other members, are collectively accountable for the performance and outcomes associated with their work, and who work together for the time required for task completion or to fulfill their responsibilities. To further your understanding of the differences between groups and teams, Self-Assessment 8.2 guides you through a simple way of determining the maturity level of a past or present team of which you were or are a member.

LO 8-3

Apply your knowledge of teams to increase your value as an employee and team player.

SELF-ASSESSMENT 8.2

Is This a Mature Work Group or a Team?

Please be prepared to answer these questions if your instructor has assigned Self-Assessment 8.2 in Connect.

1. Does your evaluation help explain why the group or team was successful or not? Explain.

2. Was (or is) there anything you could have done (or can do) to increase the maturity of this group? Explain.

3. How will this evaluation help you be a more effective group member or leader in the future?

Besides being a central component of the Organizing Framework, teams are a cornerstone of work life. This means practically all employees need to develop skills related to being good team players and building effective teams. It also means that in today's team-focused work environment, organizations need leaders who are adept at teamwork themselves and can cultivate the level of trust necessary to foster constructive teamwork.[30] To help you be more effective in the team context, let's begin by exploring what it means to be a team player. But before doing this, read the OB in Action box which describes how switching to teamwork has been essential to T-Mobile's success and competitiveness.

Team Players versus Free-Riders

Teams collaborate and perform most effectively when companies develop and encourage teamwork competencies. Five common teamwork competencies are outlined in

OB in Action

Common Scenario and Common Outcomes When many people think of call centers, they envision hordes of customer service representatives, slouching in front of screens, headsets on, semi-frantically mowing through customer calls in attempts to meet "handle time" (time spent with each caller) expectations. Most of these same people have a much clearer and even more unappealing view of what it's like to be a customer of one of these representatives. One writer described the customer experience this way: "They are forced to navigate computerized call trees and, should they get a live person, they're often treated robotically and handed from one agent or department to another if their issue is outside a rep's narrow repertoire." Combined, it is no wonder turnover for such employees exceeds that of almost every type of job, and customers are frequently frustrated and reluctant to even bother calling.

The T-Mobile Scenario The above quite accurately described T-Mobile's call centers with groups of reps toiling in less than inspiring conditions and delivering less than satisfying service. Then things changed. Reps are now organized into teams who gather in shared spaces (pods) and collaboratively solve customer issues as they see fit. More interesting still is the customers they serve are organized into pools for which particular teams are responsible.

Different Approach, Different Metrics Instead of being preoccupied with handle times per call, the teams are problem solvers and responsible for how best to improve customer retention, loyalty, and share of wallet (how much of a customer's total telecom budget goes to T-Mobile). As for customers, they know how to communicate with their appropriate team and do not suffer through call trees.

Impressive Outcomes The results have been impressive. In just three years, the new team approach cut costs to serve customers 13 percent, boosted customer loyalty measures by 50 percent, and reduced customer churn to all-time lows for the company. Better still, employee satisfaction is up, and absenteeism and turnover are down.

Motives for the Changes Like many other Industries and services, T-Mobile customers and their needs have evolved. Billing, address changes, and plan modifications can often be handled by customers themselves (self-serve online). This means customers now call and need direct service for more complex issues, and more complex issues require a more sophisticated and cooperative approach to service.

YOUR THOUGHTS?

1. Differentiate T-Mobile's previous group-based to its new team-based approach to customer service.

2. How would you contrast management challenges in the group- versus team-based approaches at T-Mobile?

3. What do you think are the key challenges for employees in the team approach?

Table 8.5, along with examples of behaviors to assist in recognition and measurement. Notice that all these competencies are action-oriented, which means being a team player is more than a state of mind: It's about doing!

Evaluating Teamwork Competencies There are at least two ways to use Table 8.5 and your knowledge of teamwork competencies. The first is as tools to enhance your self-awareness. Do you behave in these ways on your teams? The second is as a means to measure your performance and that of other members of your team.

Many of your business courses require team assignments and some may also require peer evaluations. Complete Self-Assessment 8.3 to learn about your own teamwork competencies and/or to evaluate the performance of the members of one of your teams at school (for a class, sport, club, or fraternity/sorority). Knowledge of your teamwork competencies can help determine which competencies are your strongest and those that are opportunities for improvement. You can choose to play to your strengths and/or develop your deficiencies.

TABLE 8.5 Common Teamwork Competencies

COMPETENCY	EXAMPLES OF MEMBER BEHAVIORS
1. Contributes to the team's work	• Completed work in a timely manner • Came to meetings prepared • Did complete and accurate work
2. Constructively interacts with team members	• Communicated effectively • Listened to teammates • Accepted feedback
3. Keeps team on track	• Helped team plan and organize work • Stayed aware of team members' progress • Provided constructive feedback
4. Expects high-quality work	• Expected team to succeed • Cared that the team produced high-quality work
5. Possesses relevant knowledge, skills, and abilities (KSAs) for team's responsibilities	• Possessed necessary KSAs to contribute meaningfully to the team • Applied knowledge and skill to fill in as needed for other members' roles

SELF-ASSESSMENT 8.3

Evaluate Your Team Member Effectiveness

Please be prepared to answer these questions if your instructor has assigned Self-Assessment 8.3 in Connect.

1. Which competencies are your strongest (have the highest average scores)?
2. Do these scores match your impressions of your teamwork competencies?
3. Which competency is your lowest? Describe two things you can do to further develop and display this competency.
4. Which competency do you feel low performers most often lack in the teams of which you're a member?
5. Describe the pros and cons of using this tool to do peer evaluations for team assignments in school.

Adapted from M. W. Ohland, M. L. Loughry, D. J. Woehr, L. G. Bullard, R. M. Felder, C. J. Finelli, R. A. Layton, H. R. Pomeranz, and D. G. Schmucker, "The Comprehensive Assessment of Team Member Effectiveness: Development of a Behaviorally Anchored Rating Scale for Self- and Peer Evaluation," *Academy of Management Learning & Education,* 2012, 609–630.

What Does It Mean to Be a Team Player?   Understanding and exhibiting the competencies noted in Table 8.5 is an excellent start on becoming a team player. And while everyone has her or his own ideas of the characteristics that are most important, many people likely include the three Cs of team players:

Committed

Collaborative

Competent[32]

Think of it this way: The three Cs are the "cover charge" or the bare minimum to be considered a team player. Effective team players don't just talk about or feel the three Cs—they

Social loafing, or free-riding, is common in teams, but this can be effectively overcome by applying OB knowledge and tools. Cashiers who served separate lines of customers outperformed those who served customers who waited in groups for the next available cashier.
(Left) Robert Daly/Caia Image/Glow Images; (right) MikeDotta/Shutterstock

display them. Think of someone on one of your teams who clearly displays the three Cs and someone who does not. How do the differences affect you? The team?

While there are many potential reasons some people are not team players, a particularly common and problematic one is *social loafing*.

What Is Social Loafing? *Social loafing* **is the tendency for individual effort to decline as group size increases.** To illustrate the point, consider a group or team in which you're a member and ask yourself: "Is group performance less than, equal to, or greater than the sum of its parts?" Can three people working together, for example, accomplish less than, the same as, or more than they would working separately?

All of these outcomes are possible, but the intention is for more and not less than the sum of the parts. Social loafing is a major reason for less, and this is problematic for many reasons. Social loafers produce low-quality work, which causes others to work harder to compensate, and they can also distract or disrupt the work of other team members. Such situations are made worse when loafers expect the same rewards as other members of the team, including those who picked up their slack.

As you already know, social loafing is common at school and work. One study observed checkout lines in a supermarket. One area was configured such that each cashier had a dedicated line of customers, and in another area, customers collected in a pool and went to a cashier when one became available. The results? Cashiers in the dedicated lines worked more than 10 percent faster, regardless of the length of their lines. The explanation is they couldn't rely on (loaf on) other cashiers as in the pooled configuration. The researchers also suspect the dedicated scenario may have spurred a bit of competition too.[33]

Studies of loafing in college produce useful insights. To begin, researchers in one study assumed that students would loaf in team-based assignments, and they therefore were interested in ways of reducing loafing and boosting performance. They generated project teams in three different ways. The first set of teams was created by matching students whose schedules were compatible, and who also indicated they were highly motivated to do the work. The second set of teams were comprised of students with compatible schedules but indicated they were not particularly motivated for the work. The final set of teams were allowed to self-select. The results were quite telling. The first set of teams performed the best, on both team and individual assignments, suggesting that pairing students who are motivated and available is the superior way of reducing loafing and increasing learning performance.[34]

Given that social loafing is so common and problematic, how can you guard against it?

1. Limit group size. Fewer people means fewer places to shift work or hide.
2. Accountability. Ensure members have clear roles and responsibilities, and that they need to deliver.

3. Build in feedback. Create a way that team members receive feedback, ideally both during and at the end, of a project. This will help with accountability and discouraging loafing in the first place, and it will "call them out" if they slack off.

4. Cultivate cohesion. Teams whose members are emotionally bonded are far less likely to loaf.[35]

Now let's discuss various types of teams. Understanding the differences can make you a more effective team member and leader.

Types of Teams

As the world of work becomes more complex, so too do the types of teams. We can differentiate some common ones by particular characteristics, such as:

1. Purpose of the team.
2. Duration of the team's existence.
3. Level of member commitment.

Work Teams   Work teams have a well-defined and common purpose, are more or less permanent, and require complete commitment of their members. Professional sports teams' top priority is to win games, which they hope will also lead to higher ticket sales and more television viewers. The same teams exist from season to season, and membership is a full-time, all-consuming job for each player. An audit team at work is the same: It is full of auditors who work full time auditing.

Project Teams   Project teams are assembled to tackle a particular problem, task, or project. Depending on the purpose, their duration can vary from one meeting to many years. For instance, your employer may assemble a team to brainstorm ideas for generating more business with an existing customer. This project team may be limited to only one meeting, whether virtual or face-to-face. Or, the team may be responsible not only for creating ideas for more business with that customer, but also for executing the ideas over the course of one or more years.

Members of project teams most often divide their time between the team and their primary jobs and responsibilities. They may be from the same department, product, customer, or service area in an organization, or possibly from different functional disciplines such as finance, operations, or marketing. As you may have already experienced, any given employee may be a member of multiple project teams at one time.

Cross-Functional Teams (CFTs)   *Cross-functional* **teams are created with members from different disciplines within an organization, such as finance, operations, and R&D.** Cross-functional teams can be used for any purpose, they can be work or project teams, and they may have a short or indefinite duration. New-product development is an area in which many organizations utilize cross-functional teams. Such teams often contain members with expertise in design, manufacturing, marketing, and sales.

Self-Managed Teams (SMTs)   *Self-managed teams* **have collective autonomy and responsibility to plan, manage, and execute tasks interdependently to achieve their goals.**[36] Many of these elements are normally performed by managers, but in self-managed teams, members act as their own supervisors. Self-managed teams have a defined purpose and their duration can vary, along with the level of member commitment. Cross-functional, work, and project teams can all be self-managed. SMTs are very common—the vast majority of Fortune 1000 companies have used them for many years and they represent efforts by organizations to be more flexible and meet the demands of increased complexity.[37] Instead of needing and waiting on approval from someone at headquarters, which may be in another state or country, SMT members decide and act more quickly. Leadership responsibilities often are shared and shift as the demands on and members of self-managed teams change. Outside managers and leaders maintain *indirect* accountability. This contrasts with the hierarchical or centralized types of management historically found in teams.

Self-managed does not mean workers are simply turned loose to do their own thing. Indeed, an organization embracing self-managed teams should be prepared to undergo revolutionary changes in its management philosophy, structure, staffing and training practices, as well as its reward systems. Managers sometimes resist self-managed teams, due to the perceived threat to their authority and job security.

Now that you've learned about some common team types and their characteristics, we'll turn our attention to virtual teams. Virtual teams are ever-more common and a critically important type of team with unique characteristics.

Virtual Teams

Virtual team members work across time, space, and organizational boundaries to achieve common goals. They are connected using various technologies, which enable them to utilize talent more efficiently than in a traditional office setting where work and people are tied to places.[38]

Advocates say virtual teams are very flexible and efficient because they are driven by information and skills, not by time and location. Nevertheless, virtual teams have pros and cons like every other type of team, which we will address next, along with guidance on how to use them most effectively.

Technology not only allows people to communicate where, when, and with whom they wish, but it also allows people and organizations to work without offices. What are the advantages and disadvantages for you personally of telecommuting and virtual work?
Image Source/Getty Images

Best Uses of Virtual Teams   Virtual teams and distributed workers present many potential benefits. One notable benefit is reduced real estate costs (limited or no office space). IBM was an early adopter and calculated it saved over 58 million square feet of office space, amounting to approximately $2 billion in savings.[39] Virtual teams enable organizations to leverage diverse knowledge, skills, and experience across geography and time; ability to share knowledge of diverse markets; and reduced commuting and travel expenses. The flexibility afforded by virtual teams also can reduce work–life conflicts for employees, which some employers contend makes it easier for them to attract and retain talent.[40]

Challenges and Recommendations for Virtual Teams   Virtual teams have many challenges, too. Recent research identified the five most common, which are described in Table 8.6 along with suggestions on how to overcome them. The solutions included are derived from research done with companies in *Fortune*'s 100 Best Places to Work over the period of four years.

Face Time   Researchers and consultants agree about one aspect of virtual teams—*there is no substitute for face-to-face contact*. Meeting in person is especially beneficial early in virtual team development, and team leaders are encouraged to meet even more frequently with key members.[42] Face-to-face interactions can be as simple as lunch, water-cooler conversations, social events, or periodic meetings. Whatever the case, these interactions enable people to become familiar with each other and build credibility, trust, and understanding. This reduces misunderstandings and makes subsequent virtual interactions more efficient and effective, and it also increases job performance and reduces conflict and intentions to quit.[43]

TABLE 8.6 Most Common Challenges for Virtual Teams and Recommended Solutions[41]

CHALLENGE	DESCRIPTION	RECOMMENDED SOLUTIONS FROM FORTUNE'S 100 BEST COMPANIES
Relationships	Lack of interpersonal and face-to-face interactions make building trusting relationships difficult.	Build trust by modeling candid and respectful communication. Create opportunities for members to meet face-to-face, including nonwork activities.
Communication	Communicating via technology limits nonverbal and other information commonly exchange. Feedback is limited and delayed.	Create norms of transparency and openness in all communications. Support telecommuting, and ensure all members receive the same/sufficient resources (training and technology and support).
Decision making	Biases and perceived inequities can limit information shared and impair decision making.	Train employees on effective distributed decision making, ensure employee voice, and reward efforts and success.
Leadership	Rich relationships are difficult to build at a distance. Also it's difficult to monitor performance, coach, and share leadership.	Make extra efforts to meet, get to know, support team members. Be available, responsive, and role model the behaviors you want and expect.
Diversity	Differences are difficult to appreciate or overcome, which may affect collaboration and understanding of team norms.	Initiate and support informal interventions, such as social networks and defense around shared interests. Formal interventions, diversity training and diverse hiring.

SOURCE: Eisenberg, Julia, and Aparna Krishnan. "Addressing Virtual Work Challenges: Learning From the Field." *Organization Management Journal* 15, no.2 (May 2018): 78–94. https://doi.org/10.1080/15416518.2018.1471976.

Team Interdependence

One of the most important aspects of teams is *interdependence,* or the extent to which members are dependent on each other to accomplish their own work.[44] We discuss two common forms of interdependence—task and outcome. **Task interdependence is the degree to which team members depend on each other for information, materials, and other resources to complete their job tasks.** The degree of task interdependence is determined by the degree of interaction between members and the amount of coordination required among them. There are four basic types of task interdependence, ranked by how much team member interaction and coordination are required. The types are illustrated in Figure 8.4.

1. *Pooled.* Many pharmaceutical and other sales teams illustrate pooled interdependence. Each member sells a given drug to his or her customers, which requires little or no interaction or coordination with other representatives. At the end of the month all reps' sales are added together to arrive at a team sales total.

2. *Sequential.* Manufacturing or assembly processes are typically sequential. PC manufacturing teams, for example, require that motherboards and hard drives be installed before the box can be closed and fastened.

3. *Reciprocal.* Hiring processes sometimes use reciprocal interdependence. Candidates are interviewed by members of HR and then separately interviewed by the hiring manager or members of the department. The two communicate and decide to whom an offer should be made.

4. *Comprehensive.* Product development teams often utilize comprehensive interdependence. Online games, for instance, require significant back and forth among those who create the idea, write the code, test, and market the game. It isn't just a linear or sequential process.

FIGURE 8.4   Types of Team Interdependence

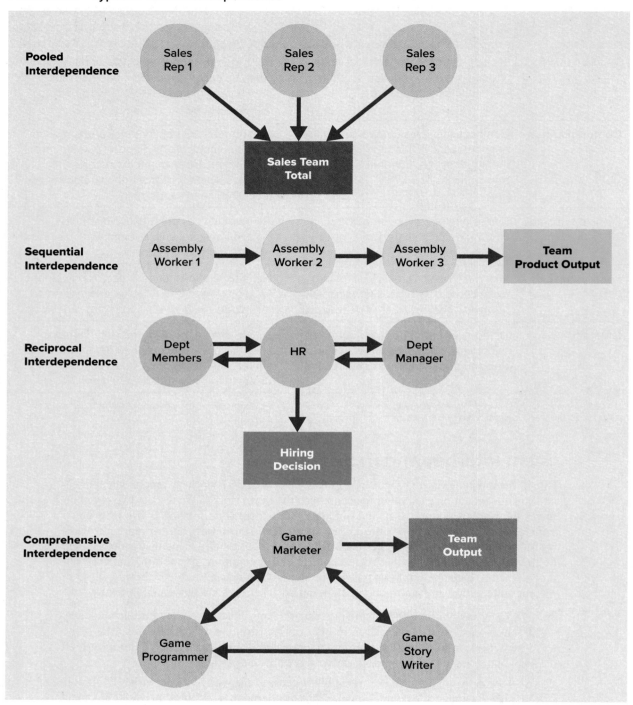

Outcome interdependence **is "the degree to which the outcomes of task work are measured, rewarded, and communicated at the group level so as to emphasize collective outputs rather than individual contributions."**[45] Outcome interdependence is determined by the extent to which team members' objectives and rewards are aligned.

Practically speaking, the type or degree of interdependence should match what is required for the team to meet its objectives.

Now let's learn about trust, which either facilitates or impedes interpersonal interactions and relationships, and thus the effectiveness of teams.

8.4 TRUST BUILDING AND REPAIR— ESSENTIAL TOOLS FOR SUCCESS

THE BIGGER PICTURE

Trust sometimes seems like a rare commodity in the world of work and you're about to see why it's so important at all levels of the Organizing Framework. Moreover, in the context of teams, trust is essential because it facilitates all interactions within and between teams. With this understanding you'll be empowered to apply your knowledge to build trust and to repair it when it has been damaged or diminished.

Trust is the willingness to be vulnerable to another person, and the belief that the other person will consider the impact of how his or her intentions and behaviors will affect you.[46] We can't overstate the value of trust in organizational life. It is the lubricant of interpersonal relationships within and between all organizational levels in the Organizing Framework, and thus it also drives performance across levels. Put simply, trusting employees provide tremendous benefits to their employers (see Figure 8.5).

LO 8-4

Build and repair trust.

FIGURE 8.5 Employer-Supportive Behaviors Enacted by Employees Based on High v. Low Trust[47]

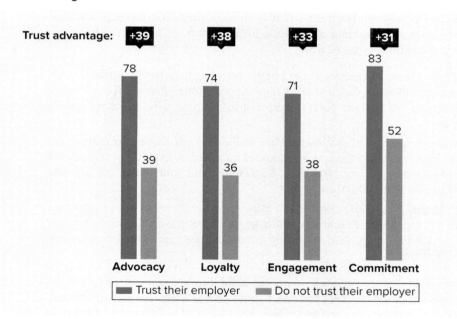

SOURCE: Edelman, R. "2019 Edelman Trust Barometer: Global Report," Edelman.com, https://www.edelman.com/sites/g/files/aatuss191/files/2019-02/2019_Edelman_Trust_Barometer_Global_Report_2.pdf (accessed May 4, 2019)

Two additional benefits of trust are faster communication and decision making. Shiona Watson, Senior Director of HR for Pepsico Australia and New Zealand, described how the trust she shares with CEO Robert Rietbroek enabled them to communicate more quickly and arrive at critical decisions more efficiently during the process of merging Smith's Snackfood Company with Pepsi.[48]

Trust can also help guard against job stress. Specifically, firefighters who trusted members of their team experienced less fatigue associated with the physical aspects of their jobs. The rationale is that trusting your coworkers boosts rather than depletes your energy—you don't have to wonder if they have your back.[49] Still other research suggests that trust in individual accounting auditors increased the likelihood that employees of the audited companies would report improper conduct (whistle-blow).[50]

Clearly, trust pays important dividends across industries, yet these have not been good times for trust in the business world. As Richard Edelman, whose company produces the famous Trust Barometer each year, said:

> The past two decades have seen a progressive destruction of trust in societal institutions, a consequence of the Great Recession, fears about immigration and economic dislocation caused by globalization and automation. Traditional power elite figures, such as CEOs and heads-of-state, have been discredited. The growth of social media platforms fully shifted people's trust from a top-down orientation to a horizontal one in favor of peers or experts.[51]

On the bright side, respondents in the trust survey reported their employers as the most trusted of institutions (government and media the lowest). Driving this, according to Edelman and his colleagues, is employees' expectation their employers will engage larger societal issues and be agents of change.[52] This in turn places much greater responsibility on organizations and their leaders than in the past, making trust even more important now and in the future. Let's increase your understanding of and ability to build trust by outlining three fundamental forms of trust.

Three Forms of Trust and How to Build Them

For our purposes in OB, we discuss three particular forms of trust—contractual, communication, and competence. The practical application for building trust is to act in ways that demonstrate each of the three types of trust:

1. *Contractual trust.* Trust of character. Do people do what they say they will do? Do managers and employees make clear what they expect of one another? Keep track of your commitments, be realistic (don't overpromise), and be sure to deliver quality work on time.

2. *Communication trust.* Trust of disclosure. How well do people share information and tell the truth? Keep team members and employees informed by explaining policies and decisions and providing accurate feedback. Be candid about your challenges and limitations. And of course, tell the truth.

3. *Competence trust.* Trust of capability. How effectively do people meet or perform their responsibilities and acknowledge other people's skills and abilities? Enhance your credibility by demonstrating good business sense, technical ability, and professionalism.[53]

Finally, if trust is a matter of give and take, it will be helpful to know how trusting you are of others. Self-Assessment 8.4 can help you learn about different aspects of your interpersonal trust. Besides improving your self-awareness, knowledge of your interpersonal trust may provide guidance for how you can more effectively build trust with others—friends, classmates, coworkers, and bosses.

Before moving on to how to repair trust, we encourage you to review and consider the advice in the Applying OB box regarding microinternships. Building your experience and skills during microinternships is an effective way of enhancing the level of competence trust future employers will have in you.

How Much Do You Trust Another?

Please be prepared to answer these questions if your instructor has assigned Self-Assessment 8.4 in Connect.

1. Which particular items in this questionnaire are most central to your idea of trust? Why?

2. Does your score accurately depict the degree to which you trust (or distrust) the target person?

3. Why do you trust (or distrust) this individual?

4. If you trust this person to a high degree, how hard was it to build that trust? Explain.

5. Given your inclination to trust others (your score on the assessment), describe three implications for your work in group assignments and project teams at school.

Applying OB

CAREER READINESS

Microinternships Can Produce Major Benefits[54]

Like more conventional internships, microinternships pay real money, and enable you to get a sense of whether you like the work and industry while you develop valuable skills and experience to add to your resume. They differ in that they are short term, outside of the typical summer internship format, and are often more flexible in terms of time and place (work can be done remotely). Microinternships are gigs more so than traditional jobs, but in some instances act like a mutual interview for future full-time employment.

Benefits to You In addition to the above benefits, microinternships can happen earlier and more frequently than traditional internships offered through career services at your university. The greater breadth, depth, and length of your experience can make you a more attractive candidate to potential employers.

Jeffrey Moss, the founder and CEO of Parker Dewey, a Chicago-based placement company and pioneer in microinternships, describes them as projects that require 5 to 40 hours over the span of a few weeks. As with other gig arrangements, employers post the specs of the projects, along with compensation, and students bid for the work.

What's in It for Employers? Motivated, cheap, and hopefully able labor and if things work out perhaps even a valuable full-time employee. Using a firm like Parker Dewey means little fuss and effort on the part of the employer, as it is Parker Dewey that facilitates the connections and handles all the administrative details, including compensation. This means virtually no involvement by the employing company's HR department.

Major Doesn't Clearly Match Interests A reason Mr. Moss started the company, and another potential benefit for you, is that such gigs can help facilitate the college-to-work transition. You may be uncertain as to your major, which often disqualifies you from formal internships where students are selected based on major and year (juniors and seniors), or your major may not match your interests. Microinternships can provide alternatives and help you overcome these hurdles. They're a low risk means of career exploration.

College Credit Too? At least in the case of Parker Dewey, which has an arrangement with more than 150 colleges and universities in the U.S., some colleges also allow credit to be earned for microinternships.

Repairing Trust

Sometimes trust is fragile and can be violated in many ways, even unwittingly. Regardless of who is responsible for eroding or damaging trust, both parties need to be active in the repair of trust. Dennis and Michelle Reina studied thousands of instances of broken trust in business and developed seven steps for regaining it. Figure 8.6 illustrates their recommendations as an upward staircase, to show how individuals must work their way back from distrust, one step at a time, to finally regain what they have lost. This seven-step process can help whether you are the perpetrator or the victim.

We conclude this section with an observation about the importance of trust for leaders from Lars Dalgaard, long-time venture entrepreneur and venture capitalist:

> The funny thing is that you're actually a stronger leader and more trustworthy if you're able to be vulnerable and you're able to show your real personality. It's a trust multiplier, and people really will want to work for you and be on a mission together with you.[55]

FIGURE 8.6 **Reina Seven-Step Model for Rebuilding Trust**

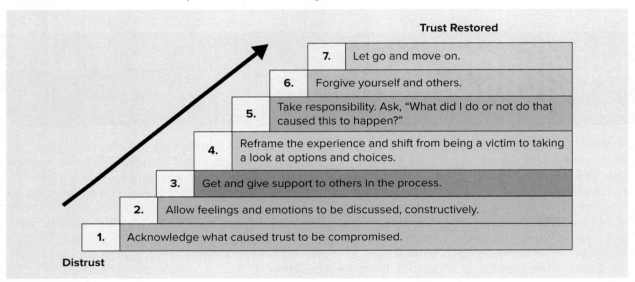

Trust Restored

7. Let go and move on.

6. Forgive yourself and others.

5. Take responsibility. Ask, "What did I do or not do that caused this to happen?"

4. Reframe the experience and shift from being a victim to taking a look at options and choices.

3. Get and give support to others in the process.

2. Allow feelings and emotions to be discussed, constructively.

1. Acknowledge what caused trust to be compromised.

Distrust

SOURCE: Reina, Dennis S., and Michelle L. Reina. *Rebuilding Trust in the Workplace: Seven Steps to Renew Confidence, Commitment, and Energy.* Oakland, CA: Berrett-Koehler Publishers, 2010.

8.5 KEYS TO TEAM EFFECTIVENESS

THE BIGGER PICTURE

You will thrive in team settings when you better understand the characteristics of high-performing teams. You can use these characteristics as facilitators to function more successfully in group and team settings. You will also benefit from the practical suggestions, supported by research and practice, with which we conclude the chapter, such as how to foster and reward collaboration and teamwork.

Characteristics of High-Performing Teams

LO 8-5

Illustrate your ability to foster team effectiveness.

As stated earlier, effective work teams enable employees to accomplish more than they could as individuals. They produce many desirable outcomes across levels of the Organizing Framework, such as innovation, safety, and saved lives, to name but a few.[56] Current research and practice have identified the following eight attributes of high-performance teams:

1. Compelling team purpose and clear goals.
2. Clear goals and responsibilities.
3. Appropriate mix of knowledge, skills, and abilities.
4. Effective incentives and motivation.
5. Trust and communication.
6. Power and empowerment.
7. Early and effective conflict resolution.
8. Norms for collaboration.[57]

You've likely noticed that nearly all of these we've covered already in this chapter, but the difference here is that true high-performing teams do all of these things. That's what makes them special and rare.

The 3 Cs of Effective Teams

With the above characteristics in mind, you might ask: How do you build a high-performing team? The short answer is to use the three Cs. (Note: These three Cs are at the *team* level, in contrast to the three Cs of effective team *players* discussed earlier that focus on the individual or team member level.) The three Cs are:

Charters and strategies

Composition

Capacity

Charters and Strategies   Both researchers and practitioners urge groups and teams to explicitly plan before tackling their tasks, early in the group development process (the storming stage). These plans should include **team charters that describe how the team will operate, for instance, how members will share information, hold members accountable, deal with conflict, and make decisions.**[58] Team charters were discussed in the Winning at Work feature at the beginning of this chapter, and since charters help team members align, this is reason enough to give them a try.[59] Teams should also create and implement **team performance strategies, deliberate plans that outline what**

exactly the team is to do, such as goal setting and defining particular member roles, tasks, and responsibilities.[60]

Given that teamwork is a fact of life and one of the skills most sought by employers, nearly 79 percent in a survey by the National Association of Colleges and Employers (just behind communication and problem-solving skills),[61] you are strongly encouraged to build your understanding and skill using team charters and strategies, while you're in college. Hone your skills now so you're ready to use them when they really count—at work. To help boost your motivation, research shows that medical students who implemented team charters reported better group dynamics and improved communication within the team. They also felt and exercised greater responsibility for their own learning, performance, development, and team performance. These outcomes are especially encouraging given that patient care, like many other services and industries, is a team-based job.[62]

Composition   *Team composition* **describes the collection of jobs, personalities, knowledge, skills, abilities, and experience levels of team members.**[63] When we think of it this way, it is no surprise that team composition can and does affect team performance. Team member characteristics should fit the responsibilities of the team if the team is to be effective. *Fit* facilitates effectiveness and *misfit* impedes it—you need the right people on your team.

Although it may seem counterintuitive, fostering functional conflict can actually enhance team effectiveness. The OB in Action box describes how.

OB in Action

Want Better Teamwork? Expect and Ensure Conflict

The title of this box may seem ridiculous or at least counterintuitive but read on and learn otherwise. First, note you'll learn much more about conflict In Chapter 10, but some experts believe a key to effective teams is tension, not harmony. One such expert is Liane Davey a team effectiveness consultant and author of *The Good Fight, You First*.

Davey criticizes leaders and other employees who describe and strive for happy and harmonious teamwork, such as the rowing crew all synchronously pulling in one direction. She argues teams that function this way are likely risk-adverse and composed of members who are overly concerned about offending other members or breaking from the status quo.

To clarify, Ms. Davey does not recommend chaos and war, but instead coaches teams to purposefully identify and benefit from tensions. Team members should expect and improve due to conflict. This is how she explains it.

1. Draw a circle and carve it up into the necessary number of wedges for each role on the team.

2. Describe the value to the team of each role, such as what does this role provide that none of the others do. It helps to consider how removing this role would negatively impact the team. Perhaps the role is unnecessary or needs to change.

3. Which stakeholders, internal and/or external to the team, does each role serve, and how? How is the effectiveness of this role determined and by whom?

4. Then, what are the most common and important ways in which this role conflicts with or causes tensions with other roles?

Davey contends doing this for each role not only clarifies them for the role players, but it helps in determining who is best to play each role for a given project. As you can see, this approach makes conflict explicit and expected, which she believes improves teamwork and outcomes. How?

The rationale is that team members will be more comfortable speaking up, calling out unsubstantiated positions, and collaborating.

YOUR THOUGHTS?

1. What are the benefits to Liane Davey's approach?

2. Identify potential shortcomings.

3. Explain why you would or would not want to be a member of a team using this approach.

Research shows that in the early stages of team development (forming and storming), teams perform better when members have a high tolerance for uncertainty (a personality trait). This same finding applies to self-managed and virtual teams, due to their relative lack of imposed direction and face-to-face communication.[64] Team research also shows that teams with members who possess high levels of extraversion and openness tended to provide better customer service than teams whose members were lower on these traits.[65]

Research on Tour de France cycling teams revealed that teams with greater diversity in tenure—with some new riders, some long-time riders, and some in between—had better team performance, measured as the number of riders finishing in Paris. What makes this finding intriguing is that diversity in terms of members' skills, previous Tour stage wins, age, and experience had no effect on team performance![66]

Finally, in the university context, top management teams (presidents, vice presidents, and chancellors) who were more diverse in terms of educational and disciplinary backgrounds generated more funding for research and improved school reputations.[67]

The bottom line: Create teams with the composition to match the desired objectives. Knowledge of OB and the Organizing Framework, in particular, can be very helpful in this regard.

Capacity   *Team adaptive capacity* **(adaptability) is the ability to make needed changes in response to demands put on the team.**[68] Like individuals and organizations, teams must adapt in order to thrive (and in some instances survive). It is fostered by team members who are both willing and able to adapt to achieve the team's objectives.

Using the 3Cs will help you build a high-performing team.
King Lawrence/Blend Images

Described in this way, team adaptive capacity is a matter of team composition—the characteristics of individual team members. Team researchers explain how effective adaptation often includes recognition of the need to change, reframing team member's skills and approach to the new demands, responding appropriately, and reflecting on the team's adaptive processes and outcomes. Considered together, it is clear that capacity is another critical element of effective teams.[69]

Collaboration and Team Rewards

Collaboration **is the act of sharing information and coordinating efforts to achieve a collective outcome.** It's safe to assume that teams whose members collaborate are more effective than those whose members don't. Collaboration is what enables teams to produce more than the sum of their parts. Many factors can influence collaboration, including how teams are rewarded. In this final section we'll explore how to foster collaboration and the role rewards can play.

Collaboration—The Lifeblood of Teamwork As interdependence increases, so too does the need for and value of collaboration. Today's business landscape, characterized by globalization, outsourcing, strategic partnering, and virtual teams, makes collaboration ever more important.[70] That said, many things can interfere with collaboration, thus it is important to:

1. **Communicate expectations.** Clarifying roles and responsibilities for each team member is essential. Identify and communicate both individual and team accountability.

2. **Set team goals.** SMART goals for teams are a good place to start, but review goals regularly as a team (weekly, monthly, or quarterly) and be sure individual roles and responsibilities align with team goals.

3. **Encourage creativity.** Create a safe environment where employees can take risks without fear of humiliation or career damage. Nurture a "can do" attitude within the team, and foster it by asking "why" or "why not" instead of saying yes or no.

4. **Build work flow rhythm.** Technology can be of great assistance. Project management software as well as other scheduling tools can help team members know exactly what they need to do and when. This may also assist in coordination efforts and help assure that interdependent needs of team members are met.

5. **Leverage team member strengths.** Set individuals up to win by identifying and utilizing their strengths. The key to realizing the benefits of the team is to appropriately utilize the strengths of its individual members.[71]

Reward Collaboration and Teamwork Rewards matter, and dissatisfaction with rewards is a common cause for suboptimal team performance. Despite the need to work collaboratively, many if not most professional service firms (law, accounting, and consulting practices) measure and reward individual contributions, such as billable hours, up-or-out promotion systems (either qualify for partner or find another job), and competition between team members.[72]

Organizations that foster the greatest collaboration and assemble the most effective teams typically use hybrid reward systems that recognize both individual and team performance. Table 8.7 provides guidance on how to reward performance in teams, based on the desired outcome (speed or accuracy) and the degree of interdependence (low, moderate, high). These guidelines can give you a tremendous head start in determining how best to reward and motivate team performance.[73]

Appropriate rewards for collaboration and teamwork motivate at both the individual and team levels, and also positively influence important outcomes across all levels in the

TABLE 8.7 Recommendations for Improving the Coordination and Motivation of Teams and Team Members

	LOW INTERDEPENDENCE	MODERATE INTERDEPENDENCE	HIGH INTERDEPENDENCE
Speed	**Relay Teams**	**Road Cycling Teams**	**Crew Teams**
	What to measure: Individual performance	**What to measure:** Individual performance	**What to measure:** Team performance
	How to measure: Managerial assessment	**How to measure:** Managerial assessment	**How to measure:** Managerial and peer assessment
	How to Reward: Competitive rewards	**How to reward:** Competitive rewards	**How to reward:** Cooperative rewards
Accuracy	**Gymnastics Teams**	**Basketball Teams**	**Synchronized Swimming Teams**
	What to measure: Individual performance	**What to measure:** Team performance	**What to measure:** Team performance
	How to measure: Managerial assessment	**How to measure:** Managerial and peer assessment	**How to measure:** Managerial and peer assessment
	How to reward: Competitive rewards	**How to reward:** Cooperative rewards	**How to reward:** Cooperative rewards

SOURCE: Gottfredson, Ryan K. "How to Get YOUR TEAMS to Work." *Industrial Management* 57, no. 4 (July/August 2015): 25–30. https://www.questia.com/read/1P3-3769151081/how-to-get-your-teams-to-work.

Organizing Framework. The following Problem-Solving Application illustrates how collaboration, teamwork, and performance management were applied in hospitals and nursing homes to improve patient and financial outcomes.

Problem-Solving Application

Hospitals and Nursing Homes Collaborate to Combat Common Foes

The Foes MRSA (methicillin-resistant Staphylococcus aureus) and CRE (carbapenem-resistant Enterobacteriaceae) are two especially resistant and dangerous bacteria, and although you can catch these bugs anywhere, the most common and problematic places are hospitals and nursing homes. When patients are infected in these facilities they are referred to as health care-associated infections (HCAIs). Some patients enter both types of facilities with these infections which need to be treated. But it also is increasingly common for patients to be infection free when admitted and then catch one of the bugs while a patient. This major problem is made even worse when infected patients are then transferred from one facility to another along with their super bugs. This means health care facilities are not islands with independent challenges contained within, but instead they are interconnected and literally share their problem bugs. And once the bugs are in a facility they spread, often rapidly and mercilessly.[74]

Costs and Responsibilities The Centers for Disease Control estimates approximately 15 percent of hospital patients and 65 percent of nursing home patients carry resistant bacteria (not all will develop infections), which result in more than 23,000 deaths.[75] Medicare is increasingly rewarding or punishing hospitals based on performance outcomes, like infection rates and readmissions. Hospitals and nursing homes therefore have both moral and financial incentives to act.[76]

Causes and Solutions   Besides rampant misuse and overuse of antibiotics, which is the fundamental cause for resistance in the first place, the transfer from facility to facility and patient to patient is largely attributed to insufficient hygiene—clinician handwashing, patient bathing, and facility cleanliness, all of which can be controlled by health care personnel, but obviously any effort needs coordination, collaboration, and commitment. One nurse may be meticulously clean, but those efforts are undermined by the first/next one that isn't so conscientious.

Many efforts and programs have been initiated to combat the spread of HCAIs, including some in Southern California and Illinois. In fact, fifty facilities (hospitals and nursing homes) are implementing a new protocol funded by the CDC in which patients are bathed with a particular antimicrobial soap, one proven to kill MRSA, CRE, and some of the other most resistant bugs.[77]

Such collaborations are unusual and difficult, as in many cases the facilities in a particular area compete daily for patients and health care dollars.

Put antibiotic prescribing practices aside, assume you are a chief nursing officer in a metropolitan hospital. Apply the 3-Step Problem-Solving Approach to help mitigate the problem of HCAIs.

Apply the 3-Step Problem-Solving Approach

Step 1:   Define the problem(s) confronting hospitals and nursing homes.

Step 2:   Identify the major causes of the problem(s).

Step 3:   Make your recommendations. Provide details.

We conclude this section with perhaps the most incredible and challenging application of teamwork—the International Space Station (ISS). ISS teamwork is literally out of this world!

OB in Action

Space Travel Requires Teams of Teams

The International Space Station (ISS) was assembled in space and has been continuously occupied since 2000. More than 230 Individuals from 18 countries have visited the station whose operations are handled by five agencies: NASA (US), Roscosmos (Russia), European Space Agency, Japanese Aerospace Exploration Agency, and the Canadian Space Agency. Control centers are located in each of these same places, which have the tremendous responsibilities and challenges of coordinating their efforts 24/7, 365, year after year, decade after decade, and through changes in political leaders and economic conditions.[78]

The individuals and teams involved in the ISS are confronted with some of the most challenging, and also fulfilling, experiences in team diversity of any workplace. Not only do the astronauts represent different countries, languages, and cultures, but the countless people around the globe are similarly diverse. The coordination of people, processes, and outcomes is enormous, all of which is made more complicated by the inevitable turnover. As with all other jobs and organizations, employees from the agencies noted above get promoted, rotate to different jobs, retire, and otherwise quit.[79]

The teams of teams manage every detail necessary to keep the ISS functional and to support the 2–13 astronauts onboard at any given time (3–6 is most common). Making matters even more complex is the growing number of commercial (nongovernment) partners who contribute to the missions. For instance, as space programs are retired, such as America's space shuttle, other means are needed to transport people and equipment. Russia's Soyouz rockets assumed much of that work, but now Dragon (by SpaceX), and CST-100 (Boeing) help. Each of these rockets has different capabilities, which makes planning and execution even more complex. Reliance on commercial partners is increasing with Orbital ATK's and Antares and Sierra Nevada's Dream Chaser also expected to begin service.[80]

This makes us wonder: How do they do it? The coordination and collaboration occur almost seamlessly, despite the complexity related to people, processes, and culture.

Dynamic Composition Safety is among the reasons astronauts' time on the ISS is limited. Imagine the time and resources required to continually prepare new members to live on the space station. Technical, physical, and cultural training requirements are immense, because all team members must effectively communicate and execute their responsibilities when on board.

Technology and Distance Communication is critical and an ever-present challenge. Ground control must communicate with both the ISS and its various locations on the ground at all times. It's not as simple as making a cellular phone call or Skyping. Distance is an obvious obstacle. NASA and its partners must overcome the "us" versus "them" dynamic between the flight crew and mission control too. In addition to language differences at both mission control and on the ISS, isolation is a problem.

One of the ISS teams gathered for a group photo.
Source: NASA

Astronauts can be on board the station for up to a year at a time. The confined spaces and lack of communication with family and friends are incredibly stressful. Thankfully, new technology enables the flight crew to communicate more frequently and privately with others on the ground.

The Ultimate Telecommuters An interesting way to think of astronauts is to think of them as the most extreme telecommuters! Most if not all the challenges discussed in this chapter are experienced by those involved in the ISS—both on the ground and in space.[81]

YOUR THOUGHTS?

Imagine you're a leader of the ISS flight crew.

1. What team challenges do you think would be most enjoyable for you?

2. What team challenges do you think would be most problematic for you?

3. What would you do to ensure the team aboard the ISS works most effectively and safely?

8.6 MAKING THE CONNECTION: HOW CAN WORKING WITH OTHERS INCREASE MY PERFORMANCE?

THE BIGGER PICTURE

You will thrive as an employee and manager by applying your knowledge of groups, teams, and trust.

As in previous chapters, we conclude this one with a number of explicit practical applications for you and for managers.

Takeaways for Me

There are five practical ways you can apply the material in this chapter:

1. **Learn which individual functions of groups are most important to you.** This knowledge can help you understand why you are more satisfied in some groups than others. Knowledge of organizational functions can help diagnose conflict and/or underperformance in some of the groups in which you are a member.

2. **Apply your knowledge of task and maintenance roles to identify ways you can make meaningful contributions to groups and teams.** If a role is missing and important, use your knowledge to fulfill it.

3. **Develop your teamwork competencies.** Table 8.5 provides examples of how to do it. These competencies will serve you in any group or team and increase your value throughout your career.

4. **Apply your knowledge to combat social loafing.** Don't let free riders add to or undermine your hard work.

5. **Pay attention to communication, support, respect, fairness, predictability, and competence to boost your trustworthiness.** Your trustworthiness will make or break you. When trust is diminished or violated, use Figure 8.6 to repair it.

Takeaways for Managers

There are six practical implications that will benefit you as a manager:

1. **Identify the important task and maintenance roles in the various teams you manage or belong to.** Be sure these important roles are fulfilled effectively (not always by you).

2. **Reduce frustrations when working in teams by understanding the group development process.** Identify the particular stage of development the group is in and apply your knowledge to advance it to the next.

3. **Evaluate those you manage in terms of the three Cs of a team player—committed, collaborative, competent.** These can help you identify top performers and underperformers.

4. **Always be mindful of trust, how trusting you are of your people and how trusting they are of you.** Managing people is infinitely more difficult when trust is an issue—never underestimate its importance. Apply the knowledge gained in this chapter to both build and repair trust (see Figure 8.6).

5. **Use team charters to set up your various teams to win.** Doing this work early can pay great dividends and avoid conflict throughout the team's existence.

6. **Ensure the tangible and intangible rewards you offer support collaboration and teamwork.**

Your work life, and life more generally, is awash in teams. Apply the OB knowledge and tools gained in this chapter to be more successful and fulfilled when you work with others.

What Did I Learn?

You learned that working with others can increase everyone's performance because groups and teams can, and often do, accomplish more than individuals. You learned that roles and norms are the building blocks of group and team behavior. We explored group development processes, along with ways to differentiate groups and teams and the characteristics of effective team players. We saw the different types of teams and the value of interdependence. You learned how to boost personal effectiveness further still by understanding trust and knowing how to repair it. Finally, we addressed the elements that foster team effectiveness and collaboration. Reinforce and consolidate your learning with the Key Points and Organizing Framework. Then challenge your mastery of the material by completing the Problem-Solving Application Case and Legal/Ethical Challenge below.

Key Points for Understanding Chapter 8

You learned the following key points:

8.1 GROUP CHARACTERISTICS

- Groups consist of two or more individuals who have low/no task dependency, are not accountable to each other, and may (not) assemble for a specified period of time.
- Both formal and informal groups are useful.
- Roles are expected behaviors for a particular job or position, and group roles set expectations for members of a group.
- Norms are shared attitudes, opinions, feelings, or actions that help govern the behaviors of groups and their members.

8.2 THE GROUP DEVELOPMENT PROCESS

- Groups often develop along five defined steps: forming, storming, norming, performing, and adjourning.

- Punctuated equilibrium is another form of group development.

8.3 TEAMS AND THE POWER OF COMMON PURPOSE

- Teams are collections of two or more individuals whose tasks are interdependent, collectively accountable for outcomes, and work together for a specified time.
- Team players are committed, collaborative, and competent.
- Common forms of teams are work, project, cross-functional, self-managed, and virtual.
- Team interdependence describes the degree to dependence between members for task completion.

8.4 TRUST BUILDING AND REPAIR—ESSENTIAL TOOLS FOR SUCCESS

- Trust is a belief that another person will consider the way his or her intentions and behaviors will affect you.
- Three common forms of trust are contractual, communication, and competence.
- Damaged trust can be repaired using a seven-step process.

8.5 KEYS TO TEAM EFFECTIVENESS

- High-performing teams are characterized by clarity, complementary skills, incentives and motivation, trust and communication, empowerment, effective conflict resolution, and collaboration.
- Charters and strategies, composition, and capacity are the three Cs of effective teams.
- Rewards and collaboration are important means of fostering team effectiveness.

8.6 HOW CAN WORKING WITH OTHERS INCREASE MY PERFORMANCE?

- Understanding groups, teams, and trust are keys to success as an employee.
- Understanding and applying your knowledge of groups, teams, and trust are keys to success as a manager.

The Organizing Framework for Chapter 8

As shown in Figure 8.7, the process of group/team dynamics leads to a large number of outcomes at all three levels in the Organizing Framework.

FIGURE 8.7 Organizing Framework for Understanding and Applying OB

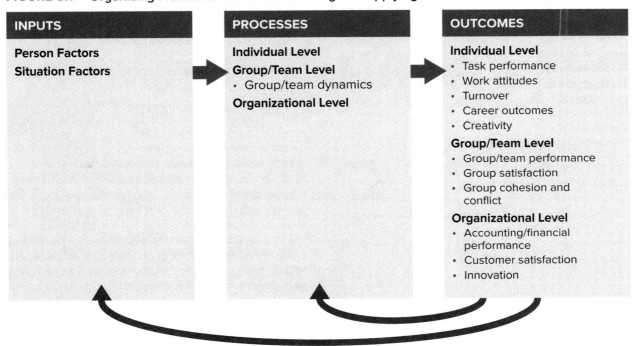

INPUTS

Person Factors
Situation Factors

PROCESSES

Individual Level
Group/Team Level
- Group/team dynamics

Organizational Level

OUTCOMES

Individual Level
- Task performance
- Work attitudes
- Turnover
- Career outcomes
- Creativity

Group/Team Level
- Group/team performance
- Group satisfaction
- Group cohesion and conflict

Organizational Level
- Accounting/financial performance
- Customer satisfaction
- Innovation

Money, Design, and Disaster

Assume you're the CEO of a company in which a single product accounts for nearly 80 percent of current sales (worth over $300 billion) and it is the fastest selling in the long and proud history of your company. The product sells for approximately $100 million, and great care was taken in its design with the strategy of ensuring it easily fit with your company's other products which have been purchased by companies around the world. However, this same product is responsible for the deaths of 346 people in just six months. The CEO is Dennis Muilenburg, the company is Boeing, and the product is the 737 Max plane. Every one of these planes sits on the ground across the globe.[82]

COSTS TO THE COMPANY

The value of the lives lost is of course immeasurable but will require compensation. The quantifiable costs are varied and potentially enormous, such as a drop in the value of the stock, massive legal liabilities from the families of the passengers, and increased scrutiny from regulators. Boeing's reputation is horribly tarnished, to say the least. Confidence in the quality and safety of Boeing's products has been deeply shaken for a range of important stakeholders, notably airline passengers who fly In Boeing's products, investors who buy the company's stock, airlines who purchase the planes, and the pilots and cabin crews who fly them.

Another stakeholder who thus far has been largely overlooked is Boeing's employees. After all it is they who built, tested, and helped certify the safety of the planes. The crashes call into question their performance, the collaboration between departments, and importantly, management oversight. In addition to the blame cast upon them, they too are concerned and deeply saddened by the loss of life due to the product failures.

HOW DID THIS HAPPEN?

Facts will no doubt continue to emerge for a long time, but now we know several relevant details. The Max was the latest model in the long line of 737s dating back to the 1960s.[83] The Max is more fuel efficient and has longer range than its predecessors, making it more attractive to airlines around the world. These gains are due primarily to larger engines, but they in turn require positioning farther forward and up than the previous models. The design modification causes the plane's nose to tilt upward in some conditions which can cause the plane to stall. To combat this potentially catastrophic event, Boeing created and installed software—Maneuvering Characteristics Augmentation System (MCAS)—to adjust the nose down. It is now clear the MCAS and its accompanying sensors did not function properly and wrestled control away from pilots and caused the crashes.[84]

Adding to the problem, it appears Boeing cut corners in the design and certification of the Max. Many experts have claimed the MCAS was a band-aid and insufficiently addressed the underlying design problems. Also insufficient was that only one sensor triggered the software, whereas most critical systems on planes have redundancies to guard against a failure in one element. It has also come to light that the Federal Aviation Association (FAA), the governmental agency responsible for certifying new planes, actually had Boeing employees play a significant role in the certification process, raising concerns of conflict of interest. To elaborate, critics have accused the FAA of having a "cozy" relationship with Boeing and allowing the airline to exert undue influence in the certification and safety testing. These certification processes also in large part determined how much training would be required by airlines and their pilots to fly the new planes.[85]

TRAINING AND COMMUNICATION

One of the key selling points of the Max was it could be easily integrated into existing fleets, in particular, minimal pilot training would be required. This would reduce costs and boost profits, making the plane more attractive to airlines. However, it appears Boeing did not appropriately train and inform pilots of the changes, new systems, and potential challenges associated with the Max, engine positioning, and MCAS.[86]

Some pilots have since commented that a lack of training and communication related to these types of changes are uncharacteristic of Boeing, meaning historically pilots could trust they would be appropriately informed and trained. Evidence for these deficiencies was revealed in black-box and flight data recordings and in subsequent simulations. These showed pilots of the doomed flights had less than a minute to respond, and when they did, were unable to regain control of the planes due to the MCAS.[87]

WHAT HAPPENED IN THE HANGARS, DESIGN ROOMS, AND IN COUNTLESS MEETINGS?

From designers, to their managers, to safety engineers, and regulators, their decision-making criteria and processes failed. Senior leadership's knowledge and involvement is yet to be revealed, but as with the emissions scandals in the auto industry in recent years, it is likely that numerous senior leaders had intimate involvement and knowledge. This could pose personal liability (legal and financial), along with the jobs and reputations of many executives. Some protestors are already calling for CEO Muilenburg to resign.

Moreover, additional information has come to light showing that Boeing engineers "believed" a key cockpit warning light was a standard feature on all new 737 Max planes. It wasn't. Only the 20 percent of airlines who had purchased the equivalent of a premium package had the working warning light. The light signaled pilots when two key sensors register different readings about the angle of the plane, which suggests there may be a malfunction with the sensors that pilots should investigate. But without the functioning light, it seems pilots of the doomed flights were unaware the sensors malfunctioned, activating the MCAS which dramatically and inappropriately corrected the angle of the planes. This scenario played out in seconds, not minutes, and seems to be a major design flaw and fundamental cause of the fatalities.[88]

This scenario was exacerbated by a lack of communication by Boeing. After learning in 2017 the lights didn't function on all planes, Boeing conducted internal tests and concluded the planes were still safe and no action was necessary. Because of this the company did not notify airlines, pilots, or the FAA.[89]

Boeing's troubles, however, are broader and deeper than the 737 Max. Production processes and practices for its 787 Dreamliner have been scrutinized for years. (Remember the battery fires that grounded those planes in 2013? The fixes were much more complex than software.)[90] Company norms were strong and clear, such that criticisms of key products were discouraged and or ignored. Numerous reports exist of employees being intimidated and, in some instances, retaliated against for speaking up. Critics, some of whom are current and former employees, claim the company values production speed over quality, and similar concerns motivated Qatar airlines to stop accepting planes from a plant in South Carolina. Many now wonder if this reflects deeply embedded cultural problems throughout Boeing and its products.[91]

CURRENT PREDICAMENT

For the Max to fly again, Boeing must develop and implement a software fix, and have this certified by the FAA, which will take several months. Many people both inside and outside the airline industry doubt that will be enough. Trust is gone. As stated by Ross Aimer, aviation consultant and former Boeing training captain: "*Boeing in the past always told the pilots and airlines exactly what was on those airplanes. . . . I have been a Boeing pilot for over 50 years and have loved their products, but they have lost my trust.*" He further said he feels Boeing was purely profit focused in these decisions. A survey showed that 53 percent of American adults would rather not fly in the 737 Max even when it is approved for service.[92]

Mr. Muilenburg realizes the magnitude of the situation and began what is sure to be a long apology and trust re-building tour.[93] But again, many experts question whether he or anyone else can do enough. Some argue Boeing will need to replace the 737 Max altogether; still, others say the flying public has short memories and such drastic action will not be required. To elaborate, sadly planes do crash, and sometimes this is due to design errors which are then corrected, and the same model of planes returns back into service.

Assume you are the board of directors at Boeing, and apply the 3-Step Problem-Solving Approach to the predicament facing the company.

APPLY THE 3-STEP PROBLEM-SOLVING APPROACH TO OB

Use the Organizing Framework in Figure 8.7 and the 3-Step Problem-Solving Approach to help identify inputs, processes, and outcomes relative to this case.

STEP 1: Define the problem.

A. Look first at the Outcomes box of the Organizing Framework to help identify the important problem(s) in this case. Remember that a problem is a gap between a desired and current state. State your problem as a gap and be sure to consider problems at all three levels. If more than one desired outcome is not being accomplished, decide which one is most important and focus on it for steps 2 and 3.

B. Cases have key players, and problems are generally viewed from a particular player's perspective. You need to determine from whose perspective—employee, manager, team, or the organization—you're defining the problem. In this case you're asked to assume the role of the board of directors for Boeing (they have ultimate responsibility for the entire organization).

C. Use details in the case to determine the key problem. Don't assume, infer, or create problems not included in the case.

D. To refine your choice, ask yourself, *why is this a problem?* Explaining why helps refine and focus your thinking. Focus on topics in the current chapter, because we generally select cases illustrating concepts specifically located within the current chapter.

STEP 2: Identify causes.

Using material from this chapter and summarized in the Organizing Framework, identify the causes of the problem you identified in Step 1? Remember, causes tend to appear in either the Inputs or Processes boxes.

A. Start by looking at the Organizing Framework (Figure 8.7) and decide which person factors, if any, are most likely causes of the defined problem. For each cause, explain why this is a cause of the problem. Asking *why* multiple times is more likely to lead you to root causes of the problem. For example, do executive characteristics help explain the problem you defined in Step 1?

B. Follow the same process for the situation factors. For each ask yourself, *why is this a cause?* By asking why multiple times you are likely to arrive at a complete and more accurate list of causes. Again, look to the Organizing Framework for this chapter for guidance. Did particular policies or practices play a role?

C. Now consider the Processes box in the Organizing Framework. Are any processes at the individual, group/team, or organizational level potential causes of your defined problem? For any process you consider, ask yourself, *why is this a cause?* Again, do this for several iterations to arrive at the root causes.

D. To check the accuracy or appropriateness of the causes, be sure to map them onto the defined problem and confirm the link or cause and effect connection.

STEP 3: Recommend solutions.

Make your recommendations for solving the problem. Consider whether you want to resolve it, solve it, or dissolve it (see Section 1.5). Which recommendation is desirable and feasible?

A. Given the causes you identified in Step 2, what are your best recommendations? Use material in the current chapter that best suits the cause. Consider the OB in Action and Applying OB boxes, because these contain insights into what others have done.

B. Be sure to consider the Organizing Framework—both person and situation factors—as well as processes at different levels.

C. Create an action plan for implementing your recommendations and be sure your recommendations map onto the causes and resolve the problem.

LEGAL/ETHICAL CHALLENGE

Who's Accountable?

Who is responsible for the performance and conduct of a team? At work it is typically the team members and the immediate manager, and to a lesser extent, the manager's manager and so on. In sports, most would agree at the very least players and coaches. In collegiate and professional sports many others are involved in creating, supporting, and contributing to the performance of the teams, such as assistant coaches, general managers and owners (in professional sports), and athletic directors, presidents, and trustees at the college level. All of them, individually and collectively, share some measure of the glory of victory and the agony of defeat. But who, if anyone, shares the responsibility for conduct off the field, court, pool, or arena? If it's misconduct, then who shares the responsibility is unclear, or at least uneven.

The National Collegiate Athletic Association (NCAA), the governing body for college sports, routinely sanctions violations of rules related to recruiting, academic eligibility, and illegal payments. Titles and wins are vacated, schools can be banned from playoff participation for a season, coaches and players are suspended for a given number of games. Nevertheless, misconduct is widespread, and at some schools and with some coaches, violations occur repeatedly, suggesting that current efforts to prevent unethical conduct in college sports are ineffective.

The most egregious misconduct sometimes qualifies as criminal, as was the horrific sex abuse case involving team physician Larry Nassar (Michigan State University and USA Gymnastics) and defensive coordinating coach Jerry Sandusky (Penn State University football). They received prison sentences of 40 to 175 years and 30 to 60 years, respectively.[94] Some misconduct qualifies as bribery and fraud and also ends up in courts. The vast majority of misconduct in college sports Is wrong, but not illegal, and therefore is left up to the NCAA, universities, and respective university leaders at all levels to monitor, prevent, and punish.

With this as background, one can appropriately argue that everyone makes mistakes. Indeed, it is part of being human. It's also reasonable to assert some mistakes should be forgiven (get a second chance); however, the larger issue in college sports is *patterns* of misconduct that exist. Patterns of misconduct occur in particular programs, universities, and with certain coaches. Nassar's and Sandusky's crimes continued for years, many people knew about it, and some of these have also suffered consequences. What about Rick Pitino? He had a prolific coaching career across college and professional teams: Hawaii, Boston University, the Knicks, Providence, Kentucky, the Celtics, and finally Louisville. He was implicated in various and multiple types of misconduct in his first position, and yet later Kentucky hired him when they were already in the process of "paying for the sins" of their previous coach. Eventually, the scandal at Louisville seemingly ended his career.[95]

Then there is Larry Brown, who was hired to coach basketball at Southern Methodist University in 2012. Like Pitino, Brown had legendary success at both the college and professional levels. But his UCLA championship team was stripped of its title because of NCAA violations, and when he later coached the University of Kansas it was banned from postseason play for a year and placed on probation for three years. If that wasn't enough, while at SMU he and the team were hit with additional NCAA sanctions for violations.[96]

With the preceding as background, the point of this Legal/Ethical Challenge is determining who should bear the consequences of such misconduct. It seems that leaders at different levels of universities reap the benefits of wins and championships, but rarely suffer the consequences of the misconduct, even misconduct they (should) have known about. Moreover, these same university officials are routinely involved in the hiring and annual reviews of these troubled coaches, athletic directors, team physicians, etc.

If you agree this is a problem that needs to be addressed, despite its intentions and efforts, the NCAA is only part of the solution. Perhaps the ultimate solution lies in the quality of university-level leadership by boards of trustees, presidents, and athletic directors.[97] The NCAA gives college presidents wide latitude to govern sports programs. They have official authority, and typically report to boards of trustees who are in effect their bosses and thus should be responsible for their conduct. What if sanctions were extended to university leaders? For instance, what if the board of trustees at a given university said that if a player is suspended, so are the coach(es) and the athletic director, without pay. If the player is dismissed, so too are the coach(es) and athletic director, and perhaps even the college president. After all, business executives and managers are fired every day when their conduct, or that of their employees, jeopardizes far less money than is at stake in major college sports programs.

While this solution may seem extreme and even unrealistic, it would certainly motivate presidents, athletic directors, and trustees to take greater responsibility for and oversight of the ethical conduct of their sports teams and programs.[98] These leaders bask in the rewards when their teams win championships, but they are able to contain or even avoid the costs of their misconduct. If both the rewards *and* the punishments extended beyond individual players, however, that behavior would likely change. It is also more likely that leaders, such as university presidents and trustees, would be more proactive. For instance, they might think twice about hiring coaches who bring not mistakes, but patterns of misconduct, with them.[99]

In the current system, if anyone pays penalties in a meaningful way, it is the players who lose postseason opportunities and scholarships, compared to a token few game suspensions for coaches who are already wealthy. So what about the other leaders—athletic directors, presidents, trustees?[100]

What Should Be Done about the Unethical Conduct in College Sports?

1. Don't change anything. The current means for dealing with misconduct, including NCAA sanctions, are sufficient. Justify.

2. Modify the NCAA authority and sanctions but keep the system more or less as it is. Explain.

3. Hold university leadership accountable—some combination of coaches, their bosses (athletic directors), their bosses (university presidents), and *their* bosses (boards of trustees). Explain.

4. Brainstorm another alternative and explain.

9

Communication in the Digital Age

After reading this chapter, you should be able to:

LO 9-1   Describe how the communication process works.

LO 9-2   Identify the key aspects of interpersonal communication.

LO 9-3   Explain how gender and age affect the communication process.

LO 9-4   Describe how using social media can increase your effectiveness at work.

LO 9-5   Explain how communication skills can increase your effectiveness.

LO 9-6   Describe the implications of communication in the digital age for you and managers.

The Organizing Framework shown in Figure 9.1 summarizes what you will learn in this chapter. You can see that communication is an important process at all three levels of OB—individual, group/team, and organizational. The quality and effectiveness of your communication is influenced greatly by person factors, such as your interpersonal, nonverbal communication, and listening skills. Of course many situation factors also influence the outcomes of your communication efforts. Your choice of medium, spoken or written words, and of course social media are increasingly important in the workplace. Collectively, these inputs impact communication across levels and outcomes in the Organizing Framework.

FIGURE 9.1 Organizing Framework for Understanding and Applying OB

INPUTS

Person Factors
- Nonverbal communication
- Active listening
- Nondefensive communication
- Empathy
- Ethical behavior
- Social media behaviors (an individual employee)
- Communication skills

Situation Factors
- Choice of medium
- HR policies (hiring and firing)
- Social media practices (managers and coworkers)

PROCESSES

Individual Level
- Communication

Group/Team Level
- Communication

Organizational Level
- Communication
- HR policies (social media policies)

OUTCOMES

Individual Level
- Task performance
- Work attitudes
- Turnover

Group/Team Level
- Group/team performance
- Group satisfaction

Organizational Level
- Accounting/financial performance
- Customer satisfaction
- Innovation
- Reputation
- Legal liability

Your communication skills are important determinants of your opportunities and effectiveness throughout your working life. Many jobs require teamwork and communication technology, meaning you are well served to enhance your understanding of communication processes and improve the many type of communication skills used in your professional life.

Hero Images Inc./Alamy Stock Photo

Winning at Work

Communication Counts in Landing a Job

As a job seeker, you are responsible for proving you're the best candidate for the job. Performing well during a job interview depends on what you say *and* how you say it! Effective communication skills enable you both to sell yourself as the best candidate and to calm your own nerves.

What You Say in a Job Interview

- *Direct the conversation.* Many people simply wait to be asked questions, but you don't need to. You can use small talk to get things started, but be brief. Also be sure you know your key selling points and guide the conversation to these. You can even state them upfront, saying, "I'd like to cover A, B, and C."

- *Pick your selling points.* Identify and focus on only your top two or three selling points. If you have little experience, focus on personal qualities or skills. If you have experience, highlight significant achievements.

- *Substantiate.* Support and illustrate your selling points with numbers and/or stories. For instance, be explicit and say you were the number one in sales, increased efficiency by 20 percent, ranked top 10 in your class, or were member of a state champion team in a sport. Also consider using stories to describe achievements (school, work, or sports), how you dealt with a challenging situation, or what you appreciated most about a particular job or experience.

- *Describe what's in it for them.* Ask not what the job will do for you, but what you can do on the job. Explain why you're a good match and why you can add value to the organization.

- *Do your homework.* Be sure to thoroughly research the company and people. Look online for information relevant to past, current, and future company events and initiatives. Use this knowledge when talking or asking questions about the company.

- *Anticipate challenging questions.* Know you will be asked, "What are your weaknesses?" The key here is to briefly identify a challenge, then discuss how you solved the problem and how it helped you grow.

How You Say It

- *Show them you'll bring it.* Express your enthusiasm and willingness to do anything, not just the most interesting stuff. Remember, enthusiasm and other positive emotions are both attractive to others and contagious. Positivity sells . . . be positive in your words, nonverbals, attitude, and emotions!

- *Smile.* It's one of the easiest ways to win people over.

- *Take your time.* Nerves can make us speak more quickly than usual. Slow yourself to a normal conversational pace. If you need time to phrase your answer, say, "That's a good question," before you respond.

- *Make eye contact.* Don't stare in the other person's eyes, but don't stare at the floor or out the window either.

- *Dress the way they dress.* Regardless of your own style or wardrobe, your choices need to match what is common at the company. The rule: Anything that distracts, diminishes.

- *Close with a handshake.* End the interview with a "thank you" and a firm handshake (don't crush bones).

- *Follow up.* At the end of the interview ask when the interviewer would like you to follow up. Then drop your interviewer a note of thanks.

Fighting Nerves

- Prepare.
- Breathe.
- Pause before answering.
- Never say you're nervous.
- Use positive self-talk and visualization.[1]

What's Ahead in This Chapter

We're about to give you practical guidance on how to communicate effectively. Communication is a critically important process at all levels of OB—individual, group, and organizational—and in most arenas of your life. We'll guide you through important elements at each level, beginning with how individuals process information. We'll also highlight the characteristics of competent communicators and show you how to more successfully communicate within and between generations and genders. We'll conclude with the most practical tips of all: the do's and don'ts of using social media in your professional life, ways to develop effective presentation and conversational skills, and suggestions for managing up.

9.1 BASIC DIMENSIONS OF THE COMMUNICATION PROCESS

THE BIGGER PICTURE

By this point in your study of OB, you probably realize that communication is a critical and dynamic *process* within the Organizing Framework. It includes a sender, a message, and a receiver; encoding and decoding; a medium; feedback; and the need to deal with "noise" or interference. You will also see why you should match the communication medium to the situation.

Irish playwright George Bernard Shaw summed up a key issue with communication in stating "the single biggest problem in communication is the illusion that it has taken place."[2]

The illusion that we have communicated when we have not can lead to catastrophic consequences, such as the 2014 sinking of the *Sewol,* a South Korean ferry. Investigators concluded that "crucial miscommunication between the crew and ship traffic controllers who could have expedited rescue" was a key cause of 293 deaths. Many of the dead were 16- and 17-year-olds on a school outing.[3]

Effective communication helps individuals, groups, and organizations to achieve their goals. Bridgewater Associates LP, the world's largest hedge fund, is trying to enhance productivity and customer service by fostering open communication. Employees are asked to "tell it like it is," according to *The Wall Street Journal.* They are "encouraged to air any gripes and concerns about the hedge fund in a digital 'issue log' that can be seen by anyone at Bridgewater. The comments usually are about bigger problems but also have included difficulties formatting e-mail." To improve individual performance, the company also gathers and disseminates feedback collected on iPads on which workers use apps to rate each other on dozens of strengths and weaknesses.[4]

TEKsystems, an IT recruiting firm, has employed a different communication strategy. The company sent 18 senior leaders to visit more than 100 of its local offices over the course of one month. The goal of these meetings was to update employees in person about what was happening in the company and its plans.[5]

These examples illustrate why communication is a critical process at all three levels in the Organizing Framework. We hope this chapter helps you develop your communication skills.

LO 9-1

Describe how the communication process works.

Defining Communication

Communication **is "the exchange of information between a sender and a receiver, and the inference (perception) of meaning between the individuals involved."**[6] It is a circular and dynamic process in which people interpret and make sense of the information they exchange. And it's a very important activity in both our personal and professional lives.[7]

A recent national survey of nearly 1,000 employers who recruit on business school campuses revealed that communication skills top the list of skills and abilities these employers will be looking for in new hires. One recruiter observed that candidates seem to have the technological skills employers are looking for. However, many recent grads seem to lack soft skills, such as communications and people skills, which tend to make the difference in an effective hire.[8]

These students are working on a class project. Note how some of them are actively involved while others appear a bit detached. Why do you think college students overestimate their communication skills?

Jacob Lund/Shutterstock

How the Communication Process Works

We all know communicating is neither simple nor clear-cut. Researchers have begun to examine it as a form of social information processing in which receivers interpret messages by cognitively processing information. This work has led to development of a perceptual model of communication that depicts it as a process in which receivers create meaning in their own minds.[9] Let us consider the parts of this process and illustrate them with an example (see Figure 9.2).

Sender, Message, and Receiver   The sender is the person or group wanting to communicate information—the message. The receiver is the person, group, or organization for whom the message is intended.

FIGURE 9.2   Communication Process in Action

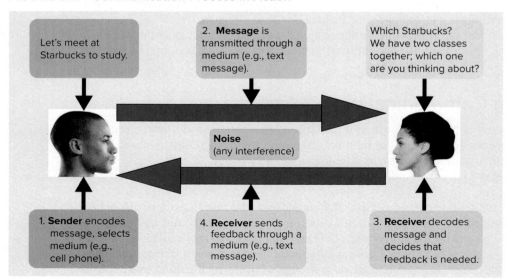

(left): Wolf/Fuse/Getty Images; (right): paffy/Shutterstock

Encoding   Communication begins when a sender encodes an idea or thought. Encoding means translating thoughts into a form or language that can be understood by others. This language becomes the foundation of the message. For example, if a professor wants to communicate with you about an assignment, he or she must first think about what information to communicate. Once the professor has resolved this issue in his or her mind (encoding), the next step is to select a medium in which to communicate.

Selecting a Medium   Managers can communicate through a variety of media. These include face-to-face conversations and meetings, telephone calls, charts and graphs, and the many digital messaging forms—e-mail, texting, voice mail, videoconferencing, Twitter, Facebook, Blackboard, and others. We discuss the best way to select a medium in the next section.

Decoding and Creating Meaning   Decoding, the process of interpreting or making sense of a message, occurs when receivers receive a message. When a professor communicates with you about an assignment, for example, you decode the message when you receive it.

The perceptual model of communication assumes the receiver creates the meaning of a message in his or her mind. This means different people can interpret the same message differently.

Feedback   The first round of feedback occurs when the original receiver expresses a reaction to the sender's message. Once the initial sender has obtained this feedback, he or she is likely to decode it and send corresponding feedback. This process continues until sender and receiver believe they have effectively communicated.

Noise   *Noise* **is anything that interferes with the transmission and understanding of a message.** There are many other sources of noise: language differences, speech impairment, illegible handwriting, inaccurate statistics, poor hearing and eyesight, environmental noises, other people talking, faulty equipment, and physical distance between sender and receiver. Noise affects all the links in the communication process. Nonverbal communication, discussed later in this chapter, also is a source of noise, as are cross-cultural differences between senders and receivers, and the physical work environment.

OB in Action

Transparency Is the Message at Skinfix

If noise is anything that interferes with the transmission and understanding of a message, what is the absence of noise? For Amy Risley, CEO of award-winning skin care company Skinfix, Inc., it's a standard of communication transparency high enough to make the company's message crystal-clear—to employees, clients, suppliers, and the industry.[10]

How does Skinfix achieve that transparency? First, not only are its products tested and recommended by impartial dermatologists; the number and percentage of natural active ingredients are also verified and listed on the packaging. "We respect our customers enough to be transparent with our formulations," says Risley. That includes not overpromising.

The company takes pride in its customers' loyalty and the high ratings its products earn as a result of rigorous testing procedures. "If it doesn't fix skin, it doesn't wear the Skinfix logo," Risley says.

Transparency also extends to information sharing among employees. Working on the principle that "a fantastic product is not the work of one—it's a collaborative effort along the way," employees absorb information from a wide variety of sources, including beauty, fashion, and dermatology, and use it to collaborate. "We don't silo teams," Risley observes. "We work across functions because we all wear many hats in a small company. Collaboration is a necessity, and one that enriches the work environment."

The company also shares sensitive information with employees, including profit and loss, cost of goods sold, and profit margin. While some managers might be cautious with these data, Risley finds that choosing "transparency over fear" has worked to the company's advantage. "We don't make a habit of sharing detailed strategies with anyone and everyone," she says, "but we do share information when it's relevant and productive . . . when we share within the industry, they share back! We learn so much from our industry friends, mentors, and contacts. It often helps us avoid pitfalls and mistakes that they have made along the way—some of which we were headed right for!"

YOUR THOUGHTS?

1. Which components of the communication process are most likely to create noise among Skinfix employees? Between employees and customers?

2. What most impresses you about Skinfix's approach to transparency? Explain.

Selecting the Right Medium

One way in which we communicate effectively is by using the medium most appropriate for the situation. That is, we match media *richness* with the situation's complexity. Let's look at how.

Media Richness *Media richness* **measures the capacity of a given communication medium to convey information and promote understanding.**[11] Media vary from rich to lean. As shown in Figure 9.3, there are three zones of communication effectiveness. Effective communication occurs when the richness of the medium is matched appropriately to the complexity of the problem or situation. The richer a medium, the better it is at conveying information.

Four factors affect communication richness:

1. **Speed of feedback:** Faster feedback offers more richness.

2. **Channel:** The visual and audio characteristics of a videoconference are richer than the limited visual aspects of a written report.

FIGURE 9.3 Selecting the Right Medium for Effective Communication

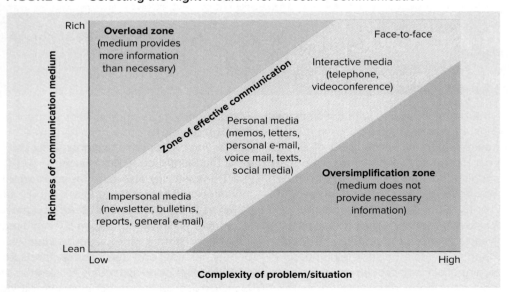

SOURCES: Daft, Richard L., and Robert H. Lengel. "The Selection of Communication Media as an Executive Skill." *Academy of Management Perspectives* 2, no. 3 (August 1998): 225–32. https://doi.org/10.5465/ame.1988.4277259; and Daft, Richard L., and Robert H. Lengel. *Information Richness: A New Approach to Managerial Behavior and Organization Design.* Texas: Texas A & M University, 1983.

The photo on the right represents a less complex situation than the one on the left. Speaking to a group of employees in an open forum is more complicated because the speaker has no idea what people might ask or how they might respond to the message. How would you suggest managers prepare for an open forum meeting?

(left): wavebreakmedia/Shutterstock; (right): LWA/Larry Williams/Getty Images

3. **Type:** Personal media such as phone calls and interpersonal speech are richer than impersonal media such as memos and group e-mails.

4. **Language source:** The natural body language and speech in a face-to-face conversation provide a richer medium than the numbers in a financial report.

Complexity of the Situation   Situations can range from low to high in complexity. Low-complexity situations are routine and predictable, such as a manager updating employees on last month's sales or calculating someone's paycheck. Highly complex situations, such as a corporate reorganization or merger, are ambiguous, hard to analyze, and often emotionally charged.

Picking the Right Medium   A two-way face-to-face conversation is the richest form of communication. It provides immediate feedback and allows participants to observe multiple cues such as body language and tone of voice. Use face-to-face in situations that are complex or that are highly important to receivers. In contrast, telephone conversations and videoconferencing are not as informative as face-to-face exchanges even though they are relatively high in richness. For example, webinars and WebEx presentations are well suited for disseminating information, but we can say from experience that they are not as good for ensuring the messaging has been understood. At the other end of the complexity scale, newsletters, reports, and general e-mail blasts are lean media and best for less complex situations. E-mail and social media messages vary in media richness: leaner if they impersonally blanket a large audience, and richer if they mix personal textual and video information that prompts quick conversational feedback.[12]

We conclude this section by noting that people have preferences for communicating in different media. Research on individual differences identified the following trends:

- Improving the level of media richness reduces the cost of information search and increases the number of options consumers consider when making choices.[13]

- Managers, not coworkers, can influence the media richness perception held by employees, particularly when it comes to e-mail messages.[14]

- Employees targeted by coworkers' negative workplace gossip are less likely to demonstrate appropriate work behaviors.[15]

9.2 COMMUNICATION COMPETENCE

THE BIGGER PICTURE

Communication competence is your ability to effectively communicate with others. Knowing that recruiters look for communication skills in college graduates, you'll be happy to learn that you can improve these skills. You will learn how you can use nonverbal communication, active listening, nondefensive communication, and empathy to enhance your communication competence.

Although there is no universally accepted definition of *communication competence,* it is a performance-based index of an individual's abilities to effectively use communication behaviors in a given context.[16]

Are you curious about your level of communication competence? Is it low, medium, or high? Find out by completing Self-Assessment 9.1. If your score is lower than you prefer, find ideas in the chapter for improving your interpersonal communication skills.

SELF-ASSESSMENT 9.1   CAREER READINESS

Assessing Your Communication Competence

Please be prepared to answer these questions if your instructor has assigned Self-Assessment 9.1 in Connect.

1. Are you happy with the results?
2. Based on your scores, what are your top three strengths and your three biggest weaknesses?
3. How might you use your strengths more effectively in your role as a student?
4. How might you improve on your weaknesses?

Let's consider four key communication skills that affect your communication competence:

- Nonverbal communication
- Active listening
- Nondefensive communication
- Empathy

Sources of Nonverbal Communication

Nonverbal communication **is communication without words.** According to communication experts "it includes observable behaviors such as facial expressions, eyes, touching, and tone of voice, as well as less obvious messages such as dress, posture, and spatial distance between two or more people."[17]

Nonverbal communication adds flavor to oral communication. That is, it helps you understand the attitudes and emotions of those with whom you are speaking, which in turn helps you more accurately interpret their message.[18]

Let's consider four key sources of nonverbal messages:

- Body movements and gestures.
- Touch.
- Facial expressions.
- Eye contact.

Body Movements and Gestures   Body movements, such as leaning forward or backward, and gestures provide nonverbal information that can either enhance or detract from the communication process. Open body positions, such as leaning backward or gesturing with palms facing up, communicate *immediacy,* a term used to represent openness, warmth, closeness, and availability for communication. A recent study suggested that the use of gestures can help in the process of learning and comprehension in both adults and children.[19] *Defensiveness* is communicated by gestures such as folding arms, crossing hands, crossing legs, or pointing at others.

Touch   Touching is another powerful nonverbal cue. People tend to touch those they like. Research reveals that women do more touching during conversations than men.[20] Touching conveys an impression of warmth and caring and can help create a personal bond between people. Be careful about using touch with people from diverse cultures, however, because norms for touching vary significantly around the world.

Facial Expressions   Facial expressions convey a wealth of information. Smiling, for instance, typically represents warmth, happiness, or friendship, whereas frowning conveys dissatisfaction or anger. Are these interpretations universal? A summary of relevant research revealed that the association between facial expressions and emotions varies across cultures.[21] A smile, for example, does not convey the same emotion in different countries. Be careful when interpreting facial expressions among diverse groups of employees.

Eye Contact   Eye contact is a strong nonverbal cue that varies across cultures. Westerners are taught at an early age to look at their parents when spoken to. In contrast, Asians are taught to avoid eye contact with a parent or superior in order to show obedience and subservience.[22] Once again, you need to be sensitive to different orientations toward maintaining eye contact with diverse employees.

Practical Tips   Here is our advice for improving your nonverbal communication skills.

Body movements, gestures, and speech

- Lean forward to show the speaker you are interested.
- Don't display slumped shoulders, downward head, flat tones, or inaudible voice, all of which convey indecisiveness or lack of confidence.
- Don't speak too fast or too slowly. Your tone of voice should match the tone of the message.
- Use paraphrasing as a mechanism to check on communication accuracy. ***Paraphrasing*** **is restating what someone else has said or written.**

Facial expressions like these can reveal the emotions behind a message, but they are easily misinterpreted. Which of these facial expressions suggest happiness, worry, and anger?

(left to right): Jack Hollingsworth/Blend Images LLC; liza54500/Shutterstock; Aaron Amat/Shutterstock; SensorSpot/Getty Images

Facial expressions

- Nod your head to show you are listening or that you agree.
- Smile and show interest.
- Don't close your eyes or tense facial muscles.

Eye contact

- Maintain eye contact and don't look away from the speaker.

Listening

***Listening* is the process of actively decoding and interpreting verbal messages.** It requires cognitive attention and information processing; simply hearing does not. There is general consensus that listening is a cornerstone skill of communication competence.

In studies that support this conclusion, active listening made receivers feel more understood. It also led people to conclude that their conversations were more helpful, sensitive, and supportive.[23] Clearly, active listening yields positive outcomes.

As children, we all were instructed to listen. However, many adults seem to suffer from poor listening skills. Why is this? For one, it takes effort and motivation to be a good listener. To communicate and perform better, we would all benefit from investing more effort into listening more effectively.

Luis Molinero/Shutterstock

Unfortunately, many of us think we are good listeners when evidence suggests just the opposite. For example, researchers estimate that typical listeners retain only 20 to 50 percent of what they hear.[24]

Why do you think we miss or lose so much of what we hear? One reason is that we have the cognitive capacity to process words at a much higher rate than people speak. This means our cognitive processes are being underutilized, leading to daydreaming and distractions. Noise is another reason. A third reason, and one you can control, is your motivation to listen and your listening style. It takes effort to actively listen. You won't be a better listener unless you are motivated to become one.

What's Your Listening Style—or Styles?   You can improve your communication competence by understanding your typical listening style. There are four styles:[25]

1. **Active—I'm fully invested.** Active listeners are "all in." That is, they are motivated to listen and give full attention when others are talking. They focus on what is being communicated and expend energy by participating in the discussion. They also use positive body language, such as leaning in or making direct eye contact, to convey their interest.

2. **Involved—I'm partially invested.** Involved listeners devote some, but not all, of their attention and energy to listening. They reflect on what is being said and halfheartedly participate in the discussion. Their use of nonverbal cues tends to be inconsistent or intermittent, and they can show nonverbal signs of interest and noninterest in the same conversation.

3. **Passive—It's not my responsibility to listen.** Passive listeners are not equal partners in a speaking-listening exchange. They assume the speaker is responsible for the quality of the interaction and believe their role is to passively take in information. Passive listeners will display attentiveness, but they can fake it at times. Overall, they don't expend much motivation or energy in receiving and decoding messages.

4. **Detached—I'm uninterested.** Detached listeners tend to withdraw from the interaction. They appear inattentive, bored, distracted, and uninterested. They may start using mobile devices during the speaking-listening exchange. Their body language will reflect lack of interest, such as slumping and avoiding direct eye contact.

Which of the four styles do you tend to use? Do you consistently use one or two styles, or does your style vary from one situation to the next? You can answer these questions by taking Self-Assessment 9.2.

Assessing Your Listening Style

Please be prepared to answer these questions if your instructor has assigned Self-Assessment 9.2 in Connect.

1. Based on your results, how would you classify your style?
2. Are you surprised by the results?
3. Identify three things you can do to improve your listening skills.

Becoming a More Effective Listener   Effective listening is a learned skill that requires effort and motivation. It comes down to *paying attention to the content of the message.* The suggestions in Table 9.1 can increase your listening skills at school, home, and work.

Researchers have now begun to study an emerging dimension of listening called *social listening,* which pertains to how we communicate and listen to others using social media and communication technologies that influence our personal engagement with others. The increase in constant interaction brought about by social media and mobile devices appears to be changing the way we react to stimuli (for example, social media posts, comments, and likes) and listen and respond to messages.[26]

TABLE 9.1   Tips for Effective Listening

TIP	EXPLANATION
Show respect.	Give everyone the opportunity to explain his/her ideas without interrupting. Actively try to help the sender convey his or her message.
Listen from the first sentence.	Turn off your internal thoughts and mentally put aside whatever you were thinking about prior to the interaction.
Be mindful.	Stay in the moment and focus on the sender. Don't try to figure out what the speaker is going to say.
Keep quiet.	Use your ears more than your mouth, and try to follow the 80/20 rule. That is, your conversation partner should speak 80 percent of the time and you should speak 20 percent.
Ask questions.	Asking questions helps you clarify what is being said, unlocks learning, and improves interpersonal bonding.
Paraphrase and summarize.	Paraphrasing repeats back to someone what you believe you just heard him or her say. Summarizing consolidates an entire conversation. Both these techniques enhance communication accuracy because they help to ensure messages are being understood correctly.
Remember what was said.	Either take notes or make an effort to log critical information into your mental computer.
Involve your body.	Use nonverbal cues to demonstrate interest and involvement.

SOURCES: Brooks, Alison Wood, and Leslie K. John. "The Surprising Power of Questions." *Harvard Business Review,* June 2018. https://hbr.org/2018/05/the-surprising-power-of-questions; Altman, Ian. "The Most Successful Entrepreneurs Possess This One Crucial Skill." *Forbes Media, LLC,* April 18, 2017. https://www.forbes.com/sites/ianaltman/2017/04/18/the-most-successful-entrepreneurs-possess-this-one-crucial-skill/#61d4f4b25d67; and Keyser, John. "Active Listening Leads to Business Success." Association for Talent Development. https://www.td.org/magazines/td-magazine/active-listening-leads-to-business-success.

Nondefensive Communication

Nondefensive communication occurs when you ask questions and make statements in an open and neutral manner. Using this approach helps the communicator gather accurate information and speak in an even-tempered tone without jumping to conclusions that may inflame the situation. Nondefensive communication also helps individuals gain the respect of their colleagues and others in an organization while strengthening personal and professional relationships. For example, if one of your coworkers acts upset, you could simply state an observation by asking the person, "Are you angry about something?" This neutral question will allow the person to explain his or her emotions without getting more upset or blaming others for the situation.[27]

Have you ever been in an auto accident? If yes, then you likely have intimate knowledge of defensiveness. In situations like this, one person often tries to blame the other while both defend themselves. Which toward-defensive styles in Table 9.2 on the next page are likely to occur in such situations?

Tom Merton/age fotostock

Defensiveness occurs when people perceive they are being attacked or threatened. Our "first responder" to defensiveness is the brain's amygdala. A neuroscience expert noted the amygdala "accesses emotional memories that identify a given stimulus as potentially threatening and triggers the emotional fear response that sets the fight-or-flight biobehavioral response in motion."[28] This reaction leads to defensive listening and destructive behaviors such as shutting down or being passive-aggressive, standing behind rules or policies, creating a diversion, or counterattacking.

Moreover, defensiveness from one person activates a similar response in the other party. All told, defensiveness from either party in an exchange fosters the exchange of inaccurate and inefficient communication.[29]

You may be surprised to learn that defensiveness is often triggered by nothing more than a poor choice of words or nonverbal posture during interactions. In the language of behavior modification, these triggers are *antecedents* of defensiveness. For example, using absolutes like "always" or "never" is very likely to create a defensive response. Try to avoid using absolutes because they are rarely true. Instead, you can increase your communication competence by avoiding the defensive antecedents and employing the positive antecedents of nondefensive communication shown in Table 9.2.

Connecting with Others via Empathy

We first mentioned empathy in Chapter 3 when discussing the components of emotional intelligence. Although researchers propose multiple types of empathy, the general consensus is that **empathy represents the ability to recognize and understand another person's feelings and thoughts.**[30] It is a reflective technique that fosters open communication.

Being empathetic requires two key actions. The first is mindfulness. Empathy necessitates that we place our attention on the feelings and emotions being displayed both verbally and nonverbally by others. The second action is to incorporate our understanding of another person's feelings and thoughts into our communications. This will lead us to use language that fits the receiver's perspective.

TABLE 9.2 Antecedents of Defensive and Nondefensive Communication

TOWARD DEFENSIVENESS		TOWARD NONDEFENSIVENESS	
Style	**Example**	**Style**	**Example**
Evaluative	"Your work is sloppy."	Descriptive	"Your work was two days late."
Controlling	"You need to . . ."	Problem solving	"What do you think are the causes of the missed deadline?"
Strategizing	"I'd like you to agree with me during the meeting so that we can overcome any challenges."	Straightforward	"Vote your conscience at the meeting. You can agree or disagree with my proposal."
Neutral	"Don't worry about missing the deadline. It's no big deal."	Empathetic	"I sense disappointment about missing the deadline. Let's figure out how we can get back on schedule."
Superior	"Listen to me; I've worked here 20 years."	Equal	"Let's figure out the causes of the missed deadline together."
Certain	"We tried this idea in the past. It just doesn't work."	Honest and open	Using I-messages: "I am angry about the way you spoke to the customer because our department looked unresponsive."

SOURCES: Gibb, R. Jack. "Defensive Communication." *Journal of Communication* 11, no. 3 (September 1961): 141–48. https://doi.org/10.1111/j.1460-2466.1961.tb00344.x; and "Reach Out: Effective Communication." *Sunday Business Post*, April 14, 2013.

Empathy leads to more effective communication and interaction because people feel heard. It also sends the message that we care about others. For example, a recent study of audiotaped performance appraisal interviews revealed that managers' empathetic communication styles were positively related to employees' intentions to change or improve their performance and to employees' perceptions of their supervisors' likeability.[31] British entrepreneur Maurice Ostro offers some advice on the importance of empathy in the OB in Action feature.

OB in Action

Empathy Is Good for Business

British entrepreneur Maurice Ostro runs his family's gem company, Ostro Minerals, and Entrepreneurial Giving, a network he founded for entrepreneurs who donate some of their profits to charity. Convinced that empathy is good for business, Ostro offers this advice:[32]

- Maintain a purpose beyond profit. Align it with your values and make it part of every day.

- Write that purpose down. Encourage employees to do likewise.

- To keep productive employees and loyal customers, "tell everyone . . . about what you're doing for those around you." Says Ostro, "Research shows that employees at a purposeful company can be up to three times more productive."

- Connect with like-minded people.

YOUR THOUGHTS?

1. Do you agree that empathy is good for business? Why or why not?

2. Can you think of any other contexts in which empathy could be useful? Discuss.

9.3 GENDER, GENERATIONS, AND COMMUNICATION

THE BIGGER PICTURE

Women and men have communicated differently since the dawn of time. So do people from varying generations. You can improve your communication competence by understanding and accommodating communication differences among men and women and various generations. This section will help you in this pursuit.

LO 9-3

Explain how gender and age affect the communication process.

Assume you are about to work with someone who made the following statement during a strategic planning meeting. "I'm not on board with the direction this decision is going. . . . No, I'm not finished. I won't back down from this position, and I'm not going to commit my team and resources to this project until we have more conclusive evidence to work with. Period." What is your impression of this person? Would it be different if the speaker's name were Mary rather than Mark?

A team of researchers examined this question and found that women who disagreed in a forceful manner like this were evaluated more negatively than men.[33] This result held for both male and female evaluators. Let's consider two explanations.

The first is *implicit cognition,* or *bias,* which was discussed in Chapter 4. Implicit cognition consists of any thoughts or beliefs that are automatically activated from memory without our conscious awareness. It causes us to make biased decisions without realizing we are doing so.[34] Lawyer and former First Lady of the United States Michelle Obama commented about this bias by noting, "No country can ever truly flourish if it stifles the potential of its women and deprives itself of the contributions of half of its citizens."[35]

The second explanation is linguistic styles. Deborah Tannen, a communication expert, defines *linguistic style* as follows:

> **Linguistic style refers to a person's characteristic speaking pattern.** It includes such features as directness or indirectness, pacing and pausing, word choice, and the use of such elements as jokes, figures of speech, stories, questions, and apologies. In other words, linguistic style is a set of culturally learned signals by which we not only communicate what we mean but also interpret others' meaning and evaluate one another as people.[36]

You can see how linguistic style helps explain communication differences between women and men and across generations. This section will increase your understanding of interpersonal communication across age and gender barriers.

Communication Patterns between Women and Men

There are two competing explanations about the origin of linguistic styles between men and women. Some researchers believe interpersonal differences between women and men are due to inherited biological differences between the sexes. This perspective, also called the evolutionary psychology or Darwinian perspective, attributes gender differences in communication to drives, needs, and conflicts associated with reproductive strategies used by women and men. The second perspective, social role theory, suggests that girls and boys are taught to communicate differently. Here is what these explanations suggest about male and female communication patterns.[37]

The Male Perspective   Males are expected to communicate more aggressively, interrupt others more than women, and hide their emotions because they have an inherent desire to possess features attractive to females. Men also see conversations as negotiations in which people try to achieve and maintain the upper hand. Thus they feel it is important to protect themselves from others' attempts to put them down or push them around. This perspective increases a male's need to maintain independence and avoid failure.[38] Although males are certainly not competing for mate selection during a business meeting, evolutionary psychologists propose that men cannot turn off the biologically based determinants of their behavior.[39]

The Female Perspective   According to social role theory, females and males learn ways of speaking while growing up. Research shows that girls learn conversational skills and habits that focus on rapport and relationships, whereas boys learn skills and habits that focus on status and hierarchies. Accordingly, women come to view communication as a network of connections in which conversations are negotiations for closeness. This orientation leads women to seek and give confirmation and support more than men.[40]

What Does Research Reveal?   Research demonstrates that women and men communicate differently in a number of ways.[41] Women are more likely to share credit for success, to ask questions for clarification, to tactfully give feedback by mitigating criticism with praise, and to indirectly tell others what to do. According to *The Wall Street Journal,* women also are "more likely to add qualifiers ('I'm not sure, but . . .') and apologies ('I'm sorry to interrupt, but . . .'). When complimented on her work, a woman is more likely to downplay it, saying she was 'lucky.'"[42] These tendencies allow women to be interrupted more than men when communicating with others.[43]

In contrast, men are more likely to boast about themselves, to bluntly give feedback, to withhold compliments, to ask fewer questions, and to avoid admitting fault or weaknesses.

Generational Differences in Communication

As discussed in Chapter 4, today's workplace often includes people from four different generations—traditionalists, baby boomers, Gen Xers, and Millennials—with Gen Zers also starting to make their mark. (Refer to Table 4.3 for additional details and characteristics.) Among the challenges in this scenario is the fact that different generations prefer different media, as discussed above, and they have different expectations and norms about communication.

The Role of Digital Devices   When it comes to communication media, Millennials and Gen Xers are more likely to love their digital devices than boomers and traditionalists. Millennials were brought up with instant messaging and texting and prefer these media over phone calls, letters, and reports. Several professional sports teams, including the NFL's Arizona Cardinals, acknowledge these trends and are making accommodations in managing their operations and players.

Women are more likely to be interrupted during this meeting attended by a group of global employees. What can women do to ensure that their voices are heard and not overrun by others during a meeting?

oneinchpunch/Shutterstock

To help his Millennial players get their "social media fix," Cardinals coach Kliff Kingsbury recently announced he planned to allow cellphone breaks during team meetings. According to Kingsbury, the breaks will come every 20 minutes—or sooner—if he sees players starting to lose interest in the meetings. "They're itching to get to those things," Kingsbury said. "We'll let them hop over there and then get back in the meeting and refocus." The Cardinals are not the only team making changes to address the popularity of digital devices. Baseball's Toronto Blue Jays recently passed a team rule restricting the amount of time players can play the popular video game "Fortnite," which seems to be keeping some team members from getting enough rest.[44]

Communication Expectations and Norms   Younger employees also are more likely to use the Internet and social media to accomplish their work tasks. However, advances in communication technology, along with scammers, have changed the approach businesspeople of all ages use to call prospective clients on the phone.

According to recent research, almost 50 percent of all phone calls are robo-called cold-calls from companies that are either real or fake. Thus, the act of cold-calling companies to seek new business may no longer be a viable communications strategy. In fact, the invention of voice mail significantly reduced the effectiveness of trying to communicate with potential clients via phone because it is no longer easy to get through to a key decision maker within any organization.[45]

Other more effective communication strategies regardless of whether you're a Millennial, Gen Zer, or Boomer may include seeking recommendations or referrals from current customers about potential new clients and e-mailing the prospects directly; networking with industry organizations and other professional groups; communicating through business or company accounts on social media such as Facebook, Twitter, Pinterest, or Instagram; and redesigning company websites to focus on selling products and services and signing up potential clients through the use of online newsletters, podcasts, sales discounts, and other business opportunities.[46]

Improving Communications between the Sexes and Generations

It's unwise to generalize any trends, preferences, or perceptions to all men, all women, or all members of a particular generation. Some men, for instance, are less likely to boast about their achievements, while some women are less likely to share the credit. Some traditionalists embrace technology and new communication practices, while not all Millennials are technological whizzes. There are always exceptions to the rule. In recognition of that fact, here are some suggestions that can enhance your communication competence:

- **Clarify communication expectations and norms.** If your manager fails to discuss these, bring the topic up. It's better to understand expectations than to guess wrong. After all, you are the one who will lose if people form negative perceptions about your communication skills and patterns.

- **Use a variety of communication tools.** Regardless of your preferred mode of communication (such as face-to-face or texting), employees from all generations should use a variety of media according to the circumstances. This avoids alienating any particular generation.

- **Be aware of implicit bias.** Don't assume, based on somebody's gender or age, that he or she only likes one mode of communication. If you find males interrupting, gently call them out. If someone is quiet in a meeting, ask for his or her opinion.

- **Make sure people get credit for their ideas and not their gender.** Sometimes a woman will propose an idea in a meeting and it's not acknowledged until a man offers the same suggestion later in the discussion. Researchers recently confirmed this scenario when study results revealed that a bump in status and leader recognition as a result of speaking up with ideas only happened for men, not women.[47]

9.4 SOCIAL MEDIA AND OB

THE BIGGER PICTURE

Employers are continually challenged to reap the benefits of social media while controlling the costs. Your own knowledge and behavior are part of the solution. In this section, you'll expand your understanding of how to use social media productively, the cost of social media, the effective use of e-mail, and ways to manage issues related to social media policies, privacy, and etiquette.

Social media use web-based and mobile technologies to generate interactive dialogue with members of a network. Social media are now woven throughout the fabric of our lives. Their use affects many subjects covered in this book, highlighting the importance of communication as an OB topic. Social media are now used by a significant proportion of people across all age groups (see Figure 9.4 for utilization rates by age).[48]

LO 9-4

Describe how using social media can increase your effectiveness at work.

These figures suggest that employers and managers are wise to utilize social media tools with employees of all generations. A communications expert put it this way:

> A social media policy should apply to *all* platforms, and ultimately everything employees post on line. Some employees may believe that while they use LinkedIn and Twitter for business purposes, they use Facebook for personal use and can, therefore, post indiscriminately. However, they are still company representatives, and inappropriate posts may damage their employer's brand, as well as their own.[49]

FIGURE 9.4 Age Distribution at the Top Social Networks

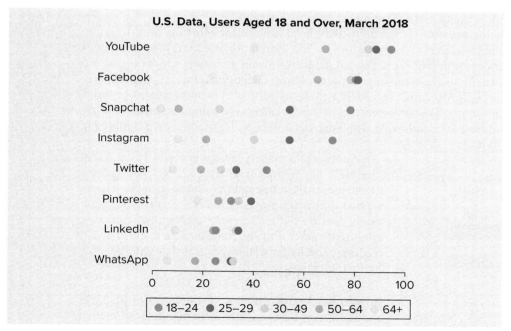

SOURCE: Marketing Charts. "Social Networking Platforms' User Demographics Update 2018. Marketing Charts LLC." Accessed June 19, 2019. https://www.marketingcharts.com/digital/social-media-82642.

The same applies to you and other employees. Everyone needs to realize the benefits and avoid the pitfalls of social media. To do this, let's begin our discussion with what experts and researchers say about the effects of social media on productivity.

Social Media and Increased Productivity

A driving force behind the use of all forms of technology at work, including social media, is to boost productivity. The key for employees, managers, and employers is to harness the potential and enhance performance at the individual, group, and organizational levels. The following quotation articulates this argument:

> [W]ork is becoming a place to collaborate, exchange ideas, and communicate with colleagues and customers. Your value as an employee will be determined not only by how well you perform your job but also by how much you contribute your knowledge and ideas back to the organization. The ways in which companies develop this culture of collaboration will become a significant competitive factor in attracting and engaging top talent in the twenty-first century.[50]

Social media is clearly a tool that can help both you and your employers realize these productivity benefits.

Employee Productivity   Evidence is mounting that social media provides a host of benefits for employees, such as

- Increased job satisfaction and better work–life balance.[51]
- Performance and retention.[52]
- More creativity and collaboration.[53]

Two studies of thousands of employees even showed that those who used five or more social networking sites had higher sales numbers than those who used only one to four.[54] This implies that more is better for salespeople! While you should be careful about drawing broad conclusions from these findings, they are revealing.

Furthermore, if you think employees' opinions matter, you'll be interested in a study by Microsoft showing that 46 percent of employees across generations and industries felt social media tools would make them more productive at work.[55]

LinkedIn, for example, is far more than an online résumé-hosting site. It is currently *the* key professional networking tool for job search. Recent surveys reveal that as many as 92 percent of recruiters use social media for hiring purposes, and, as Figure 9.5 shows, 77 percent use LinkedIn, 63 percent use Facebook, and 25 percent use Instagram, especially Millennial recruiters and those working at technology companies.[56] This means that more than three-quarters of job recruiters are using LinkedIn, and you likely use it yourself. The following Applying OB box provides guidance on optimizing LinkedIn for you.

FIGURE 9.5   Percentage of Recruiters Who Use Various Social Media

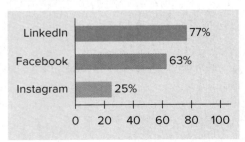

Another productivity benefit of social media is that they make digital information searchable. This capability can reduce the time employees spend trying to retrieve needed information by as much as 35 percent. What would you do with 35 percent more time in a day, month, or year?[60] Finally, consider that many of social media's benefits for employees translate into benefits for their employers.

Employer Productivity   Companies of all sizes and industries believe in the benefits of social media. Domino's, for example, gets more than 80 percent of

To use LinkedIn effectively you need to:[57]

Build a Professional LinkedIn Profile. This is only the first step, but it is essential to your success.

- Focus all sections (summary and experience) to reflect your growth over time and your responsibilities in your current job.
- Consider writing your summary and experience sections in the first person and telling a story instead of using bullet points. Describe what you've accomplished and what you can do for other employers. (Include the past but don't dwell on it—include more about what you do today.)
- Learn and use the appropriate keywords. LinkedIn's search function is effective and recruiters use it extensively. Learn what they are looking for and be sure to include these words in your profile, and in your headline as well.
- Spend the time necessary. Although obvious, think of what you want to achieve with your LinkedIn profile. Also, think of your profile as a living web page, something that evolves over time. Explain how your past experiences helped shape who you are today.[58]

Build a LinkedIn Network. Simply building a profile doesn't mean recruiters (or anybody else) will view it. You need to actively and wisely build and engage your connections. Some helpful pointers and etiquette follow:

- Think in terms of quality, not quantity. It's not a scoreboard. Make connections that are meaningful to you professionally.
- Don't invite people to your network blindly, and don't accept invitations without first learning why they reached out and how the connection might be relevant.
- Connect beyond your current industry and professional sphere. Drawing on diverse views is a key way to expand your own knowledge and grow.
- Use the personal note option for inviting others to connect.
- When inviting others, focus only on making the connection. Other business can wait.
- Be a good connection for others. Respond to messages and write recommendations for and endorse those whose skills you can confidently promote.[59]

Build a Reputation. You need to offer value to others, which in turn earns you trust and respect. This requires genuine thought and attention to what you post.

- Be a resource for others by liking (means "thanks"), commenting on (means you're interested), or sharing (means you think others also will benefit) relevant information within your network.
- Always explain why you are sharing or liking content.
- Avoid controversy, criticism, and complaints. If you can't resist doing this, then don't use LinkedIn. It can torpedo your reputation.

its sales through digital channels. The company enjoys a strong reputation as a leader in making the customer experience seamless and launched its digital ordering tools more than a decade ago. In addition to real-time tracking of orders on any mobile device, the company uses Dom the Pizza bot to allow customers to order on Facebook Messenger, Amazon's Alexa, Twitter, Apple Watches, Android Wear, and Samsung Smart TVs.[61] If deployed effectively, social media enable businesses to realize the many benefits outlined in Table 9.3.

Crowdsourcing **occurs when companies invite nonemployees to contribute to achieving particular goals and manage the input process via the Internet.** Integra Gold Corp, a mining company based in Canada, illustrates the benefits of utilizing talent and resources outside the organization to meet goals. The company acquired a firm with mineral rights and six terabytes of geological surveys used to prospect for gold.

TABLE 9.3 Social Media Benefits for Employers

BENEFIT	DESCRIPTION
Connect in real time over distance	Employees, customers, communities, suppliers, prospective talent, and many others can communicate as needed and while work is being completed.
Collaborate within and outside the organization	Linking sources of knowledge is a means for realizing the potential of employee diversity and enhancing productivity. Social media is by definition a way of connecting people virtually, so its effective implementation benefits virtual teamwork.
Expand boundaries	Social networks can become critical means for organizational innovation and effectiveness, allowing them to utilize knowledge, skills, and experience of people outside (not employed by) the organization.

SOURCE: McFarland, Lynn A., and Robert E. Ployhart. "Social Media: A Contextual Framework to Guide Research and Practice." *Journal of Applied Psychology* 100, no. 6 (2015): 1653–1677. https://dx.doi.org/10.1037/a0039244.

Integra crowdsourced the analyses of this data instead of hiring people and managing the work itself. It is offering a prize of $811,000 to whoever finds the next multimillion-ounce gold deposit.[62]

The OB in Action box describes how other well-known companies now use social media to innovate and solve problems using crowdsourcing.

OB in Action

Expanding Organizational Boundaries with Crowdsourcing at Lego, Frito-Lay

Lego Ideas is an official Lego website where fans submit original ideas for new products, via written descriptions and photos or 3D renderings. Ideas must draw 100 supporters within 60 days and then 10,000 within the next two years. Winners are chosen three times a year; their designers earn 1 percent of the toy's net revenue. Two recent winners are a Steamboat Willie replica and the Central Perk coffee shop from the TV series "Friends."[63]

The fifth winner of Frito-Lay's "Do Us a Flavor" crowdsourcing challenge, which let customers submit ideas for new potato chip flavors for a $1 million prize, is Crispy Taco. The company will also produce runners-up Fried Tomato and Everything Bagel with Cream Cheese. Frito-Lay hasn't ruled out the possibility of a sixth round.[64]

YOUR THOUGHTS

1. Describe at least two ways you crowdsource, including reading product recommendations on social media.

2. Identify a service you use or some element of your job that could benefit from crowdsourcing. Focus on how others can help you solve problems, which requires more than just soliciting their opinions.

Costs of Social Media

Lost productivity due to **cyberloafing—using the Internet at work for personal use—**is a primary concern for employers in their adoption of social media. Some studies put the cost at $85 billion per year and report that employees spend 60 to 80 percent of their time at work pretending to do actual or legitimate work.[65]

How do employees waste time on social media?

- 50 percent are talking on a cell phone or texting.
- 39 percent are surfing the Internet.

- 38 percent are on social media.
- 23 percent are sending personal e-mail.[66]

Perhaps the biggest problem with such productivity losses is that employees rarely think about them. Have you ever thought you were cheating your employer by checking Facebook, sending a tweet, or booking a trip during work hours? Did you ever think the message you sent a friend about work might be shared and give a competitor an advantage?

Then there is shopping online while at work. A recent survey by Careerbuilder found that on average 53 percent of workers planned to shop online while at work, with nearly 50 percent of them using their personal mobile devices. And it seems the greater access you have to technology at work, the more likely you are to use it to shop—68 percent of IT workers said they were likely to shop online while at work.[67]

The following Problem-Solving Application regarding fantasy football highlights the magnitude of the problem.

Problem-Solving Application

A Very Expensive Fantasy

Fantasy sports are a well-entrenched phenomenon. Tens of millions of people play, and many of them do so at work. Here are some statistics:[68]

1. The U.S. Bureau of Labor Statistics (BLS) estimates that employers should expect to lose approximately one hour of work per week for each employee who plays fantasy football.

2. The Fantasy Sports Trade Association estimates that approximately 57.4 million people in the United States and Canada play fantasy football.

3. About two-thirds of those players are employed full time, and BLS data indicates they earn an average of almost $26 an hour.

4. Given all that, the estimated price tag for productivity lost to fantasy football was close to $17 billion in 2016. For comparison, consider that the real-world NFL took in only a little more than $13 billion in revenue that same year.

Challenger, Gray & Christmas is the research firm that compiled the data on productivity lost to the distractions of fantasy sports leagues. However, its CEO, John Challenger, says there may be a plus side to all the time spent on the game, namely that—unlike online shopping or reading and writing posts on Facebook—it does get coworkers talking to each other and perhaps even helps them collaborate better at work. Creativity and morale may also get a boost, says Challenger.[69]

Assume you own a business and know many of your employees play in a fantasy league. Does this information change your attitude about access to and use of social media at work? Why or why not? What would you do in this situation?

Apply the 3-Step Problem-Solving Approach

Step 1: As a business owner, define the problem posed by employees playing fantasy football at work.

Step 2: Identify potential causes of the problem.

Step 3: As the owner, make your recommendations to remedy or at least reduce the problem defined in Step 1.

Let's explore the pros and cons of e-mail next.

Make E-mail Your Friend, Not Your Foe

E-mail is not only one of the most useful communication tools but also one of biggest drains on your productivity. Recent research suggests that the average business professional spends nearly 30 percent of the work day reading and answering mail—which translates into close to 3 hours a day reading, writing, and responding to e-mail messages.[70] If we add in some amount of nonwork e-mail, the time it consumes is truly immense! In addition, analyzing more than 52,000 e-mails at a mid-sized company, researchers found that employee communication patterns could potentially pinpoint employees who were experiencing disengagement and job burnout.[71] Most people acknowledge that e-mail is essential, but handling it effectively can make it your friend instead of your foe. See Table 9.4 for tips on managing e-mail.

Social Media Concerns and Remedies— What Companies and You Can Do

Of course *some* employees waste time. This has been and always will be true. But when it comes to social media, more than half of U.S. employers now block employees' access to social media sites at work.[72] However, evidence is growing that this strategy can backfire.

Be Careful about Blocking Access Banning access can damage employee morale and loyalty—potentially leading to even greater losses in productivity. Some experts argue, and most employees would agree, that small breaks during the workday help boost productivity. Such breaks can take the form of going outside to get a breath of fresh air, talking with a colleague over a cup of coffee, checking personal e-mail or Facebook, or checking and sending tweets.[73]

TABLE 9.4 **Tips for Managing E-mail**

TIP	DESCRIPTION
Set aside a specific time each work day to read and respond to e-mails.	Don't leave your e-mail open all day. Alerts can interrupt workflow and cause distraction.
Use the 80-20 rule.	Prioritize 20% of your e-mails and defer the other 80%.
Make decisions and respond immediately to e-mails that require a brief response.	If it takes less than 1 minute to answer an e-mail, make a decision and send a response.
Realize you don't need to reply to every e-mail.	Sometimes no reply after a certain period of time can be considered a reply.
Unsubscribe from sources you don't read.	If you find yourself routinely deleting e-mails from news alerts, e-mail subscriptions, and other sources—unsubscribe.
Organize your inbox with folders and categories.	Prioritize, sort, and file messages to keep your inbox organized.
Stop checking work e-mails at all hours.	Your brain needs time to decompress and rejuvenate—break the habit of checking your work messages at night, on weekends, and on the way to work in the morning.

SOURCE: Chua, Celestine. "11 Simple Tips to Effective Email Management." Lifehack. https://www.lifehack.org/articles/productivity/11-simple-tips-effective-email-management.html.

If these reenergizing benefits of social media breaks are not convincing enough for you or your employer, consider other potential and undesirable results of the blocking policies:

Although companies must protect their own interests when it comes to blocking employee access to social media and other websites, many experts warn the costs of blocking access could be larger than the benefits.
LDProd/Getty Images

- *They could alienate employees.* Young, old, or in between, many people are accustomed to being plugged into social sites throughout the day. Blocking their access can be off-putting. Moreover, organizations can block access on company devices, but most people have smartphones, tablets, and other devices of their own. As a result, many employees continue their typical use of social media but simply do so on their own devices—still on company time.

- *You can't have it only one way.* If employers expect employees to be connected and responsive 24/7 to work-related e-mails, such as those from managers, coworkers, clients, or suppliers, it seems only fair to also allow them to reasonably tend to their own business during work hours. This is especially true if employees work both within and outside prescribed hours (such as at home in the evenings or on weekends).

- *Blocking suggests a lack of trust.* As one tech business reporter put it: "Banning social media may send a message to your employees that you don't trust them. . . . This can cause a sharp divide in the team atmosphere you want to create."[74] It is difficult to manage and influence others without trust, and one of the basic ways of gaining trust from others is to trust them first.

In 2019, more than two dozen states either have passed or have pending legislation to prevent employers from demanding passwords and access to employees' social networking sites.[75] Whether an organization will consider adopting such practices depends in part on leaders' social media attitudes.

Phubbing and FOMO   Acts of unconscious bias, or *microaggressions,* include a number of seemingly tiny but repeated actions, like interrupting others, mispronouncing or mistaking someone's name, avoiding eye contact, or phubbing. *Phubbing* is the act of phone snubbing or ignoring those around us in order to pay attention to a mobile phone. The urge to phub others springs from the fear of missing out—FOMO—or being out of touch with something happening in our social network.[76] This is a growing phenomenon, although research shows that conversations are actually less satisfying for both parties when interrupted by a person's texting.[77]

A recent study found that employees who were phubbed by their manager felt they could no longer trust that person to keep promises or treat them fairly, which led to negative effects on their psychological preparedness to work and, predictably, on their job satisfaction and job performance.[78] Phubbing tends to be more common among younger people, who are more intimately connected to their phones, and among men, who view interruptions as less onerous than women do.[79] Even if unused, a cell phone on the table can make people feel less connected to those they are with.[80] Phubbing doesn't have to keep happening, however. The phubbed should calmly explain how they feel, and phubbers should use empathy to understand the harm their microaggression is doing to their communications and their relationships with others.[81]

Psychologists have demonstrated that FOMO causes anxiety. A recent study examined college students' anxiety levels after giving up their phones for an hour. Light users of smartphones experienced no increases in anxiety, while moderate users showed signs of increased anxiety after 25 minutes without a phone. These levels of anxiety stayed steady for the remaining time of the hour-long study. Heavy users, in contrast, revealed heightened anxiety after only 10 phone-free minutes, and their level of anxiety increased over time.[82]

FOMO is exacerbated by our habits, such as paying attention to our phones during sleep hours. One study found that 40 percent of students reported waking at night to answer phone calls, and 47 percent woke to answer text messages. Psychologists demonstrated that "people of all generations seem to have succumbed to the phenomenon."[83]

Assess and Manage Leadership's Social Media Attitudes   Consider the social media readiness of an organization to which you belong. Self-Assessment 9.3 helps you assess leadership's attitude toward social media, such as:

- How supportive management is of creating communities.
- How well the culture fosters collaboration and knowledge sharing.
- How widely social media is used to collaborate.

With this knowledge you can determine how well your own attitudes fit with those of the organization, and it may even unveil opportunities for you to improve the organization's readiness.

SELF-ASSESSMENT 9.3

Assessing Social Media Readiness

Please be prepared to answer these questions if your instructor has assigned Self-Assessment 9.3 in Connect.

1. Which of the dimensions has the highest score?
2. What are the implications for employees/members?
3. What are the implications for the organization and its interactions with stakeholders other than employees/members?
4. Which dimension is the lowest?
5. Describe two things that could be done to improve the organization's social media readiness.

If the attitudes you find are not as positive as you would like, have no fear. Attitudes can be changed. Favorable leadership attitudes open the door to developing and implementing productive social media policies.

Adopt a Social Media Policy   As the use of social media continues to grow, estimates suggest more than 80 percent of U.S. companies now have a formal social media policy, and 70 percent of these firms report taking disciplinary action against an employee for violating these policies.[84] A *social media policy* **should describe the who, how, when, and for what purposes of social media use, and the consequences for noncompliance.** One way to avoid social media missteps is to create, communicate, and enforce effective social media policies as outlined in Table 9.5. The OB in Action box describes the Coca-Cola Company's social media policy.

Privacy   Any discussion of the effective use of social media by employees or their employers must include privacy issues. People and companies have reputations, which are built over time and can be extremely consequential professionally. They can also be damaged in a variety of ways, with serious consequences including loss of employment or business, social stigma, embarrassment and stress, lost opportunities, and, of course, legal action.[86]

TABLE 9.5   Eight Elements of an Effective Social Media Policy

ELEMENT	DESCRIPTION
Create safe channels for employees to air their concerns before going online.	The key words here are *safe* and *before*. Conflicts happen, but managers and organizations should provide means by which employees' concerns are reported and handled without retaliation so they don't feel the need to take them to the Internet.
Clarify what is confidential.	Clearly explain what information employees can and cannot share online. Providing an approval process for the release of information may help too.
Outline consequences for violations.	Make it known that employees can be held responsible for what they post (such as videos of undesirable behavior on the job or in company uniform), and list the consequences.
Designate a spokesperson for online policies.	You don't want every employee fielding questions about company policies; identify a spokesperson(s) so interpretations and communications are consistent.
Discuss appropriate ways to engage others online.	It is typically a poor idea to have any and all employees responding to others' comments about the company online. Instruct them to be polite and nonconfrontational, and then to notify the designated person to respond.
Explain what is considered illegal.	It is illegal to divulge proprietary information and to violate trademarks and copyrights. The organization is responsible for educating employees on these matters.
Align social media policy with the organization's culture.	Your company's social media policy is a great place to reaffirm what you want your company culture to be, while conveying your stance on this serious topic.
Educate employees.	It's not enough to have a social media policy; it is necessary to educate and train people about it and to embed it in social media practices. (The author, for instance, could not locate a social media policy, or a person responsible for it, at his university.)

SOURCES: Carter, Rebekah. "Your Guide to Creating a Social Media Policy." Sprout Social, Inc., October 18, 2018. https://sproutsocial.com/insights/social-media-policy/; PowerDMS. "Six Elements of a Good Social Media Policy." Accessed June 19, 2019. https://www.powerdms.com/blog/six-elements-good-social-media-policy/; and Thomson, Jimmy. "How to Write a Social Media Policy for Your Company." Hootsuite Inc., May 22, 2018. https://blog.hootsuite.com/social-media-policy-for-employees/.

OB in Action

Coca-Cola's Online Social Media Principles

The Coca-Cola Company formulated its policies with the motive to "guide your participation in social media, both personally as well as when you are acting in an official capacity on behalf of the Company. It is critical we always remember who we are—the world's largest beverage company, refreshing consumers with more than 500 sparkling and still brands—and what our Company's role is in the social media community—to inspire moments of optimism and happiness and build our brands. The same considerations that apply to our messaging and communications in traditional media still apply in the online social media space, including on what you might consider 'internal' platforms."[85]

"Have fun, but be smart. Use sound judgment and common sense, adhere to the Company's values, and follow the same Company policies that you follow in the offline world. . . ." "Whether you are an authorized Company spokesperson or not, when you're talking about our Company, our brands, or our business on your personal social networks, keep in mind that:

1. Our Company's Information Protection Policy, Insider Trading Policy, and other policies still apply.

2. You are responsible for your actions. We encourage you to get online and have fun, but use sound judgment and common sense.

3. You are an important ambassador for our Company's brands, and you're encouraged to promote them as long as you *make sure you disclose that you are affiliated with the Company.* How you disclose can depend on the platform, but the disclosure should be clear and in proximity to the message itself.

4. When you see posts or commentary on topics that require subject matter expertise, such as ingredients, obesity, the Company's environmental impacts, or the Company's financial performance, avoid the temptation to respond to these directly unless you respond with approved messaging the Company has prepared for those topics. When in doubt, contact your local Public Affairs and Communications director.

5. Be conscientious when mixing your business and personal lives; be sure to know your work group's policies regarding personal use of social media at work or on Company devices."

YOUR THOUGHTS?

1. What are two benefits you see in Coca-Cola's social media policy?

2. What gaps do you notice, based on your experiences with social media at work and what you've studied in this chapter?

Social media privacy becomes even more elusive given that better than 60 percent of employees report they are connected to at least one coworker and over 40 percent with an immediate supervisor.[87] Employees are especially concerned about employers having access to personal e-mails and attachments, voice mail, text and instant messages, lists of apps on their devices, information in their mobile apps, and their location.[88]

What can employers do? Here are some recommendations:

1. Communicate what personal information from mobile devices is accessed by the employer.

2. Be sure employees understand what is accessible depending on the operating system used on their device (Apple or Android).

3. Create and communicate clear and sensible policies regarding potential employer actions regarding information on employees' mobile devices.

4. Do all of this when employees are setting up their devices, which is when they are most likely thinking about and can do something about such matters.

5. Tell employees that anything on the company's e-mail server is saved for legal purposes.

6. Use the available privacy controls.[89]

What Can You Do to Protect Yourself and Your Personal Brand (Reputation)?
First consider the recommendations above and other things you've learned in this chapter. You also may be well served to keep the arenas of your life separate in cyberspace, at least to the extent possible. Establishing and maintaining multiple accounts, and using discretion about what you post, can be quite a challenge. But think of the potential implications—your reputation and your job! If you don't know what your company's policy is, ask. The author of this book did so and was told by its IT director that the university knew which porn websites were being viewed at the fraternity houses.

Social Media Etiquette   Before leaving this section we want to raise the issue of "appropriate use." Norms of acceptable social media behavior at school, work, and socially are evolving, and it pays to be mindful of them.

Cellphones   Because they are like extensions of our hands, cellphones are with us everywhere, at dinner, at work, in class, in bed, and in the bathroom. But that doesn't mean it is okay to use them in every situation.

Here's a good test: The next time you pull out your phone, for instance, during dinner at a restaurant or when visiting with a friend, ask yourself, *Is what I'm doing or looking at going to enhance my interaction with the other person here and now?* If it isn't, don't risk being rude—put the phone away.

Videoconferencing   Skype, FaceTime, and other services are growing in popularity every year. They provide far richer communication than texts, e-mails, or even phone calls. From an employer's perspective they also save on travel costs. But effectively communicating on camera is quite different from doing so in other media. Videoconferencing has its own code of conduct for participating in meetings, as well as for interviewing for a job. The Applying OB box provides some tips for successful video interviews.

Now let's move beyond social media and learn about how to deliver killer presentations, conduct crucial conversations, and manage up.

Applying OB

CAREER READINESS

Acing a Skype Interview

Video interviews are increasingly common among companies screening job candidates. They can save time and travel costs for the company and the applicant, and they convey more information than telephone interviews. Suppose you've applied for a job and will be interviewed via Skype. How will you present yourself at your best and most professional? Here are some tips.[90]

1. **Prepare as you would for any job interview.** Learn as much as you can about the company, its structure, its mission and goals, and the position that's open. Prepare a few specific questions to ask.

2. **Select a quiet place with a well-lighted, uncluttered background.** Be sure you won't be interrupted; tell family or roommates the time and expected duration of the interview, keep pets out of the room, and put away your phone.

3. **Make the most of Skype's features.** Select an appropriate profile picture and a professional-looking profile that matches your resume, and line up any documents, like your portfolio or work samples, that you may want to share during the call. Check in advance that your equipment and settings are all in order and obtain the employer's Skype username.

4. **Dress the part from head to toe, not just from the waist up.** This will increase your confidence. Avoid bright colors, loud prints, and noisy or shiny jewelry and accessories. If you wear makeup, consider using a little more than usual. To look the interviewer in the eye, gaze straight at the camera,

With video interviews becoming more common, job seekers need to prepare for them as if they are interviewing in person.
andreypopov/123RF

not at your own image on the screen. Don't move around too much but lean forward a little to show interest and eagerness.

5. **Remember this is a real, serious interview.** The employer is investing time and energy; you should too. Be energetic and positive about your interest in the organization. Speak clearly and don't rush. Remember to ask the questions you prepared.

6. **Cover the basics.** As in an interview situation, thank the interviewer for his or her time, reiterate your interest, and ask when and how you should follow up.

9.5 COMMUNICATION SKILLS TO BOOST YOUR EFFECTIVENESS

THE BIGGER PICTURE

Presenting, crucial conversations, and managing up—master these communication skills, and they will enhance your performance and career success throughout your life. These individual-level process skills make you more effective when working with others and influence a host of outcomes at both the individual and group levels in the Organizing Framework for OB.

LO 9-5

Explain how communication skills can increase your effectiveness.

Some jobs require you to present regularly and others never. How well you present can greatly affect others' perceptions of you and your professional opportunities. We devote this section to practical skills to help make you a more effective presenter. Improving your presentation skills is always valuable, given that relatively few people are truly at ease or actually enjoy speaking or presenting to a group.

Presenting—Do You Give Reports or Do You Tell Stories?

You should probably start by answering the question in the above heading. Reports are packed with data and information and can be exhausting in their detail. Stories, in contrast, are short in all these elements but are rich in emotion and help the presenter connect with the audience.

As you learned earlier, different communication media are better than others for any given message. The challenge for you is to know what your audience wants and needs, and then to construct and deliver your presentation accordingly. It generally is more effective if you present your message more as a colorful story with emotion than as a detail-laden report. The people who organize the TED (Technology, Education, Design) talks have a five-step protocol they use to guide their presenters to deliver with impact.[91]

Step 1. Frame your story.

Step 2. Plan your delivery.

Step 3. Develop your stage presence.

Step 4. Plan your multimedia.

Step 5. Put it together.

Let's consider these steps in more detail.

Step 1—Frame Your Story   Think of your presentation as a journey and decide where you want to start and end. Consider what your audience already knows about your subject, start there, and quickly explain why it matters to you or why it should matter to them. Include only the most relevant details or points and try to bring them to life with examples.

Don't try to do too much. Don't just skim over all possible points either, but instead pick the best and dive deeper into each of those.

Beware of jargon, boasting, and mind-numbing details. Plan to end your journey with a solution, or even with a question to spur audience engagement and give them something to think about afterward.

For example, you have learned about and applied a 3-Step Problem-Solving Approach throughout this book. Perhaps your presentation might be structured similarly—what is the problem, what are potential causes or explanations, and what is your recommendation for action.

Step 2—Plan Your Delivery   There are three basic ways to deliver a talk:

1. Read it from a script.
2. Use bullet lists that outline what you will cover in each section.
3. Memorize everything you wish to say and REHEARSE.

Reading generally is ineffective. You will almost certainly lose your connection with the audience, if you ever connect in the first place. (TED forbids presenters to read.) Memorizing can work, if your audience is expected to simply sit and listen, but it takes a tremendous amount of time and practice. Unless you have your presentation completely ingrained in your memory, your audience can easily realize you are not as prepared as you hoped. If you use the bullet list approach, be sure you know not only the content for each point, but also how you want to transition from one to the next.

Amy Cuddy is a social psychologist who studies body language. She argues that the way we hold and present ourselves affects the way others perceive us and *the way we perceive ourselves.*
Astrid Stawiarz/Getty Images

Step 3—Develop Your Stage Presence   Getting your story or message right is more important than the way you stand or whether you appear nervous. Nevertheless, beware of how much you move—not too much or too little.

If you're really nervous, pay particular attention to your lower body to prevent rocking or shifting from one leg to the other. Walking around is fine, if it is natural for you. But if it is not, then you may be well served to stand in particular spots for different lengths of time or when making certain points. The nonverbal communication pointers you learned earlier in this chapter are helpful too.

Your body aside, the most important element of stage presence is eye contact! Find a handful of friendly faces around the room and deliver your talk while looking them in the eyes.

We cannot learn about presenting without addressing public speaking head-on. The following Applying OB box provides suggestions. When combined with the TED protocol, it should help you overcome your nervousness and light up the room.

As for nervousness, there are many ways to help overcome this, and many of them you've learned in this book. For instance, what you learned about self-efficacy in Chapter 3 can be especially helpful, and preparation is a critical element in building your efficacy. But perhaps one of the most useful things you can do to overcome nervousness is to realize that people expect you to be nervous. Don't make too much of it.

Journalist and women's rights activist Gloria Steinem delivers a talk at the Watermark Conference for Women. Note her use of hand gestures and eye contact with her audience. Both of these nonverbal communication elements are important in developing a stage presence.
Marla Aufmuth/Getty Images

How to Dazzle the Crowd—Tips on Public Speaking

The noted poet Maya Angelou once said, "I've learned that people will forget what you said, people will forget what you did, but people will never forget how you made them feel."[92] When you speak in public, remember that as in any conversation, you want your listeners to *feel* something. Here are some additional tips:[93]

1. *Remember they are rooting for you.* The audience most often is on your side and hopes you give a good presentation, if for no other reason than that they don't want to sit through a bad one.

2. *Know your audience.* You don't have to be an expert on your audience or know everything they know. However, know enough to make a few meaningful, audience-specific comments and show that you care and your insights are relevant for them.

3. *Compliment the audience.* Building on No. 2, make your audience feel special by acknowledging what they do and its importance. For instance, if talking to a group of executives, tell them they've worked very hard and accomplished a lot. Or, if their jobs are especially difficult and uncelebrated, such as nurses or teachers, acknowledge this and tell them how important their work is and how much it's appreciated.

4. *Be snazzy, not distracting.* Your clothes, jewelry, and any other accessories should be neat and match your audience. Don't wear a suit or dress to a construction site, or construction boots to present a keynote at a conference. Be sharp but don't wear anything that will cause people to comment. You want to exude confidence but not generate fodder for the next TMZ episode.

5. *Unshackle yourself.* If possible, and it is most often possible, lose the podium. Too often presenters shackle themselves to the podium, which is a physical barrier between you and the audience and ties you to one spot. Have you ever seen an excellent presentation and thought it would have been better still if the speaker had stayed behind the podium? Of course not.

6. *Be funny if you can, but don't try too hard.* Everybody likes to be funny, and when it works and is appropriate it's great, but when it doesn't it can be disastrous. Don't try too hard, but if you have something that you are confident will work with the audience, use it.

7. *Be gracious.* Thank the host, the audience, and the organization that invited you. Even if the content of your presentation will change their lives, it nevertheless is your privilege to have the opportunity to do so. Express your gratitude.

Step 4—Plan Your Multimedia   Don't feel compelled to use the latest and greatest technology, or any technology at all. But whatever you choose, keep it simple and don't let it distract the audience. If photos or images are appropriate, use them. People respond differently to pictures and videos, which convey emotional content better than words. However, if you use video clips, try to keep them to 60 seconds or less to prevent losing people's attention.

PowerPoint continues to be widely used, although more sophisticated programs with scaling features—zoomable user interfaces or ZUIs—are also gaining popularity. Regardless of what presentation program you use, be sure to limit the number of words per slide; make sure the font is big enough for easy reading from the back of the room; and don't read the slides out loud for your audience. While they read the slide's wording, provide some additional commentary or insight about the idea presented.[94]

Step 5—Put It Together   Be prepared far enough in advance; think weeks if possible, not days, hours, or minutes. If you practice in front of others, which is a good idea, be selective. Anybody in the practice audience role will feel compelled to give you feedback, but you need valuable feedback, not just any feedback.

Preparation aside, remember to focus on the framing and substance of your journey and don't get too wrapped up in the other steps and details. If you don't think you have a compelling story, go back to the drawing board and create one.

Lastly, be yourself. Use these steps as a guide and learn from them, but don't try to copy somebody else.

Crucial Conversations

*"**Crucial conversations** are discussions between two or more people where (1) the stakes are high, (2) opinions vary, and (3) emotions run strong."*[95] Such conversations can and do occur in all arenas of your life—school, work, and socially. Examples of relevant occasions include:

- Ending a relationship.
- Talking to a coworker or classmate who behaves offensively.
- Giving the boss or a professor feedback.
- Critiquing a classmate or colleague's work.
- Asking a roommate to move out.
- Talking to a team member who isn't keeping commitments.
- Giving an unfavorable performance review.[96]

Recall what you learned in Chapter 6 related to feedback, because it also is very helpful with most crucial conversations. The consequences of these encounters can be enormous for your job and career. Handling difficult communications effectively can prevent problems, motivate teams members, increase collaboration, and improve bottom-line results.[97]

When confronted with high-stakes interactions, you have three choices—avoid them, face them and handle them poorly, or face them and handle them well. We'll focus on the last one. But first let's explore why people often do so poorly in crucial situations, and it will also serve as a bit of review of things you've learned already.

When It Matters Most, We Often Do Our Worst

Joseph Grenny, who cowrote the book *Crucial Conversations,* said this: "When conversations turn crucial, most of us toggle between some form of silence or verbal violence: Either we withdraw from sharing our information or try to force it on others by raising our voice or overstating our point. Ironically, when it matters the most we do our very worst."[98] Our negative emotions (see Chapter 3) kick in, and the fight-or-flight response takes over.

Moreover, crucial conversations often happen unexpectedly, which means we typically are unprepared. When this happens, again, negative emotions can dominate and self-efficacy decline. Research supports this observation. According to a recent survey of more than 1,300 employees, one of three managers is unable to handle high-stakes, high pressure situations, which leave their teams less successful in business situations.[99]

Knowledge on positive emotions and positive OB can help you in crucial situations. Specifically, a good way to prepare for crucial conversations is to foster your own positive state. Then you can use the STATE technique, described next, to conduct your crucial conversations more effectively.

STATE: How to Be Effective When It's Crucial

The acronym STATE will help you address even the most difficult conversations with a plan or path to follow.

- **Share your facts.** Start with the least controversial, most persuasive elements that support what you want for yourself and for the relationship.
- **Tell your story.** Enhance what you want by describing what has happened, how you've arrived where you are, how

Many of your important conversations with coworkers, friends, and classmates are full of emotions. Applying some of the communication skills and tools described in this chapter can help you improve the outcomes of crucial and high-stakes conversations.
Bananastock/Alamy Stock Photo

you'd like to see it change, and why. It may help to add what you *don't* want personally or for the relationship.

- **Ask for others' facts and stories.** This is key to creating dialogue, which is essential if you're to have a productive crucial conversation. Don't *talk at* but instead *talk with* others. Approach all crucial conversations as two-way exchanges. Don't be accusatory, but instead simply describe the situation, the way you feel, and what you would like to see happen. Use "I" instead of "you."
- **Talk tentatively.** Keep in mind that you're telling a story, not stating facts. The facts come first, then you can add "color" or describe the impact on you via your story. In other words, don't pound the podium and talk like you're "preaching" facts.
- **Encourage testing.** Make it safe for others to share their (opposing) views. Allow them to share or test their ideas, thoughts, and feelings. Don't interrupt, steamroll, or intimidate. It is critical to maintain mutual respect during crucial conversations. One way to do this is to explain and focus on mutual purpose—what you both stand to gain. Be sure the other person respects you in order to avoid defensiveness (recall what you learned earlier in this chapter) and conflict. If it's appropriate, apologize to get back on track.[100]

Managing Up

You learned in Chapter 6 about more contemporary forms of feedback (such as 360 degree), and that knowledge is helpful here. We are going to build on that and on crucial conversations to give you some guidance on how to manage your boss.

Gauge Receptiveness to Coaching Many organizations now claim they believe in the merits of employee involvement and feedback, even upward feedback. Note that translating these values into action requires skill. For example, an HR professional was promoted to a senior position with little previous experience dealing with senior management. She focused on doing her new job well but failed to build strong relationships with her bosses, leaving her with few supporters in the executive suite. When the company went public, she "got taken out by a wave I didn't see coming," while the rest of the company's management team kept their jobs.[101] The outcome might have been different had she learned to manage her bosses.

The place to begin managing up is by assessing your manager's receptiveness. Regardless of your organization's policy or comments from senior leadership, if your manager is not receptive, you're wise to put your efforts elsewhere.[102] You can't coach a boss who doesn't want to be coached. To gauge receptiveness, you can:[103]

1. Learn your manager's view of you coaching. What are his or her expectations? What are yours?
2. Explain what's in it for him or her.
3. Ask for permission to provide coaching or feedback. For instance, "Would you mind if I share a different perspective, one that might help us solve the problem?"
4. Find out how best to deliver criticism. Learn where, when, and how your manager wants to hear criticism—in the moment, in private, via e-mail, face-to-face, or another way.
5. Ask for agreement and commitment. After the first two items in this list, confirm that your boss is interested.

A boss who is receptive to coaching is especially valuable. Be careful, however: Don't assume because you may appreciate coaching from your boss that she or he will appreciate coaching from you. Gauge your boss's receptiveness first.

Roberto Westbrook/Blend Images LLC

What to Do Next If your boss is receptive to upward feedback, follow the steps in Table 9.6. If your boss is not

TABLE 9.6   How to Manage Up

Steps	Description
Step 1—Prepare your message.	Unlike crucial conversations that often happen in the moment, attempts to manage up or coach your boss are an agreed-upon arrangement that occurs over time. Therefore, use time to your advantage and prepare. • Know what you want to accomplish. • Support your points with examples, data, or other evidence.
Step 2—Plan your delivery and tactics.	Plan the delivery of your message—the tone and choice of words that will most likely achieve your desired result. Role-playing is a very valuable practice tool—use it!
Step 3—Deliver.	When conducting the coaching conversation, be sure you know the right way to discuss problems with your boss: • *Be sensitive.* Your boss has feelings just like you, and just as you don't like to get hammered with comments about how horrible and disappointing you are, neither does your boss. • *Don't generalize behavior.* Speak to specific areas of your boss's job, specific behaviors, and specific situations. • *Provide ideas or suggestions in a polite and helpful manner.* Don't introduce your ideas as if they are the only ones that will work, or use language like "you must" or "you should."
Step 4—Follow up.	Coaching and managing both consist of more than simply providing feedback. Follow up to see how your boss has been doing in the areas discussed. Establishing a trusting relationship with your boss may position you as the "go-to" person who can pick up the slack when needed.

SOURCES: Shellenbarger, Sue. "The Right and Wrong Way to Manage Up at the Office." *The Wall Street Journal,* April 10, 2018. https://www.wsj.com/articles/the-right-and-wrong-way-to-manage-up-at-the-office-1523366792; Reynolds, Justin. "What Does It Mean to Manage Up?" TINYPulse, March 14, 2017. https://www.tinypulse.com/blog/what-does-it-mean-to-manage-up; Rosenthal, Michael. "Last Word: Constructive Criticism for Managers." Lakewood Media Group, LLC. https://trainingmag.com/content/last-word-constructive-criticism-managers/; and Patton, Carol. "Coaching Up." *Lakewood Media Group, LLC.* https://trainingmag.com/content/coaching/.

receptive, or you're preparing for your first real job in the workplace, read the table anyway. It provides helpful insight for managing others and helping others manage you.

We conclude this section with words of wisdom from Dana Rousmaniere, a contributor to the *Harvard Business Review* series on managing up:

> The most important skill to master is figuring out how to be a genuine source of help—because managing up doesn't mean sucking up. It means being the most effective employee you can be, creating value for your boss and your company. That's why the best path to a healthy relationship begins and ends with doing your job, and doing it well.[104]

9.6 MAKING THE CONNECTION: HOW CAN I BECOME A MORE EFFECTIVE COMMUNICATOR?

THE BIGGER PICTURE

Effective communication helps individuals, groups, and organizations achieve their goals. Here are some key points to consider.

Takeaways for Me

Here are six things you can do to turn this chapter's lessons into positive change in your personal and professional life.

1. **Communication is a perceptual process—what we say is not always what people hear:** Always be on the lookout for misinterpretations in your communications.

2. **You can improve your communication competence:** Follow the advice presented in Section 9.2.

3. **Miscommunication is likely to occur between men and women and across generations:** Be sensitive to these differences and try to modify your communication accordingly.

4. **The pervasiveness of social media means that to distinguish yourself, you need to be better than the rest:** Learn how to use services such as LinkedIn like the pros; the time and effort will make a difference in your job and career.

5. **Learn your employer's social media policies, and regardless of what you learn, you may be wise to keep your digital worlds separate:** Make appropriate use of mobile devices; don't be rude or embarrass yourself or others.

6. **You are always presenting when communicating. The only things that differ in a formal presentation are the number of people, the context, the objective, and the medium:** These are skills—learn, practice, improve!

Takeaways for Managers

There are eight key implications for managers.

1. **It is easy to encounter miscommunication because communication is a perceptual process:** To overcome this, try paraphrasing and summarizing what others communicate to ensure you are getting the intended message.

2. **Your choice of communication medium needs to match the complexity of the situation:** You can improve your communication by considering this requirement when choosing the best way to communicate with others.

3. **Be aware of the linguistic differences between men and women:** Failure to appreciate these nuances can lead to inaccurate attributions and conclusions about others.

4. **Assess how social media can boost your productivity and that of those you manage. Learn specifically which forms help you and how. Also learn how workplace productivity is lost via social media:** Collaborate with your employees to generate policies that are both reasonable and legally defensible. Then communicate these policies and expected practices.

5. **Get a handle on your e-mail as a way of boosting your productivity:** Part of your solution may be to use other technology, but another part is certainly being aware of your own behaviors and using discipline.

6. **Always be mindful of social media privacy.**

7. **Learn about and build your skills related to crucial conversations:** These are critical for your success when managing both down and up.

8. **Model the communication behaviors, including use of social media, you expect from those you manage:** Your own behavior is one of your most powerful means for influencing others.

What Did I Learn?

You learned that you can become a more effective communicator by understanding communication as a process that operates at all levels of the organization. You learned about the differences and similarities between genders and generations, as well as the benefits and costs of social media. You also explored how the proper approach to communication can allow you to manage up to higher levels in the organization and how to prepare for crucial conversations. Reinforce your learning with the Key Points below. Then consolidate your learning using the Organizing Framework. Challenge your mastery of the material by answering the Major Questions in your own words.

Key Points for Understanding Chapter 9

You learned the following key points.

9.1 BASIC DIMENSIONS OF THE COMMUNICATION PROCESS

- All communication involves a sender, message, and receiver.
- Noise has many sources and types and can interfere with communications.
- Media richness varies from rich to lean and helps convey information and promote understanding. It is influenced by feedback, channel, type, and language source.
- Choosing the appropriate medium is critical for effective communication.

9.2 COMMUNICATION COMPETENCE

- Communication competence refers to an individual's ability to effectively use communication behaviors in a given context.
- Nonverbal communication is a component of effective communication and includes many potential elements, such as body movements and gestures, touch, facial expressions, and eye contact.
- Listening is the process of actively decoding and interpreting verbal messages. Four common listening styles are active, involved, passive, and detached.
- The feeling of being attacked or threatened is the cause of defensive communication.
- Empathy, the ability to recognize and understand another person's feelings and thoughts, is an important communication skill.

9.3 GENDER, GENERATIONS, AND COMMUNICATION

- Linguistic style is a person's characteristic speaking pattern.
- Women and men communicate differently. Women are more likely to share credit and ask clarifying questions, and men are more likely to give blunt feedback and withhold compliments.
- Each generation has its own communication norms and preferences.
- It's a mistake to generalize anything we know about communication and apply it to entire genders or generations.

9.4 SOCIAL MEDIA AND OB

- Social media can increase employee and employer productivity.
- The use of social media at work also has many costs, some potentially significant.
- E-mail can increase teamwork and flexibility and reduce costs of paper and the distribution of information. But it also has costs: decreased productivity, information overload, and increased time and money to organize, store, and monitor.
- Social media policies help outline what is expected and what is off limits. They also help guard employers against liability and undesirable events.

- Organizations need to monitor and manage privacy in the digital space. Individuals must monitor and manage their personal brand (their reputation) and their employer's.
- Mobile technology etiquette is evolving. Different contexts and different technologies come with different norms and expectations.

9.5 COMMUNICATION SKILLS TO BOOST YOUR EFFECTIVENESS

- Effective presenters are more likely to tell stories than give reports. It is helpful to frame your story, plan the delivery, develop stage presence and multimedia, and put it all together.
- Crucial conversations are those between two or more people in which the stakes are high, opinions vary, and emotions run strong.
- Managing up is more effective if you gauge your manager's receptiveness, ask permission to provide feedback/input, prepare your message, plan your delivery and tactics, and follow up.

9.6 HOW CAN I BECOME A MORE EFFECTIVE COMMUNICATOR?

- Recognizing that what we say is not always what people hear will allow you to fine-tune your approach to communications.
- Learning to master social media will help you distinguish yourself in a good way and possibly further your career.
- Choosing the right communication medium to match the complexity of each situation will help improve your communication skills.

The Organizing Framework for Chapter 9

As shown in Figure 9.6, communication is a key individual-, group/team-, and organizational-level process. We explored a host of inputs, both person factors (nonverbal communication, active listening, empathy, communication skills, and social media behaviors) and situation factors (choice of communication medium, HR policies, and social media practices of your manager and coworkers). You learned that communication links to outcomes across the three levels of OB. At the individual level, communication relates to task performance, work attitudes, citizenship behavior/counterproductive behavior, turnover. Communication also is related to group/team performance, group satisfaction, and group cohesion and conflict. Finally, communication influences organizational outcomes such as accounting/financial performance, customer satisfaction, innovation, reputation, and legal liability.

Challenge: Major Questions for Chapter 9

You should now be able to answer the following questions. Unless you can, have you really processed and internalized the lessons in the chapter? Refer to the Key Points, Figure 9.6, the chapter itself, and your notes to revisit and answer the following major questions:

1. How can knowing about the basic communication process help me communicate more effectively?
2. What key aspects of interpersonal communication can help me improve my communication competence?
3. How do gender and age affect the communication process?
4. How can social media increase my effectiveness at work and in my career?
5. How can I increase my effectiveness using presentation skills, crucial conversations, and managing up?

FIGURE 9.6 Organizing Framework for Understanding and Applying OB

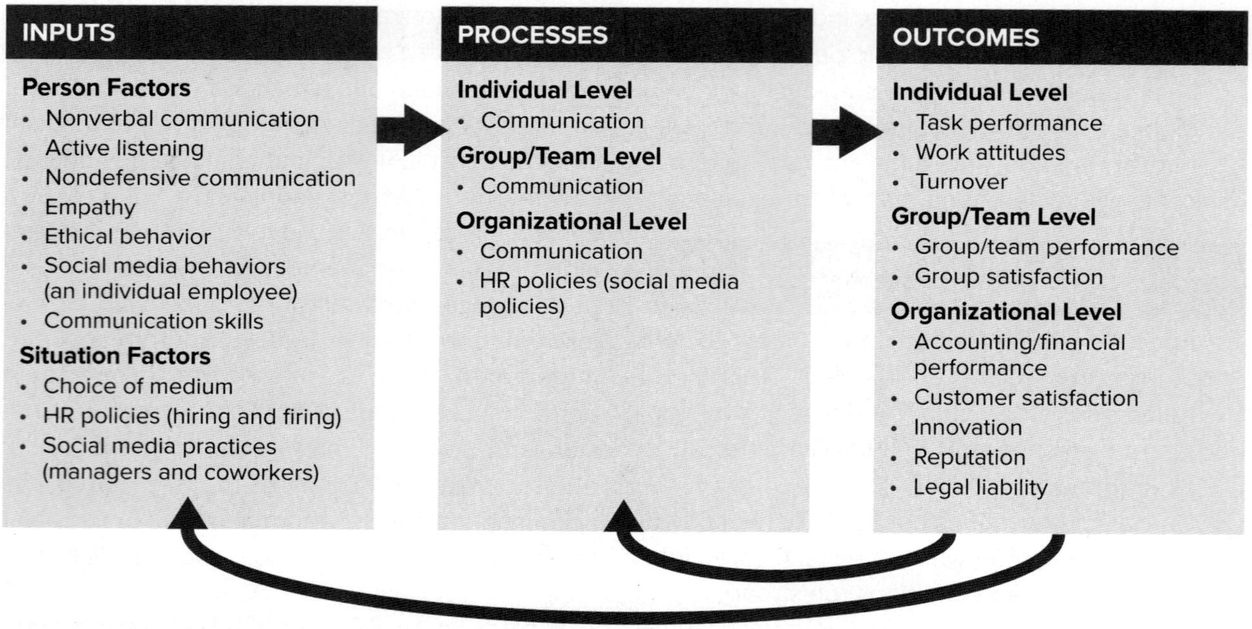

INPUTS	PROCESSES	OUTCOMES
Person Factors • Nonverbal communication • Active listening • Nondefensive communication • Empathy • Ethical behavior • Social media behaviors (an individual employee) • Communication skills **Situation Factors** • Choice of medium • HR policies (hiring and firing) • Social media practices (managers and coworkers)	**Individual Level** • Communication **Group/Team Level** • Communication **Organizational Level** • Communication • HR policies (social media policies)	**Individual Level** • Task performance • Work attitudes • Turnover **Group/Team Level** • Group/team performance • Group satisfaction **Organizational Level** • Accounting/financial performance • Customer satisfaction • Innovation • Reputation • Legal liability

United's Turbulent Communications Strategy

United Airlines is one of the world's largest airlines serving 353 destinations across five continents. The Chicago-based carrier has approximately 92,000 employees and earned more than $41 billion in revenue in 2018.[105] Oscar Munoz started as United's CEO in 2015, and by March 2017 was named "Communicator of the Year" by *PRWeek*. Unfortunately, he fell from grace a month later due to United's botched response to a flight-related incident.[106]

Let's consider how United communicated about the incident.

SUNDAY, APRIL 9: CHAOS ON FLIGHT 3411

A fully booked United flight 3411 was preparing to depart from Chicago to Louisville when gate agents realized that four airline crew members needed to get to Louisville. The gate agents asked for four volunteers to give up their seats in return for compensation. No one accepted United's offer because the flight was the last one to Louisville that evening. United then decided to enact an "involuntary de-boarding situation," in which four random passengers were directed to deplane. Three of the passengers deplaned without incident. The fourth, Dr. David Dao, refused, saying "I can't get off the plane. I have to get home. I'm a doctor. I have to get to the hospital in the morning," according to *The Sentinel News*.[107]

United employees responded to Dao by contacting the Chicago Department of Aviation Security. A scuffle broke out between the officers and Dao when they tried to forcibly remove him from the plane, resulting in a concussion, broken teeth, a broken nose, and other injuries for Dr. Dao. The bloodied image of Dr. Dao was posted on social media and rapidly spread around the world.[108]

MONDAY, APRIL 10: UNITED'S INITIAL RESPONSE

A series of communication blunders transpired the next day:

- United released a statement apologizing for the "overbook situation." The airline would later backtrack and clarify that the flight was not actually overbooked, and passengers were removed to make space for United employees.

- CEO Munoz released a public statement on Twitter calling the incident an "upsetting event," but did not address the treatment of passenger Dao. He apologized to the passengers who were involuntarily deplaned but called their removal "re-accommodation."[109] According to Sean Czarnecki of *PRWeek*, the word "re-accommodate" was then "lodged in the Internet lexicon as a United Airlines euphemism for brutally assaulting your customers."[110]

- CEO Munoz sent an internal letter to United employees blaming Dr. Dao for what happened, calling him "disruptive and belligerent." He also stated that he fully supported his employees' handling of the situation.[111] The internal letter quickly became public, which flamed the negative publicity.

News outlets compared videos of a bloodied and bruised passenger being dragged off an aircraft with United's defensive, un-empathetic, written responses.[112] The result was outrage on social media with thousands of flyers signing a petition demanding Munoz's resignation. Many also called for a boycott of United, whose slogan of "Fly the Friendly Skies" was tarnished by the incident.[113] In fact, a survey conducted by *Morning Consult* found that nearly half of the respondents said they would pick a more expensive, longer flight to avoid giving United their business.[114]

TUESDAY, APRIL 11: UNITED CHANGES COURSE

A turbulent day on Wall Street kicked off after United's initial response to the incident. The airline started the morning losing nearly $1 billion in stock value.

Munoz responded by releasing another written statement. This time he struck a different tone and took "full responsibility" for the episode and said that Dr. Dao should not have been "mistreated" the way he was. The airline also pledged to conduct a review and quickly release findings. Although the statement helped reduce the stock's slide, United still closed the day down around $250 million.[115]

WEDNESDAY, APRIL 12: MUNOZ APPEARS ON TV

On Wednesday morning, Munoz utilized another medium of communication by appearing on ABC's "Good Morning, America." His body language was solemn as he said he felt "shame" when he saw the video of Dao being dragged off the plane. "This can never—will never—happen again on a United Airlines flight. That's my premise and that's my promise," Munoz told viewers.[116]

The airline's efforts may not have been enough to turn the tide. A survey taken by LendEDU after Munoz's TV appearance found that 42 percent of Millennials, the most frequent business travelers of any generation, would still not fly with United.[117]

A TOUGH COUPLE OF WEEKS FOR MUNOZ AND UNITED

The crucial conversations spurred by flight 3411 continued for weeks after the incident. United published full-page ads in several major U.S. newspapers in late April. The ads included an apology from Munoz. "That day, corporate policies were placed ahead of shared values," said United's CEO. The ads also outlined how the airline was changing its policies to prevent the reoccurrence of such an incident.[118]

Munoz's handling of the situation took a toll on his career at United. The airline's parent company, United Continental Holdings, denied the CEO's planned promotion to chairman weeks after the incident.[119] Ironically, he too lost a seat he expected to receive.

APPLY THE 3-STEP PROBLEM-SOLVING APPROACH TO OB

Use the Organizing Framework in Figure 9.6 and the 3-Step Problem-Solving Approach to help identify inputs, processes, and outcomes relative to this case.

STEP 1: Define the problem.

A. Look first at the Outcomes box of the Organizing Framework to help identify the important problem(s) in this case. Remember that a problem is a gap between a desired and current state. State your problem as a gap, and be sure to consider problems at all three levels. If more than one desired outcome is not being accomplished, decide which one is most important and focus on it for steps 2 and 3.

B. Cases have protagonists (key players), and problems are generally viewed from a particular protagonist's perspective. In this case you're asked to assume the role of a business owner.

C. Use details in the case to determine the key problem. Don't assume, infer, or create problems that are not included in the case.

D. To refine your choice, ask yourself, *Why is this a problem?* Focus on topics in the current chapter, because we generally select cases that illustrate concepts in the current chapter.

STEP 2: Identify causes of the problem by using material from this chapter, which has been summarized in the Organizing Framework for Chapter 9 and is shown in Figure 9.6. Causes will tend to show up in either the Inputs box or the Processes box.

A. Start by looking at the Organizing Framework (Figure 9.6) and decide which person factors, if any, are most likely causes of the defined problem. For each cause, explain why this is a cause of the problem. Asking why multiple times is more likely to lead you to root causes of the problem. For example, do employee characteristics help explain the problem you defined in Step 1?

B. Follow the same process for the situation factors. For each ask yourself, *Why is this a cause?* By asking why multiple times you are likely to arrive at a more complete and accurate list of causes. Again, look to the Organizing Framework for this chapter for guidance.

C. Now consider the Processes box in the Organizing Framework. Social media policies and practices can be but are not necessarily a cause. Are any other processes at the individual, group/team, or organizational level potential causes of your defined problem? For any process you consider, ask yourself, *Why is this a cause?* Again, do this for several iterations to arrive at the root causes.

D. To check the accuracy or appropriateness of the causes, map them onto the defined problem.

STEP 3: Make your recommendations for solving the problem. Consider whether you want to resolve it, solve it, or dissolve it (see Section 1.5). Which recommendation is desirable and feasible?

A. Given the causes you identified in Step 2, what are your best recommendations? Use the material in the current chapter that best suits the cause. Remember to consider the OB in Action and Applying OB boxes, because these contain insights into what others have done that might be especially useful for this case.

B. Be sure to consider the Organizing Framework—both person and situation factors—as well as processes at different levels.

C. Create an action plan for implementing your recommendations.

Should Social Media Posts Impact Life Insurance Premiums?

Life insurance companies have traditionally used physical exams and questionnaires to determine customers' premiums, but nowadays many are viewing social media posts as well.[120] These social media posts may include customer tweets, pictures, videos, and likes/dislikes of other posts. There had been limited legal guidance on this matter until a 2019 ruling by New York's Department of Financial Services (NYFS). The NYFS ruled that insurance companies operating in the state may legally use social media posts to determine customer risk propensity.[121]

Insurers typically don't have their employees go through millions of social media posts. Instead, they use carefully crafted algorithms to browse the Internet for policyholders', or potential policyholders', posts. These algorithms speed up the processing of life insurance applications by automatically greenlighting applicants, allowing them to receive a policy without invasive medical tests or waiting weeks for a doctor's appointment.[122]

Algorithms may help speed along the processing of insurance applications, but they can also be used to illegally discriminate against certain groups of people based on built-in biases.[123] For example, the *MIT Technology Review* found algorithmic bias in systems used to rank teachers and gender-biased models for natural language processing.[124] The NYFS is trying to combat this by requiring insurers to monitor their algorithms for bias due to "race, color, creed, national origin, status as a victim of domestic violence, past lawful travel, or sexual orientation in any manner, or any other protected class."[125]

This mandate may not be enough. For starters, many insurance companies legally refuse to share details of their social media algorithms with customers. Second, if the algorithms were shared with customers, how could they be interpreted by a lay person? Dr. Jessica Baron, a tech ethics writer and reporter at TechEngage, says that "it will be very difficult for customers who are not well-versed in algorithmic bias to fight against unfair decisions made about their life insurance premiums based on data they don't even realize they're giving away."[126]

The Wall Street Journal has some advice for those who decide to share aspects of their lives online: "Don't post photos of yourself smoking on social-media sites. Do post photos of yourself running."[127] Those who decide not to utilize social media are not in the clear either. Research presented by *Forbes* shows that information about a person can be constructed from the comments of as few as eight of their online friends.[128]

If You Led an Insurance Company Based in New York, What Would You Do?

1. Utilize information gathered from social media when making life insurance premium decisions. It is legal and may also benefit some applicants.

2. Refuse to utilize information gathered from social media. It is an invasion of privacy and may lead to discrimination.

3. Invent other options and explain.

10

Managing Conflict and Negotiations

After reading this chapter, you should be able to:

LO 10-1 Describe contemporary conflict.

LO 10-2 Differentiate conventional forms of work-related conflict.

LO 10-3 Explain common forms of contemporary work-related conflict.

LO 10-4 Apply your knowledge to manage conflict.

LO 10-5 Implement your negotiation skills.

LO 10-6 Describe the implications of managing conflict and negotiations for you and managers.

The Organizing Framework in Figure 10.1 summarizes the key concepts you'll learn in this chapter. Notice that many person factors, such as personality, experience, conflict-handling styles, mindfulness, and civility influence the type, frequency, and the intensity of conflict you have in all arenas of your life. Many of these same factors influence how you negotiate. You can also expect relationship quality, leadership, organizational climate, as well as norms and practices, to shape conflict and negotiations at work. The importance of these factors notwithstanding, our primary focus in this chapter is understanding conflict and negotiation processes, and how they impact nearly every outcome in the Organizing Framework. The complexity and broad impact of conflict highlights the critical importance of managing conflict for your own satisfaction and performance at work.

FIGURE 10.1 Organizing Framework for Understanding and Applying OB

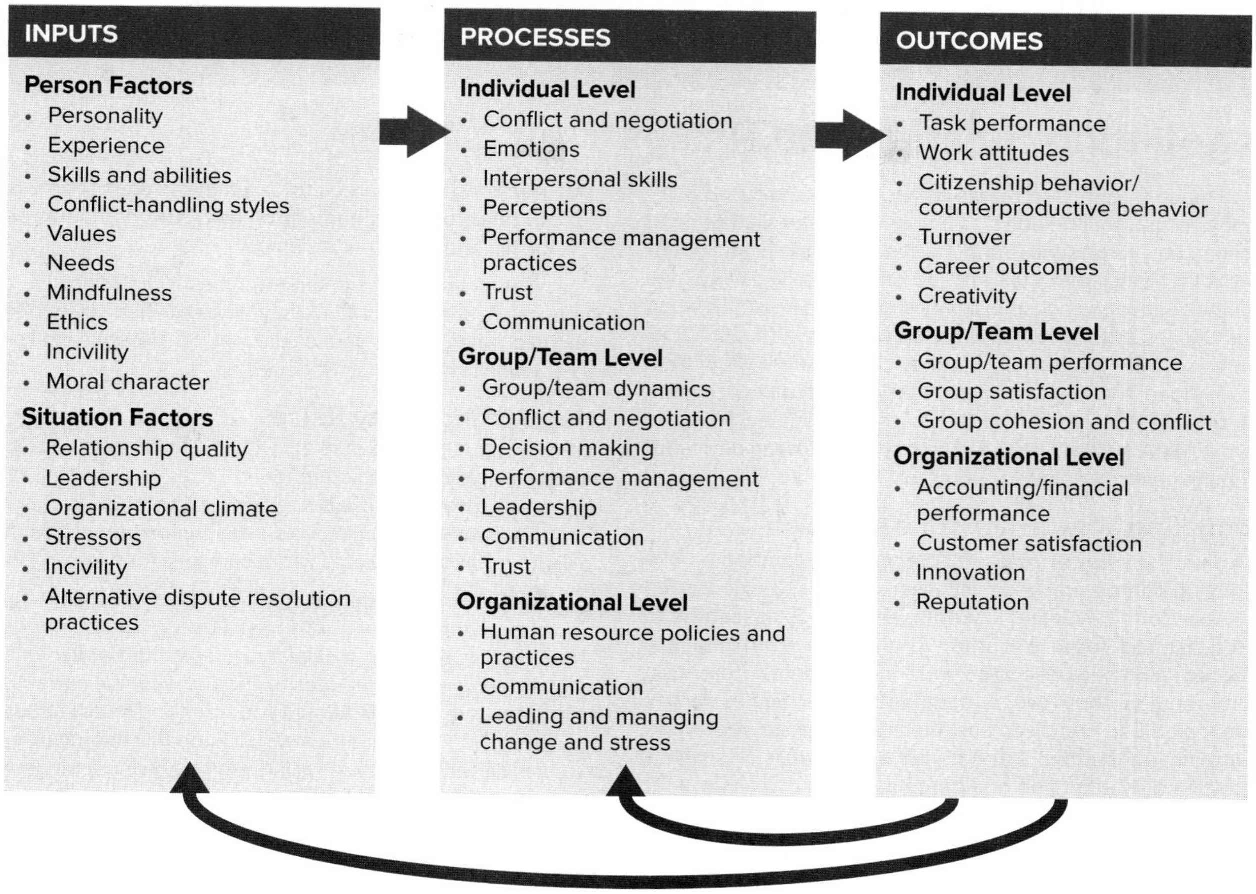

INPUTS

Person Factors
- Personality
- Experience
- Skills and abilities
- Conflict-handling styles
- Values
- Needs
- Mindfulness
- Ethics
- Incivility
- Moral character

Situation Factors
- Relationship quality
- Leadership
- Organizational climate
- Stressors
- Incivility
- Alternative dispute resolution practices

PROCESSES

Individual Level
- Conflict and negotiation
- Emotions
- Interpersonal skills
- Perceptions
- Performance management practices
- Trust
- Communication

Group/Team Level
- Group/team dynamics
- Conflict and negotiation
- Decision making
- Performance management
- Leadership
- Communication
- Trust

Organizational Level
- Human resource policies and practices
- Communication
- Leading and managing change and stress

OUTCOMES

Individual Level
- Task performance
- Work attitudes
- Citizenship behavior/ counterproductive behavior
- Turnover
- Career outcomes
- Creativity

Group/Team Level
- Group/team performance
- Group satisfaction
- Group cohesion and conflict

Organizational Level
- Accounting/financial performance
- Customer satisfaction
- Innovation
- Reputation

Winning at Work

Negotiating Salaries and Raises

A good place to start is to realize salary negotiations are not as common as you think. Recent research by Robert Half Staffing and Hiring Solutions found only 39 percent of workers attempted to negotiate salary with their last job offer. Breaking this down further by gender and age, the survey showed 46 percent of men versus 34 percent of women, 45 percent of 18–34-year-olds, 40 percent of 35–54-year-olds, and 30 percent of those 55 and older engaged in salary negotiations. Asking can pay off, as one study revealed 84 percent of those who negotiated received more pay.[1] With this in mind, experts offer the following advice for getting the best compensation you can.

Negotiating Your Salary for a New Job

- **Know the market rate.** Research what companies are paying other employees with similar jobs. Glassdoor.com, Salary.com, PayScale, LinkedIn, and Randstad can help. It's a good Idea to gather information from multiple sources. Be sure also to consider geographic differences; sometimes they are substantial. A PayScale survey revealed San Francisco has the largest year-to-year wage growth (4.9 percent at the end of 2018), while Nashville's declined by a fraction of a percent.[2]

- **Know your own value.** Can you justify asking for more than the market rate? If yes, then be prepared to justify this premium with compelling examples of your performance and accomplishments. You may also want to consider particular combinations of skills that give you an edge, such as engineering combined with project management, or experience and knowledge in hot industries, such as cybersecurity, cloud computing, or whatever is in demand in a particular city. Whether asking for premium or not, it is always a good idea to focus on how you currently do or will benefit your future or present employers.[3]

- **What's in it for them?** Of course, like everyone else you pursue particular jobs because of how they will benefit you. However, during interviews and negotiations for a new job you are best served to focus on the ways you can benefit your new employer, help the hiring manager reach her goals, and the positive impact you'll have in work teams.

- **Be honest.** Don't exaggerate your current or past pay, actual value, or accomplishments.

- **Don't go first.** Try to wait for the other person to name a number. If you must say something first, then say you want to be paid the rate of a top performer with your qualifications. If pressed for an answer, give a range and not a specific dollar figure.

- **Consider benefits, too.** Some of the most valuable parts of the compensation package may be insurance, retirement savings, vacation time, or the ability to work from home a certain percentage of time. Retirement may seem like eons away, but an employer matching a 5 percent contribution to your 401(k) plan is like giving you an extra 5 percent of pay—without an immediate tax bite.

- **Look at the long term.** If you can't get a big pay package, consider whether asking for something else that will help your long-term career, for example, a chance to work on an important assignment or have the company pay for certification or other training.

Finally, as pointed out by Kim Churches, chief executive of the American Association of University Women, when you're offered a job the company wants you to take that job. "Negotiating your salary shouldn't change their decision."[4]

Negotiating a Pay Raise

Even during robust job markets with low unemployment, 81 percent of employers estimate offering raises of 3 percent or less. This means getting a raise is largely on you, and to set yourself up to win, preparation is critical. You need information, and the following are valuable sources and techniques for acquiring it.

- **Ask current colleagues.** Peers are the best source but may also be the toughest. The best strategy is to be honest and say: "I'm not sure my salary reflects market value, so I'm checking with colleagues to find out what the current salary range is in our field. Would you be willing to talk about compensation?" Assure them you'll keep this information confidential, and, if they're willing, start by giving a range where your salary falls and asking how it compares with theirs.

- **Query former colleagues.** Ask former coworkers their thoughts on an appropriate range for your job in a company of your employer's size and industry. It may help to keep the discussion in the third person: What do you think is a competitive or appropriate salary for a solid performer doing X type of work in a company like mine (or a company like yours)?

- **Give to get.** Another effective approach is to offer your salary: "Does X dollars sound competitive with what you're making or what your company offers?"

- **Ask recruiters.** One of the very best sources is recruiters who place people in jobs and companies like yours. Salary is almost always part of their discussions. So, if you're going to build out your network, adding a recruiter or two who will share such info can be extremely valuable. But you need the relationship first. It's no use cold calling a recruiter and expecting him or her to answer your questions—that expertise is part of what recruiters get paid for!

What's Ahead in This Chapter

We continue our discussion of the group and team level in the Organizing Framework and address conflict and negotiation in this chapter. Conflict is an inevitable part of organizational life and can be both positive and negative. We explore common forms of conflict at work, such as personality and intergroup, and we'll pay significant attention to work–life conflict and incivility (bullying, cyberbullying, and harassment). We then provide practical guidance on how to manage various forms of conflict, followed by an explanation of negotiation, including types of negotiations, the role of emotions, and ethical pitfalls.

10.1 A CONTEMPORARY VIEW OF CONFLICT

THE BIGGER PICTURE

Conflict is an ever-present part of life and an important group-level process in the Organizing Framework. To help you better understand and manage conflict, we explore several common causes of conflict at school and work. Then you'll learn what it means to have too little, too much, and just enough conflict (the conflict continuum). We explain why not all conflict is bad or dysfunctional; some forms are functional or desirable. Next, we describe some desired outcomes of functional conflict.

Because conflicts occur between people, a good place to begin is for you to learn about your own tendencies for conflicts with others. You likely believe you have relatively few conflicts and are easy to get along with, which may be true. However, many of the most problematic bosses, coworkers, business partners, and classmates view themselves the same way. Test your impressions of yourself by completing Self-Assessment 10.1.

LO 10-1

Describe contemporary conflict.

SELF-ASSESSMENT 10.1

Interpersonal Conflict Tendencies

Please be prepared to answer these questions if your instructor has assigned Self-Assessment 10.1 in Connect.

1. Does your score match your perception of yourself?
2. The assessment measures how well you get along with others and how they treat you; both are sources of conflict. If you were to improve the measure, what other factors do you think should be included?

Conflict Is Everywhere and It Matters

Conflict is a pervasive part of the human experience, and at work it can manifest as a lack of cooperation, exclusion, insults, bullying, anger, and many other behaviors and emotions. It also occurs within and between levels in the Organizing Framework and can affect most of the outcomes. Among the many undesirable outcomes of conflict are reduced productivity, project failure, stress, damaged reputations, and termination.[5] It also is safe and wise to assume all forms of conflict at work are underreported.

However, it is important to realize conflict has *both* positive and negative consequences. The goal of this chapter is to help you understand how to avoid the negative consequences while also gaining from the positive outcomes. Let's begin by defining conflict, describing the conflict continuum, then explaining the difference between functional and dysfunctional conflict.

A Modern View of Conflict

Conflict is the energy created by the perceived gap between what we want and what we're experiencing, and as such, it is important to use this energy most effectively.[6]

Notice this definition describes conflict as a gap, just as we describe problems as gaps between what we want and what we have in the 3-Step Problem-Solving Approach. Also notice the word *energy*, which means conflict is more than a simple difference of opinion. You may disagree with someone and not care, but if you have no energy about it you have no conflict due to the difference. And the word *perceived* reminds us that sources of conflict can be real or imagined, just like perceptions of fairness. A lack of fairness, incidentally, perceived or real, is a major source of conflict at work. Your knowledge of OB will therefore prove useful in understanding and managing conflict.

A Conflict Continuum

Historically, management experts believed all conflict ultimately threatened management's authority, reduced productivity, and thus should be avoided or quickly resolved. Experts later recognized the inevitability of conflict and advised managers to learn to live with it. As the understanding of conflict evolved, researchers and managers realized conflict had both positive and negative outcomes, and the most productive way to think of it was in terms of *too much* conflict or *too little*. Neither is desirable.

Appropriate types and levels of conflict energize people to move in constructive directions[7] and are illustrated in Figure 10.2. The differences between types and levels of conflict lead to the distinction between functional and dysfunctional conflict discussed next.

Functional vs. Dysfunctional Conflict

The distinction between *functional conflict* and *dysfunctional conflict* pivots on whether the organization's interests are being served. **Functional conflict, commonly referred to as constructive or cooperative conflict, is characterized by consultative interactions, a focus on the issues, mutual respect, and useful give-and-take.** In such situations people often feel comfortable disagreeing and presenting opposing views. Functional conflict can foster several desirable outcomes, such as:

- Open-mindedness. When conflict is functional, people speak up, others listen, which in turn can increase engagement.
- Increased understanding and strengthened relationships. Feeling understood, even when views differ, cultivates respect and empathy. These of course facilitate productive problem solving.
- Innovation. Working through conflicts in a positive manner pushes people to consider different views than they would otherwise, which often results in new and better processes and outcomes.
- Accelerated growth. Functional conflict results in change—a break from the status quo—and improves performance across levels of OB.[8]

Hopefully, these potential benefits will motivate you and others to invest the time and energy to work through conflict rather than avoiding it.

Each of these beneficial factors is lacking in cases of **dysfunctional conflict, which are disagreements that threaten or diminish an organization's interests.**[9] A primary reason we study and manage conflict is because of its costs due to:

- Absenteeism. Conflict is a major driver of people not showing up. More conflict generates more stress, more stress results in more time off.
- Turnover. Lack of fairness, bullying, or other forms of disrespect and incivility cause people to quit altogether.
- Unionization. Again, a lack of fairness can be costly and motivate employees to organize to combat poor treatment and practices.
- Litigation. If conflict is not dealt with effectively internal to the organization, many employees will seek legal remedies which are often expensive not only in terms of money, but also time and reputations.[10]

FIGURE 10.2   Relationship between Conflict Intensity and Outcomes

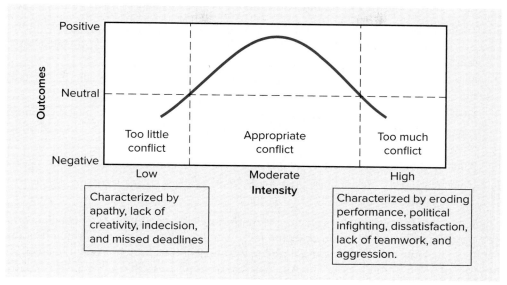

SOURCE: Donald, Carrie G., John D. Ralston, and Suzanne F. Webb. "Arbitral Views of Fighting: An Analysis of Arbitration Cases, 1989–2003." *Journal of Academic and Business Ethics* 2 (July 2009): 1–19.

These outcomes highlight the critical role of management, and your own actions, in determining whether conflict is positive or not. To effectively deal with any kind of conflict, we need to understand some of the common causes.

Common Causes of Conflict

Some causes are more common than others, and knowing these can help you and managers anticipate conflict and take steps to resolve it if it becomes dysfunctional. Table 10.1 lists several of the most common. Which have you experienced?

Proactive managers look for these early warnings and take appropriate action. For example, conflict can sometimes be reduced by making decisions on the basis of majority approval rather than striving for a consensus. However, if conflict is unnoticed or allowed to continue, it can and does escalate.

Escalation of Conflict

When conflict escalates, the exchanges intensify and conflicting parties commonly turn to destructive and negative attacks. When this happens those involved are often more about undermining or hurting the other party than advancing one's own interests. The involved

TABLE 10.1   Common Causes of Workplace Conflict[11]

Personality differences	Competing responsibilities
Irritating workplace behaviors	Change
Unmet needs at work	Poor management
Perceived inequities of resources and policies	Poor communication (including no communication)
Unclear roles and responsibilities	Differences in methods for doing work

SOURCE: Society of Human Resource Management. "Managing Workplace Conflict." Accessed July 4, 2019. https://www.shrm.org/resourcesandtools/tools-and-samples/toolkits/pages/managingworkplaceconflict.aspx.

parties also tend to take more extreme positions and becoming less flexible.[12] Common warning signs of conflict escalation are:

1. **Tactics change.** Parties move from "light tactics," such as persuasive arguments, promises, and efforts to please the other side, to "heavy tactics" that include threats, power plays, and even violence.

2. **Number of issues grows.** More issues that bother each party are raised and included in the conflict.

3. **Issues move from specific to general.** Small and specific concerns often become more vague or general and can evolve into a general dislike of or intolerance for the other party.

4. **Number of parties grows.** More people and groups are drawn into the conflict.

5. **Goals change.** Parties change their focus from "doing well" or resolving conflict to winning and even hurting the other party.[13]

Sometimes conflict will result in wanting to quit your job—you've either had enough or you don't see the people or situation changing meaningfully. When this occurs, you'll be looking for a job while still in your conflict-ridden job and will thus need to explain in an effective way why you want to leave. The Applying OB box provides some guidance.

Applying OB

You've Decided to Leave Your Job . . . How Do You Explain It During an Interview?[14]

Many of your job searches will occur while you're still employed. This means you'll often be asked during interviews, "So, why do you want to leave your current job?" There may be many specific reasons, but often it's because you're unsatisfied, perhaps due to a lack of opportunity, boring work, horrible boss, or low pay. Of course, another common reason is conflict. Whatever the reason, you need to have an effective response to this question. The following tips should help.

Acknowledge the Obvious

When you currently have a job and are interviewing for another, interviewers realize something isn't working for you and you're willing to leave. This obvious fact is often overlooked by job candidates and undermines their performance in interviews. Don't forget or feel uncomfortable with this obvious fact.

What Not to Do

Don't bash and don't ramble. You've learned already that most people believe it is best not to trash or complain about your current employer. You and many others realize this, but unfortunately in your efforts to avoid doing so you may ramble. This can be interpreted by the interviewer as

either a problem exists in your current job, and that problem might be you, or you lack clarity on what it is you are seeking. Neither is good for you. To avoid these pitfalls you need clarity.

Identify the Reasons and Create the Message

List all the reasons you want to leave, and if there are many pare the list to no more than two or three. And even if the major reason is a horrible boss or pay, it may be helpful to reflect more broadly and consider: What are my career goals? What do I like about my current and past positions? What are my relationships with coworkers like and how do these influence my job satisfaction? Then, create a short, clear sentence for each reason and practice saying them aloud. This is your script.

Frame Your Answer and Speak Confidently

Martin Yate, a career coach and HR professional, suggests framing your thinking positively rather than negatively. Instead of thinking of your current job as a troubled situation you need to explain delicately, think of your motives for leaving as reasonable and appropriate, and then talk as if they are. During the interview look the person in the eye and explain confidently the reasons you want to leave, using the script you created and practiced.

Some common scripts to consider, modify, and use are:

- There is limited room for growth, and I'm ambitious and determined. My hope is it is different here.

- I'm unable to contribute in the ways I would like and am able, and I am looking for opportunities to do so. This seems like an excellent place for me to do just that.

- Compensation is out of sync with the market and my level of skills and contributions, and this isn't going to change.

- I want to change career paths and am looking for exciting new opportunities. This appears to be just that.

- I am determined to grow my skill set and make significant contributions, and I hope to do both here.

Follow the above advice and prevent unnecessary stress and missteps during interviews.

Conflict Avoidance

Are you uncomfortable with conflict? Do you go out of your way to avoid it? If so, you're not alone. Fifty-three percent of people in one study reported "delay responding" as their first reaction to conflict, and avoidance is a key ingredient for escalation.[15] Margaret Heffernan, business executive and thought leader, described conflict and avoiding it this way:

> We train people to be expert in managing technology, numbers, finance, and the law. But this most fundamental characteristic of human interaction—conflict—is something we are somehow just supposed to figure out as we go along, but we don't. . . . Not knowing how to handle it, we prefer to ignore it and hope it goes away; unresolved conflict festers and grows. The good news is it doesn't have to be that way.[16]

This raises the question—why? Some of the most common reasons people avoid conflict are:

1. We're social. Like other social animals, groups of humans (organizations) function better without conflict. We therefore generally prefer not to cause or engage in tensions with others.

2. It's stressful. This too is a fact of life; conflict often causes stress and avoiding conflict, at least in the immediate term, may reduce stress.

3. Agreeableness is rewarded. When we go along, or at least don't disagree, with others we're generally rewarded. People like us, include us, and communications are smooth. Conflict, however, is rarely rewarded and is often accompanied by undesirable consequences, even punishment (termination).

4. Backlash. Last but not least is the fear of damaged relationships. Conflicts typically strain relationships, and if you have conflicts with a coworker with whom you work every day your worklife can be miserable.[17]

Conflict avoidance is a common reason otherwise qualified employees are passed over for management and executive positions. Avoiding making tough decisions, confronting poor performance, or challenging weak or faulty ideas are not ways to get ahead. So, what is the alternative? Table 10.2 provides six useful suggestions for constructively engaging rather than avoiding conflict.

We realize that embracing conflict or taking a more functional and constructive view can be difficult if not counterintuitive. To help convince you it is worth the effort, we explain about the payoff or benefits next.

TABLE 10.2   How to Avoid Avoiding[18]

YOUR ROLE	REASON
1. *Stop ignoring a conflict*	Ignoring or working around a conflict won't make it go away and may cause further escalation. Instead, bring both sides together to address the issues.
2. *Act decisively to improve the outcome*	Delay only causes the problem, real or perceived, to fester. Addressing a conflict in short order can help unveil misunderstandings or simple ovesights before they grow into something more or spread.
3. *Make the path to resolution open and honest*	Involve all relevant parties, collect information, and determine a desired outcome. Doing so helps resolve misunderstandings and focuses everyone on the end state instead of wallowing in the (alleged) offenses.
4. *Use descriptive language instead of evaluative*	Beware of accusations and judgmental language. Both put people on the defensive and impede progress. Instead, focus on the problem (behaviors, feelings, implications) and solution rather than the perpetrator.
5. *Make the process a team-building opportunity*	If the problem affects the team, then it may be beneficial to approach the conflict and its solution as a team. Such resolutions may improve relationships in such a way that the team functions even better than it did before the conflict.
6. *Keep the upside in mind*	Effective conflict resolution creates "success momentum." In other words, conflicts are signs along the road to the final and desired destination. Don't get bogged down and lose sight of the ultimate goal or bigger picture.

SOURCE: Duncum, Karen. "Turning Conflict into Cooperation." Bloomberg L.P., October 15, 2010. https://www.bloomberg.com/news/articles/2010-10-15/turning-conflict-into-cooperation.

Desired Outcomes of Conflict Management

It's best to view conflict management neither as a quest for agreement nor a quest for victory. Instead, frame and pursue it as an opportunity to produce positive outcomes, such as:

1. Change. Conflict is rarely productively resolved if nothing changes. Therefore, identify positive elements in the various parties' views and find a way forward—new, different, better.

2. Goal alignment. Incongruent objectives are common sources of conflict for individuals, groups, and departments, and organizations. Confronting these is an opportunity to review and realign goals to serve the parties involved.

3. Innovation. A cousin of change, innovation occurs when conflict generates new and more effective processes, products, and mindsets.[19]

Think of the above this way: if you or the person with whom you have conflict simply sticks to your position, then none of the above desirable outcomes are possible—change doesn't happen, goals are not aligned, and innovation is zero.

We therefore encourage you, when possible, to look at conflict not as a war or a battle, but instead as an *opportunity* or a *journey*.

10.2 CONVENTIONAL FORMS OF CONFLICT

THE BIGGER PICTURE

You can probably think of many types of conflicts from your own life, and you likely have a good idea what caused most of them. But in this section we focus on two of the most common and consequential types of conflict in organizations—*personality* and *intergroup*. The first occurs at the individual level and the other at the group level. Understanding both types will make you more effective at managing an extremely valuable group-level process in the Organizing Framework.

As discussed. opposition isn't necessarily a problem. It can be a constructive way of challenging the status quo and improving behaviors, processes, and outcomes.[20] New ideas, by definition, contrast with old ideas or ways of doing things. Opposition becomes an issue if it turns into dysfunctional conflict and impedes progress and performance. *Personality conflict* and *intergroup conflict* can both cause numerous undesirable outcomes across levels of the Organizing Framework for OB.

LO 10-2

Differentiate conventional forms of work-related conflict.

Personality Conflicts

Given the many possible combinations of personality traits (recall Chapter 3), it is clear why personality conflicts are inevitable. How many times have you said or heard, "I just don't like him (or her)? We don't get along." One of the many reasons for these feelings and statements is personality conflicts. We define a **personality conflict** as **interpersonal opposition based on personal dislike or disagreement.** Like other conflicts, personality conflicts can escalate if not addressed. Think of personality conflicts you've had at school or work. What were the consequences for you? The other person? Members of your team, department, or class? Did things escalate? If the source of a conflict really is personality, then dealing with such conflicts is particularly troublesome since personality traits are by definition stable and resistant to change.

Research shows conflicts over work tasks can turn into personal conflicts and escalate into bullying.[21] But they have other undesirable outcomes too, such as negative emotions related to particular coworkers and to work in general. If these feelings persist beyond work, employees can ruminate and fail to recover appropriately, resulting in poor health and strained nonwork relationships.[22]

Table 10.3 presents practical tips for both you and managers who are involved in or affected by personality conflicts. Best practices vary and items 2 through 4 in the table highlight how to proceed if the conflict is not resolved.

Conflicts between groups are another common form and are addressed next.

Intergroup Conflict

Conflict among work groups, teams, departments, and organizations is a threat to effectiveness across organizational levels, as illustrated in the Organizing Framework. Airbnb, for instance, has ongoing heated conflicts with many local governments in the United States and abroad. Hosts or owners of properties want to make money on their investments by providing accommodations for travelers, but many neighboring full-time residents and

TABLE 10.3   How to Respond When an Employee is in a Personality Conflict

FOR THE EMPLOYEE	FOR THIRD-PARTY OBSERVERS	FOR THE EMPLOYEE'S MANAGER
1. Be familiar with and *follow* company policies on diversity, discrimination, and sexual harassment.		
2. Communicate directly with the other person to resolve the perceived conflict (emphasize problem solving and common objectives, not personalities).	Do not take sides in someone else's personality conflict.	Investigate and document the conflict; if appropriate, take corrective action (feedback or behavior modification).
3. Resist dragging coworkers into the conflict.	Suggest the parties work things out for themselves in a constructive and positive way.	If necessary, attempt informal dispute resolution.
4. If dysfunctional conflict persists, seek help from direct supervisors or human resource specialists.	If dysfunctional conflict persists, refer the problem to the parties' direct supervisors.	Refer difficult conflicts to human resource specialists or hired counselors for formal resolution efforts and other interventions.

Regulators often have conflicts with various groups, such as code enforcement agencies and the owners of Airbnb properties. An increasing number of communities are limiting the use of properties, which puts owners, renters, property managers, and community agency at odds.

Scott Baker/The New York Times/Redux Pictures

local governing bodies want to limit or prevent Airbnb's penetration. They do this in a variety of ways, for example, zoning areas as residential and thus ineligible for short-term rentals.

An article in the *New York Times* described a scenario in Miami where a code compliance officer went door-to-door in an apartment building asking questions of those staying there to determine if they were in compliance. In some instances, violators were required to move out, immediately, which left the renters in a tough spot and created additional conflicts between them, their hosts, and Airbnb itself. Making matters worse, the owner of the building described in the article was fined $40,000 for violating the zoning codes! Therefore, intergroup conflict can escalate much like other forms of conflict discussed in the previous section.[23]

Because of the seemingly limitless number of groups and differences both within and between, let's provide some guidance to you on how to handle such conflicts.

How to Handle Intergroup Conflict

How have you attempted to solve conflicts between a group of which you are a member and another group? While many techniques are successful in particular situations, the contact hypothesis and creation of psychologically safe climates can help.

Contact Hypothesis   The **contact hypothesis** suggests that the more members of different groups interact, the less intergroup conflict they will experience. Those interested in improving race, international, and union–management relations typically encourage cross-group interaction. The hope is that interaction will reduce stereotyping and diminish differences. For instance, research in the IT context showed that contract employees working side-by-side with their client representatives resulted in greater cross-cultural training participation for both groups, and it also improved individual performance.[24]

Trying to understand and appreciate differing company, industry, or cultural customs is an effective way to avoid conflicts and ensure all parties are more comfortable.

Dave and Les Jacobs/Blend Images/Alamy Stock Photo

It helps to focus on the perceived security and quality of the interactions. If you and/ or your managers can make the minority (or out-group) feel there is nothing at stake (they are not being evaluated), they are more likely to feel secure and satisfied with the interaction. This reassurance can also reduce both groups' prejudices about the other. We can achieve such benefits by sharing social interests or social events where the focus is not on work, particularly the minority group's work.[25]

Creating a Psychologically Safe Climate   One especially important organizational level cause and remedy to conflict is a climate of psychological safety. A ***psychological safety climate*** **represents a shared belief among team members that it is safe to engage in risky behaviors, such as questioning current practices without retribution or negative consequences.**[26] When employees feel psychologically safe, they are more likely to speak up and present their ideas and less likely to take disagreements personally. This interaction results in increased team creativity,[27] less conflict within and between teams, and higher individual and team performance.[28] Psychological safety climates also help improve employee turnover, safe work behaviors, and job satisfaction.[29]

How can you and your employers foster a climate for psychological safety? Here are four fundamental and widely applicable practices:

1. Frame work as a learning problem, not a performance problem.
2. Practice inclusive leadership.
3. Model curiosity and ask many questions.
4. Celebrate and reinforce risk taking and differences.[30]

Find out the level of psychological safety in one of your groups, teams, or organizations by completing Self-Assessment 10.2. It's a quick, accurate, and valuable way to get a sense of this important situation factor and unit-level process. Knowing the level of psychological safety can help you understand why some conflicts occur and how you can handle them effectively.

Before leaving this section, read the Applying OB box and learn how Google determined the importance of psychological safety for team performance (as you learned in Chapter 8).

Applying OB

Psychological Safety Is Oxygen at Google[31]

Google employed its vast data and tremendous analytic skills to determine what makes an effective manager in their company. The initiative, called Project Oxygen, also helped identify the key ingredients of successful teams. By far the most important factor was psychological safety. Put simply, if people feel they won't be punished for making mistakes, it is likely they work in a psychologically safe environment. This helps people speak up and ask questions, make suggestions, and challenge the status quo. Not only do these behaviors increase individual and team performance, but they also help diminish conflict avoidance. To increase and cultivate such a climate within your team or organization, Google's Head of Industry, Paul Santagata, recommends:

1. When conflict occurs collaborate Instead of combat.
2. Emphasize empathy and respect for everyone, regardless of differences.
3. Engage rather than avoid difficult topics and conversations.
4. Anticipate counterarguments and formulate responses, but always be mindful of #1 and #2.
5. Search for win-win while being ever conscious of discouraging dissent.

Keeping this advice in mind, and putting it into practice, may increase your performance, satisfaction, and team member effectiveness.

Now let's explore work–family conflict and incivility, two forms of conflict that are growing in frequency and intensity.

10.3 FORMS OF CONFLICT INTENSIFIED BY TECHNOLOGY

THE BIGGER PICTURE

We focus our discussion on two forms of conflict: work–life conflict and incivility. You face demands at school and in other arenas of your life—work, social life, and perhaps family—and these demands can compete and sometimes cause conflicts for you. These conflicts, along with incivility, can have dramatic and undesirable effects on your personal health, well-being, opportunities, and other outcomes across all levels of the Organizing Framework.

Students, employees, and people everywhere have always experienced conflicts between the various arenas of their lives, notably between work, school, and home. But historically, various activities and their demands were confined to the physical locations in which they occurred—work happened largely at the office—but those days are ancient history. Technology has not only blurred the boundaries between these different arenas,[32] but it has also extended mistreatment to every arena. Our mobile devices and social media are ubiquitous and devastating tools for bullies and other bad actors. For these reasons we give special attention to these forms of conflict.

LO 10-3

Explain common forms of contemporary work-related conflict.

Work–Life Conflict

Work–life conflict is the perception that expectations and demands between work and nonwork roles are mutually incompatible.[33] It is important to realize conflict can go both ways—work can interfere with family and family can interfere with work. For example, suppose two managers in the same department have daughters playing on the same soccer team. One manager misses the big soccer game to attend a last-minute department meeting (work interferes with family), while the other manager skips the meeting to attend the game (family interferes with work). If you receive and respond to a text from a friend during class, this is a form of school–social life conflict, just as is skipping happy hour with friends in order to study for an exam.

These various conflicts matter because they can negatively affect important outcomes in the Organizing Framework and in your larger life, such as lower job and career satisfaction, job performance, and marital and family satisfaction. The same conflicts are linked to declines in emotional and physical health and to substance abuse.[34]

Self-Assessment 10.3 will help you see such conflicts from the point of view of others, not just your own perceptions. It can also help you identify which conflicts are the most and least serious, and this knowledge can assist in deciding what to do about them.

However, like other forms of conflict, recent research shows work–life conflicts are not all bad.[35] Answering a work-related phone call or text when having dinner with your partner, friend, or family can indeed be intrusive and undesirable, but if doing so enables you to solve a problem for a coworker or customer in real-time, then this may enhance your performance and satisfaction in the work domain. Conversely, if you take a call from your sister or a friend while you're working, this can interrupt your flow and productivity, despite pleasing them. Therefore, the real challenge for you is not to avoid or eliminate conflict, but instead to manage it in ways to realize the benefits and reduce the costs.[36] Let's explore this next.

Work–Life Balance, Harmony, Blend, Integration, or Rhythm   Business researchers and managers in America have argued for "work–life balance" since the 1980s, which suggests achieving just the right level of demands from all of life's domains is possible. Even if it is possible how would you know? This has led to more recent views and concepts—harmony, blend, integration, and rhythm—that more accurately describe our realities and the challenge facing all of us, which is to manage the competing demands from your various roles and domains effectively.[37]

Work, parenting, and life. For you, do they conflict, balance, or integrate? We have many competing demands and managing them effectively is critical for your success and well-being.
Zivica Kerkez/Shutterstock

To underscore the importance of effectively managing the boundaries between domains and your energy, 33 percent of employees reported work–life balance as their top criterion when selecting a job, above compensation and promotion opportunities.[38] Work–life conflicts are intensified by technology and the nature of our lives. As in the examples above, the boundaries between our roles and life domains are more permeable and you need to manage the interruptions from one domain into another. The responsibilities for doing this belong to both you and your employer.

Your responsibilities:

Designate time.   Tell family and friends you'll talk during your breaks, such as lunch and when you grab a snack of coffee in the afternoon. You can coordinate the latter, for instance, with the time when your kids get home from school. Do the same with work colleagues; tell them not to expect e-mails or texts from you after a certain time in the evening or on weekends. The important point here is to set and communicate the times.[39]

Designate space.   Besides managing time boundaries, if you work part- or full-time from home it is helpful to designate a particular space where work happens—an office, unused bedroom, or some other space not in front of the TV or at the dining room table—to reduce interruptions. This signals to you and others where work happens, and others should respect this space.

Share.   Parents of course have child-rearing, household, and other responsibilities. Research shows that parents, collectively and as individuals, are more satisfied at both work and home when they share the load. Moreover, spousal support is an instrumental factor for career success, according to research involving senior-level executives.[40]

The objective is not to eliminate interruptions, but instead to manage them effectively by considering time and space. As for the employer's part, balance requires flexibility and other accommodating attitudes and practices.

Employer responsibilities:

Flex space **such as telecommuting, occurs when policies enable employees to do their work from different locations besides the office (coffee shop, home, or the beach).** ***Flextime*** **is flexible scheduling, covering either the time when work must be completed (deadlines) or the limits of the workday (9–5, 10-4, or any time today).** Table 10.4 outlines some benefits of flexible hours and locations.

Family supportive culture. *An employer's family-supportive culture is more important than specific programs.* Organizational culture must support the use of family-friendly programs for employees to benefit from them. To elaborate, it's not enough to simply provide child care; employees must also feel supported and comfortable using it. The same goes for leaving work early to attend a child's sporting event or recital.

TABLE 10.4   Key Benefits of Flexible Work Policies[41]

BENEFITS	EXPLANATION
Lower expenses— higher profits	Allowing employees to work from other places requires less formal office space, which lowers real estate/rent costs, and in turn boosts profits.
Environmentally friendly	Telecommuting saves energy from both the gasoline required to get to work, and the utilities (gas, water, electric) for the office space.
Boosts productivity	Some research shows those who work remotely actually work more (lunch breaks are shorter and commuting time is short or zero).
Increased retention	Flexibility enables employees—men and women—to tend their children's needs and schedules, as well as the inevitable doctor's appointments and other commitments.

SOURCE: Castillo-Frick, Iliana. "Words of Wisdom: The Evolution of Workflex." *SHRM,* November 21, 2017. https://www.shrm.org/hr-today/news/hr-magazine/1217/pages/words-of-wisdom-the-evolution-of-workflex-castillo-frick.aspx.

Another point worth noting is that the benefit of work–life initiatives applies to women *and* men. Specifically, organizations with flexible arrangements, leaves of absence, and on-site child care are more likely to have employees (men and women) who aspire to leadership roles.[42] *Working Mother* magazine, well known for its annual list of Best Companies for Moms, recently created its first list of Best Companies for Dads. These companies work diligently to reduce the stigma long felt by (new) fathers related to benefits historically only provided to women, if at all, such as paternity leave, phased back-to-work, telecommuting, and flexible schedules. American Express provides 20 weeks paternity leave, 20 weeks for adoption leave, and paid surrogacy expenses. Bank of America, Deloitte, and EY all provide 16 weeks of paternity leave and the same amount of time for adoptions.[43]

Family friendly policies aren't just for women anymore. Organizations are increasingly realizing the value (e.g., attracting and retaining) of such benefits for male employees too.

Sorapop Udomsri/Shutterstock

The magazine's editor, Meredith Bodgas, said: "Not only does this help dads . . . it helps moms succeed both at home and work and puts them on more equal footing." Such policies are a means for organizations, like those on this list, to earn employer of choice status in the eyes of job candidates.[44]

Before moving on, a few words of caution are in order. The value of most flexible work arrangements can be undermined if your immediate supervisor isn't supportive. This is especially critical considering a survey found 29 percent of participants' bosses expect them to work even on vacation![45] Put another way, supportive policies matter, but what good is a policy if you aren't allowed to use it?[46] Your manager's own behaviors are a stronger signal and influence on behavior than most any policy, including those related to flexible work arrangements. Fully half of companies surveyed offer some sort of flexible work arrangements, yet the same companies report that only a third of employees utilize them.[47]

Cathy Engelbert, commissioner of the WNBA and former CEO of Deloitte, practices "work-life strategy." As reported in a *Time* magazine article, she "has a black belt in scheduling."[48] In one week she was in Washington, DC, Dallas, Singapore, and Madrid. She also made time to coach her daughter's lacrosse team, and later the day of the *Time* interview, she promised her son to make it home by 5 p.m. to watch an NCAA basketball game with him. Engelbert is disciplined, obviously, and sets aside 10-minute blocks for what she calls SMORs—small moments of reflection—in between meetings to consider the previous and prepare for the next.

Now let's turn our attention to a different category of conflict—incivility.

Cathy Engelbert knows a thing or two about managing the demands of her professional and personal lives. Most of her career was spent at Deloitte, living the life an auditor, manager and eventually becoming the first female CEO of a Big 4 accounting firm. She has since taken her talents to the Women's National Basketball Association, where she is now the first commissioner in the league's history. Along the way she has both modeled and established policies and behaviors supportive to women.

Joshua Roberts/Reuters/Newscom

Incivility—Treating Others Poorly Has Real Costs

Incivility **is any form of socially harmful behavior, such as aggression, interpersonal deviance, social undermining, interactional injustice, harassment, abusive supervision, and bullying.**[49] At its foundation, incivility violates norms of respect, and like other OB concepts it is perceptual and thus exists in the eyes of the abused. If you feel you've been treated disrespectfully, then you've been treated disrespectfully. This perception is what negatively affects numerous outcomes across levels of the Organizing Framework, such as lower employee engagement and job satisfaction, reduced effort and commitment, and increased stress and turnover.[50]

Incivility can be insidious, meaning it often happens in the background without notice, until it accumulates or escalates and causes others to become involved. Subtle or not, statistics regarding various forms of mistreatment are astounding and suggest a growing epidemic. It is estimated that 13 percent of executives' time at Fortune 1000 companies is spent dealing with incivility. This equates to seven weeks per year![51] Beyond the executive ranks, 98 percent of employees reported experiencing some form of incivility, and 50 percent said they had been treated rudely at least once a week![52] Statistics from the Workplace Bullying Institute, shown in Table 10.5, provide a brief glimpse of the pervasiveness and costs of the problem.

Like more conventional epidemics, incivility is contagious and being rude to one person is associated with them being rude to others. And if not addressed by managers and others, disrespectful behaviors can become embedded and create toxic cultures and negatively impact an array of stakeholders—customers, employees, and suppliers.[53]

Even more shocking is the prevalence and impact of incivility in health care. For instance, hospital workers whose supervisors mistreated them were less likely to share knowledge and information, which diminished their team's performance.[54] Another study found that almost 25 percent of physicians said incivility led to patient harm, and nearly 75 percent of those physicians said bad behavior in their team caused medical errors, even contributing to patient deaths.[55]

TABLE 10.5   Employees' Responses to and the Costs of Incivility at Work

61% of Americans are aware of abusive conduct in the workplace
71% of employer actions are harmful to targets of incivility
60 million Americans are affected by it
61% of bullies are bosses
29% of targets remain silent about their experiences
40% of targets believe they suffer adverse health because of incivility

SOURCE: Namie, Gary. "2017 WBI U.S. Workplace Bullying Survey." Workplace Bullying Institute. https://www.workplacebullying.org/wbiresearch/wbi-2017-survey/.

The appropriate and obvious next question is "why?" In order to prevent and overcome incivility we need to understand the causes.

Causes of Incivility   It's no surprise that both individuals and their employers can be the root cause of mistreatment at work (see Figure 10.3). The causes, just like the outcomes, can occur at all three levels in the Organizing Framework. Incivility, for instance, has been shown to be catastrophic to teamwork, because it undermines collaboration and individual member performance;[56] it also undermines engagement and fosters intentions to quit.[57] This means bad behavior and disrespect is truly an organizational problem, even if it starts with a single individual.

FIGURE 10.3   Causes, Forms, and Outcomes of Incivility at Work

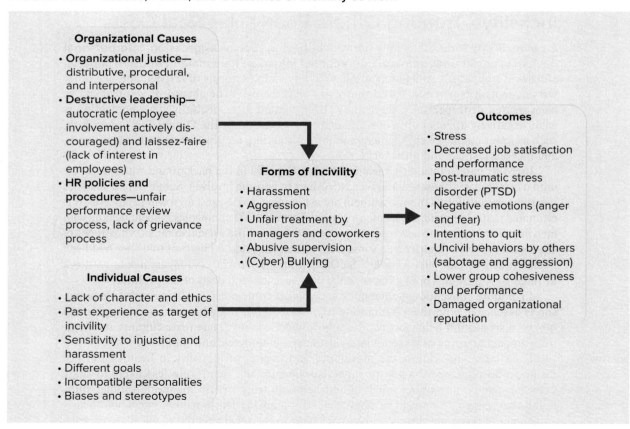

SOURCE: Singleton, R., L. A. Toombs, S. Taneja, C. Larkin, and M. G. Pryor. "Workplace Conflict: A Strategic Leadership Imperative." *International Journal of Business and Public Administration* 8 (2011): 149–56.

With this knowledge in hand, we'll address some particular forms of incivility—bullying, cyberbullying, and harassment.

Bullying **is unwelcomed behavior that occurs over a period of time and is meant to harm someone who feels powerless to respond.**[58] Bullying also occurs at multiple levels in OB and is different from other forms of mistreatment or incivility in at least three ways.[59]

1. *Bullying is usually evident to others.* Bullies at work don't have to push you down or take your lunch money, like they do in elementary school.[60] Even when the bullying is less obvious and nonviolent, coworkers are commonly aware through either gossip or other forms of communication (meetings, e-mail, and social media) that someone is being bullied.

2. *Bullying affects even those who are NOT bullied.* Research shows that employees who are simply aware of bullying of colleagues but are not themselves a target are more likely to quit their jobs. This means bullying has costs that extend well beyond the harm to the person being bullied.[61] Simply witnessing or being aware one of your colleagues is mistreated has negative effects on you.

3. *Bullying has group-level implications.* Because even those who are not targeted by bullies can be affected, bullying often negatively affects group dynamics and group satisfaction and performance,[62] important processes and outcomes in the Organizing Framework.

Given the costs of bullying, what can you and employers do? Table 10.6 provides a collection of best practices from business and research.

Cyber Bullying   Social media and mobile devices have created new avenues and weapons for bullies at school, at work, and in our social lives. Many researchers now report that virtual bullying is more common than face-to-face bullying, although the two often co-occur.[63] Making matters worse, the undesirable effects last over time. Employees who experienced cyber-bullying at work today reported greater physical and emotional distress at the end of the day *and the next morning.* And the targets are harmed both by the direct assault or event, and the *fear of future mistreatment.*[64]

Besides the fact so much of our lives and communication is online, why else might cyber-bullying be such a problem? One reason is organizations commonly have "norms of civility" for face-to-face interactions, such as meetings where people are respectful in tone, content, and nature of their communications. However, such norms are less clear or are absent via e-mail and texts. You, and employees more generally, may say and do things online differently without any ill intent. Second, nonverbal queues and information are absent and can dramatically influence the way your message is perceived. Moreover, feedback is delayed and may further

TABLE 10.6   **Anti-Bullying Strategies for Groups and Organizations**

Develop a workplace bullying policy.
Encourage open and respectful communication.
Identify and model appropriate ways for people to interact with colleagues.
Develop and communicate a system for reporting bullying.
Identify and resolve conflicts quickly and fairly to prevent escalation.
Identify the situations, policies, and behaviors likely to cause bullying or allow it to occur.
Train employees to manage conflict.
Establish and enforce clear consequences for those who engage in bullying.
Monitor and review employee relationships, with particular attention to fairness.

SOURCE: Thomas, Helena Cooper, Dianne Gardner, Michael O'Driscoll, Bevan Catley, Tim Bentley, and Linda Trenberth. "Neutralizing Workplace Bullying: The Buffering Effects of Contextual Factors." *Journal of Managerial Psychology* 28, no. 4 (2013): 384–407. https://doi.org/10.1108/JMP-12-2012-0399.

alter the intended message.[65] All of this applies before considering the shorthand language that dominates texting and the infamous autocorrect, which is either your friend or your foe.

The situation is made worse when the communications and bullying occur at work. The simple reason is that often you cannot avoid or otherwise delay or ignore responding to your boss or other (powerful) coworkers and clients. The importance and impact of cyber-bullying is captured extremely well by a group of researchers on the topic: ". . . [O]ur results suggest that the distressing effects of cyber-incivility are persistent and strong."[66]

Now let's learn about a close relative of bullying—harassment.

Harassment   Comes in many forms, but in essence ***harassment* is discrimination based on a protected class (race, gender, religion, pregnancy, age, disability), that becomes illegal when it threatens your employment or is considered intimidating, hostile, or abusive.** That is a mouthful and very "legal." It is important to note the majority of inappropriate workplace behavior does not qualify as harassment unless it is related to and targets a member of a protected class.[67] This means if you're a white American male under 40 with no disabilities, almost any form of mistreatment you experience will not qualify as harassment under the law. To be clear, any incivility is still problematic and potentially devastating, but harassment is relatively narrow in terms of legal qualifications.

Sexual harassment is a pervasive and dramatically underreported form receiving greater attention in the recent past. As stated by Johnny C. Taylor, CEO of the Society of Human Resource Management, "Given that nearly every U.S. organization (98 percent) has a sexual harassment policy, clearly the problem is bigger than policy; it's a matter of culture."[68] This means sexual harassment, like other forms of incivility we've discussed, extends beyond individuals to groups, teams, and organizations.

The costs are enormous and growing, and thanks to the #MeToo movement attention also is growing. Cases filed with the Equal Employment Opportunity Commission (EEOC) doubled in just the first year following the movement, and claims paid by employers increased from $47 million to $70 million. Regardless of your reaction to these numbers, it is important to realize that many more cases are filed outside of the EEOC, in civil courts, and many more still are unreported (approximately 70 percent). As with other forms of incivility, the target individuals and the units in which they work both suffer negative

Tarana Burke is credited with coining the term MeToo and igniting the movement in 2006. A tsunami of allegations and scandals related to sexual harassment and sexual assault in the workplace have been reported in recent years.

Chelsea Guglielmino/FilmMagic/Getty Images

consequences, as can the larger organization—damaged reputations, lost customers, and lost job candidates.[69]

Sexual harassment comes in two principal forms—*quid pro quo* and *hostile work environment*. Quid pro quo literally means "this for that." If a person in power implies or explicitly demands sex in exchange for a benefit (raise) or preventing something undesirable (termination), then this is quid pro quo. In contrast, "an intimidating or demeaning environment or situation that negatively affects a person's job performance" is considered a hostile work environment. Among the many examples are inappropriate touching, sexual jokes or comments, offensive photos or e-mails, and repeated requests for dates.[70]

A few additional details are worth knowing: (1) the harasser's conduct must be unwelcomed; (2) the victim does not have to be the target, but anyone who is affected by the conduct; and (3) any form of harassment is equally illegal and uncivil.[71]

How to combat sexual and other forms of harassment? Experts recommend:

1. **Don't make definitions and policies overly legal.** Legal terminology is good for attorneys, but it is best to create and communicate policies in simple language in terms relevant to your workplace.

2. **Use relevant examples.** Identify offensive behaviors most likely to occur in your particular workplace, whether technically illegal or not, and explain why not to do them and what employees are expected to do when they occur or are observed.

3. **Make it everyone's responsibility.** This needs to be communicated and clear channels for reporting known. Whom should you notify and how? Outside tip-lines can help.

4. **Enforce top to bottom.** Despite the high-profile cases associated with #MeToo, the fact remains that many perpetrators are people in power who are often protected. People need to believe every employee will be held accountable.[72]

Victim, Witness, or Perpetrator? Let's conclude this section by having you assess not just your experience but also your actions. Completing Self-Assessment 10.4 can help you improve your own effectiveness.

SELF-ASSESSMENT 10.4

Bullying Scale—Target and Perpetrator

Please be prepared to answer these questions if your instructor has assigned Self-Assessment 10.4 in Connect.

1. Which three example items do you most commonly experience?

2. What do you think are the causes of these examples? Try to identify causes across individual, group, and organizational levels using your OB knowledge.

3. To what extent do your most common experiences of being bullied match those you most commonly engage in?

4. Describe some things that could be done to prevent or reduce these acts of bullying.

SOURCE: Glomb, Theresa M. "Predicting Workplace Aggression: Reciprocal Aggression, Organizational, and Individual Antecedents." *International Journal of Organization Theory and Behavior* 13, no. 2 (March 2010): 249–91. https://doi.org/10.1108/IJOTB-13-02-2010-B005.

Another way to be more effective and helpful when witnessing incivility is to take the perspective of the target. Consciously think about what it is like to be him or her, walk in his or her shoes, and experience what that person is going through. It may sound trite but practicing the Golden Rule can go a long way in preventing inappropriate conduct. This simple approach can prove useful, because in the heat of conflict most parties are so focused on themselves that they never think to consider the other's view.

Remember that mistreatment has more victims than the actual target. Don't be a silent bystander. Do your part to prevent and remedy various forms of incivility at school, work, and home.

10.4 EFFECTIVELY MANAGING CONFLICT

THE BIGGER PICTURE

We extend your knowledge in this section by introducing several practical means for dealing with a variety of conflicts. Specifically, we explore ways to program or *create* functional conflict, and you'll also learn about various conflict-handling styles and when to use them. We then explore how to implement alternative forms of dispute resolution (ADR). Combined, the practical knowledge in this section will enable you to better manage conflicts and in turn influence important outcomes in the Organizing Framework.

LO 10-4

Apply your knowledge to manage conflict.

Programming Functional Conflict

Have you ever been on a team or committee that became so bogged down in details and procedures it accomplished nothing? Many of us have. These experiences are both a waste of time and frustrating. Thankfully, OB provides two programmed conflict techniques with proven track records to help break out of these ruts—*devil's advocacy* and the *dialectic method*. Let's explore each.

Devil's Advocacy   One individual is assigned the role of *devil's advocate* and identifies any potential shortcomings in the proposal. Figure 10.4 shows the steps in this approach. Note how devil's advocacy alters the usual decision-making process in steps 2 and 3 on the left-hand side of the figure.

The Dialectic Method   The *dialectic method* **involves a structured dialogue or debate of opposing viewpoints prior to making a decision.** Steps 3 and 4 in the right-hand side of Figure 10.4 set the dialectic approach apart from common decision-making processes

Pros, Cons, and Practical Advice on Programmed Conflict   It is a good idea to rotate the job of devil's advocate so no one person or group develops an undeserved negative reputation. Moreover, periodically playing the devil's advocacy role is good training for developing analytical and communication skills and emotional intelligence. The strengths of this approach are critical thinking and reality testing, but a major drawback is that the goal of "winning the debate" might overshadow the issue at hand. The dialectic method also requires more skilled training than does devil's advocacy.

Research on the relative effectiveness of the two methods ended in a tie, although both methods were more effective than consensus decision making.[73] However, another study showed that devil's advocacy produced more potential solutions and made better recommendations for a case problem than did the dialectic method.[74]

Considering this mixed evidence, you have some latitude in choosing a method for breaking the logjams that sometimes occur. It is likely that personal preference and other members' experiences may be the deciding factors in your decision. The important thing is to actively stimulate functional conflict when possible, such as when the risk of blind conformity or groupthink is high.

FIGURE 10.4 **Techniques for Stimulating Functional Conflict: Devil's Advocacy and the Dialectic Method**

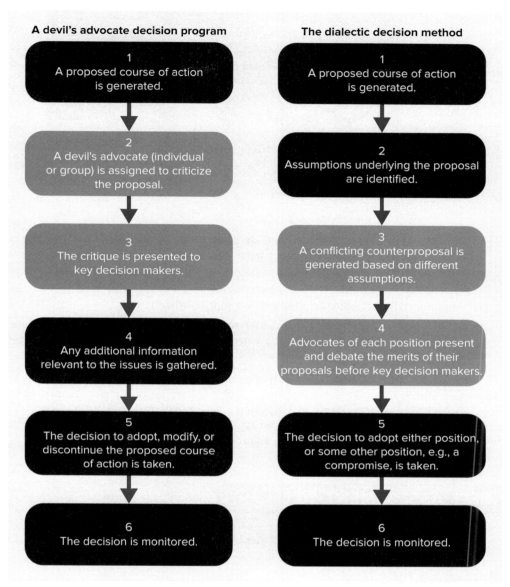

SOURCE: Cosier, Richard A., and Charles R. Schwenk. "Agreement and Thinking Alike: Ingredients for Poor Decisions." *The Executive* 4, no.1 (February 1990): 69–74.

Conflict-Handling Styles

As with the many other individual differences you've learned about, people have stable preferences or styles for handling conflicts. Figure 10.5 distinguishes five of the most common styles based on an individual's relative concern for others (*x*-axis) versus concern for self (*y*-axis). Combinations of these produce the conflict-handling styles called integrating, obliging, dominating, avoiding, and compromising.[75]

> **Integrating:** Interested parties confront the issue and cooperatively identify it, generate and weigh alternatives, and select a solution.

> **Obliging:** Tends to show low concern for yourself and a great concern for others. Such people tend to minimize differences and highlight similarities to please the other party.

FIGURE 10.5 Five Common Conflict-Handling Styles

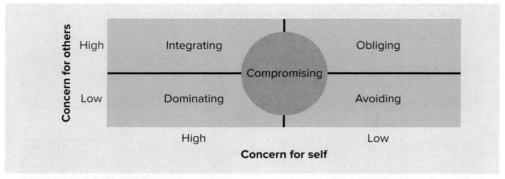

SOURCE: Rahim, M. Afzalur. "A Strategy for Managing Conflict in Complex Organizations." *Human Relations* 38, no. 1 (January 1985): 81–89. https://doi.org/10.1177/001872678503800105.

Dominating: High concern for self and low concern for others, often characterized by "I win, you lose" tactics. The other party's needs are largely ignored. This style is often called *forcing* because it relies on formal authority to force compliance.

Avoiding: Passive withdrawal from the problem and active suppression of the issue are common. We addressed the pitfalls of avoiding conflict earlier.

Compromising: Is a give-and-take approach with a moderate concern for both self and others. Compromise is appropriate when parties have opposite goals or possess equal power.

Before you learn about the characteristics of these styles and the best situations in which to use each one, take Self-Assessment 10.5 to learn your own style. Then you'll be able to see whether what you learn matches your style. Better still, you'll better understand in which conflict situations your preferred style assists you and when it hurts you. For instance, wouldn't you like to know when an *avoiding* style is most effective?

SELF-ASSESSMENT 10.5   **CAREER READINESS**

Preferred Conflict-Handling Style

Please be prepared to answer these questions if your instructor has assigned Self-Assessment 10.5 in Connect.

1. What is your style? On the surface, before reading below, does this make sense to you? Why or why not?

2. Describe a conflict you've experienced in which your conflict-handling style helped you.

3. Describe a conflict in which your style didn't serve you well. Explain why.

4. Which style do you think would have been best for that particular conflict?

SOURCE: Rahim, M. Afzalur. "A Measure of Styles of Handling Interpersonal Conflict." *Academy of Management Journal* 26, no. 2 (June 1983): 368–76. https://doi.org/10.5465/255985.

When to Apply the Various Conflict-Handling Styles   Consistent with the contingency approach described throughout this book, conflict resolution is not a "one style fits all" approach. Research and practice thankfully provide some guidance indicating which styles seem to work best in particular situations (see Table 10.7).

TABLE 10.7 Styles for Handling Conflict and the Situations where they are Appropriate and Inappropriate

STYLE	APPROPRIATE	INAPPROPRIATE
Integrating	1. Issues are complex. 2. Synthesis of ideas is needed to come up with better solutions. 3. Commitment is needed from other parties for successful implementation. 4. Time is available for problem solving. 5. One party alone cannot solve the problem. 6. Resources possessed by different parties are needed to solve their common problem.	1. Task or problem is simple. 2. Immediate decision is required. 3. Other parties are unconcerned about outcome. 4. Other parties do not have problem-solving skills.
Obliging	1. You believe that you may be wrong. 2. Issue is more important to the other party. 3. You are willing to give up something in exchange for something from the other party in the future. 4. You are dealing from a position of weakness. 5. Preserving relationship is important.	1. Issue is important to you. 2. You believe that you are right. 3. The other party is wrong or unethical.
Dominating	1. Issue is trivial. 2. Speedy decision is needed. 3. Unpopular course of action is implemented. 4. Necessary to overcome assertive subordinates. 5. Unfavorable decision by the other party may be costly to you. 6. Subordinates lack expertise to make technical decisions. 7. Issue is important to you.	1. Issue is complex. 2. Issue is not important to you. 3. Both parties are equally powerful. 4. Decision does not have to be made quickly. 5. Subordinates possess high degree of competence.
Avoiding	1. Issue is trivial. 2. Potential dysfunctional effect of confronting the other party outweighs benefits of resolution. 3. Cooling-off period is needed.	1. Issue is important to you. 2. It is your responsibility to make decision. 3. Parties are unwilling to defer. 4. Prompt attention is needed.
Compromising	1. Goals of parties are mutually exclusive. 2. Parties are equally powerful. 3. Consensus cannot be reached. 4. Integrating or dominating style is not successful. 5. Temporary solution to a complex problem is needed.	1. One party is more powerful. 2. Problem is complex enough to need problem-solving approach.

SOURCE: Rahim, M. Afzalur. "Toward a Theory of Managing Organizational Conflict." *International Journal of Conflict Management* 13, no. 3 (October 2003): 206–35. https://DOI: 10.2139/ssrn.437684.

When to Avoid Pamela Valencia, an organizational development consultant and trainer to Fortune 500 companies, recommends avoiding when:

> You decide that the conflict has no value, and that you're better off saving your time and energy for other matters. Additionally, this can be a good temporary solution if you need more time to gather facts, refocus, take a break, or simply change the setting of the conflict. However, be sure not to avoid people in your attempt to avoid conflict—don't be evasive.[76]

Why Styles Matter Because conflict is so pervasive, it is no surprise that researchers and managers have both devoted considerable attention to the topic. Key points about conflict-handling styles follow:

1. **Culture.** Conflict-handling styles are not just an individual-level phenomenon. Departments and entire organizations can develop the same styles—integrating, dominating, and avoiding. And leaders' own styles have the greatest influence in determining which style becomes embedded in the group or organization.

2. **Results.** Cooperative styles (integrating and obliging) improved new-product development performance between buyers and suppliers across several industries in Hong Kong. In contrast, uncooperative styles (dominating and avoiding) increased numerous types of conflicts and hampered new-product development. Compromising had no effect on performance in these same situations.[77] New-product development relationships are increasingly important in the global economy. Give careful consideration to the styles you use when working with such partners.

3. **Reduced turnover.** Research with nurses showed that those with high levels of emotional intelligence were more inclined to use collaborative conflict-handling styles and less likely to use accommodating styles.[78] Given the intense shortage of nurses in many parts of the world, turnover is a critical and top-of-the-mind issue for nursing managers and health care administrators alike. Therefore, reducing conflict (bullying) is an important and effective means for reducing turnover.

4. **You vs. Others.** As you learned regarding personality conflict above, it is important to consider your style versus that of the other person(s) in the conflict. Your styles might be at odds, but it might also be your personalities. The OB in Action box can shed light on this and help.

OB in Action

Maybe It's a Difference in Style, and Maybe It's Yours[79]

The following advice is useful to consider with any type of conflict, but especially if it is personal or you think it is due to differing conflict handling styles.

1. **Look in the Mirror.** First, ask yourself: How am I contributing to this conflict? It is possible "you didn't start it," but often your reaction or inaction played a role.

2. **Styles Alignment.** How does your conflict handling style influence the conflict? What do you think is the conflict handling style of the other person? Use this Information to guide your efforts.

3. **Look for the Sunshine, Not the Rain.** The other person often tries to help resolve the situation;

be sure to look for and acknowledge these efforts. It's as simple as saying, "I know we differ, and I appreciate your attempts to improve the situation."

4. **Talk!** Calmly talking to the person is generally an essential, albeit obvious, part of the solution to any conflict. (Remember, avoiding a conflict rarely makes it go away.)

5. **Keep Communicating.** Too often during conflict people avoid or otherwise limit communication and contact. Don't.

6. **Be Equitable If Not Equal.** The point is to be sure not to single out the person with whom you have a conflict, still include them in meetings, e-mails, and social activities, such as the daily

lunch group if that applies. Separation is a form of avoidance and is often viewed as punishment and escalation.

7. **Agree to Disagree.** Sometimes you just won't agree, and in some proportion of these situations you don't have to. Therefore, consider agreeing to disagree on a particular view or method, and instead focus on the outcome.

YOUR THOUGHTS?

1. Think of a conflict you've had that would benefit from each of the points above.

2. Identify a current conflict and determine which of the above applies and could help.

3. Explain which of the above tactics you would use and how you could apply them to a team on which you are a member at work or school.

In the next section you'll learn about alternative means for resolving conflicts, collectively called ADRs.

Third-Party Interventions: Alternative Dispute Resolution (ADRs)

Disputes between employees, between employees and their managers or employers, and between companies too often end up in lengthy and costly court battles. U.S. businesses spend hundreds of billions of dollars per year on *direct legal costs*, but this number is puny when compared to *indirect legal costs,* such as opportunities not pursued due to litigation concerns, disclaimers, and extra testing. All such costs are ultimately passed on to consumers in the form of higher prices.[80]

A more constructive, less expensive approach called alternative dispute resolution has grown rapidly in recent years. *Alternative dispute resolution (ADR) is a means for solving disputes using an independent third party and avoids the costs and problems associated with litigation or unilateral decision making.*[81]

The Many Forms and Progression of ADR   You may not realize it, but you already know a few forms of ADR, such as peer review, arbitration, and mediation. These techniques represent a progression of steps third parties can take to resolve conflicts, and they have the following benefits when compared to litigation:

1. **Speed.** Mediation, for example, often takes only a few hours and has a 70 to 80 percent success rate. This track record is in stark contrast to the months or even years it can take for cases to get through litigation.

2. **Low cost.** ADRs generally cost 90 percent less than litigation.

3. **Confidentiality.** ADRs provide near-complete control over what's disclosed and what's not, which contrasts with legal proceedings which are in the public record. Moreover, ADR decisions are rarely formalized like the outcomes of lawsuits, which means there is no record to be made public or to use as precedent in future conflicts.

4. **Winning solutions.** Courts decide based on the law, and their decisions are almost always win or lose, with one party writing a check to the other. ADRs, in contrast, can reach win–win solutions arranged by the parties themselves.[82]

Table 10.8 ranks forms of ADR from easiest and least expensive to most difficult and costly.

Read the nearby Problem-Solving Application case and perhaps you'll decide a form of ADR is appropriate. Whether you do or not, Wendy's clearly has a conflict.

TABLE 10.8 Different Forms of Alternative Dispute Resolution (ADR)

FORM OF ADR	DESCRIPTION
Facilitation	A third party, usually a manager, informally urges disputing parties to deal directly with each other in a positive and constructive manner.
Conciliation	A neutral third party informally acts as a communication conduit between disputing parties. This is appropriate when conflicting parties refuse to meet face-to-face. The immediate goal is to establish direct communication, with the broader aim of finding common ground and a constructive solution.
Peer Review	A panel of trustworthy coworkers, selected for their ability to remain objective, hears both sides of a dispute in an informal and confidential meeting. A decision by the review panel may or may not be binding, depending on the company's ADR policy. Membership on the peer review panel often is rotated among employees.[83]
Ombudsman	Someone who works for the organization and is widely respected and trusted by his or her coworkers, hears grievances on a confidential basis and attempts to arrange a solution. This approach, more common in Europe than in North America, permits someone to get help from above without relying on the formal chain of hierarchy.
Mediation	A neutral and trained third party guides the others to find innovative solutions to the conflict. To ensure neutrality, many organizations hire ADR qualified outsiders. Unlike an arbitrator, a mediator does *not* render a decision. It is up to the disputants to reach a mutually acceptable decision. The Equal Employment Opportunity Commission (EEOC) implemented mediation in the 1990s and cut the average time to resolution by 80 percent![84]
Arbitration	Disputing parties agree ahead of time to accept the decision of a neutral arbitrator in a formal court-like setting, often complete with evidence and witnesses. Statements are confidential, and decisions are based on the legal merits of the case. Trained arbitrators, typically from outside agencies such as the American Arbitration Association, are versed in relevant laws and case precedents. In many instances, employee arbitration is mandatory for resolving disputes. Heated debate has occurred over the past several years, however, regarding mandatory versus voluntary arbitration. On the one hand, many employers have not reaped the time and cost savings promised by arbitration and now prefer to litigate. On the other, many employees feel arbitration unfairly benefits employers, who hire skilled arbitrators whose job it is to handle such disputes.[85]

Problem-Solving Application

Food Fight on Campus[86]

A conflict between Wendy's and students at colleges across America is growing and at the root are tomatoes. Protestors are pressuring the hamburger chain to purchase its tomatoes from suppliers who participate In the Fair Food Program (FFP). This program isn't so much about food as it is the farm workers who grow, pick, process, and ship tomatoes.

Who Are the Players and What Is Their Mission?
The FFP is an initiative by the Coalition of Immokalee Workers, which is a worker-based human rights organization that originated in Immokalee, Florida. (You'll learn more about coalitions In Chapter 12.) The coalition's aim is to improve labor standards for farm workers. The goals of the coalition and the FFP are to prevent modern-day slavery,

sexual assault, harassment, unfair compensation, and other abuses rampant in the industry. Advocates of the program claim the FFP and Immokalee have had dramatic and positive effects. For instance, the program now covers about 35,000 workers, largely In Florida, and has raised standards for the tomato industry in that state from one of the lowest to nearly the best in only a decade.

For their part, FFP participants such as Subway, Whole Foods, and Trader Joe's purchase tomatoes only from farmers in the program. They also agree to pay 1 to 4 cents more per pound of tomatoes, and the growers in turn agree to pay workers at least the local minimum wage and a bonus in each paycheck; provide training regarding sexual harassment and assault; offer reasonable working conditions (shade and water) and hours, and a 24-hour independent hotline for complaints; and submit to intensive auditing by third parties.

Why the Beef with Wendy's?   Wendy's is a more recent target of these efforts as they have quit buying from Florida sources and FFP participants. Instead, the company now gets most tomatoes from farms in Mexico where labor standards are much lower. This contrasts with McDonald's, Walmart, and other major brands who buy from FFP suppliers. These factors combine to intensify the conflict. For instance, when major brands, like Wendy's, don't participate it signals to other buyers in the industry it's okay not to purchase from FFP suppliers, which is then interpreted as a lack of concern and oversight of worker well-being.

Wendy's has countered by saying it plans to purchase most of its tomatoes from greenhouse farmers In the U.S. and Canada, but this does little to alleviate the concerns of its critics. They argue conditions in greenhouses are just as inhumane as those found in non-FFP farms, and third party reviews done outside of the FFP are superficial at best.

Pressure Grows   Workers and students have pressured universities to insist Wendy's locations on their campuses sign on to the FFP or be ousted. They are in effect borrowing a page from the playbook used against Taco Bell in the early 2000s, which resulted in that company signing on and being the first major company to do so. Both companies are susceptible to this pressure, as a key segment of their customer base is people in their 20s.

The outcomes are not as simple as yes or no, participate or don't. A student boycott caused a Wendy's franchise at the University of Michigan to not renew its lease. Presumably the franchisee will relocate and purchase outside of the FFP as in the past. Mayors and local legislators in other college towns—University of Florida (Gainesville) and University of North Carolina (Chapel Hill)—have presented resolutions urging Wendy's stores on their campuses to join the FFP. Immokalee workers, along with others, are protesting in some of these same college towns.

Wendy's Is Not Alone   Costco, Publix, and Kroger do not participate in the FFP. For its part, Publix said it views the entire issue as a dispute between its suppliers and their employees, and as such it is not their business. With so many large brands not participating, the market for non-FFP tomatoes is significant, which means despite the challenges for some growers, many others still feel little pressure to ensure higher labor standards in order to sell their products.

Assume you are the CEO of Wendy's and have decided to address this conflict on behalf of the entire company. First, identify with whom the conflict exists, then apply the 3-Step Problem-Solving Approach defining the problem, identifying the causes, and what to do about it. Note: Conflict itself Is not a problem.

Apply the 3-Step Problem-Solving Approach

Step 1:   Define the problem in this case.

Step 2:   Identify the potential causes.

Step 3:   Make your recommendations.

We close this section with a reminder. The time to consider the various forms of ADR is when a conflict first arises. And regardless of the issue, you are wise to evaluate likely costs and opportunities associated with conflict before it escalates and causes legal action, fees, and anger. Once these things happen more functional or constructive outcomes are increasingly difficult.

10.5 NEGOTIATION

THE BIGGER PICTURE

Life is an endless series of negotiations. It therefore is valuable to better understand negotiation and related strategies. We discuss different forms and tactics of negotiation in this section because they are both the cause and remedy of many conflicts. You'll also notice that negotiations can influence outcomes across all three levels of the Organizing Framework.

LO 10-5

Implement your negotiation skills.

Negotiation **is a give-and-take decision-making process between two or more parties with different preferences.** Common negotiations occur over salary, flextime and hours, and job location. Negotiation is even more important today given the increasingly complex and competitive workplace, wherein you're expected to accomplish more things, in more places, with more people, which increases the value of your negotiation skills.

Before we dive into the types of negotiation and other pertinent details, it is important to address how you think of negotiation. Professor Linda Babcock of Carnegie Mellon University and author of *Ask for It: How Women Can Use the Power of Negotiation to Get What They Really Want* explains how many people think of negotiation as a form of conflict, even if only subconsciously. This means they view it in terms of "I have to win or at least avoid losing." As you learned earlier in the chapter, there are many reasons people avoid conflict which means they also are likely to avoid negotiating as frequently or as well as they should.[87]

We therefore encourage you to be mindful and not think of negotiation as a conflict. Instead, framing negotiation as an art, a skill, a task, or even a game can greatly and positively impact your attitude, approach, and outcomes. Let's move on.

Two Basic Types of Negotiation

Negotiation experts often distinguish between two fundamental types of negotiation—position-based (distributive), and interest-based (integrative). Understanding the difference has great practical value.

Position-Based vs. Interest-Based   *A distributive negotiation* **usually concerns a single issue—a "fixed pie"—in which one person gains at the expense of another.**[88] This win–lose approach is arguably the most common type of negotiation and is characterized by dividing up the pieces of a pie. Haggling over the price of a car is a position-based or distributive negotiation. You have a particular price you want, and you get it only if the seller compromises on the price he or she desires.

Many conflicts, however, bring together a variety of interests (not just the price of a car), and each party in the negotiation values those interests differently. The outcome is no longer a fixed pie distributed among all parties, but instead multiple interests are integrated into a mutually satisfying solution. Such scenarios call for *integrative negotiation,* **in which numerous interests are considered, resulting in an agreement that is satisfactory for both parties.**[89] This kind of interest-based negotiation is a more collaborative, problem-solving approach. As one group of researchers puts it, instead of dividing a pie, as in position-based negotiation, interest-based negotiations often generate win–win outcomes—one party gets the crusts and the other the fruit (the part each prefers). Interest-based negotiations may even lead to creative solutions. The parties may decide to build a pie factory together instead of negotiating over individual pies.[90]

TABLE 10.9   Key Characteristics of the Two Fundamental Forms of Negotiation

POSITION-BASED NEGOTIATION	INTEREST-BASED NEGOTIATION
Adversarial	Partner
Focus on winning	Focus on challenge to be met
Acquire the most value	Create value for all parties
Personal goal focused	Solution focused
Impose or sell your own position	Find mutual interests and satisfaction
Use salesmanship and manipulation	Make honest disclosure of respective interests
Choose between relationship and achieving goals	Emphasize relationship and substance
Yield reluctantly to other positions/interests	Be open and willing to yield
Outcomes are win–lose or compromise	Win–win collaborative outcomes are possible

SOURCE: Campbell, Kevin, and Rosemary O'Leary. "Big Ideas for Big Problems: Lessons from Conflict Resolution for Public Administration." *Conflict Resolution Quarterly* 33 (October 2015): 107–19. https://doi.org/10.1002/crq.21146.

Table 10.9 describes some key differences between conventional position-based negotiation and the more collaborative interest-based process.

Applying a Collaborative Interest-Based Approach   The collaborative, interest-based approach is explicitly based on problem solving and can be applied between two or more individuals, between an individual and a group, or between two or more groups. The following protocol is followed by renowned negotiator Christina Merchant.[91]

1. Define and frame the issue in terms of parties' interests.
2. Explain the respective interests (listen, learn, and share).
3. Explore expanding the pie (*create* value rather than claiming it).
4. Generate options.
5. Evaluate options in light of the interests described in step 1.
6. Choose the option that best meets the interests described.
7. Develop and agree on a plan of implementation.

Factors to Consider in All Negotiations   Regardless of your negotiation approach, finding areas of common ground can be difficult. Successful negotiators weigh multiple issues and gather information about which are most important to the other parties and why. Research and practice provide some helpful hints:

- **Know who you are.** Personality matters. Research shows people with high levels of agreeableness are best suited for integrative negotiations, whereas those low in this personality characteristic are better at distributive negotiations.[92] Why do you think this is?

- **Manage outcome expectations.** In most negotiations, each party has an expected outcome and compares it to the actual outcome.[93] Skilled negotiators manage expectations in advance of actual negotiations. For example, if two people paid $35,000 for a car, then the one who expected to pay $33,000 was disappointed and the one who expected to pay $37,000 was delighted. Similarly, managers will often send out a message saying, "It's been a tough year" in advance of annual reviews and salary discussions to help adjust expectations.

- **Consider the other person's outcome.**[94] Of course you negotiate for your own benefit, but it also matters how the other party fares—is he or she satisfied?

Many people say we are negotiating all the time and throughout our lives. Buying a car is one such instance. These transactions are excellent opportunities to apply your OB knowledge and improve your outcomes—more car for less money.

Adam Gault /OJO Images Ltd/Alamy Stock Photo

- **Adhere to standards of justice.**[95] Not only do the outcomes need to be perceived as fair (distributive justice), but so too do the processes by which they were attained. No one likes to be taken advantage of, which can happen when they have incomplete information. Again, think of buying a new car where the dealer knows all the numbers, and despite the best information the Web has to offer, you are still never as well informed.

- **Remember your reputation.**[96] You may "win" today only to foreclose opportunities in the future. Put another way, winning at all costs often has significant costs!

Considering these factors can help you decide whether you should pursue a particular position (you win, they lose), or if you're better off reaching an interest-based agreement that leaves both parties satisfied. The OB in Action box provides an opportunity to apply your knowledge.

OB in Action

Who Is Going to Eat More Pie, Writers or Agents?[97]

When you watch shows on TV or your device, three of the major players involved in their creation are writers, agents, and studios. Writers write, studios buy, and agents are in between making these deals happen. The Writers' Guild (a union representing thousands of writers for TV and movies) and the Association of Talent Agents (a union representing major agencies) are locked in a heated battle over the terms of their agreement that have been in place since the mid-1970's.

Issues. Writers have two principle complaints and are willing to go on strike to affect change. First, they take issue with agents "packaging" a group of writers for a given project. The agents get paid a packaging fee by the studios, in exchange for arranging all of the writers for a project, saving the studio from having to identify and negotiate with each writer individually. From the studios' perspective this is more efficient and perhaps, but not necessarily, less costly. The writers, however, argue this money should go to them and not the agents. Their position is reinforced by the claim compensation for their work is either stagnant or declining, despite the current time period being heralded as high-times for TV, due in large part to streaming service expanding the TV universe and generating demand for more content (writers and their writing).

Second, a number of major agencies (William Morris Endeavor, Creative Artists, and United Talent) are now producing their own shows, which historically has only been done by studios. This means they now generate their own content, what writers provide, which then is sold to studios. Writers claim this is a conflict of interest as they are now competing with the people who are supposed to represent them and sell their work.

Potential Actions. The contract formalizing the arrangement has expired, and if the agencies don't come around the writers have been instructed to fire agencies, work directly with studios, and do their own deals on their own terms. For their part, agencies have threatened to sue claiming it is unlawful (in some states) for writers' managers and attorneys to act as agents. Also, the agents are unwilling to give up the practices challenged by the writers.

YOUR THOUGHTS?

1. What would you do if you were representing the writers? The agencies? Explain.

2. Which conflict handling style do you think is most suitable for each representative?

3. Do you think this scenario is best suited for a distributive, integrative, or ADR approach? Explain.

Many people believe good negotiators show no emotion, like Roger Federer on the tennis court. But as you've learned, emotions are an integral part of the human experience and of almost everything we do. Let us learn how they affect negotiations next.

Emotions and Negotiations

Negotiation experts and researchers provide guidance on how to use emotions to your advantage. Remember that emotions are contagious. If you want the other party to be calm, creative, or energetic, consider showing these emotions yourself.[98]

Preparation is critical to effective negotiations. The following tips can help you prepare emotionally for an upcoming negotiation.

1. **Identify your ideal emotions.** How do you want to feel going into the negotiation? Why? Many people answer this question quickly and say, "calm but assertive," but when probed further they reveal other, if not competing, emotions. The challenge is to realize which emotions will best suit your objectives and be mindful of them while negotiating.

2. **Manage your emotions.** What can you do in advance to put yourself in the ideal emotional state? Promote positive emotions. Choose appropriately—meditation to calm you down or perhaps music that pumps you up. If you are ambushed or put on the spot, such as by an unexpected phone call or somebody stopping by your office, buy some time and say to your negotiating partner, "I just need to wrap up what I'm doing, and I'll call you back in 10 minutes." This will give you time to regain the appropriate emotional state.

3. **Know your hot buttons.** What can throw you off balance? Some people seem eternally patient, others get frustrated easily, and some negotiators try to push your hot buttons as a deliberate tactic. Know your own tendencies and be sure to manage them appropriately.

4. **Keep your balance.** Everyone loses balance occasionally. How will you regain yours if lost? Taking a break is a good idea. Stepping out, going to the restroom, or simply calling a "time-out" can provide a break in the action and enable you to regroup. These same tactics can redirect a negotiation that has gone in the wrong direction. You may also want to redirect to higher-level issues, especially if you are getting bogged down in details.

5. **Identify your takeaway emotions.** How do you want to feel when you're finished? Many people say, "relieved," which signifies the stress many of us feel while negotiating.

Others say, "satisfied," which speaks more to performance. Whatever the case for you, set goals for emotions just as you do for other outcomes in negotiations (and in the Organizing Framework).[99]

Do emotions affect position-based and interest-based negotiations differently? The answer appears to be yes. Research showed expressing emotional ambivalence—not clearly positive or clearly negative—can be detrimental in position-based negotiations. The rationale is that it invites the other side to be assertive and take advantage of you. However, in interest-based negotiations emotional ambivalence was shown to increase value creation. Being ambivalent, rather than clearly positive or negative emotionally, tends to facilitate cooperation and allow you the opportunity to integrate the negotiators' interests.[100]

Nonverbal communications also help convey your emotions during negotiations. You can smile, laugh, or flinch in reaction to a first offer, for example. These actions signal your counterpart that his or her proposal is unacceptable.[101]

Although the Winning at Work feature at the beginning of this chapter addressed negotiating salaries and pay raises, we feel the topic is so important that we offer additional insights at the end of this negotiation section. Our intention is for you to combine the knowledge you've acquired throughout the chapter to become more effective, and to this end we describe exchanges and associated scripts to help during these crucial conversations in the following Applying OB box.

Applying OB

How to Ask for More Money[102]

Knowing what to say can build your efficacy (Chapter 3) and shape a more positive attitude (Chapter 4) around your negotiations, which by themselves are likely to improve the outcomes of your efforts. The scripts below are equally useful when used via e-mail, over the phone, or face-to-face.

Salary Discussions During the Interview

Interviewer: "What's your current salary?"

Your responses: "I'm not really comfortable sharing that information. I would prefer to focus on the value I can add to this company and not what I'm paid at my current job." (Note: Such questions are increasingly illegal In many states.)

Interviewer: "What's your expected salary?"

Your response: "I want this move to a be a big step forward for me in terms of both responsibility and compensation."

Note: If a prospective employer seems hung up on or overly determined to learn your current pay and expectations, this may be a red flag, suggesting they are trying to underpay and get a bargain. Beware.

Getting More After Receiving an Offer: The Counter Offer

Josh Doody, author of *Fearless Salary Negotiation,* recommends considering four elements when determining your counter request: (1) salary offered, (2) your minimum acceptable salary (your walk away number), (3) your perception of how bad they want you to accept, and (4) how bad you need/want the job.

Prospective employer: The company offered you $45,000.

My response: "I appreciate the offer. I however feel $50,000 would more accurately reflect the importance and expectations for this position, especially considering my qualifications and experience."

If you're fortunate enough to have an actual offer from another company, then consider saying:

"Thank you for this offer. As I mentioned during the interview process, I'm speaking with multiple companies. If you're able to adjust your offer to $50,000, then I would be eager to accept."

The company's counter will likely be somewhere in between, in which case Doody recommends anticipating these amounts and creating a script. For instance, using the example above, if the company comes back with $49,000 accept outright.

If the company comes back with a lower number and seems firm, consider accepting that number along with something else of value to you, such as vacation time, working from home, or a signing bonus. Identify and prioritize your preferences so you know the appropriate order and value. For example:

> Company: "The best we can do is $47,500."
>
> Your response: "I understand that is the most you can offer in terms of salary, but if you can add in an extra week of vacation time, then I'm on board."

If they say, no, then move to your second most valuable benefit, perhaps working from home one day per week or a $4,000 signing bonus. Once they agree, you're finished. Don't try for more.

Asking for a Raise

Typically, the motive for asking is you feel your value to the company has increased over time and is not reflected in your salary. Put differently, your salary was set some time ago, and now you have more experience and have made real contributions. Doody recommends making the request via e-mail.

> "Boss, during our next meeting I would like to discuss compensation. It has been X period of time since I was hired or received a raise, and I would like to revisit my compensation now that I'm contributing more to the company. I've done some research and it appears the mid-point for this job in this industry is $Y. I thus would like to request a pay raise to (insert target amount)."

It is a good idea to include your accomplishments and justification for the raise in addition to the market value of the job. Realize, however, *the raise is for you, not the job*.

"Always remember, your talent Is precious, and you deserve to be compensated for It. Learning to foster conversations about compensation is a vital skill that yields rewards."

Now let's close this section and chapter with a discussion of ethics and negotiations.

Ethics and Negotiations

Many people believe ethical negotiations are impossible, as individuals are self-interested and will lie or otherwise deceive the other party the vast majority of the time in order to get their desired outcome. (See Table 10.10 for a list of common questionable and unethical

TABLE 10.10 Questionable and Unethical Tactics in Negotiations

TACTIC	DESCRIPTION/CLARIFICATION/RANGE
Lies	Subject matter for lies can include limits, alternatives, the negotiator's intent, authority to bargain, other commitments, acceptability of the opponent's offers, time pressures, and available resources.
Puffery	Among the items that can be puffed up are the value of one's payoffs to the opponent, the negotiator's own alternatives, the costs of what one is giving up or is prepared to yield, importance of issues, and attributes of the products or services.
Deception	Acts and statements may include promises or threats, excessive initial demands, careless misstatements of facts, or asking for concessions not wanted.
Weakening the opponent	The negotiator here may cut off or eliminate some of the opponent's alternatives, blame the opponent for his own actions, use personally abrasive statements to or about the opponent, or undermine the opponent's alliances.
Strengthening one's own position	This tactic includes building one's own resources, including expertise, finances, and alliances. It also includes presentations of persuasive rationales to the opponent or third parties (e.g., the public, the media) or getting mandates for one's position.
Nondisclosure	Includes partial disclosure of facts, failure to disclose a hidden fact, failure to correct the opponents' misperceptions or ignorance, and concealment of the negotiator's own position or circumstances.
Information exploitation	Information provided by the opponent can be used to exploit his weaknesses, close off his alternatives, generate demands against him, or weaken his alliances.
Maximization	Includes demanding the opponent make concessions that result in the negotiator's gain and the opponent's equal or greater loss. Also entails converting a win–win situation into win–lose.

negotiation tactics.) Accordingly, most negotiation research focuses on and shows that unethical tactics may have short term benefits but generally long-term costs, notably, reduced trustworthiness and financial gains, as well as increased motivation by the deceived to retaliate.[103] But reality isn't that simple. Like many other processes and outcomes in the Organizing Framework, the causes of unethical negotiation behaviors can be both person and situation factors.

Person Factors and Ethical Negotiations.   Personality has been extensively studied and linked to first impressions of and satisfaction with negotiation partners, distributive and integrative negotiation success, and speed of reaching final agreements, among others. An especially relevant individual difference is *moral character,* **which represents an individual's general tendency to think, feel, and behave in ways associated with ethical and unethical behavior.**[104] As such, the assumption is that people with high moral character are less likely to use the questionable tactics (see Table 10.10) and will instead have more ethical and positive negotiation related attitudes, motives, and behaviors.[105]

Situation Factors and Ethical Negotiations.   However, as you know by now, situation factors often influence person factors to produce outcomes different from what you might expect. The same is true for negotiations. Incentives and dysfunctional competition—where one party goes to any means to win—can influence otherwise well-intentioned ethical negotiators. Also interesting is that groups tend to lie more often than individuals, which suggests you may want to be especially careful when negotiating between teams, departments, or organizations.[106] The rationale is the responsibility (guilt) is shared or diffused among many people, as would any potential consequences.

Well, What's the Answer?   After considering all of this, you're likely still left wondering—how do I determine what is ethical and what is not during negotiations? Sadly, the answer isn't simple either, but research provides three criteria to consider.[107]

1. *Intent.* If the deception is pro-social (benefits the target) it may be considered ethical, whereas if information is withheld for your personal benefit then you have likely crossed the line. When or why might you do deceive someone for their benefit? To build goodwill, show good faith, because you're generous, or because the other person may indeed benefit more than you.

2. *Content.* Modifying your emotions to achieve a better outcome is viewed by many as more acceptable than it is to change, omit, or lie about information. For instance, faking great disappointment with the process, offer, or outcome, or alternatively pretending to like the person illustrate deceptive emotions. Information can be manipulated by providing false prices or dollar amounts (the most you'll pay or the least you'll accept), or actually fabricating false information or lying about facts. Put more simply, change your emotions but not the facts.

3. *Activity.* Lies of omission occur when one fails to reveal relevant information, and lies of commission are just that, lies, as we commonly understand them—offering false information. "The car's transmission is like new," when in fact it isn't and has never been serviced is a lie of commission. A lie of omission would be not telling the buyer that the transmission has problems when you know it does.

One last thing to consider. Assume you're searching for a job and have no offers in hand. Would you still tell a prospective employer you *do* have concrete offers? Or, assume you've been offered the job and the salary is $60,000. Would you say you have another and higher offer, even if you didn't, in an attempt to get the other party to boost the salary? Are these tactics ethical? It might be worth answering these questions for yourself.

Let's close the chapter with some practical and pointed applications.

10.6 MAKING THE CONNECTION: HOW CAN MANAGING CONFLICT AND NEGOTIATING GIVE ME AN ADVANTAGE?

THE BIGGER PICTURE

We conclude this chapter with a number of practical applications for managing conflict and negotiations to improve your effectiveness as both an employee and manager.

Takeaways for Me

We highlight eight practical nuggets for you.

LO 10-6

Describe the implications of managing conflict and negotiations for you and managers.

1. **Realize that not all conflict is bad or should be avoided.** Some amount of functional conflict is desirable and can help you develop as an individual. Be especially mindful of this if you run your own business or wish to do so someday. Conflict can lead to growth.

2. **Be sure to tend to dysfunctional conflict and don't allow it to escalate, costing you jobs and relationships.**

3. **Personality conflicts are almost certain to happen.** Table 10.3 can be helpful in dealing with them.

4. **Be mindful of work–school–family conflicts.** The way you manage them can dramatically affect your personal fulfillment and flourishing in life. Do what you can to balance demands from the various arenas of your life and look for companies that are also mindful of this and have family-friendly policies *and leaders.*

5. **Beware of the many forms of incivility at work.** Don't underestimate their causes and effects. Beyond what your employer requires through policies and practices, civility, like ethical conduct, starts with the behavior of individuals. Table 10.6 can help clarify what to do.

6. **Use your knowledge of conflict-handling styles and your own preferences to be more effective when dealing with groups and teams.** Table 10.7 is an excellent guide to which style to use in a given situation.

7. **Continue to expand your knowledge and skill using interest-based negotiations.** Doing so can help you avoid and overcome the resistance common in position-based negotiations. You're often better off to approach the other parties as partners than adversaries.

8. **The knowledge and tools in this chapter are essential if you hope to manage people effectively.** Apply your knowledge and build your skills!

Takeaways for Managers

We provide seven practical steps for you as a manager.

1. **Distinguish between conflict states and conflict processes.** Doing so will make you more effective at avoiding and remedying conflict as a manager.

2. **Managing intergroup conflict can make or break your own opportunities and successes.** Perhaps the single best way to prevent such conflicts, as well as to deal with them, is to create a psychologically safe climate.

3. **Beware of the many forms of incivility at work.** As a manager you are responsible for knowing what is happening, intervening, and following up. Do not underestimate how destructive incivility is to individuals, your team, and your larger organization. Not only the targets suffer. Your own actions are the single most powerful tool you have. Don't tolerate bad behavior. Use Table 10.6 as a guide.

4. **Utilize devil's advocacy and the dialectic method to arrive at better decisions and be more inclusive.**

5. **Use your knowledge of conflict-handling styles and of your own preferences to become more effective when dealing with groups and teams.** Table 10.7 is an excellent guide for which style to use in a given situation.

6. **Become familiar with the alternative dispute resolution choices and use the appropriate remedy** (Table 10.8).

7. **Taking an interest-based approach to negotiating with those you manage, and more generally with those with whom you work, can improve their level of trust in you and thereby boost your effectiveness.**

To summarize, conflict and negotiations are affected by and in turn influence many elements in the Organizing Framework. They can determine your personal satisfaction and performance throughout your professional life. Apply your knowledge of conflict and negotiation to realize its true value and enhance your own effectiveness.

What Did I Learn?

In this chapter you learned that by managing conflict and applying sound principles in negotiation, you gain an advantage in working for better outcomes at work, school, and home, and across all levels of organizations. Reinforce and consolidate your learning with the Key Points and Organizing Framework. Then challenge your mastery of the material by completing the Problem-Solving Application Case and Legal/Ethical Challenge.

Key Points for Understanding Chapter 10

You learned the following key points:

10.1 A CONTEMPORARY VIEW OF CONFLICT

- Conflict is the energy created by the perceived gap between what we want and what we're experiencing.
- Conflict can be either functional or dysfunctional.
- People avoid conflict for many reasons; however, doing so can cause it to escalate.

10.2 CONVENTIONAL FORMS OF CONFLICT

- Common forms of conflict are personality and intergroup.
- Personality conflicts can be overcome with or without the help of others.
- Contact and safety climates can help prevent intergroup conflict.

10.3 FORMS OF CONFLICT INTENSIFIED BY TECHNOLOGY

- Work–life conflict is the perception expectations and demands between work and nonwork roles are mutually incompatible.
- Designate time, designate space, and share responsibilities to help overcome work–life conflict.

- Incivility (bullying and harassment) has negative consequences not only for targeted employees but also for coworkers who witness it.

10.4 EFFECTIVELY MANAGING CONFLICT

- Functional conflict can be fostered using programmed conflict, devil's advocacy, and the dialectic method.
- Five common conflict-handling styles are integrating, obliging, dominating, avoiding, and compromising.
- Forms of alternative dispute resolution (ADR) include facilitation, conciliation, peer-review, ombudsman, mediation, and arbitration.

10.5 NEGOTIATION

- Negotiation is a give-and-take decision-making process involving two or more parties with different preferences.
- Position-based negotiation focuses on a single issue and dividing a fixed pie.
- Interest-based negotiation seeks agreements that serve both parties varied interests.
- Emotions and ethics affect negotiations.

10.6 HOW CAN MANAGING CONFLICT AND NEGOTIATING GIVE ME AN ADVANTAGE?

- Understanding and dealing with conflict is critical to your job and career success.
- An inability to manage conflict is a common reason managers don't succeed or advance to higher levels of responsibility.

The Organizing Framework for Chapter 10

As shown in Figure 10.6, you learned that conflict is an inevitable part of organizational life and serves as an especially important group/team-level process in the Organizing Framework. The way you manage conflict can influence outcomes across all levels of OB. You also learned the process of negotiation is a valuable tool for preventing and managing conflict, as well as achieving goals.

FIGURE 10.6 Organizing Framework for Understanding and Applying OB

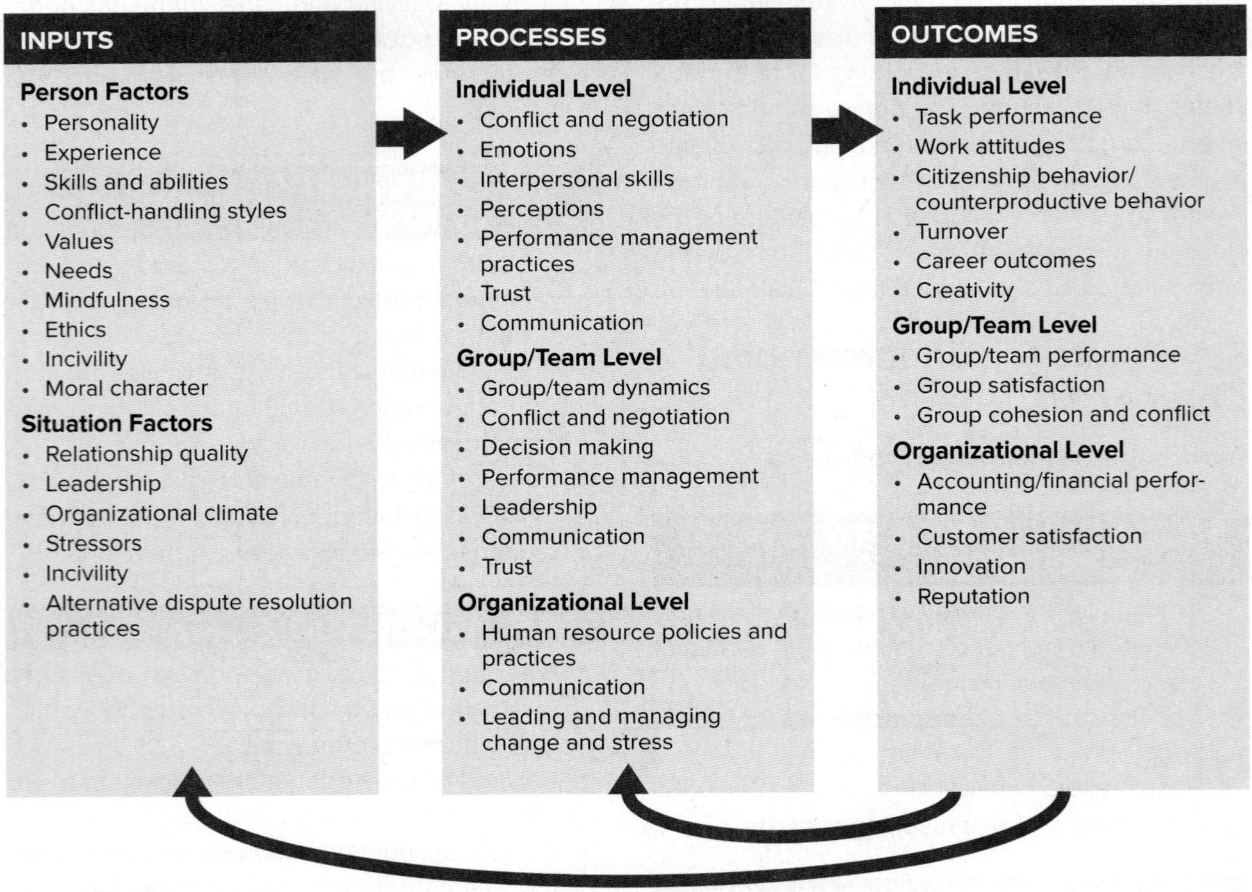

INPUTS	PROCESSES	OUTCOMES
Person Factors • Personality • Experience • Skills and abilities • Conflict-handling styles • Values • Needs • Mindfulness • Ethics • Incivility • Moral character **Situation Factors** • Relationship quality • Leadership • Organizational climate • Stressors • Incivility • Alternative dispute resolution practices	**Individual Level** • Conflict and negotiation • Emotions • Interpersonal skills • Perceptions • Performance management practices • Trust • Communication **Group/Team Level** • Group/team dynamics • Conflict and negotiation • Decision making • Performance management • Leadership • Communication • Trust **Organizational Level** • Human resource policies and practices • Communication • Leading and managing change and stress	**Individual Level** • Task performance • Work attitudes • Citizenship behavior/counterproductive behavior • Turnover • Career outcomes • Creativity **Group/Team Level** • Group/team performance • Group satisfaction • Group cohesion and conflict **Organizational Level** • Accounting/financial performance • Customer satisfaction • Innovation • Reputation

With Trouble Comes Conflict, and with Conflict Comes Trouble

Facebook's meteoric growth and central role in revolutionizing social media has been overshadowed in recent years by its many controversies, such as the company's role related to influencing the presidential election in 2016, the improper harvesting and use of nearly 90 million user accounts by Cambridge Analytica, and the widespread concerns by users and regulators that the company insufficiently protects its more than 2.2 billion users' data and privacy. These issues are significant, as they can and have cost the company users, advertising revenues, damage to its reputation, along with fines and restriction from regulators. Adding to the troubles, top level executives like Mark Zuckerberg and Sheryl Sandberg's conduct has been questioned on ethical grounds for how they've responded.[108]

PRECIOUS JEWELS, NOW COSTLY CONFLICT

However, the issues that grab fewer headlines but perhaps signal other significant troubles are the departures of key executives of companies Facebook has acquired, notably Instagram and WhatsApp. Facebook bought Instagram in 2012 for $1 billion, when it had only a few employees and about 30 million users. It now has 1 billion users and an estimated value of $100 billion if it were independent. WhatsApp was purchased in 2014 for $19 billion at a time when it had approximately 50 employees and about 450 million users. Just two years later the number was over 1 billion users. These acquisitions have been central to Facebook's strategy and growth, but the founders of these two companies (Jan Koum and Brian Acton of WhatsApp, and Kevin Systom and Mike Krieger of Instagram) have all left in the period of a few months, signaling conflict and trouble at the social networking icon.[109]

HARMONIOUS AUTONOMY

The founders of both Instagram and WhatsApp stayed in place for several years after their companies were acquired, which is not the norm given many cash out and leave. They however were allowed to run their companies much as they had, maintaining autonomy and the ability to creatively realize their visions for the companies they created. For WhatsApp founders, Koum and Acton, their passion was the privacy of communication. WhatsApp's encrypted messaging service exploded in parts of the world where messaging services were either expensive or social networks like Facebook had not penetrated. Mr. Koum, in particular, valued secure communication due to his upbringing in the Soviet Union where everyone was monitored all of the time. The founders continued to develop WhatsApp's end-to-end encryption after the Facebook acquisition, avoided advertising, and maintained offices separate from Facebook's campus. In fact, WhatsApp's offices do not even bear the company's name; how about that for dedication to privacy?

As for Instagram, Systom and Krieger also preserved considerable autonomy over the app and grew advertising revenues to $6 billion in 2018. The app is growing and is particularly popular with younger people. Despite the controversies consuming Facebook and Zuckerberg, the founders' relationship with Zuckerberg seemed harmonious and was often touted by Zuckerberg and others as a model for how to acquire and work with small tech companies.

ZUCKERBERG ASSERTS CONTROL

Facebook, fairly or not, is equated with its founder, Mr. Zuckerberg, who maintains control and largely determines the direction and structure of the company he founded. And therein lies the source of many of the conflicts. Zuckerberg envisions integrating Facebook's apps (Messenger, WhatsApp, and Instagram) which will require the sharing of user data between the products in ways not done previously. Part of this effort has included reorganizing senior management and installing Adam Mosseri as VP of product design at Instagram, a role previously filled by the founders. But it didn't stop there. Zuckerberg also inserted Chris Cox, Facebook's chief product officer, between him and Systom and Krieger, which many internal to Instagram viewed as a move to put a trusted "Facebook first" person in place to control the direction and guard against the departure of the founders.

CONFLICTS GROW AND FOUNDERS EXIT

Instagram's founders increasingly disagreed with Zuckerberg and other Facebook executives during meetings, and although historically quite cordial, the disagreements became more severe and spilled over onto internal message boards. As for WhatsApp, Zuckerberg is determined for the app to start using advertising and making money, which requires sharing user data between the apps. Koum had taken issue with how data was used by social media companies, especially by Facebook, and abruptly resigned. As one reporter put it: "Instead of changing his values, Mr. Koum is leaving Facebook."[110] His departure was further complicated due to his seat on Facebook's board of directors (he resigned).

In the period of only a few months all of the founders of these crown jewel acquisitions had left. Although some of the motives were unique to individual executives, they appeared to share a growing dissatisfaction with Zuckerberg and the direction of the company. Power and decision making were shifting away to others and becoming more centralized. It is likely the departing executives felt their objections would not prevail and resistance would be futile.

THE PROBLEM IS BIGGER AND THE CONFLICTS MORE NUMEROUS

The problem is not just confined to WhatsApp and Instagram. Justin Rosenstein (creator of the "like" button), Chamath Palihapitiya (head of user growth), and Sandy Parakilas (platform operations manager) have all left. They, too, have taken issue with protection of data and privacy, the use of the platforms to manipulate thought and behavior, as well as the lack of personal accountability by executives. Their issues reflect a growing concern across the industry about increased growth and connectivity, but at what cost. Zuckerberg and other social media executives are being pressed to justify if not alter their own values, or at least the practices of their companies, related to data protection, usage, and privacy.[111]

Some view the conflicts and departures of key executives as pushback against Zuckerberg's mission for Facebook, to "make the world more open and connected." Increasingly, as described in this case, important players both inside and outside the company are taking issue with the means for reaching this end. Zuckerberg, as the founder and face of the company, is now forced to confront challenges and genuine conflict on many fronts, and how effectively he does this will determine the direction, path, and outcomes for years to come.

Assume you are Mark Zuckerberg, and you can go back in time before the departures of these key executives. Apply the knowledge and tools in this chapter and the 3-Step Problem-Solving Approach to determine how you would deal with the conflicts described above.

APPLY THE 3-STEP PROBLEM-SOLVING APPROACH TO OB

Use the Organizing Framework in Figure 10.6 and the 3-Step Problem-Solving Approach to help identify inputs, processes, and outcomes relative to this case.

STEP 1: Define the problem.

A. Look first at the Outcomes box of the Organizing Framework to help identify the important problem(s) in this case. Remember that a problem is a gap between a desired and current state. State your problem as a gap and be sure to consider problems at all three levels. If more than one desired outcome is not being accomplished, decide which one is most important and focus on it for steps 2 and 3.

B. Cases have key players, and problems are generally viewed from a particular player's perspective. You need to determine from whose perspective—employee, manager, team, or the organization—you're defining the problem. In this case you're asked to assume the role of CEO Mark Zuckerberg.

C. Use details in the case to determine the key problem. Don't assume, infer, or create problems not included in the case.

D. To refine your choice, ask yourself, *why is this a problem?* Explaining why helps refine and focus your thinking. Focus on topics in the current chapter, because we generally select cases illustrating concepts specifically located within the current chapter.

STEP 2: Identify causes.

Using material from this chapter and summarized in the Organizing Framework, identify the causes of the problem you identified in Step 1. Remember, causes tend to appear in either the Inputs or Processes boxes.

A. Start by looking at the Organizing Framework (Figure 10.6) and decide which person factors, if any, are most likely causes of the defined problem. For each cause, explain why this is a cause of the problem. Asking *why* multiple times is more likely to lead you to root causes of the problem. For example, do executive characteristics help explain the problem you defined in Step 1?

B. Follow the same process for the situation factors. For each ask yourself, *why is this a cause?* By asking why multiple times you are likely to arrive at a complete and more accurate list of causes. Again, look to the Organizing Framework for this chapter for guidance. Did particular policies or practices play a role?

C. Now consider the Processes box in the Organizing Framework. Are any processes at the individual, group/team, or organizational level potential causes of your defined problem? For any process you consider, ask yourself, *why is this a cause?* Again, do this for several iterations to arrive at the root causes.

D. To check the accuracy or appropriateness of the causes, be sure to map them onto the defined problem and confirm the link or cause and effect connection.

STEP 3: Recommend solutions.
Make your recommendations for solving the problem. Consider whether you want to resolve it, solve it, or dissolve it (see Section 1.5). Which recommendation is desirable and feasible?

A. Given the causes you identified in Step 2, what are your best recommendations? Use material in the current chapter that best suits the cause. Consider the OB in Action and Applying OB boxes, because these contain insights into what others have done.

B. Be sure to consider the Organizing Framework—both person and situation factors—as well as processes at different levels.

C. Create an action plan for implementing your recommendations and be sure your recommendations map onto the causes and resolve the problem.

LEGAL/ETHICAL CHALLENGE

Arbitrate or Litigate? Employees Now Have a Choice

If you haven't actually been involved in arbitration, then you might be surprised to know you have likely agreed to this form of alternative dispute resolution (ADR) many times without knowing it. Most cell phone, cable, Internet, online shopping, and credit card agreements have contained arbitration clauses for quite some time. In the fine print of their service agreements are buried the words, "The company may elect to resolve any claim by individual arbitration." This means you agree to be bound by the decision of a third party, often hired by the company against which you have a complaint. You cannot take matters to court, which also means you cannot band together with coworkers in a class action suit.[112]

Arbitration agreements are frequently included in employment contracts with little or no room to negotiate the terms. The potential benefit of maintaining the confidentiality of the matters and people involved can be negated by the inability to appeal decisions. Moreover, the confidentiality element (also governed by nondisclosure agreements—NDAs) has come under fire most recently for shielding the perpetrators of sexual harassment and assault, such as those disclosed in the #MeToo movement.

Google, along with Adobe and Intuit, made headlines when they eliminated forced arbitration for all employee disputes. This is seen as a tectonic event. Such agreements typically give the employer an enormous advantage, as they have skill and experience in arbitrating, as well as financial resources, that

employees typically lack. For instance, research shows employees on average receive larger settlements in court than in arbitration.[113]

Changes at tech, and other, companies have been motivated by protests over mandatory arbitration protecting executives and their employers from the embarrassment and costs associated with sexual harassment. This is viewed as a victory for employees who can now more effectively pursue claims of discrimination, wage theft and overtime issues, or many other employee-employer disputes.[114]

However, it is important to recall the benefits of arbitration: time, cost, and confidentiality (sometimes names and offenses are best left out of public view). And Google did not eliminate mandatory arbitration for its contract workers who comprise approximately half of its workforce.

What Should Be Done?

1. Nothing. Allow companies to include arbitration agreements in employment contracts as they choose. Explain your reasoning.

2. Modify the arbitration agreements to better protect employees. Explain your recommended modifications.

3. Do away with arbitration agreements in employment contracts just as Google and other companies have done. Justify.

4. Create and explain other alternatives.

11

Decision Making and Creativity

After reading this chapter, you should be able to:

LO 11-1   Compare rational and nonrational models of decision making.

LO 11-2   Describe eight decision-making biases.

LO 11-3   Explain evidence-based decision making.

LO 11-4   Compare the four styles of decision making.

LO 11-5   Describe how to assess the ethics of decision making.

LO 11-6   Outline the basics of group decision making.

LO 11-7   Explain how creativity relates to decision making.

LO 11-8   Describe the implications of decision making and creativity for you and managers.

Throughout this book we encourage you to use the Organizing Framework to solve problems, a skill recruiters say college graduates need.[1] The goal of this chapter is to further help you develop your problem-solving skills. The Organizing Framework in Figure 11.1 summarizes what you will learn in this chapter. Although the chapter focuses on decision making, which is an individual- and group/team-level process, a host of person and situation factors influence it. Figure 11.1 further shows that many other individual, group/team, and organizational level processes impact how we make decisions. We will touch on many of these in the sections to come. Finally, take note of how the various decision-making processes affect numerous individual, group/team, and organizational level outcomes.

FIGURE 11.1   Organizing Framework for Understanding and Applying OB

INPUTS	PROCESSES	OUTCOMES
Person Factors • Intuition • Judgmental heuristics • Decision-making styles • Ethical values • Personality • Self-efficacy • National culture **Situation Factors** • Decision situation • Organizational culture • Organizational climate	**Individual Level** • Rational/nonrational decision making • Ethical decision making • Creativity **Group/Team Level** • Rational/nonrational decision making • Groupthink • Minority dissent • Consensus • Creativity **Organizational Level** • Evidence-based decision making • Creativity	**Individual Level** • Task performance • Career outcomes • Creativity **Group/Team Level** • Group/team performance • Group cohesion and conflict **Organizational Level** • Accounting/financial performance • Legal liability • Innovation • Customer satisfaction

Decision making and problem solving affect all aspects of our lives. Consider the success of a basketball team. Here we see a coach meeting with her team to discuss strategies to defeat the opposing team. Making effective decisions during the game can make the difference between winning and losing.
Randy Faris/Corbis/Getty Images

Winning at Work

How to Practice Critical Thinking for Decision Making

We make decisions every day. Some are minor—bring the umbrella or not? Others are consequential, like your choice of career, and others can be life-changing. This chapter explores types of decisions, useful models and tools for management decision making, and logical biases and other problems that can get in the way of making good decisions.

One skill that underlies all good decision making, however, and one you can begin practicing right now, is critical thinking, the application of logic and reasoning to problem solving. Here are some tips:

1. **Get all available facts.** Decisions made in the absence of facts are often flawed, based on biased thinking or guesswork, or overly reliant on emotional responses to an uncertain situation. Getting reliable factual information from several different sources is an essential first step.

2. **Understand your motive.** This means being clear about whether you've sought objective information or merely validation of what you already believe. If you're looking for validation, you're not thinking critically, and you need to ask yourself why. You may be heading for a biased decision.[2]

3. **Reconsider the facts.** Look objectively at the facts. If you are basing your decision on some unavoidable assumptions, for instance, ask yourself how valid they are in light of objective reality. How often do circumstances like yours lead to the outcome you're hoping for? Learning about probability (the measure of an event's likelihood of occurring) can help you avoid many of the cognitive biases this chapter will discuss.[3]

4. **Expect to be wrong.** Realize that no one is right all the time. (Most of us are wrong surprisingly often.) Instead of seeing this as a roadblock, use it to avoid the mistake of overconfidence. Ask for and listen to others' opinions, reconsider your own logic, and be open to the possibility that you could change your mind.[4]

5. **Choose your course of action.** If you've collected facts, looked at them objectively, made sure you're not just confirming your own opinion, and listened carefully to input from others, you're ready to make a decision as grounded in critical thinking as possible.

Another useful idea that roughly parallels these suggestions is the "six thinking hats" strategy popularized by Edward De Bono.[5] The six hats are symbols in a step-by-step decision process that asks you to imagine putting on a different-colored hat for each step. The white hat is first and calls for you to focus on the available facts and keep your thinking free of bias, just as white is free of color. Next, the black hat allows you to think negatively and assess which ideas won't work, followed by the yellow hat, which focuses on the positive (think sunshine) and the potential for opportunity.

Like the shoots of a new plant, the next hat is green for creativity and insights from outside-the-box thinking, while red, suggesting hearts, puts emotion in the picture so you can test your intuition and feelings. The last hat is blue like the sky and signals it's time to put all ideas together into an action plan that will fly. One advantage of De Bono's strategy is that sequentially imagining the six hats helps keep members of decision-making groups focused on the same step at the same time. And it offers a good blueprint for individuals making decisions, too.

Six different colored hats symbolize a popular step-by-step decision process.
YolLusZam1802/Shutterstock

What's Ahead in This Chapter

We contrast rational and nonrational decision making and explain why it's important to understand both. We also show you eight decision-making biases and the benefits of evidence-based decision making. We explain why companies are leveraging big data and utilizing artificial intelligence to make decisions. Next we discuss general decision-making styles and ethical decision making. We conclude by distinguishing the pros and cons of group decision making, group problem-solving techniques, and the process of creativity. All this information will help you improve your ability to make decisions.

11.1 RATIONAL AND NONRATIONAL MODELS OF DECISION MAKING

THE BIGGER PICTURE

Decision making is a key process within the Organizing Framework for Understanding and Applying OB. The process varies along a continuum of rational to nonrational. Four steps in making rational decisions are (1) identify the problem, (2) generate alternative solutions, (3) evaluate alternatives and select a solution, and (4) implement and evaluate the solution. Examples of nonrational models include (1) satisficing and (2) intuition.

Decision making matters deeply in your personal and work life. Let's consider the impact of decisions made by a few college graduates during the interview process. One job applicant took a nonemergency call on his smartphone 15 minutes into the interview. Do you think this decision made a positive impression? Another decided to bring his father into a 45-minute interview: The recruiter was shocked. Paula Welch, a Cigna HR representative, similarly noted how one recent grad asked his father to call and negotiate a higher salary after the son received a job offer. Here's another decision: A college senior brought her cat to the interview in a cage and then proceeded to play with it during the interview. The end results of these decisions were negative for all the applicants.[6]

Decision making entails identifying and choosing from among alternate solutions that lead to a desired state of affairs. The above examples illustrate how decisions affect your chances of getting a job after graduation, but successful decision making has much broader applications. Among organizations, for example, *Fortune* concluded, "Decision making at even the most basic level has slowed materially over the past five to 10 years."[7] Slower decision making leads to increased costs, lower efficiency, and lower customer satisfaction.[8] In sum, individuals, teams, and organizations are well served to improve their decision-making skills.

Before discussing rational and nonrational models of decision making, we set the context by discussing two ways of thinking that affect the way we make decisions.

LO 11-1

Compare rational and nonrational models of decision making.

Two Ways of Thinking

In his book *Thinking, Fast and Slow,* Daniel Kahneman, a professor who received the 2002 Nobel Prize in economics, described two kinds of thinking, which he labeled System 1 and System 2.[9]

System 1—Intuitive and Largely Unconscious Thought   System 1 is our automatic, instinctive, and emotional mode of decision making. It is fast because it relies on mental shortcuts that create intuitive solutions to problems as they come up, for example, when we hit the brakes at the sight of another car's brake lights or pause when we detect anger in someone's voice.

System 2—Analytical and Conscious Thought   System 2 is our slow, logical, deliberate mode of decision making. It helps us identify when our intuition is wrong or when our emotions are clouding our judgment. It requires more cognitive effort than System 1 and is used when contemplating a discrete task such as parallel parking or how to best climb a tree.

Both Systems Have Value   There are pros and cons to both systems of thinking. For example, System 1 thinking forms first impressions and judgments, which may be automatic but may lead us to jump to conclusions that may or may not be accurate. It can also lead to poor follow-through on plans because it focuses on immediate payoffs, which distract us from considering the long-term implications of our decisions.[10]

When System 1 runs into difficulties, we can call on System 2 thinking for a more methodical approach to a specific situation or problem. System 2 thinking typically gets involved only when we encounter something unexpected that System 1 thinking can't answer. In addition, System 2 thinking can be time consuming, especially when we don't have the cognitive energy or attention required to think through a situation. For example, suppose you were looking to purchase a new phone. Comparing two different smartphones to determine their features and price points requires attention to detail and may take longer than a quick decision that occurs using System 1 thinking.[11]

What do you do when you see the rear brake lights like this light up? Do you think about stepping on the brake, or do you automatically hit the brakes? This automatic process is an example of System 1 thinking.

Ingram Publishing

Rational Decision Making: Managers Make Logical and Optimal Decisions

The *rational model of decision making* **explains how managers** *should* **make decisions.** It assumes that managers are completely objective and possess all information for their decisions. In this model, decisions thus demonstrate excellent logic and promote the organization's best interests.

Four generic stages are associated with rational decision making (see Figure 11.2). We discuss each one next.

Stage 1: Identify the Problem or Opportunity—Determining the Actual versus the Desirable   We defined a *problem* in Chapter 1 as a difference or gap between an actual and a desired situation. By now you know that problem identification is the first step in solving any type of problem. In addition to making decisions to solve problems, however, managers also have to make decisions about optimizing opportunities. An **opportunity is a situation in which results that exceed goals and expectations are possible.** For example, U.S. medical schools must prepare to graduate more than 12,000 more medical students each year over the next decade. This opportunity, however, will require some tough decisions because the number of funded medical residencies has been frozen by the federal government since 1997. Residencies are the three to seven years of additional on-the-job training that medical students need before they can practice medicine on their own. Without Congress approving the additional funding for more medical residencies, the Association of American Medical Colleges predicts a shortage of as many as 121,000 doctors by 2030.[12]

FIGURE 11.2   The Four Stages in Rational Decision Making

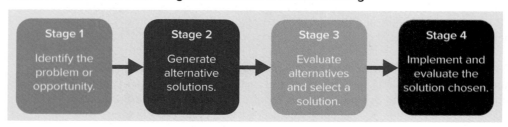

Stage 1: Identify the problem or opportunity. → Stage 2: Generate alternative solutions. → Stage 3: Evaluate alternatives and select a solution. → Stage 4: Implement and evaluate the solution chosen.

McGraw-Hill Global Education Holdings, LLC

Whether you face a problem or an opportunity, the goal is always the same: to make improvements that change conditions from their current state to a more desirable one. This requires you to diagnose the cause of the problem, or the nature of the opportunity.

Stage 2: Generate Alternative Solutions—Both the Obvious and the Creative

For many people generating solutions is the exciting part of decision making, the step where you get to be creative, think outside the box, and share your ideas about how things should be done. *Brainstorming,* for instance, is a common technique (discussed later in the chapter) that both individuals and groups use to generate potential solutions. A research study of 400 strategic decisions revealed that managers struggled during brainstorming because of three key decision-making blunders:[13]

1. **Rushing to judgment.** Managers simply make decisions too quickly without considering all relevant information.

2. **Selecting readily available ideas or solutions.** Managers take the easy solution without rigorously considering alternatives. This can happen when emotions about the problem are running high.

3. **Making poor allocation of resources to study alternate solutions.** Managers don't invest the resources to properly study the problem and the alternate courses of action.

Decision makers thus are encouraged to slow down and use System 2 thinking (analytical and conscious) when making decisions. This should lead them to identify a broader set of alternatives and potential solutions.[14]

Stage 3: Evaluate Alternatives and Select a Solution—Ethics, Feasibility, and Effectiveness

In the third stage, evaluate your alternatives on several criteria. Costs and quality are important, but you should also consider the following questions: (1) Is it ethical? (If not, don't consider it.) (2) Is it feasible? (If time is an issue, costs are high, resources are limited, new technology is needed, or customers are resistant, for instance, then the alternative is not feasible.) (3) Will it remove the causes and solve the problem?

Stage 4: Implement and Evaluate the Solution Chosen

After the solution has been implemented, stakeholders need to evaluate how effectively it solves the problem. If effective, it should eliminate or significantly reduce the difference between the problem state and the desired outcome. If not, either the problem was incorrectly identified or the solution was inappropriately conceived or executed. Management can return to the first step, problem identification. If the problem was correctly identified, management should consider implementing one of the untried solutions. This process can continue until all feasible solutions have been tried or the problem has changed. System 2 thinking is needed to effectively work through this stage.

What Are the Pros and Cons of the Rational Model?

The rational model is prescriptive. It outlines a logical process managers *should* use, assuming they are *optimizing* when making decisions. **Optimizing means solving problems by producing the best possible solution based on a set of highly desirable conditions**—having complete information, leaving emotions out of the decision-making process, honestly and accurately evaluating all alternatives, having abundant and accessible time and resources, and having people willing to implement and support decisions. Practical experience, of course, tells us that these conditions are all rarely met, and assumptions to the contrary are unrealistic. Social scientist Herbert Simon earned the 1978 Nobel Prize for his work on decision making. He put it this way: "The assumptions of perfect rationality are contrary to fact. It is not a question of approximation; they do not even remotely describe the processes that human beings use for making decisions in complex situations."[15]

That said, there are three benefits of trying to follow a rational process as closely as is realistically possible:

- **Quality.** The quality of decisions may be enhanced, in the sense that they follow more logically from all available knowledge and expertise.

- **Transparency.** Rationality makes the reasoning behind a decision transparent and available to scrutiny.

- **Responsibility.** The rational model discourages decision makers from acting on suspect considerations (such as personal advancement or avoidance of bureaucratic embarrassment) and therefore encourages more responsible decisions.[16]

Nonrational Models of Decision Making: Decision Making Does Not Follow an Orderly Process

Nonrational models of decision making explain how managers actually make decisions. These models typically build on assumptions that decision making is uncertain, that decision makers do not possess complete information, and that managers struggle to make optimal decisions. The choice to text while driving is an example of nonrational decision making.

According to recent statistics, 9 percent of all U.S. fatal crashes involve texting while driving, and texting while driving increases by *400 percent* a driver's time spent with their eyes off the road. At 55 mph, that's enough time to travel the length of a football field.[17] Psychologist Dan Ariely noted, "This behavior embodies the way we're capable of doing things that can kill us without thinking about the long-term consequences."[18] Two nonrational models that might explain this behavior are Herbert Simon's *normative* model and the *intuition* model.

Do you text and drive? Many of us do even in light of the fact that about 25 percent of all automobile accidents involve the use of a cell phone. Sadly, the American Automobile Association estimates that 11 teens die every day from texting and driving. What can you do to reduce the extent to which you text and drive?

kali9/Getty Images

Simon's Normative Model: "Satisfactory Is Good Enough" Herbert Simon proposed the normative model to describe the process that managers actually use when making decisions. This process is guided by a decision maker's bounded rationality.

***Bounded rationality* represents the notion that decision makers are "bounded" or restricted by a variety of constraints when making decisions.** Lack of information is a prime example of a decision-making constraint. Would you invest $500 million in the face of bounded rationality? General Motors did.

GM invested more than $500 million in the car-hailing service Lyft. GM management concluded that Lyft could help the automaker prepare for a time when people will want self-driving cars. What will the market be for such cars? When will that market become viable? Will the government block this market due to safety concerns? As of today, no one really knows, but both companies see the world changing quickly and wanted to prepare for the future.[19]

In addition to lack of information, bounded rationality is caused by any personal characteristics and internal and external resources that reduce rational decision making. Personal characteristics include personality and the limited capacity of the human mind. Consider gender: Males tend to make riskier decisions than females.[20] Examples of internal resources are the organization's human and social capital, financial resources, technology, plant and equipment, internal processes and systems, and the time available. External resources include factors the organization cannot directly control, such as employment levels in the community, capital availability, and government policies.[21]

Ultimately, bounded rationality leads managers to obtain manageable rather than optimal amounts of information as described in the OB in Action feature. This practice makes it difficult for managers to identify all possible alternate solutions. In the long run, the constraints of bounded rationality cause decision makers to fail to evaluate all potential alternatives, thereby causing them to *satisfice.*

OB in Action

Improving an Airport Terminal under Bounded Rationality

How do you make a decision that will affect the future when you don't know what will happen a week or a year from now? Making choices in the face of incomplete information—that is, under the constraints of bounded rationality—is a challenging situation we face all the time, in our personal and professional lives. For example, Charles Darwin, whose scientific mind shaped the theory of evolution, was so confounded by the decision whether to marry and have children or remain single that he made a list of pros and cons for each option. (He opted to marry.)[22]

If you are looking for a decision-making strategy that's more reliable than subjectively comparing pros and cons, consider the intensive collaborative and interdisciplinary technique called "design charrette," in which decision makers gather as a group and divide their problem into multiple parts, each of which is taken over by a small but diverse group that works to find a solution. The groups then reassemble, each presents its work to the others, and a process of giving feedback, making revisions, and regrouping begins that lasts until a decision has

been made.[23] The word *charrette* is French for cart and refers to the wheeled container that was used to gather students' assignments in the classrooms of 19th-century France.[24] Here are some recent examples of the charrette strategy in use.

- Consultants from MIG Inc., charged with planning a major update to the passenger terminal at California's Hollywood Burbank Airport, recently held the first of several planned meetings with local residents and other stakeholders to discuss what they would like to see in the new design. About 80 people attended and split into small groups to offer their ideas, which will be refined in more charrette workshops to follow.[25]

- Design students at the University of Kentucky, University of Cincinnati, and Western Kentucky University provided input to a building industry design charrette intended to develop environmentally sustainable and extreme weather-resistant home-construction materials.[26]

- The Board of Selectmen in Rye, NH, held a design charrette including themselves, town residents, and consultants from a local non-profit group to discuss ways to improve the town center and bring the community together by attracting both young families and older residents. The meeting was inspired by residents, who suggested the charrette idea to the board.[27]
- Drexel University's departments of design and architecture have hosted charrettes for several years. Most recently, an interdisciplinary design charrette was organized to discuss transforming the urban landscape of Philadelphia by closing selected single streets and redesigning them to increase, rather than limit, public access to the business and facilities now located there. Students from all majors were invited to participate in an effort aimed at "reconceiving the street as a truly public space."[28]

YOUR THOUGHTS?

1. How do you think design charrettes help decision makers working under bounded rationality?

2. What other applications of design charrettes can you think of? What would make the strategy most successful in those situations?

Satisficing **consists of choosing a solution that meets some minimum qualifications and thus is "good enough."** Satisficing resolves problems by producing solutions that are satisfactory, as opposed to optimal. Finding a radio station to listen to in your car is a good example of satisficing. You cannot optimize because it is impossible to listen to all stations at the same time. You thus stop searching for a station when you find one playing a song you like or do not mind hearing.

The Intuition Model: "It Just Feels Right" *Intuition* **consists of judgments, insights, or decisions that "come to mind on their own, without explicit awareness of the evoking cues and of course without explicit evaluation of the validity of these cues."**[29] We all have the ability to use intuition.

> **EXAMPLE** Ignoring recommendations from advisers, Ray Kroc purchased the McDonald's brand from the McDonald brothers: "I'm not a gambler and I didn't have that kind of money, but my funny bone instinct kept urging me on."[30] Zachary Bodish bought a poster for a 1958 exhibition of ceramics by Pablo Picasso for $14.44 at an Ohio thrift store. He had a hunch it might be worth much more. Turns out the piece was actually signed by Picasso, and Bodish sold it for $7,000."[31]

The use of intuition does not always lead to blockbuster decisions such as those by Ray Kroc and Zachary Bodish, however. To enhance your understanding of the role of intuition in decision making, this section reviews a model of intuition and discusses the pros and cons of using intuition to make decisions.

A Model of Intuition   Figure 11.3 presents a model of intuition. Note that it shows two forms of intuition:

1. A *holistic hunch* **is a judgment based on the subconscious integration of information stored in memory.** People using holistic intuition may not be able to explain why they want to make a certain decision except that the choice "feels right." This reflects System 1 thinking (intuitive and largely unconscious).

2. *Automated experience* **represents a choice based on a familiar situation and a partially subconscious application of learned information related to it.** For example, when you have years of experience driving a car, you react to a variety of situations without conscious analysis. Apple co-founder, the late Steve Jobs, arguably one of the most important entrepreneurs in the last 40 years, attributed his success to intuition, saying that "intuition is a very powerful thing, more powerful than intellect, in my opinion. That had a big impact on my work."[32]

FIGURE 11.3 **A Model of Intuition**

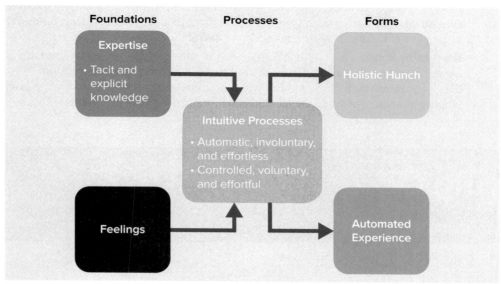

SOURCES: Kahneman, Daniel, and Gary Klein. "Conditions for Intuitive Expertise: A Failure to Disagree." *American Psychologist* 64, no. 6 (September 2009): 515–26. https://DOI: 10.1037/a0016755; Sadler-Smith, Eugene, and Erella Shefy. "The Intuitive Executive: Understanding and Applying 'Gut Feel' in Decision-Making." *Academy of Management Executive* 18, no. 4 (2004): 76–91; and Miller, C. Chet, and R. Duane Ireland. "Intuition in Strategic Decision Making: Friend or Foe in the Fast-Paced 21st Century?" *Academy of Management* 19, no. 1 (February 2005). https://doi.org/10.5465/ame.2005.15841948.

In Figure 11.3, you can see that intuition is represented by the two distinct processes we just described. One is automatic, involuntary, and mostly effortless. The second is quite the opposite in that it is controlled, voluntary, and effortful. For example, when you are trying to answer one of the Your Thoughts? questions at the end of the OB in Action boxes, an answer may pop into your mind based on your recollection of what you've read (an automatic process). But upon further reflection (a controlled process), you may decide your initial thought was wrong and that you need to go back and reread some material to arrive at another answer. This in turn may cause novel ideas to come to mind, and the two processes continue.

These intuitive processes are influenced by two sources: expertise and feelings (see Figure 11.3). **Expertise is an individual's combined *explicit knowledge* or information that can easily be put into words, and *tacit knowledge* or information we gain through experience that is difficult to express and formalize.**

EXAMPLE Tim Cook uses a combination of explicit and tacit knowledge when making business decisions as Apple's CEO. When Steve Jobs was still running the company, Cook was instrumental in setting up Apple's plan of using contract manufacturers to make products faster and in larger quantities than Apple's own factories while keeping costs relatively low. This strategy also meant that Apple's competitors had to fight for the small amount of factory capacity left to build their own products, which gave Apple a serious lead in getting products to market (and to waiting consumers) faster than the rest. As Apple crossed the trillion-dollar valuation mark recently, Cook continues to be a driving force in technology as well as a champion for data privacy, human rights, and the ethical use of artificial intelligence.[33]

- **Pros and Cons of Using Intuition.** There are two benefits of using intuition to make decisions. (1) It can speed up the decision-making process, which is valuable when you are under time constraints.[34] (2) It is useful when resources are limited. On the downside, however, intuition is subject to the same types of biases associated with rational decision making, biases we discuss in the next section. In addition, the decision maker may have difficulty convincing others that the intuitive decision makes sense, so a good idea may be ignored.

- **What Is the Bottom Line on Intuition?** We believe intuition and rationality are complementary and that managers should attempt to use both when making decisions.[35] We thus encourage you to use intuition when making decisions. You can develop your intuitive awareness by using the recommendations in the Applying OB box.

Applying OB

Tips for Improving Your Intuition

- **Trust your intuitive judgments.** The 80-20 rule says if you have 80 percent of the relevant information, your intuition can fill in the remaining 20 percent.
- **Seek feedback.** Confirm your intuitive judgments by asking trusted others for feedback.
- **Test your intuitive success rate.** Think back over the last year and assess how many times you relied on your intuition. What was your success rate? If your intuition was wrong, assess why and try to use this knowledge in the future.
- **Try visualizing solutions.** This will help engage System 1 thinking to activate your intuition. And relax—worry and anxiety will hinder it.
- **Challenge your intuition.** Rather than automatically accepting your intuitive thoughts, challenge them. Test your intuition by thinking of counterarguments. Then challenge those counterarguments.[36]

- **Improving Your Intuitive Awareness.** Do you think being intuitive is a good thing? Would you like to become more intuitive? If yes, you will find Self-Assessment 11.1 valuable.

SELF-ASSESSMENT 11.1

Assessing Your Intuition

Please be prepared to answer these questions if your instructor has assigned Self-Assessment 11.1 in Connect.

1. What is your assessed level of intuitiveness? Do you agree with this assessment?

2. What are the two highest-ranked items driving your intuition? When do you tend to use these characteristics?

3. What are the two lowest-ranked items that detract from your intuition? When do they get in the way of your making intuitive decisions?

11.2 DECISION-MAKING BIASES: RULES OF THUMB OR "HEURISTICS"

THE BIGGER PICTURE

All of us use *heuristics* when making decisions. By better understanding the nature of these various rules of thumb, you can improve your ability to make more rational decisions. Heuristics fall into eight categories: availability bias, representativeness bias, confirmation bias, anchoring bias, overconfidence bias, hindsight bias, framing bias, and escalation of commitment bias.

Ever had a hard time explaining why you made a particular decision? That's normal. All of us use shortcuts or "rules of thumb" when making decisions. Academics call these shortcuts judgmental heuristics, pronounced "hyur-*ris*-tiks." *Judgmental heuristics are cognitive shortcuts or biases that are used to simplify the process of making decisions.*[37]

There are both pros and cons to the use of heuristics.[38] Because these shortcuts derive from knowledge gained from past experience, they can help managers make decisions. At the same time, however, they can lead to bad decisions, particularly by people facing time constraints, such as physicians and other health care professionals. For example, diagnostic errors affect more than 12 million Americans each year. According to a recent study of malpractice claims, more than 53 percent of the claims were related to inaccurate diagnoses and treatment. Some researchers estimate that more than $100 billion may be wasted annually in the U.S. as a result of inaccurate diagnoses.[39] We suspect heuristics are partly to blame for these outcomes because physicians and other health care professionals don't have the time to consider all of a patient's symptoms when making diagnoses.[40]

Here are eight biases that commonly affect decision making:

1. Confirmation bias
2. Overconfidence bias
3. Availability bias
4. Representativeness bias
5. Anchoring bias
6. Hindsight bias
7. Framing bias
8. Escalation of commitment bias

Knowledge about these biases or heuristics can help you to avoid using them in the wrong situation or being blinded by not knowing you are in fact using them.

1. **Confirmation bias.** *Confirmation bias pertains to how we selectively gather information* and has two components. The decision maker (1) subconsciously decides something even before investigating why it is the right decision—for example, making a snap decision to purchase a particular smartphone—and (2) seeks information that supports or confirms the decision while discounting information that does not.[41] This bias leads us to collect information that supports our beliefs or views.

2. **Overconfidence bias.** *Overconfidence bias results in overestimating our skills relative to those of others,* such as our driving ability, **and overestimating the**

accuracy of our predictions. This bias grows in strength when people are asked moderate to extremely difficult questions rather than easy ones. (See the Problem-Solving Application on the California wildfire.) Recent research suggests that individuals who believe they are "better-than-average" and in better social standing than others can fall prey to this bias.[42] Our advice: Don't assume that overconfident and assertive people have the best recommendations.

Problem-Solving Application

Overconfidence Bias Partly to Blame for California Wildfire

In late November 2018, a wildfire took hold in a dangerously dry area of California's Sierra Nevada foothills. Possibly sparked by the malfunction of an electrical power line that initially affected a single customer, it soon burst out of control. Later known as the Camp Fire, the blaze became the deadliest and most destructive in California's history. Before being contained two weeks later, it had roared through 154,000 acres of land and destroyed the entire town of Paradise. At least 85 people were killed, and hundreds left homeless; nearly 16,000 buildings were burned.[43]

Biases on the part of PG&E's management team contributed to the disastrous Camp Fire in California that killed 85 people, left hundreds homeless, and destroyed the entire town of Paradise.
Justin Sullivan/Getty Images

The malfunctioning tower, left in place 25 years longer than intended, belonged to Pacific Gas & Electric (PG&E), a utility company with a history of safety problems. According to the *New York Times*, "Five of the 10 most destructive fires in California since 2015 have been linked to PG&E's electrical network. Regulators have found that in many fires, PG&E violated state law or could have done more to make its equipment safer." The company's interim CEO admitted errors and promised change, but Governor Gavin Newsom told an interviewer that the company, which recently filed for bankruptcy under the burden of responsibility for tens of billions of dollars of damage from the fire, could not be trusted.[44]

State investigators probing earlier disasters that implicated PG&E, including many hundreds of fires, heard from employees that the company routinely looked the other way when they complained about outdated equipment and flawed reports. Finding the company had spent millions of dollars less on operations and maintenance than authorized, California's Public Utilities Commission concluded it was prioritizing the bottom line over safety. PG&E was also accused of undertaking repairs and improvements only after a fire or

explosion had occurred, instead of conducting needed maintenance on a timely basis. "Some people believe that you run equipment to failure," said one former state regulator. "They believe 'run to failure' to save money. This [the Camp Fire] is the danger of run to failure." The company had earlier announced some steps to incentivize safety but they were short-lived, and at the time of the Camp Fire it was in court, pushing back against legal principles that would hold the utility liable for damage caused by its equipment even when it acted properly.[45]

PG&E, which has already come through one bankruptcy proceeding, was also fighting to expand the protection of a new law allowing utilities to pay for the costs of fires by raising fees to customers. The company and other utilities claim that their rates will increase anyway because banks will be less willing to lend them money, and that climate change and increased development of remote areas have made fires more likely and harder to fight. Meanwhile the company's stock dropped 60 percent, its credit rating was downgraded, and it may face criminal charges relating to the fire if it is found to have behaved in a "reckless" manner. It is now seeking new directors and advice on preventing future disasters.[46]

Apply the 3-Step Problem-Solving Approach

Step 1: Define the problem in this example.

Step 2: Identify the causes. How did overconfidence and any other biases contribute to this disaster?

Step 3: Make your recommendations about what PG&E should do differently in the future to avoid such disasters.

---

3. **Availability bias.** The *availability heuristic* **is a decision maker's tendency to base decisions on information readily available in memory.** Because the information is recent, we overestimate its importance. The problem, of course, is that recent information is not necessarily the best or most accurate. The availability bias can be fueled by the news media, which emphasize negative or unusual events like school shootings and plane crashes and often cause us to overestimate their frequency.[47]

4. **Representativeness bias.** We use the representativeness heuristic when we estimate the probability of an event's occurrence based on our impressions about similar occurrences. *Representativeness bias* **leads us to look for information that supports previously formed stereotypes.**[48] A manager, for example, may hire a graduate from a particular university because the past three people hired from this university turned out to be good performers. In this case, the "school attended" criterion is being used to facilitate complex information processing associated with employment interviews. However, this shortcut can result in a biased decision.[49]

5. **Anchoring bias.** Is the population of Mexico greater than 40 million? What's your best guess about the population of Canada? If your answer to the second question was influenced by the number *40 million* suggested by the first question, you were affected by the anchoring bias. *Anchoring bias* **occurs when decision makers are influenced by the first information they receive about a decision, even if it is irrelevant.** Initial information, impressions, data, feedback, or stereotypes anchor our subsequent judgments and decisions.[50]

6. **Hindsight bias.** Imagine you are taking an OB course that meets Tuesdays and Thursdays, and your professor gives unannounced quizzes each week. It's the Monday before a class, and you are deciding whether to study for a potential quiz or watch *Monday Night Football.* Two of your classmates have decided to watch the game rather than study because they don't think there will be a quiz the next day. The next morning you walk into class and the professor says, "Take out a sheet

Some people are afraid of flying because they overestimate the chances of being in a plane crash. Plane crashes are actually low-probability events. In 2017, there were more than 35 million commercial jet takeoffs with only 1 fatal accident.

AF archive/Alamy Stock Photo

New England Patriots quarterback Tom Brady being interviewed after his victory in Super Bowl 53 at Mercedes-Benz Stadium in Atlanta on February 3, 2019. Many of us fall prey to the hindsight bias when we evaluate the success or failure of plays called by quarterbacks.

Jamie Squire/Getty Images

of paper for the quiz." You turn to your friends and say, "I knew we were going to have a quiz; why did I listen to you?" **Hindsight bias occurs when knowledge of an outcome influences our belief about the probability that we could have predicted the outcome earlier.** The danger of this bias is that, in retrospect, we get overconfident about our foresight, which leads to bad decisions.[51] For example, an investor may look at the sudden death of an important CEO as something that should have been expected because the individual was experiencing severe health issues recently.[52]

7. **Framing bias.** *Framing bias* **relates to the manner in which a question is posed or framed. It leads us to change the way we interpret alternatives.** For example, customers have been found to prefer meat that is framed as "85 percent lean" instead of "15 percent fat," although, of course, the two mean the same thing. In general, people view choices more favorably when they are framed in terms of gains rather than losses.[53] You would be more likely to invest in a product that had a 60 percent chance of success rather than a 40 percent chance of failure. Try framing your decision questions in alternate ways to avoid this bias.

6. **Escalation of commitment bias.** *Escalation of commitment bias* **is the tendency to hold to an ineffective course of action even when it is unlikely the bad situation can be reversed.** Would you invest more money in an old or broken car? The Drug Enforcement Administration and the Pentagon continued to spend on a spy plane for use in Afghanistan that was supposed to be completed in 2012 at a cost of $22 million, even though the project had missed every projected delivery date. By 2016, it had not yet left the ground, and total payouts had reached more than $86 million.[54]

Researchers recommend the following actions to reduce the escalation of commitment:

- Set minimum targets for performance, and have decision makers compare their performance against these targets.
- Regularly rotate managers in key positions throughout a project.
- Encourage decision makers to become less ego-involved with a project.
- Make decision makers aware of the costs of persistence.[55]

11.3 EVIDENCE-BASED DECISION MAKING

THE BIGGER PICTURE

You can improve the quality of your decisions by looking for the best evidence and the best available data to make, inform, or support them. This section of the chapter will help you understand the role of evidence in decision making and the move toward big data and artificial intelligence.

Evidence-based decision making **is the process of conscientiously using the best available data and evidence when making managerial decisions.** It holds the promise of helping avoid the decision-making biases discussed earlier and improving performance while reducing costs. Proponents also believe evidence-based decision making can help in the use of "big data" to market and sell products and services.

Consider the applications to farming and cruising.

LO 11-3

Explain evidence-based decision making.

EXAMPLE The Riensche family has been farming 12,000 acres in Iowa for six generations. Recently they signed up with Bayer's Climate Corp. for a data analysis service, which among other things, helped reduce the seed they use by 6 percent and fertilizer by 11 percent—all while growing the best crops they've ever planted. Ben Riensche, the most recent family member to manage the farm, still has his grandfather's spiral notebooks that meticulously list crop and egg yields. Before data analysis,

More and more farmers are signing up for data analysis services, which can provide them with important data that can help them manage their crops more efficiently and make decisions based on solid evidence.
Nolanberg11/Shutterstock

Carnival Corporation's CEO and President, Arnold Donald, holds a Medallion tracking device.
Rick Wilking/Newscom

Riensche says, "there was no secret sauce other than just keeping notes and making field observations. Now we have all these digital tools." Climate Corp. and its competitors use information supplied by farmers who subscribe to their services and feed it into software programs that predict combinations of seeds, fertilizer, and sprays to maximize yield and revenues.[56]

EXAMPLE Carnival Cruise Lines has introduced a tracking device on its Princess cruise ships to help the company collect and analyze passenger data and preferences. The Medallion is a wearable device the size of a poker chip worn on the wrist or around the neck that syncs to each passenger's information stored in the cloud. Not only does this technology allow for quicker check-ins and boarding, it also helps the company track each guest's interaction with various digital and gaming experiences created to enhance their sea-going adventures. In addition, the data-tracking system includes avatars called Tagalongs that accompany each passenger around the ship, appearing on nearby digital screens and on the more than 3,000 digital devices that cruisers bring along on their trips. The company expects digital tracking and data collection to enhance passengers' cruise experiences while helping the company zero in on making decisions to entice passengers to book for future vacations.[57]

Using Evidence to Make Decisions

Managers use evidence or data in three different ways: to make a decision, to inform a decision, and to support a decision. Here is what a team of researchers had to say about how we use data to make decisions.

"Evidence is used to *make* a decision whenever the decision follows directly from the evidence." For example, if you wanted to purchase a particular used car such as a Toyota

Prius based on price and color, you would obtain data from the Internet and classified ads and then choose the seller offering the lowest-priced red Prius. "Evidence is used to *inform* a decision whenever the decision process combines hard, objective facts with qualitative inputs, such as intuition or bargaining with stakeholders." For instance, when firms are hiring new college graduates, objective data about their past experience, education, and participation in student organizations is relevant input to the hiring decision. Nonetheless, subjective impressions garnered from interviews and references are typically combined with these objective data to make a final decision. These two uses of evidence are clearly positive and should be encouraged. The same cannot be said about using evidence to support a decision.

"Evidence is used to *support* a decision whenever the evidence is gathered or modified for the sole purpose of lending legitimacy to a decision that has already been made."[58] This application of evidence has both positive and negative effects. On the positive side, evidence collected after the fact can be used to convince an external audience that the organization is following a sound course of action in a complex and ambiguous decision context. This can lead to confidence and goodwill about how a company is responding to environmental events. On the negative side, the practice can stifle employee involvement and input because people will come to believe that management is going to ignore evidence and just do what it wants. In summary, because this practice has both pros and cons, management needs to carefully consider when (if ever) it might be appropriate to ignore disconfirming evidence and push its own agenda or decisions.

Big Data: The Next Frontier in Evidence-Based Decision Making

Researchers suggest that data creation has doubled in size every two years over the past decade, and by 2025 the digital universe will grow to more than 163 zettabytes (ZB) or one trillion gigabytes. This equates to *ten times* the 16 ZBs of data generated in 2016.[59] The term **big data reflects the vast quantity of data available for decision making.** It also encompasses the collection, sorting, and analysis of that information, and the techniques to do so.[60] The analysis of big data has already revolutionized all aspects of our lives, and companies are scrambling to hire qualified employees for the job.

According to the U.S. Bureau of Labor Statistics, the demand for people with data analytic skills will increase by 27 percent between 2016 and 2026.[61] Guess who is responding to this need? Universities. More universities are offering majors in data analytics to fill the more than 2.7 million data and analytics positions that will be available in the U.S. workforce by 2020.[62] These degrees will train people to use quantitative and statistical tools to analyze and interpret big data. Do you think you are suited for this career?

Managers and companies that effectively utilize big data, such as organizations in the health care industry (see the OB in Action box), are expected to gain competitive advantage. Big data creates value in the following ways:

- It can make information more transparent and usable.
- It allows organizations to measure and collect all types of performance information, enabling them to implement initiatives to enhance productivity.
- It enhances decision making at all levels of the organization.
- It can be used to develop new products or services.[63]

One problem with big data is that private or sensitive information is more easily obtained, which means it can be leaked to others. In a recent survey of senior managers, the respondents ranked cybersecurity breaches as the single greatest data threat their companies face.[64]

OB in Action

Big Data Helps Advance the Health Care Industry

Health care today is being revolutionized by the application of big data to many medical challenges, especially the uncovering of hidden patterns and correlations that can lead to better diagnosis and treatment of new and existing diseases. It was recently estimated that investments in big data by the health care and pharmaceutical industries would total $4.7 billion for 2018 and would grow 12 percent a year over the next several years, reaching more than $7 billion by 2021. Health care providers around the world already report reductions in cost, patient wait times, and emergency room visits, with improved patient outcomes and revenues.[65]

Big data thus has the potential not only to transform the way health care providers operate as businesses, allowing them to become more efficient and reduce costs and errors. It can also speed and improve the way they treat and care for their patients.[66] Here are just a few examples:[67]

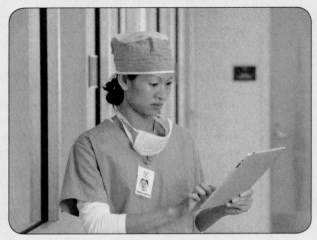

The health care industry continues to be revolutionized by the use of big data to assist doctors and other professionals in improving patient care and outcomes.
Ariel Skelley/Blend Images LLC

- A company called Ginger.io gathers smartphone data from users with mental illness, providing a mobile platform that allows experienced health care professionals to deliver better and more personalized care to those patients.

- PeraHealth uses proprietary data sets and a graphic tool called the Rothman Index, which combines vital signs, lab results, and other live patient data, to help identify patients who might be at risk for certain complications before they occur, and to suggest which patients might need intensive-care treatment.

- RDMD, a health care start-up, uses artificial intelligence tools to sift big data from medical records of cases of rare diseases. It is then able to market the data to pharmaceutical companies to help advance the search for treatments and cures.

- Seattle Children's Hospital has adopted a system to mine big data about patients to almost instantly find reliable diagnoses and customized treatments that used to require days or even weeks of work poring over thousands of bits of information.

YOUR THOUGHTS?

1. Can you think of any other applications for big data in health care decision making? What kinds of companies or organizations might be interested in such tools?

2. What drawbacks, if any, might arise from the collection and use of big data in medical settings?

3. Do you foresee any privacy concerns in medical applications of big data? How should the health care industry safeguard patients' individual privacy?

Artificial Intelligence: Teaching Machines to Make Decisions

New technologies are changing our world. Consider that Alphabet's Waymo division recently launched the United States' first commercial self-driving taxi service and China's Xinhau News is using the first artificial intelligence–driven news anchor.[68]

***Artificial intelligence (AI)* is a form of computing that allows machines to perform cognitive functions,** such as acting or reacting to inputs, similar to the way humans do.[69]

There are three key ways that AI can help managers enhance business operations: automating business processes, gaining insight through data analysis, and engaging with customers and employees.[70] Back-office administrative tasks and other financial activities lend themselves to automation and are considered the "least smart" type of AI activity. For example, updating customer files with address changes; replacing lost or stolen credit cards; and managing customer communications are all tasks that can be handled by automated systems fueled by AI.

AI can also be used to gain business insights by creating algorithms that can be used to detect patterns in vast amounts of data and actually interpret their meaning. This type of task is a more moderate level of AI activity utilized by many organizations. For example, by using these algorithms, machine learning can predict what product or service a specific type of customer is likely to buy; detect financial or insurance claim fraud in real time; automate personalized targeting of digital ads on websites; and analyze warranty data to identify safety or quality problems in manufactured products.

Another way managers and organizations can use AI in business operations is through customer and employee engagement. This application may include chatbots, a form of artificial intelligence that simulates conversations with humans. These AI tools can also offer 24/7 customer service to provide answers to basic, technical questions—in the customer's natural language; product and service recommendation systems for retailers that increase shopper personalization, engagement, and sales; and company internal websites for answering employee questions about technology, benefits, HR policies, and even ethics. For example, LEADx developed a coaching bot called "Coach Amanda" that provides tips, guidance, videos, and texts that managers can consult for advice in real time. Ken Ryzner told the *Wall Street Journal* that Coach Amanda has helped him run richer brainstorming sessions with colleagues by suggesting he ask more questions.[71]

Coach Amanda, LEADx's AI tool and coaching bot, provides tips, guidance, videos, and texts that managers can consult for advice in real time.

Courtesy of LEADx

With increasing computing power and the ability to harness vast amounts of data, managers need to decide how best to utilize artificial intelligence as part of their business strategies.[72] Companies that utilize AI effectively recognize machine learning alone is not the key to gaining competitive advantage. Research suggests companies that decide to automate certain activities as a way to eliminate jobs may be losing their competitive edge.[73] In contrast, companies that automate processes and shift employees to more value-added job tasks may see significant returns on their AI and human collaboration efforts in terms of increasing revenues, retaining employees, and sparking innovation.[74]

The rise of AI and machine learning is not without challenges, however. Sometimes humans pose situations in which machine learning must choose between two actions with negative or unpleasant consequences and ask what the device should do.[75] For example, in a recent study, researchers asked participants about several real-world events that involved "poor decisions" on the part of AI software that could be attributed to human biases. Can AI be racist, sexist, or possibly spread hate? Or, were the algorithms created by humans who have inherent biases when it comes to such "moral violations"? This study and others suggest the relationship between AI and humans is a complex one that needs continuing study.[76]

11.4 FOUR DECISION-MAKING STYLES

THE BIGGER PICTURE

Your decision-making style reflects the manner in which you use information to make decisions. It's an input in the Organizing Framework. Knowing the four general styles of decision making will help you understand how your managers and coworkers are making their decisions; and it will help you know yourself that much better too. The four decision-making styles are directive, analytical, conceptual, and behavioral.

LO 11-4

Compare the four styles of decision making.

We make countless decisions on a daily basis—what to wear, what to eat, what route to take driving to school, whether to confront a negative colleague. These decisions are guided by our decision-making style. A **decision-making style** is the way an individual perceives and comprehends stimuli and the general manner in which he or she chooses to respond to such information.[77] A team of researchers developed a model of decision-making styles based on the idea that styles vary along two dimensions: value orientation and tolerance for ambiguity.[78]

Value Orientation and Tolerance for Ambiguity

Value orientation is the extent to which an individual focuses on either task and technical concerns or people and social concerns when making decisions. Some people, for instance, are very task-focused at work and do not pay much attention to people issues, whereas others are just the opposite.

The second dimension pertains to a person's *tolerance for ambiguity*. This characteristic indicates the extent to which a person needs structure or control in his or her life. Some people desire a lot of structure. They have a low tolerance for ambiguity and find ambiguous situations stressful and psychologically uncomfortable. Others do not have a high need for structure and can thrive in uncertain situations; their tolerance for ambiguity is high. Imagine the ambiguity faced by Andrés Sepúlveda as he worked to rig political campaigns across Latin America. He and his team of hackers "stole campaign strategies, manipulated social media to create false waves of enthusiasm and derision, and installed spyware in oppositions offices, all to help Peña Nieto get elected president of Mexico," according to *Bloomberg Businessweek*. Ambiguous situations can energize people like Sepúlveda with a high tolerance for ambiguity. He is currently serving a 10-year prison term for his actions.[79]

When we combine the dimensions of value orientation and tolerance for ambiguity, they form four styles of decision making: directive, analytical, conceptual, and behavioral (see Figure 11.4). Let's look at each of these.

The Directive Style: Action-Oriented Decision Makers Who Focus on Facts

People with a *directive* style have a low tolerance for ambiguity and are oriented toward task and technical concerns when making decisions. They are efficient, logical, practical, and systematic in their approach to solving problems. Directive decision makers are action oriented and decisive and like to focus on facts. In their pursuit of speed and results, however, they tend to be autocratic, exercise power and control, and focus on the short run.

FIGURE 11.4 Decision-Making Styles

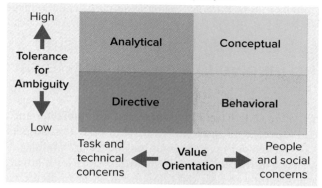

SOURCE: Rowe, Alan J., and Richard O. Mason. *Managing with Style: A Guide to Understanding, Assessing, and Improving Decision Making.* San Francisco: Jossey-Bass, 1987.

Amazon CEO Jeff Bezos uses a directive style. Bezos is known to be decisive, makes decisions quickly, and pivots at breakneck speed when a strategy or course of action needs to be revised. According to Bezos, "Every day at Amazon is Day 1," which means he expects Amazon employees to embrace the characteristics of a start-up company—an organization that can shift its focus quickly to adjust to changing customer and market trends.[80]

The Analytical Style: Careful and Slow Decision Makers Who Like Lots of Information

People with the analytical style have a much higher tolerance for ambiguity and tend to overanalyze a situation. They like to consider more information and alternatives than do those with a directive style. Analytical individuals are careful decision makers who take longer to make decisions but who also respond well to new or uncertain situations. They can often be autocratic.

IBM CEO Ginni Rometty appears to have an analytical style. She and her management team must analyze business and technology trends worldwide to determine the best course of action for increasing company revenues and moving the company forward in an

IBM CEO Ginni Rometty uses her analytic style to gather relevant data and evaluate business and technology trends worldwide to assist in making critical decisions for her organization.

Justin Sullivan/Getty Images

era of digital disruption. As CEO, Rometty has shifted IBM's focus from computers to cloud computing, blockchain technology, big data, and artificial intelligence.[81]

The Conceptual Style: Intuitive Decision Makers Who Involve Others in Long-Term Thinking

People with a conceptual style have a high tolerance for ambiguity and tend to focus on the people or social aspects of a work situation. They take a broad perspective on problem solving and like to consider many options and future possibilities. Conceptual types adopt a long-term view and rely on intuition and discussions with others to acquire information. They also are willing to take risks and are good at finding creative solutions to problems. On the downside, however, a conceptual style can foster an idealistic and indecisive approach to decision making. Netflix CEO Reed Hastings exhibits this style of decision making.[82]

The Behavioral Style: Highly People-Oriented Decision Makers

The behavioral style is the most people-oriented of the four. People with this style work well with others and enjoy social interactions in which opinions are openly exchanged. Behavioral decision makers are supportive, are receptive to suggestions, show warmth, and prefer verbal to written information. Although they like to hold meetings, they prefer to avoid conflict and can be too concerned about others. This can lead behavioral types to adopt a conflict-avoidance approach to decision making and to have a hard time saying no. Madeline Bell, CEO of Children's Hospital of Pennsylvania, uses this decision-making style successfully by identifying and engaging the key people who need to be on board with major decisions made at one of the top children's hospitals in the country.[83]

Which Style Are You?

Research reveals that very few people have only one dominant decision-making style. Rather, most managers have characteristics that fall into two or three styles. Studies also show that decision-making styles vary by age, occupation, personality type, gender, and country.[84] It's important to understand your decision-making style because it affects the quality of your decisions and team performance.[85] Self-Assessment 11.2 will enhance your understanding about your decision-making style.

SELF-ASSESSMENT 11.2	CAREER READINESS

What Is My Decision-Making Style?

Please be prepared to answer these questions if your instructor has assigned Self-Assessment 11.2 in Connect.

1. Do you agree with your results? Explain.
2. Which of these styles is most important in your role as a student and in your current job?
3. Based on your answer to question 2, what might you do to modify your decision-making style?

11.5 A ROAD MAP TO ETHICAL DECISION MAKING

THE BIGGER PICTURE

Sometimes you may find yourself confused about the ethics of a situation. One way to gain some certainty is to graph the situation with a decision tree, which provides a framework for ethical decision making.

Although research tells us that ethical behavior is related to inputs such as personality, values, locus of control, and a culture and climate for ethics,[86] there are few tools for helping individuals to navigate through ethical dilemmas or challenges. An approach suggested by Harvard Business School Professor Constance Bagley can help fill the gap. Bagley recommends a *decision tree* to help managers make ethical decisions.[87]

A ***decision tree*** **is a graphical representation of the process underlying decisions,** and it shows the consequences of making various choices. You can follow Bagley's decision tree, shown in Figure 11.5, by asking the following questions about your decision:

LO 11-5

Describe how to assess the ethics of decision making.

FIGURE 11.5 An Ethical Decision Tree

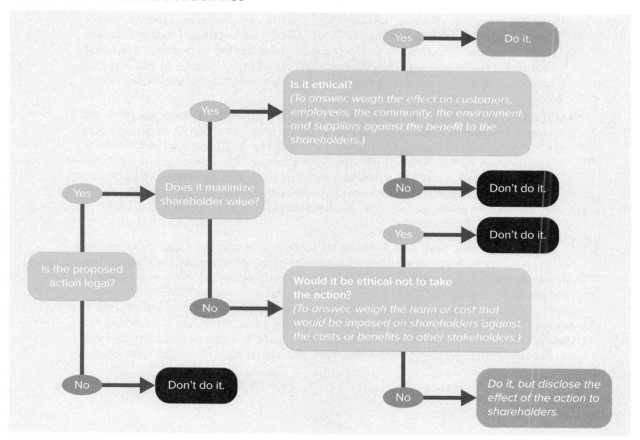

SOURCE: Bagley, Constance E. "The Ethical Leader's Decision Tree." *Harvard Business School Publishing,* February 2003. https://hbr.org/2003/02/the-ethical-leaders-decision-tree.

Unethical decision making by the parent company of the University of Phoenix may have cost the for-profit education company dearly in terms of student enrollment over the past several years.

Kristoffer Tripplaar/Alamy Stock Photo

1. **Is the proposed action legal?** This may seem like a common-sense question, but some managers and companies fail to ask it. Owners of Purdue Pharma, maker of the highly addictive opioid drug OxyContin, recently faced fraud charges in New York as a result of transferring funds from the company to various family trusts in an effort to shield company assets from ongoing litigation.[88]

2. **If "yes," does the proposed action maximize shareholder value?** A decision maximizes shareholder value when it increases profits for an organization, because these profits are eventually distributed to shareholders. Regardless of shareholder value, however, the decision tree shows that managers still need to consider the ethical implications of each decision or action.

3. **If the decision maximizes shareholder value, the decision maker then considers whether or not the action is ethical.** Managers should answer this question by weighing the effect of the action on an organization's other key constituents (customers, employees, the community, the environment, suppliers) against the benefit to the shareholders. For example, Apollo Education Group, the parent company of for-profit University of Phoenix, has been the subject of both state and federal investigations that allege the company used aggressive and deceptive recruiting, advertising, and financial aid practices. Negative perceptions of the University of Phoenix may also be to blame for the substantial drop in student enrollment, more than 70 percent between 2010 and 2017.[89]

4. **If the decision does not maximize shareholder value, then the decision maker should consider whether it would be ethical not to take the proposed action.** If an action would not directly benefit shareholders, consider whether it would be ethical *not* to take it. The decision for the Apollo Education Group to continue to use existing, possibly unethical practices could also have an impact on other stakeholders, such as University of Phoenix employees. A recent Glassdoor survey revealed that only 30 percent of the school's employees would recommend working at the university to a friend or acquaintance.[90]

The decision tree cannot provide a quick formula that managers and organizations can use to evaluate every ethical question. Ethical decision making is not always clear-cut and is affected by cross-cultural differences and organizational culture and climate. Organizations are encouraged to conduct ethics training and to increase awareness about cross-cultural issues when the work engages people with mixed cultural backgrounds.[91] That said, the decision tree does provide a framework for considering the trade-offs between managerial and corporate actions and managerial and corporate ethics. Try using this decision tree the next time you are faced with a significant ethical question or problem.

11.6 GROUP DECISION MAKING

THE BIGGER PICTURE

You've probably seen both good and poor results from a group decision. OB confirms that group decisions can lead to mixed results. It identifies five potential advantages and four disadvantages. Knowing them arms you with information to help you maximize the advantages and minimize the disadvantages. In this section you will find contingency recommendations for working with groups in decision making and three helpful group problem-solving techniques: brainstorming, the nominal group technique, and computer-aided decision making.

Aristotle was an early proponent of group decision making. He concluded that "when there are many who contribute to the process of deliberation, each can bring his share of goodness and more prudence . . . some appreciate one part, some another, and all together appreciate all."[92] Aristotle is suggesting that group decision making is more effective when individuals in the group share and aggregate their information. As you well know, this does not always happen when groups make decisions. This section will help you learn about decision making in groups so you can achieve Aristotle's proposed benefits.

LO 11-6

Outline the basics of group decision making.

Aristotle (384-322 BC) was a Greek philosopher and scientist. His writings span many subjects and he highly believed in the value of using logic and empirical data when making decisions.

QEDimages/Alamy Stock Photo

Advantages and Disadvantages of Group Decision Making

We often have to decide whether to make a decision alone or to consult with others. The following list of advantages and disadvantages can help you decide what to do.

Advantages   These five advantages are most likely to be found when the group has experience with the issue at hand, and when it is diverse in terms of characteristics such as personalities, gender, attitudes, and experience.[93]

- **Greater pool of knowledge.** A group possesses more information and knowledge than one individual acting alone.
- **Different approaches to a problem.** Individuals with different backgrounds and experiences bring varied perspectives to diagnosing and solving problems.
- **Greater commitment to a decision.** Participation and a voice in decision making are more likely to result in commitment to a decision. This in turn leads group members to accept and feel responsible for implementing a proposed solution.
- **Better understanding of decision rationale.** Participating in a decision increases group members' understanding about why the decision is being made and what must occur to implement it. This in turn reduces miscommunication among people.
- **More visible role modeling.** Less experienced group members learn about group dynamics and how to solve problems.[94]

Disadvantages   The disadvantages of group-aided decision making relate to group dynamics and interpersonal interactions.[95]

- **Social pressure.** The desire to look good in front of others, particularly the boss, leads to conformity and stifles creativity.
- **A few dominant participants.** The quality of a group's decision can be influenced by a few vocal people who dominate the discussion. This is particularly problematic when the vocal person is perceived as a powerful individual.
- **Goal displacement.** When the group is evaluating alternatives, secondary considerations such as winning an argument, getting back at a rival, or trying to impress the boss can override the primary goal of solving a problem. ***Goal displacement* occurs when the primary goal is overridden by a secondary goal.**[96]
- **Groupthink.** ***Groupthink* is "a mode of thinking that people engage in when they are deeply involved in a cohesive in-group, when members' strivings for unanimity override their motivation to realistically appraise alternative courses of action."**[97] Groupthink is thoroughly discussed in the next section.

Groupthink

The term *groupthink,* defined above, originated from an analysis of the decision-making processes underlying the war in Vietnam and other U.S. foreign policy fiascos. Groupthink happens when members fail to exercise sufficient reality testing and moral judgment due to pressures from the group. If they passively ignore the danger, modern managers can all too easily become victims of groupthink. Consider the group of 14 teachers and other staff members in an Idaho school district who decided to dress up as ethnic stereotypes for Halloween recently and followed that up with an impersonation of a Mexican border wall. Despite being taken down from Facebook, these photos quickly went viral and sparked outrage both locally and nationally. "We are better than this," said the school superintendent—all 14 individuals were placed on administrative leave.[98]

As you might imagine, groupthink negatively affects group performance and is often driven by high levels of cohesiveness.[99] ***Cohesiveness* or a sense of "we-ness" tends to override individual differences and motives.** Members of groups tend to be cohesive for two fundamental reasons: (1) they like and enjoy each other's company and (2) they need each other to achieve a common goal. You can see how cohesiveness is a double-edged sword in its effects on group-level outcomes in the Organizing Framework. It can help you and your team reduce conflict, but it can also reduce performance if it limits questioning and critical thinking and results in groupthink.[100] How do you avoid groupthink? First, know the symptoms.

Symptoms of Groupthink   There are eight common symptoms of groupthink. The more that are present in a situation, the higher the probability that groupthink will occur.

1. *Invulnerability.* An illusion that the group cannot make a mistake breeds excessive optimism and risk taking.

2. *Inherent morality.* Assuming the group is highly moral encourages members to ignore ethical implications.

3. *Rationalization.* Members protect their personal or "pet" ideas and assumptions.

4. *Stereotyped views of opposition.* The group may underestimate opponents.

5. *Self-censorship.* Keeping ideas and questions to yourself stifles critical debate.

6. *Illusion of unanimity.* Members' silence can be interpreted to mean consent.

7. *Peer pressure.* Be careful when the loyalty of dissenters is questioned.

8. *Mindguards.* Self-appointed protectors can shut out adverse information.[101]

Prevention Is Better than Treatment   Prevention is better than treatment or cure when dealing with groupthink. Table 11.1 provides excellent recommendations for removing barriers to minority dissent. **Minority dissent occurs when group members feel comfortable disagreeing with other group members.** Research reveals that minority dissent is positively related to participation in decision making and job satisfaction.[102]

Are you working on any project teams at school or work? If yes, you may be interested in assessing the level of minority dissent and participation in decision making. Results from Self-Assessment 11.3 can help you to improve your effectiveness within these teams.

TABLE 11.1   Techniques for Preventing Groupthink

1. Each member of the group should be assigned the role of critical evaluator or dissenter. This role requires the active voicing of objections and doubts.

2. Top-level executives should not use policy committees to rubber-stamp decisions that have already been made.

3. Different groups with different leaders should explore the same policy questions.

4. Managers should encourage subgroup debates and bring in outside experts to introduce fresh perspectives.

5. Someone should be given the role of devil's advocate when discussing major alternatives. This person tries to uncover every conceivable negative factor.

6. Once a consensus has been reached, everyone should be encouraged to rethink his/her position to check for flaws.

SOURCES: Thibodeaux, Wanda. "How to End Groupthink and Encourage Your Team to Be Creative." Mansueto Ventures, December 10, 2018. https://www.inc.com/wanda-thibodeaux/how-to-end-groupthink-encourage-your-team-to-be-creative.html; Price, Dom. "Need Fresh Ideas? 5 Ways to Disrupt Groupthink." Mansueto Ventures, October 23, 2018. https://www.inc.com/dom-price/need-fresh-ideas-5-ways-to-disrupt-groupthink.html; and Janis, Irving L. "Victims of Groupthink." *Political Psychology* 12, no. 2 (June 1991): 247–78. https:// DOI: 10.2307/3791464.

Practical Contingency Recommendations for Group Decision Making

There are three practical considerations in decision making.

1. **Routine and frequency:** If the decision occurs frequently and is of a routine nature, such as deciding on promotions or who qualifies for a loan, use groups because they tend to produce more consistent decisions than do individuals.

2. **Time constraints:** Given time constraints, let the most competent individual, rather than a group, make the decision.

3. **Information and communication:** In the face of environmental threats such as time pressure and potential serious effects of a decision, groups use less information and fewer communication channels. This increases the probability of a bad decision.

Reaching Consensus: The Goal of Group Problem-Solving Techniques

Groups asked to make decisions must generally reach a consensus. According to a decision-making expert, a **consensus "is reached when all members can say they either agree with the decision or have had their 'day in court' and were unable to convince the others of their viewpoint. In the final analysis, everyone agrees to support the outcome."**[103] This definition indicates that consensus does not require unanimous agreement, because group members may still disagree with the final decision but are willing to work toward its success. They must honestly and accurately communicate with each other when trying to reach a consensus.

Practical Problem-Solving Techniques

Decision-making experts have developed a host of problem-solving techniques to aid in problem solving. Three we discuss here are (1) brainstorming, (2) the Delphi technique, and (3) decision support systems.

Brainstorming: A Tool for Generating Ideas **_Brainstorming_ helps groups generate multiple ideas and alternatives for solving problems.** Developed by advertising executive A. F. Osborn, brainstorming can apply in a variety of contexts.[104] They include solving problems, developing creative ideas for new products, removing performance roadblocks, and developing action plans to achieve goals. Brainstorming sessions begin by asking participants to silently generate ideas or solutions, which then are collected either in public or anonymously and summarized in some fashion (such as on a whiteboard or a flip chart).

> **TIP** It's good to collect the ideas/solutions anonymously if the issue is emotional, political, or highly salient/sensitive to some group members.[105]

At a second session group members critique and evaluate the alternatives. Today, many brainstorming sessions are conducted electronically. ***Electronic brainstorming,*** **sometimes called *brainwriting*, allows participants to submit their ideas and alternatives over the Internet.** Webinars and other virtual collaboration tools such as MeetingRoom. io, MURAL, and Appear.in work well for this purpose.[106]

Managers are advised to follow the seven rules for brainstorming used by IDEO, a product design company (see Table 11.2).

Brainstorming is an effective technique for generating new ideas/alternatives, and research reveals that people can be trained to improve their brainstorming skills.[107]

The Delphi Technique The Delphi technique was originally developed by the RAND Corp. for technological forecasting.[108] It now serves as a multipurpose planning tool. **The *Delphi technique* is a group process that generates anonymous ideas or judgments from physically dispersed experts in multiple rounds of brainstorming.**

This technique is useful when face-to-face discussions are impractical, when disagreements and conflict are likely to impair communication, when certain individuals might severely dominate group discussion, and when groupthink is a probable outcome of the group process.[109]

Decision Support Systems The increased globalization of organizations, the existence of big data, and the advancement of information technology have led to the development of decision support systems. ***Decision support systems (DSS)*** **are "computer-based interactive systems that help decision makers to use data and models to solve unstructured problems."**[110] For example, Best Buy, Google, GE, Intel, and Microsoft all use internal intranets to obtain input for their DSS from employees. Both Best Buy and Google found DSS systems helpful in estimating the demand for new products and services.[111] They also improve information processing and decision making within virtual teams.[112]

TABLE 11.2 Seven Rules for Brainstorming

RULE	DETAILS
1. Defer judgment.	Don't criticize during the initial stage of generating ideas. Avoid phrases such as "We've never done it that way," "It won't work," "It's too expensive," and "Our manager will never agree."
2. Build on the ideas of others.	Encourage participants to extend others' ideas by avoiding "buts" and using "ands."
3. Encourage wild ideas.	Encourage out-of-the-box thinking. The wilder and more outrageous the ideas, the better.
4. Go for quantity over quality.	Guide participants to generate and write down as many new ideas as possible. Focusing on quantity encourages people to think beyond their favorite ideas.
5. Be visual.	Use different colored pens (e.g., red, purple, blue) to write on big sheets of flip chart paper, whiteboards, or poster board that is put on the wall.
6. Stay focused on the topic.	Appoint a facilitator to keep the discussion on target.
7. Keep to one conversation at a time.	Set ground rules that no one interrupts another person, dismisses someone's ideas, shows disrespect, or otherwise behaves rudely.

SOURCES: IDEO. "Effective Brainstorming Techniques." Accessed May 22, 2019. https://www.ideou.com/pages/brainstorming; Shellenbarger, Sue. "Tactics to Spark Creativity." *The Wall Street Journal*, April 2, 2013. https://www.wsj.com/articles/SB10001424127887323611604578398342398991844; "How Entrepreneurs Come Up With Great Ideas." *The Wall Street Journal*, April 29, 2013. https://www.wsj.com/articles/SB10001424127887324445904578283792526004684; and Lehrer, Jonah. "How To Be Creative." *The Wall Street Journal*, March 12, 2012. https://www.wsj.com/articles/SB10001424052970203370604577265632205015846.

11.7 CREATIVITY

THE BIGGER PICTURE

Can you become more creative if you need to? As a manager, can you improve the creativity of your group? The answer to both questions is yes. When you consider creativity from an OB perspective, you will see it as both a process and an outcome (see the Organizing Framework in Figure 11.1). The process aspect of creativity includes four key behaviors: problem formulation/definition, preparation/information gathering, idea generation, and idea evaluation/validation. You can increase creativity by following some practical recommendations.

Creativity is defined here as the process of producing "new and useful ideas concerning products, services, processes, and procedures."[113] Being creative can be as simple as locating a new place to hang your car keys or as complex as developing a pocket-size microcomputer. You can create something new, combine or synthesize existing things, or improve or change things. Recent research suggests that creativity and curiosity are much more important to organizations than previously thought. Cultivating creativity at all levels helps managers and leaders adapt to uncertain market conditions and other external pressures. When our curiosity is triggered, we think more deeply about decisions and come up with more creative solutions.[114]

Let's consider a model of creativity to gain some insight into ways you can increase your own creativity and, as a manager, do the same for your employees.

A Model of Creativity

Figure 11.6 illustrates a model of creativity. You can see that it flows nicely from the Organizing Framework for Understanding and Applying OB in that a combination of person factors and situation factors influence creative performance behaviors, which in turn affect creative outcome effectiveness. Let's explore this model, starting with a discussion of the difference between creative performance behaviors and creative outcome effectiveness.

Creative Performance Behaviors Produce Creative Outcome Effectiveness *Creative performance behaviors* are four key behaviors that drive the production of creative outcomes. *Creative outcome effectiveness* is "the joint novelty and usefulness (quality) of a product or service" as judged by others.[115]

Researchers believe the four behaviors constituting *creative performance behaviors* unfold according to the following sequence.[116]

* **Problem formulation/definition.** Problem formulation is the familiar Step 1 in our 3-Step

FIGURE 11.6   A Model of Creativity

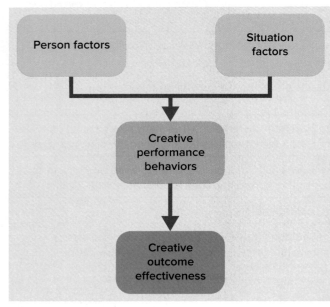

McGraw-Hill Global Education Holdings, LLC

Problem-Solving Approach. The practice of accurately defining the problem will enhance your creativity, and it requires System 1 thinking (System 1 thinking is intuitive and mainly unconscious).

- **Preparation/information gathering.** The preparation stage reflects the notion that creativity starts from a base of knowledge. Experts suggest that creativity arises from the convergence of tacit and explicit knowledge. Lowell Wood, the most prolific inventor in U.S. history—he holds 1,761 patents, many more than Thomas Alva Edison—is inventor in residence at Intellectual Ventures.

Lowell Wood obtained his 1,761st patent in August 2018, passing Thomas Edison as the all-time most prolific inventor from the United States.

Alex Wong/Getty Images

EXAMPLE Wood is an astrophysicist, a self-taught paleontologist, and a computer scientist. He works hard at being creative. In commenting about his time studying in college and graduate school, he told a writer from *Bloomberg Businessweek* that he "often failed or received the lowest score on the first exam given in a particular course and improved his marks through repetition and intense effort." He credits his ability to find creative solutions to problems to the amount of reading he does. He religiously reads three dozen academic journals from varying fields of study. He got this habit from chemist and author Linus Pauling. Wood asked Pauling how he comes up with all his great ideas. Pauling said, "There's really nothing to it all. You just read, and you remember what you read."[117]

As Lowell Wood's career demonstrates, preparation/information gathering consists of intentionally and actively searching for new information related to a problem.

- **Idea generation.** Generating ideas requires making new mental connections about the task or problem at hand. This behavior is emphasized in brainstorming and calls for System 1 thinking.

- **Idea evaluation/validation.** Selecting the most creative and promising idea from among multiple options relies on System 2 thinking (System 2 thinking is analytical and mainly conscious).

Drivers of Creative Performance Behaviors   Figure 11.6 shows that person factors and situation factors go into producing the four creative performance behaviors (and they are inputs in the Organizing Framework of OB). Here is a summary of person factors and situation characteristics, identified through research, that drive creative performance behaviors:

- **Person factors.** Creativity starts with motivation and domain-relevant knowledge. Like Lowell Wood, people need to be motivated to apply their knowledge and capabilities to create new ideas, new products, and solutions to all sorts of problems.[118] Other drivers of creativity include the Big Five personality dimensions, self-efficacy, national culture, willingness to tolerate ambiguity, and proactive personality.[119]

- **Situation factors.** High-commitment work systems promote creative behavior. *High-commitment work systems* **rely on selective hiring, comprehensive training, comparatively high pay, pay contingent on performance, and good benefits.**[120] We suspect that high-performance work systems demonstrate a form of social support for employees, leading them to put more effort into creative

This Google office in London illustrates the type of "cozy" work environment that promotes creativity. Would you find this office distracting, or do you think it would increase your creative performance?

View Pictures/Universal Images Group/Getty Images

behaviors. Other important situation factors include interpersonal diversity, time pressure, positive relationships with supervisors and coworkers, mutual accountability among group members, and spatial configuration of work settings.[121] For example, many organizations, such as Google, Zappos, Salesforce.com, and Etsy, are designing the work environment to encourage casual conversations among employees who don't generally work together. A *Wall Street Journal* reporter noted that these companies do this by "squeezing workers into smaller spaces so they are more likely to bump into each other." They also are "installing playful prompts, like trivia games, to get workers talking in traditional conversational dead zones, such as elevators."[122]

Organizational culture and climate also contribute to the expression of creative behaviors.[123] Self-Assessment 11.4 measures *creativity climate*. If you are curious about whether a current or former employer has a climate for creativity, complete this assessment.

SELF-ASSESSMENT 11.4

Assessing Climate for Creativity

Please be prepared to answer these questions if your instructor has assigned Self-Assessment 11.4 in Connect.

1. What items most and least contributed to the company's creative climate?

2. Based on your results and suggestions in the Applying OB box below, what would you do to increase the level of creativity in this organization?

Practical Recommendations for Increasing Creativity

While some consultants recommend hypnotism as a good way to increase employees' creativity, we prefer suggestions derived from research and practical experience. The first recommendation is to effectively manage the four creative performance behaviors. Another is to allow yourself to enjoy boredom. According to experts, "when we experience boredom, two areas of the brain may be busy working closely together—the executive network, which solves problems, and the so-called default network, which takes over when your brain isn't involved with something external. The result is enhanced creativity."[124] This suggests that doing "nothing," such as "just sitting in a café, strolling in the park, lying on the beach, or even staring into space while everyone else is running busily, may be one of the most important creative things we can do," according to management expert Manfred Kets de Vries.[125] Research also has uncovered some practical tips that all of us can use to increase our creativity.

Applying OB

Tips for Sparking Creativity

You can often renew your creativity simply by shaking up your routine. These tips offer a quick and powerful creative boost.[126]

1. **Change your commute.** Take a different route to work or walk part of the way. If you work at home, take a walk before you start.
2. **Listen to noise.** Research by a Chinese university found that a moderate level of noise, not silence, makes people more productive.[127] Listen to music or an ambient-noise app like Coffivity (wear headphones if you have coworkers).
3. **Move your lunch.** Go somewhere new for lunch. If you work at home, prepare a new dish or invite someone over.
4. **Change your workspace.** Instead of your home office, park at the kitchen counter or a coffee shop. In an office environment, ask to borrow an unused space.
5. **Try a creativity exercise.** Pick an everyday object like a coffeepot and write a few sentences about what it reminds you of.

There is one final issue to consider. Should organizations use extrinsic rewards such as pay and promotions to enhance creativity? While it seems like common sense to do this, research reveals rewards have conflicting effects on creative behavior. When rewards make people feel like they are being controlled, they can reduce creativity. On the other hand, when rewards provide information about what is important and valued, they can increase creativity. Putting it all together, a team of researchers concluded, "The effects of rewards on creative performance depend on the nature of rewards and the context in which the rewards are being offered."[128] This tells us managers should not use a "one size fits all" approach when linking rewards to creative behavior.[129]

11.8 MAKING THE CONNECTION: HOW CAN I MASTER DECISION-MAKING AND CREATIVITY SKILLS?

THE BIGGER PICTURE

Developing effective decision-making skills takes practice and can be influenced by a person's creativity. Here are some key points to consider.

LO 11-8

Describe the implications of decision making and creativity for you and managers.

Takeaways for Me

Here are seven things you can do to turn this chapter's lessons into positive change in your personal and professional life.

1. **Work on developing your critical thinking and problem-solving skills:** You might begin by trying to solve all the problem-solving application boxes and cases in this book. You can also take an active role in case discussions in other classes.

2. **Practice identifying problems at work:** Consider recommending alternative solutions to your manager.

3. **Examine past decisions that turned out poorly and consider whether you were influenced by any of the eight decision-making biases:** Use awareness of these biases to avoid automatically applying them in the future.

4. **Assess your decision-making style:** Consider its impact on your teamwork at school and on the job.

5. **Use the ethical decision-making tree when you try to solve the legal/ethical challenges at the end of each chapter in the book.**

6. **Use the guidelines for brainstorming whenever you brainstorm with others.**

7. **Find ways to apply the tips for sparking creativity.**

Takeaways for Managers

There are six key implications for managers.

1. **Recognize that your decision-making skills affect your career progression as well as influence a variety of important individual, group, and organizational outcomes.**

2. **Use awareness of decision-making biases to help you avoid them.**

3. **Analyze the strengths and weaknesses of your decision-making style:** Then try to build on your strengths.

4. **Consider how you might use big data in your managerial role:** If you lack the statistical background to make this happen, you might take an internal training class or look for one online.

5. **Train your employees to effectively conduct brainstorming sessions.**

6. **Consider how you can spark creativity among your team by applying the model of creativity:** Remember, creative behavior from your team will positively affect a host of important outcomes.

What Did I Learn?

You learned that it is critical to master the skills of both decision making and creativity and that you have tools and techniques available to you to do just that. Reinforce your learning with the Key Points below. Consolidate your learning using the Organizing Framework. Then challenge your mastery of the material by answering the Major Questions in your own words.

Key Points for Understanding Chapter 11

You learned the following key points.

11.1 RATIONAL AND NONRATIONAL MODELS OF DECISION MAKING

- There are two fundamental ways of thinking. System 1 is more intuitive and unconscious, and System 2 is more analytical and conscious.
- The rational model explains how managers *should* make decisions.
- The four stages of rational decision making are (1) identify the problem or opportunity, (2) generate alternative solutions, (3) evaluate alternatives and select a solution, and (4) implement and evaluate the solution chosen.
- Nonrational models explain how managers *actually* make decisions. Two nonrational models are the normative model and the intuitive model.
- According to the normative model, decision makers are guided by bounded rationality, which represents the fact that decision makers are "bounded" or restricted by different constraints. This limitation leads to satisficing.

- There are two types of intuition: holistic hunches and automated experiences. Intuition is represented by two distinct processes: one is automatic and the second is controlled, and there are two sources of intuition: expertise and feelings.

11.2 DECISION-MAKING BIASES: RULES OF THUMB OR "HEURISTICS"

- Decision-making bias results from the use of judgmental heuristics. The eight biases are (a) confirmation, (b) overconfidence, (c) availability, (d) representativeness, (e) anchoring, (f) hindsight, (g) framing, and (h) escalation of commitment.

11.3 EVIDENCE-BASED DECISION MAKING

- The goal of evidence-based decision making is to conscientiously use the best data when making decisions.
- Evidence-based decision making has three purposes: to make decisions, to inform decisions, and to support decisions.
- Big data denotes the vast quantity of data available for decision making. It makes information more transparent and usable, allows organizations to measure and collect many types of performance data, allows the segmentation of customers, and can help in developing new products.
- Artificial intelligence (AI) is a form of computing that allows machines to perform cognitive functions, such as acting or reacting to inputs, similar to the way humans do. AI can help managers enhance business operations by automating business processes, gaining insight through data analysis, and engaging with customers and employees.

11.4 FOUR DECISION-MAKING STYLES

- The model of decision-making styles is based on the idea that styles vary along two dimensions: value orientation and tolerance for ambiguity.
- There are four styles of decision making: analytical, conceptual, behavioral, and directive.

11.5 A ROAD MAP TO ETHICAL DECISION MAKING

- A decision tree is a graphical representation of the process underlying decisions.
- The ethical decision tree is a structured approach for making ethical decisions.
- Answering a series of questions in the tree leads to a recommended decision.

11.6 GROUP DECISION MAKING

- There are both pros and cons to using groups in the decision-making process.
- The advantages include (1) a greater pool of knowledge, (2) different approaches to a problem, (3) greater commitment to decisions, and (4) more visible role modeling.
- The disadvantages to using groups include (1) social pressure to make particular decisions, (2) dominance by a few people, (3) goal displacement, and (4) groupthink.
- Groupthink reduces the quality of decisions and is caused by high levels of cohesiveness among group members that overrides individual differences.
- Seven symptoms of groupthink help predict its occurrence.
- A contingency approach can help in deciding whether to include groups in the decision-making process.
- Three common problem-solving tools are brainstorming, the Delphi technique, and decision support systems (DSS).

11.7 CREATIVITY

- Creativity is the process of using imagination and skill to develop a new or unique product, object, process, or thought.
- Four creative performance behaviors to increase your creativity are problem formulation/definition, preparation/information gathering, idea generation, and idea evaluation/validation.
- Creative behaviors are influenced by a host of person factors and situation factors.

11.8 HOW CAN I MASTER DECISION-MAKING AND CREATIVITY SKILLS?

- Work on developing your critical thinking and problem-solving skills, which will be essential to your professional success.
- Examine previous poor decisions and consider whether you were influenced by any of the decision-making biases discussed in this chapter.
- Evaluate your decision-making style and determine whether it will help or hinder you in your professional career.

The Organizing Framework for Chapter 11

You learned that decision making is a key process at both the individual and group/team levels, and it is affected by a host of person factors such as intuition, decision making styles, personality, and self-efficacy. Decision making also is influenced by situation factors associated with the decision situation, organizational culture, and organizational climate. As shown in Figure 11.7, a number of additional processes affect outcomes associated with decision making. Decision making is associated with the individual outcomes of task performance, career outcomes, and creativity. At the group level, it affects group/team performance and group cohesion and conflict. Finally, decision making affects an organization's overall financial performance, innovation, and customer satisfaction.

Challenge: Major Questions for Chapter 11

You should now be able to answer the following questions. Unless you can, have you really processed and internalized the lessons in the chapter? Refer to the Key Points, Figure 11.7, the chapter discussion, and your notes to revisit and answer the following major questions:

1. How can I integrate rational and nonrational models of decision making?

2. It's hard to be rational. What biases get in the way?

3. How can I more effectively use evidence-based decision making?

4. How do I decide to decide?

5. How can I assess the ethics of my decisions?

6. What are the pros and cons of group decision making and the various problem-solving tools?

7. How can I increase my own creative behavior and that of my employees?

FIGURE 11.7 Organizing Framework for Understanding and Applying OB

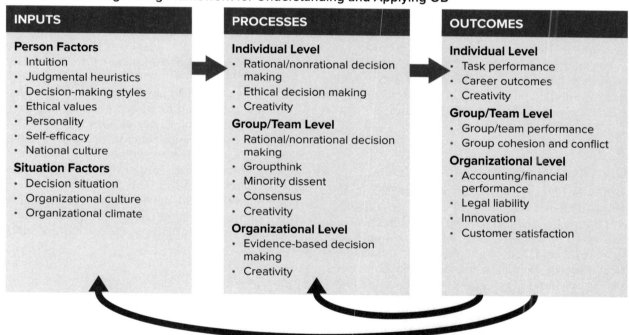

INPUTS	PROCESSES	OUTCOMES
Person Factors • Intuition • Judgmental heuristics • Decision-making styles • Ethical values • Personality • Self-efficacy • National culture **Situation Factors** • Decision situation • Organizational culture • Organizational climate	**Individual Level** • Rational/nonrational decision making • Ethical decision making • Creativity **Group/Team Level** • Rational/nonrational decision making • Groupthink • Minority dissent • Consensus • Creativity **Organizational Level** • Evidence-based decision making • Creativity	**Individual Level** • Task performance • Career outcomes • Creativity **Group/Team Level** • Group/team performance • Group cohesion and conflict **Organizational Level** • Accounting/financial performance • Legal liability • Innovation • Customer satisfaction

Airbus Decides to Permanently Land the A380

Airbus SE is Europe's largest aircraft manufacturer with revenues exceeding $71 billion in 2018. Boeing, the company's chief rival, dominated the long-haul market with its flagship, double-decker 747 aircraft for decades. In 2005 Airbus unveiled its A380 aircraft with a range of 8,000 nautical miles to challenge Boeing's dominance of this important market. The four-engine A380 superjumbo is certified for up to 853 passengers, making it the world's largest passenger aircraft.

We want you to consider how the decision-making process led Airbus in 2019 to cease production of the A380. Overall, the company expects to have sold 251 planes by the time it ceases production in 2021, well under its breakeven target.[130] The decision to stop production also means a reduction of about 3,500 jobs, and the company will not recoup the roughly $25 billion it invested in the aircraft project.[131]

CHANGING MARKET DEMANDS

Airbus began development of the A380 in the 1990s. The manufacturer believed it had identified an opportunity: as air travel increased there would be a need for larger aircraft. Airports in hub cities, such as London, Tokyo, and New York, only had so much capacity. So a massive aircraft that could seat a large number of passengers seemed like an ideal solution.[132]

The gigantic aircraft was a hit with airplane enthusiasts, but the industry was experiencing three unexpected changes. First, bilateral and multilateral agreements eased airport congestion. Traditionally, countries granted each other landing rights for a fixed number of flights per week to a fixed destination. Then came "Open Skies" agreements that provided unrestricted access to all airports.[133] These agreements facilitated the growth of secondary airports so passengers could take advantage of lower fare tickets. "The A380 was better suited to 1995, before air routes fragmented," said Richard Aboulafia, an aviation expert.[134] For example, London was no longer the premier destination in the UK with cities such as Manchester becoming hubs of their own.[135]

Second, Airbus grossly misjudged future passenger preferences. The company's initial research in the 1990s focused on Boeing's 747, which offered fewer flights, but more capacity on each one. The A380 launched more than a decade after this research was conducted. Passenger preferences had actually switched to wanting more flight times by the time the A380 went into service. Business travelers needed flexibility for flight departures between popular destinations, and this often meant more flights with each not operating at full capacity.[136] An airline strategist told *Bloomberg* that the A380 was "Too costly to fly anything but near full, and unusable on any less dense sectors."[137]

Finally, many airlines have turned to smaller, fuel-efficient aircraft, such as Boeing's 787 Dreamliner. "As smaller, more efficient planes flood the market . . . [it kills] the case for larger aircraft," according to the *New York Times*.[138] The two-engine Dreamliner has a lightweight carbon fiber body with significantly less fuel cost than the A380. The Dreamliner is much smaller than the A380, but that works out just fine in an era where each flight consists of fewer passengers who demand flexibility in the number of flights available to them.[139]

THE PRODUCTION PROCESS

Airbus had trouble delivering the first A380s on time and within budget because the manufacturer realized it had underestimated the complexity of wiring the aircraft and it used a multinational design team. Airbus is in fact a partnership between different European nations. This results in different designers, using different software, making group decisions on the design of aircraft. Multinational representation at Airbus went all the way to the upper echelons of the company until 2006. In fact, the manufacturer was led by French and German co-CEOs throughout the development of the A380. The superjumbo, dubbed the "Eighth Wonder of the World," represented all that was great about the European Union, including shared leadership.[140] "From its inception, the A380 was a grand European project," according to *Bloomberg*.[141]

This pride may have interfered in the production group's decision-making processes. "Airbus stumbled into this production fiasco because of overconfidence in its own abilities," company veterans told *The Wall Street Journal*. These issues also caused the goal of the project to shift. Steven Udvar-Hazy, a pioneer of aircraft leasing, told the *Journal* that the A380 went from its original goal of hub-to-hub transport during congested times to pure ". . . political ambition to outdo Boeing Co.'s 747 jumbo jet as the world's largest airliner."[142]

EMIRATES IMPACTS DECISION MAKING AT AIRBUS

Emirates Airlines is known as the chief sponsor of the A380 and ordered more than 160 units, far more than any other carrier.[143] The Dubai-based airline also placed an order for 20 additional planes in January 2018, giving life to the floundering program. Emirates canceled the order a year later when it was not able to secure price and performance concessions from engine-maker Rolls-Royce.[144] The cancellation was the last straw for Airbus. "As a result of this decision we have no substantial A380 backlog and hence no basis to sustain production, despite all our sales efforts with other airlines in recent years," former Airbus CEO Tom Enders said.[145] Airbus was thus forced to terminate production of an aircraft that could not match its popular appeal with revenues.

APPLY THE 3-STEP PROBLEM-SOLVING APPROACH TO OB

STEP 1: Define the problem.

A. Look first at the Outcomes box of the Organizing Framework in Figure 11.7 to help identify the important problem(s) in this case. Remember that a problem is a gap between a desired and a current state. State your problem as a gap, and be sure to consider problems at all three levels. If more than one desired outcome is not being accomplished, decide which one is most important and focus on it for steps 2 and 3.

B. Cases have protagonists (key players), and problems are generally viewed from a particular protagonist's perspective. Take the perspective of a member of the task force investigating this problem.

C. Use details in the case to identify the key problem. Don't assume, infer, or create problems that are not included in the case.

STEP 2: Identify causes of the problem by using material from this chapter, summarized in the Organizing Framework shown in Figure 11.7. Causes will appear in either the Inputs box or the Processes box.

A. Start by looking at the Organizing Framework to identify which person factors, if any, are most likely causes to the defined problem. For each cause, ask yourself, *Why is this a cause of the problem?* Asking why multiple times is more likely to lead you to root causes of the problem.

B. Follow the same process for the situation factors.

C. Now consider the Processes box shown in Figure 11.7. Consider concepts listed at all three levels. For any concept that might be a cause, ask yourself, *Why is this a cause?* Again, do this for several iterations to arrive at root causes.

C. To check the accuracy or appropriateness of the causes, map them onto the defined problem.

STEP 3: Make your recommendations for solving the problem. Consider whether you want to resolve it, solve it, or dissolve it (see Section 1.5). Which recommendation is desirable and feasible?

A. Given the causes identified in Step 2, what are your best recommendations? Use the content in Chapter 11 or one of the earlier chapters to propose a solution.

B. You may find potential solutions in the OB in Action boxes and Applying OB boxes within this chapter. These features provide insights into what other individuals or companies are doing in relationship to the topic at hand.

C. Create an action plan for implementing your recommendations.

Should Colleges Expel Students Whose Parents Cheated to Get Them In?

The largest academic fraud scandal to date occurred in March 2018. Federal prosecutors charged 50 individuals with a variety of crimes, including money laundering. Wealthy television actresses, corporate executives, hedge fund managers, and others are said to have paid $25 million to college officials to secure slots for their children.[146]

How Did the Scandal Work?

The admissions scheme had two parts. The first involved college athletic departments admitting some children as athletes, even if they did not play a sport. Some of the college coaches were accused of taking bribes. The second involved testing centers inflating some students' SAT and ACT scores or having someone else take the tests for the students.[147] Indicted college officials and parents will have their day in court, but affected universities have a difficult decision to make when it comes to students who were admitted as part of the scheme.

The University of Southern California (USC) is one institution involved with the charges, and it is reviewing the status of students associated with the scandal. The school said on Twitter, "Following the review, we will take the proper action related to their status, up to revoking admission or expulsion."[148] USC has also placed holds on these students' accounts, which restricts them from registering for classes or acquiring transcripts.[149]

Are There Innocent Bystanders?

Evidence suggests that some of the students associated with the scandal were innocent bystanders. William Singer, a college admissions consultant who ran the whole scheme, was recorded on a call saying that "most of the kids" did not know their scores were inflated after leaving the testing center. Further, some of the students who were falsely classified as elite athletes did not know that their applications were doctored. One USC student, for example, confronted his parents about receiving e-mails regarding practices and team events for track and field: He was admitted to USC as a track and field athlete. The student, who never participated in that sport, did not know his parents arranged his fraudulent admission.[150] "Your heart goes out to these kids who in some ways seem like innocent pawns of their parents' machinations," says Amy Sepinwall, a University of Pennsylvania professor of law and business ethics.[151]

What Should Universities Do?

One solution is to investigate each student associated with the scandal. Students who are determined to have benefited from the scheme would be booted and those who are found to be innocent get to stay. However, some of the cases are not that simple. According to *Bloomberg*, students often exaggerate and pad their resumes during the admissions cycle. So universities will have to determine which of these particular cases warrant action. For example, Singer sometimes created whole athletic careers that didn't exist. Such was the case for a student admitted to Stanford's sailing team who had never sailed. For others, Singer advised parents to exaggerate their kids' existing athletic accomplishments.[152]

The impacted universities have difficult decisions to make. They may come under harsh criticism if they don't take action against coddled students of the rich and famous. Sadly, expulsion can ruin the lives of students whose only crime was having parents who cheated.

If You Led a University and Found Out That Some of Your Admitted Students Were Associated with the Admissions Scandal, What Would You Do?

1. Expel them whether or not they knew what their parents were doing. These students are the beneficiaries of an alleged crime and allowing them to stay enrolled sends a poor message to other students.

2. Only expel them if they were actively involved in the scheme. It would not be fair to ruin the life of a student who did not know what his or her parents were up to.

3. Force students involved in the scandal to re-apply, whether or not they knew what their parents had done. Expel them if they don't meet the criteria for admissions based on their legitimate applications.

4. Invent other options and explain.

12

Power, Influence, and Politics

After reading this chapter, you should be able to:

LO 12-1 Understand the basic forms of power.

LO 12-2 Understand how to empower yourself and others.

LO 12-3 Describe and implement various influence tactics.

LO 12-4 Differentiate and apply the main forms of organizational politics.

LO 12-5 Determine how to implement effective impression management.

LO 12-6 Describe the implications of power, influence, and politics for you and managers.

This chapter focuses on particular means for influencing others, and thus the concepts in this chapter are especially important group/team-level processes in the Organizing Framework for Understanding and Applying OB (see Figure 12.1). The reason for this bold assertion is that you are being influenced by and attempting to influence others every day of your life, especially at work. Thus, understanding and applying knowledge related to power, influence, empowerment, political tactics, and impression management are extremely valuable to your success. You'll see support for this claim in the Organizing Framework, where power and influence relate to most outcomes across all levels of OB. Many different person and situation factors are related to power and influence, but our primary focus is on understanding the power and influence processes themselves and the numerous outcomes they affect.

FIGURE 12.1 Organizing Framework for Understanding and Applying OB

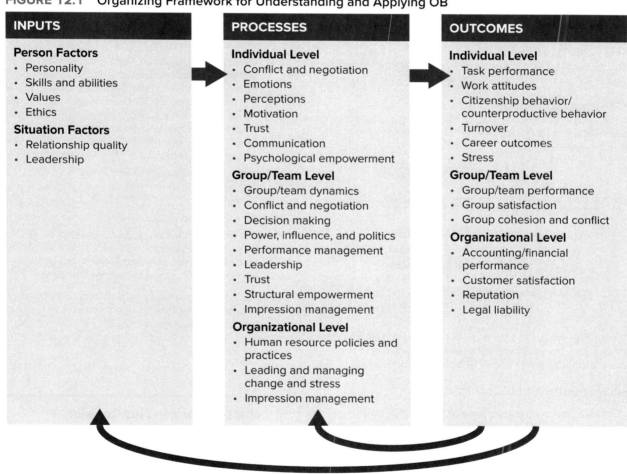

INPUTS	PROCESSES	OUTCOMES
Person Factors	**Individual Level**	**Individual Level**
• Personality	• Conflict and negotiation	• Task performance
• Skills and abilities	• Emotions	• Work attitudes
• Values	• Perceptions	• Citizenship behavior/
• Ethics	• Motivation	counterproductive behavior
Situation Factors	• Trust	• Turnover
• Relationship quality	• Communication	• Career outcomes
• Leadership	• Psychological empowerment	• Stress
	Group/Team Level	**Group/Team Level**
	• Group/team dynamics	• Group/team performance
	• Conflict and negotiation	• Group satisfaction
	• Decision making	• Group cohesion and conflict
	• Power, influence, and politics	**Organizational Level**
	• Performance management	• Accounting/financial
	• Leadership	performance
	• Trust	• Customer satisfaction
	• Structural empowerment	• Reputation
	• Impression management	• Legal liability
	Organizational Level	
	• Human resource policies and practices	
	• Leading and managing change and stress	
	• Impression management	

Winning at Work

Make Meetings Work for You

As one business writer stated: "If you had to identify, in one word, the reason why the human race has not achieved, and never will achieve, its full potential, that word would be 'meetings.'"[1] This cynical and humorous quote resonates with employees everywhere. You've probably never heard anyone plead for more meetings. One estimate is the average worker spends 21 percent of their work hours in meetings and 25 percent of that is wasted. Managers suffer too. A study conducted by the Society of Human Resource Management found 71 percent of managers said meetings were generally unproductive, and 65 percent claimed meetings kept them from productive work.[2] Yet despite the pain, we know people need to meet, and when managed effectively, groups and teams of people can accomplish great things. We therefore give you practical tools to get the most out of your meetings, your colleagues, and your time. Doing so will not only help combat boredom and frustration, but also increase your influence with others, and in turn improve your performance and that of your colleagues.

Common Complaints

A survey by Accountemps revealed the following most common complaints about meetings, ranked by the percentage of respondents who indicated each:

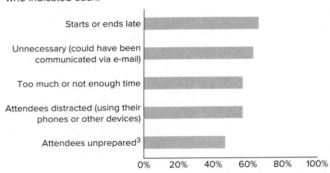

Making all of this worse is the fact that managers and others who initiate meetings think they are far, far more productive than those who attend them, 79 percent versus 57 percent, respectively.

How to Improve Meetings

1. *Make and distribute an agenda.* Do more than simply state purpose, day, time, and location. Tell participants specifically what they need to do to prepare.

2. *Set and communicate a goal for the meeting.* Explain in advance what you want to accomplish by the time you conclude the meeting, such as a decision or plan of action. Tell participants your goal again at the beginning of the meeting.

3. *Assign responsibilities.* Assign roles and responsibilities for the meeting itself, and then assign follow-up or next steps.[4]

4. *Limit the participants.* Some research concludes no more than eight people should be invited, and that when a meeting exceeds this number more people are likely to check out and free-load.[5]

5. *Choose carefully.* Too often only one, two, or a few people dominate meetings. If you or one other person is simply conveying information to the others, with no genuine interaction or decisions

required, then consider sending an e-mail. Otherwise, invite people with the appropriate knowledge and responsibilities to contribute, and be sure they do. (See #3 above—assign and communicate roles and expectations for their contributions.)[6]

6. *Set a time limit.* Some experts suggest that meetings be limited to no more than 45 minutes. There are at least two benefits to this practice: (1) people typically schedule calendar items to begin on the hour, and a 45-minute limit gives them time to get to and prepare for their next appointment; and (2) tasks expand to fill the time you give them, and allowing only 45 minutes will help keep you disciplined and on task.[7]

7. *Match complaints with solutions.* Establish the expectation that someone who raises an issue or complaint must also provide a potential solution.

8. *Control the conversation.* Some people ramble, others complain without offering solutions, and still others wander off on tangents. You don't want to be rude, but you must control the meeting. To a rambler, say: "Interesting comment, Taylor. Let's talk about it after the meeting." Complainer: "Robin, we've heard your issue. What solution do you recommend?" Tangents: "Sylvia, you've taken the discussion off the agenda. Is there something we're missing or something bothering you?"[8]

9. *Be concise.* Tell everyone you expect comments that are concise and on topic, then reinforce this by modeling the same behavior.

10. *Stick to a schedule.* Start on time and end on time.

11. *Ask for input.* You can use your knowledge of feedback and ask those who attend your meetings, "What two or three things made the meeting effective?" and "What are two or three ways we can make future meetings more effective?"

Greg Caimi, a partner at Bain Consulting and author of the firm's time management study, said, "If time really was money, and accounted for in the same way, many companies would be running huge deficits."[9] Treat *your* time, and that of others, like money and don't run deficits!

What's Ahead in This Chapter

The purpose of this chapter is to give you a tool kit for navigating the eternal and ubiquitous world of influence in organizational life. We explore the interrelated topics of power, empowerment, influence and persuasion, organizational politics, and impression management. These topics are in the group and team section of the book because they are about influencing others—individuals *and* groups. They are important group-level processes in the Organizing Framework for Applying and Understanding OB. The way you influence others affects their response and your effectiveness. Appropriate, skilled, and ethical use of the knowledge in this chapter will not only help set you apart from your peers, but also close the gap between you and those with more experience and bigger titles.

12.1 POWER AND ITS BASIC FORMS

THE BIGGER PICTURE

You try to influence people all day, every day of your life, sometimes with great effort and other times without even being aware. And others are doing the same to you. To influence people, you draw on various types of power depending on the situation. You might simply tell a subordinate to do what you want, or you might inspire a coworker with your charismatic personality and persuasive prowess. The way you choose to influence others, and the types of power you use, can have important implications for the responses you get. We will help you gain and apply different forms of power to boost your effectiveness at managing outcomes across the levels of the Organizing Framework for OB.

Power is the discretion and the means to enforce your will over others.[10] Given this definition power is all about influencing others. The more influence you have, the more powerful you are, and vice versa. The well-known phrase—"power tends to corrupt, and absolute power corrupts absolutely"—is undoubtedly true in some instances. However, like it or not, power is a fact of organizational life and you are wise to understand and use it effectively and ethically. The following quote captures the idea well:

> Power must be used because managers must influence those they depend on. Power also is crucial in the development of managers' self-confidence and willingness to support subordinates. From this perspective, power should be accepted as a natural part of any organization. Managers should recognize and develop their own power to coordinate and support the work of subordinates; it is powerlessness, not power, that undermines organizational effectiveness.[11]

To make our discussion of power more practical, we distinguish five common forms or bases of power.

Five Bases of Power

The five common bases of power are: legitimate, reward, coercive, expert, and referent. (See Figure 12.2.) Each represents a different approach to influencing others and has advantages and drawbacks. Let's learn more.

Legitimate Power   Legitimate power is what most people think of as authority and is anchored to a formal position or job. Thus, **managers who obtain compliance primarily by using their formal authority to make decisions have *legitimate power.*** Legitimate power may be used positively or negatively.

- *Positive legitimate power* focuses constructively on job performance. The CBS board of directors utilized this form of power when it ousted CEO Les Moonves and refused to pay his $120 million severance package. The board claimed Mr. Moonves

LO 12-1

Understand the basic forms of power.

FIGURE 12.2   The Five Bases of Power

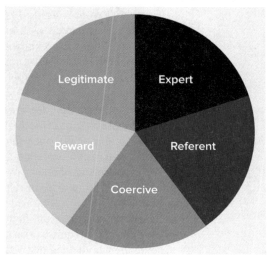

lied and attempted to cover up multiple allegations related to sexual misconduct, thus violating company policies and his contractual obligations.[12] The board asserted its legitimate power by punishing the CEO, which also sent a strong signal to the rest of the organization that policies are enforced consistently—even at the top.

- *Negative legitimate power,* in contrast, tends to be threatening and demeaning to those being influenced. Sometimes this is simply an exercise in building the power holder's ego, such as the many U.S. politicians who have used their legislative position power to name various "monuments" after themselves. While a road here and a library there are quite common, the late Robert Byrd from West Virginia had more than 30 monuments named after him.[13] Citizens of Florida are considering banning such practices. They are seeking to amend the state's constitution and prevent city, county, and state officials from naming taxpayer-funded facilities after elected officials.[14]

Recent ethics research found that powerful chief financial officers (CFOs), when compared to those who are less powerful, were more likely to negotiate short-term compensation incentives and manage company earnings in order to increase their pay and receive the funds sooner, rather than vesting over longer periods of time.[15] For instance, they are more likely to arrange for cash and stock bonuses to be paid over three rather than five years. If you recall the time value of money from finance, you'd rather have your entire annual salary paid today instead of divided up with some paid each month. The idea is you could invest that large sum and earn additional income over and above the value of your salary. CFOs certainly understand this and may tend to use their legitimate power for their personal benefit.

Can you think of your own examples of both positive and negative legitimate power?

Reward Power   Individuals or organizations have ***reward power* if they can obtain compliance by promising or granting rewards valued by the other party.** As you learned in Chapter 6, pay-for-performance plans and positive reinforcement practices rely on reward power. The relationship between Barnes & Noble and Starbucks, along with other alliances, is an excellent example of reward power. Books and coffee are a wonderful combination for many people, and this partnership enables one party to help combat the extinction of brick and mortar bookstores, while at the same time providing books to customers without having to invest in inventory and manage the operation.[16]

Coercive Power   The ability to **make threats of punishment and deliver actual punishment reflects *coercive power*.** The Federal Trade Commission (FTC) filed a lawsuit against DeVry University, one of the largest for-profit colleges in the United States. The FTC charged the company falsely claimed 90 percent of its graduates gained employment within six months of graduation and earned 15 percent higher salaries a year after graduation than graduates of all other colleges.[17]

Expert Power   **Valued knowledge or information gives an individual *expert power*** over those who need such knowledge or information. One way the power of supervisors is enhanced stems from knowing about work assignments and pay raises before their employees do. Perhaps the most common source of expert power for employees more generally is that derived from past experience and performance.

Referent Power   ***Referent power* is derived from personal characteristics and social relationships that effectively gain others' compliance.** Charisma is commonly associated with referent power, but you do not need to be the life of the party to possess such power. In Asian cultures, for instance, characteristics such as age, gender, or family name are sources of social status and referent power. One often overlooked and underestimated source of referent power is your network of relationships. Assume a coworker calls and asks whether you can help her with a project. You tell her you don't have the knowledge or skill yourself, but that Susan, a member of another department whom you happen to know, can provide the help your coworker requires. You make the introduction. Because you introduced your coworker to someone who helped her, you have referent power by virtue of your relationships.

Mattel partnered with Warner Bros. to produce a movie leveraging the iconic Barbie doll to sell other products and promote positivity and confidence for girls and young women. Margot Robbie was cast to play Barbie.

(Left): Keith Homan/Shutterstock; (right): Samir Hussein/WireImage/Getty Images

Referent power drives the success of a number of marketing schemes, such as those used by Tupperware and Mary Kay. These companies and others use independent contractors to throw home parties to display and sell goods to friends and families. More generally, referral programs are examples of referent power. Airbnb provides dollar credits for referring friends who then use its services, and Marriott Reward members can earn up to 50,000 points when up to five referrals book with one of the hotels in the same calendar year. Referrals pay in the beauty and cosmetics industry too. Ulta Beauty awards $15 toward your next salon treatment when you gift $15 to someone else.[18]

Reputation is another aspect of referent power. Many companies hire new CEOs in part to reap the benefits of the executive's reputation. Mattel, the toy maker, has truly put this to the test by hiring three CEOs since 2015. Ynon Kreiz was the latest expected to reverse the continuing decline in company revenues over the past several years. Amazon and the collapse of Toys-R-Us and other brick-and-mortar retailers have made things especially difficult for toy companies. As with other CEO replacements, Mattel is hoping the change and Kreiz's reputation in television production will woo investors by connecting the company's products with movies featuring its products, such as a movie including Barbie, its iconic doll.[19]

Referent power is also a major means for converting your social media connections and reputation into influence—and money. The following Applying OB box illustrates how "influencers" do just this via Instagram.

Applying OB

Follow Me—All the Way to the Bank

Social media has come a long way in a few short years, so much so that "social media influencer" is a genuine career path with many earning annual incomes similar to more conventional professions. For instance, micro-influencers (up to 50,000 followers) can earn a few thousand dollars per post, and those with up to a million followers might earn $10,000 per post.[20]

There are the elite influencers on YouTube and Instagram who make many millions of dollars a year. Whether you are micro or elite,[21] the fundamental reasons for success are the same—referent and expert power.

Referent power for social media influencers is reflected in influencers' reputations, often their celebrity status in sports or movies. People like celebrities, they want to emulate them, and sometimes they identify with a character or the team on which one plays. These forms of conventional celebrity result in name recognition and attention and thus followers on social media.

Yet other influencers' power is derived from their expertise or relevance to particular areas of interest for followers, the largest of which are fashion, fitness, and gaming. Some of the highest paid influencers are gamers—such as DanTDM, VanossGaming, and PewDiePie—who reveal their tricks of the trade on various games on YouTube and earn over $10 million per year.[22]

Selena Gomez, the most-followed person on Instagram, reportedly gets paid $550,000 per sponsored post, while Kylie Jenner earns $400,000, and Cristiano Ronaldo adds to his goal scoring fortune by earning about the same as Jenner.[23]

Just like other types of relationships, social media influencers rely on their authenticity to build follower trust and commitment. Followers come to rely on the influencers for sound, honest, and valuable advice and recommendations, which is what keeps them coming back and buying![24]

Now that you've learned about the five bases of power, complete Self-Assessment 12.1 to identify which bases you prefer to use. Answering the associated questions will help you understand how the various forms of power can both help and hurt you when trying to influence others.

SELF-ASSESSMENT 12.1   CAREER READINESS

What Kind of Power Do I Prefer?

Please be prepared to answer these questions if your instructor has assigned Self-Assessment 12.1 in Connect.

1. Which of the five bases of power do you prefer to use?
2. Describe how your preferred form of power helps you at school, at work, and socially.
3. Which of the five bases is your least preferred? What are the implications for you at school, at work, and socially?
4. What two specific things can you do to increase your expert power? And what two things to increase your referent power?

Adapted from T. R. Hinkin and C. A. Schriesheim, "Development and Application of New Scales to Measure the French and Raven (1959) Bases of Social Power," *Journal of Applied Psychology,* 1989, 567, American Psychological Association.

Position vs. Personal Power

The first three forms of power—legitimate, reward, and coercive—are often referred to as *position power* **because the source of influence is associated with a particular job or position within an organization.** Managers, for instance, have legitimate, reward, and coercive power because they control your pay, work assignments, hiring and firing, and evaluations. In contrast, expert and referent are forms of *personal power,* **which you possess independent of your position or job.** (See Figure 12.3.)

These two general sources of power frequently collide when you are promoted and must manage the people who just yesterday were your peers. The following Applying OB box offers good advice.

FIGURE 12.3   Bases of Power: Position and Personal

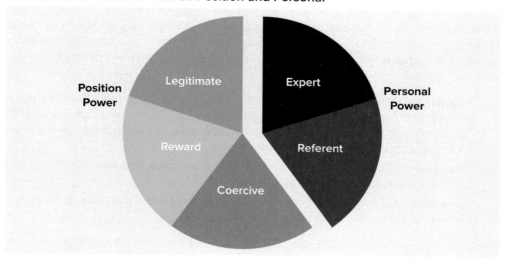

Applying OB

From Teammate to Manager: Taking Charge

If you've been promoted to manage your group, you suddenly have more legitimate power. But to be an effective manager you need to exercise that power carefully, in a way that doesn't alienate but instead motivates your former peers.

What do Sam Hazen at HCA Healthcare[25] and Tony Lowings of Kentucky Fried Chicken[26] have in common? Certainly not their companies' products and services. Both were promoted within their companies to the role of CEO and likely confronted the challenges of becoming everyone's boss, including other executives who had been their peers. Such transitions are often difficult for the promoted and those passed over. Of course, thousands if not millions of workers are promoted every day, and they too face challenges similar to those of executives. The following advice can help you influence former peers who are now subordinates, while at the same time making the transition *easier on you and them*.

1. *It's awkward . . . admit it.* Be honest and don't act as if it is no big deal or it isn't awkward. Be vulnerable, ask for others' help and input, rather than acting as though all the necessary knowledge and answers came along with your new title.
2. *Communicate boundaries.* Be sure to consider and communicate boundaries. You need to determine what you can talk about and share, and what you can't or would rather not. Your former peers may be able to continue to confide in you as

before, but not always. And it is very likely there will be things about your new role you cannot and should not share with them. Figure it out and tell them.[27]
3. *Meet one-on-one.* Meet with all your new direct reports, especially those who were your peers and are your friends. Doing this regularly can not only help you set goals and communicate expectations, but will also provide opportunities for them to learn what you think of them and their work, now that you're their manager.[28]
4. *Don't show off.* It might be tempting to strengthen your leadership role with an aggressive, dominating style, overseeing every detail; however, that approach can generate resentment.
5. *Do accept responsibility.* Don't try to remain buddies if it will undermine your ability to get the job done. Collaborate when it's the best way to accomplish goals, but not to save a friendship.
6. *Do your homework.* Work with your new supervisor to define goals for yourself and your team. Strengthen your network of mentors to improve your management skills. Meet with your staff to go over your vision and expectations. Setting a direction for the team enhances your credibility (via expert power).
7. *Pay attention to team members' concerns.* Show them how meeting the group's goals will put them on track toward meeting their own needs.[29]

Power, but for What Purpose?

Asserting power is a necessary and sometimes even a subconscious activity in our lives. However, we often overlook the potential outcomes. People tend to have three primary reactions to our attempts to manage and otherwise influence them—resistance, compliance, and commitment.

- **Resistance.** You know what resistance is, but have you ever thought of the many forms and degrees? People can simply be indifferent, be passive-aggressive or actively resist. They can also purposefully undermine or even sabotage your efforts. The degree and form of resistance thus matter.
- **Compliance.** Those who comply do only what is expected, nothing more. They exert no extra effort and provide no extra input.
- **Commitment.** Those who are committed believe in the cause and often go above and beyond to ensure its success.

These outcomes are obviously different, and the differences matter! One factor that certainly can affect others' responses is how ethically or responsibly you utilize any form of power.

Using Power Ethically and Effectively   People who do not use their power responsibly risk losing it. This has been shown time and again in political uprisings and the ouster of government leaders, as well as in the persistent waves of scandals in business and the resulting downfall of executives. For instance, as of late 2018 the #MeToo movement had toppled over 200 men in positions of power due to allegations of sexual assault and harassment.[30]

Research is mounting that shows pro-social employees who ascend to leadership positions, and use their position to benefit the group instead of themselves, outperform pro-self individuals (those who become leaders and use the position to benefit themselves). These same pro-social leaders also were more effective at fostering contributions from their teams.[31]

As a senior level commander, General Wesley Clark needed to influence people all the time. Of course he had considerable position power as a general, which in many instances enabled him to get others to comply with his wishes and orders. However, he also knew that sometimes he needed others to actually buy-in and commit. He therefore chose the bases of power accordingly to be more effective.

John Thys/AFP/Getty Images

For managers who want to avoid the potential pitfalls and wield power responsibly, a step in the right direction is understanding the difference between commitment and mere compliance. Responsible managers strive to use power for the good of others, rather than simply for personal gain. Retired General Wesley Clark, former NATO commander, put it this way:

> Sometimes threatening works, but it usually brings with it adverse consequences—like resentment and a desire to get even in some way. People don't like to be reminded that they are inferior in power or status. And so, in business, it is important to motivate through the power of shared goals, shared objectives, and shared standards.[32]

As Clark describes, sometimes you only need someone to comply, but at other times you need genuine commitment. Choose the types of power you use accordingly.

How Do the Five Bases of Power Relate to Commitment and Compliance?
Research, practice, and perhaps your own experiences reveal that, as shown in Figure 12.4:

- Reward, coercive, and *negative* legitimate power tend to produce *compliance* (and sometimes resistance).
- *Positive* legitimate power, expert power, and referent power tend to foster *commitment*.

Once again, commitment is superior to compliance because it is driven by internal or intrinsic motivation. Committed employees tend to be self-starters who do not require close supervision. Intrinsically motivated self-starters are success factors in today's flatter, team-oriented organizations. In contrast, employees who merely comply require frequent jolts of power from the boss to keep them going.

Although most of our discussion thus far has focused on how an individual's power influences other individuals, the same concepts apply between organizations. For instance, research shows that organizations can influence their suppliers and their suppliers' suppliers. Companies that engage in socially responsible management practices, such as those related to fair labor (reasonable hours and employee rights) and fair trade (sustainable farming and packaging), can most effectively get members of their supply chain to adopt these practices if they share their own expertise, knowledge, and training. Trying to coerce, reward, and require (legitimate) suppliers to adopt such practices is likely to result in resistance and wasted time and efforts.[33]

FIGURE 12.4   Bases of Power: Commitment vs. Compliance

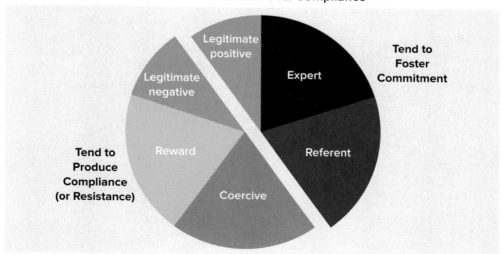

Bases of Power and Outcomes in the Organizing Framework Research gives us some insights into how different bases of power affect important outcomes in the Organizing Framework, such as job performance, job satisfaction, and turnover. These relationships are illustrated in Figure 12.5.

- Expert and referent power have a generally positive effect.
- Reward and legitimate power have a slightly positive effect.
- Coercive power has a slightly negative effect.

Now that you have a clearer sense of what power is and how it operates, let's learn about how sharing power can actually increase your own power.

FIGURE 12.5 Bases of Power and Effectiveness of Outcomes

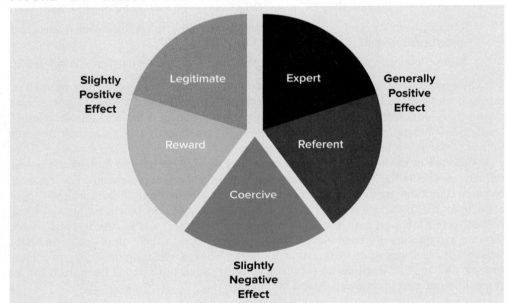

12.2 POWER SHARING AND EMPOWERMENT

THE BIGGER PICTURE

How much do you like being told what to do? Chances are you didn't like it as a kid and like it even less as an adult at work. Thankfully, many managers and organizations are looking to employees to solve problems and make decisions, instead of always telling them what to do and how to do it. This increased participation and sharing of authority is the result of empowerment. We explore different forms of empowerment (structural and psychological), various degrees of empowerment, and ways to foster it in individuals, teams, and organizations.

Empowerment consists of efforts to "enhance employee performance, well-being, and positive attitudes."[34] Empowerment has been shown to favorably influence many outcomes in the Organizing Framework, such as job satisfaction, organizational commitment, performance, turnover, and employee stress.[35]

In addition to these benefits, empowerment is becoming a necessity. Time-management research done by two researchers at Harvard showed the CEOs in their study spent nearly 25 percent of their time on e-mail![36] This means no individual, executive or not, can accomplish all the necessary tasks alone. You must share the load. To help in this effort, research and practice related to empowerment have focused on two general forms—*structural* and *psychological.*

Structural Empowerment

Structural empowerment **transfers authority and responsibilities from management to employees.** Some popular ways to do this are via the job design and job characteristics forms of motivation. Managers and their employers can boost employee empowerment by changing policies, procedures, job responsibilities, and team designs. Any of these that increase the effectiveness of employee decision making are likely also to increase their performance, well-being, and job-related attitudes. To better understand and apply this knowledge about empowerment, it is necessary to think about the issue correctly.

Thinking the Right Way about Empowerment   Effective empowerment does *not* include giving decision-making authority to just any employee in every situation. That would be both foolish and irresponsible, and it would not be empowerment. Instead, decision-making authority and other broader responsibilities should be shared only with those who are competent to do what is necessary. There are two pitfalls to avoid:

1. Empowerment is *not a zero-sum game* in which one person's gain is another's loss. Sharing power via empowerment is a means of increasing your own power. Think of it this way: you cannot be everywhere, all the time, with all the answers. But if you allow competent others to act, then you've increased your reach and your influence. This means authoritarian managers who view employee empowerment as a threat to their own power are missing the point because of their win–lose thinking.

2. Empowerment is *a matter of degree,* not an either–or proposition. Figure 12.6 illustrates how power can be shifted to the hands of nonmanagers step by step. The

FIGURE 12.6   The Evolution of Power from Domination to Delegation

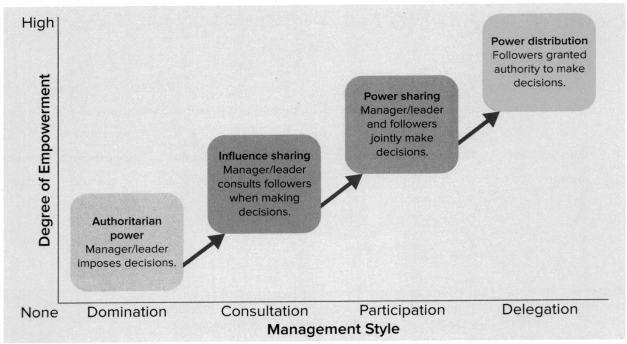

overriding goal is to increase productivity and competitiveness in organizations. Each step in this evolution increases the power of organizational contributors who traditionally were told what, when, and how to do things.

Sharing Power to Increase Your Power and Performance   A common element of empowerment is pushing decision-making authority to lower levels and is illustrated in Figure 12.6. At the level of least empowerment, managers and leaders practice domination, characterized as authoritarian power wherein they make all of the decisions and then hand them down to employees. Next is consultation which occurs when employees are asked for their input, but managers ultimately make the decisions themselves. Participation takes place when managers and employees jointly identify problems *and* solutions—power is shared more or less evenly. Finally, delegation occurs when managers turn over decision-making authority to employees and remove themselves from the process altogether. It is important to note that one level of empowerment is not necessarily better than another. Like many other things related to OB, the degree of power sharing should match the needs of the situation and the capabilities of the individuals or teams involved.[37]

Homewood Suites, part of Hilton Hotels, offers a 100 percent money-back guarantee if a guest isn't satisfied. Any employee from housekeeper to manager can make good on that guarantee—no manager's approval is needed. And the guest doesn't have to go through a chain of command to have a complaint resolved. "The return we get on every dollar refunded is 20 to 1," based on repeat business and referrals from those refunded guests, said former executive Frank Saitta. The return on engaged employees "is much higher."[38]

Not to be outdone, Ritz Carlton allows employees up to $2,000 to remedy a customer related incident. That's right, employees don't need approval and there is no limit on the number of customers a given employee can assist with $2,000 awards, which can include gifts, upgrades, and free nights. Wholesale club standout Costco is legendary for its return policy. Customers don't need a receipt and there is no time limit. Employees have the latitude to accept items, make exchanges, or do whatever else they deem necessary to resolve customer issues.[39]

As part of their efforts to compete for guests' business, Hilton and Ritz-Carlton both provide considerable levels of empowerment for employees to enable them to satisfy guests as they see appropriate. No manager approval needed.

(Left): Lester Balajadia/Shutterstock; (right): Max_Ryazanov/Shutterstock

With your understanding of structural empowerment in hand, let's move on and learn about psychological empowerment.

Psychological Empowerment

Psychological empowerment occurs when we feel a sense of:

Meaning—Belief that your work values and goals align with those of your manager, team, or employer.

Competence—Personal evaluation of your ability to do the job.

Self-determination—Sense that you have control over your work and its outcomes.

Impact at work—Feeling your efforts make a difference and affect the organization.[40]

How Do Structural and Psychological Empowerment Differ?   While structural empowerment draws on job design and characteristics, psychological empowerment is related to self-efficacy and intrinsic motivation.[41] "It is less concerned with the actual transition of authority and responsibility but instead focuses on employees' perceptions or cognitive states regarding empowerment."[42] Put simply, if you feel your work has meaning, you are competent, and you have some control (self-determination), then you are very likely to feel highly efficacious and perform at a high level.

It therefore is necessary to do more than simply delegate responsibilities if you wish to psychologically empower others. For instance, assume you're a janitor and you clean sinks and do it very well. Would you feel empowered if your manager said, "Because you clean the sinks so well, now I'd like you to clean the toilets too." Empowered? No. Where is the sense of meaning or impact? This is simply delegating more work to you (similar to simple job enlargement in Chapter 5). Put plainly, don't feel too confident you're empowering others if they don't actually feel empowered.

Psychological Empowerment at the Team and Organizational Levels   Both research and practice show the same four elements that empower individuals—meaning, competence, self-determination, and impact—also foster psychological empowerment in teams.[43] Moreover, the benefits to individuals also apply to teams and organizations—higher performance and satisfaction[44] and more positive emotions within the team.[45]

Toyota has successfully empowered teams for decades. In the company's manufacturing facilities, for example, teams are expected to identify and solve problems as they

Simply giving employees more responsibilities or tasks does not mean they will feel empowered. Would you feel empowered if your manager allowed you to clean toilets because you've done such an excellent job of cleaning sinks?

BlueSkyImage/Shutterstock

occur and not simply pass them along to management to fix. Employees are further encouraged to make efficiency and quality-improvement suggestions to management. These are typically reviewed by management, but the problems are often assigned to employee teams charged with identifying and implementing solutions. Toyota's practices have been so effective that they have been adopted not only by other auto companies, but also by manufacturers in many other industries the world over.

Since we've explored different forms of empowerment and its various degrees and levels, let's conclude this section with a discussion of how to increase or develop empowerment in individuals, teams, and organizations.

How to Empower Individuals, Teams, and Organizations

Empowering others is not simple, but what makes it easier is the same levers operate across all levels of an organization. Figure 12.7 illustrates some key inputs to empowering others and their resulting outcomes. Notice how many are elements in the Organizing Framework.

Empowerment Inputs   Structural empowerment is an input to psychological empowerment. This makes sense because job characteristics, policies, and practices can either facilitate or impede feelings of empowerment for individuals and teams. In one case, hospital policies and practices were changed (structural empowerment) which helped nurse leaders find greater meaning in their jobs, provided more participative decision making,

FIGURE 12.7   Inputs and Outcomes of Psychological Empowerment Across Organizational Levels

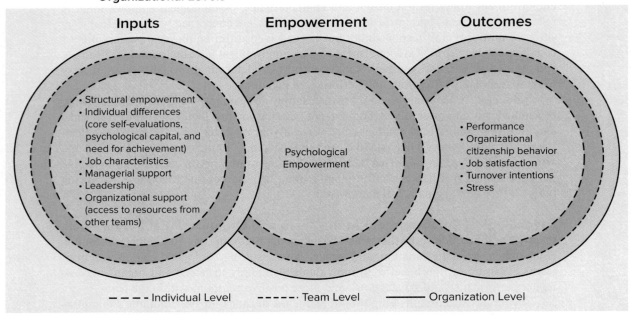

SOURCE: Maynard, M. Travis, Lucy L. Gilson, and John E. Mathieu. "Empowerment—Fad or Fab? A Multilevel Review of the Past Two Decades of Research." *Journal of Management* 38, no. 4 (2012): 1231–1281. https://doi.org/10.1177/0149206312438773.

and reduced bureaucracy. These changes in turn increased the nurses' feelings of psychological empowerment and their actual empowering behaviors.[46]

Also helpful to enhancing empowerment is the extent to which employees have positive self-evaluations, such as core self-evaluations and positive psychological capital (Chapters 3 and 7, respectively). Your knowledge of motivation also is helpful to understanding and fostering empowerment across levels of the Organizing Framework. Job characteristics, for instance, that generate intrinsic motivational states (sense of meaningfulness and responsibility) clearly can help, along with empowering leadership (Chapter 13). Finally, if teams have access to resources such as the people and ideas in other teams, then they too are more likely to be empowered.

Empowerment Outputs   Like many of the topics covered in this book, empowerment is valuable because it positively influences performance for individuals, teams, and organizations. But the benefits extend beyond performance and include citizenship behaviors, job satisfaction, turnover intentions, and creativity. Empowerment also reduces stress for individuals and teams.[47]

To help your empowerment efforts, we turn our attention in the next section to particular tools for influencing others. But before moving on, apply your new knowledge in the following Problem-Solving Application.

Problem-Solving Application

Empowering a Team of Your Peers[48]

Jennifer was a highly regarded and top-performing marketing associate at an international pharmaceutical company. Due to her exceptional performance and other skills and abilities, she was promoted to manager. This transition meant she was now the supervisor of her former peers.

Her first assignment was a new product to be launched in a foreign market. To formulate and ultimately execute a successful product launch, Jennifer and her team needed to gather market data, learn and share information about the competition, analyze financial details, coordinate with other product managers, hire and work with an advertising agency, and secure regulatory approval.

Jennifer had personal experience and success doing most of these things, but now she had to do them on a much larger scale and in the context of a team she managed. As a high performer, she was determined to get all the details right. Therefore, when any element was late, done poorly, or just not up to her expectations, she stepped in and did it herself. Her work life quickly expanded to 15-hour days and weekends.

Jennifer's involvement in so many aspects of the product launch prevented her from mentoring and developing her team members in the ways they clearly needed. They seemed to lack a sense of accountability, knowing that if their work wasn't up to speed the boss would step in and complete or correct it. Jennifer noticed this and feared her team was not learning to produce high-quality work on its own. Not only would this hurt the current project, but other departments and teams would come to know it and be less willing to work with them in the future, damaging Jennifer's own performance and that of her team.

Jennifer was extremely reluctant to go to her boss for help, because she had been told she'd earned her new position, and it was a test for another role with still greater responsibility.

Assuming you are Jennifer, what would you do?

Apply the 3-Step Problem Solving Approach

Step 1: Define the problem in the case.

Step 2: Identify the potential causes.

Step 3: Recommend what you would do if you were Jennifer.

12.3 EFFECTIVELY INFLUENCING OTHERS

THE BIGGER PICTURE

How do you get others to do as you wish? Do you attempt to dazzle them with your knowledge and logical arguments? Or do you prefer a less direct approach, such as promising to return the favor? Whatever approach you use, the crux of the matter is social influence. Many of our interpersonal interactions are attempts to influence others, including parents, bosses, coworkers, professors, friends, spouses, and children. Let's start sharpening your influence skills by exploring influence tactics and their effective and ethical application.

LO 12-3

Describe and implement various influence tactics.

In a perfect world other people's interests would align with your own and everyone would move forward as one. However, the world isn't perfect, and we often find a rather messy situation in which self-interests override the collective mission of the department or organization. Personal and hidden agendas are pursued, political coalitions are formed, false impressions are made, and people end up working against rather than with each other. Managers, and you, need to guide diverse individuals, all with their own interests, to pursue common objectives. At stake in this tug-of-war between individual and collective interests is effectiveness at the personal, group, and organizational levels. Your tools for managing such challenges are *influence tactics*.

Common Influence Tactics

Influence tactics **are conscious efforts to affect and change behaviors in others.** The nine most common ways people try to influence their bosses, coworkers, and subordinates are listed in Table 12.1, beginning with the most frequently used.

TABLE 12.1   9 Common Influence Tactics

INFLUENCE TACTIC	DESCRIPTION
1. Rational persuasion	Trying to convince someone with reason, logic, or facts.
2. Inspirational appeals	Trying to build enthusiasm by appealing to others' emotions, ideals, or values.
3. Consultation	Getting others to provide insights, experience or information you can use in planning and making decisions.
4. Ingratiation	Getting someone in a good mood prior to making a request. Being friendly and helpful and using praise, flattery, or humor. A particular form of ingratiation is "brownnosing."
5. Personal appeals	Referring to friendship and loyalty when making a request.
6. Exchange	Making explicit or implied promises and trading favors.
7. Coalition tactics	Getting others to support your efforts to persuade someone.
8. Pressure	Demanding compliance or using intimidation or threats.
9. Legitimating tactics	Basing a request on authority or right, organizational rules or policies, or explicit/implied support from superiors.

SOURCE: Plouffe, Christopher R., Willy Bolander, Joseph A. Cote, and Bryan Hochstein. "Does the Customer Matter Most? Exploring Strategic Frontline Employees' Influence of Customers, the Internal Business Team, and External Business Partners." *Journal of Marketing* 80, no. 1 (January 2016): 106–123. https://doi.org/10.1509/jm.14.0192.

Claire Foy used personal power and soft tactics to close the pay gap between her and her male counterpart, Matt Smith, on the Netflix blockbuster, *The Crown*. This contrasts with her character, the Queen of England, who in real life has varying degrees of position power and the ability to use hard tactics, along with those used by Foy.

Pictorial Press Ltd/Alamy Stock Photo

These are considered *generic* influence tactics because they can be used in all directions—up (your boss), down (your subordinates), and sideways (your peers). Research has shown this ranking to be fairly consistent regardless of direction, which means you are likely to attempt to influence everyone the same way. And more generally, it means rational persuasion is the most common tactic we employ and encounter.

Actress Claire Foy, who portrayed Queen Elizabeth in the first two seasons of *The Crown*, was effectively influential when she protested about the difference in pay between her and the male counterpart in the show. She said, "I'd been working on that show for two years . . . (and) loved everybody on it. And then I realized, there's been a big, fat, dirty secret that nobody's ever talked about." She shared that she felt the need to be vocal about the pay gap for the sake of her fellow actresses. "But then there was also that thing [of being] an inadvertent spokesperson . . . Why did it have to be me? I could have said nothing. And I think everyone would have preferred that. But I thought, if I do that, I will be cheating myself and all the other women I know."[49] It worked! Foy's pay was adjusted to match that of her male co-star (Matt Smith), and Netflix, the show's creator, subsequently reviewed and closed similar types of pay disparities in other shows.[50]

Hard vs. Soft Tactics   Some refer to the first five influence tactics—rational persuasion, inspirational appeals, consultation, ingratiation, and personal appeals—as **"soft" tactics because they are friendlier than, and not as coercive as, the last four tactics—** exchange, coalition, pressure, and legitimating tactics, which are **"hard" tactics because they exert more overt pressure.**

Which Do I Use Most? Least?   When you read the list of tactics, each probably means something to you. Which do you most commonly use? Knowing the answer can help you better choose the appropriate tactic for any given situation and thus increase the chance of achieving your desired outcome. The next step to realizing these benefits is to complete Self-Assessment 12.2. Be sure to answer the associated questions to increase the value of your knowledge.

Which Influence Tactics Do I Use?

Please be prepared to answer these questions if your instructor has assigned Self-Assessment 12.2 in Connect.

1. Is your rational persuasion score the highest? Regardless, give some specific examples of ways you use this tactic.

2. Which tactic is your least preferred (lowest score)? Provide examples of situations of when and how you may use this tactic.

Some organizations routinely, if not masterfully, apply the same tactics as individuals. The following OB in Action box illustrates how Amazon obtains tax and other concessions from city and state governments in exchange for locating its facilities within their borders.

OB in Action

Hard Sell... Amazon Style

Amazon made headlines in early 2019 when it backed out of plans to build a second headquarters in New York City. NYC was a finalist in a field of many cities and states that engaged in an intense courtship to lure Amazon. Like others, the city offered billions of dollars of tax incentives in exchange for the company employing thousands of workers and the associated economic benefits, such as real estate development and sale, retail sales and taxes, along with employees' payroll and income taxes.

Although many legislators, business people, and others saw the concessions as justifiable and a victory, still others objected. The dissenters protested that rich subsidies should not be given to the world-dominating Amazon. Their rationale: The company is extremely successful and can pay its own way.

The company has a history of extracting concessions from city and state governments in exchange for the perceived benefits of locating Amazon facilities within their borders. Some estimates put the figure at nearly $2.5 billion, and they are tough or even ruthless in the process. For instance, the company closed its only Texas warehouse when the state pressured the company to pay over $250 million dollars in back taxes. Texas ultimately ended its pursuit of the taxes in return for more warehouses. In South Carolina, Amazon threatened to halt hiring unless it was given generous tax exemptions; the state eventually went Amazon's way.[51]

Such tactics and exchanges are nothing new and not unique to Amazon. Companies and governments at all levels have been doing such deals for ages, even in New York City. The Hudson Yards real estate development reportedly received approximately $6 billion in tax breaks, and the incentives didn't stop there. Some tenants in the development, such as BlackRock (the world's biggest money manager), which has over $5 trillion under management, also received tax credits in the tens of millions to occupy the space.[52] Again, opponents of the incentives argue that the companies can certainly pay their way. And these arguments are countered with companies effectively saying: "Give us what we want, or we'll leave and take our jobs elsewhere."[53]

YOUR THOUGHTS?

1. Make the case for granting tax and other incentives to companies.

2. Argue against such concessions.

3. Now assume you are Jeff Bezos, CEO of Amazon, and decide what you would do: continue with such practices, stop, or something else. Justify your position.

Match Tactics to Desired Outcomes

Research and practice provide some useful lessons about the relative effectiveness of influence tactics. Rely on the core. *Core influence tactics*–rational persuasion, consultation, collaboration, and inspirational appeals–are most effective at building commitment. Do not rely on pressure and coalition tactics. In one study, managers who were not very effective at using downward influence relied most heavily on inspiration (an effective tactic), ingratiation (a moderately effective tactic), and pressure (an ineffective tactic). More generally, you are well served to:

- **Be believable and trustworthy.** Credible people tend to be the most persuasive.
- **Consult rather than legitimate.** Some employees are more apt to accept change when managers rely on a consultative strategy and are more likely to resist change when managers use a legitimating tactic.
- **Expect little from schmoozing.** Ingratiation improved short-term sales goal achievement but reduced it in the long term. Schmoozing can help today's sales but not tomorrow's.
- **Be subtle.** Subtle flattery and agreement with the other person's opinion (forms of ingratiation) were shown to increase the likelihood executives would win recommendations to sit on boards.
- **Learn to influence.** Research with corporate managers of a supermarket chain showed influence tactics can be taught and learned. Managers who received 360-degree feedback on two occasions regarding their influence tactics showed an increased use of core influence tactics.

These insights are helpful, but what is the bottom line? There is no one best influence tactic. Customers may respond more favorably to one tactic while internal team members and external business partners are influenced by another.[54] You need to understand *and* effectively apply a range of influence tactics to be effective. But, thankfully, you can learn and improve influence tactics to move resisters to compliance and move those who are compliant to commitment.

Influence in Virtual Teams

Work is increasingly done from a distance and mediated by technology, so it's worth knowing which influence tactics are used most in virtual teams and how. The most common (in order of use) are: pressure, legitimating, rational persuasion, consultation, and personal appeals. These tactics obviously overlap with those used in face-to-face interactions. However, putting the word *urgent* in the subject line of an e-mail or typing the entire (short) message there provides a quick jolt of pressure, as does marking a message as high priority. Highlighting text is another way of focusing attention and asserting pressure.

Reducing ambiguity emerged as a unique influence tactic in virtual teams. Virtual team members do three things to reduce ambiguity:[55]

1. *Share information.* Of course we share information face-to-face as well, but in virtual teams sharing ensures members have the information necessary to complete their work or fulfill a request. This differs from rational persuasion since it is not meant to persuade someone to act,[56] but instead it helps overcome the lack of nonverbal and other cues in face-to-face interactions that communicate useful information.

2. *Create accountability.* Accountability is often more explicit in virtual interactions because a written record is created. Clarifying and confirming performance expectations, such as deliverables and timelines, are important examples of accountability.

3. *Provide examples.* Attachments and screen sharing are common ways in which virtual team members share examples. Again, examples are not a form of rational persuasion intended to convince a team member of a particular position, but instead are a means for clarifying intended messages and providing guidance.

Let's not forget emoticons, which convey friendliness or soften an otherwise stern text or e-mail message. You can further enhance your ability to persuade others by understanding and applying the six principles of persuasion described next.

Cialdini's Six Principles of Persuasion

Experiments by Robert Cialdini and others have identified six principles for influencing people.[57] They are based on the idea that people have fundamental responses, and if your efforts align with these responses your influence increases. Read and learn about the following to see what you think.

Robert Cialdini is one of the world's foremost authorities on influence. His principles are based in research and proven in practice. You too can benefit from the application of these principles in every arena of your life—in school, at work, and socially.
Courtesy of INFLUENCE AT WORK

1. *Liking.* People tend to like those who like them. Learning about another person's likes and dislikes through conversations builds friendship bonds. Sincere and timely praise, empathy, and recognition also help.

2. *Reciprocity.* The societal norm that says good and bad deeds should be repaid in kind is virtually universal. Managers who act unethically and treat employees with disrespect should expect the same in return, and their employees are likely to treat each other and their customers unethically and with disrespect. Managers need to be positive and constructive role models and be fair-minded to benefit from the principle of reciprocity.

3. *Social proof.* People tend to follow the lead of those most like themselves, and role models and peer pressure are powerful cultural forces in social settings. Managers are advised to build support for workplace changes by first gaining the enthusiastic support of informal leaders who will influence their peers.

4. *Consistency.* People tend to do what they commit to, especially publicly or to others. A manager who can elicit a verbal commitment from an employee has taken an important step toward applying influence and persuasion.

5. *Authority.* People tend to defer to and respect credible experts. Too many managers and professionals take their own expertise for granted, as did one hospital's physical therapy staff that grew frustrated by the lack of follow-through by patients. No matter how much these professionals emphasized the importance of continuing therapy, many patients stopped once they returned home. An investigation of the causes revealed patients were unaware of the professional/clinical qualifications of their therapists, and once diplomas and certifications were hung on the walls in the clinic, patient compliance increased a remarkable 34 percent![58]

6. *Scarcity.* People want items, information, and opportunities that have limited availability. Special opportunities and privileged information are influence-builders for managers.

Cialdini says that when one or more principles naturally exist in a situation, using them together can produce an additive effect. Because there are ethical implications to using your influence, your goals need to be worthy and your actions need to be sincere and genuine.

Apply Your Knowledge

We conclude this section by giving you an opportunity to apply your knowledge in a familiar scenario and recognize that effective influence starts with a plan. Follow these steps to create your own influence plan.

Step 1: Set a goal and get a clear idea of what you want to achieve. It helps if achieving clearly requires someone else's effort or agreement.

Step 2: Identify the person or persons who can help you achieve that goal.

Step 3: Decide what type of influence outcome—compliance or commitment—you want or need from the person(s) identified in Step 2.

Step 4: Decide which bases of power and tactics are most appropriate for the influence outcome you desire. (Be realistic about which are available to you.)

Step 5: Explicitly describe how you will apply the bases of power and tactics you chose.

Apply this approach to the following scenario. Assume your goal is to get a job in the product development group at Salesforce, a leader in cloud-based customer relationship management services and No. 2 on *Fortune*'s 2019 list of Best Companies to Work For.[59]

To achieve this goal, you'll want to learn more about the organization and its decision makers. Fortunately, you learn that two years ago Salesforce hired Arica, who went to your school. You plan to contact her on LinkedIn in the hope she will share her experiences and put you in touch with the hiring manager in product development.

You do not need Arica's enthusiastic *commitment* to your employment efforts, since she doesn't even know you. But what you would like is her *compliance* with your request for more information and an introduction to the product development group manager. She is probably willing to do this, if for no other reason than she is an alumna of your school, and you were very charming in your e-mail and phone communications. Now you need to decide which of the bases of power and influence tactics you have available with Arica, and which of these are most appropriate for gaining her compliance.

We hope the practical tools you've gained in this section piqued your interest and you are motivated to learn more about how you can influence others to affect processes and outcomes in the Organizing Framework. Let's continue to build your knowledge and skills and focus on political tactics next.

12.4 POLITICAL TACTICS AND HOW TO USE THEM

THE BIGGER PICTURE

Politics are not all bad. To make this point, and to increase your effectiveness at school, at work, and socially, we explore this important and interesting topic in terms of causes, tactics, and levels. You'll learn how to manage politics in your favor. All this will help you better understand and manage this ever-present aspect of organizational life and key group-level process in the Organizing Framework.

Before we learn about organizational politics, let's get a sense of how political you are by completing Self-Assessment 12.3. This is another one of those personal attributes, similar to trust, about which people often think more highly of themselves than others do. It therefore could be quite interesting to have some friends complete this same assessment in terms of *how they see you*, especially considering this particular self-assessment also taps into ethics and manipulation.

SELF-ASSESSMENT 12.3   CAREER READINESS

How Political Am I?

Please be prepared to answer these questions if your instructor has assigned Self-Assessment 12.3 in Connect.

1. Does your score accurately capture your tendencies in organizational politics? Why or why not?

2. Do you think a true organizational politician would complete the assessment honestly? Explain.

3. Given knowledge of your political tendencies, describe how they could both help or hurt you at school, at work, and in your career.

Organizational Politics—The Good and the Bad

When you hear the word *politics,* what comes to mind? The President, a deadlocked Congress, or a conniving boss or coworker? Whatever the case, it is unlikely a smile comes to your face. Likewise, people typically view organizational politics as consisting of negative or counterproductive behaviors such as manipulation, controlling of information, and undermining. But it is important to realize that organizational politics also include positive outcomes, such as restoring justice, providing opportunities and resources for followers, and affecting change.[60] If you understand organizational politics you can realize the benefits and avoid or manage the shortcomings.

Organizational politics **are intentional actions to improve individual or organizational interests.** This definition clearly allows for positive behaviors and outcomes, but our primary focus in OB is the use of influence to further *self-interests,* especially when these interests conflict with those of the organization. Managers are endlessly challenged to achieve a workable balance or alignment between employees and organizational interests.

When Are Politics Good?   Positive uses of politics can occur when actions help an organization adapt, such as when the organization's leadership, policies, practices, and/or strategies may be taking the organization in the wrong direction. In these situations, if an individual or coalition operates counter to the organization's goals, policies, or practices it may ultimately be positive for the organization. Such instances of political action by employees and other groups have exploded in the past few years. See the OB in Action box for an example.

OB in Action

Turning Politics Upside Down . . . Employees Rule!

Influence has historically been top down—employers say, employees do. The past few years, however, have seen a growing trend of employee activism, wherein the rank and file have asserted themselves to change the policies and practices of their employers. For instance, 20,000 Google employees walked out in the summer of 2018 protesting against the company's protection of executives accused of sexual harassment. This was followed by additional actions. In one instance employees took issue with the company's contract with the Pentagon for which it was developing software for drone strike targeting. And in another they applied pressure to alter practices pertaining to the treatment of minority workers and contractors.

Claire Stapleton, marketing manager at YouTube (owned by Google) and organizer of the employee protests, explained that Google's own technology (Google Docs and Groups) helped facilitate this political action. Employees are now organized, committed, and determined to shape the direction of the company.[61]

This adds to concerns expressed by Googlers about building a search engine censoring product for the Chinese government. And such efforts are not unique to Google. Along with employees from Microsoft and Amazon, they've signed petitions protesting the uses of their work, and some employees have expressed their objections even more strongly—they've quit!

An engineer from artificial intelligence start-up Clarifai quit when he learned the project he was working on was for the U.S. Defense Department.[62]

Again, this is part of a larger trend in which employees want transparency regarding the customers and applications of their work.

YOUR THOUGHTS?

1. Do employees have the right to know all details related to their work, such as who the customer is and what the intended uses are?

2. Does your opinion change if the nature of the work is confidential or otherwise protected, as in the case of products, services, or technology related to national security? Justify your answer.

3. Assume you're an employee and have concerns about such matters regarding your own work. What would you do? Explain.

When Are Politics Bad?   Organizational politics can negatively affect outcomes across all three levels in the Organizing Framework. At the individual level, politics can increase stress and turnover intentions and reduce job satisfaction, organizational commitment, and organizational citizenship behaviors. Undesirable effects on the group and organizational levels include wasted time and resources, diverted decision-maker attention, and restricted and distorted information flow among decision makers.[63]

Uncertainty and Political Behavior

The causes of political behavior occur at all three levels of the Organizing Framework. For instance, negative emotions and a lack of trust are the strongest individual- and group/team-level causes, and a perceived lack of justice is the strongest organizational-level driver of political behavior.[64] Underlying most of these causes is a more fundamental or root cause—uncertainty. Uncertainty drives a great deal of political behavior, and research outlines five common sources of uncertainty within organizations:

1. Unclear objectives.
2. Vague performance measures.
3. Ill-defined decision processes.
4. Strong individual or group competition.[65]
5. Any type of change.

Reflecting items 1–4, unfair performance management procedures and outcomes are major determinants of uncertainty. So too is a lack of trust in your boss or a coworker. Individuals and organizations that do not treat their employees with respect, or that create "cut-throat" cultures, also motivate political activity. Related to the fifth factor, many changes at work increase uncertainty and employees' efforts to protect their interests (status, opportunities, and resources)—in other words, politics.

Frequently Used Political Tactics

Anyone who has worked in an organization has firsthand knowledge of blatant politicking. Although there are many different ways to describe and categorize political tactics, Table 12.2 shows some of the most commonly used political tactics and a description of each.

TABLE 12.2   Most Commonly Used Political Tactics

TACTIC	DESCRIPTION
1. Building a network of useful contacts	Cultivating a support network both inside and outside the organization
2. Using "key players" to support initiatives	Getting prior support for a decision or issue; building others' commitment via participation
3. Making friends with power brokers	Teaming up with powerful people who can get results
4. Bending the rules to fit the situation	Interpreting or (not) enforcing rules to serve your own interests
5. Using self-promotion	Blowing your own horn, but not doing the same for others' accomplishments
6. Creating a favorable image (also known as *impression management,* discussed next)	Dressing for success; adhering to organizational norms and drawing attention to your successes and influence; taking credit for others' accomplishments
7. Praising others (ingratiation)	Making influential people feel good (brownnosing)
8. Attacking or blaming others	Avoiding or minimizing association with failure; scapegoating; reducing competition for limited resources
9. Using information as a political tool	Withholding or distorting information; obscuring an unfavorable situation by overwhelming superiors with information

SOURCE: Allen, Robert W., Dan L. Madison, Layman W. Porter, Patricia A. Renwick, and Bronston T. Mayes. "Organizational Politics: Tactics and Characteristics of Its Actors." *California Management Review* 22, no. 1 (October 1979): 77–83. https://doi.org/10.2307/41164852.

The World Economic Forum brings leaders from many domains from around the globe. A wide variety of political tactics are used by attendees to influence awareness, policy, and action.

Jason Alden/Bloomberg/Getty Images

The World Economic Forum in Davos, Switzerland, has become one of the premier events on the planet for building political influence via networking. Leaders from politics, business, government, and many other arenas meet with the goal of improving the state of the world. Individuals are selling products, services, ideas, and themselves by utilizing many of the tactics listed in Table 12.2, such as networking, making friends with influential others, associating with power brokers, making a favorable impression, and praising others.[66]

You may view some of the tactics in Table 12.2 very favorably, such as building a network of useful contacts. Many management experts and career counselors agree it is wise to build, maintain, and use networks both inside and outside your organization. This is a positive use of politics. However, let's explore another common and not-so-positive political tactic—blaming others.

Blame and Politics

You may have noticed that politicking often occurs when things don't work out; that is, in situations of underperformance, scandal, or otherwise unethical conduct. People often look to assign blame, in part, to help preserve their influence with others. Research in the United States showed 70 percent of employees tend to assign blame for failures in one of three ways:

1. Blame others
2. Blame self
3. Deny blame[67]

Blame occurs across levels of OB. Goldman Sachs, for instance, was embroiled in allegations of looting nearly $3 billion from a Malaysian government investment fund, known as 1MDB. Some reports show Goldman has gone to great lengths to aggressively shift responsibility to one "rogue" partner, Tim Leissner, who they say duped a large number of Goldman employees across levels and over time.

In efforts to discredit Leissner, the company went so far as to create a PowerPoint presentation for U.S. authorities wherein it alleged he was married to two women at once, converted to Islam at least twice to impress Muslim women he was dating, and received a mail-order PhD from a defunct university. It is worth noting that those with knowledge of the campaign against Leissner question the evidence supporting the allegations, and they point out that Goldman's CEO and compliance department were aware of his actions. The courts will sort out the legal implications, but regardless of those outcomes this is a clear and common example of an organization blaming employees for mistakes attributed to the organization.[68]

Counterintuitively, blaming ourselves can be useful in some situations. Consider serial entrepreneurs who may fail in one venture yet go on to start another. Research suggests it is critical for them to accurately identify the appropriate reason for their business failures, such as industry conditions or personal strategy or leadership. If they mistakenly attributed blame to the industry, they are likely to start their next venture in a different industry but repeat the same personal errors (strategy or leadership) and fail again. In contrast, if blaming the industry is correct, then they are likely to start their next venture in the same industry and use what they learned from failure.[69] Assigning blame correctly is important not only to preserve your influence, but also to help guide your future behavior.

Three Levels of Political Action

Figure 12.8 illustrates three levels of political action: the individual level, the coalition level, and the network level. At the individual level, we pursue our self-interests. The political aspects of coalitions and networks are not so obvious, however, and thus require a bit of explanation.

Coalition-Level Politics A *coalition* is an informal group bound together by the *active* pursuit of a *single* issue. Coalitions may or may not coincide with formal group membership. When the coalition's target issue has been resolved (when a sexually harassing supervisor is fired, for example), the coalition disbands. Political coalitions have "fuzzy boundaries," meaning they are fluid in membership, flexible in structure, and temporary in duration.[70] Coalitions are a potent political force within and between organizations.

A very interesting coalition was developed between food delivery service UberEats of London and one of its largest clients, McDonald's. UberEats couriers decided to strike and picket next to McDonald's employees, both demanding higher pay. Employees of both companies have long felt powerless against their enormous and resource rich employers, but by banding together for a common cause, expanding to multiple cities, and including employees of other client restaurants, they may have greater influence. For example, the food delivery service companies know McDonald's views delivery as a key to its future growth. Although nothing has changed yet, the pressure is clearly on.[71]

FIGURE 12.8 Levels of Political Action in Organizations

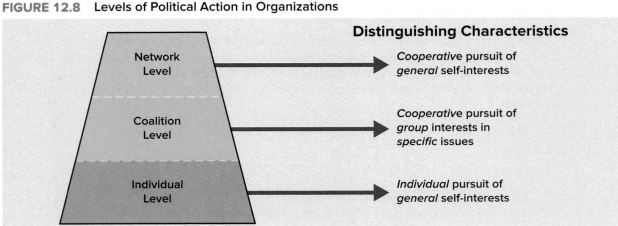

The past few years have seen an increase in student activism and the application of multiple political tactics to influence change. See the following OB in Action box.

OB in Action

Fed Up, Rise Up, Affect Change... Students Take Action

Students of Marjory Stoneman Douglas High School in Parkland, Florida, garnered tremendous attention, support, and influence when they rallied against gun violence in schools after 17 students and teachers were killed at their school in 2018. Student representatives went to Washington, DC, were interviewed on *60 Minutes* and NPR, and were featured in *Time* and *Teen Vogue*.[72] The ensuing March for Our Lives campaign is associated with a number of changes in gun policies across the country, such as 67 gun-control measures, a historic surge in youth voting in the 2018 midterm elections, and eight states passing extreme risk protection measures. What began as a coalition is now a formal organization with chapters in 200 cities across America.[73]

These events and actions helped motivate numerous companies to break ties with the National Rifle Association (NRA). Delta and American Airlines halted agreements to provide discounts to NRA members, and MetLife stopped providing discounted insurance rates for NRA members' boats, RVs, and motorcycles. And not surprisingly, the NRA then advised its members not to use the services and products of these companies.[74] Political action can and often does work in both directions. Yet still other companies—Walmart, Meijer, and L. L. Bean—stopped selling certain guns and put limits on the purchase of others.

However, there is another angle. FedEx, for instance, continued its NRA member discounts and said, the company "has never set or changed rates for any of our millions of customers around the world in response to their politics, beliefs or positions on issues."[75]

More generally, such activities are part of a larger trend in American business, which is that organizations and their leaders are increasingly expected to

March for Our Lives is an excellent example of students organizing to affect change.

The Asahi Shimbun/Getty Images

actively engage social and political causes. Due in part to social media, executives and the companies they run are pressured to confront issues they could historically avoid. They now are making such choices on ethical grounds or organizational values. For example, Dick's no longer sells guns and CVS has stopped selling tobacco products.[76]

YOUR THOUGHTS?

1. Should companies take action on what many see as political matters? Explain your position.

2. If you were the CEO of American Airlines, justify your decision to stop offering discounts to NRA members.

3. Now assume you are CEO of a competing airline that also has agreements to provide discounts to NRA members. Justify honoring those commitments and continuing to grant discounts.

Network-Level Politics　In terms of organizational politics, *networks are people-oriented, while coalitions are issue-oriented.* Networks have broader and longer-term agendas than do coalitions. The Time's Up movement, initiated by some powerful women in Hollywood (Reese Witherspoon and Shonda Rimes), is an excellent and recent example of network-level politics. The mission of this movement is "that everyone, every human being, deserves a right to earn a living, to take care of themselves, to take care of their families, free of the impediments of harassment and sexual assault and discrimination. In short—fairness, safety, and equity in the workplace," said Christy Haubegger, one of the founders of Time's Up.[77]

By focusing on more general characteristics at work, Time's Up is an example of network-level politics; it differs from the #MeToo movement which focuses specifically on sexual violence.

Before moving on, remember you need to match political activity to the appropriate level to meet your objectives. No particular tactic or level is good or bad, rather it is how effectively either assists in meeting your goals that matters. Now let's explore directly how to use politics to your benefit.

Using Politics to Your Advantage

We close this section by highlighting the point that people's *perceptions* of politics (POP) matter, not just actual acts of politics. As perceptions, POPs are subjective evaluations of the extent to which "the work environment is characterized by coworkers and supervisors who demonstrate such self-serving behavior,"[78] and these perceptions matter. POPs have been linked to many undesirable outcomes in the Organizing Framework, such as:

- Decreased job satisfaction, organizational commitment, and commitment.
- Increased stress, frustration, and turnover intentions.[79]

Do these results suggest managers should attempt to stop people from being political? Good luck. Organizational politics cannot be eliminated, but political behavior can and should be managed to keep it constructive.

Not Too Much and Not Too Little   An individual's degree of political engagement is a matter of personal values, ethics, and temperament. People who are either strictly nonpolitical or highly political generally pay a price for their behavior. The former may experience slow promotions and feel left out, while the latter may run the risk of being called self-serving and lose credibility. People at both ends may be considered poor team players.

A moderate amount of prudent political behavior is generally considered a survival tool in organizational life. And it is worth noting that the reason politics has a bad name is due to politicians and their behavior. Politics is not inherently bad; the problem is the way politics is practiced.

How to Build Support for Your Ideas   Our discussion of politics might leave you asking, "What should I do? How do I avoid the bad and take advantage of the good?" Here are eight recommendations backed by research and practice:

1. Create a simple one-liner that captures your idea.
2. Get your idea on the agenda. Describe how it addresses an important need or objective and look for ways to make it a priority.
3. Score small wins early and broadcast them widely. Results build momentum and make it easier for other people to commit.
4. Form alliances with people who have the power to decide, fund, and implement.
5. Persist and continue to build support. Persuading others is a process, not an event.
6. Respond and adjust. Be flexible and accepting of other people's input; the more names supporting your idea, the more likely you are to succeed.
7. Lock it in. Anchor the idea to the organization through budgets, job descriptions, incentives, and other operating procedures.
8. Secure and allocate credit. You don't want your idea to be hijacked, nor do you want to blow your own horn. You need others to sing your praises to ensure you get the credit you deserve.[80]

Now we turn our attention to a specific form of influence—impression management. Doing this effectively is key to your job and career opportunities and success.

12.5 IMPRESSION MANAGEMENT

THE BIGGER PICTURE

We all want to look good in the eyes of others, and to do this we often engage in impression management. Like the other topics discussed in this chapter, impression management consists of techniques for influencing others in all arenas of life. To help you manage your own impressions, we define impression management and discuss what it means to make good impressions, as well as how to make positive impressions during job interviews and effective apologies. You will see how practical knowledge in this area helps boost your effectiveness across levels of outcomes in the Organizing Framework.

We pursue the basic human desire to impress others not only because it makes us feel good about ourselves, but also because others can often provide what we desire, such as a job, a good grade, or a date. Many of our attempts to influence others in such ways are impression management.

LO 12-5

Determine how to implement effective impression management.

What Is Impression Management?

Impression management is any attempt to control or manipulate the images related to a person, organization, or idea.[81] It encompasses speech, behavior, and appearance and can be aimed at anyone—parents, teachers, peers, employees, and customers are all fair game. For instance, by positioning themselves as socially responsible, companies can create positive impressions with many stakeholders, such as potential customers, and in turn boost sales.[82] Let's dive into good and bad impressions in more detail.

Good Impressions

Research conducted in the context of job interviews shows that impressions are formed very quickly and often subtly. Interviewers gather information about job candidates based on their handshake, smile, and manner of dress. All this information is communicated before any questions have been asked or answered. These same factors were also related to ultimate job offers. The following Applying OB box provides additional guidance.

How to Make a Killer First Impression   You've undoubtedly heard the saying, "You have only one chance to make a good first impression." Some argue people judge you within one second of meeting you. Researchers tested this belief and found that after viewing only a microsecond of a video of a political candidate, subjects predicted

Etiquette Gets You Hired

As much as jobs, careers, and technology change, some things remain the same. Notably, the interview is still the most critical determinant in hiring decisions. You therefore want to do what you can to get the interview and perform well once you do. One important determinant of your performance is presenting the appropriate image, and etiquette is a key contributor to this. Those involved in the hiring process may consciously assess your etiquette as a part of your image, or they will subconsciously consider it. Either way, etiquette matters.

First, what is etiquette? Interview etiquette is "the customary code of polite behavior that prospective employees adhere to (or should adhere to) during interactions with recruiters, hiring managers, and other members of an organization throughout the interview process."[84]

Interesting research found interviewees' etiquette had similar importance to answer quality and perceived person–organization fit. The same research also found etiquette serves to amplify the positive effects of high-quality answers to interview questions. And last but certainly not least, etiquette also predicted more job offers, more than self-promotion or ingratiation!

The bottom line? Etiquette matters. The following are elements of etiquette you should carefully consider and practice.

1. I address interviewers by their formal titles when first meeting them.
2. I dress formally for interviews—dark business suit—versus dressing more casually.
3. I carry a portfolio/notepad to the interview.
4. I extend my hand first when meeting the interviewer.
5. I provide a firm handshake to the interviewer.
6. I provide the interviewer with an extra copy of my resume at the time of the interview.
7. I keep my cell phone silenced and out of sight during the interview.
8. I exchange business cards with the interviewer.
9. I thank the interviewer for his or her time at the end of the interview.
10. I follow up with a thank you note (e-mail is acceptable) after the interview.[85]

These are simple enough, be sure to implement them.

---

with 70 percent accuracy who would win an election. Table 12.3 provides recommendations to help you overcome the pressure and ensure that people's snap judgments of you are favorable.

Reciprocity and Impression Management Recall our discussion of reciprocity earlier in this chapter ("Cialdini's six Principles of Persuasion") and the benefits of giving in order to receive. Research tells us that when a CEO makes positive comments about another executive and the other executive's company, Wall Street analysts give more favorable reports of both the CEO and the company even when they come up short of earnings forecasts.[83] Put another way, saying something positive in the media means Wall Street analysts are likely to be more forgiving if your performance is low. This is obviously a powerful form of influence—one that really pays.

Favorable Upward Impression Management Tactics On a positive note, both research and practice have revealed numerous forms of upward impression management techniques which can be put in three categories:[86]

1. *Job-focused*—tactics that present information about your job performance in a favorable light.
2. *Supervisor-focused*—praise and favors for your supervisor.
3. *Self-focused*—an image of yourself as a polite and nice person.

Recent work highlights two additional ways of impressing your boss. The first is to associate yourself with so-called stars, those on the fast track who already have the attention of management. The second is to work on key projects that need help or refinement.

TABLE 12.3 How to Make a Killer First Impression

ACTION	DESCRIPTION
Set goals	When you're preparing for an event (a meeting, social event, or conference), think of whom you'd like to meet and what you'd like to achieve from that introduction. Then plan your energy, introduction, and comments accordingly.
Consider your ornaments	We're not talking about Christmas trees or party favors, but instead about your jewelry, makeup, and clothes. This advice is for both men and women. Many people will draw conclusions from the type of watch you wear and how well it aligns with your clothes (sporty, gaudy, trendy). Makeup and jewelry are judged similarly. Be sure they match your personality and your intended message.
Remember your body speaks	We've all heard body language makes a difference, so pay attention to nonverbals. Find a way to video yourself in a social setting. Use this evidence to help manage your body language habits in the future.
Bust bad moods and bad days	If you're in a bad mood before an important event, find a way to snap out of it—play some of your favorite music, work out, go shopping—or reschedule (or stay home). People will pick up on your mood, and you don't want your body language to convey: "Hello, my name is Bad Mood Bob."
Be interested to be interesting	The best way to appear interesting is *to appear interested.* People tend to like people who like them; at least this is a good place to start. Rather than blather on about yourself, an excellent way to show interest is to ask questions about the other person. You may be able to do research ahead of time about the person or persons you'll meet, and make it part of your goal to ask them about what you learned.

SOURCE: Adapted from V. Van Petten, "5 Ways to Make a Killer First Impression," *Forbes,* November 2, 2011, http://www.forbes.com/sites/yec/2011/11/02/5-ways-to-make-a-killer-first-impression/.

In both instances, managers have more positive emotions about the employee and perceive him or her as more promotable.[87]

What are your own tendencies for using favorable impression management? Self-Assessment 12.4 will help you understand the types of impression management—job-, supervisor-, and self-focused—you use in work settings. Be sure to answer the accompanying questions to get the most from your knowledge.

SELF-ASSESSMENT 12.4 CAREER READINESS

Your Impression Management—How and Who

Please be prepared to answer these questions if your instructor has assigned Self-Assessment 12.4 in Connect.

1. Are you better suited for "Hollywood," or are you better described as safe or a free agent?
2. What are the benefits of your impression management tendencies?
3. What are the drawbacks?
4. Look at all the items in the assessment and select the two that could be most useful to you. Describe specifically how you could use them.
5. What about ethical considerations? Which items potentially raise ethical flags for you? Why and why not?

Let's be clear: a moderate amount of upward impression management is a necessity, but not all forms are effective and none are effective all the time. Ingratiation, for instance, can slightly improve your performance appraisal results and make your boss like you significantly more. Engage in too little impression management and busy managers are liable to overlook some of your valuable contributions when they make job assignment, pay, and promotion decisions. But do too much and you run the risk of being branded a "schmoozer," a "phony," and other unflattering characterizations by your coworkers. Consider, for instance, that the application of noticeable flattery and ingratiation can backfire by embarrassing the target person and damaging your credibility.[88]

Impression Management and Job Interviews

Job interviews probably epitomize our experiences of impression management, as there are few other instances in which we are more determined to make a good impression. Researchers provide a number of insights we highlight next.

Deception Detection   Many people are deceptive in interviews, and interviewers' abilities to detect such tactics vary greatly. One study found that experienced interviewers were no better at detecting deception than novices.[89]

Ethics aside, bending the truth in an interview can cause an organization to hire the wrong person for the job. Deception that leads to bad hires can be very costly. Organizations are wise to train their interviewers to identify the common impression management tactics used in interviews, such as self-promotion, image repair, image protection, and image creation. This is the first step in making them aware of the deceptive techniques candidates often use.[90]

Other research shows that both interviewers and coworkers are especially poor at knowing whether a candidate is honest and humble, qualities increasingly valued in the workplace. Employees lacking these characteristics are known to engage in more counterproductive work behaviors and have lower performance.[91] Of course, we encourage you to be ethical, present your true self, and use the other knowledge in this chapter (and book) to be more influential and impress interviewers.

Tattoos may also be part of your impression during an interview. Read the OB in Action box and find out.

OB in Action

Is Your Ink an Asset, a Liability, or Just Colorful?

The frequency and perceptions of tattoos has changed dramatically over time. For perspective, a survey of over 9,000 people in 18 countries revealed some interesting insights about prevalence and attitudes based on age and country. Notably,

- 38% of respondents had at least one tattoo.
- 45% of those 30–49 years old did, vs. 32% of those 14–29.
- 72% don't regret getting inked.
- 75% of those with tattoos have more than one.
- Italy, Sweden, and the U.S. are the most tattooed of the countries represented, with 48 percent, 47 percent, and 46 percent, respectively.

- Tattooed Americans are more likely than people in other countries to have multiple tatts (the median is 4).[92]
- In most countries the prevalence of tattoos is quite similar for men and women.

Not long ago health researchers found associations between youths' tattoos and sexual activity, alcohol and drug use, eating disorders and suicide. But more

Are tattoos a non-issue or a hindrance during job interviews? Could they help your prospects?

Frare Davis/Rubberball/Getty Images

current evidence suggests otherwise and shows ink and piercings (other than in one's ears) are now mainstream. However, nearly as many people today as in 2008 still think such associations exist.[93]

Although health risks related to tattoos and piercings persist, such as hepatitis C and infections due to tainted ink, regulation of tattoo studios varies dramatically from state to state.[94] But what matters more for OB is what such forms of body art say about you, and how others' impressions affect your job and career opportunities.

Perceptions and Stereotypes

The reality is that, depending on who sits across the table from you in an interview, your body art could make a difference. As one HR writer put it, one sees your tatts and concludes you're an unreliable renegade, while another may see you as creative and expressive, a person to whom younger customers will relate.[95] But one recent study suggests there are no hiring, wage, or earnings differences between inked and non-inked candidates.[96]

What Do Hiring Managers Think?

Before rushing out to the tattoo studio on the way to your next job interview, it is important to consider the nature of your tattoo(s) and other body art. Some are more obvious and potentially more offensive than others. Some research has found biases against candidates with tatts. Many of the old stereotypes, like tatts being associated with gang membership, still linger and can cost you job offers and higher starting salaries. The authors of this study explain that hiring managers have limited information about candidates during the recruiting process, and as a result may resort to or be influenced by such stereotypes. Specifically, applicants with extreme tattoos were viewed as less competent and committed. And manager ink was related to the views of candidates. Managers with tatts viewed candidates with tatts more favorably, and those without tended to discount the value of candidates with body art.[97]

Worth Considering

It's also worth considering the industry in which you want to work. If you're an athlete without ink you're in a puny minority (only 14 percent), and the same goes for primary school teachers. Nearly 60 percent have at least one tatt according to research by the Harris group.[98]

Finally, an employer can establish a dress code requiring employees to cover body art, but at the moment no laws exist governing such policies and practices.[99]

YOUR THOUGHTS?

1. Assume you're a hiring manager, how would you perceive a candidate's body art? Explain.

2. Would you allow it to influence your decisions? Explain.

3. If approximately 40 percent of adults in the U.S. have tattoos, then explain the implications of hiring versus not hiring those with Ink.

Interviewers' Attempts to Impress You There's another angle on the story—interviewers are trying to impress interviewees. Especially in tight labor markets, employers compete intensely for top talent. This means they must impress candidates in order to attract and hire the best, representing the organization favorably with a broad range of tactics, including:

- Verbal—what they say and how they say it.
- Nonverbal—laughing, smiling, leaning in.
- Artifactual—dress, appearance of interview venue, visual and promotional items.
- Administrative—timing of communication, confirmation that application was received, feedback, and follow-up.[100]

Ethics and Impression Management

It's one thing to cast yourself in the best possible light, but it is quite another to lie. Therefore, the ethics of impression management focuses on the gray area in between. One way to help decide whether your favorable light is "too bright" (has gone too far) is to imagine you have to explain what you said or did on the evening news. Would you be comfortable with portraying that same impression to the entire community? Would people who know you well, friends or coworkers (past and present), agree? Asking and answering these two questions can help you navigate the ethics of impression management. Research provides some guidance and interesting details to consider.

A study of more than 600 companies surpassing $100 million in revenues showed that unfavorable analyst comments prompted the CEOs to say their companies do have policies and practices that are in shareholders' best interests. Related research showed that CEOs also routinely said their own compensation plan was aligned with shareholder interests, although in both instances they regularly misrepresented the issues.[101] For example, their companies often made job and R&D cuts that undermined the long-term health of the company (counter to shareholder interests), and their personal compensation often increased even when the share price of their company plummeted.

Consider this story of impression management from a large bank:

EXAMPLE After 7 pm, people would open the door to their office, drape a spare jacket on the back of their chair, lay a set of glasses down on some reading material on their desk—and then go home for the night. The point of this elaborate gesture was to create the illusion that they were just out grabbing dinner and would be returning to burn the midnight oil.[102]

No one is always right. Sometimes an apology is necessary to save, repair, or even enhance the impressions others have of you. Let's look at how best to do this.

Apologies

One way to remedy or at least reduce the impact of bad impressions, negative uses of power, or poor performance is an apology. Apologies are a form of trust repair in which we acknowledge an offense and usually offer to make amends. It is a widely held norm in the U.S. and other cultures (such as in Japan) to apologize when our action, or lack of action, causes harm to another, whether intentionally or not.

And while harm can be perceived or actual, it is always real to those harmed. Apologies are effective to the extent they restore trust and positively affect your ability to influence the offended party in the future.[103] To help ensure the effectiveness of your apologies, make sure they include the following four characteristics:

1. Acknowledgment of wrongdoing.
2. Acceptance of responsibility.
3. Expression of regret.
4. Promise the offense will not be repeated.[104]

Deep and public bows are a sign of apology in Japanese cultures, as illustrated in the photos of executives of Takada (defective airbags) and Toshiba (pattern of overstated profits). Public apologies by leaders can either make or break the public relations and reputation of organizations. For example, Kentucky Fried Chicken (KFC) once ran out of chicken in the United Kingdom, which resulted in the temporary closure of 900 restaurants there. The company responded with humor and took out a full-page ad in London newspapers showing its emblematic bucket with the letters in its logo rearranged to read—FCK—along with an explanation and assurances it wouldn't happen again. Risky, but it was effective.[106]

Another example was PWC's mistake in the Best Picture category at the 2017 Oscars. The company was responsible for the voting process and listed the wrong winner. Participants in the ceremony intervened in real time and rectified the situation.[107] The company briefly explained what happened, apologized, and then made and explained numerous changes to ensure it wouldn't happen again.[108]

Executives from some of Japan's largest companies have issued very public apologies; among them were Shigehisa Takada, the CEO of Takata, the maker of defective airbags responsible for the recall of over 60 million vehicles worldwide. Electronics giant Toshiba overstated profits by more than a billion dollars over a number of years. Its CEO, Hisai Tanaka, resigned along with a number of board members.[105]
(Left): Nippon News/Aflo Co. Ltd./Alamy Stock Photo; (right): epa european pressphoto agency b.v./Alamy Stock Photo

It also is helpful to consider that a failure to apologize, or to do so in a timely manner, can turn a bad situation worse and damage how others see you.

You are now far better equipped to influence people in many arenas of life. We close this chapter with a reminder: You typically have more power than you think and don't need a fancy title or corner office. We encourage you to be more purposeful and accurate in your application of power, empowerment, influence, politics, and impression management. Doing so will dramatically increase your effectiveness across levels of the Organizing Framework. Besides, you'll get your way more often!

Let's conclude the chapter with a few pointed applications of the knowledge and tools from this chapter.

12.6 MAKING THE CONNECTION: HOW CAN I APPLY POWER, INFLUENCE, AND POLITICS TO INCREASE MY EFFECTIVENESS?

THE BIGGER PICTURE

We conclude this chapter with a number of practical applications of power, empowerment, influence, politics, and impression management. Use your new knowledge and tools to improve your effectiveness as both an employee and manager.

LO 12-6

Describe the implications of power, influence, and politics for you and managers.

The following applications should help increase your own influence and increase your performance and opportunities throughout your career.

Takeaways for Me

Here are five practical applications.

1. **Be mindful that the power you use affects whether people resist, comply, or actually commit to your wishes.**
2. **Use both position and personal power.** You'll find the most influential and successful people you work with, even those with big titles and considerable position power, derive much of their effectiveness by using personal power.
3. **Develop your referent power.** You can use your (social) network to help others, which in turn builds your own power. If someone that has helped you in the past called you today and asked for assistance, would you provide it? Of course you would. This illustrates the power of reciprocity and shows helping others enhances your power and influence.
4. **Increase your understanding and expand your use of influence tactics and political tactics (see Table 12.1).** Match the tactic to the situation and boost your effectiveness.
5. **To make more favorable impressions in your professional life, follow the advice in Table 12.3.**

Takeaways for Managers

There are five very important practical tools for managers.

1. **Do not rely (heavily) on your position power.** Use it when you need to, but if you consistently rely on it to get things done you will dramatically undermine your power and influence with others.
2. **Identify and develop your particular sources of personal power.** Even those with substantial position power (like executives) get ahead in the long term by effectively blending it with personal power.
3. **Use both structural and psychological empowerment to more effectively manage others.** When done well, empowerment can supercharge the performance of those you manage and in turn your own. Besides, even if you're a superhero, you can't do everything yourself—share your power to build your power.
4. **Learn about and apply a larger variety of influence and political tactics.** Don't get stuck playing your preferred tactics, such as rational persuasion, again and again across all situations. Choose the right tactic for the situation to build your effectiveness.
5. **Don't be afraid to apologize.** Willingness to apologize builds credibility and influence with those you manage.

What Did I Learn?

You learned your effectiveness can be increased by applying power, influence, politics, and impression management. You learned the bases of power, common influence tactics, the causes of politics, and which forms are most effective in different situations. You also learned sharing power and empowering others are important means for building your own influence and improving your performance. Reinforce and consolidate your learning with the Key Points and Organizing Framework. Then challenge your mastery of the material by completing the Problem-Solving Application Case and Legal/Ethical Challenge.

Key Points for Understanding Chapter 12

You learned the following key points.

12.1 POWER AND ITS BASIC FORMS

- Power is the discretion and the means to enforce your will over others.
- The five main bases of power are legitimate, reward, coercive, expert, and referent.
- The first three bases are considered forms of position power, and the last two are forms of personal power.
- The bases of power we use often determine whether others will resist, comply, or commit to our wishes.

12.2 POWER SHARING AND EMPOWERMENT

- Empowerment consists of efforts to enhance employee performance, well-being, and positive attitudes.
- Structural empowerment transfers authority and responsibilities from management to employees.

- Power sharing can occur on a continuum from domination to consultation, participation, and finally delegation.
- Psychological empowerment occurs when employees feel a sense of meaning, competence, self-determination, and impact.

12.3 EFFECTIVELY INFLUENCING OTHERS

- Influence tactics are conscious efforts to affect and change behaviors in others.
- Sharing information, creating accountability, and providing examples are common influence tactics used by virtual teams.
- Six principles of persuasion are liking, reciprocity, social proof, consistency, authority, and scarcity.

12.4 POLITICAL TACTICS AND HOW TO USE THEM

- Organizational politics are intentional acts to improve individual or organizational interests.
- Competition and uncertainty are major causes of political actions.
- Political action occurs at three levels—individual, coalition, and network.

12.5 IMPRESSION MANAGEMENT

- Impression management is any attempt to control or manipulate the images related to a person, organization, or idea.
- Impression management is especially important in job interviews, but beware of deception as well as interviewers' attempts to impress you.
- Effective apologies are more than simply say "sorry."

12.6 HOW CAN I APPLY POWER, INFLUENCE, AND POLITICS TO INCREASE MY EFFECTIVENESS?

- Understanding and applying a broader array of influence makes you more effective in all jobs, levels, and career stages.
- How you influence subordinates is a key determinant of whether they resist, comply, or commit with your wishes.

The Organizing Framework for Chapter 12

As shown in Figure 12.9, you learned practical tools to help influence others—power, empowerment, influence, politics, and impression management. Collectively, these tools represent important group-level processes. And the way you use these tools often determines whether people resist, comply with, or actually commit to your wishes. You learned how using these tools relates to individual-level outcomes, such as performance, attitudes, well-being, (counter)productive citizenship behaviors, turnover, and career outcomes. Power and influence are also associated with satisfaction, cohesion, and conflict at the group/team level, and with survival, financial performance, customer satisfaction, and reputation at the organizational level. Beyond this, you explored the notion of empowerment and how sharing power with others can increase your own power and influence.

FIGURE 12.9 The Organizing Framework for Understanding and Applying OB

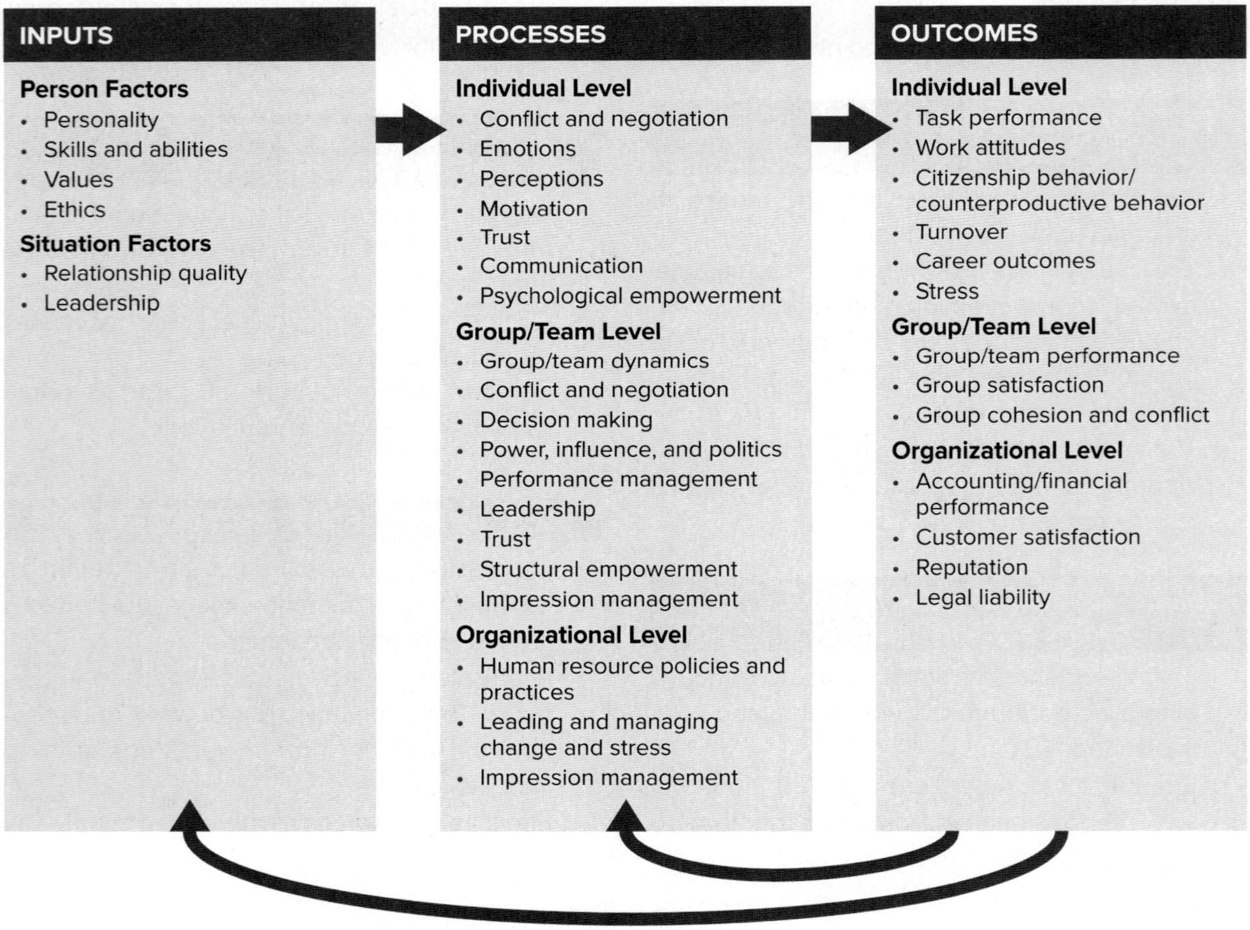

INPUTS	PROCESSES	OUTCOMES
Person Factors • Personality • Skills and abilities • Values • Ethics **Situation Factors** • Relationship quality • Leadership	**Individual Level** • Conflict and negotiation • Emotions • Perceptions • Motivation • Trust • Communication • Psychological empowerment **Group/Team Level** • Group/team dynamics • Conflict and negotiation • Decision making • Power, influence, and politics • Performance management • Leadership • Trust • Structural empowerment • Impression management **Organizational Level** • Human resource policies and practices • Leading and managing change and stress • Impression management	**Individual Level** • Task performance • Work attitudes • Citizenship behavior/ counterproductive behavior • Turnover • Career outcomes • Stress **Group/Team Level** • Group/team performance • Group satisfaction • Group cohesion and conflict **Organizational Level** • Accounting/financial performance • Customer satisfaction • Reputation • Legal liability

#MeToo—Just Do It!

Business events that move to strip clubs, e-mails in your own inbox about parts of your body, lewd and vulgar comments, and more commonly but similarly troubling—unfair pay and promotion practices. These are a subset of complaints revealed in a survey conducted by female employees at Nike. The findings illustrated systematic sexual harassment and discrimination.

Supporting these claims are a long history of complaints to HR and leaders within the company about inappropriate behavior by a number of male leaders. Women comprise nearly 50% of the company's workforce, but occupy only 38% of management level and 29% of vice president positions.[109]

Female employees shared these results with CEO Mark Parker in an effort not only to improve the situation for women at Nike, but also to improve Nike. Their efforts provide yet another example of how employees are organizing and wielding power and influence to change leadership, culture, and practices at their employers.[110]

HOW DID THIS HAPPEN?

The allegations and evidence are wide-ranging, but many attribute misconduct not only to the perpetrators, but also to their superiors who have tolerated or looked the other way. For instance, numerous implicated executives are linked to former company president Trevor Edwards. His charismatic personality and stellar performance had taken him to the heights of the organization, and many believed he was next in line for the CEO job. But many senior leaders who ascended the ranks were largely male and considered a part of an elite group—F.O.T., or Friends of Trevor.[111]

Although Nike claims the behaviors were the actions of an insulated few, and has since fired at least 11 executives as a result, the fact remains that many individuals in power destroyed relationships and undermined the careers of others. Complicit were HR policies, practice, and people who failed to sufficiently act on and provide consequences for inappropriate behavior. These detrimental actions eroded performance, trust, and a sense of justice, along with fostering conflict and a culture many describe as discriminatory and abusive to women.

THE COSTS

In addition to damaging the careers of the terminated executives, widespread misconduct exposes the company to tremendous legal liability, reputational damage, investor pressure, and the alienation of women both inside and outside the company. Expanding product offerings for female customers is a major component of the company's strategy. Particularly troublesome for the remaining leaders is the likelihood of a class action lawsuit, in which more than 500 employees will seek compensation from Nike for sexual harassment, pay discrimination, and unfair promotion practices.[112]

REACTIONS

CEO Parker and the remaining senior leadership team have responded in several ways. Parker directly and publicly acknowledged the problems and apologized to employees in a town hall meeting, established a complaint hotline, set up unconscious bias training, required specific training for managers, appointed Nike's first chief diversity and inclusion officer, revamped its pay structure and provided raises for approximately 7500 employees, or 10% of its global workforce. Nike also has adopted a gender-blind resume review process, and is tying bonuses more prominently to overall company performance.[113]

Part of Parker's apology included, "I apologize to the people on her team who were excluded, and I apologize if some of those same people felt they had no one to turn to . . . I want everyone at Nike to know their voices do matter and your bravery is making us better."[114] But even after all of the company's corrective actions, Parker and others feel the work is far from finished.

Assume you are CEO Parker and you want to: (1) make amends with the important stakeholders involved, and (2) put Nike on a positive track for the future. Drawing on what you learned in this chapter what else would you do?

APPLY THE 3-STEP PROBLEM-SOLVING APPROACH TO OB

Use the Organizing Framework in Figure 12.9 and the 3-Step Problem-Solving Approach to help identify inputs, processes, and outcomes relative to this case.

STEP 1: Define the problem.

A. Look first at the Outcomes box of the Organizing Framework to help identify the important problem(s) in this case. Remember a problem is a gap between a desired and current state. State your problem as a gap and be sure to consider problems at all three levels. If more than one desired outcome is not being accomplished, decide which one is most important and focus on it for steps 2 and 3.

B. Cases have key players, and problems are generally viewed from a particular player's perspective. You need to determine from whose perspective—employee, manager, team, or the organization—you're defining the problem. In this case you're asked to assume the role of CEO Mark Parker.

C. Use details in the case to determine the key problem. Don't assume, infer, or create problems not included in the case.

D. To refine your choice, ask yourself, *why is this a problem?* Explaining why helps refine and focus your thinking. Focus on topics in the current chapter, because we generally select cases illustrating concepts in the current chapter.

STEP 2: Identify causes.

Using material from this chapter and summarized in the Organizing Framework, identify the causes of the problem you identified in Step 1. Remember, causes tend to appear in either the inputs or Processes boxes.

A. Start by looking at the Organizing Framework (Figure 12.9) and decide which person factors, if any, are most likely causes of the defined problem. For each cause, explain why this is a cause

of the problem. Asking *why* multiple times is more likely to lead you to root causes of the problem. For example, do executive characteristics help explain the problem you defined in Step 1?

B. Follow the same process for the situation factors. For each ask yourself, *why is this a cause?* By asking why multiple times you are likely to arrive at a more complete and accurate list of causes. Again, look to the Organizing Framework for this chapter for guidance. Did particular policies or practices play a role?

C. Now consider the Processes box in the Organizing Framework. Are any processes at the individual, group/team, or organizational level potential causes of your defined problem? For any process you consider, ask yourself, *why is this a cause?* Again, do this for several iterations to arrive at the root causes.

D. To check the accuracy or appropriateness of the causes, be sure to map them onto the defined problem and confirm the link or cause and effect connection.

STEP 3: Recommend solutions.

Make your recommendations for solving the problem. Consider whether you want to resolve it, solve it, or dissolve it (see Section 1.5). Which recommendation is desirable and feasible?

A. Given the causes you identified in Step 2, what are your best recommendations? Use material in the current chapter that best suits the cause. Consider the OB in Action and Applying OB boxes, because these contain insights into what others have done.

B. Be sure to consider the Organizing Framework—both person and situation factors—as well as processes at different levels.

C. Create an action plan for implementing your recommendations, and be sure your recommendations map onto the causes and resolve the problem.

LEGAL/ETHICAL CHALLENGE

If You Work Here, You Can't Eat Meat![115]

Vegetarians might rejoice, but meat-eating WeWork employees may lament that the company will no longer serve or pay for red meat, poultry, or pork at company functions. Companies have the right to determine what they pay for, such as the food and beverages at functions

and what employee expenses they reimburse. Miguel McKelvey, co-founder and CEO of the office sharing company, justified this new policy in the name of the environment, claiming that avoiding meat can have a larger environmental impact than driving a hybrid car, and the anticipated reduction in meat consumption by WeWork employees alone will save over 15 million animals in just a few years. McKelvey argued further the policy is intended to heighten the awareness and accountability of the company's 6,000 employees.

Critics, however, note this is just another example of employers imposing the values of their leaders on employees. For instance, Hobby Lobby refuses to pay for employees' birth control, Koch Industries distributes messages encouraging employees about how to vote, and IBM made a short-lived attempt to ban employees from using ride-sharing apps.

Some policies are better aligned with business objectives and cost savings. For instance, GE incentivized employees to quit smoking in order to improve health and cut costs, and Scotts Miracle-Gro took it a step further and adopted a policy of not hiring smokers altogether.

When questioned about imposing his views on WeWork employees, McKelvey explains he sees it as part of a leader's responsibility today. "Companies have greater responsibility to their team members and to the world these days . . . We're the ones with the power. Large employers are the ones that can move the needle on issues."

What Would You Do?

1. Assume you are the founder of a company, and also assume you are fine with imposing your values on your employees. Name one value and how would you ensure employees comply? Also justify your decision.

2. Argue against such practices, explaining why and how imposing your values can negatively affect employees and your business.

3. Take a completely different course of action and explain.

13

Leadership Effectiveness

After reading this chapter, you should be able to:

LO 13-1 Describe how an integrated model of leadership helps you become an effective leader.

LO 13-2 Explain how using trait theories can improve your leadership skills.

LO 13-3 Describe four categories of leadership behaviors.

LO 13-4 Describe two theories of contingency leadership.

LO 13-5 Describe how to use transformational leadership to work with others.

LO 13-6 Compare more recent approaches to leadership theory.

LO 13-7 Describe the implications of leadership effectiveness for you and managers.

The Organizing Framework shown in Figure 13.1 summarizes what you will learn in this chapter. It shows a greater number of total inputs and processes than past chapters. This indicates that effective leadership is not a simple activity. It requires that individuals possess a host of person factors including specific traits, skills, and experience. It further requires an understanding of how a variety of situation factors such as organizational culture and structure affect individual, group/team, and organizational level processes.

Figure 13.1 shows there are five key forms of individual level leadership you will learn about. They are: task-oriented leadership, relationship-oriented leadership, passive leadership, transformational leadership, and leader-member exchange. Each of these types of leadership rely on different types of leader behavior and they all in turn affect a number of individual, group/team, and organizational-level outcomes. The large number of outcomes shown in Figure 13.1 underscores the importance of leadership. Research demonstrates that effective leadership impacts individual, group/team, and organizational performance.

FIGURE 13.1 Organizing Framework for Understanding and Applying OB

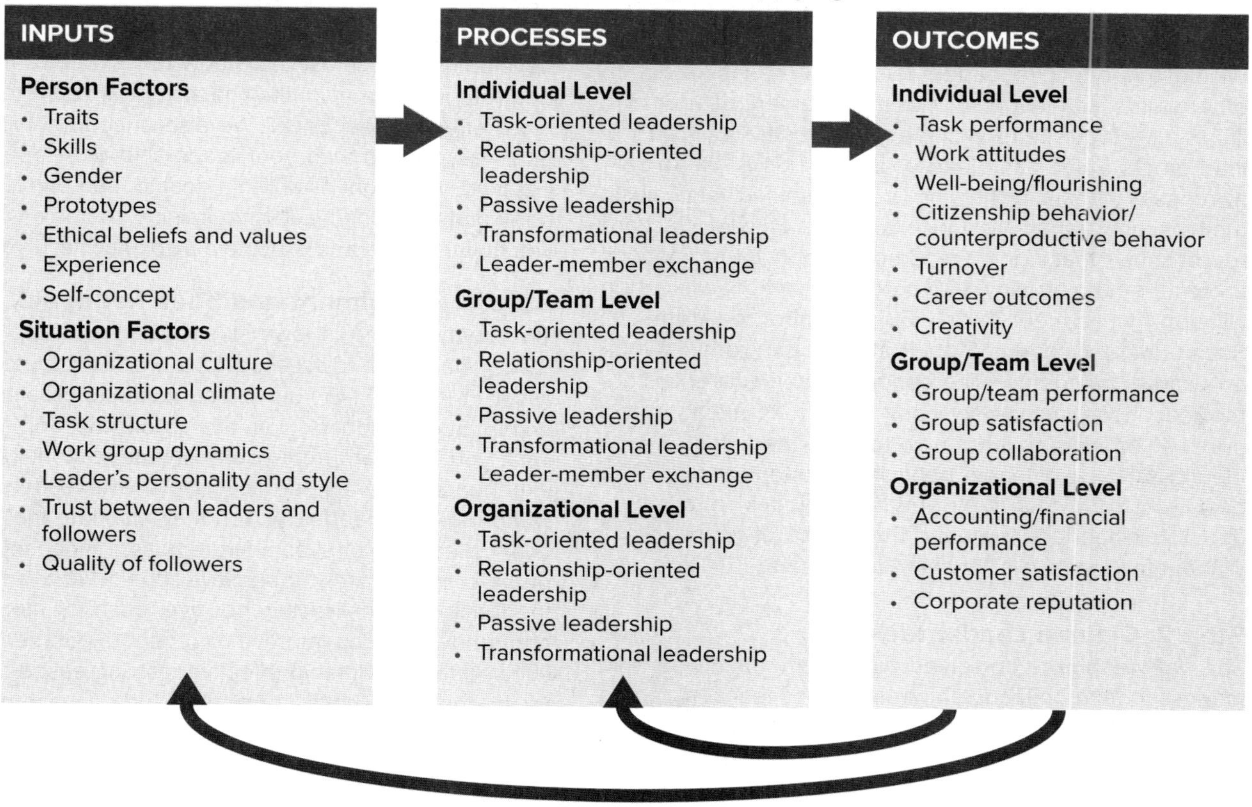

INPUTS	PROCESSES	OUTCOMES
Person Factors	**Individual Level**	**Individual Level**
• Traits	• Task-oriented leadership	• Task performance
• Skills	• Relationship-oriented leadership	• Work attitudes
• Gender	• Passive leadership	• Well-being/flourishing
• Prototypes	• Transformational leadership	• Citizenship behavior/counterproductive behavior
• Ethical beliefs and values	• Leader-member exchange	• Turnover
• Experience	**Group/Team Level**	• Career outcomes
• Self-concept	• Task-oriented leadership	• Creativity
Situation Factors	• Relationship-oriented leadership	**Group/Team Level**
• Organizational culture	• Passive leadership	• Group/team performance
• Organizational climate	• Transformational leadership	• Group satisfaction
• Task structure	• Leader-member exchange	• Group collaboration
• Work group dynamics	**Organizational Level**	**Organizational Level**
• Leader's personality and style	• Task-oriented leadership	• Accounting/financial performance
• Trust between leaders and followers	• Relationship-oriented leadership	• Customer satisfaction
• Quality of followers	• Passive leadership	• Corporate reputation
	• Transformational leadership	

Winning at Work

Learning to Lead

Leadership effectiveness is more a function of your behavior than a set of traits you are born with. This means leadership skills can be learned, a conclusion supported by research.[1]

Step 1: How Can I Begin the Learning Process?

We believe effective leaders lead from the inside out. In other words, self-leadership, or management of your own life, is a prerequisite for being a good leader. How can you lead others if you can't lead yourself? This is where self-awareness matters, by helping you understand your values, motives, and behaviors. For example, a Hewlett Packard report shows that women tend not to apply for promotions unless they are already 100 percent qualified, while men will apply while meeting only 60 percent of requirements. Such underestimations of their abilities can reduce women's career outcomes.[2] The benefits of self-awareness are the reason we include so many Self-Assessments in this book. If you want to learn how to lead, the first step is to identify the type of leader behaviors you tend to use.[3] The best way to do this is by getting feedback from others about your leadership during the course of your career.[4] Without feedback, it is very hard to improve.

Step 2: Claim a Leader Identity

The way we think of ourselves, our *identity,* affects our willingness to take on leadership roles. This means that to be a leader, you need to see yourself authentically as a leader, even in a small way.[5] You can do this in three ways. The first is to take a direct approach, in which you refer to yourself as a leader of some group, project, or task or engage in typical leadership acts. For example, if you are meeting with a student group to complete an assignment, you can walk into the meeting with an agenda and then start running the meeting. The second way to see yourself as a leader is to stake indirect claims of leadership, such as sitting at the head of the table for a meeting, mentioning your relationship with recognized leaders, or dressing the part.[6] The third way entails acting or behaving in ways that meet people's expectations about effective leadership. For example, many people perceived that effective leaders use styles that emphasize empowerment, fairness, compassion, and supportiveness. You are more likely to be perceived as a leader if you display these styles.

Step 3: Develop a Learning Goal Orientation

In Chapter 6 we discussed the difference between learning goals and performance goals. Learning goals promote learning because they focus on what we can learn from both success and failure, and they encourage us to seek input, guidance, and coaching from effective leaders. We encourage you to set learning goals associated with leadership development, such as "learn how to run better meetings," "learn to improve my influence skills," or "learn to provide more effective feedback." We also encourage you to set goals associated with your leadership development. For instance, you might establish a goal to read one leadership book or attend one leadership training course a year. Once you do this, make and execute a plan to achieve your goals.

Step 4: Experiment and Seek Feedback

Try experimenting in low-risk situations with the different leader behaviors discussed later in this chapter.[7] Next, assess the impact of your experimental approach to leadership. Seek feedback from those you trust and reflect on what you can learn from your many educational and work experiences. It's very hard to improve your leadership skills without getting feedback. You may also find that some of your colleagues, or even a future boss, may be reluctant to provide accurate and honest feedback. If you feel your feedback is unrealistically positive, push for more details about how you can improve. A recent experimental study showed that leadership effectiveness increased over time for students who consistently reflected on what they could learn from their experiences.[8]

What's Ahead in This Chapter

Improving your leadership skills will enhance both your personal and professional life. The good news is that leadership is available to all. Genetics and privilege neither guarantee leadership abilities, nor are they required. We are about to help you navigate the many theories of leadership, grasp how leadership traits and behaviors can be learned and developed, identify and apply styles of leadership, and finally apply what you learn about leadership to being a better leader and follower and more effective at any level in an organization.

13.1 MAKING SENSE OF LEADERSHIP THEORIES

THE BIGGER PICTURE

You're about to learn why leadership is both an input and a process in the Organizing Framework for Understanding and Applying OB. Organizations can't really start or sustain operations without leadership. You'll acquire an overall model of leadership that integrates the many leadership theories that have been proposed. Then you'll hone your understanding of effective leadership and parse the difference between leading and managing.

"If your actions inspire others to dream more, learn more, do more and become more, you are a leader."

—John Quincy Adams

LO 13-1

Describe how an integrated model of leadership helps you become an effective leader.

Adams's words underscore the value of leadership. Whether at home or work, effective leadership matters! A recent study spanning 18,000 firm-years revealed that the impact of individual chief executives on corporate financial performance has increased over the last 60 years.[9]

Leadership is "a process whereby an individual influences a group of individuals to achieve a common goal."[10] As Adams suggested, you do not need to have a formal position of authority to be a leader. Anyone who exerts influence over others in the pursuit of organizationally relevant matters is a leader.

This definition underscores the broad impact leaders have on organizations. Consider that employee disengagement in the United States costs $483 billion to $605 billion each year, and ineffective leadership is a key driver of disengagement.[11] Researchers also have estimated that half of all managers around the world are incompetent or ineffective.[12] Those are pretty discouraging statistics. Further, results from a recent global survey of more than 9,000 leaders from 31 countries suggested these negative trends are not going away. In fact, 80 percent of respondents said that leadership was a very important issue and that "21st-century leaders" face unique challenges to address critical new competencies, such as leading through change, understanding digital and AI-driven technologies, and embracing ambiguity and uncertainty.[13]

The topic of leadership has generated more OB-related research than any other topic except motivation, so there are far too many leadership theories to cover in this one chapter. Instead we have created a model that integrates the major theories. We begin there and then focus on theories that have received some level of research support.

An Integrated Model of Leadership

Figure 13.2 presents an integrated model of leadership. Starting at the far right of the model, you see that leadership effectiveness is the outcome we explain in this chapter. The center of the model shows this outcome is influenced by four types of leadership behavior: *task-oriented, relationship-oriented, passive,* and *transformational.* Effective

FIGURE 13.2 An Integrated Model of Leadership

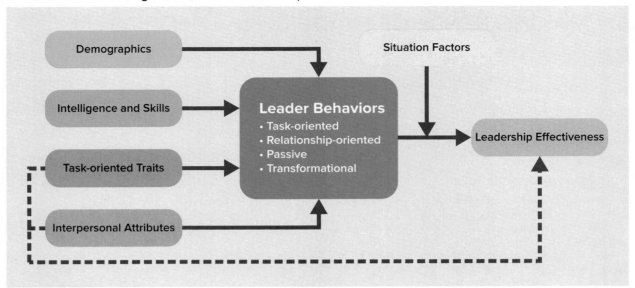

McGraw-Hill Global Education Holdings, LLC

leadership also is affected by a combination of task-oriented traits and interpersonal attributes (the left side of the model). Recall from Chapter 3 that individual differences significantly affect performance, and they vary from relatively fixed (cognitive ability) to somewhat flexible (self-efficacy). For example, a recent study of 19,000 people found that gender predicted leadership potential over the past 25 years—men were more likely than women to become leaders—although that result is slowly beginning to change.[14]

Do singers (from left: Macklemore, Mary Lambert, Madonna, Ryan Lewis, Queen Latifah) exert leadership when they perform? Would a group of well-known singers like this exert more influence than one singer performing alone? Why or why not?

Kevin Winter/WireImage/Getty Images

Moreover, Figure 13.2 shows how demographic characteristics such as gender and age, task-oriented traits, and interpersonal attributes influence an individual's use of leader behaviors. The final component in leadership effectiveness, situation factors, suggests that different situations call for different leader behaviors. That is, effective leadership requires using the right behavior at the right time.

What Is the Difference between Leading and Managing?

Bernard Bass, a leadership expert, concluded, "Leaders manage and managers lead, but the two activities are not synonymous."[15] Broadly speaking, managers typically perform functions associated with planning, investigating, organizing, and control, and leaders focus on influencing others. Leaders inspire others, provide emotional support, and try to get employees to rally around a common goal. Leaders also play a key role in *creating* a vision and strategic plan for an organization. Managers, in turn, are charged with *implementing* the vision and plan. We can draw several conclusions from this division of labor.

First, good leaders are not necessarily good managers, and good managers are not necessarily good leaders. Second, effective leadership requires effective managerial skills at some level. For example, Nissan's former CEO, Carlos Ghosn, was arrested in Tokyo for allegedly underreporting his income by millions of dollars over the last decade.[16] In contrast, both Beth Ford, CEO of Land O'Lakes, and Chip Bergh, CEO of Levi Strauss, are recognized for their use of good managerial skills when implementing corporate strategies.[17]

Do you want to lead others or understand what makes a leader tick? Then take Self-Assessment 13.1. It provides feedback on your readiness to assume a leadership role and can help you consider how to prepare for a formal leadership position.

SELF-ASSESSMENT 13.1	CAREER READINESS

Assessing Your Readiness to Assume a Leadership Role

Please be prepared to answer these questions if your instructor has assigned Self-Assessment 13.1 in Connect.

1. Do you agree with your results?
2. If you scored below 60 and desire to become a leader, what might you do to increase your readiness to lead?
3. What is your biggest take-away from these results?

13.2 TRAIT THEORIES: DO LEADERS POSSESS UNIQUE TRAITS AND PERSONAL CHARACTERISTICS?

THE BIGGER PICTURE

Trait theories attempt to identify personal characteristics that differentiate leaders from followers. They represent inputs within the Organizing Framework. After identifying key traits established by research, we discuss the role of gender and perceptions in determining what it takes to be an effective leader.

LO 13-2

Explain how using trait theories can improve your leadership skills.

Trait theory is the successor to what was once called the "great man" theory of leadership. This approach was based on the assumption that leaders such as Abraham Lincoln, Martin Luther King Jr., and Angela Merkel are born with some innate ability to lead. In contrast, trait theorists believe leadership traits are not inborn but can be developed through experience and learning. The **trait approach attempts to identify personality characteristics or interpersonal attributes that differentiate leaders from followers.**

What Core Traits Do Leaders Possess?

Researchers have attempted to identify leadership traits for nearly 100 years. It has been a frustrating pursuit that has not led to a consistent answer. Some have claimed that effective leaders are taller, bald, or wear glasses.[18] But if instead you believe in drawing conclusions based on science, OB researchers offer you a statistical technique called meta-analysis. A *meta-analysis* is a statistical procedure that effectively computes an average relationship between two variables. Table 13.1 is a summary of what we know from this research. Note the emphasis on task-orientation and the expansion into interpersonal attributes.[19]

TABLE 13.1   Key Task-Oriented Traits and Interpersonal Attributes

POSITIVE TASK-ORIENTED TRAITS	POSITIVE/NEGATIVE INTERPERSONAL ATTRIBUTES
• Intelligence	• Extraversion (+)
• Conscientiousness	• Agreeableness (+)
• Open to Experience	• Communication Skills (+)
• Emotional Stability	• Emotional Intelligence (+)
	• Narcissism (−)
	• Machiavellianism (−)
	• Psychopathy (−)

All the traits and interpersonal attributes listed in Table 13.1 have been defined elsewhere in this book except for the "dark triad" traits of narcissism, Machiavellianism, and psychopathy.[20]

- *Narcissism* **consists of "a self-centered perspective, feelings of superiority, and a drive for personal power and glory."**[21] Individuals with this trait have inflated views of themselves, fantasize about being in control of everything, and like to attract the admiration of others. It's thus not surprising that narcissists tend to emerge as leaders, even though they can promote counterproductive work behaviors from others.[22]

- *Machiavellianism* **is the use of manipulation, a cynical view of human nature, and a moral code that puts results over principles.** It's not surprising that individuals who believe everyone lies to get what they want and that it's necessary to cheat to get ahead are less likely to garner support from others.

- *Psychopathy* **is characterized by a lack of concern for others, impulsive behavior, and a lack of remorse or guilt when your actions harm others.** This type of person is toxic at work.

We can draw two more conclusions from Table 13.1. First, when selecting leaders, it's more useful to consider personality than intelligence.[23] Second, displaying the "dark triad" traits at work can lower your performance ratings and even get you demoted or fired.[24]

What Role Does Emotional Intelligence Play in Leadership Effectiveness?

Recall from Chapter 3 that *emotional intelligence* is the ability to manage yourself and your relationships in mature and constructive ways. Scientific evidence supports two conclusions about emotional intelligence and leadership:[25]

1. **Emotional intelligence is an input to transformational leadership.** In other words, emotional intelligence helps managers effectively enact the behaviors associated with transformational leadership, discussed later in this chapter.

2. **Emotional intelligence has a small, positive, and significant association with leadership effectiveness.** This suggests that emotional intelligence will help you lead more effectively, but it is not the secret elixir of leadership effectiveness.

Angela Merkel has been Germany's Chancellor for nearly 15 years. Which positive traits does she likely possess?
Leon Neal/Getty Images

Bashar al-Assad, Syria's long-serving president, has been linked to chemical bombings that have killed thousands of people, including children. Do you think al-Assad possesses any of the "dark side" traits?
Joseph Eid/Getty Images

Do Women and Men Display the Same Leadership Traits?

The increase in the number of women in the workforce has generated much interest in understanding the similarities and differences between female and male leaders. Research reveals the following four conclusions:

1. Men were observed to display more task leadership and women more relationship leadership.[26]

2. Women used a more democratic or participative style than men, and men used a more autocratic and directive style.[27]

3. Female leadership was associated with more cohesion, cooperative learning, and participative communication among team members.[28]

4. Peers, managers, direct reports, and judges/trained observers rated women executives as more effective than men. Men rated themselves as more effective than women evaluated themselves.[29]

How Important Are Knowledge and Skills?

Knowledge and skills are extremely important! Table 13.2 identifies the four basic skills leaders need, according to researchers.

Do Perceptions Matter?

Perceptions do matter, according to implicit leadership theory. *Implicit leadership theory* **proposes that people have beliefs about how leaders should behave and what they should do for their followers.** These beliefs are summarized in a *leadership prototype*.[30] A *leadership prototype* **is a mental representation of the traits and**

Speaker of the House of Representatives Nancy Pelosi is the first woman in U.S. history to hold this leadership position. In fact, Pelosi has held the Speaker's position twice. As Speaker, Pelosi is third in the line (after the President and Vice President) of succession to the presidency. It would seem that Pelosi possesses the positive traits associated with leadership effectiveness.
Mark Wilson/Getty Images

TABLE 13.2 Four Basic Skills for Leaders

WHAT LEADERS NEED	AND WHY
Cognitive abilities to identify problems and their causes in rapidly changing situations.	Leaders must sometimes devise effective solutions in short time spans with limited information.
Interpersonal skills to influence and persuade others.	Leaders need to work well with diverse people.
Business skills to maximize the use of organizational assets.	Leaders increasingly need business skills as they advance up through an organization.
Strategic skills to draft an organization's mission, vision, strategies, and implementation plans.	Strategic skills matter most for individuals in the top ranks in an organization.

SOURCE: Mumford, Troy V., Michael A. Campion, and Frederick P. Morgeson. "Leadership Skills Strataplex: Leadership Skill Requirements across Organizational Levels." *Leadership Quarterly* 18 (2007): 154–66. https://doi:10.1016/j.leaqua.2007.01.005.

behaviors people believe leaders possess. For example, a recent study identified a leadership prototype of physically imposing men: that they possess leadership ability and thus are granted greater status.[31]

We tend to perceive someone as a leader who exhibits traits or behaviors consistent with our prototypes. The person you voted for in the 2016 presidential election most likely exhibited traits contained in your leadership prototype. A pair of researchers recently investigated leadership prototypes regarding facial appearance. Here is what they found:

> People prefer leaders with dominant, masculine-looking faces in times of war and conflict, yet they prefer leaders with more trustworthy, feminine faces in peacetime. In addition, leaders with older-looking faces are preferred in traditional knowledge domains, whereas younger-looking leaders are preferred for new challenges.[32]

As this study's results suggest, we all need to be mindful that our prototypes can bias our evaluation of leaders.

As result of their extensive behavioral research, Jim Kouzes and Barry Posner developed a leadership model based on five common behaviors leaders exemplify that reflect honesty and integrity: (1) Model the way—establish principles about the way people should be treated; (2) inspire a shared vision—believe you can make a difference and envision what your organization can become; (3) challenge the process—look for ways to shake things up to improve the organization; (4) enable others to act—foster collaboration and build teams that engage others; and (5) encourage the heart—recognize the contributions of others.[33]

What Are the Take-Aways from Trait Theory?

Trait theory offers us four conclusions.

1. **We cannot ignore the implications of leadership traits.** Traits play a central role in the way we perceive leaders, and they do ultimately affect leadership effectiveness. For example, the Cardiac Rhythm Disease Management Group within Medtronic Inc. identified nine types of traits and skills necessary for leaders (such as giving clear performance feedback and being courageous). The company then designed a leadership development program to help its employees learn and apply these traits.[34]

   More companies are using management development programs to build a pipeline of leadership talent. Total U.S. spending by organizations for leadership training was $87.6 billion for 2018, a 6 percent decrease from the previous year.[35]

2. **The positive and "dark triad" traits shown in Table 13.1 suggest the qualities you should cultivate and avoid if you want to assume a leadership role in the future.** Personality tests, discussed in Chapter 3, and other trait assessments can help evaluate your strengths and weaknesses on these traits. The website for this book contains a host of tests you can take for this purpose.

3. **Organizations may want to include personality and trait assessments in their selection and promotion processes.** For example, Nina Brody, head of talent for Take Care Health Systems in Conshohocken, Pennsylvania, used an assessment tool to assist in hiring nurses, doctors, medical assistants, and others with traits that fit the organization's culture.[36] Of course, companies should match only valid leadership traits.

4. **A global mind-set is an increasingly valued task-oriented trait.** As more companies expand their international operations and hire more culturally diverse people for domestic operations in the United States, they want to enhance employees' global mind-set.[37] A **global mind-set is the belief in one's ability to influence dissimilar others in a global context.** For example, MasterCard and InterContinental Hotels Group implemented leadership development programs aimed at enhancing employees' cross-cultural awareness and ability to work with people from different countries.[38]

13.3 BEHAVIORAL THEORIES: WHICH LEADER BEHAVIORS DRIVE EFFECTIVENESS?

THE BIGGER PICTURE

Behavioral style theories identify key leader behaviors believed to affect leadership effectiveness. We'll focus on four leader behaviors confirmed to differentiate effective from ineffective leaders: task-oriented behavior, relationship-oriented behavior, passive leadership, and transformational leadership.

LO 13-3

Describe four categories of leadership behaviors.

As you might expect, leaders rely on many different types of behaviors to influence others and to accomplish goals. This realization spurred the *behavioral styles approach,* which attempts to identify the unique behaviors displayed by effective leaders.

Researchers have boiled down the unique leader behaviors into four categories: task-oriented, relationship-oriented, passive, and transformational (see Figure 13.2). This section discusses the first three, while transformational leadership is discussed later in the chapter.

Task-Oriented Leader Behavior

The primary purpose of task-oriented behaviors is to assist others in accomplishing their goals and those of the work unit.[39] Although a host of behaviors fall under this category, such as planning, clarifying, monitoring, and problem solving, researchers have mainly studied two: initiating structure and transactional leadership.[40]

Initiating Structure   Researchers at Ohio State University defined *initiating structure* as leader behavior that organizes and defines what group members should be doing to maximize output. You witness this behavior style when someone organizes a team meeting for a class project or seeks input from a knowledgeable source to help guide the team's work. This form of leadership has a moderately strong positive relationship with measures of leadership effectiveness.[41]

Transactional Leadership   *Transactional leadership* focuses on clarifying employees' role and task requirements and providing followers with positive and negative rewards contingent on performance. Transactional leadership includes the fundamental managerial activities of setting goals, monitoring progress toward goal achievement, and rewarding and punishing people for their level of goal accomplishment.[42] You can see that transactional leadership is based on using rewards and punishment to drive motivation and performance. Research supports a positive association between transactional leadership and leader effectiveness and group performance.[43]

Dabo Swinney, head football coach at Clemson University, uses task-oriented leadership (see the OB in Action Box). His teams have won two national championships in recent years, attesting to his effectiveness as a leader.[44]

OB in Action

Dabo Swinney Uses Task-Oriented Leadership to Reclaim the Championship for Clemson

After a drought of almost 40 years, college football coach Dabo Swinney recently restored Clemson University's Tigers to the national championship in a dramatic upset that some observers have called a game for the ages. Later, in his speech on the White House lawn following the celebration traditionally offered to the winning team, Swinney outlined his approach to coaching the team to victory. It's not a coincidence that in doing so he also described the values many task-oriented leaders live by. Here are the highlights:

1. "Run your race in such a way as to win."

2. Quoting George Washington Carver, Swinney said, "Do the common things in an uncommon way, and you will command the respect of the world."

3. His next point was a reminder that life consists not of just the big moments, like winning championships and visiting the White House, but also of all the little moments in between and how we live them.

4. "Continue to be 'all in.' Continue to apply 'best is the standard.' Continue to be a person of excellence in everything you do."

5. Swinney concluded by reminding his team that their achievements "pale in comparison to the daily commitments it took to get there."[45]

Indeed, the entire campus and the town of Clemson, South Carolina, have prospered dramatically since Swinney was hired in 2008 and began steadily reviving the football team's fortunes. More and better students are applying to the university, donations to all its teams are growing, new construction is under way across the campus, and salaries in town are inching up.[46] Swinney's leadership approach must be working: The Tigers won the national championship again in January 2019.[47]

YOUR THOUGHTS?

1. In what ways do Swinney's five points exemplify task-oriented leader behavior?

Clemson University football coach Dabo Swinney celebrates his team's NCAA College Football Championship in 2019.
Michael Zagaris/Getty Images

2. What aspects of initiating structure and transactional leadership can you find in the five points?

3. What aspects of Swinney's approach do you see as most applicable to a business organization, and why?

Relationship-Oriented Leader Behavior

The purpose of relationship-oriented leadership is to enhance employees' skills and create positive work relationships among coworkers and between the leader and his/her employees.[48] OB researchers have investigated the impact of four relationship-oriented behaviors:

- Consideration
- Empowerment
- Servant-leadership
- Ethical leadership

Consideration   *Consideration* **is leader behavior that creates mutual respect or trust and prioritizes group members' needs and desires.** Consideration promotes social interactions and identification with the team and leader. In fact, researchers at Ohio State (who identified consideration) initially proposed that a high-initiating structure, high-consideration style would be the best style of leadership. While research results did not support this bold prediction, considerate leader behavior has a moderately strong positive relationship with measures of leadership effectiveness.[49]

What use do you make of initiating structure and consideration when interacting with student peers or work colleagues? Which of these two types of leader behavior is a strength, an opportunity, or a weakness for you? You can answer these questions by taking Self-Assessment 13.2.

SELF-ASSESSMENT 13.2   CAREER READINESS

Assessing Your Task- and Relationship-Oriented Leader Behavior

Please be prepared to answer these questions if your instructor has assigned Self-Assessment 13.2 in Connect.

1. Are you better at using initiating structure or consideration?
2. Looking at your two lowest scores for each type of leader behavior, suggest ways to improve your leadership.

Empowering Leadership   To explain the positive effects of empowering leadership, we need to define two terms. *Empowering leadership* **represents the leader's ability to create perceptions of psychological empowerment in others.** *Psychological empowerment,* **employees' belief that they have control over their work, is believed to drive intrinsic motivation.**[50]

Marc Benioff, co-founder and CEO of Salesforce, has learned to be an empowering leader. A business analyst who tracks Salesforce for Pivotal Research says Benioff "knows he can be a force for good and a force for change."[51]

Leaders increase their followers' psychological empowerment by engaging in behaviors that enhance perceptions of meaning, self-determination or choice, competence, and impact. Let's consider how Benioff creates psychological empowerment at Salesforce, the tech company he co-founded 20 years ago.

- **Leading for meaningfulness.** Managers lead for meaningfulness by *inspiring* their employees and *modeling* desired behaviors. One way to do this is by helping employees to identify their passions at work and creating an exciting organizational vision employees feel connected to. Benioff demonstrated this when he campaigned vigorously for Proposition C in San Francisco, a measured that called on companies in the city with revenue over $50 million to pay a tax toward homeless programs. In addition to spending $8 million to help pass the bill, Benioff convened meetings with local business leaders, nonprofit organizations, and experts on homelessness before the election. He also tweeted about the proposed legislation more than 50 times to show his support. Despite strong opposition from several high-profile tech companies headquartered in San Francisco, Prop C passed easily.[52]

Salesforce co-founder Marc Benioff is an empowering leader. Inspiring employees and modeling desired behaviors, Benioff has made valuable contributions not only to his staff but also to his San Francisco community.

Tim Mosenfelder/Getty Images

- **Leading for self-determination or choice.** Managers lead for choice by *delegating* meaningful assignments and tasks. When Benioff took a two-week vacation—unplugged and unreachable—he had a lot of time to meditate and had a revelation: He's too busy. In addition to running a 30,000-person company, a full-time endeavor for most people, Benioff is also deeply involved in philanthropy, mentoring other business leaders, and making his voice heard on various social and political issues. He decided to promote Keith Block, Saleforce's chief operating officer, to become co-CEO of the company. According to Benioff, the move was a "divide and conquer strategy," virtually unheard of in the software industry.[53]

- **Leading for competence.** Leading for competence means *supporting* and *coaching* employees. Managers first need to make sure employees have the knowledge needed to successfully perform their jobs. Deficiencies can be handled through training and mentoring. Managers can also combine positive feedback and sincere recognition with challenging tasks to fuel employees' intrinsic motivation. On their first day at Salesforce, new employees spend the afternoon doing service work, as part of the company's "giving back" culture.[54]

- **Leading for progress.** Managers lead for progress by *monitoring* and *rewarding* others. Over the past several years, Benioff directed Salesforce to spend more than $6 million dollars to ensure that all employees were paid fairly, regardless of gender, race, or ethnicity. In addition, he announced he would not hold meetings unless 30 percent of the attendees were women, a strategy he believed would make it likelier that female employees would be seen as leaders and improve their opportunities for promotion within the company.[55]

Research supports the use of empowering leadership. It fosters psychological empowerment, which in turn improves outcomes such as intrinsic motivation, creativity, career self-efficacy and satisfaction, performance, and team collaboration.[56]

Servant-Leadership   The term *servant-leadership* was coined in 1970 by Robert Greenleaf, who believed great leaders act as servants and make the needs of others, including employees, customers, and community, their first priority. **Servant-leadership focuses on increased service to others rather than to oneself.**[57] Because the focus of servant-leadership is on serving others, servant-leaders are less likely to engage in self-serving behaviors that hurt others. Embedding servant-leadership into an organization's culture requires actions as well as words.

> **EXAMPLE** Afni, Inc., a global customer contact services provider, launched a leadership development program aimed at enhancing both servant and empowering leadership. Heather Cushing, senior manager of leadership development, said the

TABLE 13.3 Characteristics of the Servant-Leader

SERVANT-LEADERSHIP CHARACTERISTICS	DESCRIPTION
1. Listening	Servant-leaders focus on listening to identify and clarify the needs and desires of a group.
2. Empathy	Servant-leaders try to empathize with others' feelings and emotions. An individual's good intentions are assumed even when he or she performs poorly.
3. Healing	Servant-leaders strive to make themselves and others whole in the face of failure or suffering.
4. Awareness	Servant-leaders are aware of their own strengths and limitations.
5. Persuasion	Servant-leaders rely more on persuasion than on positional authority when making decisions and trying to influence others.
6. Conceptualization	Servant-leaders take the time and effort to develop broader-based conceptual thinking. They seek an appropriate balance between a short-term, day-to-day focus and a long-term, conceptual orientation.
7. Foresight	Servant-leaders have the ability to foresee outcomes of a current course of action or situation.
8. Stewardship	Servant-leaders assume they are stewards of the people and resources they manage.
9. Commitment to the growth of people	Servant-leaders commit to people beyond their immediate work role. They foster an environment that encourages personal, professional, and spiritual growth.
10. Interest in building community	Servant-leaders strive to create a sense of community both within and outside the work organization.

SOURCES: Spears, Larry C. "Character and Servant Leadership: Ten Characteristics of Effective, Caring Leaders." *The Journal of Virtues & Leadership* 1, no. 1 (2010): 25–30; and Spears, Larry C. *Reflections on Leadership: How Robert K. Greenleaf's Theory of Servant-Leadership Influenced Today's Top Management Thinkers.* New Jersey: John Wiley & Sons, Inc., 1995.

goal of the program is to help managers "exhibit an attitude of servant-hood, caring for the coaching and development of each level reporting up through them." Afni wants managers to empower "others to reach their full potential, while also inspiring teamwork and loyalty and improving employee engagement."[58]

Servant-leadership is expected to promote leadership effectiveness because it focuses on providing support and growth opportunities to employees. As you may recall from our discussion of perceived organizational support (POS) in Chapter 2, people generally reciprocate with increased effort toward collective performance when they feel supported. Servant-leaders have the characteristics listed in Table 13.3.

Does your current manager display the traits shown in Table 13.3? If yes, you are likely to be happier, more productive, more creative, and more willing to go above and beyond your role. This is precisely what researchers have uncovered.[59] Self-Assessment 13.3 measures the extent to which you possess a serving orientation. Results from the assessment will enhance your understanding of what it takes to really be a servant-leader.

Bono, lead singer of the Irish band U2, is a good example of a servant-leader. Here is what reporter Ellen McGirt had to say about him.

EXAMPLE In 2005 he started the One campaign, a volunteer-led movement to influence lawmakers to commit resources to funding programs that truly change the lives of the poor—from Pepfar (which continues to provide lifesaving antiretroviral drugs); to the Global Fund, the Geneva-based not-for-profit that finances select local programs fighting AIDS, TB, malaria; to Gavi, a public-private partnership that provides needed vaccines to kids. Bono's motto is adapted from St. Francis, who said, "Go into the world to preach the gospel, and if necessary, use words." Bono commented that "It's about being useful, and that's what I want to be."[60]

Ethical Leadership   OB scholars are interested in studying ethical leadership. *Ethical leadership* **represents normatively appropriate behavior that focuses on being a moral role model.** This includes communicating ethical values to others, rewarding ethical behavior, and treating followers with care and concern.[61]

Ethical leadership is clearly driven by personal factors related to our beliefs and values. It also has a reciprocal relationship with an organization's culture and climate. In other words, an ethical culture and climate promote ethical leadership, and ethical leadership in turn promotes an ethical culture and climate. Although ethical leadership is a relatively new area of study in OB, research already shows that it is positively related to employee job satisfaction, organizational commitment, organizational citizenship behavior, motivation, and task performance. It also is negatively associated with job stress, counterproductive work behavior, and intentions to quit.[62] It appears that ethical leadership has many positive benefits.

Abusive Supervision

Although most managers exhibit positive behavior toward their direct reports and others in the organization, there are some who demonstrate abusive behavior in the workplace. *Abusive supervision* **is the sustained display of hostile verbal and nonverbal behavior by managers.**[63] Examples of such behavior can include telling subordinates their ideas are stupid; criticizing them in front of colleagues and other managers; reminding them of past errors and missteps; and giving them the silent treatment.[64]

Research suggests that abusive supervision affects more than 13 percent of U.S. workers, although that percentage may be understated because of employees' fear of retaliation if they speak up. Abusive supervision may also increase job dissatisfaction, manifest as retaliatory behavior on the part of the abused worker, decrease productivity and innovation, and actually encourage abused employees to act out or demonstrate the same bad behavior as their supervisors to colleagues and others outside of work. In addition, costs of abusive supervision to organizations are estimated at nearly $24 billion annually.[65]

Research suggests the reasons for supervisors' abusive behavior may vary.[66] Regardless of the reasons, organizations can implement strategies to eliminate abusive behavior including

- An anonymous tip line that employees can call to report abuse.
- Written company policies prohibiting abusive behavior.
- Acknowledgment by senior managers that there is no place for abusive behavior in the company's culture.[67]

Unfortunately, not all supervisors and managers recognize such inappropriate behavior, as described in the OB in Action feature.

OB in Action

Abusive Leadership at a Pharmacy

It's hard to imagine a leader taking abuse of employees to the extreme lengths that a court case alleges Joyce Fogleman did. According to a federal suit filed by a former employee, in the "sexually hostile work environment" at J&S Professional Pharmacy in West Frankfort, Illinois, Fogleman, who has been the pharmacy's president and owner for almost 25 years, demanded employees line up and kiss her on the mouth to receive their pay checks, used public spanking as a disciplinary measure, often went about the workplace naked; and made comments about employees' physical attributes in front of other employees and customers. The former employee had worked at J&S for 12 years and was under the supervision of Fogleman's sister at the time. She claims that after seeking medical and psychiatric help to deal with high blood pressure, anxiety, and depression as a result of the situation at work, she was unlawfully fired in March 2017.[68]

Fogleman, who has supported many local charities and won various local business awards, told *Newsweek* that the claims in the suit were "just crazy," "totally bogus," and "ridiculous," and that the alleged events

"Never happened."[69] Her company employs 13 people and has annual revenues of nearly $5 million.[70] Fogleman also said the former employee bringing suit, Wendy Blades, was not fired, but Blades says not only that she was let go in retaliation but also that she was not the only victim of abuse. At least one other employee backs her claims.[71]

Meanwhile, Workforce.com made Fogleman its first nominee for the "worst boss of 2019."[72] If the allegations against her are true, her performance will be hard to top.

YOUR THOUGHTS?

1. If Blades is being truthful, do Fogleman's alleged actions fit the definition of abusive leadership? Why or why not?

2. How might Fogleman clear her name if she is innocent? What would she need to do?

3. What do you think would be the likely outcome for J&S Pharmacy if Fogleman were found guilty? Why?

What Are the Take-Aways from Behavioral Theory?

There are four points to remember about behavioral theory.

1. **Behavior is more important than traits when it comes to leaders' effectiveness.**[73] Our mantra for leaders is, "Every behavior matters."

2. **Leader behaviors can be systematically improved and developed.**[74] Organizations should continue to invest in leadership development programs.

3. **There is no one best style of leadership.** The effectiveness of a particular leadership style depends on the situation at hand.

4. **Abusive supervision takes it toll on employees, managers, and the overall organization.** Leaders at all levels of the company must recognize abusive behavior and work together to eliminate it.[75]

13.4 CONTINGENCY THEORIES: DOES THE EFFECTIVENESS OF LEADERSHIP DEPEND ON THE SITUATION?

THE BIGGER PICTURE

Proponents of contingency leadership believe the effectiveness of leadership behaviors depends on the situation. Makes common sense! Contingency theories help managers recognize when they should use particular types of leader behavior. Two that have been widely researched are Fred Fiedler's *contingency model* and Robert House's *path-goal theory*.

Contingency leadership theories grew out of the realization that there is no single "best" style of leadership. **Contingency theories propose that the effectiveness of a particular style of leader behavior depends on the situation.** As situations change, different styles become appropriate. As you will learn, however, the application of contingency theories is more complicated than it appears.

Let's examine two contingency theories: Fiedler's contingency model and House's path-goal theory.

LO 13-4

Describe two theories of contingency leadership.

Fiedler's Contingency Model

The oldest contingency-based theory was developed by Fred Fiedler. He labeled the model **contingency theory because it is based on the premise that a leader's effectiveness is contingent on the extent to which the leader's style matches characteristics of the situation at hand.** To understand how this matching process works, we'll consider the key leadership styles Fiedler identified and the situational variables that constitute what he labeled *situational control.*[76]

Two Leadership Styles: Task Orientation and Relationship Orientation
Fiedler believed leaders have one dominant or natural leadership style that is resistant to change—either task-motivated or relationship-motivated. Recall these two orientations from our earlier discussion in this chapter. Task-motivated leaders focus on accomplishing goals, whereas relationship-motivated leaders are more interested in developing positive relationships with followers. Fiedler developed the **least preferred coworker (LPC) scale to measure the extent to which an individual takes a task- or relationship-based approach toward leadership.** The scale asks you to evaluate a coworker you least enjoy working with on 16 pairs of opposite characteristics (such as friendly/unfriendly and tense/relaxed). High scores on the survey (high LPC) indicate that an individual is relationship-motivated, and low scores (low LPC) suggest a task-motivated style.

Three Dimensions of Situational Control   Situational control refers to the amount of control and influence the leader has in her or his immediate work environment. There are three dimensions of situational control: *leader–member relations, task structure,* and *position power.*

- **Leader–member relations describe the extent to which the leader has the support, loyalty, and trust of the work group.** This dimension is the most important component of situational control. Good leader–member relations suggest that the leader can depend on the group, thus ensuring members will try to meet the leader's goals and objectives.

- **Task structure measures the amount of structure contained within tasks performed by the work group.** For example, a managerial job contains less structure than that of a bank teller. Because there are guidelines for the way structured tasks should be completed, the leader has more control and influence over employees performing such tasks. This dimension is the second-most important component of situational control.

- **Position power is the leader's formal power to reward, punish, or otherwise obtain compliance from employees.**

The dimensions of situational control vary independently, forming eight combinations in which control varies from high to low (see Figure 13.3). High control implies that the leader's decisions will produce predictable results because the leader has the ability to influence work outcomes. Low control implies that the leader's decisions may not influence work outcomes because the leader has very little influence.

When Is Each Style Most Effective?   No leadership style is effective in all situations. Figure 13.3 illustrates when task- and relationship-motivated leadership are expected to be most effective.

- Task-oriented leadership should be most effective in either *high-control* (situations I–III in Figure 13.3) or *low-control* situations (situation VIII).
- Relationship-oriented leadership should be most effective in situations of *moderate control* (situations IV–VII in Figure 13.3).

FIGURE 13.3   Representation of Fiedler's Contingency Model

Situational Control	High-Control Situations			Moderate-Control Situations				Low-Control Situations
Leader–Member Relations	Good	Good	Good	Good	Poor	Poor	Poor	Poor
Task Structure	High	High	Low	Low	High	High	Low	Low
Position Power	Strong	Weak	Strong	Weak	Strong	Weak	Strong	Weak
Situation	I	II	III	IV	V	VI	VII	VIII
Optimal Leadership Style	Task-Motivated Leadership			Relationship-Motivated Leadership				Task-Motivated Leadership

SOURCE: "Situational Control and a Dynamic Theory of Leadership." In *Managerial Control and Organizational Democracy,* edited by Bert T. King, Siegfried Streufert, and Fred Edward Fiedler. Washington: V. H. Winston, 1978.

What should you do if your dominant leadership style does not match the situation? Then, Fiedler suggests, it is better to move to a more suitable situation than to try to change your leadership style. This response is different from that of the behavioral styles approach, which assumes we can learn different leader behaviors. Fiedler believes people cannot change their leadership style. Do you agree with this proposition?

Take-Aways from Fiedler's Model Although research provides only partial support for Fiedler's model and the LPC scale,[77] there are three key take-aways.

1. *Leadership effectiveness goes beyond traits and behaviors.* The fit between a leader's style and the situational demands is influential. For example, a recent study found that companies with task-oriented CEOs achieved greater financial performance (higher return on assets) when the company had a relationship-focused culture, whereas firms with relationship-oriented CEOs had higher firm performance in task-focused cultures.[78]

2. *Organizations should attempt to hire or promote people whose leadership styles fit or match situational demands.* Bookseller Barnes & Noble has gone through a series of CEOs over the past several years as the company's founder can't seem to find a candidate with the right leadership skills he desires (see the Problem-Solving Application box).

3. *Leaders need to modify their style to fit a situation.* A recent study found that too much task-oriented leader behavior was viewed negatively by employees, whereas excessive relationship leadership was not. Leaders need to experiment with finding the appropriate amount of leadership to exhibit in different situations.[79]

Problem-Solving Application

Barnes & Noble Seeks a Leader

Struggling to halt losses from both its online business and its brick-and-mortar stores, the venerable bookseller Barnes & Noble is now trying to find a CEO who can stay in the job for a while. With five CEOs at the helm in the last five years, the company has suffered through chaos and uncertainty while trying to retain its 600 remaining U.S. stores in the face of a long decline. Barnes & Noble's financial troubles have been caused mainly by the market-dominating success of Amazon and, ironically, a minor resurgence of independent bookstores.[80]

Most recently, Barnes & Noble fired CEO Demos Parneros, under whose leadership the company's shares dropped 32 percent in value, over unspecified violations of company policy that were later revealed to be sexual harassment claims and bullying. Parneros, formerly a 30-year veteran of Staples, Inc., has denied any misconduct and blames the company for disapproving of his business decisions, including a failed plan to sell the company. His countersuit claims defamation and breach of contract. The company's founder and long-time chair, Leonard Riggio, whom Parneros calls "volatile," "erratic and unprofessional," and someone who "refuses to relinquish control," has said the company must "heal" and will begin the search for a CEO yet again. The company also calls Parneros' characterization of Riggio "lies and mischaracterizations," though some industry analysts believe Riggio has been heavy-handed and lacks a vision for the company's future.[81] A group of leaders will oversee the chain in the meantime, including its chief financial officer, chief merchandising offer, and vice president of stores.[82]

The CEO who preceded Parneros, Ronald Boire, was let go after less than a year in the job, on the grounds that he was not a "good fit" for the company.[83] Boire's tenure had been marked by an expansion of non-book offering such as games and toys and by the introduction of workshops in coding and 3D printing. All these were to bolster a focus on "learning, personal growth and development [that] fits with our brand," Boire told a *New York Times* interviewer. But the company still racked up losses, especially since the Nook, Barnes & Noble's entry into the e-book reader market, has stumbled badly, costing the firm more money than it earned.[84]

Boire had followed Michael Huseby, who resigned in 2015, and William Lynch, who left in 2013. After Boire's departure, Riggio postponed his retirement to serve as interim CEO, a job he may find himself filling once more.

Apply the 3-Step Problem-Solving Approach

Step 1: Identify the problem in this case.

Step 2: Identify the cause of the problem. What leadership concepts or theories should Barnes & Noble apply when choosing its next CEO?

Step 3: Make your recommendation. Do you think Barnes & Noble's recent history will make it even more difficult to recruit a new CEO?

House's Path-Goal Theory

A second popular contingency-based theory, proposed by Robert House in the 1970s and revised in 1996, is **path-goal theory, which holds that leader behaviors are effective when employees view them as a source of satisfaction or as paving the way to future satisfaction.** Leaders are expected to do this by (1) reducing roadblocks that interfere with goal accomplishment, (2) providing the guidance and support employees need, and (3) linking meaningful rewards to goal accomplishment.[85]

House's revised model is presented in Figure 13.4. You can see that leadership effectiveness is influenced by the interaction between eight leadership behaviors (see Table 13.4) and a variety of contingency factors.

The mountaineering guide (pulling the climber up) exemplifies path-goal leadership. His job is to reduce roadblocks during an ascent and to provide coaching and support during the journey. Of the two climbers, who do you think has the most fun? Who has the greatest sense of accomplishment?

Javier Perini CM/Image Source

What Determines Leadership Effectiveness? The Match between Leadership Behavior and Contingency Factors Figure 13.4 shows that two contingency factors—employee characteristics and environmental factors—can cause some leadership behaviors to be more effective than others.

FIGURE 13.4   Representation of House's Revised Path-Goal Theory

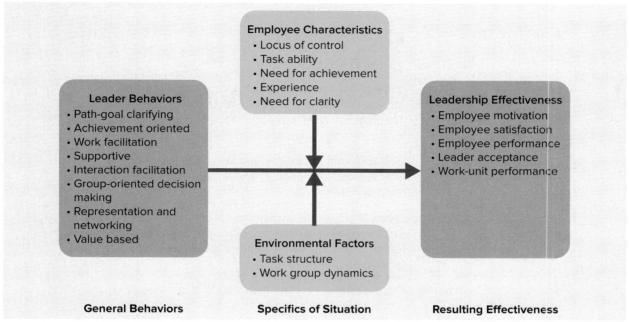

McGraw-Hill Global Education Holdings, LLC

Putting the Theory into Action   To better understand how these contingency factors influence leadership effectiveness, we consider locus of control (see Chapter 3), an employee characteristic, and task structure, an environmental factor.

EXAMPLE **Locus of control** can be internal or external.

Internal. Employees with an internal locus of control are

- More likely to prefer participative or achievement-oriented leadership because they believe they have control over the work environment.
- Unlikely to be satisfied with directive leader behaviors that exert additional control over their activities.

External. Employees with an external locus

- Tend to view the environment as uncontrollable, preferring the structure provided by supportive or directive leadership.

EXAMPLE **Task structure** can be low or high.

Low. Low task structure occurs when

- Employees are not clear about their roles or performance expectations and have high role ambiguity.

Directive and supportive leadership should help employees experiencing role ambiguity.

High. High task structure occurs when

- Employees work on routine and simple tasks.

Directive leadership is likely to frustrate such employees. Supportive leadership is most useful in this context.

TABLE 13.4 Categories of Leader Behavior in Revised Path-Goal Theory

LEADER BEHAVIORS	WHAT IT MEANS
Path-goal–clarifying behaviors	Clarifying employees' performance goals; providing guidance on how employees can complete tasks; clarifying performance standards and expectations; use of positive and negative rewards contingent on performance
Achievement-oriented behaviors	Setting challenging goals; emphasizing excellence; demonstrating confidence in employees' abilities
Work-facilitation behaviors	Planning, scheduling, organizing, and coordinating work; providing mentoring, coaching, counseling, and feedback to assist employees in developing their skills; eliminating roadblocks; providing resources; empowering employees to take actions and make decisions
Supportive behaviors	Showing concern for the well-being and needs of employees; being friendly and approachable; treating employees as equals
Interaction-facilitation behaviors	Resolving disputes; facilitating communication; encouraging the sharing of minority opinions; emphasizing collaboration and teamwork; encouraging close relationships among employees
Group-oriented decision-making behaviors	Posing problems rather than solutions to the work group; encouraging group members to participate in decision making; providing necessary information to the group for analysis; involving knowledgeable employees in decision making
Representation and networking behaviors	Presenting the work group in a positive light to others; maintaining positive relationships with influential others; participating in organizational social functions and ceremonies; doing unconditional favors for others
Value-based behaviors	Establishing a vision, displaying passion for it, and supporting its accomplishment; demonstrating self-confidence; communicating high-performance expectations and confidence in others' abilities to meet their goals; giving frequent positive feedback

SOURCE: House, Robert J. "Path-Goal Theory of Leadership: Lessons, Legacy, and a Reformulated Theory." *The Leadership Quarterly* 7, no. 3 (Autumn 1996): 323–52. https://doi.org/10.1016/S1048-9843(96)90024-7.

Does the Revised Path-Goal Theory Work?   There are not enough direct tests of House's revised path-goal theory to draw overall conclusions. Nonetheless, the theory offers us three key points.

1. *Use more than one style of leadership.* Effective leaders use multiple types of leader behavior. Familiarize yourself with the eight types of leader behavior outlined in path-goal theory and try new behaviors when the situation calls for them.

2. *Help employees achieve their goals.* Clarify the paths to goal accomplishment and remove any obstacles that may impair an employee's ability to achieve his or her goals.

3. ***Modify your leadership style to fit various employee and environmental characteristics.*** Remember that a small set of employee characteristics (ability, experience, and need for independence) and environmental factors (task characteristics of autonomy, variety, and significance) are relevant contingency factors.[86]

Applying Contingency Theories

Although researchers and practitioners support the logic of contingency leadership, its practical applications have not been clearly developed. A team of researchers proposed a general strategy managers can use across a variety of situations, however. It has five steps.[87] To describe them, let's use the examples of a head coach of a sports team and a sales manager.

Step 1: Identify important outcomes. Managers must first identify the goals they want to achieve. For example, the head coach may have games to win or wish to avoid injury to key players, whereas a sales manager's goal might be to increase sales by 10 percent or reduce customers' complaints by half.

Step 2: Identify relevant leadership behaviors. Next managers need to identify the specific types of behaviors that may be appropriate for the situation at hand. The list in Table 13.4 is a good starting point. A head coach in a championship game, for instance, might focus on achievement-oriented and work-facilitation behaviors. In contrast, a sales manager might find path-goal–clarifying, work-facilitation, and supportive behaviors more relevant for the sales team. Don't try to use all available leadership behaviors. Rather, select the one or two that appear most helpful.

Step 3: Identify situational conditions. Fiedler and House both identify a set of potential contingency factors to consider, but there may be other practical considerations. For example, a star quarterback on a football team may be injured, which might require the team to adopt a different strategy for winning the game. Similarly, the need to manage a virtual sales team with members from around the world will affect the types of leadership most effective in this context.

Step 4: Match leadership to the conditions at hand. There are too many possible situational conditions for us to provide specific advice. This means you should use your knowledge about organizational behavior to find the best match between your leadership styles and behaviors and the situation at hand. The coach whose star quarterback is injured might use supportive and values-based behaviors to instill confidence that the team can win with a different quarterback. Our sales manager also might find it useful to use the empowering leadership associated with work-facilitation behaviors and avoid directive leadership.

Step 5: Decide how to make the match. Managers can use guidelines from either contingency theory or path-goal theory: change the person in the leadership role or change his or her behavior. It is not possible to change the head coach in a championship game. This means the head coach needs to change his or her style or behavior to meet the specific challenge. In contrast, the organization employing the sales manager might move him or her to another position because the individual is too directive and does not like to empower others. Or the sales manager could change his or her behavior, if possible.

13.5 TRANSFORMATIONAL LEADERSHIP: HOW DO LEADERS TRANSFORM EMPLOYEES' MOTIVES?

THE BIGGER PICTURE

Transformational leaders use a combination of charisma, interpersonal skills, and leader behaviors to transform followers' goals, motives, and behavior. Four key behaviors they adopt are inspirational motivation, idealized influence, individualized consideration, and intellectual stimulation. We discuss a process by which these behaviors help produce positive outcomes.

LO 13-5

Describe how to use transformational leadership to work with others.

Transformational leadership represents a broad type of leader behavior that goes beyond task and relational leadership. Its origins date to the 1940s, when German sociologist Max Weber discussed the pros and cons of charismatic leadership.[88] *Charisma* **is a form of interpersonal attraction that inspires acceptance, devotion, and enthusiasm.** Weber's initial ideas were examined and then incorporated into different models of transformational leadership during the 1970s and '80s. The dominant model of transformational leadership was proposed by a renowned OB scholar, Bernard Bass.[89] Bass believed transformational leaders used key leader behaviors to influence others.

A Model of Transformational Leadership

Transformational leaders **transform their followers to pursue organizational goals over self-interests.** They do this by appealing to followers' self-concepts—their values, motives, and personal identity. There are *four key behaviors of transformational leaders:* inspirational motivation, idealized influence, individualized consideration, and intellectual stimulation. Figure 13.5 provides a sketch of the way transformational leaders rely on the four behaviors. Let's look at each in more detail.

Inspirational Motivation   "Let me share a vision that elevates us to a greater good." *Inspirational motivation,* **which includes the use of charisma, relies on an attractive vision of the future, emotional arguments, and demonstrated optimism and enthusiasm.** A vision is "a realistic, credible, attractive future for your organization."[90] According to Burt Nanus, a leadership expert, the right vision unleashes human potential because it serves as a beacon of hope and common purpose. It does this by attracting commitment, energizing workers, creating meaning in employees' lives, establishing a standard of excellence, promoting high ideals, and bridging the gap between an organization's present problems and its future goals and aspirations.

> **EXAMPLE** Netflix co-founder and CEO Reed Hastings motivates employees by stepping back and letting them make decisions, which empowers them to acquire knowledge and share this knowledge with others at all levels of the organization.[91]

FIGURE 13.5   A Transformational Model of Leadership

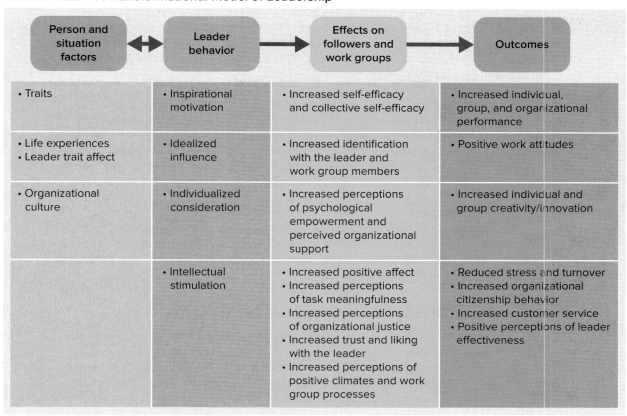

Person and situation factors	Leader behavior	Effects on followers and work groups	Outcomes
• Traits	• Inspirational motivation	• Increased self-efficacy and collective self-efficacy	• Increased individual, group, and organizational performance
• Life experiences • Leader trait affect	• Idealized influence	• Increased identification with the leader and work group members	• Positive work attitudes
• Organizational culture	• Individualized consideration	• Increased perceptions of psychological empowerment and perceived organizational support	• Increased individual and group creativity/innovation
	• Intellectual stimulation	• Increased positive affect • Increased perceptions of task meaningfulness • Increased perceptions of organizational justice • Increased trust and liking with the leader • Increased perceptions of positive climates and work group processes	• Reduced stress and turnover • Increased organizational citizenship behavior • Increased customer service • Positive perceptions of leader effectiveness

SOURCE: Waldman, David A., and Francis J. Yammarino. "CEO Charismatic Leadership: Levels-of-Management and Levels-of-Analysis Effects." *The Academy of Management Review* 24, no. 2 (April 1999): 266–85. https: DOI: 10.2307/259082; and Knippenberg, Daan van, and Sim B. Sitkin. "A Critical Assessment of Charismatic—Transformational Leadership Research: Back to the Drawing Board?" *The Academy of Management Annals* 7, no. 1 (January 2013): 1–60. https://doi.org/10.1080/19416520.2013.759433.

Idealized Influence   "Let me demonstrate how to work hard and do the right thing." The focus of ***idealized influence* is to instill pride, respect, and trust within employees.** Managers do this by sacrificing for the good of the group, being a role model, and displaying high ethical standards.

> **EXAMPLE** Netflix's core philosophy is "people over process." According to Hastings, the company's top core value is encouraging employees to make decisions independently that will foster a creative and collaborative environment.[92]

Individualized Consideration   "Let me provide tangible support to help you reach your goals." The individualized consideration part of transformational leadership is about relationships. Specifically, ***individualized consideration* consists of behaviors that provide support, encouragement, empowerment, and coaching to employees.** To enact these behaviors, leaders must pay special attention to the needs of their followers and search for ways to help them develop and grow. Spend time talking with people about their interests and identify new learning opportunities for them.

Reed Hastings, Netflix's co-founder and CEO, exhibits transformational leadership skills that help him encourage employees to make decisions independently and empower them to create a collaborative and creative work environment.

Ethan Miller/Getty Images

EXAMPLE More than a decade ago, Hastings and the former chief talent officer put together a slide presentation famously known as Netflix's Culture Deck, which lays out the company's expectations when it comes to employee behavior. Although not for everyone, this approach to shaping organizational culture and promising freedom, transparency, and responsibility has garnered Netflix a strong level of job satisfaction from its employees.[93]

Intellectual Stimulation "Let's establish challenging and meaningful goals." The intellectual component of transformational leadership is more task-oriented. **Intellectual stimulation behavior encourages employees to question the status quo and to seek innovative and creative solutions to organizational problems.** If effectively challenged, employees are more likely to view organizational problems as "my problems" and proactively attempt to overcome performance roadblocks.

EXAMPLE One of Netflix's underlying corporate values is "challenge everything," which leads everyone—both managers and employees—to question tasks and processes, try new things, make mistakes, try other things, and learn from good and bad outcomes. This collaborative approach reinforces the company's commitment to keeping employees intellectually engaged.[94]

How Does Transformational Leadership Work?

Figure 13.5 showed on the left-hand side that transformational leader behavior is first influenced by both person and situation factors. On the person factor side of the equation, research reveals that transformational leaders tend to have personalities that are more extroverted, agreeable, and proactive and less neurotic than nontransformational leaders. They also have higher emotional intelligence[95] and tend to be female.[96] Leader trait affect, which represents a person's tendency to feel either positive or negative, also influences how well we use transformational leadership, because positive people are more likely to engage in transformational leadership than negatively oriented individuals.[97]

Finally, Figure 13.5 also shows that organizational culture influences the extent to which leaders are transformational. Cultures that are adaptive and flexible rather than rigid and bureaucratic are more likely to foster the opportunity for leaders to demonstrate transformational leadership.

The third column from the left in Figure 13.5 reveals that the use of transformational leadership creates immediate positive effects on followers and work groups. These in turn generate the additional positive outcomes shown in the fourth column of Figure 13.5 like individual, group, and organizational performance; organizational commitment; organizational citizenship behaviors; reduced turnover intentions; and safety behaviors.[98] By and large, research supports the linkages the figure shows.[99]

Have you worked for a transformational leader? Self-Assessment 13.4 measures the extent to which a current or former manager used transformational leadership. It also gives you a good idea about the specific behaviors you need to exhibit if you want to lead in a transformational manner.

SELF-ASSESSMENT 13.4

Assessing Your Boss's Transformational Leadership

Please be prepared to answer these questions if your instructor has assigned Self-Assessment 13.4 in Connect.

1. What could your manager have done to be more transformational?

2. What three behaviors can you exhibit to increase your application of transformational leadership?

Implications for Managers Support for transformational leadership underscores five important managerial implications.

- **The establishment of a positive vision of the future—inspirational motivation—should be considered a first step in applying transformational leadership.** Why? Because the vision represents a long-term goal, and it is important for leaders to begin their influence attempts by gaining agreement and consensus about where the team or organization is headed.[100] It also is critical to widely communicate the vision among the team or entire organization.[101] People can't get excited about something they don't know about or don't understand.

- **The best leaders are not just transformational.** Effective leaders also rely on other task-oriented and relationship-oriented behaviors, and they avoid a laissez-faire or "wait-and-see" style. Use all types of leader behavior discussed in this chapter, when appropriate.

- **Transformational leadership affects outcomes at the individual, group, and organizational levels.**[102] Managers can use the four types of transformational leadership shown in Figure 13.5 (second column from left) as a vehicle to improve a host of important outcomes.

- **Transformational leadership works virtually.** If you lead geographically dispersed people, focus on how you can display the four transformational leader behaviors in your e-mails, tweets, webinars, and conference calls.[103]

- **Transformational leaders can be ethical or unethical.** While ethical transformational leaders enable employees to enhance their self-concepts, unethical ones select or produce obedient, dependent, and compliant followers.

Managers need to be more like Optimus Prime and his fellow transformers. That is, managers can be more effective by morphing their leadership styles to fit the situation at hand. Why do you think some people struggle with changing their leadership style across situations?

Gustavo Caballero/Getty Images

13.6 ADDITIONAL PERSPECTIVES ON LEADERSHIP

THE BIGGER PICTURE

You are about to discover how leader–member exchange theory, humility, and characteristics of good followers can help you achieve your career aspirations.

LO 13-6

Compare more recent approaches to leadership theory.

Three additional perspectives on leadership deserve attention:

- Leader–member exchange (LMX) theory.
- The use of humility.
- A follower perspective.

The Leader–Member Exchange (LMX) Model of Leadership

Leader–member exchange (LMX) theory differs considerably from the theories already discussed because it focuses on the *quality of relationships* between managers and subordinates, as opposed to their behaviors or traits. It also does not assume that leader behavior is characterized by a stable or average leadership style.

Leader–member exchange (LMX) theory is based on the assumption that leaders develop unique one-to-one relationships (exchanges) with each of the people reporting to them. Behavioral scientists call this sort of relationship a *vertical dyad* (a dyad is something with two parts). The forming of vertical dyads is said to be a naturally occurring process, resulting from the leader's attempt to delegate and assign work roles. Two distinct types of LMX relationships are expected to evolve, in-groups and out-groups.[104]

In-Group vs. Out-Group Exchanges   LMX relationships are based on the leader's attempt to delegate and assign work roles. This process results in two types of leader–member dyads.

- **In-group exchange: Creating trust and mutual obligation.** High in-group exchanges, also called high LMX, are characterized by a partnership of reciprocal influence, mutual trust, respect and liking, and a sense of common fate. These relationships become more social over time.
- **Out-group exchange: Creating more formality in expectations and rewards.** Out-group exchanges, also known as low LMX relationships, tend to focus on the economic exchange between leaders and followers. They tend to be more formal and revolve around negotiating the relationship between performance and pay. They do not create a sense of mutual trust, respect, or common fate.[105]

Does the Quality of an LMX Matter?   Whether an LMX is high or low influences many important outcomes contained in the Organizing Framework. For example, a high LMX is associated with individual-level behavioral outcomes such as task performance, turnover, organizational citizenship, counterproductive behavior, and attitudinal outcomes such as organizational commitment, job satisfaction, and justice.[106] An effective leader will treat

These two photos illustrate a core aspect of LMX theory. Leaders and followers with a positive "in-group exchange" tend to get along better and experience less conflict. In contrast, out-group exchanges are more likely to have a negative tone and more conflict.

(Left): Fuse/Corbis/Getty Images; (right): John Lund/Nevada Wier/Blend Images/Getty Images

employees fairly in terms of assigning projects that are both challenging and interesting to all group members in an effort to keep them on track to achieve success, both on an individual and group level.

Differential treatment of team members (due to LMXs of different quality) can be problematic.[107] For example, a leader who plays favorites with employees she likes by continuously giving them the top projects while ignoring others in the group may discover she is not only fostering a negative and hostile work environment, but her behavior may border on abusive supervision, a topic discussed earlier in the chapter, which could have severe consequences in terms of personal as well as organizational success.[108] Recent research suggests that leaders perceived by subordinates to feel remorse about such low LMX or abusive treatment may actually improve relationships with their employees.[109]

The above findings underscore how important it is for you to have a high LMX with your boss. We'll offer solutions for fixing a low LMX below, but for now let's consider how LMXs are formed.

How Are LMX Relationships Formed?

The quality of an LMX is influenced by three categories of variables: follower characteristics, leader characteristics, and interpersonal relationship variables.[110]

1. **Follower characteristics.** Leaders tend to create higher LMXs with employees they perceive as possessing competence, positive personalities, agreeableness, conscientiousness, and extraversion. Do you possess these characteristics?

2. **Leader characteristics.** Leaders who use transactional and transformational leadership tend to have higher LMXs. Not surprisingly, so do extroverted and agreeable leaders.

3. **Interpersonal relationship variables.** Far too many interpersonal factors affect an LMX for us to discuss here, so we note three that have the greatest impact on a leader-member relationship. High LMXs tend to occur when the parties:

   - Trust each other.
   - Perceive themselves as similar in terms of interests (both like sports or action movies), values (both value honesty), and attitudes (both want work-life balance).
   - Like each other.

Your dyadic relationship with your boss changes over time. A team of researchers concluded this happens because the variables that affect LMX interact and accumulate over time.[111] For example, your author has had relationships with bosses that changed from good to bad, and then back to good. This tells us that you should not easily give up on trying to improve a low LMX.

Managerial and Personal Implications of LMX Theory   Here are three important managerial and personal implications of LMX theory.

- **Expectations matter.** Leaders are encouraged to establish high-performance expectations for *all* their direct reports, because favoritism and differential treatment lead to negative outcomes. Leaders should also communicate their view of relationships with their team.[112]

- **Diversity still counts.** Personality and demographic similarity between leaders and followers may be associated with higher LMXs, but managers should avoid creating a homogenous work environment just for the sake of having positive relationships with their direct reports. Diversity's many benefits are too powerful to be ignored.

- **The initiative is yours.** Positive actions can improve a poor LMX (see the Applying OB box). Take the lead rather than waiting for your boss to change the relationship. Self-Assessment 13.5 will help you diagnose the quality of your relationship with a boss and discover how you can improve it.

SELF-ASSESSMENT 13.5

Assessing Your Leader–Member Exchange

Please be prepared to answer these questions if your instructor has assigned Self-Assessment 13.5 in Connect.

1. Are you surprised by the results? Explain.
2. Based on your results, what do you think are the key causes of your LMX with your boss? Be specific.

Applying OB

Tips for Improving the Quality of a Leader–Member Exchange

Your boss needs your contributions to achieve his or her goals as a manager, and you need information, direction, and support from your boss. But when it comes to managing the relationship between you, you're the one who's in charge.[113]

1. *Stay focused on your department's goals and remain positive about your ability to accomplish your own goals.* An unsupportive boss is just another obstacle to be overcome.
2. *Be careful about the emotions you show at work.* Anger generally is not a good emotion to display. Too much positivity can also be interpreted as unrealistic or silly. Emotions should be appropriate for the situation at hand.[114]

3. *Work on improving your relationship with your manager.* Begin by examining the level of trust between you and then try to improve it by frequently and effectively communicating. You can also increase trust by following through on your commitments and achieving your goals.[115]
4. *Learn what your boss believes are the desired characteristics of a good performer.* Too many people fail to clarify expectations with their managers. For example, there are generational differences about what is appropriate dress at work. Violating these beliefs can land you in a poor LMX.[116]

The Power of Humility

Humility is a relatively stable trait grounded in the belief that "something greater than the self exists."[117] Although some think it is a sign of weakness or low self-esteem, nothing could be further from the truth.

Humble leaders tend to display five key qualities valued by employees: high self-awareness, openness to feedback, appreciation of others, low self-focus, and appreciation of the greater good.[118] Adam Robinson, co-founder of Hireology, a talent management consulting firm, says one of the top leadership qualities companies are looking for in new hires or when promoting new leaders is humility. "Humble leaders appreciate their employees' strengths and trust them to do effective work to help move the company forward," according to Robinson.[119]

Although the scientific study of humility is relatively new, it has shown proven benefits for this trait. For example, a study of more than 146 employee teams in China, Portugal, and Singapore revealed that workers felt optimistic, resilient, and engaged when the boss was humble.[120] Another study conducted in China demonstrated cascading positive effects of CEO humility across two organizational levels. CEO humility positively influenced employee engagement, commitment, and performance.[121]

We don't tend to see professional athletes as humble, but this one surely is recognized for this attribute. Larry Fitzgerald is a wide receiver for the Arizona Cardinals. He has been selected for the Pro Bowl 11 times and currently ranks second in all-time receiving yards per game in NFL history. Despite these achievements, he does not assume he is good enough for the Hall of Fame. He is recognized for continually working on improving his game, being "nice" to opposing players, and being involved with charity and community-based organizations.
Christian Petersen/Getty Images

What can we conclude about humility in the context of OB? First, try to be more humble by changing the focus of your accomplishment from "me" to "we." Share credit with others. Second, a humble style is better than an arrogant or complacent one.[122] Third, an organization's culture can promote humility. Employee-owned construction company TDIndustries does so with its agreed-upon set of cultural norms: "No rank in the room, everyone participates—no one dominates, and listen as an ally." Employees also strive to be on a first-name basis with everyone.[123]

The Role of Followers in the Leadership Process

All the theories discussed in this chapter have been leader-centric. That is, they focused on understanding leadership effectiveness from the leader's point of view. We conclude the chapter by discussing the role of followers in the leadership process.

To start, note how leaders and followers are closely linked. You cannot lead without having followers, and you cannot follow without having leaders. Each needs the other, and the quality of the relationship determines how we behave as followers. This is why both leaders and followers must focus on developing a mutually rewarding and beneficial relationship.

Let's consider some possible types of followers and the steps you can take to be a better follower.

What Do Leaders Want from Followers?   Followers vary in terms of the extent to which they commit to, comply with, or resist a leader's influence attempts. For example, one researcher identified three types of followers: helpers, independents, and rebels.[124]

- *Helpers* show deference to and comply with the leadership.
- *Independents* distance themselves from the leadership and show less compliance.
- *Rebels* show divergence from the leader and are least compliant.

Leaders obviously want followers who are:

1. Productive
2. Reliable
3. Honest
4. Cooperative
5. Proactive
6. Flexible

Leaders do not benefit from followers who hide the truth, withhold information, fail to generate ideas, are unwilling to collaborate, provide inaccurate feedback, or are unwilling to take the lead on projects and initiatives.[125]

What Do Followers Want from Leaders?   Followers seek, admire, and respect leaders who foster three emotional responses in others:

- Significance
- Community
- Excitement

That is, followers want organizational leaders who make them feel what they do at work is important and meaningful, who foster a sense of unity that encourages people to treat others with respect and dignity and to work together, and who make them feel engaged and energized at work.[126]

How Can I Become a Better Follower?   A pair of OB experts developed a four-step process for followers to use in managing the leader–follower relationship.[127]

1. **Understand your boss.** Gain an appreciation for your manager's leadership style, interpersonal style, goals, expectations, pressures, and strengths and weaknesses. One way is to ask him or her these seven questions:[128]

    a. How would you describe your leadership style? Does it change when you are under pressure?

    b. When would you like me to approach you with questions or information? Are any situations off-limits (like social events)?

    c. How do you want me to communicate with you?

    d. Do you have any preferred or unique ways of working?

    e. Are there behaviors or attitudes you won't tolerate? What are they?

    f. What is your approach to giving feedback?

    g. How can I help you?

2. **Understand your own style, needs, goals, expectations, and strengths and weaknesses.**

3. **Conduct a gap analysis between the understanding you have about your boss and the understanding you have about yourself.**

4. **Build on mutual strengths and adjust or accommodate your boss's divergent style, goals, expectations, and weaknesses.**[129] For example, you might adjust your style of communication in response to your boss's preferred method for receiving information. Or if the boss prefers participative decision making, consult him or her in all decisions regardless of your own style. Most managers are pushed for time, energy, and resources and are more likely to appreciate followers who save rather than cost them these. Avoid using your manager's time discussing trivial matters.

13.7 MAKING THE CONNECTION: WHAT DOES IT TAKE TO BE AN EFFECTIVE LEADER?

Becoming an effective leader is a challenging process for anyone and involves continuously learning about yourself, as well as others. Here are some key points to consider.

Takeaways for Me

LO 13-7

Describe the implications of leadership effectiveness for you and managers.

Here are six things you can do to turn this chapter's lessons into positive change in your personal and professional life.

1. **Give some thought to whether you want a managerial or leadership role in your career:** It's not for everyone. For example, if you don't like to participate in meetings, this role is not for you. Self-Assessment 13.1 was created to help you with this decision.

2. **The more you look and act like someone's prototype of a leader, the more he or she will see you that way:** This implies you should seek to understand your employer's expectations of leadership.

3. **Experiment with the full repertoire of leadership behaviors at school and work:** Reflecting on this experience will help you understand the situational aspect of leadership.

4. **Try being more transformational at meetings:** You can do this by demonstrating the four key behaviors underlying transformational leadership.

5. **Take responsibility for your relationship with your boss:** You can improve this relationship by following our recommendations about being a good follower.

6. **Get feedback on your leadership:** It's the only way to improve.

Takeaways for Managers

There are seven key implications for managers.

1. **Take stock of the task-oriented traits and interpersonal attributes needed to lead.**

2. **Find out how others are assessing your leadership:** You won't get promoted if people perceive you lack leadership ability.

3. **Experiment with a contingency approach toward leadership:** This requires you to gain perspective about the different leadership behaviors your followers may need.

4. **Being mindful can improve your leadership skills:** Revisit our discussion of mindfulness in Chapter 7 and incorporate mindfulness techniques into your leadership.

5. **Try to develop positive relationships with all your followers.**

6. **Be a good follower to your boss.**

7. **Get feedback on your leadership:** It's the only way to improve

What Did I Learn?

You learned that being an effective leader requires appropriate leadership behavior that you can learn and develop. The integrated model of leadership allows you to understand the many factors contributing to leadership effectiveness. You also learned the importance of being a good follower. Reinforce your learning with the Key Points below. Consolidate your knowledge by using the Organizing Framework. Then challenge your mastery of the material by answering the Major Questions in your own words.

- Emotional intelligence contributes to transformational leadership and is positively associated with leader effectiveness.
- There are both similarities and differences in the leadership traits possessed by men and by women.
- Leaders need four key skills: cognitive abilities, interpersonal skills, business skills, and strategic skills.
- People hold mental prototypes of effective and ineffective leaders.

Key Points for Understanding Chapter 13

You learned the following key points.

13.1 MAKING SENSE OF LEADERSHIP THEORIES

- You do not need to have a formal position of authority to lead.
- Figure 13.2 shows an integrated model of leadership. The extent to which people effectively use the four key leader behaviors—task-oriented, relationship-oriented, passive, and transformational—is a function of demographic characteristics, intelligence and skills, task-oriented traits, and interpersonal attributes.
- Effective leadership requires effective managerial skills at some level.

13.2 TRAIT THEORIES: DO LEADERS POSSESS UNIQUE TRAITS AND PERSONAL CHARACTERISTICS?

- Table 13.1 summarizes the positive task-oriented traits and positive/negative interpersonal attributes leaders possess.

13.3 BEHAVIORAL THEORIES: WHICH LEADER BEHAVIORS DRIVE EFFECTIVENESS?

- Four categories of leader behavior are task-oriented, relationship-oriented, passive, and transformational.
- Task-oriented leadership includes the use of initiating structure and transactional leadership.
- Relationship-oriented leadership includes the use of consideration, empowerment, servant leadership, and ethical leadership.
- Followers experience psychological empowerment when leaders create perceptions of meaningfulness, self-determination or choice, competence, and impact.
- Servant-leadership focuses on increased service to others rather than ourselves. Servant-leaders display the characteristics in Table 13.3.
- Ethical leadership focuses on doing the right thing and establishing norms of ethical behavior.
- Abusive leadership is demoralizing and counterproductive to both employees and the overall organization. Avoid it!

13.4 CONTINGENCY THEORIES: DOES THE EFFECTIVENESS OF LEADERSHIP DEPEND ON THE SITUATION?

- Contingency theories are based on the idea that the effectiveness of leadership depends on the situation at hand.
- Fiedler believes leadership effectiveness depends on an appropriate match between leadership style and situational control. Leaders are either task- or relationship-oriented, and the situation is composed of leader–member relationships, task structure, and position power.
- House's path-goal theory holds that leader behaviors are effective when employees view them as a source of satisfaction or as paving the way to future satisfaction. In this respect, leaders exhibit eight styles or categories of leader behavior. In turn, the effectiveness of these styles depends on various employee characteristics and environmental factors.
- Researchers suggest a five-step approach for applying contingency theories.

13.5 TRANSFORMATIONAL LEADERSHIP: HOW DO LEADERS TRANSFORM EMPLOYEES' MOTIVES?

- Transformational leaders motivate employees to pursue organizational goals above their own self-interests.
- Transformational leaders rely on four unique types of leader behavior: inspirational motivation, idealized influence, individualized consideration, and intellectual stimulation.
- Person and situation factors influence the extent to which people use transformational leadership.
- The use of transformational leadership has positive effects on followers and work groups. In turn, these positive effects foster positive individual, group, and organizational performance.

13.6 ADDITIONAL PERSPECTIVES ON LEADERSHIP

- The LMX model revolves around the development of dyadic relationships between managers and their direct reports. These leader–member exchanges result in either in-group or out-group relationships.
- Humility is a stable trait associated with the belief that something is more important than the self. Humble leaders exhibit five key qualities: high self-awareness, openness to feedback, appreciation of others, low self-focus, and appreciation of the greater good.
- It is hard for leaders to be effective if they have poor followers. Leaders want followers who are productive, reliable, honest, cooperative, proactive, and flexible. People are more likely to be positive followers when the leader creates feelings of significance, community, and excitement.
- To improve the relationship with a boss, followers should first understand the boss. Second, followers should understand their own style, needs, goals, expectations, and strengths and weaknesses. Third, they should conduct a gap analysis between the understandings they have about their boss and about themselves. Finally, followers can build on mutual strengths and adjust to or accommodate the leader's different style, goals, expectations, and weaknesses.

13.7 WHAT DOES IT TAKE TO BE AN EFFECTIVE LEADER?

- Give some thought to whether you want a managerial or leadership role in your career—it's not for everyone.
- Experiment with various leadership behaviors—this will help you understand the situational aspect of leadership.
- Find out how others assess your leadership skills—it's the only way to improve.

The Organizing Framework for Chapter 13

As shown in Figure 13.6, you learned a host of person and situation factors that influence the leadership processes identified in the figure. You also understand the breadth and power of leadership by looking at the Outcomes box of the framework. Here you see the individual-, group/team-, and organizational-level outcomes affected by leadership.

Challenge: Major Questions for Chapter 13

You now should be able to answer the following questions. Unless you can, have you really processed and internalized the lessons in the chapter? Refer to the Key Points, Figure 13.6, the chapter itself, and your notes to revisit and answer the following major questions:

1. How does having an integrated model of leadership help me become an effective leader?
2. How can I use trait theories to improve my ability to lead?
3. Do effective leaders behave in similar ways?
4. How do I know when to use a specific leader behavior?
5. How can I use transformational leadership when working with others?
6. How can more recent approaches to leadership improve my effectiveness at work?

FIGURE 13.6 The Organizing Framework for Understanding and Applying OB

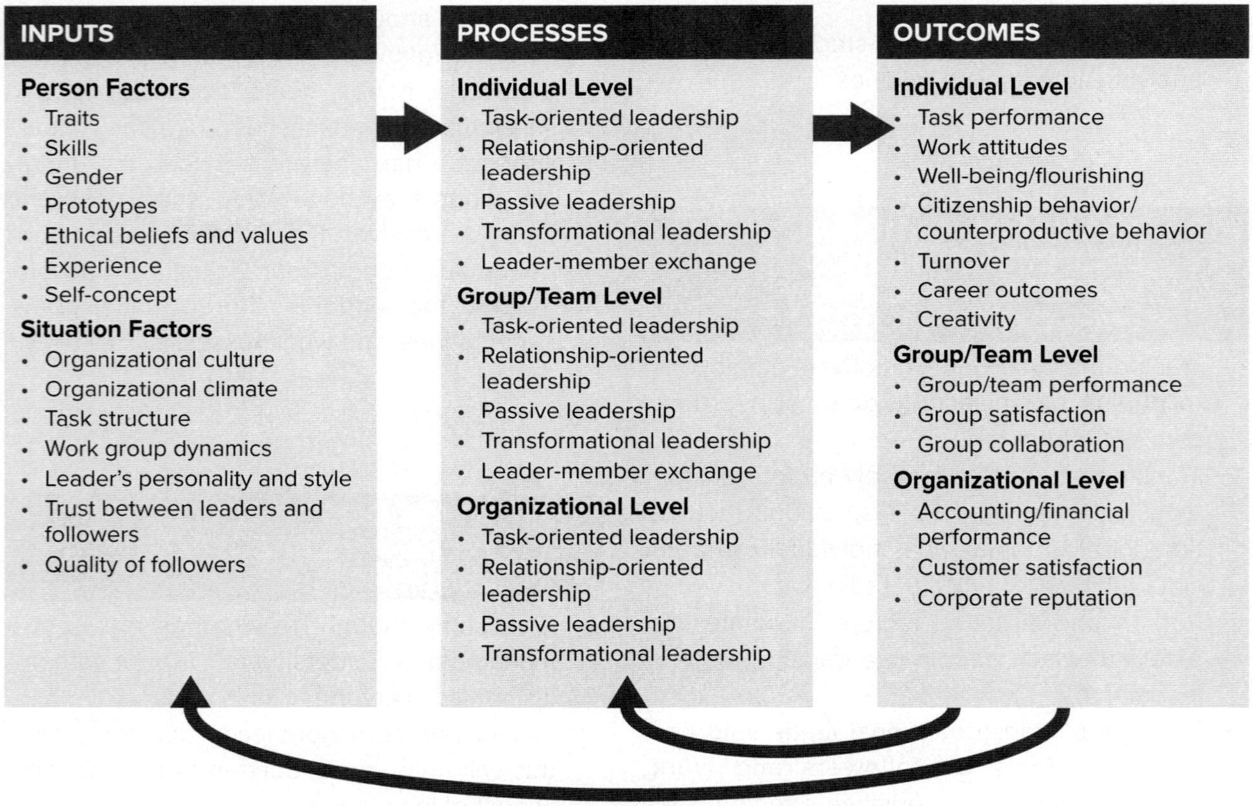

INPUTS	PROCESSES	OUTCOMES
Person Factors • Traits • Skills • Gender • Prototypes • Ethical beliefs and values • Experience • Self-concept **Situation Factors** • Organizational culture • Organizational climate • Task structure • Work group dynamics • Leader's personality and style • Trust between leaders and followers • Quality of followers	**Individual Level** • Task-oriented leadership • Relationship-oriented leadership • Passive leadership • Transformational leadership • Leader-member exchange **Group/Team Level** • Task-oriented leadership • Relationship-oriented leadership • Passive leadership • Transformational leadership • Leader-member exchange **Organizational Level** • Task-oriented leadership • Relationship-oriented leadership • Passive leadership • Transformational leadership	**Individual Level** • Task performance • Work attitudes • Well-being/flourishing • Citizenship behavior/counterproductive behavior • Turnover • Career outcomes • Creativity **Group/Team Level** • Group/team performance • Group satisfaction • Group collaboration **Organizational Level** • Accounting/financial performance • Customer satisfaction • Corporate reputation

Leadership Matters!

Elon Musk is widely regarded as one of the most successful entrepreneurs in history.[130] He became a billionaire by age 31 after founding and selling several successful start-ups—most notably the company that would later be known as Paypal. In 2004 Musk invested $6.3 million into Tesla Motors and soon after became the company's CEO.[131]

Musk has a keen ability to express ideas and get people excited about them and has garnered praise for his inspiring and visionary leadership.[132] Author Dale Buss argues that "...a huge part of Musk's motivational quiver is to come up with and continually express other-worldly goals that appeal to the passions of his employees as well as to his own ambitions."[133] Todd Maron, Tesla's former general counsel, said Musk is "someone who empowers you to be better than you think you can be," adding that "he has extraordinarily high standards, and so he pushes you to be your absolute best." Another former employee described Musk as "the smartest person I have ever met," adding, "I can't tell you how many times I prepared a report for him and he asked a question that made us realize we were looking at the problem completely wrong."[134]

MUSK'S LEADERSHIP STYLE AND BEHAVIOR

Some have criticized Musk's aspirations to change the world as outlandish and his ideas as unachievable, but Musk doesn't believe in impossibilities. Says author Christopher Davenport, "People are always telling him he can't do it. But he doesn't like to hear it can't be done. He categorically rejects that. It's all about, 'How can we do it?'"[135] A recent example of Musk's stubbornness is the production of the Model 3. After the company revealed the concept to the public and locked in production dates, Musk called a meeting to tell executives he had a dream that the entire production process had been fully automated. In other words, vehicle production would require no humans from start to finish. He wanted to make the dream a reality, he wanted to do it with the Model 3, and he wanted to begin production four months ahead of Tesla's original schedule. What followed were several months of what former executives and employees describe as a familiar pattern: executives told Musk his idea wasn't achievable, he disagreed, and engineers resigned when they realized they couldn't reason with him.[136]

Musk eventually conceded that his idea for fully automated production of the Model 3 was a nonstarter, and he and his workers scrambled to get production back on track by working 80–100 hour weeks.[137] Customers waited months past delivery dates for their vehicles and took to social media to lambast the company. Further, many of the Model 3s that were delivered needed costly and time-consuming repairs.[138] Musk would later refer to the ordeal as "production hell."[139]

Some blame Musk's inability to delegate for Tesla's problems and for the recent exodus of more than 36 VPs and other high-ranking executives.[140] Musk wants things done his way down to the tiniest detail and often rejects industry best practices along with advice from his senior leadership. For example, Musk once instituted a new workflow management method against the advice of his production workers. The employees secretly reverted to Toyota's Kanban method when Musk's technique ultimately slowed production.[141] Author Barry Enderwick believes Musk's micromanaging style "...displays a fundamental misunderstanding of what leadership means. No one person can do everything at a company."[142]

Others blame Musk's mental health for his downward spiral and describe him as emotionally unstable and fragile. Musk developed a reputation on the production floor for openly ridiculing, insulting, and bullying workers who fell short of performance targets. He appeared extremely sensitive to skeptics, often reassigning workers who questioned his ideas to new departments, uninviting them to important meetings, and even firing them. Musk also displayed frequent emotional reactions to isolated customer complaints on social media. As a former employee recalls, "Some customer would tweet some random complaint, and then we would be ordered to drop everything and spend a week on some problem affecting one loudmouth in Pasadena, rather than all the work we're supposed to do to support the thousands of customers who didn't tweet that day."[143]

Musk's recent public appearances and social media posts have raised consumer concerns about his ability to deliver on his promises and successfully run his companies. In one instance, he angrily tweeted that a diver sent to rescue a trapped Thai boys' soccer team was a pedophile after Musk's offer to assist with the rescue was declined. The diver filed a defamation lawsuit against Musk for this damaging and unsubstantiated claim.[144] As another example, Musk chose to smoke marijuana during an appearance on "The Joe Rogan Experience" podcast.[145] In August 2018, in what would prove the most financially damaging of his social media choices to date, Musk tweeted that he was taking Tesla private and had secured the funding to do so. As a result of his tweet, the company's shares skyrocketed 11 percent in one day. Musk had not actually secured funding to take Tesla private and the SEC charged him with securities fraud. He settled the case and agreed to pay a $40 million fine to the SEC, step down as Tesla's chairperson, and allow others in the company to regulate his social media activity.[146] A few months after reaching the settlement, Musk gave a *60 Minutes* interview and said "I do not respect the SEC." While it is not illegal for Musk to criticize the regulatory agency, experts agree it's an unwise choice, both in terms of his relationship with the agency and his ability to attract board members to his companies.[147]

WHAT'S NEXT FOR ELON MUSK?

Musk's quirkiness, overconfidence, and volatility resemble the attributes and behaviors of other famous entrepreneurs—most notably, Steve Jobs.[148] As consumers we allow for and even expect a certain amount of idiosyncrasy in our leaders. Yale School of Management's Dr. Jeffrey Sonnenfeld argues that some measure of hubris is necessary for entrepreneurs to succeed, saying, "The odds are against them succeeding rationally, so they have to have an unrealistic sense of their own efficacy to beat the odds." But Sonnenfeld also notes that Musk is likely to "take himself and the company off a cliff" if he doesn't dial things back.[149]

Tesla recently unveiled its new electric vehicle—the Model Y crossover—to lukewarm reception. Pre-orders started immediately and required a $2,500 initial payment—$1,000 more than the company had charged customers to reserve the Model 3. Market analysts see this increase as cause for concern about the company's cash position and predict that initial orders for the Model Y will be much lower than they were for the Model 3.[150]

As for that tweet that cost him $40 million in SEC fines and his position as chairman of Tesla's board, Musk says it was "worth it."[151]

APPLY THE 3-STEP PROBLEM-SOLVING APPROACH TO OB

STEP 1: Define the problem.

A. Look first at the Outcomes box of the Organizing Framework in Figure 13.6 to help identify the important problem(s) in this case. Remember that a problem is a gap between a desired and a current state. State your problem as a gap, and be sure to consider problems at all three levels. If more than one desired outcome is not being accomplished, decide which one is most important and focus on it for steps 2 and 3.

B. Cases have protagonists (key players), and problems are generally viewed from a particular protagonist's perspective. Identify the perspective from which you're defining the problem.

STEP 2: Identify causes of the problem by using material from this chapter, summarized in the Organizing Framework shown in Figure 13.6. Causes will appear in either the Inputs box or the Processes box.

A. Start by looking at Figure 13.6 to identify which person factors, if any, are most likely causes to the defined problem. For each cause, ask yourself, *Why is this a cause of the problem?* Asking why multiple times is more likely to lead you to root causes of the problem.

B. Follow the same process for the situation factors.

C. Now consider the Processes box shown in Figure 13.6. Consider concepts listed at all three levels. For any concept that might be a cause, ask yourself, *Why is this a cause?* Again, do this for several iterations to arrive at root causes.

D. To check the accuracy or appropriateness of the causes, map them onto the defined problem.

STEP 3: Make your recommendations for solving the problem. Consider whether you want to resolve it, solve it, or dissolve it (see Section 1.5). Which recommendation is desirable and feasible?

A. Given the causes identified in Step 2, what are your best recommendations? Use the content in Chapter 13 or one of the earlier chapters to propose a solution.

B. You may find potential solutions in the OB in Action boxes and Applying OB boxes within this chapter. These features provide insights into what other individuals or companies are doing in relationship to the topic at hand.

C. Create an action plan for implementing your recommendations.

Should Store Managers Force Employees to Pierce Kids' Ears Against Their Wishes?

A former Claire's employee in Edmonton, Canada, is calling out the accessories chain for its piercing policies.

Raylene Marks believes store employees should respect children's boundaries with regard to their bodies. She described a recent distressing situation in which a 7-year-old child's mother continually pressured her to allow Marks to pierce her ears.

"The girl pleaded and sobbed for 30 minutes not to be pierced" . . . "Despite mom saying, 'Honey, we can go home whenever you want,' she was not letting her daughter go home. She was putting a great deal of pressure on her daughter to go through with the piercing," said Marks. She added that the child was "articulate, smart and well aware of herself and her body" and "expressed that she didn't want us touching her, that we were standing too close, that she was feeling uncomfortable." Marks says the child "made it clear she no longer wanted to get her ears pierced."

The mother eventually left the store without forcing her child to have her ears pierced. Marks later informed her manager that she would not have consented to do the piercing without the child's express consent to and comfort with the procedure. Marks says her manager told her the job required her to pierce children's ears even if they were being physically restrained by guardians and in clear distress.

Policy 509 in the company's manual states that "We reserve the right to refuse an ear piercing if a successful one cannot be done," but Marks says the policy makes no mention of physical restraint or employees' rights to refuse to pierce due to child welfare concerns.

Marks quit her job at Claire's after the conversation with her manager. She says any subsequent refusals of this sort would have resulted in her being disciplined and potentially fired. Marks has written an open letter to the company asking them to "Please do better" and update their policy to address children's domain over their bodies. She says corporate has since informed her that they are reviewing and revising their policy and investigating how Marks' store manager handled the incident.[152]

What Would You Recommend to Claire's Regarding Their Store Policies on Piercing?

1. Claire's policy doesn't specifically address child consent, but it is ambiguous enough to allow for employees to use discretion in such cases without fear of termination. Marks' manager simply interpreted the policy incorrectly. Claire's should do a better job training their managers in the application of company policies.

2. Stores should be allowed to come up with their own policies and parents should be left to parent as they see fit. The manager wasn't breaking any laws or violating company policy, therefore she was correct in telling Marks that her job would have required her to pierce without the child's consent. Claire's should not have to revise its policy.

3. Claire's should revise its policy to clearly address child safety concerns. No child should be forced to be pierced against their will, and employees should have the discretion to refuse to pierce children's ears for these reasons.

4. Invent other options.

PART THREE

Organizational Processes

Organizational Culture, Socialization, and Mentoring

After reading this chapter, you should be able to:

LO 14-1   Describe the three levels and four functions of organizational culture.

LO 14-2   Explain how to characterize an organization's culture.

LO 14-3   Describe the process of culture change in an organization.

LO 14-4   Explain the three-phase model of organizational socialization.

LO 14-5   Describe how mentoring can foster personal and professional success.

LO 14-6   Describe the implications of organizational culture, socialization, and mentoring for you and managers.

The Organizing Framework in Figure 14.1 summarizes what you will learn in this chapter. Two person factors—human and social capital—and four situation factors—culture types, leader behavior, organizational climate, and human resource practices and policies—influence key processes at the individual, group, and organizational levels. In turn, these key processes support positive outcomes at all three levels. Concepts we discuss in this chapter have greater impact on individual and organizational outcomes than on group ones.

FIGURE 14.1   Organizing Framework for Understanding and Applying OB

INPUTS	PROCESSES	OUTCOMES
Person Factors • Human capital • Social capital **Situation Factors** • Culture types • Leader behavior • Organizational climate • Human resource practices and policies	**Individual Level** • P-O fit • Socialization • Mentoring **Group/Team Level** • Group dynamics • Department/unit culture **Organizational Level** • Culture • Socialization • Mentoring	**Individual Level** • Work attitudes • Employee behaviors • Career outcomes • Task performance • Turnover **Group/Team Level** • Group/team performance • Group cohesion and conflict **Organizational Level** • Accounting/financial performance • Customer service/satisfaction • Innovation • Product/service quality • Operational efficiency

The Walt Disney Company was founded in 1923 by brothers Walt and Roy Disney. The company is much more than its theme parks. Today Disney is a diversified multinational mass media and entertainment company headquartered in Burbank, California. The company has a long reputation of having a strong culture aimed at being innovative and a fun place to work. In recognition of this theme, the Walt Disney Company was ranked as the 4th Most Admired Company in 2019 by *Fortune*. Here we see a manifestation of the company's culture in front of Cinderella's Castle at Walt Disney World, Orlando, Florida. Thousands of families visit their theme parks to have fun and enjoy the outstanding service provided by employees. The strong customer-driven culture established by the Disney brothers is alive and well. This chapter will help you understand how companies like Disney create such cultures.

Ilene MacDonald/Alamy Stock Photo

Winning at Work

How Would I Assess Person–Organization Fit (P–O) When Applying for Jobs?

Fitting in is important to everyone. When I was 7, my father put me on a baseball team composed of 8- and 9-year-old boys. He thought it would be good for my development, but I was smaller and less skilled than the other boys, and they treated me like an outsider who didn't fit in. It did not help that I was the coach's son. I hated the experience.

I also experienced a lack of fit at some of my early job positions. I valued things others did not and believed people were engaging in counterproductive actions. Some of my peers loved the job, the boss, and the work environment. They could not understand why I wasn't happy, but I felt disengaged and started looking for a new job. That experience opened my eyes to the importance of "fitting in" at work.

What Does It Mean to Fit?

***Person–environment fit (P–E)* is "the compatibility between an individual and a work environment that occurs when their characteristics are well matched."[1]** Although there are many types of fit, we are interested in ***person–organization fit (P–O),* which reflects the extent to which your personality and values match the climate and culture in an organization.** P–O fit matters because good fit is associated with more positive work attitudes and task performance, lower intentions to quit, and less stress.[2] The process of assessing fit begins during the recruiting phase. Your goal should be to discover whether you and the job or the organization are a good fit for each other.[3]

Fitting in at work is like doing a puzzle. When the pieces fit in the right pattern, all is well.
Lawrence Manning/Corbis/Punchstock

How Can I Assess P–O Fit?

Assessing P–O fit will take some effort on your part. First, evaluate your strengths, weaknesses, and values. Next, do the same for the company or department at hand by researching it online or talking with current employees. Now prepare a set of diagnostic questions to ask during the interview.[4]

Julian Pscheid, COO of Emerge Interactive, says, "The best candidates will go as far as reflecting on our core values—which are posted on our website. This is also an early way to screen for a values match."[5]

How Can I Improve My Level of Fit?

- Find ways to build your strengths into your work role. Talk to your boss about how to redesign or modify your job to incorporate your strengths.

- Decide whether weaknesses are affecting your performance. If they are, seek developmental opportunities, coaching, or mentoring. If that does not work, find another role.

- Assess any misalignment between your values and those endorsed by the company. You can do this by writing down your five most important values and comparing them to your employer's stated values. If they don't overlap and you can't accept the discrepancy, it's time to move on.

- If you don't fit at one job or location, consider a lateral move to another department. You may just need a different role or boss.[6]

> ### What's Ahead in This Chapter
>
> This chapter begins your study of macro-level organizational behavior from the perspective of the organization as a whole. We start by exploring the foundation of organizational culture so you can understand its drivers and functions. Next, we review the four key types of organizational culture and consider their relationships with various outcomes. This is followed by a discussion of ways managers can change organizational culture. Finally, we discuss how socialization and mentoring serve to embed organizational culture, and we focus on how you can use knowledge of these processes to enhance your career success and happiness.

14.1 THE FOUNDATION OF ORGANIZATIONAL CULTURE: UNDERSTANDING ITS DRIVERS AND FUNCTIONS

THE BIGGER PICTURE

Although you may have a small impact on your employer's organizational culture, you undoubtedly are affected by it. Culture affects outcomes at the individual, group, and organizational level. You are about to learn what creates organizational culture and how culture affects other organizational processes. You also will identify the three levels that constitute culture and the functions it serves for organizations.

The saying "Culture eats strategy for breakfast" was attributed to management expert Peter Drucker. But no one takes that quote more seriously than T-Mobile CEO John Legere. Holding the top spot at the wireless carrier for the past seven years, Legere has turned the company's culture upside down, starting with his signature magenta-colored T-Mobile wardrobe. Legere has transformed himself from a "suit" in the corner office to a charismatic leader who spends time with his 50,000 employees at offices around the country and connects with customers via social media every day.[7] Others agree with Legere's emphasis on organizational culture.

LO 14-1

Describe the three levels and four functions of organizational culture.

Alan Murray, *Fortune* editor, studied the annual Best Companies to Work For lists and concluded that great companies don't just provide "free food, generous benefits, and nap pods (although those clearly don't hurt)." He believes that culture is the essence of what makes great companies. "Today's workers are looking for a corporate culture that values them and their contributions," he said.[8]

Richard Branson—entrepreneur, philanthropist, and founder of the Virgin Group—also believes in the power of corporate culture. According to Branson, "there is no magic formula for great company culture. The key is just to treat your staff how you would like to be treated."[9]

One of our primary goals in this chapter is to help you understand how managers can use organizational culture as a competitive advantage. We start by considering the foundation of organizational culture.

Defining Culture and Exploring Its Impact

Organizational culture is defined as "the set of shared, taken-for-granted implicit assumptions that a group holds and that determines how it perceives, thinks about, and reacts to its various environments."[10] This definition highlights four important characteristics of organizational culture:

- **Shared concept.** Organizational culture consists of beliefs and values shared among a group of people.

- **Learned over time.** Culture is passed to new employees through the processes of socialization and mentoring, discussed later in this chapter.

FIGURE 14.2   Drivers and Flow of Organizational Culture

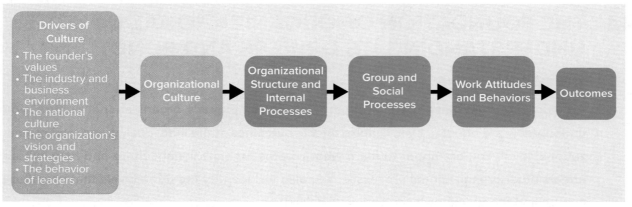

SOURCE: Ostroff, Cheri, Angelo J. Kinicki, and Rabiah S. Muhammad. "Organizational Culture and Climate." In *Handbook of Psychology,* edited by Irving B. Weiner, 619–76. Hoboken, NJ: John Wiley & Sons, Inc., 2013.

- **Influences behavior at work.** Its influence on behavior is the reason "culture eats strategy for breakfast."
- **Affects outcomes at multiple levels.** Culture affects outcomes at the individual, group/team, and organizational levels.

Figure 14.2 provides a conceptual framework for understanding the drivers and effects of organizational culture. Five elements drive organizational culture:

- The founder's values.
- The industry and business environment.
- The national culture.
- The organization's vision and strategies.
- The behavior of leaders.

In turn, organizational culture influences the type of organizational structure a company adopts and a host of internal processes (including human resource practices) it implements in pursuit of its goals. These organizational characteristics then affect a variety of group and social processes.[11] This sequence ultimately affects employees' work attitudes and behaviors and a variety of organizational outcomes. All told, Figure 14.2 tells us that organizational culture has a wide span of influence, ultimately influencing many individual, group, and organizational outcomes.[12] Once again, this is the reason culture eats strategy for breakfast.

The Three Levels of Organizational Culture

Organizational culture operates on three levels:

1. Observable artifacts.
2. Espoused values.
3. Basic underlying assumptions.

These levels differ in their visibility and resistance to change, and each one influences another. Let's look at them one by one.

Level 1: Observable Artifacts   At the most visible level, culture consists of observable artifacts. *Artifacts* **are the physical manifestation of an organization's culture.** They include:

- Acronyms.
- Manner of dress.
- Awards.

- Myths and stories told about the organization.
- Published lists of values.
- Observable rituals and ceremonies.
- Special parking spaces.
- Pictures and images handing on walls.

Zappos and its parent company Amazon put a different spin on organizational artifacts: the companies offer a "quit" bonus to employees who no longer want to work for them.
Helen H. Richardson/Getty Images

At Facebook, for example, the word *hack* is pasted all around offices. It symbolizes "the hacker way" of pursuing continuous improvement and challenging the status quo.[13] Zappos and its parent company Amazon have a different take on artifacts: offering a "quit bonus" to employees who no longer want to work for the online giant. Started by Zappos more than a decade ago and continued after Amazon bought the company, the quit bonus pays employees up to $5,000 to leave the company. According to an Amazon spokesperson, "In the long-term, staying somewhere you don't want to be isn't healthy for our employees or our company." The catch? Once an employee accepts the offer to quit, they can never work at Amazon again.[14] Artifacts are easier to change than the less visible aspects of organizational culture.

Level 2: Espoused Values

Values were defined in Chapter 2 as abstract ideals that guide our thinking and behavior across all situations. In the context of organizational culture, we distinguish between values that are espoused and values that are enacted.

- ***Espoused values* are the explicitly stated qualities and norms preferred by an organization.** They are generally established by the founder of a new or small company and by the top management team in a larger organization. Most companies have a short list. For example, eyewear company Warby Parker has four espoused values: (1) treat customers the way you would like to be treated; (2) create an environment where employees can think big, have fun, and do good; (3) serve the community; and (4) going green is good.[15]

Because espoused values are explicitly communicated to employees, managers hope they will directly influence employee behavior. But people do not always automatically "walk the talk." Leadership at Patagonia recognized this gap and made a key strategic change to align its stated values with its actions.

> **EXAMPLE** Patagonia, one of the world's most environmentally conscious companies, recently stopped selling its popular fleece vests to financial firms on Wall Street that invested in companies and other financial ventures that did not engage in sustainable business practices. The company said it shifted the focus of its corporate sales program to "mission-driven companies that prioritize the planet."[16]

- ***Enacted values* are the qualities and norms that are exhibited or converted into employee behavior.** These are values employees ascribe to an organization based on their observations of what occurs on a daily basis. As at Patagonia, managers should reduce gaps between espoused and enacted values because they can significantly influence employee attitudes and organizational performance.

A survey from the Ethics Resource Center showed that employees were more likely to behave ethically when management set a good behavioral example and kept its promises and commitments.[17] This finding was underscored by another study of

129 mergers. Employees were more productive and post-merger performance was higher when employees believed that behavior was consistent with the newly formed firm's espoused values.[18]

Level 3: Basic Underlying Assumptions

Basic underlying assumptions are **organizational values so taken for granted over time that they become assumptions guiding organizational behavior.** Underlying assumptions are employees' deep-seated beliefs about their company and are the core of organizational culture. As you might expect, they are highly resistant to change. Consider the way some companies reinforce a core belief in sustainability (see the OB in Action box).

Sustainability is "a company's ability to make a profit without sacrificing the resources of its people, the community, and the planet."[19] Achieving sustainability is sometimes called "being green" and has become a priority for many companies in recent years. In addition to helping reduce a company's global footprint, sustainability can also provide organizations with a competitive advantage when it comes to overall business strategies and financial success.[20] For example, Kering SA, a French conglomerate that owns luxury goods companies such as Gucci, Saint Laurent, and Alexander McQueen, demonstrates its commitment to sustainability by sourcing more than 40 percent of its products from certifiable sources. In addition, Kering's sustainability commitment extends to more diversity among its top management and board of directors. More that 60 percent of the company's board of directors are women, far more than the gender makeup of most large corporations. Kering was recently named to the second spot on the 2019 Global 100—a list of large firms across the globe ranked on their performance in reducing waste, increasing gender diversity among leadership, realizing revenues from clean products, and forging overall sustainability practices.[21]

OB in Action

Being vs. Becoming Sustainable

Ceres, a sustainability nonprofit organization that seeks to "tackle the world's biggest sustainability challenges," recently published a web-based analysis of more than 600 large, publicly traded companies in the United States that examined their performance on 20 key areas of sustainability leadership. Ceres found some encouraging results in the group, which included Citi, Coca-Cola, CVS Health, Gap, Inc., General Mills, Intel, Kellogg, Nike, and PepsiCo:

- Nearly two-thirds of the companies plan to reduce their greenhouse gas emissions.
- More than half have adopted formal water-management policies.
- Almost half are committed to protecting their workers' rights.

While a great deal more remains to be done, "We have reached a turning point," said Amy Augustine, senior director of the Ceres Company

Goods by Natura Brasil are made from sustainable products.
Florian Kopp/Newscom

Network and co-author of the report. "It is no longer just about raising the ceiling. It is about lifting the floor. The time has come for bold and scalable solutions, not just from a few leading companies, but from companies in all sectors and of all sizes who need to transition from making commitments to taking concrete actions."[22]

What does sustainability look like in action?

- Started by college-student siblings in an entrepreneurship program and partially funded on Kickstarter, New York–based Fair Harbor Clothing makes affordable boardshorts and swimwear of polyester spun from recycled plastic bottles. "I started my company because I saw all of the issues with single use plastic waste and the effect that it has been having on our environment," said Jake Danehy, cofounder and CEO. "Our objective was to create an awesome product that people loved, and show the positive things we can create out of recycled materials."[23]

- NaturaBrasil, an award-winning global cosmetics company that recently expanded to the United States, was founded in Brazil in 1969 with a mission to "build a better world through our commitment to transparency, sustainability and well-being." A certified B corporation (meeting the highest standards of social and environmental performance), NaturaBrasil makes hair and skin care products, perfumes, soaps, and creams from natural Brazilian ingredients and works closely with more than 30 local communities in the Amazon region to "develop sustainable business models that benefit the forest."[24]

YOUR THOUGHTS?

1. What do you think was the driving force behind Fair Harbor's and NaturaBrasil's efforts to found sustainable, profitable businesses?

2. What might differentiate the cultures of firms like these from the ones in Ceres' study?

3. What challenges face a company trying to become a sustainable business, as opposed to being founded as a sustainable business?

The Four Functions of Organizational Culture

An organization's culture fulfills four important functions (see Figure 14.3):

1. Establish organizational identity.
2. Encourage collective commitment.
3. Ensure social system stability.
4. Act as sense-making device.

To help bring these four functions to life, let's consider how each has taken shape at Southwest Airlines. Southwest has grown to serve more customers domestically than any other airline and has achieved 46 consecutive years of profitability. The company has been on *Fortune*'s list of Most Admired Companies in the World for 25 consecutive years, and it was named to Glassdoor's Best Places to Work list for a 10th consecutive time.[25]

Function 1: Culture Provides Employees with an Organizational Identity
The identity of Southwest Airlines employees is focused on the belief that employee satisfaction and customer loyalty are more important than corporate profits. Gary Kelly, Southwest's CEO, highlighted this theme by noting, "Our people are our greatest asset and they deserve all the credit for our continued success."[26]

Southwest reinforces this identity by demonstrating in a variety of ways that it truly cares about its employees. The company's catastrophe fund, for instance, is based on voluntary contributions for distribution to employees experiencing serious personal difficulties. Its profit-sharing program paid out $544 million in 2018, adding

FIGURE 14.3   Four Functions of Organizational Culture

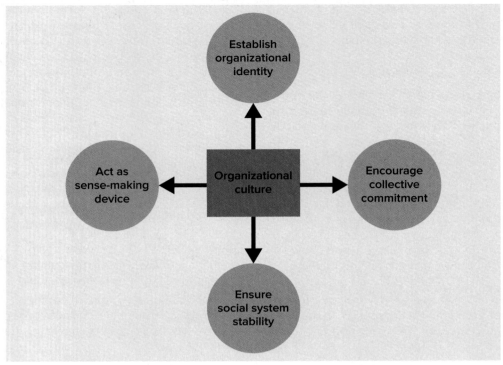

SOURCE: Smircich, Linda. "Concepts of Culture and Organizational Analysis." *Administrative Science Quarterly 28*, no. 3 (1983): 339–58. https://DOI: 10.2307/2392246.

about 10.8 percent to each employee's compensation.[27] Southwest's people-focused identity also is reinforced by the fact that it is an employer of choice. The company received 342,664 resumes for 7,207 job openings in 2016. It also was rated as providing outstanding opportunities for women, Hispanics, and members of the LGBTQ community.[28]

Function 2: Culture Facilitates Collective Commitment   The mission of Southwest Airlines is "dedication to the highest quality of customer service delivered with a sense of warmth, friendliness, individual pride, and company spirit."[29] This commitment to serving others is endorsed by the company's more than 58,000 employees. Southwest consistently lands at the top of the list for best customer service among domestic airlines and has received the lowest ratio of complaints by passengers based on statistics maintained by the U.S. Department of Transportation over the last 30 years. Commitment to service doesn't just apply to customers at Southwest. Employees volunteered more than 190,000 hours to local and national nonprofit organizations in 2018.[30]

Function 3: Culture Promotes Social System Stability   Social system stability is the extent to which the work environment is perceived as positive and reinforcing, and the extent to which conflict and change are effectively managed. Southwest is noted for its philosophy of having fun, holding parties, and celebrating. For example, staff in each city

This photo demonstrates Southwest's culture. Employees are having fun in an airport terminal to lighten what can be a frustrating experience for passengers. Do you think these employees can lift the spirits of the travelers in the background?

Glenn Asakawa/Denver Post/Getty Images

in which the firm operates are given a budget for parties. The company also uses a variety of performance-based awards and service awards to reinforce employees' efforts. Its positive and enriching environment is supported by the lowest turnover rates in the airline industry.[31]

Function 4: Culture Shapes Behaviors by Helping Members Make Sense of Their Surroundings   Making sense of the surroundings is what helps employees understand why the organization does what it does and how it intends to accomplish its long-term goals. Keeping in mind that Southwest's leadership originally viewed ground transportation as its main competitor in 1971, employees understand why the airline's primary vision is to be the best short-haul, low-fare, high-frequency, point-to-point carrier in the United States. Employees know they must achieve exceptional performance, such as turning a plane around in 20 minutes, because they must keep costs down to compete against Greyhound and automobiles. In turn, the company reinforces the value it places on outstanding customer service and high performance by using performance-based awards and profit sharing. Employees own about 10 percent of the company stock.[32]

14.2 THE IMPACT OF ORGANIZATIONAL CULTURE TYPES ON OUTCOMES

THE BIGGER PICTURE

Do you think companies rated on *Fortune*'s List of 100 Best Places to Work might have unique cultures? How do we know what type of culture exists at these companies or your current employer? In this section you will learn about the four types of culture defined by the competing values framework. You will also discover the extent to which these four culture types are related to important outcomes.

LO 14-2

Explain how to characterize an organization's culture.

To learn how different types of culture relate to outcomes, we need a way to classify culture types. While the complexity of culture makes agreement on a set of types difficult to reach, academics have proposed and scientifically tested three different frameworks. The *competing values framework* we discuss here is the most widely used. It also was named one of the 40 most important frameworks in the study of organizations and has been shown to be a valid approach for classifying organizational culture.[33] We will also discuss relationships among culture types and outcomes.

Identifying Culture Types with the Competing Values Framework

The **competing values framework (CVF) provides a practical way for managers to understand, measure, and change organizational culture.** It identifies four fundamental types of organizational culture—clan, adhocracy, hierarchy, and market—all shown in Figure 14.4.[34]

The CVF was developed by a team of researchers trying to classify different ways to assess organizational effectiveness. Their research showed that measures of organizational effectiveness varied along two fundamental dimensions or axes. One axis described whether an organization focuses its attention and efforts on internal dynamics and employees, or outward to its external environment and its customers and shareholders. The second axis measured an organization's preference for flexibility and discretion over control and stability. Combining these two axes creates four types of organizational culture, each with different core values and different sets of criteria for assessing organizational effectiveness.

Figure 14.4 shows the strategic direction associated with each cultural type (collaborate, create, and so on), along with the means and goals it pursues. Each type has different characteristics, and while one type tends to dominate in any given organization, it is the mix of types that creates competitive advantage. We begin our discussion of culture types in the upper-left-hand quadrant of the CVF.

FIGURE 14.4 The Competing Values Framework

Culture varies along two axes of competing values: flexibility and discretion vs. stability and control, and internal focus and integration vs. external focus and differentiation. This leads to four categories of organizations, each with its own unique character.

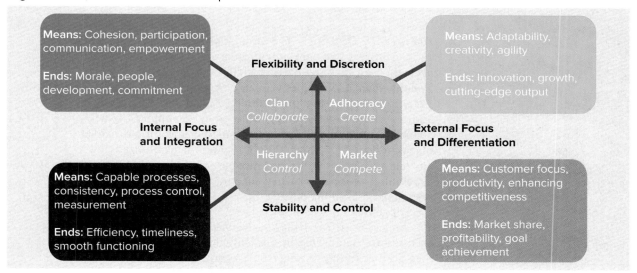

SOURCE: Cameron, Kim S., Robert E. Quinn, Jeff Degraff, and Anjan V. Thakor. *Competing Values Leadership: Creating Value in Organizations.* Northampton, MA: Edward Elgar Publishing, 2007.

Clan Culture   A company with a **clan culture** has an internal focus and values flexibility rather than stability and control. It resembles a family-type organization that achieves effectiveness by encouraging collaboration, trust, and support among employees. This type of culture is very employee-focused and strives to instill cohesion through consensus and job satisfaction, and commitment through employee involvement and development.[35] Clan organizations devote considerable resources to hiring and developing their employees, and they view customers as partners. Collaborating is this culture's strategy.

EXAMPLE Blake Mycoskie, founder of Toms Shoes, the company famous for its "buy-one-give one" model, came back from a year sabbatical with a deep resolve to take care of his own employees in addition to giving shoes and backpacks to others in need. Mycoskie and his managers have made a concerted effort to implement practices to make their employees' lives more fulfilling and balanced. Employee-friendly practices include flexible work schedules, generous paid paternity leave, and no-meeting Mondays. In addition, Toms is committed to better aligning its organizational culture with the company's overall mission by getting employees involved in charitable activities. For example, as part of a "Happy Helping Hour" each month, employees work with a charitable organization in a philanthropic activity, such as preparing care packages for women in domestic abuse shelters.[36]

EXAMPLE Property and casualty insurance company Acuity has been consistently ranked as a top employer by *Forbes, Fortune,* and the American Business Awards and strongly endorses a clan culture. On the occasion of his 20th year as president and CEO of the company, Ben Salzmann remarked, "We have a tremendous team of staff and agents who are committed to doing what is right for our customers and

Clan culture is on full display at Toms Shoes with management making a concerted effort to implement practices to make employees' lives more fulfilling and balanced.

Yonhap News/YNA/Newscom

working toward our mutual success. I simply could not ask to work with better people." Employees have generous perks and are empowered to participate in the way the company is run. The end result is profitability and an enviably low 2 percent turnover rate.[37]

Adhocracy Culture The term *adhocracy* reflects an organization with less structure and bureaucracy. It also reflects a management team focused on responding to problems rather than avoiding them. Companies with an **adhocracy culture have an external focus and value flexibility.** Creation of new products and services is their strategy, which they accomplish by being adaptable, creative, and fast to respond to changes in the marketplace. Adhocracy cultures do not rely on the centralized power and authority relationships that are part of market and hierarchical cultures (see below). They encourage and empower employees to take risks, think outside the box, and experiment with new ways of getting things done.

An article in *The Wall Street Journal* noted that adhocracy cultures are decreasing in the United States as many companies are becoming risk-averse. The downside of this trend is that a certain amount of reasonable risk taking is necessary to create new businesses, products, and ultimately jobs. On the positive side, however, risk taking is still occurring in industries such as technology and energy, and in coastal cities such as San Francisco and Boston and college towns like Boulder, Colorado, and Austin, Texas.[38]

EXAMPLE As part of its mission, Menlo Innovations, a software development company, is strongly committed to "restoring joy to technology," by offering employees an open, active office environment conducive to being collaborative and taking risks (and encouraging babies and dogs to be part of the office); by partnering with clients to provide effective business solutions; and by maintaining a strict 40-hour workweek for all.[39]

Market Culture Companies with a **market culture have a strong external focus and value stability and control.** Competition is their strategic thrust. They have a strong desire to deliver results and accomplish goals, and because they are focused on the external environment, customers and profits take precedence over employee development and satisfaction. Managers' major goal is to improve productivity, profits, and customer satisfaction.

EXAMPLE Grupo Bimbo is the world's largest bakery company. Bimbo managers operate in a low-margin business and thus focus heavily on execution. "Profits depend heavily on getting the right amount of highly perishable products to stores at the right moment and at a reasonable cost. . . . For instance, [the company] uses tricycle delivery bikes in urban areas of China where streets are too narrow for trucks, a practice it first implemented in Latin America," according to a *Harvard Business Review* author.[40] Grupo Bimbo operates 171 plants and delivers more than 10,000 products to 22 countries.

Imagine having to deliver over 10,000 products to 22 countries. Do you think this takes a lot of planning and detailed execution? Bimbo's market-based culture contributes to this effort.

Scott Olson/Getty Images

EXAMPLE Publix Super Markets, the largest employee-owned supermarket chain in the United States, was ranked *Fortune's* 12th of 100 best places to work in 2019. The company is highly customer-focused and trains and rewards employees to provide friendly and helpful service.[41] According to a recent American Customer Satisfaction Index, Publix had the highest customer satisfaction score of any company in the retail sector.[42]

Hierarchy Culture   Control is the strategy within a hierarchy culture. The **hierarchy culture has an internal focus, which produces a more formalized and structured work environment, and values stability and control over flexibility.** This orientation leads to the development of reliable internal processes, the extensive use of measurement, and the implementation of a variety of control mechanisms. Effectiveness is likely to be measured in terms of efficiency, timeliness, quality, safety, and reliability in producing and delivering products and services.[43]

EXAMPLE McDonald's relies on the benefits of a hierarchical structure to effectively manage its vast business operations throughout the world. However, that doesn't mean that top management is content with the status quo. The company has made several key changes to the company's organization and culture in an effort to shake things up, including moving the corporate offices from suburban Chicago to the city in an effort to attract younger employees; implementing self-ordering kiosks at many stores; and reshaping the company's structure to create a sense of urgency and agility across various departments.[44]

Cultural Types Represent Competing Values The four cultural types include some opposing core values. The internal values associated with clan and hierarchy can conflict with the external ones associated with adhocracy and market cultures. Similarly, the flexibility and discretion associated with clan and adhocracy cultures are at odds with the stability and control values endorsed by companies with hierarchy and market cultures.

These conflicts matter because an organization's success may depend on its ability to act on core values associated with competing cultural types. While this is difficult to pull off, it can be done. Video game developer Activision Blizzard is a good example.

OB in Action

Activision Blizzard Integrates Clan and Adhocracy Cultures

If you like video games, you've probably played one from Activision Blizzard, a leading developer of blockbusters like Call of Duty, World of Warcraft, and Guitar Hero. Despite some recent weakening in its player base and competition from new entries like Fortnite, Activision remains a strong performer, with hundreds of millions of monthly active users and record sales and earnings in 2018. It ranks 96th on *Forbes'* list of 100 best places to work for 2019, with more than 5,000 employees worldwide.[45]

Activision's culture appears to be a combination of all four culture types, but with an emphasis on clan and adhocracy (see Figure 14.5). One employee described it this way: "We are lucky to work in a business where imagination, creativity, and play aren't only encouraged, they're required."[46] Bobby Kotick, Activision Blizzard CEO, reinforced this belief by saying, "Everything we do starts with our employees' talent, inspired creativity, and commitment to excellence." The culture is noted for being inspirational, creative, and fun.[47]

FIGURE 14.5   Graph of Activision's Culture

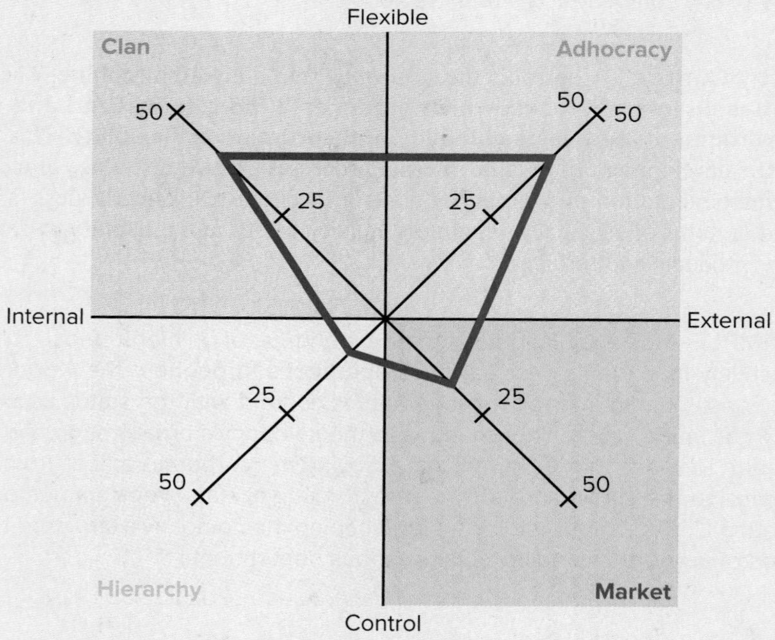

Based on multiple articles describing the work environment at Activision Blizzard.
McGraw-Hill Global Education Holdings, LLC.

Clan Dominates One of the company's mantras is "Gamers + gaming = fun." "Activision Blizzard is a community of people who love to have fun together, and our employee camaraderie is fueled by our passion for gameplay," according to the company's website."[48] This cultural characteristic is reinforced via the Gaming Zone. *Great Place to Work* described the Gaming Zone as "the heart of Activision Blizzard's headquarters. Employees are encouraged to play games during their breaks, and the company regularly hosts tournaments and biweekly get-togethers like Gaming Zone Game Night, where employees play video games together."[49]

Personal development is encouraged. For example, Activision Blizzard Studio Summit is an annual event at which game development teams meet to discuss experiences and learn from each other. *Great Place to Work* noted that "development teams share their combined knowledge and annual findings across a variety of disciplines, including audio and talent, art, design, animation, programming, and production."[50] Other developmental activities include a Master's in the Business of Activision (the company's self-made MBA program) and Blizzard Academy, where experts teach specialized classes.[51]

Other clan-related characteristics include a host of positive employee perks such as company-paid health benefits, a wellness program, free food and beverages, massage therapy, and work–life balance programs.[52]

Adhocracy Dominates Creativity is at the core of Activision's success. "Bringing Activision Blizzard's franchises to our audiences is a massive, complex, and very creative process," says CEO Kotick. "I think of our teams as symphony orchestras, because they work hard to bring so many details together in perfect harmony."[53]

The company uses its Cultural Enrichment Series to foster innovation and creativity. Part of the series consists of TED-type talks called Activisionaries. "This speaker and concert series features inspirational leaders, entrepreneurs, world-class athletes, military leaders, best-selling authors, musicians, and others. The events not only provide intellectual stimulation and consistent opportunities for community-gathering, but also instill a sense of creativity that inspires and guides our culture."[54]

YOUR THOUGHTS?

1. What is the cultural thread that enables Activision to have a culture dominated by clan and adhocracy?

2. Do you think Activision's cultural profile is the best one for a company whose strategic goal is to grow its business? Explain.

3. Would you like to work at Activision? Why or why not?

Are you curious about the type of culture that exists in a current or past employer? Do you wonder whether you possess person–organization fit? Self-Assessment 14.1 allows you to consider these questions.

SELF-ASSESSMENT 14.1

What Is the Organizational Culture at My Current Employer?

Please be prepared to answer these questions if your instructor has assigned Self-Assessment 14.1 in Connect.

1. How would you describe the organizational culture?

2. Do you think this type of culture is best suited to help the company achieve its strategic goals? Explain.

Outcomes Associated with Organizational Culture

Both managers and academic researchers believe organizational culture can influence outcomes at the individual, group, and organizational levels of the OB Organizing Framework. A team of researchers tested this hypothesis by conducting a meta-analysis of more than 38,000 organizational units and 616,000 individuals: An organizational unit is either an organization as a whole or departments in different organizations. Figure 14.6 summarizes the findings.[55]

Figure 14.6 illustrates the strength of relationships among nine organizational outcomes and the four culture types. As you probably expected, culture is positively associated with a variety of outcomes. Most relationships were of moderate strength, meaning they are important to today's managers. Closer examination of Figure 14.6 leads to the following six conclusions:

1. **Organizational culture is related to organizational effectiveness.** This means an organization's culture can be a source of competitive advantage.

2. **Employees have more positive work attitudes when working in organizations with clan cultures.** Employees clearly prefer to work in organizations that value flexibility over stability and control, and those that are more concerned with satisfying employees' needs than with customer or shareholder desires.

FIGURE 14.6 Correlates of Clan, Adhocracy, Market, and Hierarchy Organizational Cultures

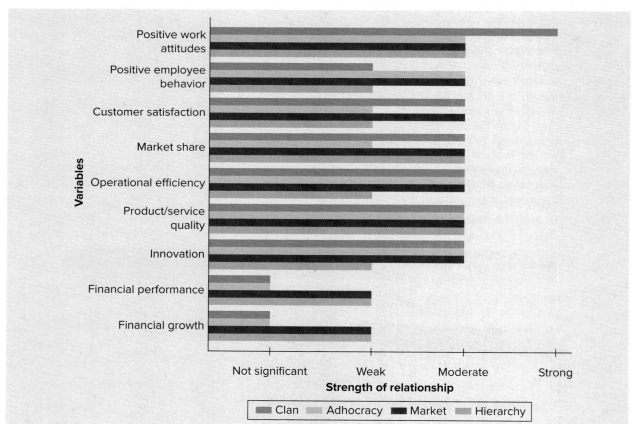

SOURCE: Results were based on A. Ou, C. Hartnell, A. Kinicki, E. Karam, & D. Choi, "Culture in Context: A Meta-Analysis of the Nomological Network of Organizational Culture." Presentation as part of a symposium, titled "Connecting Culture and Context: Insights from Organizational Culture Theory and Research," at the 2016 National Academy of Management Meeting in Anaheim.

3. **Clan and market cultures are more likely to deliver higher customer satisfaction and market share.** We suspect this result holds because the positive employee attitudes associated with clan cultures motivate employees to provide better customer service.

4. **Operational outcomes, quality, and innovation are more strongly related to clan, adhocracy, and market cultures than to hierarchical ones.** Managers should avoid the use of too many rules and procedures—hierarchical characteristics—when trying to improve these outcomes.

5. **An organization's financial performance (profit and revenue growth) is not strongly related to organizational culture.** Only market and hierarchy cultures were associated with financial outcomes. Managers should not expect to immediately increase financial performance when they try to change their organization's culture. This underscores the conclusion that culture change needs time to take hold.

6. **Companies with market cultures tend to have more positive organizational outcomes.** Managers should make their cultures more market oriented.

Subcultures Matter

Thus far we have discussed organizational culture as if a company possessed a single homogeneous culture. Most don't. Rather, organizations develop subcultures.[56]

Two OB scholars describe organizational subcultures as consisting of "distinctive clusters of ideologies, cultural forms [clan, adhocracy, market, hierarchy], and other practices that identifiable groups of people in an organization exhibit." They tend to vary from a company's overall culture, "either intensifying its understandings and practices or diverging from them."[57] Subcultures tend to form along the following lines, often leading to noticeably different cultures:

- Functional/occupational groups
- Geographical areas
- Products, markets, or technology
- Divisions or departments
- Levels of management—senior management versus supervisors
- Work role—firefighter versus salesperson[58]

While subcultures develop naturally, senior leaders should link them with "common goals, common language, and common procedures for solving problems," according to OB expert Edgar Schein.[59] You don't want *highly* different subcultures to develop, because they can lead groups to focus on different goals, customers, or values, which lowers unit and organizational performance.[60] Such culture clashes frequently happen when subcultures within an organization interpret rules differently based on their levels within the organization. Research shows that failure to integrate subcultures within high-risk industries such as oil and gas may lead to a gap in their ability to interpret and enact safety rules, leading to different levels of rule compliance.[61]

14.3 MECHANISMS OR LEVERS FOR CULTURE CHANGE

THE BIGGER PICTURE

Some people suggest that culture change takes years, whereas others believe leadership actions can change culture more quickly. Yet others contend that culture evolves and managers should not attempt to manage it. Where do you stand? We believe culture can and should be nurtured and developed so it aligns with a company's vision and strategic plan. You will learn about 12 mechanisms or levers you can use to implement culture change. We discuss them in the context of the managerial role, but knowing these techniques helps you at any level in the organization.

LO 14-3

Describe the process of culture change in an organization.

Edgar Schein, who has written a great deal about organizational culture, believes the creation and management of culture is a leader's most important role.[62] We agree, because culture can be a source of competitive advantage. You may not think organizational culture is important to you now while you're still in school. However, after graduation when you're out in the real world looking for a job and trying to decide which company to pursue in your job search, you will want to learn about the company's culture and why (or why not) it would be the ideal place to start or continue your professional career.

Consider companies like Apple, Google, and Facebook. As suggested by Figure 14.2, the cultures at these companies were first formed by their founders—Steve Jobs at Apple, Larry Page and Sergey Brin at Google, and Mark Zuckerberg at Facebook. Over time, the founders embedded or reinforced their desired cultures by adopting specific types of organizational structure and implementing a host of human resource practices, policies, and procedures. It is not an easy task to change an organization's culture, but let us look at how it can be done.

First let's review four truths about culture change.

Sergey Brin (left) and Larry Page met as Ph.D. students at Stanford. They created the first version of the algorithm underlying searches while students, and then incorporated Google after graduation. Today, Brin is president of Alphabet, Inc., Google's parent company, and Page is the CEO. Although Google is somewhat secretive about the number of searches it conducts, the best estimate is more than 5 billion a day.
Matthew Staver/Bloomberg/Getty Images

1. **Leaders are the architects and developers of organizational culture.** This suggests that culture is not determined by fate. It is formed and shaped by the ongoing behavior of everyone who works at a company. John Mackey, co-founder and CEO of Whole Foods Market, believes creating a healthy culture starts with strong leadership. According to Mackey, "If you are lucky enough to be someone's employer, then you have a moral obligation to make sure people do look forward to coming to work in the morning."[63]

2. **Changing culture starts with targeting one of the three levels of organizational culture—observable artifacts, espoused values, or basic underlying assumptions.** The fastest way to start a culture change project is through the use of observable artifacts. For example, if you wanted to foster a market culture, you could post graphs of performance metrics around the office to reinforce the value of high performance. That said, culture will not change in a significant way unless managers are able to change basic underlying assumptions.[64] It takes time to alter this deep-seated component of culture.

3. **The current culture probably closely aligns with the organization's vision and strategic plan.** Remember the quote "culture eats strategy for breakfast" whenever you pursue culture change. An organization's culture must be consistent with its vision and strategic goals. **A *vision* is a long-term goal that describes what an organization wants to become. A *strategic plan* outlines the organization's long-term goals and the actions necessary to achieve them.**

> **EXAMPLE** Although culture change is an organizationwide process, it must start at the top. At Novelis, an industrial aluminum company in Atlanta, Georgia, several culture initiatives failed because one leader in particular was reluctant to support the process, according to the company's HR director. The company began to see real results once leadership committed to the culture shift within the organization. It's important that every member of the executive team align around the same goals or the change won't take hold.[65]

4. **A structured approach works best when implementing culture change.** Our experience as consultants tells us that culture change frequently meets with resistance. People become accustomed to the culture they know and prefer to leave things as they are. Chapter 16 outlines several techniques you can use to overcome such resistance.

Let's now consider the specific methods or techniques managers can use to change an organization's culture.

12 Mechanisms or Levers for Creating Culture Change

OB experts have proposed 12 mechanisms or levers for changing organizational culture. These levers can be pushed to create a preferred type of culture or they can be pulled to reduce a particular culture type. Changing culture amounts to pushing and pulling these levers to create a culture profile that is best suited to help an organization achieve its goals. Any of these levers can be used to foster any of the culture types previously discussed. Table 14.1 shows the relationship between these levers and the three levels of organizational culture.[66] Let's consider how these levers can be used to create culture change.

1. Formal Statements Formal statements of organizational philosophy, mission, vision, values, and materials can embed culture when used for recruiting, selection, and socialization. They represent observable artifacts.

> **EXAMPLE** Equipment manufacturer Caterpillar has a vision of "a world in which all people's basic needs—such as shelter, clean water, sanitation, food and reliable power—are fulfilled in an environmentally sustainable way and a company that improves the quality of the environment and the communities where we live and work."

> **EXAMPLE** The vision of the Alzheimer's Association is quite simply "a world without Alzheimer's disease."[67]

2. Design of Physical Space, Work Environments, and Buildings Physical spacing among people and buildings and the location of office furniture are different ways to send messages about culture. For example, an open office environment is more appropriate for an organization that wants to foster collaboration and innovation.

TABLE 14.1   12 Mechanisms for Changing Organizational Culture

MECHANISM	LEVEL OF ORGANIZATIONAL CULTURE		
	Observable Artifact	Espoused Value	Basic Assumption
1. Formal statements	X	X	
2. Design of physical space, work environments, and buildings	X		X
3. Slogans, language, acronyms, and sayings	X	X	
4. Deliberate role modeling, training programs, teaching, and coaching by others	X	X	X
5. Explicit rewards, status symbols, and promotion criteria	X	X	X
6. Stories, legends, or myths about key people and events	X	X	X
7. Organizational activities, processes, or outcomes		X	X
8. Leader reactions to critical incidents and organizational crises			X
9. Rites and rituals	X	X	X
10. Work flow and organizational structure	X		X
11. Organizational systems and procedures	X	X	X
12. Organizational goals and criteria throughout employee cycle (hire to retire)	X	X	X

EXAMPLE Instagram's New York office is picture perfect to post on its own social media site. From the two-floor high living plant wall complete with modern, inviting chairs that add a pop of color to the giant mirror located at the top floor's stairwell and the most popular corner for selfies, the office is designed to be functional, flexible, and fun.[68]

3. Slogans, Language, Acronyms, and Sayings Corporate slogans, acronyms, and specialized language often have a profound effect on the organization over time because they are easy to remember and repeat.

EXAMPLE The New England Patriots have a tradition that started in 2003 when then-linebacker Tedy Bruschi uttered two words, "Awww yeah," at a pre-season practice. After a win over the Philadelphia Eagles early that season, Bruschi asked his teammates a question in the locker room that has become a Patriots ritual after every victory: "How do we feel about a victory?" The team responded: "Awww yeah," and a tradition began that continues today. After Bruschi retired, several other Patriots stepped up to ask the question in the team's locker room after a win—with a resounding response from their teammates. The Patriots recently filed a request with the U.S. Patent and Trademark Office to trademark "Awww yeah" for use on sporting apparel and entertainment services.[69] What type of cultures are reinforced by these slogans and sayings?

4. Deliberate Role Modeling, Training Programs, Teaching, and Coaching by Others   Companies such as Experian, one of the largest crediting-reporting services in the world, use collaboration to model and empower organizational change through networking. Justin Hastings, Experian North America's chief human resource office, sees his role as "not only to supply, maintain and retain talent, but to make sure those people are motivated and see real meaning and value in their work."[70]

> **EXAMPLE** Hastings believes that organizational change doesn't happen top-down or bottom-up in an organization but rather it tends to move side-to-side, as a result of horizontal connections among colleagues throughout the company. According to Hastings, "You can't just build a culture from the top down. To be authentic, you have to build your culture organically, through informal networks." He cites employees who participate in the "Le Tour de Experian" bike rides to benefit charity. He explains employees ride in the event to do some good and to have fun, but he noticed they were also building strong bonds across company boundaries. These bonds with others in the organization result in collaborations that have created value for Experian, its customers, and its employees.[71]

5. Explicit Rewards, Status Symbols, and Promotion Criteria   Because they are meaningful and visible, reward systems have a strong impact on employees and are one of the strongest ways to embed organizational culture. For example, team-based rewards reinforce a clan culture, while individual rewards are better suited for market cultures. Dan Price, CEO of Gravity Payments, a credit card processing company, made a decision several years ago that has significantly affected the company's culture.

Recognizing that "people should come first," Gravity Payments CEO Dan Price slashed his $1.1 million salary and raised his employees' pay to a minimum of $70,000 annually, which has allowed employees to save for retirement and, in some instances, buy their first home.
Matthew Ryan Williams/Redux Pictures

EXAMPLE Dan Price's 120 employees at Gravity Payments in Seattle were stunned a few years ago when Price announced he was raising their salaries to a minimum of $70,000 a year, partly by slashing his $1.1 million pay to the same level. Since his decision, despite several bumps in the road (i.e., several key employees quitting and his brother threatening to sue him), Price says the company has more than doubled its business and added 80 more employees. Price says his employees are now in a better position to buy their first home, save for retirement, and raise their families because they make a decent salary. "The purpose of an organization is to make the humans' lives better . . . People should come first," Price says.[72] What type of culture is promoted by this decision?

6. Stories, Legends, or Myths About Key People and Events   Storytelling is a powerful way to send messages to others about the values and behaviors the organization desires. Stories reinforce characteristics of the desired culture.

EXAMPLE According to myth, Steve Chen and Chad Hurley came up with the idea for YouTube when they tried to upload video to the web they had taken at a dinner party but failed. Although the founders admit the story is largely embellished, it underscores how stories can influence organizational culture.[73]

EXAMPLE With her elderly father snowed in, a woman called a local Trader Joe's in Pennsylvania to see if they could deliver groceries to her stranded father. The company rep said they normally don't make deliveries but would make an exception. Thirty minutes later, groceries were delivered to the woman's elderly father free of charge, demonstrating Trader Joe's strong commitment to its customers.[74] What type of culture does this action reinforce?

7. Organizational Activities, Processes, or Outcomes   Leaders pay special attention to activities, processes, and outcomes they can measure and control. This behavior sends strong messages to employees about acceptable norms and behavior. For example. if you want to create an adhocracy culture, then managers would pay attention to innovation processes and outcomes such as number of patents or number of ideas submitted to suggestion systems.

EXAMPLE Susan T. Carroll, chief regional executive officer at Inova Health System, recognized health care practitioners encounter vast amounts of data that can be used to improve patient outcomes, but too much data can make culture change difficult, if not impossible. As a result, she focused the new company culture on a narrow, measurable goal: do no harm to patients. By creating a simple, measurable goal that employees could support, she enabled widespread change across the organization.[75]

EXAMPLE GM CEO Mary Barra is trying to move the company culture toward a higher level of hierarchy and market. She started this change by establishing a vision of GM as "the world's most valued automotive company," and by measuring its achievement of this vision via strategic goals to improve customer satisfaction, quality, and financial results. To reinforce this strategic and cultural shift, she told the company's top 300 executives, "If you're not in line with this vision . . . you don't need to be here."[76]

8. Leader Reactions to Critical Incidents and Organizational Crises   Neuroscience research shows that people learn and pay attention to the emotions leaders exhibit. Positive emotions spread, but negative emotions travel faster and farther.[77] Market cultures, for example, are reinforced by showing positive emotions after landing a new customer or negative emotions such as anger after losing a customer because of bad service. Consider how executives at Starbucks responded to a crisis eroding feelings of respect and inclusiveness, both of which reinforce clan culture.

EXAMPLE Executives at Starbucks responded quickly when two black men were arrested at a company store in Philadelphia for loitering, and video of the two being led off in handcuffs went viral. A local resident filmed the incident and posted it on Twitter, writing "The police were called because these men hadn't ordered anything. They were waiting for a friend to show up, who did as they were taken out in hand-cuffs for doing nothing."[78]

Responding to the public outcry about the incident, Starbucks CEO Kevin Johnson in a statement called the incident "reprehensible," and said the video shot by customers was "hard to watch and not representative of our Starbucks Mission and Values."[79] Johnson also announced that Starbucks would close down 8,000 U.S. stores for an afternoon of racial bias training for nearly 175,000 employees. Howard Schultz, Starbucks' chairman, realizes that a four-hour training session on racial bias "is not going to solve racial inequity. . . but we have to start the conversation."[80]

9. Rites and Rituals   *Rites and rituals* **are the planned and unplanned activities and ceremonies used to celebrate important events or achievements.** Consider how managers at Thumbtack reinforce several culture types at once.

EXAMPLE When Thumbtack, an online service that matches customers with local pro-fessional services, was a start-up 10 years ago, CEO Marco Zappacosta cooked lunch for the team. As the company grew, the founders made room in their budget for an in-house chef who fed the team lunch at a big table in the middle of the office. Today, with more than 300 employees at its San Francisco headquarters, Thumbtack's single chef has grown to a culinary team of 10 that makes lunch from scratch for everyone to nur-ture both body and spirit. Chef April Word says, "If someone gets to eat their favorite thing for lunch, they're going to be jazzed, even if they had a meeting that didn't go well. They're going to be happy because their belly's happy and it gave them something to laugh or talk about." Facilitating both clan and adhocracy cultures, this lunch ritual helps form relationships and create ideas while enjoying a tasty meal with colleagues.[81]

10. Work Flow and Organizational Structure   Work flow is the way work gets done—work flow and organizational structure are the way reporting relationships are orga-nized. Both can become tools for changing organizational culture. For example, encourag-ing brainstorming meetings to solve problems reinforces an adhocracy culture, whereas having weekly progress meeting encourages both market and hierarchy cultures.

EXAMPLE Implementing clinical workflow changes and giving patients alternative medications to opioids may help reduce readmission rates, length of stay, and cost of care according to a recent study at Vanderbilt University Medical Center. Noting that the care transition plan from in-hospital care to out-of-hospital care seemed to be where patients were most vulnerable for opioid abuse, the research team developed a treatment pathway that combined pharmacy services, clinical education, and pain man-agement consultations in an effort to increase collaboration and communication across the care team. As a result of the workflow changes and increased collaboration, the readmission rates for patients in the study were significantly reduced.[82] These work flow changes would serve to move the culture in the direction of hierarchy and market.

11. Organizational Systems and Procedures   Companies are increasingly using electronic networks as a tool to promote different types of cultures. Disney, for example, has invested over $1 billion in big data technology to identify the best way to provide cus-tomer service, a characteristic of market cultures.[83]

EXAMPLE Disco is an artificial intelligence tool that helps employers build a culture of appreciation and recognition to improve employee retention and productivity through the use of technology and analytics. In addition, companies can assign a recognition emoji to each of their company values guiding recognition of employee achievements to align with company priorities.[84]

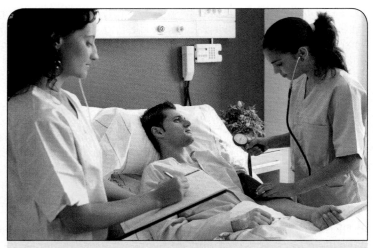

Implementing workflow changes, increasing collaboration among the care team, and giving patients alternative medications to opioids may help reduce readmission rates, length of stay, and cost of care.

Javier Larrea/Pixtal/age fotostock

EXAMPLE Lifesize Communications, a videoconferencing company in Austin, Texas, uses an internal online network to promote collaboration (clan) and increased sales (market). A salesperson recently wanted advice about how to sell a product against a competitor. To get ideas, the salesperson logged onto the network to access content posted by a Lifesize partner in South Africa. The content describes an approach the partner used to win business against that competitor.[85]

12. Organizational Goals and Criteria throughout the Employee Cycle An organization's culture is reflected in the goals it pursues. For example. the clan-type cultures in companies such as Google and Zappos are reinforced by goals like increasing employee development, satisfaction, or involvement. Walmart has decided to foster more of an adhocracy and market culture in response to its strategic goal of growing revenue and market share.

EXAMPLE With the goal of offering grocery home delivery in more than 100 U.S. cities (covering nearly 40 percent of all U.S. households), Walmart recently partnered with several same-day delivery companies. This strategic move is the company's attempt to tackle one of the biggest challenges in retail: the "last mile" of delivering goods to customers who order online. Walmart's aggressive expansion plans into grocery home delivery is in response to Amazon's purchase of Whole Foods, which offers home delivery for online grocery orders.[86]

Managers have many mechanisms at their disposal to change organizational culture for the better. But what happens when managers are the reason the culture needs to change? See the Problem-Solving Application feature for more details.

Problem-Solving Application

Sprouts Farmers Market: The Best Culture, or the Worst?

Founded in 2015, Arizona-based Sprouts Farmers Market is a fast-growing organic grocery chain that prides itself on its community ties, nutrition-education efforts, philanthropic commitments, and concern for people with learning disabilities, food scarcity, and other needs. Its website advertises "Good Food.

Good People," and the company offers an enormous variety of nearly 19,000 fresh and healthy fruits, vegetables, meat, dairy, and fish items that are local, seasonal, natural or organic, gluten-free, non-GMO, and grass-fed or fresh caught. Deli and bakery goods, vitamins, and beer and wine are available too. Nearly 3 million customers visit its 300-plus stores around the country each week, and Instacart orders placed online are filled within an hour.[87]

The company promises customers a friendly, well-trained staff eager to answer questions and offer samples, and new employees are assured of training, plenty of opportunities, and generous benefits.[88] In 2018, Sprouts was the only Arizona-based company to earn a place on *Fortune*'s list of the world's most admired companies, ranking high on social responsibility, people management, quality of products/services, and quality of management.[89]

That same year, however, Sprouts came in sixth on a much less prestigious list—the nation's worst companies to work for, based on a *USA Today* analysis of current and former employees' reviews on the job-listing site Glassdoor.com. Only 36 percent of the employees who posted about Sprouts on Glassdoor would recommend working there, and the company's overall rating was only 2.6 stars of a possible 5 (the average rating is 3.4). The negative factor in many of Sprouts' reviews was company management, including what *USA Today* called "dozens" of complaints about "immaturity" and high manager turnover that left workers unsure about what to expect on the job. The report cited a Glassdoor expert who said "company culture" was first among the top three reasons for employee satisfaction (the other two were "career opportunities and trust in senior leadership").[90]

Apply the 3-Step Problem-Solving Approach

Step 1: Define the problem Sprouts appears to be facing.

Step 2: Identify the causes of the problem. What OB concepts help explain why there are such differing perceptions of the company's culture?

Step 3: Make your recommendation about which lever(s) for creating culture change might help solve Sprouts' apparent problem.

Remember Person–Organization Fit   Now that we have described the four key types of organizational culture and the mechanisms managers can use to change culture, it's time to reflect on your person–organization (P–O) fit. Recall that P–O fit reflects the extent to which your personality and values match the climate and culture in an organization. Your P–O fit matters because it links to your work attitudes and performance.[91]

Do you have a preference for one of the four types of culture in the CVF? Use Self-Assessment 14.2 to explore this topic.

SELF-ASSESSMENT 14.2

What Type of Organizational Culture Do I Prefer?

Please be prepared to answer these questions if your instructor has assigned Self-Assessment 14.2 in Connect.

1. In rank order, what are your preferred culture types?
2. To what extent does your preferred culture type affect your job satisfaction?

14.4 EMBEDDING ORGANIZATIONAL CULTURE THROUGH THE SOCIALIZATION PROCESS

THE BIGGER PICTURE

Organizational culture spreads by means of a learning process. That is, people teach each other about the values and norms the organization values and rewards. Organizational socialization is one mechanism underlying this learning process. All of us have been socialized at one time or another. It's a natural aspect of starting a new job at any company, and it ultimately affects your work attitudes and performance. You will learn about a three-phase model of organizational socialization and practical lessons based on socialization research.

LO 14-4

Explain the three-phase model of organizational socialization.

Organizational socialization is "the process by which individuals acquire the knowledge, skills, attitudes, and behaviors required to assume a work role."[92] This definition highlights that organizational socialization is a key mechanism by which organizations embed their cultures, particularly in new employees. In short, organizational socialization turns outsiders into fully functioning insiders by promoting and reinforcing the organization's core values and beliefs. This section introduces a three-phase model of organizational socialization and examines the practical application of socialization research.

Imagine the feelings this new employee might have about starting a job. What emotions might she be experiencing? Excitement? Worry? Challenge? How can companies help new employees begin to fit in during the first few weeks of employment?

Ingram Publishing/age fotostock

A Three-Phase Model of Organizational Socialization

Anyone's first year in a complex organization can be confusing. There is a constant swirl of new faces, strange jargon, conflicting expectations, and apparently unrelated events. Many organizations treat new members in a rather haphazard, sink-or-swim manner. For example, a recent Gallup survey revealed that only 12 percent of the respondents felt their organizations did a great job of introducing new employees to organizational socialization.[93] This is unfortunate because unstructured socialization is associated with decreased learning, performance, and satisfaction.[94] It also leads to increased turnover.[95] There is a better way.

Organizational behavior researcher Daniel Feldman has proposed a three-phase model of organizational socialization that promotes deeper understanding of this important process. As illustrated in Figure 14.7, the three phases are:

1. Anticipatory socialization
2. Encounter
3. Change and acquisition

Each phase has associated perceptual and social processes. Feldman's model also specifies behavioral and affective outcomes that reveal how well the individual has been socialized. The entire three-phase sequence may take from a few weeks to a year to complete, depending on individual differences and the complexity of the situation. Let's look at each phase.

FIGURE 14.7 Model of Organizational Socialization

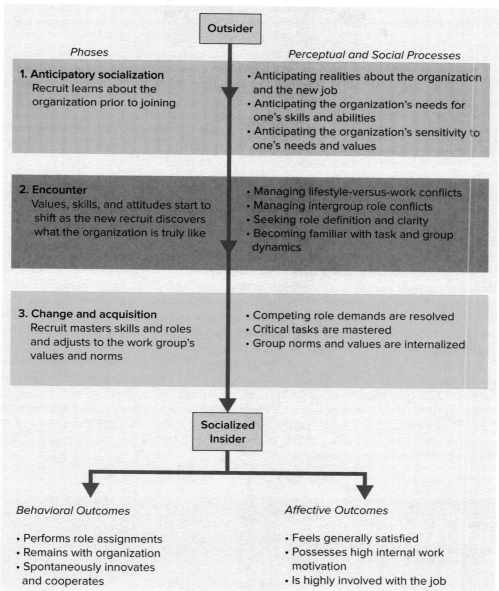

SOURCE: Feldman, Daniel Charles. "The Multiple Socialization of Organization Members." *The Academy of Management Review* 6, no. 2 (1981): 309–18. https:// DOI: 10.2307/257888.

Phase 1: Anticipatory Socialization   The *anticipatory socialization phase* **occurs before an individual actually joins an organization.** During this phase people acquire information about different careers, occupations, professions, and organizations that can come from many sources. An organization's current employees are a powerful source of information. So are the Internet, social media, internships, and job fairs.

Unrealistic expectations about the nature of the work, pay, and promotions are often formulated during Phase 1. Because employees with unrealistic expectations are more likely to quit their jobs in the future, organizations should offer realistic job previews. A *realistic job preview (RJP)* **gives recruits a realistic idea of what lies ahead by presenting both positive and negative aspects of the job.**

EXAMPLE Comcast uses RJPs that consist of three components found on the company's job website. The first part is a description of the job and its responsibilities. The second part is a video "job trailer" that runs an average of three minutes and follows an employee through his or her day showing the types of tasks that occur on an actual workday for the position the applicant is applying for. The final part of the RJP is the application process, which involves creating a profile, applying for the position, and then following through several more steps as the application goes through the Comcast HR system.[96]

Research revealed that realistic job previews were related to higher performance and lower attrition from the recruitment process. RJPs also lowered job applicants' initial expectations and led to lower turnover among those who were hired.[97]

Phase 2: Encounter   The next phase begins when the employment contract has been signed. During the *encounter phase* **employees come to learn what the organization is really like.** It is a time for reconciling unmet expectations and making sense of a new work environment. Many companies use a combination of orientation and training programs to socialize employees during the encounter phase. Onboarding is one such technique. *Onboarding* **programs help employees to integrate, assimilate, and transition to new jobs by making them familiar with corporate policies, procedures, culture, and politics and by clarifying work-role expectations and responsibilities.**[98] One corporate survey revealed that nearly 66 percent of organizations say onboarding practices have been underutilized and only 40 percent say onboarding is effective at retaining new hires.[99]

There is no set way to onboard a new employee. The OB in Action box illustrates a variety of methods used at different organizations. Video gaming company Riot Games, *Fortune's* 39th best place to work in 2016, has an interesting approach to onboarding. If within the first 60 days new hires decide the company is not a good fit, Riot Games pays them 10 percent of their annual salary, up to $25,000, to quit.[100] Zappos similarly pays new employees a month's salary if they believe they are a bad fit after participating in the company's four-week onboarding program.[101]

OB in Action

Companies Use Different Approaches to Onboard Employees

The first day on the job can be filled with boring paperwork regarding benefits and dull presentations about the company's history, mission, and values. While these activities are important, some companies try to find more creative ways for employees to spend their first few days and weeks at work.

Netflix Nourishes Its Culture   At Netflix, new hires are introduced to helpful coworkers as well as executive managers, and they are given a significant level of responsibility from the start. The company communicates its values with plenty of resources focused on its cultural diversity and inclusiveness programs.[102]

Consulting Firm Protiviti Puts New Hires in Groups   A *Fortune* reporter stated, "The company ushers in new hires in batches, then sends them on a journey through Passport to Protiviti, a program that integrates them into the environment as they collaborate as teams, work with peer advisers, and meet regularly with leaders."[103]

Twitter Offers Lots of Support   Before they reach their desk on the first day, new Twitter employees have had breakfast with the CEO and been given their company e-mail address, a company T-shirt, and a celebratory bottle of wine. They go on to a tour of the office and attend a group training session, after which they can settle into their workspaces, conveniently located near key colleagues who can help and answer questions. A new-hire happy hour with senior leadership takes place once a month.[104]

NCR Corp. Relies Heavily On an Online Portal   Electronics and computer hardware maker NCR Corp. has a year-long onboarding process that starts with an online portal. *HR Magazine* noted that this enables "new hires to interact with one another with built-in social networking capabilities tied to virtual learning platform CorpU. Managers can assign an onboarding plan for each new hire, track his or her progress, and solicit feedback about the individual's performance." HR also partnered with the company's "marketing staff to make the portal design appealing and fun, as well as to ensure a consistent branded experience for all employees," according to *HR Magazine*. Employees reported positive attitudes about their onboarding experiences.[105]

YOUR THOUGHTS?

1. Which of these onboarding methods is most appealing to you? Why?

2. Which of these onboarding methods is least appealing to you? Why?

3. How do these companies' onboarding programs compare to experiences you may have had when starting a new job, or even when arriving on campus?

Phase 3: Change and Acquisition   The *change and acquisition phase* requires **employees to master important tasks and roles and adjust to their work group's values and norms.** Mastery will occur only when employees have a clear understanding about their roles and are effectively integrated within the work unit. Being successful in Phase 3 also requires employees to have a clear understanding of the use of social media. It is easy for you to create problems for yourself by not being aware of expectations regarding surfing, texting during meetings, and use of company equipment for personal messages. Experts suggest setting ground rules on the first day of employment, coaching employees on norms, and discussing how guidelines have changed.[106]

Table 14.2 presents a list of paired socialization processes or tactics organizations use to help employees through this adjustment process.

To what extent have you been adequately socialized? If your socialization level is high, then all is well. If it is medium to low, you may need to find a mentor. We discuss mentoring in the next section. Take a moment to complete Self-Assessment 14.3. It measures the extent to which you have been socialized into your current work organization.

SELF-ASSESSMENT 14.3

Have You Been Adequately Socialized?

Please be prepared to answer these questions if your instructor has assigned Self-Assessment 14.3 in Connect.

1. What is your level of socialization? Are you surprised by the results?

2. Based on your results and what you have learned about socialization, what advice would you provide to your organization to improve its socialization process?

Practical Applications of Socialization Research

Research suggests four practical guidelines for managers.

1. Managers should avoid a haphazard, sink-or-swim approach to organizational socialization, because formalized and proactive socialization tactics positively affect new hires.[107]

2. More organizations today use socialization tactics to reinforce a culture that promotes ethical behavior. Managers should consider how they might best set expectations for ethical behavior during all three phases of the socialization process.[108]

TABLE 14.2 Socialization Tactics

Examples in each row illustrate one or the other of the alternatives. Which one appears in the example?

ALTERNATIVE TACTICS AND DESCRIPTION			WHICH IS THIS AN EXAMPLE OF?
Collective	**vs.**	**Individual**	**Example**
Grouping newcomers and exposing them to a common set of experiences.		Treating each newcomer individually and exposing him or her to more or less unique experiences.	All new hires attend an orientation session on the same day.
Formal	**vs.**	**Informal**	**Example**
Segregating a newcomer from regular organization members during a defined socialization period.		No effort to clearly distinguish a newcomer from more experienced members.	Army recruits must attend boot camp before they are allowed to work alongside established soldiers.
Sequential	**vs.**	**Random**	**Example**
The newcomer completes a fixed progression of steps culminating in his or her new role.		No clear steps are given and progression is ambiguous or dynamic.	Doctors must follow a sequence from medical school to internship to residency before they are allowed to practice on their own.
Fixed	**vs.**	**Variable**	**Example**
Management setting a timetable for the assumption of the role.		Management setting no timetable and relying on contingencies for assumption of the role.	American university students typically spend one year apiece as freshman, sophomores, juniors, and seniors.
Serial	**vs.**	**Disjunctive**	**Example**
The newcomer is socialized over time with the help of an experienced organization member.		The newcomer is not provided a role model.	A buddy system is used during orientation.
Investiture	**vs.**	**Divestiture**	**Example**
The affirmation of a newcomer's incoming global and specific role identities and attributes.		The denial and stripping away of the newcomer's existing sense of self and the reconstruction of self in the organization's image.	During police training, cadets are required to wear uniforms and maintain an immaculate appearance; they are addressed as "officer" and told they are no longer ordinary citizens but representatives of the police force.

SOURCE: Ashforth, Blake. *Role Transitions in Organizational Life: An Identity-Based Perspective.* Mahwah, NJ: Routledge, 2000.

3. Support for stage models is mixed. Although there are different stages of socialization, they are not identical in order, length, or content for all people or jobs.[109] Managers should use a contingency approach to organizational socialization. In other words, keep in mind that different techniques are appropriate for different people at different times.

4. Research finds that expatriates, workers who take an assignment in a foreign country, experienced different socialization activities than other newcomers. In turn, these different experiences affected their long-term success and job satisfaction.[110]

Regardless of how well your employee handles the socialization process, you can improve your own socialization experience. The Applying OB box provides recommendations for improving three skills essential for success at a new job.

Applying OB

CAREER READINESS

Key Skills Needed for Success in a New Job[111]

1. *Introducing yourself to strangers.* Don't assume others will not want to meet you or are too busy to spend time with you. As a new employee you are expected to reach out and meet people. Gain confidence in this activity by practicing your opening lines. It helps to write them down, rehearse, and experiment with different approaches. Preparing a list of initial questions to ask people will help you demonstrate interest and motivation. When talking with others, try to make them feel heard, valued, and respected. People will remember this more than specific details about yourself. Finally, write down what you learn about others and consult it when you are next going to meet them.

2. *Remembering people's names.* Neuroscientists have shown that we encode and remember names differently than other details about people, such as their faces, jobs, or family status. This tells us that weak neural connections exist between someone's face and name. You can overcome this drawback by using a few key techniques:
   a. Make a commitment to pay attention to people when you first meet them.
   b. Repeat the name in your mind several times and use it during the conversation.
   c. Write down the name as soon as you can to increase recall.
   d. Create a mental picture that provides a clue to the person's name, because we remember things or objects better than names. For example, when meeting Angelo, picture an angel.

   e. Use cheat sheets before going to events or meetings. Review the names and backgrounds of people you expect to see during such encounters.

3. *Asking good questions.* Research shows "the more questions new employees ask and the more help they seek, the better they perform . . . question askers are also more satisfied in new jobs and more committed to new organizations."[112] The learning point is that most new employees do not ask enough questions. Here are a few ideas for asking better questions:
   a. Be clear in your mind about what you want. The clearer you are, the easier it is to ask the right questions.
   b. Find the best person to answer your questions. If it is someone you just met, ask him or her whether you can contact them later for advice.
   c. There are no dumb questions coming from new employees. Just ask what is on your mind.
   d. Ask pointed questions. If you want a specific piece of information, ask a closed question such as, "When is the report due?" If you want more detailed information, ask an open-ended question such as, "What is the process for completing an expense report?"
   e. Show appreciation and gratitude to those who answer your questions.
   f. Find a "newbie buddy," a peer who can be your initial "go-to" person for questions.

14.5 EMBEDDING ORGANIZATIONAL CULTURE THROUGH MENTORING

THE BIGGER PICTURE

Mentoring is another mechanism for embedding organizational culture because mentors play a key role in socializing newcomers. This section can help you understand how to benefit from mentoring, which ultimately should help you obtain career satisfaction and promotions.

LO 14-5

Describe how mentoring can foster personal and professional success.

The modern word *mentor* derives from Mentor, the name of a wise and trusted counselor in Greek mythology. Terms typically associated with mentoring include *teacher, sponsor, peer,* and *coach.* Sometimes people use the words *mentor* and coach interchangeably. Note, however, there is a difference between terms as they relate to a working relationship.

Mentoring is the process of forming and maintaining intensive and lasting developmental relationships between a variety of developers (people who provide career and psychosocial support) and a junior person (the protégé, if male, or protégée, if female).[113] **Coaching is a process that focuses on improving an individual's behavior and performance to resolve work issues or handle specific aspects of the job and may be short term.**[114]

Mentoring can serve to embed an organization's culture when developers and the protégé/protégée work in the same organization for two reasons. First, mentoring contributes to creating a sense of oneness by promoting the acceptance of the organization's core values throughout the organization. Second, the networking aspect of mentoring also promotes positive interpersonal relationships.

Not only is mentoring valuable as a tactic for embedding organizational culture, but research suggests it can significantly influence the protégé/protégée's future career.[115] This section reviews the functions of mentoring, the role of human and social capital in mentoring, and the personal implications of mentoring.

Mentoring is the process of forming and maintaining lasting developmental relationships between colleagues. It can serve to embed an organization's culture because it can create a sense of oneness by promoting the acceptance of the organization's core values throughout the organization.
Onoky/Image Source

Functions of Mentoring

Kathy Kram, a Boston University researcher, conducted in-depth interviews with 18 pairs of senior and junior managers. As a by-product of this study, Kram identified two general functions of the mentoring process—career and psychosocial—that occur over four phases. Table 14.3 provides examples of these functions.

Five *career functions* that enhanced career development were:

1. Sponsorship
2. Exposure and visibility
3. Coaching
4. Protection
5. Challenging assignments

Four *psychosocial functions* were:

1. Role modeling
2. Acceptance and confirmation
3. Counseling
4. Friendship

Four Phases of Mentoring   The four phases of mentoring are initiation, cultivation, separation, and redefinition. The *initiation* phase lasts 6 to 12 months and starts during the encounter phase of socialization. Mentors socialize new employees about the values, norms, and expectations associated with the organization's culture during this phase. If you don't get connected to a mentor during this period of employment, we suggest

TABLE 14.3   Examples of Career and Psychosocial Functions of Mentoring

FUNCTIONS	EXAMPLES	
Career		
Sponsorship	Mentor advocates for protégé/protégée, possibly putting reputation on the line by suggesting him/her for challenging projects or additional assignments.	
Exposure and visibility	Mentor introduces protégé/protégée to industry colleagues at professional meetings and offers suggestions for other networking opportunities.	
Coaching	Mentor provides advice to protégé/protégée regarding development of additional skills to expand job experience portfolio.	
Protection	Mentor defends actions/decisions of protégé/protégée to others while at the same time providing him/her with constructive feedback regarding actions/decisions.	
Challenging assignments	Mentor encourages protégé/protégée to take on projects outside his/her comfort zone in effort to gain more experience and expand career opportunities.	
Psychosocial		
Role modeling	Mentor works with protégé/protégée to think critically about specific situations that might occur in work/personal contexts and provides advice.	
Acceptance and confirmation	Mentor helps protégé/protégée develop a sense of competence and self-identity.	
Counseling	Mentor provides advice to protégé/protégée about positive and negative relationships with others in the organization.	
Friendship	Mentor and protégé/protégée build relationship on mutual respect, loyalty, and trust that may help both individuals in their professional and personal lives.	

SOURCES: Porter, Jane. Yes, You Need A Mentor, But A Sponsor Will Really Boost Your Career. *Mansueto Ventures, LLC.,* September 23, 2014. https://www.fastcompany.com/3036037/yes-you-need-a-mentor-but-a-sponsor-will-really-boost-your-career; "NextGen Voices: Quality Monitoring," *Science,* October 201 and Bradford, Laurence. 8 Tips For An Amazing Mentor Relationship. *Forbes Media LLC.,* January 31, 2018. https://www.forbes.com/sites/laurencebradford/2018/01/31/8-tips-for-an-amazing-mentor-relationship/#14b22bba21e2.

actively seeking someone out. The *cultivation* phase spans two to five years and entails the protégé/protégée receiving a host of career and psychosocial guidance. Your ability to learn the ropes and master the tasks during this phase is essential for future promotions. In the *separation* phase you detach from your mentor and become more autonomous. During the *redefinition* phases, you and your mentor start interacting as peers.[116]

Benefits of Mentoring   Mentoring leads to more positive outcomes for the protégé/protégée when several conditions are present, some of which the protégé cannot control.

- Both mentor and protégé/protégée possess emotional intelligence.
- The mentoring relationship is formal rather than informal.[117]
- The mentor is skilled at coaching, is a good role model, and possesses social capital.[118]
- The protégé/protégée possesses high levels of human and social capital—discussed in the next section.[119]

Human and Social Capital Enhance the Benefits of Mentoring

Human Capital   **Human capital is the productive potential of an individual's knowledge, skills, and experiences.** *Potential* is the operative word in this definition. When you are hungry, money in your pocket is good because it has the potential to buy a meal. Likewise, a protégé/protégée with the right combination of knowledge, skills, and motivation to excel possesses human capital with the potential to give the organization a competitive advantage. Developing your human capital not only enables you to more effectively do your job, but it also makes you more attractive to mentors, who have options when selecting protégé/protégées. You may find this surprising, but a recent study showed that lack of sleep depletes your human capital and lowers performance.[120] Get the proper amount of sleep to perform at your best.

Scripps Health, a nonprofit health care system in San Diego and the 41st best place to work in 2018 according to *Fortune,* helps employees develop human capital by providing career coaching and administering scholarships, tuition reimbursement, and discounts for courses offered by universities that have partnerships with the company. In 2018, Scripps invested more than $35 million in employee training and provided an additional $1.33 million in tuition reimbursement and scholarships.[121]

Social Capital   **Social capital is the productive potential resulting from relationships, goodwill, trust, and cooperative effort.** Again, the word *potential* is key. Social capital helps you during the anticipatory phase of socialization. For example, a national survey of recruiters revealed that 74 percent found the highest-quality job applicants were employee referrals. Referrals also tend to stay longer at their jobs, a result of better P–O fit.[122]

Social capital is beneficial beyond the early stages of your career, particularly when you are developing trusting relationships with others. Trusting relationships lead to more job and business opportunities, faster advancement, greater capacity to innovate, and more status and authority.[123] In addition, social capital can also lead to a form of learning called **network intelligence, which draws on the knowledge of your social network,**[124] as described in the following example.

EXAMPLE   LinkedIn co-founder Reid Hoffman solved a major business problem when he was running PayPal by drawing on the knowledge of his social network. When the company was trying to launch services in Japan, PayPal continued to run into legal issues and major delays. Hoffman called eight friends with good connections in Japan and three of them mentioned the same Japanese entrepreneur. One introduction from

Reid Hoffman, co-founder of LinkedIn
Tony Avelar/AP Images

one of his connections, and Hoffman was discussing the situation with the Japanese businessman. The businessman found a consultant who obtained a letter from the Japanese financial services agency that gave PayPal the go-ahead to launch its services. Shortly thereafter, PayPal Japan was up and running, and Hoffman added the Japanese entrepreneur to his social network as a friend and collaborator.[125]

The moral of the story is that it pays to have a rich network of good relationships. Social capital helps make that possible. The Applying OB box provides some strategies for you to consider as you begin to build your own network and seek mentors to help you along the way.

Applying OB

Key Strategies for Cultivating a Network and a Mentoring Relationship

Here are four key strategies to consider as you begin to build your network and seek a mentor:

1. **Build a broad developmental network because the number and quality of your contacts influences your career success.** In doing this, keep in mind the comments of two networking experts: "Relationships are living, breathing things. Feed, nurture, and care about them; they grow. Neglect them; they die."[126] Invest time in your developmental relationships.

2. **Seek consistency or congruence between your career goals and the type of developmental network at your disposal.** This alignment has a big influence on job and career satisfaction. For example, if you are interested in a job in finance, try to develop relationships with people with a finance background. If you want to start your own business one day, try to network with a diverse group of people. This should help broaden your understanding of what it takes to start a business.

3. **A mentor's willingness to provide career and psychosocial assistance depends on the protégé/protégée's ability and potential and the quality of the interpersonal relationship.**[127] This point underscores the value of building your human and social capital.

4. **Develop a mentoring plan.** Experts suggest your plan should include the following steps:[128]
   - Base your mentoring goals on what you want to learn, and then prioritize them.
   - Identify people who are skilled or experienced in areas where you want to improve. Don't overlook your peers; they are a good source of functional, technical, and organizational knowledge.
   - Decide how best to build a relationship with your targeted individuals.
   - Figure out how you can provide value to your mentor. Because mentoring is a two-way street, others are more likely to help you if they see some value in assisting you to pursue your career goals.
   - Recognize when it is time to move on. Mentors are not forever. If you believe your mentor is ineffective or harming more than helping, find a new mentor. It's easy to become stuck with one mentor. Expanding your horizons will not only benefit you, but it can help the mentor develop his or her mentoring skills as well.

Are you being adequately mentored? If not, you are more likely to experience adverse work attitudes, performance, and career outcomes. Self-Assessment 14.4 was created so you can take stock of your level of mentoring.

SELF-ASSESSMENT 14.4

Assessing My Level of Mentoring

Please be prepared to answer these questions if your instructor has assigned Self-Assessment 14.4 in Connect.

1. What is your level of mentoring?

2. After identifying your three lowest-scoring items in the survey, propose steps you can take to improve your level of mentoring.

3. How will you evaluate the success of these steps?

14.6 MAKING THE CONNECTION: HOW CAN I USE THESE CONCEPTS TO FIT, DEVELOP, AND PERFORM?

For an organization to be successful, managers must constantly evaluate its corporate culture, recognize how the organization socializes new employees into that culture, and foster an environment of mentoring at all levels. Here are some key points to consider.

Takeaways for Me

LO 14-6

Describe the implications of organizational culture, socialization, and mentoring for you and managers.

Here are seven things you can do to turn this chapter's lessons into positive change in your personal and professional life.

1. **Person–organization fit matters:** It's important to assess your level of fit with current and future employers. Use the recommendations discussed in the Winning at Work feature at the start of the chapter to help in this effort.

2. **Departments or work units contain subcultures:** Be sure to assess your fit at this level, too.

3. **Awareness of the 12 mechanisms for changing culture provides insight you can use to help your employer move its culture in a desired direction.**

4. **If you are not getting what you need to perform a new job, stop and ask for guidance:** Too many companies take an ad hoc approach toward socialization, which adversely affects your level of success.

5. **You can continually upgrade your human and social capital:** Take ownership for enhancing your skills, abilities, and developmental networks as well as your interpersonal relationships if you want to experience career advancement throughout your life; you get what you give.

6. **Don't contact mentors only when you want something:** Build and maintain relationships by continuing to have regular contact with people in your developmental network.

7. **Proficiency with social networking tools such as Twitter, LinkedIn, and Facebook will help you find jobs throughout your career.**

Takeaways for Managers

There are six key implications for managers.

1. **Managing organizational culture is one of the most important aspects of your job:** Remember, culture eats strategy for breakfast.

2. **Culture is important because it performs four key functions for employees:** Use this knowledge to help employees reach their maximum potential.

3. **Consider the extent to which your unit's culture is fostering the type of work environment needed to help you achieve department goals:** If the culture is conflicting with your strategies or goals, consider using one of the 12 mechanisms for changing culture.

4. **Assess the extent to which your unit's culture is consistent with the company's overall culture:** Make changes as needed.

5. **Take an active role in socializing employees:** It's good for you and your employer.

6. **We all benefit from mentoring:** Spend time developing your own human and social capital. You never know when a new opportunity will arise.

What Did I Learn?

You learned that organizational culture helps managers to create competitive advantage. You examined the function and types of culture and considered how managers can change culture. Finally, you now know that socialization and mentoring are two processes organizations use to embed organizational culture. As an employee you realize how to use this knowledge to understand your employer's culture and how best to fit in. Reinforce what you learned with the Key Points below. Then consolidate your learning using the Organizing Framework. Finally, challenge your mastery of this chapter by answering the Major Questions in your own words.

Key Points for Understanding Chapter 14

You learned the following key points.

14.1 THE FOUNDATION OF ORGANIZATIONAL CULTURE: UNDERSTANDING ITS DRIVERS AND FUNCTIONS

- Culture is a shared concept that we learn over time. It also influences our behavior at work and outcomes at multiple levels.
- The three levels of organizational culture are observable artifacts, espoused values, and basic underlying assumptions.
- Espoused values are the explicitly stated values and norms an organization prefers. Enacted values, in contrast, are the values and norms we actually see in employee behavior.
- Four functions of organizational culture are to establish organizational identity, encourage collective commitment, ensure social system stability, and act as a device for sense-making.

14.2 THE IMPACT OF ORGANIZATIONAL CULTURE TYPES ON OUTCOMES

- The competing values framework identifies four types of organizational culture. A clan culture has an employee focus. Adhocracy and market cultures have external foci that emphasize innovation/growth and market share/profitability, respectively. Hierarchical cultures are internally focused on efficiency and smooth functioning.
- There are six conclusions about outcomes associated with organizational culture: (1) culture is related to the way an organization measures its effectiveness; (2) employees are more satisfied and committed to companies with clan cultures; (3) clan and market cultures are more likely to deliver higher customer satisfactions and market share; (4) operational outcomes, quality, and innovation are more strongly related to clan, adhocracy, and market cultures; (5) an organization's financial performance is not strongly related to culture; and (6) companies with market cultures tend to have more positive organizational outcomes.
- Subcultures should be integrated with a company's overall culture.

14.3 MECHANISMS OR LEVERS FOR CULTURE CHANGE

- Here are four key points about culture change. First, leaders are the architects and developers of organizational culture. Second, the process of culture change begins with targeting the three layers of culture. Third, culture needs to be aligned with a company's vision and strategic plan. Finally, a structured approach works best when implementing culture change.

- Managers can change organizational culture in 12 ways.
- Good person–organization fit is associated with positive work attitudes and performance.

14.4 EMBEDDING ORGANIZATIONAL CULTURE THROUGH THE SOCIALIZATION PROCESS

- Socialization is a key mechanism organizations use to embed their organizational cultures. It turns outsiders into fully functioning insiders.
- The three-phase model of socialization proposes that anticipatory socialization, encounter, and change and acquisition take place.
- Six opposite pairs of socialization tactics are collective versus individual, formal versus informal, sequential versus random, fixed versus variable, serial versus disjunctive, and investiture versus divestiture.

14.5 EMBEDDING ORGANIZATIONAL CULTURE THROUGH MENTORING

- Mentoring helps embed organizational culture in two ways. First, it contributes to creating a sense of oneness by promoting acceptance of the organization's values. Second, the socialization aspect of mentoring promotes a sense of membership.
- Mentoring has two general functions: career and psychosocial.
- Mentoring occurs in four phases: initiation, cultivation, separation, and redefinition.
- The human and social capital of both parties enhance the benefits of mentoring.

- There are four important personal implications of effective mentoring. First, build a broad developmental network because the number and quality of your contacts influences your career success. Second, seek consistency or congruence between your career goals and the type of developmental network at your disposal. Third, a mentor's willingness to provide career and psychosocial assistance depends on the protégé/protégée's ability and potential and the quality of the interpersonal relationship. Finally, develop a mentoring plan.

14.6 HOW CAN I USE THESE CONCEPTS TO FIT, DEVELOP, AND PERFORM?

- Assessing your level of fit with current and future employers is important to your overall success.
- Stopping to ask for guidance in a new job is an important strategy for personal and professional development.
- Managing organizational culture is one of the most important aspects of any manager's job.

The Organizing Framework for Chapter 14

As shown in Figure 14.8, you learned that two person factors and four situation factors influence individual, group/team, and organizational processes. You now understand the power of organizational culture, having considered many outcomes related to it. The Outcomes box shows five individual-, two group/team-, and five organizational-level outcomes influenced by culture, socialization, and mentoring.

Challenge: Major Questions for Chapter 14

You now should be able to answer the following questions. Unless you can, have you really processed and internalized the lessons in the chapter? Refer to the Key Points, Figure 14.8, the chapter itself, and your notes to revisit and answer the following major questions:

1. What is culture and why is it helpful to understand its layers and functions?
2. How are different types of organizational culture related to important outcomes?
3. What mechanisms or levers can I use to implement culture change?
4. How can I integrate the findings of socialization research with the three phases of socialization?
5. How can I use mentoring to foster personal and professional success?

FIGURE 14.8 Organizing Framework for Understanding and Applying OB

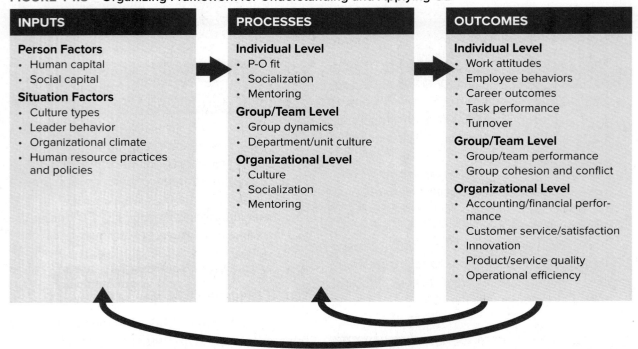

Cultures Clash at Ford

Ford Motor Company revolutionized the auto manufacturing industry more than 100 years ago with the invention of the assembly line, but lately the company is struggling to remain attractive to investors. Ford has experienced costly recalls and lost hundreds of millions of dollars from its international businesses in recent years.[129] New tariffs on steel and aluminum have eaten up $1 billion of Ford's profits, and Moody's has downgraded the company's credit rating to one level above "junk" status. By the fall of 2018, Ford's stock price hit a nine-year low.[130] Meanwhile, rival manufacturers are inching closer to delivering on new technologies like fully autonomous and connected automobiles, and Ford needs to reinvent itself to have any chance of surviving, let alone thriving, in its rapidly shifting competitive environment. But can a massive, entrenched, 116-year-old company change itself? Executive Chairman Bill Ford believes it can, and in May 2017 he brought on CEO James Hackett to make it happen.

Hackett planned to drastically alter the way Ford operated.[131] Specifically, he wanted to change Ford's culture to one that was more open-minded, creative, and adaptable so that it would be better equipped to respond to rapidly shifting market demands.[132] Stakeholders had high expectations for Hackett's ability to deliver. In the two decades he spent as CEO of Steelcase, Inc.—an office furniture company—Hackett was a strong proponent of "design thinking." This approach to problem solving focuses on the customer—what goes through their minds and how they experience a product.[133] At Steelcase, Hackett's teams of sociologists, anthropologists, and technology experts used design thinking to transform the company from a cubicle designer to a trailblazer in today's open, collaborative workspaces.[134] Hackett was hired to bring design thinking to Ford, overhaul its culture, and reinvent the approach the automaker took to creating its products.[135]

Hackett made some noticeable changes right away. He reduced the number of people reporting directly to him from 18 to 8 and decreased the frequency of meetings with them to allow them more time for creative thinking and decision making. He hired 28-year-old Clare Braun as his chief of staff, calling her a "reverse mentor" who would help him understand how people under 30 were thinking. Hackett also made waves by removing a plaque that commemorated former CEO Alan Mulally's "One Ford" plan. Mulally's plan had been credited with repairing Ford's culture and

saving profits ten years earlier, but Hackett wanted to make the point that old approaches only continue to work if the past and future were identical. The space on the wall became dedicated to drawing, mapping, and diagramming out Ford's strategy for competing in its new reality.[136]

Hackett favors collaboration over traditional top-down management. Many of his efforts to change the culture inside Ford's corporate offices have centered around removing hierarchies to generate creative discussions across functional areas.[137] For example, Hackett launched "Team Edison" to focus exclusively on electric vehicles. The cross-functional team occupies an open space inside one of Ford's former Detroit factories and, according to director Darren Palmer, knew that to succeed they needed to "be willing to challenge every truth and every process we had developed over the course of our careers." Hackett has encouraged the team to generate ideas from multiple viewpoints. According to Palmer, "On any given day you can find yourself sitting next to someone working to market our electric vehicles, someone looking at the profit potential of our electric vehicles, or be on a coffee break with someone involved in our charging strategy."[138]

FRUSTRATIONS WITH HACKETT

By mid-2018, approximately one year after Hackett took over, Ford's profits were down around $1 billion. Key stakeholders were growing increasingly anxious and impatient with the fact they still didn't understand exactly what was going on or how Hackett planned to change the company.[139]

Analysts began criticizing Hackett for failing to articulate a compelling vision for exactly where he planned to take Ford. Morgan Stanley analyst Adam Jonas said what little Hackett had communicated was "vague and unstructured" compared to Ford's industry competitors. One journalist said Hackett used "fuzzy terms more common to urbanists and businesspeople, and talking with him can feel like taking a college philosophy seminar after a few bong rips."[140] Issues with Hackett's communication were present inside the company as well, where executives were often calling upon Braun, Hackett's chief of staff, to translate Hackett's diagrams and cryptic messages after meetings.[141] Ford dealership owners also expressed concerns about communications from corporate headquarters.

Jack Madden, owner of a Ford dealership in Norwood, Massachusetts, said "There's been a lot less exposure to senior management . . . There's just not enough information flowing down to dealers about where the company's headed."[142]

One thing Hackett did make clear was that reorganizing and reinventing Ford would require that the company become leaner in both its product offerings and its workforce. Hackett moved quickly and explicitly to slash Ford's unprofitable vehicles and ventures. He announced in early 2018 that the company would discontinue five of its sedans to focus on SUVs and trucks.[143] Ford also announced in 2019 that it was closing its oldest factory in Brazil and pulling out of its South American commercial truck business.[144] Hackett has been less transparent on how and when he plans to trim Ford's workforce. While the need for some job cuts within Ford is not disputed, the manner in which Hackett has communicated about the impending layoffs has been heavily scrutinized. Experts believe that vague statements about layoffs, along with a long process, have the potential to negatively impact employee morale. Employees may feel undue stress and begin job searching and underperforming if they worry about losing their jobs.[145]

IS FORD TURNING A CORNER?

Ford reported first quarter earnings in 2019 that far outpaced investors' expectations.[146] Around the same time, Hackett gave what some felt was his most straightforward statement to date. He told analysts that Ford's two previous CEOs had allowed the company's costs to incrementally increase so much that the company had to, as one article put it, "stop the bleeding before it could start showing gains from herculean efforts to turn the company around." Hackett reported that by the end of 2018, the company had finally been able to put a stop to the spending and level off structural expenses. Hackett said the company would be able to move much more quickly to deliver new products to the market now that this problem had been solved.[147] Ford has announced it will make substantial investments in electric vehicles, and Hackett recently told CNBC that drivers should expect a "big surprise" on the horizon.[148]

Still, it's likely that Hackett will continue to mystify Ford's stakeholders. In an industry looking for a savior with a clear, concise plan of action, Hackett operates more like a coach. He favors using things like TED talks and Socratic exercises to slowly draw creativity and organic solutions from his people, rather than handing down personal dictates.[149] Hackett's quirky style is closer to that of a tech CEO than an auto industry leader, which he sees as particularly important in Ford's situation. Ford's competitors are no longer limited to other auto manufacturers and now include Silicon Valley. Hackett thinks Ford's best shot is to start thinking like a tech start-up, saying, "Corporations tend to reward action over thinking ... But the truth is ... you'll find the companies that didn't do the deep thinking and acted quickly have to redo things."[150]

Hackett acknowledges that it has been difficult for his executive team to adjust to him and his penchant for design thinking, but he believes they are starting to see the method to his madness.[151] One member of his team said recently that they believe "People will look back in a few years and say, 'I understand now.'"[152]

APPLY THE 3-STEP PROBLEM-SOLVING APPROACH TO OB

STEP 1: Define the problem.

A. Look first at the Outcomes box of the Organizing Framework in Figure 14.8 to help identify the important problem(s) in this case. Remember that a problem is a gap between a desired and a current state. State your problem as a gap, and be sure to consider problems at all three levels. If more than one desired outcome is not being accomplished, decide which one is most important and focus on it for steps 2 and 3.

B. Cases have protagonists (key players), and problems are generally viewed from a particular protagonist's perspective. Identify the perspective from which you're defining the problem.

STEP 2: Identify causes of the problem by using material from this chapter, summarized in the Organizing Framework shown in Figure 14.8. Causes will appear in either the Inputs box or the Processes box.

A. Start by looking at Figure 14.8 to identify which person factors, if any, are most likely causes to the defined problem. For each cause, ask yourself, *Why is this a cause of the problem?* Asking why multiple times is more likely to lead you to root causes of the problem.

B. Follow the same process for the situation factors.

C. Now consider the Processes box shown in Figure 14.8. Consider concepts listed at all three levels. For any concept that might be a cause, ask yourself, *Why is this a cause?* Again, do this for several iterations to arrive at root causes.

D. To check the accuracy or appropriateness of the causes, map them onto the defined problem.

STEP 3: Make your recommendations for solving the problem. Consider whether you want to resolve it, solve it, or dissolve it (see Section 1.5). Which recommendation is desirable and feasible?

A. Given the causes identified in Step 2, what are your best recommendations? Use the content in Chapter 14 or one of the earlier chapters to propose a solution.

B. You may find potential solutions in the OB in Action boxes and Applying OB boxes within this chapter. These features provide insights into what other individuals or companies are doing in relationship to the topic at hand.

C. Create an action plan for implementing your recommendations.

LEGAL/ETHICAL CHALLENGE

Should the Citadel Change Its Socialization Practices?

The Citadel—The Military College of South Carolina—was founded in 1842. It has a student body of about 2,300 undergraduates (2,121 males and 171 females) and about 1,000 graduate students. The college's vision is "achieving excellence in the education and development of principled leaders." Its "primary purpose has been to educate undergraduates as members of the South Carolina Corps of Cadets and to prepare them for post-graduate positions of leadership through academic programs of recognized excellence supported by the best features of a military environment. The cadet lifestyle provides a structured environment that supports growth and development of each student's intellect, discipline, physical fitness, and moral and ethical values."[153]

In socializing new students, the Citadel uses the divestiture approach reviewed in Table 14.2. In this method, organizations attempt to strip away a newcomer's existing sense of self and reorient it into one that conforms to the institution's image. College President Lt. General John Rosa said, "The cadet system is based on common uniform and standardization of cadets in appearance, actions, and privileges is essential to the military system."[154]

A newly admitted female student requested to wear a traditional Muslim headscarf, called a hijab. President Rosa said the school respects students' religious views, but could not accommodate a request that would disrupt the school's core principles. "Uniformity is the cornerstone of this four-year leader development model," said Rosa. The school does make accommodations for prayer and dietary needs.[155]

The student's parents considered legal action because the Citadel is a public university. She ultimately chose to pursue naval officer training at Norwich University after the school honored her request to wear the hijab with her uniform. Norwich President Richard Schneider said in a statement to the higher education community, "As educators of future leaders, it is our duty to matriculate a diverse student body that reflects our society . . . Norwich prepares traditional students and the young men and women of our corps of cadets to welcome and respect diversity and to be inclusive of all people."[156]

Solving the Dilemma

Assuming you were the president of the Citadel, what would you do?

1. The college has the right to determine its own mission, culture, and socialization techniques. I would deny the request because such action is consistent with the Citadel's mission, culture, and method of socialization.

2. The college is a public institution and it needs to be more open-minded when it comes to supporting diversity. I would accommodate the woman based on religious considerations.

3. I would deny the request because the Citadel is a military school. The prospective student knew this coming in, and she should not have applied if she could not abide by the dress code for religious reasons.

4. Invent other options.

Ferenc Szelepcseny/Shutterstock

After reading this chapter, you should be able to:

LO 15-1   Describe the basics of organizational effectiveness.

LO 15-2   Describe the characteristics of an organization.

LO 15-3   Describe the seven types of organizational structure.

LO 15-4   Explain the relationship between contingency design and internal alignment.

LO 15-5   Describe the importance of innovation in any organization.

LO 15-6   Explain how to assess an organization's effectiveness.

LO 15-7   Describe the implications of organizational design, effectiveness, and innovation for you and managers.

The Organizing Framework shown in Figure 15.1 summarizes what you will learn in this chapter. The influences on key processes at the individual, group, and organizational levels are three person factors (attitudes about freelancing, goal orientation and P–O fit) and six situation factors (organizational structure, organizational culture, organizational climate, organizational vision and values, contingency factors, and office design). The greater number of situation rather than person factors impacting processes reveals that situation factors play a more important role in explaining the OB outcomes discussed in this chapter. However, OB processes affect outcomes at all three levels.

FIGURE 15.1 Organizing Framework for Understanding and Applying OB

INPUTS	PROCESSES	OUTCOMES
Person Factors • Attitudes about freelancing • Goal orientation • P-O fit **Situation Factors** • Organizational structure • Organizational culture • Organizational climate • Organizational vision and values • Contingency factors • Physical environment	**Individual Level** • Decision making **Group/Team Level** • Postmortems of failure • Decision making • Communication **Organizational Level** • Organizational learning • Human resource policies, practices, and procedures • Communication • Balanced scorecard • Strategy maps • Innovation system	**Individual Level** • Job satisfaction • Performance • Creativity **Group/Team Level** • Group/team performance • Innovation **Organizational Level** • Accounting/financial performance • Innovation

These two photos are great representations of how organizational design and innovation have changed over the years. The photo of workers on the left depicts a typical department in the early 1900s. Note the linear set of desks and the seriousness with which people are working. If you look toward the left edge of this photo you will see managers in the aisle watching over the workers. Organizations tended to be structured more hierarchically and relied on more managerial oversight. In contrast, modern day offices tend to be more open, which encourages more spontaneous interactions among coworkers. Research shows that creativity and innovation are enhanced by spontaneous interactions.

SOURCE: (Left): Library of Congress Prints & Photographs Division [LC-DIG-hec-29780]; (right): Robert Daly/Caia Image/Getty Images

Winning at Work

Working Virtually Takes Special Preparations

A recent report by careers website Flexjobs reveals that 3.9 million U.S. workers—nearly 3 percent of the workforce, including freelancers—now work from home at least two or three days a week. That's a 115 percent increase from 2005, and the number is expected to keep growing, as companies large and small both hire more freelancers and extend more flexible work arrangements to a larger pool of their in-house employees.[1] Some estimates suggest that as much as a third to half the U.S. workforce could be working remotely in just the next few years.[2] If you haven't already had the experience of working from home, your odds of doing so soon are increasing all the time.

Why Is It Hard to Work Virtually?

Although you can work virtually from almost anywhere, most virtual work is done at home. Three primary issues make this challenging. The first is the need for personal contact and social interaction. Many of us enjoy the social contact and camaraderie that comes with working in an office. Second, many people have difficulty creating boundaries between their work and home life. Finally, it takes discipline to work from home. There are no managers or colleagues around to prompt you to get things done.

Tips for Working Virtually

1. **Separate work life from home life.** You need dedicated space to work, free of clutter and distractions (like the TV). It should feel like an office, be well lit, and allow for privacy. One expert suggested that you "establish 'do not disturb' guidelines, work hours, break times, and a policy on handling personal matters . . . no doing dishes or laundry or taking out the trash during work hours . . . treat your home office as if it were a 'real' office located somewhere else."[3]

2. **Set your work hours.** Too much flexibility can lead to distractions and wasted time. Commit to specific hours just as if you were going to an office. Otherwise you may find yourself putting off your work or working around the clock to make up for it.

3. **Establish and maintain a morning routine.** You want your morning routine to put you into a productive mind-set. Business writer Shannon Cyr recommends that virtual workers should "take a shower, get dressed, brush your teeth, make the bed, exercise, make coffee, eat breakfast, or meditate. Regardless of what you do to start your day, the trick is to remain consistent in your routine so you give your brain a signal it's time to start the workday."[4]

4. **Set expectations with family and friends.** Talk to family and friends about your need to minimize distractions while working from home. You need to be left alone. It must be clear that working from home doesn't mean you are available to answer personal questions any more than if you worked at an office. Interruptions should be allowed for important issues.

5. **Establish goals and to-do lists.** A list of things you need to get done will help you focus on the work and avoid distractions or the tendency to procrastinate. Your author, Angelo Kinicki, works virtually and starts every day with a prioritized list of things to accomplish.

6. **Communicate with people in your professional network.** Out of sight, out of mind. Proactive communication with your network is essential if you are working virtually. This obviously includes your boss and coworkers, but also customers, vendors, and personal contacts. We recommend that you make an effort to lunch with work colleagues and others in your network.

7. **Get the desired level of human interaction.** Schedule time to meet face-to-face with coworkers and friends. You will have to make a special effort because you are the one away from the office.

8. **Know yourself before saying yes.** Working virtually is not for everyone. It takes self-motivation, flexibility, emotional intelligence, and sensitivity to what others need.[5] If you don't have these skills, it may be better to say no to telecommuting.

What's Ahead in This Chapter

This second chapter on macro OB highlights the way organizational structure and design affect organizational-level outcomes. We begin by exploring the basic foundation of an organization and then review seven basic ways organizations are structured. Next, we review the contingency approach to organizational design and explore innovation and the ways in which you can foster it. We conclude by discussing the four basic effectiveness criteria used by organizations.

15.1 UNDERSTANDING ORGANIZATIONAL BEHAVIOR

THE BIGGER PICTURE

Organizations have common characteristics. Understanding how these characteristics dynamically interact will help you contribute to organizational success. It will also assist you in finding an employer whose structure and culture fit with your values and needs. We begin this chapter by providing an overview of the basics of organizational effectiveness.

Organizational behavior scholars attempt to understand why organizations do what they do by treating organizations like individual entities. They isolate organizational characteristics or features such as culture, climate, and structure and determine how they dynamically work together to affect organizational performance or effectiveness.

LO 15-1

Describe the basics of organizational effectiveness.

This chapter provides an overview regarding the impact of two organizational characteristics—organizational structure and innovation—on organizational effectiveness. This awareness is fundamental to navigating your way through organizational life and to understanding how and why managers implement organizational change. To guide our journey into organizational effectiveness, consider that all organizations have three things in common.

First, all organizations have a form or structure that acts like a fingerprint. An organization's structure enables us to understand who reports to whom and how information is expected to flow across organizational levels. For example, the federal government in the U.S. is structured around many hierarchical levels, which can cause slow decision making and duplication of efforts. This structure is one reason why the federal government has a fingerprint of being sluggish and bureaucratic. In contrast, W.L. Gore, one of the 200 largest privately held firms in the U.S., has a very different organizational fingerprint. It is known as an innovative and nimble firm that uses a flatter structure to create the products it sells to the medical, pharmaceutical and biology, oil and gas, automotive, aerospace and semiconductor industries.

Second, all organizations share the desire to be effective. For many firms this amounts to making money and satisfying employees, customers, and shareholders. For others, such as nonprofit firms like the Red Cross or United Way, their goals include feeding and housing the homeless and others in need. The point is that all organizations desire to be effective in one way or another. Finally, all organizations generally find that innovation is needed to remain in business. Innovation is a key driver of long-term organizational performance.

Figure 15.2 provides a broad illustration of the basic process underlying organizational effectiveness. It primarily highlights the role of organizational structure and innovation. Starting at the far right of the diagram is the outcome of organizational effectiveness. You will learn that a tool called the *Balanced Scorecard* is a good method for understanding the criteria managers use to define organizational success. You will also learn that organizational effectiveness is fundamentally driven by the way managers design

FIGURE 15.2   The Basics of Organizational Effectiveness

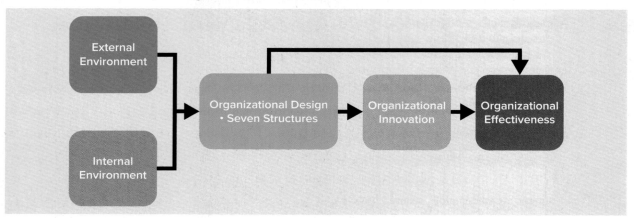

an organization. Organizational design represents an organization's fingerprint or structure and is generally built around one of seven different structures. Choosing the best structure entails considering how an organization's external and internal environments influence an organization's mission, vision, and goals. You will learn that this is called *contingency design.* Figure 15.2 further shows that organizational design influences organizational innovation and ultimately organizational effectiveness.

15.2 THE FOUNDATION OF AN ORGANIZATION

THE BIGGER PICTURE

Whether they are for-profit, nonprofit, or mutual benefit, organizations possess some common characteristics. The better you understand these foundations, the better prepared you will be to perform at any level of the organization. You'll explore these commonalities and more, such as the difference between closed and open systems and the way organizations can become learning organizations. As a necessary springboard for this chapter, we formally define the term *organization,* clarify the meaning of organization charts, and explore two open-system perspectives of organizations.

What Is an Organization?

From a design perspective, an *organization* is "a system of consciously coordinated activities or forces of two or more persons."[6] Earlier in this book, the everyday understanding of organization was adequate for our discussions. But this formal definition is especially helpful now because the phrase "consciously coordinated" underscores the importance of organizational design.

Embodied in the *conscious coordination* aspect of this definition are four common denominators of all organizations: coordination of effort, aligned goals, division of labor, and a hierarchy of authority.[7]

- **Coordination of effort** is achieved through formulation and enforcement of policies, rules, and regulations.
- **Aligned goals** start with the development of a companywide strategic plan. These strategic goals are then cascaded down through the organization so employees are aligned in their pursuit of common goals.
- **Division of labor** occurs when the common goals are pursued by individuals performing separate but related tasks.
- **Hierarchy of authority,** also called the chain of command, is a control mechanism dedicated to making sure the right people do the right things at the right time. Historically, managers have maintained the integrity of the hierarchy of authority by adhering to the unity of command principle. **The unity of command principle specifies that each employee should report to only one manager.** Otherwise, the argument goes, inefficiency would prevail because of conflicting orders and lack of personal accountability. As you will learn in this chapter, this philosophy of managing and structuring organizations has been replaced by more dynamic approaches.[8]

When operating in concert, the four foundational factors—coordination of effort, aligned goals, division of labor, and a hierarchy of authority—enable an organization to come to life and function.

LO 15-2

Describe the characteristics of an organization.

Organization Charts

An organization chart is a graphic representation of formal authority and division of labor relationships. Within each box is the name and title of a current position holder. Informally, we can think of an *organization chart* as a family tree. To organization theorists, however, organization charts reveal much more. The partial organization chart in Figure 15.3 shows four basic dimensions of organizational structure: (1) hierarchy of authority (who reports to whom), (2) division of labor, (3) spans of control, and (4) line and staff positions.

Hierarchy of Authority   As Figure 15.3 illustrates, an organization has an unmistakable structure or chain of command. Working from bottom to top, the 10 directors report to the two executive directors who report to the president who reports to the chief executive officer. Ultimately, the chief executive officer answers to the hospital's board of directors. The chart in Figure 15.3 shows strict unity of command up and down the line. A formal hierarchy of authority also delineates the official communication network and speaks volumes about compensation. Research shows that the difference in pay between successive layers tends to increase over time.[9]

Division of Labor   Our sample organization chart indicates extensive division of labor. Immediately below the hospital's president, one executive director is responsible for general administration, while another is responsible for medical affairs. Each of these two specialties is further subdivided, as indicated by the next layer of positions. At each successively lower level in the organization, jobs become more specialized.

FIGURE 15.3   Sample Organization Chart for a Hospital (Executive and Director Levels Only)

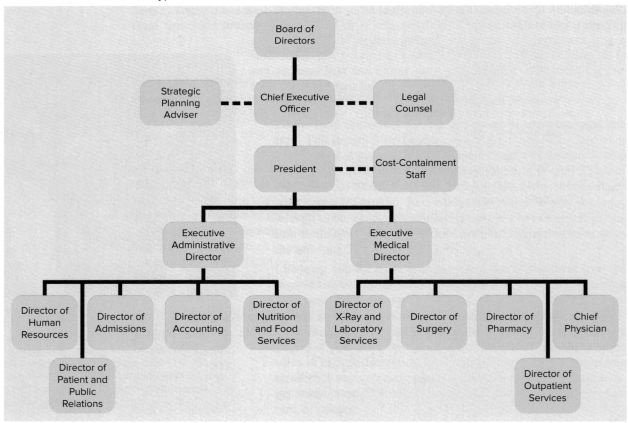

Spans of Control *Span of control* **describes the number of people reporting directly to a given manager.** Spans of control can range from narrow to wide. For example, the president in Figure 15.3 has a narrow span of control of two. (Staff assistants usually are not included in a manager's span of control.) Narrow spans of control tend to create "taller" or more hierarchical organizations. In contrast, a wide span of control leads to a "flat" organization. The executive administrative director in Figure 15.3 has a wider span of control of five. Historically, spans of 7 to 10 people were considered best. More recently, however, corporate restructuring and improved communication technologies have increased the typical span of control.[10]

Although there is no consensus regarding the optimal span of control, managers should consider four factors when establishing spans of control: organizational size, managers' skill level, organizational culture, and managerial responsibilities. Let's consider each of these factors.[11]

1. **Organizational size.** Larger organizations tend to have narrower spans of control and more organizational layers, whereas smaller ones have a wider span of control. Costs tend to be higher in organizations with narrow spans due to the increased expense of having more managers. Communication also tends to be slower in narrow spans because information must travel throughout multiple organizational layers.

2. **Skill level.** Complex tasks require more managerial input, thereby suggesting a narrow span of control. Conversely, routine tasks do not require much supervision, leading to the use of a wider span of control.

3. **Organizational culture.** Narrow spans of control are more likely in companies with a hierarchical culture because they focus on internal integration and stability and control—recall Figure 14.4. In contrast, wider spans of control are more likely to be found in companies that desire flexibility and discretion, cultures characterized as clan or adhocracy. Wider spans also complement cultures that desire greater worker autonomy and participation.

4. **Managerial responsibilities.** The most senior-level executives tend to have narrower spans of control than middle managers because their responsibilities are broader in scope and more complex. It's important to consider the breadth of a person's responsibilities when deciding his or her span of control.

Line and Staff Positions The organization chart in Figure 15.3 also distinguishes between line and staff positions. Line managers such as the president, the two executive directors, and the various directors occupy formal decision-making positions within the chain of command. Line positions generally are connected by solid lines on organization charts. Dotted lines indicate staff relationships. *Staff employees* **do background research and provide technical advice and recommendations to their line managers.** *Line managers* **generally have the authority to make decisions for their units.** For example, the cost-containment specialists in the sample organization chart merely advise the president on relevant matters. Apart from supervising the work of their own staff assistants, they have no line authority over other organizational members. Modern trends such as cross-functional teams and matrix structures, discussed later in this chapter, are blurring the distinction between line and staff.

An Open-System Perspective of Organizations

To better understand how organizational models have evolved over the years, we need to know the difference between closed and open systems. A *closed system* **is a self-sufficient entity.** It is "closed" to the surrounding environment. In contrast, an *open system* **depends on constant interaction with the environment for survival.** The distinction between closed and open systems is a matter of degree. Because every worldly system is partly closed and partly open, the key question is: How great a role does the environment play in the functioning of the system? For instance, a battery-powered clock is a relatively closed system. Once the battery has been inserted, the clock performs its

Whole Foods Market is putting increased pressure on farms like this to produce products that are Responsibly Grown. This organic farm of green and red lettuce would need to meet Whole Foods standards if it wants to sell produce to the company. Do you think it is fair for chains like Whole Foods to create additional standards that increase a farmer's costs?

Ingram Publishing

time-keeping function hour after hour until the battery goes dead. The human body, on the other hand, is a highly open system because it requires a constant supply of life-sustaining oxygen from the environment. Nutrients and water also are imported from the environment. Open systems are capable of self-correction, adaptation, and growth, thanks to feedback from the environment.

Whole Foods Market's approach to the growing and selling of organic food is good example of an open system. John Mackey, cofounder and CEO of Whole Foods Market, believes this industry can benefit from systems thinking. "Organic has grown stale. Its guidelines prohibit the use of synthetic fertilizers and pesticides, which is a good thing," he says. But they don't address all the burgeoning issues—from excessive water usage to the treatment of migrant laborers—facing agriculture today. And once farmers are certified as organic, Mackey believes they have little incentive to improve their practices. Whole Foods thus decided to take a more open-systems approach by implementing a new system called Responsibly Grown. The program measures factors such as energy conservation, waste reduction, and farm-worker welfare. As you might imagine, many local organic growers are angry about these changes, claiming they will increase their costs. Whole Foods has made some small adjustments to the program based on this feedback, but Mackey is staying with it. He firmly believes an open-systems approach is better for consumers and the planet. In addition, with Amazon's recent purchase of Whole Foods, it remains to be see what impact the acquisition will have on Mackey's strong commitment to responsible growing and sustainability practices.[12]

Historically, management theorists downplayed the environment because they used closed-system thinking to characterize organizations as either well-oiled machines or highly disciplined military units. They believed rigorous planning and control would eliminate environmental uncertainty. But that approach proved unrealistic. Drawing on the field of general systems theory that emerged during the 1950s, organization theorists suggested a more dynamic model for organizations.[13] The resulting open-system model likened organizations to the human body. Accordingly, the model in Figure 15.4 reveals the organization to be a living organism that transforms inputs into various outputs. (Notice the similarity to the Input, Process, and Outcome features of the Organizing Framework for Understanding and Applying OB.) The outer boundary of the organization is permeable. People, information, capital, and goods and services move back and forth across this boundary.

Moreover, each of the five organizational subsystems—goals and values, technical, psychosocial, structural, and managerial—is dependent on the others. Feedback about such things as sales and customer satisfaction enables the organization to self-adjust and survive despite uncertainty and change. In effect, the organization is alive.

Learning Organizations

In recent years, organizational theorists have extended the open-system model by adding a "brain" to the "living body." Organizations are said to have humanlike cognitive functions, such as the abilities to perceive and interpret, solve problems, store information,

FIGURE 15.4 The Organization as an Open System

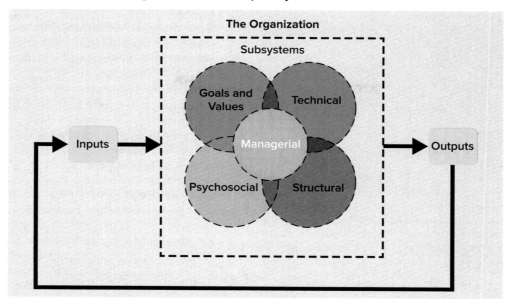

SOURCE: Kast, Fremont E., and James E. Rosenzweig. *Organization and Management: A System and Contingency Approach,* 4th ed. New York: McGraw-Hill, 1986.

and learn from experience. This realization has led to a stream of research that examines the process by which organizations learn. Peter Senge, a professor at the Massachusetts Institute of Technology, popularized the term *learning organization* in his best-selling book *The Fifth Discipline.* He described a learning organization as "a group of people working together to collectively enhance their capacities to create results that they truly care about."[14] A practical interpretation of these ideas results in the following definition. A *learning organization* **proactively creates, acquires, and transfers knowledge and changes its behavior on the basis of new knowledge and insights.**[15]

We want to understand how organizations learn because organizational learning is positively associated with organizational performance and innovation, a topic we discuss later in this chapter.[16] Researchers have shown that organizations learn by using five independent subprocesses (see Figure 15.5): information acquisition, information distribution, information interpretation, knowledge integration, and organizational memory.[17] Let us consider how these processes work.

FIGURE 15.5 The Process of Organizational Learning

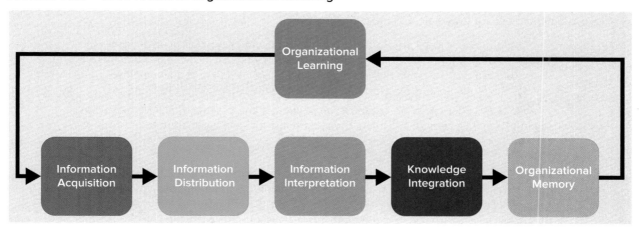

This unit of firefighters has to rely on organizational learning to effectively fight fires. It has to work as a team while adjusting to factors such as weather, temperature, and breadth of the fire. Fire units also are known for having postmortems after a fire to discuss the lessons learned.

Eric Schultz/The Huntsville Times/AP Images

Step 1: Information Acquisition

Information acquisition, also known as *scanning,* is "the process through which an organization obtains information from internal and external sources."[18] Because this is the first step of learning, organizations should cast a wide net in their acquisition of information. For example, discussions about past success and failure, called postmortems, are critical sources of information.

Step 2: Information Distribution

Information distribution consists of the processes or systems that people, groups, or organizational units use to share information among themselves. For example, Jill Nelson, the founder of Ruby, a virtual receptionist service in Oregon, asks employees to discuss their mistakes at weekly staff meetings. Nelson commented, "We discuss the mistakes and what the employees learned from them. The sharing of this information sends the message that it's OK to make a low-stakes mistake—as long as you learn from it and share your lesson with others."[19]

Step 3: Information Interpretation
This step is all about making sense of the information organizations have acquired and distributed. In this process people are affected by the perceptual biases discussed in Chapter 4 and the decision-making biases reviewed in Chapter 11.

Step 4: Knowledge Integration
Knowledge integration occurs when information is shared and accumulated across different parts of an organization. This provides more and better information for making decisions. This step can be accomplished by having postmortems in which different people or groups present their ideas about an opportunity or problem. The point is to seek consensus about what the learned information means.

Step 5: Organizational Memory
Learning will not last unless the organization finds a method to save it. Knowledge needs to be put into some type of repository or organizational memory if it is to be used in the future. Organizational memory is not an object. According to a team of OB experts, it is the combined processes of "encoding, storing, and retrieving the lessons learned from an organization's history, despite the turnover of personnel."[20]

What Can Be Done to Improve Organizational Learning? We have three recommendations for improving organizational learning.

1. Improve on the five steps just discussed. You might begin by using a survey to assess the extent to which your organization is already following these steps. Self-Assessment 15.1 was created so that you could make this assessment on a current or former employer. You can use the results to target organizational changes aimed at improving learning.

2. Realize that leader behavior, organizational climate, and organizational culture drive organizational learning.[21] If leaders do not support a vision and culture that promote the value of learning, it won't happen.

   EXAMPLE U.S. Army leaders understand this conclusion. In the 1990s, the Army coined the acronym VUCA (volatile, uncertain, complex, and ambiguous) to describe the post–Cold War operational environment it faced. To respond to this new reality, the Army moved from a threat-based force to a capability-based force, which required the organization to leverage technology, align organizational structures, and establish a learning organization. Learning strategies included war game simulations; new concepts in tactical combat training; and a progressive system of professional education to prepare leaders for the organizational change.[22]

3. We can all be role models of learning from failure. **Failure occurs when an activity fails to deliver its expected results or outcomes.** Unfortunately, failure or mistakes are generally feared and penalized, which creates an environment of risk aversion. Bill Gates, co-founder of Microsoft, concludes, "It's fine to celebrate success, but it's more important to heed the lessons of failure. How a company deals with mistakes suggests how well it will bring out the best ideas and talents of its people, and how effectively it will respond to change."[23]

SELF-ASSESSMENT 15.1

Are You Working for a Learning Organization?

Please be prepared to answer these questions if your instructor has assigned Self-Assessment 15.1 in Connect.

1. To what extent is the company a learning organization? Are you surprised by the results?

2. Identify the three items receiving the lowest ratings. Propose solutions for improving on these three areas.

Suggestions in the Applying OB box guide the way to learning from failure.

Applying OB

Learning from Failure

1. **Conduct postmortems.** Demonstrate leadership and maturity by owning your mistake, even if it's hard. Then start at the beginning and consider everything that occurred during the project, reflecting on why it failed or a goal was missed. You may need to collect data, and you can also use the Organizing Framework to brainstorm potential causes of the failure. Reflect on what you learned regarding each of these factors:
   a. Customers.
   b. The organization's vision, strategy, culture, climate, and internal processes.
   c. Yourself and those who worked on the project.
   d. Group dynamics.
   e. Organizational leadership and politics.[24]
2. **Share the learning with others.** The real value of failure comes from sharing our experiences with others.[25] This is a form of "sharing best practices" in which knowledge about what led to failure identifies the best practice. Following this suggestion also destigmatizes failure and can reduce our fear of it.[26] This lesson is valuable because self-preservation and fear of failure are big obstacles to innovation.[27]
3. **Consider your goal orientation.** In Chapter 6 we defined two goal orientations that influence the way we work and our willingness to learn from failure. A *performance goal orientation* is aimed at demonstrating competence or avoiding perceptions of incompetence. People with this orientation are less likely to take the risks needed for innovation. In contrast, a *learning or mastery orientation* focuses on learning and growing. For those with this orientation, failure is just another way to learn and develop. Employees should adopt more of a learning goal orientation if they want to increase their learning from failure.[28]

15.3 ORGANIZATIONAL DESIGN

THE BIGGER PICTURE

An organization's design or structure is like a fingerprint. It uniquely identifies an organization and provides information about how things get done. You will learn about seven fundamental types of organizational structures, and the implications for you at any level of the organization.

LO 15-3

Describe the seven types of organizational structure.

Organizational design sets "the structures of accountability and responsibility used to develop and implement strategies, and the human resource practices and information and business processes that activate those structures."[29] The general idea behind the study of organizational design is that organizations are more effective or successful when their structure supports the execution of corporate strategies. Keep in mind that there is no one best structure for a company. Companies tend to change structure in response to changes in the marketplace or in their strategic goals. Consider the case of McDonald's Corporation.

EXAMPLE McDonald's recently changed its corporate structure, eliminating U.S. regional offices and implementing a "field office" approach, which resulted in layoffs at the company's corporate level. Chris Kempczinski, McDonald's USA President, says the new structure "is a significant shift in how we will incentivize our team, resource our system, and even how we operate here at home office to better support our franchisees and restaurants." The restructuring is expected to contribute to the company's plan to cut $500 million in general and administrative costs by the end of 2019.[30]

Our consulting experience tells us that too many companies attempt structural changes to solve performance problems. For example, Sony restructured nine times between 1994 and 2009.[31] A McKinsey & Co. survey of 1,890 executives supports a similar conclusion; only 8 percent experienced positive results after making structural changes. This finding is also consistent with a study of 57 reorganizations by consulting firm Bain & Co., which demonstrated that most reorgs had no effect, and some led to *lower* organizational performance.[32]

This section and the next provide information about how managers can increase their chances of choosing an effective organizational design. The same information will allow you to better understand which structure your employer adopts—and how you can better function and perform within that structure.

We begin by reviewing three broad categories of organizational structure and then turn to the seven fundamental types of designs found in the workplace today. The following section then identifies when these structures may be most effective.[33]

Three Categories

Our changing world means businesses develop new forms of organization to respond to emerging business opportunities. Management professor Richard L. Daft defined three eras that each contributed its own broad category of organization and focus (see Table 15.1).

TABLE 15.1   Categories and Eras of Organizational Design

CATEGORY	ERA	FOCUS	TYPE
1. Traditional	Mid-1800s through 1970s	Self-contained within organization's boundaries	• Functional • Divisional • Matrix
2. Horizontal	1980s	Team- and process-oriented	• Horizontal
3. Open	Since mid-1990s	Opened beyond organization's boundaries	• Hollow • Modular • Virtual

SOURCE: N. Anand and R. L. Daft, "What Is the Right Organizational Design?" *Organizational Dynamics*, June 2007, 329–344.

Traditional Design   Organizations defined by a traditional approach tend to have functional, divisional, and/or matrix structures. Each of these structures relies on a vertical hierarchy and attempts to define clear departmental boundaries and reporting relationships.

> **Historical Forces:** Industrialization, mass production, and related capitalization. Mid-1800s through 1970s.

> **Rationale:** With industrialization and mass production, organizations were able to achieve great economies of scale by specializing the application of labor to specific and standardized functions.

Horizontal Design   Organizations defined by a horizontal approach work hard to flatten hierarchy and organize people around specific segments of the work flow. A horizontal structure, sometimes called a team or process structure, relies on a horizontal work flow and attempts to dissolve departmental boundaries and reporting relationships as much as possible.

> **Historical Forces:** Increased complexity and increasingly rapid development cycles for new products. 1980s.

> **Rationale:** The traditional approach of dividing up work according to functions, products, and customers frustrates managers who want to focus on bringing people together, without internal boundaries keeping them apart. If you want people to share knowledge, collaborate, and continually improve the way things are done, a horizontal design is a good option.

Open Design   Organizations defined by an open approach tend to have hollow, modular, or virtual structures. Each of these structures relies on leveraging technology and structural flexibility to maximize potential value through outsourcing and external collaboration.

> **Historical Forces:** Rapid technological improvements (including the Internet and mobile phones) and the rise of emerging economies (China and India) with pools of skilled workers willing to work for less than those in developed economies. Since mid-1990s.

> **Rationale:** Open designs help organizations respond more rapidly to customer and market changes. They also potentially reduce costs and increase innovation.

The rationale of open systems led Jack Welch, former CEO of GE, to coin the term *boundaryless organization.* **A *boundaryless organization* is one in which "management has largely succeeded in breaking down barriers between internal levels, job functions, and departments, as well as reducing external barriers between the association [organization] and those with whom it does business."**[34] This type of structure is fluid and flexible and relies on telecommuting between geographically dispersed people using various technological tools such as texting, e-mail, social media, and other virtual methods of communication.[35] It is most appropriate for businesses in fast-changing industries or environments.

All the structural forms outlined in Table 15.1 are in use today. Let's consider each design and an illustrative example.

Seven Types of Organizational Structures

The following seven types of organizational structure cover almost all organizations. We provide historical background, with examples and schematic diagrams for each.

Functional Structure **A *functional structure* groups people according to the business functions they perform, for example, manufacturing, marketing, and finance.** A manager is responsible for the performance of each of these functions, and employees tend to identify strongly with their particular function, such as sales or engineering.

> **EXAMPLE** The organization chart previously shown in Figure 15.3 illustrates a functional structure. Responsibility at this hospital is first divided into administrative and medical functions, and within each category, directors are responsible for each of the functions. This arrangement puts together people who are experts in the same or similar activities. As a small company grows and hires more production workers, salespeople, and accounting staff, it typically groups them with a supervisor who understands their function.

Some organizations have concluded that using a functional structure divides people too much, ultimately creating silos within the organization. This detracts from the extent to which employees collaborate and share best practices across functions.

FUNCTIONAL STRUCTURE
Work is organized into separate vertical functions, such as finance, sales, production, and human resources.

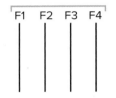

Divisional Structure **In a *divisional structure,* employees are segregated into organization groups based on industries, products or services, customers or clients, or geographic regions.** The divisional structure is sometimes called a product structure or profit center approach.

> **EXAMPLE** Consumer-products giant Procter & Gamble recently reorganized its division structure from 10 to 6 divisional units: Beauty; Baby and Feminine Care; Fabric and Home Care; Family Care and New Ventures; Grooming; and Health Care. The company's CEO said the reorganization will help P&G increase its agility in dealing with ongoing global volatility and competitive disruption.[36]

As with functional structures, some organizations have concluded that using a divisional structure can also create silos within the organization.

DIVISIONAL STRUCTURE
Work is organized into separate vertical divisions, which may focus on products or services, customers or clients, or even geography.

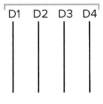

Matrix Structure Organizations use matrix structures when they need stronger horizontal alignment or cooperation in order to meet their goals. **A *matrix structure* combines a vertical structure with an equally strong horizontal overlay.** Functional and divisional chains of command form a grid with two command structures, one shown vertically by function and the other shown horizontally by product line, brand, customer group, or geographic region.

EXAMPLE Starbucks is highly committed to the matrix structure. The design allows the company's three product-based divisions (coffee and related products, baked goods, and merchandise) to intersect with functional groups (such as HR, finance, and marketing) and three global geographic divisions (Americas; China and Asia-Pacific; and Europe, Middle East, and Africa). In the U.S., Starbucks further divides its geographic divisions into four regional sectors. The matrix structure allows Starbucks to improve the customer experience and its overall financial performance.[37]

A matrix structure can also provide a reasonable counterbalance among important stakeholders, but applying it to an organization is not easy. Matrix organizations can be complex and confusing without an extra layer of collaboration and integration to effectively implement the structure. Jay Galbraith, an expert on the subject, noted that matrix structures frequently fail because management fails to create complementary and reinforcing changes to the organization's IT systems, human resource procedures (performance appraisals, rewards, selection criteria), planning and budgeting processes, organizational culture, internal processes, and so on. He concluded, "Organization structures do not fail; managements fail at implementation."[38] This type of structure is increasingly being used by companies expanding into international markets.[39]

MATRIX STRUCTURE
The matrix can be used with a variety of vertical and horizontal elements. Shown here are four different functions (F1, F2, and so on) interlinked to four product lines (P1, P2).

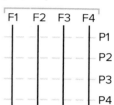

Horizontal Structure In a *horizontal structure,* teams or **work groups, either temporary or permanent, are created to improve collaboration and work on common projects.**

The horizontal approach to organizational design tends to focus on work processes. A process consists of every task and responsibility needed to meet a customer need, such as developing a new product or filling a customer order. Completing a process requires input from people in different functions, typically organized into a cross-functional team (described in Chapter 8). W.L. Gore & Associates is a good example of a company that has successfully implemented this structure (see the OB in Action box).

HORIZONTAL STRUCTURE
Several flexible teams— T1–T4—organize around the horizontal work flow or processes. Some vertical functions remain, but they are minimized.

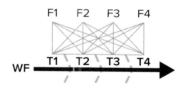

OB in Action

W.L. Gore & Associates Operates with a Horizontal Design

W.L. Gore is a technologically driven company that focuses on product innovation. It develops and manufactures products that provide highly reliable performance in varied environments ranging from the surface of Mars to the inside of the human heart. Today, Gore has more than $3 billion in annual revenue and 9,500 employees working in more than 25 countries.[40]

The company has been profitable every year since its founding in 1958, and it was ranked among *Fortune*'s 100 Best Places to Work every year from 1998 to 2017. It has also been cited as a "best workplace" in China, France, Germany, Italy, Spain, and Sweden.[41]

Culture and Values Founder Bill Gore wanted a company free of bureaucracy and a command and control style of leadership. To support this culture, the company promotes the following values:[42]

- **Belief in the individual**—employees are encouraged to trust and believe in each other.
- **Power of small teams**—a team-based structure with minimum hierarchy is used.
- **All in the same boat**—employees are part owners through a stock plan.
- **Long-term view**—investments are based on long-term payoffs.

Organizational Structure Gore's structure is consistent with its strategy and culture. It has a team-based "lattice" organization. The company website describes the structure as one with "no traditional organizational charts, no chains of command, nor predetermined channels of communication." Employees, who are called associates, are accountable to the members of their multidisciplined teams. "Teams organize around opportunities and leaders emerge," according to the corporate website.[43]

Associates are not hired for specific jobs. The corporate website indicates employees are "hired for general work areas. With the guidance of their sponsors (not bosses) and a growing understanding of opportunities and team objectives, associates commit to projects that match their skills. All of this takes place in an environment that combines freedom with cooperation and autonomy with synergy."[44]

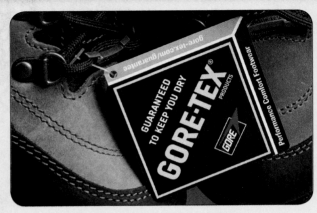

Focusing on product innovation, W.L. Gore links organizational strategy, culture, and structure.

Carolyn Jenkins/Alamy Stock Photo

Sponsors help associates adjust to this flexible work environment by providing feedback on performance and by assisting in internal networking.

YOUR THOUGHTS?

1. What type of people would like to work at Gore given its structure and culture?
2. Would this type of structure enhance or reduce organizational learning? Discuss your rationale.
3. Do you think this type of structure would work in most organizations? Explain.

The final three types of structures are all examples of open organizations. Before learning about them in more detail, find out how well suited you are for telecommuting by completing Self-Assessment 15.2. Telecommuting is a common practice in companies that use open designs.

SELF-ASSESSMENT 15.2

What Is Your Preference for Telecommuting?

Please be prepared to answer these questions if your instructor has assigned Self-Assessment 15.2 in Connect.

1. Do you prefer telecommuting or a traditional work environment?
2. What bothers you most about telecommuting?
3. How might managers assess an employee's preference for telecommuting during a job interview?

Hollow Structure   A *hollow structure,* also known as a *network structure,* is designed around a central core of key functions and outsources other functions to outside companies or individuals who can do them cheaper or faster. An athletic shoe company, for example, might decide it can excel at developing new designs, owing to its design talent and knowledge of the market. Then it might find outsourcing partners to handle other activities such as manufacturing, order taking, shipping, and managing employee benefits. The more processes that are outsourced, the more the resulting organization is "hollow"—and focused on what it does best.

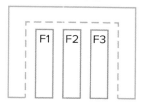

HOLLOW STRUCTURE Within the organization, a number of functions are outsourced.

EXAMPLE Herman Miller, the furniture company, goes outside the organization for design expertise. CEO Brian Walker explained the advantages: "This external network ensures that we are always taking a fresh look at problems faced by our customers without subjecting [them] to our own filters. If you have only an internal design staff, even an enormously talented one, you are inherently limited by their existing world view and experiences. Our ability to tap into a broader outside network lets us . . . get a fresh perspective on existing or emerging problems." The company also uses other organizations for manufacturing; Walker says the company is "more . . . an integrator than a manufacturer," which makes it less resistant to new product ideas because it doesn't have to change manufacturing processes itself.[45]

A hollow structure is useful when an organization is faced with strong price competition and there are enough companies to perform the required outsourced processes.

The growing number of hollow structures has increased demand for freelance workers. This has created an online industry that helps companies hire people for micro-tasks or short-term assignments (see the Problem-Solving Application).

Problem-Solving Application

Gig Workers Are a Growing Force in the Labor Market

More than 40 percent of U.S. workers, male and female, are now doing outsourced part-time, freelance, or "gig" work, according to Deloitte's 2018 Global Human Capital Trends study.[46] *Harvard Business Review* puts the current number of independent contractors in North America and Western Europe at 150 million, and many people believe that in the future nearly everyone will do at least some freelancing, from management consulting and writing to errand-running and taxi driving.[47]

Some gig workers are filling gaps between regular jobs, while others view freelancing as a job in itself and are not looking for a traditional career. These workers enjoy the autonomy and variety that contingent work can bring. In the United States almost two-thirds of them are between 18 and 44; close to half have a bachelor's or graduate degree and bring skills and experience to the table. "The vast majority are folks who easily could go get [traditional full-time] jobs somewhere," says Lori Williams, a vice president at software developer Gigster, whose 80 employees work with 1,000 freelancers. "They've chosen this lifestyle." Each new assignment can be an opportunity for a freelancer to learn new skills; gigs offering little financial or other compensation can often be turned down.[48]

Gig work has clear downsides, however. Hiring on a project basis saves hollow-structure companies money; they benefit from not having to offer freelancers costly benefits like medical insurance, retirement plans, paid vacations, or professional development. Freelancers' workflow can be uneven, and working alone requires self-discipline and can be isolating. Technology is so deeply embedded in the so-called gig economy that one observer notes, "Gig workers don't have human bosses. They work for *apps.*"[49]

Apply the 3-Step Problem-Solving Approach

Step 1: Define the problem that is leading companies to rely on the gig economy.

Step 2: Identify the causes of the problem. What OB theories or concepts explain why some people want to work as freelancers?

Step 3: Recommend steps organizations can take to motivate, monitor, and compensate freelancers.

Modular Structure A modular organization, like a hollow organization, uses outsourcing. But instead of outsourcing processes, it outsources production of parts of a product, such as components of a jet or subroutines of a software program. **In a *modular structure,* the company assembles product parts, components, or modules provided by external contractors.** The modular organization also is responsible for ensuring that the parts meet quality requirements, that they arrive in a timely fashion, and that the organization is capable of efficiently combining the parts into the final whole. This design is useful when a company can identify product modules and create design interfaces that allow it to assemble parts into a working order.

> **EXAMPLE** A good example is Boeing, in the production of its 787 Dreamliner. Instead of using a traditional aviation manufacturing process of building an aircraft from the ground up, Boeing engaged a global group of suppliers to build some of the plane's subassemblies off site and then deliver them to Boeing for final assembly. According to the company, nearly 45 major companies have been involved in building the 787's fuselage, engines, bulkhead, and other components. This approach helps keep the assembly process efficient and lowers the number of parts a company needs to keep on hand, thus reducing inventory.[50]

MODULAR STRUCTURE
The main part of the organization (M) is structured and managed to make it easy to plug in vendors for well-defined functions (F1 through F3) as parts of the business process.

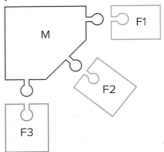

Virtual Structure The concept of virtual organizations originated in the 1990s as an outgrowth of the benefits of information technology. A **virtual structure is one whose members are geographically apart, usually working with e-mail and other forms of information technology, but that generally appears to customers as a single, unified organization with a real physical location.**

> **EXAMPLE** Scopic Software, a web and app developer, has more than 200 employees working in over 30 countries. Headquartered in the U.S., the company believes great software developers can be found in every part of the world, and talent

These employees are conducting final assembly of a Boeing 787 airplane in the Everett, Washington, plant. The company used a global network of suppliers to build some of the plane's components and then deliver them to Boeing for integration and final assembly. This is a classic example of a modular structure.
Wang Ying/Xinhua/Alamy Stock Photo

shouldn't be limited by location and time zone. According to the Careers page on its website, "Scopic's entirely virtual structure means you can work from anywhere, whether it's a café, in bed, or on the road." The company encourages flexible hours so employees can set their work schedule to accommodate their lifestyle and spend more time with family and friends. To stay connected, Scopic's team members use real-time tools like Slack and Skype to facilitate communication and software tools to track productivity.[51]

The primary benefits of virtual structures such as Scopic Software are the ability to tap into a wider talent pool, to get things done more quickly, and to reduce costs because there is less need for physical facilities and travel budgets.

Today, virtual structures are classified into two types: internal and networked.[52]

1. **Internal virtual structures.** Internal virtual structures coordinate the work of geographically dispersed employees working for one organization, such as those at Scopic Software. This structure primarily relies on the use of information technology, but it also requires managers to consider three key issues:

   - **Do I have the right people?** Not everyone is suited to work virtually, as you may have learned from taking Self-Assessment 15.2. Managers must consider the personal characteristics, needs, and values of their people who might work virtually. For example, research about effective virtual leaders revealed that constant feedback, clear communications, reliability, and trust were key competencies required to be a successful manager of virtual teams.[53]

   - **How often should people get together?** There is no clear answer to this question. Our recommendation is to use a contingency approach. More frequent contact is needed at the start of a project, and we suggest holding regular milestone meetings online.

   - **What type of technology should be used to coordinate activities?** Remote workers can stay connected with a host of technologies. The choice depends on their skills and the resources at hand.

2. **Networked virtual structures.** Networked virtual structures establish a collaborative network of independent firms or individuals to create a virtual entity. The networked individuals or companies join forces because each possesses core competencies needed for a project or product. This structure is used in the movie/entertainment industry. For example, writers, producers, actors, and studios join forces to make a movie, not as one legal entity, but rather as a collaborative network. Once again, a variety of information technologies coordinates the efforts of different members within the network.

   Now that we have reviewed all seven designs, consider Table 15.2. It lists the pros and cons for each design and suggests situations when each may be most effective.

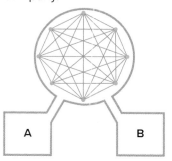

VIRTUAL STRUCTURE
One or more companies (here we show companies A and B) create or manage a wide network of virtually connected employees, represented by the dots, for a specific business process that otherwise appears as a traditional company.

TABLE 15.2 Seven Structures of Organizational Design

STRUCTURE	BEST FOR	PROS	CONS
Functional F1 F2 F3 F4	Small companies, some large government organizations and divisions of large companies.	Clear roles and responsibilities.	Coordination and communication lapses across functional silos; most companies use dotted line or other informal means to combat this potential limitation.
Divisional D1 D2 D3 D4	Large companies with separate divisions built on different technologies, geographies, or different bases of customers.	Clear roles and responsibilities. Greater product focus, accountability, and flexibility for workers in each division than in a functional structure.	Coordination and communication lapses across divisional silos; most companies use dotted line or other informal means to combat this potential limitation.
Matrix F1 F2 F3 F4 P1 P2 P3 P4	Organizations, increasingly including international ones, looking to avoid problems associated with silos by using a formal level of horizontal integration.	Lines of formal authority along two dimensions, such as functional/product or product/region, that allow organizations to work more cohesively.	Inadequate processes to ensure success. Potential for conflict when employees report to two bosses if those managers fail to coordinate.
Horizontal F1 F2 F3 F4 WF T1 T2 T3 T4	Companies needing greater efficiency or flexibility to rapidly respond to customer needs.	Rapid communication and reduction in cycle time for work done; greater flexibility; faster organizational learning; improved responsiveness to customers.	Potential conflicts between processes and nonprocess functions; neglect of nonprocess parts of the organization; reduced opportunities for functional specialization.
Hollow F1 F2 F3	Companies facing heavy price competition with pressure to cut costs; companies with options outside the organization that can perform required processes.	Lower cost of entry and overhead; access to best sources of specialization and technology; market discipline that leads to supplier competition and innovation; potential for further cost reduction and quality improvement.	Loss or decrease of in-house skills, of internal capacity to innovate, and of control over supply; costs of transitioning to hollow state; need for higher monitoring to align incentives; danger of being supplanted by suppliers.
Modular M F1 F2 F3	Organizations that can specify the nature of product modules and design interfaces to multiple vendors and join them.	Potential for cost savings, greater responsiveness, and competence beyond the organization's boundaries; ability to switch vendors for best fit and product improvement.	A high proportion of products unsuitable to chunking into modules; poorly specified interfaces; slow or poor-quality collaborators.
Virtual A B	Companies that need to explore a new market opportunity by partnering with other organizations or rapidly deploy a new potential business model.	Ability to respond nimbly to market opportunity; ability to provide product extension or one-stop-shop service; low exit costs if initial opportunity vanishes.	High level of communication necessary to avoid redundancy; low trust and coordination among widely distributed employees; failure to promote strong employee loyalty or organizational identification.

SOURCE: Anand, N., and Richard L. Daft. "What Is the Right Organizational Design?" *Organizational Dynamics* 36, no. 4 (2007): 329–344. https://doi:10.1016/j.orgdyn.2007.06.001.

15.4 CONTINGENCY DESIGN AND INTERNAL ALIGNMENT

THE BIGGER PICTURE

The previous section showed that no one structure is appropriate for all organizations. This section reviews five contingency factors to consider when choosing an organizational design. We also discuss the need to align several organizational characteristics in this process and show how you can use this knowledge to enhance your personal and career outcomes.

There is no one best form of structure for an organization. The choice of structure is instead based on considering a host of contingency factors and internal organizational characteristics. This section helps show how this is done by discussing the concept of contingency organization design. According to the **contingency approach to organization design, organizations tend to be more effective when they are structured to fit the demands of the situation, and when the structure is aligned with internal activities and actions of the organization.**[54] The demands of the situation consist of five contingency factors.

LO 15-4

Explain the relationship between contingency design and internal alignment.

Contingency Factors

Experts suggest that managers should consider five key contingency factors when making decisions about organization design: strategy and goals, market uncertainty, decision-making processes, technology, and size.[55]

Strategy and Goals   An organization's strategy is the cornerstone of its decision about the most appropriate design. Because setting a corporate strategy requires an organization to decide how it will compete given both internal and external considerations, organizational design must be developed in tandem with establishing strategy. For example, if a company has a strategy to grow by developing and selling new products or services, a flatter or more horizontal structure may be more effective. In general, more complex organizational designs are needed as companies pursue strategies to add products, services, markets, or geographic expansion.

Market Uncertainty   The level of market uncertainty the organization faces helps determine the level of formalization it needs. Organizations such as Intel and Facebook that operate in dynamic markets need less formalized structures. Horizontal or open structures are more appropriate in this case because they allow quicker responses to marketplace threats and opportunities. Organizations may need to change their structure due to marketplace changes such as new competitors, alternate products, or customer preferences.

Decision-Making Processes   Decision-making processes span a continuum from centralized to

Selecting the best organizational design is akin to putting together a puzzle. The organization's strategy, market uncertainty, decision-making processes, technology, and size must fit together like this puzzle.

Adam Gault/OJO Images/age fotostock

decentralized. ***Centralized decision making* occurs when key decisions are made by top management. *Decentralized decision making* occurs when important decisions are made by middle- and lower-level managers.** A landmark study by a pair of British behavioral scientists, Tom Burns and G. M. Stalker, found a relationship between decision-making processes and organizational structure. In the course of their research, Burns and Stalker drew a very instructive distinction between what they called *mechanistic* and *organic* organizations.

***Mechanistic organizations* are rigid bureaucracies with strict rules, narrowly defined tasks, top-down communication, and centralized decision making.** A mechanistic organization generally would have one of the traditional organizational designs described in the preceding section and a hierarchical culture. The "orderliness" of this structure is expected to produce reliability and consistency in internal processes, resulting in higher efficiency, quality, and timeliness.

***Organic organizations* are flexible networks of multitalented individuals who perform a variety of tasks.** Organic organizations are more likely to use decentralized decision making and horizontal or open designs.[56]

Burns and Stalker discovered that one type was not superior to the other. Each type had its appropriate place, depending on the environment.[57] When the environment was relatively stable and certain, the successful organizations tended to be *mechanistic*. When the environment was unstable and uncertain, the successful ones tended to be *organic*.[58]

Technology Technology consists of the information technology, equipment, tools, and processes needed to transform inputs to outputs. It allows products and services to be created and distributed and lets companies use big data in making decisions. Experts suggest that the use of big data "will change organizational structures as organizations pursue the opportunities presented."[59] This implies that the technology a company uses is a key consideration in deciding the best way to organize in pursuit of strategic goals.

Size Size is measured by the number of employees, volume of sales, amount of assets, and geographical locations. Larger size generally requires more complex organizational designs.

Internal Alignment

The choice of best organizational form requires more than just considering the five contingency factors. Organizations perform more effectively when various internal organizational-level characteristics are aligned and mutually reinforcing. For example, if a company wants to grow through innovative product offerings (strategy), then it probably needs a less hierarchical structure coupled with an adhocracy and market culture. It also would help to have rewards tied to innovation and to employ people with high amounts of human and social capital. Can you see the alignment that exists among strategy, culture, structure, human resources practices, and employees' capabilities?

In contrast, if a company wants to reduce costs by improving internal processes (strategy), it would benefit from a more horizontal structure coupled with a hierarchical and clan culture. This combination would be enhanced if rewards were linked to cost reduction or efficiency, and if employees were knowledgeable about internal process control. Again, you can see that alignment is needed across internal characteristics for organizations to achieve higher performance. Although academics and consultants don't completely agree on the list of internal characteristics that need to be aligned, it is safe to recommend the following for inclusion:[60]

1. Strategy.
2. Structure.
3. Organizational culture.
4. Internal processes.
5. Human resource practices, policies, and procedures.
6. Employees' human and social capital.

What Does This Mean to Me?

There are both short and long-term implications to consider.

Short-Term Implications

How many times have you sat in a lecture hall or classroom structured like the top photo? The experience is quite different from a small group meeting in which participants interact in a less formal fashion. Both contexts have their place, and our behavior is affected by the structure of a the learning environment.

(Top): Aaron Roeth Photography;
(Bottom): Hero Images/Getty Images

- **Structure affects your behavior and performance.** Imagine taking a class in which the seats are arranged in a stair-step, theater-style set of rows in which chairs are bolted to the ground. You can swivel in your chair, but your position is set. Now consider how this structure affects your interactions with other students. You will tend to speak with others on either side and will struggle to do group work with four to five people. It's inconvenient to turn and observe someone speaking from the back of the room. This structure also stops instructors from walking into the audience and interacting with students as in a talk show. Contrast this with a classroom with a flat floor and round tables with five or six students at each. Interactions and group work are both easier and more efficient. You can move to another table if you want. The instructor can easily walk around and interact with everyone. The point is that structure affects behavior. The value of understanding the various types of organization design is that you can work around their strengths and limitations.

- **You may want to start your own company.** Yesterday, the owner of an appliance repair company came to the home of your author to fix an ice maker and dishwasher. He has 15 employees. When asked how he structured his small company, he said everyone reports to him, but this structure is getting overwhelming and he needs someone to focus on getting new customers. He is the only person doing this, but he also has to do repairs on certain types of equipment like those in our home, leaving him less time to cultivate new business. We discussed how he might use a divisional structure based on having offices in cities within the Phoenix metropolitan area and creating incentives for those who bring in new customers. He was thankful for the free advice. You need to know about various organizational designs if you ever start your own company.

- **Person–organization (P-O) fit matters.** In Chapter 14 we defined P-O fit as the extent to which your personality and values match the climate and culture in an organization. You also learned that P-O fit is related to a host of important outcomes such as job satisfaction, engagement, commitment, performance, and turnover. You will be happier, healthier, and more productive when you fit.[61] For example, if you prefer autonomy, flexibility, and empowerment, then you probably won't fit into a company with a mechanistic structure. You would be much happier with an organic type of structure.[62] Knowledge about organization design can help you find a work environment that fits.

Long-Term Implications   Decisions about organizational design generally are made by senior leaders and consultants in medium and large firms. We have participated in this process and it can get quite complicated. Assuming you want to move up the managerial hierarchy, the day will come when you have to provide input on organizational designs that can help your employer meets its strategic goals. Our discussion here will help.

15.5 ORGANIZATIONAL INNOVATION

THE BIGGER PICTURE

Managers agree that the ability to innovate affects long-term success, and you will undoubtedly be asked to help your employer achieve this. This section provides insights into the ways organizations approach the goal of innovation. After discussing approaches toward innovation pursued by companies, we review the need to create an innovation system and summarize the influence of office design on innovation and performance.

We live in a time of technological advancement that is creating transformative changes in the way we live, work, and play. Organizations are feeling both the opportunity and the pinch of this reality. Consider the situation faced by executives at Gap. Sales at the global retailer have slumped, and the company has too many stores. An industry expert further concluded, "Every retailer is competing for a shrinking pool of customers who lately spend more of their money on meals or services, such as manicures and travel. Still, they demand greater value and discounts from their clothing purchases."[63] Despite the company's promises to innovate, Gap recently announced it would close more than 200 underperforming stores and spin off its Old Navy brand to a separate company.[64]

Is Gap an anomaly or is the need to innovate widespread? It's widespread! Results from a recent survey of nearly 700 leaders revealed that although 85 percent of them said innovation is important, more than three-quarters of them focus on incremental changes in their businesses instead. In addition, close to 60 percent of the leaders said innovation is a slow process—taking a year or longer to create new products.[65]

Innovation "is the creation of something new that makes money; it finds a pathway to the consumer."[66] This definition underscores that innovations must be both novel and useful. We now take a closer look at innovation and the way organizations foster it. You will learn that innovation is more likely to occur when organizations create and support a system of innovation, which includes tailoring the characteristics of the physical environment.

Approaches toward Innovation

We can classify innovations by crossing their type with their focus, producing four distinct types (see Figure 15.6).

The Type of Innovation   Managers often need to improve a product or service they offer in response to competition or customer feedback. This response often amounts to a technological innovation. Or managers may need to improve the process by which a product is made or a service is offered. This need typically leads to a process improvement.

More specifically, a *product innovation* **is a change in the appearance or functionalilty/performance of a product or a service or the creation of a new one.** Apple has made ten generations of iPhones that each added new features or functionality, such as camera features, screen size, and Siri voice control system. Apple CEO Tim Cook revealed that Apple has sold about 1.5 billion iPhones as of the end of 2018.[67] PepsiCo's

FIGURE 15.6 Approaches Toward Innovation

		Focus of Innovation	
		Improvement	**New Directions**
Type of Innovation	**Product**	**Apple iPhone** • Ten generations/versions since first introduced in June 2007	**Driverless Cars** • Major automobile manufacturers and Google
	Process	**3-D Printing** • Alcoa's use of 3-D printing in its manufacturing process	**Home Construction** • Panelized homes

creation of Mountain Dew Kickstart is another example: higher juice content, fewer calories, new flavors. This new drink generated over $200 million in two years.[68]

A *process innovation* **is a change in the way a product or a service is conceived, manufactured, or distributed.** Alcoa's use of 3-D printing in its manufacturing process of jet engine components is a great example. *Fortune* contrasted Alcoa's old and new manufacturing processes: "In the past, Alcoa built a die using a process called subtractive machining. It's similar to sculpture: Start with a material—in this case, steel—then whittle it down into the shape you need. Ten to 30 weeks later, the company ended up with a custom die that it would then use to cast the needed engine part. Today Alcoa pairs computer-aided design, or CAD, with 3-D printing to construct the die from a computer file, layer by layer. A process that once took half a year could be completed in two to eight weeks, allowing the company to dramatically increase its output." The new process reduced manufacturing costs by 25 percent.[69]

The Focus of the Innovation The focus continuum measures the scope of the innovation. **Improvement innovations enhance or upgrade an existing product, service, or process.** These types of innovations are often incremental and are less likely to generate significant amounts of new revenue at one point in time. As is true for products like Apple's iPhone and PepsiCo's Mountain Dew, however, improvement innovations can produce significant revenue if the results are highly different from past products or services.

In contrast, **new-direction innovations take a totally new or different approach to a product, service, process, or industry.** These innovations focus on creating new markets and customers and rely on developing breakthroughs and inventing things that didn't already exist. Experimental driverless cars are a new-direction innovation, and most major automobile manufacturers are exploring their market potential. Some industry experts, including Christoph Grote, head of BMW's advanced technologies group, believe this innovation might change the entire industry. "The next 10 years will bring more change than the last 30," he said.[70]

Three-D printing, also known as additive manufacturing, is used to create a three-dimensional object by having a computer control the successive layers of material that comprise an object. Some people believe that 3-D printing will create a third industrial revolution.
Zoonar GmbH/Cylonphoto/Alamy Stock Photo

The housing industry has experienced a new-direction innovation that changes the process of constructing homes. The traditional way of building a home is called "stick-built." Architectural plans are given to a general contractor, who then hires subcontractors to build the home in phases, starting with pouring the foundation and framing the structure. The process is time consuming, filled with quality issues, and expensive. The new alternative is "panelized homes," in which all components of a house are prefabricated at a climate-controlled factory and then shipped to the building site for construction. The weather-tight shell usually can be assembled in a matter of days.[71] An industry study compared results of these two constructions processes for a 2,600-square-foot home and found that panelized homes "required 26 percent less lumber, wasted 76 percent less materials, and needed just over a third of the man-hours that would be used in a comparable stick-built house."[72]

An example of building a panelized home. Note the section of a home being raised so that it can be assembled with additional prefabricated walls. As you can imagine, homes can be built more quickly using this innovative method of construction.

Acontadini/E+/Getty Images

An Innovation System: The Supporting Forces for Innovation

Innovation won't happen as a matter of course. It takes dedicated effort and resources, and the process must be nurtured and supported. Organizations do this best by developing an innovation system. An **innovation system** is **"a coherent set of interdependent processes and structures that dictates how the company searches for novel problems and solutions, synthesizes ideas into a business concept and product designs, and selects which projects get funded."**[73] Research and practice have identified seven components of an innovation system: innovation strategy; committed leadership; innovative culture and climate; required structure and processes; necessary human capital; human resource policies, practices, and procedures; and appropriate resources (see Figure 15.7).[74] These must be aligned and integrated for innovation to blossom, hence the dual-headed arrows in Figure 15.7.

Create an Innovation Strategy Many companies fail in their improvement efforts because they lack an innovation strategy.[75] An *innovation strategy,* which amounts to a plan for being more innovative, requires a company to integrate its innovation activities into its business strategies. This integration encourages management to invest resources in innovation and generates employee commitment to innovation across the organization.

Corning is a diverse company that used its expertise in glassmaking to become a global manufacturer of specialty components needed for electronic displays, life sciences instruments, and telecommunications systems among others. According to a writer for the *Harvard Business Review,* "The company's business strategy focuses on selling 'keystone components' that significantly improve the performance of customers' complex system products. Executing this strategy requires Corning to be at the leading edge of glass and materials science so that it can solve exceptionally challenging problems for customers and discover new applications for its technologies. That requires heavy investments in

FIGURE 15.7 Components of an Innovation System

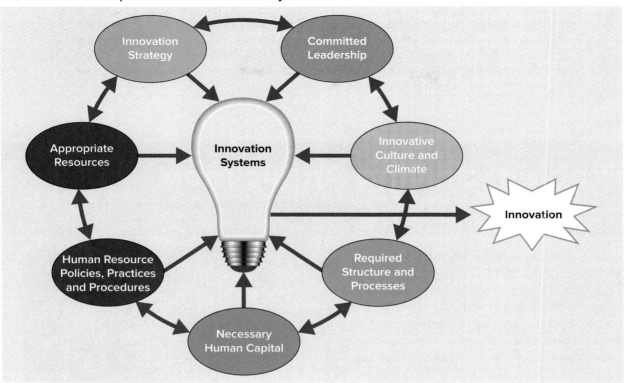

long-term research."[76] The company spearheads these innovation efforts via a centralized R&D laboratory in upstate New York.

Commitment from Senior Leaders   One of the biggest lessons we have learned from our consulting experience is that the achievement of strategic goals is unlikely without real commitment from senior leaders. Microsoft CEO Satya Nadella knows this lesson well. He is currently driving innovation by using empathy. His message to employees when he took over as CEO in 2014: Empathy leads to understanding and collaboration, which helps innovation push its way toward helpful, new products.

> **EXAMPLE** A Microsoft engineer who is deaf had difficulty Skyping with her parents in India because the fuzzy video made it difficult for her to read their lips. She always had to ask them to turn off the lights in the background so she could focus better on their faces. She kept wondering, "Why can't we build technology that can do this for us instead?" So the engineer came up with the idea of a background-blurring feature, which has since been integrated into Skype and Microsoft Teams.[77]

Foster an Innovative Culture and Climate   A recent survey by the Boston Consulting Group identified risk-averse culture as the key obstacle to innovation.[78] Academic research also supports the conclusion that an innovative culture and climate are associated with the creation of new ideas and products.[79] These findings reflect the fact that innovation requires experimentation, failure, and risk taking, and these are all aspects of an organization's culture. Many senior leaders understand this link.

Nike co-founder Philip Knight says he learned early on in business to expect setbacks and failure as part of trying to innovate. "The only time you must not fail is the last time you try," he says. The founder of Honda Motor, Soichiro Honda, explained the link between innovation, success, and failure as follows: "Success represents the 1 percent of your work which results from the 99 percent that is called failure."[80]

Managers can create an innovative culture and climate by using the 12 mechanisms for creating culture change discussed in Chapter 14. These concerted efforts should facilitate the creation of values, norms, and rewards that support risk taking, adaptability, agility, and psychological safety to speak up and provide criticism.[81]

Problem-Solving Application

Can AMD Innovate without Risk?

AMD is a global maker of high-performance computing and graphic technology for gaming, tech platforms, and data management systems used by hundreds of millions of end-user consumers. Based in California and Texas and currently under the leadership of president and CEO Lisa Su, the company is celebrating 50 years in the computing industry. Second only to Intel, AMD has been described as a company that "always springs back with a vengeance, thanks in part to its commitment to innovation, willingness to try something different technologically, and maybe with a chip on its shoulder wanting to prove it has what it takes."[82]

AMD has weathered many years of industry ups and downs. Along the way it contributed to some significant technology milestones, like the increasing capacity and declining costs of computer processors. Now, however, the company is posting lower revenues (down almost 23 percent in the first quarter of 2019), mirroring lower revenues in the computing and graphics industry generally.[83]

The company has also been losing executive talent to Intel and other tech companies. Its senior

The computer chip developed by AMD
Anatolii Mazhora/Shutterstock

vice president of global computing and graphics sales, its graphics chip architect, and its senior director of product marketing are all recent departures. Promotions from within have so far filled the gaps.[84]

AMD's stated goal is "to provide increasing compute and graphics power to more and more people globally, enabling the next generation of global problem solvers." However, the company is "more focused on execution than taking huge risks," according to an analyst.[85]

Apply the 3-Step Problem-Solving Approach

Step 1: Define the problem AMD faces as it celebrates 50 years in business.

Step 2: Identify the causes of the problem. What OB theories or concepts help explain them?

Step 3: Recommend what AMD's leaders should to do ensure its continued success.

Have you worked for a company that has an innovative climate? Are you wondering what it takes to create such a climate? If yes, take the innovation climate Self-Assessment 15.3.

How Innovative Is the Organizational Climate?

Please be prepared to answer these questions if your instructor has assigned Self-Assessment 15.3 in Connect.

1. What is the level of innovation? Are you surprised by the results? Explain.
2. Select the three lowest survey item scores. Use the content of these items to recommend what the company could do to become more innovative.

Required Structure and Processes Organizational structure and internal processes can promote innovation if they foster collaboration, cross-functional communication, and agility. Our earlier discussion of organizational design suggests that organic structures are better suited for innovation than mechanistic ones. For example, Juniper Networks, a leader in computer network integration, concluded that its "formal organizational structure was not conducive to the types of rich interactions and conversations required for innovation to thrive." Vince Molinaro, executive vice president of worldwide sales, commented, "We were not integrating diverse expertise and experience across engineering, infrastructure, and sales teams the way we could when we were a small company." Juniper changed its structure.[86]

In Chapter 1, we defined organizational processes as an organization's capabilities in management, internal processes, and technology that turn inputs into outcomes. Processes play a critical role in innovation. The design and consulting firm IDEO, for example, employs a unique process when it helps companies to innovate (see the OB in Action box). **Crowdsourcing, defined as "the practice of obtaining needed services, ideas, or content by soliciting contributions from a large group of people" typically via the Internet,** is being used by more companies to help innovate. For example, Procter & Gamble's crowdsourcing platform, Connect + Develop, has enabled the company to establish more than 2,000 successful agreements with innovation partners around the world. LEGO Ideas crowdsourcing platform has been a hit with adult LEGO fans for more than a decade, with 26,000 ideas submitted for new LEGO products and 23 new products launched.[87] More research is being done on the effectiveness of crowdsourcing and suggests that it is positively associated with firm performance.[88]

OB in Action

Design Thinking Your Way to Innovative Solutions

IDEO (pronounced "EYE-dee-oh") is a unique, award-winning, and highly respected and influential global design firm. It is responsible for such innovative products as the first mouse for Apple, heart defibrillators that walk a user through the steps, and TiVo's "thumbs up–thumbs down" button. An intense focus on end-user behavior is the foundation of all the company does and is embedded in the three steps of its design thinking. The steps are inspiration, ideation, and implementation.

- **Inspiration.** As defined by David Kelley, IDEO's legendary founder, inspiration is the problem or opportunity that motivates the search for solutions.

- **Ideation.** Ideation is the process of generating, developing, and testing ideas.

- **Implementation.** The final step, implementation, links the problem's solution to people's lives.

Observing user behavior and working with proto-types are important aspects of each step. They help IDEO's diverse problem-solving teams both define client problems and gauge the effectiveness of their solutions.

Thinking Like a Designer   The company's consulting approach to products, services, processes, and strategy brings together what is desirable from a human point of view with what is technologically feasible and economically viable. It also allows people who are trained as designers to use creative tools to address a vast range of challenges. The goal: to tap into abilities we all have that are overlooked by more conventional problem-solving practices. Thinking like a designer relies on one's ability "to be intuitive, to recognize patterns, to construct ideas that are emotionally meaningful as well as functional, and to express ourselves through means beyond words or symbols."[89]

Beyond Product Design   IDEO's design thinking has been so successful that many nonbusiness and nonproduct organizations are now engaging the company. For instance, it is working with the City of Los Angeles to design a revolutionary voting system for its 5 million registered voters. The system must be "useful and accessible to all types of voters: those who are vision and hearing impaired, in wheelchairs, have learning disabilities, are unfamiliar with technology, speak languages other than English—voters of all ages and backgrounds."[90] IDEO's Ann Kim also sees an opening to help with very human problems like sleeplessness and loneliness. "Science has surfaced the myriad of ways we can cultivate emotional and mental well-being—all of which are new channels for design," she says. "You don't have to have a doctor or nurse to help people. Designers are healers, too."[91]

As an Organization   IDEO has more than 700 employees in 9 offices, both in major U.S. cities and overseas in London, Munich, Shanghai, Singapore, and Tokyo.[92] The firm has an organic design, the result of merging four design companies. Its current structure builds on project teams and a flat hierarchy, in support of individual autonomy and creativity.[93]

YOUR THOUGHTS?

1. What is appealing to you about IDEO?

2. To what extent does IDEO's approach to design force companies to use the seven components of an innovation system (see Figure 15.7)? Explain.

Finally, a team of experts suggested that organizations can foster innovation by focusing on four agility techniques.[94]

1. **Place more emphasis on people than on processes and tools.** Innovation initiatives or projects should be built around motivated individuals who are empowered to get the job done and have the resources to do it.

2. **Be responsive to change rather than following a detailed plan.** It helps to create project plans, but don't spend large amounts of time trying to identify each and every task to be completed. Tasks frequently change as situations evolve. Teams thus need the freedom to diverge from project plans if the situation or customer requires it. Alaska Airlines is following this recommendation. As the airline grew and revenues rose, it became more bureaucratic, with employees following a heavily scripted operations playbook. This rigid approach tied employees' hands when it came to pivoting to address customer service issues. Recognizing the problem, Alaska Airlines returned to its culture of giving employees autonomy and encouraging them to make decisions independently.[95]

3. **Develop and test prototypes rather than focusing on documentation.** People learn more and are happier when they observe their ideas being applied in real market conditions. Teams should experiment with products and services on a small scale to see whether customers like them. If they do, keep the new ideas; otherwise, it's back to the drawing board. For example, PepsiCo originally designed SunChips to be one-inch square and to break into pieces when eaten. When the company pilot-tested the product in focus groups, people said they preferred products that were smaller than one inch. PepsiCo concluded the chips were too big and changed its molds and production processes.[96]

4. **Collaborate with customers rather than adhering to rigid contracts.** Customers often don't know what they want. Adhering to fixed contracts and deliverables rather than

adjusting to customer preferences can reduce innovation when employees get too focused on budgets and specifications. Constant collaboration with customers will keep work focused on what they ultimately value.[97]

Develop the Necessary Human Capital   We defined human capital in Chapter 14 as the productive potential of an individual's knowledge and actions: a person factor in the Organizing Framework. Research has identified several employee characteristics that can help organizations innovate. For example, innovation has been positively associated with the individual characteristics associated with creativity, creative-thinking skills, intrinsic motivation, the quality of the relationship between managers and employees, and international work experience.[98]

> **EXAMPLE**   Cornerstone OnDemand, an HR software company, recognizes people get stuck in routines and put creativity aside. To get people away from their everyday routines, the company hosts an annual "hackathon" that takes place over a 24-hour period. People from all departments work alone or in teams to develop and pitch ideas they think will help move the company forward. According to Cornerstone's chief technology officer, there is only one rule: "You cannot work on activities related to your day job; only new thinking and new ideas are allowed."[99]

Human Resource Policies, Practices, and Procedures   Human resource policies, practices, and procedures need to be consistent with and reinforce the other six components of an innovation system. Companies that know this are more likely to be innovative and to have higher financial performance.[100] For example, the practice of bringing people from different disciplines together to both brainstorm and train is a good way to foster the collaboration needed for innovation. The University of Michigan's Biointerfaces Institute "locates materials scientists, chemical engineers, biomechanical engineers, and medical researchers near each other. The resulting collaborations led to the creation of a blood test that both captures and cultures cancer cells for speedier cancer diagnoses," according to a writer for *Training*.[101]

A company's performance management and incentive system are often at odds with an innovation culture and climate. For example, GE changed its well-known annual performance review process to make it more consistent with driving innovation and attracting younger employees. In the past, the company ranked all employees and then eliminated the bottom 10 percent. This process has been replaced with a more nurturing approach including an app, PD@GE, to help employees, managers, and teammates share feedback for continuous improvement.[102] Companies also need to align their reward and recognition systems with innovation-related goals. Research shows that receipt of extrinsic rewards is associated with both creativity and innovation.[103]

Appropriate Resources   Organizations need to put their money where their mouths are. If managers want innovation, they must dedicate resources to its development. Resources can include people, dollars, time, energy, knowledge, and focus. Heineken, for example, spent $2 million on training employees in beer basics to help them innovate.[104]

Office Design

Office designs have gone through radical changes in the past 15 years. In an effort to reduce costs, to promote cooperative behavior and camaraderie, to increase productivity, and to create more transparency in what we do, many companies have adopted open-office design. Unlike traditional designs in which people have their own offices, open-plan designs offer shared work space that accommodates anywhere from two to several hundred people. *The Washington Post* reported that 70 percent of today's organizations use some amount of open office space. All told, our personal space at work is predicted to decrease from 2010 levels of 225 square feet to under 100 square feet in the near future.[105]

This photo is quite typical for an open office environment. What are the pros and cons to working in this area? Would you prefer this office design or a traditional office with a door?

Cathy Yeulet/123RF

For us, the question is whether the move to open-office designs is leading to positive individual, group, and organizational outcomes. What is your opinion? Here are some findings from OB research:

- Privacy, defined as the ability to control incoming stimulation and interpersonal contact and to limit outgoing information, is reduced in an open-plan office.[106]

- Few office cubicle dividers are tall enough to block the noise and distractions that limit people's ability to focus at work. The resulting overstimulation is stressful for many people.[107]

- Spatially dense work environments (in which employees are crowded) have been found to promote cooperative behavior and productivity, but they can also be detrimental to individual, group, and organizational performance.[108]

- Attitudes about personal space are culturally bound around the world. "Germans allocate an average of 320 square feet per employee; Americans an average of 190. For workers in India and China, the figures are 70 and 50 square feet respectively," according to a writer in the *Harvard Business Review*. Both Indian and Chinese workers rated their work environments highly in terms of their ability to concentrate and work without disruption, but this is not true in the United States.[109]

The above results demonstrate both positive and negative effects of open-office designs. So what is management to do? For one, recognize that people have preferences. For example, some people enjoy the social interaction of the workplace, while others find the work environment too distracting to be productive and would rather work in a quiet environment. Second, remember that open offices are not inherently good or bad when it comes to innovation, collaboration, or performance. All told, we agree with these conclusions by a team of office design professionals.

The key to successful work spaces is to empower individuals by giving them choices that allow control over their work environment. When they can choose where and how they work, they have more capacity to draw energy and ideas from others and be re-energized by moments of solitude. Providing the ability to move easily between group time and individual private time, create a rhythm—coming together to think about a problem and then going away to let ideas gestate—that is essential to the modern organization.[110]

15.6 ASSESSING ORGANIZATIONAL EFFECTIVENESS

THE BIGGER PICTURE

Organizations that measure and monitor their progress in achieving goals outperform those that do not. The type of goals companies seek to achieve essentially define their mission and vision. The purpose of this section is to discuss the effectiveness criteria organizations use.

LO 15-6

Explain how to assess an organization's effectiveness.

Do you think top managers would like to have easy-to-read graphics that contain the latest information about sales, quality problems, employee turnover, and the like, aggregated from data pulled in real time from corporate software? The technology to track all these metrics exists and is called a *dashboard,* like the instrument panel in a car.

Bob Parsons, founder of GoDaddy, believed in dashboards. "Measure everything of significance. Anything that is measured and watched improves," he said.[111] Larry Bossidy, former CEO of both Honeywell International and AlliedSignal, similarly noted, "When I see companies that don't execute, the chances are that they don't measure, don't reward, and don't promote people who know how to get things done."[112]

In several chapters we emphasized the value of evidence-based management—the use of real-world data rather than assumptions or hunches in making managerial decisions. The dashboard is a tool that can help you manage this way. Two professors from Harvard, Robert Kaplan and David Norton, have applied the dashboard idea in their *balanced scorecard* and *strategy maps.* These tools help companies establish their strategies and goals and provide a vehicle for assessing organizational effectiveness. Hundreds of companies around the globe have used them.[113]

The Balanced Scorecard: A Dashboard-Based Approach to Measuring Organizational Effectiveness

Kaplan and Norton note, "The balanced scorecard (BSC) translates an organization's vision and strategy into a comprehensive set of performance measures that provides the framework for a strategic measurement and management system." It "retains an emphasis on achieving financial objectives, but also includes the performance drivers of these financial objectives."[114] The BSC provides managers with a comprehensive view of the organization in terms of four perspectives: (1) financial, (2) customer, (3) internal business processes, and (4) learning and growth, which looks at employee welfare and development.

"Think of the balanced scorecard as the dials and indicators in an airplane cockpit," say Kaplan and Norton. For a pilot, "reliance on one instrument can be fatal. Similarly, the complexity of managing an organization today requires that managers be able to view performance in several areas simultaneously."[115]

Four Perspectives Underlying the Balanced Scorecard The process of creating a balanced scorecard requires managers to establish goals and measures for all four perspectives. Let's look at each one.

1. **Financial Perspective: How Do We Look to Shareholders?** Corporate financial strategies and goals generally fall into two buckets: revenue growth and productivity growth. Revenue growth goals might focus on increasing revenue from both new and existing customers. Equipment manufacturer John Deere, for instance, is pursuing new revenue by developing software services and machine learning algorithms that provide information

and guidance to farmers in the field. It is doing this to offset a recent decrease in revenue.[116] Productivity metrics such as revenue per employee or total output produced divided by number of employees are common organization-level goals. We can also measure productivity in terms of costs. For example, Gap recently announced plans to close more than 200 underperforming retail stores to decrease costs and improve profitability.[117]

2. **Customer Perspective: How Do Customers See Us?** Many companies view customers as one of their most important constituents. The balanced scorecard translates this belief into measures such as market share, customer acquisition, customer retention, customer satisfaction/loyalty, product/service quality, response time—the time between order and delivery—and percentage of bids won. Part of Amazon's success, for example, is its response time and pricing. The general idea behind the customer perspective is that companies will acquire and retain more customers, thereby growing market share, when they provide high-quality products and services people want, and in a timely manner.[118]

Management at the the Four Seasons resort chain places high emphasis on customer satisfaction and loyalty. To achieve the goal of providing the quietest rooms in the industry, a *Fortune* reporter noted the company built facilities such that "no plumbing touches concrete. To encourage personalized service [the CEO], gave everyone from parking attendants on up the authority to act instantly when a guest makes a request."[119]

These pilots monitor the dials and gauges in the cockpit to safely navigate a plane. A balanced scorecard is akin to the dials and gauges in a cockpit. They inform managers as to the status of achieving their goals.

Vladimir Maravic/Vetta/Getty Images

3. **Internal Business Process Perspective: What Must We Excel At?** The internal business perspective focuses on "what the organization must excel at" to effectively meet its financial objectives and customers' expectations. A team of researchers has identified four critical high-level internal processes that managers are encouraged to measure and manage:

- Innovation.
- Customer service and satisfaction.
- Operational excellence, which includes safety and quality.
- Good corporate citizenship.[120]

These processes influence productivity, efficiency, quality, safety, and a host of other internal metrics. Companies tend to adopt continuous improvement programs in pursuit of upgrades to their internal processes. Consider how Graycor Industrial Constructors (Graycor) attempts to meet its goal of safety and quality.

EXAMPLE Chicago–based Graycor Industrial Constructors sets a safety standard of zero incidents led by its tenet: "Nothing is more important than safety. Not production, not sales, not profits." As part of the general contractor's safety and health program, all company leaders and project team supervisors—from general foremen to company president—must complete job site-specific safety training, which includes the Occupational Safety and Health Administration's (OSHA) 30-hour course, incident investigation, task safety planning, and hazard recognition. One way the North American builder encourages its employees to participate in the safety process is through a "good catch" program, set up to motivate field workers and managers to share lessons learned to prevent an incident from occurring. Graycor, founded in 1921, was named one of America's safest companies in 2018 by *EHS Today*.[121]

Cotopaxi, an outdoor apparel company, makes corporate citizenship its top criterion for evaluating organizational effectiveness. As part of its mission the company funds global poverty alleviation, moves people to do good, and inspires adventure through innovative outdoor products and experiences.[122] According to *Bloomberg Businessweek,* "Cotopaxi is one of about 1,700 businesses worldwide that have registered as a benefit corporation, or B Corp, a legal category for corporations that hew to the concept of a double bottom line, in which financial goals don't take precedence over social ones."[123] The company gives 1 percent of its profits to organizations focused on poverty alleviation around the world.[124]

In an industrial project's "topping out," Graycor Industrial Constructors safely hoisted and placed a roof weighing approximately 170 tons as a major milestone during an environmental retrofit project the general contractor completed at a coal-fired power plant in the United States.
Courtesy of Graycor Industrial Constructors Inc.

4. **Learning and Growth Perspective: Can We Continue to and Create Value?** The learning and growth perspective focuses on providing employees with the capabilities, resources, and work environment they need to achieve customer, internal business processes, and financial goals. It's the foundation of all other goals in a scorecard. Typical metrics in this perspective are employee satisfaction/engagement, employee retention, employee productivity, training budget per employee, technology utilization, and organizational climate and culture. Many are tracked with employee surveys to gauge attitudes and opinions.

Based on theories and research discussed throughout this book, you might expect your job satisfaction, engagement, and performance to be higher if you work for a company that truly cares about the innovation and learning perspective. Are you curious about whether a current or former employer is committed to this perspective? You can find out by completing Self-Assessment 15.4.

SELF-ASSESSMENT 15.4

Assessing the Learning and Growth Perspective of the Balanced Scorecard

Please be prepared to answer these questions if your instructor has assigned Self-Assessment 15.4 in Connect.

1. Where does the company stand in terms of commitment to innovation and learning? Are you surprised by the results?

2. Use the three highest and three lowest scores to identify the strengths and weaknesses of this company's commitment to innovation and learning.

3. Based on your answer to question 2, suggest three ways management can improve its commitment to innovation and learning.

Strategy Mapping: Visual Representation of the Path to Organizational Effectiveness

Have you ever worked for a company that failed to effectively communicate its vision and strategic plan? If yes, then you know how it feels to be disengaged because you don't know how your work contributes to organizational effectiveness. Kaplan and Norton recognized this common problem and developed a tool called the strategy map.

A **strategy map** is a "visual representation of a company's critical objectives and the crucial relationships among them that drive organizational performance." Maps show relationships among a company's strategic goals. This helps employees understand how their work contributes to their employer's overall success.

We created an illustrative strategy map for Dr Pepper Snapple Group in Figure 15.8. Starting with learning and growth, the arrows in the diagram show the logic that connects

FIGURE 15.8 Sample Strategy Map for Dr Pepper Snapple Group

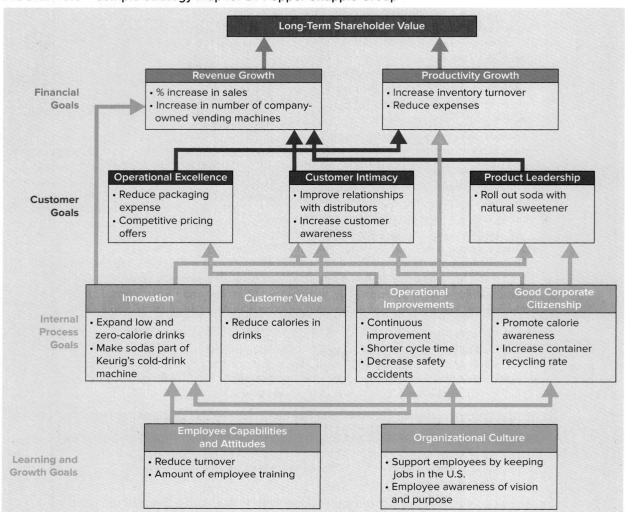

SOURCES: The Shelby Report. "Dr Pepper Snapple Group To Boost Container Recycling, And More..." Accessed June 14, 2019. https://www.theshelbyreport. com/2016/02/12/dr-pepper-snapple-group-to-boost-container-recycling-and-more/.; Choi, Candice. "Dr Pepper to Test Naturally Sweetened Sodas." Advantage Business Marketing, February 13, 2014. https://www.manufacturing.net/news/2014/02/dr-pepper-test-naturally-sweetened-sodas.; Gasparro, Annie, and Mike Esterl. "Keurig Reels In Dr Pepper for Its Coming Soda Machine." *The Wall Street Journal,* January 7, 2015. https://www.wsj.com/articles/keurig-reels-in-dr-pepper-for-its-coming-soda-machine-1420590475.; Frizell, Sam. Coke and Pepsi Pledge to Cut Calories. *TIME USA,* LLC., September 23, 2014. https://time.com/3422724/coca-cola-pepsi-dr-pepper-snapple-soda-calories/.; Esterl, Mike. "How Dr Pepper Cuts Costs. And Keeps Cutting." *The Wall Street Journal,* February 21, 2016. https://www.wsj.com/articles/how-dr-pepper-cuts-costs-and-keeps-cutting-1456110339.; and Keurig Dr Pepper, Inc. "Vision—Call to Breakthrough ACTION."

goals to internal processes, to customers, to financial goals, and finally to the long-term goal of providing shareholder value. For example, you can see that organizational culture affects the internal process goals related to innovation, operational improvements, and good corporate citizenship. This causal structure provides a strategic road map of how the company plans to achieve organizational effectiveness.

You can also detect which of the four perspectives is most important to Dr Pepper Snapple by counting the number of goals in each perspective. For this strategy map, there are four, five, eight, and four goals for the financial, customer, internal processes, and learning and growth perspectives, respectively. You can also see that internal process goals affect eight other goals—count the number of arrows coming from internal process goals. All told, the beauty of a strategy map is that it enables leaders to present a strategic road map to employees on one page. It also provides a clear statement about the criteria used to assess organizational effectiveness. The strategy map for Dr Pepper Snapple Group may be changing in the near future because the company was recently purchased by Keurig Green Mountain, a merger that will create a new beverage giant with $11 billion in sales and combines the Dr Pepper, 7UP, and Keurig's single-serve coffee brands.[125]

15.7 MAKING THE CONNECTION: HOW CAN UNDERSTANDING ORGANIZATIONAL DESIGN, EFFECTIVENESS, AND INNOVATION HELP ME SUCCEED?

Regardless of their size, organizations possess common characteristics such as structure and innovation, which impact their overall effectiveness. Here are some key points to consider.

Takeaways for Me

Here are six things you can do to turn this chapter's lessons into positive change in your personal and professional life.

1. **Take the time to learn from failure in both your personal and work life:** It helps to adopt a learning or mastery goal orientation.

2. **Structure affects your behavior and performance:** If you feel your employer's organizational structure is constraining your effectiveness, try to find a solution for overcoming the barrier.

3. **Person–organization fit matters when it comes to organizational design:** This means you need to understand the pros and cons of the seven organizational designs so you can assess whether a particular work environment is going to fit.

4. **Build your human and social capital so you can help your organization innovate.**

5. **If your office environment does not suit your work style, talk to your boss about changes that would make things better.**

6. **Try to establish goals at work that take the four perspectives in the balanced scorecard:** This will be more effective if your goals flow from those of your boss.

Takeaways for Managers

There are seven key implications for managers.

1. **Do what you can to help your organization learn:** Be seen as someone who promotes learning rather than someone who hides from failure and constructive feedback.

2. **Formalize the process of learning from failure within your work unit.**

3. **Familiarize yourself with the pros and cons of the seven core organizational designs:** This will enable you to participate in related discussions at work.

4. **Assess the extent to which your organization's current structure is based on the alignment of the six key internal organizational-level characteristics:** If they are not aligned, present a proposal to someone higher in the managerial chain about improving this alignment.

5. **Foster innovation by focusing on how you can enhance an innovation system:** Improve those factors under your control.

6. **Talk to your team about the office design:** Find out how everyone feels about it and ask for recommendations about how it might be improved.

7. **Use the balanced scorecard as a framework for setting goals for your work unit:** Apply strategy mapping as a mechanism to show how your goals flow upward from the learning and growth perspective to the financial perspective.

LO 15-7

Describe the implications of organizational design, effectiveness, and innovation for you and managers.

What Did I Learn?

You learned that your knowledge of organizational design, effectiveness, and innovation gives you the ability to help both you and an organization to achieve desired goals. Reinforce your learning with the Key Points below. Then consolidate your learning with the Organizing Framework. Finally, challenge your mastery of the material by answering the Major Questions in your own words.

Key Points for Understanding Chapter 15

You learned the following key points.

15.1 UNDERSTANDING ORGANIZATIONAL BEHAVIOR

- All organizations have three things in common: a form or structure, a desire to be effective, and the need to innovate.
- An organization's structure acts like a fingerprint, helping us understand who reports to whom and how information flows across organizational levels.
- An organization's effectiveness amounts to making money (for-profit firms) or helping those in need (nonprofit organizations) and satisfying employees, customers, and shareholders.
- All organizations need to innovate to remain in business. Innovation is a key driver of long-term organizational performance.

15.2 THE FOUNDATION OF AN ORGANIZATION

- Coordination of effort, aligned goals, division of labor, and hierarchy of authority are four common denominators of all organizations.
- There is no consensus about the optimal span of control. In setting the span of control, managers should consider the organization's size, the skill level needed to complete tasks, the organization's culture, and managerial responsibilities.
- Closed systems, such as a battery-powered clock, are relatively self-sufficient. Open systems, such as the growing and selling of organic food, are highly dependent on the environment for survival. Organizations are open systems.
- A learning organization proactively creates, acquires, and transfers knowledge and changes its behavior on the basis of new knowledge and insights.
- Figure 15.5 illustrates the five-step process underlying organizational learning.

15.3 ORGANIZATIONAL DESIGN

- There are three broad types of organizational design: traditional, horizontal, and open. Each has a different focus and is associated with specific types of structure.
- Organizations are structured in seven basic ways. Traditional designs include (1) functional structures, in which work is divided according to function; (2) divisional structures, in which work is divided according to product or customer type or location; and (3) matrix structures, with dual-reporting lines based on product and function. Organizations also may be designed (4) horizontally, with cross-functional teams responsible for entire processes. Organization design can reduce barriers between organizations, by means of (5) hollow organizations, which outsource functions; (6) modular organizations, which outsource the production of a product's components; and (7) virtual organizations, which temporarily combine the efforts of members of different companies to complete a project.
- Table 15.2 summarizes the pros and cons of each of the seven types of organizational design.

15.4 CONTINGENCY DESIGN AND INTERNAL ALIGNMENT

- There is no one best form of structure for an organization. Organizations are more effective when they are structured to fit the demands of the situation.
- Managers should consider five key contingency factors when making decisions about organizational design: strategy and goals, market uncertainty, decision-making processes, technology, and size.
- Six organizational characteristics—strategy; structure; organizational culture; internal processes; human resource practices, policies, and procedures; and employees' human and social capital—need to be aligned and mutually reinforcing when selecting an effective organizational design.
- There are both short- and long-term benefits to knowing about organizational design.

15.5 ORGANIZATIONAL INNOVATION

- Innovation is the creation of something new and useful that gets commercialized.
- Crossing the types of innovation with the focus of the innovation results in four approaches toward innovation.
- Innovations can produce new products or new processes and can vary in focus from improvement to new directions.
- An innovation system's seven components are an innovation strategy, commitment from senior leaders, an innovative culture and climate, required structure and processes, necessary human capital, appropriate resources, and human resource policies, practices, and procedures.
- Office design affects innovation and employee performance.

15.6 ASSESSING ORGANIZATIONAL EFFECTIVENESS

- The balanced scorecard is a dashboard approach to measuring organizational effectiveness. It is based on the use of four key perspectives to measure organizational effectiveness.
- The four perspectives underlying the balanced scorecard are financial, customer, internal business process, and learning and growth.
- A strategy map is a visual representation of a company's strategic goals and the relationships among them.

15.7 HOW CAN UNDERSTANDING ORGANIZATIONAL DESIGN, EFFECTIVENESS, AND INNOVATION HELP ME SUCCEED?

- Learning from failure in your personal and work life can help you adopt a learning orientation.
- Familiarizing yourself with the pros and cons of the seven core organizational designs will give you confidence to participate in related discussions at work.
- Using the balanced scorecard framework to set goals for your work unit will provide a comprehensive look at what the organization is trying to accomplish.

The Organizing Framework for Chapter 15

As shown in Figure 15.9, more situation than person factors serve as inputs to a host of processes across all three organizational levels. These processes in turn affect outcomes across the individual, group, and organizational levels.

FIGURE 15.9 Organizing Framework for Understanding and Applying OB

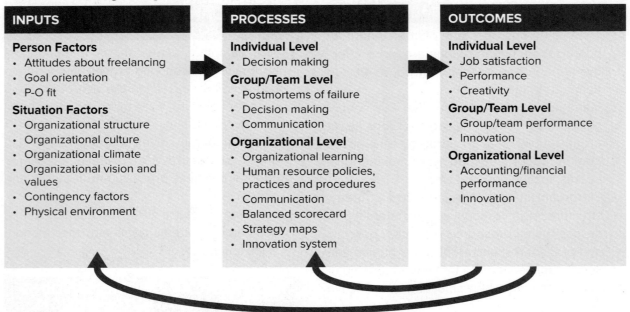

Challenge: Major Questions for Chapter 15

You now should be able to answer the following questions. Unless you can, have you really processed and internalized the lessons in the chapter? Refer to the Key Points, Figure 15.9, the chapter itself, and your notes to revisit and answer the following major questions:

1. How can knowledge about an organization's foundation help me in my career?

2. What are the seven basic ways in which organizations are structured, and how do these structures relate to the organization's purpose?

3. How can I use knowledge about contingent organization design and internal alignment to improve my satisfaction and performance?

4. How can I support my employer's attempts to innovate?

5. What does its choice of ways to measure its effectiveness tell me about an organization?

Barnes & Noble Faces Its Last Chapter

Barnes & Noble is the largest bookstore chain in the United States having sold more than 6.7 billion books since going public in 1993. Leonard Riggio, the bookseller's chairman, started with a single Manhattan location and now operates 627 stores in all 50 states. The New York–based company has approximately 26,000 employees.[126]

Barnes & Noble has fallen on hard times. The bookseller has experienced declining revenues, resulting in increased debt from $84 million in 2017 to $178 million in 2018.[127] The company also was forced to lay off its entire full-time staff of 1,800 employees in February 2018 to alleviate some of the mounting financial pressure.[128] These financial pressures have taken a toll on the bookseller's stock, which plunged more than 60 percent between 2015 and 2018.[129] Let's explore the causes of Barnes & Noble's downfall.

THE RETAIL BOOKSTORE INDUSTRY HAS EVOLVED

Barnes & Noble was once vilified as a behemoth that drove local bookstores out of business. The bookselling giant grew at the turn of the century with the number of independent bookstores falling 43 percent from 1995 to 2009, according to the American Booksellers Association.[130] This growth was fueled by the increased development of malls and shopping centers.

The company's fortunes changed with two critical, yet conflicting, events. First, the success of online retailers, such as Amazon, has led to the decline of storefront traffic, which Barnes & Noble relies on as a primary revenue source. Second, independent bookstores are making a comeback, aided by increased customer interest in localization and a curated experience. In fact, the number of independent store locations has increased 67 percent between 2009 and 2018.[131]

STAGNATION AND CONFUSION AT BARNES AND NOBLE

So why is Barnes & Noble failing in an industry that is growing in the face of Amazon? Its flagship Union Square location in New York City provides a clue. "The CD and DVD sections, which still occupy a sizable chunk of store space, are often deserted and unmanned," according to Andria Cheng, a *Forbes* contributor. Customers don't seem to have a reason to come into a Barnes and Noble like they would a niche independent bookstore. The national bookseller doesn't have a unique experience to offer; on the contrary, it seems to offer too much of everything. "Elsewhere in the store, alongside bestsellers, signed copies and books . . . are more examples of mismatched merchandise: journals, toys, candles and diffuser sets, tea and chocolate selections," says Cheng.[132]

Business Insider compared New York's Barnes & Noble with Amazon stores and found Barnes & Noble to be "like a dollar store" and that "the grab-bag inventory strategy makes the store seem confused and desperate." The Amazon store, on the other hand, resembled "the future of chain retail."[133] In the end, Barnes & Noble doesn't seem to know what it stands for, and what it wants to be, according to *Forbes*.[134]

WHO'S ATOP THE HIERARCHY?

It's difficult to come up with an effective strategy when you don't have a leader. Chairman Leonard Riggio stepped down as CEO of Barnes & Noble in 2002. The company had stable leadership for another decade, first led by Stephen Riggio (Leonard's younger brother) and then by William Lynch. Lynch is credited with launching the company's electronic bookstore and introducing its electronic book reader, the Nook.[135] Lynch stepped down in 2013, launching a turbulent time for company leadership with five chief executives leaving between 2013 and 2018.[136]

Some of the turnover atop the organization can be attributed to Chairman Riggio. Riggio is notorious for micromanaging his CEOs. An analyst at Gabelli & Company told *The New York Times* that, "Anyone who joins there knows that the chairman is very hands on."[137] For example, Riggio fired former-CEO Ronald Boire less than one year into Boire's tenure. The chairman simply stated that Boire "was not a good fit for the organization" and declined to provide additional commentary after letting him go in 2016.[138] Riggio then hired Demos Parneros as chief executive. Parneros was fired for misconduct a year later and is now suing Barnes & Noble for wrongful termination.[139]

The organization's skyrocketing CEO turnover rate has caught the attention of external stakeholders. For example, book-publishing executives expressed concerns to Riggio about continuing management instability at the retail giant and the direction of the business, according to *The Wall Street Journal*. Publishers argue that Barnes & Noble needs to have a strategy to drive performance. This is especially important when Amazon is competing with it digitally and in stores, and small bookstores are nipping at its heels. "I expressed frustration that if they had a plan, we didn't know it," a publishing executive who met with Riggio told the *Journal*.[140]

Riggio disputes claims that Barnes & Noble is mired in a leadership crisis. "I have a big stake in the business, I founded it and I've been here forever, so I think there's a lot of stability that comes with that . . . If we're without a leader, I'm it," Riggio told *The New York Times*.[141] The chairman and interim CEO firmly believes he is the innovative leader the company currently needs. "We have a lot of work that needs to get done, and I think I bring the necessary leadership," he told *Publishers Weekly*.

Riggio's strategy is for Barnes & Noble to become an innovative storefront bookstore. The new store in Columbia, Maryland, is a prime example. It features a contemporary design, USB and electricity ports in the café, and "book theaters," which offer a 360-degree in-the-round browsing experience. Riggio believes these types of retail outlets are the way of the future. He also believes that the company will succeed with better merchandising and a coherent pricing strategy.[142]

Riggio doesn't appreciate having his strategy questioned, which is evident by the number of CEOs he's lost in a short amount of time. Only time will tell if Reggio's vision and strategy will fix what ails Barnes & Noble.

APPLY THE 3-STEP PROBLEM-SOLVING APPROACH TO OB

STEP 1: Define the problem.

A. Look first at the Outcomes box of the Organizing Framework in Figure 15.9 to help identify the important problem(s) in this case. Remember that a problem is a gap between a desired and a current state. State your problem as a gap, and be sure to consider problems at all three levels. If more than one desired outcome is not being accomplished, decide which one is most important and focus on it for steps 2 and 3.

B. Cases have protagonists (key players), and problems are generally viewed from a particular protagonist's perspective. Take the perspective of Barnes & Noble employees.

STEP 2: Identify causes of the problem by using material from this chapter, summarized in the Organizing Framework shown in Figure 15.9. Causes will appear in either the Inputs box or the Processes box.

A. Start by looking at Figure 15.9 to identify which person factors, if any, are most likely causes to the defined problem. For each cause, ask yourself, *Why is this a cause of the problem?* Asking why multiple times is more likely to lead you to root causes of the problem.

B. Follow the same process for the situation factors.

C. Now consider the Processes box shown in Figure 15.9. Consider concepts listed at all three levels. For any concept that might be a cause, ask yourself, *Why is this a cause?* Again, do this for several iterations to arrive at root causes.

D. To check the accuracy or appropriateness of the causes, map them onto the defined problem.

STEP 3: Make your recommendations for solving the problem. Consider whether you want to resolve it, solve it, or dissolve it (see Section 1.5). Which recommendation is desirable and feasible?

A. Given the causes identified in Step 2, what are your best recommendations? Use the content in Chapter 15 or one of the earlier chapters to propose a solution.

B. You may find potential solutions in the OB in Action boxes and Applying OB boxes within this chapter. These features provide insights into what other individuals or companies are doing in relationship to the topic at hand.

C. Create an action plan for implementing your recommendations.

Does Tax-Exempt Status for Universities Make Them Good Organizational Citizens?

You learned that the balanced scorecard identifies four categories of organizational effectiveness criteria. Community-related measures of effectiveness, such as good corporate citizenship, are one component of the internal business process perspective. This challenge considers the issue of community-related effectiveness.

Surely universities and colleges are good for society, but could they do better? Consider the issue of federal income taxation. According to the Association of American Universities (AAU), "the vast majority of private and public universities and colleges are tax-exempt entities as defined by the Internal Revenue Code . . . because of their educational purposes—purposes that the federal government has long recognized as fundamental to fostering the productive and civic capacities of citizens."[143] The AAU further notes that "income for activities that are substantially related to the purpose of an institution's tax exemption, charitable contributions received, and investment income are not subject to federal income tax."[144]

Local Community Uproar

Princeton University is New Jersey's only Ivy League school. Its $22.7 billion endowment is the fourth largest in the United States.[145] Not only has Princeton not paid income taxes on investment income from this endowment, but it has also been exempt from property taxes. This property tax exemption is problematic for the local Princeton community because residents end up paying more in taxes to make up the difference. "Those with the least resources . . . [are] subsidizing the nonpayment of some of the wealthiest property owners, namely Princeton University," according to the town's former mayor.[146]

Local homeowners filed suit against Princeton University in 2011, challenging the tax-exempt status of the school. The 27 plaintiffs were low-income, disabled, or retirees. Bruce Afran, an attorney who represented the residents, told *The Wall Street Journal* that, "We don't want Princeton to just be a preserve of the well-off . . . so we designed this lawsuit to try to stabilize the tax base, to give these more disadvantaged families a chance to keep up."[147] The university settled the lawsuit in 2016 by agreeing to pay $18.2 million over six years. However, the question of future property tax liability remains unresolved.[148]

Congress Gets Involved

Congress passed a federal budget bill in 2018 that targets 35 colleges and universities that have large endowments. The law enacts a 1.4% excise tax on annual endowment income for institutions with assets greater than $500,000 per full-time student. Yale University is one of the institutions impacted by this law because it has a total of $2 million per full-time student. Therefore, the university will have to pay an estimated $30.8 million on its 2018 endowment income. The tax will surely cause budgeting challenges for Yale and other affected institutions, an expert on endowments told the *Yale Daily News*. Yale is lobbying Congress to repeal the law.[149]

If You Were a Lawmaker Evaluating the Tax-Exempt Status of Princeton and Yale, How Would You Vote?

1. I would continue to give universities tax-exempt status on both endowments and property taxes. Universities most likely spend the tax-exempt money on scholarships, buildings, and funding research. All these expenditures provide value to society, suggesting that universities are good citizens.

2. I would vote for tax-exempt status on investment income for the same reasons noted above, but not for the property taxes. Everyone else has to pay property taxes, and if colleges and universities paid them too, the funds would directly help the members of the surrounding community by reducing their tax burden. This is good citizenship.

3. I would revoke the tax-exempt status of investment income and collect property taxes from the universities. Being a good corporate citizen necessitates that these institutions pay taxes like businesses and individuals do.

4. Invent other options.

16

Managing Change and Stress

After reading this chapter, you should be able to:

LO 16-1   Understand the major forces of organizational change.

LO 16-2   Apply knowledge of various models to effectively manage change.

LO 16-3   Outline and manage major causes of resistance to change.

LO 16-4   Explain both the benefits and problems associated with stress.

LO 16-5   Use OB knowledge and tools to manage change and stress.

LO 16-6   Describe the implications of managing stress and change for you and managers.

We conclude the book with how to manage change and stress. These organization-level processes (see Figure 16.1) are fitting ways to conclude our OB journey, because they either influence or are influenced by everything else you've learned. For instance, effectively managing change involves person and situation inputs, as well as numerous processes at the individual, group, and organizational levels. Similarly, the success of change initiatives is measured in terms of outcomes across the three levels of OB. We discuss stress along with change because change is one of the most common and significant causes of employee stress. Managing change effectively will not only reduce the stress in your life, but also help you stand out from the competition throughout your career.

FIGURE 16.1   Organizing Framework for Understanding and Applying OB

INPUTS	PROCESSES	OUTCOMES
Person Factors • Personality • Demographics • Skills and abilities • Values • Needs • Ethics • Stressors **Situation Factors** • Relationship quality • Leadership • Human resource problems/ prospects • Managerial behavior/ decisions • Culture (organizational) • Technology • Market forces • Social, political, and regulatory pressures • Stressors • Organizational mission and vision • Strategy	**Individual Level** • Emotions • Cognitive appraisals • Coping strategies • Perceptions • Motivation • Trust • Communication **Group/Team Level** • Group/team dynamics • Conflict and negotiation • Decision making • Power, influence, and politics • Performance management • Leadership • Trust **Organizational Level** • Human resource policies and practices • Culture • Organizational design and effectiveness • Leading and managing change and stress • Trust	**Individual Level** • Task performance • Work attitudes • Well-being • Citizenship behavior/ counterproductive behavior • Resistance to change • Turnover • Career outcomes • Stress (physical and emotional) • Accidents **Group/Team Level** • Group/team performance • Group satisfaction • Group cohesion and conflict • Resistance to change **Organizational Level** • Survival • Accounting/financial performance • Organizational performance • Customer satisfaction • Innovation • Reputation

Winning at Work

To Move or Not to Move, That Is the Question

Throughout your career you'll likely have many jobs in many locations, and some of the most appealing may require you to relocate. Such opportunities can be very exciting and the decision to pack and go easy. However, depending on you (your age and career goals), the job (responsibilities and future promotion prospects), your life (proximity to family and your partner's career), and the distance (another state or country), the decision may be quite challenging. Relocation decisions often require you to balance professional and personal benefits and costs. The following considerations may help.

1. **Think Big.** This means consider your larger career and life goals. Who do you want to become and what do you want to accomplish professionally? What sort of life do you want outside of work? How would the move impact you as a partner and how will the move affect your partner? If you have children or plan to have children, what are the implications for them and for you as their parent? In short, consider your happiness within and between your professional and personal lives.

2. **Keep a Foot in Each Place.** Some moves, especially those that are international, can disconnect you from your previous network. Though you'll presumably build new relationships and skills in your new location, it may be important also to work hard at preserving those ties in your original location. Plan for this, including who you'll communicate with, how, and how often. It may be wise to plan periodic return trips to the other office, and/or make attempts to attend important events at the old location, even if you have to pay for it yourself.

3. **Next Job.** You're relocating for a new position and the opportunities you expect it to provide. What opportunities will likely be available to you because of the position you're relocating for? Consider whether the move and associated cost (personal, social and professional) is worth it.

4. **Is there a Parachute?** Sometimes things don't work out, you're miserable, your family is miserable, or the job and location just don't meet your expectations. Can you come back to your old position? Is there another attractive position within the company you could

reasonably expect to obtain? Or, will you be on your own to find a new job with a different company? Some organizations provide employees a "leave of absence" or a trial period and will even hold the old position, but this is relatively rare (consider negotiating for this). And if moving expenses were covered in the relocation package, then you might have to pay back some portion should you have a change of heart.

5. **Your Partner.** If you currently have a partner this will likely be a major factor in your consideration. What about his or her job and career? Are there opportunities for both of you? Does one need to make a compromise, and if so, is it temporary or long-term? You may not be able to definitively answer these questions, but they should be thoroughly explored and discussed.

6. **Children.** They of course matter too, especially depending on their ages, schools, friends, and family. Experts recommend talking to them as well, but how much you weigh their input and consider them in the decision is a deeply personal matter.[1]

What's Ahead in This Chapter

You've heard the statement: "The only constant in life is change." Now we want you to think about what this fact might mean for your job and career. We created this chapter not only to help you figure this out, but also to give you practical knowledge and tools to help manage change at different levels in the Organizing Framework for OB. We'll explore common forces or drivers for change, as well as learn about some popular models for understanding and managing change. Because it's normal for people to resist change, it helps to learn why and what you can do about it. Since change is a major cause of stress at work, and in your life as a whole, we help you understand both its positive and negative aspects. The chapter concludes with suggestions for managing resistance, stress, and change more generally.

16.1 FORCES FOR CHANGE

THE BIGGER PICTURE

There are a great many potential forces for organizational change. In order for you to understand and manage them more effectively, we organize them into two broad categories—external and internal.

Before we dive into a discussion of the forces for change, we'd like you to assess your own attitudes toward change. Remember that attitudes are tendencies to respond either favorably or unfavorably to a given object or situation. Complete Self-Assessment 16.1 to learn about your general attitudes toward change, and use what you learn in this chapter to help strengthen an already positive attitude or improve one that is not.

SELF-ASSESSMENT 16.1   CAREER READINESS

Assessing Your Attitudes toward Change at Work

Please be prepared to answer these questions if your instructor has assigned Self-Assessment 16.1 in Connect.

1. What is your overall attitude? Are you surprised?
2. Think of three examples from school or work that are consistent with your score.
3. Now think of a clearly negative attitude you held toward a particular change. What made this response different from or similar to your general attitudes toward change?
4. Describe two specific ways you can improve your attitudes toward change. (Hint: Draw on what you learned about attitudes.)

SOURCE: Adapted from V. D. Miller, J. R. Johnson, and J. Grau, "Antecedents and Willingness to Participate in a Planned Organizational Change," *Journal of Applied Communication Research*, 1994, 22: 59–80.

Now that you have a sense of your own attitudes toward change, consider this question about organizations: How do they know when they should change? What cues should they look for? Although there is no perfect answer to this question, a good place to start is to consider the forces for change. We categorize them into external and internal forces to make them easier to understand and remember (see Figure 16.2).

External Forces

External forces for change **originate outside the organization.** They can either present new opportunities for the organization to realize and grow, or they can cause its ultimate demise. The advent of smartphones created an opportunity that Apple seized and converted into a market-dominating platform with the iPhone. This same opportunity

FIGURE 16.2   External and Internal Forces for Change

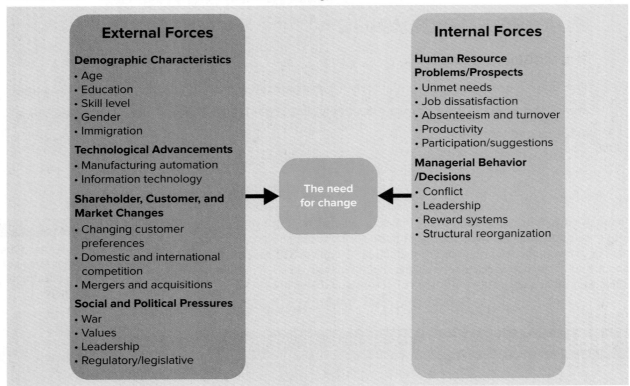

caused the downfall of the BlackBerry as a dominant mobile phone player. Video streaming has been meteoric for Netflix, Hulu, and others, but it crushed and eliminated Blockbuster and other video stores. Ride sharing—Lyft and Uber—have not eliminated taxis but it has upended the industry around the world. Let us now consider the four key external forces for change:

1. Demographic characteristics.
2. Technological advancements.
3. Shareholder, customer, and market changes.
4. Social, political, and regulatory.

Demographic Characteristics   As shown in Figure 16.3, Asians are now the fastest-growing immigrant group in the United States, surpassing Latin Americans (including those from Mexico).[2] Millennials (those born between 1981 and 1996) should pass Baby Boomers as the largest generation in the U.S. population by 2019, and they are already the largest generation in the workforce (35 percent of the total). Another interesting statistic—20 percent of U.S. citizens live in multigenerational households, a trend that exists across racial groups and is nearly as high as it was in 1950![3] Demographic factors like these are motivating organizations to change benefits and aspects of the work environment in order to attract, motivate, and retain diverse employees. This has caused organizations to change many aspects of their business, from the products and services they offer, how they are delivered, to how they attract, hire, and retain employees.

Persistently high unemployment levels among young people around the world are creating a strong force for change felt by governments and organizations alike. Many believe much of the unrest in the Middle East and Europe is fueled by a younger population that cannot find meaningful employment opportunities.

FIGURE 16.3   Racial Demographic Trends in the United States: 1965–2065

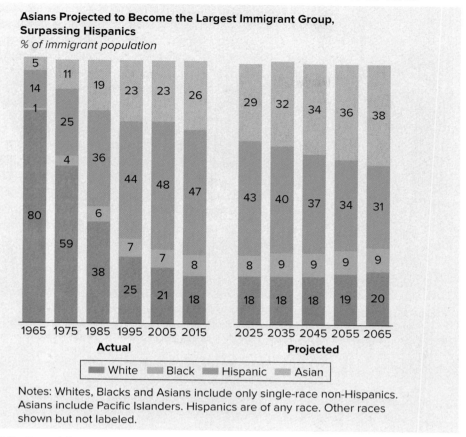

Asians Projected to Become the Largest Immigrant Group, Surpassing Hispanics
% of immigrant population

Legend: White, Black, Hispanic, Asian

Notes: Whites, Blacks and Asians include only single-race non-Hispanics. Asians include Pacific Islanders. Hispanics are of any race. Other races shown but not labeled.

SOURCES: Pew Research Center estimates for 1965–2015 based on adjusted census data; Pew Research Center. "Modern Immigration Wave Brings 59 Million to U.S., Driving Population Growth and Change Through 2065: Views of Immigration's Impact on U.S. Society Mixed." Washington, DC, 2015.

Technological Advancements   Technology continues to be a common means for improving productivity, competitiveness, and customer service. The effect of social media, for instance, cannot be overstated as it has changed every dimension of our lives. Virtual reality (VR) has already begun to revolutionize medicine, for example, by enabling physicians to see 3-D images of tumors and organs without cutting the patient open. Microsoft HoloLens VR allows medical students to virtually inspect parts of the human anatomy in less than half the time required by students using only cadavers. The scalability of such applications is impactful too, as the growing global population will require far more clinicians to be trained, in more and sometimes remote places, and VR may be part of the answer.[4]

Drones are doing much more than delivering packages and taking aerial videos of your favorite hike or beach. They are also delivering blood and other emergency supplies. Zipline is helping the government of Rwanda provide medical care to residents who are isolated due to distance or a lack of infrastructure, such as roads, clinics, and hospitals. Expertise and supplies are going to those in need via drone, rather than patients traveling to find care.[5]

Chipotle, the fresh-Mex restaurant chain, is utilizing technology to further boost its robust sales and fuel its tremendous growth. For instance, technology is used to build customer loyalty. Chipotle, like others in the industry, now generates a significant and growing proportion of their sales from online orders—up 64 percent from a year earlier when they accounted for 13 percent of total sales in early 2019. The company has partnered with Venmo, a digital wallet, to facilitate sales and build customer loyalty. Chipotle has taken it

Chipotle Mexican Grill has taken an especially effective approach to online orders. The app is only one component, as they have also created a "second line" behind the counter to fill these orders. This prevents the growing online sales from negatively impacting the quality and speed of service delivered to in-store customers.

BestStockFoto/Shutterstock

a step further and installed separate food preparation lines to serve digital orders. The reasoning is two-pronged—to meet the growing demand and avoid slowing down and eroding the experience of in-store customers.[6]

Each of these may present job and career opportunities for you. OB will certainly play a central role in the level of success individuals and organizations will have with each trend. Put another way, it is people who design and use such technological tools, interpret the data, formulate a plan, and then apply it effectively.

Shareholder, Customer, and Market Changes   Increased shareholder activism is one of the most significant forces for change public companies have faced in the past several years. Shareholders have pressed organizations to be more efficient, respond to legal lapses, address privacy issues and hacks, and justify executive compensation packages. Wall Street firm Janna Partners and CalSTRS, the enormous California public school teachers' pension fund wrote a letter to Apple insisting it explore and address the detrimental effects of its products on children. In the letter, Jana stated: "we believe the long-term health of its youngest customers and the health of the society, our economy, and the company itself are inextricably linked."[7]

Social, Political, and Regulatory   Uber continues to battle regulators, governments, unions, and others regarding business practices, infringement on taxi services and licenses, and employee versus contractor status of its drivers. These challenges are routinely in the news, including its especially consequential conflict with the London Transit Authority. Taxi drivers, the famous black cabs, face some of the most stringent qualifications of any in the world. They have argued Uber's drivers have unfair advantage and are circumventing

Regulators can be major forces for change, either helping or hurting a company or industry. Uber, for instance, has battled regulators across the globe, perhaps most notably in London. Decisions by regulators there could have significant consequences locally and globally if other cities and countries adopt similar policies.

Anthony Devlin/PA Images/Alamy Stock Photo

the same requirements they must meet. If the Authority revokes Uber's license to operate in the city, which it has done in the past, the company will lose one of its largest and most lucrative markets in the world.[8]

Cross cultural and cross boarder differences can also drive change. Tech companies often face tougher regulations and big fines in Europe, such as the billions of dollars European Union regulators have levied against Google,[9] and the Indian government's potentially severe restrictions on what Amazon and Walmart can sell on their sites in the country.[10]

Internal Forces

***Internal forces for change* come from inside the organization.** Internal forces for change come from both human resource problems and managerial behavior and decisions.

Human Resource Problems or Prospects   Human resource challenges stem from employee perceptions regarding the way they are treated at work and the match between individual and organization needs and desires. Dissatisfaction is a symptom of unmet needs or mistreatment and most often requires attention from company leadership and may signal a need for change. Similarly, unusual levels of absenteeism, work slowdowns, strikes, and turnover can be powerful internal forces for change. American Airlines' on-time performance, for instance, took a hit when mechanics slowed the pace of their work due to a lack of progress in contract negotiations.[11] To help combat these challenges, leaders and managers of change should encourage employee participation early and throughout the change process.

Both internal (employees) and external (investors) forces can lead to changes in senior leadership, as described in the OB in Action box.

OB in Action

The C-Suite Revolving Door

The saying "the only constant is change" also applies to the CEO's office. The top bosses at some companies seem to turn over as frequently as call center employees. Toy maker Mattel changed CEOs three times between 2015 and 2019. Seemingly none has been able to stem losses and achieve profitability, let alone new growth.[12]

The Top Turns Fast and Often Investors' desire for improved performance has spurred a dramatic increase in CEO change as a means for such improvements. Outplacement firm Challenger, Gray, & Christmas reported a 25 percent increase in top executive turnover from 2017 to 2018,[13] and this increase occurred in a relatively strong economy.

Reasons for Turnover Of course, there are many reasons CEOs leave—retirement, other opportunities, #MeToo and other questionable conduct,[14] and even illness and death. Sadly, Sergio Marchionne, who was credited with saving or at least reviving Fiat and Chrysler, died due to complications of shoulder surgery.[15] But research provides some measure of support for CEO change and performance improvement, such as that changes aligning with sound organizational strategy are more likely to generate gains, specifically, when a CEO is replaced due to differences with the Board's view on appropriate organizational strategy.[16]

Gains Are Not Quick The same research showed that the best performing companies often suffered stock price declines In the first year after the CEO's departure, but the prices rebounded and matched the competition in about three years.[17] The same companies typically tied the new CEO's compensation to long-term incentives, rather than short-term quarterly metrics, and they also tended to limit stock buy-backs (a very common way of improving short-term earnings per share). Companies and new CEOs who were successful also increased investment In the business (capital expenditures) by 36 percent annually, much higher than average.[18]

YOUR THOUGHTS?

1. What are your thoughts about removing CEOs in order to boost organizational performance?

2. Assume you're on the board of directors, what three elements of CEO performance would you consider most important when deciding whether to force a CEO out?

3. What are three potential drawbacks to CEO turnover?

Managerial Behaviors and Decisions Excessive interpersonal conflict between managers and their subordinates or the board of directors can be a sign that change is needed, as can misconduct. 2018 alone saw numerous CEOs ousted or resign due to alleged or actual misconduct. Martin Sorrell, founder and CEO of one of the world's largest advertising and marketing firms, WPP, stepped down due to allegations of misconduct, and Brian Krzanich, former CEO of Intel, left after it was learned he had a consensual relationship with a subordinate. No scandal, no abuse, but such relationships violate company policies.[19]

Andrew Mason, founder and former CEO of Groupon, was fired due to his strategy and the firm's underperformance. Mason had decided to take the firm aggressively into selling goods and not just coupons for discounts with local merchants. These actions, combined with a disappointing international expansion, led the board to conclude that his decisions and direction were not right for the company. For his part, Mason said: "After

Changes in an organization's strategy can cause leadership to make a wide array of other changes, including removing senior leaders. This can even happen to founders, as was the case with Andrew Mason at Groupon.

Christoph Soeder/dapd/AP Images

four and a half intense and wonderful years as CEO of Groupon, I've decided I'd like to spend more time with my family. Just kidding—I was fired today."[20]

When leadership at the top changes, it is common for incoming executives to clean house and insert their own team. Airbus, the European aerospace pioneer (more than just airplanes), appointed a new CEO in early 2019, Guillaume Faury. His work was cut out for him, as the company continues to face intense competition from the likes of Boeing, and the challenges of overcoming bribery and corruption allegations. Faury is expected to change things, and to do this he brought in his own executive team.[21]

Now that you have a sense of the various forces of change, let's explore some of the common forms of change and models used to both understand and manage change more effectively.

16.2 TYPES AND MODELS OF CHANGE

THE BIGGER PICTURE

This section provides insights into general types of organizational changes, as well as reviews of Lewin's change model, a systems model of change, Kotter's eight steps for leading organizational change, and the organizational development approach. Each serves as an organizational-level tool for managing outcomes across the levels of our Organizing Framework for Understanding and Applying OB.

LO 16-2

Apply knowledge of various models to effectively manage change.

To manage change effectively, a contingency approach suggests you'd be wise to have a variety of approaches or change management tools and use the one best suited for a particular change. We provide such knowledge and tools in this section. Let's start our discussion by looking at three general types of changes.

Three General Types of Change

A useful high-level way to organize and think about change is in terms of its degree of complexity, cost, and uncertainty, and classify it as either adaptive, innovative, or radically innovative (see Figure 16.4).

1. ***Adaptive change* reintroduces a familiar practice either in a different unit or in the same unit at a different point in time.** Adaptive changes are the least complex, costly, and uncertain. Allowing the market research group to operate on flextime, after allowing the sales group to do so, is an example of adapting the scheduling practices in one group based on those in another. Adaptive changes are not particularly threatening to employees because they are at least somewhat familiar.

2. ***Innovative change* introduces a practice that is new to the organization** and is midway on the continuum of complexity, cost, and uncertainty. If competitors in your industry utilize shared office space, but your company hasn't, then doing so qualifies as innovative change. Innovative changes bring more uncertainty and cause more concern than adaptive changes.

FIGURE 16.4 Generic Typology of Organizational Change

3. **Radically innovative change introduces a practice new to the industry** and is at the high end of the continuum of complexity, cost, and uncertainty. The introduction of the sharing economy has been a radical change for many industries, such as transportation (Uber and Lyft) and housing (Airbnb).

Driverless cars are and will be radically innovative for multiple industries. Many players are obvious and already involved. For instance, taxi companies will likely still exist but without drivers, as will the likes of Uber, Lyft, and other ride sharing companies. Automobile and technology companies are already deeply invested, but what about others? Who else? It's easy to see how health care providers could dispatch vehicles to transport patients to appointments, but what will this mean for the legal driving age and car ownership?

Furthermore, as change moves from adaptive to radical it requires and results in an increasingly profound role for people, processes, and culture.[22] Therefore, if you want to radically innovate you had better understand and apply OB.

Now that you have a way of describing and classifying types of change, we will explore several models to help you understand and manage change more effectively.

Lewin's Change Model

Most models of organizational change originated from the landmark work of social psychologist Kurt Lewin. Lewin developed a three-stage model of planned change that explained how to initiate, manage, and stabilize the change process.[23] The three stages are *unfreezing*, *changing*, and *refreezing* (see Figure 16.5).

Unfreezing The focus of the unfreezing stage is creating motivation to change. The most common, but not necessarily most effective, way of communicating a convincing reason to change is to demonstrate current practices are less than ideal. Data related to employee or customer satisfaction, or showing market share gains made by competitors, is often used. The driverless car example above will require unfreezing for, among others, consumers. Some claim the end of conventional car ownership is quickly coming. Purchasing, maintaining, insuring, and keeping a personal car is on the way out.[24]

Changing Because change calls for learning and doing things differently, this stage entails providing employees with new information, new behavioral models, new processes or procedures, new equipment, new technology, or new ways of getting the job done.

How does management know what to change? There is no simple answer to this question. Organizational change can be aimed at improvement or growth, or it can focus on solving a problem such as poor customer service or low productivity. Change also can be targeted at different levels in an organization. The point to keep in mind is that change should be targeted at some type of desired end-result. The Organizing Framework for Understanding and Applying OB is a good tool to use for identifying specific targets or purposes for change.

FIGURE 16.5 Lewin Model of Change

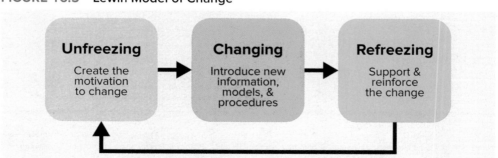

Refreezing The goal of refreezing is to support and reinforce the change. Managers support change by helping employees integrate the new behavior or attitude into their accustomed way of doing things. They can first give employees a chance to exhibit the new behaviors or attitudes. Once this happens, positive reinforcement can encourage the desired change. More specifically, continuous reinforcement with extrinsic rewards (recognition, feedback, bonuses) is useful early in the change process. This helps establish clear links between the desired new behaviors and the reinforcing reward or recognition. And don't forget role modeling. Walking the talk of change is arguably the most powerful way to get others to follow.

A Systems Model of Change

The systems approach to change is based on the notion that any change, no matter how large or small, has ripple effects. Promoting an individual to a new work group affects group dynamics in both the old and new groups. Creating project or work teams may necessitate revamping compensation practices. These examples illustrate that *change creates additional change.*

A systems model of change is similar to the systems framework used in the Organizing Framework but a bit more complex (see Figure 16.6). This systems model of change

FIGURE 16.6 Systems Model of Change

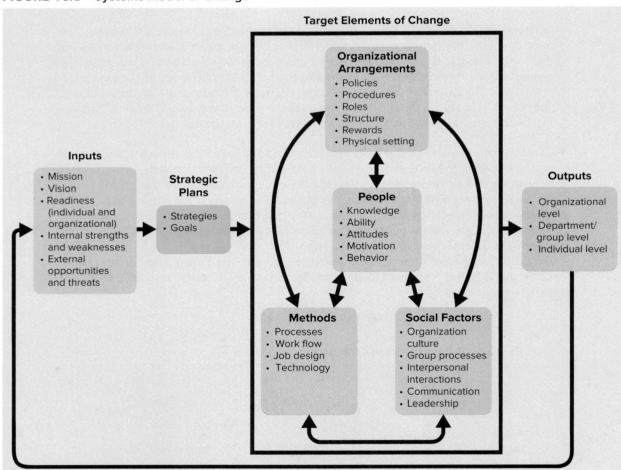

SOURCES: Fuqua, D. R. and Kurpius, D. J., "Conceptual Models in Organizational Consultation," *Journal of Counseling and Development,* July–August 1993, 602–618; and Nadler, David A., and Michael L. Tushman. "Organizational Frame Bending: Principles for Managing Reorientation." *Academy of Management Executive* 3, no. 3 (1989): 194–204. https://pdfs.semanticscholar.org/3250/e8a8f2f99c94e362fabcb2147a8ec1395d6e.pdf.

includes inputs, strategic plans, target elements of change, and outputs. It is a very practical approach that can diagnose *what* to change and *how* to evaluate the success of a change effort. Let's explore its individual components.

Inputs   The starting point for organizational change should be asking and answering the question: "Why change?" Leaders need to be clear about the overarching motive or reason for change, and elements in the inputs box in Figure 16.6 can help. For instance, it is wise to ensure the intended changes align with the organization's mission, vision, and resulting strategic plan.[25]

Mission statements express the reason an organization exists. Some examples of clear and effective mission statements follow:

- Instagram—"To capture and share the world's moments."[26]
- TED (Technology, Entertainment, and Design)—"Spread ideas."[27]
- Patagonia—"Build the best product, cause no unnecessary harm, use business to inspire and implement solutions to the environmental crisis."[28]
- Sweetgreen—"To inspire healthier communities by connecting people to real food."[29]

All well and good, you say, but how does an organization create an effective mission? Sally Jewell, former CEO of REI, the outdoor clothing and equipment retailer, describes how she and her team of 150 leaders went about formulating a mission for the company. The details are in the Applying OB box.

Applying OB

How to Formulate a Meaningful Mission Statement

Missions are big-picture, long term, and existential. These qualities mean they are often quite general, but they cannot be too general, because that would make them abstract and meaningless. Sally Jewell, when CEO of outdoor clothing and adventure retailer REI, followed a very useful and repeatable process when refining the company's mission. She began by assembling a representative team of leaders. It's best to be inclusive rather than exclusive here, because engaging people in the process helps ensure their interests are reflected in the mission and they will be more likely to "live it." Then she asked team members:

1. Why does our organization exist? Ask this question three to five times to get a deeper, richer view.
2. What would happen if our organization went away?
3. Why do I devote my creative energies to this organization?
4. Compile and consolidate the answers to these questions.[30]

This process resulted in REI's mission statement: "To inspire, educate, and outfit for a lifetime of outdoor adventure and stewardship."[31]

Another input in the systems model of change is *vision,* **which is a compelling future state for an organization.** Missions typically imply little or nothing about change and instead define the organization's overall purpose. Effective visions, in contrast, describe a highly desirable future and outline how the organization will get there, such as which markets, services, products, and people will be involved, and how all these elements

Patagonia, an outdoor clothing and equipment retailer, was one of the first to adopt a vision focused on the environment and employee well-being.

lentamart/Shutterstock

align with the organization's values. Interface Inc., a world leader in sustainability and commercial interiors, captures all these and more in its vision:

Interface will become the first name in commercial and institutional interiors worldwide through its commitment to **people, process, product, place, and profits.** We will strive to create an organization wherein all people are accorded unconditional respect and dignity; one that allows each person to continuously learn and develop. We will focus on product (which includes service) through constant emphasis on process quality and engineering, which we will combine with careful attention to our customers' needs so as always to deliver superior value to our customers, thereby maximizing all stakeholders' satisfaction. We will honor the places where we do business by endeavoring to become the first name in industrial ecology, a corporation that cherishes nature and restores the environment. Interface will lead by example and validate by results, including profits, leaving the world a better place than when we began, and we will be restorative through the power of our influence in the world.[32]

The following OB in Action box describes how founder of TOMS Shoes Blake Mycoskie's compelling vision has motivated him and now many others to build giving into their business models.

OB in Action

Changing the World with Shoes and Much More

Vision for Change The Idea for "Tomorrow's Shoes"—now known as TOMS—was born In 2006 during a trip to Argentina. This is when founder and now serial entrepreneur Blake Mycoskie saw the impact a pair of shoes could make for kids without them. He quickly realized that giving one pair to one person was not enough; after all, where and how would they get their next pair? This is where the idea of "buy one-give one" was born. Sell a pair of shoes to someone who can afford them, and then use part of the proceeds to make a pair to give to someone that can't. [33]

Impact Besides being cool and trendy, the vision of "improving lives" made the shoes even more appealing to customers, as well as employees and suppliers. Sales have since exploded, but perhaps the better measure is more than 60 million pairs of shoes have been donated.[34] Mycoskie is quick to point out, however, that shoes are simply a vehicle or means for realizing his vision for changing

A vision for change and doing well by doing good has always been a fundamental driving force for entrepreneur Blake Mycoskie.

Gary Gershoff/Getty Images

people's lives. He has since applied the make-one-give-one practice in other ways, such as coffee, more than 250,000 weeks' supply of clean drinking water, and over 360,000 pairs of glasses or medical treatments to restore sight.[35]

YOUR THOUGHTS?

1. How or why is Mycoskie's vision of "improving lives" compelling to you?

2. Think of one other product or service you think could improve lives.

3. What do you think are the challenges with a business using a buy-one-make-one model?

4. Related to #3, why do you think we don't see more companies doing this? After all, Mycoskie and TOMS have been incredibly successful.

Readiness for change **is the strength of our beliefs and attitudes about the extent to which changes are needed and our capacity to successfully implement them.** Readiness can be an individual or an organization-level input.[36] Put another way, effective change at work requires both the employees and the employer have high readiness and are willing and able to change. Readiness has four components:

1. Necessity for change.
2. Top-management support for change efforts.
3. Personal ability to cope with changes.
4. Perceived personal consequences of change.

The first two pertain to an organization's readiness and the last two to your readiness. Self-Assessment 16.2 will help you gauge your own readiness for change. You can also use it to measure the readiness of an organization to which you belong.

SELF-ASSESSMENT 16.2 — CAREER READINESS

What Is Your Readiness for Change?

Please be prepared to answer these questions if your instructor has assigned Self-Assessment 16.2 in Connect.

1. Focusing on your personal readiness, which component is higher?
2. Describe how you think this affects how you deal with this change? Think of how it affects you and your interactions with coworkers.
3. Of the two organizational readiness components, which is the lowest?
4. How do you think this result will affect the success of the particular change? Be specific.
5. Given what the readiness measure tells you, what do you recommend to improve your readiness and your organization's readiness?

Strategic Plans A strategic plan outlines an organization's long-term direction and the actions necessary to achieve planned results. Among other tools, strategic plans can use SWOT analysis to identify strengths, weaknesses, opportunities, and threats. In the process model of change, SWOT analysis provides input by helping managers develop an organizational strategy for reaching their desired change goals, such as higher profits, customer satisfaction, quality, or return on investment, acceptable levels of turnover and employee satisfaction.

Target Elements of Change   Target elements of change are the components of an organization that can be changed. In the systems model they essentially represent levers managers can push and pull to influence various aspects of an organization. The target elements of change can also help diagnose problems and identify change-related solutions. Figure 16.6 illustrates four target elements:

1. Organizational arrangements.
2. Social factors.
3. Methods.
4. People.

Each target element of change contains a subset of more detailed organizational features, all of which are OB topics covered in this book and included in the Organizing Framework.

There are two final issues to keep in mind about the target elements. First, the double-headed arrows in the figure are intended to communicate that change ripples across an organization. Changing a reward system, for instance, to reinforce team rather than individual performance (an organizational arrangement) is likely to change organizational culture (a social factor). Second, the "people" component is at the center of the target elements of the change box because all organizational change ultimately affects employees—and vice versa. This means organizational change is more likely to succeed when managers proactively consider the impact of change on employees.

Outputs   Goals or results are the final piece of the process model of change and should be consistent with an organization's strategic plan. Figure 16.6 indicates that change can be directed at the individual, group, or organizational level, and change efforts are more complicated and challenging to manage when targeted at the organizational level. This is because organizational-level changes are more likely to affect more than one of the target elements of change shown in the model.

Now that you've learned the details of the systems approach to change, we shift our focus to one of the most popular approaches to organizational change since the 1990s—Kotter's eight steps.

Kotter's Eight-Step Organizational Change Process

John Kotter, a world-renowned expert in leadership and change management, believes organizational change most often fails not because of inadequate planning but because of ineffective implementation. To help overcome this challenge, he proposed an eight-step process for leading change (see Figure 16.7). This approach differs from the systems model in that it does not help diagnose the need for change or the targets of change. It is somewhat like Lewin's model, however, as it also guides managers through a sequential process. For instance, you could map Kotter's first four steps onto Lewin's "unfreezing," steps 5, 6, and 7 onto "changing," and step 8 onto "refreezing."

The value of Kotter's approach is its recommendations about specific behaviors and activities. Notice that vision and strategy are central components, as in the systems model. But Kotter insists the steps need to be followed in sequence and none can be skipped. It therefore requires a tremendous commitment of time, money, and people to implement Kotter's eight steps. This approach can prove very challenging for most organizations, and particularly for individuals, to implement. Its hurdles, however, are partially overcome by our final approach to change—organizational development (OD).

Creating Change through Organizational Development (OD)

One way to think of organizational development (OD) is to approach the organization as if it were a sick patient: "Diagnose" its ills, prescribe and implement an "intervention," and

FIGURE 16.7 Eight Steps to Leading Organizational Change

STEP	DESCRIPTION
1. Establish a sense of urgency.	Unfreeze the organization using a compelling reason why change is needed.
2. Create the guiding coalition.	Create a team with appropriate knowledge and enough power to lead change.
3. Develop a vision and strategy.	Create a vision to inspire and a strategic plan to guide the change process.
4. Communicate the change vision.	Implement a communication strategy and "overcommunicate" the new vision and strategic plan.
5. Empower broad-based action.	Eliminate obstacles (processes and people) and encourage risk taking and creative problem solving.
6. Generate short-term wins.	Plan for and create short-term "wins" or improvements. Recognize and reward people who contribute to the wins.
7. Consolidate gains and produce more change.	Allow guiding coalition to use credibility from short-term wins to create more change. Additional people are brought into the change process as change cascades throughout the organization. Attempts are made to energize the change process.
8. Anchor new approaches in the culture.	Reinforce the changes by highlighting connections between new behaviors and processes and organizational success. Embed these in performance management and other processes—hiring, promotion, and leadership development and succession.

SOURCE: Kotter, John P. *Leading Change.* Boston: Harvard Business School Press, 1996.

"evaluate" progress or effectiveness. If the evaluation reveals that positive change has not occurred, this information provides feedback you can use to refine the diagnosis or consider the extent to which the intervention was effectively implemented or appropriate in the first place (see Figure 16.8).

FIGURE 16.8 Organizational Development Processes

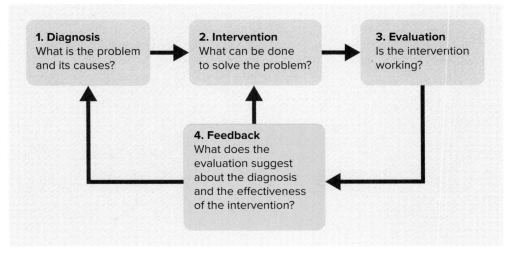

SOURCE: French, Wendell L., and Cecil Bell. *Organization Development: Behavioral Interventions for Organizational Improvement.* Englewood Cliffs, NJ: Prentice Hall, 1978.

Let's improve your understanding by exploring each of these components in more detail.

1. ***Diagnosis:*** *What is the problem and its causes?* Many means can be used to answer this question: interviews, surveys, meetings, and direct observation. We recommend the 3-Step Problem-Solving Approach and the Organizing Framework to help. The target elements in the systems model of change can also be useful. For example, you might ask, "To what extent does the structure or the reward system contribute to the problem?"

2. ***Intervention:*** *What can be done to solve the problem?* The treatment or intervention represents the changes being made to solve the problem and are based on the causes. If the cause of low-quality service is poor teamwork, then team building might be a useful intervention. No single intervention is best in all circumstances—the best solution depends on the situation.

3. ***Evaluation:*** *Is the intervention working?* Evaluation requires measurement and the measures must match the problem. If the problem is job performance you are highly unlikely to properly evaluate teamwork or quality of service if you measure only sales volume. The final evaluation should compare measures of effectiveness obtained before and after the intervention.

4. ***Feedback:*** *What does the evaluation suggest about the diagnosis and the effectiveness of the intervention?* If the evaluation reveals the intervention worked, then the OD process is complete and you can consider how best to "refreeze" the changes. However, a negative evaluation means one of two things: either (1) the initial diagnosis was wrong, or (2) the intervention was inappropriate or not implemented effectively. Negative evaluations generally require you to collect more information about steps 1 and 2 in the OD process shown in Figure 16.8.

Now that we've explored a number of key models of change, let's learn about something that affects almost every change, regardless of the model or approach—resistance.

16.3 UNDERSTANDING RESISTANCE TO CHANGE

THE BIGGER PICTURE

You can't think about change without also thinking about resistance. If you are going to effectively manage change you need to understand and manage resistance. Your ability to do this is fundamental to your effectiveness in managing this important organizational-level process and its many related outcomes in the Organizing Framework for Understanding and Applying OB.

Resistance to change is any thought, emotion, or behavior that does not align with actual or potential changes to existing routines. People can resist both actual and imagined events, and both individuals and groups can resist. If you think about change in terms of influence, you can assume people will either comply, commit, or resist.[37] This perspective leads many people to conclude that resistance to change represents a failed influence attempt. And while resistance can indeed doom change initiatives, we are going to challenge this assumption and approach resistance in a different and more useful way to help you gain more compliance and commitment to change.

To better understand the nature of resistance to change, you can learn about the level of your own dispositional resistance to change by completing Self-Assessment 16.3. Knowing this about yourself will help you manage your own tendencies and better recognize them in others. Both insights will make you more successful with organizational change throughout your career.

SELF-ASSESSMENT 16.3 — CAREER READINESS

Assessing Your Resistance to Change

Please be prepared to answer these questions if your instructor has assigned Self-Assessment 16.3 in Connect.

1. Which of the four components is highest?
2. Given your answer to question 1, what are the potential implications if your manager changes?
3. Describe two things you can do to help reduce the negative impact of your attribute with the lowest score.
4. Describe two things you can do to help reduce the negative impact of your attribute with the second-lowest score.

SOURCE: Adapted with permission from S. Oreg, "Resistance to Change: Developing an Individual Differences Measure," *Journal of Applied Psychology* 88, no. 4, 682.

A Dynamic View of Resistance

Many managers of change see resistance as employees pursuing their own interests, if not actively undermining the interests of the manager or larger organization. Accordingly, the cause of resistance resides solely with the individual employee, a narrow view of resistance. In contrast, some of the most widely recognized change experts argue that resistance does

FIGURE 16.9 Dynamic Model of Resistance to Change and Its Causes

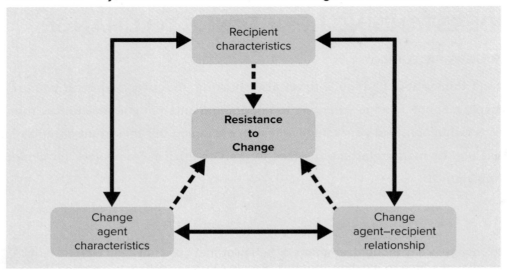

not reside within the individual but instead is a result of the context in which change occurs.[38] Resistance is caused by an interaction between change recipients, change agents, and the relationships between the two. This is a more complex and systems approach to resistance, one that is dynamic and illustrated in Figure 16.9.

Causes of Resistance to Change

Figure 16.9 presents a model of resistance characterized by a dynamic interaction among three causes, rather than being caused solely by irrational and stubborn recipients of change. Recipients resist partly based on their perceptions of change, which are very much influenced by the attitudes and behaviors exhibited by change agents and the level of trust in the relationship between change agents and recipients. Similarly, change agents' actions and perceptions are affected by the recipients' actions and inactions and the quality of relationships with recipients.[39] Let's consider each cause of resistance.

Recipient Characteristics   Recipient characteristics include perceptions and a variety of individual differences that help explain actions (engaging in new behaviors) and inactions (failing to engage in new behaviors). Six of the most common recipient characteristics are:[40]

1. *Dispositional resistance to change.* Individuals with high **dispositional resistance to change, a stable personality trait, are "less likely to voluntarily initiate changes and more likely to form negative attitudes toward the changes [they] encounter."**[41]

2. *Surprise and fear of the unknown.* When innovative or radically different changes are introduced without warning, affected employees often become fearful of the implications. The same is true when managers announce new goals without explaining specifically how the goals will be achieved. Imagine how you would feel if your boss said your department was going to increase sales by 25 percent without hiring any new employees. Unrealistic or unclear goals commonly contribute to resistance.

3. *Fear of failure.* Many changes cause employees to doubt their capabilities. Self-doubt erodes self-confidence and performance, and it also impedes personal growth and development.

4. *Loss of status and/or job security.* Changes that threaten to alter power bases or eliminate jobs can trigger strong resistance. Empowerment programs, when done well, will

often shift responsibilities from managers to others, which can result in some feeling threatened and resisting. Restructurings can include downsizing, and employees rarely if ever support changes costing their jobs.

5. *Peer pressure.* Someone who is not directly affected by a change may actively resist it to protect the interests of friends and coworkers.

6. *Past success.* Success can breed complacency. It also can foster a stubbornness to change because people come to believe what has worked in the past will work in the future.

Change Agent Characteristics *A change agent is someone who is a catalyst in helping organizations deal with old problems in new ways.* Change agents can be external consultants or internal employees, and their characteristics can include actions or inactions. For instance, opaque planning and a lack of participation and compassion during implementation can undermine a change agent's effectiveness. But in a more positive light, research shows supportive change agents (managers) who communicate timely and useful change-related information, clarify change-related expectations for employees and from employees, and foster trust are more likely to have employees who perceived the change positively and champion or commit rather than simply comply.[42]

More generally, change agents play an important role in helping others make sense of the changes—why is it happening, how will it affect them, and what does it mean for the future of the company and their own jobs and careers?[43] Therefore, the role of change agent can be extremely important, and we want you and other change agents to avoid some common mistakes. Table 16.1 outlines five. Enhance your own effectiveness by becoming aware of and avoiding these pitfalls.

TABLE 16.1   Common Pitfalls Effective Change Agents Should Avoid

Decisions that disrupt cultural traditions or group relationships. Whenever individuals are transferred, promoted, or reassigned, cultural and group dynamics are often thrown into disequilibrium. Resistance increases because of the uncertainty associated with dealing with new team members and their expectations.
Personality conflicts. Change agents who display narcissism, excessive ego, lack of fairness, or any of the traits of bad leaders are likely to engender resistance from recipients.
Lack of tact or poor timing. Undue resistance can occur because change agents introduce change in an insensitive manner or at an awkward time. They should not only "sell" the benefits of the change but also explain why it is strategically important to the organization's success and must occur at a particular time.
Poor leadership style. Research shows people are less likely to resist change when the change agent uses transformational leadership and makes the change about the organization and the employees, rather than about the leader him- or herself.[44]
Failing to legitimize change. Active, honest communication and aligned reward systems help recipients understand and believe in the value of changes. Change agents must also explain how change will lead to positive personal and organizational benefits. They need a clear understanding about how recipients' jobs will change and how they will be rewarded.[45] For example, an employee is unlikely to support a change effort he or she perceives as requiring more work and more pressure without a commensurate increase in pay.

Change Agent–Recipient Relationship   In general, resistance is reduced when change agents and recipients have a positive, trusting relationship. Trust consists of mutual faith in others' intentions and behavior. Mutual mistrust can doom to failure an otherwise well-conceived change.[46] Managers who trust their employees make the change process an open, honest, and participative affair. Employees who trust management are more willing to expend extra effort and take chances with something different.

16.4 THE GOOD AND THE BAD OF STRESS

THE BIGGER PICTURE

This section addresses an outcome associated with almost every change—stress. Change can be desirable or undesirable for you, but either results can be stressful. Realizing this helps you understand the benefits and reduce the costs of stress, which will enable you to be better equipped to effectively manage change as well as other possible outcomes across levels of the Organizing Framework. To help your efforts, we will define stress, and introduce a model to help explore the components of the stress process to improve your personal effectiveness.

LO 16-4

Explain both the benefits and problems associated with stress.

Everyone experiences stress regardless of age or stage of their career. The American Psychological Association (APA) report—*Stress in America 2018*—found Millennials reported the most stress, followed by generations Z, X, Boomers, then older adults. Figure 16.10 shows the major sources of stress for the youngest members of the workforce—Generation Z (approximately 17–24 years old)—compared to adults overall. On the upside, those in Gen Z are also the most likely to seek professional help for mental health issues.[47]

The APA has also begun tracking what they call "emerging sources of stress"—personal debt, housing instability, discrimination, and hunger/getting enough to eat (see Figure 16.10).

The National Institute for Occupational Safety and Health (NIOSH) defines **job stress "as the harmful physical and emotional responses that occur when the requirements of the job do not match the capabilities, resources, or needs of the worker."**[48] This definition implies stress can mean different things to different people. It also describes stress as an interaction between person and situation factors, as illustrated in the Organizing Framework you've applied throughout this book. It therefore is helpful to think of both factors as potential causes and remedies for stress. But before we explain this relationship in more detail we must recognize that not all stress is bad.

Stress—Good and Bad

Think of ways stress generates positive emotions, like excitement instead of anxiety. This type of stress can motivate you to prepare and perform during an interview or presentation at school or work. Positive stress adds to the excitement and fun of a first date or causes you to take the game-winning shot. We call **stress associated with positive emotions and outcomes *eustress* (good stress).**

However, the stress garnering the most attention is the bad kind, the kind epidemic at work and so costly to employees and employers alike. Some studies estimate job stress costs the U.S. economy more than $300 billion per year,[49] and to make matters worse, research shows levels of job stress have increased 20 percent since the 1980s!

Of the potential sources of work stress, which do you think is the biggest? Your BOSS! Thirty-five percent of respondents in another study reported it was not only the actions of the boss—a lack of fairness, a narcissistic personality—but also his or her

FIGURE 16.10 Sources of Stress

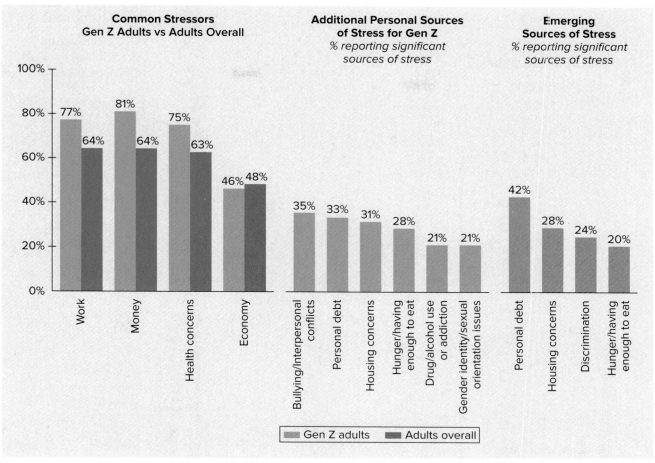

SOURCE: American Psychological Association. "Stress in America: Generation Z." October, 2018. https://www.apa.org/news/press/releases/stress/2018/stress-gen-z.pdf.

own stress. Much like you learned about emotions, stress too is contagious.[50] Perhaps it is no surprise then that:

- 76% said job stress negatively impacted their personal relationships.
- 66% lost sleep because of it.
- 16% have quit their jobs.[51]

These details make clear stress is inevitable, which means your efforts should be directed at understanding and managing stress, not escaping it altogether.

A Model of Job Stress

Figure 16.11 presents a comprehensive model of job stress. It originates from psychology and health research and practice and can help you understand and manage your stress more effectively.

Potential Stressors   The model begins with four potential types of **stressors, factors that produce stress.** The four types are:

1. **Individual level.** Job demands are the most common individual-level stressors, but work overload, unclear or conflicting expectations, everyday hassles, perceived lack of control over events occurring in the work environment, and job characteristics can also be problematic.[52] One of the heaviest stressors is job loss, which negatively affects

FIGURE 16.11   Model of Job Stress

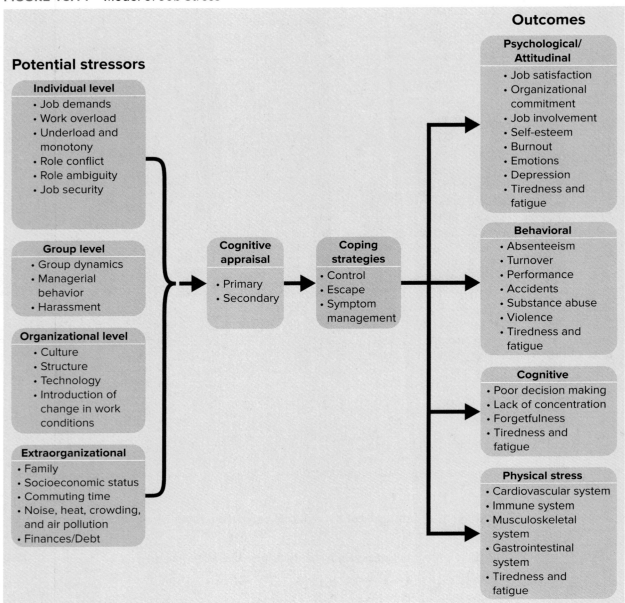

every aspect of people's lives—financial, professional, health, and interpersonal relationships. If you lack opportunities for advancement, fear being laid off, or work at a job that is not in your desired career path, you too are likely to be stressed.

2. **Group level.** As noted above, bad managers create stress for employees by (1) exhibiting inconsistent behaviors, (2) failing to provide support, (3) showing lack of concern, (4) giving inadequate direction, (5) creating a high-productivity environment, and (6) focusing on negatives while ignoring good performance. Sexual harassment experiences and bullying represent other group-level stressors. And let's not forget annoying coworkers, one of the most common and problematic sources of group-level stress.[53]

3. **Organizational level.** Organizational culture can also be a stressor. For instance, a high-pressure environment that fuels employee fear about performing up to standard can increase the stress response. Jobs on Wall Street have long been known for such pressure, and the long hours expected from employees generate their own version of stress-inducing organizational cultures in many tech companies.[54]

4. **Extra-organizational.** Extra-organizational stressors originate outside the organization. For instance, conflicts associated with balancing school with career or family life are stressful. Socioeconomic status—a combination of relative income, education, and occupation—is another extra-organizational stressor. Stress is higher for people with lower socioeconomic status.[55]

Can you relate? Demands of work and other arenas of our lives can indeed be overwhelming and negatively impact our performance and well-being.

Stokkete/Shutterstock

Fatigue v. Tiredness *Fatigue* **is a prolonged state of physical and mental exhaustion that cannot simply be remedied by a good night's sleep.** In fact, a sign of fatigue is its persistence despite sleep, and it is often accompanied by feelings of depression and/or anxiety, confusion, and difficulties concentrating and staying organized, whereas *tiredness* **is typically physical and short-term and is resolved by rest and sleep.**[56]

Too much work and a lack of sleep contribute to both. Americans now work an average of 48 hours per week compared to only 38 in 1976.[57] Research estimates that 43 percent of workers are sleep-deprived—don't get the recommended 7 to 9 hours per night—and it is worse for those who work nights or long and/or irregular shifts. The associated problems are numerous and not limited to your performance and health (depression, obesity, and cardiovascular disease) as shown in Figure 16.11, but also affect your economic well-being and safety:[58]

- Lost productivity of $1,200 to $3,100 per employee per year. Multiply this times the approximately 50 percent of your company's employees and the numbers become very large—1,000 employees X $3,100/employee = $3,100,000 in lost productivity in one company!

- Three times more likely to have an auto accident, and 5,000 people died due to drowsy driving in 2014.

It is estimated that losing just two hours of sleep impairs your judgment and reaction time to the same degree as having three beers.[59] Other research translates fatigue into lost productivity costing 10 times more than absenteeism,[60] and many times more than *presenteeism*, **which occurs when employees show up but are sick or in no condition to work productively.**[61]

In case you're not moved by these research findings, let's make this more real. All employees are tired sometimes, and too many are seemingly tired often or always. Although this obviously affects productivity to varying degrees depending on the person and the job, sometimes fatigue is dangerous if not catastrophic or even deadly. Imagine the potential consequences for a tired and fatigued boat captain, pilot, bus driver, or surgeon! If individuals doing these jobs aren't overly concerned, certainly their employers, coworkers, customers, and patients are and should be.

What can you and your employer do?

1. **Staffing.** Maintain adequate staffing to cover the workload. This is especially necessary for companies that have downsized, because they are likely to simply spread the same amount of work across a smaller number of employees.

2. **Scheduling.** Consider overtime and commuting time when scheduling workers, to help ensure they have enough time between shifts to obtain sufficient rest and sleep. Be wary of disrupting people's circadian rhythms with crazy shift-work schedules—nights, days, and back again.

3. **Environment.** Light, sound, temperature, and other workplace elements can have subtle yet meaningful effects on worker fatigue. For too long these elements were taken for granted, but many managers and employers have found employees greatly appreciate the ability to make their spaces "their own."

4. **Education.** Educate workers to better manage their sleep and the factors that can affect it. Covering sleep-disorder screening under employer-provided insurance may also help, since many people have underlying clinical/health problems that reduce the quantity and quality of sleep.[62]

Now that we've covered the causes of stress on the left side of our Model of Job Stress in Figure 16.11, let's move to how you process and cope with stress, beginning with cognitive appraisals.

Cognitive Appraisals   You've undoubtedly heard the expression: "It's not what happens to you but the way you respond that matters." This sentence essentially describes cognitive appraisal, the process by which you evaluate the meaning of events and demands in your life. Put another way, what makes stressors actually stressful is the way you think about them. Two types of appraisals influence whether you experience a particular stressor as stress, and the degree to which it is stressful.

1. *Primary appraisals* **are your perceptions of whether a stressor is irrelevant, positive, or negative.** Negative primary appraisals are the most relevant to our current discussion because they imply we perceive a situation or stressor as harmful, threatening, or challenging.

2. *Secondary appraisals* **are your perceptions of how able you are to cope with a given demand.** During secondary appraisals we consider which coping strategies are available and most likely to help resolve the stressful situation.

Combined, these appraisals influence our choice of coping strategies and in turn the subsequent outcomes.

Coping Strategies   Coping strategies are specific behaviors and cognitions (thoughts) we use to manage a situation. The appropriateness and thus the success of any particular type of coping depends on the person and situation factors.[63] People use a combination of three approaches to cope with stressors and stress (see Figure 16.11). The first, called a *control strategy*, **consists of behaviors and cognitions that directly anticipate or solve problems.** A control strategy has a take-charge tone. Examples include talking to your professor or boss about workload if you feel overwhelmed with your responsibilities or confronting someone who is spreading negative rumors. Some research shows health and other benefits from control coping. People are more apt to use control coping when they possess high self-esteem, self-efficacy, and problem-solving skills.[64]

Escape strategies **are those in which you avoid or ignore stressors.** These strategies can be beneficial if you have no control over the stressors or their causes. If the president of your company is an unpredictable and unlikable individual but is not your direct supervisor, then it is best not to attempt control coping but instead to avoid stressful encounters with him or her.

Symptom management strategies **focus on reducing the symptoms of stress** and include relaxation, meditation, medication, and exercise. A vacation can be a good way to reduce the symptoms of stress. The author of this book finds walking or playing with his dog beneficial.

Stress Outcomes   Stress has psychological, attitudinal, behavioral, cognitive, and physical health outcomes. Besides your own personal experiences, a large body of research supports the negative effects of perceived stress on many aspects of our lives.[65] Workplace stress is associated with undesirable effects on many outcomes in the Organizing Framework for Understanding and Applying OB:

- Decreases in job satisfaction, organizational commitment, organizational citizenship behavior, positive emotions, and performance.
- Increases in emotional exhaustion, burnout, absenteeism, and turnover.[66]

The undesirable effects extend beyond these, however. Stress is linked to many counterproductive behaviors, such as yelling, verbal abuse, and violence toward others. It is associated with frequent drinking and the taking of illicit drugs.[67] These stress outcomes are costly to individuals and organizations alike. Moreover, abundant research shows stress also negatively affects our physical, psychological, and physical health in almost every way imaginable.[68]

We think it is stressful to think about all these problems! We close this section with some advice on how to deal with a particularly difficult stressor—underperformance and failure.

Confronting and Overcoming Failures

We all have experiences at school and work wherein we underperform, whether doing horribly on a test or presentation, providing an unclear answer to our boss, blowing it with a customer, making poor job choices, or losing our temper with a classmate or coworker. Some have little consequence (low score on a single homework assignment) while others can be very problematic (taking a bad job or losing a key customer). Since failure is universal, it is helpful to consider how to deal with such inevitable experiences, how to recover from them, and how to use them as agents of change for the future.

First, when you consider a particular experience a failure, it is important not to hide from it. The surest way of not failing is not trying. Where would that mindset get you, or the rest of the human race for that matter? Of course, no one is going to say to celebrate failure, but the more typical and damaging reaction is to hide it from yourself and others. One career expert explains it this way: it is every employee's responsibility to anticipate and avoid mistakes when possible, but also to make things go right when they do occur.[69]

Experts recommend reflecting on the experience, then acting. For instance:

Talk About It. That's right, instead of avoiding it, talk to your colleagues and/or boss to gain their insights and learn. Instead of ranting or being defensive, ask: "I had a bad experience, can you help me with this?" The goal is to get another's perspective, and at the same time show your vulnerability, willingness to own your mistakes, and determination to learn and grow. Moreover, research suggests such behaviors can develop closer, more productive relationships, especially when compared to leaders and other employees who present themselves as perfect or flawless, which tends to be perceived as inauthentic.[70]

Fail Productively. Many failures are due to complex interactions between people and situations, in other words OB. And many times, it is the complexity and not your fault. Neither you nor anyone else can possibly control the outcomes all of the time but recognizing this and being vigilant can help improve processes, your approach, and make you more effective over time. For instance, clinicians in emergency departments and critical care units have extensive training and skills and use processes to guide them, but sometimes bad things still happen to patients. Productive failure can also occur when doing something new and when no one has previous experience or knowledge on how best to succeed, such as a new product, new technology, or a novel process. Failure will likely be common. This doesn't mean you shouldn't try, as this is the heart of change, innovation, and growth.[71]

Choose Your Audience. Of course, it not only matters how you frame your failure, but who you share it with. Early in your career or a particular job it is admittedly more difficult, but the important takeaway is to find someone you trust, someone who will appreciate your situation and experience, and genuinely help you to change and grow. Consider sharing experiences at lunch with coworkers, or perhaps at happy hour with friends not in your company or industry. Or this could be an especially good time and reason to get a mentor.[72]

Read and heed the advice provided in the following Applying OB box to learn how to address interview questions aimed at failure.

Applying OB

"Tell me about a time when you . . . experienced failure, or when things didn't work out."

This is one of the most common behavioral interview questions. We're asked those questions because prospective employers want to know how you'll respond when things go sideways when you work for them.

They ask such questions knowing full well we all make mistakes, things go wrong, we fail. Sometimes it is entirely our fault, sometimes it is not, but most always we are expected to do something about it and do our best to improve in the future. One career expert describes failures in this way: it is every employee's responsibility to anticipate and avoid mistakes when possible, but also to make things right when they do occur.[73]

When asked such a question, it is wise to think of and share a past challenge, rather than one that is pending or just happened. Why? Because you can better show and explain the

1. Context and what happened.
2. What you did in response including who you may have consulted.
3. How it helped you develop.
4. Why you are unlikely to make a similar mistake in the future.[74]

This is about change and development. Put differently, look at and communicate failures in terms of opportunities for change and growth. Not only will this make you more successful in interviews, but it will help you cope with what can be painful experiences.

Now that you've learned a great deal of knowledge about change and stress, let's conclude the chapter with some useful and practical applications.

16.5 EFFECTIVE CHANGE AND STRESS MANAGEMENT

THE BIGGER PICTURE

Since organizational change has implications for nearly every element of the Organizing Framework, it is an excellent opportunity to consolidate and apply the knowledge gained throughout the book. OB provides practical tools to make you a more effective manager of change. Specifically, we'll describe how to apply the systems model you learned about earlier for strategic planning and diagnosis, and provide advice on how to overcome resistance to change and manage stress. We conclude with some practical tips for successful change management.

Applying the Systems Model of Change—Strategic Planning and Diagnosis

LO 16-5

Use OB knowledge and tools to manage change and stress.

There are two ways to apply the systems model of change. The first is as an aid during the strategic planning process (why change?), and the second is to help identify the necessary targets of change (change what and how?). Together, these uses can assist leaders and managers in formulating and implementing effective organizational change (see Figure 16.6).

Use the following Problem-Solving Application to apply the systems model of change for diagnosing problems and identifying the targets for change.

Problem-Solving Application

HBO + TNT + TBS + CNN + ETC = NEW AT&T[75]

There are more than 26 characters in the alphabet soup created in the merger between AT&T and Time Warner, given the latter included HBO, TNT, TBS, CNN, Warner Bros. movie studio, and other assets. AT&T finally prevailed in its efforts to acquire Time Warner for over $85 billion, which required it to win a suit filed by the Justice Department seeking to block the merger. AT&T argued that such a marriage would not be anti-competitive and limit choice for consumers, but by combining the companies it was necessary to be competitive in a radically different landscape that blurs the previous lines between content and distribution. This merger says a lot about AT&T's strategy for dealing with these challenges and how it plans to grow in the future.

History and Additional Motives for the Marriage
Telecom companies have historically offered cable, telephone, and mobile services, however now, AT&T not only needs to compete with Verizon and T-Mobile/Sprint, but also the likes of Netflix, Hulu, Amazon, Google, Facebook, and Apple, many of whom create content *and* provide distribution. The future is now, and it requires telecom companies to combat the millions of people who have cut the cable cord while at the same time attracting the millions that sign up for streaming services.

Some experts claim these changes are essential to the survival of a company like AT&T, and as a result the company is expected to be more attractive to investors and consumers. Moreover, if AT&T's larger portfolio attracts more eyeballs it will also attract more advertisers and boost revenues and profits further still.

What Is Required to Realize the Value? The merger expands the products and customer bases of all of the brands involved in the merger, but this complexity also requires masterful change leadership. Many of these assets, notably HBO, have long and very successful histories. The challenge will be minimizing conflict and fostering collaboration and cohesiveness among employees (nearly 270,000 in the combined company), processes (decision making, HR, technology, and communication), and products (streaming, content, technology, mobile, and cable). This therefore represents an enormous leadership challenge.

Leading the Change Efforts John Stankey, an AT&T executive who was immediately put in charge of Warner Media, put it simply: "If you don't make a change, you're not going to get any change in the product." In this spirit he quickly made a number of senior leadership moves. He brought in Robert Greenblatt who had a long successful career at NBC and Showtime, and effectively offered him his dream opportunity, as he will now oversee HBO, considered the crown jewel of the acquisition, along with Warner's planned streaming service. Also joining the team is Jeff Zucker (formerly chief at CNN) who will not only oversee larger business than he did at his previous job, but also lead a portfolio AT&T sees as especially important to its strategy and future. However, the shakeup also includes departures, such as Richard Plepler who worked at HBO for more than two decades and has been its chief executive and face of the company for the past several years, and David Levy the president of Turner Broadcasting. Neither was fired but both left presumably because there were clear signals their roles would be much smaller in the new company, which would mean their previous considerable autonomy and influence would be diminished.

Potential Obstacles With regulators seemingly out of the way, the new and existing leadership has many things to tend to. For instance, Mr. Stankey's leadership style has been questioned. Critics say he is quite opaque in communicating his thoughts and plans, which has been quite frustrating to many employees. And given the enormous task ahead, the skills of many leaders will be put to the test. Among the many challenges will be to reduce conflict, foster collaboration, and integrate cultures. Competitors certainly won't relent and are likely to respond with their own efforts, such as Apple's planned streaming service, alliances between content providers and telcos like Netflix and T-Mobile, and Comcast's acquisition of many of 20th Century Fox's assets. Reputations of the brands and their associated leaders will undoubtedly both help and hurt in the merger process, as will employee resistance. Employees that are dissatisfied with their situation in the new company may resist the changes or even quit, while those who are happy and satisfied may see new opportunities and commit.

Assume you are Mr. Stankey. Apply the 3-Step Problem-Solving Approach to identify the problems, causes, and potential solutions included In the case.

Apply the 3-Step Problem-Solving Approach

Step 1: Define the problems facing John Stankey and the new merged AT&T-Time Warner company.

Step 2: Identify the potential causes.

Step 3: Make your recommendations.

How to Overcome Resistance to Change

We've noted resistance is a form of feedback and managers need to understand why it is occurring before trying to overcome it. They can do this by considering the extent to which the three sources of resistance shown in Figure 16.9 are contributing to the problem.

Respond to Employee Characteristics   Employees are more likely to resist change when they perceive its personal costs outweigh the benefits. If this is the case, managers are advised to:

1. Provide employees with as much information as possible about the change.
2. Inform employees about the reasons for the change.
3. Conduct meetings to address employees' questions about the change.
4. Provide employees the opportunity to discuss how the proposed change might affect them.

Improve Change Agent–Employee Relationships   The four recommendations described will also improve the agent–recipient relationship by enhancing the level of trust between the parties.

When Jim Weber took over as CEO of Brooks Sports, the maker of the running shoes, the company was languishing. In its long history, the company endured two bankruptcies and multiple owners. He desperately needed to productively alter relationships with both employees and customers. At the time he took the helm the company had expanded from a specialty running shoe company to one also selling cleats, tennis shoes, and cross-trainers at a variety of price points, but often cheap. He scrapped everything except its one profitable and eternal line—high-end running shoes developed for elite runners. Since these changes the company has experienced consistent and phenomenal growth for many years. Although it still pales in comparison to the largest players in the market—Nike, Adidas, Asics, and New Balance—it is number one with its target. Specifically, it is the top brand in specialty retailers devoted to running, first or second most popular in the Boston Marathon over the past few years, and Olympic runners wore more Brooks' shoes than any other, including Nike.[76]

To achieve this, Mr. Weber has had to convince employees such changes were in their best interest—the future depended on it. The R&D people had to be pushed to apply their talents to different types of runners, rather than simply creating the best materials and products. This meant everyone at the company had to engage customers and market in

Jim Weber had many challenges to overcome when he became CEO of Brooks. He chose to focus on shoes for elite runners, which required enormous changes for many employees. His efforts have paid off, as the company now leads in this category.

(Left): Courtesy of Brooks Sports, Inc.; (right): Miet Astlen/Shutterstock

ways they hadn't before. And now, to continue the growth, Weber and Brooks' employees must convince non-elite runners of the value in shelling out premium prices for their shoes. Appeal to more than the running nerds, but the much larger running herds and penetrate the athleisure market, including the tens of millions of non-elite but often serious runners.[77]

Implement Organizational Processes and Practices

For starters, managers should not assume people are consciously resisting change. Second, using the Organizing Framework can be very helpful. Resistance to organizational changes is often caused by some obstacle in the work environment, such as job design or performance management practices that make the change difficult or counter to an employee's self-interests. If employees, for example, are still rewarded for doing their jobs the old way, then it is unrealistic or even foolish to expect them to do their jobs differently.

Soliciting and using feedback about the changes can be invaluable to achieving desired change outcomes, and change agents should not be afraid to modify the targeted elements of change or their approach toward change if people are resisting for valid reasons.

Take a Contingency Approach to Overcoming Resistance

As you have learned throughout this book, effective managers apply the knowledge and tools that match the requirements of the situation (one size does not fit all). A similar contingency approach is recommended for avoiding or overcoming resistance to change. You and other change agents are likely to be more successful if you follow the six strategies:

1. Inspire. Do the best you can to describe a vivid and compelling vision of what the changed organization will look like, and equally important, what role you see those who report to you playing and the value they can provide.

2. Recognize progress, not just outcomes. Many if not most organizational changes occur over long periods of time, which means changes will include multiple steps along the way. Observe and recognize people for their efforts, and don't wait for ultimate performance outcomes. This is similar to Kotter's advice from earlier in the chapter to create and celebrate small wins. Don't simply wait for performance metrics at the end of the quarter, the year, or until the merger is close and the cultures or systems integrated.

3. Expect mistakes. Expect them, tell your people you expect them, and don't panic when they happen. Treat them as learning opportunities, which means you need to analyze and identify what to do and what not to do in the future.

4. Model, measure, and reward collaboration. A common sign of resistance is a lack of collaboration, and one way to overcome this is to apply what you learned in Chapter 6 to make collaboration part of the performance expectations. Communicate, model, measure, and reward collaboration.

5. Positivity. As you learned previously, we tend pay attention to negative events, experiences, and emotions more than positive ones, and this is especially common in the context of organizational change. It therefore can be an excellent and productive opportunity to exercise mindfulness, and for you and employees to identify and reflect on the positive elements of the change.

6. Goals and time. Just as you learned in Chapter 6, setting SMART goals and being sure to include a time element will help focus people's efforts and actually change. It is better to set a deadline and need to change it, rather than not setting one at all.[78]

As you can easily see, understanding and managing resistance can indeed reduce stress indirectly. But now let's look at how to manage stress directly.

How to Manage Stress

Because stress influences many outcomes across levels of the Organizing Framework, it is not surprising that organizations are increasingly implementing a variety of stress-reduction programs to help employees cope. Let's explore some that may benefit you, other employees, and your employer.

Stress-Reduction   It's best if both you and your employer make efforts to reduce stress. Some common, widely applicable, and effective ones are:

- Provide and encourage employees to utilize stress-management and wellness resources—mediation and yoga.
- Take regular breaks, we all need them, and volumes of research show productivity increases.
- Exercise, socialize, hobbies, and play. Get employees to regularly do other things.

Walk the talk and lead by example. If managers actively tend to their stress and follow the above recommendations, then employees are more likely to do the same.[79]

But what has proven to be one of the most effective stress-reduction techniques is cognitive restructuring.[80]

The ABCDEs of Cognitive Restructuring   Many positive OB tools can help you avoid and reduce stress, such as fostering positive emotions, using mindfulness, flourishing, and developing a positive organizational climate. In addition, the following five-step process of cognitive restructuring can help you to stop thinking pessimistically about an event or problem. It's called the ABCDEs:[81]

A—Name the event or problem. For example:

My roommate is going to move out, and I can't afford to pay the rent by myself.

B—List your beliefs about the event or problem.

I don't have any prospects for a new roommate, and I may have to move back home and quit school. I could ask my parents for money, but they really can't afford to pay my rent or I could move to a lower-priced single apartment in a bad part of town.

C—Identify the consequences of your beliefs.

I'm going to move back home for spring semester and will return in the fall.

D—Formulate a counterargument to your initial thoughts and beliefs. Pessimistic thoughts are generally overreactions, so the first step is to correct inaccurate or distorted thoughts.

I have not reviewed my expenses closely, and I may be able to afford the apartment. Even if I can't afford the apartment right now, I could get a part-time job to cover the additional expenses or I could advertise on Craigslist or in the school newspaper for a new roommate. I don't have to accept a bad roommate, but the worst-case scenario is I will have to cover the added expenses for one semester.

E—Describe how energized and empowered you feel at the moment.

I'm motivated to find a new roommate and/or get a part-time job. I have taken care of myself throughout college and there is no reason I can't continue to resolve this short-term problem.

Research and practice show this technique works well over time. The key is to stay with your ABCDEs and not to expect instantaneous results.

Before moving on, read the Applying OB box for another means for dealing with stress.

Applying OB

How Do You Spell Stress Relief? R-A-N-T![82]

In chapters 3 and 7 you learned about emotions and how to use and manage them at work. One way to deal with stress is to blow off steam, or RANT! Releasing your emotions and associated energy can be an effective means for relieving stress. To clarify, the following are ways to productively express your frustrations without losing control and allowing your emotions to cause additional problems. Here's how:

1. **Never Rant via E-mail.** If you're even the slightest bit concerned about how it will be perceived, then don't send it. At the very least, leave it until the next day, review it again, tone it down, and/or have somebody else review it first. If you're still concerned skip the e-mail and find another, more productive path.

2. **Not the Target, but Instead Your Friend.** Ranting isn't ranting unless someone is listening. Although your boss or coworker may be the source of your disgust, frustration, or need to rant, you'll be better served to share your emotionally

charged thoughts with a friend, preferably not one who also works at your company. An expert provides a helpful script to use when asking someone to help: "I need to get something off my chest. You don't have to actually listen. Please wait until I'm done and agree with everything I say." This may help satisfy your need to be heard and agreed with without causing damage to relationships at work.

3. **Back Stage, Not on Stage.** It is wise to avoid ranting in public. The potential for your rant to come back to haunt you Is high, especially because of the possibility for someone in the crowd to record it.

4. **Purging, Not Problem Solving.** Ranting is an emotional release that reduces stress. It's for you. Don't rant expecting to solve problems with somebody else. Emotions often do play a role in problem solving, but ranting is different.

Pulling It All Together—Change Management Tips for Managers

We conclude the chapter and book by asking you to return to the Organizing Framework. You realize now how both person and situation inputs can have a major impact on what needs to change, how it needs to change, and the ultimate success of any change initiatives. And you know process always matters, such that employees react more positively to changes that are personally undesirable, even job cuts, when the process by which they are formulated and implemented is perceived as fair. To be clear, employees may still be unhappy, but not as unhappy as if changes were implemented in ways they perceived as unfair.

Applying OB

Five Tips for Effective Change[83]

We can safely predict your future is going to include change and related stress. While accepting change is neither simple nor easy, here are our best tips to help stack the deck in your favor and improve your chances for success. While some tips specifically address the manager's role, all will help you at any level of the organization.

1. **Set realistic change goals.** Leaders of change often think big and bold. This is fine so long as the objectives are realistic and attainable for the situation and organization. As you learned previously, SMART goals are challenging but attainable.
2. **Ensure senior leader involvement and commitment.** CEOs and other senior leaders must be *visibly* involved in change initiatives. They cannot simply sit in their ivory tower and dictate change. They need to be planners, cheerleaders, and doers. This kind of deep involvement will help shape employee perceptions and beliefs that leaders are serious about the changes and they care about employees
3. **Walk the talk.** Change can be difficult, even scary, for many employees. It is beneficial if managers and leaders change first. This means when employees are asked to make sacrifices (give pay concessions, work overtime, take on additional responsibilities), leaders and managers make them first and in-kind. Leaders and managers of change need to make their actions visible and make them count.
4. **Be clear on "why."** Everyone wants to know why the changes are happening. What are the motives, what will be the personal impact, and what role will individuals play in shaping the outcomes? Your organization must avoid the situation in which "the lower you go, the less you know." Everyone responsible for and affected by the change must clearly understand why it is happening. Understanding is fundamental to building commitment to change and reducing resistance. Communicate.
5. **Align performance management practices.** It is difficult, even foolish, to expect your salespeople to give full attention to selling your company's new product if the bulk of their compensation is still focused on the old product. It is necessary not only to align goals, but to also align recognition and other rewards with the change-related goals.

Effective managers of change therefore carefully consider the relevant inputs *and* processes for any given change effort, because these are critical determinants of outcomes in the Organizing Framework. Moreover, the outcomes in the Organizing Framework likely overlap with the goals of a given change, such as employee satisfaction, team performance, and organizational reputation. You therefore may want to start with the end in mind, as suggested in the following Applying OB box that details five tips to successful change management.

Let's now pull it altogether and conclude not only our exploration of change and stress, but also the larger journey in OB, with some practical tips.

16.6 MAKING THE CONNECTION: HOW CAN I APPLY OB AND SHOW WHAT I'VE LEARNED?

THE BIGGER PICTURE

We close the chapter and book with practical applications related to change, stress, and the management of each. As with the previous chapters, use your new knowledge and tools to improve your effectiveness as both an employee and manager.

LO 16-6

Describe the implications of managing stress and change for you and managers.

Takeaways for Me

Here are five practical implications for you.

1. **Learn about and be mindful of your own attitudes toward change.** If you have a negative approach, you are more likely to resist change and expect negative experiences and outcomes. A more positive attitude, in contrast, means you're more likely to frame change as a challenge or an opportunity.

2. **Pay attention to and utilize your knowledge of the internal and external forces of change.** This will enable you to understand, manage, and perform within the context of change.

3. **Change is complex.** Using your knowledge of the types of change as well as the different models can help you understand and perform better during the many changes you will undoubtedly face in your career.

4. **Resistance is a given.** Apply your knowledge from Figure 16.9 to understand the different causes of resistance and use this to reduce your resistance as well as that of others.

5. **Understand and apply your knowledge of occupational stress and coping** (see Figure 16.11). Cognitive restructuring is an especially effective tool—learn it and use it. This will greatly improve your performance and satisfaction at work and in life.

Takeaways for Managers

There are seven practical implications for managers.

1. **Taking a more strategic approach to change will help you get ahead in your professional life.** To do this, consider both internal and external forces for change.

2. **Consider the complexity, cost, and perceived threat associated with the different types of change—adaptive, innovative, and radical** (see Figure 16.4).

3. **Not all changes are alike, which means you'll need different tools to be effective.** The models outlined in this chapter should help you better understand and manage the various changes you'll be confronted with in your professional life.

4. **Utilize the systems model (see Figure 16.6) for both planning and diagnosing change.** When you are planning change, it will help ensure you consider important elements you might not otherwise.

5. **Employee resistance will make or break your effectiveness as a manager and viewing resistance as a dynamic process with several different sources is a good starting point.** Then, utilize the knowledge within this chapter to help reduce and overcome resistance.

6. **Stress affects your performance and that of those you manage.** Be aware of your stress and manage it effectively in order to better manage others.

7. **The final Applying OB box provides five tips for managing change effectively–learn them and use them!**

Parting Words for Change and OB

Whether you work for someone else or run your own business, your ability to effectively manage change will benefit you throughout your career. It is a challenge, but the rewards are enormous if you can do it well. The knowledge and tools we've provided here can give you a competitive edge on other employees and managers.

And don't forget that managing change is about *doing*. Perhaps Charlie Strong, currently the head football coach for the University of South Florida, put it best in 2014 when he was hired at the University of Texas and outlined his expectations for players, particularly the team's leaders: "They can lead the new culture or be run over by it. . . . I don't want to talk about things. I'd rather do things. We just talked. Now it's time to do."[84]

We wrote this book to help you perform better at work, at school, and in life more generally. You've gained an enormous amount of knowledge throughout this book and course, and you've had many opportunities to apply the knowledge. We encourage you to continue learning *and* applying your knowledge, because it is the application of what you know that will help you get ahead. We hope you enjoyed your journey and wish you the very best both professionally and personally.

What Did I Learn?

You learned change and stress will be two companions throughout your professional life. You learned how you can apply OB to help recognize and respond appropriately to drivers of change and to manage both the positive and negative aspects of stress for greater effectiveness. Reinforce and consolidate your learning with the Key Points and Organizing Framework. Then challenge your mastery of the material by completing the Problem-Solving Application Case and Legal/Ethical Challenge.

Key Points for Understanding Chapter 16

You learned the following key points.

16.1 FORCES FOR CHANGE

- Forces for change can be categorized as external and internal.
- External forces are demographic, technological, shareholder and market, social, political, and regulatory.
- Internal forces often pertain to human resources and managerial behavior and decisions.

16.2 TYPES AND MODELS OF CHANGE

- Three general types of change—adaptive, innovative, and radically innovative—differ in complexity, cost, and uncertainty.
- Lewin's change model proposes three stages: unfreezing, changing, and refreezing.
- A systems model of change includes inputs, strategic plans, target elements of change, and outputs.
- Kotter's eight-step model of change requires organizations to move through each step sequentially.
- An organizational development (OD) approach to change consists of diagnosing, intervening, evaluating, and feeding the evaluation back to assess change effectiveness.

16.3 UNDERSTANDING RESISTANCE TO CHANGE

- Resistance to change is any thought, emotion, or behavior that does not align with actual or potential changes to existing routines.
- Dynamic perspectives of resistance describe it as an interplay of change recipient characteristics, change agent characteristics, and the relationship between the two.

16.4 THE GOOD AND THE BAD OF STRESS

- Job stress contains both harmful physical and emotional elements.
- Stressors can occur at multiple levels—individual, group, organizational, and extra-organizational.
- Primary and secondary are the two common forms of cognitive appraisal.
- Common coping strategies are control, escape, and symptom management.

16.5 EFFECTIVE CHANGE AND STRESS MANAGEMENT

- The systems model of change provides multiple targets for effective change management.
- Education and communication, involvement, negotiation, and coercion are among the many means for overcoming resistance to change.
- Stress Is managed most effectively when employers and employees take action.

16.6 HOW CAN I APPLY OB AND SHOW WHAT I'VE LEARNED?

- Your attitudes towards change can make or break you as an employee and manager.
- Identifying the factors that influence resistance can help you as an employee and manager.
- Manage your stress and remember It is contagious.

FIGURE 16.12 Organizing Framework for Understanding and Applying OB

INPUTS	PROCESSES	OUTCOMES
Person Factors • Personality • Demographics • Skills and abilities • Values • Needs • Ethics • Stressors **Situation Factors** • Relationship quality • Leadership • Human resource problems/prospects • Managerial behavior/decisions • Culture (organizational) • Technology • Market forces • Social, political, and regulatory pressures • Stressors • Organizational mission and vision • Strategy	**Individual Level** • Emotions • Cognitive appraisals • Coping strategies • Perceptions • Motivation • Trust • Communication **Group/Team Level** • Group/team dynamics • Conflict and negotiation • Decision making • Power, influence, and politics • Performance management • Leadership • Trust **Organizational Level** • Human resource policies and practices • Culture • Organizational design and effectiveness • Leading and managing change and stress • Trust	**Individual Level** • Task performance • Work attitudes • Well-being • Citizenship behavior/counter-productive behavior • Resistance to change • Turnover • Career outcomes • Stress (physical and emotional) • Accidents **Group/Team Level** • Group/team performance • Group satisfaction • Group cohesion and conflict • Resistance to change **Organizational Level** • Survival • Accounting/financial performance • Organizational performance • Customer satisfaction • Innovation • Reputation

The Organizing Framework for Chapter 16

As shown in Figure 16.12, you learned that the process of leading and managing change and stress at the organizational level often includes a range of inputs, processes, and outcomes across all levels of the organization.

Toys R Amazon, Walmart, and Others, but Not Us

Toys-R-Us has long been known as a marquee toy retailer with giant 40,000-square-foot stores and nearly every item desired or imaginable for children (and some adults). A large percentage of Americans, as well as customers in international markets, can recall visiting a Toys-R-Us store.

Sadly however, even icons fail, especially when confronted with nearly $5 billion of debt, fierce online competition from Amazon and Walmart, changing customer preferences (video games instead of conventional toys), and technology (e-commerce). Not even 3 billion dollars in annual sales could surmount these challenges.

Toys R Us is yet another iconic retailer to suffer due to changes in technology, customer preferences, and new competitors.

Daysi Calavia-Robertson/Newsday/Getty Images

SEALED FATE

Some argue the company's fate was sealed back in 2005 when Bain Capital took the company private and buried it in debt to do so. Toys R Us never shed this burden.[85] The Toys R Us scenario is a familiar one. In the years prior to the great recession (2006–2008), private equity firms (PE), like Bain and KKR, went shopping for retailers. They took the companies private by borrowing money for the purchase and planned to achieve high returns by making them more efficient, selling off parts, or both, and in a period of a few years take them public again. (Note: PE firms generally collect large fees associated with taking the companies public.)

However, the recession eroded the value of the retailer's real estate and at the same time e-commerce exploded onto the market. Online sales have more than quadrupled since 2007. For perspective, Neiman Marcus, another PE-, debt-plagued retailer reaped 34 percent of total sales online in 2017. These same factors also spurred the demise of other well-known brands, like Gymboree, Payless Shoes, and Sports Authority.[86]

To compete online requires massive investments in technology and support, people, all while selling products at lower margins. In summary, competition is up, debt is up, expenses for creating an online channel go up, and profits go down—a tough scenario for any retailer.[87] Many have responded by only investing in safe bets and cutting products and people, which in turn has limited merchandise and degraded service.

For its part, Toys R Us tried bankruptcy in September 2017 to salvage the company but doing this before the holiday shopping season (when it collects a large percentage of annual revenue) hurt more than helped. Company leadership and other employees were in survival mode instead of executing and boosting sales when it needed them most. The poor timing was made even worse as it scared customers away, as they were concerned that toys couldn't be returned, and gift cards redeemed.[88]

COMPETITORS POUNCED

Knowing Toys R Us was on the ropes, Walmart, Target, and Amazon cut prices during the holiday season and took an ever greater share of sales. For instance, competitors sold some toys at a loss in order to get the business. This practice isn't sustainable, normally, but each of these large competitors sells many, many other products besides toys. As such, they could compensate with sales from other products while Toys R Us couldn't. It sells only toys.[89]

Concerns spread and a domino effect ensued. Many toy suppliers delayed shipments fearing they might not be paid if the company went bankrupt, and creditors also tightened terms making things even worse.

WHERE NOW?

All is not lost. Yes, the company did technically go away—over 700 U.S. stores closed and nearly 33,000 employees lost their jobs, but a new company, Tru Kids Brands, has emerged in 2019. Investors bought Toys R Us trademarks, private toy and baby brands, its famous mascot (Geoffrey the Giraffe), Babies R Us, and other assets. The new CEO, Richard Barry, formerly the chief marketing officer of Toys R Us, hired many of the former company's leaders but none of its stores and associated employees.[90]

Many industry experts note that although the major competitors are indeed formidable, the demise of Toys R Us leaves a notable gap in the market. Many people still need or at least desire to shop in an actual toy store, and this is especially true during the holidays. It's nostalgic.[91]

NEW TEAM . . . NEW APPROACH

Time will tell, but at the time this case was written it is clear it will involve new employees, new stores, and a new strategy to go along with the new name.

Assume you are the new CEO Richard Barry and apply the 3-Step Problem-Solving Approach to chart a path forward for Tru Kids Brands.

APPLY THE 3-STEP PROBLEM-SOLVING APPROACH TO OB

STEP 1: Define the problem.

A. Look first at the Outcomes box of the Organizing Framework in Figure 16.12 to help identify the important problem(s) in this case. Remember, a problem is a gap between a desired and a current state. State your problem as a gap and be sure to consider problems at all three levels. If more than one desired outcome is not being accomplished, decide which one is most important and focus on it for steps 2 and 3.

B. Cases have key players, and problems are generally viewed from a player's perspective. You need to determine from whose perspective—employee, manager, team, or the organization—you're defining the problem. As in other cases, whether you choose the individual or organizational level in this case can make a difference. In this case you're asked to assume the role of new CEO Richard Barry.

C. Use details in the case to determine the key problem. Don't assume, infer, or create problems that are not explicitly included in the case itself. Only use what Is provided in the case.

D. To refine your choice, ask yourself, *why is this a problem?* Explaining why helps refine your thinking. Focus on topics in the current chapter, because we generally select cases that illustrate concepts in the current chapter.

STEP 2: Identify causes.
Using material from this chapter and summarized in the Organizing Framework, identify what are the causes of the problem you identified in Step 1. Remember, causes tend to appear in either the Inputs or Processes boxes.

A. Start by looking at Figure 16.12 to identify which person factors, if any, are most likely causes of the defined problem. For each cause explain why or how It causes the problem. Asking why multiple times is more likely to lead you to root causes of the problem. In this case, for instance, how do competitors factor in to your decisions? What about the value of the brand? Expertise of leadership?

B. Follow the same process for the situation factors. For each ask yourself, *why is this a cause?* By following the process of asking why multiple times, you are likely to arrive at a more complete and accurate list of causes. Again, look to the Organizing Framework for guidance.

C. Now consider the Processes box shown in Figure 16.12. Consider concepts listed at all three levels. For any concept that might be a cause, ask yourself, *why is this a cause?* Again, do this for several iterations to arrive at root causes.

D. To check the accuracy or appropriateness of the causes, be sure to map them onto the defined problem and confirm the link or cause and effect connection.

STEP 3: Recommend solutions.
Make your recommendations for solving the problem. Consider whether you want to resolve it, solve it, or dissolve it (see Section 1.5). Which recommendation is desirable and feasible?

A. Given the causes identified in Step 2, what are your best recommendations? Use material in the current chapter that best suits the cause. Remember to consider the OB in Action and Applying OB boxes, because these contain insights into what others have done.

B. Be sure to consider the Organizing Framework—both person and situation factors, as well as processes at different levels.

C. Create an action plan for implementing your recommendations and be sure your recommendations map onto the causes and resolve the problem.

Can Employers Ethically Force You to Change and Be Healthy?

Healthy employees provide many benefits for employers: improved employee engagement and performance, attracting and retaining talent, job satisfaction, thriving culture and morale, and reduced health care costs. In fact, many leaders now view employee wellness as a fundamental part of business strategy and competitiveness.[92] it therefore is no surprise employers are using both carrots (incentives) and sticks (penalties) to motivate healthier employee lifestyles. These efforts have raised legal and ethical considerations regarding the means used to gain employee compliance.

Carrots and Sticks

Many programs offer incentives for employee participation. The most common is reduced health insurance premiums if employees participate in health screening, stress reduction, nutrition counseling, weight loss, smoking cessation, exercise, or other employer-sponsored programs. Many more employers (some estimate 60 percent) are penalizing employees for not meeting health standards or participating in wellness programs. Common penalties are increased health care premiums or surcharges for smokers or for those who are obese, and in some instances health expenses are not reimbursed if employees do not adopt a healthier lifestyle. At the extreme, some employers are linking employment offers to health behaviors, refusing to hire smokers or insisting current smokers must quit to remain employed.[93]

Truly Voluntary or Actually Coercive?

Employers often argue wellness and the associated carrots and sticks benefit all stakeholders. Opponents, however, are concerned the carrot approaches are actually coercive rather than voluntary.[94] The incentives and expectations may be so strong as to induce employees to engage in activities, such as strenuous exercise, that are unhealthy for those who are out of shape or have underlying conditions.[95] Others worry that stick programs and their associated penalties may be a form of harassment, and employees who choose not to participate may be stigmatized and in effect penalized. What about otherwise healthy employees, for whom participation in any type of program may not actually matter?

Some critics see employer-sponsored wellness as a "slippery slope" that may lead to employers' governing other nonwork activity, such as eating fast food or participating in extreme sports.[96] Particular concerns arise when employers set consequences tied to outcomes and not simply to participation. Of course, measurable outcomes make sense, but what about those who try but don't meet the desired standard? Is it fair to deny them discounts or penalize them with higher premiums?

Although Equal Employment Opportunity Commission (EEOC) policy largely governs the legal parameters, the reality is employers will continue to use carrots and sticks to foster employee health and wellness.[97]

Putting the EEOC aside, can employers fairly provide consequences (incentives or penalties) for employees who do not comply with their wellness standards, including participation in wellness programs?

What Is Your Position?

1. No. Employers should not provide positive or negative consequences for employees' health status. Justify.

2. Yes. Employers can provide incentives but not penalties. Justify.

3. Yes. Employers can provide both incentives and penalties. Justify.

4. Create and describe other possible alternatives for motivating employee wellness.

CHAPTER NOTES

CHAPTER 1

1. A. Glusker, "Why People Skills Are So Important—And How You Can Polish Yours to Shine," *Forbes*, June 8, 2018, https://www.forbes.com/sites/anneglusker/2018/06/08/why-people-skills-are-so-important-and-how-you-can-polish-yours-to-a-shine/#72c5e6022458.
2. S. Adams, "The College Degrees and Skills Employers Most Want in 2015," *Forbes*, April 15, 2015, http://www.forbes.com/sites/susanadams/2015/04/15/the-college-degrees-and-skills-employers-most-want-in-2015/print/.
3. "What Are Soft Job Skills and Why Are They Important?" *CareerBuilder.com*, July 9, 2018, https://www.careerbuilder.com/advice/what-are-soft-job-skills-and-why-are-they-important.
4. Inspired by and adapted from C. Ellers, "Resume Keywords to Use: Step-by-step Guide," *Zetsy*, October 25, 2018, https://zety.com/blog/resume-keywords.
5. Anne Glusker, "Why People Skills Are So Important—And How You Can Polish Yours to a Shine," *Forbes Media LLC*, June 8, 2018, https://www.forbes.com/sites/anneglusker/2018/06/08/why-people-skills-are-so-important-and-how-you-can-polish-yours-to-a-shine/#77124fc62458.
6. As quoted in P. LaBarre, "The Industrialized Revolution," *Fast Company*, November 2003, 116, 118.
7. T. Eurich, "What Self-Awareness Really Is (and How to Cultivate It)," *Harvard Business Review*, January 4, 2018, https://hbr.org/2018/01/what-self-awareness-really-is-and-how-to-cultivate-it.
8. J. Zenger and J. Folkman, "We Like Leaders Who Underrate Themselves," *Harvard Business Review*, November 10, 2015, https://hbr.org/2015/11/we-like-leaders-who-underrate-themselves.
9. C. Esimai, "Great Leadership Starts with Self-Awareness," *Forbes*, February 15, 2018, https://www.forbes.com/sites/ellevate/2018/02/15/self-awareness-being-more-of-what-makes-you-great/#5f6a841340dd.
10. Burck, Charles, Larry Bossidy, and Ram Charan. *Execution: The Discipline of Getting Things Done*. London: Random House, 2011.
11. T. Eurich, "What Self-Awareness Really Is (and How to Cultivate It)," *Harvard Business Review*, January 4, 2018, https://hbr.org/2018/01/what-self-awareness-really-is-and-how-to-cultivate-it.
12. Adapted using R. Hougaard, J. Carter, and M. Afton, "Self-Awareness Can Help Leaders More Than an MBA," *Harvard Business Review*, January 12, 2018, https://hbr.org/2018/01/self-awareness-can-help-leaders-more-than-an-mba-can; and A. K. Tjan, "5 Ways to Become More Self-Aware," *Harvard Business Review*, February 11, 2015, https://hbr.org/2015/02/5-ways-to-become-more-self-aware.
13. S. Vozza, "These Are the Five Soft Skills Recruiters Want Most," *FastCompany*, January 26, 2018, https://www.fastcompany.com/40520691/these-are-the-five-soft-skills-recruiters-want-most.
14. M. S. Rao, "Myths and Truths about Skills," *T+D*, May 7, 2012.
15. M. Curtin, "10 Skills Employers Will Want the Most in 2020," *businessinsider.com*, January 4, 2018, https://www.businessinsider.com/10-skills-employers-will-want-the-most-in-2020-2018-1.
16. S. Vozza, "These Are the Five Soft Skills Recruiters Want Most," *FastCompany*, January 26, 2018: https://www.fastcompany.com/40520691/these-are-the-five-soft-skills-recruiters-want-most.
17. Megan Elliott, "5 Essential Skills College Grads Need to Get a Decent Job," Showbiz Cheat Sheet, May 1, 2015, https://www.cheatsheet.com/money-career/5-skills-todays-college-grads-need-to-get-a-job.html/?a=viewall.
18. Melanie Curtin, "10 Skills Employers Will Want the Most in 2020," *Insider Inc.*, January 4, 2018, https://www.businessinsider.com/10-skills-employers-will-want-the-most-in-2020-2018-1?IR=T.
19. "What Are Soft Skills and Why Are They Important?" *CareerBuilder*, July 9, 2018, https://www.careerbuilder.com/advice/what-are-soft-job-skills-and-why-are-they-important.
20. N. Scheiber, "A.I. as Talent Scout: Unorthodox Hires, and Maybe Lower Pay," *The New York Times*, December 6, 2018, https://www.nytimes.com/2018/12/06/business/economy/artificial-intelligence-hiring.html: see also C. Scivicque, "What You Really Need to Get Promoted," *Ivy Exec Blog*, https://www.ivyexec.com/executive-insights/2014/show-soft-skills-get-promoted/.
21. Adapted from R. Ryan, "How to Ace Your Next Job Interview," *Talent Development*, February 10, 2016, https://www.td.org/Publications/Blogs/Career-Development-Blog/2016/02/How-to-Ace-Your-Next-Job-Interview.
22. Roxanne Hori, "Why Soft Skills Matter," *Bloomberg L.P.*, December 5, 2012, https://www.bloomberg.com/news/articles/2012-12-05/why-soft-skills-matter.
23. C. Scivicque, "What You Really Need to Get Promoted," *Ivy Exec Blog*, https://www.ivyexec.com/executive-insights/2014/show-soft-skills-get-promoted/; see also R. Patterson, "Hard Skills vs. Soft Skills: Why You Need Both to Succeed," *collegeinfogeek.com*, March 25, 2019, https://collegeinfogeek.com/hard-vs-soft-skills/.
24. B. Rothenberg and C. Clarey, "Review Finds 'Tsunami' of Fixed Matches in Lower Level Tennis," *The New York Times*, April 25, 2018, https://www.nytimes.com/2018/04/25/sports/tennis/tennis-anti-corruption-report.html.
25. "Performance Enhancing Drugs in Sports Fast Facts," CNN, May 7, 2018, https://www.cnn.com/2013/06/06/us/performance-enhancing-drugs-in-sports-fast-facts/index.html.
26. B. Y. Lee, "A Doping Scandal in Bridge? The World's Top Player Fails Drug Test," *forbes.com*, March 4, 2019, https://www.forbes.com/sites/brucelee/2019/03/04/a-doping-scandal-in-bridge-the-worlds-top-player-fails-drug-test/#56852a6a7450.
27. M. Dreyer, "Rampant Chinese Cheating Exposed at the Boston Marathon," *supchina.com*, April 21, 2019, https://supchina.com/2019/04/21/rampant-chinese-cheating-exposed-at-the-boston-marathon/.
28. E. M. Anderman, "Why Students at Prestigious High Schools Still Cheat on Exams," *The Conversation*, February 15, 2018, http://theconversation.com/why-students-at-prestigious-high-schools-still-cheat-on-exams-91041.
29. "What Impact Is Technology Having on Student Cheating?" *The NYU Dispatch*, February 26, 2018, https://wp.nyu.edu/ispatch/2018/02/26/what-impact-is-technology-having-on-student-cheating/.
30. "What Impact Is Technology Having on Student Cheating?" *The NYU Dispatch*, February 26, 2018, https://wp.nyu.edu/dispatch/2018/02/26/what-impact-is-technology-having-on-student-cheating/.
31. E. Whitford, "Study: Students Worldwide Pay to Cheat," *Inside Higher Education*, September 4, 2018, https://www.insidehighered.com/quicktakes/2018/09/04/study-students-worldwide-pay-cheat.
32. L. McKenzie, "Learning Tool of Cheating Aid," *Inside Higher Education*, May 14, 2018, https://www.insidehighered.com/news/2018/05/14/professors-warned-about-popular-learning-tool-used-students-cheat; see also E. B. Cadloff, "How Do You Solve a Problem Like Contract Cheating?" *University Affairs*, April 4, 2018, https://www.universityaffairs.ca/news/news-article/solve-problem-like-contract-cheating/.
33. E. L. Green and K. Benner, "Louisiana School Made Headlines for Sending Black Kids to Elite Colleges. Here's the Reality," *The New York Times*, November 30, 2018, https://www.nytimes.com/2018/11/30/us/tm-landry-college-prep-black-students.html.
34. G. Chen, "When Teachers Cheat: The Standardized Test Controversies," *Public School Review*, August 6, 2018, https://www.publicschoolreview.com/blog/when-teachers-cheat-the-standardized-test-controversies.
35. K. Nails, "Ousted Dean, False Rankings Data, AG Probe: A Guide to the Temple Business School Scandal," *The Inquirer*, July 17, 2018, http://www.philly.com/philly/education/temple-business-school-dean-data-fox-moshe-porat-explainer-20180717.html.
36. "College Admissions Scandal: Your Questions Answered," *The New York Times*, March 14, 2019, https://www.nytimes.com/2019/03/14/us/college-admissions-scandal-questions.html?action=click&module=RelatedCoverage&pgtype=Article&region=Footer; See also J. Medina and K. Taylor, "L.A.'s Elite on Edge as Prosecutors Pursue More Parents in Admissions Scandal," *The New York Times*, May 1, 2019, https://www.nytimes.com/2019/05/01/us/college-admissions-scandal.html?emc=edit_na_20190501&nl=breaking-news&nlid=49995115ing-news&ref=cta.
37. C. Tejada, "Nissan Workers in Japan Falsified Emissions Tests, Review Says," *The New York Times*, July 9, 2018, https://www.nytimes.com/2018/07/09/business/nissan-falsified-emissions-inspections.html.
38. C. Ornstein and K. Thomas, "Top Cancer Researcher Fails to Disclose Corporate Financial Ties in Major Research Journals," *The New York Times*, September 8, 2018, https://www.nytimes.com/2018/09/08/health/jose-baselga-cancer-memorial-sloan-kettering.html?nl=top-stories&nlid=49995115ries&ref=headline.
39. Z. Wichter, "Southwest Airlines Mechanics Approve Contract, Ending Long Impasse," *The New York Times*, May 21, 2019, https://www.nytimes.com/2019/05/21/business/southwest-airlines-mechanics-contract.html?nl=todaysheadlines&emc=edit_th_190522.
40. "You Asked, We Answered: Why Didn't Any Wall Street CEOs Go to Jail After the Financial Crisis? It's Complicated," *Marketplace.org*, https://features.marketplace.org/why-no-ceo-went-jail-after-financial-crisis/ (accessed June 14, 2019).

41. K. Scannell and R. Milne, "Who Was Convicted Because of the Global Financial Crisis," *ft.com,* August 9, 2017, https://www.ft.com/content/de173cc6-7c79-11e7-ab01-a13271d1ee9c.

42. J. Eaglesham, "Missing: Stats on Crisis Convictions," *The Wall Street Journal,* May 13, 2012.

43. CNBC LLC, "Bernanke: More Execs Should Have Gone to Jail," https://www.cnbc.com/2015/10/04/bernanke-more-bank-execs-should-have-been-jailed-for-financial-crisis.html (accessed June 28, 2019).

44. J. Strasburg and J. Chung, "Investors Exit Fund Dogged by Probe," *The Wall Street Journal,* February 15, 2013.

45. M. Goldstein and A. Stevenson, "In Insider Trading Settlement, Steven Cohen Will Be Free to Manage Outside Money in Two Years," *The New York Times,* January 8, 2016, http://www.nytimes.com/2016/01/09/business/dealbook/sec-and-steven—cohen-reach-settlement-in-insider-trading-case.html?_r=0.

46. K. Burton, "Steven Cohen Needs to Prove Himself to Wall Street All Over Again," *Bloomberg Businessweek,* February, 2018, https://www.bloomberg.com/news/articles/2018-02-01/steve-cohen-needs-to-prove-himself-to-wall-street-all-over-again; see also Bloomberg Billionaires Index, May 22, 2019, https://www.bloomberg.com/billionaires/profiles/steven-a-cohen/.

47. K. J. M. Baker, "What Do We Do with These Men?" *The New York Times,* April 27, 2018, https://www.nytimes.com/2018/04/27/opinion/sunday/metoo-comebacks-charlie-rose.html.

48. A. Carlsen, M. Salam, C. C. Miller, D. Lu, A. Ngu, J. K. Patel, and Z. Wichter, "#MeToo Brought Down 201 Powerful Men. Nearly Half of Their Replacements Are Women," *The New York Times,* October 29, 2018, https://www.nytimes.com/interactive/2018/10/23/us/metoo-replacements.html.

49. Inspired by Editorial Board, "It's Time for Pharmaceutical Companies to Have Their Tobacco Moment," *The New York Times,* February 24, 2019, https://www.nytimes.com/2019/02/24/opinion/drug-prices-congress.html.

50. W. Pavlo, "Pharma Boy Martin Shkreli and His Prison Troubles," *Forbes.com,* March 11, 2019, https://www.forbes.com/sites/walterpavlo/2019/03/11/pharma-boy-martin-shkreli-and-his-prison-troubles/#6a38a7e71404.

51. R. Khan, "Whistleblower: Warrior, Sabateur, or Snitch?" *Forbes,* July 5, 2018, https://www.forbes.com/sites/roomykhan/2018/07/05/whistleblower-saboteur-or-snitch/#39a75a856362.

52. "SEC Announces Its Largest-Ever Whistleblower Awards," Securities and Exchange Commission, March 19, 2018, https://www.sec.gov/news/press-release/2018-44.

53. P. Schroeder, "U.S. SEC Awards Merrill Lynch Whistleblowers a Record $83 Million," Reuters, March 19, 2018, https://www.reuters.com/article/us-usa-sec-whistleblower/u-s-sec-awards-merrill-lynch-whistleblowers-a-record-83-million-idUSKBN1GV2MT.

54. L. Berlin, "J. P. Morgan Chase Whistleblower: 'Essentially Suicide' to Stand Up to Bank," *The Huffington Post,* August 5, 2012, http://www.huffingtonpost.com.au/entry/linda-almonte-jpmorgan-chase-whistleblower_n_1478268.

55. P. Danner, "Regulators Slap JPMorgan Chase," *San Antonio Express News,* July 8, 2015, http://www.expressnews.com/business/local/article/Regulators-slap-JPMorgan-Chase-6373817.php.

56. M. Bazerman and A. Tenbrunsel, "Ethical Breakdowns: Good People Often Let Bad Things Happen, Why?" *Harvard Business Review,* April 2011, http://www.hbs.edu/faculty/Pages/item.aspx?num=39125.

57. B. Tepper, "When Managers Pressure Employees to Behave Badly: Toward a Comprehensive Response," *Business Horizons 53,* 2010, 591–598.

58. D. L. McCabe, K. D. Butterfield, and L. K. Trevino, "Academic Dishonesty in Graduate Business Programs: Prevalence, Causes, and Proposed Action," *Academy of Management Learning & Education,* 2006, 294–305.

59. Pamela Babcock, "Spotting Lies," *SHRM,* October 1, 2003, https://www.shrm.org/hr-today/news/hr-magazine/pages/1003babcock.aspx. Also see D. Macsai, ". . . And I Invented Velcro," *BusinessWeek,* August 4, 2008, 15.

60. J. T. O'Donnell, "85 Percent of Job Applicants Lie on Resumes. Here's How to Spot a Dishonest Candidate," *Inc.,* July 17, 2017, https://www.inc.com/jt-odonnell/staggering-85-of-job-applicants-lying-on-resumes-.html.

61. D. Papandrea, "The Biggest Resume Lies to Avoid," Monster Worldwide Inc., https://www.monster.com/career-advice/article/the-truth-about-resume-lies-hot-jobs (accessed December 16, 2018).

62. Based on M. C. Gentile, "Keeping Your Colleagues Honest," *Harvard Business Review,* March 2010.

63. Loren Gary, "Want Better Results? Boost Your Problem-Solving Power," *Harvard Business Review,* October 1, 2004, https://hbr.org/product/want-better-results-boost-your-problem-solving-power/U0410A-PDF-ENG.

64. T. Judge and C. Zapata, "The Person-Situation Debate Revisited, Effect of the Situation Strength and Trait Activation on the Validity of The Big Five Personality Traits in Predicting Job Performance," *Academy of Management Journal,* 2015, 1149–1179.

65. M. N., Conley and G. Saucier, "An Initial Broad-Level Mapping of Personality-Situation Contingencies in Self-Report Data," *Personality and Individual Differences,* 2019, 166–172.

66. S. Kim and S. Yun, "The Effect of Coworker Knowledge Sharing on Performance and Its Boundary Conditions: An Interactional Perspective," *Journal of Applied Psychology,* 2015, 575–582.

67. James R. Terborg, "Interactional Psychology and Research on Human Behavior in Organizations," *The Academy of Management Review* 6, no. 4 (October 1981): 569–76. https://DOI: 10.2307/257635.

68. J. Weber, "Mars Inc. CEO Grant Reid Is Thinking a Hundred Years Ahead," *Bloomberg.com,* January 23, 2019, https://www.bloomberg.com/news/features/2019-01-23/mars-inc-ceo-grant-reid-is-thinking-a-hundred-years-ahead; along with C. Thompson, "The Company Behind Some of the Most Popular Candies in the World Is Quietly Taking Over the Pet-Care Industry," *businessinsider.com,* June 13, 2018, https://www.businessinsider.com.au/mars-plans-to-grow-products-services-expand-digitally-2018-6.

69. M. C. Bush and C. Tkaczyk, "100 Best Companies to Work For," *Fortune,* 2019, 57–80.

70. M. Moskowitz and R. Levering, "The 100 Best Companies to Work For," *Fortune,* March 15, 2015, 152.

71. M. Moskowitz and R. Levering, "The 100 Best Companies to Work For," *Fortune,* March 15, 2015, 152.

72. J. Weber, "Mars Inc. CEO Grant Reid Is Thinking a Hundred Years Ahead," *Bloomberg.com,* January 23, 2019, https://www.bloomberg.com/news/features/2019-01-23/mars-inc-ceo-grant-reid-is-thinking-a-hundred-years-ahead.

73. J. Weber, "Mars Inc. CEO Grant Reid Is Thinking a Hundred Years Ahead," *Bloomberg.com,* January 23, 2019, https://www.bloomberg.com/news/features/2019-01-23/mars-inc-ceo-grant-reid-is-thinking-a-hundred-years-ahead.

74. Mars.com, https://www.mars.com/news-and-stories/media-resources/mars-volunteer-program (accessed March 10, 2019).

75. J. Weber, "Mars Inc. CEO Grant Reid Is Thinking a Hundred Years Ahead," *Bloomberg.com,* January 23, 2019, https://www.bloomberg.com/news/features/2019-01-23/mars-inc-ceo-grant-reid-is-thinking-a-hundred-years-ahead.

76. M. Moskowitz, R. Levering, O. Akhtar, E. Fry, C. Leahey, and A. Vandermey, "The 100 Best Companies to Work For," *Fortune,* February 4, 2013, 73–82.

77. J. Weber, "Mars Inc. CEO Grant Reid Is Thinking a Hundred Years Ahead," *Bloomberg.com,* January 23, 2019, https://www.bloomberg.com/news/features/2019-01-23/mars-inc-ceo-grant-reid-is-thinking-a-hundred-years-ahead.

78. G. Bhardwaj, A. Crocker, J. Sims, and R. D. Wang, "Alleviating the Plunging-In Bias, Elevating Strategic Problem-Solving," *Academy of Management Learning and Education,* 2018, 17(3): 279–301.

79. R. L. Ackoff, "On the Use of Models in Corporate Planning," *Strategic Management Journal,* 1981, 353–359. See also R. Kreitner, *Management,* 9th ed. (New York: Houghton-Mifflin, 2002), 271.

80. N. Morgan, "Are You Getting the Best Solutions for Your Problems?" *Harvard Business Review,* January 1, 2002, http://cb.hbsp.harvard.edu/cb/web/he/product_view.seam?R5C0201D-PDF-ENG&T5EC&C5SEARCH&CS505149d1977477612e265fff9eb8043c2 (accessed March 5, 2013).

81. M. P. Lynch, "Leave My iPhone Alone: Why Our Smartphones are Extensions of Ourselves," *The Guardian,* February 19, 2016, https://www.theguardian.com/technology/2016/feb/19/iphone-apple-privacy-smart-phones-extension-of-ourselves.

82. A. Perrin, "About a Quarter of U.S. Adults Say They Are 'Almost Constantly' Online," Pew Research Center, March 14, 2018, http://www.pewresearch.org/fact-tank/2018/03/14/about-a-quarter-of-americans-report-going-online-almost-constantly/.

83. A. Smith, "Walmart Adopts Bring-Your-Own-Device Policy," *SHRM.org,* October 26, 2018, https://www.shrm.org/resourcesandtools/legal-and-compliance/employment-law/pages/walmart-bring-your-own-device-policy.aspx.

84. R. Haridy, "The Right to Disconnect: The New Laws Banning After-Hours Work Emails," *Newatlas.com,* August 14, 2018, https://newatlas.com/right-to-disconnect-after-work-emails/55879/.

85. M. Thomas, "Vacation Policy in Corporate America Is Broken," *Harvard Business Review,* June 26, 2015, https://hbr.org/2015/06/vacation-policy-in-corporate-america-is-broken.

86. L. Nagele-Piazza, "Tips for Managing Workers' After-Hours Use of Mobile Devices," *SHRM.org,* June 15, 2018, https://www.shrm.org/resource-sandtools/legal-and-compliance/employment-law/pages/tips-for-managing-worker-after-hours-use-of-mobile-devices.aspx.

87. "Mere Expectation of Checking Work Email After Hours Harms Health of Workers and Families," *Eurekalert.org,* August 10, 2018, https://vtnews.vt.edu/articles/2018/08/pamplin-employer-emailexpectations.html.

88. C. Breen, "Elizabeth Holmes and Theranos Are Back in the News. Here's What You Need to Know About the Story. Holmes Said Theranos Would Revolutionize Health Care. That Never Happened," *thelily.com,* March 20, 2019, https://www.thelily.com/elizabeth-holmes-and-theranos-are-back-in-the-news-heres-what-you-need-to-know-about-the-story/.

89. J. Carreyrou, *Bad Blood: Secrets and Lies in a Silicon Valley Startup* (New York: Alfred A. Kopf, 2018).

90. J. Carreyrou, *Bad Blood: Secrets and Lies in a Silicon Valley Startup* (New York: Alfred A. Kopf, 2018).

91. J. Carreyrou, *Bad Blood: Secrets and Lies in a Silicon Valley Startup* (New York: Alfred A. Kopf, 2018); and C. Breen, "Elizabeth Holmes and Theranos Are Back in the News. Here's What You Need to Know About the Story. Holmes Said Theranos Would Revolutionize Health Care. That Never Happened," *thelily.com,* March 20, 2019, https://www.thelily.com/elizabeth-holmes-and-theranos-are-back-in-the-news-heres-what-you-need-to-know-about-the-story/.

92. J. Carreyrou, *Bad Blood: Secrets and Lies in a Silicon Valley Startup* (New York: Alfred A. Kopf, 2018).

CHAPTER 2

1. W. Thibodeaux, "How to Overcome the 3 Big Issues Killing Worker Engagement," *Inc.,* September 27, 2018, https://www.inc.com/wanda-thibodeaux/whats-actually-making-your-workers-disengaged-and-how-to-inspire-them.html?cid=search; J. Hayes, "Want to Improve Employee Engagement and Morale? Start By Addressing This 1 Huge Issue," *Inc.,* September 21, 2018, https://www.inc.com/julian-hayes-ii/70-percent-of-employees-are-distracted-at-work-its-costing-you-money-heres-how-to-fix-it.html?cid=search; C. Skaggs, "How to Be a More Engaged Employee," *Glassdoor.com,* January 5, 2018, https://www.glassdoor.com/blog/engaged-employee/; B. Gleeson, "5 Powerful Steps to Improve Employee Engagement," *Forbes,* October 15, 2017, https://www.forbes.com/sites/brentgleeson/2017/10/15/5-powerful-steps-to-improve-employee-engagement/#7cbe4645341d; M. E. Slater, "6 Steps to Take When You're Not Feeling Engaged at Work," *Monster.com,* https://www.monster.com/career-advice/article/6-steps-take-not-engaged-at-work-0316; and T. Chamorro-Premuzic and L. Garrad, "How to Tell Your Boss That You're Not Engaged at Work," *Harvard Business Review,* October 18, 2017, https://hbr.org/2017/10/how-to-tell-your-boss-that-youre-not-engaged-at-work.

2. B. Gleeson, "5 Powerful Steps to Improve Employee Engagement," *Forbes,* October 15, 2017, https://www.forbes.com/sites/brentgleeson/2017/10/15/5-powerful-steps-to-improve-employee-engagement/#7cbe4645341d.

3. See S. H. Schwartz, "An Overview of the Schwartz Theory of Basic Values," *Online Readings in Psychology and Culture,* December 1, 2012, 8, http://dx.doi.org/10.9707/2307-0919.1116.

4. See A. K. Döring, S. H. Schwartz, J. Cieciuch, P. J. F. Groenen, V. Glatzel, J. Harasimczuk, N. Janowicz, M. Nyagolova, E. R. Scheefer, M. Allritz, T. L. Milfont, and W. Bilsky, "Cross-Cultural Evidence of Value Structure and Priorities in Childhood," *British Journal of Psychology,* November 2015, 675–699; and W. Bilsky, T. Gollan, S. Roccas, H. Grad, M. L. M. Teixeira, M. Rodriguez, I. S. Gallo, and L. Segal-Caspi, "On the Relative Importance of Personal Values," *Journal of Individual Differences,* 2015, 119–129.

5. Company website, "Careers at Airbnb," https://careers.airbnb.com, (accessed February 25, 2019); and R. Brooks, "10 Companies with Core Values That Actually Reflect Their Culture," February 8, 2018, https://peakon.com/blog/workplace-culture/best-company-core-values/.

6. J. Desjardins, "Meet Generation Z: The Newest Member of the Workforce," *Visual Capitalist,* February 14, 2019, https://www.visualcapitalist.com/meet-generation-z-the-newest-member-to-the-workforce/; and R. Tanner, "15 Influential Events That Shaped Generation Y," May 12, 2018, https://managementisajourney.com/15-influential-events-that-shaped-generation-y-infographic/.

7. E. G. Dunn, "Not Enough Cooks," *Bloomberg Businessweek,* November 23–29, 2015, 67.

8. A. Lancaster, "3 Ways Restaurants Are Measuring Employee Satisfaction," *Restaurant Business Online,* September 6, 2017, https://www.restaurant-businessonline.com/workforce/3-ways-restaurants-are-measuring-employee-satisfaction#page=2.

9. L. Festinger, *A Theory of Cognitive Dissonance* (Palo Alto: Stanford University Press, 1957).

10. I. Ajzen, "The Theory of Planned Behavior," *Organizational Behavior and Human Decision Processes,* 1991, 188.

11. R. Abrams, "McDonald's Workers Across the U.S. Stage #MeToo Protests," *The New York Times,* September 18, 2018, https://www.nytimes.com/2018/09/18/business/mcdonalds-strike-metoo.html.

12. Rachel Abrams, "McDonald's Workers Across the U.S. Stage #MeToo Protests," *The New York Times,* September 18, 2018. https://www.nytimes.com/2018/09/18/business/mcdonalds-strike-metoo.html.

13. Rachel Abrams, "McDonald's Workers Across the U.S. Stage #MeToo Protests," *The New York Times,* September 18, 2018, https://www.nytimes.com/2018/09/18/business/mcdonalds-strike-metoo.html.

14. J. Gassam, "McDonald's Employees Strike to Protest Sexual Misconduct," *Forbes,* September 20, 2018, https://www.forbes.com/sites/janicegassam/2018/09/20/mcdonalds-employees-strike-to-protest-sexual-misconduct-how-to-prevent-misconduct-at-your-company/#6bd9a89b2b13.

15. C. Dewberry and D. J. R. Duncan, "An Application of the Theory of Planned Behavior to Student Retention," *Journal of Vocational Behavior,* August 2018, 100–110.

16. A. Buhmann and P. S. Brønn, "Applying Ajzen's Theory of Planned Behavior to Predict Practitioners' Intentions to Measure and Evaluate Communication Outcomes," *Corporate Communications: An International Journal,* August 2018, 377–391; and Y. Yang, J. N. Choi, and K. Lee, "Theory of Planned Behavior and Different Forms of Organizational Change Behavior," *Social Behavior and Personality* 46, no. 10 (2018), 1657–1672.

17. S. Kim, Y.A. Park, and L. Headrick, "Daily Micro-Breaks and Job Performance: General Work Engagement as a Cross-Level Moderator," *Journal of Applied Psychology* July 2018, 772–786.

18. S. Judd, E. O'Rourke, and A. Grant, "Employee Surveys Are Still One of the Best Ways to Measure Engagement," *Harvard Business Review,* March 14, 2018, https://hbr.org/2018/03/employee-surveys-are-still-one-of-the-best-ways-to-measure-engagement.

19. J. P. Meyer and L. Herscovitch, "Commitment in the Workplace: Toward a General Model," *Human Resource Management,* Autumn 2001, 301.

20. L. Wang, K. S. Law, M. J. Zhang, Y. N. Li, and Y. Liang, "It's Mine! Psychological Ownership of One's Job Explains Positive and Negative Workplace Outcomes of Job Engagement," *Journal of Applied Psychology,* February 2019, 229–246.

21. D. M. Rousseau, S. D. Hansen, and M. Tomprou, "A Dynamic Phase Model of Psychological Contract Processes," *Journal of Organizational Behavior,* November 2018, 1081–1098.

22. "Fortune 2019 100 Best Companies to Work For: Hilton," http://fortune.com (accessed February 22, 2019); and Great Place to Work, "Hilton—Hospitality for All," https://www.greatplacetowork.com (accessed February 22, 2019).

23. "Fortune 2019 100 Best Companies to Work For: Salesforce," http://fortune.com (accessed February 22, 2019); and A. McBride, "How Salesforce Philanthropy Chief Ebony Frelix Connects with People," *San Francisco Chronicle,* September 25, 2018, www.sfchronicle.com.

24. "Fortune 2019 100 Best Companies to Work For: Cisco," http://fortune.com (accessed February 22, 2019); and R. Hackett, "How Cisco Encourages Everyone to Innovate," *Fortune,* February 14, 2019, http://fortune.com/2019/02/14/best-companies-cisco-innovation/.

25. William A. Kahn, "Psychological Conditions of Personal Engagement and Disengagement at Work," *Academy of Management Journal* 33, no. 4 (December 1990): 692–724.

26. W. A. Macy, B. Schneider, K. M. Barbera, and S. A. Young, *Employee Engagement: Tools for Analysis, Practice, and Competitive Advantage* (West Sussex, UK: Wiley-Blackwell, 2009), 20.

27. Aon, "2018 Trends in Global Employee Engagement," https://www.aon.com/2018-global-employee-engagement-trends/index.html.

28. B. Schneider, A. B. Yost, A. Kropp, C. Kind, and H. Lam, "Workforce Engagement: What It Is, What Drives It, and Why It Matters for Organizational Performance," *Journal of Organizational Behavior,* May 2018, 462–480.

29. M. Hernandez and C. L. Guarana, "An Examination of the Temporal Intricacies of Job Engagement," *Journal of Management,* May 2018, 1711–1735.

30. S. Sonnentag, E. J. Mojza, E. Demerouti, and A. B. Bakker, "Reciprocal Relations between Recovery and Work Engagement: The Moderating Role of Job Stressors," *Journal of Applied Psychology,* July 2012, 842–853.

31. J. Harter, "Employee Engagement on the Rise in U.S.," August 26, 2018, https://news.gallup.com/poll/241649/employee-engagement-rise.aspx.

32. A. Kohll, "Your Employee Engagement Strategy Needs More Wellness," *Forbes,* July 30, 2018, https://www.forbes.com/sites/alankohll/2018/07/30/your-employee-engagement-strategy-needs-more-wellness/#25bae0c242b5; and L. Venz, A. Pundt, and S. Sonnentag, "What Matters for Work Engagement? A Diary Study on Resources and the Benefits of Selective Optimization with Compensation for State Work Engagement," *Journal of Organizational Behavior,* January 2018, 26–38.

33. A. Bonner, "Use Ritz-Carlton's Gold Standards to Boost Customer Service," June 29, 2018, https://eyecareleaders.com/customer-service-ritz-carlton/.

34. Ed Frauenheim, "The Secrets of One of Texas's Best Companies to Work For," *Fortune Media IP Limited,* March 20, 2018, http://fortune.com/2018/03/20/the-secrets-of-one-of-texass-best-companies-to-work-for/.

35. Ed Frauenheim, and Great Place to Work. "How T-Mobile Became One of the Best Workplaces in New York," *Fortune Media IP Limited,* July 17, 2018, http://fortune.com/2018/07/17/t-mobile-became-one-of-the-best-workplaces-in-new-york/.

36. Clifton Leaf, "Move Over, Gym Memberships. The Hot New Employee Perk Involves Spitting Into a Cup." *Fortune Media IP Limited,* April 19, 2018, http://fortune.com/2018/04/19/levi-strauss-ceo-dna-testing/.

37. REI, "Pay and Benefits," https://rei.jobs/portal/11/docs/rei-pay-and-benefits.pdf (accessed February 22, 2019).

38. H. R. Young, David R. Glerum, W. Wang, and D. L. Joseph, "Who Are the Most Engaged at Work? A Meta-Analysis of Personality and Employee Engagement," *Journal of Organizational Behavior,* December 2018, 1330–1346.

39. M. M. Joy and M. J. Chiramel, "Importance of Perceived Organizational Support in Controlling Employee Withdrawal Behaviors," *International Journal of Engineering Technology, Management and Applied Sciences,* 2016, 37–41; and L. Rhodes and R. Eisenberger, "Perceived Organizational Support: A Review of the Literature," *Journal of Applied Psychology,* August 2002, 698–714.

40. P. C. Smith, L. M. Kendall, and C. L. Hulin, *The Measurement of Satisfaction in Work and Retirement* (Skokie, IL: Rand-McNally, 1969).

41. D. B. Kline, "A Majority of U.S. Workers Are Actually Satisfied with Their Jobs," *USA Today,* September 7, 2018, https://www.usatoday.com/story/money/careers/employment-trends/2018/09/03/labor-day-majority-workers-satisfied-jobs-survey/37670201/.

42. SHRM, "SHRM Survey: Equity and Openness Are Key Contributors to Job Satisfaction; Employee Job Satisfaction Remains High," https://www.shrm.org/about-shrm/press-room/press-releases/pages/shrm-survey-equity-and-openness-are-key-contributors-to-job-satisfaction.aspx (accessed May 22, 2019).

43. E. F. Stone, "A Critical Analysis of Social Information Processing Models of Job Perceptions and Job Attitudes," in *Job Satisfaction: How People Feel about Their Jobs and How It Affects Their Performance,* ed. C. J. Cranny, P. Cain Smith, and E. F. Stone (New York: Lexington Books, 1992), 21–52.

44. J. P. Wanous, T. D. Poland, S. L. Premack, and K. S. Davis, "The Effects of Met Expectations on Newcomer Attitudes and Behaviors: A Review and Meta-Analysis," *Journal of Applied Psychology,* June 1992, 288–297.

45. Results can be found in J. Cohen-Charash and P. E. Spector, "The Role of Justice in Organizations: A Meta-Analysis," *Organizational Behavior and Human Decision Processes,* November 2001, 278–321.

46. A. M. Nofal, N. Nicolau, and N. Symeonidou, "Biology and Management: A Review, Critique, and Research Agenda," *Journal of Management,* January 2018, 7–31; and W. D. Li, K. C. Stanek, Z. Zhang, D. S. Ones, and M. McGue, "Are Genetic and Environmental Influences on Job Satisfaction Stable over Time? A Three-Wave Longitudinal Twin Study," *Journal of Applied Psychology,* November 2016, 1598–1619.

47. S. D. Riza, Y. Ganzach, and Y. Liu, "Time and Job Satisfaction: A Longitudinal Study of the Differential Roles of Age and Tenure," *Journal of Management,* September 2018, 2558–2579.

48. See C. Dormann and D. Zapf, "Job Satisfaction: A Meta-Analysis of Stabilities," *Journal of Organizational Behavior,* August 2001, 483–504.

49. D. Cyranoski, "The CRISPR-baby Scandal: What's Next for Human Gene-Editing," *Nature,* February 26, 2019, https://www.nature.com; A. Ramzy and S. Wee, "Scientist Who Edited Babies' Genes Is Likely to Face Charges in China," *The New York Times,* January 21, 2019, https://www.nytimes.com; P. Rana and W. Fan, "Chinese Gene-Editing Experiment Loses Track of Patients, Alarming Technology's Inventors," *The Wall Street Journal,* December 28, 2018, https://www.wsj.com.

50. "Telecommuting Trend Data (updated July 2018)," https://globalworkplaceanalytics.com/telecommuting-statistics.

51. S. Mautz, "A 2-Year Stanford Study Shows the Astonishing Productivity Boost of Working from Home," *Inc.,* April 2, 2018, https://www.inc.com/scott-mautz/a-2-year-stanford-study-shows-astonishing-productivity-boost-of-working-from-home.html; and S. Lynch, "Why Working from Home Is a 'Future-looking Technology,'" *Stanford Business Insights,* June 22, 2017, https://www.gsb.stanford.edu/insights/why-working-home-future-looking-technology.

52. B. Braccio Hering, "5 Best Practices for Your Telecommuters," *Flexjobs.com,* April 26, 2017, https://www.flexjobs.com/employer-blog/best-practices-for-telecommuters/; and M. R. Barrick and M. K. Mount, "The Big Five Personality Dimensions and Job Performance: A Meta-Analysis," *Personnel Psychology,* Spring 1991, 21.

53. S. P. Brown, "A Meta-Analysis and Review of Organizational Research on Job Involvement," *Psychological Bulletin,* September 1996, 235–255.

54. Bamboo HR Blog, "What People Really Want from Onboarding," October 3, 2018, https://www.bamboohr.com/blog/onboarding-infographic/?utm_source=Par-Bnusly-Ref&utm_medium=referral&utm_campaign=10-surprising-employee-retention-statistics-you-need-to-know-blog.

55. A. Golden, "Some Companies Encourage Employees to Disconnect During Vacation," *NBC News,* March 10, 2017, https://www.nbcnews.com/nightly-news/some-companies-encouraging-employees-disconnect-during-vacation-n732116.

56. Suzanne Lucas, "Netflix Has a New Sexual Harassment Policy. It's Like 7th Grade on Steroids," Inc.com, June 14, 2018. https://www.inc.com/suzanne-lucas/netflix-has-a-new-sexual-harassment-policy-its-like-7th-grade-on-steroids.html?cid=search.

57. K. Timpf, "Report: Netflix Bans Employees from Looking at Each Other for More Than Five Seconds," *National Review,* June 14, 2018, https://www.nationalreview.com/2018/06/netflix-five-second-staring-rule/; K. Gurchiek, "Don't Look! Reports of Netflix's 'No Staring' Rule Raise Harassment Questions," *Society for Human Resource Management,* June 22, 2018, https://www.nationalreview.com/2018/06/netflix-five-second-staring-rule/; and S. Lucas, "Netflix Has a New Sexual Harassment Policy. It's

Like 7th Grade," *Inc.,* June 14, 2018, https://www.inc.com/suzanne-lucas/netflix-has-a-new-sexual-harassment-policy-its-like-7th-grade-on-steroids.html?cid=search.

58. Y. H. Chun, S. Choi, and M. Song, "Analyzing the Link Between Job Satisfaction and Performance in Educational Institutions," *International Journal of Public Administration,* August 2018, 1–16.

59. Y. H. Chun, S. Choi, and M. Song, "Analyzing the Link Between Job Satisfaction and Performance in Educational Institutions," *International Journal of Public Administration,* August 2018, 1–16.

60. Dennis W. Organ, "The Motivational Basis of Organizational Citizenship Behavior," *Research in Organizational Behavior* 12 (1990): 43–72.

61. D. W. Organ, "The Motivational Basis of Organizational Citizenship Behavior," in *Research in Organizational Behavior,* ed. B. M. Staw and L. L. Cummings (Greenwich, CT: JAI Press, 1990), 46.

62. A. C. Klotz, M. C. Bolino, H. Song, and J. Stornelli, "Examining the Nature, Causes, and Consequences of Profiles of Organizational Citizenship Behavior," *Journal of Organizational Behavior,* June 2018, 629–647.

63. P. S. Thompson and M. C. Bolino, "Negative Beliefs About Accepting Coworker Help: Implications for Employee Attitudes, Job Performance, and Reputation," *Journal of Applied Psychology,* August 2018, 842–866.

64. S. J. Motowidlo and H. J. Kell, "Job Performance," in *Handbook of Psychology* (Vol. 12), ed. N. W. Schmitt and S. Highhouse (Hoboken, NJ: John Wiley & Sons 2012).

65. J. Bilski, "Workers Gone Wild: 7 Outrageous Cases of Employee Fraud," *CFO Daily News,* July 13, 2018, http://www.cfodailynews.com/workers-gone-wild-7-outrageous-cases-of-employee-fraud/.

66. Z. E. Zhou, E. M. Eatough, and D. R. Wald, "Feeling Insulted? Examining End-of-Work Anger as a Mediator in the Relationship Between Daily Illegitimate Tasks and Next-Day CWB," *Journal of Organizational Behavior,* October 2018, 911–921.

67. "The High Costs of Staff Turnover," *The Economist,* September 20, 2018, https://www.economist.com/business/2018/09/20/the-high-costs-of-staff-turnover.

68. L. Jiang and L. M. Lavaysse, "Cognitive and Affective Job Security: A Meta-Analysis and a Primary Study," *Journal of Management,* July 2018, 2307–2342.

69. R. Maurer, "Why Are Workers Quitting Their Jobs in Record Numbers?" *Society for Human Resource Management,* December 12, 2018, https://www.shrm.org/resourcesandtools/hr-topics/talent-acquisition/pages/workers-are-quitting-jobs-record-numbers.aspx.

70. J. M. Rosenberg, "How to Deal with and Prevent Mass Employee Turnover at Your Small Business," *Inc.,* August 16, 2018, https://www.inc.com/associated-press/how-to-deal-with-prevent-mass-employee-turnover.html?cid=search.

71. See M. Krasman, "Three Must-Have Onboarding Elements for New and Relocated Employees," *Employment Relations Today,* July 2015, 9–14; and "A Signature New-Hire Experience," http://mycareer.deloitte.com/us/en/life-at-deloitte/leadership/learning-and-development/a-signature-new-hire-experience (accessed June 24, 2014).

72. M. C. Sturman, L. Shao, and J. H. Katz, "The Effect of Culture on the Curvilinear Relationship between Performance and Turnover," *Journal of Applied Psychology,* January 2012, 46–62.

73. J. M. Rosenberg, "How to Deal with and Prevent Mass Employee Turnover at Your Small Business," *Inc.,* August 16, 2018, https://www.inc.com/associated-press/how-to-deal-with-prevent-mass-employee-turnover.html?cid=search.

74. Y. Lai, G. Saridakis, and S. Johnstone, "Human Resource Practices, Employee Attitudes and Small Firm Performance," *International Small Business Journal,* June 2017, 470–494.

75. M. S. Sohail and J. Jang, "Understanding the Relationships among Internal Marketing Practices, Job Satisfaction, Service Quality and Customer Satisfaction: An Empirical Investigation of Saudi Arabia's Service Employees," *International Journal of Tourism Sciences,* March 2017, 67–85.

76. Y. G. T. van Rossenberg, Howard J. Klein, K. Asplund, K. Bentein, et al., "The Future of Workplace Commitment: Key Questions and Directions," *European Journal of Work and Organizational Psychology,* March 2018, 153–167.

77. "About Us," https://corporate.walmart.com/our-story (accessed April 16, 2019).

78. Walmart Inc. "Walmart Core Values," https://careers.walmart.com/values (accessed May 22, 2019).

79. Rachel Abrams, "Walmart Is Accused of Punishing Workers for Sick Days," *The New York Times,* June 1, 2017, https://www.nytimes.com/2017/06/01/business/walmart-workers-sick-days.html.

80. R. Abrams, "Walmart Is Accused of Punishing Workers for Sick Days," *The New York Times,* June 1, 2017, https://www.nytimes.com/2017/06/01/business/walmart-workers-sick-days.html.

81. Vanessa Romo, "Federal Commission Sues Walmart for Alleged Discrimination Against Pregnant Employees," *NPR,* September 21, 2018, https://www.npr.org/2018/09/21/650620184/federal-commission-sues-walmart-for-alleged-discrimination-against-pregnant-empl.

82. CBS Broadcasting Inc. "Customers Angry Walmart Greeter with Cerebral Palsy May Lose Job After Policy Change," https://philadelphia.cbslocal.com/2019/02/21/customers-angry-that-disabled-walmart-greeter-may-lose-his-job-after-policy-change/ (accessed May 22, 2019).

83. See D. Hembree, "CEO Pay Skyrockets to 361 Times That of the Average Worker," *Forbes*, May 22, 2018, https://www.forbes.com/sites/dianahembree/2018/05/22/ceo-pay-skyrockets-to-361-times-that-of-the-average-worker/#11be9b00776d; and S. Butler-Young, "Making Sense of Why Walmart's CEO Earns 1,200 Times the Pay of Its Median Employee," *Footwear News*, April 23, 2018, https://footwearnews.com/2018/business/retail/walmart-ceo-doug-mcmillon-salary-compensation-2018-1202553529/.

84. Jonathan Tasini, "Why Walmart's Bait and Switch Matters," *CNN*, January 13, 2018, https://edition.cnn.com/2018/01/13/opinions/sams-club-walmart-corporate-greed-tasini-opinion/index.html.

85. Jill Disis, "Walmart Is Raising Its Minimum Wage and Handing Out Tax Cut Bonuses," *CNN*, January 11, 2018, https://money.cnn.com/2018/01/11/news/companies/walmart-minimum-wage-increase/index.html.

86. J. Tasini, "Why Walmart's Bait and Switch Matters," *CNN*, January 13, 2018, https://edition.cnn.com/2018/01/13/opinions/sams-club-walmart-corporate-greed-tasini-opinion/index.html.

87. M. Corkery, "Walmart's Bumpy Day: From Wage Increase to Store Closings," *The New York Times*, January 11, 2018, https://www.nytimes.com/2018/01/11/business/walmart-wages-tax-cuts.html.

88. J. Goodheart, "Ten Thousand Laid-Off Workers Later, Sam's Club 'Transforms' Its Business," *Fast Company*, February 15, 2018, https://www.fastcompany.com/40530984/ten-thousand-laid-off-workers-later-sams-club-transforms-its-business.

89. M. Corkery, "Walmart's Bumpy Day: From Wage Increase to Store Closings," *The New York Times*, January 11, 2018, https://www.nytimes.com/2018/01/11/business/walmart-wages-tax-cuts.html.

90. P. Mourdoukoutas, "Minimum Wage Hikes Won't Solve Walmart's Customer Service Problem," *Forbes*, March 18, 2018, https://www.forbes.com/sites/panosmourdoukoutas/2018/03/18/minimum-wage-hikes-wont-solve-walmarts-customer-service-problem/#34fea3201e09.

91. Panos Mourdoukoutas, "Minimum Wage Hikes Won't Solve Walmart's Customer Service Problem," *Forbes Media LLC*, March 18, 2018, https://www.forbes.com/sites/unicefusa/2019/04/25/born-a-refugee-baby-mohammad-is-growing-up-healthy-thanks-to-unicef/#5880187e56ea.

92. P. Mourdoukoutas, "Minimum Wage Hikes Won't Solve Walmart's Customer Service Problem," *Forbes*, March 18, 2018, https://www.forbes.com/sites/panosmourdoukoutas/2018/03/18/minimum-wage-hikes-wont-solve-walmarts-customer-service-problem/#34fea3201e09.

93. "Walmart Core Values," https://careers.walmart.com/values, accessed April 16, 2019.

94. Susanna Kim, "NJ Town Tax Collector's Office Accused of Abusing Worker With 'Wall of Shame,'" *ABC News Internet Ventures*, March 11, 2014, https://abcnews.go.com/US/gov-jay-inslee-signs-bill-making-washington-1st/story?id=63189512.

95. Bill Borden, "Point Boro Tax Official Named in Lawsuit to Retire June 1," *Patch Media*, April 16, 2014, https://patch.com/new-jersey/pointpleasant/point-boro-tax-official-named-in-lawsuit-to-retire-june-1.

96. S. Kim, "NJ Town Tax Collector's Office Accused of Abusing Worker with 'Wall of Shame,'" *ABC News*, March 11, 2014, http://abcnews.go.com/Business/nj-boss-sued-abuse-urn-ashes-problem-employees/story?id=22862773.

CHAPTER 3

1. Adapted from E. Moore, "How to Answer the 50 Most Common Interview Questions: Parts 1-4," *Glassdoor.com*, October 6, 2017, https://www.glassdoor.com/blog/most-common-interview-questions-1/.

2. Adapted from R. Maurer, "Recruiters Need to Be Ready to Answer these Candidate Questions," *SHRM.org*, March 21, 2018, https://www.shrm.org/ResourcesAndTools/hr-topics/talent-acquisition/Pages/Recruiters-Prepare-Answer-Candidate-Questions.aspx.

3. R. Plomin, J. DeFries, V. Knopik, and J. Neiderhiser. "Top 10 Replicated Findings from Behavioral Genetics," *Perspectives in Psychological Science*, 2016, 3–23.

4. D. A. Briley and E. M. Tucker-Drob, "Genetic and Environmental Continuity in Personality Development: A Meta-Analysis," *Psychological Bulletin*, June 23, 2014, 1–29.

5. T. A. Judge and C. Zapata, "The Person-Situation Debate Revisited: Effect of Situational Strength and Trait Activation on the Validity of the Big Five Personality Traits in Predicting Job Performance," *Academy of Management Journal*, 2015, 1149–1179.

6. B. Hyacinth, "Employees Don't Leave Companies, They Leave Managers," *LinkedIn.com*, December 27, 2017, https://www.linkedin.com/pulse/employees-dont-leave-companies-managers-brigette-hyacinth/.

7. Adapted from B. Hyacinth, "Employees Don't Leave Companies, They Leave Managers," *LinkedIn.com*, December 27, 2017, https://www.linkedin.com/pulse/employees-dont-leave-companies-managers-brigette-hyacinth/.

8. P. Agnello, R. Ryan, and K. Yusko, "Implications of Modern Intelligence Research for Assessing Intelligence in the Workplace," *Human Resource Management Review*, 2015, 47–55.

9. S. Kanazawa, "Evolutionary Psychology and Intelligence Research," *American Psychologist*, May–June 2010, 279–289.

10. B. Azar, "People Are Becoming Smarter—Why?" *APA Monitor*, June 1996, 20.

11. A. Suarez, "21 Celebrities with Surprisingly High IQs," *Hollywood.com*, June 5, 2013, http://www.hollywood.com/celebrities/celebrities-with-surprisingly-high-iqs-60471366/#/ms-22545/11.

12. H. Gardner, *Frames of Mind: The Theory of Multiple Intelligences*, 10th ed. (New York: Basic Books, 1993). See also H. Gardner, *Intelligence Reframed: Multiple Intelligences for the 21st Century* (New York: Basic Books, 2000); and B. Fryer, "The Ethical Mind: A Conversation with Psychologist Howard Gardner," *Harvard Business Review*, March 2007, 51–56.

13. A. Smith, "Benefits of Being a Multilingual CEO: 10 Successful Entrepreneurs Who Speak Multiple Languages," *CEO World Magazine*, July 24, 2015, http://ceoworld.biz/2015/07/24/benefitsof-being-a-multilingual-ceo-10-successful-entrepreneurs-who-speakmultiple-languages.

14. D. Sacks, "Patagonia CEO Rose Marcario Fights the Fights Worth Fighting," *Fast Company*, January 1, 2015, http://www.fastcompany.com/3039739/creative-conversations/patagonia-ceo-rose-marcario-fights-the-fights-worth-fighting.

15. H. A. A. Popkin, K. Knowles, L. Aratani, and S. Marwan, "The World's Top 50 Women in Tech," *Forbes.com*, December 12, 2018, https://www.forbes.com/top-tech-women/#6d0a40654df0.

16. Grace Holliday, "Anne-Marie Imafidon: 'My Dream in Life Is to Be a Hermit'" *Guardian News & Media Limited*, October 27, 2018, https://www.theguardian.com/lifeandstyle/2018/oct/27/anne-marie-imafidon-computer-scientist-work-life-balance.

17. L. Sheahan, A. While, and J. Bloomfield, "An Exploratory Trial Exploring the Use of a Multiple Intelligences Teaching Approach (MITA) for Teaching Clinical Skills to First Year Undergraduate Nursing Students," *Nurse Education Today*, 2015, 1148–1154.

18. Robert J. Sternberg, "WICS: A Model of Leadership in Organizations," *Academy of Management Learning & Education* 2, no. 4 (December 2003): 386–401, https://DOI: 10.5465/AMLE.2003.11902088.

19. S. Randazzo, "A Plaintiffs' Lawyer with Eye for Big Settlements," *The Wall Street Journal*, March 3, 2016, http://www.wsj.com/ articles/a-plaintiffs-lawyer-with-eye-for-big-settlements-1457001002.

20. L. Denworth, "Do Brain-Changing Games Really Work?" *Psychology Today*, July 14, 2017, https://www.psychologytoday.com/us/blog/brain-waves/201707/do-brain-changing-games-really-work.

21. T. Lewis, "Here's What the Science Really Says About Whether Brain Training Helps Keep You Sharp," *Business Insider*, January 29, 2016, http://www.businessinsider.com.au/science-of-brain-training-2016-1.

22. K. Richardson and S. Norgate, "Does IQ Really Predict Job Performance?" *Applied Developmental Science*, 2015, 153–169.

23. S. Weems, "Three Things to Know About 'Brain-Training' Programs," *Psychology Today*, February 2, 2018, https://www.psychologytoday.com/us/blog/feed-your-head/201802/three-things-know-about-brain-training-programs.

24. C. Goodbread, "Ryan Fitzpatrick: Wonderlic-Score Questions Are My Least Favorite," *NFL.com*, October 8, 2015, http://www.nfl.com/news/story/0ap3000000552415/article/ryan-fitzpatrick-wonderlicscore-questions-are-my-least-favorite; see also C. Bennett, "Ryan Fitzpatrick: 5 Fast Facts You Need to Know," *Heavy.com*, August 11, 2015, http://heavy.com/sports/2015/08/ryan-fitzpatrick-football-nfl-quarterbackcollege-career-stats-bio-wife-smart-wonderlic-geno-smith/.

25. J. Smith, "6 NFL Players with Genius IQs," *Cheatsheet.com*, October 3, 2017, https://www.cheatsheet.com/sports/nfl-players-with-genius-iqs.html/.

26. M. Tracy, "Let Us Tell You What Else Clemson's Christian Wilkins Does," *The New York Times*, December 27, 2018, https://www.nytimes.com/2018/12/27/sports/clemson-christian-wilkins-.html.

27. C. Crouse, "On NFL Draft Day, a New IQ Test Takes Top Position in Player Scouting," *CNBC.com*, April 26, 2018, https://www.cnbc.com/2018/04/26/on-nfl-draft-day-new-iq-test-takes-top-position-in-player-scouting.html.

28. R. Klemko, "What Analytics Say About Baker Mayfield," *SI.com*, March 22, 2018, https://www.si.com/nfl/2018/03/22/baker-mayfield-advance-analytics-nfl-draft-oklahoma-pff.

29. R. Plomin, J. DeFries, V. Knopik, and J. Neiderhiser, "Top 10 Replicated Findings from Behavioral Genetics," *Perspectives in Psychological Science*, 2016, 3–23. See also C. J. Hopwood, M. B. Donnellan, D. M. Blonigen, R. F. Krueger, M. McGue, W. G. Iacono, and S. A. Burt, "Genetic and Environmental Influences on Personality Trait Stability and Growth During the Transition to Adulthood: A Three-Wave Longitudinal Study," *Journal of Personality and Social Psychology*, January 17, 2011, 1–12.

30. The landmark report is J. M. Digman, "Personality Structure: Emergence of the Five-Factor Model," *Annual Review of Psychology* 41, 1990, 417–440. Also see P. Warr, D. Bartram, and A. Brown, "Big Five Validity: Aggregation Method Matters," *Journal of Occupational and Organizational Psychology*, September 2005, 377–386.

31. Data from S. V. Paunonen et al., "The Structure of Personality in Six Cultures," *Journal of Cross-Cultural Psychology*, May 1996, 339–353.

32. For supporting evidence see D. P. Schmitt, J. Allik, R. R. McCrae, and V. Benet-Martinez, "The Geographic Distribution of Big Five Personality Traits," *Journal of Cross-Cultural Psychology*, March 2007, 173–212.

33. B. A. Macaluso, "15 Things You Should Know About Ruth Bader Ginsburg," *Mentalfloss.com*, December 25, 2018, http://mentalfloss.com/article/76804/15-things-you-should-know-about-ruth-bader-ginsburg.

34. M. DeFelice, "5 of Ruth Bader Ginsburg's Qualities We Can Emulate for Success in Work and Life," *Forbes*, July 2, 2018, https://www.forbes.com/sites/manondefelice/2018/07/02/5-of-ruth-bader-ginsburgs-qualities-we-can-emulate-for-success-in-work-life/#2743d9ac7fe7.

35. T. S. Bateman and M. J. Crant, "The Proactive Component of Organizational Behavior: A Measure and Correlates," *Journal of Organizational Behavior* 14, March 1993, 103–118. See also J. P. Thomas, D. S. Whitman, and V. Chockalingam, "Employee Proactivity in Organizations: A Comparative Meta-Analysis of Emergent Proactive Constructs," *Journal of Occupational & Organizational Psychology*, June 2010, 275–300.

36. W. Li, D. Fay, M. Frese, and P. Harms, "Reciprocal Relationships between Proactive Personality and Work Characteristics: A Latent Change Score Approach," *Journal of Applied Psychology*, September 2014, 948–965.

37. T. J. Maurer and E. F. Chapman, "Relationship of Proactive Personality with Life Satisfaction During Late Career and Early Retirement," *Journal of Career Development*, 2018 (45), 345–360.

38. R. Fujioka, "How Bill Gates, Larry Page, and Mark Zuckerberg All Thrive as Introverts," *Inc. Magazine*, February 23, 2016, http://www. inc.com/russ-fujioka/how-bill-gates-larry-page-and-mark-zuckerbergall-thrive-as-introverts.html.

39. Z. Zhang, M. Wang, and J. Shi, "Leader-Follower Congruence in Proactive Personality and Work Outcomes: The Mediating Role of Leader Member Exchange," *Academy of Management Journal*, 2012, 111–130.

40. J. Dikkers, P. G. Jansen, A. de Lange, C. Vinkenburg, and D. Kooij, "Proactivity, Job Characteristics, and Engagement: A Longitudinal Study," *Career Development International*, 2010, 59–77; T. Kim, A. H. Hon, and J. M. Crant, "Proactive Personality, Employee Creativity, and Newcomer Outcomes: A Longitudinal Study," *Journal of Business Psychology*, 2009, 93–103; and J. M. Crant, "The Proactive Personality Scale as a Predictor of Entrepreneurial Intentions," *Journal of Small Business Management*, 1996, 42–50.

41. A. Lawrence, "Tennis Pro Finds a New Way to Serve," *Fortune*, April 25, 2015, 41–45.

42. C. Smith, "Interesting Khan Academy Statistics and Facts (2019)—By the Numbers," *DMR*, January 28, 2019, https://expandedramblings.com/index.php/kahn-academy-statistics-and-facts/.

43. C. E Vize, K. L. Colisson, J. D. Miller, and D. R. Lynam, "Examining the Effects of Controlling of Shared Variance Among the Dark Triad Using Meta-Analytic Structural Equation Modeling," *European Journal of Personality*, 2018 (32), 46–61.

44. S. Braun, N. Aydin, D. Frey, and C. Peus, "Leader Narcissism Predicts Malicious Envy and Supervisor Targeted Counterproductive Work Behavior: Evidence from a Field Experiment," *Journal of Business Ethics*, 2016 (151), 725–741.

45. B. Eddy, "3 Steps to Identifying a Narcissist," *Psychology Today*, August 1, 2018, https://www.psychologytoday.com/us/blog/5-types-people-who-can-ruin-your-life/201808/3-steps-identifying-narcissist.

46. N. Schutte, G. Blickle, R. E. Frieder, A. Wihler, F. Schnitzler, J. Heupel, and I. Zettler, "The Role of Interpersonal Influence in Counterbalancing Psychopathic Personality Trait Facets at Work," *Journal of Management*, 2018 (44), 1338–1368.

47. T. Judge and C. Zapata, "The Person-Situation Debate Revisited: Effect of Situation Strength and Trait Activation on the Validity of the Big Five Personality Traits in Predicting Job Performance," *Academy of Management Journal*, 2015, 1149–1179.

48. M. R. Barrick and M. K. Mount, "The Big Five Personality Dimensions and Job Performance: A Meta-Analysis," *Personnel Psychology*, Spring 1991, 21. See also I. S. Oh, G. Wang, and M. K. Mount, "Validity of Observer Ratings of the Five-Factor Model of Personality Traits: A Meta-Analysis," *Journal of Applied Psychology*, December 13, 2010, 1–12.

49. M. Gensowski, "The 3 Personality Traits Affect What You Earn—But Only After 40," *Harvard Business Review*, April 24, 2018, https://hbr.org/2018/04/these-3-personality-traits-affect-what-you-earn-but-only-after-age-40.

50. S. Woo, M. Chae, A. Jebb, and Y. Kim, "A Closer Look at the Personality-Turnover Relationship: Criterion Expansion, Dark Traits, and Time," *Journal of Management*, 2016, 357–385. See also D. Choi, I. Oh, and A. Colbert, "Understanding Organizational Commitment: A Meta-Analytic Examination of the Roles of the Five-Factor Model of Personality and Culture," *Journal of Applied Psychology*, 2015, 1542–1567.

51. S. Woo, M. Chae, A. Jebb, and Y. Kim, "A Closer Look at the Personality-Turnover Relationship: Criterion Expansion, Dark Traits, and Time," *Journal of Management*, 2016, 357–385.

52. H. R. Young, D. R. Glenrum, W. Wang, and D. L. Joseph, "Who Are the Most Engaged at Work? A Meta-Analysis of Personality and Employee Engagement," *Journal of Organizational Behavior*, 2018, 1330–1346.

53. T. Chamorro-Premuzic, "Managing Yourself: Ace the Assessment," *Harvard Business Review*, July–August 2015, 118–121.

54. T. Chamorro-Premuzic, "Managing Yourself: Ace the Assessment," *Harvard Business Review*, July–August 2015, 118–121.

55. D. Meinert, "Heads Up: Personality Assessments Are Being Used More Often in the Hiring Process. But What Do They Really Tell You?" *HR Magazine*, June 2015, 88–98. See also I. S. Oh, G. Wang, and M. K. Mount, "Validity of Observer Ratings of the Five-Factor Model of Personality Traits: A Meta-Analysis," *Journal of Applied Psychology*, December 13, 2010, 1–12. For details on test bias, see H. Aguinis, S. A. Carpenter, and C. A. Pierce, "Revival of Test Bias Research in Pre-Employment Testing," *Journal of Applied Psychology*, 2010, 648–680. For a discussion and advice on using pre-employment tests see T. Minton-Eversole, "Avoiding Bias in Pre-Employment Testing," *HR Magazine*, December 2010, 77–80.

56. D. Meinert, "Heads Up: Personality Assessments Are Being Used More Often in the Hiring Process. But What Do They Really Tell You?" *HR Magazine*, June 2015, 88–98.

57. K. McNulty, "There Is No Place for the MBTI in Organizations," *LinkedIn.com*, September 10, 2018, https://www.linkedin.com/pulse/youre-enfp-im-leo-perfect-well-hit-off-keith-mcnulty/.

58. Z. Simsek, C. Heavey, and J. F. Veiga, "The Impact of CEO Core Self-Evaluation on the Firm's Entrepreneurial Orientation," *Strategic Management Journal*, 2010, 110–119.

59. J. Debusscher, J. Hofmans, and F. DeFruyt, "The Effect of State Core Self-Evaluations on Task Performance, Organizational Citizenship Behavior, and Counterproductive Work Behavior," *European Journal of Work and Organizational Psychology*, 2016, 301–315.

60. F. Giblin and B. Lakey, "Integrating Mentoring and Social Support Research within the Context of Stressful Medical Training," *Journal of Social and Clinical Psychology*, 2010, 771–796.

61. Adapted from L. Debter, "Meet the Unknown Immigrant Billionaire Betting Her Fortune to Take On Musk in Space," *Forbes.com*, July 12, 2018, https://www.forbes.com/sites/forbesdigitalcovers/2018/07/11/meet-the-unknown-immigrant-billionaire-betting-her-fortune-to-take-on-musk-in-space/#2aeefeb5f0da.

62. See P. C. Earley and T. R. Lituchy, "Delineating Goal and Efficacy Effects: A Test of Three Models," *Journal of Applied Psychology*, February 1991, 81–98.

63. See P. Tierney and S. M. Farmer, "Creative Self-Efficacy: Its Potential Antecedents and Relationship to Creative Performance," *Academy of Management Journal*, December 2002, 1137–1148.

64. W. S. Silver, T. R. Mitchell, and M. E. Gist, "Response to Successful and Unsuccessful Performance: The Moderating Effect of Self-Efficacy on the Relationship between Performance and Attributions," *Organizational Behavior and Human Decision Processes*, June 1995, 286–299.

65. Taken from D. L. Ferris, H. Lian, D. J. Brown, F. X. J. Pang, and L. M. Keeping, "Self-Esteem and Job Performance: The Moderating Role of Self-Esteem Contingencies," *Personnel Psychology*, 2010, 561–593.

66. F. Giblin and B. Lakey, "Integrating Mentoring and Social Support Research within the Context of Stressful Medical Training," *Journal of Social and Clinical Psychology*, 2010, 771–796.

67. W. J. McGuire and C. V. McGuire, "Enhancing Self-Esteem by Directed Thinking Tasks: Cognitive and Affective Positivity Asymmetries," *Journal of Personality and Social Psychology*, June 1996, 1124.

68. T. Huddleston, "Uber CEO: It's Time for Tech Founders to 'Take Responsibility for the Content on Your Platform,'" CNBC, November 28, 2018, https://www.cnbc.com/2018/11/27/uber-ceo-khosrowshahi-silicon-valley-needs-to-take-responsibility.html.

69. For an overall review of research on locus of control, see P. E. Spector, "Behavior in Organizations as a Function of Employee's Locus of Control," *Psychological Bulletin*, May 1982, 482–497.

70. C. Wu, M. Griffin, and S. Parker, "Developing Agency through Good Work: Longitudinal Effects of Job Autonomy and Skill Utilization on Locus of Control," *Journal of Vocational Behavior*, 2015, 102–108.

71. Adapted from S. Craig, "DealBook: A Female Wall Street Financial Chief Avoids Pitfalls that Stymied Others," *The New York Times*, November 9, 2010.

72. D. Joseph, J. Jin, D. Newman, and E. O'Boyle, "Why Does Self-Reported Emotional Intelligence Predict Job Performance? A Meta-Analytic Investigation of Mixed EI," *Journal of Applied Psychology*, 2015, 298–342.

73. For a current review see D. Joseph, J. Jin, D. Newman, and E. O'Boyle, "Why Does Self-Reported Emotional Intelligence Predict Job Performance? A Meta-Analytic Investigation of Mixed EI," *Journal of Applied Psychology*, 2015, 298–342. See the box titled "Get Happy Carefully" in D. Goleman, R. Boyatzis, and A. McKee, "Primal Leadership: The Hidden Driver of Great Performance," *Harvard Business Review*, Special Issue: Breakthrough Leadership, December 2001, 49.

74. J. Bonazzo, "New Report Details How Uber's Scandalous 2017 Led to Travis Kalanick's Downfall," *Observer.com,* March 12, 2018, https://observer.com/2018/03/uber-travis-kalanick-business-insider/.

75. Adapted from E. Newcomer, and B. Stone, "The Fall of Travis Kalanick," *Bloomberg BusinessWeek,* January 22, 2018, 46–51. See also K. Leland, "Why Uber CEO is a Toxic Boss and Must Go," *Inc.,* June 13, 2017, https://www.inc.com/karen-tiber-leland/how-uber-ceo-travis-kalanicks-toxic-boss-behaviors-could-cost-him-the-company.html. See also A. Griswold, "There Would Be No Uber without Travis Kalanick," Quartz, June 22, 2017, https://qz.com/1011300/uber-ceo-travis-kalanick-pissed-people-off-and-it-made-the-company-great/.

76. D. Joseph, J. Jin, D. Newman, and E. O'Boyle, "Why Does Self-Reported Emotional Intelligence Predict Job Performance? A Meta-Analytic Investigation of Mixed EI," *Journal of Applied Psychology,* 2015, 298–342.

77. C. Wilderom, Y. Hur, U. Wiersma, P. Van den Berg, and J. Lee, "From Manager's Emotional Intelligence to Objective Store Performance: Through Store Cohesiveness and Sale-Directed Employee Behavior," *Journal of Organizational Behavior,* 2015, 825–844.

78. M. Parke, M. Seo, and E. Sherf, "Regulating and Facilitating: The Role of Emotional Intelligence in Maintaining and Using Positive Affect for Creativity," *Journal of Applied Psychology,* 2015, 917–934.

79. D. H. M. Pelt, D. Van der Linden, and M. P. Born, "How Emotional Intelligence Might Get You the Job: The Relationship Between Trait Emotional Intelligence and Faking Personality Tests," *Human Performance,* 2018 (31), 33–54.

80. R. Carucci, "Is Your Emotional Intelligence Authentic, or Self-Serving?" *Harvard Business Review,* May 23, 2018, https://hbr.org/2018/05/is-your-emotional-intelligence-authentic-or-self-serving.

81. Elle Kaplan, "EQ Can Make You Wealthy and Successful, According to Science—Here's How to Build Yours," *CNBC LLC,* January 16, 2018, https://www.cnbc.com/2018/01/16/ceo-elle-kaplan-eq-can-make-you-successful-according-to-science.html.

82. L. Kroll and K. A. Dolan, "Forbes 400 Richest People 2018," *Forbes.com,* October 3, 2018, https://www.forbes.com/profile/tilman-fertitta/#534d0364271b.

83. D. Goleman and M. Nevarez, "Boost Your Emotional Intelligence with These 3 Questions," *Harvard Business Review,* August 16, 2018, http://web.b.ebscohost.com.proxyau.wrlc.org/ehost/pdfviewer/pdfviewer?vid=7&sid=c4333be5-dd2f-4a62-ae32-dc385b3920a1%40pdc-v-sessmgr02.

84. The pros and cons are debated in the point-counterpoint, "Is Emotional Intelligence a Good Measure of Leadership Ability?" *HR Magazine,* November 2015, 22–23.

85. M. Fugate, A. J. Kinicki, and G. E. Prussia, "Employee Coping with Organizational Change: An Examination of Alternative Theoretical Perspectives and Models," *Personnel Psychology,* 2008, 1–36.

86. U. Ulsheger, J. Lang, A. Schewe, and F. Zijlstra, "When Regulating Emotions at Work Pays Off: A Diary and an Intervention Study on Emotion Regulation and Customer Tips in Service Jobs," *Journal of Applied Psychology,* 2015, 263–277.

87. G. Van Kleef, H. van den Berg, and M. Heerdink, "The Persuasive Power of Emotions: Effects of Emotional Expressions on Attitude Formation and Change," *Journal of Applied Psychology,* 2015, 1124–1142.

88. M. Wypych, J. Matuszewski, and W. Dragan, "Roles of Impulsivity, Motivation, and Emotion Regulation in Procrastination—Path Analysis and Comparison Between Students and Non-Students," *Frontiers in Psychology,* June 5, 2018, https://www.frontiersin.org/articles/10.3389/fpsyg.2018.00891/full.

89. R. S. Lazarus, *Emotion and Adaptation* (New York: Oxford University Press, 1991), chapters 6, 7.

90. K. L. Wang and M. Groth, "Buffering the Negative Effects of Employee Surface Acting: The Moderating Role of Employee-Customer Relationship Strength and Personalized Services," *Journal of Applied Psychology,* 99, 2014, 341–350.

91. K. Gurchiek, "How Does Your Workplace Handle Crying at Work?" *SHRM.com,* December 12, 2018, https://www.shrm.org/hr-today/news/hr-news/pages/crying-at-work-how-does-your-culture-handle-it.aspx.

92. S. Shellenbarger, "When the Boss Is a Screamer," *The Wall Street Journal,* August 15, 2012.

93. J. Bauer and P. Spector, "Discrete Negative Emotions and Counterproductive Work Behavior," *Human Performance,* 2015, 307–331.

94. A. Rafaeli, A. Erez, S. Ravid, R. Derfler-Rozin, D. Treister, and R. Scheyer, "When Customers Exhibit Verbal Aggression, Employees Pay Cognitive Costs," *Journal of Applied Psychology,* 2012, 931–950.

95. D. Geddes and R. R. Callister, "Crossing the Line(s): A Dual Threshold Model of Anger in Organizations," *Academy of Management Review,* 2007, 721–746.

96. V. Salem, "How to Ride the Emotions of Your First Job Search," *Monster.com,* https://www.monster.com/career-advice/article/how-to-ride-emotions-first-job-search (accessed January 10, 2019).

97. "About Us," https://www.papajohns.com/company/ (accessed June 11, 2019).

98. "Papa John's: Revenue 2007-2018 | Statistic," *Statista,* https://www.statista.com/statistics/221441/papa-johns-total-revenue/ (accessed June 08, 2019).

99. J. Valinsky, "Papa John's Founder John Schnatter Kicked Out of His Office," *CNN Business,* July 16, 2018, https://money.cnn.com/2018/07/16/news/companies/papa-johns-office/.

100. A. Wolfson, "The Rise and Fall of John Schnatter: His Mouth Was His Own Worst Enemy," *Louisville Courier Journal,* July 18, 2018, https://www.courier-journal.com/story/news/2018/07/15/papa-johns-founder-john-schnatter-mouth-his-own-worst-enemy/778278002/.

101. A. Bingham, "Papa John's CEO Says 'Obamacare' Will Up Pizza Price," *ABC News,* August 09, 2012, https://abcnews.go.com/Politics/OTUS/papa-johns-john-schnatter-obamacare-pizza-prices/story?id=16962891.

102. M. Eltagouri, "Papa John's Founder Will Step down as CEO after Criticizing National Anthem Protests in the NFL," *The Washington Post,* December 21, 2017, https://www.washingtonpost.com/news/business/wp/2017/12/21/papa-johns-founder-replaced-as-ceo-weeks-after-blaming-the-nfl-for-sagging-pizza-sales/?utm_term=.678b0ca98527.

103. K. Belson, "N.F.L. and Papa John's Part Ways in Wake of C.E.O. Commentary," *The New York Times,* February 27, 2018, https://www.nytimes.com/2018/02/27/sports/football/nfl-papa-johns.html.

104. N. Kirsch, "Papa John's Founder Used N-Word On Conference Call," *Forbes,* July 13, 2018, https://www.forbes.com/sites/noahkirsch/2018/07/11/papa-johns-founder-john-schnatter-allegedly-used-n-word-on-conference-call/#3e87ee744cfc.

105. T. Hsu, "Papa John's Founder, John Schnatter, to Leave Board After Nasty Leadership Fight," *The New York Times,* March 05, 2019, https://www.nytimes.com/2019/03/05/business/papa-johns-john-schnatter.html.

106. J. Chrisman, "Papa John Is Getting Evicted From Company Headquarters," *Thrillist,* July 16, 2018, https://www.thrillist.com/news/nation/papa-johns-john-schnatter-evicted-from-office.

107. "Save Papa Johns," https://savepapajohns.com/ (accessed June 09, 2019); J. Wattles and J. Valinsky, "John Schnatter Files Lawsuit against Papa John's," *CNNMoney,* July 26, 2018, https://money.cnn.com/2018/07/26/news/companies/papa-johns-lawsuit-john-schnatter/index.html; and A. Wolfson, "'Papa John' Schnatter Has Sent a Love Letter to His Former Employees," *Louisville Courier Journal,* August 22, 2018, https://www.courier-journal.com/story/news/2018/08/21/john-schnatter-publishes-open-letter-papa-johns-employees/1053597002/.

108. N. Kirsch, "John Schnatter Resigns From Papa John's Board, Ends Lawsuits," *Forbes,* March 05, 2019, https://www.forbes.com/sites/noahkirsch/2019/03/05/john-schnatter-resigns-from-papa-johns-board-ends-lawsuits/#4a8830bf2b0d.

109. J. Fantozzi, "John Schnatter's Stock Sales Trim His Papa John's Stake to 19%," *Nation's Restaurant News,* May 23, 2019, https://www.nrn.com/quick-service/john-schnatter-s-stock-sales-trim-his-papa-john-s-stake-19.

110. "Papa John's, Restaurants by Country 2017-2018 | Statistic," *Statista,* https://www.statista.com/statistics/816446/number-of-papa-johns-restaurants-by-country/ (accessed June 09, 2019).

111. J. Maze, "Papa John's Has a Franchisee Problem," *Restaurant Business,* February 20, 2019, https://www.restaurantbusinessonline.com/financing/papa-johns-has-franchisee-problem.

112. J. Berke and S. Gould, "This Map Shows Every US State Where Pot Is Legal," *Business Insider,* January 4, 2019, https://www.businessinsider.com/legal-marijuana-states-2018-1.

113. J. Reidy and D. Hewick, "Are Employer Drug-Testing Programs Obsolete?" *SHRM.org,* May 23, 2018, https://www.shrm.org/hr-today/news/hr-magazine/0618/pages/are-employer-drug-testing-programs-obsolete.aspx.

114. K. J. Russo, M. Van Oot, and A. C. Zangara, "What Vermont's Recreational Marijuana Law Means for Employers," *SHRM.org,* June 26, 2018, https://www.shrm.org/resourcesandtools/legal-and-compliance/state-and-local-updates/pages/what-vermont-recreational-marijuana-law-means-for-employers.aspx.

115. J. Reidy and D. Hewick, "Are Employer Drug-Testing Programs Obsolete?" *SHRM.org,* May 23, 2018, https://www.shrm.org/hr-today/news/hr-magazine/0618/pages/are-employer-drug-testing-programs-obsolete.aspx.

116. R. Maurer, "Eating Poppy-Seed Bagels and Other Excuses for Failing Workplace Drug Tests," *SHRM.org,* November 13, 2018, https://www.shrm.org/ResourcesAndTools/hr-topics/talent-acquisition/Pages/Common-Excuses-Failing-Workplace-Drug-Tests.aspx.

CHAPTER 4

1. M. Singer, "2018 Recruiter Nation Survey: The Tipping Point and the Next Chapter in Recruiting," *Jobvite.com,* November 8, 2018, https://www.jobvite.com/jobvite-news-and-reports/2018-recruiter-nation-report-tipping-point-and-the-next-chapter-in-recruiting/.

2. Lauren Durfy, "Recruitment and Social Media Connection," *PostBeyond. com,* September 18, 2018, https://www.jobvite.com/jobvite-news-and-reports/2018-recruiter-nation-report-tipping-point-and-the-next-chapter-in-recruiting/.

3. "More than Half of Employers Have Found Content on Social Media That Caused Them Not to Hire a Candidate, According to Recent Career-Builder Survey," *PRNewswire,* August 9, 2018, https://www.prnewswire.com/news-releases/more-than-half-of-employers-have-found-content-on-social-media-that-caused-them-not-to-hire-a-candidate-according-to-recent-careerbuilder-survey-300694437.html.

4. Leslie Kwoh, "Beware: Potential Employers Are Watching You," *The Wall Street Journal,* October 29, 2012, https://www.wsj.com/articles/SB10000872396390443759504577631410093879278?ns=prod/accounts-wsj.

5. M. Singer, "2018 Recruiter Nation Survey: The Tipping Point and the Next Chapter in Recruiting," *Jobvite.com,* November 8, 2018, https://www.jobvite.com/jobvite-news-and-reports/2018-recruiter-nation-report-tipping-point-and-the-next-chapter-in-recruiting/; "10 Things You Should Never Post on Social Media," *College Grad,* https://collegegrad.com/blog/10-things-you-should-never-post-on-social-media (accessed March 11, 2019).

6. E. Rosch, C.B. Mervis, W.D. Gray, D. M. Johnson, and P. Boyes-Braem, "Basic Objects in Natural Categories," *Cognitive Psychology,* 1976, 383.

7. D. M. Amodio and K. G. Ratner, "A Memory Systems Model of Implicit Social Cognition," *Current Directions in Psychological Science,* June 2011, 143–148.

8. K. Kindelan, "Weight Watchers Rebrands as WW and Puts the Focus on Wellness, Not Just Dieting," *ABC News,* September 25, 2018, https://abcnews.go.com/GMA/Wellness/weight-watchers-rebrands-ww-puts-focus-wellness-dieting/story?id=58065632.

9. This figure is based on discussion in E. Hehman, Clare A. M. Sutherland, J. K. Flake, and M. L. Slepian, "The Unique Contributions of Perceiver and Target Characteristics in Person Perception," *Journal of Personality and Social Psychology,* October 2017, 513–529; C. N. Macrae and S. Quadflieg, "Perceiving People," in S. T. Fiske, D. T. Gilbert, and G. Lindzey, eds., *Handbook of Social Psychology* (New York: John Wiley & Sons, 2010), 428–463; and M. Snyder and A. A. Stukas, Jr., "Interpersonal Processes: The Interplay of Cognitive, Motivational, and Behavioral Activities in Social Interaction," in J. T. Spence, J. M. Darley, and D. J. Foss, eds., *Annual Review of Psychology* (Palo Alto, CA: Annual Review, 1999), 273–303.

10. Conclusions about perceiver characteristics were derived from E. Hehman, Clare A. M. Sutherland, J. K. Flake, and M. L. Slepian, "The Unique Contributions of Perceiver and Target Characteristics in Person Perception," *Journal of Personality and Social Psychology,* October 2017, 513–529; C. N. Macrae and S. Quadflieg, "Perceiving People," in S. T. Fiske, D. T. Gilbert, and G. Lindzey, eds., *Handbook of Social Psychology* (New York: John Wiley & Sons, 2010), 428–463; and M. Snyder and A. A. Stukas, Jr., "Interpersonal Processes: The Interplay of Cognitive, Motivational, and Behavioral Activities in Social Interaction," in J. T. Spence, J. M. Darley, and D. J. Foss, eds., *Annual Review of Psychology* (Palo Alto, CA: Annual Review, 1999), 273–303.

11. Conclusions about target characteristics were derived from E. Hehman, Clare A. M. Sutherland, J. K. Flake, and M. L. Slepian, "The Unique Contributions of Perceiver and Target Characteristics in Person Perception," *Journal of Personality and Social Psychology,* October 2017, 513–529; C. N. Macrae and S. Quadflieg, "Perceiving People," in S. T. Fiske, D. T. Gilbert, and G. Lindzey, eds., *Handbook of Social Psychology* (New York: John Wiley & Sons, 2010), 428–463; and M. Snyder and A. A. Stukas, Jr., "Interpersonal Processes: The Interplay of Cognitive, Motivational, and Behavioral Activities in Social Interaction," in J. T. Spence, J. M. Darley, and D. J. Foss, eds., *Annual Review of Psychology* (Palo Alto, CA: Annual Review, 1999), 273–303.

12. "A Tattoo Won't Hurt Your Job Prospects," *Harvard Business Review,* November–December 2018, 30–31.

13. J. H. Langlois, L. Kalakanis, A. J. Rubenstein, A. J. Larson, M. Hallam, and M. Smoot, "Maxims or Myths of Beauty? A Meta-Analytic and Theoretical Review," *Psychological Bulletin* 126, no. 3 (2000): 390–423. https://DOI: 10.1037//0033-2909.126.3.390.

14. William W. Maddux, Peter H. Kim, Tetsushi Okumura, and Jeanne Brett, "Why *'I'm Sorry'* Doesn't Always Translate," *Harvard Business Review,* June 1, 2012, https://hbr.org/product/why-im-sorry-doesnt-always-translate/F1206B-PDF-ENG.

15. D. Rodneck, "What Practices Could You Implement to Increase Cultural Sensitivity and Acceptance in the Workplace?" *Small Business Chronicle,* https://smallbusiness.chron.com/practices-could-implement-increase-cultural-sensitivity-acceptance-workplace-16661.html (accessed March 5, 2019); "Seven Practices You Can Implement to Increase Cultural Awareness in the Workplace," *DeakinCo.com,* September 22, 2017, https://www.deakinco.com/media-centre/news/seven-practices-you-can-implement-to-increase-cultural-awareness-in-the-workplace.

16. N. M. Wessels, J. Zimmermann, J. C. Biesanz, and D. Leising, "Differential Associations of Knowing and Liking with Accuracy and Positivity Bias in Person Perception," *Journal of Personality and Social Psychology,* October 2018, 1–12; R. S. Rubinstein, J. Jussim, and S. T. Stevens, "Reliance on Individuating Information and Stereotypes in Implicit and Explicit Person Perception," *Journal of Experimental Social Psychology,* March 2018, 54–70.

17. M. Hebl, C. L. Nittrouer, A. R. Corrington, and J. M. Madera, "How We Describe Male and Female Job Applicants Differently," *Harvard Business Review,* September 27, 2018, https://hbr.org/2018/09/how-we-describe-male-and-female-job-applicants-differently.

18. P. Dwivedi, A. Joshi, and V. F. Misangyi, "Gender-Inclusive Gatekeeping: How (Mostly Male) Predecessors Influence the Success of Female CEOs," *Academy of Management Journal,* April 2018, 379–404.

19. C. H. Tinsley and R. J. Ely, "What Most People Get Wrong about Men and Women," *Harvard Business Review,* May-June 2018, 114–121.

20. "33 Companies Who Use Skype to Take Online Job Interviews," *WebEmployed.com,* March 28, 2018, https://www.webemployed.com/companies-online-job-interviews-skype/.

21. Marcel Schwantes, "The Job Interview Will Soon Be Dead. Here's What the Top Companies Are Replacing It With," *Mansueto Ventures,* March 6, 2017, https://www.inc.com/marcel-schwantes/science-81-percent-of-people-lie-in-job-interviews-heres-what-top-companies-are-.html.

22. S. McLaren, "8 Innovative Ways Companies Are Using Virtual Reality to Recruit," *LinkedIn.com,* July 18, 2017, https://business.linkedin.com/talent-solutions/blog/future-of-recruiting/2017/8-innovative-ways-companies-are-using-virtual-reality-to-recruit.

23. Leadership characterization was studied by J. S. Phillips and R. G. Lord, "Schematic Information Processing and Perceptions of Leadership in Problem-Solving Groups," *Journal of Applied Psychology,* August 1982, 486–492.

24. C. M. Judd and B. Park, "Definition and Assessment of Accuracy in Social Stereotypes," *Psychological Review,* 1993, 110. Emphasis added.

25. B. J. Lyons, L. R. Martinez, E. N. Ruggs, M. R. Hebl, A. M. Ryan, K. R. O'Brien, and A. Roebuck, "To Say or Not to Say: Different Strategies of Acknowledging a Visible Disability," *Journal of Management,* May 2018, 1980–2007.

26. "Cancer Stat Facts: Cancer of Any Site," https://seer.cancer.gov/statfacts/html/all.html (accessed March 6, 2019).

27. M. Feuerstein, A. K. Gehrke, B. T. McMahon, and M. C. McMahon, "Challenges Persist under Americans with Disabilities Act Amendment Act: How Can Oncology Providers Help?" *Journal of Oncology Practice,* June 2017, 543–551.

28. D. Kanze, L. Huang, Mark A. Conley, and E. T. Higgins, "We Ask Men to Win and Women Not to Lose: Closing the Gender Gap in Startup Funding," *Academy of Management Journal,* April 2018, 586–614; S. Keck and L. Babcock, "Who Gets the Benefit of the Doubt? The Impact of Causal Reasoning Depth on How Violations of Gender Stereotypes Are Evaluated," *Journal of Organizational Behavior,* March 2018, 276–291; K. B. Coffman, C. L. Exley, and M. Niederle, "When Gender Discrimination Is Not about Gender," Harvard Business School Working Paper, No. 18-054, January 2018; and L. Rosenthal and M. Lobel, "Stereotypes of Black American Women Related to Sexuality and Motherhood," *Psychology of Women Quarterly,* September 2016, 414–427.

29. H. Yan, "This Is Why Everyday Racial Profiling Is So Dangerous," *CNN,* May 11, 2018, https://www.cnn.com/2018/05/11/us/everyday-racial-profiling-consequences-trnd/index.html.

30. "Physiological & Psychological Impact of Racism and Discrimination for African-Americans," American Psychological Association, https://www.apa.org/pi/oema/resources/ethnicity-health/racism-stress (accessed March 6, 2019); and D. M. Amodio and J. K. Swencionis, "Proactive Control of Implicit Bias: A Theoretical Model and Implications for Change," *Journal of Personality and Social Psychology,* June 2018, 255–275.

31. C. von Hippel, E. K. Kalokerinos, K. Haanterä, and H. Zacher, "Age-Based Stereotype Threat and Work Outcomes: Stress Appraisals and Rumination as Mediators," *Psychology and Aging,* February 2019, 68–84.

32. D. W. Sue, S. Alsaidi, M. N. Awad, E. Glaeser, C. Z. Calle, and N. Mendez, "Disarming Racial Microaggressions: Microintervention Strategies for Targets, White Allies, and Bystanders," *American Psychologist,* January 2019, 128–142.

33. M. Ignatova, "New Report: Women Apply to Fewer Jobs Than Men, But Are More Likely to Get Hired," *LinkedIn Talent Blog,* March 5, 2019, https://business.linkedin.com/talent-solutions/blog/diversity/2019/how-women-find-jobs-gender-report.

34. Kelley's model is discussed in detail in H. H. Kelley, "The Processes of Causal Attribution," *American Psychologist,* February 1973, 107–128.

35. R. Pishghadam and H. Abbasnejad, "Introducing *Emotioncy* as an Invisible Force Controlling Causal Decisions: A Case of Attribution Theory," *Polish Psychological Bulletin,* 2017, 129–140.

36. K. Cherry, "How the Self-Serving Bias Protects Self-Esteem," https://www.verywellmind.com/what-is-the-self-serving-bias-2795032 (accessed March 11, 2019).

37. See S. E. Moss and M. J. Martinko, "The Effects of Performance Attributions and Outcome Dependence on Leader Feedback Behavior Following Poor Subordinate Performance," *Journal of Organizational Behavior,* May 1998, 259–274.

38. H. Gehlbach and C. C. Vriesema, "Meta-Bias: A Practical Theory of Motivated Thinking," *Educational Psychology Review,* November 2018, 1–21.

39. C. Zillman, "There Are the 12 Fortune 500 Companies with Zero Women on Their Boards," *Fortune,* May 22, 2018, https://business.linkedin.com/talent-solutions/blog/diversity/2019/how-women-find-jobs-gender-report; and C. Post and K. Byron, "Women on Boards and Firm Financial Performance: A Meta-Analysis," *Academy of Management Journal,* October 2015, 1546–1571.

40. D. DeZube, "Bye Bye Boomers: Who Will Fill Your Workforce Gap?" *Monster,* https://hiring.monster.com/hr/hr-best-practices/recruiting-hiring-advice/strategic-workforce-planning/baby-boomer-workforce-gap.aspx (accessed March 7, 2019); and R. Fry, R. Igielnik, and E. Patten, "How Millennials Today Compare with Their Grandparents 50 Years Ago," *Fact Tank* (Pew Research Center), March 16, 2018, http://www.pewresearch.org/fact-tank/2018/03/16/how-millennials-compare-with-their-grandparents/#!14.

41. J. Vespa, D. M. Armstrong, and L. Medina, "Demographic Turning Points for the United States: Population Projections for 2020 to 2060," https://www.census.gov/content/dam/Census/library/publications/2018/demo/P25_1144.pdf (accessed March 7, 2019).

42. Irving B. Weiner, Neal W. Schmitt, and Scott Highhouse, *Handbook of Psychology: Industrial and Organizational Psychology,* (New Jersey: John Wiley & Sons, Inc., 2012).

43. H. Collingwood. "Who Handles a Diverse Work Force Best?" *Working Women,* 1996.

44. Irving B. Weiner, Neal W. Schmitt, and Scott Highhouse, *Handbook of Psychology: Industrial and Organizational Psychology,* (New Jersey: John Wiley & Sons, Inc., 2012).

45. Results can be found in D. A. Harrison, D. A. Kravitz, D. M. Mayer, L. M. Leslie, and D. Lev-Arey, "Understanding Attitudes Toward Affirmative Action Programs in Employment: Summary and Meta-Analysis of 35 Years of Research," *Journal of Applied Psychology,* September 2006, 1013–1036.

46. V. Strauss, "What You Should Know about Race-Based Affirmative Action and Diversity in Schools," *The Washington Post,* July 3, 2018, https://www.washingtonpost.com/news/answer-sheet/wp/2018/07/03/what-you-should-know-about-race-based-affirmative-action-and-diversity-in-schools/?utm_term=.61f2269e1edc; and K. W. Phillips, T. L. Dumas, and N. P. Rothbard, "Diversity and Authenticity," *Harvard Business Review,* March–April 2018, 132–136.

47. L. Shen, "Some Female Leaders Aren't Huge Fans of California's New Law Requiring Women on Boards," *Fortune,* October 4, 2018, http://fortune.com/2018/10/03/women-boards-california/.

48. Ann. M. Morrison, *The New Leaders: Leadership Diversity in America,* (New Jersey: John Wiley & Sons, Inc., 1992).

49. M. Sawhney, "3 Keys for Making Products and Marketing for All," *Forbes,* June 19, 2018, https://www.forbes.com/sites/mohanbirsawhney/2018/06/19/3-keys-for-making-products-and-marketing-for-all/#4d3c214c38a3.

50. Mark Wilson, "What You're Getting Wrong About Inclusive Design," *Mansueto Ventures LLC,* April 4, 2018, https://www.fastcompany.com/90166413/what-youre-getting-wrong-about-inclusive-design.

51. M. Sawhney, "3 Keys for Making Products and Marketing for All," *Forbes,* June 19, 2018, https://www.forbes.com/sites/mohanbirsawhney/2018/06/19/3-keys-for-making-products-and-marketing-for-all/#4d3c214c38a3.

52. D. Vinjamuri, "Diversity in Advertising Is Good Marketing," *Forbes,* December 11, 2015, https://www.forbes.com/sites/davidvinjamuri/2015/12/11/diversityinadsisgoodmarketing/#7c889e7d4248.

53. "The 2018 DiversityInc Top 50 Companies for Diversity: #1: Johnson & Johnson," https://www.diversityinc.com/di_top_50/ (accessed March 8, 2019).

54. R. J. Ely and D. A. Thomas, "Cultural Diversity at Work: The Effects of Diversity Perspectives on Work Group Processes and Outcomes," *Administrative Science Quarterly,* 2001, 243. Emphasis added.

55. D. R. Avery, P. F. McKay, S. Tonidandel, S. D. Volpone, and M. A. Morris, "Is There Method to the Madness? Examining How Racioethnic Matching Influences Retail Store Productivity," *Personnel Psychology,* 2012, 167–199.

56. R. G. Netemeyer, C. M. Heilman, and J. G. Maxham III, "Identification with the Retail Organization and Customer-Perceived Employee Similarities: Effects on Customer Spending," *Journal of Applied Psychology,* September 2012, 1049–1058.

57. See Bureau of Labor Statistics, "Table 39: 2018 Median Weekly Earnings of Full-Time Wage and Salary Workers by Detailed Occupation and Sex," https://www.bls.gov/cps/cpsaat39.htm (accessed March 8, 2019); and N. Bach, "Getting an MBA Won't Save You from the Pay Gap If You're a Woman or Minority," *Fortune,* February 7, 2019, http://fortune.com/2019/02/06/mba-graduates-pay-gap-women-minorities/.

58. H. Aguinis, Y. H. Ji, and H. Joo, "Gender Productivity Gap among Star Performers in STEM and Other Scientific Fields," *Journal of Applied Psychology,* December 2018, 1283–1306.

59. See A. H. Eagly and L. L. Carli, *Through the Labyrinth* (Boston: Harvard Business School Press, 2007).

60. See Catalyst, "Women CEOs of the S&P 500," January 24, 2019, https://www.catalyst.org/research/women-ceos-of-the-sp-500/; and Bureau of Labor Statistics, "Table 39: Median Weekly Earnings of Full-Time Wage and Salary Workers by Detailed Occupation and Sex," for years 2018, 2009, and 1999, https://www.bls.gov (accessed March 8, 2019).

61. G. Knobler, "Women's Underrepresentation in the Judiciary," https://www.representwomen.org (accessed March 8, 2019); Catalyst, "Pyramid: Women in S&P 500 Companies," July 11, 2019, https://www.catalyst.org/research/women-in-sp-500-companies/; E. D. Herman, "Redefining Representation: The Women of the 116th Congress," *The New York Times,* January 14, 2019, https://www.nytimes.com/interactive/2019/01/14/us/politics/women-of-the-116th-congress.html; and J. Napolitano, "Women Earn More College Degrees and Men Still Earn More Money," *Forbes,* September 4, 2018, https://www.forbes.com/sites/janetnapolitano/2018/09/04/women-earn-more-college-degrees-and-men-still-earn-more-money/#1578fbf139f1.

62. Alice Hendrickson Eagly, and Linda Lorene Carli, *Through the Labyrinth: The Truth about How Women Become Leaders,* (Boston Massachusetts: Harvard Business Press, 2007).

63. J. Vespa, D. M. Armstrong, and L. Medina, "Demographic Turning Points for the United States: Population Projections for 2020 to 2060," https://www.census.gov/content/dam/Census/library/publications/2018/demo/P25_1144.pdf (accessed March 8, 2019).

64. M. Toossi, "A Look at the Future of the U.S. Labor Force to 2060," https://www.bls.gov/spotlight/2016/a-look-at-the-future-of-the-us-labor-force-to-2060/pdf/a-look-at-the-future-of-the-us-labor-force-to-2060.pdf (accessed March 8, 2019).

65. U.S. Equal Employment Opportunity Commission, "Performance and Accountability Report for Fiscal Year 2017," https://www.eeoc.gov/eeoc/plan/2017par.cfm (accessed March 10, 2019).

66. Bureau of Labor Statistics, "Table 37: Median Weekly Earnings of Full-Time Wage and Salary Workers by Selected Characteristics," https://www.bls.gov/cps/cpsaat37.pdf (accessed March 10, 2019).

67. GLAAD Media Reference Guide and Glossary of Terms. New York: GLAAD. https://www.glaad.org/reference/lgbtq.

68. F. Newport, "In U.S., Estimate of LGBT Population Rises to 4.5%," May 22, 2018, https://news.gallup.com/poll/234863/estimate-lgbt-population-rises.aspx.

69. Human Rights Campaign Foundation, "A Workplace Divided: Understanding the Climate for LGBTQ Workers Nationwide," https://www.hrc.org/resources/a-workplace-divided-understanding-the-climate-for-lgbtq-workers-nationwide (accessed March 10, 2019).

70. Human Rights Campaign Foundation, "LGBTQ Equality at the Fortune 500," https://www.hrc.org/resources/lgbt-equality-at-the-fortune-500, and "Employment," https://www.hrc.org/state-maps/employment (accessed March 10, 2019).

71. "Does the Americans with Disabilities Act (ADA) Provide a List of Conditions That Are Covered under the Act," *Society for Human Resource Management,* July 16, 2018, https://www.shrm.org/resourcesandtools/tools-and-samples/hr-qa/pages/cms_011495.aspx.

72. Bureau of Labor Statistics, "Persons with a Disability: Labor Force Characteristics Summary—2018," February 26, 2019, https://www.bls.gov/news.release/disable.nr0.htm.

73. T. Prasad, "How Microsoft Is Changing the Face of Disability Employment: It Has Never Been More Important," October 26, 2018, https://www.popsugar.com/smart-living/Interview-Microsoft-About-Disability-Inclusion-45326888.

74. R. Jenkins, "Why Generational Diversity Is the Ultimate Competitive Advantage," *Inc.,* https://www.inc.com/ryan-jenkins/why-generational-diversity-is-the-ultimate-competitive-advantage.html (accessed March 12, 2019); and M. Dimock, "Defining Generations: Where Millennials End and Generation Z Begins," *Fact Tank,* January 17, 2019, http://www.pewresearch.org/fact-tank/2019/01/17/where-millennials-end-and-generation-z-begins/.

75. For a review of generational research, see S. Lyons and L. Kuron, "Generational Differences in the Workplace: A Review of the Evidence and Directions for Future Research," *Journal of Organizational Behavior,* February 2014, 139–157.

76. K. Elsbury, "Five Proven Tactics for Hiring and Retaining Millennial Employees," *Forbes,* March 1, 2018, https://www.forbes.com/sites/yec/2018/03/01/five-proven-tactics-for-hiring-and-retaining-millennial-employees/#42e1e0752deb.

77. Lindsay Gellman, and Justin Baer, "Goldman Sachs Sweetens Deal for Young Bankers," *The Wall Street Journal,* November 5, 2015, https://www.wsj.com/articles/goldman-sachs-brings-back-junior-banker-program-1446753898.

78. U.S. Census Bureau, "Table 2: Educational Attainment of the Population 25 Years and Over, by Selected Characteristics, 2018," https://www.census.gov (accessed March 11, 2019).

79. Bureau of Labor Statistics, "Table 6: Wage and Salary Workers Paid Hourly Rates with Earnings at or below the Prevailing Federal Minimum Wage, by Educational Attainment, 2017 Annual Averages," https://www.bls.gov (accessed March 11, 2019).

80. F. M. McKee-Ryan and J. Harvey, "'I Have a Job, But . . .': A Review of Underemployment," *Journal of Management,* July 2011, 962–996.

81. "Building Tomorrow's Talent: Collaboration Can Close Emerging Skills Gap," *Bloomberg Next,* https://www.bna.com/uploadedFiles/BNA_V2/Micro_Sites/2018/Future_of_Work/Workday%20Bloomberg%20Build-Tomorrow-Talent_FINAL.pdf (accessed March 12, 2019); and S. Florentine, "Class of 2018: This Year's Grads Not Seen as a Skills Gap Solution," *CIO,* June 11, 2018, https://www.cio.com/article/3280101/class-of-2018-this-years-grads-not-seen-as-a-skills-gap-solution.html.

82. U.S. Department of Education, National Center for Education Statistics, *The Condition of Education 2018* (NCES 2018-144) (accessed March 11, 2019).

83. R. Diemart, "32 Million American Adults Can't Read: Why Literacy Is the Key to Growth," https://medium.com/@OneYoungWorld_/32-million-american-adults-cant-read-why-literacy-is-the-key-to-growth-818996739523 (accessed March 11, 2019).

84. These barriers were taken from discussions in A. S. Pruitt, C. Brinkworth, J. Young, and K. L. Aponte, "5 Things We Learned about Creating a Successful Workplace Diversity Program," *Harvard Business Review,* March 30, 2018, https://hbr.org/2018/03/5-things-we-learned-about-creating-a-successful-workplace-diversity-program; A. Morrison, *The New Leaders* (San Francisco: Jossey-Bass, 1996); M. Loden, *Implementing Diversity* (New York: McGraw-Hill, 1995); and E. E. Spragins, "Benchmark: The Diverse Work Force," *Inc.,* January 1993, 33.

85. Anne Tergesen, "To Age Well, Change How You Feel About Aging," *The Wall Street Journal,* October 19, 2015, https://www.wsj.com/articles/to-age-well-change-how-you-feel-about-aging-1445220002.

86. J. A. Gonzalez and A. DeNisi, "Cross-Level Effects of Demography and Diversity Climate on Organizational Attachment and Firm Effectiveness," *Journal of Organizational Behavior,* January 2009, 24.

87. A. Rattan and C. S. Dweck, "What Happens after Prejudice Is Confronted in the Workplace? How Mindsets Affect Minorities' and Women's Outlook on Future Social Relations," *Journal of Applied Psychology,* June 2018, 676–687.

88. J. Ludema and A. Johnson, "Avoid Risk, Make Innovation Possible; Psychological Safety as the Path to High Performance," *Forbes,* September 24, 2018, https://www.forbes.com/sites/amberjohnson-jim-ludema/2018/09/24/avoid-risk-make-innovation-possible-psychological-safety-as-the-path-to-high-performance/#6346c0043223.

89. "Hostile Work Environment & Discrimination Settlements," *Forensic Notes,* https://www.forensicnotes.com/eeoc-settlements/ (accessed March 11, 2019).

90. "Beyond the Clichés: Top-Rated Workplaces by Millennials," *Indeed.com,* June 12, 2018, http://blog.indeed.com/2018/06/12/top-rated-workplaces-millennials/.

91. K. Zimmerman, "Here Are the Best Companies for Millennials," *Forbes,* September 12, 2018, https://www.forbes.com/sites/kaytiezimmerman/2018/09/12/here-are-the-best-companies-for-millennials/#558019403783.

92. "Profit Sharing," *Delta News Hub,* February 15, 2019, https://news.delta.com/tags/profit-sharing; Kaytie Zimmerman, "Here Are the Best Companies for Millennials," *Forbes,* September 12, 2018, https://www.forbes.com/sites/kaytiezimmerman/2018/09/12/here-are-the-best-companies-for-millennials/#558019403783; "Beyond the Clichés: Top-Rated Workplaces by Millennials," *Indeed.com,* June 12, 2018, http://blog.indeed.com/2018/06/12/top-rated-workplaces-millennials/.

93. M. A. McCord, D. L. Joseph, L. Y. Dhanani, and J. M. Beus, "A Meta-Analysis of Sex and Race Differences in Perceived Workplace Mistreatment," *Journal of Applied Psychology,* February 2018, 137–163.

94. "Employee Networks at American Express," https://www.americanexpress.com (accessed March 12, 2019); "Cisco Employee Resource Organizations," https://www.cisco.com (accessed March 12, 2019).

95. "The 2018 DiversityInc Top 50 Companies for Diversity: AT&T," https://www.diversityinc.com/att/ (accessed March 12, 2019); S. Shinneman, "AT&T CEO Doubles Down on 'Tolerance Is for Cowards' Comments," https://www.bizjournals.com/dallas/news/2017/05/17/at-t-ceo-doubles-down-on-tolerance-is-for-cowards.html (accessed March 12, 2019).

96. B. Larmer, "Why Does Japan Make It So Hard for Working Women to Succeed?" *The New York Times Magazine,* October 17, 2018, https://www.nytimes.com.

97. This discussion is based on R. R. Thomas, Jr., *Redefining Diversity* (New York: AMACOM, 1996).

98. J. Stensland, "Former Big 5 Employee Who Claimed Racism Gets $165,000 in Settlement," *Whidbey News-Times,* September 21, 2018, https://www.whidbeynewstimes.com; "Big 5 to Pay $165,000 to Settle EEOC Race Discrimination Lawsuit," September 19, 2018, https://www.jdsupra.com/legalnews/big-5-to-pay-165-000-to-settle-eeoc-39417/.

99. P. Brinkmann and K. Arnold, "Darden to Pay $2.85 Million to Settle 'Old White Guys' Discrimination Suit," *Orlando Sentinel,* May 3, 2018, https://www.orlandosentinel.com/business/brinkmann-on-business/os-bz-darden-eeoc-settlement-20180503-story.html.

100. K. Flaim, "How Baird Learns from Millennials on Staff," *Fortune,* February 14, 2019, http://fortune.com/2019/02/14/best-companies-baird-millennial-mentors/.

101. "Defend Your Research: Women Benefit When They Downplay Gender," *Harvard Business Review,* July–August 2018, 30–31.

102. ACLU, "Know Your Rights: Transgender People and the Law," https://www.aclu.org/know-your-rights/transgender-people-and-law (accessed March 12, 2019); "LGBTQ Equality at the Fortune 500," https://www.hrc.org/resources/lgbt-equality-at-the-fortune-500 (accessed March 12, 2019).

103. A. E. Jackson, "20 Companies That Champion LGBTQ Equality Hiring Now," *Glassdoor,* June 6, 2018, https://www.glassdoor.com/blog/companies-lgbtq-equality/.

104. A. de Vogue and Z. Cohen, "Supreme Court Allows Transgender Military Ban to Go into Effect," *CNN,* January 22, 2019, https://www.cnn.com/2019/01/22/politics/scotus-transgender-ban/index.html.

105. P. Morse, "What Brands Can Learn from Target's Approach to Hispanic Marketing," *Mobile Marketing Watch,* December 21, 2017, https://mobilemarketingwatch.com/brands-can-learn-targets-approach-hispanic-marketing-74245/.

106. A. E. Jackson, "6 Companies Offering Returnship Programs," *Glassdoor,* November 9, 2017, https://www.glassdoor.com/blog/6-companies-offering-returnship-programs/.

107. Shaw Industries, "Diversity: A Foundation for Our Business," https://shawinc.com (accessed March 12, 2019); "The Best Employers for Latinos 2018: Arthrex," *Latino Leaders* magazine, https://www.latinoleader-smagazine.com (accessed March 12, 2019); and M. Estrada, P. R. Hernandez, and P. W. Schultz, "A Longitudinal Study of How Quality Mentorship and Research Experience Integrate Underrepresented Minorities in STEM Careers," *CBE Life Sciences Education,* Spring 2018, https://www.lifescied.org.

108. Michael Bloomberg, "The Fellowship Initiative," JPMorgan Chase & Co, https://www.jpmorganchase.com/corporate/About-JPMC/the-fellowship-initiative.htm.

109. B. T. Parton, "Connecting High Schoolers to Apprenticeships," *School Administrator,* August 2018; and S. Harris, "Drilling Down into the Skills Gap," *Training,* March/April 2013, 22–23.

110. Forbes Coaches Council, "14 Smart Strategies to Prepare Your Company for an Aging Workforce," *Forbes,* October 25, 2018, https://www.forbes.com/sites/forbescoachescouncil/2018/10/25/14-smart-strategies-to-prepare-your-company-for-an-aging-workforce/#534763936a94; and G. M. McEvoy and M. J. Blahana, "Engagement or Disengagement? Older Workers and the Looming Labor Shortage," *Business Horizons,* September–October 2001, 50.

111. J. Green, "Chowing Down on Boomers' Brains," *Bloomberg Business Week,* January 15–21, 2016, https://www.chegg.com/homework-help/chowing-boomers-brainsvikram-ravinder-little-nervous-faced-b-chapter-15-problem-1bcn-solution-9781259732669-exc.

112. C. Garden, *Opinion Analysis: Federal Age-Discrimination Law Applies to All Public Employees, SCOTUS Blog,* November 6, 2018, https://www.scotusblog.com/2018/11/opinion-analysis-federal-age-discrimination-law-applies-to-all-public-employees/; H. Fischer, "US Supreme Court Says Mount Lemmon Fire District Can Be Sued for Age Discrimination," *Tuscon.com,* November 6, 2018, https://tucson.com/news/local/us-supreme-court-says-mount-lemmon-fire-district-can-be/article_9ad583e2-0ccd-5bf6-a51b-d9d71dfc6804.html; and "Mount Lemmon Fire District v. Guido," *Oyez,* March 1, 2019, www.oyez.org/cases/2018/17-587.

113. D. Brown, "Google Diversity Annual Report 2018," *Google,* https://diversity.google/annual-report/ (accessed March 11, 2019).

114. M. Burrage-Sims, "2017 Employer Information Report," *Apple,* December 31, 2017, https://www.apple.com/diversity/pdf/2017-EEO-1-Consolidated-Report.pdf.

115. M. Williams, "Facebook 2018 Diversity Report: Reflecting on Our Journey," *Facebook Newsroom,* July 12, 2018, https://newsroom.fb.com/news/2018/07/diversity-report/.

116. A. Hensel, "Pinterest Misses 2018 Hiring Goal for Underrepresented Minorities in Tech Roles, Hits Other Targets," *Venture Beat,* January 14, 2019, https://venturebeat.com/2019/01/14/pinterest-misses-2018-hiring-goal-for-underrepresented-minorities-in-tech-roles-hits-other-targets/.

117. J. Griffin, "Two Years Ahead of Schedule, Intel's Diversity & Inclusion Campaign Has Major Traction," *Forbes,* December 3, 2018, https://www.forbes.com/sites/jillgriffin/2018/12/03/two-years-ahead-of-schedule-intels-diversity-inclusion-campaign-has-major-traction/#3fac548a16fd.

118. Heather R. Huhman, "STEM Fields and the Gender Gap: Where Are the Women?" *Forbes Media LLC,* June 20, 2012, https://www.forbes.com/sites/work-in-progress/2012/06/20/stem-fields-and-the-gender-gap-where-are-the-women/#18914fca41ba.

119. CareerBuilder, LLC, "New CareerBuilder and Emsi Analysis Finds College Degrees Are Not Keeping Up with Demand in Critical Area," https://www.careerbuilder.com/share/aboutus/pressreleasesdetail.aspx?sd=3%2F3%2F2016&id=pr937&ed=12%2F31%2F2016 (accessed May 30, 2019).

120. B. Flavin, "Women in Computer Science: 6 Assumptions to Avoid," *Rasmussen College,* February 21, 2018, https://www.rasmussen.edu/degrees/technology/blog/women-in-computer-science-assumptions-to-avoid/.

121. C. Jones, "Girls Draw Even with Boys in High School STEM Classes, But Still Lag in College and Careers," *EdSource,* March 12, 2017, https://edsource.org/2017/girls-now-outnumber-boys-in-high-school-stem-but-still-lag-in-college-and-career/578444.

122. "State of Girls and Women in STEM," *National Girls Collaborative Project,* https://ngcproject.org/statistics (accessed March 11, 2019).

123. Bonnie Marcus, "The Lack Of Diversity in Tech is a Cultural Issue," *Forbes Media LLC,* August 12, 2015, https://www.forbes.com/sites/bonniemarcus/2015/08/12/the-lack-of-diversity-in-tech-is-a-cultural-issue/#38f03e5c79a2.

124. Vauhini Vara, "Inside Pinterest's Plans to Fix Its Diversity Problem," *Fast Company,* October 12, 2015, https://www.fastcompany.com/3051659/inside-pinterests-plans-to-fix-its-diversity-problem.

125. K. Williams, "Women in Tech: How to Attract and Retain Top Talent," *Indeed,* November 6, 2018, http://blog.indeed.com/2018/11/06/women-in-tech-report/.

126. Kieran Snyder, "The ResumeGgap: Are Different Gender Styles Contributing to Tech's Dismal Diversity?" *Fortune Media IP Limited,* March 26, 2015, http://fortune.com/2015/03/26/the-resume-gap-women-tell-stories-men-stick-to-facts-and-get-the-advantage/.

127. J. Biswas, "Nurse Sues Hospital, Saying It Obeyed Patient Who Didn't Want a Black Caregiver," *ABC News,* August 16, 2018, https://abcnews.go.com/US/nurse-sues-hospital-obeyed-patient-black-carer/story?id=57216585.

128. NBCUniversal Media, LLC, "Suit: Michigan Hospital Honored Patient's Request for No Black Nurse," https://www.nbcchicago.com/news/local/suit-hospital-honored-patients-request-for-no-black-nurse-491214811.html (accessed May 30, 2019).

129. American Medical Association, "AMA Principles of Medical Ethics," https://www.ama-assn.org/sites/ama-assn.org/files/corp/media-browser/code-of-medical-ethics-chapter-1.pdf (accessed March 11, 2019).

130. B. Trogen and A. Caplan, "When a Patient Is a Bigot, What Can a Doctor Do?" *Chicago Tribune,* June 29, 2017, https://www.chicagotribune.com/news/opinion/commentary/ct-doctors-bigot-patients-discrimination-perspec-20170629-story.html.

131. J. Karoub, "Hospitals Often Appease Bigotry," *The Arizona Republic,* February 24, 2013.

132. Staff, "The Patient Is Racist (or Sexist). Now What?" *Medpage Today,* April 5, 2018, https://www.medpagetoday.com/hospitalbasedmedicine/generalhospitalpractice/72169.

CHAPTER 5

1. L. Youngkin, "How to Negotiate the Raise You Deserve," *Forbes,* April 10, 2018, https://www.forbes.com/sites/laurayoungkin/2018/04/10/how-to-negotiate-the-raise-you-deserve/#4f06fc7b277c.

2. S. Florentine and J. Camp, "The Do's and Don'ts of Negotiating a Raise," *CIO,* July 19, 2018, https://www.cio.com/article/2438603/careers-staffing-10-mistakes-to-avoid-when-negotiating-a-raise.html.

3. S. Florentine and J. Camp, "The Do's and Don'ts of Negotiating a Raise," *CIO,* July 19, 2018, https://www.cio.com/article/2438603/careers-staffing-10-mistakes-to-avoid-when-negotiating-a-raise.html.

4. Sharon Florentine, and Jim Camp, "The Do's and Don'ts of Negotiating a Raise," *IDG Communications,* July 19, 2018, https://www.cio.com/article/2438603/careers-staffing-10-mistakes-to-avoid-when-negotiating-a-raise.html.

5. J. Doody, "How to Negotiate Beyond the Raise You Were Offered," *Glassdoor.com,* April 30, 2018, https://www.glassdoor.com/blog/how-to-negotiate-beyond-the-raise-you-were-offered/.

6. Aaron M. Schmidt, James W. Beck, and Jennifer Z. Gillespie, "Motivation," in *Handbook of Psychology,* Vol. 12, *Industrial and Organizational Psychology,* edited by Irving B. Weiner, Walter C. Borman, Daniel R. Ilgen, and Richard J. Klimoski, 311–40 (New Jersey: John Wiley & Sons, Inc., 2003).

7. Aaron M. Schmidt, James W. Beck, and Jennifer Z. Gillespie, "Motivation," in *Handbook of Psychology,* Vol. 12, *Industrial and Organizational Psychology,* edited by Irving B. Weiner, Walter C. Borman, Daniel R. Ilgen, and Richard J. Klimoski, 311–40 (New Jersey: John Wiley & Sons, Inc., 2003).

8. "Southwest Airlines Employees Earn $544 Million in 2018 Profit Sharing," February 13, 2019, http://investors.southwest.com; and D. Campbell, J. Case, and B. Fotsch, "More than a Paycheck," *Harvard Business Review,* January–February 2018, 118–124.

9. K. Woolley and A. Fishbach, "It's About Time: Earlier Rewards Increase Intrinsic Motivation," *Journal of Personality and Social Psychology,* June 2018, 877–890; and J. R. Hackman, G. R. Oldham, R. Janson, and K. Purdy, "A New Strategy for Job Enrichment," *California Management Review,* Summer 1975, 58.

10. "30-under-30: Kory and Mallory Stevens–Taft," *Forbes,* www.forbes.com, accessed March 25, 2019; "About Us," https://taftclothing.com, accessed March 25, 2019; M. Pineda, "How Taft Footwear Plans to Become NBA Players' Favorite Shoe Off the Court, with a Little Help from Social Media," *CNBC,* September 30, 2018, https://www.cnbc.com/2018/09/28/how-taft-footwear-became-nba-players-favorite-shoeoff-the-court.html; and T. Popomaronis, "How This Remarkable Couple Bootstrapped Their Startup to Millions in Under 3 years," *Forbes,* https://www.forbes.com, August 9, 2017.

11. A review of content and process theories of motivation is provided by "Motivation in Today's Workplace: The Link to Performance," *Research Quarterly* (Society for Human Resource Management), Second Quarter 2010, 1–9.

12. See D. McGregor, *The Human Side of Enterprise* (New York: McGraw-Hill, 1960).

13. See L. Lawter, R. E. Kopelman, and D. J. Prottas, "McGregor's Theory X/Y and Job Performance: A Multilevel, Multi-Source Analysis," *Journal of Managerial Issues,* April 2015, 84–101; and S. Gürbüz, F. Sahin, and O. Köksal, "Revisiting Theory X and Y: A Multilevel Analysis of the Effects of Leaders' Managerial Assumptions on Followers' Attitudes," *Management Decision,* 2014, 1888–1906.

14. For a complete description of Maslow's theory, see A. H. Maslow, "A Theory of Human Motivation," *Psychological Review,* July 1943, 370–396.

15. "14 Companies with Incredible Employee Perks," *Salary.com,* April 19, 2018, https://www.salary.com/articles/14-companies-with-incredible-employee-perks/.

16. T. Rowe, "5 Ways to Motivate Small Business Staff," https://www.theselfemployed.com/start_ups/5-ways-motivate-small-business-staff/ (accessed March 22, 2019).

17. D. C. McClelland, *Human Motivation* (New York: Guilford Press, 1985).

18. O. Kauppila, "How Does It Feel and How Does It Look? The Role of Employee Motivation in Organizational Learning Type," *Journal of Organizational Behavior,* October 2018, 941–955; and C. L. Burk and B. S. Wiese, "Professor or Manager? A Model of Motivational Orientations Applied to Preferred Career Paths," *Journal of Research in Personality,* August 2018, 113–132.

19. L. A. Mark, "Why Restaurateur Cameron Mitchell Always Says Yes," *Forbes,* December 5, 2018, https://www.forbes.com/sites/loisaltermark/2018/12/05/why-restaurateur-cameron-mitchell-always-says-yes/#2a44734f45de; and P. Kavilanz, "Once a Teenage Runaway, He Now Owns a $300 Million Restaurant Empire," *CNN Business,* May 18, 2018, https://www.cnn.com/2018/09/30/success/cameron-mitchell-restaurants/index.html.

20. Cameron Mitchell Restaurants, "Message From Cameron," https://cameronmitchell.com/careers/message-from-cameron/ (accessed May 30, 2019).

21. "My American Dream," *People,* February 22, 2016, 93.

22. Lois Alter Mark, "Why Restaurateur Cameron Mitchell Always Says Yes," *Forbes Media, LLC,* December 5, 2018, https://www.forbes.com/sites/loisaltermark/2018/12/05/why-restaurateur-cameron-mitchell-always-says-yes/#2f906a8545de.

23. Cameron Mitchell Restaurants, "Careers," https://cameronmitchell.com/careers (accessed May 30, 2019).

24. H. Ozcelik and S. G. Barsade, "No Employee an Island: Workplace Loneliness and Job Performance," *Academy of Management Journal,* December 2018, 2343–2366.

25. R. M. Ryan and E. L. Deci, "Self-Determination Theory and the Facilitation of Intrinsic Motivation, Social Development, and Well-Being," *American Psychologist,* January 2000, 68–78.

26. E. L. Deci, R. Koestner, and R. M. Ryan, "A Meta-Analytic Review of Experiments Examining the Effects of Extrinsic Rewards on Intrinsic Motivation," *Psychological Bulletin,* November 1999, 627–668.

27. C. Scott Rigby and R. M. Ryan, "Self-Determination Theory in Human Resource Development: New Directions and Practical Considerations," *Advances in Developing Human Resources,* May 2018, 133–147; and A. Thibault-Landry, R. Egan, L. Crevier-Braud, L. Manganelli, and J. Forest, "An Empirical Investigation of the Employee Work Passion Appraisal Model Using Self-Determination Theory," *Advances in Developing Human Resources,* May 2018, 148–168.

28. Isabel Thottam, "10 Companies with Awesome Training and Development Programs," Monster Worldwide, https://www.monster.com/career-advice/article/companies-with-awesome-training-development-programs.

29. K. Rogers, "Do Your Employees Feel Respected?" *Harvard Business Review,* July–August 2018, 62–71.

30. I. Thottam, "10 Companies with Awesome Training and Development Programs," *Monster,* https://www.monster.com/career-advice/article/companies-with-awesome-training-development-programs (accessed March 22, 2019).

31. E. Spencer, "How to Grow and Scale a Culture Like 23andMe," *Forbes,* July 18, 2018, https://www.forbes.com/sites/erinspencer1/2018/07/18/how-to-grow-scale-a-culture-like-23andme/#4e3ff1922b79.

32. F. Herzberg, B. Mausner, and B. B. Snyderman, *The Motivation to Work* (New York: John Wiley & Sons, 1959).

33. Frederick Herzberg, *One More Time: How Do You Motivate Employees?* (Boston Massachusetts: Harvard Business Review, 2003).

34. "REI Is a Best Place to Work," https://www.rei.com/about-rei/100-best-companies (accessed March 22, 2019); "Jerry Stritzke: A Conversation about Store Hourly Pay and Benefits," https://newsroom.rei.com (accessed March 22, 2019); and A. Cain, "The Best Way to Stand Out in a Job Interview at One of the Most Beloved Companies in America," *Business Insider,* February 27, 2018, https://www.businessinsider.com/rei-jobs-biggest-mistake-2018-2.

35. N. El-Bawab, "More Millennials Are Demanding These Workplace Perks," *CNBC,* February 7, 2019, https://www.cnbc.com/2019/02/07/millennials-are-demanding-these-workplace-perks.html; and A. D. Wright, "Employers Say Accommodating Millennials Is a Business Imperative," *Society for Human Resource Management,* April 26, 2018, https://www.shrm.org/resourcesandtools/hr-topics/employee-relations/pages/accommodating-millennials-is-a-business-imperative.aspx.

36. M. Boyle and Bloomberg, "Walmart to Pay Hourly Workers for Sick Leave in Overhaul of Employment Policies," *Forbes,* February 1, 2019, http://fortune.com/2019/02/01/walmart-to-pay-hourly-workers-for-sick-leave-in-overhaul-of-employment-policies/.

37. K. Gibson, "Walmart Offers Paid Sick Leave to Its 1.1 Million Hourly Workers," *CBS News,* February 1, 2019, https://www.cbsnews.com/news/walmart-sick-leave-policy-offered-to-11-million-hourly-workers/.

38. Kate Gibson, "Walmart Offers Paid Sick Leave to Its 1.1 Million Hourly Workers," *CBS Interactive Inc.,* February 1, 2019, https://www.cbsnews.com/news/walmart-sick-leave-policy-offered-to-11-million-hourly-workers/.

39. "Bernie Sanders Stands Up for Walmart Workers," Yahoo! Finance Video, February 5, 2019, https://finance.yahoo.com/video/bernie-sanders-stands-walmart-workers-180646570.html.

40. Rep. Ro Khanna and M. Perrone, "American Workers Need Congress to Stand Up to Amazon and Walmart," *The Hill,* February 28, 2019, https://thehill.com/blogs/congress-blog/economy-budget/431867-american-workers-need-congress-to-stand-up-to-amazon-and.

41. J. Herron, "Walmart Introduces Paid Time-Off for Sickness and Other Absences," *USA Today,* February 3, 2019, https://www.usatoday.com/story/money/2019/02/03/walmart-workers-can-now-earn-paid-time-off-sick-days/2762856002/.

42. E. Chuck, "Poultry Workers, Denied Bathroom Breaks, Wear Diapers: Oxfam Report," *NBC News,* https://www.nbcnews.com/business/business-news/poultry-workers-denied-bathroom-breaks-wear-diapers-oxfam-report-n572806 (accessed March 22, 2019).

43. H Xu, M. Strode, and A. Withers, "Poultry Processing Workers Still Face High Number of Injuries," Midwest Center for Investigative Reporting, June 28, 2018, https://investigatemidwest.org/2018/06/28/poultry-processing-workers-still-face-high-number-of-injuries/.

44. P. Lowe, "Tyson Foods Promises Better Conditions and Safety for Meat Workers," *NPR,* https://www.npr.org/sections/the-salt/2017/04/26/525736888/tyson-foods-promises-better-conditions-and-safety-for-meat-workers (accessed March 22, 2019).

45. M. Valentine, "When Equity Seems Unfair: The Role of Justice Enforceability in Temporary Team Coordination," *Academy of Management Journal,* December 2018, 2018–2105; and M. D. Baer, J. B. Rodell, R. K. Dhensa-Kahlon, J. A. Colquitt, K. P. Zipay, R. Burgess, and R. Outlaw, "Pacification or Aggravation? The Effects of Talking About Supervisor Unfairness," *Academy of Management Journal,* October 2018, 1764–1788.

46. "New PayScale Study Reveals Employees' Perceptions about Pay Fairness and Transparency Are Five Times More Impactful on Engagement Than Actual Compensation," November 17, 2017, https://www.globenewswire.com/news-release/2017/11/07/1176260/0/en/New-PayScale-Study-Reveals-Employees-Perceptions-About-Pay-Fairness-and-Transparency-are-Five-Times-More-Impactful-on-Engagement-Than-Actual-Compensation.html.

47. For a thorough review of organizational justice theory and research, see R. Cropanzano, D. E. Rupp, C. J. Mohler, and M. Schminke, "Three Roads to Organizational Justice," in G. R. Ferris, ed., *Research in Personnel and Human Resources Management* (vol. 20) (New York: JAI Press, 2001), 269–329.

48. "Fortune 100 Best Companies to Work For 2019: #16: Baird," http://fortune.com/best-companies/baird/ (accessed March 22, 2019); and R. Levering, "The 100 Best Companies to Work For 2016," *Fortune,* March 15, 2016, 147.

49. J. A. Colquitt, D. E. Conlon, M. J. Wesson, C. O. L. H. Porter, and K. Y. Ng, "Justice at the Millennium: A Meta-Analytic Review of 25 Years of Organizational Justice Research," *Journal of Applied Psychology,* June 2001, 426.

50. R. C. Huseman, J. D. Hatfield, and E. W. Miles, "A New Perspective on Equity Theory: The Equity Sensitivity Construct," *Academy of Management Review,* April 1987, 222–234.

51. G. Jeon and D. A. Newman, "Equity Sensitivity versus Egoism: A Reconceptualization and New Measure of Individual Differences in Justice Perceptions," *Journal of Vocational Behavior,* August 2016, 138–155; and H. J. R. Woodley, J. S. Bourdage, B. Ogunfowora, and B. Nguyen, "Examining Equity Sensitivity: An Investigation Using the Big Five and HEXACO Models of Personality," *Frontiers in Psychology,* January 2016.

52. Y. Han, G. Sears, and H. Zhang, "Revising the 'Give and Take' in LMX," *Personnel Review,* March 2018, 555–571; and J. S. Bourdage, A. Goupal, T. Neilson, E. R. Lukacik, and N. Lee, "Personality, Equity Sensitivity, and Discretionary Workplace Behavior," *Personality and Individual Differences,* January 2018, 144–150.

53. V. Khoreva and A. Tenhiälä, "Gender Differences in Reactions to Injustice," *Journal of Managerial Psychology,* April 2016, 790–804.

54. M. Mooijman and J. Graham, "Unjust Punishment in Organizations," *Research in Organizational Behavior,* November 2018, 95–106; and D. B. Whiteside and L. J. Barclay, "When Wanting to Be Fair Is Not Enough: The Effects of Depletion and Self-Appraisal Gaps on Fair Behavior," *Journal of Management,* November 2018, 3311–3335.

55. Michael Ramsay Bashshur, and Burak Oc, "When Voice Matters: A Multilevel Review of the Impact of Voice in Organizations," *Journal of Management* 41, no. 5 (November 2014): 1530–554. https://doi.org/10.1177/0149206314558302.

56. M. Zetline, "Salesforce Employees Objected to Its Immigration Work. CEO Marc Benioff's Response Was Brilliant," *Inc.,* November 26, 2018, https://www.inc.com/minda-zetlin/salesforce-ethical-humane-office-marc-benioff-kara-swisher-employee-activism.html?cid=search.

57. M. L. Frazier and W. M. Bowler, "Voice Climate, Supervisor Undermining, and Work Outcomes: A Group-Level Examination," *Journal of Management,* March 2015, 841–863.

58. M. van Dijke, D. De Cremer, G. Langendijk, and C. Anderson, "Ranking Low, Feeling High: How Hierarchical Position and Experienced Power Promote Prosocial Behavior in Response to Procedural Justice," *Journal of Applied Psychology,* February 2018, 164–181.

59. David Gelles, "The C.E.O. Who Stood Up to President Trump: Ken Frazier Speaks Out," *The New York Times Company,* February 19, 2018, https://www.nytimes.com/2018/02/19/business/merck-ceo-ken-frazier-trump.html.

60. C. Rubino, D. R. Avery, P. F. McKay, Brenda L. Moore, D. C. Wilson, M. S. Van Driel, L. A. Witt, D. P. McDonald, "And Justice for All: How Organizational Justice Climate Deters Sexual Harassment," *Personnel Psychology,* Winter 2018, 519–544.

61. C. Porath and C. Pearson, "You're Rude Because Your Boss Is Rude," *Harvard Business Review,* https://hbr.org/2013/01/youre-rude-because-your-boss-is (accessed March 22, 2019); and D. McMahan, "How to Handle Bad Customer Service . . . Without Holding a Grudge," *NBC News,* March 12, 2018, https://www.nbcnews.com/better/business/how-handle-bad-customer-service-grace-ncna854806.

62. B. M. Galla, J. Amemiya, and M. T. Wang, "Using Expectancy-Value Theory to Understand Academic Self-Control," *Learning and Instruction,* December 2018, 22–33; H. Dai, B. J. Dietvorst, B. Tuckfield, K. L. Milkman, and M. E. Schweitzer, "Quitting When the Going Gets Tough: A Downside of High Performance Expectations," *Academy of Management Journal,* October 2018, 1667–1691; and M. S. Giarratana, M. Mariani, and I. Weller, "Rewards for Patents and Inventor Behaviors in Industrial Research and Development," *Academy of Management Journal,* February 2018, 264–292.

63. "U.S. Navy Enlistment Bonuses," https://www.navy.com/bonus (accessed March 25, 2019).

64. M. Moskowitz and R. Levering, "The 100 Best Companies to Work For," *Fortune,* February 3, 2014, 96.

65. Michael Cooper, "The Chicago Symphony Goes on Strike Over Pension Plan," *The New York Times Company,* March 11, 2019, https://www.nytimes.com/2019/03/11/arts/music/chicago-symphony-orchestra-strike.html.

66. Cooper Michael, "The Chicago Symphony Goes on Strike Over Pension Plan," *The New York Times Company,* March 11, 2019, https://www.nytimes.com/2019/03/11/arts/music/chicago-symphony-orchestra-strike.html.

67. M. Di Nunzio, "Strike by CSO Musicians Leads to Concert Cancellations Through March 16," *Chicago Sun Times,* March 12, 2019, https://chicago.suntimes.com/news/strike-by-cso-musicians-leads-to-concert-cancelations-riccardo-muti-symphony-center/.

68. E. Bachman, "Put Your Money Where Your Mouth Is: Tying Executives' Bonuses to Diversity Initiatives," *Forbes,* June 7, 2018, https://www.forbes.com/sites/ericbachman/2018/06/07/put-your-money-where-your-mouth-is-tying-executives-bonuses-to-diversity-initiatives/#34a7b79f731f.

69. Payscale, *2019 Compensation Best Practices: Executive Summary,* https://www.payscale.com/cbpr (accessed March 25, 2019); and L. Bodell, "It's Time to Put Performance Reviews on Notice," *Forbes,* April 27, 2018, https://www.forbes.com/sites/lisabodell/2018/04/27/why-performance-reviews-are-irrelevant-today/#2709bdcc4b63.

70. S. Miller, "Employees Have High Hopes for Bonuses This Year," *Society for Human Resource Management,* January 14, 2019, https://shrm.org/resourcesandtools/hr-topics/compensation/pages/employees-high-hopes-for-bonuses.aspx.

71. Cathryn Creno, "Program Helps Students Succeed," *The Arizona Republic,* November 27, 2012, https://www.pressreader.com/usa/the-arizona-republic/20121127/281702612007686.

72. G. H. Seijts and G. P. Latham, "Knowing When to Set Learning versus Performance Goals," *Organizational Dynamics,* 2012, 1–6.

73. See E. A. Locke and G. P. Latham, "Building a Practically Useful Theory of Goal Setting and Task Motivation," *American Psychologist,* September 2002, 705–717.

74. S. Shellenbarger, "The Downside of Carrying the Most Weight at Work," *The Wall Street Journal,* January 29, 2019, https://www.wsj.com/articles/the-downsides-of-carrying-the-most-weight-at-work-11548776660?mod=searchresults&page=3&pos=3.

75. "Statistics & Facts about the Volkswagen Diesel Scandal," https://www.statista.com/topics/3253/volkswagen-diesel-scandal-us-focus/ (accessed March 25, 2019).

76. J. Ewing, A. Stevenson, and M. Goldstein, "Ex-VW Chief Knew of Diesel Scheme Years Earlier Than He Admitted, S.E.C. Says," *The New York Times,* March 15, 2019, https://www.nytimes.com/2019/03/15/business/volkswagen-winterkorn-sec-fraud.html; and "VW Fights Investors as Diesel-Scandal Cost Could Top $35 Billion," *Fortune,* September 8, 2018, http://fortune.com/2018/09/08/volkswagen-vw-diesel-scandal/.

77. T. Ballard, J. B. Vancouver, and A. Neal, "On the Pursuit of Multiple Goals with Different Deadlines," *Journal of Applied Psychology,* November 2018, 1242–1264.

78. A. Kelso, "KFC Announces Major Plastics Pledge, Achievement of Antibiotics Goal," *Forbes,* January 24, 2019, https://www.forbes.com/sites/aliciakelso/2019/01/24/kfc-announces-major-plastics-pledge-achievement-of-antibiotics-goal/#1355d8c04b72.

79. E. Pofeldt, "Memphis' Goal: To Grow Revenue at Minority-Owned Firms by $50M in Five Years," *Forbes,* February 20, 2019, https://www.forbes.com/sites/elainepofeldt/2019/02/20/memphiss-goal-to-grow-revenue-at-minority-owned-firms-by-50m-in-five-years/#7a0e0c196a68.

80. M. R. Parke, J. M. Weinhardt, A. Brodsky, S. Tangirala, and S. E. DeVoe, "When Daily Planning Improves Employee Performance: The Importance of Planning Type, Engagement, and Interruptions," *Journal of Applied Psychology,* March 2018, 300–312.

81. John Bowe, Marisa Bowe, and Sabin C. Streeter, *Gig: Americans Talk about Their Jobs at the Turn of the Millennium,* (New York: Crown Publishers, 2000).

82. For a review, see S. K. Parker, "Beyond Motivation: Job and Work Design for Development, Health, Ambidexterity, and More," *Annual Review of Psychology,* 2014, 661–691.

83. A review of these approaches is provided by S. Hornung, D. M. Rousseau, J. Glaser, P. Angerer, and M. Weigl, "Beyond Top-Down and Bottom-Up Work Redesign: Customizing Job Content through Idiosyncratic Deals," *Journal of Organizational Behavior,* February 2010, 187–215; and G. R. Oldham and J. R. Hackman, "Not What It Was and Not What It Will Be: The Future of Job Design," *Journal of Organizational Behavior,* February 2010, 463–479.

84. George De Albert Babcock, and Reginald Trautschold, *The Taylor System in Franklin Management* (New York: The Engineering Magazine Company, 1917).

85. See the related discussion in S. Wagner-Tsukamoto, "An Institutional Economic Reconstruction of Scientific Management: On the Lost Theoretical Logic of Taylorism," *Academy of Management Review,* January 2007, 105–117; and P. R. Lawrence, "The Key Job Design Problem Is Still Taylorism," *Journal of Organizational Behavior,* February 2010, 412–421.

86. This type of program was developed and tested by M. A. Campion and C. L. McClelland, "Follow-Up and Extension of the Interdisciplinary Costs and Benefits of Enlarged Jobs," *Journal of Applied Psychology,* June 1993, 339–351.

87. See B. K. Tarus, "Effects of Job Rotation Strategy on High Performance Workplace in Lake Victoria North Water Services Board, Kenya," *International Journal of Business and Management,* 2014, 139–146.

88. E. Moore, "7 Companies with Amazing Office Rotation Options," *Glassdoor.com,* November 29, 2017, https://www.glassdoor.com/blog/companies-with-office-rotation-options/.

89. Stephanie Vozza, "Why This CEO Lets Other Executives Do His Job For a Day," *Fast Company,* January 11, 2017, https://www.fastcompany.com/3066911/why-this-ceo-trades-jobs-with-other-execs.

90. S. M. Heathfield, "6 Keys to Successful Job Rotation," *The Balance,* September 17, 2018, https://www.thebalancecareers.com/keys-to-successful-job-rotation-1918167.

91. "Who We Are," https://hotdogmarketing.net (accessed March 25, 2019); M. Tabaka, "These Founders Couldn't Afford Traditional Employee Benefits, So They Did Something Even Better," *Inc.,* July 11, 2018, https://www.inc.com/marla-tabaka/these-founders-couldnt-afford-traditional-employee-benefits-so-they-did-something-even-better.html?cid=search.

92. Definitions of the job characteristics model were adapted from J. R. Hackman and G. R. Oldham, "Motivation through the Design of Work: Test of a Theory," *Organizational Behavior and Human Performance,* August 1976, 250–279.

93. L. A. Wegman, B. J. Hoffman, N. T. Carter, J. M. Twenge, and N. Guenole, "Placing Job Characteristics in Context: Cross-Temporal Meta-Analysis of Changes in Job Characteristics Since 1975," *Journal of Management,* January 2018, 352–386.

94. W. G. M. Oerlemans and A. B. Bakker, "Motivating Job Characteristics and Happiness at Work: A Multilevel Perspective," *Journal of Applied Psychology,* November 2018, 1230–1241.

95. A. E. Jackson, "14 Awesome Companies with Unlimited Vacation," *Glassdoor,* March 7, 2019, https://www.glassdoor.com/blog/cool-companies-offering-unlimited-vacation/; and D. Burkus, "How Adobe Structures Feedback Conversations," *Harvard Business Review,* July 20, 2017, https://hbr.org/2017/07/how-adobe-structures-feedback-conversations.

96. Productivity studies are reviewed in R. E. Kopelman, *Managing Productivity in Organizations* (New York: McGraw-Hill, 1986).

97. P. Petrou, E. Demerouti, and W. B. Schaufeli, "Crafting the Change: The Role of Employee Job Crafting Behaviors for Successful Organizational Change," *Journal of Management,* May 2018, 1766–1792.

98. S. Achor, A. Reece, G. R. Kellerman, and A. Robichaux, "9 Out of 10 People Are Willing to Earn Less Money to Do More Meaningful Work," *Harvard Business Review,* November 6, 2018, https://hbr.org/2018/11/9-out-of-10-people-are-willing-to-earn-less-money-to-do-more-meaningful-work.

99. P. F. Bruning and M. A. Campion, "A Role-Resource Approach-Avoidance Model of Job Crafting: A Multimethod Integration and Extension of Job Crafting Theory," *Academy of Management Journal,* April 2018, 499–522; and M. Tims, D. Derks, and A. B. Bakker, "Job Crafting and Its Relationships with Person-Job Fit and Meaningfulness: A Three-Wave Study," *Journal of Vocational Behavior,* February 2016, 44–53.

100. J. Amortegui, "Want a Job You Love? Stop Looking and Job Craft It," *Forbes,* January 22, 2016, https://www.forbes.com/sites/womensmedia/2016/01/22/want-a-job-you-love-stop-looking-and-job-craft-it/#162e4e9d1ed7; and S. Shellenbarger, "Feeling Stuck? Write Yourself a New Job Description," *The Wall Street Journal,* August 12, 2015, D1, D2.

101. Y. Rofcanin, A. Berber, S. Koch, and L. Sevinc, "Job Crafting and I-deals: A Study Testing the Nomological Network of Proactive Behaviors," *International Journal of Human Resource Management,* 2016, 2695–2726; and S. Hornung, D. M. Rousseau, J. Glaser, P. Angerer, and M. Weighl, "Beyond Top-Down and Bottom-Up Work Redesign: Customizing Job Content through Idiosyncratic Deals," *Journal of Organizational Behavior,* February 2010, 188.

102. "Idea Watch: Why You Should Rotate Office Seating Assignments," *Harvard Business Review,* March–April 2018, 22–24; and C. C. Rosen, D. J. Slater, C.-H. Chang, and R. E. Johnson, "Let's Make a Deal: Development and Validation of the Ex Post I-Deals Scale," *Journal of Management,* March 2013, 709–742.

103. "Working at RSM: Culture of Flexibility," https://rsmus.com/careers/working-at-rsm/culture-of-flexibility.html (accessed March 26, 2019); and T. Hopke, "Go Ahead, Take a Few Months Off," *HRMagazine,* September 2010, 71–74.

104. P. M. Bal, "Why Do Employees Negotiate Idiosyncratic Deals? An Exploration of the Process of I-deal Negotiation," *New Zealand Journal of Employment Relations,* January 2018, 2–18; and C. Liao, S. J. Wayne, and D.M. Rousseau, "Idiosyncratic Deals in Contemporary Organizations: A Qualitative and Meta-Analytical Review," *Journal of Organizational Behavior,* February 2016, S9–S29.

105. See "Our Fulfillment Centers," *Aboutamazon.com,* https://www.about-amazon.com/amazon-fulfillment/our-fulfillment-centers (accessed March 20, 2019); and "Amazon's Fulfillment Network," *Aboutamazon.com,* https://www.aboutamazon.com/working-at-amazon/amazons-fulfillment-network (accessed April 2, 2019).

106. See E. Feinberg, "How Amazon Is Investing in Customer Experience by Reimagining Retail Delivery," *Forbes*, January 4, 2018, https://www.forbes.com/sites/forbescommunicationscouncil/2018/01/04/how-amazon-is-investing-in-customer-experience-by-reimagining-retail-delivery/#5c78fd7f2c2e; and B. Morgan, "Costco Takes Top Spot In Online Customer Satisfaction over Amazon," *Forbes*, February 27, 2019, https://www.forbes.com/sites/blakemorgan/2019/02/27/costco-takes-top-spot-in-online-customer-satisfaction-over-amazon/#1290d33949a7.

107. See L. Feiner, "Amazon Is the Most Valuable Public Company in the World after Passing Microsoft," *CNBC*, January 7, 2019, https://www.cnbc.com/2019/01/07/amazon-passes-microsoft-market-value-becomes-largest.html; and A. Levy, "The 7 Largest E-Commerce Companies in the World," *The Motley Fool*, December 26, 2018, https://www.fool.com/investing/2018/12/26/the-7-largest-e-commerce-companies-in-the-world.aspx.

108. S. Liao, "Amazon Warehouse Workers Skip Bathroom Breaks to Keep Their Jobs, Says Report," *The Verge*, April 16, 2018, https://www.theverge.com/2018/4/16/17243026/amazon-warehouse-jobs-worker-conditions-bathroom-breaks.

109. A. Semuels, "What Amazon Does to Poor Cities," *The Atlantic*, February 1, 2018, https://www.theatlantic.com/business/archive/2018/02/amazon-warehouses-poor-cities/552020/.

110. N. Godlewski, "Amazon Working Conditions: Urinating in Trash Cans, Shamed to Work Injured, List of Employee Complaints," *Newsweek*, September 12, 2018, https://www.newsweek.com/amazon-drivers-warehouse-conditions-workers-complains-jeff-bezos-bernie-1118849.

111. C. Lieber, "Bernie Sanders Called Out Jeff Bezos for Poor Treatment of Amazon Workers. In a Rare Move, the Company Fired Back," *Vox*, August 30, 2018, https://www.vox.com/2018/8/30/17797786/amazon-warehouse-conditions-bernie-sanders.

112. S. Liao, "Amazon Warehouse Workers Skip Bathroom Breaks to Keep Their Jobs, Says Report," *The Verge*, April 16, 2018, https://www.theverge.com/2018/4/16/17243026/amazon-warehouse-jobs-worker-conditions-bathroom-breaks.

113. E. Fox, "Amazon Reportedly Has Scoreboards to Shame Its Workers," *Vanity Fair*, March 8, 2016, https://www.vanityfair.com/news/2016/03/amazon-warehouse-theft.

114. I. A. Hamilton and Á. Cain, "Amazon Warehouse Employees Speak Out about the 'Brutal' Reality of Working during the Holidays, When 60-Hour Weeks Are Mandatory and Ambulance Calls Are Common," *Business Insider*, February 19, 2019, https://www.businessinsider.com/amazon-employees-describe-peak-2019-2.

115. A. Semuels, "What Amazon Does to Poor Cities," *The Atlantic*, February 1, 2018, https://www.theatlantic.com/business/archive/2018/02/amazon-warehouses-poor-cities/552020/.

116. Alana Semuels, "What Amazon Does to Poor Cities," *The Atlantic Monthly Group*, February 1, 2018, https://www.theatlantic.com/business/archive/2018/02/amazon-warehouses-poor-cities/552020/.

117. I. A. Hamilton and Á. Cain, "Amazon Warehouse Employees Speak Out about the 'Brutal' Reality of Working during the Holidays, When 60-Hour Weeks Are Mandatory and Ambulance Calls Are Common," *Business Insider*, February 19, 2019, https://www.businessinsider.com/amazon-employees-describe-peak-2019-2.

118. Alana Semuels, "What Amazon Does to Poor Cities," *The Atlantic Monthly Group*, February 1, 2018, https://www.theatlantic.com/business/archive/2018/02/amazon-warehouses-poor-cities/552020/.

119. I. A. Hamilton and Á. Cain, "Amazon Warehouse Employees Speak Out about the 'Brutal' Reality of Working during the Holidays, When 60-Hour Weeks Are Mandatory and Ambulance Calls Are Common," *Business Insider*, February 19, 2019, https://www.businessinsider.com/amazon-employees-describe-peak-2019-2.

120. A. Bhattarai, "Amazon Is Doling Out Raises of as Little as 25 Cents an Hour in What Employees Call 'Damage Control,'" *The Washington Post*, September 24, 2018, https://www.washingtonpost.com/business/2018/09/24/it-feels-like-damage-control-amazon-warehouse-workers-say-company-is-quietly-doling-out-small-raises/?noredirect=on&utm_term=.57415d467603.

121. K. Weise, "Some Amazon Workers Are Fuming About Their Raise," *The New York Times*, October 9, 2018, https://www.nytimes.com/2018/10/09/technology/amazon-workers-pay-raise.html.

122. Alana Semuels, "What Amazon Does to Poor Cities," *The Atlantic Monthly Group*, February 1, 2018, https://www.theatlantic.com/business/archive/2018/02/amazon-warehouses-poor-cities/552020/.

123. A. Semuels, "What Amazon Does to Poor Cities," *The Atlantic*, February 1, 2018, https://www.theatlantic.com/business/archive/2018/02/amazon-warehouses-poor-cities/552020/.

124. A. Semuels, "What Amazon Does to Poor Cities," *The Atlantic*, February 1, 2018, https://www.theatlantic.com/business/archive/2018/02/amazon-warehouses-poor-cities/552020/.

125. See N. Bomey and K. Tyko, "Sears Store Closing List: 142 More Sears, Kmart Locations Closing in Chapter 11 Bankruptcy," *USA Today*, October 15, 2018, https://www.usatoday.com/story/money/2018/10/15/sears-holdings-bankruptcy-store-closures/1645971002/; and L. Zumbach, "Sears Slashed More Than 50,000 Jobs Last Year," *Chicago Tribune*, March 23, 2018, https://www.chicagotribune.com/business/ct-biz-sears-employee-cuts-store-closures-0324-story.html.

126. R. Beals, "Bankrupt Sears Can Give $25.3 Million in Bonuses to Top Employees, Court Says," *MarketWatch*, December 15, 2018, https://www.marketwatch.com/story/bankrupt-sears-can-give-253-million-in-bonuses-to-top-employees-court-says-2018-12-15.

127. M. Segarra, "How Companies Like Toys R Us Get Approval to Pay Executive Bonuses During Bankruptcy," *Marketplace*, April 10, 2018, https://www.marketplace.org/2018/04/10/business/how-companies-toys-r-us-get-approval-pay-executive-bonuses-during-bankruptcy.

128. R. Beals, "Bankrupt Sears Can Give $25.3 Million in Bonuses to Top Employees, Court Says," *MarketWatch*, December 15, 2018, https://www.marketwatch.com/story/bankrupt-sears-can-give-253-million-in-bonuses-to-top-employees-court-says-2018-12-15.

129. David Dayen, "Sears Adds Further Insult to Its Workers—Bankruptcy Bonuses for Execs," *The American Prospect*, December 17, 2018, https://prospect.org/article/sears-adds-further-insult-its-workers-bankruptcy-bonuses-execs.

130. Mike Spector, and Tom McGinty, "The CEO Bankruptcy Bonus," *The Wall Street Journal*, January 27, 2012. https://www.wsj.com/articles/SB10001424053111903703604576584480750545602.

CHAPTER 6

1. J. Stone, "5 Tips for Being Productive, Not Busy," *SHRM.org*, January 10, 2019, https://blog.shrm.org/blog/5-tips-for-being-productive-not-busy.

2. T. Bradberry, "11 Things Ultra-Productive People Do Differently," *Forbes*, May 13, 2015, http://www.forbes.com/sites/travisbradberry/2015/05/13/11-things-ultra-productive-people-do-differently/print/. See also T. Bradberry, "Want to Be More Productive? Never Touch Things Twice," *LinkedIn*, October 14, 2015, https://www.linkedin.com/pulse/productivity-hacks-want-more-productive-never-touch-things-bradberry.

3. J. Rampton, "15 Ways to Increase Your Productivity at Work," *Inc.com*, February 4, 2015, http://www.inc.com/john-rampton/15-ways-to-increase-productivity-at-work.html.

4. J. Stone, "5 Tips for Being Productive, Not Busy," *SHRM.org*, January 10, 2019, https://blog.shrm.org/blog/5-tips-for-being-productive-not-busy.

5. Adapted from J. Stone, "5 Tips for Being Productive, Not Busy," *SHRM.org*, January 10, 2019, https://blog.shrm.org/blog/5-tips-for-being-productive-not-busy.

6. Adapted from A. J. Kinicki, K. J. L. Jacobson, S. J. Peterson, and G. E. Prussia, "Development and Validation of the Performance Management Behavior Questionnaire," *Personnel Psychology*, 2013, 1–45.

7. D. Schleicher, H. M. Baumann, D. W. Sullivan, P. E. Levy, D. C. Hargrove, and B. A Barros-Rivera, "Putting the System into Performance Management Systems: A Review and Agenda for Performance management Research," *Journal of Management*, 2018, 44, 2209–2245.

8. E. D. Pulakos, R. Mueller-Hanson, and S. Arad, "The Evolution of Performance Management: Searching for Value," Annual Review of Organizational Psychology and Organizational Behavior," *Annual Reviews*, 2019, 6, 249–271.

9. E. D. Pulakos, R. Mueller-Hanson, and S. Arad, "The Evolution of Performance Management: Searching for Value," Annual Review of Organizational Psychology and Organizational Behavior," *Annual Reviews*, 2019, 6, 249–271.

10. C. Groscurth, "Great Managers Can Fix Broken Performance Management Systems," *Gallup Business Journal*, June 14, 2015, http://www.gallup.com/businessjournal/183770/great-managers-fix-broken-performance-management-systems.aspx.

11. D. Schleicher, H. M. Baumann, D. W. Sullivan, P. E. Levy, D. C. Hargrove, and B. A Barros-Rivera, "Putting the System into Performance Management Systems: A Review and Agenda for Performance management Research," *Journal of Management*, 2018, 44, 2209–2245.

12. D. Schleicher, H. M. Baumann, D. W. Sullivan, P. E. Levy, D. C. Hargrove, and B. A Barros-Rivera, "Putting the System into Performance Management Systems: A Review and Agenda for Performance management Research," *Journal of Management*, 2018, 44, 2209–2245.

13. M. Yate, "Your Career Q&A: Defensive and Offensive Tactics for Career Success," *SHRM.com*, January 2, 2018, https://www.shrm.org/resourcesandtools/hr-topics/organizational-and-employee-development/pages/your-career-qa-defensive-and-offensive-career-tactics.aspx.

14. B. Wigert and J. Harter, "Re-Engineering Performance Management," Gallup, 2018, https://www.gallup.com/workplace/238064/re-engineering-performance-management.aspx.

15. W. F. Cascio, "Global Performance Management Systems," in I. Bjorkman and G. Stahl, eds., *Handbook of Research in International Human Resources Management* (London, UK: Edward Elgar Ltd., 2006), 176–196. See also E. D. Pulakos, *Performance Management: A New Approach for Driving Business Results* (West Sussex, UK: Wiley-Blackwell, 2009).

16. J. Light, "Human Resource Executives Say Reviews Are Off Mark," *The Wall Street Journal,* November 7, 2010.

17. Adapted from B. Wigert and J. Harter, "Re-Engineering Performance Management," Gallup, 2018, https://www.gallup.com/workplace/238064/re-engineering-performance-management.aspx.

18. B. Wigert and A. Mann, "Give Performance Reviews that Actually Inspire Employees," Gallup, September 25, 2017, https://www.gallup.com/workplace/236135/give-performance-reviews-actually-inspire-employees.aspx.

19. E. Bank, "Reinventing Performance Management at Deloitte," *Talent Development,* January 13, 2015, https://www.td.org/Publications/Blogs/Learning-Executive-Blog/2016/01/Reinventing-Performance-Management-at-Deloitte.

20. M. Buckingham and A. Goodall, "Reinventing Performance Management," *Harvard Business Review,* April 2015, https://hbr.org/2015/04/reinventing-performance-management.

21. E. Bank, "Reinventing Performance Management at Deloitte," *Talent Development,* January 13, 2015, https://www.td.org/Publications/Blogs/Learning-Executive-Blog/2016/01/Reinventing-Performance-Management-at-Deloitte.

22. E. Bank, "Reinventing Performance Management at Deloitte," *Talent Development,* January 13, 2015, https://www.td.org/Publications/Blogs/Learning-Executive-Blog/2016/01/Reinventing-Performance-Management-at-Deloitte.

23. K. Fenty, "Employee Performance Management Needs a Promotion," Forrester Research Group, February 2018, https://www.workday.com/en-us/forms/reports/employee-performance-management-needs-a-promotion.html.

24. K. Fenty, "Employee Performance Management Needs a Promotion," Forrester Research Group, February 2018, https://www.workday.com/en-us/forms/reports/employee-performance-management-needs-a-promotion.html; B. Wigert and J. Harter, "Re-Engineering Performance Management," Gallup, 2018, https://www.gallup.com/workplace/238064/re-engineering-performance-management.aspx.

25. P. Cappelli and A. Tavis, "HR Goes Agile," *Harvard Business Review,* March-April 2018, https://hbr.org/2018/03/the-new-rules-of-talent-management.

26. C. Groscurth, "Managers Could Do a Lot Better at Performance Management," *Gallup Business Journal,* June 30, 2015, http://www.gallup.com/businessjournal/183821/managers-lot-better-performance-management.aspx.

27. National Center for Education Statistics, https://nces.ed.gov/fastfacts/display.asp?id=40.

28. D. Morisano, J. B. Hirsh, J. B. Peterson, R. O. Pihl, and B. M. Shore, "Setting, Elaborating, and Reflecting on Personal Goals Improves Academic Performance," *Journal of Applied Psychology,* March 2010, 255.

29. S. Bhargava and H. Pradhan, "Effect of Goal Orientation on Job Performance," *Journal of Management Research,*" April–June 2018, 90–101.

30. W. Craig, "Why Communicating Company Goals is Key for Employee Growth," *Forbes.com,* August 14, 2018, https://www.forbes.com/sites/williamcraig/2018/08/14/why-communicating-company-goals-is-key-for-employee-growth/#1d31c0063b85.

31. From E. D. Pulakos, R. A. Mueller-Hanson, R. S. O'Leary, and M. M. Meyrowitz, "Building a High-Performance Culture: A Fresh Look at Performance Management," *SHRM Foundations Effective Practice Guidelines Series,* July 24, 2012, 9.

32. T. Sitzmann and S. K. Johnson, "The Best Laid Plans: Examining the Condition under Which a Planning Intervention Improves Learning and Reduces Attrition," *Journal of Applied Psychology,* September 2012, 967–981.

33. Adapted from C. Downing, N. Capriola, and S. Greller, "Preventing Credit Card Fraud: A Goal-Setting and Prompting Intervention to Increase Cashiers' ID-Checking Behavior," *Journal of Organizational Behavior Management,* 2018, 38, 335–344.

34. Adapted from, "Total Rewards Model," *WorldatWork,* 2015, https://www.worldatwork.org/aboutus/html/aboutus-whatis.jsp.

35. E. R. Shell, "The Employer-Surveillance State," *The Atlantic,* October 15, 2018, https://www.theatlantic.com/business/archive/2018/10/employee-surveillance/568159/.

36. D. L. Tomczak, L. A. Lanzo, and H. Aguinis, "Evidence-based Recommendations for Employee Performance Monitoring," *Business Horizons,* 2018, 61, 251–259.

37. L. Katz, "Monitoring Employee Productivity: Proceed with Caution," *SHRM,* June 1, 2015, https://www.shrm.org/publications/hrmagazine/editorialcontent/2015/0615/pages/0615-employee-monitoring.aspx

38. L. Katz, "Monitoring Employee Productivity: Proceed with Caution," *SHRM,* June 1, 2015, https://www.shrm.org/publications/hrmagazine/editorialcontent/2015/0615/pages/0615-employee-monitoring.aspx.

39. M. Schlanenstein, "UPS Crunches Data to Make Routes More Efficient, Save Gas," *Bloomberg Businessweek,* October 30, 2013, http://www.bloomberg.com/news/articles/2013-10-30/ups-uses-big-data-to-make-routes-more-efficient-save-gas.

40. D. L. Tomczak, L. A. Lanzo, and H. Aguinis, "Evidence-based Recommendations for Employee Performance Monitoring," *Business Horizons,* 2018, 61, 251–259.

41. L. Katz, "Monitoring Employee Productivity: Proceed with Caution," *SHRM,* June 1, 2015, https://www.shrm.org/publications/hrmagazine/editorialcontent/2015/0615/pages/0615-employee-monitoring.aspx.

42. D. L. Tomczak, L. A. Lanzo, and H. Aguinis, "Evidence-based Recommendations for Employee Performance Monitoring," *Business Horizons,* 2018, 61, 251–259.

43. C. E. Thiel, A. E. MacDougall, and Z. Bagdasarov, "Big (Benevolent) Brother: Overcoming the Drawbacks of Employee Monitoring Through Ethical Administration," *Organizational Dynamics,* 2018.

44. Tribune Media, "March Madness Could Cost Employers $4 Billion in Productivity," *WGNO.com,* March 14, 2018, https://wgno.com/2018/03/14/march-madness-could-cost-employers-4-billion-in-productivity/.

45. M. Dewhurst, M. Guthridge, and E. Mohr, "Motivating People: Getting Beyond Money," *McKinsey Quarterly,* November 2009, 2; K. Shaw, "GPS Tracking of Employee Devices: How Much Is Too Much?" *OnLabor.org,* May 8, 2017, https://onlabor.org/gps-tracking-of-employee-devices-how-much-is-too-much/.

46. Adapted from D. L. Tomczak, L. A. Lanzo, and H. Aguinis, "Evidence-based Recommendations for Employee Performance Monitoring," *Business Horizons,* 2018, 61, 251–259.

47. E. D. Pulakos, R. Mueller-Hanson, and S. Arad, "The Evolution of Performance Management: Searching for Value" (Annual Review of Organizational Psychology and Organizational Behavior), *Annual Reviews,* 2019, 6, 249–271.

48. A. Bryant, "He's Not Bill Gates, or Fred Astaire," *The New York Times,* February 14, 2010.

49. J. Zenger and J. Folkman, "We Like Leaders Who Underrate Themselves," *Harvard Business Review,* November 10, 2015, https://hbr.org/2015/11/we-like-leaders-who-underrate-themselves.

50. B. Wigert and J. Harter, "Re-Engineering Performance Management," Gallup, 2018, https://www.gallup.com/workplace/238064/re-engineering-performance-management.aspx.

51. Christopher D. Lee, "Management Tools," *SHRM,* November 01, 2006, https://www.shrm.org/hr-today/news/hr-magazine/pages/1106managementtools.aspx.

52. Anne D'innocenzio, and Rachel Beck, "Wal-Mart CEO Talks Leadership, Life," Associated Press, February 6, 2011.

53. V. Lipman, "65% of Employees Want More Feedback (So Why Don't They Get It?)," *Forbes.com,* August 8, 2016, https://www.forbes.com/sites/victorlipman/2016/08/08/65-of-employees-want-more-feedback-so-why-dont-they-get-it/#5d992f2c914a.

54. B. Huisman, N. Saab, J. Van Driel, and P. Van den Broek, "Peer Feedback on Academic Writing: Undergraduate Students' Peer Feedback Role, Peer Feedback Perceptions, and Essay Performance," *Assessment & Evaluation in Higher Education,* 2018, 43, 955–968.

55. Interview with Zappos employee Lori Johnson on April 17, 2019.

56. S. Heathfield, "Find Out How Zappos Reinforces Its Company Culture," *TheBalanceCareers.com,* September 21, 2018, https://www.thebalancecareers.com/zappos-company-culture-1918813.

57. E. D. Pulakos, *Performance Management: A New Approach for Driving Business Results* (West Sussex, UK: Wiley-Blackwell, 2009), 15; and interview with Zappos employee Lori Johnson on April 17, 2019.

58. E. D. Pulakos, *Performance Management: A New Approach for Driving Business Results* (West Sussex, UK: Wiley-Blackwell, 2009), 15; and interview with Zappos employee Lori Johnson on April 17, 2019.

59. For complete details, see P. M. Podsakoff and J.-L. Farh, "Effects of Feedback Sign and Credibility on Goal Setting and Task Performance," *Organizational Behavior and Human Decision Processes,* August 1989, 45–67.

60. S. Berinato, "Negative Feedback Rarely Leads to Improvement," *Harvard Business Review,* January–February, 2018, 1–3.

61. Adapted from T. Eurich, "The Right Way to Respond to Negative Feedback," *Harvard Business Review,* May 31, 2018, https://hbr.org/2018/05/the-right-way-to-respond-to-negative-feedback.

62. Adapted from J. Miller, "Four Steps to Giving Effective Feedback at Work," *Forbes.com,* October 25, 2018, https://www.forbes.com/sites/forbeshumanresourcescouncil/2018/10/25/four-steps-to-giving-effective-feedback-at-work/#15cb517368ec.

63. These disadvantages are based on N. R. F. Maier, "Assets and Liabilities in Group Problem Solving: The Need for an Integrative Function," *Psychological Review,* July 1967, 239–249; and C. R. Sunstein and R. Hastie, "The New Science of Group Decision Making," *Harvard Business Review,* December 2014, 91–98.

64. For a comprehensive collection of articles and research related to feedback, see "Guide to Giving Effective Feedback," *Harvard Business Review*, February 9, 2011.

65. S. Denning, "The Netflix Pressure-Cooker: A Culture that Drives Performance," *Forbes.com*, October 26, 2018, https://www.forbes.com/sites/stephaniedenning/2018/10/26/the-netflix-pressure-cooker-a-culture-that-drives-performance/#2275a16a151a.

66. B. Wigert and J. Harter, "Re-Engineering Performance Management," Gallup, 2018, https://www.gallup.com/workplace/238064/re-engineering-performance-management.aspx.

67. A. Reitman and S. Benatti, "Mentoring versus Coaching: What's the Difference," *Training and Development*, August 8, 2014, https://www.td.org/Publications/Blogs/Human-Capital-Blog/2014/08/Mentoring-Versus-Coaching-Whats-the-Difference.

68. Mark Wayland, "Providing Positive Feedback to Your Sales Stars," *Association for Talent Development (ATD)*, August 17, 2012, https://www.td.org/insights/effective-coaching-connections.

69. B. Wigert and J. Harter, "Re-Engineering Performance Management," Gallup, 2018, https://www.gallup.com/workplace/238064/re-engineering-performance-management.aspx.

70. A. Konrad, "This VC Firm is Gifting Founders 1% of Every Dollar Invested to Spend on Coaching and Mental Health," *Forbes.com*, September 10, 2018, https://www.forbes.com/sites/alexkonrad/2018/09/10/vc-firm-pledges-1-percent-to-founder-health/#701a63572ec1.

71. Adapted from B. Wigert and J. Harter, "Re-Engineering Performance Management," Gallup, 2018, https://www.gallup.com/workplace/238064/re-engineering-performance-management.aspx.

72. "Coaching in a Business Environment," *SHRM Templates*, March 21, 2013.

73. I. Fulmer and W. Walker, "More Bang for the Buck? Personality Traits as Moderators of Responsiveness to Pay-for-Performance," *Human Performance*, 2015, 40–65.

74. A. Goodnough, "Kaiser Permanente's New Medical School Will Waive Tuition for Its First 5 Classes," *The New York Times*, February 19, 2019, https://www.nytimes.com/2019/02/19/health/kaiser-medical-school-free-.html.

75. J. Del Rey, "Andreesen Horowitz Schools You on Your Phony Startup Metrics," *Re/code*, August 22, 2015, http://recode.net/2015/08/22/andreessen-horowitz-schools-you-on-your-phony-startup-metrics/; see also "16 Startup Metrics," *Andreesen Horowitz*, http://a16z.com/2015/08/21/16-metrics/; L. Gannes. "Andreessen and Mixpanel Call for an End to 'Bullshit Metrics,'" *All Things D*, December 17, 2012, http://allthingsd.com/20121217/andreessen-and-mixpanel-call-for-an-end-to-bullshit-metrics/, accessed April 12, 2013.

76. Adapted from B. McKay, "The Six Most Effective Social Media Metrics to Understand Your Campaign's Success," *Forbes.com*, July 14, 2018, https://www.forbes.com/sites/forbesagencycouncil/2017/07/14/the-six-most-effective-social-media-metrics-to-understand-your-campaigns-success/#2b2b8d9c64cb.

77. L. Gannes, "Andreessen and Mixpanel Call for an End to 'Bullshit Metrics,'" *All Things D*, December 17, 2012, http://allthingsd.com/20121217/andreessen-and-mixpanel-call-for-an-end-to-bullshit-metrics/ (accessed April 12, 2013).

78. Convenience Store News, "QuikTrip Makes Inaugural List of Best Millennial Workplaces," http://www.csnews.com/industry-news-and-trends/corporate-store-operations/quiktrip-makes-inaugural-list-best-millennial-workplaces (accessed June 14, 2019).

79. C. Weaver, "Treatment Woes Can Bolster Hospital's Profit," *The Wall Street Journal*, April 16, 2016, http://www.wsj.com/articles/SB10001424127887324345804578426693303833964.

80. D. Agarwal, J. Bersin, and G. Lahiri, "New Rewards: Personalized, Agile, and Holistic," *Deloitte Insights*, March 28, 2018, https://www2.deloitte.com/insights/us/en/focus/human-capital-trends/2018/personalized-incentives-talent-management-strategies.html.

81. © 2014 Angelo Kinicki and Mel Fugate.

82. M. C. Bush and S. Lewis-Kulin, "100 Best Companies to Work For 2018," *Fortune*, March 1, 2018, 53–78; M. Bush and C. Tkaczyk, "100 Best Companies to Work for 2019," *Fortune*, March 1, 2019, 57–80.

83. "How We Do It: Performance Management Tips from the Top," *McKinsey Quarterly*, 2018, 2, 52–59.

84. Hilcorp company website, Hilcorp.com.

85. "Taking Aim with Talent How to Lead a People-First Company," *McKinsey Quarterly*, no. 2 (2018): 52–59, https://www.mckinsey.com/~/media/McKinsey/McKinsey%20Quarterly/Digital%20Newsstand/2018%20Issues%20McKinsey%20Quarterly/Q2-2018_McK-Quarterly-Full-Issue.ashx.

86. A. Colquitt, "A Pleasant Death of Performance-Based Pay," *Administration*, August 31, 2015, http://www.hrps.org/blogpost/1297410/225487/A-Pleasant-Death-of-Performance-Based-Pay.

87. Adapted from J. Carpenter, "Millions Spent on Incentives Failed to Get Better Teachers in High-Need HISD Schools," *Houston Chronicle*, December 7, 2018, https://www.houstonchronicle.com/news/education/article/Millions-spent-on-incentives-failed-to-get-better-13450913.php.

88. P. Gooderman, M. Fenton-O'Creevy, R. Croucher, and M. Brookes, "A Multilevel Analysis of the Use of Individual Pay-for-Performance Systems," *Journal of Management*, April 2018, 1479–1504.

89. J. Han, K. Bartol, and S. Kim, "Tightening Up the Pay-for-Performance Linkage: Roles of Contingent Reward Leadership and Profit-Sharing in the Cross-Level Influence of Individual Pay-for-Performance," *Journal of Applied Psychology*, 2015, 417–430.

90. "Variable Pay Trends into 2018: Who Gets It, What Types and Why?" *Payscale.com*, April 30, 2018, https://www.payscale.com/compensation-today/2018/04/variable-pay-trends.

91. A. J. Nyberg, M. A. Maltarich, D. Abdusalam, S. M. Essman, and O. Cragun, "Collective Pay for Performance: A Cross-Disciplinary Review and Meta-Analysis," *Journal of Management*, 2018, 44, 2433–2472.

92. "Variable Pay Trends into 2018: Who Gets It, What Types and Why?" *Payscale.com*, April 30, 2018, https://www.payscale.com/compensation-today/2018/04/variable-pay-trends.

93. "Variable Pay Trends into 2018: Who Gets It, What Types and Why?" *Payscale.com*, April 30, 2018, https://www.payscale.com/compensation-today/2018/04/variable-pay-trends.

94. L. Brunelli, "What Is a Per-Piece Pay Rate or Piecework?" *TheBalanceCareers.com*, September 9, 2018, https://www.thebalancecareers.com/what-is-per-piece-work-3542479.

95. S. Strauss, "Get Your Gig: Here Are the 9 Best Sites to Visit for Freelance or Contract Work," *USAToday.com*, July 12, 2018, https://www.usatoday.com/story/money/columnist/strauss/2018/07/12/strauss-column-gig-economy/773914002/.

96. S. Rossman, "Girl Scout Cookies Sales Start Today, The Popular Cookie Is . . .", *USAToday.com*, January 3, 2018, https://www.usatoday.com/story/news/nation-now/2018/01/03/girl-scout-cookie-sales-start-today-best-selling-cookie/1000299001/.

97. Forbes Business Development Council, "Nine Commission Structures That Will Keep Your Sales Team Motivated," *Forbes.com*, August 1, 2018, https://www.forbes.com/sites/forbesbusinessdevelopmentcouncil/2018/08/01/nine-commission-structures-that-will-keep-your-sales-team-motivated/#671b7dda4cd8.

98. Forbes Media LLC, "Nine Commission Structures That Will Keep Your Sales Team Motivated," https://www.forbes.com/sites/forbesbusinessdevelopmentcouncil/2018/08/01/nine-commission-structures-that-will-keep-your-sales-team-motivated/#671b7dda4cd8 (accessed June 14, 2019).

99. K. Maas, "Do Corporate Social Performance Targets in Executive Compensation Contribute to Corporate Social Performance?" *Journal of Business Ethics*, 2018, 148, 573–585.

100. Adapted from S. Miller, "Study: Keys to Effective Performance Pay," *Society for Human Resource Management*, December 15, 2010.

101. E. D. Pulakos, R. Mueller-Hanson, and S. Arad, "The Evolution of Performance Management: Searching for Value" (Annual Review of Organizational Psychology and Organizational Behavior), *Annual Reviews*, 2019, 6, 249–271.

102. See E. L. Thorndike, *Educational Psychology: The Psychology of Learning*, Vol. II (New York: Columbia University Teachers College, 1913).

103. See B. F. Skinner, *The Behavior of Organisms* (New York: Appleton-Century-Crofts, 1938).

104. G. C. Hazan and D. Mattioli, "BP Links Pay to Safety in Fourth Quarter," *The Wall Street Journal*, October 19, 2010.

105. W. Neuman, "Flights at JFK Sit on Tarmac for Hours," *The New York Times*, December 29, 2010.

106. D. Gilbertson, "Allegiant Air Fined $225,000 for Keeping Planes Too Hot During Tarmac Delays," *USAToday.com*, October 5, 2018, https://www.usatoday.com/story/travel/flights/todayinthesky/2018/10/05/allegiant-fined-225-k-dot-hot-planes-during-tarmac-delays/1534101002/.

107. R. Channick, "Study: Rule to Prevent Tarmac Delays Backfires for Airline Passengers," *ChicagoTribune.com*, January 5, 2016, https://www.chicagotribune.com/business/ct-tarmac-delays-0105-biz-20160104-story.html.

108. Kaiser Family Foundation, "2018 Employer Health Benefits Survey," *KFF.org*, October 3, 2018, https://www.kff.org/report-section/2018-employer-health-benefits-survey-summary-of-findings/.

109. B. C. Skaggs, C. C. Manz, M. C. B. Lyle, and C. L. Pearce, "On the Folly of Punishing A While Hoping for A: Exploring Punishment in Organizations," *Journal of Organizational Behavior*, March 2018, 812–815.

110. S. Jayachandran, "Lottery-Like Prizes Coax Savings. What's the Risk in Expanding Them?" *The New York Times*, December 21, 2018, https://www.nytimes.com/2018/12/21/business/lotteries-savings-accounts.html.

111. S. Jayachandran, "Lottery-Like Prizes Coax Savings. What's the Risk in Expanding Them?" *The New York Times*, December 21, 2018, https://www.nytimes.com/2018/12/21/business/lotteries-savings-accounts.html.

112. M. Egan, "The Two-Year Wells Fargo Horror Story Just Won't End," *MoneyCNN.com*, September 7, 2018, https://money.cnn.com/2018/09/07/news/companies/wells-fargo-scandal-two-years/index.html.

113. S. Cowley and J. A. Kingson, "Wells Fargo to Claw Back $75 Million from Two Former Executives," *The New York Times*, April 10, 2017, https://www.nytimes.com/2017/04/10/business/wells-fargo-pay-executives-accounts-scandal.html.

114. M. Egan, "The Two-Year Wells Fargo Horror Story Just Won't End," *MoneyCNN.com*, September 7, 2018, https://money.cnn.com/2018/09/07/news/companies/wells-fargo-scandal-two-years/index.html.

115. G. Morgenson, "Wells Fargo Forced Unwanted Auto Insurance on Borrowers," *The New York Times*, July 27, 2017, https://www.nytimes.com/2017/07/27/business/wells-fargo-unwanted-auto-insurance.html.

116. E. Wolff-Mann, "Every Wells Fargo Consumer Scandal Since 2015: A Timeline," *YahooFinance.com*, August 8, 2018, https://finance.yahoo.com/news/every-wells-fargo-consumer-scandal-since-2015-timeline-194946222.html.

117. S. Cowley and J. A. Kingson, "Wells Fargo to Claw Back $75 Million from Two Former Executives," *The New York Times*, April 10, 2017, https://www.nytimes.com/2017/04/10/business/wells-fargo-pay-executives-accounts-scandal.html.

118. Elizabeth C. Tippett, "How Wells Fargo Encouraged Employees to Commit Fraud," The Conversation Media Group Ltd., October 7, 2016, https://theconversation.com/how-wells-fargo-encouraged-employees-to-commit-fraud-66615.

119. M. Corkery and S. Cowley, "Wells Fargo Warned Workers Against Sham Accounts, but 'They Needed a Paycheck,'" *The New York Times*, September 16, 2016, https://www.nytimes.com/2016/09/17/business/dealbook/wells-fargo-warned-workers-against-fake-accounts-but-they-needed-a-paycheck.html.

120. *CBS This Morning*, January 25, 2019.

121. R. Merle, "After Years of Apologies for Customer Abuses, Wells Fargo CEO Tim Sloan Suddenly Steps Down," *The Washington Post*, March 28, 2019, https://www.washingtonpost.com/business/2019/03/28/wells-fargo-ceo-tim-sloan-step-down-immediately/?utm_term5.27bf62d146f8.

122. Adapated from S. Milligan, "Are Salary Histories History?" *HR Magazine*, March 2018, 54–59.

CHAPTER 7

1. J. Rogers and C. Ciaccia, "NASA's Insight Mars Lander Arrives on the Red Planet, Ends Successful Journey," *Foxnews.com*, November 26, 2018, https://www.foxnews.com/science/nasas-insight-mars-lander-set-for-seven-minutes-of-terror-as-it-prepares-to-land-on-red-planet.

2. Adapted from E. H. Jensen, "Contagious Positivity: The Secret Weapon of Successful Leaders," *LinkedIn*, July 20, 2018, https://www.linkedin.com/pulse/contagious-positivity-secret-weapon-successful-emil-hauch-jensen/.

3. F. Luthans and B. J. Avolio, "The 'Point' of Positive Organizational Behavior," *Journal of Organizational Behavior*, 2009, 291–307.

4. M. Meyer, "The Evolution and Challenges of the Concept of Organizational Virtuousness in Positive Organizational Scholarship," *Journal of Business Ethics*, 153, 2018, 245–264.

5. Kim Cameron and Jane Dutton, *Positive Organizational Scholarship: Foundations of a New Discipline* (San Francisco: Berrett-Koehler Publishers, 2003).

6. Kim Cameron and Jane Dutton, *Positive Organizational Scholarship: Foundations of a New Discipline* (San Francisco: Berrett-Koehler Publishers, 2003).

7. B. L. Fredrickson and T. Joiner, "Reflections on Positive Emotions and Upward Spirals," *Perspectives on Psychological Science*, March 2018, 194–199.

8. J. Halbesleben and A. Wheeler, "To Invest or Not? The Role of Coworker Support and Trust in Daily Reciprocal Gain Spirals of Helping Behavior," *Journal of Applied Psychology*, September 2015, 1628–1650.

9. M. Meyer, "The Evolution and Challenges of the Concept of Organizational Virtuousness in Positive Organizational Scholarship," *Journal of Business Ethics*, 153, 2018, 245–264.

10. S. Koeppen, "'Not Letting Each Other Quit': Two Women Hold Hands, Motivate One Another to Finish Pittsburgh Marathon," *Pittsburgh.CBSlocal.com*, May 7, 2019, https://pittsburgh.cbslocal.com/2019/05/07/marathon-finishers-hold-hands/.

11. M. Meyer, "The Evolution and Challenges of the Concept of Organizational Virtuousness in Positive Organizational Scholarship," *Journal of Business Ethics*, 153, 2018, 245–264.

12. Kim Cameron, Carlos Mora, Trevor Leutscher, and Margaret Calarco, "Effects of Positive Practices on Organizational Effectiveness," *The Journal of Applied Behavioral Science* 47, no. 3 (August 2011): 266–308. https://DOI:10.1177/ 0021886310395514.

13. M. Meyer, "The Evolution and Challenges of the Concept of Organizational Virtuousness in Positive Organizational Scholarship," *Journal of Business Ethics*, 153, 2018, 245–264.

14. A. Whillans, "Time for Happiness," *Harvard Business Review*, January 2019, https://hbr.org/cover-story/2019/01/time-for-happiness.

15. G. Spreitzer and K. Cameron, "Applying the POS Lens to Bring Out the Best in Organizations," *Organizational Dynamics*, 2012, 85–88.

16. See P. M. Gollwitzer, "Implementation Intentions," *American Psychologist*, July 1999, 493–503.

17. See S. Pinker, "Mind & Matter: An Attitude of Gratitude Brings Better Health," *The Wall Street Journal*, December 19–20, 2015, C2.

18. Research on generosity is discussed by S. Begley, "Stingy Brain, Generous Brain," *Mindful*, August 2016, 20–22.

19. E. Bernstein, "An Emotion We Need More Of," *The Wall Street Journal*, March 22, 2016.

20. See E. Bernstein, "An Emotion We Need More Of," *The Wall Street Journal*, March 22, 2016, D1, D4.

21. See R. Hanson and R. Mendius, *Buddha's Brain* (Oakland, CA: New Harbinger Publications, 2009).

22. G. Spreitzer and C. Porath, "Creating Sustained Performance," *Harvard Business Review*, January–February 2012, 3–9.

23. Adapted from G. Spreitzer and C. Porath, "Creating Sustained Performance," *Harvard Business Review*, January–February 2012, 3–9.

24. E. Fry and M. Heimer, "Change the World," *Fortune*, September 2018, 60–78.

25. A. Bryant, "Three Good Hires? He'll Pay More for One Who's Great," *The New York Times*, March 13, 2010, http://www.nytimes.com/2010/03/14/business/14corners.html? pagewanted=all&_r=0, accessed April 1, 2013.

26. K. Gurchiek, "Chief Relaxation Officer, Fairy Godmother: Job Titles Get Creative," *SHRM.org*, March 29, 2018, https://www.shrm.org/hr-today/news/hr-news/pages/chief-relaxation-officer-fairy-godmother-job-titles-get-creative.aspx.

27. A. Hirsch, "Doing Well by Doing Good," *SHRM.org*, January 5, 2019, https://www.shrm.org/hr-today/news/all-things-work/Pages/Doing-Well-by-Doing-Good.aspx.

28. M. Heimer, "Doing Well by Doing Good: 5 Stocks to Buy for 2019," *Yahoo Finance*, December 5, 2018, https://finance.yahoo.com/news/doing-well-doing-good-5-135901765.html?soc_src=social-sh&soc_trk=ma.

29. Walmart.com, https://corporate.walmart.com/2016grr/enhancing-sustainability/moving-toward-a-zero-waste-future (accessed January 27, 2019).

30. V. Chang, P. Kuo, and P. Wai, "Doing Well by Doing Good: Linking Access with Quality," *The American Journal of Surgery*, 2015, 457–462.

31. R. Derousseau, "Good Behavior, Heavenly Returns," *Fortune*, September 1, 2018, 45–48.

32. R. Derousseau, "Good Behavior, Heavenly Returns," *Fortune*, September 1, 2018, 45–48.

33. A. Sorkin, "A Fund to Feel Good About," *The New York Times*, June 15, 2018, 7.

34. M. C. Bush and S. Lewis-Kulin, "100 Best Companies to Work For 2018," *Fortune*, March 2018, 53–78. And M. C. Bush and C. Tkaczyk, "100 Best Companies to Work For 2019," *Fortune*, March 2019, 57–80.

35. R. Feloni, "15 Major Companies That Treat Employees Well, Value Their Customers, and Put Their Communities First," *BusinessInsider.com*, January 30, 2018, https://www.businessinsider.com/best-companies-of-2017-ranking-just-capital-2018-1.

36. Michael Blanding, "Amazon vs. Whole Foods: When Cultures Collide," *Harvard Business School Working Knowledge*, May 14, 2018, https://hbswk.hbs.edu/item/amazon-vs-whole-foods-when-cultures-collide.

37. Barbara L. Fredrickson, *Positivity* (New York: Three Rivers Press, 2009).

38. X. Zheng, W. Zhu, H. Zhao, and C. Zhang, "Employee Well-Being in Organizations: Theoretical Model, Scale Development, and Cross-Cultural Validation," *Journal of Organizational Behavior*, 2015, 621–644.

39. S. Barsade and O. O'Neill, "Manage Your Emotional Culture," *Harvard Business Review*, January–February 2016, https://hbr.org/2016/01/manage-your-emotional-culture.

40. O. Siu, F. Cheung, and S. Lui, "Linking Positive Emotions to Work Well-Being and Turnover Intention among Hong Kong Police Officers: The Role of Psychological Capital," *Journal of Happiness Studies*, 2015, 367–380.

41. Barbara L. Fredrickson, *Positivity* (New York: Three Rivers Press, 2009).

42. D. Barnes, N. Ponder, and C. Hopkins, "The Impact of Perceived Customer Delight on the Frontline Employee," *Journal of Business Research*, 2015, 433–441.

43. A. Knight and N. Eisenkraft, "Positive Is Usually Good, Negative Is Not Always Bad: The Effects of Group Affect on Social Integration and Task Performance," *Journal of Applied Psychology*, 2015, 1214–1227.

44. A. Shrira, E. Bodner, and Y. Pagli, "Positivity Ratio of Flourishing Individuals: Examining the Moderation Effects of Methodological Variations and Chronological Age," *The Journal of Positive Psychology*, 2016, 109–123.

45. A. Shrira, E. Bodner, and Y. Pagli, "Positivity Ratio of Flourishing Individuals: Examining the Moderation Effects of Methodological Variations and Chronological Age," *The Journal of Positive Psychology*, 2016, 109–123.

46. See D. Goleman, Focus: *The Hidden Driver of Excellence* (New York: Harper Collins, 2013).

47. John W. Michel, Michael Tews, and David Allen, "Fun in the Workplace: A Review and Expanded Theoretical Perspective," *Human Resource Management Review* 29, no. 1 (March 2019): 98–110. https://doi.org/10.1016/j.hrmr.2018.03.001.

48. J. W. Michel, M. J. Tewes, and D. G. Allen, "Fun in the Workplace: A Review and Expanded Theoretical Perspective," *Human Resource Management Review*, 29, 2019, 98–110.

49. E. Chester, "Southwest Airlines Is Dead Serious about Employee Fun," *ericchester.com,* https://ericchester.com/southwest-airlines-is-dead-serious-about-employee-fun/. Downloaded January 6, 2019.

50. Adapted from J. W. Michel, M. J. Tewes, and D. G. Allen, "Fun in the Workplace: A Review and Expanded Theoretical Perspective," *Human Resource Management Review*, 29, 2019, 98–110.

51. Adapted from J. W. Michel, M. J. Tewes, and D. G. Allen, "Fun in the Workplace: A Review and Expanded Theoretical Perspective," *Human Resource Management Review*, 29, 2019, 98–110.

52. Advice in this section comes from B. L. Fredrickson, *Positivity* (New York: Three Rivers Press, 2009).

53. Brian Pinelli, "In Pole Vault, Sam Kendricks Is a Team Player," *The New York Times Company,* July 4, 2018, https://www.nytimes.com/2018/07/04/sports/pole-vault-sam-kendricks.html.

54. Advice in this section comes from B. L. Fredrickson, *Positivity* (New York: Three Rivers Press, 2009).

55. Jon Kabat-Zinn, "Mindfulness-Based Interventions in Context: Past, Present, and Future," *Clinical Psychology Science and Practice* 10, no. 2 (June 2003): 144–56. http://dx.doi.org/10.1093/clipsy.bpg016.

56. F. C. M. Geisler, M. N. Becholdt, N. Oberlander, and M. Schacht-Jablonowsky, "The Benefits of a Mindfulness Exercise in a Performance Situation," *Psychological Reports*, 121, 853–876.

57. A. Walton, "Yoga and Meditation Continue to Gain Popularity in the US," *Forbes.com,* November 8, 2018, https://www.forbes.com/sites/alicegwalton/2018/11/08/yoga-and-meditation-continue-to-gain-popularity-in-the-u-s/#4f67068d3782.

58. Fidelity, "Making Well-Being Work," *Fidelity.com,* https://workplace.fidelity.com/sites/default/files/nbgh-wellness-survey-results.pdf.

59. InsightTimer website, *InsightTimer.com* (accessed January 6, 2019).

60. M. Levin, "Why Google, Nike, and Apple Love Mindfulness Training, and How You Can Easily Love It Too," *Inc.com,* June 12, 2017, https://www.inc.com/marissa-levin/why-google-nike-and-apple-love-mindfulness-training-and-how-you-can-easily-love-html.

61. A. LaVito, "Meditation App Headspace on Track to Double Corporate Clients, Bring Mindfulness to Work," *CNBC.com,* Sunday, September 2, 2018, https://www.cnbc.com/ 2018/09/02/companies-are-turning-to-headspace-to-help-their-workers-meditate.html.

62. David Gelles, "Mark Bertolini of Aetna on Yoga, Meditation and Darth Vader," The New York Times Company, September 21, 2018, https://www.nytimes.com/2018/09/21/business/mark-bertolini-aetna-corner-office.html.

63. C. Connley, "The Surprising Way Office Yoga Helped This CEO Raise the Minimum Wage of His Company," *CNBC.com,* Friday, October 12, 2018, https://www.cnbc.com/2018/10/12/aetna-how-office-yoga-helped-one-ceo-raise-his-companys-minimum-wage.html.

64. Angelica LaVito, "Meditation App Headspace on Track to Double Corporate Clients, Bring Mindfulness to Work," *CNBC LLC,* September 2, 2018, https://www.cnbc.com/2018/09/02/companies-are-turning-to-headspace-to-help-their-workers-meditate.html.

65. D. J. Good, C. J. Lyddy, T. M. Glomb, J. E. Bono, K. W. Brown, M. K. Duffy, R. A Baer, J. A Brewer, and S. W. Lazar, "Contemplating Mindfulness at Work: An Integrative Review," *Journal of Management*, 43, 114–142.

66. J. DeMers, "5 Successful Business Leaders That Have Used Meditation to Improve Productivity, Creativity, and Business Acumen," *Businessinsider.com,* April 3, 2018, https://www.businessinsider.com/5-successful-leaders-that-have-used-meditation-to-be-more-productive-2018-4.

67. D. J. Good, C. J. Lyddy, T. M. Glomb, J. E. Bono, K. W. Brown, M. K. Duffy, R. A Baer, J. A Brewer, and S. W. Lazar, "Contemplating Mindfulness at Work: An Integrative Review," *Journal of Management*, 43, 114–142.

68. His Holiness The Dalai Lama, and Laurens van den Muyzenberg, *The Leader's Way: The Art of Making the Right Decisions in Our Careers, Our Companies, and the World at Large* (New York: Crown Publishing Group, 2009).

69. See S. Hickman, "Am I Doing This Right?" *Mindful,* August 2016, 36–37; J. Kabat-Zinn, *Wherever You Go There You Are* (New York: Hyperion Books, 1994); R. Hanson and R. Mendius, *Buddha's Brain: The Practical Neuroscience of Happiness, Love, and Wisdom* (Oakland, CA: New Harbinger Publications, 2009); and His Holiness the Dalai Lama and L. V. D. Muyzenberg, *The Leader's Way* (New York: Broadway Books, 2009).

70. J. J. Arch and M. G. Craske, "Mechanisms of Mindfulness: Emotion Regulation Following a Focused Breathing Induction," *Behavior Research and Therapy,* 2006, 1849–1858; and D. M. Levy, J. O. Wobbrock, A. W. Kaszniak, and M. Ostergren, "The Effects of Mindfulness Meditation Training on Multitasking in a High-Stress Information Environment," *Graphics Interface,* May 2012, 45–52.

71. R. Hanson and R. Mendius, *Buddha's Brain: The Practical Neuroscience of Happiness, Love, and Wisdom* (Oakland, CA: New Harbinger Publications, 2009).

72. S. L. Shapiro, L. E. Carlson, J. A. Astin, and B. Freedman, "Mechanisms of Mindfulness," *Journal of Clinical Psychology,* March 2006, 373–386.

73. See C. Morey-Nase, "Mind Where You Walk," *Mindful,* August 2016, 72–76; and His Holiness the Dalai Lama and L. V. D. Muyzenberg, *The Leader's Way* (New York: Broadway Books, 2009).

74. See K. Kennedy, "Meditation Made Easy," *The ArizonaRepublic,* March 7, 2016, 1d, 3d.

75. R. Bachman, "The Gym Class Where You Never, Ever Sweat," *The Wall Street Journal,* March 23, 2016, D1, D2.

76. T. Pitichat, R. Reichard, A. Kea-Edwards, E. Middleton, and S. M. Norman, "Psychological Capital for Leader Development," *Journal of Leadership & Organizational Studies,* February 2018, 25, 47–62.

77. S. A. Davis, C. E. Fretwell, and M. Scharaeder, "Enhancing Expatriate Success: A Psychological Capital Perspective," *Organization Development Journal,* Summer 2018, 36, 39–48.

78. A. Newman, D. Ucbasaran, F. Zhu, and G. Hirst, "Psychological Capital: A Review and Synthesis," *Journal of Organizational Behavior,* 2014, 120–138.

79. J. Ahmad, M. R. Athar, R. I. Azam, M. R. W. Hamstra, and M. Hanif, "A Resource Perspective on Abusive Supervision and Extra-Role Behaviors: The Role of Subordinates' Psychological Capital," *Journal of Leadership and Organizational Studies,* 2019, 26, 73–86.

80. V. E. Jancenelle, "Organizational Psychological Capital During Earnings Conference Calls: Mitigating Shareholders' Sell-Off in the Face of Earnings Surprises," *Journal of Leadership and Organizational Studies,* 2018, 25, 469–480.

81. J. B. Avey, F. Luthans, and S. M. Jensen, "Psychological Capital: A Positive Resource for Combating Employee Stress and Turnover," *Human Resource Management,* September–October 2009, 677–693.

82. M. Helft, "Silicon Valley's Stealth Power," *Fortune,* February 27, 2014, http://money.cnn.com/2014/02/27/technology/ben-horowitz.pr.fortune/.

83. Miguel Helft, "Silicon Valley's Stealth Power," *Fortune Media IP Limited,* February 27, 2014, https://fortune.com/ 2014/02/27/silicon-valleys-stealth-power/.

84. H. P. Madrid, M. T. Diaz, S. Leka, and P. I. Leiva, "A Finer Grained Approach to Psychological Capital and Work Performance," *Journal of Business Psychology,* 2018, 33, 461–477.

85. K. Strauss, K. Niven, C. McClelland, and B. Cheung, "Hope and Optimism in the Face of Change: Contributions to Task Adaptivity," *Journal of Business Psychology,* 2015, 733–745.

86. K. Thompson, G. Lemmon, and T. Walter, "Employee Engagement and Positive Psychological Capital," *Organizational Dynamics,* 2015, 185–195.

87. J. B. Avey, F. Luthans, and S. M. Jensen, "Psychological Capital: A Positive Resource for Combating Employee Stress and Turnover," *Human Resource Management,* September–October 2009, 682.

88. A. Rego, K. C. Yam, B. P. Owens, J. S. P. Story, M. Cunha, D. Bluhm, and M. P. Lopes, "Conveyed Leader PsyCap Predicting Leader Effectiveness Through Positive Energy," *Journal of Management,* April 2019, 45, 1689–1712; and J. B. Avey, F. Luthans, and S. M. Jensen, "Psychological Capital: A Positive Resource for Combating Employee Stress and Turnover," *Human Resource Management,* September–October 2009, 682.

89. K. Thompson, G. Lemmon, and T. Walter, "Employee Engagement and Positive Psychological Capital," *Organizational Dynamics,* 2015, 185–195.

90. "The Importance of Addressing Resilience in the Workplace: An Interview with Kathy Gerwig," *American Journal of Health Promotion,* March 1, 2018, 832–833.

91. CEO Roundtable of the American Heart Association, "Resilience in the Workplace: An Evidence Review and Implications for Practice," American Heart Association, May 2018, http://ceoroundtable.heart.org/wp-content/uploads/ 2018/05/ucm_496856.pdf.

92. "The Importance of Addressing Resilience in the Workplace: An Interview with Kathy Gerwig," *American Journal of Health Promotion,* March 1, 2018, 832–833.

93. CEO Roundtable of the American Heart Association, "Resilience in the Workplace: An Evidence Review and Implications for Practice," American Heart Association, May 2018, http://ceoroundtable.heart.org/wp-content/uploads/ 2018/05/ucm_496856.pdf.

94. J. B. Avey, F. Luthans, and S. M. Jensen, "Psychological Capital: A Positive Resource for Combating Employee Stress and Turnover," *Human Resource Management,* September–October 2009, 681.

95. D. L. Devitt and D. L. Schacter, "An Optimistic Outlook Creates a Rosy Past: The Impact of Episodic Simulation on Subsequent Memory," *Psychological Science,* June 2018, 29, 936–946.

96. F. Luthans, J. B. Avey, B. J. Avolio, and S. J. Peterson, "The Development and Resulting Performance Impact of Positive Psychological Capital," *Human Resource Development Quarterly,* Spring 2010, 41–66.

97. F. Luthans, J. B. Avey, B. J. Avolio, and S. J. Peterson, "The Development and Resulting Performance Impact of Positive Psychological Capital," *Human Resource Development Quarterly,* Spring 2010, 41–66.

98. J. B. Avey, R. J. Reichard, F. Luthans, and K. H. Mhatre, "Meta-Analysis of the Impact of Positive Psychological Capital on Employee Attitudes, Behaviors, and Performance," *Human Resource Development Quarterly*, 2011, 127–152. See also M. H. Jafri, "Psychological Capital and Innovative Behavior: An Empirical Study on Apparel Fashion Industry," *The Journal Contemporary Management Research*, 2012, 42–52.

99. S. Lavy and H. Littman-Ovadia, "My Better Self: Using Strengths at Work and Work Productivity, Organizational Citizenship Behavior, and Satisfaction," *Journal of Career Development*, February 25, 2016, http://jcd. sagepub.com/content/early/2016/02/24/0894845316634056. abstract.

100. C. Harzer and W. Ruch, "The Application of Signature Character Strengths and Positive Experiences at Work," *Journal of Happiness Studies*, 2013, 965–983.

101. B. Allan and R. Duffy, "Examining Moderators of Signature Strengths Use and Well-being: Calling in Signature Strengths Level," *Journal of Happiness Studies*, 2014, 323–337.

102. N. Dvorak, C. Deweese, and B. Ott, "Why Clifton Strengths Help Managers Lead Winning Teams," *Gallup.com*, November 30, 2018, https://www.gallup.com/workplace/245093/why-cliftonstrengths-helps-managers-lead-winning-teams.aspx.

103. J. Asplund and G. Elliot, "Employees Who Use Their Strengths Outperform Those Who Don't," Gallup, October 8, 2015, http://www.gallup.com/businessjournal/186044/employees-strengths-outperform-don. aspx.

104. J. Asplund and G. Elliot, "Employees Who Use Their Strengths Outperform Those Who Don't," Gallup, October 8, 2015, http://www.gallup.com/businessjournal/186044/employees-strengths-outperform-don. aspx.

105. Peter Flade, Jim Asplund, and Gwen Elliot, "Employees Who Use Their Strengths Outperform Those Who Don't," Gallup, Inc., October 8, 2015. https://www.gallup.com/workplace/236561/employees-strengths-out-perform-don.aspx.

106. N. S. Schutte and J. M. Malouff, "The Impact of Signature Character Strengths Interventions: A Meta-Analysis," *Journal of Happiness Studies*, 2019, 20, 1179–1196.

107. J. Asplund and G. Elliot, "Employees Who Use Their Strengths Outperform Those Who Don't," Gallup, October 8, 2015, http://www.gallup.com/businessjournal/186044/employees-strengths-outperform-don. aspx.

108. S. V. Marinova, X. Cao, and H. Park, "Constructive Organizational Values Climate and Organizational Citizenship Behaviors: A Configurational View," *Journal of Management*, May 2019, 45, 2045–2071.

109. T. M. Probst, "Organizational Safety Climate and Supervisory Safety Enforcement: Multilevel Explorations of the Causes of Accident Underreporting," *Journal of Applied Psychology*, November 2015, 1899–1907.

110. K. Alfes, A. D. Shantz, and A. Ritz, "A Multilevel Examination of the Relationship Between Role Overload and Employee Subjective Health: The Buffering Effect of Supportive Climates," *Human Resource Management*, March 2018, 57, 659–673.

111. See M. Priesemuth, M. Schminke, M. L. Ambrose, and R. Folger, "Abusive Supervision Climate: A Multiple-Mediation Model of Its Impact on Group Outcomes," *Academy of Management Journal*, October 2014, 1513–1534; and D. Meinert, "Scared Stiff: Do You Have a Workplace Culture of Fear?" *HR Magazine*, December 2015/January 2016, 12.

112. D. Galarza, "How Sweetgreen Got to $1 Billion," *Eater.com*, November 15, 2018, https://www.eater.com/2018/11/15/ 18096104/sweetgreen-1-billion-unicorn-tech-company-lifestyle-brand.

113. A. Kohll, "How to Build a Positive Company," *Forbes.com*, August 14, 2018, https://www.forbes.com/sites/alankohll/2018/08/14/how-to-build-a-positive-company-culture/#8fdf8d349b5b.

114. A. Kohll, "How to Build a Positive Company," *Forbes.com*, August 14, 2018, https://www.forbes.com/sites/alankohll/2018/08/14/how-to-build-a-positive-company-culture/#8fdf8d349b5b.

115. S. V. Marinova, X. Cao, and H. Park, "Constructive Organizational Values Climate and Organizational Citizenship Behaviors: A Configurational View," *Journal of Management*, May 2019, 45, 2045–2071; see also R. Fehr and M. J. Gelfand, "The Forgiving Organization: A Multilevel Model of Forgiveness at Work," *Academy of Management Review*, October 2012, 664–688.

116. Ryan Fehr and Michele J. Gelfand, "The Forgiving Organization: A Multilevel Model of Forgiveness at Work," *Academy of Management Review* 37, no. 4 (October 2012): 664–88. https://doi.org/10.5465/amr.2010.0497.

117. A. Peticca-Harris, "Managing Compassionately? Managerial Narratives about Grief and Compassion," *Human Relations*, March 2019, 72, 588–612.

118. G. Seijts, J. Gandz, M. Crossan, and M. Reno, "Character Matters: Character Dimensions' Impact on Leader Performance and Outcomes," *Organizational Dynamics*, January 2015, 65–74.

119. See R. R. Kehoe and P. M. Wright, "The Impact of High-Performance Human Resource Practices on Employees' Attitudes and Behaviors," *Journal of Management*, February 2013, 366–391.

120. R. Eisenberger and F. Stinglhamber, *Perceived Organizational Support: Fostering Enthusiastic and Productive Employees* (Washington, DC: APA, 2011); and J. D. Nahrgang, F. P. Morgeson, and D. A. Hofmann, "Safety at Work: A Meta-Analytic Investigation of the Link between Job Demands, Job Resources, Burnout, Engagement, and Safety Outcomes," *Journal of Applied Psychology*, January 2011, 71–94.

121. M. C. Bush and S. Lewis-Kulin, "100 Best Companies to Work For 2018," *Fortune*, March 2018, 53–78; and M. C. Bush and C. Tkaczyk, "100 Best Companies to Work For 2019," *Fortune*, March 2019, 57–80.

122. D. Gelles, "Marc Benioff of Salesforce: 'Are We Not All Concerned?'" *The New York Times*, June 15, 2018, https://www.nytimes.com/2018/06/15/business/marc-benioff-salesforce-corner-office.html.

123. K. Cameron, D. Bright, and A. Caza, "Exploring the Relationships between Organizational Virtuousness and Performance," *American Behavioral Scientist*, February 2004, 767.

124. See C. Ostroff, A. J. Kinicki, and R. S. Muhammad, "Organizational Culture and Climate," in I. B. Weiner, N. W. Schmitt, and S. Highhouse, eds., *Handbook of Psychology*, vol. 12, 2nd ed. (Hoboken, NJ: Wiley, 2012), 643–676.

125. See "Lying Less Linked to Better Health, New Research Finds," http://www.apa.org/news/press/releases/2012/08/lying-less.aspx, August 4, 2012 (accessed April 27, 2016).

126. Cameron, Kim S., and Arran Caza. "Organizational and Leadership Virtues and the Role of Forgiveness." *Journal of Leadership & Organizational Studies* 9, no. 1 (August 2002): 33–48. https://doi.org/10.1177/107179190200900103.

127. D. Cole, "The Healing Power of Forgiveness," *The Wall Street Journal*, March 21, 2016, R8.

128. F. Luthans, "The Need for Meaning of Positive Organizational Behavior," *Journal of Organizational Behavior*, September 2002, 695–706.

129. M. P. Seligman, *Flourish* (New York: Free Press, 2011).

130. B. L. Fredrickson and M. F. Losada, "Positive Affect in the Complex Dynamics of Human Flourishing," *American Psychologist*, 2005, 678–686.

131. C. L. M. Keyes and E. J. Simoes, "To Flourish or Not: Positive Mental Health and All-Cause Mortality," *American Journal of Public Health*, November 2012, 2164–2172; M. P. Seligman, *Flourish* (New York: Free Press, 2011).

132. See K. Cameron, C. Mora, T. Leutscher, and M. Calarco, "Effects of Positive Practices on Organizational Effectiveness," *The Journal of Applied Behavioral Science*, September 2011, 266–308; and M. Losada and E. Heaphy, "The Role of Positivity and Connectivity in the Performance of Business Teams," *American Behavioral Scientist*, February 2004, 740–765.

133. R. Knoesen and L. Naude, "Experiences of Flourishing and Languishing During the First Year at University," *Journal of Mental Health*, 27, 2018, 269–278.

134. Adapted from D. Brin, "Make You Job Candidates Happier," *SHRM.org*, January 14, 2019, https://www.shrm.org/resourcesandtools/hr-topics/talent-acquisition/pages/make-your-job-candidates-happier-in-2019.aspx.

135. Adapted from D. Brin, "Make You Job Candidates Happier," *SHRM.org*, January 14, 2019, https://www.shrm.org/resourcesandtools/hr-topics/talent-acquisition/pages/make-your-job-candidates-happier-in-2019.aspx.

136. Adapted from D. Brin, "Make You Job Candidates Happier," *SHRM.org*, January 14, 2019, https://www.shrm.org/resourcesandtools/hr-topics/talent-acquisition/pages/make-your-job-candidates-happier-in-2019.aspx.

137. Adapted from D. Brin, "Make You Job Candidates Happier," *SHRM.org*, January 14, 2019, https://www.shrm.org/resourcesandtools/hr-topics/talent-acquisition/pages/make-your-job-candidates-happier-in-2019.aspx.

138. B. A. Wallace, "Mental Balance and Well-Being: Building Bridges between Buddhism and Western Psychology," *American Psychologist*, October 2006, 696.

139. M. E. P. Seligman, *Flourish* (New York: Free Press, 2011).

140. S. Cohen and T. A. Wills, "Stress, Social Support, and the Buffering Hypothesis," *Psychological Bulletin*, September 1985, 310–357.

141. M. E. P. Seligman, *Flourish* (New York: Free Press, 2011).

142. V. E. Frankl, *Man's Search for Meaning* (New York: Pocket Books, 1959).

143. M. E. P. Seligman, *Flourish* (New York: Free Press, 2011).

144. M. C. Bush and S. Lewis-Kulin, "100 Best Companies to Work For 2018," *Fortune*, March 2018, 53–78; and M. C. Bush and C. Tkaczyk, "100 Best Companies to Work For 2019," *Fortune*, March 2019, 57–80.

145. M. C. Bush and S. Lewis-Kulin, "100 Best Companies to Work For 2018," *Fortune*, March 2018, 53–78; and M. C. Bush and C. Tkaczyk, "100 Best Companies to Work For 2019," *Fortune*, March 2019, 57–80.

146. Kimley-Horn and Associates, Inc. "WHY KIMLEY-HORN?" https://www.kimley-horn.com/about-us/why-kimley-horn/ (accessed July 1, 2019).

147. M. E. P. Seligman, *Flourish* (New York: Free Press, 2011).

148. M. C. Bush and S. Lewis-Kulin, "100 Best Companies to Work For 2018," *Fortune*, March 2018, 53–78; and Crowe Horvath website, https://www.crowe.com/careers/why-crowe.

149. L. Freifeld, "Training Magazine Ranks 2018 Training Top 125 Organizations," *TrainingMagazine.com*, February 13, 2018, https://trainingmag.com/training-magazine-ranks-2018-training-top-125-organizations/.

150. S. Moghe, "Opioid History: From 'Wonder Drug' to Abuse Epidemic," *CNN.com*, October 14, 2016, https://www.cnn.com/2016/05/12/health/opioid-addiction-history/ index.html.

151. S. Moghe, "Opioid History: From 'Wonder Drug' to Abuse Epidemic," *CNN.com*, October 14, 2016, https://www.cnn.com/2016/05/12/health/opioid-addiction-history/ index.html.

152. S. Moghe, "Opioid History: From 'Wonder Drug' to Abuse Epidemic," *CNN.com*, October 14, 2016, https://www.cnn.com/2016/05/12/health/opioid-addiction-history/ index.html.

153. S. Moghe, "Opioid History: From 'Wonder Drug' to Abuse Epidemic," *CNN.com*, October 14, 2016, https://www.cnn.com/2016/05/12/health/opioid-addiction-history/ index.html.

154. S. Moghe, "Opioid History: From 'Wonder Drug' to Abuse Epidemic," *CNN.com*, October 14, 2016, https://www.cnn.com/2016/05/12/health/opioid-addiction-history/ index.html.

155. L. Skarnulis, "Oxycontin: Pain Relief vs. Abuse," *Webmd.com*, n.d., https://www.webmd.com/pain-management/features/oxycontin-pain-relief-vs-abuse#1.

156. B. Meier, "Sacklers Directed Efforts to Mislead Public About OxyContin, Court Filing Claims," *The New York Times*, January 15, 2019, https://www.nytimes.com/2019/01/15/health/sacklers-purdue-oxycontin-opioids.html.

157. M. Scutari, "Toxic Gifts? Coming to Terms with Sackler Family Philanthropy," *Inside Philanthropy*, March 12, 2018, https://www.insidephilanthropy.com/home/2018/3/12/sackler-family-philanthropy-controversial-gifts.

158. S. Moghe, "Opioid History: From 'Wonder Drug' to Abuse Epidemic," *CNN.com*, October 14, 2016, https://www.cnn.com/2016/05/12/health/opioid-addiction-history/ index.html.

159. M. Scutari, "Toxic Gifts? Coming to Terms with Sackler Family Philanthropy," *Inside Philanthropy*, March 12, 2018, https://www.insidephilanthropy.com/home/2018/3/12/sackler-family-philanthropy-controversial-gifts.

160. A. Van Zee, "The Promotion and Marketing of OxyContin: Commercial Triumph, Public Health Tragedy," *American Journal of Public Health*, February 2009, 99, 221–226.

161. A. Van Zee, "The Promotion and Marketing of OxyContin: Commercial Triumph, Public Health Tragedy," *American Journal of Public Health*, February 2009, 99, 221–226.

162. R. Frehse and T. Marco, "Opioid Maker Purdue Pharma Fights to Prevent Documents Involving Sackler Family from Going Public," *CNN.com*, January 30, 2019, https://www.cnn.com/2019/01/30/health/purdue-pharma-stay-bn/ index.html.

163. Barry Meier, "Sacklers Directed Efforts to Mislead Public About OxyContin, Court Filing Claims," The New York Times Company, January 15, 2019, https://www.nytimes.com/2019/01/15/health/sacklers-purdue-oxycontin-opioids.html.

164. S. Moghe, "Opioid History: From 'Wonder Drug' to Abuse Epidemic," *CNN.com*, October 14, 2016, https://www.cnn.com/2016/05/12/health/opioid-addiction-history/index.html.

165. S. Moghe, "Opioid History: From 'Wonder Drug' to Abuse Epidemic," CNN.com, October 14, 2016, https://www.cnn.com/2016/05/12/health/opioid-addiction-history/ index.html.

166. CBS News, "Family Behind OxyContin Maker Engineered Opioid Crisis, Massachusetts AG Says," January 24, 2019, https://www.cbsnews.com/news/purdue-pharma-lawsuit-massachusetts-attorney-general-blames-sackler-family-for-creating-opioid-crisis-oxycontin/.

167. "Workers with Criminal Records," *SHRM.org*, May 17, 2018, https://www.shrm.org/hr-today/trends-and-forecasting/research-and-surveys/pages/second-chances.aspx.

168. J. C. Taylor, "They've Paid Their Debt: Now Let's Help People with Criminal Records Get Back to Work," *SHRM.org*, January 28, 2019, https://blog.shrm.org/blog/they-ve-paid-their-debt-now-let-s-help-people-with-criminal-records- get-bac.

169. "Workers with Criminal Records," *SHRM.org*, May 17, 2018, https://www.shrm.org/hr-today/trends-and-forecasting/research-and-surveys/pages/second-chances.aspx.

170. R. Mauer, "'Ban the Box' Turns 20: What Employers Need to Know," *SHRM.org*, November 12, 2018, https://www.shrm.org/resourcesandtools/hr-topics/talent-acquisition/pages/ban-the-box-turns-20-what-employers-need-to-know.aspx.

CHAPTER 8

1. T. Sverdrup and V. Schei, "'Cut Me Slack': The Psychological Contracts as a Foundation for Understanding Team Charters," *Journal of Applied Behavioral Science*, 2015, 451–478.

2. S. H. Courtright, B. W. McCormick, S. Mistry, and J. Wang, "Quality Charters or Quality Members? A Control Theory Perspective on Team Charters and Team Performance," *Journal of Applied Psychology*, 102, 1462–1470.

3. Adapted from P. Hunsaker, C. Pavett, and J. Hunsaker, "Increasing Student-Learning Team Effectiveness with Team Charters," *Journal of Education for Business*, 2011, 127–138; and J. R. Aaron, W. C. McDowell, and A. O. Herdman, "The Effect of Team Charter on Student Team Behaviors," *Journal of Education for Business*, 89, 90–97.

4. Human Society International, "2018 Annual Report," https://www.hsi.org/wp-content/uploads/2019/05/Annual-report-2018-HSI.pdf (accessed July 2, 2019).

5. S. H. Courtright, B. W. McCormick, S. Mistry, and J. Wang, "Quality Charters or Quality Members? A Control Theory Perspective on Team Charters and Team Performance," *Journal of Applied Psychology*, 102, 1462–1470; see also P. Hunsaker, C. Pavett, and J. Hunsaker, "Increasing Student-Learning Team Effectiveness with Team Charters," *Journal of Education for Business*, 2011, 127–138.

6. T. A. O'Neill and E. Salas, "Creating High Performance Teamwork in Organizations," *Human Resource Management Review*, 2018, 28, 325–331.

7. B. Nemeth, "Group v. Team: What's the Difference?" *Sessionlab.com*, January 13, 2018, https://www.sessionlab.com/blog/working-with-groups-and-teams/.

8. B. Nemeth, "Group v. Team: What's the Difference?" *Sessionlab. com*, January 13, 2018, https://www.sessionlab.com/blog/working-with-groups-and-teams/.

9. Adapted from B. Nemeth, "Group v. Team: What's the Difference?" *Sessionlab.com*, January 13, 2018, https://www.sessionlab.com/blog/working-with-groups-and-teams/.

10. See R. Cross, N. Nohria, and A. Parker, "Six Myths about Informal Networks—and How to Overcome Them," *MIT Sloan Management Review*, Spring 2002, 67–75; and C. Shirky, "Watching the Patterns Emerge," *Harvard Business Review*, February 2004, 34–35.

11. "The Top 10 Most Followed Celebrities on Instagram in 2019, *BigBangram.com*, https://bigbangram.com/blog/the-top-10-most-followed-celebrities-on-instagram-in-2018.

12. G. Tucker, "Why Companies Should Stay Connected with Ex-Employees," *SHRM.org*, March 19, 2018, https://www.shrm.org/hr-today/news/hr-magazine/0418/pages/corporate-alumni-programs-mean-never-having-to-say-goodbye.aspx.

13. G. Tucker, "Why Companies Should Stay Connected with Ex-Employees," *SHRM.org*, March 19, 2018, https://www.shrm.org/hr-today/news/hr-magazine/0418/pages/corporate-alumni-programs-mean-never-having-to-say-goodbye.aspx.

14. T. Driskell, J. E. Driskell, C. S. Burke, and E Salas, "Team Roles: A Review and Integration," *Small Group Research*, 48, 2017, 482–511.

15. Ann Porteus, "Roles People Play in Groups," Stanford University, https://web.stanford.edu/group/resed/resed/staffresources/RM/training/grouproles.html (accessed April 4, 2019).

16. D. Weis, "Giving Employees Permission to Fail Is a Formula for Innovation at 3M," *AEM.org*, June 21, 2018, https://www.aem.org/giving-employees-permission-to-fail-is-a-formula-for-innovation-at-3m/.

17. A. Ross, "Why Did Google Abandon 20% for Innovation?" *HRZone.com*, June 3, 2015, https://www.hrzone.com/lead/culture/why-did-google-abandon-20-time-for-innovation.

18. C. L. Pedersen, "How to Use 20% Time to Manage Pet Projects," *Nature.com*, January 17, 2019, https://www.nature.com/articles/d41586-019-00179-w.

19. T. G. Weiser and A. B. Haynes, "Ten Years of the Surgical Safety Checklist," *British Journal of Surgery*, May 17, 2018, 105, 927–929; and World Health Organization, *Surgical Safety Checklist and Manual*, 2015, http://who.int/patientsafety/safesurgery/ss_checklist/en/.

20. T. G. Weiser and A. B. Haynes, "Ten Years of the Surgical Safety Checklist," *British Journal of Surgery*, May 17, 2018, 105, 927–929.

21. T. G. Weiser and A. B. Haynes, "Ten Years of the Surgical Safety Checklist," *British Journal of Surgery*, May 17, 2018, 105, 927–929; and R. Schwendimann, C. Blatter, M. Lüthy, G. Mohr, T. Girard, S. Batzer, E. Davis, and H. Hoffmann, "Adherence to the WHO Surgical Safety Checklist: An Observational Study in a Swiss Academic Center," *Patient Safety in Surgery*, March 12, 2019, 23, 1–6.

22. R. Schwendimann, C. Blatter, M. Lüthy, G. Mohr, T. Girard, S. Batzer, E. Davis, and H. Hoffmann, "Adherence to the WHO Surgical Safety Checklist: An Observational Study in a Swiss Academic Center," *Patient Safety in Surgery*, March 12, 2019, 23, 1–6.

23. N. R. Quigley, C. G. Collins, C. B. Gibson, and S. K. Parker, "Team Performance Archetypes: Toward a New Conceptualization of Team Performance Over Time," *Group & Organization Management*, August 2018, 787–824.

24. See B. W. Tuckman, "Developmental Sequence in Small Groups," *Psychological Bulletin*, June 1965, 384–399; and B. W. Tuckman and M. A. C. Jensen, "Stages of Small-Group Development Revisited," *Group & Organization Studies*, December 1977, 419–427.

25. J. L. Farh, C. Lee, and C. I. C. Farh, "Task Conflict and Team Creativity: A Question of How Much and When," *Journal of Applied Psychology,* 2010, 1173–1180.

26. J. Ewing, "Volkswagen's New C.E.O. Is an Outsider: That's an Asset, and a Liability," *The New York Times,* April 12, 2018, https://www.nytimes.com/2018/04/12/business/volkswagen-chief.html.

27. D. Courpasson and D. Younes, "Double or Quits: Understanding the Links Between Secrecy and Creativity in a Project Development Process," *Organization Studies,* 2018, 39, 271–295.

28. Adapted from J. M. O'Connor, "14 Ways for Business Leaders to Build Team Cohesion," *Forbes.com,* December 28, 2018, https://www.forbes.com/sites/forbescoachescouncil/2018/12/28/14-ways-for-business-leaders-to-build-team-cohesion/#4e13dd1857f4.

29. J. Moore, "How 3 Companies Used Disruptive Innovation to Transform Their Industries," *Ideadrop.com,* November 16, 2017, https://ideadrop.co/how-3-companies-used-disruptive-innovation-to-transform-their-industries/.

30. J. E. Mathieu, P. T. Gallagher, M. A. Domingo, and E. A. Klock, "Embracing Complexity: Reviewing the Past Decade of Team Effectiveness Research," *Annual Review of Organizational Psychology and Organizational Behavior,* 6, 2019, 17–46.

31. Matthew Dixon, "Reinventing Customer Service," *Harvard Business Review,* December 2018, https://hbr.org/2018/11/reinventing-customer-service.

32. *Harvard Business Essentials: Creating Teams with an Edge* (Boston, MA: Harvard Business School Press, 2004).

33. J. Wang and Y. P. Zhou, "Impact of Queue Configuration on Service Time: Evidence from a Supermarket," *Management Science,* July 2018, 64, 3055–3075.

34. L. M. Harding, "Students of a Feather 'Flocked' Together: A Group Assignment Method for Reducing Free-riding and Improving Group and Individual Learning Outcomes," *Journal of Marketing Education,* 40, 2018, 117–127.

35. Inspired by K. Dower, "Stop Social Loafing: 6 Ways to Get Everyone Working," *rapidstartleadership.com,* https://www.rapidstartleadership.com/social-loafing/. Accessed May 1, 2019.

36. N. C. Magpili and P. Pazos, "Self-Managing Team Performance: A Systematic Review of Multilevel Input Factors," *Small Group Research,* 49, 2018, 3–33.

37. N. C. Magpili and P. Pazos, "Self-Managing Team Performance: A Systematic Review of Multilevel Input Factors," *Small Group Research,* 49, 2018, 3–33.

38. J. Ferrell and K. Kline, "Facilitating Trust and Communication in Virtual Teams," *People & Strategy,* 41, Spring 2018, 30–35; and adapted from "Developing and Sustaining High-Performing Work Teams," *SHRM.org,* March 27, 2019, https://www.shrm.org/resourcesandtools/tools-and-samples/toolkits/pages/developingandsustaininghigh-performance-workteams.aspx.

39. D. Wilkie, "Why Are Companies Ending Remote Work?" *SHRM.org,* May 7, 2019, https://www.shrm.org/resourcesandtools/hr-topics/employee-relations/pages/drawbacks-to-working-at-home-.aspx.

40. J. Eisenberg and A. Krishnan, "Addressing Virtual Work Challenges: Learning from the Field," *Organization Management Journal,* 15, 2018, 78–94.

41. Julia Eisenberg and Aparna Krishnan, "Addressing Virtual Work Challenges: Learning From the Field," *Organization Management Journal* 15, no. 2 (May 2018): 78–94. https://doi.org/10.1080/15416518.2018.1471976.

42. J. Ferrell and K. Kline, "Facilitating Trust and Communication in Virtual Teams," *People & Strategy,* 41, Spring 2018, 30–35.

43. E. Martinez-Mareno, A. Zornoza, P. Gonzalez-Navarro, and L. F. Thompson, "Investigating Face-to-Face and Virtual Teamwork over Time: When Does Early Task Conflict Trigger Relationship Conflict?" *Group Dynamics: Theory, Research, and Practice,* 2012, 159–171.

44. S. Courtright, G. Thurgood, G. Stewart, and A. Pierotti, "Structural Interdependence in Teams: An Integrative Framework and Meta-Analysis," *Journal of Applied Psychology,* 2015, 1825–1846.

45. S. Courtright, G. Thurgood, G. Stewart, and A. Pierotti, "Structural Interdependence in Teams: An Integrative Framework and Meta-Analysis," *Journal of Applied Psychology,* 2015, 1829.

46. M. Baer, R. Dhensa-Kahlon, J. Colquitt, J. Rodell, R. Outlaw, and D. Long, "Uneasy Lies the Head That Bears the Trust: The Effects of Feeling Trusted on Emotional Exhaustion," *Academy of Management Journal,* 2015, 1637–1657.

47. R. Edelman, "2019 Edelman Trust Barometer: Global Report," *Edelman.com,* https://www.edelman.com/sites/g/files/aatuss191/files/2019-02/2019_Edelman_Trust_Barometer_Global_Report_2.pdf (accessed May 4, 2019).

48. T. Cowie, "That Fizz Effect," *HRM Magazine,* May 2018, 30.

49. M. J. Burtscher, B. Meyer, K. Jonas, S. Freese, and G. Troster, "A Time to Trust? The Buffering Effect of Trust and Its Temporal Variations in the Context of High-Reliability Teams," *Journal of Organizational Behavior,* 38, 2018, 1099–1112.

50. A. B. Wilson, C. McNellis, and C. K. Latham, "Audit Firm Tenure, Auditor Familiarity, and Trust: Effect on Auditee Whistleblowing Reporting Intentions," *International Journal of Auditing,* 22, 2018, 113–130.

51. R. Edelman, "2019 Edelman Trust Barometer: Global Report," *Edelman.com,* https://www.edelman.com/sites/g/files/aatuss191/files/2019-02/2019_Edelman_Trust_Barometer_Global_Report_2.pdf (accessed May 4, 2019).

52. R. Edelman, "2019 Edelman Trust Barometer: Global Report," *Edelman.com,* https://www.edelman.com/sites/g/files/aatuss191/files/2019-02/2019_Edelman_Trust_Barometer_Global_Report_2.pdf (accessed May 4, 2019).

53. R. Hastings, "Broken Trust Is Bad for Business," *Society of Human Resource Management,* March 7, 2011.

54. Adapted from R. Maurer, "Microinternships Offer New College-to-Career Path," *SHRM.org,* April 19, 2019, https://www.shrm.org/resourcesandtools/hr-topics/talent-acquisition/pages/microinternships-offer-new-college-to-career-path.aspx.

55. A. Bryant, "Lars Dalgaard: Build Trust by Daring to Show that You're Human," *The New York Times,* October 17, 2015, http://www.nytimes.com/2015/10/18/business/lars-dalgaard-build-trust-by-daring-to-show-that-youre-human.html.

56. T. A. O'Neill and E. Salas, "Creating High Performance Teamwork in Organizations," *Human Resource Management Review,* 2018, 28, 325–331.

57. Adapted from "Developing and Sustaining High-Performing Work Teams," *SHRM.org,* March 27, 2019, https://www.shrm.org/resourcesandtools/tools-and-samples/toolkits/pages/developingandsustaining-high-performanceworkteams.aspx.

58. C. Curry, "Managing Conflict in Global Teams," *Training,* January/February 2016, http://web.a.ebscohost.com.access.library.unisa.edu.au/ehost/pdfviewer/pdfviewer?vid=6&sid=d82496f2-0036-407c-8177-a25b4767d243%40sessionmgr4005&hid=4209.

59. C. Edmonds, "Team Charters Align Goals," *peopledevelopmentmagazine.com,* February 19, 2019, https://peopledevelopmentmagazine.com/2019/02/19/team-charters-align-goals/.

60. Based on J. E. Mathieu and T. L. Ra, "Laying the Foundation for Successful Team Performance Trajectories: The Roles of Team Charters and Performance Strategies," *Journal of Applied Psychology,* 2009, 90–103.

61. "Employers Want to See These Attributes on Students' Resumes," *naceweb.org,* December 12, 2018, https://www.naceweb.org/talent-acquisition/candidate-selection/employers-want-to-see-these-attributes-on-students-resumes/.

62. R. W. Doughterty, C. C. Wyles, W. Pawlina, and N. Lachman, "'The Team is More than the Sum of Its Parts': Implementation of Charters to Improve Team Dynamics in an Anatomy Course," *theasiapacificscholar.org,* 3, January 2, 2018, 6–14.

63. "Employers Want to See These Attributes on Students' Resumes," *naceweb.org,* December 12, 2018, https://www.naceweb.org/talent-acquisition/candidate-selection/employers-want-to-see-these-attributes-on-students-resumes/.

64. C. Cheng, R. Y. J. Chua, M. W. Morris, and L. Lee, "Finding the Right Mix: How the Composition of Self-Managing Multicultural Teams' Cultural Value Orientation Influences Performance over Time," *Journal of Organizational Behavior,* 2012, 389–411.

65. M. S. Prewett, M. I. Brown, A. Goswami, and N. D. Christiansen, "Effects of Team Personality Composition on Member Performance: A Multilevel Perspective," *Group & Organization Management,* 43, 2018, 316–348.

66. J. Prinz and P. Wicker, "Diversity Effects on Team Performance in the Tour de France," *Team Performance Management,* 2016, 22–35.

67. F. Hattke and S. Blaschke, "Striving for Excellence: The Role of Top Management Team Diversity in Universities," *Team Performance Management,* 2015, 121–138.

68. Adapted from S. E. Frick, K. A. Fletcher, P. S. Ramsey, and W. L. Boswell, "Understanding Team Maladaptation Through the Lens of the Four R's of Adaptation," *Human Resource Management Review,* 28, 2018, 411–422.

69. S. E. Frick, K. A. Fletcher, P. S. Ramsey, and W. L. Boswell, "Understanding Team Maladaptation Through the Lens of the Four R's of Adaptation," *Human Resource Management Review,* 28, 2018, 411–422.

70. N. Hill and K. Bartol, "Empowering Leadership and Effective Collaboration in Geographically Dispersed Teams," *Personnel Psychology,* 2016, 159–198.

71. Adapted from K. Goldstein, "Fostering Team Collaboration," *Leadership Excellence Essentials,* January 2016, http://web.a.ebscohost.com.access.library.unisa.edu.au/ehost/pdfviewer/pdfviewer?vid=46&sid=d82496f2-0036-407c-8177-a25b4767d243%40session mgr4005&hid=4209.

72. J. S. Smock, "Meaningful Compensation for Practice and Industry Team Leaders (and Teams)—How Important Is It?" *managinpartnerforum.org,* March 30, 2018, http://www.managingpartnerforum.org/tasks/sites/mpf/assets/image/MPF%20FEATURED%20ARTICLE%20-%20Compensation%20for%20Law%20Firm%20Team%20Leaders%20-%20SMOCK%20-%203-30-18.pdf; and H. Gardner, "When Senior Managers Won't Collaborate," *Harvard Business Review,* March 2015, https://hbr.org/2015/03/when–senior-managers-wont-collaborate.

73. R. K. Gottfredson, "How to Get Your Teams to Work," *Industrial Management*, July/August 2015, 25–30.

74. A. Gorman, "Hospitals Look to Nursing Homes to Help Stop Drug-Resistant Infections," *npr.org*, April 2, 2019, https://www.npr.org/sections/health-shots/2019/04/02/707842736/enter-title.

75. A. Gorman, "Hospitals Look to Nursing Homes to Help Stop Drug-Resistant Infections," *npr.org*, April 2, 2019, https://www.npr.org/sections/health-shots/2019/04/02/707842736/enter-title.

76. B. McKay, "Rochester Hospitals Unite to Defeat a Common Foe: C. Difficile," *The Wall Street Journal*, February 15, 2016, http://www.wsj.com/articles/rochester-hospitals-unite-to-defeat-a-common-foe-c-difficile-1455592271.

77. A. Gorman, "Hospitals Look to Nursing Homes to Help Stop Drug-Resistant Infections," *npr.org*, April 2, 2019, https://www.npr.org/sections/health-shots/2019/04/02/707842736/enter-title.

78. Adapted from D. Howell, "International Space Station: Facts, History, and Tracking," *Space.com*, February 8, 2018, https://www.space.com/16748-international-space-station.html.

79. Adapted from D. Howell, "International Space Station: Facts, History, and Tracking," *Space.com*, February 8, 2018, https://www.space.com/16748-international-space-station.html.

80. D. Howell, "International Space Station: Facts, History, and Tracking," *Space.com*, February 8, 2018, https://www.space.com/16748-international-space-station.html.

81. T. Sharp, "International Space Station: Facts, History, and Tracking," *Space.com*, April 5, 2016, http://www.space.com/16748-international-space-station.html. See also K. E. Keeton, L. L. Schmidt, K. J. Slack, and A. A. Malka, "The Rocket Science of Teams," *Industrial and Organizational Psychology*, March 2012, 32–35.

82. Z. Wichter, "What You Need to Know After Deadly Boeing 737 Max Crashes," *The New York Times*, April 30, 2019, https://www.nytimes.com/interactive/2019/business/boeing-737-crashes.html; and P. Ausick, "How Much Does a Boeing 737 Max Cost?" *247wallst.com*, March 11, 2019, https://247wallst.com/aerospace-defense/2019/03/11/how-much-does-a-boeing-737-max-cost-2/.

83. J. Nicas and J. Creswell, "Boeing's 737 Max: 1960's Design, 1990s Computing Power and Paper Manuals," *The New York Times*, April 8, 2019, https://www.nytimes.com/2019/04/08/business/boeing-737-max-.html.

84. Z. Wichter, "What You Need to Know After Deadly Boeing 737 Max Crashes," *The New York Times*, April 30, 2019, https://www.nytimes.com/interactive/2019/business/boeing-737-crashes.html.

85. Z. Wichter, "What You Need to Know After Deadly Boeing 737 Max Crashes," *The New York Times*, April 30, 2019, https://www.nytimes.com/interactive/2019/business/boeing-737-crashes.html.

86. Z. Wichter, "What You Need to Know After Deadly Boeing 737 Max Crashes," *The New York Times*, April 30, 2019, https://www.nytimes.com/interactive/2019/business/boeing-737-crashes.html.

87. Z. Wichter, "What You Need to Know After Deadly Boeing 737 Max Crashes," *The New York Times*, April 30, 2019, https://www.nytimes.com/interactive/2019/business/boeing-737-crashes.html.

88. D. Gelles and N. Kitroeff, "Boeing Believed a 737 Max Warning Light Was Standard. It Wasn't," *The New York Times*, May 5, 2019, https://www.nytimes.com/2019/05/05/business/boeing-737-max-warning-light.html.

89. D. Gelles and N. Kitroeff, "Boeing Believed a 737 Max Warning Light Was Standard. It Wasn't," *The New York Times*, May 5, 2019, https://www.nytimes.com/2019/05/05/business/boeing-737-max-warning-light.html.

90. C. Isidore, "Boeing Will Keep Building New 737 Max Planes as it Scrambles to Get Them Back in the Air," *CNN.com*, March 15, 2019, https://www.cnn.com/2019/03/14/business/boeing-to-keep-building-737-max/index.html.

91. N. Kitroeff and D. Gelles, "Claims of Shoddy Production Draw Scrutiny to a Second Boeing Jet," *The New York Times*, April 20, 2019, https://www.nytimes.com/2019/04/20/business/boeing-dreamliner-production-problems.html.

92. Zach Wichter, "What You Need to Know After Deadly Boeing 737 Max Crashes," *The New York Times Company*, April 30, 2019, https://www.nytimes.com/interactive/2019/business/boeing-737-crashes.html.

93. N. Kitroeff, "Boeing Chief Seeks to Reassure Shareholders on Safety of the 737 Max Jets," *The New York Times*, April 29, 2019, https://www.nytimes.com/2019/04/29/business/boeing-737-max-annual-meeting.html.

94. V. Ryckaert, "Larry Nassar Case: What You Need to Know About the Abuser of More than 150 Young Athletes," *USAToday.com*, January 25, 2018, https://www.usatoday.com/story/news/nation-now/2018/01/25/larry-nassar-usa-gymnastics-sex-abuse-what-we-know/1066355001/.

95. V. Mather, "The Fall of Rick Pitino: One Scandal Too Many," *The New York Times*, September 27, 2017, https://www.nytimes.com/2017/09/27/sports/pitino-louisville-scandals.html.

96. T. Durkee, "NCAA Didn't Consider Larry Brown's History of Infractions in SMU Case," *Sporting News*, September 29, 2015, http://www.sportingnews.com/ncaa-basketball-news/4656662-larry-brown-smu-infractions-ncaa-penalty-ucla-kansas-violations.

97. M. Powell, "The Most Honest Man in College Basketball Is Going to Prison," *The New York Times*, May 3, 2019, https://www.nytimes.com/2019/05/03/sports/college-basketball-trial.html; and C. Turner, "Conflicts of Interest in the Intercollegiate Athletics Management Structure—The Impetus for Nullification of Presidential Authority," *United States Sports Academy*, February 9, 2015, http://thesportjournal.org/article/conflicts-of-interest-in-the-intercollegiate-athletics-management-structure-the-impetus-for-nullification-of–presidential-authority/.

98. M. Powell, "The Most Honest Man in College Basketball Is Going to Prison," *The New York Times*, May 3, 2019, https://www.nytimes.com/2019/05/03/sports/college-basketball-trial.html.

99. T. Durkee, "NCAA Didn't Consider Larry Brown's History of Infractions in SMU Case," *Sporting News*, September 29, 2015, http://www.sportingnews.com/ncaa-basketball-news/4656662-larry-brown-smu-infractions-ncaa-penalty-ucla-kansas-violations.

100. E. Graney, "Scandals Never Out of Season in College Basketball," *Las Vegas Review Journal*, October 6, 2015, http://www.reviewjournal.com/opinion/columns-blogs/ed-graney/scandals-never-out-season-college-basketball.

CHAPTER 9

1. Alison Doyle, "16 Things to Say in a Job Interview," *The Balance/Careers*, updated February 27, 2019, https://www.thebalancecareers.com/what-to-say-in-a-job-interview-4158527; Catherine Conlan, "What to Say at a Job Interview," *Monster.com*, https://www.monster.com/career-advice/article/best-things-say-in-interview/ (accessed March 25, 2019); and M. Civiello, "Communication Counts in Landing a Job," *Training & Development*, February 2009, 82–83.

2. George Bernard Shaw (playwright and critic).

3. J. Bacon, "Miscommunication Added to Chaos as Ferry Sank," *USA Today*, April 20, 2014, http://usat.ly/1kNTGGv (accessed April 3, 2019).

4. Rob Copeland and Bradley Hope, "Bridgewater, World's Largest Hedge Fund, Grapples with Succession," *The Wall Street Journal*, March 16, 2016, https://www.wsj.com/articles/bridgewater-worlds-largest-hedge-fund-grapples-with-succession-1458144347.

5. R. Levering, "The 100 Best Companies to Work for 2016," *Fortune*, March 15, 2016, 143–165.

6. James L. Bowditch, Anthony F. Buono, and Marcus M. Stewart. *A Primer on Organizational Behavior*, 4th ed. (New York: John Wiley & Sons, 1997).

7. Y.-C. Huang and S.-H. Lin, "An Inventory for Assessing Interpersonal Communication Competence of College Students," *British Journal of Guidance & Counselling*, July–August 2018, 385–401; and C. Johansson, V. D. Miller, and S. Hamrin, "Conceptualizing Communicative Leadership," *Corporate Communications: An International Journal*, April 2014, 147–165.

8. "Employers Seek Communication Skills in New Hires," January 1, 2018, https://www.mba.com/mbas-and-business-masters/articles/your-career-path/employers-seek-communications-skills.

9. See R. S. Wyer, Jr., and L. J. Shrum, "The Role of Comprehension Processes in Communication and Persuasion," *Media Psychology*, April 2015, 163–195.

10. Kevin Daum, "This Skin Care CEO Shows How Your Business Communication Should Be As Clear Your Pores," Mansueto Ventures, October 26, 2018, https://www.inc.com/kevin-daum/this-skin-care-ceo-shows-how-your-business-communication-should-be-as-clear-your-pores.html.

11. R. L. Daft and R. H. Lengel, "Information Richness: A New Approach to Managerial Behavior and Organizational Design," in *Research in Organizational Behavior*, ed. B. M. Staw and L. L. Cummings (Greenwich, CT: JAI Press, 1984), 196.

12. For a good discussion see A. M. Kaplan and M. Haenlein, "Users of the World, Unite! The Challenges and Opportunities of Social Media," *Business Horizons*, January–February 2010, 59–68.

13. M. Maity, M. Dass, and P. Kumar, "The Impact of Media Richness on Consumer Information Search and Choice," *Journal of Business Research*, June 2018, 36–45.

14. X. Armengol, V. Fernandez, P. Simo, and J. M. Sallan, "An Examination of the Effects of Self-Regulatory Focus on the Perception of the Media Richness: The Case of E-Mail," *International Journal of Business Communication*, October 2017, 394–407.

15. L.-Z. Wu, T. A. Birtch, F. F. T. Chang, and H. Zhang, "Perceptions of Negative Workplace Gossip: A Self-Consistency Theory Framework," *Journal of Management*, May 2018, 1873–1898.

16. A. R. Sanchez, A. Pico, and L. B. Comer, "Salespeople's Communication Competence: A Study of the Mexican Market," *Journal of Business & Economic Studies*, Spring 2010, 1–19.

17. Conflict Resolution Education, "What Is Nonverbal Communication? Non-verbal Communication for Educators," https://creducation.net/resources/nonverbal_communication/what_is_nonverbal_communication.html (accessed June 19, 2019).

18. J. A. Hall, T. G. Horgan, and N. A. Murphy, "Nonverbal Communication," *Annual Review of Psychology,* January 2019, 271–294.

19. N. Dargue and N. Sweller, "Not All Gestures Are Created Equal: The Effects of Typical and Atypical Iconic Gestures on Narrative Comprehension," *Journal of Nonverbal Behavior,* September 2018, 327–345.

20. Related research is summarized by J. A. Hall, "Male and Female Nonverbal Behavior," in *Multichannel Integrations of Nonverbal Behavior,* ed. A. W. Siegman and S. Feldstein (Hillsdale, NJ: Lawrence Erlbaum, 1985), 195–226; and M. J. Simmering, J. Bryan Fuller, L. E. Marler, S. S. Cox, and R. J. Bennett, "Tactile Interaction Norms and Positive Workplace Touch," *Journal of Managerial Issues,* Spring 2013, 132–153.

21. D. Marinova, S. K. Singh, and J. Singh, "Frontline Problem-Solving Effectiveness: A Dynamic Analysis of Verbal and Nonverbal Cues," *Journal of Marketing Research,* April 2018, 178–192; and D. B. Rane, "Effective Body Language for Organizational Success," *Journal of Soft Skills,* 2010, 17–26.

22. Norms for cross-cultural eye contact are discussed by C. Engholm, *When Business East Meets Business West: The Guide to Practice and Protocol in the Pacific Rim* (New York: John Wiley & Sons, 1991).

23. G. Itzchakov, K. G. DeMarree, A. N. Kluger, and Y. Turjeman-Levi, "The Listener Sets the Tone: High-Quality Listening Increases Attitude Clarity and Behavior-Intention Consequences," *Personality and Social Psychology Bulletin,* May 2018, 762–778; and S. E. Spataro and J. Bloch, "'Can You Repeat That?' Teaching Active Listening in Management Education," *Journal of Management Education,* April 2018, 168–198.

24. See J. Keyser, "Active Listening Leads to Business Success," *T+D,* July 2013, 26–28.

25. This discussion is based on C. G. Pearce, I. W. Johnson, and R. T. Barker, "Assessment of the Listening Styles Inventory: Progress in Establishing Reliability and Validity," *Journal of Business and Technical Communication,* January 2003, 84–113.

26. M. C. Stewart and C. L. Arnold, "Defining Social Listening: Recognizing an Emerging Dimension of Listening," *International Journal of Listening,* May 2018, 85–100.

27. L. Girardin, "3 Non-Defensive Tricks for Dealing with Tricky Coworkers," https://www.govloop.com/community/blog/3-non-defensive-tricks-dealing-tricky-coworkers/ (accessed March 29, 2019).

28. L. Leanna Holmer, "Understanding and Reducing the Impact of Defensiveness on Management Learning: Some Lessons from Neuroscience," *Journal of Management Education* 38, no. 5 (October 2014): 618–41. https://doi.org/10.1177/1052562913505568.

29. J. R. Gibb, "Defensive Communication," *Journal of Communication,* 1961, 141–148.

30. See D. Goleman, *Focus: The Hidden Driver of Excellence* (New York: HarperCollins Publishers, 2013).

31. A. L. Meinecke and S. Kauffeld, "Engaging the Hearts and Minds of Followers: Leader Empathy and Language Style Matching During Appraisal Interviews," *Journal of Business and Psychology,* July 2018, 1–17.

32. Kevin Daum, "This Entrepreneur and Son of a Holocaust Survivor Proves Empathy Can Lead to Business Success," Mansueto Ventures, June 15, 2018, https://www.inc.com/kevin-daum/this-entrepreneur-son-of-a-holocaust-survivor-proves-empathy-can-lead-to-business-success.html.

33. I. I. Szymanska and B. A. Rubin, "Gender and Relationship Differences in the Perceptions of Male and Female Leadership," *Gender in Management: An International Journal,* June 2018, 254–281; and N. Ellemers, "Gender Stereotypes," *Annual Review of Psychology,* 2018, 275–298.

34. D. G. Smith, J. E. Rosenstein, and M. C. Nikolov, "The Different Words We Use to Describe Male and Female Leaders," *Harvard Business Review,* May 25, 2018, https://hbr.org/2018/05/the-different-words-we-use-to-describe-male-and-female-leaders; and H. Murphy, "Who's the Boss? Research Reveals Unconscious Gender Bias," *The New York Times,* April 24, 2018, https://www.nytimes.com.

35. K. Daum, "23 Inspiring Quotes from Strong Businesswomen," *Inc.,* https://www.inc.com/kevin-daum/inspiring-quotes-from-strong-businesswomen.html (accessed March 29, 2019).

36. D. Tannen, "The Power of Talk: Who Gets Heard and Why," in R. J. Lewicki and D. M. Saunders, eds., *Negotiation: Readings, Exercises, and Cases,* 3rd ed. (Boston: Irwin/McGraw-Hill, 1999), 160–173.

37. See A. H. Eagly and W. Wood, "The Origins of Sex Differences in Human Behavior," *American Psychologist,* June 1999, 408–423.

38. See D. Tannen, "The Power of Talk: Who Gets Heard and Why," in R. J. Lewicki and D. M. Saunders, eds., *Negotiation: Readings, Exercises, and Cases,* 3rd ed. (Boston: Irwin/McGraw-Hill, 1999), 160–173.

39. For a thorough review of the evolutionary explanation of sex differences in communication, see A. H. Eagly and W. Wood, "The Origins of Sex Differences in Human Behavior," *American Psychologist,* June 1999, 408–423.

40. See A. H. Eagly and W. Wood, "The Origins of Sex Differences in Human Behavior," *American Psychologist,* June 1999, 408–423.

41. S. R. Stryker, "Language Barriers to Gender Equity in Senior Executive Leadership," *Journal of Management Policy and Practice,* June 2018, 111–120; and W. H. Locander and D. M. Ladik, "CEO Tweet Behavior: The Use of Metaphors and Gendered Communication Style," *Journal of Managerial Issues,* Winter 2017, 365–379.

42. Joanne Lipman, "Women at Work: A Guide for Men," *The Wall Street Journal,* December 12, 2014, https://www.wsj.com/articles/women-at-work-a-guide-for-men-1418418595.

43. T. Burrell, "The Science Behind Interrupting: Gender, Nationality and Power, and the Roles They Play," *Post Magazine,* March 14, 2018, https://www.scmp.com/magazines/post-magazine/long-reads/article/2137023/science-behind-interrupting-gender-nationality.

44. Scooby Axson, "Cardinals' Kliff Kingsbury Allowing Cellphone Breaks During Team Meetings," Meredith Corporation, March 27, 2019, https://www.si.com/nfl/2019/03/27/arizona-cardinals-kliff-kingsbury-meeting-cellphone-breaks.

45. G. James, "It's Official: Cold-Calling Is Dead and Buried," *Inc.,* January 12, 2019, https://www.inc.com.

46. G. James, "It's Official: Cold-Calling Is Dead and Buried," *Inc.,* January 12, 2019, https://www.inc.com; and G. James, "The 10-Minute Website Tweak That Increases Sales," *Inc.,* January 7, 2019, https://www.inc.com.

47. S. R. Martin, "Research: Men Get Credit for Voicing Ideas, but Not Problems. Women Don't Get Credit for Either," *Harvard Business Review,* https://hbr.org/2017/11/research-men-get-credit-for-voicing-ideas-but-not-problems-women-dont-get-credit-for-either (accessed April 2, 2019); and J. Lipman, "Women at Work: A Guide for Men," *The Wall Street Journal,* December 12/13, 2014, C1, C2.

48. Data taken from A. Smith and M. Anderson, "Social Media Use in 2018," March 1, 2018, https://www.pewinternet.org/2018/03/01/social-media-use-in-2018/.

49. "Why Your Business Needs a Social Media Policy and Eight Things It Should Cover," *Forbes,* https://www.forbes.com/sites/forbeshumanresourcescouncil/2017/05/25/why-your-business-needs-a-social-media-policy-and-eight-things-it-should-cover/#7e5b805d5264 (accessed April 3, 2019).

50. C. Jeanne Meister, and Karie Willyerd, *The 2020 Workplace: How Innovative Companies Attract, Develop, and Keep Tomorrow's Employees Today* (New York: Harper Collins, 2010).

51. S. Baer, "Social Media Proves to Boost Employee Engagement," *Forbes,* February 13, 2018, https://www.forbes.com/sites/forbesagencycouncil/2018/02/13/social-media-proves-to-boost-employee-engagement/#2d5a2bcc4db5.

52. S. S. Cetinkaya and M. Rashid, "The Effect of Social Media on Employees' Job Performance: The Mediating Role of Organizational Structure," *Journal of Organizational Psychology,* November 2018, 103–125.

53. L. Bizzi, "Employees Who Use Social Media for Work Are More Engaged—But Also More Likely to Leave Their Jobs," *Harvard Business Review,* May 17, 2018, https://hbr.org/2018/05/employees-who-use-social-media-for-work-are-more-engaged-but-also-more-likely-to-leave-their-jobs.

54. J. Meister, "Want to Be a More Productive Employee? Get on Social Networks," *Forbes,* April 18, 2013, http://www.forbes.com/sites/jeannemeister/2013/04/18/want-to-be-a-more-productive-employee-get-on-social-networks/ (accessed April 3, 2019); and T. Kunsman, "25 Social Selling Statistics That Matter for Sales Teams and Beyond," *Everyone Social,* October 30, 2018, https://everyonesocial.com/blog/social-selling-statistics/.

55. M. C. Long, "How Social Media Actually Boosts Efficiency in an Office Environment," *AdWeek,* May 10, 2018, https://www.adweek.com/digital/how-social-media-actually-boosts-efficiency-in-an-office-environment/.

56. Jobvite, "2018 Recruiter Nation Survey: The Tipping Point—The Next Chapter in Recruiting," November 2018, https://www.jobvite.com/jobvite-news-and-reports/2018-recruiter-nation-report-tipping-point-and-the-next-chapter-in-recruiting/; and Society for Human Resource Management, "Using Social Media for Talent Acquisition," September 20, 2017, https://www.shrm.org/hr-today/trends-and-forecasting/research-and-surveys/pages/social-media-recruiting-screening-2015.aspx.

57. Adapted from T. Burriss, "Maximize the Value of LinkedIn by Connecting and Engaging," *T+D,* March 15, 2016, https://www.td.org/Publications/Blogs/Career-Development-Blog/2016/03/Maximize-the-Value-of-LinkedIn-by-Connecting-and-Engaging.

58. T. Burriss, "How to Build an Eye-Catching LinkedIn Profile," *T+D,* February 4, 2016, https://www.td.org/Publications/Blogs/Career-Development- Blog/2016/02/How-to-Build-An-Eye-Catching-LinkedIn-Profile.

59. R. Ryan, "How to Write a LinkedIn Headline That Gets You Noticed," *Forbes,* March 7, 2019, https://www.forbes.com/sites/robin-ryan/2019/03/07/how-to-write-a-linkedin-headline-that-gets-you-noticed/#3e978f2a2d7e; and A. George, "3 Ways to Be a Better LinkedIn Connection," *Inc.,* February 11, 2019, https://www.inc.com/amy-george/3-ways-to-be-a-better-linkedin-connection.html?cid=search.

60. J. Meister, "Want to Be a More Productive Employee? Get on Social Networks," *Forbes,* https://www.forbes.com/sites/jeannemeister/2013/04/18/want-to-be-a-more-productive-employee-get-on-social-networks/#39a92ab5753d (accessed April 3, 2019).

61. "18 Companies with Brilliant Digital Strategies," *Econsultancy,* February 26, 2019, https://econsultancy.com/how-digital-helped-dominos-overtake-pizza-hut/; P. Robles, "How Digital Helped Domino's Overtake Pizza Hut," *Econsultancy,* February 22, 2018, https://econsultancy.com/how-digital-helped-dominos-overtake-pizza-hut/.

62. G. De Vynck, "Crowdsourcing Is Canadian Miner's Answer to Slumping Gold," *Bloomberg,* June 23, 2015, http://www.bloomberg.com/news/articles/2015-06-23/gold-crowdsourcing-is-miner-s-answerto-slumping-price.

63. Company website, https://ideas.lego.com/guidelines, and https://ideas.lego.com/blogs (accessed April 2, 2019).

64. L. Jackson, "Cashing In on Americans' No-Rules Approach to Snacking," *The Motley Fool,* August 25, 2018, https://www.fool.com/investing/2018/08/25/cashing-in-on-americans-no-rules-approach-to-snack.aspx; and "Marketer's Brief: Lay's 'Do Us a Flavor' Is Over, But Quirky Flavors Aren't," *AdAge,* July 18, 2018, https://adage.com/article/marketers-brief/marketer-s-lay-s-a-flavor/314259/.

65. C. Zakrzewski, "The Key to Getting Workers to Stop Wasting Time Online," *The Wall Street Journal,* https://www.wsj.com/articles/the-key-to-getting-workers-to-stop-wasting-time-online-1457921545 (accessed April 3, 2019); and K.-Y. Koay and P. Chin-Hooi Soh, "Should Cyberloafing Be Allowed in the Workplace?" *Human Resource Management International Digest,* October 2018, 4–6.

66. C. Conner, "Wasting Time at Work: The Epidemic Continues," *Forbes,* https://www.forbes.com/sites/cherylsnappconner/2015/07/31/wasting-time-at-work-the-epidemic-continues/#76c722f51d94 (accessed April 3, 2019).

67. "Careerbuilder: 53% of Employees Are Using Time at Work to Shop Online, Increase from Last Year, Finds Annual CareerBuilder Survey," http://www.careerbuilder.com/share/aboutus/pressreleasesdetail.aspx?ed=12%2F31%2F2016&id=pr978&sd=11%2F22%2F2016 (accessed April 3, 2019).

68. B. Darrow, "Employers Pay the Real Cost of Fantasy Football," *Fortune,* August 30, 2016, http://fortune.com/2016/08/30/why-fantasy-football-costs-money/.

69. "Does Fantasy Football Sack Productivity?" press release, Challenger, Gray & Christmas, August 30, 2016, http://www.challengergray.com/press/press-releases/fantasy-football-could-cost-17b-worth-it.

70. C. C. Rosen, L. S. Simon, R. S. Gajendran, R. E. Johnson, H. W. Lee, and S.-H. Lin, "Boxed in by Your Inbox: Implications of Daily E-Mail Demands for Managers' Leadership Behaviors," *Journal of Applied Psychology,* January 2019, 19–33.

71. C. P. Estévez-Mujica and E. Quintane, "E-mail Communication Patterns and Job Burnout," *PLoS ONE,* March 8, 2018, 1–25.

72. S. Holtz, "The Debate about Blocking Social Media in the Workplace," *Monster,* https://hiring.monster.com/hr/hr-best-practices/workforce-management/employee-performance-management/blocking-social-media-us.aspx (accessed April 3, 2019).

73. M. C. Long, "How Social Media Actually Boosts Efficiency in an Office Environment," *AdWeek,* May 10, 2018, https://www.adweek.com/digital/how-social-media-actually-boosts-efficiency-in-an-office-environment/.

74. Stephanie Vozza, "Why Banning Facebook at Work Is a Stupid Move," Entrepreneur Media, Inc., September 30, 2013, https://www.entrepreneur.com/article/228641.

75. National Conference of State Legislatures, "Access to Social Media Usernames and Passwords," March 15, 2019, http://www.ncsl.org/research/telecommunications-and-information-technology/employer-access-to-social-media-passwords-2013.aspx.

76. N. Goodman, "Micro-Aggressions and Phubbing in the Age of FoMO," *Training,* https://trainingmag.com/trgmag-article/micro-aggressions-and-phubbing-age-fomo (accessed April 3, 2019).

77. J. Ducharme, "'Phubbing' Is Hurting Your Relationships. Here's What It Is," *Time,* March 29, 2018, http://time.com/5216853/what-is-phubbing/.

78. N. Goodman, "Micro-Aggressions and Phubbing in the Age of FoMO," *Training,* https://trainingmag.com/trgmag-article/micro-aggressions-and-phubbing-age-fomo (accessed April 3, 2019).

79. N. Goodman, "Micro-Aggressions and Phubbing in the Age of FoMO," *Training,* https://trainingmag.com/trgmag-article/micro-aggressions-and-phubbing-age-fomo (accessed April 3, 2019); and J. Ducharme, "'Phubbing' Is Hurting Your Relationships. Here's What It Is," *Time,* March 29, 2018, http://time.com/5216853/what-is-phubbing/.

80. J. Ducharme, "'Phubbing' Is Hurting Your Relationships. Here's What It Is," *Time,* March 29, 2018, http://time.com/5216853/what-is-phubbing/.

81. N. Goodman, "Micro-Aggressions and Phubbing in the Age of FoMO," *Training,* https://trainingmag.com/trgmag-article/micro-aggressions-and-phubbing-age-fomo (accessed April 3, 2019); and J. Ducharme, "'Phubbing' Is Hurting Your Relationships. Here's What It Is," *Time,* March 29, 2018, http://time.com/5216853/what-is-phubbing/.

82. K. Weir, "(Dis)connected," *Monitor on Psychology,* March 2017, 42–48.

83. K. Weir, "(Dis)connected," *Monitor on Psychology,* March 2017, 42–48.

84. "Managing and Leveraging Workplace Use of Social Media," *Society for Human Resource Management,* https://www.shrm.org/resourcesandtools/tools-and-samples/toolkits/pages/managingsocialmedia.aspx (accessed April 3, 2019).

85. The Coca-Cola Company, "Social Media Principles." https://www.coca-colacompany.com/stories/online-social-media-principles, (accessed June 19, 2019).

86. J. Oravec, "Deconstructing 'Personal Privacy' in an Age of Social Media: information Control and Reputation Management Dimensions," *International Journal of the Academic Business World* 6, Spring 2012, 95–101.

87. G. Schmidt and K. O'Connor, "Fired for Facebook: Using NLRB Guidance to Craft Appropriate Social Media Policies," *Business Horizons,* 2015, 571–579.

88. Kathy Gurchiek, "Workers Using Own Devices for Work Expect Employers to Respect Their Privacy," SHRM, July 20, 2015, https://www.shrm.org/resourcesandtools/hr-topics/technology/pages/why-byod-and-privacy-are-important.aspx

89. Adapted from K. Gurchiek, "Workers Using Own Devices for Work Expect Employers to Respect Their Privacy," *Society for Human Resource Management,* July 20, 2015, https://www.shrm.org/hrdisciplines/technology/pages/why-byod-and-privacy-are-important.aspx.

90. J. Robbins, "How to Ace Your interview on Skype," *blogs.skype.com,* April 3, 2018, https://blogs.skype.com/tips/2018/04/03/how-to-ace-your-interview-on-skype/; "The New Secrets to Rocking Your Skype Interview," *The Muse.com,* https://www.themuse.com/advice/the-new-secrets-to-rocking-your-skype-interview (accessed March 30, 2019); P. Loretto, "How to Ace a Skype Interview," *The Balance Careers.com,* January 21, 2019, https://www.thebalancecareers.com/learn-how-to-ace-a-skype-interview-1986906.

91. C. Anderson, "How to Give a Killer Presentation," *Harvard Business Review,* https://hbr.org/2013/06/how-to-give-a-killer-presentation (accessed April 3, 2019).

92. "Top 20 Public Speaking Quotes," Institute of Public Speaking, https://www.instituteofpublicspeaking.com/public-speaking-tips/top-20-public-speaking-quotes/ (accessed March 30, 2019).

93. A. Bryant, "How to Speak in Public," *The New York Times,* https://www.nytimes.com/guides/year-of-living-better/how-to-speak-in-public (accessed April 3, 2019); B. Liu, "5 Simple Ways to Become a More Impressive Public Speaker," *Inc.,* June 30, 2015, http://www.inc.com/betty-liu/5-easy-ways-to-improve-your-stage-presence.html; and J. Moore, "How Anyone Can Become a Good Public Speaker," *Time,* April 1, 2015, http://time.com/3758692/become-good-public-speaker.

94. A. Bryant, "How to Speak in Public," *The New York Times,* https://www.nytimes.com/guides/year-of-living-better/how-to-speak-in-public (accessed April 3, 2019); and P. Armstrong, "Stop Using PowerPoint, Harvard University Says It's Damaging Your Brand and Your Company," *Forbes,* July 5, 2017, https://www.forbes.com/sites/paularmstrongtech/2017/07/05/stop-using-powerpoint-harvard-university-says-its-damaging-your-brand-and-your-company/#213ede7e3e65.

95. Kerry Patterson, Joseph Grenny, Ron McMillan, and Al Switzler, *Crucial Conversations: Tools for Talking When Stakes Are High* (New York: McGraw-Hill Education, 2012).

96. K. Patterson, J. Grenny, R. McMillan, and S. Switzler, *Crucial Conversations: Tools for Talking When Stakes Are High* (New York: McGraw-Hill, 2012).

97. D. Stam D. van Knippenberg, B. Wisse, and A. N. Pieterse, "Motivation in Words: Promotion- and Prevention-Oriented Leader Communication in Times of Crisis," *Journal of Management,* September 2018, 2859–2887; and D. W. Robertson, "Training Resilient Leaders during Times of Change," *Leadership Excellence,* August 2018, 16–18.

98. Joseph Grenny, "How Can We Significantly Improve Bottom-Line Results?" Association for Talent Development, March 16, 2015, https://www.td.org/insights/how-can-we-significantly-improve-bottom-line-results.

99. "The Manager Effect: 1 Out of 3 Managers Can't Handle High-Stakes Situations and as a Result, Their Teams Are Less Successful," *PR Newswire,* November 13, 2018, https://www.prnewswire.com.

100. Adapted from K. Patterson, J. Grenny, R. McMillan, and S. Switzler, *Crucial Conversations: Tools for Talking When Stakes Are High* (New York: McGraw-Hill, 2012), 154.

101. Sue Shellenbarger, "The Right and Wrong Way to Manage Up at the Office," *The Wall Street Journal,* April 10, 2018, https://www.wsj.com/articles/the-right-and-wrong-way-to-manage-up-at-the-office-1523366792; Justin Reynolds, "What Does It Mean to Manage Up?" TINYPulse, March 14, 2017, https://www.tinypulse.com/blog/what-does-it-mean-to-manage-up; Michael Rosenthal, "Last Word: Constructive Criticism for Managers," Lakewood Media Group, LLC, https://trainingmag.com/content/last-word-constructive-criticism-managers/; and Carol Patton, "Coaching Up," *Lakewood Media Group,* LLC, https://trainingmag.com/content/coaching/.

102. J. Brady, "Managing Up: Is Upwards Feedback Too Great a Challenge for Leadership?" *Journal of Applied Linguistics and Professional Practice,* December 2018, 34–55; and E. Leonard, "Managing Up as a Positive, Collaborative Approach," *Reference & User Services Quarterly,* Winter 2018, 70–72.

103. Adapted from M. Rosenthal, "Constructive Criticism for Managers," *Training,* July/August 2013, 64; and C. Patton, "Coaching Up," *Training,* July/August 2013, 29–31.

104. D. Rousmaniere, "What Everyone Should Know about Managing Up," *Harvard Business Review,* https://hbr.org/2015/01/what-everyone-should-know-about-managing-up.

105. "United Airlines Annual Form 10-K for Year Ended December 31, 2018," http://ir.united.com/investor-relations (accessed March 27, 2019).

106. M. Castillo, "United CEO Oscar Munoz Was Recently Named 'Communicator of the Year' by PR Week," *CNBC,* https://www.cnbc.com/2017/04/11/united-ceo-oscar-munoz-recently-named-communicator-of-the-year.html (accessed March 27, 2019).

107. Ashley Sutter, "Shelby Woman on United Flight Says Incident Was Avoidable," *The Sentinel News,* April 14, 2017, https://www.sentinelnews.com/content/shelby-woman-united-flight-says-incident-was-avoidable.

108. C. Zdanowicz and E. Grinberg, "Passenger Dragged Off Overbooked United Flight," *CNN,* April 10, 2018, https://www.cnn.com/2017/04/10/travel/passenger-removed-united-flight-trnd/index.html.

109. E. McCann, "United's Apologies: A Timeline," *The New York Times,* April 14, 2017, https://www.nytimes.com/2017/04/14/business/united-airlines-passenger-doctor.html.

110. S. Czarnecki, "Timeline of a Crisis: United Airlines," *PRWeek,* June 6, 2017, https://www.prweek.com/article/1435619/timeline-crisis-united-airlines.

111. N. Khomami and J. Lartey, "United Airlines CEO Calls Dragged Passenger 'Disruptive and Belligerent,'" *The Guardian,* April 11, 2017, https://www.theguardian.com/world/2017/apr/11/united-airlines-boss-oliver-munoz-says-passenger-belligerent.

112. C. Zdanowicz and E. Grinberg, "Passenger Dragged Off Overbooked United Flight," *CNN,* April 10, 2018, https://www.cnn.com/2017/04/10/travel/passenger-removed-united-flight-trnd/index.html.

113. N. Khomami and J. Lartey, "United Airlines CEO Calls Dragged Passenger 'Disruptive and Belligerent,'" *The Guardian,* April 11, 2017, https://www.theguardian.com/world/2017/apr/11/united-airlines-boss-oliver-munoz-says-passenger-belligerent.

114. J. Passy, "Survey: Nearly Half of Young Americans Say They Won't Fly United Anymore," *MarketWatch,* April 21, 2017, https://www.marketwatch.com/story/nearly-half-of-young-americans-wont-fly-united-anymore-2017-04-21.

115. S. Czarnecki, "Timeline of a Crisis: United Airlines," *PRWeek,* June 6, 2017, https://www.prweek.com/article/1435619/timeline-crisis-united-airlines.

116. E. McCann, "United's Apologies: A Timeline," *The New York Times,* April 14, 2017, https://www.nytimes.com/2017/04/14/business/united-airlines-passenger-doctor.html.

117. J. Passy, "Survey: Nearly Half of Young Americans Say They Won't Fly United Anymore," *MarketWatch,* April 21, 2017, https://www.marketwatch.com/story/nearly-half-of-young-americans-wont-fly-united-anymore-2017-04-21.

118. C. Thompson, "United's CEO Bought a Full Page Ad in Dramatic Apology for Passenger Dragged Off Plane," *Business Insider,* April 27, 2017, https://www.businessinsider.com/united-ceo-apologizes-in-ad-for-passenger-dragged-from-flight-2017-4.

119. B. Meier, "Oscar Munoz Won't Get Planned Promotion to Chairman of United," *The New York Times,* April 21, 2017, https://www.nytimes.com/2017/04/21/business/united-airlines-ceo.html?_r=0.

120. Jessica Baron, "Life Insurers Can Use Social Media Posts to Determine Premiums, As Long As They Don't Discriminate," *Forbes Media, LLC,* February 4, 2019, https://www.forbes.com/sites/jessicabaron/2019/02/04/life-insurers-can-use-social-media-posts-to-determine-premiums/#60e5fd6023ce.

121. L. Scism, "New York Insurers Can Evaluate Your Social Media Use—If They Can Prove Why It's Needed," *The Wall Street Journal,* January 30, 2019, https://www.wsj.com/articles/new-york-insurers-can-evaluate-your-social-media-useif-they-can-prove-why-its-needed-11548856802.

122. A. Chen, "Why the Future of Life Insurance May Depend on Your Online Presence," *The Verge,* February 7, 2019, https://www.theverge.com/2019/2/7/18211890/social-media-life-insurance-new-york-algorithms-big-data-discrimination-online-records.

123. J. Baron, "Life Insurers Can Use Social Media Posts to Determine Premiums, As Long As They Don't Discriminate," *Forbes,* February 4, 2019, https://www.forbes.com/sites/jessicabaron/2019/02/04/life-insurers-can-use-social-media-posts-to-determine-premiums/#4b99378023ce.

124. W. Knight, "Biased Algorithms Are Everywhere, and No One Seems to Care," *MIT Technology Review,* July 12, 2017, https://www.technologyreview.com/s/608248/biased-algorithms-are-everywhere-and-no-one-seems-to-care/.

125. J. Baron, "Life Insurers Can Use Social Media Posts to Determine Premiums, As Long As They Don't Discriminate," *Forbes,* February 4, 2019, https://www.forbes.com/sites/jessicabaron/2019/02/04/life-insurers-can-use-social-media-posts-to-determine-premiums/#4b99378023ce.

126. Jessica Baron, "Life Insurers Can Use Social Media Posts to Determine Premiums, As Long As They Don't Discriminate," *Forbes Media, LLC,* February 4, 2019, https://www.forbes.com/sites/jessicabaron/2019/02/04/life-insurers-can-use-social-media-posts-to-determine-premiums/#60e5fd6023ce.

127. L. Scism, "New York Insurers Can Evaluate Your Social Media Use—If They Can Prove Why It's Needed," *The Wall Street Journal,* January 30, 2019, https://www.wsj.com/articles/new-york-insurers-can-evaluate-your-social-media-useif-they-can-prove-why-its-needed-11548856802.

128. J. Baron, "Life Insurers Can Use Social Media Posts to Determine Premiums, As Long As They Don't Discriminate," *Forbes,* February 4, 2019, https://www.forbes.com/sites/jessicabaron/2019/02/04/life-insurers-can-use-social-media-posts-to-determine-premiums/#4b99378023ce.

CHAPTER 10

1. R. Maurer, "Salary Negotiations Aren't Happening as Much as You Think," *SHRM.org,* February 20, 2018, https://www.shrm.org/resourcesandtools/hr-topics/talent-acquisition/pages/salary-negotiations-are-not-happening.aspx.

2. Adapted from G. Moran, "These Are the Salary Trends You Need to Know Before Your Next Negotiation," *FastCompany.com,* February 25, 2019, https://www.fastcompany.com/90309036/these-are-the-salary-trends-you-need-to-know-before-your-next-negotiation; and "7 Negotiating Tricks to Get the Salary You Deserve in 2016," *Business Insider,* January 10, 2016, http://www.businessinsider.com.au/tips-to-negotiate-your-salary-2015-12#/#keep-silent-until-the-interview-process-is-over-1.

3. Adapted from G. Moran, "These Are the Salary Trends You Need to Know Before Your Next Negotiation," *FastCompany.com,* February 25, 2019, https://www.fastcompany.com/90309036/these-are-the-salary-trends-you-need-to-know-before-your-next-negotiation; and "7 Negotiating Tricks to Get the Salary You Deserve in 2016," *Business Insider,* January 10, 2016, http://www.businessinsider.com.au/tips-to-negotiate-your-salary-2015-12#/#keep-silent-until-the-interview-process-is-over-1.

4. Eilene Zimmerman, "How to Benchmark Your Salary," CBS Interactive Inc., July 23, 2009, https://www.cbsnews.com/news/how-to-benchmark-your-salary/.

5. Adapted from Society of Human Resource Management, "Managing Workplace Conflict," *SHRM.org,* https://www.shrm.org/resourcesandtools/tools-and-samples/toolkits/pages/managingworkplaceconflict.aspx (accessed March 23, 2019).

6. Adapted from N. Regier, *Conflict Without Casualties* (Berrett-Koehler, 2017), as cited in D. Meinert, "Why Workplace Conflict Can Be Healthy," *SHRM.org,* April 18, 2017, https://www.shrm.org/hr-today/news/hr-magazine/0517/pages/why-workplace-conflict-can-be-healthy.aspx.

7. D. Meinert, "Why Workplace Conflict Can Be Healthy," *SHRM.org,* April 18, 2017, https://www.shrm.org/hr-today/news/hr-magazine/0517/pages/why-workplace-conflict-can-be-healthy.aspx.

8. Adapted from C. Coats, "Workplace Conflict: Friend or Foe?" *Forbes.com,* October 16, 2018, https://www.forbes.com/sites/forbescoachescouncil/2018/10/16/workplace-conflict-friend-or-foe/#4d5d4af7549d.

9. G. R. Massey and P. L. Dawes, "The Antecedents and Consequence of Functional and Dysfunctional Conflict between Marketing Managers and Sales Managers," *Industrial Marketing Management,* 2007, 1118–1129. See also S. Alper, D. Tjosvold, and K. S. Law, "Interdependence and Controversy in Group Decision Making: Antecedents to Effective Self-Managing Teams," *Organizational Behavior and Human Decision Processes,* April 1998, 33–52.

10. Adapted from Society of Human Resource Management, "Managing Workplace Conflict," *SHRM.org,* https://www.shrm.org/resourcesandtools/tools-and-samples/toolkits/pages/managingworkplaceconflict.aspx (accessed March 23, 2019).

11. Society of Human Resource Management, "Managing Workplace Conflict," https://www.shrm.org/resourcesandtools/tools-and-samples/toolkits/pages/managingworkplaceconflict.aspx (accessed July 4, 2019).

12. C. E. Thiel, J. Harvey, S. Courtright, and B. Bradley, "What Doesn't Kill You Makes You Stronger: How Teams Rebound from Early-Stage Relationship Conflict," *Journal of Management,* 45, 2019, 1623–1659.

13. "General Information on Escalation," International Online Training Program on Intractable Conflict, Conflict Research Consortium, University of Colorado, http://www.colorado.edu/conflict/peace/problem/escalation.htm, accessed June 12, 2013.

14. Inspired by M. Yate, "Your Career Q&A: How to Explain Why You Want to Leave a Job," *SHRM.org*, January 16, 2019, https://www.shrm.org/resourcesandtools/hr-topics/organizational-and-employee-development/pages/your-career-qa-how-to-explain-why-you-want-to-leave-a-job.aspx.; and "How to Explain Your Reasons for Leaving a Job," *Indeed.com*, https://www.indeed.com/career-advice/interviewing/how-to-explain-your-reasons-for-leaving-a-job, downloaded February 19, 2019.

15. C. Hanson, "Viewpoint: The Art and Science of Conflict Management," *SHRM.org*, August 7, 2018, https://www.shrm.org/resourcesandtools/hr-topics/employee-relations/pages/viewpoint-the-art-and-science-of-conflict-management.aspx.

16. Cynthia B. Hanson, "Viewpoint: The Art and Science of Conflict Management," *SHRM*, August 7, 2018, https://www.shrm.org/resourcesandtools/hr-topics/employee-relations/pages/viewpoint-the-art-and-science-of-conflict-management.aspx.

17. Adapted from Managing Mental Health Matters, "Why Dealing with Conflict is Difficult," Centre for Mental Health in the Workplace, October 2018, https://www.workplacestrategiesformentalhealth.com/mmhm/pdf/articles/Why_Dealing_with_Conflict_is_Difficult.pdf.

18. Karen Duncum, "Turning Conflict into Cooperation," Bloomberg L.P., October 15, 2010, https://www.bloomberg.com/news/articles/2010-10-15/turning-conflict-into-cooperation.

19. D. Adams, "Positive and Negative Consequences of Conflict in Organizations," *Chron.com*, March 6, 2019, https://smallbusiness.chron.com/positive-negative-consequences-conflict-organizations-10254.html.

20. C. E. Thiel, J. A. Griffith, J. H. Hardy, D. R. Peterson, and S. Connelly, "Let's Look at This Another Way: How Supervisors Can Help Subordinates Manage the Threat of Relationship Conflict," *Journal of Leadership and Organizational Studies*, 25, 368–380.

21. J. Leon-Perez, F. Medina, A. Arenas, and L. Munduate, "The Relationship between Interpersonal Conflict and Workplace Bullying," *Journal of Managerial Psychology*, 2015, 250–263.

22. I. Martinez-Corts, E. Demerouti, A. Bakker, and M. Boz, "Spillover of Interpersonal Conflicts from Work into Nonwork: A Daily Diary Study," *Journal of Occupational Health Psychology*, 2015, 326–337.

23. T. Mzezewa, "Airbnb and Miami Beach Are at War. Travelers Are Caught in the Crossfire," *The New York Times*, March 9, 2019, https://www.nytimes.com/2019/03/09/travel/airbnb-miami-beach-war.html.

24. A. Presbitero and L. S. Toledano, "Global Team Members' Performance and the Roles of Cross-Cultural Training, Cultural Intelligence, and Contact Intensity: The Case of Global Teams in IT Offshoring Sector," *The International Journal of Human Resource Management*, 2018, 29, 2188–2208.

25. G. Boccato, D. Capozza, E. Trifiletti, and G. Di Bernardo, "Attachment Security and Intergroup Contact," *Journal of Applied Social Psychology*, 2015, 629–647.

26. H. Deng, K. Leung, C. K. Lam, and X. Huang, "Slacking Off in Comfort: A Dual-Pathway Model for Psychological Safety Climate," *Journal of Management*, 2019, 45, 1114-1144.

27. Q. Zhou and W. Pan, "A Cross-Level Examination of the Process Linking Transformational Leadership and Creativity: The Role of Psychological Safety Climate," *Human Performance*, 2015, 405-424.

28. J. Wang, K. Lueng, and F. Zhou, "Dispositional Approach to Psychological Climate: Relationships between Interpersonal Harmony Motives and Psychological Climate for Communication Safety," *Human Relations*, 2014, 489–515.

29. A. Nixon, J. Lanz, A. Manapragada, V. Bruk-Lee, A. Schantz, and J. Rodriguez, "Nurse Safety: How Is Safety Climate Related to Affect and Attitude?" *Work & Stress*, 2015, 401–419.

30. Created from *Re:Work*, "Understanding Team Effectiveness," *Google.com*, https://rework.withgoogle.com/print/guides/5721312655835136/, as cited in A. S. Hirsch, "Working with People Who Avoid Conflict," *SHRM.org*, September 12, 2018, https://www.shrm.org/resourcesandtools/hr-topics/employee-relations/pages/working-with-people-who-avoid-conflict.aspx; and J. Wang, K. Lueng, and F. Zhou, "Dispositional Approach to Psychological Climate: Relationships between Interpersonal Harmony Motives and Psychological Climate for Communication Safety," *Human Relations*, 2014, 489–515.

31. Adapted from A. S. Hirsch, "Working with People Who Avoid Conflict," *SHRM.org*, September 12, 2018, https://www.shrm.org/resourcesandtools/hr-topics/employee-relations/pages/working-with-people-who-avoid-conflict.aspx.

32. E. M. Hunter, M. A Clark, and D. S. Carlson, "Violating Work-Family Boundaries: Reactions to Interruptions at Work and Hom," *Journal of Management*, 2019, 45, 1284–1308.

33. I. Spieler, S. Scheibe, and C. S. Robnagel, "Keeping Work and Private Life Apart," Age-Related Differences in Managing the Work-Nonwork Interface," *Journal of Organizational Behavior*, 39, 2018, 12334-1251.

34. I. Spieler, S. Scheibe, and C. S. Robnagel, "Keeping Work and Private Life Apart," Age-Related Differences in Managing the Work-Nonwork Interface," *Journal of Organizational Behavior*, 39, 2018, 12334-1251.

35. E. M. Hunter, M. A. Clark, ad D. S. Carlson, "Violating Work-Family Boundaries: Reactions to Interruptions at Work and Home," *Journal of Management*, 45, 2019, 1284–1308.

36. E. M. Hunter, M. A. Clark, ad D. S. Carlson, "Violating Work-Family Boundaries: Reactions to Interruptions at Work and Home," *Journal of Management*, 45, 2019, 1284–1308.

37. R. Montanez, "The Highest-Rated Companies for Work-Life Balance in 2018," *Forbes.com*, October 1, 2018, https://www.forbes.com/sites/rachelmontanez/2018/10/01/the-2018-highest-rated-companies-for-work-life-balance/#34651ce07cb1.

38. R. Montanez, "The Highest-Rated Companies for Work-Life Balance in 2018," *Forbes.com*, October 1, 2018, https://www.forbes.com/sites/rachelmontanez/2018/10/01/the-2018-highest-rated-companies-for-work-life-balance/#34651ce07cb1.

39. Adapted from E. M. Hunter, M. A. Clark, ad D. S. Carlson, "Violating Work-Family Boundaries: Reactions to Interruptions at Work and Home," *Journal of Management*, 45, 2019, 1284–1308.

40. "Flexible Work Plans Key to Retention," *HR Magazine*, December 2010, 105.

41. Iliana Castillo-Frick, "Words of Wisdom: The Evolution of Workflex," *SHRM*, November 21, 2017, https://www.shrm.org/hr-today/news/hr-magazine/1217/pages/words-of-wisdom-the-evolution-of-workflex-castillo-frick.aspx.

42. C. Fritz and D. Van Knippenberg, "Gender and Leadership Aspiration: The Impact of Work-Life Initiatives," *Human Resource Management*, 57, 2018, 855–868.

43. K. Gurchiek, "'Best Companies for Dads' Spotlights Exemplary Support for Working Fathers," *SHRM.org*, December 6, 2018, https://www.shrm.org/resourcesandtools/hr-topics/behavioral-competencies/global-and-cultural-effectiveness/pages/best-companies-for-dads-support-working-fathers.aspx.

44. Kathy Gurchiek, "'Best Companies for Dads' Spotlights Exemplary Support for Working Fathers," *SHRM*, December 6, 2018, https://www.shrm.org/resourcesandtools/hr-topics/behavioral-competencies/global-and-cultural-effectiveness/pages/best-companies-for-dads-support-working-fathers.aspx.

45. R. Montanez, "The Highest-Rated Companies for Work-Life Balance in 2018," *Forbes.com*, October 1, 2018, https://www.forbes.com/sites/rachelmontanez/2018/10/01/the-2018-highest-rated-companies-for-work-life-balance/#34651ce07cb1.

46. S. C. Paustian-Underdahl and J. R. B. Halbesleben, "Examining the Influence of Climate, Supervisor Guidance, and Behavioral Integrity on Work-Family Conflict: A Demands and Resources Approach," *Journal of Organizational Behavior*, 2014, 447–463.

47. R. Maurer, "Flexwork Participation Lagging," *HR Magazine*, April 2015, 75.

48. B. Luscombe, "How Deloitte CEO Cathy Engelbert Rose to the Top," *Time*, March 22, 2018, http://time.com/5210505/how-deloitte-ceo-cathy-engelbert-rose-to-the-top/.

49. M. Houshmand, J. O'Reilly, S. Robinson, and A. Wolff, "Escaping Bullying: The Simultaneous Impact of Individual and Unit-Level Bullying on Turnover Intentions," *Human Relations*, 65, 2012, 901–918.

50. T. Vahle-Hinz, A. Baethge, and R. Van Dick, "Beyond One Work Day? A Daily Diary Study on Causal and Reverse Effects Between Experienced Workplace Incivility and Behaving Rude Towards Others," *European Journal of Work and Organizational Psychology*," 28, 2019, 272–285; and A. Murrell, "Stopping the Downward Spiral of Workplace Incivility," *Forbes.com*, July 16, 2018, https://www.forbes.com/sites/audreymurrell/2018/07/16/stopping-the-downward-spiral-of-workplace-incivility/#4967a87954ef.

51. C. Porath and C. Pearson, "The Price of Incivility—Lack of Respect Hurts Morale and the Bottom Line," *Harvard Business Review*, January–February 2013, 115–121.

52. C. Porath and C. Pearson, "The Price of Incivility—Lack of Respect Hurts Morale and the Bottom Line," *Harvard Business Review*, January–February 2013, 115–121.

53. T. Vahle-Hinz, A. Baethge, and R. Van Dick, "Beyond One Work Day? A Daily Diary Study On Causal and Reverse Effects Between Experienced Workplace Incivility and Behaving Rude Towards Others," *European Journal of Work and Organizational Psychology*," 2019, 28, 272–285; and A. Murrell, "Stopping the Downward Spiral of Workplace Incivility," *Forbes.com*, July 16, 2018, https://www.forbes.com/sites/audreymurrell/2018/07/16/stopping-the-downward-spiral-of-workplace-incivility/#4967a87954ef.

54. M. Sharifirad, "Can Incivility Impair Teams' Creative Performance Through Paralyzing Employees' Knowledge Sharing? A Multi-Level Approach," *Leadership and Organization Development Journal*, 2016, 200–225.

55. C. Porath, T. Fould, and A. Erez, "How Incivility Hijacks Performance: It Robs Cognitive Resources, Increases Dysfunctional Behavior, and Infects Team Dynamics and Functioning," *Organizational Dynamics*, 2015, 258–265.

56. C. Porath, T. Fould, and A. Erez, "How Incivility Hijacks Performance: It Robs Cognitive Resources, Increases Dysfunctional Behavior, and Infects Team Dynamics and Functioning," *Organizational Dynamics*, 2015, 258–265.

57. M. Coetzee and J. Van Dyk, "Workplace Bullying and Turnover Intention: Exploring Work Engagement as a Mediator," *Psychological Reports*, 2018, 121, 375–392.

58. L. Nagele-Piazza, "Workplace Bullying and Harassment: What's the Difference?" *SHRM.org,* March 28, 2018, https://www.shrm.org/resourcesandtools/legal-and-compliance/state-and-local-updates/pages/workplace-bullying.aspx.

59. S. Einarsen, A. Skogstad, E. Rorvik. A. B. Lande, and M. B. Nielsen, "Climate for Conflict Management, Exposure to Workplace Bullying and Work Engagement: A Moderated Mediation Analysis," *The International Journal of Human Resource Management*, 29, 2018, 549–570.; and M. Houshmand, J. O'Reilly, S. Robinson, and A. Wolf, "Escaping Bullying," *Human Relations*, July 12, 2012, 901–918.

60. S. Valentine and G. Fleischman, "From Schoolyard to Workplace: The Impact of Bullying on Sale and Business Employees' Machiavellianism, Job Satisfaction, and Perceived Importance of an Ethical Issue," *Human Resource Management*, 57, 2018, 293–305.

61. S. Branch and J. Murray, "Workplace Bullying: Is Lack of Understanding the Reason for Inaction?" *Organizational Dynamics*, 2015, 287–295.

62. S. Branch and J. Murray, "Workplace Bullying: Is Lack of Understanding the Reason for Inaction?" *Organizational Dynamics*, 2015, 287–295.

63. D. P. Ford, "Virtual Harassment: Media Characteristics' Role in Psychological Health," *Journal of Managerial Psychology* 28, 2013, 408–428.

64. Y. Park, C. Fritz, and S. M. Jex, "Daily Cyber Incivility and Distress: The Moderating Roles of Resources at Work and Home," *Journal of Management*, 44, 2018, 2535–2557; and D. P. Ford, "Virtual Harassment: Media Characteristics' Role in Psychological Health," *Journal of Managerial Psychology* 28, 2013, 408–428.

65. Y. Park, C. Fritz, and S. M. Jex, "Daily Cyber Incivility and Distress: The Moderating Roles of Resources at Work and Home," *Journal of Management*, 44, 2018, 2535–2557.

66. Y. Park, C. Fritz, and S. M. Jex, "Daily Cyber Incivility and Distress: The Moderating Roles of Resources at Work and Home," *Journal of Management*, 44, 2018, 2554.

67. EEOC, "Harassment," *EEOC.gov,* https://www.eeoc.gov/laws/types/harassment.cfm (accessed April 9, 2019).

68. Johnny C. Taylor, "#MeToo: Where Was HR?" *SHRM,* January 30, 2018, https://www.shrm.org/hr-today/news/hr-magazine/0218/pages/metoo-where-was-hr.aspx.

69. C. R. Feldblum and S. P. Masling, "Convincing CEOs to Make Harassment Prevention a Priority," *SHRM.org,* November 19, 2018, https://www.shrm.org/resourcesandtools/hr-topics/employee-relations/pages/convincing-ceos-to-make-harassment-prevention-a-priority.aspx.

70. EEOC, "Harassment," EEOC.gov, https://www.eeoc.gov/laws/types/harassment.cfm (accessed April 9, 2019).

71. Society of Human Resource Management, "What Are the Different Types of Sexual Harassment?" *SHRM.org,* January 12, 2018, https://www.shrm.org/resourcesandtools/tools-and-samples/hr-qa/pages/typesofsexualharassment.aspx.

72. J. A. Segal, "Strengthen Your Harassment Complaint Process," *HR Magazine,* April 2018, 64–65; and J. A. Segal, "Upgrade Your Anti-Harassment Policy," *HR Magazine,* March 2018, 64–65.

73. See J. S. Valacich and C. Schwenk, "Devil's Advocacy and Dialectical Inquiry Effects on Face-to-Face and Computer-Mediated Group Decision Making," *Organizational Behavior and Human Decision Processes,* August 1995, 158–173.

74. See D. M. Schweiger, W. R. Sandberg, and P. L. Rechner, "Experiential Effects of Dialectical Inquiry, Devil's Advocacy, and Consensus Approaches to Strategic Decision Making," *Academy of Management Journal,* December 1989, 745–772.

75. T. Yasir, J. Qi, A. Umair, and T. Anum, "Antecedents of Frontline Manager Handling Relationship Conflicts," *International Journal of Conflict management*, 29, 2018, 2–23.

76. Pamela Valencia, "Trouble Is Brewing," Association for Talent Development, April 2015, https://www.td.org/magazines/td-magazine/trouble-is-brewing.

77. P. K. Lam and K. S. Chin, "Managing Conflict in Collaborative New Product Development: A Supplier Perspective," *International Journal of Quality and Reliability Management,* 2007, 891–907.

78. J. Morrison, "The Relationship between Emotional Intelligence Competencies and Preferred Conflict Handling Styles," *Journal of Nursing Management,* August 2008, 974–983.

79. Adapted from the American Management Association, "Answers to Personality Conflicts," January 24, 2019, https://www.amanet.org/articles/answers-to-personality-conflicts/.

80. F. Aquila, "Taming the Litigation Beast," *Bloomberg Businessweek,* April 6, 2010.

81. K. Shonk, "What is Alternative Dispute Resolution?" Harvard Law School Program on Negotiation, December 27, 2018, https://www.pon.harvard.edu/daily/dispute-resolution/what-is-alternative-dispute-resolution/.

82. P. Holtzman, "Why Litigate When You Can Mediate?" *HR Magazine,* September 2015, 86–87.

83. For more, see M. M. Clark, "A Jury of Their Peers," *HR Magazine,* January 2004, 54–59.

84. P. Holtzman, "Why Litigate When You Can Mediate?" *HR Magazine,* September 2015, 86–87.

85. For an excellent description of the pros and cons from both employee and employer perspectives, see C. D. Coleman, "Is Mandatory Employment Arbitration Living Up to Its Expectations? A View from the Employer's Perspective," *ABA Journal of Labor & Employment Law,* Winter 2010, 227–239. The EEOC website also has excellent additional information on ADR techniques: http://www.eeoc.gov/federal/adr/typesofadr.cfm.

86. Adapted from N. Scheiber, "Why Wendy's Is Facing Campus Protests (It's All About the Tomatoes)," *The New York Times,* March 7, 2019, https://www.nytimes.com/2019/03/07/business/economy/wendys-farm-workers-tomatoes.html; and Coalition of Immokalee Workers webpage, https://ciw-online.org/about/ (accessed March 31, 2019).

87. A. C. Shilton, "How to Be an Ace Salary Negotiator (Even if You Hate Conflict)," *The New York Times,* August 10, 2018, https://www.nytimes.com/2018/08/10/smarter-living/how-to-negotiate-salary.html.

88. J. Sebenius, "Why a Behavioral Theory of Labor Negotiation Remains a Triumph at 50 but the Labels 'Distributive' and 'Integrative' Should Be Retired," *Negotiation Journal,* October 2015, 335–347.

89. K. Campbell and R. O'Leary, "Big Ideas for Big Problems: Lessons from Conflict Resolution for Public Administration," *Conflict Resolution Quarterly,* Winter 2015, http://onlinelibrary.wiley.com/doi/10.1002/crq.21146/abstract. See also P. L. Stockli and C. Tanner, "Are Integrative or Distributive Outcomes More Satisfactory? The Effects of Interest-Based versus Value-Based Issues on Negotiator Satisfaction," *European Journal of Social Psychology,* 2014, 202–208.

90. J. Graham, L. Lawrence, and W. Requejo, "Inventive Negotiation: Getting Beyond Yes," *Organizational Dynamics,* 2015, 35–46.

91. Adapted from K. Campbell and R. O'Leary, "Big Ideas for Big Problems: Lessons from Conflict Resolution for Public Administration," *Conflict Resolution Quarterly,* Winter 2015, http://onlinelibrary.wiley.com/doi/10.1002/crq.21146/abstract.

92. N. Dimotakis, D. E. Conlon, and R. Ilies, "The Mind and Heart (Literally) of the Negotiator: Personality and Contextual Determinants of Experiential Reactions in Economic Outcomes in Negotiation," *Journal of Applied Psychology,* 2012, 183–193.

93. L. Schiff, "Revisiting 'Win-Win' Negotiation: It's Still a Losing Game," *Forbes,* March 13, 2013, http://www.forbes.com/sites/jimcamp/2013/03/11/revisiting-win-win-negotiation-its-still-a-losing-game/ (accessed August 19, 2013).

94. C. Porath and C. Pearson, "The Price of Incivility—Lack of Respect Hurts Morale and the Bottom Line," *Harvard Business Review,* January–February 2013, 115–121.

95. C. Porath and C. Pearson, "The Price of Incivility—Lack of Respect Hurts Morale and the Bottom Line," *Harvard Business Review,* January–February 2013, 115–121.

96. N. A. Welsh, "The Reputational Advantages of Demonstrating Trustworthiness: Using the Reputation Index with Law Students," *Negotiation Journal,* January 2012, 117–141.

97. Adapted from J. Koblin, "Hollywood Upended as Unions Tell Writers to Fire Agents," *The New York Times,* April 12, 2019, https://www.nytimes.com/2019/04/12/business/media/hollywood-writers-agents-fire.html.

98. G. A. Van Kleef and S. Cote, "Emotional Dynamics in Conflict and Negotiation: Individual, Dyadic, and Group Processes," *Annual Review of Organizational Psychology and Organizational Behavior,* 5, 2018, 437–464.

99. Adapted from K. Leary, J. Pillemer, and M. Wheeler, "Negotiating with Emotion," *Harvard Business Review,* January–February 2013, 96–103. See also A. Wood Brooks, "Emotion in the Art of Negotiation," *Harvard Business Review,* December 2015, 57–64.

100. N. Rothman and G. Northcraft, "Unlocking Integrative Potential: Expressed Emotional Ambivalence and Negotiation Outcomes," *Organizational Behavior and Human Decision Processes,* 2015, 65–76.

101. G. A. Van Kleef and S. Cote, "Emotional Dynamics in Conflict and Negotiation: Individual, Dyadic, and Group Processes," *Annual Review of Organizational Psychology and Organizational Behavior,* 5, 2018, 437–464.

102. Eileen Hoenigman Meyer, "Salary Negotiation Scripts for Any Job," *Glassdoor,* April 1, 2019, https://www.glassdoor.com/blog/salary-negotiation-scripts-for-any-job/.

103. B. Gunia, "Ethics in Negotiation: Causes and Consequences," *Academy of Management Perspectives,* 33, 2019, 3–11.

104. Lily Morse and Taya R. Cohen, "Moral Character in Negotiation," *Academy of Management Perspectives* 33, no. 1 (February 2019): 12–25. https://doi.org/10.5465/amp.2017.0051.

105. L. Morse, and T. R. Cohen, "Moral Character in Negotiation," *Academy of Management Perspectives*, 33, 2019, 12–25.

106. M. R. Rees, A. E. Tenbrunsel, and M. H. Bazerman, "Bounded Ethicality and Ethical Fading in Negotiations: Understanding Unintended Unethical Behavior," *Academy of Management Perspectives*, 33, 2019, 26–42.

107. J. P. Gaspar, R. Methasani, and M. Schweitzer, "Fifty Shades of Deception: Characteristics and Consequences of Lying to Negotiators," *Academy of Management Perspectives*, 33, 2019, 62–81.

108. S. Frenkel, N. Confessore, C. Kang, M. Rosenberg, and J. Nicas, "Delay, Deny, and Deflect: How Facebook's Leaders Fought Through Crisis," *The New York Times*, November 14, 2018, https://www.nytimes.com/2018/11/14/technology/facebook-data-russia-election-racism.html.

109. M. Isaac, "When Zuckerberg Asserted Control, Instagram's Founders Chafed," *The New York Times*, September 25, 2018, https://www.nytimes.com/2018/09/25/technology/instagram-cofounders-resign-zuckerberg.html.

110. S. Frenkel and C. Metz, "WhatsApp Co-Founder Leaving Facebook Amid User Data Disputes," *The New York Times*, April 30, 2018, https://www.nytimes.com/2018/04/30/technology/whatsapp-facebook-jan-koum.html.

111. N. Bowles, "Facebook Made Him a Billionaire. Now He's a Critic," *The New York Times*, March 21, 2018, https://www.nytimes.com/2018/03/21/technology/brian-acton-facebook-critic.html.

112. J. Silver-Greenberg and R. Gebeloff, "Arbitration Everywhere, Stacking the Deck of Justice," *The New York Times*, October 31, 2015, http://www.nytimes.com/2015/11/01/business/dealbook/arbitration-every-where-stacking-the-deck-of-justice.html?_r=0.

113. R. Mabud, "Google Put an End to Forced Arbitration—And Why That's So Important," *Forbes.com*, February 26, 2019, https://www.forbes.com/sites/rakeenmabud/2019/02/26/worker-organizing-results-in-big-change-at-google/#19e2ba954399.

114. R. Mabud, "Google Put an End to Forced Arbitration—And Why That's So Important," *Forbes.com*, February 26, 2019, https://www.forbes.com/sites/rakeenmabud/2019/02/26/worker-organizing-results-in-big-change-at-google/#19e2ba954399.

CHAPTER 11

1. M. Rowh, "Transferable Skills for College Students," *College Xpress*, https://www.collegexpress.com/articles-and-advice/career-search/articles/career-success-after-college/transferable-skills-college-students-secret-getting-job/ (accessed April 16, 2019).

2. R. Jenkins, "How to Improve Generation Z's Critical Thinking Skills," *Inc.*, June 27, 2018, https://www.inc.com/ryan-jenkins/2-simple-steps-for-improved-critical-thinking.html?cid=search//.

3. W. Frick, "3 Ways to Improve Your Decision Making," *Harvard Business Review*, January 22, 2018, https://hbr.org/2018/01/3-ways-to-improve-your-decision-making.

4. M. Plummer, "Top Universities Struggle to Develop One of Today's Most In-Demand Skills. Here's How You and Your Company Can," *Inc.*, February 26, 2019, https://www.inc.com/matt-plummer/top-universities-struggle-to-develop-one-of-todays-most-in-demand-skills-heres-how-you-your-company-can.html?cid=search.

5. Organization website, De Bono Group, http://www.debonogroup.com/six_thinking_hats.php (accessed April 2, 2019); H. Schacter, "What Colour Hat Do You Wear in Meetings," *The Globe and Mail*, April 21, 2018, https://www.theglobeandmail.com/business/careers/management/article-what-colour-hat-do-you-wear-in-meetings/.

6. P. Davidson, "Watch Interview Behavior," *The Arizona Republic*, May 15, 2013, CL1.

7. Adapted from I. Janis, *Groupthink*, 2nd ed. (Boston: Houghton Mifflin, 1982, 174–175. Also see J. M. Wellen and M. Neale, "Deviance, Self-Typicality, and Group Cohesion: The Corrosive Effects of the Bad Ales on the Barrel," *Small Group Research*, 2006, 165–186.

8. G. P. Hodgkinson and E. Sadler-Smith, "The Dynamics of Intuition and Analysis in Managerial and Organizational Decision Making," *Academy of Management Perspectives*, November 2018, 473–492.

9. D. Kahneman, *Thinking, Fast and Slow* (New York: Farrar, Straus and Giroux, 2011).

10. V. A. Thompson, G. Pennycook, D. Trippas, and J. St. B. T. Evans, "Do Smart People Have Better Intuitions?" *Journal of Experimental Psychology*, July 2018, 945–961; and J. Okoli and J. Watt, "Crisis Decision-Making: The Overlap between Intuitive and Analytical Strategies," *Management Decisions*, May 2018, 1122–1134.

11. D. Kahneman, "Of 2 Minds: How Fast and Slow Thinking Shape Perception and Choice [Excerpt]," *Scientific American*, https://www.scientificamerican.com/article/kahneman-excerpt-thinking-fast-and-slow/ (accessed April 16, 2019); and A. Ranadive, "What I Learned from 'Thinking, Fast and Slow,'" https://medium.com/leadership-motivation-and-impact/what-i-learned-from-thinking-fast-and-slow-a4a47cf8b5d5 (accessed April 16, 2019).

12. AAMC News, "New Research Shows Increasing Physician Shortages in Both Primary and Specialty Care," April 11, 2018, https://news.aamc.org/press-releases/article/workforce_report_shortage_04112018/.

13. This study was conducted by P. C. Nutt, "Expanding the Search for Alternatives During Strategic Decision Making," *Academy of Management Executive*, November 2004, 13–28.

14. Adapted from I. Janis, *Groupthink*, 2nd ed. (Boston: Houghton Mifflin, 1982, 174–175. Also see J. M. Wellen and M. Neale, "Deviance, Self-Typicality, and Group Cohesion: The Corrosive Effects of the Bad Ales on the Barrel," *Small Group Research*, 2006, 165–186.

15. Herbert A. Simon, "Rational Decision Making in Business Organizations," *The American Economic Review* 69, no. 4 (September 1979): 493–513.

16. G. G. Marchisotti, M. L. C. Domingos, and R. L. De Almeida, "Decision-Making at the First Management Level: The Interference of the Organizational Culture," *Human and Social Management*, May/June 2018, 1–26.

17. "Texting and Driving Statistics 2019," *The Zebra*, January 2, 2019, https://www.thezebra.com/texting-and-driving-statistics/.

18. Kirsten Weir, "Totally Irrational," *Monitor on Psychology* 47, no. 3 (March 2016): 31.

19. A. Alaniz, "How the Lyft IPO Will Benefit General Motors," *GM Authority*, March 1, 2019, http://gmauthority.com/blog/2019/03/how-the-lyft-ipo-will-benefit-general-motors/; and M. Wayland, "GM-Lyft Relationship? It's Complicated," *Automotive News*, December 11, 2017, https://www.autonews.com/article/20171211/MOBILITY/171219939/gm-lyft-relationship-it-s-complicated.

20. C. To, G. J. Kilduff, L. Ordoñez, and M. Schweitzer, "Going for It on Fourth Down: Rivalry Increases Risk Taking, Physiological Arousal, and Promotion Focus," *Academy of Management Journal*, August 2018, 1281–1306.

21. Bounded rationality is discussed by A. R. Memati, A. M. Bhatti, M. Maqsal, I. Mansoor, and F. Naveed, "Impact of Resource Based View and Resource Dependence Theory on Strategic Decision Making," *International Journal of Business Management*, December 2010, 110–115; and H. A. Simon, *Administrative Behavior*, 2nd ed. (New York: Free Press, 1957).

22. Joshua Rothman, "The Art of Decision-Making," *The New Yorker*, January 14, 2019, https://www.newyorker.com/magazine/2019/01/21/the-art-of-decision-making.

23. Joshua Rothman, "The Art of Decision-Making," *The New Yorker*, January 14, 2019, https://www.newyorker.com/magazine/2019/01/21/the-art-of-decision-making.

24. "The Residence of the Future to Be Designed in Lexington, Kentucky, Sponsored by VANHOOSECO," *PR Newswire*, May 9, 2019, https://www.prnewswire.com/news-releases/the-residence-of-the-future-to-be-designed-in-lexington-kentucky-sponsored-by-vanhoo-seco-300847591.html.

25. Anthony Clark Carpio, "Hollywood Burbank Airport Gathers Input Regarding Replacement Terminal," *L.A. Times*, March 29, 2019, https://www.latimes.com/socal/burbank-leader/news/tn-blr-me-replacement-terminal-charrette-20190329-story.html.

26. "The Residence of the Future to Be Designed in Lexington, Kentucky, Sponsored by VANHOOSECO," *PR Newswire*, May 9, 2019, https://www.prnewswire.com/news-releases/the-residence-of-the-future-to-be-designed-in-lexington-kentucky-sponsored-by-vanhooseco-300847591.html.

27. Erin Hayes, "Rye Charrette to Re-imagine Town Center," *Seacostonline.com*, updated May 16, 2019, https://www.seacoastonline.com/news/20190514/rye-charrette-to-re-imagine-town-center.

28. "2019 Charrette: Re-Imagining Streets as Pedestrian Spaces," Drexel University, March 11, 2019, https://drexel.edu/westphal/news-events/news/2019/March/charrette-april-2019/.

29. Daniel Kahneman and G. Klein, "Conditions for Intuitive Expertise: A Failure to Disagree." *American Psychologist* 64, no. 6 (September 2009): 515–26. https://doi: 10.1037/a0016755.

30. C. Chet Miller and R. Duane Ireland, "Intuition in Strategic Decision Making: Friend or Foe in the Fast-Paced 21st Century?" *The Academy of Management Executive* 19, no. 1 (February 2005): 19–30.

31. B. Herzog, "Best of Luck: Why Good Fortune Isn't Just a Game of Chance," *Southwest Magazine*, October 2015, 59–61.

32. Ruth Umoh, "Steve Jobs Attributed His Success to Intuition— Here's How to Use Yours," *CNBC LLC*, May 23, 2018, https://www.cnbc.com/2018/05/23/how-to-trust-your-intuition-like-apple-co-founder-steve-jobs.html.

33. C. Mui, "Tim Cook Is Right—We Must Not Shrink from This Moment," *Forbes*, October 26, 2018, https://www.forbes.com/sites/chunka-mui/2018/10/26/tim-cook-is-right-we-must-not-shrink-from-this-moment/#3d4c7374b916; M. Weinberger, "The Rise of Apple CEO Tim Cook, the Leader of the First $1 Trillion Company in the U.S.," *Business Insider*, August 2, 2018, https://www.businessinsider.com/the-rise-of-apple-ceo-tim-cook-2016-1; Z. Mejia, "Tim Cook: Listening to Steve Jobs Rather Than My Friends Was 'the Best Decision of My Life,'" *CNBC*, June 2018, https://www.cnbc.com/2018/06/20/tim-cook-says-joining-apple-was-the-best-decision-of-his-life.html.

34. J. Haden, "How Experts Make Smart, Fast Decisions: A Nobel Prize Winning Economist Reveals When to Trust Your Intuition and Instinct," *Inc.,* December 10, 2018, https://www.inc.com/jeff-haden/how-experts-make-smart-fast-decisions-a-nobel-prize-winning-economist-reveals-when-to-trust-your-intuition-instinct.html.

35. K. C. Williams, "Business Intuition: The Mortar among the Bricks of Analysis," *Journal of Management Policy and Practice,* December 2012, 48–65.

36. L. Colan, "How to Use Your Intuition to Make Faster Decisions," *Inc.,* April 4, 2018, https://www.inc.com/lee-colan/how-to-use-your-intuition-to-make-faster-decisions.html?cid=search; J. Stillman, "Science: Your Anxiety Is Killing Your Intuition," *Inc.,* October 25, 2017, https://www.inc.com/jessica-stillman/science-stress-silences-your-gut-instincts.html?cid=search; and E. Sadler-Smith and E. Shefy, "The Intuitive Executive: Understanding and Applying 'Gut Feel' in Decision Making," *Academy of Management Executive,* November 2004, 88.

37. Biases associated with using shortcuts in decision making are discussed by A. Tversky and D. Kahneman, "Judgment under Uncertainty: Heuristics and Biases," *Science,* September 1974, 1124–1131.

38. J. J. Starns and Q. Ma, "Response Biases in Simple Decision Making: Faster Decision Making, Faster Response Execution, or Both?" *Psychonomic Bulletin & Review,* August 2018, 1535–1541.

39. Society to Improve Diagnosis in Medicine, "Frequently Asked Questions," https://www.improvediagnosis.org/facts/ (accessed April 16, 2019); and R. Hanscom, M. Small, and A. Lambrecht, "Diagnostic Accuracy: Room for Improvement," https://coverys.com/PDFs/Coverys_Diagnostic_Accuracy_Report.aspx (accessed April 16, 2019).

40. M. Castellucci, "Diagnostic Errors are Largest Contributor to Medical Malpractice Claims," *Modern Healthcare,* March 13, 2018, https://www.modernhealthcare.com/article/20180313/NEWS/180319965/diagnostic-errors-are-largest-contributor-to-medical-malpractice-claims.

41. C. W. Von Bergen and M. S. Bressler, "Confirmation Bias in Entrepreneurship," *Journal of Management Policy and Practice,* September 2018, 74–84.

42. J. M. Logg, U. Haran, and D. A. Moore, "Is Overconfidence a Motivated Bias? Experimental Evidence," *Journal of Experimental Psychology,* October 2018, 1445–1465; and I. B. S. Mahdi and M. B. Abbes, "Risk and Inefficiency: Behavioral Explanation through Overconfidence in Islamic and Conventional Banks," *Managerial Finance,* June 2018, 688–703.

43. J. Bacon, "Five Things to Know a Dozen Days into California's Horrific Camp Fire," *USA Today,* November 19, 2018, https://www.usatoday.com/story/news/nation/2018/11/19/california-fire-look-camp-fire-12-days/2056034002/; C. Lombardo, "Northern California Camp Fire Contained," *NPR,* November 25, 2018, https://www.npr.org/2018/11/25/670652466/northern-california-camp-fire-contained.

44. I. Penn, P. Eavis, and J. Glanz, "How PG&E Ignored Fire Risks in Favor of Profits," The New York Times, March 18, 2019, https://www.nytimes.com/interactive/2019/03/18/business/ pge-california-wildfires.html.

45. I. Penn, P. Eavis, and J. Glanz, "How PG&E Ignored Fire Risks in Favor of Profits," *The New York Times,* March 18, 2019, https://www.nytimes.com/interactive/2019/03/18/business/pge-california-wildfires.html.

46. I. Penn, "As Fires Ravaged California, Utilities Lobbied Lawmakers for Protection," *The New York Times,* January 5, 2019, https://www.nytimes.com/2019/01/05/business/energy-environment/california-wildfire-electric.html.

47. M. I. H. Lindeman, A. M. Durik, and G. J. Hall, "Sometimes Less Is More: The Role of Subjective Task Experience in Self-Generated Value Interventions," *Social Psychology of Education,* April 2018, 371–381.

48. M. H. Bazerman, *Judgment in Managerial Decision Making* (Hoboken, NJ: John Wiley & Sons, 2006), 9.

49. M. Kang and M. J. Park, "Employees' Judgment and Decision Making in the Banking Industry: The Perspective of Heuristics and Biases," *International Journal of Bank Marketing,* February 2019, 382–400.

50. L. Meub and T. Proeger, "Are Groups 'Less Behavioral'? The Case of Anchoring," *Theory and Decision,* August 2018, 117–150.

51. I. von der Beck, U. Cress, and A. Oeberst, "Is There Hindsight Bias without Real Hindsight? Conjectures Are Sufficient to Elicit Hindsight Bias," *Journal of Experimental Psychology,* March 2019, 88–99; and J. Groß and T. Pachur, "Age Differences in Hindsight Bias: A Meta-Analysis," *Psychology and Aging,* January 2019, 1–17.

52. J. Chen, "Hindsight Bias," *Investopedia,* March 19, 2018, https://www.investopedia.com/terms/h/hindsight-bias.asp.

53. M. Gearon, "Cognitive Biases—Framing Effect," *Medium,* December 22, 2018, https://medium.com/@michaelgearon/cognitive-biases-framing-effect-e37d45012dc5.

54. J. Davidson, "DEA Drug Fighting Plane Doesn't Fly, But Costs Soar," *The Washington Post,* https://www.washingtonpost.com/news/powerpost/wp/2016/03/30/dea-drug-fighting-plane-doesnt-fly-but-costs-soar/?utm_term=.db37e0bc4c8c (accessed April 16, 2019).

55. See J. Ross and B. M. Staw, "Organizational Escalation and Exit: Lessons from the Shoreham Nuclear Power Plant," *Academy of Management Journal,* August 1993, 701–732.

56. Andrew Noel, "A Bumper Crop of Information," *Bloomberg Businessweek,* March 18, 2019, https://www.scribd.com/article/401923809/A-Bumper-Crop-Of-Information.

57. J. Gaudiosi, "Your Personal Avatar Can Now Board a Cruise Ship with You," *Wired,* January 3, 2019, https://www.wired.com/story/carnival-medallion-cruise-tagalong-avatar/.

58. Peter M. Tingling and Michael J. Brydon, "Is Decision-Based Evidence Making Necessarily Bad?" *MIT Sloan Management Review* Summer 2010, https://sloanreview.mit.edu/article/is-decision-based-evidence-making-necessarily-bad/.

59. B. Griffiths, "Data Growth and the Network," https://www.scc.com/scc-insights/data-growth-network/ (accessed April 17, 2019).

60. A. Mohamed, M. K. Najafabadi, Y. B. Wah, E. A. K. Zaman, and R. Maskat, "The State of the Art and Taxonomy of Big Data Analytics: View from New Big Data Framework," *Artificial Intelligence Review,* February 2019, 1–49.

61. "Operations Research Analysts," *Occupational Outlook Handbook,* https://www.bls.gov/ooh/math/operations-research-analysts.htm#tab-6 (accessed April 17, 2019).

62. S. Colino, "8 College Majors with Great Job Prospects," *US News & World Report,* September 11, 2018, https://www.usnews.com/education/best-colleges/articles/2018-09-11/8-college-majors-with-great-job-prospects.

63. A. Merendino, S. Dibb, M. Meadows, L. Quinn, D. Wilson, L. Simkin, and A. Canhoto, "Big Data, Big Decisions: The Impact of Board Level Decision-Making," *Journal of Business Research,* December 2018, 67–78; and S. Blake-Plock, "Where's the Value in Big Data?" *Forbes,* April 14, 2017, https://www.forbes.com/sites/forbestechcouncil/2017/04/14/wheres-the-value-in-big-data/#463623d430da.

64. C. Harvey, "Big Data Pros and Cons," *Datamation,* August 9, 2018, https://www.datamation.com/big-data/big-data-pros-and-cons.html.

65. "Big Data in the Healthcare & Pharmaceutical Industry: 2018–2030: Opportunities, Challenges, Strategies & Forecasts," *PR Newswire,* July 26, 2018, https://www.prnewswire.com/news-releases/big-data-in-the-healthcare--pharmaceutical-industry-2018-2030--opportunities-challenges-strategies--forecasts-300687336.html.

66. "Top Benefits of Big Data in the Healthcare Industry," *Business Wire,* February 7, 2018, https://www.businesswire.com/news/home/20180207005640/en/Top-Benefits-Big-Data-Healthcare-Industry-Quantzig.

67. B. Morgan, "Healthcare Innovation: 10 Recent Examples of Powerful Innovation in Healthcare," *Forbes,* March 12, 2019, https://www.forbes.com/sites/blakemorgan/2019/03/12/healthcare-innovation-10-recent-examples-of-powerful-innovation-in-healthcare/#5412f88457dc; and K. Rands, "5 Companies Using Big Data to Disrupt Healthcare," *CIO,* October 30, 2017, https://www.cio.com/article/3235445/5-companies-using-big-data-to-disrupt-healthcare.html.

68. See K. Schwab, "Why Business Must Step Up to Shape the Next Industrial Revolution," *Fortune,* January 1, 2019, 45–46.

69. "Big Data vs. Artificial Intelligence," *Datamation,* https://www.datamation.com/big-data/big-data-vs.-artificial-intelligence.html (accessed April 17, 2019).

70. Artificial intelligence and its impact on the workplace are discussed in E. Sage-Gavin, M. Vazirani, and F. Hintermann, "Getting Your Employees Ready for Work in the Age of AI," *MITSloan Management Review,* February 27, 2019, https://sloanreview.mit.edu/article/getting-your-employees-ready-for-work-in-the-age-of-ai/; and T. H. Davenport and R. Ronanki, "Artificial Intelligence for the Real World," *Harvard Business Review,* January–February 2018, 108–116.

71. S. Shellenbarger, "Robots That Manage the Managers," *The Wall Street Journal,* April 16, 2019, A11.

72. G. Anthes, "Artificial Intelligence Poised to Ride a New Wave," *Communications of the ACM,* July 2017, 19–21; and S. Makridakis, "The Forthcoming Artificial Intelligence (AI) Revolution: Its Impact on Society and Firms," *Futures,* 2017, 46–60.

73. M. H. Jarrahi, "Artificial Intelligence and the Future of Work: Human–AI Symbiosis in Organizational Decision Making," *Business Horizons* July–August 2018, 577–586.

74. B. J. Grosz and P. Stone, "A Century-Long Commitment to Assessing Intelligence and Its Impact on Society," *Communications of the ACM,* December 2018, 68–73; and H. J. Wilson and P. R. Daugherty, "Collaborative Intelligence: Humans and AI Are Joining Forces," *Harvard Business Review,* July–August 2018, 114–123.

75. D. L. Parnas, "The Real Risks of Artificial Intelligence," *Communications of the ACM,* October 2017, 27–31.

76. D. B. Shank and A. DeSanti, "Attributions of Morality and Mind to Artificial Intelligence after Real-World Moral Violations," *Computers in Human Behavior,* September 2018, 401–411; and J. Keating and I. Nourbakhsh, "Viewpoint: Teaching Artificial Intelligence and Humanity," *Communications of the ACM,* February 2018, 29–32.

77. Definition derived from A. J. Rowe and R. O. Mason, *Managing with Style: A Guide to Understanding, Assessing, and Improving Decision Making* (San Francisco: Jossey-Bass, 1987).

78. See A. J. Rowe and R. O. Mason, *Managing with Style: A Guide to Understanding, Assessing, and Improving Decision Making* (San Francisco: Jossey-Bass, 1987).

79. E. Gallagher, "Interview with Colombian Hacker Andrés Sepúlveda," *Medium,* February 8, 2018, https://medium.com/@erin_gallagher/interview-with-colombian-hacker-andr%C3%A9s-sep%C3%BAlveda-f985fe860f7f; and J. Robertson, M. Riley, and A. Willis, "How to Hack an Election," *Bloomberg Businessweek,* April 4, 2016.

80. E. Larson, "How Jeff Bezos Uses Faster, Better Decisions to Keep Amazon Innovating," *Forbes,* September 24, 2018, https://www.forbes.com/sites/eriklarson/2018/09/24/how-jeff-bezos-uses-faster-better-decisions-to-keep-amazon-innovating/#690f7f7a7a65.

81. H. Merry, "InterConnect Keynote: Ginni Rometty," https://www.ibm.com/blogs/internet-of-things/ginni-rometty-interconnect-cloud/ (accessed April 17, 2019); and H. P. Levy, "IBM's Ginni Rometty on Leading Through Disruption," October 17, 2018, https://www.gartner.com/smarterwithgartner/ibms-ginni-rometty-on-leading-through-disruption/.

82. D. Pontefract, "The Netflix Decision Making Model Is Why They're So Successful," *Forbes,* February 4, 2019, https://www.forbes.com/sites/danpontefract/2019/02/04/the-netflix-decision-making-model-is-why-theyre-so-successful/#15f76e3173bc.

83. "Four Essential Leadership Behaviors," http://fcpacompliancereport.com/2017/05/12539/ (accessed April 17, 2019); and "Why They Serve: Madeline Bell," https://www.chop.edu/giving/our-campaign/why-they-serve-madeline-bell (accessed April 17, 2019).

84. F. Jiang, S. Ananthram, and J. Li, "Global Mindset and Entry Mode Decisions: Moderating Roles of Managers' Decision-Making Style and Managerial Experience," *Management International Review,* June 2018, 413–447.

85. M. Geisler and C. M. Allwood, "Relating Decision-Making Styles to Social Orientation and Time Approach," *Journal of Behavioral Decision Making,* July 2018, 415–429.

86. S. R. Valentine, D. Hollingworth, and P. Schultz, "Data-based Ethical Decision Making, Lateral Relations, and Organizational Commitment: Building Positive Workplace Connections through Ethical Operations," *Employee Relations,* October 2018, 946–963; and J. McManus, "Hubris and Unethical Decision Making: The Tragedy of the Uncommon," *Journal of Business Ethics,* April 2018, 169–185.

87. The decision tree and resulting discussion are based on C. E. Begley, "The Ethical Leader's Decision Tree," *Harvard Business Review,* February 2003, 18–19.

88. J. S. Hopkins and S. Randazzo, "Purdue's Sackler Family Accused of Fraud in Transfers of Opioid Profits," *The Wall Street Journal,* March 28, 2019, https://www.wsj.com/articles/new-york-attorney-general-files-new-allegations-against-opioid-maker-purdue-pharma-and-sackler-family-owners-11553781600.

89. S. Stebbins, E. Comen, M. B. Sauter, and C. Stockdale, "Bad Reputation: America's Top 20 Most-Hated Companies," *USA Today,* February 12, 2018, https://www.usatoday.com/story/money/business/2018/02/01/bad-reputation-americas-top-20-most-hated-companies/1058718001/.

90. S. Stebbins, E. Comen, M. B. Sauter, and C. Stockdale, "Bad Reputation: America's Top 20 Most-Hated Companies," *USA Today,* February 12, 2018, https://www.usatoday.com/story/money/business/2018/02/01/bad-reputation-americas-top-20-most-hated-companies/1058718001/.

91. J. C. Blewitt, J. M. Blewitt, and J. Ryan, "Business Forums Pave the Way to Ethical Decision Making: The Mediating Role of Self-Efficacy and Awareness of a Value-Based Educational Institution," *Journal of Business Ethics,* April 2018, 235–244.

92. Cass R. Sunstein and Reid Hastie, "Making Dumb Groups Smarter," *Harvard Business Review,* December, 2014, https://hbr.org/2014/12/making-dumb-groups-smarter.

93. T. Connolly, L. Ordóñez and S. Barker, "Judgment and Decision Making," in N. W. Schmitt and S. Highhouse, eds., *Handbook of Psychology,* 2nd ed., vol. 12 (Hoboken, NJ: Wiley, 2013), 493–522.

94. These advantages are based on N. R. F. Maier, "Assets and Liabilities in Group Problem Solving: The Need for an Integrative Function," *Psychological Review,* July 1967, 239–249.

95. These disadvantages are based on N. R. F. Maier, "Assets and Liabilities in Group Problem Solving: The Need for an Integrative Function," *Psychological Review,* July 1967, 239–249; and C. R. Sunstein and R. Hastie, "The New Science of Group Decision Making," *Harvard Business Review,* December 2014, 92.

96. C. R. Sunstein and R. Hastie, "Smarte: The New Science of Group Decision Making," *Harvard Business Review,* December 2014, 92.

97. Irving Lester Janis, *Groupthink: Psychological Studies of Policy Decisions and Fiascoes* (Boston: Houghton Mifflin, 1982).

98. E. Sherman, "A Tone-Deaf Halloween Costume Decision by Some Teachers Shows the Danger of Groupthink," *Inc.,* November 5, 2018, https://www.inc.com/erik-sherman/this-group-of-teachers-made-a-disastrous-decision-heres-how-to-avoid-doing-same.html?cid=search; and "Report: 14 Middleton School Staffers on Leave after Costume Controversy," *Idaho News,* November 2, 2018, https://idahonews.com/news/local/middleton-school-superintendent-says-staff-halloween-costumes-were-poor-decision.

99. A. Bonime-Blanc and D. A. Disparte, "Pale, Stale, and Male: Does Board Diversity Matter?" *Risk Management,* September 2018, 20–24.

100. A. Hill, "Why Groupthink Never Went Away," *Financial Times,* May 7, 2018, https://ft.com.

101. Adapted from I. Janis, *Groupthink,* 2nd ed. (Boston: Houghton Mifflin, 1982), 174–175. See also J. M. Wellen and M. Neale, "Deviance, Self-Typicality, and Group Cohesion: The Corrosive Effects of the Bad Apples on the Barrel," *Small Group Research,* April 2006, 165–186.

102. B. Oc, M. R. Bashshur, and C. Moore, "Head Above the Parapet: How Minority Subordinates Influence Group Outcomes and the Consequences They Face for Doing So," *Journal of Applied Psychology,* January 2019, 1–17.

103. Glenn M. Parker, *Team Players and Teamwork: The New Competitive Business Strategy* (San Francisco: Wiley, 1990).

104. A. F. Osborn, *Applied Imagination: Principles and Procedures of Creative Thinking,* 3rd ed. (New York: Scribners, 1979).

105. H. Gregersen, "Better Brainstorming," *Harvard Business Review,* March-April 2018, 65–71.

106. "3 Helpful Tools for Virtual Brainstorming," https://remote.co/helpful-tools-virtual-brainstorming/ (accessed April 17, 2019); and W. Burns, "The Demons of Traditional Brainstorming Are Slain with Brainwriting," *Forbes,* https://www.forbes.com/sites/willburns/2016/08/16/the-demons-of-traditional-brainstorming-are-slain-with-brainwriting/#317961e82b6d (accessed April 17, 2019).

107. D. K. Hassan, "Potentiating the Innovation Capacity of Brainstorming Testing Approaches in Architecture Education Medium," *International Journal of Technology and Design Education,* May 2018, 1–20; and B. R. Johnson and C. J. D'Lauro, "After Brainstorming, Groups Select an Early Generated Idea as Their Best Idea," *Small Group Research,* April 2018, 177–194.

108. See N. C. Dalkey, D. L. Rourke, R. Lewis, and D. Snyder, *Studies in the Quality of Life: Delphi and Decision Making* (Lexington, MA: Lexington Books, 1972).

109. An application of the Delphi technique can be found in A. Graefe and J. S. Armstrong, "Comparing Face-to-Face Meetings, Nominal Groups, Delphi and Prediction Markets on an Estimating Task," *International Journal of Forecasting,* January–March 2011, 183–195.

110. A.-M. Suduc, M. Bîzoi, M. Cioca, and F. G. Filip, "Evolution of Decision Support Systems Research Field in Numbers," *Informatica Economica,* 2010, 78.

111. See P. Dvorak, "Best Buy Taps 'Prediction Market'; Imaginary Stocks Let Workers Forecast Whether Retailer's Plan Will Meet Goals," *The Wall Street Journal,* September 16, 2008, B1.

112. E. Turban, T.-P. Liang, and S. P. J. Wu, "A Framework for Adopting Collaboration 2.0 Tools for Virtual Group Decision Making," *Group Decision Negotiations,* March 2011, 137–154.

113. J. Zhou and C. E. Shalley, "Deepening Our Understanding of Creativity in the Workplace: A Review of Different Approaches to Creativity Research," in S. Zedeck, ed., *Handbook of Industrial and Organizational Psychology* (Washington, DC: American Psychological Association, 2011), 275–302.

114. F. Gino, "The Business Case for Curiosity," *Harvard Business Review,* September–October 2018, 48–57.

115. T. Montag, C. P. Maertz, Jr., and M. Baer, "A Critical Analysis of the Workplace Creativity Criterion Space," *Journal of Management,* July 2012, 1369.

116. This discussion is based on T. Montag, C. P. Maertz, Jr., and M. Baer, "A Critical Analysis of the Workplace Creativity Criterion Space," *Journal of Management,* July 2012, 1362–1386.

117. Ashlee Vance, "How An F Student Became America's Most Prolific Inventor: Lowell Wood Broke Edison's Patent Record and Helped Bring Down the Soviet Union," Bloomberg L.P., October 20, 2015, https://www.bloomberg.com/features/2015-americas-top-inventor-lowell-wood/.

118. Y.-Q. Zhu, D. G. Gardner, and H.-G. Chen, "Relationships Between Work Team Climate, Individual Motivation, and Chemistry," *Journal of Management,* May 2018, 2094–2115.

119. J. L. Schoen, J. L. Bowler, and M. C. Schilpzand, "Conditional Reasoning Test for Creative Personality: Rationale, Theoretical Development, and Validation," *Journal of Management,* April 2018, 1651–1677.

120. I. Jeong and S. J. Shin, "High-Performance Work Practices and Organizational Creativity During Organizational Change: A Collective Learning Perspective," *Journal of Management,* March 2019, 909–925.

121. O. A. Acar, M. Tarakei, and D. van Knippenberg, "Creativity and Innovation Under Constraints: A Cross-Disciplinary Integrative Review," *Journal of Management,* January 2019, 96–121.

122. R. E. Silverman, "The Science of Serendipity in the Workplace," *The Wall Street Journal,* April 30, 2013, https://www.wsj.com/articles/SB1000142 412788732379810457845508121 8505870.

123. C. Bouquet, J.-L. Barsoux, and M. Wade, "Bring Your Breakthrough Ideas to Life," *Harvard Business Review,* November–December 2018, 102–113.

124. Boogaard, K. "20 of the Most Creative Companies to Work For Right Now," *The Muse,* https://www.themuse.com/advice/20-of-the-most-creative-companies-to-work-for-right-now, accessed April 17, 2019; and Elizabeth Bernstein, "Why a Little Boredom Could Be Good for Your Relationship," *The Wall Street Journal,* February 22, 2016, https://www.wsj.com/articles/why-a-little-boredom-could-be-good-for-your-relation-ship-1456167350.

125. Manfred F. R. Kets de Vries, "Doing Nothing and Nothing to Do: The Hidden Value of Empty Time and Boredom," INSEAD Institut privé d'enseignement supérieur, July–September 2015.

126. N. Cole, "7 Ways to Give Your Creativity Muscle a Quick Jolt," *Inc.,* March 8, 2018, https://www.inc.com/nicolas-cole/want-to-hack-your-creativity-muscle-here-are-7-ways-to-give-yourself-a-quick-jolt.html?cid=search; C. DiRisio, "5 Easy Ways to Spark Creativity When You Feel Stuck," *Inc.,* October 5, 2017, https://www.inc.com/quora/5-easy-ways-to-spark-creativity-when-you-feel-stuck.html?cid=search; and K. Holst, "Feeling Uninspired? How to Spark Creativity When You Work from Home," *Inc.,* March 4, 2019, https://www.inc.com/karen-holst/feeling-uninspired-how-to-spark-creativity-when-you-work-from-home.html?cid=search.

127. K. Holst, "Feeling Uninspired? How to Spark Creativity When You Work from Home," *Inc.,* March 4, 2019, https://www.inc.com/karen-holst/feel-ing-uninspired-how-to-spark-creativity-when-you-work-from-home.html?cid=search.

128. Muhammad Abdur Rahman Malik, Arif N. Butt, and Jin Nam Choi, "Rewards and Creative Performance: Moderating Effects of Creative Self-Efficacy, Reward Importance, and Locus of Control," *Journal of Organizational Behavior* 36, no. 1 (January 2015): 59–74. https://doi.org/10.1002/job.194.

129. See J. Mueller, S. Melwani, J. Loewenstein, and J. J. Deal, "Reframing the Decision-Makers' Dilemma: Towards a Social Context Model of Creative Idea Recognition," *Academy of Management Journal,* February 2018, 94–110; and M. S. Giarratana, M. Mariani, and I. Weller, "Rewards for Patents and Inventor Behaviors in Industrial Research and Development," *Academy of Management Journal,* February 2018, 264–292.

130. "Airbus Reports Strong Full-Year 2018 Results, Delivers on Guidance (press release)," https://www.airbus.com/newsroom/press-releases/en/2019/02/airbus-reports-strong-fullyear-2018-results-delivers-on-guidance.html (accessed April 7, 2019); and R. Wall and D. Michaels, "How Airbus's A380 Went from Wonder to Blunder," *The Wall Street Journal,* April 1, 2019, https://www.wsj.com/articles/how-airbuss-a380-went-from-wonder-to-blun-der-11550599532.

131. B. Katz and B. Kammel, "Airbus Will Stop Making the World's Largest Passenger Jet," *Bloomberg,* February 14, 2019, https://www.bloomberg.com/news/articles/2019-02-14/airbus-buries-a380-flagship-drawing-curtain-on-jumbo-jet-era.

132. H. Gosai, "Airbus A380: The Plane That Tried," *Airline Geeks,* April 27, 2018, https://airlinegeeks.com/2018/04/27/airbus-a380-the-plane-that-tried/.

133. US Airlines for Open Skies, "What Are Open Skies Agreements?" http://openskiescoalition (accessed April 7, 2019).

134. J. Ewing, "Airbus A380, Once the Future of Aviation, May Cease Pro-duction," January 15, 2018, https://www.nytimes.com/2018/01/15/business/airbus-a380-emirates.html.

135. H. Gosai, "Airbus A380: The Plane That Tried," *Airlines Geeks,* April 27, 2018, https://airlinegeeks.com/2018/04/27/airbus-a380-the-plane-that-tried/.

136. H. Gosai. "Airbus A380: The Plane that Tried," *Airline Geeks,* April 27, 2018, https://airlinegeeks.com/2018/04/27/airbus-a380-the-plane-that-tried/.

137. B. Katz and B. Kammel, "Airbus Will Stop Making the World's Largest Passenger Jet," *Bloomberg,* February 14, 2019, https://www.bloomberg.com/news/articles/2019-02-14/airbus-buries-a380-flagship-drawing-curtain-on-jumbo-jet-era.

138. J. Ewing, "Airbus A380, Once the Future of Aviation, May Cease Produc-tion," *The New York Times,* January 15, 2018, https://www.nytimes.com/2018/01/15/business/airbus-a380-emirates.html.

139. B. Katz and B. Kammel, "Airbus Will Stop Making the World's Largest Passenger Jet," *Bloomberg,* February 14, 2019, https://www.bloomberg.com/news/articles/2019-02-14/airbus-buries-a380-flagship-drawing-curtain-on-jumbo-jet-era.

140. R. Wall and D. Michaels, "How Airbus's A380 Went from Wonder to Blunder," *The Wall Street Journal,* April 1, 2019, https://www.wsj.com/articles/how-airbuss-a380-went-from-wonder-to-blunder-11550599532.

141. B. Katz and B. Kammel, "Airbus Will Stop Making the World's Largest Passenger Jet," *Bloomberg,* February 14, 2019, https://www.bloomberg.com/news/articles/2019-02-14/airbus-buries-a380-flagship-drawing-curtain-on-jumbo-jet-era.

142. Robert Wall, and Daniel Michaels, "How Airbus's A380 Went from Wonder to Blunder," *The Wall Street Journal,* February 19, 2019, https://www.wsj.com/articles/how-airbuss-a380-went-from-wonder-to-blunder-11550599532.

143. B. Katz and B. Kammel, "Airbus Will Stop Making the World's Largest Passenger Jet," *Bloomberg,* February 14, 2019, https://www.bloomberg.com/news/articles/2019-02-14/airbus-buries-a380-flagship-drawing-curtain-on-jumbo-jet-era.

144. "Airbus A380 Superjumbo, How It Happened and What Went Wrong," *Bloomberg,* https://www.bloomberg.com/news/features/2019-02-14/airbus-a380-superjumbo-how-it-happened-and-what-went-wrong (accessed April 1, 2019).

145. Benjamin D. Katz and Benedikt Kammel, "Airbus Will Stop Making the World's Largest Passenger Jet," Bloomberg L.P., February 14, 2019, https://www.bloomberg.com/news/articles/2019-02-14/airbus-buries-a380-flagship-drawing-curtain-on-jumbo-jet-era.

146. G. Korte, "College Admissions Scandal: What Did the Students Know about 'the Side Door,' and What Should Happen Next?" *USA Today,* March 18, 2019, https://www.usatoday.com/story/news/educa-tion/2019/03/18/college-admissions-scam-what-did-students-know-what-should-happen/3164580002/; and M. Burke, "USC Students Linked to Admissions Scandal Can't Enroll in Classes, Get Transcripts, University Says," *NBC News,* March 19, 2019, https://www.nbcnews.com/news/us-news/usc-students-linked-admissions-scandal-can-t-enroll-classes-get-n983656.

147. "Here's How the F.B.I. Says Their Parents Cheated to Get Their Kids into Elite Colleges," *The New York Times,* March 12, 2019, https://www.nytimes.com/2019/03/12/us/admissions-scandal.html.

148. M. Burke, "USC Students Linked to Admissions Scandal Can't Enroll in Classes, Get Transcripts, University Says," *NBC News,* March 19, 2019, https://www.nbcnews.com/news/us-news/usc-students-linked-admis-sions-scandal-can-t-enroll-classes-get-n983656.

149. B. Pascus, "USC May Expel Students Associated with College Admis-sions Scandal," *CBS News,* March 19, 2019, https://www.cbsnews.com/news/college-admissions-scandal-usc-admissions-scam-explusion-lori-loughlin-olivia-jade/.

150. N. Feldman, "Expel the Students? It's Not an Easy Choice for Duped Colleges," *Bloomberg,* March 14, 2019, https://www.bloomberg.com/opinion/articles/2019-03-14/college-admissions-scandal-should-students-be-expelled.

151. G. Korte, "College Admissions Scandal: What Did the Students Know about 'the Side Door,' and What Should Happen Next?" *USA Today,* March 18, 2019, https://www.usatoday.com/story/news/education/2019/03/18/college-admissions-scam-what-did-students-know-what-should-happen/3164580002/.

152. N. Feldman, "Expel the Students? It's Not an Easy Choice for Duped Colleges," *Bloomberg,* March 14, 2019, https://www.bloomberg.com/opinion/articles/2019-03-14/college-admissions-scandal-should-students-be-expelled.

CHAPTER 12

1. Dave Barry quoted in A. Buzzese, "Make Your Meetings Work for You," *Arizona Republic,* May 5, 2013, D6.

2. D. Meinert, "7 Steps to Running Better Meetings," *SHRM.org,* October 30, 2018, https://www.shrm.org/hr-today/news/hr-magazine/1118/pages/7-steps-to-running-better-meetings.aspx.

3. D. Meinert, "7 Steps to Running Better Meetings," *SHRM.org,* October 30, 2018, https://www.shrm.org/hr-today/news/hr-magazine/1118/pages/7-steps-to-running-better-meetings.aspx.

4. A. Buzzese, "Make Your Meetings Work for You," *Arizona Republic,* May 5, 2013, D6.

5. D. Meinert, "7 Steps to Running Better Meetings," *SHRM.org,* October 30, 2018, https://www.shrm.org/hr-today/news/hr-magazine/1118/pages/7-steps-to-running-better-meetings.aspx.

6. D. Meinert, "7 Steps to Running Better Meetings," *SHRM.org,* October 30, 2018, https://www.shrm.org/hr-today/news/hr-magazine/1118/pages/7-steps-to-running-better-meetings.aspx.

7. A. Buzzese, "Make Your Meetings Work for You," *Arizona Republic,* May 5, 2013, D6

8. A. Gallo, "The Seven Imperatives to Keeping Meetings on Track," *Har-vard Business Review,* December 20, 2013, https://hbr.org/2013/12/the-seven-imperatives-to-keeping-meetings-on-track/.

9. "Busy CEOs Spend Nearly One Day Each Week Managing Communica-tions, Two Days In Meetings," *Bain.com,* May 6, 2014, http://www.bain.com/about/press/press-releases/Busy-ceos-spend-nearly-one-day-each-week-managing-communications.aspx.

10. R. Sturm and J. Antonakis, "Interpersonal Power: A Review, Critique, and Research Agenda," *Journal of Management*, January 2015, 136–163.

11. A. D. Wright, "Survey: Nonprofits Fall Short on Ethics," *HR Magazine*, May 2008, 24; and R. Riney, "Heal Leadership Disorders," *HR Magazine*, May 2008, 62–66.

12. E. Lee and R. Abrams, "CBS Says Les Moonves Will Not Receive $120 Million Severance," *The New York Times*, December 17, 2018, https://www.nytimes.com/2018/12/17/business/media/les-moonves-cbs-severance.html.

13. S. Forbes, "Deficit Size Egos," *Forbes*, April 11, 2011, https://www.forbes.com/forbes/2011/0328/billionaires-11-fact-comment-steve-forbes-deficit-size-egos.html#2ae063151d87.

14. J. Turner, "Voters May Get to Ban Politicians Naming Things After Themselves," *OrlandoSentinel.com*, March 27, 2018, https://www.orlandosentinel.com/news/politics/political-pulse/os-state-naming-politicians-20180327-story.html.

15. D. Collins, G. Fleishman, S. Kaden, and J. M. Sanchez, "How Powerful CEOs Camouflage and Exploit Equity-Based Incentive Compensation," *Journal of Business Ethics*, 153, 2018, 591–613.

16. K. Leonard, "Examples of Successful Strategic Alliances," *Chron.com*, February, 4, 2019, https://smallbusiness.chron.com/examples-successful-strategic-alliances-13859.html.

17. D. Douglas-Gabriel, "Federal Trade Commission Sues DeVry University for Deceptive Advertising," *The Washington Post*, January 27, 2016, https://www.washingtonpost.com/news/grade-point/wp/2016/01/27/federal-trade-commission-sues-devry-university-for-deceptive-advertising/.

18. Extole, "An Epic List of 75 Best Referral Programs for 2018," *Extole.com*, https://www.extole.com/blog/an-epic-list-of-75-besties-referral-programs-for-2018/.

19. R. Derousseau, "4 Stocks that Could Soar under New CEOs," *Fortune.com*, January 27, 2019, http://fortune.com/2019/01/27/4-stocks-that-could-soar-under-new-ceos/.

20. C. Lieber, "How and Why Do Influencers Make So Much Money?" *Vox.com*, November 28, 2018, https://www.vox.com/the-goods/2018/11/28/18116875/influencer-marketing-social-media-engagement-instagram-youtube.

21. R. Romis, "The Influencer Blueprint: Find, Maximize and Profit with Brand Partners," *Forbes.com*, August 27, 2018, https://www.forbes.com/sites/forbesagencycouncil/2018/08/27/the-influencer-blueprint-find-maximize-and-profit-with-brand-partners/#4302938f5af5.

22. "25 of the Highest-Paid Social Media Influencers," *Izea.com*, April 5, 2018, https://izea.com/2018/04/05/highest-paid-social-media-influencers/.

23. "25 of the Highest-Paid Social Media Influencers," *Izea.com*, April 5, 2018, https://izea.com/2018/04/05/highest-paid-social-media-influencers/.

24. R. Romis, "The Influencer Blueprint: Find, Maximize and Profit with Brand Partners," *Forbes.com*, August 27, 2018, https://www.forbes.com/sites/forbesagencycouncil/2018/08/27/the-influencer-blueprint-find-maximize-and-profit-with-brand-partners/#4302938f5af5.

25. A. Baxter, "HCA Healthcare CEO to Retire, COO Promoted," *HealthExec.com*, September, 11, 2018, https://www.healthexec.com/topics/leadership/hca-healthcare-ceo-retire-coo-promoted.

26. "Tony Lowings Promoted to KFC Division CEO, Effective January 1, 2019," *MarketWatch.com*, September 28, 2018, https://www.marketwatch.com/press-release/tony-lowings-promoted-to-kfc-division-ceo-effective-january-1-2019-09-28.

27. Adapted from M. Markey, "Three Tasks to Ease the Transition from Peer to Manager," *Forbes.com*, November 6, 2018, https://www.forbes.com/sites/forbeshumanresourcescouncil/2018/11/06/three-tasks-to-ease-the-transition-from-peer-to-manager/#5223058b6ea7.

28. Adapted from M. Markey, "Three Tasks to Ease the Transition from Peer to Manager," *Forbes.com*, November 6, 2018, https://www.forbes.com/sites/forbeshumanresourcescouncil/2018/11/06/three-tasks-to-ease-the-transition-from-peer-to-manager/#5223058b6ea7.

29. E. Garone, "Managing Your Former Peers Takes Extra Effort," *The Wall Street Journal*, March 10, 2008, http://online.wsj.com/news/articles/SB12049012131471.

30. A. Carlsen, M. Salam, C. Cain Miller, D. Lu, A. Ngu, J. K. Patel, and Z. Wichter, "#MeToo Brought Down 201 Powerful Men. Nearly Half of Their Replacements Are Women," *The New York Times*, October 29, 2018, https://www.nytimes.com/interactive/2018/10/23/us/metoo-replacements.html?nl=top-stories&nlid=49995115ries&ref=cta.

31. A. Harrell and B. Simpson, "The Dynamics of Pro Social Leadership: Power and Influence in Collective Action Groups," *Social Forces*, March 2016, 1283–1308.

32. W. Clark, "The Potency of Persuasion," *Fortune*, November 12, 2007, 48.

33. D. Marshall, L. McCarthy, M. Claudy, and P. McGrath, "Piggy in the Middle: How Direct Customer Power Affects First-Tier Suppliers' Adoption of Socially Responsible Procurement Practices and Performance," *Journal of Business Ethics*, 154, 2019, 1081–1102.

34. M. T. Maynard, L. L. Gilson, and J. E. Mathieu, "Empowerment—Fad or Fab? A Multilevel Review of the Past Two Decades of Research," *Journal of Management*, 2012, 1–51.

35. D. Simonet, A. Narayan, and C. Nelson, "A Social-Cognitive Moderated Mediated Model of Psychological Safety and Empowerment," *The Journal of Psychology*, 2015, 818–845.

36. M. Lansat, "An Analysis of CEOs' Schedules Scrutinized 60,000 Hours and Found Email Is an Even Bigger Time Sink than People Realize," *BusinessInsider.com*, June 28, 2018, https://www.businessinsider.co.za/email-dangerous-time-sink-for-ceos-study-2018-6.

37. A. Lee, S. Willis, and A. W. Tian, "When Empowering Employees Works, and When it Doesn't," *HBR.org*, March 2, 2018, https://hbr.org/2018/03/when-empowering-employees-works-and-when-it-doesnt.

38. A. Fox, "Raising Engagement," *HR Magazine*, May 2010, 39. See also "How May We Help You?" *Inc.*, March 2011, 63.

39. B. Morgan, "10 Companies That Arm Employees with Tools to Fix Customer Problems," *Forbes.com*, March 14, 2018, https://www.forbes.com/sites/blakemorgan/2018/03/14/10-companies-that-arm-employees-with-tools-to-fix-customer-problems/#bd4f0354a301.

40. Y. Woon Chung, "Workplace Ostracism and Workplace Behaviors: A Moderated Mediation Model of Perceived Stress and Psychological Empowerment," *Anxiety, Stress, and Coping*, 31, 2018, 304–317.

41. Y. Li, F. Wei, S. Ren, and Y. Di, "Locus of Control, Psychological Empowerment and Intrinsic Motivation Relation to Performance," *Journal of Managerial Psychology*, 2015, 422–438.

42. M. Travis Maynard, Lucy L. Gilson, and John E. Mathieu, "Empowerment—Fad or Fab? A Multilevel Review of the Past Two Decades of Research," *Journal of Management* 38, no. 4 (2012): 1231–281. https://doi.org/10.1177/0149206312438773.

43. M. T. Maynard, J. E. Mathieu, L. L. Gilson, E. H. O'Boyle, and K. P. Cigularov, "Drivers and Outcomes of Team Psychological Empowerment: A Meta-Analytic Review and Model Test," *Organizational Psychological Review*, 3, 2012, 101–137.

44. M. M Luciano, J. E. Mathieu, and T. M. Ruddy, "Leading Multiple Teams: Average and Relative External Leadership Influences on Team Empowerment and Effectiveness," *Journal of Applied Psychology*, 2014, 322–331.

45. M. M Luciano, J. E. Mathieu, and T. M. Ruddy, "Leading Multiple Teams: Average and Relative External Leadership Influences on Team Empowerment and Effectiveness," *Journal of Applied Psychology*, 2014, 322–331.

46. M. Macphee, V. S. Dahinten, S. Hejazi, H. Lachinger, A. Kazanjian, A. McCutcheon, J. Skelton-Green, and L. O'Brien-Pallas, "Testing the Effects of an Empowerment-Based Leadership Development Programme: Part 1—Leader Outcomes," *Journal of Nursing Management*, 2014, 4–15.

47. M. Macphee, V. S. Dahinten, S. Hejazi, H. Lachinger, A. Kazanjian, A. McCutcheon, J. Skelton-Green, and L. O'Brien-Pallas, "Testing the Effects of an Empowerment-Based Leadership Development Programme: Part 1—Leader Outcomes," *Journal of Nursing Management*, 2014, 4–15.

48. Adapted from R. Ashkenas, "First-Time Managers, Don't Do Your Teams' Work for Them," *Harvard Business Review*, September 21, 2015, https://hbr.org/2015/09/first-time-managers-dont-do-your-teams-work-for-them.

49. Hayley Fitzpatrick, "Claire Foy Addresses the Gender Pay Gap in Hollywood and 'The Crown'," *ABC News Internet Ventures*, January 10, 2019, https://abcnews.go.com/GMA/Culture/claire-foy-addresses-gender-pay-gap-hollywood-crown/story?id=60284140.

50. K. Fitzpatrick, "The Crown Gender-Pay Gap Made Netflix Investigate Other Salaries, Too," *Vanityfair.com*, February 9, 2019, https://www.vanityfair.com/hollywood/2019/02/netflix-pay-gap?verso=true.

51. A. R. Sorkin, M. de la Merced, and J. Condliffe, "How Amazon Is Squeezing Cities Across American," DealBook Briefing, *The New York Times*, March 4, 2019, NYT.com.

52. M. Haag, "Amazon's Tax Breaks and Incentives Were Big. Hudson Yards' Are Bigger," *The New York Times*, March 9, 2019, https://www.nytimes.com/2019/03/09/nyregion/hudson-yards-new-york-tax-breaks.html.

53. K. Weise, M. Fernandez, and J. Eligon, "Amazon's Hard Bargain Extends Far Beyond New York," *The New York Times*, March 3, 2019, https://www.nytimes.com/2019/03/03/technology/amazon-new-york-politics-jobs.html.

54. C. Plouffe, W. Bolander, J. Cote, and B. Hochstein, "Does the Customer Matter Most? Exploring Strategic Frontline Employees' Influence of Customers, the Internal Business Team, and External Business Partners," *Journal of Marketing*, January 2016, 106–123.

55. M. Wadsworth and A. Blanchard, "Influence Tactics in Virtual Teams," *Computers and Human Behavior*, 2015, 386–393.

56. M. Wadsworth and A. Blanchard, "Influence Tactics in Virtual Teams," *Computers and Human Behavior*, 2015, 386–393.

57. "The Uses (and Abuses) of Influence," *Harvard Business Review*, July–August 2013, 76–81. Also adapted from R. B. Cialdini, "Harnessing the Science of Persuasion," *Harvard Business Review*, October 2001, 72–79.

58. "The Uses (and Abuses) of Influence," *Harvard Business Review*, July–August 2013, 77.

59. M. C. Bush and C. Tkaczyk, "Fortune's 100 Best Companies to Work For 2019," *Fortune*, March 1, 2019, https://www.greatplacetowork.com/best-workplaces/100-best/2019.

60. G. R. Ferris, B. P. Ellen III, C. P. McAllister, and L. P. Maher, "Reorganizing Organizational Politics Research: A Review of the Literature and Identification of Future Research Directions," *Annual Review of Organizational Psychology and Organizational Behavior*, 6, 2019, 299–323.

61. F. Manjoo, "Why the Google Walkout Was a Watershed Moment in Tech," *The New York Times*, November 7, 2018, https://www.nytimes.com/2018/11/07/technology/google-walkout-watershed-tech.html.

62. K. Conger and C. Metz, "Tech Workers Now Want to Know What Are We Building This For?" *The New York Times*, October 7, 2018, https://www.nytimes.com/2018/10/07/technology/tech-workers-ask-censorship-surveillance.html.

63. M. Kreutzer, J. Walter, and L. Cardinal, "Organizational Control as Antidote to Politics in the Pursuit of Strategic Initiatives," *Strategic Management Journal*, 2015, 1317–1337.

64. G. R. Ferris, B. P. Ellen III, C. P. McAllister, and L. P. Maher, "Reorganizing Organizational Politics Research: A Review of the Literature and Identification of Future Research Directions," *Annual Review of Organizational Psychology and Organizational Behavior*, 6, 2019, 299–323.

65. G. R. Ferris, B. P. Ellen III, C. P. McAllister, and L. P. Maher, "Reorganizing Organizational Politics Research: A Review of the Literature and Identification of Future Research Directions," *Annual Review of Organizational Psychology and Organizational Behavior*, 6, 2019, 299–323.

66. R. Blumenstein and K. Safdar, "Business Leaders, Policy Makers Gather in Davos," *The Wall Street Journal*, January 24, 2016, http://www.wsj.com/articles/business-leaders-policy-makers-gather-in-davos-for-world-economic-forum-1453292480.

67. B. Dattner and R. Hogan, "Can You Handle Failure?" *Harvard Business Review*, April 2011.

68. M. Goldstein, E. Flitter, and K. Kelly, "Goldman Sachs's Tactic in Malaysian Fraud Case: Smear an Ex-Partner," *The New York Times*, January 16, 2019, https://www.nytimes.com/2019/01/16/business/goldman-malaysia-1mdb-leissner.html.

69. J. Eggers and L. Song, "Dealing with Failure: Serial Entrepreneurs and the Costs of Changing Industries Between Ventures," *Academy of Management Journal*, 2015, 1785–1803.

70. An excellent historical and theoretical perspective of coalitions can be found in W. B. Stevenson, J. L. Pearce, and L. W. Porter, "The Concept of 'Coalition' in Organization Theory and Research," *Academy of Management Review*, April 1985, 256–268.

71. E. Mellino, "UberEats Workers May Have Accidentally Found the Company's Achilles Heel," *Forbes.com*, October 4, 2018, https://www.forbes.com/sites/emilianomellino/2018/10/04/ubereats-workers-may-have-accidentally-found-the-companys-achilles-heel/#6972a5c16555.

72. E. Witt, "The March for Our Lives Presents a Radical New Model for Youth Protest," *The New Yorker*, March 25, 2018, https://www.newyorker.com/news/dispatch/the-march-for-our-lives-presents-a-radical-new-model-for-youth-protest.

73. L. Beckett, "Parkland One Year On: What Victories Have Gun Control Advocates Seen?" *TheGuardian.com*, February 14, 2019, https://www.theguardian.com/us-news/2019/feb/14/parkland-school-shooting-anniversary-gun-control-victories.

74. C. Morris, "Delta, REI, and Now Yeti Coolers. Here's a List of Brands Cutting Ties with the NRA," *Fortune.com*, April 23, 2018, http://fortune.com/2018/04/23/yeti-coolers-cuts-ties-with-nra-boycott-complete-list/.

75. Pamela N. Danziger, "When Corporate Social Responsibility Veers Into Political Action: Safe Or Sorry?" *Forbes Media LLC*, March 12, 2018, https://www.forbes.com/sites/pamdanziger/2018/03/12/when-corporate-social-responsibility-veers-into-political-action-safe-or-sorry/#13f20aab257d.

76. P. Danziger, "When Corporate Social Responsibility Veers into Political Action: Safe Or Sorry?" *Forbes.com*, March 12, 2018, https://www.forbes.com/sites/pamdanziger/2018/03/12/when-corporate-social-responsibility-veers-into-political-action-safe-or-sorry/#13f20aab257d.

77. Alix Langone, "#MeToo and Time's Up Founders Explain the Differences between the 2 Movements—And How They're Alike," *TIME USA, LLC*, March 22, 2018, http://time.com/5189945/whats-the-difference-between-the-metoo-and-times-up-movements/.

78. G. R. Ferris, B. P. Ellen III, C. P. McAllister, and L. P. Maher, "Reorganizing Organizational Politics Research: A Review of the Literature and Identification of Future Research Directions," *Annual Review of Organizational Psychology and Organizational Behavior*, 6, 2019, 299–323.

79. G. R. Ferris, B. P. Ellen III, C. P. McAllister, and L. P. Maher, "Reorganizing Organizational Politics Research: A Review of the Literature and Identification of Future Research Directions," *Annual Review of Organizational Psychology and Organizational Behavior*, 6, 2019, 299–323.

80. Adapted from "Best Practices for Managing Organizational Politics," *Nonprofit World*, July–August 2010.

81. H. Zhao and R. C. Liden, "Internship: A Recruitment and Selection Perspective," *Journal of Applied Psychology*, 2011, 221–229.

82. M. S. Kim, D. T. Kim, and J. I. Kim, "CSR for Sustainable Development: CSR Beneficiary Positioning and Impression Management Motivation," *Corporate Social Responsibility and Environmental Management*, 2014, 14–27.

83. J. D. Westphal, S. Hyun, M. L. McDonald, and M. L. A. Hayward, "Helping Other CEOs Avoid Bad Press: Social Exchange and Impression Management Support among CEOs in Communications with Journalists," *Administrative Science Quarterly*, June 2012, 217–268.

84. Michael Tews, Kathryn Stafford, and John W. Michel, "Interview Etiquette and Hiring Outcomes," *International Journal of Selection and Assessment* (December 2018): 1–12. https://doi.org/10.1111/ijsa.12228.

85. M. Tews, K. Stafford, and J. W. Michel, "Interview Etiquette and Hiring Outcomes," *International Journal of Selection and Assessment*, 26, 2018, 164–175.

86. M. C. Bolino, K. M. Kacmar, W. H. Turnley, and J. B. Gilstrap, "A Multi-Level Review of Impression Management Motives and Behaviors," *Journal of Management*, 34, 2008, 1080–1109.

87. D. Long, M. Baer, J. Colquitt, R. Outlaw, and R. Dhensa-Kahlon, "What Will the Boss Think? The Impression Management Implications of Supportive Relationships with Star and Project Peers," *Personnel Psychology*, 2015, 463–498.

88. M. C. Bolino, K. M. Kacmar, W. H. Turnley, and J. B. Gilstrap, "A Multi-Level Review of Impression Management Motives and Behaviors," *Journal of Management*, 34, 2008, 1080–1109.

89. J. S. Bourdage, N. Roulin, and R. Tarraf, "'I (might be) Just that Good': Honest and Deceptive Impression Management in Employment Interviews," *Personnel Psychology*, 71, 597–632.

90. J. S. Bourdage, N. Roulin, and R. Tarraf, "'I (might be) Just that Good': Honest and Deceptive Impression Management in Employment Interviews," *Personnel Psychology*, 71, 597–632.

91. J. Bourdage, J. Wiltshire, and K. Lee, "Personality and Workplace Impression Management: Correlates and Implications," *Journal of Applied Psychology*, 2015, 537–546.

92. "Global Tattoo Survey Results," *Daliaresearch.com*, May 16, 2018, https://daliaresearch.com/wp-content/uploads/2018/05/2018-05-16_Pressrelease_Tattoo_Survey.pdf.

93. M. Newman, "Report: More Young People Have Tattoos and Piercings than Ever Before," *USAToday*, September 20, 2017, https://www.indystar.com/story/news/nation-now/2017/09/20/young-people-tattoos-and-piercings-report/686360001/.

94. M. Mercer, "Explosion in Tattooing, Piercing Tests State Regulators," Pew Research, June 14, 2017, https://www.pewtrusts.org/en/research-and-analysis/blogs/stateline/2017/06/14/explosion-in-tattooing-piercing-tests-state-regulators.

95. D. Wilkie, "What Are an Applicant's Tattoos Telling Potential Employers?" *SHRM.org*, September 18, 2018, https://www.shrm.org/ResourcesAndTools/hr-topics/employee-relations/Pages/tattoos-at-work.aspx.

96. M. T. French, K. Mortensen, and A. R. Timming, "Are Tattoos Associated with Employment and Wage Discrimination? Analyzing the Relationships between Body Art and Labor Market Outcomes," *Human Relations*, August 7, 2018, https://journals.sagepub.com/doi/abs/10.1177/0018726718782597.

97. C. A. Henle, T. H. Shore, and A. Marshall, "Body Art as a Source of Employment Discrimination," *Academy of Management Proceedings*, July 9, 2018, https://journals.aom.org/doi/10.5465/AMBPP.2018.12589abstract?utm_source=newsletter&utm_medium=email&utm_campaign=newsletter_axiosfutureofwork&stream=future-of-work.

98. D. Wilkie, "What Are an Applicant's Tattoos Telling Potential Employers?" *SHRM.org*, September 18, 2018, https://www.shrm.org/ResourcesAndTools/hr-topics/employee-relations/Pages/tattoos-at-work.aspx.

99. D. Wilkie, "What Are an Applicant's Tattoos Telling Potential Employers?" *SHRM.org*, September 18, 2018, https://www.shrm.org/ResourcesAndTools/hr-topics/employee-relations/Pages/tattoos-at-work.aspx.

100. A. Wilhelmy, M. Kleinmann, C. Konig, K. Melchers, and D. Truxillo, "How and Why Do Interviewers Try to Make Impressions on Applicants? A Qualitative Study," *Journal of Applied Psychology*, 2016, 313–332.

101. J. D. Westphal and M. E. Graebner, "A Matter of Appearances: How Corporate Leaders Manage the Impressions of Financial Analysts about the Conduct of Their Boards," *Academy of Management Journal*, 2010, 15–43.

102. S. Friedman, "What Do You Really Care About? What Are You Most Interested In?" *Fast Company*, March 1999, 90.

103. K. T. Dirks, P. H. Kim, D. L. Ferrin, and C. D. Cooper, "Understanding the Effects of Substantive Responses on Trust Following Transgression," *Organizational Behavior and Decision Processes*, 2011, 87–103.

104. K. T. Dirks, P. H. Kim, D. L. Ferrin, and C. D. Cooper, "Understanding the Effects of Substantive Responses on Trust Following Transgression," *Organizational Behavior and Decision Processes*, 2011, 87–103.

105. N. Smith, "Corporate Japan Needs to Do More Than Apologize," *Bloomberg*, February 3, 2016, http://www.bloomberg.com/view/articles/2016-02-03/saying-sorry-isn-t-enough--in-corporate-japan.

106. B. Morgan, "10 Powerful Examples of Corporate Apologies," *Forbes.com*, October 24, 2018, https://www.forbes.com/sites/blakemorgan/2018/10/24/10-powerful-examples-of-corporate-apologies/#44d61d9f40de.

107. B. Morgan, "10 Powerful Examples of Corporate Apologies," *Forbes.com*, October 24, 2018, https://www.forbes.com/sites/blakemorgan/2018/10/24/10-powerful-examples-of-corporate-apologies/#44d61d9f40de.

108. D. McNary, "After Oscars Mishap, PricewaterhouseCoopers Tightens Envelop Procedures," *Variety.com*, January 22, 2018, https://variety.com/2018/film/news/oscars-new-envelope-procedures-pricewaterhousecoopers-1202672294/.

109. J. Creswell, K. Draper, and R. Abrams, "At Nike, Revolt Led by Women Leads to Exodus of Male Executives," *The New York Times*, April 28, 2018, https://www.nytimes.com/2018/04/28/business/nike-women.html.

110. S. Cowley, "Nike Will Raise Wages for Thousands after Outcry Over Inequality," *The New York Times*, July 23, 2018, https://www.nytimes.com/2018/07/23/business/nike-wages-raises.html.

111. J. Creswell, K. Draper, and R. Abrams, "At Nike, Revolt Led by Women Leads to Exodus of Male Executives," *The New York Times*, April 28, 2018, https://www.nytimes.com/2018/04/28/business/nike-women.html.

112. R. Greenfield and E. Novy-Williams, "Nike Gets Tripped Up While Trying to Change Its Culture," *Bloomberg BusinessWeek*, August 30, 2018, https://www.bloomberg.com/news/articles/2018-08-30/nike-gets-tripped-up-while-trying-to-change-its-culture.

113. S. Cowley, "Nike Will Raise Wages for Thousands after Outcry Over Inequality," *The New York Times*, July 23, 2018, https://www.nytimes.com/2018/07/23/business/nike-wages-raises.html.

114. Kevin Draper and Julie Creswell, "Nike's CEO Vows Changes After Claims of Workplace Harassment and Bias," The New York Times Company, May 5, 2018, https://www.nytimes.com/2018/05/05/business/mark-parker-nike.html.

115. David Gelles, "Memo from the Boss: You're a Vegetarian Now," The New York Times Company, July 20, 2018, https://www.nytimes.com/2018/07/20/business/wework-vegetarian.html.

CHAPTER 13

1. H. B. Cohen, "An Inconvenient Truth about Leadership Development," *Organizational Dynamics*, 2019, 8–15.

2. J. Zenger, "The Confidence Gap in Men and Women: Why It Matters and How to Overcome It," *Forbes*, April 8, 2018, https://www.forbes.com/sites/jackzenger/2018/04/08/the-confidence-gap-in-men-and-women-why-it-matters-and-how-to-overcome-it/#c834ba53bfa1.

3. M. Buckingham, "Leadership Development in the Age of the Algorithm," *Harvard Business Review*, June 2012, 86–94.

4. See D. A. Garvin and J. D. Margolis, "The Art of Giving and Receiving Advice," *Harvard Business Review*, June 2012, 146–154.

5. R. S. Peterson and K. O'Connor, "Time to Rethinking Bringing Your Whole Self to Work?" *Forbes*, April 1, 2019, https://www.forbes.com/sites/lbsbusinessstrategyreview/2019/04/01/time-to-rethink-bringing-your-whole-self-to-work/#3db7e9f67b68; and D. Meinert, "Fake It Till You Make It," *HR Magazine*, October 2015, 19.

6. These steps are based on S. J. Ashford and D. S. DeRue, "Developing as a Leader: The Power of Mindful Engagement," *Organizational Dynamics*, April–June 2012, 146–154.

7. Peter Bregman, "To Develop Leadership Skills, Practice in a Low-Risk Environment," *Harvard Business Review*, April 5, 2019, https://hbr.org/2019/04/to-develop-leadership-skills-practice-in-a-low-risk-environment.

8. D. S. DeRue, J. D. Nahrgang, J. R. Hollenbeck, and K. Workman, "A Quasi-Experimental Study of After-Event Reviews and Leadership Development," *Journal of Applied Psychology*, September 2012, 997–1015.

9. T. J. Quigley and D. C. Hambrick, "Has the 'CEO Effect' Increased in Recent Decades? A New Explanation for the Great Rise in America's Attention to Corporate Leaders," *Strategic Management Journal*, June 2015, 821–830.

10. P. G. Northouse, *Leadership: Theory and Practice*, 6th ed. (Thousand Oaks, CA: Sage, 2012), 3.

11. C. Robinson, "The Real Cost of Employee Disengagement," *Shiftboard*, February 14, 2018, https://www.shiftboard.com/blog/real-cost-employee-disengagement/.

12. See J. Hogan, R. Hogan, and R. B. Kaiser, "Management Derailment," in S. Zedeck, ed., *APA Handbook of Industrial and Organizational Psychology* (Washington, DC: American Psychological Association, 2011), 555–575.

13. *Leading the Social Enterprise: Reinvent with a Human Focus*, 2019 Deloitte Global Human Capital Trends, https://www2.deloitte.com (accessed April 19, 2019).

14. K. L. Badura, E. Grijalva, D. A. Newman, T. T. Yan, and G. Jeon, "Gender and Leadership Emergence: A Meta-Analysis and Explanatory Model," *Personnel Psychology*, Autumn 2018, 335–367.

15. B. M. Bass and R. Bass, *The Bass Handbook of Leadership: Theory, Research, and Managerial Applications*, 4th ed. (New York: Free Press, 2008), 654.

16. "The Best and Worst CEOs of 2018," *24/7 Wall Street*, December 5, 2018, https://247wallst.com/special-report/2018/12/05/the-best-and-worst-ceos-of-2018/2/.

17. L. Dishman, "These Are the Best and Worst Leaders of 2018," *Fast Company*, December 19, 2018, https://www.fastcompany.com/90278934/these-are-the-best-and-worst-leaders-of-2018.

18. D. Akst, "Flex the Muscles of Leadership," *The Wall Street Journal*, March 12–13, 2016, C4.

19. These results are based on K. Landay, P. D. Harms, and M. Credé, "Shall We Serve the Dark Lords? A Meta-Analytic Review of Psychopathy and Leadership," *Journal of Applied Psychology*, January 2019, 183–196; J. M. Hoobler, C. R. Masterson, S. M. Nkomo, and E. J. Michel, "The Business Case for Women Leaders: Meta-Analysis, Research Critique, and Path Forward," *Journal of Management*, July 2018, 2473–2499; and P. J. Fuller, B. M. Galvin, and B. E. Ashforth, "Larger Than Life: Narcissistic Organizational Identification in Leadership," *Organizational Dynamics*, January–March 2018, 8–16.

20. See S. M. Spain, P. Harms, and J. M. Lebreton, "The Dark Side of Personality at Work," *Journal of Organizational Behavior*, February 2014, S41–S60.

21. B. M. Galvin, D. A. Waldman, and P. Balthazard, "Visionary Communication Qualities as Mediators of the Relationship between Narcissism and Attributions of Leader Charisma," *Personnel Psychology*, Autumn 2010, 510.

22. B. Nevicka, A. E. M. Van Vianen, A. H. B. De Hoogh, and B. C. M. Voorn, "Narcissistic Leaders: An Asset or a Liability? Leader Visibility, Follower Responses, and Group-Level Absenteeism," *Journal of Applied Psychology*, July 2018, 703–723.

23. R. E. Frieder, G. Wang, and I.-S. Oh, "Linking Job-Relevant Personality Traits, Transformational Leadership, and Job Performance via Perceived Meaningfulness at Work: A Moderated Mediation Model," *Journal of Applied Psychology*, March 2018, 324–333; and W. Lam, C. Lee, M. S. Taylor, and H. H. Zao, "Does Proactive Personality Matter in Leadership Transitions? Effects of Proactive Personality on New Leader Identification and Responses to New Leaders and Their Change Agendas," *Academy of Management Journal*, February 2018, 245–263.

24. See J. Hogan, R. Hogan, and R. B. Kaiser, "Management Derailment," in S. Zedeck, ed., *APA Handbook of Industrial and Organizational Psychology* (Washington, DC: American Psychological Association, 2011). Also see M. F. R. Kets de Vries, "Coaching the Toxic Leader," *Harvard Business Review*, April 2014, 101–109; and M. B. Smith, J. C. Wallace, and P. Jordan, "When the Dark Ones Become Darker: How Promotion Focus Moderates the Effects of the Dark Triad on Supervision Performance Ratings," *Journal of Organizational Behavior*, February 2016, 236–254.

25. D. S. Whitman, "Emotional Intelligence and Leadership in Organizations: A Meta-Analytic Test of Process Mechanisms," dissertation submitted for Doctor of Philosophy, Florida International University, 2009; and F. Walter, R. H. Humphrey, and M. S. Cole, "Unleashing Leadership Potential: Toward an Evidence-Based Management of Emotional Intelligence," *Organizational Dynamics*, July–September 2012, 212–219.

26. V. K. Gupta, S. Han, S. C. Mortal, S. Silveri, and D. B. Turban, "Do Women CEOs Face Greater Threat of Shareholder Activism Compared to Male CEOs? A Role Congruity Perspective," *Journal of Applied Psychology*, February 2018, 228–236.

27. H. McLaughlin, J. Silvester, D. Bilimoria, S. Jané, K. Sealy, K. Peters, H. Möltner, M. Huse, and J. Göke, "Women in Power: Contributing Factors That Impact on Women in Organizations and Politics; Psychological Research and Best Practice," *Organizational Dynamics*, July–September 2018, 189–199.

28. P. Dwivedi, A. Joshi, and V. F. Misangyi, "Gender-Inclusive Gatekeeping: How (Mostly Male) Predecessors Influence the Success of Female CEOs," *Academy of Management Journal*, April 2018, 379–404.

29. I. I Szymakska and B. A. Rubin, "Gender and Relationship Differences in the Perceptions of Male and Female Leadership," *Gender in Management: An International Journal*, June 2018, 254–281.

30. Implicit leadership theory is discussed by B. M. Bass and R. Bass, *The Bass Handbook of Leadership: Theory, Research, and Managerial Applications*, 4th ed. (New York: Free Press, 2008), 46–78; and J. S. Mueller, J. A. Goncalo, and D. Kamdar, "Recognizing Creative Leadership: Can Creative Idea Expression Negatively Relate to Perceptions of Leadership Potential?" *Journal of Experimental Social Psychology*, 47, 2001, 494–498.

31. See A. W. Lukaszewski, Z. L. Simmons, C. Anderson, and J. R. Roney, "The Role of Physical Formidability in Human Social Status Allocation," *Journal of Personality and Social Psychology*, March 2016, 385–406.

32. Vugt, Mark Van, and Allen E. Grabo. "The Many Faces of Leadership: An Evolutionary-Psychology Approach." *Current Directions in Psychological Science* 24, no. 6 (December 2015): 484–89. https://doi.org/10.1177/0963721415601971.

33. For more information on Kouzes and Posner's leadership model and their extensive research, see "Our Approach," *The Leadership Challenge,* https://www.leadershipchallenge.com (accessed April 22, 2019).

34. M. Buck and M. Martin, "Leaders Teaching Leaders," *HR Magazine,* September 2012, 60–62.

35. "2018 Training Industry Report," *Training,* https://trainingmag.com/trg-mag-article/2018-training-industry-report/ (accessed April 21, 2019).

36. D. Zielinski, "Effective Assessments," *HR Magazine,* January 2011, 61–64.

37. M. Javidan, A. Bullough, and R. Dibble, "Mind the Gap: Gender Differences in Global Leadership Self-Efficacies," *Academy of Management Perspectives,* February 2016, 59–73.

38. M. Weinstein, "World-Class Leaders," *Training,* May/June 2012, 18–21.

39. G. Yukl, "Effective Leadership Behavior: What We Know and What Questions Need More Attention," *Academy of Management Perspectives,* November 2012, 69.

40. D. S. DeRue, J. D. Nahrgang, N. Wellman, and S. E. Humphrey, "Trait and Behavioral Theories of Leadership: An Integration and Meta-Analytic Test of Their Relative Validity," *Personnel Psychology,* 2011.

41. T. A. Judge, R. F. Piccolo, and R. Ilies, "The Forgotten Ones? The Validity of Consideration and Initiating Structure in Leadership Research," *Journal of Applied Psychology,* February 2004, 36–51.

42. A definition and description of transactional leadership is provided by B. M. Bass and R. Bass, *The Bass Handbook of Leadership: Theory, Research, and Managerial Applications,* 4th ed. (New York: Free Press, 2008), 618–648.

43. D. S. DeRue, J. D. Nahrgang, N. Wellman, and S. E. Humphrey, "Trait and Behavioral Theories of Leadership: An Integration and Meta-Analytic Test of Their Relative Validity," *Personnel Psychology,* 2011.

44. G. Sapakoff, "Dabo Swinney's First Order of Clemson Spring Practice Business: Find New Leaders," *The Post and Courier,* February 27, 2019, https://www.postandcourier.com/columnists/dabo-swinney-s-first-order-of-clemson-spring-practice-business/article_fb887f00-392d-11e9-938c-6fe8fcc97897.html.

45. M. Given, "5 Leadership Secrets Shared by Clemson's Dabo Swinney During His White House Speech," *Inc.,* June 14, 2017, https://www.inc.com/matt-given/5-leadership-secrets-shared-by-clemsons-dabo-swinney-during-his-white-house-spee.html.

46. J. Tamny, "Dabo Swinney, the Clemson Tigers, and the Genius of Rising Inequality," *Forbes,* September 23, 2018, https://www.forbes.com/sites/johntamny/2018/09/23/dabo-swinney-the-clemson-tigers-and-the-genius-of-rising-inequality/#4ffc360e4cc4.

47. J. Boozell, "Clemson Dominates Alabama for Second College Football Playoff Title, Third National Championship," *NCAA.com,* January 8, 2019, https://www.ncaa.com/news/football/article/2019-01-08/clemson-dominates-alabama-second-college-football-playoff-title.

48. G. Yukl, "Effective Leadership Behavior: What We Know and What Questions Need More Attention," *Academy of Management Perspectives,* November 2012, 69.

49. T. A. Judge, R. F. Piccolo, and R. Ilies, "The Forgotten Ones? The Validity of Consideration and Initiating Structure in Leadership Research," *Journal of Applied Psychology,* February 2004, 36–51.

50. M. T. Maynard, L. L. Gilson, and J. E. Mathieu, "Empowerment—Fad or Fab? A Multilevel Review of the Past Two Decades of Research," *Journal of Management,* July 2012, 1231–1281.

51. S. Fiegerman, "Forget Bezos. Marc Benioff Is Having a Moment," *CNN Business,* October 4, 2018, https://www.cnn.com/2018/10/03/tech/marc-benioff-profile/index.html.

52. A. Levy, "Salesforce's Marc Benioff Unplugged for Two Weeks, and Had a Revelation That Could Change the Tech Industry," *CNBC,* January 5, 2019, https://www.cnbc.com/2018/12/30/salesforce-marc-benioff-talks-tech-ethics-time-magazine-and-vacation.html.

53. I. A. Hamilton, "Marc Benioff Says Ditching His iPhone and iPad on Holiday Helped Him Make a Huge Decision about Salesforce's Future," *Business Insider,* January 7, 2019, https://www.businessinsider.com/marc-benioff-hired-keith-block-as-salesforce-co-ceo-after-ditching-phone-2019-1.

54. B. Mikel, "To Keep Its 30,000 Employees Happy, Salesforce Offers a Refreshing, But Peculiar Perk," *Inc.,* June 25, 2018, https://www.inc.com/betsy-mikel/new-salesforce-employees-dont-actually-work-on-their-first-day-they-get-to-do-this-instead.html.

55. M. Schwantes, "The CEO of Salesforce Found Out His Female Employees Were Paid Less Than Men. His Response Is a Priceless Leadership Lesson," *Inc.,* July 26, 2018, https://www.inc.com/marcel-schwantes/the-ceo-of-salesforce-found-out-female-employees-are-paid-less-than-men-his-response-is-a-priceless-leadership-lesson.html.

56. P. Schilpzand, L. Houston, and J. Cho, "Not Too Tired to Be Proactive: Daily Empowering Leadership Spurs Next-Morning Employee Proactivity as Moderated by Nightly Sleep Quality," *Academy of Management Journal,* December 2018, 2367–2387; J. Zhu, Z. Liao, K. C. Yam, and R. E. Johnson, "Shared Leadership: A State-of-the-Art Review and Future Research Agenda," *Journal of Organizational Behavior,* September 2018, 834–852; and A. Lee, S. Willis, and A. W. Tian, "Empowering Leadership: A Meta-Analytics Examination of Incremental Contribution, Mediation, and Moderation," *Journal of Organizational Behavior,* March 2018, 306–325.

57. An overall summary of servant-leadership is provided by L. C. Spears, *Reflections on Leadership: How Robert K. Greenleaf's Theory of Servant-Leadership Influenced Today's Top Management Thinkers* (New York: Wiley, 1995).

58. Weinstein, Margery. "The Secret Sauce for a Better Boss." *Lakewood Media Group, LLC,* https://trainingmag.com/secret-sauce-better-boss/.

59. See Z. Chen, J. Zhu, and M. Zhou, "How Does Servant Leader Fuel the Service Fire? A Multilevel Model of Servant Leadership, Individual Self-Identity, Group Competition Climate, and Customer Service Performance," *Journal of Applied Psychology,* March 2015, 511–121; and S. J. Peterson, B. M. Galvin, and D. Lange, "CEO Servant Leadership: Exploring Executive Characteristics and Firm Performance," *Personnel Psychology,* 2012, 565–596.

60. McGirt, Ellen. "Bono: I Will Follow." Fortune Media IP Limited, March 24, 2016. http://fortune.com/bono-u2-one/.

61. C. E. Thiel, J. H. Hardy III, D. R. Peterson, D. T. Welsh, and J. M. Bonner, "Too Many Sheep in the Flock? Span of Control Attenuates the Influence of Ethical Leadership," *Journal of Applied Psychology,* December 2018, 1324–1334.

62. C. Moore, D. M. Mayer, F. F. T. Chiang, C. Crossley, M. J. Karlesky, and T. A. Birtch, "Leaders Matter Morally: The Role of Ethical Leadership in Shaping Employee Moral Cognition and Misconduct," *Journal of Applied Psychology,* January 2019, 123–145.

63. B. J. Tepper, "Consequences of Abusive Supervision," *Academy of Management Journal,* 43, 178.

64. M. H. Tu, J. E. Bono, C. Shum, and L. LaMontagne, "Breaking the Cycle: The Effects of Role Model Performance and Ideal Leadership Self-Concepts on Abusive Supervision Spillover," *Journal of Applied Psychology,* July 2018, 689–702; and H. Park, J. M. Hoobler, J. Wu, R. C. Liden, J. Hu, and M. S. Wilson, "Abusive Supervision and Employee Deviance: A Multifoci Justice Perspective," *Journal of Business Ethics,* December 2017, 1–19.

65. "Study: Abusive Supervisors Impact Victims and Coworkers Alike," https://hr.blr.com/whitepapers/Staffing-Training/Leadership/Study-Abusive-supervisors-impact-victims-and-cowor (accessed April 21, 2019); J. Zhu and B. Zhang, "The Double-Edged Sword Effect of Abusive Supervision on Subordinates Innovative Behavior," *Frontiers in Psychology,* January 2019, 66; and H. Park, J. M. Hoobler, J. Wu, R. C. Liden, J. Hu, and M. S. Wilson, "Abusive Supervision and Employee Deviance: A Multifoci Justice Perspective," *Journal of Business Ethics,* December 2017, 1–19.

66. L. Yu, M. K. Duffy, and B. J. Tepper, "Consequences of Downward Envy: A Model of Self-Esteem Threat, Abusive Supervision, and Supervisory Self-Improvement," *Academy of Management Journal,* December 2018, 2296–2318.

67. C. Woolston, "Bad Bosses: Dealing with Abusive Supervisors," *Knowable Magazine,* https://www.knowablemagazine.org/article/society/2018/bad-bosses-dealing-abusive-supervisors (accessed April 21, 2019); and S. G. Taylor, M. D. Griffith, A. K. Vadera, R. Folger, and C. R. Letwin, "Breaking the Cycle of Abusive Supervision: How Disidentification and Moral Identity Help the Trickle-Down Change Course," *Journal of Applied Psychology,* January 2019, 164–182.

68. M. L. Nestel, "Pharmacy Boss Allegedly Forced Employees to Kiss Her for Their Paychecks, Get Spanked for Punishment, Lawsuit Says," *Newsweek,* December 11, 2018, https://www.newsweek.com/pharmacy-js-professional-pharmacy-joyce-fogleman-wendy-blades-spankings-kiss-1253777; and "West Frankfort Business Owner Sued for Sexual Harassment," WSILTV, December 27, 2018, http://www.wsiltv.com/story/39639959/west-frankfort-business-owner-sued-for-sexual-harassment.

69. M. L. Nestel, "Pharmacy Boss Allegedly Forced Employees to Kiss Her for Their Paychecks, Get Spanked for Punishment, Lawsuit Says," *Newsweek,* December 11, 2018, https://www.newsweek.com/pharmacy-js-professional-pharmacy-joyce-fogleman-wendy-blades-spankings-kiss-1253777.

70. "J&S Professional Pharmacy," D&B Hoovers, http://www.hoovers.com/company-information/cs/company-profile.j___s_professional_pharmacy.94dd023d1717663d.html?aka_re=1#financials-anchor (accessed April 14, 2019).

71. M. L. Nestel, "Pharmacy Boss Allegedly Forced Employees to Kiss Her for Their Paychecks, Get Spanked for Punishment, Lawsuit Says," *Newsweek,* December 11, 2018, https://www.newsweek.com/pharmacy-js-professional-pharmacy-joyce-fogleman-wendy-blades-spankings-kiss-1253777.

72. J. Hyman, "The 1st Nominee for the Worst Employer of 2019 is … the Philandering Pharmacist," *Workforce.com,* December 11, 2018, https://www.workforce.com/2018/12/11/the-1st-nominee-for-the-worst-employer-of-2019-is-the-philandering-pharmacist/.

73. See D. S. DeRue, J. D. Nahrgang, N. Wellman, and S. E. Humphrey, "Trait and Behavioral Theories of Leadership: An Integration and Meta-Analytic Test of Their Relative Validity," *Personnel Psychology,* 2011, 7–52.

74. See S. T. Hannah and B. J. Avolio, "Ready or Not: How Do We Accelerate the Developmental Readiness of Leaders?" *Journal of Organizational Behavior,* November 2010, 1181–1187.

75. A. K. Khan, S. Moss, S. Quratulain, and I. Hameed, "When and How Subordinate Performance Leads to Abusive Supervision: A Social Dominance Perspective," *Journal of Management,* September 2018, 2801–2826.

76. For more on this theory, see F. E. Fiedler, "A Contingency Model of Leadership Effectiveness," in *Advances in Experimental Social Psychology,* vol. 1, ed. L. Berkowitz (New York: Academic Press, 1964); and F. E. Fiedler, *A Theory of Leadership Effectiveness* (New York: McGraw-Hill, 1967).

77. See L. H. Peters, D. D. Hartke, and J. T. Pohlmann, "Fiedler's Contingency Theory of Leadership: An Application of the Meta-Analysis Procedures of Schmidt and Hunter," *Psychological Bulletin,* March 1985, 274–285; and C. A. Schriesheim, B. J. Tepper, and L. A. Tetrault, "Least Preferred Co-Worker Score, Situational Control, and Leadership Effectiveness: A Meta-Analysis of Contingency Model Performance Predictions," *Journal of Applied Psychology,* August 1994, 561–573.

78. C. A. Hartnell, A. J. Kinicki, L. S. Lambert, M. Fugate, and P. D. Corner, "Do Similarities of Differences between CEO Leadership and Organizational Culture Have a More Positive Effect on Firm Performance? A Test of Competing Predictions," *Journal of Applied Psychology,* June 2016, 846–861.

79. See L. S. Lambert, B. J. Tepper, J. C. Carr, D. T. Holt, and A. J. Barelka, "Forgotten but Not Gone: An Examination of Fit between Leader Consideration and Initiating Structure Needed and Received," *Journal of Applied Psychology,* September 2012, 913–930.

80. N. Meyersohn, "Barnes & Noble Is Overrun with Problems," *CNN Businesss.com,* September 6, 2018, https://money.cnn.com/2018/09/06/news/companies/barnes-and-noble-books-amazon/index.html.

81. N. Meyersohn, "Barnes & Noble Is Overrun with Problems," *CNN Businesss.com,* September 6, 2018, https://money.cnn.com/2018/09/06/news/companies/barnes-and-noble-books-amazon/index.html; and T. Hsu and A. Alter, "Barnes & Noble Says Former CEO Demos Parneros Was Fired for Sexual Harassment," *The New York Times,* August 28, 2018, https://www.nytimes.com/2018/08/28/business/barnes-noble-ceo-sexual-harassment-lawsuit.html.

82. C. Wang, "Barnes & Noble Fires CEO Demos Parneros for Violating Company Policies," *CNBC,* July 3, 2018, https://www.cnbc.com/2018/07/03/barnes--noble-fires-ceo-demos-parneros.html.

83. C. Wang, "Barnes & Noble Fires CEO Demos Parneros for Violating Company Policies," *CNBC,* July 3, 2018, https://www.cnbc.com/2018/07/03/barnes--noble-fires-ceo-demos-parneros.html.

84. A. Alter, "Ronald D. Boire Steps Down as Chief of Barnes & Noble," *The New York Times,* August 16, 2016, https://www.nytimes.com/2016/08/17/business/media/ronald-d-boire-steps-down-as-chief-of-barnes-noble.html.

85. B. Y. Farhan, "Application of Path-Goal Leadership Theory and Learning Theory in a Learning Organization," *Journal of Applied Business Research,* January/February 2018, 13–22.

86. J. T. Bickle, "Developing Remote Training Consultants as Leaders—Dialogic/Network Application of Path-Goal Leadership Theory in Leadership Development," *Performance Improvement,* October 2017, 32–39.

87. The steps were developed by H. P. Sims Jr., S. Faraj, and S. Yun, "When Should a Leader Be Directive or Empowering? How to Develop Your Own Situational Theory of Leadership," *Business Horizons,* March–April 2009, 149–158.

88. M. Weber, *The Theory of Social and Economic Organization* (New York: Oxford University Press, 1947).

89. A historical review of transformational leadership is provided by D. V. Knippenberg and S. B. Sitkin, "A Critical Assessment of Charismatic–Transformational Leadership Research: Back to the Drawing Board?" *Academy of Management Annals,* 2013, 1–60.

90. B. Nanus, *Visionary Leadership* (San Francisco: Jossey-Bass, 1992), 8.

91. A. Quito, "Netflix's CEO Says There Are Months When He Doesn't Have to Make a Single Decision," *Quartz,* April 19, 2018, https://qz.com/work/1254183/netflix-ceo-reed-hastings-expounds-on-the-netflix-culture-deck-at-ted-2018/.

92. "Netflix Culture," https://jobs.netflix.com/culture (accessed April 21, 2019).

93. "Learning from Netflix: How to Build a Culture of Freedom and Responsibility," *Knowledge@Wharton,* May 29, 2018, https://knowledge.wharton.upenn.edu/article/how-netflix-built-its-company-culture/.

94. R. Jenkins, "3 Ways Netflix Created a Culture of High-Performing Employees," *Inc.,* September 5, 2018, https://www.inc.com/ryan-jenkins/this-is-how-netflix-built-a-culture-of-highly-motivated-employees.html.

95. Supportive results can be found in P. D. Harms and M. Credé, "Emotional Intelligence and Transformational and Transactional Leadership: A Meta-Analysis," *Journal of Leadership & Organizational Studies,* February 2010, 5–17.

96. See A. Eagly, M. C. Johannesen-Schmidt, and M. L. van Engen, "Transformational, Transactional, and Laissez-Faire Leadership Styles: A Meta-Analysis Comparing Women and Men," *Psychological Bulletin,* July 2003, 569–591.

97. See D. L. Joseph, L. Y. Dhanani, W. Shen, B. C. McHugh, and M. A. McCord, "Is a Happy Leader a Good Leader: A Meta-Analytic Investigation of Leader Trait Affect and Leadership," *Leadership Quarterly,* August 2015, 558–577.

98. See S. Clarke, "Safety Leadership: A Meta-Analytic Review of Transformational Leadership and Transactional Leadership Styles as Antecedents of Safety Behavior," *Journal of Occupational and Organizational Psychology,* March 2013, 22–49; G. Wang, I.-S. Oh, S. H. Courtright, and A. E. Colbert, "Transformational Leadership and Performance across Criteria and Levels: A Meta-Analytic Review of 25 Years of Research," *Group & Organizational Management,* 2011, 223–270; and D. A. Waldman, M. Z. Carter, and P. W. Hom, "A Multi-Level Investigation of Leadership and Turnover Behavior," *Journal of Management,* September 2015, 1724–1744.

99. B. J. Tepper, N. Dimotakis, L. S. Lambert, J. Koopman, F. K. Matta, H. M. Park, and W. Goo, "Examining Follower Responses to Transformational Leadership from a Dynamic, Person–Environment Fit Perspective," *Academy of Management Journal,* August 2018, 1343–1368; and J. Vergauwe, B. Wille, J. Hofmans, R. B. Kaiser, and F. De Fruyt, "The Double-Edged Sword of Leader Charisma: Understanding the Curvilinear Relationship Between Charismatic Personality and Leader Effectiveness," *Journal of Personality and Social Psychology,* January 2018, 110–130.

100. Visionary leadership is studied by C. A. Hartnell and F. O. Walumbwa, "Transformational Leadership and Organizational Culture," in N. M. Ashkanasy, C. P. M. Wilderom, and M. F. Peterson, eds., *The Handbook of Organizational Culture and Climate,* 2nd ed. (Thousand Oaks, CA: Sage, 2011), 225–248.

101. Communicating visions is discussed by A. M. Carton and B. J. Lucas, "How Can Leaders Overcome the Blurry Vision Bias? Identifying an Antidote to the Paradox of Vision Communication," *Academy of Management Journal,* December 2018, 2106–2129; and Y. Berson, N. Halevy, B. Shamir, and M. Erez, "Leading from Different Psychological Distances: A Construal-Level Perspective on Vision Communication, Goal Setting, and Follower Motivation," *The Leadership Quarterly,* 2015, 143–155.

102. D. K. Goodwin, "Lincoln and the Art of Transformative Leadership," *Harvard Business Review,* September–October 2018, 126–134.

103. T. Whitford and S. A. Moss, "Transformational Leadership in Distributed Work Groups: The Moderating Role of Follower Regulatory Focus and Goal Orientation," *Communication Research,* December 2009, 810–837.

104. See F. Dansereau Jr., G. Graen, and W. Haga, "A Vertical Dyad Linkage Approach to Leadership within Formal Organizations," *Organizational Behavior and Human Performance,* February 1975, 46–78.

105. Based on J. H. Dulebohn, W. H. Bommer, R. C. Liden, R. L. Brouer, and G. R. Ferris, "A Meta-Analysis of Antecedents and Consequences of Leader-Member Exchange: Integrating the Past with an Eye toward the Future," *Journal of Management,* November 2012, 1715–1759.

106. J. Seo, J. D. Nahrgang, M. Z. Carter, and P. W. Hom, "Not All Differentiation Is the Same: Examining the Moderating Effects of Leader-Member Exchange Configurations," *Journal of Applied Psychology,* May 2018, 478–495; and R. Martin, G. Thomas, A. Legood, and S. Dello Russo, "Leader-Member Exchange (LMX) Differentiation and Work Outcomes: Conceptual Clarification and Critical Review," *Journal of Organizational Behavior,* February 2018, 151–168.

107. A. Yu, F. K. Matta, and B. Cornfield, "Is Leader–Member Exchange Differentiation Beneficial or Detrimental for Group Effectiveness? A Meta-Analytic Investigation and Theoretical Integration," *Academy of Management Journal,* June 2018, 1158–1188.

108. H. H. M. Tse, C. K. Lam, J. Gu, and X. S. Lin, "Examining the Interpersonal Process and Consequence of Leader–Member Exchange Comparison: The Role of Procedural Justice Climate," *Journal of Organizational Behavior,* October 2018, 922–940.

109. D. L. Haggard and H. M. Park, "Perceived Supervisor Remorse, Abusive Supervision, and LMX," *Journal of Organizational Behavior,* December 2018, 1252–1267.

110. G. Wang, C. H. Van Iddekinge, L. Zhang, and J. Bishoff, "Meta-Analytic and Primary Investigations of the Role of Followers in Ratings of Leadership Behavior in Organizations," *Journal of Applied Psychology,* January 2019, 70–106.

111. X. Huang, E. Xu, and L. Huang, "Nonlinear Consequences of Promotive and Prohibitive Voice for Managers' Responses: The Roles of Voice Frequency and LMX," *Journal of Applied Psychology,* October 2018, 1101–1120.

112. Z. Liao, W. Liu, X. Li, and Z. Song, "Give and Take: An Episodic Perspective on Leader-Member Exchange," *Journal of Applied Psychology,* January 2019, 34–51; and J. D. Mackey, C. P. McAllister, L. P. Maher, and G. Wang, "Leaders and Followers Behaving Badly: A Meta-Analytic Examination of Curvilinear Relationships Between Destructive Leadership and Followers' Workplace Behaviors," *Personnel Psychology,* June 2018, 3–47.

113. S. M. Heathfield, "10 Tips to Help You Get Along With Your Boss," *The Balance,* October 1, 2018, https://www.thebalancecareers.com/get-along-with-boss-1919375.

114. A. Kinicki, "How Can You Improve Your Work Image?" *Arizona Republic,* September 7, 2014, E6.

115. S. M. Heathfield, "10 Tips to Help You Get Along With Your Boss," *The Balance,* October 1, 2018, https://www.thebalancecareers.com/get-along-with-boss-1919375.

116. A. Kinicki, "How Can You Improve Your Work Image?" *Arizona Republic,* September 7, 2014, E6.

117. A. Y. Ou, D. A. Waldman, and S. J. Peterson, "Do Humble CEOs Matter? An Examination of CEO Humility and Firm Outcomes," *Journal of Management,* March 2018, 1147–1173.

118. L. Wang, B. P. Owens, J. Li, and L. Shi, "Exploring the Affect Impact, Boundary Conditions, and Antecedents of Leader Humility," *Journal of Applied Psychology,* September 2018, 1019–1038.

119. A. Robinson, "The Most Successful Companies Have Humble Leaders. Here's Why," *Inc.,* November 2, 2018, https://www.inc.com/adam-robinson/this-1-leadership-quality-will-motivate-your-employees-to-do-great-work.html.

120. A. Rego, B. Owens, K. C. Yam, D. Bluhm, M. Pina de Cunha, A. Silard, L. Gonçalves, M. Martins, A. Volkmann Simpson, and W. Liu, "Leader Humility and Team Performance: Exploring the Mediating Mechanisms of Team PsyCap and Task Allocation Effectiveness," *Journal of Management,* March 2019, 1009–1033.

121. J. Hu, B. Erdogan, K. Jiang, T. N. Bauer, and S. Liu, "Leader Humility and Team Creativity: The Role of Team Information Sharing, Psychological Safety, and Power Distance," *Journal of Applied Psychology,* March 2018, 313–323.

122. A. C. Weidman, J. T. Cheng, and J. L. Tracy, "The Psychological Structure of Humility," *Journal of Personality and Social Psychology,* January 2018, 153–178.

123. R. Levering, "The 100 Best Companies to Work for 2016," *Fortune,* March 15, 2016, 160.

124. See B. M. Bass and R. Bass, *The Bass Handbook of Leadership: Theory, Research, and Managerial Applications,* 4th ed. (New York: Free Press, 2008).

125. See L. Bossidy, "What Your Leader Expects of You and What You Should Expect in Return," *Harvard Business Review,* April 2007, 58–65.

126. See R. Goffee and G. Jones, "Followership: It's Personal, Too," *Harvard Business Review,* December 2001, 148.

127. This checklist was proposed by J. J. Gabarro and J. P. Kotter, "Managing Your Boss," *Harvard Business Review,* January 2005, 2–11.

128. Partially based on S. Vozza, "How to Be a Good Follower (And Why It's a Skill You Need)," *Fast Company,* February 21, 2018, https://www.fastcompany.com/40544722/how-to-be-agood-follower-and-why-its-a-skill-you-need; and B. Dattner, "Forewarned Is Forearmed," *BusinessWeek,* September 1, 2008, 50.

129. M. Alvesson and M. Blom, "Beyond Leadership and Followership: Working with a Variety of Modes of Organizing," *Organizational Dynamics,* January–March 2019, 28–37.

130. D. Buss, "For Insights into Elon Musk's Leadership of Tesla, Look at How He Leads SpaceX, Author Says," *Forbes,* August 31, 2018, https://www.forbes.com/sites/dalebuss/2018/08/31/for-insights-into-elon-musks-leadership-of-tesla-look-at-how-he-leads-spacex-author-says/#6ad83fb763a4.

131. C. Duhigg, "Dr. Elon & Mr. Musk: Life Inside Tesla's Production Hell," *Wired,* December 13, 2018, https://www.wired.com/story/elon-musk-tesla-life-inside-gigafactory/.

132. J. Wingard, "Elon Musk and the Pitfalls of Creative Leadership," *Forbes,* April 10, 2019, https://www.forbes.com/sites/jasonwingard/2019/04/10/elon-musk-and-the-pitfalls-of-creative-leadership/#6317b78f3f3e.

133. Dale Buss, "For Insights Into Elon Musk's Leadership Of Tesla, Look At How He Leads SpaceX, Author Says." *Forbes Media LLC,* August 31, 2018, https://www.forbes.com/sites/dalebuss/2018/08/31/for-insights-into-elon-musks-leadership-of-tesla-look-at-how-he-leads-spacex-author-says/#2aea54f263a4.

134. Charles Duhigg, "Dr. Elon & Mr. Musk: Life Inside Tesla's Production Hell." Condé Nast, December 13, 2018, https://www.wired.com/story/elon-musk-tesla-life-inside-gigafactory/.

135. Dale Buss, "For Insights Into Elon Musk's Leadership Of Tesla, Look At How He Leads SpaceX, Author Says." *Forbes Media LLC,* August 31, 2018, https://www.forbes.com/sites/dalebuss/2018/08/31/for-insights-into-elon-musks-leadership-of-tesla-look-at-how-he-leads-spacex-author-says/#2aea54f263a4.

136. C. Duhigg, "Dr. Elon & Mr. Musk: Life Inside Tesla's Production Hell," *Wired,* December 13, 2018, https://www.wired.com/story/elon-musk-tesla-life-inside-gigafactory/.

137. C. Duhigg, "Dr. Elon & Mr. Musk: Life Inside Tesla's Production Hell," *Wired,* December 13, 2018, https://www.wired.com/story/elon-musk-tesla-life-inside-gigafactory/.

138. R. Mitchell, "As Tesla Struggles to Exit 'Production Hell,' Buyers Complain of Delivery Limbo," *Los Angeles Times,* September 14, 2018, https://www.latimes.com/business/autos/la-fi-hy-tesla-sales-delivery-problems-20180912-story.html.

139. S. Fairyington, "What We Can Learn About How NOT to Lead From Elon Musk," *Thrive Global,* January 10, 2019, https://thriveglobal.com/stories/elon-musk-leadership-style-hamper-tesla-growth-lessons-tips/.

140. C. Duhigg, "Dr. Elon & Mr. Musk: Life Inside Tesla's Production Hell," *Wired,* December 13, 2018, https://www.wired.com/story/elon-musk-tesla-life-inside-gigafactory/.

141. L. Kolodny, "Elon Musk's Extreme Micromanagement Has Wasted Time and Money at Tesla, Insiders Say," *CNBC,* October 19, 2018, https://www.cnbc.com/2018/10/19/tesla-ceo-elon-musk-extreme-micro-manager.html.

142. B. Enderwick, "What Elon Musk Gets Wrong About Leadership," *Medium,* August 24, 2018, https://medium.com/s/story/what-elon-musk-gets-wrong-about-leadership-b97794a0e330.

143. Charles Duhigg, "Dr. Elon & Mr. Musk: Life Inside Tesla's Production Hell." Condé Nast, December 13, 2018, https://www.wired.com/story/elon-musk-tesla-life-inside-gigafactory/.

144. C. Duhigg, "Dr. Elon & Mr. Musk: Life Inside Tesla's Production Hell," *Wired,* December 13, 2018, https://www.wired.com/story/elon-musk-tesla-life-inside-gigafactory/.

145. M. Castillo, "Elon Musk May Have Violated Tesla's Business Conduct Policy by Smoking Weed," *CNBC,* September 7, 2018, https://www.cnbc.com/2018/09/07/elon-musk-may-have-violated-tesla-conduct-policy-by-smoking-weed.html.

146. J. Wingard, "Elon Musk and the Pitfalls of Creative Leadership," *Forbes,* April 10, 2019, https://www.forbes.com/sites/jasonwingard/2019/04/10/elon-musk-and-the-pitfalls-of-creative-leadership/#6317b78f3f3e.

147. J. McGregor, "Elon Musk, The Say-Anything CEO," *The Washington Post,* December 13, 2018, https://www.washingtonpost.com/business/2018/12/13/elon-musk-say-anything-ceo/?utm_term=.9eaf03d4ee48.

148. A. Pressman, "Data Sheet—Why Elon Musk's Visionary Leadership Falls Short," *Fortune,* November 8, 2018, http://fortune.com/2018/11/08/data-sheet-elon-musk-tesla-chairman-robyn-denholm/.

149. Stephanie Fairyington, "What We Can Learn about How NOT to Lead from Elon Musk," Thrive Global, January 10, 2019, https://thriveglobal.com/stories/elon-musk-leadership-style-hamper-tesla-growth-lessons-tips/.

150. D. Hull, "Tesla Sinks After Model Y Unveiling Rekindles Concerns over Cash," *Bloomberg,* March 14, 2019, https://www.bloomberg.com/news/articles/2019-03-15/elon-musk-reveals-tesla-model-y-crossover-to-start-at-39-000.

151. C. Duhigg, "Dr. Elon & Mr. Musk: Life Inside Tesla's Production Hell," *Wired,* December 13, 2018, https://www.wired.com/story/elon-musk-tesla-life-inside-gigafactory/.

152. Jen Juneau, "Claire's Employee Quits, Calls Out Policy After Refusing to Pierce a Non-Consenting Child's Ears." Meredith Corporation, April 10, 2019, https://people.com/parents/claires-employee-quits-after-child-doesnt-consent-ear-piercing-policy/.

CHAPTER 14

1. A. L. Kristof-Brown, R. D. Zimmerman, and E. C. Johnson, "Consequences of Individuals' Fit at Work: A Meta-Analysis of Person-Job, Person-Organization, Person-Group, and Person-Supervisor Fit," *Personnel Psychology,* Summer 2005, 281.

2. W. Lam, Y. Huo, and Z. Chen, "Who Is Fit to Serve? Person–Job/Organization Fit, Emotional Labor, and Customer Service Performance," *Human Resource Management,* November 2017, 483–497.

3. Fit perceptions during recruiting were examined by B. W. Swider, R. D. Zimmerman, and M. R. Barrick, "Searching for the Right Fit: Development of Applicant Person-Organization Fit Perceptions During the Recruitment Process," *Journal of Applied Psychology,* May 2015, 880–893.

4. See C. Boho, "How to Find the Right Cultural Fit," *Arizona Republic,* November 15, 2015.

5. Mansueto Ventures. "8 Entrepreneurs Share How They Weed Out Job Candidates Based on Cultural." Accessed May 22, 2019, https://www.inc.com/entrepreneurs-organization/8-proven-ways-to-identify-job-candidates-with-a-strong-cultural-fit.html?cid=search.

6. These suggestions are based on A. Kinicki, "It's Important to Fit in with Fellow Workers," *Arizona Republic,* May 31, 2015.

7. R. Feloni, "T-Mobile's CEO Says Reinventing Himself Was Key to Transforming the Company's Culture," *Business Insider,* https://www.businessinsider.com/t-mobile-ceo-john-legere-company-culture-2016-10 (accessed May 2, 2019).

8. Alan Murray, "The Pinnacles and Pitfalls of Corporate Culture," Fortune Media IP Limited, March 3, 2016, http://fortune.com/2016/03/03/best-companies-to-work-for-editors-desk/.

9. "Virgin Group in Numbers," https://www.virgin.com (accessed May 2, 2019); and C. Paton, "37 Company Culture Quotes That Will Inspire Your Team," https://blog.enplug.com/37-company-culture-quotes (accessed May 2, 2019).

10. Edgar H. Schein, "Culture: The Missing Concept in Organization Studies," *Administrative Science Quarterly* 41, no. 2 (1996): 229–40. https://DOI: 10.2307/2393715.

11. I. S. Oh, J. H. Han, B. Holtz, Y. J. Kim, and S. Kim, "Do Birds of a Feather Flock, Fly, and Continue to Fly Together? The Differential and Cumulative Effects of Attraction, Selection, and Attrition on Personality-Based Within-Organization Homogeneity and Between-Organization Heterogeneity Progression over Time," *Journal of Organizational Behavior,* December 2018; and W. Vleugels, R. De Cooman, M. Verbruggen, and O. Solinger, "Understanding Dynamic Change in Perceptions of Person–Environment Fit: An Exploration of Competing Theoretical Perspectives," *Journal of Organizational Behavior,* November 2018.

12. E. H. Follmer, D. L. Talbot, A. L. Kristof-Brown, S. L. Astrove, and J. Billsberry, "Resolution, Relief, and Resignation: A Qualitative Study of Responses to Misfit at Work," *Academy of Management Journal,* April 2018, 440–465.

13. M. Helft and J. Hempel, "Inside Facebook," *Fortune,* March 19, 2012, 113–122.

14. R. Umoh, "Why Amazon Pays Employees $5,000 to Quit," *CNBC,* https://www.cnbc.com/2018/05/21/why-amazon-pays-employees-5000-to-quit.html, May 21, 2018.

15. "Culture: We Have a Couple of Ground Rules at Warby Parker," https://www.warbyparker.com (accessed May 2, 2019).

16. A. Otani, "Patagonia Triggers a Market Panic over New Rules on Its Power Vests," *The Wall Street Journal,* April 8, 2019, https://www.wsj.com/articles/patagonia-triggers-a-market-panic-over-new-rules-on-its-power-vests-11554736920.

17. Results are discussed in "Executing Ethics," *Training,* March 2007, 8.

18. See M. Cording, J. S. Harrison, R. E. Hoskisson, and K. Jonsen, "Walking the Talk: A Multistakeholder Exploration of Organizational Authenticity, Employee Productivity, and Post-Merger Performance," *Academy of Management Perspectives,* February 2014, 38–56.

19. A. Fox, "Get in the Business of Being Green," *HR Magazine,* June 2008, 45–46.

20. S. Cantele and A. Zardini, "Is Sustainability a Competitive Advantage for Small Businesses? An Empirical Analysis of Possible Mediators in the Sustainability–Financial Performance Relationship," *Journal of Cleaner Production,* May 2018, 166–176.

21. "Sustainability: Our Strategy," https://www.kering.com/en/sustainability/ (accessed May 2, 2019); and K. Strauss, "The Most Sustainable Companies in 2019," *Forbes,* January 22, 2019, https://www.forbes.com/sites/karstenstrauss/2019/01/22/the-most-sustainable-companies-in-2019/#216203c56d7d.

22. Ceres, "Companies Show Signs of Progress, But New Ceres Analysis Calls for More Action on Sustainability Commitments," https://www.ceres.org/news-center/press-releases/companies-show-signs-progress-new-ceres-analysis-calls-more-action (accessed May 22, 2019).

23. E. Chhabra, " How Two Young Entrepreneurs Are Tackling the Plastic Problem with Swimwear," *Forbes,* June 13, 2018, https://www.forbes.com/sites/eshachhabra/2018/06/13/how-two-young-entrepreneurs-are-tackling-the-plastic-problem-with-swimwear/#50f840216422; and M. Peretz, "5 Companies Who Succeed by Prioritizing Sustainability Over Profits," *Forbes,* December 12, 2017, https://www.forbes.com/sites/marissaperetz/2017/12/12/5-companies-who-succeed-by-prioritizing-sustainability-over-profits/#1ebf92935585.

24. Company website, www.naturabrasil.com (accessed April 29, 2019); and M. Peretz, "5 Companies Who Succeed by Prioritizing Sustainability Over Profits," *Forbes,* December 12, 2017, https://www.forbes.com/sites/marissaperetz/2017/12/12/5-companies-who-succeed-by-prioritizing-sustainability-over-profits/#1ebf92935585.

25. "Southwest Corporate Fact Sheet," https://www.swamedia.com/pages/corporate-fact-sheet (accessed May 2, 2019); and "Southwest Airlines Reports Fourth Quarter and Annual Profit; 46th Year of Profitability," *PRNewswire,* January 24, 2019, https://www.prnewswire.com/news-releases/southwest-airlines-reports-fourth-quarter-and-annual-profit-46th-consecutive-year-of-profitability-300783458.html.

26. "Southwest Airlines Employees Earn $544 Million in 2018 Profit Sharing," February 13, 2019, http://investors.southwest.com/news-and-events/news-releases/2019/02-13-2019-195947063.

27. "Southwest Airlines Employees Earn $544 Million in 2018 Profit Sharing," February 13, 2019, http://investors.southwest.com/news-and-events/news-releases/2019/02-13-2019-195947063.

28. Human Rights Campaign Foundation, "Corporate Equality Index 2019," https://assets2.hrc.org/files/assets/resources/CEI-2019-FullReport.pdf?_ga=2.29417855.1901208044.1556308587-1780781685.1556308587 (accessed May 2, 2019); and C. Smith, "30 Interesting Southwest Airlines Statistics and Facts (2019): By the Numbers," *DMR,* January 28, 2019, https://expandedramblings.com/index.php/southwest-airlines-statistics-facts/.

29. Southwest Airlines Co. "About Southwest: The Mission of Southwest Airlines." Accessed May 22, 2019, https://www.southwest.com/html/about-southwest/index.html.

30. "Southwest Airlines Highlights Corporate Citizenship Through 2018 One Report," *PRNewswire,* April 22, 2019, https://www.prnewswire.com/news-releases/southwest-airlines-highlights-corporate-citizenship-through-2018-one-report-300835050.html; and O. Blanco, "Best and Worst Airlines According to Consumer Reports Readers," *Consumer Reports,* March 13, 2018, https://www.consumerreports.org/airline-travel/best-and-worst-airlines/.

31. T. Avakian, "Here's What It's Like to Work for Southwest, One of Glassdoor's Best Places to Work for 10 Years in a Row," *Travel + Leisure,* February 26, 2019, https://www.travelandleisure.com/airlines-airports/working-for-southwest-airlines-career.

32. D. Dahl, "Why Do Southwest Airlines Employees Always Seem So Happy?" *Forbes,* https://www.forbes.com/sites/darrendahl/2017/07/28/why-do-southwest-airlines-employees-always-seem-so-happy/#312fc6e359b0 (accessed May 2, 2019).

33. See C. Ostroff, A. J. Kinicki, and R. S. Muhammad, "Organizational Culture and Climate," in I. B. Weiner, N. W. Schmitt, and S. Highhouse, eds., *Handbook of Psychology,* vol. 12, 2nd ed. (Hoboken, NJ: Wiley, 2013), 643–676.

34. A thorough description of the CVF is provided in K. S. Cameron, R. E. Quinn, J. Degraff, and A. V. Thakor, *Competing Values Leadership* (Northampton, MA: Edward Elgar, 2006).

35. Y. Li, M. Wang, D. D. Van Jaarsveld, G. K. Lee, and D. G. Ma, "From Employee-Experienced High-Involvement Work System to Innovation: An Emergence-Based Human Resource Management Framework," *Academy of Management Journal,* October 2018, 2000–2019; and C. G. L. Nerstad, R. Searle, M. Cerne, A. Dysvik, M. Skerlavaj, and R. Scherer, "Perceived Mastery Climate, Felt Trust, and Knowledge Sharing," *Journal of Organizational Behavior,* May 2018, 429–447.

36. L. Buchanan, "Why This Company's Mission Includes No-Meeting Mondays," *Inc.,* https://www.inc.com/magazine/201605/leigh-buchanan/toms-employee-culture-programs.html (accessed May 2, 2019).

37. Acuity, "Ben Salzmann Marks 20 Years as Acuity CEO," https://www.acuity.com/about/media-center/in-the-news/2019/ben-salzmann-marks-20-years-as-acuity-ceo (accessed May 22, 2019).

38. B. Casselman, "Risk-Averse Culture Infects U.S. Workers, Entrepreneurs," *The Wall Street Journal,* June 3, 2013, A1, A14.

39. Company website, "Our Mission," https://menloinnovations.com/our-way (accessed May 2, 2019).

40. Mauro F. Guillén and Esteban García-Canal, "Execution as Strategy." *Harvard Business Review,* October, 2012, https://hbr.org/2012/10/execution-as-strategy.

41. "Fortune's 100 Best Companies: #12 Publix Super Markets," http://fortune.com/best-companies/publix-super-markets/ (accessed May 2, 2019).

42. G. Acosta, "Why Publix Is America's Most Popular Retailer," *Retail Leader,* February 27, 2018, https://retailleader.com/why-publix-americas-most-popular-retailer.

43. See A. Srinivasan and B. Kurey, "Creating a Culture of Quality," *Harvard Business Review,* April 2014, 23–26.

44. A. Thompson, "McDonald's Organizational Structure & Its Characteristics—An Analysis," *Panmore Institute,* February 26, 2019, http://panmore.com/mcdonalds-organizational-structure-analysis; and S. Oches, "Inside the Plan to Fix McDonald's," *QSR Magazine,* May 2018, https://www.qsrmagazine.com/reports/inside-plan-fix-mcdonalds.

45. "Fortune 100 Best: 96 Activision Blizzard," http://fortune.com/best-companies/activision-blizzard/ (accessed May 2, 2019); and Keith Noonan, "Why the Best Is Yet to Come for Activision Blizzard," *The Motley Fool.com,* March 30, 2019, https://www.fool.com/investing/2019/03/30/why-the-best-is-yet-to-come-for-activision-blizzar.aspx.

46. "Careers: You are Only as Great as the Characters on Your Team," *Activision.com,* https://www.activision.com/careers (accessed May 5, 2016).

47. M. Osako, "Activision Blizzard Recognized on Fortune's 100 Best Companies to Work For List in 2016," *Activision.com*, http://investor.activision.com (accessed May 5, 2016).

48. Blizzard Entertainment, Inc., "Why Activision Blizzard?" http://www.activisionblizzard.com/careers (accessed May 22, 2019).

49. Great Place to Work, "Great Place to Work 2016," Greatplacetowork.com, http://reviews.greatplacetowork.com/activision-blizzard (accessed May 22, 2019).

50. Great Place to Work, "Great Place to Work 2016," Greatplacetowork.com, http://reviews.greatplacetowork.com/activision-blizzard (accessed May 22, 2019).

51. "Life at Activision: Leveling Up," *Activisionblizzard.com,* http://www.activisionblizzard.com/careers (accessed May 5, 2016).

52. "Great Place to Work 2016," *Greatplacetowork.com,* http://reviews.greatplacetowork.com/activision-blizzard (accessed May 5, 2016).

53. "King of Fun," *Fortune,* March 15, 2016, 14.

54. Great Place to Work, "Great Place to Work 2016," Greatplacetowork.com, http://reviews.greatplacetowork.com/activision-blizzard (accessed May 22, 2019).

55. See A. Ou, C. Hartnell, A. Kinicki, E. Karam, and D. Choi, "Culture in Context: A Meta-Analysis of the Nomological Network of Organizational Culture" presentation as part of a symposium, Connecting Culture and Context: Insights from Organizational Culture Theory and Research, at the 2016 National Academy of Management Meeting in Anaheim, California.

56. See C. Ostroff, A. J. Kinicki, and R. S. Muhammad, "Organizational Culture and Climate," in *Handbook of Psychology,* vol. 12, 2nd ed., I. B. Weiner, N. W. Schmitt, and S. Highhouse, eds. (Hoboken, NJ: Wiley, 2013), 643–676.

57. Harrison Miller Trice and Janice M. Beyer, *The Cultures of Work Organizations.* (Englewood Cliffs, NJ: Prentice Hall, 1993).

58. See E. H. Schein, *Organizational Culture and Leadership,* 4th ed. (San Francisco: Wiley, 2010), 259–271; and D. Losonci, R. Kasa, K. Demeter, B. Heidrich, and I. Jenei, "The Impact of Shop Floor Culture and Subculture on Lean Production Practices," *International Journal of Operations and Production Management,* 37(2), 2017, 205–225.

59. E. H. Schein, *Organizational Culture and Leadership,* 4th ed. (San Francisco: Wiley, 2010), 271.

60. V. Bush, A. J. Bush, J. Oakley, and J. E. Cicala, "The Sales Profession as a Subculture: Implications for Ethical Decision Making," *Journal of Business Ethics,* 2017, 549–565; and K. Bezrukova, S. M. B. Thatcher, K. A. Jehn, and C. S. Spell, "The Effects of Alignments: Examining Group Faultlines, Organizational Cultures, and Performance," *Journal of Applied Psychology,* January 2012, 77–92.

61. E. A. Lofquist, P. K. Dyson, and S. N. Trønnes, "Mind the Gap: A Qualitative Approach to Assessing Why Different Sub-Cultures within High-Risk industries Interpret Safety Rule Gaps in Different Ways," *Safety Science,* 2017, 241–256.

62. E. H. Schein, *Organizational Culture and Leadership* (San Francisco: Jossey-Bass, 2010).

63. John Mackey in C. Wright, "10 Culture Quotes to Inspire Leadership," *HuffPost,* https://www.huffpost.com/entry/10-culture-quotes-to-inspire-leadership_b_5976aa21e4b0c6616f7ce4c4 (accessed May 2, 2019).

64. R. E. Quinn and A. J. Thakor, "Creating a Purpose-Driven Organization," *Harvard Business Review,* July–August 2018, 78–85.

65. Partners in Leadership, "3 Top Executives Spill Their Secrets on How to Successfully Manage Workplace Culture," *Inc.,* March 9, 2018, https://www.inc.com/partners-in-leadership/these-3-executives-successfully-guided-companywide-culture-shifts-heres-how.html.

66. The 12 mechanisms were based on material contained in E. H. Schein, "The Role of the Founder in Creating Organizational Culture," *Organizational Dynamics,* Summer 1983, 13–28.

67. Caterpillar. "Vision, Mission, Strategy, & Principles." Accessed May 22, 2019. https://www.caterpillar.com/en/company/sustainability/vision-mission-strategy.html; and Alzheimer's Association. "Alzheimer's Vision." Accessed May 22, 2019. https://www.alz.org/dm/fy13-sustainer-ask/general-a.html.

68. M. Cheng, "How Instagram Made Its New York Office Highly Instagrammable," *Inc.,* August 22, 2018, https://www.inc.com/michelle-cheng/how-instagram-made-its-new-york-office-highly-instagrammable.html.

69. J. Haden, "The New England Patriots Like These 2 Words So Much, They Applied for a Trademark," *Inc.,* January 29, 2019, https://www.inc.com/jeff-haden/new-england-patriots-say-same-2-words-after-every-win-trademarked-phrase.html.

70. Greg Satell, *How Experian's Networked Culture Drives Innovation,* Mansueto Ventures, April 6, 2019, https://www.inc.com/greg-satell/how-experians-networked-culture-drives-innovation.html.

71. Greg Satell, *How Experian's Networked Culture Drives Innovation,* Mansueto Ventures, April 6, 2019, https://www.inc.com/greg-satell/how-experians-networked-culture-drives-innovation.html.

72. N. Kristof, "Opinion: The $70,000-a-Year Minimum Wage," *The New York Times,* March 30, 2019, https://www.nytimes.com/2019/03/30/opinion/sunday/dan-price-minimum-wage.html; and J. Ludema and A. Johnson, "Gravity Payment's Dan Price on How He Measures Success after His $70K Experiment," *Forbes,* August 28, 2018, https://www.forbes.com/sites/amberjohnson-jimludema/2018/08/28/gravity-payments-dan-price-on-how-he-measures-success-after-his-70k-experiment/#3b7df17174b6.

73. C. Dillow, "Corporate Creation Myths, and Why We Need Them," *Fast Company,* https://www.fastcompany.com (accessed May 2, 2019).

74. "This Trader Joe's Customer Service Story Will Make Your Day," *Survey Junkie,* March 1, 2018, https://blog.surveyjunkie.com/this-trader-joes-customer-service-story-will-make-your-day/.

75. Partners in Leadership, "3 Top Executives Spill Their Secrets on How to Successfully Manage Workplace Culture," *Inc.,* March 9, 2018, https://www.inc.com/partners-in-leadership/these-3-executives-successfully-guided-companywide-culture-shifts-heres-how.html.

76. R. Feloni, "GM CEO Mary Barra Said the Recall Crisis of 2014 Forever Changed Her Leadership Style," *Business Insider,* November 14, 2018, https://www.businessinsider.com/gm-mary-barra-recall-crisis-leadership-style-2018-11; and J. B. White, "GM CEO Looks to Switch Gears, Set Strategy," *The Wall Street Journal,* September 30, 2014, B1.

77. See W. J. Becker and R. Cropanzano, "Organizational Neuroscience: The Promise and Prospects of an Emerging Discipline," *Journal of Organizational Behavior,* October 2010, 1055–1059.

78. Kelly McCleary, and Amir Vera, "A Video of Black Men Being Arrested at Starbucks. Three Very Different Reactions," *CNN,* April 16, 2018, https://edition.cnn.com/2018/04/14/us/philadelphia-police-starbucks-arrests/index.html.

79. "Starbucks CEO Calls Arrest of Men at Philadelphia Store 'Reprehensible,'" *CNN,* April 15, 2018, https://www.cnn.com/2018/04/15/us/starbucks-statement-philadelphia-arrest/index.html.

80. S. Hyken, "Starbucks Closes 8,000 Stores for Racial Bias Training—Is It Enough?" *Forbes,* June 1, 2018, https://www.forbes.com/sites/shephyken/2018/06/01/starbucks-closes-8000-stores-for-racial-bias-training-is-it-enough/#3d04119e2831.

81. Workopolis, "The Daily Ritual That These 3 Companies Have in Common," WP Online Holdings Limited, July 14, 2017, https://hiring.workopolis.com/article/daily-ritual-3-companies-common/.

82. J. Bresnick, "Workflow Changes May Improve Patient Safety, Cut Hospital Stays," *Health IT Analytics,* https://healthitanalytics.com/news/workflow-changes-may-improve-patient-safety-cut-hospital-stays (accessed May 2, 2019).

83. "Disney Uses Big Data, IoT and Machine Learning to Boost Customer Experience," *Forbes,* https://www.forbes.com/sites/bernardmarr/2017/08/24/disney-uses-big-data-iot-and-machine-learning-to-boost-customer-experience/#65bd694b3387 (accessed May 2, 2019); and C. Palmeri and B. Faries, "Big Mickey Is Watching," *Bloomberg Businessweek,* March 7, 2014, 22–23.

84. C. BasuMallick, "5 Ways Technology Can Help Build a Strong Company Culture," *HR Technologist,* December 4, 2018, https://www.hrtechnologist.com/articles/culture/5-ways-technology-can-help-build-a-strong-company-culture/.

85. "Lifesize: Communication for the Modern Workplace," https://lifesize.com/en/why-lifesize (accessed May 2, 2019); and D. Zielinski, "Group Learning," *HR Magazine,* May 2012, 49.

86. N. Bose, "Walmart Partners with Four More Grocery Delivery Companies," *Reuters,* January 19, 2019, https://www.reuters.com/article/us-walmart-services/walmart-partners-with-four-more-grocery-delivery-companies-idUSKCN1PB2K9.

87. Company website, www.sprouts.com (accessed April 30, 2019).

88. Company website, www.sprouts.com (accessed April 30, 2019).

89. "Sprouts Farmers Market," http://fortune.com/worlds-most-admired-companies/sprouts-farmers-market/ (accessed April 30, 2019).

90. G. Suneson and S. Stebbins, "What Are the Worst Companies to Work for? New Report Analyzes Employee Reviews," *USA Today,* June 15, 2018, https://www.usatoday.com/story/money/business/2018/06/15/worst-companies-to-work-for-employee-reviews/35812171/.

91. See B. W. Swider, R. D. Zimmerman, and M. R. Barrick, "Searching for the Right Fit: Development of Applicant Person-Organization Fit Perceptions During the Recruitment Process," *Journal of Applied Psychology,* May 2015, 880–893; and A. L. Kristof-Brown, J. Y. Seong, D. S. Degeest, W-W. Park, and D-S. Hong, "Collective Fit Perceptions: A Multilevel Investigation of Person-Group Fit with Individual-Level and Team-Level Outcomes," *Journal of Organizational Behavior,* October 2014, 969–989.

92. A. M. Ellis, S. S. Nifadkar, T. N. Bauer, and B. Erdogan, "Newcomer Adjustment: Examining the Role of Managers' Perception of Newcomer Proactive Behavior During Organizational Socialization," *Journal of Applied Psychology,* June 2017, 993–1001.

93. "Study Finds that a Bad Onboarding Experience May Disengage New Hires," *Human Resources Today,* http://www.humanresourcestoday.com/2018/onboarding/?open-article-id=8855796&article-title=must-read-articles-to-reinvigorate-your-onboarding-experience&blog-domain=clearcompany.com&blog-title=clearcompany-hrm (accessed May 3, 2019).

94. C. Caldwell and R. Peters, "New Employee Onboarding—Psychological Contracts and Ethical Perspectives," *Journal of Management Development,* January 2018, 27–39.

95. P. D. Gupta, S. Bhattacharya, P. Sheorey, and P. Coelho, "Relationship Between Onboarding Experience and Turnover Intention: Intervening Locus of Control and Self-Efficacy," *Industrial and Commercial Training,* 2018, no. 2, 61–80.

96. "Comcast Launches Video 'Job Trailers' in Their Job Descriptions," *ONGIG,* https://blog.ongig.com/video-job-descriptions/comcast-launches-video-job-trailers-in-their-job-descriptions (accessed May 3, 2019).

97. F. Boag-Munroe, "Recent Police Recruits' Existing Knowledge of the Police and Organisational Commitment," *Journal of Police and Criminal Psychology,* April 2018, 1–11; and C.-L. Yen, "The Tradeoff between Fit Perceptions across Recruitment Stages by New Job Seekers," *International Journal of Contemporary Hospitality Management,* October 2017, 2610–2628.

98. Onboarding programs are discussed in D. Robb, "New-Hire Onboarding Portals Provide a Warmer Welcome," *HR Magazine,* December 2015/January 2016, 58–60; and L. A. Korver, "Make It or Break It: Onboarding for Mid-Career Leaders," *Training,* March/April 2016, 12–13.

99. Human Capital Institute, "Talent Pulse: Onboarding Outcomes," http://www.hci.org (accessed May 3, 2019).

100. R. Levering, "The 100 Best Companies to Work for 2016," *Fortune,* March 15, 2016, 154.

101. K. Vasel, "New Job Not Working Out? Your Employer May Pay You to Leave," *CNN,* October 3, 2018, https://www.cnn.com/2018/09/30/success/companies-pay-unhappy-workers-to-leave/index.html.

102. V. Fitoussi, "Top 10 Employee Onboarding Programs," Sapling.com, March 1, 2019, https://www.saplinghr.com/blog/top-employee-onboarding-programs.

103. "Protiviti: At This Consulting Firm, a Restless Pursuit to Solve Problems Drives Excellence," *Fortune,* March 15, 2016, https://customcontentonline.com/download/160315-protiviti-pdf/.

104. V. Fitoussi, "Top 10 Employee Onboarding Programs," Sapling.com, March 1, 2019, https://www.saplinghr.com/blog/top-employee-onboarding-programs.

105. Drew Robb, "New-Hire Onboarding Portals Provide a Warmer Welcome," *HR Magazine,* December 2015/January 2016, https://www.questia.com/read/1P3-3884137661/new-hire-onboarding-portals-provide-a-warmer-welcome.

106. H. R. Rafferty, "Social Media Etiquette: Communicate Behavioral Expectations," *SHRM,* March 24, 2010, http://www.shrm.org.hrdisciplines/technology/Articles/Pages/SocialMediaEtiquette.aspx.

107. S. S. Nifadkar, "Filling in the 'Blank Slate': Examining Newcomers' Schemas of Supervisors During Organizational Socialization," *Journal of Management,* October 2018, 1–28; and S. Livi, A. Theororou, M. Rullo, L. Cinque, and G. Alessandri, "The Rocky Road to Prosocial Behavior at Work: The Role of Positivity and Organizational Socialization in Preventing Interpersonal Strain," *PLOS ONE,* March 1, 2018, 1–14.

108. M. Karambelkar and S. Bhattacharya, "Onboarding Is a Change: Applying Change Management Model ADKAR to Onboarding," *Human Resource International Digest,* July 2017, 5–8; and J. D. DeBode, K. W. Mossholder, and A. G. Walker, "Fulfilling Employees' Psychological Contracts: Organizational Socialization's Role," *Leadership & Organization Development Journal,* January 2017, 42–55.

109. A review of stage model research can be found in B. E. Ashforth, *Role Transitions in Organizational Life: An Identity-Based Perspective* (Mahwah, NJ: Lawrence Erlbaum Associates, 2001).

110. "Smoothing the Transition: How Onboarding Helps Expatriate Workers," *Development and Learning in Organizations,* March 2017, 29–31.

111. These suggestions were based on K. Rollag, "Managing Yourself: Succeed in New Situations," *Harvard Business Review,* December 2015, 112–115; and K. Rollag, "Success in New Situations: Five Key Skills," *Psychology Today,* September 29, 2015, https://www.psychologytoday.com/blog/being-good-being-new/201509/success-innew-situations-five-key-skills (accessed May 7, 2016).

112. Keith Rollag, "Managing Yourself: Succeed in New Situations," *Harvard Business Review* 93, no. 1 (2015): 112–15.

113. This definition is based on the network perspective of mentoring proposed by M. Higgins and K. Kram, "Reconceptualizing Mentoring at Work: A Developmental Network Perspective," *Academy of Management Review,* April 2001, 264–288.

114. A. Reitman and S. Benatti, "Mentoring versus Coaching: What's the Difference?" https://www.td.org/insights/mentoring-versus-coaching-whats-the-difference (accessed May 3, 2019).

115. J. Sills: "NextGen Voices: Quality Mentoring," *Science,* October 5, 2018, 22–24.

116. See related discussion in M. Block and K. L. Florczak, "Mentoring: An Evolving Relationship," *Nursing Science Quarterly,* April–June 2017, 100–104.

117. The first three conclusions were derived from J. Dickson, K Kirkpatrick-Husk, D. Kendall, J. Longabaugh, A. Patel, and S. Scielzo, "Untangling Protégé Self-Reports of Mentoring Functions: Further Meta-Analtyic Understanding," *Journal of Career Development,* August 2014, 263–281. and R. Opengart and L. Bierema, "Emotionally Intelligent Mentoring: Reconceptualizing Effective Mentoring Relationships," *Human Resource Development Review,* September 2015, 234–258.

118. See S. N. Colakoglu, and O. Gokus, "Mentoring Functions' Relationship with Socialization Facets and Stages: A Conceptual Framework," *Journal of Organizational Culture, Communications and Conflict,* June 2015, 1–13.

119. J. A. Felício, E. Couto, and J. Caiado, "Human Capital, Social Capital and Organizational Performance," *Management Decision,* March 2014, 350–364.

120. C. M. Barnes, K. Jiang, and D. P. Lepak, "Sabotaging the Benefits of Our Own Human Capital: Work Unit Characteristics and Sleep," *Journal of Applied Psychology,* February 2016, 209–221.

121. "100 Best Companies to Work For: Scripps Health," http://fortune.com/best-companies/2018/list/filtered?searchByName=scripps%20health (accessed May 3, 2019); and "Fortune Names Scripps to National Best Companies List for 11th Straight Year," February 15, 2018, https://www.scripps.org/news_items/6309-fortune-names-scripps-to-national-best-companies-list-for-11th-straight-year.

122. See M. Feffer, "New Connections," *HR Magazine,* April 2015, 46–52.

123. Z. Wang, L. Chen, Y. Duan, J. Du, "Supervisory Mentoring and Newcomers' Work Engagement: The Mediating Role of Basic Psychological Need Satisfaction," *Social Behavior and Personality,* October 2018, 1745–1760.

124. R. Hoffman, C. Yeh, and B. Casnocha, "Learn from People, *Not* Classes," *Harvard Business Review,* March–April 2019, 50–51.

125. R. Hoffman, C. Yeh, and B. Casnocha, "Learn from People, *Not* Classes," *Harvard Business Review,* March–April 2019, 50–51.

126. R. Hoffman and B. Casnocha, "The Real Way to Build a Network," *Fortune,* February 6, 2012, 30.

127. See L. T. Eby, J. R. Durley, S. C. Evans, and B. R. Ragins, "Mentors' Perceptions of Negative Mentoring Experiences: Sale Development and Nomological Validation," *Journal of Applied Psychology,* March 2008, 358–373.

128. D. Sitar, "5 Tips to Learn from a Mentor When You Don't Want to Ask for Their Time," *Inc.,* January 26, 2019, https://www.inc.com/dana-sitar/how-to-find-a-mentor-without-bothering-everybody-you-respect.html; and G. Kawasaki, "Managing Yourself: The Art of Evangelism," *Harvard Business Review,* May 2015, 108–111.

129. I. Thibodeau, "Ford to Cut Jobs, Idle Plants, Change Lineup in Europe, *Detroit News,* January 10, 2019, https://www.detroitnews.com/story/business/autos/ford/2019/01/10/ford-announces-belt-tightening-europe/2534466002/.

130. See N. Boudette, "Ford, an Automaker at a Crossroads, Seeks Cuts and Partners," *The New York Times,* October 5, 2018, https://www.nytimes.com/2018/10/05/business/ford-motor-cars.html; and M. Huffman, "Ford to Downsize Its Workforce in Major Reorganization Plan," *Consumer Affairs,* October 10, 2018, https://www.consumeraffairs.com/news/ford-to-downsize-its-workforce-in-major-reorganization-plan-101018.html.

131. M. Martinez, "The Tension Rises at Ford," *Automotive News,* October 15, 2018, https://www.autonews.com/article/20181015/OEM/181019765/the-tension-rises-at-ford.

132. C. Rogers, "Ford's New CEO Has a Cerebral Style—and to Many, It's Just Baffling," *The Wall Street Journal,* August 14, 2018, https://www.wsj.com/articles/fords-new-ceo-has-a-cerebral-styleand-to-many-its-baffling-1534255714.

133. M. Martinez, "The Tension Rises at Ford," *Automotive News,* October 15, 2018, https://www.autonews.com/article/20181015/OEM/181019765/the-tension-rises-at-ford.

134. J. Useem, "Why Ford Hired a Furniture Maker as CEO," *The Atlantic,* March 2019, https://www.theatlantic.com/magazine/archive/2019/03/ford-ceo-jim-hackett-ux-design-thinking/580438/.

135. M. Martinez, "The Tension Rises at Ford," *Automotive News,* October 15, 2018, https://www.autonews.com/article/20181015/OEM/181019765/the-tension-rises-at-ford.

136. C. Rogers, "Ford's New CEO Has a Cerebral Style—and to Many, It's Just Baffling," *The Wall Street Journal,* August 14, 2018, https://www.wsj.com/articles/fords-new-ceo-has-a-cerebral-styleand-to-many-its-baffling-1534255714.

137. P. Howard, "CEO Jim Hackett Pushing Future for Ford Team as Investors Watch with Caution," *Detroit Free Press,* January 28, 2018, https://www.freep.com/story/money/cars/ford/2018/01/26/ceo-jim-hackett-pushing-ford-team-investors-watch-caution/1045218001/.

138. Darren Palmer, "The Stakes Are High: Inside the Team Developing Ford's New Generation of Electric Vehicles," Ford Motor Company, https://corporate.ford.com/articles/propulsion-choices/new-generation-electric-vehicles.html.

139. J. Muller, "Ford CEO James Hackett, under Fire from Wall Street, Shows Forbes the Early Fruits of His Turnaround Plan," *Forbes,* September 6, 2018, https://www.forbes.com/sites/joannmuller/2018/09/06/ford-ceo-james-hackett-under-fire-from-wall-street-shows-forbes-the-early-fruits-of-his-turnaround-plan/#4cbcf6b35b6f.

140. Phoebe Wall Howard, "CEO Jim Hackett Pushing Future for Ford Team as Investors Watch with Caution," www.freep.com, January 28, 2018, https://www.freep.com/story/money/cars/ford/2018/01/26/ceo-jim-hackett-pushing-ford-team-investors-watch-caution/1045218001/.

141. C. Rogers, "Ford's New CEO Has a Cerebral Style—and to Many, It's Just Baffling," *The Wall Street Journal,* August 14, 2018, https://www.wsj.com/articles/fords-new-ceo-has-a-cerebral-styleand-to-many-its-baffling-1534255714.

142. Michael Martinez, "The Tension Rises at Ford: Dealers Wonder: Where's the Company Headed?" Crain Communications, Inc., October 15, 2018, https://www.autonews.com/article/20181015/OEM/181019765/the-tension-rises-at-ford.

143. I. Thibodeau, "Only Mustang, Focus Crossover to Survive Ford Car Cuts," *Detroit News,* April 25, 2018, https://www.detroitnews.com/story/business/autos/ford/2018/04/25/ford-cutting-car-lineup-earnings/34244867/.

144. M. Rochabrun, "Ford to Close Oldest Brazil Plant, Exit South America Truck Biz," *Reuters,* February 19, 2019, https://www.reuters.com/article/us-ford-motor-southamerica-heavytruck/ford-to-close-oldest-brazil-plant-exit-south-america-truck-biz-idUSKCN1Q82EB.

145. M. Martinez, "The Tension Rises at Ford," *Automotive News,* October 15, 2018, https://www.autonews.com/article/20181015/OEM/181019765/the-tension-rises-at-ford.

146. J. Rosevear, "Why Shares of Ford Motor Company Are Surging Today," *Yahoo Finance,* April 26, 2019, https://finance.yahoo.com/news/why-shares-ford-motor-company-150900673.html.

147. K. Naughton, "Ford, Hackett Feel Wall Street's Pain over Slow-Motion Turnaround," *Automotive News,* January 24, 2019, https://www.autonews.com/executives/ford-hackett-feel-wall-streets-pain-over-slow-motion-turnaround.

148. Y. Li, "Ford CEO Says a 'Big Surprise' Coming Next Year with Electric Vehicles," *CNBC,* January 13, 2019, https://www.cnbc.com/2019/01/13/ford-ceo-says-a-big-surprise-coming-next-year-with-electric-vehicles.html.

149. P. Howard, "CEO Jim Hackett Pushing Future for Ford Team as Investors Watch with Caution," *Detroit Free Press,* January 28, 2018, https://www.freep.com/story/money/cars/ford/2018/01/26/ceo-jim-hackett-pushing-ford-team-investors-watch-caution/1045218001/.

150. Christina Rogers, "Ford's New CEO Has a Cerebral Style—and to Many, It's Baffling," *The Wall Street Journal,* August 14, 2018, https://www.wsj.com/articles/fords-new-ceo-has-a-cerebral-styleand-to-many-its-baffling-1534255714.

151. J. Muller, "Ford CEO James Hackett, under Fire from Wall Street, Shows Forbes the Early Fruits of His Turnaround Plan," *Forbes,* September 6, 2018, https://www.forbes.com/sites/joannmuller/2018/09/06/ford-ceo-james-hackett-under-fire-from-wall-street-shows-forbes-the-early-fruits-of-his-turnaround-plan/#4cbcf6b35b6f.

152. P. Howard, "CEO Jim Hackett Pushing Future for Ford Team as Investors Watch with Caution," *Detroit Free Press,* January 28, 2018, https://www.freep.com/story/money/cars/ford/2018/01/26/ceo-jim-hackett-pushing-ford-team-investors-watch-caution/1045218001/.

153. The Citadel, "The Citadel's Mission Statement," http://www.citadel.edu/root/mission-statement (accessed May 22, 2019).

154. Associated Press, "Military School Denies Muslim's Request to Wear Headscarf," *VOA News,* May 10, 2016, https://www.voanews.com/a/military-school-in-us-denies-muslim-student-request-to-wear-headscarf/3323479.html.

155. D. Farrington, "Citadel Military College Says Prospective Student Can't Wear Hijab," *NPR,* May 10, 2016, https://www.npr.org/sections/thetwoway/2016/05/10/477534442/citadel-military-college-says-prospective-student-cant-wear-hijab.

156. Wilson Ring, "Norwich University Officials Say Yes to Student's Hijab," *Burlington Free Press,* June 1, 2016, https://www.burlingtonfreepress.com/story/news/local/vermont/2016/06/01/norwich-university-officials-say-yes-students-hijab/85256268/.

CHAPTER 15

1. Michael Guta, "3.9 Million Americans—Including Freelancers—Now Work from Home at Least Half the Week," *Small Business Trends,* April 2, 2018, https://smallbiztrends.com/2018/04/2018-remote-work-statistics.html.

2. "Fifty Percent of U.S. Workforce Will be Remote by 2020; ULTATEL's Cloud-Based Technology Paves the Way," *PR Newswire,* February 14, 2018, https://markets.businessinsider.com/news/stocks/fifty-percent-of-u-s-workforce-will-be-remote-by-2020-ultatel-s-cloud-based-technology-paves-the-way-1015773617.

3. John Egan, "10 Tips for Telecommuting Success," *Huffington Post,* December 6, 2017, https://www.huffpost.com/entry/10-tips-for-telecommuting_b_5433833.

4. Shannon Cyr, "Tips for Effective Telecommuting," Virtual Vocations, Inc., https://www.virtualvocations.com/blog/telecommuting-survival/tips-for-effective-telecommuting/ (accessed May 6, 2019).

5. M. M. Biro, "Telecommuting Is the Future of Work," *Forbes,* http://www.forbes.com/sites/meghanbiro/2014/01/12/telecommuting-is-the-future-of-work/#50598553758f (accessed May 6, 2019).

6. C. I. Barnard, *The Functions of the Executive* (Cambridge, MA: Harvard University Press, 1938), 73.

7. Drawn from E. H. Schein, *Organizational Psychology,* 3rd ed. (Englewood Cliffs, NJ: Prentice Hall, 1980), 12–15. See also, J. R. Mueller, "Alternative Organizational Design and Its Impact on the Future of Work," *Journal of Strategic Innovation and Sustainability,* January 2014, 48–58.

8. See J. R. Mueller, "Alternative Organizational Design and Its Impact on the Future of Work," *Journal of Strategic Innovation and Sustainability,* January 2014, 48–58.

9. See V. Smeets and F. Warzynski, "Too Many Theories, Too Few Facts: What the Data Tell Us about the Link between Span of Control, Compensation, and Career Dynamics," *Labour Economics,* August 2008, 688–704.

10. See C. E. Thiel, J. H. Hardy III, D. R. Peterson, D. T. Welsh, and J. M. Bonner, "Too Many Sheep in the Flock? Span of Control Attenuates the Influence of Ethical Leadership," *Journal of Applied Psychology,* December 2018, 1324–1334; and A. Acharya, R. Lieber, L. Seem, and T. Welchman, "How to Identify the Right 'Spans of Control' for Your Organization," *McKinsey & Co.,* December 2017, https://www.mckinsey.com/business-functions/organization/our-insights/how-to-identify-the-right-spans-of-control-for-your-organization.

11. This discussion is based on K. Remenova, Z. Skorkova, and N. Jankelova, "Span of Control in Teamwork and Organizational Structure," *Montenegrin Journal of Economics,* June 2018, 155–165; and P. Graves, "What Kinds of Factors Should Determine How Many Direct Reports a Manager Supervises?" *HR Magazine,* July 2013, 19.

12. "Organic Produce," https://www.wholefoodsmarket.com/department/produce (accessed May 6, 2019); H. Peterson, "'I Ultimately Am Not Afraid to Get Fired': Leaked Audio Captures Whole Foods CEO John Mackey Describing Clashes with Amazon," *Business Insider,* June 13, 2018, https://www.businessinsider.com/whole-foods-ceo-john-mackey-clashes-with-amazon-2018-6; A. Salzman, "Amazon's Unnatural Approach with Whole Foods," *Barron's,* March 12, 2018, https://www.barrons.com/articles/amazons-unnatural-approach-with-whole-foods-1520887207; and B. Kowitt, "John Mackey: The Conscious Capitalist," *Fortune,* August 20, 2015, http://fortune.com/2015/08/20/whole-foods-john-mackey/.

13. A management-oriented discussion of general systems theory can be found in K. E. Boulding, "General Systems Theory—The Skeleton of Science," *Management Science,* April 1956, 197–208. For more recent systems-related ideas, see A. J. Kinicki, K. J. L. Jacobson, B. M. Galvin, and G. E. Prussia, "A Multi-Systems Model of Leadership," *Journal of Leadership & Organizational Studies,* May 2011, 133–149.

14. R. M. Fulmer and J. B. Keys, "A Conversation with Peter Senge: New Development in Organizational Learning," *Organizational Dynamics,* Autumn 1998, 35.

15. This definition was based on D. A. Garvin, "Building a Learning Organization," *Harvard Business Review,* August 1998, 35.

16. K. Kim, K. E. Watkings, and Z. Lu, "The Impact of a Learning Organization: Focusing on Knowledge Performance and Financial Performance," *European Journal of Training and Development,* no. 2, 2017, 177–193.

17. L. G. Flores, W. Zheng, D. Rau, and C. H. Thomas, "Organizational Learning: Subprocess Identification, Construct Validation, and an Empirical Test of Cultural Antecedents," *Journal of Management,* March 2012, 643.

18. L. G. Flores, W. Zheng, D. Rau, and C. H. Thomas, "Organizational Learning: Subprocess Identification, Construct Validation, and an Empirical Test of Cultural Antecedents," *Journal of Management,* March 2012, 643.

19. Robert Biswas-Diener, "Embracing Errors," *SHRM,* January 1, 2012, https://www.shrm.org/hr-today/news/hr-magazine/pages/0112tools.aspx.

20. L. G. Flores, W. Zheng, D. Rau, and C. H. Thomas, "Organizational Learning: Subprocess Identification, Construct Validation, and an Empirical Test of Cultural Antecedents," *Journal of Management,* March 2012, 643.

21. E.-E. Halmaghi, "From the Traditional Organization to the Learning Organization," *Journal of Defense Resources Management,* 9 (2), 2018, 98–103; and D. Heaton, "Consciousness Development for the Learning Organization," *The Learning Organization,* September 2017, 401–407.

22. G. Forsythe, K. Kuhla, and D. Rice, "Can You Do VUCA? 5 Key Strategies for Success," *Chief Executive*, January 23, 2018, https://chiefexecutive.net/5-key-strategies-success/.

23. Roy Saunderson, "Talent Tips: Oops! Learning from Our Mistakes,"/it/Training,/xit/December 2012, 63. *Lakewood Media Group, LLC*, https://trainingmag.com/content/talent-tips-oops-learning-our-mistakes/.

24. R. Abed, "Billionaire Charlie Munger Says Admitting Failure Is Key to Success. Here Are 5 Ways to Embrace Failure," *Inc.*, March 29, 2019, https://www.inc.com/robbie-abed/want-happiness-success-take-this-simple-advice-from-warren-buffetts-right-hand-man.html?cid=search; J. Birkinshaw and M. Haas, "Increase Your Return on Failure," *Harvard Business Review*, May 2016, 88–93.

25. A. Darabi, T. L. Arrington, and E. Sayilir, "Learning from Failure: A Meta-Analysis of the Empirical Studies," *Educational Technology Research & Development*, October 2018, 1101–1118; and M. Stein and M. Muzzin, "Learning from Failure: Insights from a University and STARBASE ONE Partnership Program," *Science and Children*, April/May 2018, 62–65.

26. F. Gino and B. Staats, "Why Organizations Don't Learn," *Harvard Business Review*, November 2015, 111–118.

27. L. Freifeld, "Fear of Failure Hampers Innovation," *Training*, May/June 2015, 6.

28. I. C. Chadwick and J. L. Raver, "Motivating Organizations to Learn: Goal Orientation and Its Influence on Organizational Learning," *Journal of Management*, March 2015, 957–986.

29. Royston Greenwood and Danny Miller. "Tackling Design Anew: Getting Back to the Heart of Organizational Theory," Academy of *Management Perspectives*, (2010): 78–88. https://pdfs.semanticscholar.org/015c/eb09b8bf9f28f400e08945f059cd11ef3978.pdf?_ga=2.144156860.860095876.1560356081-1108834537.1560356081.

30. Heather Hartel, "McDonald's Reveals Corporate Restructure, Layoffs," *Chicago Business Journal*, June 12, 2018. https://www.bizjournals.com/chicago/news/2018/06/12/mcdonalds-reveals-corporate-restructure-layoffs.html.

31. D. Ishneet, and G. Sonam, "Organizational Restructuring and Collaborative Creativity: The Case of Microsoft and Sony," *Journal of Business Strategy*, March 2015, 53–65.

32. See M. C. Mankins and P. Rogers, "The Decision-Driven Organization," *Harvard Business Review*, June 2010, 56–57; and "Full Speed Ahead," *HR Magazine*, March 2011, 18.

33. The following discussion is based on N. Anand and R. L. Daft, "What Is the Right Organizational Design?" *Organizational Dynamics*, 2007, 329–344.

34. WebFinance Inc., "Boundaryless Organization," http://www.businessdictionary.com/definition/boundaryless-organization.html (accessed June 14, 2019).

35. O. Durden, "The Structure of a Boundaryless Organization," *Chron.com*, December 10, 2018, https://smallbusiness.chron.com/structure-boundaryless-organization-2764.html.

36. A. Al-Muslim, "P&G Moves to Streamline Its Structure," *The Wall Street Journal*, November 8, 2018, https://www.wsj.com/articles/p-g-moves-to-streamline-its-structure-1541713822.

37. P. Meyer, "Starbucks Coffee's Organizational Structure & Its Characteristics," *Panmore Institute*, February 14, 2019, http://panmore.com/starbucks-coffee-company-organizational-structure.

38. J. R. Galbraith, *Designing Matrix Organizations That Actually Work* (San Francisco: Jossey-Bass, 2009), ix.

39. M. Sytch, F. Wohlgezogen, and E. J. Sajac, "Collaborative by Design? How Matrix Organizations See/Do Alliances," *Organization Science*, November–December 2018, 1130–1148.

40. Company website, https://www.gore.com/about/the-gore-story (accessed May 6, 2019).

41. Company website, https://www.gore.com/about/the-gore-story (accessed May 6, 2019).

42. "Fundamental Beliefs," https://www.gore.com/about/our-beliefs-and-principles (accessed May 6, 2019).

43. "Our Culture," https://www.gore.com/about/culture (accessed May 6, 2019).

44. "Our Culture," https://www.gore.com/about/culture (accessed May 6, 2019).

45. P. Lawrence, "Herman Miller's Creative Network," interview with Brian Walker, *BusinessWeek*, February 15, 2008, http://www.businessweek.com/stories/2008-02-15/herman-millers-creative-networkbusinessweek-business-news-stock-market-and-financial-advice.

46. S. Milligan, "Gig Workers Challenge Old Order," *SHRM.org*, January 26, 2019, https://www.shrm.org/hr-today/news/all-things-work/pages/gig-workers-challenge-old-order.aspx.

47. J. Frazer, "How the Gig Economy Is Reshaping Careers for the Next Generation," *Forbes*, February 15, 2019, https://www.forbes.com/sites/johnfrazer1/2019/02/15/how-the-gig-economy-is-reshaping-careers-for-the-next-generation/#2ac7d9ed49ad; and S. Milligan, "Gig Workers Challenge Old Order," *SHRM.org*, January 26, 2019, https://www.shrm.org/hr-today/news/all-things-work/pages/gig-workers-challenge-old-order.aspx.

48. S. Milligan, "Gig Workers Challenge Old Order," *SHRM.org*, January 26, 2019, https://www.shrm.org/hr-today/news/all-things-work/pages/gig-workers-challenge-old-order.aspx.

49. J. Frazer, "How the Gig Economy Is Reshaping Careers for the Next Generation," *Forbes*, February 15, 2019, https://www.forbes.com/sites/johnfrazer1/2019/02/15/how-the-gig-economy-is-reshaping-careers-for-the-next-generation/#2ac7d9ed49ad.

50. Wikipedia. "Boeing 787 Dreamliner." Accessed June 14, 2019. https://en.wikipedia.org/wiki/Boeing_787_Dreamliner.

50. P. Kavilanz, "Dreamliner: Where in the World Its Parts Come From," *CNN Business*, https://money.cnn.com/2013/01/18/news/companies/boeing-dreamliner-parts/index.html (accessed October 1, 2019); and "Boeing 787 Dreamliner Family Passes 1 Million Passenger Flights," https://www.boeing.com/commercial/787/dreamliner/#/1-million (accessed May 6, 2019).

51. "Working at Scopic," https://scopicsoftware.com/careers/, accessed May 6, 2019; and "How Do the Top 10 Biggest Virtual Companies in the World Make It Work?" Scopic Software Blog, February 1, 2018, https://scopicsoftware.com/blog/about-scopic/how-virtual-companies-work/.

52. The following discussion is based on K. Reimer and N. Vehring, "Virtual or Vague? A Literature Review Exposing Conceptual Differences in Defining Virtual Organizations in IS Research," *Electronic Markets*, 2012, 267–282.

53. N. S. Maduke, H. Edwards, D. Greenwood, A. Osborne, S. O. Babatunde, "Analysis of Competencies for Effective Virtual Team Leadership in Building Successful Organisations," *Benchmarking: An International Journal*, March 2018, 696–712; and S. J. Han, C. Chae, P. Macko, W. Park, and M. Beyerlein, "How Virtual Team Leaders Cope with Creativity Challenges," *European Journal of Training and Development*, vol. 41, no. 3, 2017, 261–276.

54. Contingency design is discussed by P. R. Lawrence, and J. W. Lorsch, *Organization and Environment* (Cambridge, MA: Harvard University Press, 1967).

55. This discussion is partly based on L. Donaldson and G. Jofee, "Fit—The Key to Organization Design, *Journal of Organization Design*, December 2014, 38–45.

56. F. Mallén, R. Chiva, J. Alegre, and J. Guinot, "Organicity and Performance in Excellent HRM Organizations: The Importance of Organizational Learning Capability," *Review of Managerial Science*, July 2016, 463–485.

57. B. Moore and A. Brown, "The Application of TQM: Organic or Mechanistic?" *International Journal of Quality & Reliability Management*, August 2006.

58. Details of this study can be found in T. Burns and G. M. Stalker, *The Management of Innovation* (London: Tavistock, 1961). Also see S. A. Al-Abbadi, "Market Environment and Centralized Decision-Making and Their Impact on the Effectiveness of Organizations," *International Business Research*, 2015, 129–142.

59. G. Slinger and R. Morrison, "Will Organization Design Be Affected by Big Data?" *Journal of Organizational Design*, December 2014, 17.

60. See J. R. Galbraith, "The Evolution of Enterprise Organization Designs," *Journal of Organization Design*, August 2012, 1–13; "McKinsey 7s Framework," *Wikipedia*, https://en.wikipedia.org/wiki/McKinsey_7S_Framework, last modified March 14, 2019; and I. M. H. Smirat and M. N. M. Shariff, "Strategy, Structure, and Family Firm Performance: The Relationships of the Resource-Based View and the Contingency Approach," *Australian Journal of Business and Management Research*, June 2014, 1–8.

61. N. Eva, S. Sendjaya, D. Prajogo, A. Cavanagh, and M. Robin, "Creating Strategic Fit: Aligning Servant Leadership with Organizational Structure and Strategy," *Personnel Review*, February 2018, 166–186.

62. See S. B. Dust, C. J. Resick, and M. B. Mawritz, "Transformational Leadership, Psychological Empowerment, and the Moderating Role of Mechanistic-Organic Contexts," *Journal of Organizational Behavior*, April 2014, 413–433.

63. Lindsey Rupp, "Resuscitating Gap," *Bloomberg Businessweek*, April 22, 2016, https://www.bloomberg.com/news/articles/2016-04-21/gap-goes-back-to-basics-in-yet-another-bid-for-growth.

64. Y. J. Yu, "Gap Announces Plan to Close More Than 200 Stores in the Next Two Years," *Today*, March 1, 2019, https://www.today.com/style/gap-announces-plan-close-more-200-stores-next-two-years-t149677.

65. CB Insights, "State of Innovation Report," https://www.cbinsights.com/research-state-of-innovation-report (accessed May 6, 2019).

66. A. Fisher, "America's Most Admired Companies," *Fortune*, March 17, 2008, 66.

67. "Global Apple iPhone Sales from 3rd Quarter 2007 to 4th Quarter 2018 (in millions of units)," *Statista*, https://www.statista.com/statistics/263401/global-apple-iphone-sales-since-3rd-quarter-2007/ (accessed May 6, 2019).

68. A. Ignatius, "How Indra Nooyi Turned Design Thinking into Strategy," *Harvard Business Review*, September 2015, 83–84.

69. Ben Geier, "Using 3-D Printing to Make Jet Engines," *Fortune Media IP Limited,* November 13, 2014, http://fortune.com/2014/11/13/3-d-printing-jet-engines-alcoa/.

70. B. Dumaine, "The Ultimate Driving Machine Prepares for a Driverless World," *Fortune,* March 1, 2016, 126.

71. A. Josephson, "The Pros and Cons of Prefab Homes," *Smart Asset,* August 13, 2018, https://smartasset.com/mortgage/the-pros-and-cons-of-prefab-homes.

72. Ken Hamey, "Panelized Homes: Factory-Built Components Assembled on Site," Builders Digital Experience, LLC, http://www.newhomesource.com/resourcecenter/articles/panelized-homes-factory-built-components-assembled-on-site (accessed June 14, 2019).

73. Gary P. Pisano, "You Need an Innovation Strategy," *Harvard Business Review,* June 2015, https://hbr.org/2015/06/you-need-an-innovation-strategy.

74. D. Añón Higón, J. Gómez, and P. Vargas, "Complementarities in Innovation Strategy: Do Intangibles Play a Role in Enhancing Firm Performance?" *Industrial and Corporate Change,* October 2017, 865–886; and R. Sharmelly, "Crafting a Winning Innovation Strategy," *Strategic Direction,* March 2017, 8–11.

75. See M. S. S. Jajja, V. R. Kannan, S. A. Brah, and S. Z. Hassan, "Linkages between Firm Innovation Strategy, Suppliers, Product Innovation, and Business Performance," *International Journal of Operations & Production Management,* August 2017, 1054–1075; and G. P. Pisano, "You Need an Innovation Strategy," *Harvard Business Review,* June 2015, 46.

76. Gary P. Pisano, "You Need an Innovation Strategy," *Harvard Business Review,* June 2015, https://hbr.org/2015/06/you-need-an-innovation-strategy.

77. S. Ray, "Empathy and Innovation: How Microsoft's Cultural Shift Is Leading to New Product Development," February 13, 2019, https://news.microsoft.com/innovation-stories/empathy-innovation-accessibility/.

78. J. Birkinshaw and M. Haas, "Increase Your Return on Failure," *Harvard Business Review,* May 2016, 88–93.

79. M. Tian, P. Deng, Y. Zhang, M. P. Salmador, "How Does Culture Influence Innovation? A Systematic Literature Review," *Management Decision,* May 2018, 1088–1107; and D. Cropley and A. Cropley, "Innovation Capacity, Organisational Culture and Gender," *European Journal of Innovation,* August 2017, 493–510.

80. Jenny Luna, "Philip Knight: 'For an Entrepreneur, Every Day Is a Crisis'." Mansueto Ventures, December 8, 2017, https://www.inc.com/stanford-business/philip-knight-for-an-entrepreneur-every-day-is-a-crisis.html (accessed May 6, 2019); and Jim Ludema and Amber Johnson, "Failure Is 99% of the Work: How to Fail Fast on the Way to Spectacular Innovation," Forbes Media LLC, February 18, 2019, https://www.forbes.com/sites/amberjohnson-jimludema/2019/02/18/failure-is-99-of-the-work-how-to-fail-fast-on-the-way-to-spectacular-innovation/#250135f24c1e.

81. J. Euchner, "Creating a Culture of Innovation," *Research-Technology Management,* November–December 2017, 10–11; and G. Manso, "Creating Incentives for Innovation," *California Management Review,* November 2017, 18–32.

82. Patrick Moorhead, "AMD's 50th Anniversary Reminds Us Why the Company Matters," *Forbes Media LLC,* May 2, 2019, https://www.forbes.com/sites/patrickmoorhead/2019/05/02/amds-50th-anniversary-reminds-us-why-the-company-matters/#43819ebd5818.

83. "AMD Reports First Quarter 2019 Financial Results," *Yahoo Finance,* April 30, 2019, https://finance.yahoo.com/news/amd-reports-first-quarter-2019-202000154.html.

84. P. Alcorn, "AMD Exec Resigns, Company Moves 7nm Chip Production To TSMC (Update)," Tomshardware.com, August 28, 2018, https://www.tomshardware.com/news/amd-moves-to-tsmc-7nm,37703.html.

85. Patrick Moorhead, "AMD's 50th Anniversary Reminds Us Why the Company Matters," *Forbes Media LLC,* May 2, 2019, https://www.forbes.com/sites/patrickmoorhead/2019/05/02/amds-50th-anniversary-reminds-us-why-the-company-matters/#43819ebd5818.

86. Rob Cross, Chris Ernst, Dimitris Assimakopoulos, and Dan Ranta, "Investing in Boundary-Spanning Collaboration to Drive Efficiency and Innovation," *Organizational Dynamics* 44, (2015): 204–216. http://www.chrisernst.org/wp-content/uploads/2015/06/Boundary-Spanning-Collaboration.pdf.

87. Deloitte, "The Three Billion Enterprise Crowdsourcing and the Growing Fragmentation of Work," https://www2.deloitte.com/content/dam/Deloitte/de/Documents/Innovation/us-cons-enterprise-crowdsourcing-and-growing-fragmentation-of-work%20(3).pdf (accessed May 6, 2019); and "Celebrating 10 Years of Crowdsourcing and Co-Creation with LEGO Fans," November 8, 2018, https://www.lego.com/en-my/aboutus/news-room/2018/november/ideas-10th-anniversary/.

88. K. B. Wilson, V. Bhakoo, and D. Samson, "Crowdsourcing: A Contemporary Form of Project Management with Linkages to Open Innovation and Novel Operations," *International Journal of Operations & Production Management,* June 2018, 1467–1494; and M. Wilson, K. Robson, and E. Botha, "Crowdsourcing in a Time of Empowered Stakeholders: Lessons from Crowdsourcing Campaigns," *Business Horizons,* March–April 2017, 247–253.

89. IDEO, "IDEO on Design Thinking," http://sds.parsons.edu/designmanagement/ideo-on-design-thinking/ (accessed June 14, 2019).

90. IDEO, "One Device for All," http://idea.com/work/one-device-for-all, project date 2015, (accessed May 24, 2016).

91. Mark Wilson, "The 9 Big Design Trends of 2019," *Fast Company & Inc.,* December 19, 2018, https://www.fastcompany.com/90281299/the-9-big-design-trends-of-2019.

92. Company website, www.ideo.com (accessed May 6, 2019).

93. F. Dobbin, "High Commitment Practices," lecture, Harvard University, October 10, 2012, as referenced in *Wikipedia* article, "IDEO."

94. These suggestions are based on D. K. Rigby, J. Sutherland, and H. Takeuchi, "Embracing Agility," *Harvard Business Review,* May 2016, 41–50.

95. R. Gulati, "Structure That's Not Stifling," *Harvard Business Review,* May–June 2018, https://hbr.org/2018/05/structure-thats-not-stifling.

96. A. Ignatius, "How Indra Nooyi Turned Design Thinking into Strategy," *Harvard Business Review,* September 2015, 81–85.

97. Techniques for building agility are also discussed by S. Winby and C. G. Worley, "Management Processes for Agility, Speed, and Innovation," *Organizational Dynamics,* July–September 2014, 225–234.

98. T. Wang and C. D. Zatzick, "Human Capital Acquisition and Organizational Innovation: A Temporal Perspective," *Academy of Management Journal,* February 2019, 99–116.

99. C. Coy, "3 Ways to Grow a Culture of Creativity and Innovation," *TLNT,* July 19, 2018, https://www.tlnt.com/3-ways-to-grow-a-culture-of-creativity-and-innovation/.

100. T. Kraśnicka, W. Glód, M. Wronka-Pośpiech, "Management Innovation, Pro-Innovation Organisational Culture and Enterprise Performance: Testing the Mediation Effect," *Review of Managerial Science,* July 2018, 737–769; and R. Nanda and M. Rhodes-Kropf, "Financing Risk and Innovation," *Management Science,* April 2017, 901–918.

101. Gail Dutton, "A Eureka! Moment,"/it/Training,/xit/January/February 2016, 114–115. *Lakewood Media Group, LLC,* https://trainingmag.com/trgmag-article/eureka-moment/ (accessed June 14, 2019).

102. L. Bodell, "It's Time to Put Performance Reviews on Notice," *Forbes,* April 27, 2018, https://www.forbes.com/sites/lisabodell/2018/04/27/why-performance-reviews-are-irrelevant-today/#5a356c3b4b63.

103. See B. Gerhart and M. Fang, "Pay, Intrinsic Motivation, Extrinsic Motivation, Performance, and Creativity in the Workplace: Revisiting Long-Held Beliefs," *Annual Review of Organizational Psychology,* 2015, 489–521.

104. D. Meinert, "Wings of Change," *HR Magazine,* November 2012, 30–36.

105. J. Pochepan, "This Office Design Trend Is Causing a Privacy Crisis. Here's What It Means to You," *Inc.,* February 14, 2018, https://www.inc.com/jeff-pochepan/this-office-design-trend-is-causing-a-privacy-crisis-heres-what-it-means-for-you.html.

106. D. DePaoli and A. Ropo, "Creative Workspaces—a Fad or Making Real Impact?" *Journal of Corporate Real Estate,* September 2017, 157–167; and B. Haynes, L. Suckley, and N. Nunnington, "Workplace Productivity and Office Type: An Evaluation of Office Occupier Differences Based on Age and Gender," *Journal of Corporate Real Estate,* April 2017, 111–138.

107. C. M. Lindberg, K. Srinivasan, B. Gilligan, J. Razjouyan, J. Lee, B. Najafi, K. J. Canada, M. R. Mehl, F. Currim, S. Ram, M. M. Lunden, J. H. Heerwagen, K. Kampschroer, and E. M. Sternberg, "Effects of Office Workstation Type on Physical Activity and Stress," *Occupational Environment Medicine,* September 2018, 689–695; and M. Yadav, J. Kim, D. Cabrera, and R. de Dear, "Auditory Distraction in Open-Plan Office Environments: The Effect of Multi-Talker Acoustics," *Applied Acoustics,* November 2017, 68–80.

108. E. N. Yunus and E. Ernawati, "Productivity Paradox? The Impact of Office Redesign on Employee Productivity," *International Journal of Productivity and Performance Management,* September 2018; and C. B. Danielsson and T. Theorell, "Office Employees' Perception of Workspace Contribution: A Gender and Office Design Perspective," *Environment and Behavior,* April 2018, 1–32.

109. Christine Congdon, Donna Flynn, and Melanie Redman, "Balancing "We" and "Me": The Best Collaborative Spaces Also Support Solitude," *Harvard Business Review,* October 2014, https://hbr.org/2014/10/balancing-we-and-me-the-best-collaborative-spaces-also-support-solitude.

110. Christine Congdon, Donna Flynn, and Melanie Redman, "Balancing "We" and "Me": The Best Collaborative Spaces Also Support Solitude," *Harvard Business Review,* October 2014, https://hbr.org/2014/10/balancing-we-and-me-the-best-collaborative-spaces-also-support-solitude.

111. "6 Benefits to Building Your Dashboard Today," http://guidingmetrics.com/benefits-of-metrics/6-benefits-to-building-your-dashboardtoday/ (accessed May 6, 2019).

112. Larry Bossidy, and Ram Charan. *Execution: The Discipline of Getting Things Done* (New York: Crown Business, 2002).

113. See K. A. Al-Tarawneh, "The Possibility of Applying the Balanced Scoreboard: A Tool of Evaluating the Strategic Performance of the Jordanian," *Academy of Marketing Studies Journal*, January 2018, 1–25; J. Kopia, A, Kompalla, M. Buchmüller, and B. Heinemann, "Performance Measurement of Management System Standards Using the Balanced Scorecard," *Amfiteatru Economic*, November 2017, 981–1002; A. H. Aly and M. E. Mansour, "Evaluating the Sustainable Performance of Corporate Boards: The Balanced Scorecard Approach," *Managerial Auditing Journal*, February 2017, 167–195; and A. Aščić and Z. Skelo, "Utilization of Balanced Scorecard as a Management Tool in Statistical Institutes," *Sarajevo Business and Economics Review*, 2017, 181–201.

114. Robert S. Kaplan and David P. Norton, *The Balanced Scorecard: Translating Strategy into Action* (Boston, MA: Harvard Business School Press, 1996).

115. Robert S. Kaplan and David P. Norton, *The Balanced Scorecard: Translating Strategy into Action* (Boston, MA: Harvard Business School Press, 1996).

116. B. Marr, "The Incredible Ways John Deere Is Using Artificial Intelligence to Transform Farming," *Forbes*, March 9, 2018, https://www.forbes.com/sites/bernardmarr/2018/03/09/the-incredible-ways-john-deere-is-using-artificial-intelligence-to-transform-farming/#5f44454d330d.

117. Y. J. Yu, "Gap Announces Plan to Close More than 200 Stores in the Next Two Years," *Today*, March 1, 2019, https://www.today.com/style/gap-announces-plan-close-more-200-stores-next-two-years-t149677.

118. R. S. Kaplan and D. P. Norton, *The Balanced Scorecard: Translating Strategy into Action* (Boston, MA: Harvard Business School Press, 1996), 61–91.

119. Dinah Eng, "How the Founder of Four Seasons Stumbled Into the Hotel Business," *Fortune Media IP Limited*, March 29, 2016, http://fortune.com/2016/03/29/four-seasons-hotels-isadore-sharp/.

120. See R. S. Kaplan and D. P. Norton, "Having Trouble with Your Strategy? Then Map It," *Harvard Business Review*, September–October 2000, 167–176.

121. D. Blanchard and S. Valentic, "America's Safest Companies 2018: Graycor Industrial Constructors," *EHS Today*, November 7, 2018, https://www.ehstoday.com/americas-safest-companies-awards/americas-safest-companies-2018-graycor-industrial-constructors.

122. "What We Do," https://www.cotopaxi.com/pages/gear-for-good (accessed May 6, 2019).

123. Lindsey Kartochwill, "Outdoor Gear Maker Cotopaxi Stitches Its Social Goals into Every Backpack," *Bloomberg Businessweek*, April 25, 2016, https://www.pressreader.com/australia/bloomberg-businessweek-asia/20160425/282381218725695.

124. "The Cotopaxi Foundation," https://www.cotopaxi.com/pages/foundation (accessed May 6, 2019).

125. Zacks, "Why Is Keurig Dr Pepper (KDP) Up 11.2% Since Last Earnings Report?" *Nasdaq*, March 30, 2019, https://www.nasdaq.com/article/why-is-keurig-dr-pepper-kdp-up-112-since-last-earnings-report-cm1122425; and L. Hirsch, "K-Cup Maker Keurig Bets Big on Beverages, Buying Dr Pepper Snapple," *CNBC*, January 31, 2018, https://www.cnbc.com/2018/01/29/dr-pepper-snapple-and-keurig-green-mountain-to-merge.html.

126. "About B&N," http://www.barnesandnobleinc.com/about-bn/ (accessed April 17, 2019); and A. Alter and T. Hsu, "As Barnes & Noble Struggles to Find Footing, Founder Takes Heat," *The New York Times*, August 12, 2018, https://www.nytimes.com/2018/08/12/business/media/barnes-noble-leonard-riggio.html.

127. A. Cheng, "Barnes & Noble's Problem Is No Longer Just Amazon," *Forbes*, September 6, 2018, https://www.forbes.com/sites/andriacheng/2018/09/06/barnes-nobles-problem-is-no-longer-about-amazon/#21e4ca0444d0.

128. C. Quackenbush, "Barnes & Noble Is Laying Off Workers Amid Declining Sales," *Fortune*, February 13, 2018, http://fortune.com/2018/02/13/barnes-noble-layoff-workers-declining-sales/.

129. A. Alter and T. Hsu, "As Barnes & Noble Struggles to Find Footing, Founder Takes Heat," *The New York Times*, August 12, 2018, https://www.nytimes.com/2018/08/12/business/media/barnes-noble-leonard-riggio.html.

130. A. Alter and T. Hsu, "As Barnes & Noble Struggles to Find Footing, Founder Takes Heat," *The New York Times*, August 12, 2018, https://www.nytimes.com/2018/08/12/business/media/barnes-noble-leonard-riggio.html.

131. A. Alter and T. Hsu, "As Barnes & Noble Struggles to Find Footing, Founder Takes Heat," *The New York Times*, August 12, 2018, https://www.nytimes.com/2018/08/12/business/media/barnes-noble-leonard-riggio.html.

132. A. Alter and T. Hsu, "As Barnes & Noble Struggles to Find Footing, Founder Takes Heat," *The New York Times*, August 12, 2018, https://www.nytimes.com/2018/08/12/business/media/barnes-noble-leonard-riggio.html.

133. Chris Meadows, "Barnes & Noble Lays Off Hundreds of Experienced Employees, May Not Be Long for This World," Teleread, February 14, 2018. https://teleread.org/2018/02/14/barnes-noble-lays-off-hundreds-of-experienced-employees-may-not-be-long-for-this-world/.

134. A. Cheng, "Barnes & Noble's Problem Is No Longer Just Amazon," *Forbes*, September 6, 2018, https://www.forbes.com/sites/andriacheng/2018/09/06/barnes-nobles-problem-is-no-longer-about-amazon/#21e4ca0444d0.

135. J. Bosman, "Chief Leaves Barnes & Noble After Losses on E-Readers," *The New York Times*, https://www.nytimes.com/2013/07/09/business/barnes-nobles-chief-executive-resigns.html (accessed April 17, 2019).

136. J. Trachtenberg. "Publishers Are Tiring of Revolving Door in Barnes & Noble's C-Suite," *The Wall Street Journal*, August 10, 2018, https://www.wsj.com/articles/publishers-are-tiring-of-revolving-door-in-barnes-nobles-c-suite-1533895200.

137. A. Alter and T. Hsu, "As Barnes & Noble Struggles to Find Footing, Founder Takes Heat," *The New York Times*, August 12, 2018, https://www.nytimes.com/2018/08/12/business/media/barnes-noble-leonard-riggio.html.

138. A. Alter, "Ronald D. Boire Steps Down as Chief of Barnes & Noble," *The New York Times*, August 16, 2016, https://www.nytimes.com/2016/08/17/business/media/ronald-d-boire-steps-down-as-chief-of-barnes-noble.html?action=click&module=inline&pgtype=Article&region=Footer.

139. J. Trachtenberg, "Barnes & Noble Details Why Former CEO Demos Parneros Was Fired," *The Wall Street Journal*, October 30, 2018, https://www.wsj.com/articles/barnes-noble-details-why-former-ceo-demos-parneros-was-fired-1540935642.

140. J. Trachtenberg, "Publishers Are Tiring of Revolving Door in Barnes & Noble's C-Suite," *The Wall Street Journal*, August 10, 2018, https://www.wsj.com/articles/publishers-are-tiring-of-revolving-door-in-barnes-nobles-c-suite-1533895200.

141. Alexandra Alter and Tiffany Hsu, "As Barnes & Noble Struggles to Find Footing, Founder Takes Heat," *The New York Times Company*, August 12, 2018, https://www.seattletimes.com/business/barnes-founder-is-confident-of-turnaround/.

142. J. Milliot, "Len Riggio Says He's Ready to Lead B&N Through the Holidays," *Publishers Weekly*, September 28, 2018, https://www.publishersweekly.com/pw/by-topic/industry-news/bookselling/article/78177-len-riggio-says-he-s-ready-to-lead-b-n-through-the-holidays.html.

143. The Association of American Universities (AAU), "Tax Exemption for Universities and Colleges: Internal Revenue Code Section 501(c) (3) and Section 115," http://www.aau.edu/workarea/downloadasset.aspx?id=14246 (accessed June 14, 2019).

144. The Association of American Universities (AAU), "Tax Exemption for Universities and Colleges: Internal Revenue Code Section 501(c) (3) and Section 115," http://www.aau.edu/workarea/downloadasset.aspx?id=14246 (accessed June 14, 2019).

145. K. King, "Princeton University Settles Tax Suit Filed by Local Homeowners." *The Wall Street Journal*, October 17, 2016, https://www.wsj.com/articles/princeton-university-settles-tax-suit-filed-by-local-homeowners-1476742298; and C. Huckabee, "Princeton Will Pay $18 Million to Settle Suit Over Property-Tax Exemption," *The Chronicle of Higher Education*, October 17, 2016, https://www.chronicle.com/blogs/ticker/princeton-will-pay-18-million-to-settle-suit-over-property-tax-exemption/115119.

146. K. King, "Princeton University Settles Tax Suit Filed by Local Homeowners," *The Wall Street Journal*, October 17, 2016, https://www.wsj.com/articles/princeton-university-settles-tax-suit-filed-by-local-homeowners-1476742298.

147. Kate King, "Princeton University Settles Tax Suit Filed by Local Homeowners," *The Wall Street Journal*, October 17, 2016, https://www.wsj.com/articles/princeton-university-settles-tax-suit-filed-by-local-homeowners-1476742298?ns=prod/accounts-wsj.

148. K. King, "Princeton University Settles Tax Suit Filed by Local Homeowners," *The Wall Street Journal*, October 17, 2016, https://www.wsj.com/articles/princeton-university-settles-tax-suit-filed-by-local-homeowners-1476742298; and C. Huckabee, "Princeton Will Pay $18 Million to Settle Suit Over Property-Tax Exemption," *The Chronicle of Higher Education*, October 17, 2016, https://www.chronicle.com/blogs/ticker/princeton-will-pay-18-million-to-settle-suit-over-property-tax-exemption/115119.

149. S. Cho and L. Arvanitis, "University Prepares for Endowment Tax," *Yale Daily News*, November 8, 2018, https://yaledailynews.com/blog/2018/11/08/university-prepares-for-endowment-tax-2/.

CHAPTER 16

1. Adapted from R. Knight, "How to Decide Whether to Relocate for a Job," *Harvard Business Review*, December 3, 2018, https://hbr.org/2018/12/how-to-decide-whether-to-relocate-for-a-job.

2. D. Cohn and A. Caumont, "10 Demographic Trends That Are Shaping the US and the World," *Pew Research Center*, March 31, 2016, http://www.pewresearch.org/fact-tank/2016/03/31/10-demographic-trends-that-are-shaping-the-u-s-and-the-world/.

3. A. Cilluffo and D. Cohn, "7 Demographic Trends Shaping the U.S. and the World in 2018," Pew Research Center, April 25, 2018, http://www.pewresearch.org/fact-tank/2018/04/25/7-demographic-trends-shaping-the-u-s-and-the-world-in-2018/.

4. A. Zaleski, "VR Gets Real in the OR," *Fortune*, January 1, 2019, 27–28.

5. T. Jackson, "Forget Pie in the Sky, Drones are Saving Lives," *Fortune*, January 1, 2019, 40–41.

6. CNBC.com video, https://www.cnbc.com/video/2019/03/12/chipotle-teams-up-with-venmo-to-encourage-loyalty-program-sign-ups.html (accessed March 12, 2019).

7. Andrew Ross Sorkin, "BlackRock's Message: Contribute to Society, or Risk Losing Our Support," *The New York Times,* January 15, 2018, https://www.nytimes.com/2018/01/15/business/dealbook/blackrock-laurence-fink-letter.html.

8. K. Wiggins, "Uber's London License Is under Threat," *Bloomberg.com,* February 13, 2019, https://www.bloomberg.com/news/articles/2019-02-13/uber-s-london-license-under-threat-as-cab-drivers-fight-back.

9. A. Sarariano, "Google Fined $1.7 Billion by E.U. for Unfair Advertising Rules," *The New York Times,* March 20, 2019, https://www.nytimes.com/2019/03/20/business/google-fine-advertising.html?emc=edit_th_190321&nl=todaysheadlines&nlid=499951150321.

10. V. Goel, "India Curbs Power of Amazon and Walmart to Sell Products Online," *The New York Times*, December 26, 2018, https://www.nytimes.com/2018/12/26/technology/india-amazon-walmart-online-retail.html.

11. T. Reed, "American Airlines Encounters Labor Slowdowns Due to Slow Pace of Contract Talks," *Forbes.com,* July 14, 2018, https://www.forbes.com/sites/tedreed/2018/07/14/american-airlines-encounters-labor-slowdowns-due-to-slow-pace-of-contract-talks/#62249fe63cdb.

12. Adapted from R. Derousseau, "The Hidden Upside to CEO Drama," *Fortune,* February 1, 2019, 45–48.

13. Adapted from R. Derousseau, "The Hidden Upside to CEO Drama," *Fortune,* February 1, 2019, 45–48.

14. Adapted from R. Derousseau, "The Hidden Upside to CEO Drama," *Fortune,* February 1, 2019, 45–48.

15. N. E. Boudette and E. Povoledo, "Sergio Marchionne, Who Revived Fiat and Chrysler, Dies at 66," *The New York Times,* July 25, 2018, https://www.nytimes.com/2018/07/25/business/sergio-marchionne-dies-fiat-chrysler.html.

16. Adapted from R. Derousseau, "The Hidden Upside to CEO Drama," *Fortune,* February 1, 2019, 45–48.

17. Adapted from R. Derousseau, "The Hidden Upside to CEO Drama," *Fortune,* February 1, 2019, 45–48.

18. Adapted from R. Derousseau, "The Hidden Upside to CEO Drama," *Fortune,* February 1, 2019, 45–48.

19. K. Strauss, "The 10 Biggest CEO Departures in 2018," *Forbes.com,* December 18, 2018, https://www.forbes.com/sites/karstenstrauss/2018/12/18/the-10-biggest-ceo-departures-of-2018/#34de40e21ef7.

20. Evelyn M. Rusli, Geoffrey A. Fowler, and John Letzing, "Struggling Groupon Ousts Its Quirky CEO," *The Wall Street Journal,* February 28, 2013, https://www.wsj.com/articles/SB10001424127887324662404578332084043537590.

21. S. Pfeifer, "Faury Gears Up to Take the Controls at Airbus," *FinancialTimes.com,* February 15, 2019, https://www.ft.com/content/f9b3cbe6-311a-11e9-ba00-0251022932c8.

22. C. Hopp, D. Antons, J. Kaminski, and T. O. Salge, "What 40 Years of Research Reveals about the Difference Between Disruptive and Radical Innovation," *Harvard Business Review*, April 9, 2018, https://hbr.org/2018/04/what-40-years-of-research-reveals-about-the-difference-between-disruptive-and-radical-innovation.

23. B. Burnes, "Understanding Resistance to Change—Building on Coch and French," *Journal of Change Management,* 2015, 92–116.

24. K. Swisher, "Owning a Car Will Soon Be as Quaint as Owning a Horse," *The New York Times,* March 22, 2019, https://www.nytimes.com/2019/03/22/opinion/end-of-cars-uber-lyft.html.

25. L. R. Hearld and J. A. Alexander, "Governance Processes and Change within Organizational Participants of Multi-Sectoral Community Health Care Alliances: The Mediating Role of Vision, Mission, Strategy Agreement and Perceived Alliance Value," *American Journal of Community Psychology*, 2014, 185–197.

26. E. M. Rusli, "Even Facebook Must Change," *The Wall Street Journal,* January 30, 2013, B1, B7, http://online.wsj.com/news/articles/SB10001424127887323829504578272233666653120.

27. L. Kolowich, "17 Truly Inspiring Company Vision and Mission Statement Example," *Hubspot,* January 27, 2019, https://blog.hubspot.com/marketing/inspiring-company-mission-statements.

28. L. Kolowich, "17 Truly Inspiring Company Vision and Mission Statement Example," *Hubspot,* January 27, 2019, https://blog.hubspot.com/marketing/inspiring-company-mission-statements.

29. L. Kolowich, "17 Truly Inspiring Company Vision and Mission Statement Example," *Hubspot,* January 27, 2019, https://blog.hubspot.com/marketing/inspiring-company-mission-statements.

30. Adapted from J. Mackey and R. Sisodia, *Conscious Capitalism* (Boston, MA: Harvard Business School Publishing, 2013), 46.

31. Adapted from J. Mackey and R. Sisodia, *Conscious Capitalism* (Boston, MA: Harvard Business School Publishing, 2013), 46.

32. Interface, Inc., "Company Perspectives," https://www.referenceforbusiness.com/history2/69/Interface-Inc.html (accessed June 14, 2019).

33. L. Handley, "Blake Mycoskie: Sole Trader to Serial Philanthropist," *CNBC.com,* November 6, 2018, https://www.cnbc.com/blake-mycoskie--sole-trader-to-serial-philanthropist/.

34. L. Handley, "Blake Mycoskie: Sole Trader to Serial Philanthropist," *CNBC.com,* November 6, 2018, https://www.cnbc.com/blake-mycoskie--sole-trader-to-serial-philanthropist/.

35. B. Mycoskie, "The Founder of TOMS on Reimagining the Company's Mission," *Harvard Business Review,* January–February 2016, https://hbr.org/2016/01/the-founder-of-toms-on-reimagining-the-companys-mission.

36. A. E. Rafferty, N. L. Jimmieson, and A. A. Armenakis, "Change Readiness: A Multilevel Review," *Journal of Management* 39, 2013, 110–135.

37. I. Cinite and L. E. Duxbury, "Measuring the Behavioral Properties of Commitment and Resistance to Organizational Change," *Journal of Applied Behavioral Science*, 54, 2018, 113–139.

38. B. Burnes, "Understanding Resistance to Change—Building on Coch and Branch," *Journal of Change Management,* 2015, 92–116.

39. C. J. Grimolizzi-Jensen, "Organizational Change: Effect of Motivational Interviewing on Readiness to Change," *Journal of Change Management,* 18, 54–69.

40. Adapted from R. J. Marshak, *Covert Processes at Work* (San Francisco, CA: Berrett-Koehler Publishers, 2006); and A. S. Judson, *Changing Behavior in Organizations: Minimizing Resistance to Change* (Cambridge, MA: Blackwell, 1991).

41. M. Fugate and G. Soenen, "Predictors and Processes Related to Employees' Change-Related Compliance and Championing," *Personnel Psychology*, 71, 2018, 109–132.

42. M. Fugate and G. Soenen, "Predictors and Processes Related to Employees' Change-Related Compliance and Championing," *Personnel Psychology*, 71, 2018, 109–132.

43. A. Kraft, J. L. Sparr, and C. Peus, "Giving and Making Sense about Change: The Back and Forth Between Leaders and Employees," *Journal of Business Psychology*, 33, 71–87.

44. See D. M. Harold, D. B. Fedor, S. Caldwell, and Y. Liu, "The Effects of Transformational and Change Leadership on Employees' Commitment to Change: A Multilevel Study," *Journal of Applied Psychology,* March 2008, 346–357.

45. See R. H. Miles, "Accelerating Corporate Transformations (Don't Lose Your Nerve!)," *Harvard Business Review,* January–February 2010, 69–75, http://hbr.org/2010/01/accelerating-corporate-transformations-dont-lose-your-nerve/ar/1.

46. T. Thundiyil, D. Chiaburu, I. Oh, G. Banks, and A. Peng, "Cynical About Change? A Preliminary Meta-Analysis and Future Research Agenda," *Journal of Applied Behavioral Science*, 2015, 429–450.

47. American Psychological Association, "Stress in American—Generation Z," October 2018, https://www.apa.org/news/press/releases/stress/2018/stress-gen-z.pdf.

48. U.S. Department of Health & Human Services, "Stress . . . At Work," https://www.cdc.gov/niosh/docs/99-101/default.html (accessed June 14, 2019).

49. American Psychological Association, "Work Stress," http://www.apaexcellence.org/resources/special-topics/work-stress (accessed January 11, 2019).

50. V. Lipman, "Workplace Trend: Stress Is on the Rise," *Forbes.com,* January 9, 2019, https://www.forbes.com/sites/victorlipman/2019/01/09/workplace-trend-stress-is-on-the-rise/#4c38083a6e1b.

51. V. Lipman, "Workplace Trend: Stress Is on the Rise," *Forbes.com,* January 9, 2019, https://www.forbes.com/sites/victorlipman/2019/01/09/workplace-trend-stress-is-on-the-rise/#4c38083a6e1b.

52. See J. D. Nahrgang, F. P. Morgeson, and D. A. Hoffman, "Safety at Work: A Meta-Analytic Investigation of the Link between Job Demands, Job Resources, Burnout, Engagement, and Safety Outcomes," *Journal of Applied Psychology,* January 2011, 71–94; and S. Ohly and C. Fritz, "Work Characteristics, Challenge Appraisal, Creativity, and Proactive Behavior: A Multi-Level Study," *Journal of Organizational Behavior,* May 2010, 543–565.

53. C. K. Goodman, "Survey: Most Americans Stressed Out about Work," *Dallas Morning News*, April 21, 2013, D2.

54. S. Denning, "How Stress Is the Business World's Silent Killer," *Forbes.com*, May 4, 2018, https://www.forbes.com/sites/stephaniedenning/2018/05/04/what-is-the-cost-of-stress-how-stress-is-the-business-worlds-silent-killer/#2ec913946e06.

55. See R. A. Clay, "Stressed in America," *Monitor on Psychology*, January 2011, 60–61.

56. M. Guta, "What Is Fatigue and Why Does It Plague Your Small Business Team?" *Smallbiztrends.com*, February 5, 2019, https://smallbiztrends.com/2019/02/workplace-fatigue.html.

57. M. Guta, "What Is Fatigue and Why Does It Plague Your Small Business Team?" *Smallbiztrends.com*, February 5, 2019, https://smallbiztrends.com/2019/02/workplace-fatigue.html.

58. National Safety Council Report, "Fatigue—You're More than Just Tired," https://www.nsc.org/work-safety/safety-topics/fatigue (accessed February 12, 2019).

59. National Safety Council Report, "Fatigue—You're More than Just Tired," https://www.nsc.org/work-safety/safety-topics/fatigue (accessed February 12, 2019).

60. A. Luksyte, D. Avery, and G. Yeo, "It Is Worse When You Do It: Examining the Interactive Effects of Coworker Presenteeism and Demographic Similarity," *Journal of Applied Psychology*, 2015, 1107–1123.

61. S. B. Gingerich, E. L. D. Seaverson, and D. R. Anderson, "Association Between Sleep and Productivity Loss Among 598,676, Employees from Multiple Industries," *American Journal of Health Promotion*, 32, 2018, 1091–1094.

62. Adapted from D. Meinert, "Sleepless in Seattle . . . and Cincinnati and Syracuse," *HR Magazine*, October 2012, 55–58.

63. R. Wright, C. Mohr, R. Sinclair, and L. Yang, "Sometimes Less Is More: Directed Coping with Interpersonal Stressors at Work," *Journal of Organizational Behavior*, 2015, 786–805.

64. A. Kurtovic, I. Vukovic, and M. Gajic, "The Effects of Control on University Students' Mental Health: Possible Mediation through Self-Esteem and Coping," *The Journal of Psychology*, 2018, 152, 341–357; aee also J. D. Kammeyer-Mueller, T. A. Judge, and B. A. Scott, "The Role of Core Self-Evaluations in the Coping Process," *Journal of Applied Psychology*, January 2009, 177–195.

65. M. F. Dollard and J. A. Gordon, "Evaluation of a Participatory Risk Management Work Stress Intervention," *International Journal of Stress Management*, 2014, 27–42.

66. Supportive results can be found in R. Ilies, N. Dimotakis, and I. E. De Pater, "Psychological and Physiological Reactions to High Workloads: Implications for Well-Being," *Personnel Psychology*, Summer 2010, 407–436; and E. R. Crawford, J. A. LePine, and B. L. Rich, "Linking Job Demands and Resources to Employee Engagement and Burnout: A Theoretical Extension and Meta-Analytic Test," *Journal of Applied Psychology*, September 2010, 834–848.

67. See M. R. Frone, "Are Work Stressors Related to Employee Substance Use? The Importance of Temporal Context in Assessments of Alcohol and Illicit Drug Use," *Journal of Applied Psychology*, January 2008, 199–206.

68. T. Wright, "More than Meets the Eye: The Role of Employee Well-Being in Organizational Research," *Oxford Handbook of Positive Psychology and Work* (Oxford, UK: Oxford University Press, 2010), 143–154.

69. M. Yale, "Accounting for 'Failure' to Prospective Employers," *SHRM.org*, September 26, 2017, https://www.shrm.org/resourcesandtools/hr-topics/organizational-and-employee-development/pages/accounting-for-a-failure-to-prospective-employers.aspx.

70. O. Babur, "Talking About Failure Is Crucial for Growth. Here's How to Do It Right," *The New York Times*, August 17, 2018, https://www.nytimes.com/2018/08/17/smarter-living/talking-about-failure-is-crucial-for-growth-heres-how-to-do-it-right.html.

71. O. Babur, "Talking About Failure Is Crucial for Growth. Here's How to Do It Right," *The New York Times*, August 17, 2018, https://www.nytimes.com/2018/08/17/smarter-living/talking-about-failure-is-crucial-for-growth-heres-how-to-do-it-right.html.

72. O. Babur, "Talking About Failure Is Crucial for Growth. Here's How to Do It Right," *The New York Times*, August 17, 2018, https://www.nytimes.com/2018/08/17/smarter-living/talking-about-failure-is-crucial-for-growth-heres-how-to-do-it-right.html.

73. Adapted from M. Yate, "Accounting for 'Failure' to Prospective Employers," *SHRM.org*, September 26, 2017, https://www.shrm.org/resourcesandtools/hr-topics/organizational-and-employee-development/pages/accounting-for-a-failure-to-prospective-employers.aspx.

74. Adapted from M. Yate, "Accounting for 'Failure' to Prospective Employers," *SHRM.org*, September 26, 2017, https://www.shrm.org/resourcesandtools/hr-topics/organizational-and-employee-development/pages/accounting-for-a-failure-to-prospective-employers.aspx.

75. Adapted from E. Lee and J. Koblin, "AT&T Assembles a Media Team, Joining a Battle with Giants," *The New York Times*, March 4, 2019, https://www.nytimes.com/2019/03/04/business/media/att-warner-greenblatt.html.

76. S. A. Ward, "Growing at an Athleisurely Pace," *Bloomberg Businessweek*, January 8, 2018, 42-45.

77. S. A. Ward, "Growing at an Athleisurely Pace," *Bloomberg Businessweek*, January 8, 2018, 42-45.

78. S. K. Hayashi, "Strategies for Managing Employees Who Resist," *Forbes.com*, March 17, 2017, https://www.forbes.com/sites/forbescoachescouncil/2017/03/17/strategies-for-managing-employees-who-resist-change/#176a88ae6c71.

79. Adapted from D. Wilkie, "What Managers Can Do to Ease Workplace Stress," *SHRM.org*, April 26, 2018, https://www.shrm.org/ResourcesAndTools/hr-topics/employee-relations/Pages/how-managers-can-help-stressed-workers-.aspx.

80. Results are presented in K. M. Richardson and H. R. Rothstein, "Effects of Occupational Stress Management Intervention Programs: A Meta-Analysis," *Journal of Occupational Health Psychology*, January 2008, 69–93.

81. These steps were based on a discussion in L. Dzubow, "Optimism 101," *The Oprah Magazine*, April 2011, 130.

82. Adapted from C. Richards, "A 4-Step Guide to Ranting Productively," *The New York Times*, May 22, 2018, https://www.nytimes.com/2018/05/22/your-money/how-to-rant-productively.html.

83. Adapted from V. Lipman, "New Study Explores Why Change Management Fails—and How to (Perhaps) Succeed," *Forbes*, September 4, 2013, http://www.forbes.com/sites/victorlipman/2013/09/04/new-study-explores-why-change-management-fails-and-how-to-perhaps-succeed/.

84. Jeffrey Kahn, "Report: Texas Football in for Major Culture Change under Charlie Strong," Bleacher Report, Inc., January 15, 2014, https://bleacherreport.com/articles/1923529-texas-football-in-for-major-culture-change-under-charlie-strong.

85. N. Bomey, "5 Reasons Toys R Us Failed to Survive Bankruptcy," *USAToday.com*, March 18, 2018, https://www.usatoday.com/story/money/2018/03/18/toys-r-us-bankruptcy-liquidation/436176002/.

86. P. Wahba, "Retail Reckoning," *Fortune*, May 1, 2018, 76–81.

87. P. Wahba, "Retail Reckoning," *Fortune*, May 1, 2018, 76–81.

88. N. Bomey, "5 Reasons Toys R Us Failed to Survive Bankruptcy," *USAToday.com*, March 18, 2018, https://www.usatoday.com/story/money/2018/03/18/toys-r-us-bankruptcy-liquidation/436176002/.

89. N. Bomey, "5 Reasons Toys R Us Failed to Survive Bankruptcy," *USAToday.com*, March 18, 2018, https://www.usatoday.com/story/money/2018/03/18/toys-r-us-bankruptcy-liquidation/436176002/.

90. S. Min, "Toys R Us Plots a 2nd Act with New Look, New Name," *Moneywatch*, February 12, 2019, https://www.cbsnews.com/news/toys-r-us-coming-back-under-new-name/.

91. D. Green, "Toys R Us Is Being Revived, but It Probably Won't Be the Store You Remember," *Businessinsider.com*, February 13, 2019, https://www.businessinsider.com/toys-r-us-revival-wont-be-like-old-store-2019-2.

92. N. Beheshti, "Adopt These 4 Trends in Corporate Wellness to Gain a Competitive Edge," *Forbes.com*, December 28, 2018, https://www.forbes.com/sites/nazbeheshti/2018/12/28/adopt-these-4-trends-in-corporate-wellness-to-gain-a-competitive-edge-in-2019/#1ce585a37c3d.

93. W. Koch, "Workplaces Ban Not Only Smoking, But Smokers Themselves," *USA Today*, January 6, 2012, http://usatoday30.usatoday.com/money/industries/health/story/2012-01-03/health-care-jobs-no-smoking/52394782/1.

94. Fisher Phillips, "3 Options for Providing Wellness Program Incentives in 2019 . . . And Beyond," *Fisherphillips.com*, December 14, 2018, https://www.fisherphillips.com/resources-alerts-3-options-for-providing-wellness-program-incentives.

95. J. Sorrell, "Ethics: Employer-Sponsored Wellness Programs for Nurses: The Ethics of Carrots and Sticks," *The Online Journal of Issues in Nursing*, January 5, 2015.

96. F. Cavico and B. Mujtaba, "Health and Wellness Policy Ethics," *International Journal of Health Policy and Management*, 2013, 111–113.

97. J. D. Arendshorst and L. X. Gionnette, "2019 Wellness Program Incentives Affected by Final EEOC Rules," *The National Law Review*, January 17, 2019, https://www.natlawreview.com/article/2019-wellness-program-incentives-affected-final-eeoc-rules.

Bold page numbers indicate definitions. *Italic* page numbers indicate material in figures, illustrations, or tables.

A

ABCDEs of cognitive restructuring, 669–670
absenteeism, 382
abusive supervision The sustained display of hostile verbal and nonverbal behavior by managers, **521**–522
academic fraud, 12, 462
access-and-legitimacy perspective Recognition that the organization's markets and constituencies are culturally diverse, **140**
accountability
    in groups versus teams, 299, *299*
    in performance management, 206
accounting. *See* financial performance
accuracy, of feedback, 221
achievement
    in acquired needs theory, 166
    in PERMA, 287
acquired needs theory States that three needs—achievement, affiliation, and power—are the key drivers of employee behavior, **165**–168, *166*
acronyms, and organizational culture change, 568–569, *568*
action plans, in goal setting, 210
active listening, 346
adaptability (team adaptive capacity) The ability to make needed changes in response to demands put on the team, **323**–324
adaptive change Reintroduces a familiar practice either in a different unit or in the same unit at a different point in time, **646**, *646*
adhocracy culture One that has an external focus and values flexibility, **560**, 562–563, *564*, 565
adjourning, in group development, 307
ADR (alternative dispute resolution) A means for solving disputes using an independent third party and avoids the costs and problems associated with litigation or unilateral decision making, **405**–407, *406*
affective component of an attitude Our feelings or emotions about a given object or situation, **50**
affiliation, in acquired needs theory, 166, 168

affirmative action An intervention aimed at giving management a chance to correct an imbalance, injustice, mistake, or outright discrimination that occurred in the past, **137**–138
African Americans, 141, 142, *641*
age
    communication styles and, 351–352
    in diversity management, 151–152
    social media use, *353*
    stereotypes, 130
    values and, 47
    workforce trends, 142–144, *143*
age discrimination, 151–152
agreeableness, *88*, 93
AI (artificial intelligence) A form of computing that allows machines to perform cognitive functions, **440**–441
alignment of goals, 597
alternative dispute resolution (ADR) A means for solving disputes using an independent third party and avoids the costs and problems associated with litigation or unilateral decision making, **405**–407, *406*
altruism, 258
ambiguity
    reducing in virtual teams, 483
    tolerance for, 442
Americans with Disabilities Act Prohibits discrimination against those with disabilities and requires organizations to reasonably accommodate an individual's disabilities, **142**
amplifying effect Positive practices from one individual result in additional positive practices by others, which spur positivity in others, which generate other positive outcomes, **254**–255
amusement (emotion), *263*
analytical style (decision making), 443–444, *443*
analytical thought, 425–426
anchoring bias Occurs when decision makers are influenced by the first information they receive about a decision, even if it is irrelevant, **435**
anger management, 111–112, *112*
antecedents, in communication, 348, *349*
anti-bullying strategies, *397*
anticipatory socialization Information gathered and expectations formed before an individual actually joins an organization, **575**, *575*

apologies, 498–499
appeals process, 178
appearance, in person perception, 127
applicant tracking software (ATS), 3
arbitration, *406*, 421
artifacts The physical manifestation of an organization's culture, **552**–553
artificial intelligence (AI) A form of computing that allows machines to perform cognitive functions, **440**–441
Asians, 141, 640, *641*
Ask for It: How Women Can Use the Power of Negotiation to Get What They Really Want (Babcock), 408
assimilation, in diversity management, 149
ATS (applicant tracking software), 3
attention The process of becoming consciously aware of someone or something, **124**
attitudes Our feelings or opinions about people, places, and objects and range from positive to negative, **48**
    cognitive dissonance and, 50–51
    components of, 50
    employee surveys of, 49, 54
    implications of, 70
    intention and, 51–53, *51*
    job satisfaction outcomes, 64–65
    Organizing Framework, *42*
    versus values, *48*, 49
    workplace, 48, 54–59
attribution theory, 132–133, *133*
authority, in persuasion, 484
automated experience A choice based on a familiar situation and a partially subconscious application of learned information related to it, **430**
autonomy
    as innate need, 168, 169
    in job characteristics model, 189
availability bias A decision maker's tendency to base decisions on information readily available in memory, **435**
avoiding style (conflict management), 402, *403*
awe, *263*

B

baby boomers, 47, 143, *143*, 152, 658
balanced scorecard (BSC), 595, 625–627
basic underlying assumptions Organizational values so taken for granted over time that they become assumptions guiding organizational behavior, **554**

behavior
  causal attribution, 132–134, *132, 133*
  job satisfaction outcomes, 66–68
  organizational culture effects on, 557
  reinforcement and consequences, 236–242, *237*
  Theory of Planned Behavior, 51–53, *51*
behavioral component of an attitude The way we intend or expect to act toward someone or something, **50**
behavioral style (decision making), *443,* 444
behavioral styles
  approach Attempts to identify the unique behaviors displayed by effective leaders, **516**
behaviorism, 236
bias
  in attribution, 134
  communication and, 350, 352
  in decision making, 433–436
  in performance management, 204
big data The vast quantity of data available for decision making, 439–440, 614
Big Five Personality Dimensions: Extroversion, agreeableness, conscientiousness, emotional stability, and openness to experience, **88**–89, *88,* 93
blame, as political tactic, *488,* 489–490
blindness, in unethical behavior, *18*
bodily-kinesthetic intelligence, *84*
body movements, in communication, 345
body shape, in person perception, 126
bonuses, 197, 242
boredom, and creativity, 455
bottom-up job design, 185, *185,* 189–190
boundaries, in team charter, 298
boundaryless organization One in which management has largely succeeded in breaking down barriers between internal levels, job functions, and departments, as well as reducing external barriers between the association [organization] and those with whom it does business, **606**
bounded rationality Represents the notion that decision makers are "bounded" or restricted by a variety of constraints when making decisions, **429**–430
brainstorming, 427, 450–451, *451*
brainwriting (electronic brainstorming) Allows participants to submit their ideas and alternatives over the Internet, **451**

breathing meditations, 271–272
broaden-and-build theory, 254–255, 283–284
BSC (balanced scorecard), 595, 625–627
buffering effect The reduction of the impact of negative events and stressors through positive practices and resources, **255**
bullying Unwelcomed behavior that occurs over a period of time and is meant to harm someone who feels powerless to respond, 397–398, *397*
business skills, in leaders, *514*
busyness, versus productivity, 200

C

career planning, 203
categorization, in stereotyping, 130
category-based knowledge, 125–126, 129
causal attributions Suspected or inferred causes of behavior, **132**–134, *132, 133*
celebrations, as rewards, 242
centralized decision making Occurs when key decisions are made by top management, **614**
central tendency, *215*
chain of command, 597
change
  diversity management and, 147
  employee relocation, 638
  external forces for, 639–643, *640*
  internal forces for, *640,* 643–645
  Kotter's process, 652, *653*
  Legal/Ethical Challenge, 678
  Lewin's model, 647–648, *647*
  organizational development approach, 652–654, *653*
  Organizing Framework, *637*
  Problem-Solving Application, 665–666
  resistance to, 655–657, *656*
  self-assessment, 639, 651
  systems model, 648–652, *648*
  types of, 646–647, *646*
change agent Someone who is a catalyst in helping organizations deal with old problems in new ways, **657**
  common pitfalls of, *657*
  relationship with employees, 667–668
change and acquisition phase Socialization phase which requires employees to master important tasks and roles and adjust to their work group's values and norms, *575,* **577**

change management
  implications of, 672–673
  overcoming resistance, 666–668
  Problem-Solving Case, 676–677
  stress management and, 669–670
  systems model application, 665–666
  tips for managers, 670–671
character strengths, 277–278, *277*
charisma A form of interpersonal attraction that inspires acceptance, devotion, and enthusiasm, **530**
cheating, 11–12, 17–18, 462–463
clan culture One that values internal focus and flexibility rather than stability and control, **559**–560, *559,* 562–563, 564, *564,* 565
closed system A self-sufficient entity, **599**–600
coaching A customized process between two or more people with the intent of enhancing learning and motivating change or improving an individual's behavior and performance to resolve work issues or handle specific aspects of the job and may be short term, **224, 580**
  as mentoring function, *581*
  organizational culture change and, *568,* 569
  in performance management, 206, 224–225
  self-efficacy and, *99*
coalition An informal group bound together by the active pursuit of a single issue, **490**
coalition-level politics, 490–491, *490*
coalition tactics, *480*
coercive power Power to make threats of punishment and deliver actual punishment, **468,** 474
cognitive abilities, in leaders, *514*
cognitive appraisals of stress, 661–662
cognitive bias, 434–435
cognitive categories Groups of objects that are considered equivalent, **124**
cognitive component of an attitude Our beliefs or ideas about an object or situation, **50**
cognitive dissonance The psychological discomfort a person experiences when simultaneously holding two or more conflicting cognitions (ideas, beliefs, values, or emotions), 50-**51**
cognitive load, 126
cognitive restructuring, 669–670
cohesiveness A sense of "we-ness" that tends to override individual differences and motives, **448**–449

collaboration The act of sharing information and coordinating efforts to achieve a collective outcome, 324–327, 668

commitment
  bases of power and, 473, *473*
  in organizational culture, 556

common sense, limits of, 7

communication competence A performance-based index of an individual's abilities to effectively use communication behaviors in a given context, **344**

communication The exchange of information between a sender and a receiver, and the inference (perception) of meaning between the individuals involved, **339**
  as change agent pitfall, *657*
  crucial conversations, 367–368
  empathy and, 348–349
  gender differences in, 350–351, 352
  generational differences in, 351–352
  implications of, 370–371
  in job interviews, 338
  Legal/Ethical Challenge, 377
  listening, 346–347, *346*, *347*
  nondefensive, 348, *349*
  nonverbal, 344–346, *345*, 412
  Organizing Framework, *337*
  presentations, 364–366
  Problem-Solving Application Case, 375–376
  process of, 340–341, *340*
  self-assessment, 344, 347
  social media, 353–363
  in team collaboration, 324
  transparency in, 341–342
  upward feedback, 368–369, *369*
  in virtual teams, *315*

communication trust, 318

comparison, in equity theory, 175

compassion A shared value that drives people to help others who are suffering, **281**

compensation. *See* pay and benefits

competence, as innate need, 168

competence trust, 318, 319

competing values framework (CVF) Provides a practical way for managers to understand, measure, and change organizational culture, **558–565**, *559*

compliance, and bases of power, 473, *473*

comprehensive task interdependence, 315

compromising style (conflict management), 402, *403*

conceptual style (decision making), *443*, 444

conciliation, *406*

confidence, in giving feedback, 218

confirmation bias Pertains to how we selectively gather information, **433**

conflict management
  alternative dispute resolution, 405–407, *406*
  programmed conflict techniques, 400, *401*
  self-assessment, 402
  styles of, 401–405, *402*, *403*

conflict The energy created by the perceived gap between what we want and what we're experiencing, **381–382**, 383
  avoidance of, 385, *386*
  causes of, 383, *383*
  contemporary types of, 391–399
  continuum of, 382, *383*
  conventional types of, 387–390
  escalation of, 383–384
  functional versus dysfunctional, 382
  Legal/Ethical Challenge, 421
  as opportunity, 386
  Organizing Framework, *379*
  Problem-Application Case, 419–421
  self-assessment, 381, 392
  in teamwork, 322

conscientiousness, *88*, 93

conscious thought, 425–426

consensus (in attribution theory) Compares an individual's behavior with that of his or her peers, **132**, *133*

consensus (in decision making) When all members can say they either agree with the decision or have had their 'day in court' and were unable to convince the others of their viewpoint. In the final analysis, everyone agrees to support the outcome, **450**

consequences
  contingent, 237–239, *237*
  law of effect, 236
  in team charter, 298

conservation, in value theory, 44, 45, 46

consideration Leader behavior that creates mutual respect or trust and prioritizes group members' needs and desires, **518**

consistency, in persuasion, 484

consistency Judges whether the individual's performance on a given task is consistent over time, **132**, *133*

constructive (functional or cooperative conflict) Characterized by consultative interactions, a focus on the issues, mutual respect, and useful give-and-take, **382**, 400

consultation (influence tactic), *480*

contact hypothesis Suggests that the more members of different groups interact, the less intergroup conflict they will experience, **388**

content theories of motivation Based on the idea that an employee's needs influence his or her motivation, **164**
  acquired needs theory, 165–168, *166*
  motivator-hygiene theory, 169–171
  need hierarchy theory, 164–165, *165*
  self-determination theory, 168–169
  theory comparison, *172*
  Theory X and Theory Y, 164

contingency approach Calls for using the OB concepts and tools that best suit the situation, instead of trying to rely on "one best way," **5**, 211, *211*, 668

contingency approach to organization design Organizations tend to be more effective when they are structured to fit the demands of the situation, and when the structure is aligned with internal activities and actions of the organization, **613**–615

contingency theories of leadership Propose that the effectiveness of a particular style of leader behavior depends on the situation, **523**
  application of, 529
  Fiedler's model, 523–525, *524*
  path-goal theory, 526–529, *526*, *527*, *528*

continuous reinforcement (CRF) A reinforcement schedule in which every instance of a target behavior is reinforced, **239–240**

contractual trust, 318

contrast effect, *215*

control strategy Behaviors and cognitions that directly anticipate or solve problems, **662**

cooperative (functional or constructive) Characterized by consultative interactions, a focus on the issues, mutual respect, and useful give-and-take, **382**, 400

coordination of effort, 597

core self-evaluations (CSEs) Four narrow and positive individual traits: (1) generalized self-efficacy, (2) self-esteem, (3) locus of control, and (4) emotional stability, **96**, *96*
  emotional stability, *88*, 93, 101, 102
  locus of control, 100–101
  practical considerations, 102–103

glossary/subject index

functional conflict (constructive or cooperative conflict) Characterized by consultative interactions, a focus on the issues, mutual respect, and useful give-and-take, **382**, 400

functional structure Groups people according to the business functions they perform, for example, manufacturing, marketing, and finance, **606**, *612*

fundamental attribution bias Tendency to attribute another person's behavior to his or her personal characteristics, rather than to situation factors, **134**

G

gaze, in person perception, 125, 126
gender
    communication and, 350–351, 352
    in person perception, 126
    stereotypes, 130
    workplace diversity trends, 140–141
generational differences
    communication, 351–352
    diversity management and, 152
    stress levels, 658
    values, 47
    workforce, 142–144, *143*
genetic factors, in job satisfaction, 62
Gen Xers, *143*, 152, 658
Gen Y. *See* Millennials
Gen Zers, 47, *143*, 144, 658
gestures, in communication, 345
gig workers, 609–610
glass ceiling An invisible but absolute barrier that prevents women from advancing to higher-level positions, **140–141**
global mind-set The belief in one's ability to influence dissimilar others in a global context, **515**
goal commitment, 209, *209*
goal displacement Occurs when the primary goal is overridden by a secondary goal, **448**
goals and goal setting
    alignment of, in organizations, 597
    in career planning, 203
    in change management, 668, 671
    contingency approach, 211, *211*
    emotional reactions to, 110
    goal-setting process, 208–211, *209*
    hope and, 274
    ill-conceived, *18*
    organizational culture change and, *568*, 572
    performance and, 184
    performance versus learning goals, 207–208

in person perception, 125
    reasonable, 222
    self-efficacy and, *99*
    SMART goals, *208*, 209
    in team collaboration, 324
goal-setting theory, 182–183
goal specificity Indicates whether a goal has been quantified, **183**
The Good Fight, You First (Davey), 322
government regulations, as force for change, 642–643
gratitude, 256, *263*
group cohesiveness The degree to which members feel part of the collective or "we" of the group, 307, **307**
group decision making
    advantages, disadvantages, 448
    goal of, 450
    groupthink in, 448–449, *449*
    problem-solving techniques for, 450–451
    self-assessment, 450
group-level stressors, 659, *660*
group role A set of shared expected behaviors for members of the group as a whole, **301**–302
groups Collections of two or more individuals with low or no task dependency, who are not accountable to each other for their work, and who may or may not assemble for a specified period of time, **299**
    decision making in, 447–451
    development models, 305–308, *305*
    formal versus informal, 300
    implications of, 328–329
    Organizing Framework, *297*
    roles and norms in, 300–304, *302*, *303*
    self-assessment, 302
    versus teams, 299–300, *299*
groupthink A mode of thinking that people engage in when they are deeply involved in a cohesive in-group, when members' strivings for unanimity override their motivation to realistically appraise alternative courses of action, **44**8–449, *449*

H

halo effect, *215*
harassment Discrimination based on a protected class (race, gender, religion, pregnancy, age, disability), that becomes illegal when it threatens your employment or is considered intimidating, hostile, or abusive, **398**–399

hard skills The technical expertise and knowledge to do a particular task or job function, **7**, *10*
helpers, followers as, 537
HERO (hope, efficacy, resilience, and optimism), 273
hierarchy culture One that has an internal focus, which produces a more formalized and structured work environment, and values stability and control over flexibility, **561**, *564*
hierarchy of authority, 597, 598
high-commitment work systems Rely on selective hiring, comprehensive training, comparatively high pay, pay contingent on performance, and good benefits, **453**
high-school dropouts, 144
hindsight bias Occurs when knowledge of an outcome influences our belief about the probability that we could have predicted the outcome earlier, 435–**436**
hiring process
    candidates with criminal records, 294
    core self-evaluation use, 103
    employment tests, 93–95
    etiquette and, 494
    perception and, 122, 128
    rejection of job candidates, 284–285
    requirements for, 9
    salary question, 249
    social media use, 122, 354, *354*
Hispanics, 141, 142, 150, *641*
holistic hunch A judgment based on the subconscious integration of information stored in memory, **430**
hollow structure (network structure) Designed around a central core of key functions and outsources other functions to outside companies or individuals who can do them cheaper or faster, **609**, *612*
hope Believing the future will be better than the present and that you have some power to make it happen, **256**
    components of, 273–274
    developing, 276
    as frequent positive emotion, *263*
    in psychological capital, 273
horizontal loading, 186
horizontal structure A structure in which teams or work groups, either temporary or permanent, are created to improve collaboration and work on common projects, 605, *605*, **607**–608, *612*
hostile work environments, 75, 146, 399

human capital The productive potential of an individual's knowledge, skills, and experiences, **582**

human resources
as force for change, 643
innovation and, 623

humility, in leaders, 537

hygiene factors Include company policy and administration, technical supervision, salary, interpersonal relationships with supervisors, and working conditions. They cause a person to move from a state of no dissatisfaction to dissatisfaction, **170**, 171

I

idea evaluation/validation, 453

idea generation, 453

idealized influence To instill pride, respect, and trust within employees, **531**

identity
in organizational culture, 555–556
in team charter, 298

idiosyncratic deals (i-deals) Employment terms individuals negotiate for themselves, taking myriad forms from flexible schedules to career development, 186, **191**

illegal behavior, versus unethical, 13–14

implicit cognition Any thoughts or beliefs that are automatically activated from memory without our conscious awareness, **128**, 350, 352

implicit leadership theory Proposes that people have beliefs about how leaders should behave and what they should do for their followers, **514**

impression management Any attempt to control or manipulate the images related to a person, organization, or idea, **493**
apologies, 498–499
ethics and, 497–498
first impressions, 493–494, *495*
job interviews and, 494, 496–497
as political tactic, *488*
reciprocity and, 494
self-assessment, 495
upward impression management, 494–496

improvement innovations Enhance or upgrade an existing product, service, or process, **617**

inadequacy, as negative emotion, *112*

incivility Any form of socially harmful behavior, such as aggression,

interpersonal deviance, social undermining, interactional injustice, harassment, abusive supervision, and bullying, **395**
bullying, 397–398, *397*
causes and outcomes of, 396, *396*
harassment, 398–399
pervasiveness and cost of, *396*

include/exclude, in diversity management, 148

inclusive design, 139

independent contractors, 609–610

independents, followers as, 537

indirect blindness, *18*

individual differences (IDs) The many attributes, such as traits and behaviors, that describe each of us as a person, *77*, **79**
core self-evaluations, 96–103, *96*
emotional intelligence and, *108*
fixed versus flexible, 79–80, *80*
implications of, 114
intelligence, 82–86
Organizing Framework, 77
personality, 87–95
positive psychological capital, 273–276
recipient characteristics, 656–657
signature strengths, 277–278, *277*

individualized consideration Consists of behaviors that provide support, encouragement, empowerment, and coaching to employees, **531**

individual-level politics, *490*

individual-level stressors, 659, *660*

inferences, in stereotyping, 130

influence tactics Conscious efforts to affect and change behaviors in others, **480**
common, *480*, 481–482
effective use of, 483
implications of, 500
impression management, 493–499
Organizing Framework, *465*
persuasion principles, 484
self-assessment, 482
using in influence plan, 485
in virtual teams, 483–484

informal group A group whose overriding purpose in getting together is friendship or a common interest, **300**

information acquisition (scanning), 602

information distribution, 602

information exploitation, *413*, *488*

information gathering (creative behavior), 453

information interpretation, 602

ingratiation, *480*, *488*, 496

in-group exchange, 534, *535*

initiating structure Leader behavior that organizes and defines what group members should be doing to maximize output, **516**

innate needs, 168

innovation system A coherent set of interdependent processes and structures that dictates how the company searches for novel problems and solutions, synthesizes ideas into a business concept and product designs, and selects which projects get funded, **618**, *619*

innovation The creation of something new that makes money; it finds a pathway to the consumer, **616**
culture and climate for, 619–620
failure and, 619
human capital for, 623
human resource practices for, 623
implications of, 629
leadership commitment, 619
in office design, 623–624, *624*
organizational structure and processes for, 621–623
Problem-Solving Application, 620
resources for, 623
self-assessment, 621
types and focus of, 616–617, *617*

innovative change Introduces a practice that is new to the organization, **646**, *646*

inputs, in equity theory, 174

inspiration, *263*, 668

inspirational appeals, *480*

inspirational motivation Includes the use of charisma, relies on an attractive vision of the future, emotional arguments, and demonstrated optimism and enthusiasm, **530**

institutional power, 166

instructional feedback, 218–219, *219*

instrumentality The perceived relationship between performance and outcomes, **179**, 180

integrating style (conflict management), 401, *403*

integrative negotiation Negotiation in which numerous interests are considered, resulting in an agreement that is satisfactory for both parties, **408**–409, *409*

intellectual stimulation Encourages employees to question the status quo and to seek innovative and creative solutions to organizational problems, **532**

intelligence An individual's capacity for constructive thinking, reasoning, and problem solving, **82**

genetics in, 82
multiple intelligences, 83–84, *84*
practical intelligence, 84–85
testing, in sports, 86
training or improving, 85–86

intentions The end point or goal you want to achieve; they drive your behavior, 51–53, *51*, **256**

interactional justice The quality of the interpersonal treatment people receive when procedures are implemented, **175**, *177*

interactional perspective States that behavior is a function of interdependent person and situation factors, **24**

interest (emotion), *263*

interest-based negotiation, 408–409, *409*

intergroup conflict, 387–390

intermittent reinforcement A reinforcement schedule in which some but not all instances of a target behavior are reinforced, **240**

internal alignment, 614

internal business perspective, 626–627

internal factors Factors within a person (such as ability), **132**, *133*

internal forces for change Forces that come from inside the organization, *640*, **643**–645

internal locus of control A belief that one can control the events and consequences that affect their lives, **101**

internal virtual structures, 611

interpersonal intelligence, *84*

interpersonal skills, 8, *514*

interpersonal treatment, 176

intervention, in organizational development, 654

interviews
communication in, 338
etiquette in, 494
explanation for leaving current job, 384–385
impression management and, 494, 496–497
questions on failure, 664
questions to answer and ask, 78
tips for, 9
virtual, 129, 363

intrapersonal intelligence, *84*

intrinsic motivation Inspired by the positive internal feelings that are generated by doing well, **162**, 168

intrinsic rewards Self-granted awards, such as psychic rewards, **226**

introversion, 89, 90

intuition Consists of judgments, insights, or decisions that come to

mind on their own, without explicit awareness of the evoking cues and of course without explicit evaluation of the validity of these cues, **430**
improving, 432
model of, 430–431, *431*
pros and cons of, 431–432
self-assessment, 432

intuitive thought, 425–426

involved listening, 346

isolation, in diversity management, 149

glossary/subject index

mediation, *406*

meditation techniques, 271-272, *272*

medium of communication, 341, 342-343, *342*

meetings, 466

memory, in social perception, 124-125

men
communication patterns, 350-351
family leave for, 394
leadership traits, 514

mental abilities, 142

mentoring The process of forming and maintaining intensive and lasting developmental relationships between a variety of developers (people who provide career and psychosocial support) and a junior person (the protégé, if male, or protégée, if female), **580**
benefits of, 582
developmental networks for, 583-584
functions and phases of, 580-582, *581*
human and social capital and, 582-583
implications of, 585
Organizing Framework, *549*
self-assessment, 584

message, in communication, 340, *340*

meta-analysis, 512

met expectations The difference between what an individual expects to receive from a job, such as good pay and promotional opportunities, and what she or he actually receives, **61**

#MeToo movement, 15-16, 398, 472, 503-504

MI (multiple intelligences), 83-84, *84*

microaggressions, 359

microinternships, 319

Millennials (Gen Y)
best companies for, 146
digital device use, 351-352
generational differences and, 143-144, *143*, 152
population of, 640
stress levels, 658
values of, 47
workplace benefits desired, 171

mindfulness The awareness that emerges through paying attention on purpose, in the present moment, and nonjudgmentally to the unfolding of experience moment by moment, **268**, *268*
benefits of, 270-271
in building self-awareness, 6
business use of, 269-270
practicing, 271-272

self-assessment, 271

minority dissent Occurs when group members feel comfortable disagreeing with other group members, **449**

mission statements An expression of the reason an organization exists, **649**
organizational change and, 567, 649
in team charter, 298

modular structure One in which the company assembles product parts, components, or modules provided by external contractors, **610**, *612*

moral character An individual's general tendency to think, feel, and behave in ways associated with ethical and unethical behavior, **414**

motivated blindness, *18*

motivating factors (motivators) Include achievement, recognition, characteristics of the work, responsibility, and advancement. They cause a person to move from a state of no satisfaction to satisfaction, **170**, 171

motivational feedback, 218-219, *219*

motivation The psychological processes that underlie the direction, intensity, and persistence of behavior or thought, **162**
content theories, 164-172
extrinsic versus intrinsic, 162
implications of, 192
as job satisfaction outcome, 64
to manage others, 5, 6
Organizing Framework, *160*
Problem-Solving Application Case, 195-196
process theories, 173-184
through job design, 185-191
values and, 46, *46*

motivator-hygiene theory Proposes that job satisfaction and dissatisfaction arise from two different sets of factors—satisfaction comes from *motivating factors* and dissatisfaction from *hygiene factors*, **169**-172

motivators (motivating factors) Include achievement, recognition, characteristics of the work, responsibility, and advancement. They cause a person to move from a state of no satisfaction to satisfaction, **170**

multiple intelligences (MI), 83-84, *84*

musical intelligence, *84*

mutual adaptation, 149

Myers-Briggs Type Indicator (MBTI), 94

myths, in organizational culture change, *568*, 570

narcissism Having a grandiose sense of self-importance; requiring or even demanding excessive admiration; having a sense of entitlement; lacking empathy; and tending to be exploitative, manipulative, and arrogant, **92, 513**

naturalist intelligence, *84*

need fulfillment models, 61

need hierarchy theory States that motivation is a function of five basic needs: physiological, safety, love, esteem, and self-actualization, **164**-165, *165*

needs Physiological or psychological deficiencies that arouse behavior, **61**, 125, **164**

negative emotions
awareness of, 257
balance with positive, 264
management of, 110, *112*
strategies to avoid, 266-267

negative reinforcement The process of strengthening a desired behavior by contingently withdrawing something displeasing, **237**, 238, *238*

negotiation A give-and-take decision-making process between two or more parties with different preferences, **408**
emotions and, 411-413
ethics and, 413-414, *413*
factors to consider, 409-410
implications of, 415-416
Organizing Framework, *379*
of pay raises, 161, 380, 413
of salaries, 380, 412-413
types of, 408-409, *409*

networked virtual structures, 611

network-level politics, *490*, 491-492

network structure (hollow structure) Designed around a central core of key functions and outsources other functions to outside companies or individuals who can do them cheaper or faster, **609**, *612*

new-direction innovations Take a totally new or different approach to a product, service, process, or industry, **617**-618

noise Anything that interferes with the transmission and understanding of a message, **341**

nondefensive communication, 348, *349*

nondisclosure, in negotiation, *413*

glossary/subject index

Problem-Solving Application Case, 633–634

strategy mapping for, 627–628, *628*

organizational identity, 555–556

organizational justice, 175

organizational-level stressors, 659, *660*

organizational memory, 602

organizational politics Intentional actions to improve individual or organizational interests, **486**

behavior drivers, 487–488

common tactics, 488–490, *488*

implications of, 500

Organizing Framework, *465*

political action levels, 490–492, *490*

positive and negative, 486–487

Problem-Solving Application Case, 503–504

self-assessment, 486

using, 492

organizational practices The procedures, policies, practices, routines, and rules that organizations use to get things done, **281**, 668

organizational processes

in change management, 668

innovation and, 621–623

organizational culture change and, *568*, 570

organizational socialization The process by which individuals acquire the knowledge, skills, attitudes, and behaviors required to assume a work role, **574**

application of, 577–579

implications of, 585

Legal/Ethical Challenge, 591

Organizing Framework, *549*

self-assessment, 577

tactics of, *578*

three-phase model of, 574–577, *575*

tips for improving, 579

organizational structure. *See* organizational design

organizational systems and procedures, *568*, 572

organization A system of consciously coordinated activities or forces of two or more persons, **597**

common characteristics, 597

learning organizations, 600–603, *601*

line versus staff positions in, 599

open-system perspective, 599–600, *601*

spans of control in, 599

organization charts, 598–599, *598*

Organizing Framework. *See also specific topics*

basic version, 27–29, *27*

summary version, 31–33, *32*

using for problem solving, 29–30

outcome interdependence The degree to which the outcomes of task work are measured, rewarded, and communicated at the group level so as to emphasize collective outputs rather than individual contributions, **316**

out-group exchange, 534

outputs, in equity theory, 174

overconfidence bias Results in overestimating our skills relative to those of others and overestimating the accuracy of our predictions, **433**–435

overqualification, 144

overvaluation, in unethical behavior, *18*

P

paraphrasing Restating what someone else has said or written, **345**

passive listening, 346

path-goal theory Holds that leader behaviors are effective when employees view them as a source of satisfaction or as paving the way to future satisfaction, **526**–529, *526, 527, 528*

pay and benefits. *See also* rewards

desired by Millennials, 171

Legal/Ethical Challenge, 197, 249

pay raise negotiation, 161, 380, 413

as performance management focus, 204

Problem-Solving Applications, 171–172, 180

salary negotiations, 380, 412–413

variable pay, 233–235, *233, 234*

pay for performance Merit and/or bonus pay based on individual-, group-, or organization-level measures and involving individual, group, or organization rewards, **233**–235, *233, 234*

peer pressure, 304, 657

peer review, *406*

people management, as sought-after skill, *8*

people with disabilities, 142

perceived behavioral control, *51*, 53

perceived organizational support (POS) The extent to which employees believe their organization values their contributions and genuinely cares about their well-being, **59**

perceiver, in person perception, 125–126, *126*

perception A cognitive process that enables us to interpret and understand our surroundings, **123**

of feedback, 221–222

in hiring process, 122, 128

implications of, 153

leadership and, 129, 514–515

performance appraisals and, 128–129

person perception model, 125–129, *126*

of politics, 492

stages of, 123–125, *124*

stereotypes in, 130–131

performance

credibility and, 10

employee engagement and, 57–58

goals effects on, 184

job satisfaction and, 66

personality effects on, 93

positivity and, 252

reinforcement schedules and, 241–242, *242*

underperformance and failures, 663

verbal recognition and, 171

performance appraisals

diversity management and, 147

perception and, 128–129

typical scenario, *204*

versus performance management, 201

Performance Conversations: An Alternative to Appraisals (Lee), 217

performance evaluation The process of comparing performance at some point in time to a previously established expectation or goal, **214**–216, *215*

performance goals Goals that garner a specific end result, **207**

performance management (PM) A set of processes and managerial behaviors that include defining, monitoring, measuring, evaluating, and providing consequences for performance expectations, **201**

coaching in, 206, 224–225

common uses of, 202–203

effective, 201–202, *202*, 206

feedback in, 217–224

goal setting in, 207–211

implications of, 243–244

monitoring and evaluating in, 212–216, *215*

Organizing Framework, *199*

pay for performance in, 233–235, *233, 234*

pitfalls of, 203–205

Problem-Solving Application Case, 247–249

reinforcement and consequences in, 236–242

rewards in, 226–232

versus performance appraisals, 201

performance monitoring Measuring, tracking, or otherwise verifying progress and ultimate outcomes, 212–214, *212*

performance norms, in team charter, 298

performing, in group development, 307

PERMA (positive emotions, engagement, relationships, meaning, and achievement), **283**

personal appeals, *480*

personal competence, *105*

personality conflict Interpersonal opposition based on personal dislike or disagreement, **387**, *388*, *657*

personality testing, 93–95, *95*

personality The combination of relatively stable physical, behavioral, and mental characteristics that gives individuals their unique identities, **87**

Big Five Dimensions of, 88–89, *88*, 93

Dark Triad, 92, 513

as diversity layer, 136

"ideal employee," 95

introversion, 89, 90

leadership traits, 512–513, *512*

liking and fit in, 87

performance and, 93

proactive, 89–92

self-assessment, 88

personal power A source of influence independent of position or job, 166, **470**, *471*

person–environment fit (P-E) The compatibility between an individual and a work environment that occurs when their characteristics are well matched, **550**

person factors Infinite characteristics that give individuals their unique identities, **24**. *See also specific factors*

in creative performance behaviors, 453

in employee engagement, 57

in negotiation, 414

in Organizing Framework, 27, 31, *32*

in problem solving, 26

in transformational leadership, *531*

person memory, 125

person–organization fit (P-O) The extent to which your personality and values match the climate and culture in an organization, **550**, 573, 615

person perception model, 125–129

person-situation distinction, 24–26

persuasion principles, 484

P-E (person–environment fit) The compatibility between an individual and a work environment that occurs when their characteristics are well matched, **550**

phubbing, 359

physical abilities, 142

physical attractiveness, in person perception, 127

PM. *See* performance management

politics. *See* organizational politics

pooled task interdependence, 315

portable skills Relevant in every job, at every level, and throughout your career, **8**

position-based negotiation, 408, *409*

position power A source of influence associated with a particular job or position within an organization; also a leader's formal power to reward, punish, or otherwise obtain compliance from employees, **470**, *471*, **524**

positive deviance Successful performance that dramatically exceeds the norm in a positive direction, **255–256**, *256*, 257

positive emotions. *See* positivity

positive organizational behavior (positive OB) The focus on positive human characteristics that can be measured, developed, effectively managed for performance improvement, **253**

amplifying effect in, 254–255

benefits of, 255–259

buffering effect in, 255

challenges of, 259–260

for employee positivity, *257*

flourishing in, *251*, 283–287

framework for, 254, *254*

implications of, 288–289

mindfulness and, 268–272

organizational climate, 279–282

Organizing Framework, 251

performance and, 252

positive emotions and, 261–267, *263*

positive psychological capital in, 273–276

positivity effect in, 255

Problem-Solving Application, 260

Problem-Solving Application Case, 292–294

signature strengths in, 277–278, *277*

positive psychological capital (PsyCap) Considerable levels of hope, efficacy, resilience, and optimism (HERO); **273**

developing, 273–276

self-assessment, 276

positive reinforcement The process of strengthening a behavior by contingently presenting something appealing, **237**

positivity

balance with negativity, 264

benefits of, 262

contagious aspect, 262

in employees, 257, *257*

most frequent positive emotions, *263*

performance and, 252

resistance to change and, 668

as resource, 261–262

self-assessment, 267

strategies for increasing, 256–257, 265–267

positivity effect The attraction of all living systems toward positive energy and away from negative energy, or toward that which is life giving and away from that which is life depleting, **255**

POS (perceived organizational support) The extent to which employees believe their organization values their contributions and genuinely cares about their well-being, **59**

P-O (person–organization fit) The extent to which your personality and values match the climate and culture in an organization, **550**, 573, 615

power The discretion and the means to enforce your will over others, **467**

in acquired needs theory, 166, 168

bases (forms) of, 467–470, *467*, *473*, *474*

commitment versus compliance, 473, *473*

empowerment, 475–479, *476*

ethical and effective use of, 472–473

implications of, 500

influence tactics, 480–485, *485*

Organizing Framework, *465*

outcomes of, 472, 474, *474*

political tactics, 486–492

position versus personal power, 470–471, *471*

self-assessment, 470

practical intelligence The ability to solve everyday problems by utilizing knowledge gained from experience in order to purposefully adapt to, shape, and select environments, **84**–85

praise, as political tactic, *488*

prejudice, 145

preparation/information gathering (creative behavior), 453

presentations, 364–366

presenteeism Occurs when employees show up but are sick or in no condition to work productively, **661**

pressure (influence tactic), *480*

pride, *263*

primary appraisals Perceptions of whether a stressor is irrelevant, positive, or negative, **662**

privacy, and social media, 360–362

proactive personality An attribute of someone relatively unconstrained by situational forces and who effects environmental change. Proactive people identify opportunities and act on them, show initiative, take action, and persevere until meaningful change occurs, **89**

  in entrepreneurs, 91–92, *91*

  in managers, 90

  self-assessment, 90

problem Difference or gap between an actual and a desired state or outcome, **21**

problem formation/definition (creative behavior), 452–453

Problem-Solving Application

  age discrimination, 151–152

  change, 665–666

  cognitive bias, 434–435

  conflict resolution, 406–407

  description of, 23

  emotional intelligence, 106

  employee benefits, 171–172, 180

  empowerment, 479

  expectancy theory, 180, 182

  innovation, 620

  leadership, 525–526

  organizational culture change, 572–573

  organizational design, 609–610

  positive organization behavior, 260

  rewards, 232

  sexual harassment, 52, 65–66

  social media costs, 357–358

  teams, 325–326

  technology and performance, 33–34

Problem-Solving Application Cases

  change management, 676–677

  communication, 375–376

  company values, 73–74

  conflict, 419–421

  controversial spokesperson, 117–118

  decision making, 460–461

  description of, 23

  diversity management, 157–158

  fraud, 39–40

  leadership, 543–544

  motivation, 195–196

  organizational behavior, 292–294

organizational culture, 589–591

organizational effectiveness, 633–634

organizational politics, 503–504

performance management, 247–249

teams, 332–334

problem solving A systematic process for closing gaps between an actual and a desired situation, **21**

  OB applied to, 26

  Organizing Framework, 29

  person-situation distinction in, 24–26

  practice scenario, 34–35

  selecting solution, 29–30

  self-assessment, 23

  skills reinforcement tools, 23

  as sought-after skill, *8*

  3-Step Approach, 21–22, 31

procedural justice The perceived fairness of the process and procedures used to make allocation decisions, **175**, *177*

process innovation A change in the way a product or a service is conceived, manufactured, or distributed, **616**

process theories of motivation Describe *how* various person factors and situation factors in the Organizing Framework affect motivation, **173**

  equity/justice theory, 173–178, *174, 177*

  expectancy theory, 178–182, *179, 181*

  goal-setting theory, 182–184

procrastination, 110

product design, inclusive, 139

product innovation A change in the appearance or functionality/performance of a product or a service or the creation of a new one, **616**

productivity

  social media and, 354–356

  versus business, 200

  worker fatigue and, 661

project teams, 313. *See also* teams

promotions

  diversity and, 146

  organizational cultural change and, *568,* 569

  requirements for, 9–10

  skills and job level, *10*

prosocial behaviors Positive acts performed without the expectation of anything in return, **255**

PsyCap. *See* positive psychological capital

psychological capital. *See* positive psychological capital

psychological contracts An individual's perception about the

reciprocal exchange between him- or herself and another party, **55**

psychological empowerment Employees' belief that they have control over their work; believed to drive intrinsic motivation, **518**

psychological empowerment Occurs when employees feel a sense of meaning, competence, self-determination, and impact at work. Reflects employees' belief that they have control over their work, **477**

psychological safety climate A shared belief among team members that it is safe to engage in risky behaviors, such as questioning current practices without retribution or negative consequences, **389–390**

psychological safety The extent to which people feel free to express their ideas and beliefs without fear of negative consequences, **146**

psychopathy A lack of guilt, remorse or concern for others when their own actions do others harm, **92, 513**

public speaking, 364–366

puffery, in negotiation, *413*

punctuated equilibrium Form of group development in which groups establish periods of stable functioning until an event causes a dramatic change in norms, roles, and/or objectives; the group then establishes and maintains new norms of functioning, returning to equilibrium, **308**, *308*

punishment The process of weakening behavior through either the contingent presentation of something displeasing or the contingent withdrawal of something positive, **238–239**

purpose. *See* meaningfulness

Q

quality improvement, and self-efficacy, *99*

quid pro quo sexual harassment, 399

R

race

  in person perception, 127–128

  stereotypes, 130

  workforce diversity trends, 141–142

racial discrimination, 130, 142, 159

resistance to change, 655
rewards, 227
school–non-school conflict, 392
signature strengths, 278
social media, 360
team maturity, 309
team member effectiveness, 311
telecommuting, 608
trust, 319
values, 47
self-awareness, 5, 6, *105*
self-determination theory Assumes that three innate needs influence our behavior and well-being—the needs for competence, autonomy, and relatedness, **168**–169
self-efficacy A person's belief about his or her chances of successfully accomplishing a specific task, **97**
application at work, *99*
developing, 276
managerial implications, 99
model of, 97–98, *97*
in psychological capital, 273, 274
self-enhancement, 44, *44*, 46
self-esteem General belief about your self-worth, **99**–100
self-managed teams (SMTs) Teams with collective autonomy and responsibility to plan, manage, and execute tasks interdependently to achieve their goals, **313**–314
self-management, *99*, *105*
self-promotion, *488*
self-serving bias Tendency to take more personal responsibility for success than for failure, **134**
self-transcendence, 44, *44*, 46
semantic memory, 125
sender, in communication, 340, *340*
sequential task interdependence, 315
serenity, *263*
servant-leadership Focuses on increased service to others rather than to oneself, **519**–521, *520*
sexual harassment
pervasiveness and costs of, 398–399
Problem-Solving Application, 52, 65–66
Problem-Solving Application Case, 503–504
types of, 399
sexual orientation, 142, 150
shareholders
balanced scorecard and, 625–626
decision making and, 446
as force for change, 642–643
sick-leave pay, 171–172
signature strengths Positive human traits that influence thoughts, feelings, and behaviors and provide a

sense of fulfillment and meaning, 277–278, *277*
Simon's normative model, 428–430
situational control, 523–524
situation factors All the elements outside us that influence what we do, the way we do it, and the ultimate results of our actions, **24**
in communication, 343
in contingency perspective, 5
in creative performance behaviors, 453–454
in employee engagement, 57
in negotiation, 414
in Organizing Framework, 27, *32*
in person perception, *126*, 127
in person-situation distinction, 24–26
in problem solving, 26
Problem-Solving Application, 33–34
six thinking hats strategy, 424
skills
desired by employers, *8*
hard vs. soft, 7–8
job level correlation, *10*
lacking in college graduates, 144
for leaders, *514*
skill variety, in job characteristics model, 188
Skype interviews, 363
slippery slope, *18*
slogans, and organizational culture change, 568–569, *568*
SMART goals An acronym for specific, measurable, attainable, results oriented, and time bound, *208*, **209**
SMTs (self-managed teams) Teams with collective autonomy and responsibility to plan, manage, and execute tasks interdependently to achieve their goals, **313**–314
social capital The productive potential resulting from relationships, goodwill, trust, and cooperative effort, **582**–583
social competence, *105*
social context, in person perception, 127
social interactions, 265
socialization. *See* organizational socialization
social loafing The tendency for individual effort to decline as group size increases, **312**–313, *312*
social media policy Describes the who, how, when, and for what purposes of social media use, and the consequences for noncompliance, **360**, 361–362, *361*
cyber-bullying, 397–398

social media The use of web-based and mobile technologies to generate interactive dialogue with members of a network, **353**
blocking access to, 359
as communication platform, 352
costs of, 356–357
effective use of, 353–354, 355
email management, 358, *358*
employer benefits, *356*
etiquette, 362–363
hiring process and, 122, 354, *354*
leader's attitudes toward, 360
Legal/Ethical Challenge, 377
policy for, 360, 361–362, *361*
privacy issues, 360–362
Problem-Solving Application, 357–358
productivity and, 354–356
referent power of influencers, 469–470
reputation and, 362
self-assessment, 360
use by age, *353*
social perception. *See* perception
social proof, 484
social responsibility, 259
social role theory, 350, 351
social support The amount of perceived helpfulness we derive from social relationships, **286**
social system stability, 556–557
soft skills Relate to our human interactions and include both interpersonal skills and personal attributes, 7–8, *8*, *10*
spans of control The number of people reporting directly to a given manager, **599**
spatial intelligence, *84*
spokesperson, controversial, 117–118
spot rewards, 241–242
staff employees Perform background research and provide technical advice and recommendations to their line managers, **599**
staffing, and worker fatigue, 661
stage presence, for presentations, 365
STATE technique, 367–368
stereotypes An individual's set of beliefs about the characteristics or attributes of a group, **130**
as diversity management barrier, 145
formation and maintenance, 130–131
managerial challenges, 131
Organizing Framework, *121*
types of, 130
storming, in group development, 306
storytelling, in organizational culture change, *568*, 570

glossary/subject index

thought processes
  critical thinking, *8*, 424
  intuitive versus analytical, 425–426
360-degree feedback Individuals compare perceptions of their own performance with behaviorally specific (and usually anonymous) performance information from their manager, subordinates, and peers, **21**5–216
3-Step Problem Solving Approach, 21–22, 31
time duration, of groups versus teams, 299, *299*
tiredness Typically physical and short-term and is resolved by rest and sleep, **660**
tolerance
  for ambiguity, 442
  in diversity management, 149
top-down job design, 185, *185*, 186–189
total rewards Rewards encompassing not only compensation and benefits, but also personal and professional growth opportunities and a motivating work environment that includes recognition, job design, and work–life balance, **230**, *230*
touch, in communication, 345
traditionalist generation, *143*, 152
training and development
  core self-evaluation use, 103
  organizational culture change and, *568*, 569
  self-efficacy and, *99*
trait approach Attempts to identify personality characteristics or interpersonal attributes that differentiate leaders from followers, **512**
transactional leadership Focuses on clarifying employees' role and task requirements and providing followers with positive and negative rewards contingent on performance, **516**
transformational leadership Leaders who transform their followers to pursue organizational goals over self-interests, **530**–533, *531*
transgender Applies to anyone whose gender identity or gender expression is different from sex at birth, **150**
transparency
  in communication, 341–342
  in performance monitoring, 214
trust The willingness to be vulnerable to another person, and the belief that the other person will consider the impact of how his or her

intentions and behaviors will affect you, **317**
  benefits of, 317–318, *317*
  in giving negative feedback, 223
  in group cohesiveness, 307
  in high-quality connections, 265
  repairing, 320, *320*, 498–499
  self-assessment, 319
  types of, 318

U

unconscious thought, 425–426
underemployment Working at jobs that require less education than attained, **144**
underperformance, coping with, 663
unethical behavior
  causes of, 17, *18*
  cheating, 11–12, 17–18
  confronting, 20
  by job applicants, 18–19
  in negotiations, 413–414, *413*
  versus illegal, 13–14
unfreezing stage of change, 647, *647*
unions, 382, 642–643
unity of command principle Specifies that each employee should report to only one manager, **597**
upward spirals of positivity Positive behaviors, feelings, and attitudes that generate the same in others in a continually reinforcing process, **262**, *264*

V

valence Describes the positive or negative value people place on outcomes, **180**
value attainment Satisfaction that results from the perception that a job allows for fulfillment of an individual's important values, **62**
value orientation, 442
values Abstract ideals that guide our thinking and behavior across all situations, **44**
  dynamics of, 47
  generational differences in, 47
  implications of, 70
  Legal/Ethical Challenge, 504–505
  in organizational climate, 280–281
  in organizational commitment, 55
  in organizational culture, 553–554, 562–563
  Organizing Framework, *42*
  Problem-Solving Application Case, 73–74

Schwartz's theory, 44–47, *44*, *46*
  self-assessment, 47
  versus attitudes, *48*, 49
variable pay, 233–235, *233*, *234*
variable rewards, 242
verbal recognition, 171
vertical dyad, 534
vertical loading, 188
virtual interviews, 129, 363
virtual reality (VR), 641
virtual structure One whose members are geographically apart, usually working with e-mail and other forms of information technology, but that generally appears to customers as a single, unified organization with a real physical location, **610**–611, *612*
virtual teams Teams that work across time, space, and organizational boundaries to achieve common goals, 314, **314**, *315*, 483
virtual work, 594, 608
virtuousness What individuals and organizations aspire to be when they are at their very best, **282**
vision A long-term goal that describes what an organization wants to become, **567**, **649**
  in leadership, 511, 530
  in organizational change, 567, 649–651
  in team charter, 298
voice climate Climate in which employees are encouraged to freely express their opinions and feelings, **178**
voice The discretionary or formal expression of ideas, opinions, suggestions, or alternative approaches directed to a specific target inside or outside of the organization with the intent to change an objectionable state of affairs and to improve the current functioning of the organization, **177**
VR (virtual reality), 641

W

walking meditation, 272, *272*
waypower The ability to see one or more paths to achieve a goal, even when faced with adversity, **274**
well-being The combined impact of five elements—positive emotions, engagement, relationships, meaning, and achievement (PERMA), **283**

whistle-blowers, 16–17, 41

willpower The determination to achieve a goal, **274**

withdrawal cognitions An individual's overall thoughts and feelings about quitting, **65**

women
on boards of directors, 138
career-family balance, 147
career navigation help, 150
communication patterns, 350–351
family leave for, 394

glass ceiling, 140–141
leadership traits, 514
work flow, and organizational culture change, *568*, 571–572

work–life conflict The perception that expectations and demands between work and nonwork roles are mutually incompatible, **39**1–394

workplace attitudes An outcome of various OB-related processes, including leadership, **48**

employee engagement, 43, 56–59
employee surveys of, 54
job satisfaction (*See* job satisfaction)
organizational commitment, 54–56
perceived organization support, 59

workspace
change over time, *593*
open office design, 623–624, *624*
organizational culture change and, 567, *568*

work teams, 313. *See also* teams

glossary/subject index

name index

name index

name index

company index

company index